P9-BII-130

# OPERATIONS MANAGEMENT

Meeting Customers' Demands

## McGraw-Hill/Irwin Series: Operations and Decision Sciences

OPERATIONS MANAGEMENT

Bowersox and Closs
**Logistical Management: *The Integrated Supply Chain Process***
*First Edition*

Chase, Aquilano, and Jacobs
**Operations Management for Competitive Advantage**
*Ninth Edition*

Chu, Hottenstein, and Greenlaw
**PROSIM for Windows**
*Third Edition*

Cohen and Apte
**Manufacturing Automation**
*First Edition*

Davis, Aquilano, and Chase
**Fundamentals of Operations Management**
*Third Edition*

Dobler and Burt
**Purchasing and Supply Management**
*Sixth Edition*

Flaherty
**Global Operations Management**
*First Edition*

Fitzsimmons and Fitzsimmons
**Service Management: *Operations, Strategy, Information Technology***
*Third Edition*

Gray and Larson
**Project Management: *The Managerial Process***
*First Edition*

Hill
**Manufacturing Strategy: *Text & Cases***
*Third Edition*

Hopp and Spearman
**Factory Physics**
*Second Edition*

Knod and Schonberger
**Operations Management**
*Seventh Edition*

Lambert and Stock
**Strategic Logistics Management**
*Third Edition*

Leenders and Fearon
**Purchasing and Supply Chain Management**
*Eleventh Edition*

Moses, Seshadri, and Yakir
**HOM Operations Management Software for Windows**
*First Edition*

Nahmias
**Production and Operations Analysis**
*Fourth Edition*

Nicholas
**Competitive Manufacturing Management**
*First Edition*

Olson
**Introduction to Information Systems Project Management**
*First Edition*

Pinedo and Chao
**Operations Scheduling**
*First Edition*

Sanderson and Uzumeri
**Managing Product Families**
*First Edition*

Schroeder
**Operations Management: *Contemporary Concepts and Cases***
*First Edition*

Simchi-Levi, Kaminsky, and Simchi-Levi
**Designing and Managing the Supply Chain: *Concepts, Strategies, and Case Studies***
*First Edition*

Sterman
**Business Dynamics: *Systems Thinking and Modeling for a Complex World***
*First Edition*

Stevenson
**Production/Operations Management**
*Sixth Edition*

Vollmann, Berry, and Whybark
**Manufacturing Planning & Control Systems**
*Fourth Edition*

Zipkin
**Foundations of Inventory Management**
*First Edition*

QUANTITATIVE METHODS AND MANAGEMENT SCIENCE

Bodily, Carraway, Frey, Pfeifer
**Quantitative Business Analysis: *Casebook***
*First Edition*

Bodily, Carraway, Frey, Pfeifer
**Quantitative Business Analysis: *Text and Cases***
*First Edition*

Bonini, Hausman, and Bierman
**Quantitative Analysis for Business Decisions**
*Ninth Edition*

Hesse
**Managerial Spreadsheet Modeling and Analysis**
*First Edition*

Hillier, Hillier, Lieberman
**Introduction to Management Science: *A Modeling and Case Studies Approach with Spreadsheets***
*First Edition*

S E V E N T H   E D I T I O N

# OPERATIONS MANAGEMENT

## Meeting Customers' Demands

**Edward M. Knod, Jr.**
*Western Illinois University*

**Richard J. Schonberger**
*Schonberger & Associates, Inc., and University of Washington*

Boston Burr Ridge, IL Dubuque, IA Madison, WI New York San Francisco St. Louis
Bangkok Bogotá Caracas Kuala Lumpur Lisbon London Madrid Mexico City
Milan Montreal New Delhi Santiago Seoul Singapore Sydney Taipei Toronto

*McGraw-Hill Higher Education*

*A Division of The* ***McGraw-Hill*** *Companies*

**Operations Management: Meeting Customers' Demands**

Published by McGraw-Hill, an imprint of The McGraw-Hill Companies, Inc. 1221 Avenue of the Americas, New York, NY, 10020. Copyright © 2001, 1997, 1994, 1991, 1988, 1985, 1981, by The McGraw-Hill Companies, Inc. All rights reserved. No part of this publication may be reproduced or distributed in any form or by any means, or stored in a data base or retrieval system, without the prior written consent of The McGraw-Hill Companies, Inc., including, but not limited to, in any network or other electronic storage or transmission, or broadcast for distance learning.
Some ancillaries, including electronic and print components, may not be available to customers outside the United States.

This book is printed on acid-free paper.

1 2 3 4 5 6 7 8 9 0 DOC/DOC 0 9 8 7 6 5 4 3 2 1

ISBN 0-07-232059-1

Publisher: *Jeffrey J. Shelstad*
Executive editor: *Richard T. Hercher, Jr.*
Senior development editor: *Wanda Zeman*
Marketing manager: *Zina Craft*
Senior project manager: *Pat Frederickson*
Production supervisor: *Susanne Riedell*
Senior coordinator freelance design: *Gino Cieslik*
Supplement coordinator: *Carol A. Bielski and Joyce Chappetto*
Media technology producer: *Ed Przyzycki*
Front cover photo: *© 2000 Michael Voltattorni*
Compositor: *Interactive Composition Corporation*
Typeface: *10/12 Times Roman*
Printer: *R. R. Donnelley & Sons Company*

**Library of Congress Cataloging-in-Publication Data**

Knod, Edward M.
Operations management : meeting customers' demands / Edward M. Knod, Richard J. Schonberger.—7th ed.
p. cm.
Includes bibliographical references (p.) and index.
ISBN 0-07-232059-1 (alk. paper)
1. Production management. I. Schonberger, Richard. II. Title.

TS155 .K697 2001
658.5—dc21 00-064739

www.mhhe.com

# PREFACE

The field of operations management (OM) has changed a great deal, especially during the last quarter century. The same can be said about the vehicles for teaching OM and about the requisite skills that the student must possess in order to take full advantage of the delivery systems. At its heart, this revision is all about addressing those changes—all of them. First, we consider subject content and then turn to format.

## Content

In our view, a revision should accomplish two things relative to subject content. First, *promising* new ideas need to be introduced. Second, and equally important, dominant themes in the subject matter need to be identified and nurtured.

In OM—maybe in any field of study—the new ideas, or the more revolutionary changes, are perhaps easier to capture. At a minimum, we add sections that define and briefly describe the more promising new tools or concepts and try to appropriately append them to the existing body of knowledge. New three-letter acronyms are often part of the package. But space and time are limited so we don't go too far; the new idea might turn out to be short-lived and amount to little more than a historical footnote in years ahead. Just as new products must prove themselves on supermarket shelves, new ideas must pan out before they earn a lasting place in our books and seminars.

Dominant themes present a greater challenge. We think that they not only ought to help define success within the OM field but should apply to business or company success across the board. Moreover, they ought to be unifying, readily embraced by people throughout the firm. Finally, dominant themes ought to crop up frequently throughout the book as various OM topics are considered; that is, they have a wide base of what might be called "natural relevance."

What are today's dominant themes and how do we treat them in *Operations Management,* 7th Edition? A very brief discussion of each follows:

- Wherever one turns for business advice, the message is clear: A customer-centered orientation is the formula for successful planning, implementation, and improvement activities in today's companies. Our subtitle, *Meeting Customers' Demands,* marks the continuation of the focus on customers that has been a hallmark of this book. In this edition, we have further developed and amplified our discussions of specific ways by which OM activities result in greater value for both internal and external customers.
- Rather like a corollary to the first point, the issue of defining or recognizing what customers value and where they expect to obtain that value is another dominant theme. Some observers think the quality movement has peaked, but we have a different view: Quality still matters, but thanks to the TQM movement, quality is much better today. Somewhat akin to the satisfied need in Maslow's hierarchy, it no longer "motivates" as it once did. Take it away, however, and customers' wrath will descend with a vengeance. Today, rapid response, flexibility, and better service are in the spotlight. And despite the booming economy, cost pressures appear to be as strong as ever. Our posture? Operate as if your customer wants it better *and* faster *and* cheaper . . . *and* served with a smile!
- Cross- or multifunctional cooperation is a way of life in successful companies. True, functional silos continue to exist in far too many companies, but hopefully their days are numbered. As a function or activity, operations management cannot and should not stand alone. OM must mesh with accounting, engineering, finance, marketing, information technology, human resources, and so forth. Time pressures mandate information sharing—in the form of common databases and round-the-table human interaction. We simply don't have time for sequential iterations of passing papers back and forth. In this book, we strive to highlight the necessary interactions and echo W. E. Deming's call for organizational constancy of purpose.
- Our overarching theme continues to be the Principles of Operations Management. The principles serve to bind the chapters and parts together. We've deliberately elected the "trade version" that includes Principle 16—Market every improvement. We tell companies to brag about their successes, so why not tell students the same thing? Also, in this edition, we incorporate some feedback on use of the principles as measures of business success.

## Format

Although we made some changes to the book's organization, perhaps the most significant format change is that this edition makes more extensive use of technology for delivery of materials. End users have ready access to the book, the CD-ROM, and the Internet-based materials.

## *The Book*

Just as operations interrelates with the rest of the organization, the activities and tools that make up operations management interrelate with one another. The field is not linear or sequential in practice, and it shouldn't be portrayed as such in a book. Therefore, we retain the *wholeness approach* that we have used in previous editions.

You will not, for instance, find concepts like just-in-time, setup, and lead time confined to a single chapter. In similar fashion, the impacts of strategy, capacity planning, design, quality, and responsiveness, for example, appear throughout the book. When you study *Operations Management,* 7th Edition, you will make five passes through the subject of OM. Each of the five parts goes a bit deeper into the field, opening new layers of content that serve to illustrate, refine and—perhaps most descriptively—build upon concepts that have been mentioned in earlier parts.

Part I is the foundation. It provides basic definitions, reviews the role that OM plays in organizational strategy and dynamic competitiveness, and presents basic principles that ought to govern operations wherever they occur throughout the organization.

Part II addresses the core OM responsibility that every organization must accomplish: assess demands, prepare capacity to serve those demands, and ensure that orders are fulfilled in ways that meet customers' requirements. In one sense, Part II is an overview of OM's key role in customer-oriented, value-adding supply chains.

Part III makes an even deeper pass, delving further into the transformation processes used to accomplish the broad-level OM responsibility described in Part II. Again, the emphasis is on giving customers what they want.

In Part IV, the focus is on key resources. People, materials, and facilities and equipment are inputs to the processes defined in Part III; these resources are the ingredients for successful operations.

Part V presents an in-depth look at the basic modes of operations. Concepts learned in previous parts apply to all modes; but customer demands regarding volume, variety, and magnitude of outputs serve to define specific OM techniques most appropriate for each setting.

## *The CD-ROM*

A CD-ROM accompanies your book. On it you will find several portions of the material that we have prepared to assist you in your study of OM. Much of the material is organized in a chapter-by-chapter fashion to integrate closely with *Operations Management,* 7th Edition. PowerPoint® slides, review exercises designed to stimulate your thinking during review, video clips, and quizzes are included for all chapters. Some chapters also contain Excel® spreadsheet programs and data sets that may be used for designated exercises in the chapter or the chapter supplements.

Other material pertains more to multiple chapters (e.g., a part in the book), to the book as a whole, or to other ancillary materials. Case studies are an example for most of the cases relate to material addressed in more than one chapter of the book. The McGraw-Hill/Irwin Operations Management Video Series contains more than two dozen videos that portray various OM concepts. Because the videos may also relate to multiple chapters, video clips are likewise applicable to various topics.

### *Internet-based Materials*

The OM Center, an Operations Management support web site edited and maintained by Byron Finch, is an excellent source for additional information about OM. The site contains over 50 company tours, links to business news and OM publications, announcements and other related materials. The address is http://www.mhhe.com/business/opsci/pom/.

The authors also maintain a web site that contains support materials oriented specifically to this book and CD-ROM material. You may access that site through the OM Center, and will want to bookmark both sites. Look for interesting tidbits on the book-support site. What we post will depend to some extent on the feedback we get from our users.

## Acknowledgments

First, we would like to thank our publication team at McGraw-Hill/Irwin:

Richard T. Hercher, Jr., Executive Editor; Wanda Zeman, Senior Development Editor; Pat Frederickson, Senior Project Manager; and Carol Bielski, Supplements Producer. Without the dedication and talents of these professionals and their colleagues, most of the "good things" about this book and the supporting package simply would not exist.

Second, we want to acknowledge the insights offered by those who critiqued our work. Reviewers' contributions stand out, for they usually reflect an in-depth study of the book and experience as an adopter. They have tasted the product, so to speak. Reviewers for this, the seventh edition include; Gordon M. Amsler, Damodar Y. Golhar, Abe Feinberg, Corinne M. Karuppan, John Klocinski, Henry Maddux, David L. Rainey, Roger L. Salstrom, Michael S. Spencer, Keith Starcher, and Madjid Tavana.

Many other individuals have contributed to this work through the years. They reviewed earlier editions of the book, made significant suggestions or shared special expertise in various disciplines, or prepared ancillary materials. They include S. Keith Adams, John Anderson, Jay Bandyopadhyay, Thomas Billesbach, Charles F. Bimmerle, Joseph Biggs, Karen Brown, James J. Browne, Ashok Chandrashekar, Sohail S. Chaudhry, Ed Davis, Keith Denton, Sudhakar Deshmukh, Joseph DeVoss, Jim Dier, Les Digman, Shad Dowlatshahi, Ike C. Ehie, Jim Gilbert, Paul Graham, Gary Green, James R. Gross, John Hael, Bob Hall, Ray M. Haynes, Gajanan Hegde, Ralph Hocking, Mark Ippolito, Vaidyanathan Jayaraman, H. Thomas Johnson, Steve Kline, Ray Lankford, John J. Lawrence, Sang Lee, Farzad Mahmoodi, Dennis McLeavey, Daniel McNamara, John Milleville, Farhad Moeeni, Russ Morey, Jerry Murphy, David Osborne, Taeho Park, James Patterson, Henry Person, James A. Pope, Farhad Raiszadeh, Steve Replogle, Rajeev Sawhney, Victor E. Sower, R. Stansbury Stockton, Robert T. Sumichrast, Rhae M. Swisher, Jr., Edward Thode, Edward Walker, Norman Ware, Roy

Williams, and Paul Wyman. Individually and collectively, these people helped us create a better product. We sincerely appreciate their numerous contributions.

Finally, we thank the end users. They keep us on our toes! Seminar attendees and corporate adopters, you are an important link to the contemporary world of OM in practice. Your letters, e-mail, and other feedback are sincerely appreciated. Students, you are our bridge to the future . . . and while you may not think so at exam time, we do have your best interest at heart. We close with a few comments just for you.

## Note to the Student

First, welcome to a new field of study! At the top of the preface, we alluded to change; perhaps the best use for this note is to offer a perspective: A quarter century ago, most of the topics that you will study in this book didn't exist. Maybe you're thinking, "Fine, I didn't exist either! Now that we've discussed ancient history, let's move on. . . ." Okay, we will.

Twenty-five *weeks* before this note was written, some of the goods and services (e.g., software and network support) that we are using to create materials to support this book did not exist. And, within the twenty-five *days* before this note was written, some of the organizations mentioned in this book had structural changes; they bought another company, sold a business unit or spun it off into a new company, or merged some facet of their operations. Finally, let's stick our neck out just a little and suggest that within the twenty-five *hours* before this note was written, some manager in most if not all companies mentioned herein either consummated or at least contemplated changes to strategic partnership alliances that will affect company operations.

We can turn this exercise around, take a future orientation, and personalize it a bit. If you have an Internet news service, change your keyword or search phrase options to include "operations," "outsourcing," and "partnership." Check your e-mail for the next few days. If you don't have a service, log on to your favorite business news outlet tomorrow and note the newly announced business alliances. Try keeping a tally for the next 25 days. Care to guess what sort of changes will occur within the next half-year (roughly, 25 weeks)? How about where you will be and what you will be doing in 25 months? One thing is certain; 25 years from now, this course will be in your ancient history!

*If we convince you of nothing else, we hope that you will view your study of operations management this term as a snapshot, a bump on the temporal continuum. Don't think that you will master the field; you won't. Change will see to that.*

Your instructor is a fundamental part of your snapshot; the material we have prepared is another. What we offer is a description of OM as it has evolved and a statement of how it is practiced in leading companies today . . . a descriptive look at the past and a prescriptive view of the present.

In keeping with the times, we are demanding more of you now than we demanded of those students who used earlier editions. You need sharper writing skills, for we ask you to write more in your responses to exercises. You need stronger mathematics skills, for we have beefed up the quantitative content of the book. And you need more computer skills; we expect you to be able to use the Internet and to have basic-level understanding of PowerPoint® and Excel®.

Absorb the materials we've put together, and then move on. It's up to you to raise the bar. Good luck in your OM studies . . . during the upcoming term and in the years ahead!

**Edward M. Knod, Jr., Springfield, Illinois**
**Richard J. Schonberger, Seattle, Washington**

# CONTENTS IN BRIEF

# C O N T E N T S

PART V

## Operations Modes: In-depth Analysis

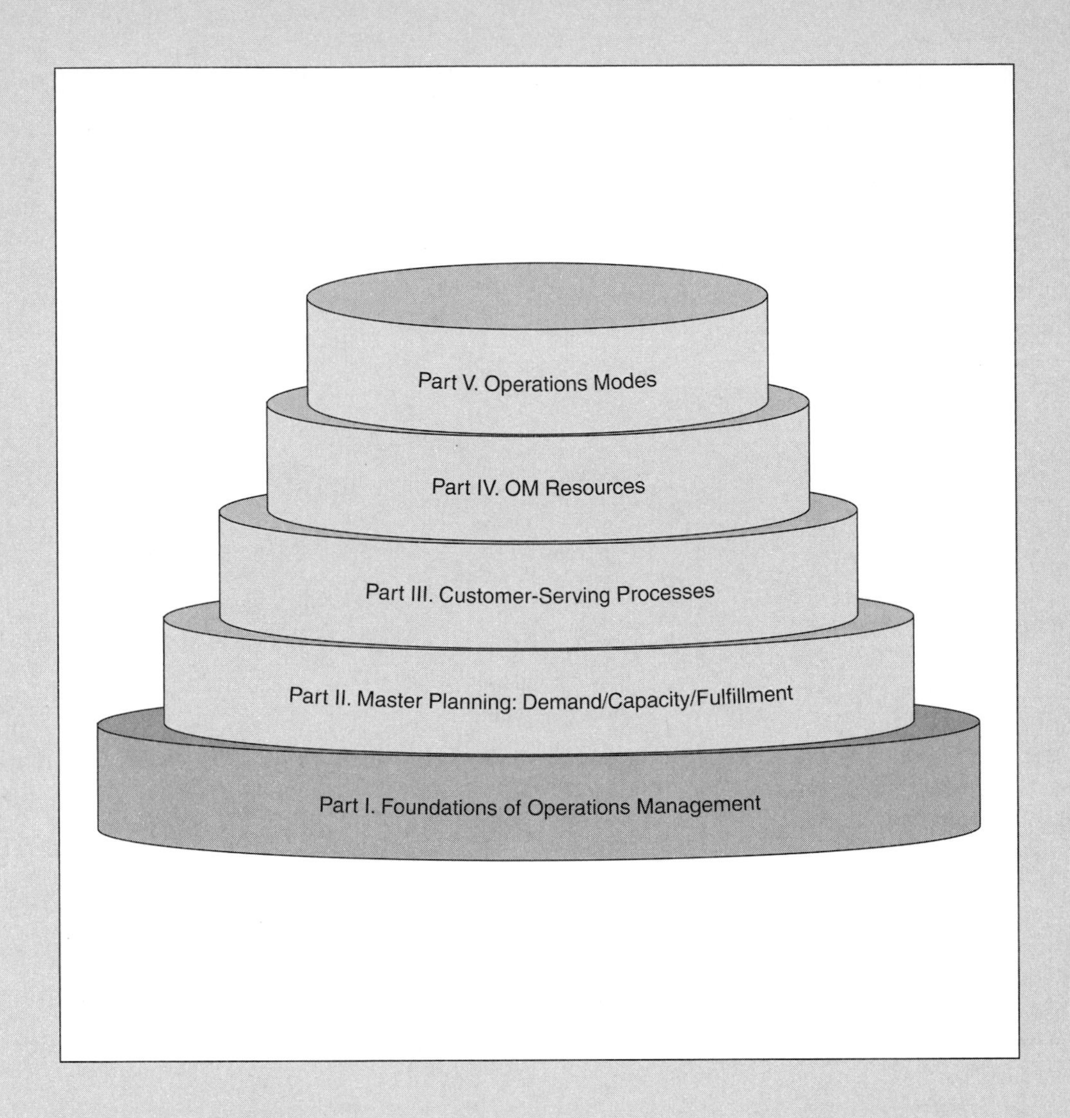
Part V. Operations Modes
Part IV. OM Resources
Part III. Customer-Serving Processes
Part II. Master Planning: Demand/Capacity/Fulfillment
Part I. Foundations of Operations Management

PART I

# FOUNDATIONS OF OPERATIONS MANAGEMENT



As we noted in the preface, Part I represents the first pass at operations management; it lays the foundation for the field and presents an overview of OM as it is practiced by leading companies today. The broad aims are to understand what the business world means by the word *operations;* to examine operations management as it fits within the broader business structure; to understand how operations strategies and operations management contribute to dynamic competitiveness; and to introduce fundamental principles that serve to guide operations managers as they plan, implement, and improve OM strategies.

**Points to ponder:** To survive in the world of commerce, a company needs some type of distinctive competency or competitive advantage. Then once attained, that advantage must be sustained. Otherwise, new ones must be developed. In either scenario, operations are the key to success . . . or failure.

CHAPTER 1

# OPERATIONS MANAGEMENT: INTRODUCTORY CONCEPTS

Innovative. Productive. Competitive. Profitable. These are but a few of the adjectives that observers use to describe successful companies, firms that appear with regularity in news articles.[1] Generally, the reputations are deserved in that these organizations—large and small, foreign and domestic, manufacturers and services providers—can post impressive arrays of numbers to justify the praise they receive. Regardless of company size or industry, however, a look beneath the accolades and the numbers usually reveals elements of a common foundation. A pattern of activities emerges, one that suggests, in turn, an underlying core value or organizational culture: *These companies are focused on their customers. They provide goods and services that their customers want, and they do so in ways that attract new customers and compel existing ones to come back for more.*

Those sought-after goods and services flow from the operations of the successful provider businesses. They are the outputs of carefully planned and executed transformation processes that are, in turn, anchored by a set of proven principles of operations management (OM). Of course, multitudes of not-so-successful firms also produce output goods and services, and they might also claim to listen to their customers. But something is missing. Frequently, the root causes of the deficiencies can be traced to poorly managed operations.

In this book, we suggest how organizations ought to conduct operations in order to position themselves as leaders, certainly in the commerce of their communities and perhaps on an even grander scale—as world-class leaders in the increasingly competitive global marketplace. This introductory chapter defines operations management and addresses OM contributions to the success of any organization. We also examine the position that OM plays in customer-focused chains of supply and consumption that form the lifeblood of commerce. We conclude with a few reasons why you—the reader—will benefit from the study of OM.

## What Is "OM"?

Frequently, students beginning a course in operations management (OM) have some difficulty pinning down just what it is that they will be studying. Part of the trouble lies in previous experience—what the students have read or heard about the word *operations* doesn't match the apparent subject matter of the course. Confusion stems from the multiple and potentially conflicting definitions of "operations" that have emerged in the literature of various fields of study and from the ways the word is used in contemporary business.

When we add the word *management,* other concerns arise, prompted perhaps by awareness of various academic program offerings within the college or university curriculum. A student who has completed a management course or two might ask, "How does OM fit within the broader field of management itself?" And regardless of one's chosen field of study, it's quite natural to wonder, "How will what I learn in this course affect my other studies and my career in general?"

Frankly, complete answers to these two questions are beyond the reach of this book, this course, and even your college experiences. That fact doesn't get us—your authors and your instructor—off the hook, however, for we can make a start. We contend that OM is relevant to any business career and to most if not all careers outside the business world. In the chapters ahead, we build our case. In this section, our aim is much more modest; we tackle the fundamental question, "Just what is OM?"

## *Operations*

An Internet search for the term *operations* will return tens of thousands of "hits," and on some search engines, a suggestion that we narrow the target inquiry. We might even be presented with suggested options for refinement of the search. Whether we explore further or not, the exercise serves a purpose. It opens our minds to the multitude of ways that people think about operations. If we eliminate nonbusiness and nonorganizational examples from the Internet search, and perhaps add some "old-fashioned" review of business news and literature, we are still able to identify several ways in which the word *operations* is used in contemporary business and organizational settings. It might refer to:

1. OVERALL BUSINESS ACTIVITY. In these cases the word *operations* is used as a near-synonym for *business.* A news article that discusses Daimler-Chrysler's South American operations, for example, refers to the entirety of that company's business activities in one geographical region.

2. PRIMARY BUSINESS ACTIVITY. When preparing financial statements, accountants use the term *operations* to refer to a company's primary ongoing business activities. Without going into detail, we note briefly that **earnings from operations,** a key figure on the income statement, is the amount by which revenue from the sales of the company's output goods and services exceeds the costs of providing those outputs. The idea is to separately identify the operating income from other earnings—interest and dividend income, for example.

3. DEPARTMENT WITHIN AN ORGANIZATION. *Operations* is the name often given to one of the main component parts or functional departments of an organization and is usually identifiable on an organization chart, perhaps similar to the abbreviated version shown in Exhibit 1-1A. This department or area is typically responsible for generating most of the revenue-producing outputs of the organization; that is, it is charged with production of goods or delivery of services destined for use by external customers. In this context, the term *operations* refers to *where* in the company certain types of work occur.

## Exhibit 1-1 Concepts of Operations

**A. Operations as an organizational department**

Acme Company

M. Alverez
C.E.O

L. Shin
V.P. Engineering

J. Thompson
V.P. Operations

P. van Zeer
V.P. Marketing

B. Jones
Chief Financial Officer

**B. Operations as transformation processes**

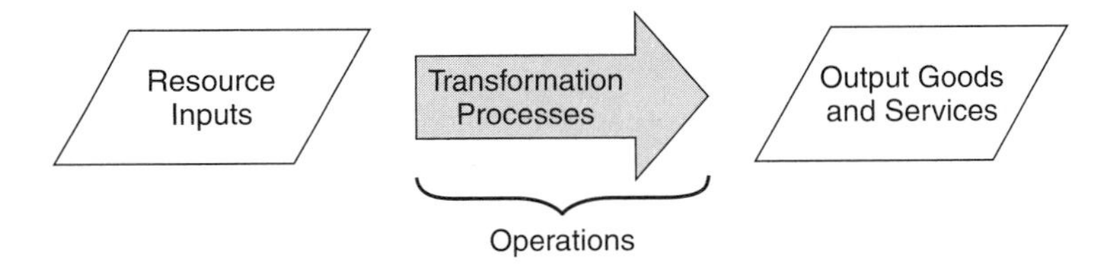


**C. An operation as a part of a job sequence**

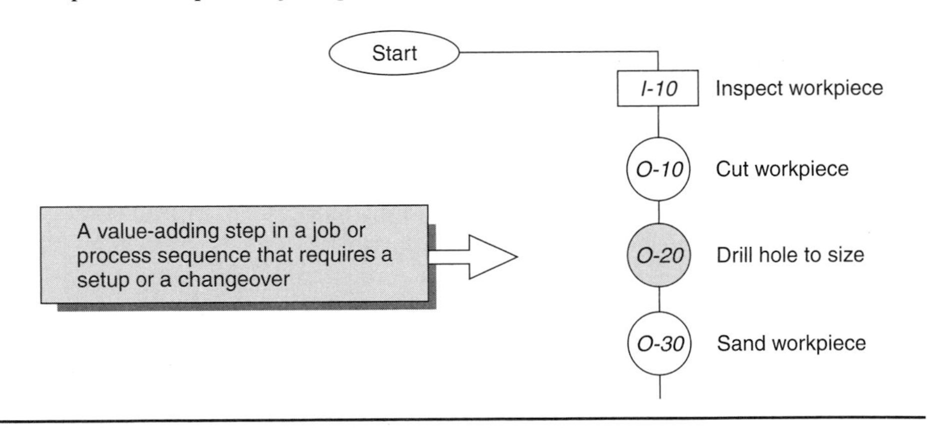


A **process** is a unique set of elements, conditions, or causes that collectively produce a given outcome or set of results.

4. Transformation processes. The word *operations* is also used to denote the processes that transform resources (inputs) into goods and services (outputs), as Exhibit 1-1B illustrates. Rather than defining a department in the organization where certain activities occur, the word "operations" in this case refers *to the activities themselves*. In this context, operations are more closely linked to the actual work that people

accomplish and to the relationships that exist in the workforce. To clarify a bit, we note that:

- A somewhat specific sequence of activities (operations) defines each process. A restaurant, a retail store, or a professional office might have dozens of transformation processes; large manufacturers might have tens of thousands.
- Each transformation process yields output goods or services for some customer. That customer, the intended recipient of process output, can be either an internal one (a fellow employee) or an external one.
- Operations occur throughout the organization, in *any* office, shop, or department, wherever input-to-output transformations take place. Therefore—and this is a key point—*everyone* in the organization has at least one customer to serve and is responsible for the transformation processes that form the provider-customer linkage.

5. VALUE-ADDING STEPS IN A JOB SEQUENCE. A fifth usage of the word *operations* has its origins in the industrial and manufacturing engineering disciplines and follows conventions established in the early parts of the 20th century. Detailed study of a transformation process involves identification and evaluation of each step in the job sequences that make up the process. Typically, many of the activities that occur in such a sequence add no value to the output. Moves, delays, storage, and even inspections are included in this class. Those steps that *do* add value are referred to as operations.

To illustrate, Exhibit 1-1C shows a segment of a flowchart of steps needed to make a small wooden toy; additional details would be provided but are not essential for our purposes. The chart segment shows an initial inspection of the workpiece followed by three operations that each add value to the workpiece.[2] The shaded operation, designated O-20, specifies that a hole is to be drilled in the workpiece. To perform operation O-20, the operator would usually need to perform a setup—preparation of the required machine (here, a drill press) by locating and inserting the proper tool (the correct drill bit). Even a small job such as the creation of a toy might entail several dozen operations.

**Setup** (or, **changeover**) Changing the setting or configuration of a machine, production line or cell, or process in order to produce a new product or service.

The OM student should be familiar with all of these uses of the word *operations.* The first, however, is rather straightforward and serves mainly to define the enterprises of a specific company rather than a field of study—we needn't pursue it further at this time.

The second, while company-specific to an extent, is fundamental to the understanding of financial statements, and is therefore useful to any business student or practitioner. But further discussion is beyond our scope and is appropriately reserved for accounting studies.

As to the third use, we note that many organizations do not have a functional component called operations per se, but there is almost always some area within the company where the bulk of output-producing activities takes place. Identify the company's primary outputs, determine the people charged with carrying out the transformations needed to create or provide those outputs, and you've probably identified those personnel who work in the company's operations area. Later in this chapter, we more fully explore the operations area within the context of the broader organization.

Most of our attention will be directed at the last two meanings of the word *operations*. Indeed, when we seek to explain what operations managers do, we usually wind up talking about their attention to transformation processes. Furthermore, efforts to improve those processes—our focus throughout this book—have a simple yet powerful aim: Eliminate non-value-adding steps and streamline the value-adding ones.

### *Management*

Popular definitions of management are plentiful. Typically, they contain some reference to desirable traits and skills that good managers possess . . . such things as goal-oriented behavior, leadership capabilities, communications and analytical skills, fiduciary loyalty to owners, and concern for employees and the environment. Operations managers are no different from any other group in that these characteristics make them more competent and more valuable as employees.

Definitions of management also usually contain lists of tasks designed to describe what managers do. Rather than devote much effort to the creation of an exhaustive list, we note that any work-related activity that a manager performs serves one or more of three general and overlapping duties: creating, implementing, and improving. (See Exhibit 1-2.)

- *Creating*. Planning, designing, forecasting, staffing, organizing, research, and development are among the generic activities that managers use to build and maintain customer-serving capacity. Facility planning and layout; design of order-processing, quality-assurance, and output-delivery systems; workforce training; and materials and component sourcing are examples of OM tasks that have a substantial creative component.
- *Implementing*. When managers allocate or assign, authorize, fund or budget, schedule, direct, or empower subordinates to carry out these types of duties, emphasis shifts from creating to implementing—putting plans into action. During implementation, managers and employees perform monitoring and controlling activities. Customer feedback, process output metrics, and other signals trigger adjustments in transformation processes.

**Exhibit 1-2 Basic Management Duties**

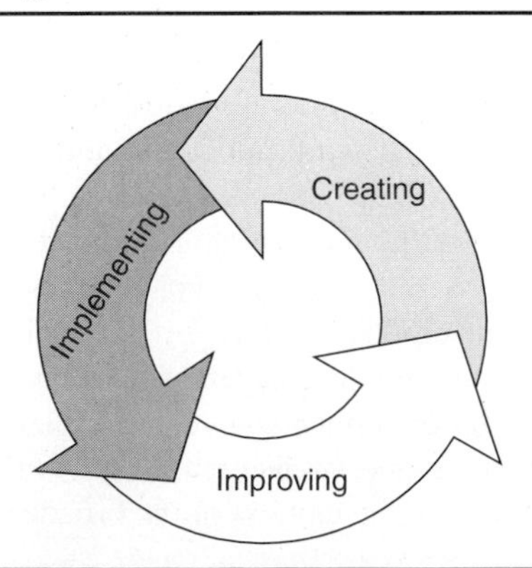

- *Improving.* The aims of these process adjustments are twofold: First, improve outputs. Environmental factors (new or revised customer needs, challenges from competitors, social and regulatory pressures, new technologies, and so forth) often necessitate improvements to output goods and services. Second, eliminate wasteful activities. Even in an ideal state of "perfect outputs"—outputs that needn't be altered—competitive forces would still mandate improvements in the ways those outputs are created.

**Waste**
Anything that does not add value to output goods and services. (Getting waste out of processes is a theme that receives attention throughout this book . . . further attention later in this chapter, for instance.)

Exhibit 1-2 suggests that the management duties are iterative. Improvements occur in response to—or better yet, in anticipation of—signals for changes; managers start the cycle again. They create revised plans, new designs, better processes, and so on. Get rid of some wasteful steps, improve some value-adding operations, listen to customers, monitor processes, and so on.

### *Operations Management*

We are now ready to combine the multipart definition of operations with our deliberately generic creating-implementing-improving view of management. Thus; **operations management** is the set of activities for creating, implementing, and improving processes that transform resource inputs into output goods and services. OM activities may be appropriately applied anywhere in organizations and may target any level of effort from a single step in a job sequence to the entirety of company activity.

Usually, it serves a purpose to identify some specific area of a company that is responsible for the bulk of the activities that result in the fabrication and delivery of the company's primary outputs, and that area might properly be called *operations.* However, it is a serious mistake to assume that operations management is applicable to that area alone. Furthermore, our definition of operations management suggests a rather inclusive set of people who might be called operations managers. We address these concerns next when we further explore operations within the organizational context.

## Operations in the Organization

Whether identified as a separate department or not, operations *as a functional activity* must exist in all organizations; some sort of output-generating transformations must be present. In this section, we examine the operations function within the organizational context. After a brief look at company growth and organization structure issues, we focus more closely on the nature of transformation processes, then turn our attention to operations managers—the people responsible for output goods and services.

### *Operations and Other Functional Responsibilities*

We've noted the need for an operations function in all organizations. Equally basic are three other functions; one takes care of money, another design, and the third, demand. Whether the organization is private or public, manufacturing or service, these four functions are present; they are called *line* functions, and managers must see to their accomplishment. In very small start-up companies, the line functions are indistinct and

## EXHIBIT 1-3 Management's Functional Responsibilities

**A. Line management functions: Start-up company**

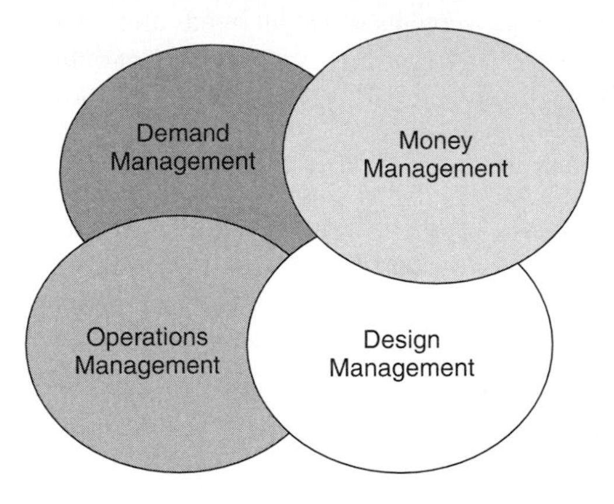


**B. Line and staff functional activities**

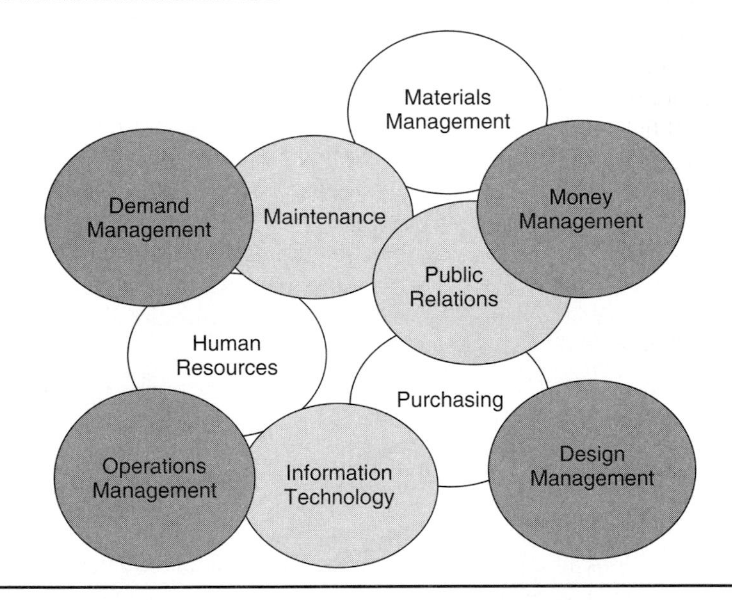


overlapping, as portrayed in Exhibit 1-3A. Quite likely, the two or three founding entrepreneurs share key line responsibilities. As the organization grows, the line functions often form the basis for the first departments, and a functional organizational structure—such as that shown in Exhibit 1-1A—emerges. The boxes on the organization chart might be called finance, research and development, marketing, and operations; or perhaps accounting, design, sales, and production.

Organizational growth ushers in the need for additional types of special skills, and other departments form. Usually, they appear on organization charts as new boxes—human resources, purchasing, materials management, maintenance, information technology, public relations, and so on. These specialized groups are called *staff* departments; they provide support to the line groups. But growth brings problems. The functional boxes truly act like boxes, and cooperation among the functions—line and staff—deteriorates, causing a drop-off in service to customers. The problem is well recognized, and in recent years practitioners and theorists alike have criticized the functional organizational structure. Some of the major complaints suggest that such a structure:

The terms *line* and *staff* have military roots but have become mainstream management terminology. We use them from time to time in later chapters.

- Restricts information flow and/or lengthens information channels thereby delaying response times.
- Facilitates "turf-protection" battles, which lead to inefficient resource allocation.
- Slows decision making, thus lengthening work throughput times.
- Inhibits formation of provider-customer linkages, affecting both internal and external customers.
- Thwarts the efforts of cross-functional teams.

We might shun the ubiquitous functional box-style organization chart in favor of a less formal representation of the functional activities needed for a given project or used by a specific product group, perhaps something like Exhibit 1-3B. Even if we were willing to change the picture from time to time to reflect changing resource requirements, however, we would still fail to completely portray the mechanics by which a top-notch company uses teams, task forces, and other cross-functional groups to satisfy its customers. In fact, some argue that organizational relationships are just too complex to be adequately captured on any sort of chart, but we shall leave that debate to others. We can gain deeper understanding of operations in organizations with a closer look at transformations.

## *Transformations for Goods and Services*

When we think of operations as transformation processes—the fourth definition of operations—and expand Exhibit 1-1B, the result might look something like Exhibit 1-4. First, let's consider the big picture. The company as a whole transforms input resources (examples are depicted on the next page in Exhibit 1-4) into output goods and services for external customers. That's what pays the bills. But equally important to an understanding of operations management is what goes on within the organization. Each functional area conducts its own operations—transformations that yield goods and services for other departments, the internal customers. These relationships among the functions are essentially provider-customer linkages; each area consumes resources as it provides outputs to other organizational entities. Human resources personnel provide training classes (services) and procedures manuals (products) to personnel throughout the organization, for example. Likewise, maintenance associates might provide care for highly specialized or expensive equipment (services) and consumable supplies like photocopier toner (goods).

The *Economist* defines a service as "anything sold in trade that could not be dropped on your foot."

Actually, outputs form a continuum; most are part good and part service. Pure examples at either end—total service or pure goods—are rare. The main differences are

**EXHIBIT 1-4 Transformation Processes**

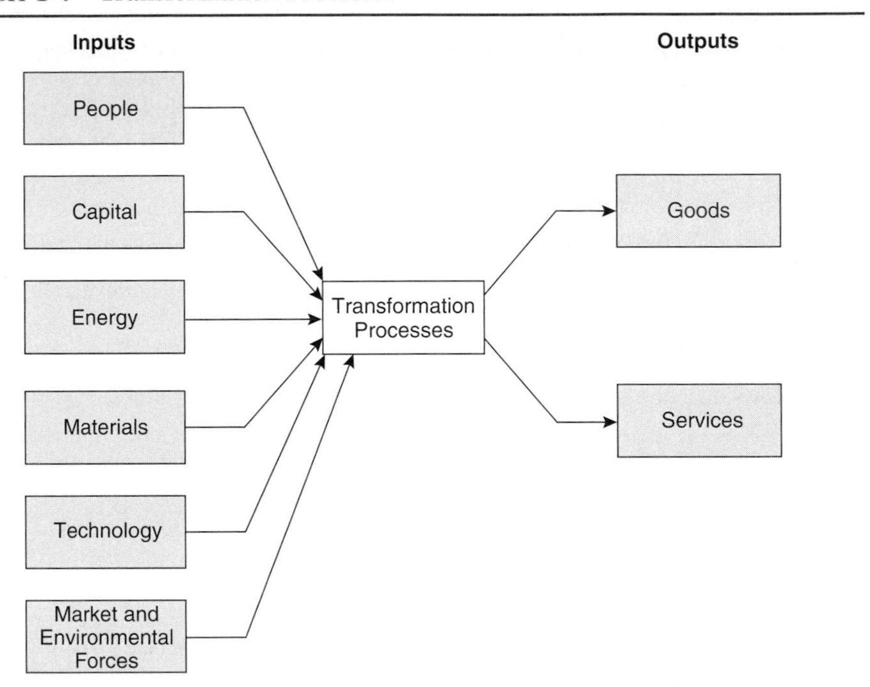


fairly obvious. We can store goods, whereas we consume services as they are provided. Services such as design, janitorial, and freight handling are closely tied to tangible goods: It is tangible items that are designed, maintained, and shipped. In human services, however, it is the client who is transformed. Despite the differences between the two classes of outputs, transformation processes are much the same for both. The following list highlights some of the main commonalties and differences for both goods and services.

**Commonalities**

- Entail customer satisfaction as a key measure of effectiveness.
- Include common measures of satisfaction (e.g., quality and speed).
- Employ the same set of standard process-improvement tools.
- Benefit from both individual initiative and teamwork.
- Can be either prescheduled or provided on demand.
- Require demand forecasting.
- Require design of both the product and the process.
- Can involve routing the product through more than one process.
- Depend on location and arrangement of resources for success.
- Can be provided in either high or low volume and be standard or customized.
- Involve purchase of materials, supplies, and services.
- Require maintenance of equipment, tools, and skills.
- Are subject to automation.

- Are affected by do-it-yourself trends.
- May be either commercial or nonprofit.
- Are shaped by an operations strategy, dovetailing with business strategy.

**Differences**
- Goods may be stored; services are consumed during delivery.
- Goods are transformed from other goods; in services, sometimes the clients themselves are transformed.

Each line in the list includes an object of operations management: satisfaction, forecasting, purchasing, automation, and so forth. They have to be planned for, implemented, and improved. In view of the many commonalities—those listed and others—we treat OM for goods and services together rather than in separate chapters or sections. Where the differences have an impact, we discuss how and why.

The "transformation process" view of operations provides valuable insights mostly about similarities of various OM activities. But, we certainly don't want to give the impression that there are no differences, especially when we consider several rather distinct environments or modes in which operations are conducted.

## *Operations Modes*

Experience is the best teacher, they say. Have you had enough experience, in your personal life if not work life, to relate to the full spectrum of operating environments? Perhaps so—as a trip to a shopping mall illustrates:

- Low on cash? The 24-hour automatic teller at the branch bank in the mall's parking lot, an example of *continuous service* operations, can solve that problem.
- A dedication plaque in a courtyard or atrium of the mall reveals its opening date, construction costs, and other information—reminders that the planning and building of a mall is a massive one-of-a-kind *project* that consists of many smaller operations.
- Inside the mall is a shop offering interior decorating services. Each decorating job, though smaller in scale, shares with the mall the uniqueness of a one-of-a-kind effort typical of *job operations.*
- We may stop for a soft drink, the product of a *continuous production* process at the manufacturer's plant. An accompanying cookie is the result of *batch* production in a bakery.
- *Assembly lines* or *cells* have provided the televisions and computers available in the electronics store and the shoes and clothing in the department store.

The mall trip yields examples from five modes of operations. Those who provide society with shopping malls, cookies, or decorating services have their own types of transformation processes. Tools used to manage these various operations differ

**EXHIBIT 1-5 Operations Modes and Characteristic Focus**

| Process Overview | Functional | Functional | Mixed | Product | Product |
|---|---|---|---|---|---|
| **Volume** | **Lowest (one item)** | **Very low** | **Moderate** | **High** | **Highest** |
| **Variety/Flexibility** | **Highest** | **Highest** | **Moderate** | **Low** | **Lowest** |
| 1. Project. | Construction<br>Computer network installation<br>R&D effort | | | | |
| 2. Job. | | Tool-and-die shop<br>Repair services<br>Portfolio review | | | |
| 3. Batch. | | | Heavy equipment<br>Printing services<br>Cement mixing | | |
| 4. Repetitive. | | | | Auto assembly<br>License processing<br>School registration | |
| 5. Continuous. | | | | | Steel mill<br>Brewery<br>24-hour laundry |

depending on the particular operations mode and its focus. The modes of operations differ along three dimensions: process overview, volume of outputs, and required variety/flexibility. The axes or borders in Exhibit 1-5 show how the three dimensions collectively serve to define each of the five modes. Examples of each appear within the center of the table. Let's look more closely at each mode and its focus.

1. *Project.* Building construction, computer network installation, and research and development (R&D) are one-of-a-kind endeavors, commonly called projects. With large numbers of diverse activities in process at one time, operations management tends to be

*A building under construction illustrates a project mode of operations with unique features and one-of-a-kind large-scale output.*

chopped up. An overview of the process sees functions (design, site planning, budgeting, etc.), rather than the end product itself. Keeping all these functions and their activities straight is a matter of good planning and control of project sequence and timing. Typically, resources—people and equipment—are quite flexible, since they must be able to adapt to the unique features of the given project and contribute differently as the project rolls along.

2. *Job.* The job mode spans the service sector and much of the manufacture of tooling and component parts. Volumes are very low: the few customers at a single table in a restaurant, a police officer on the job at a single traffic accident, a single TV set in for repair, a die set produced in a tool and die shop, or five assemblies of a certain circuit board. Though volumes are low, many different jobs are in various stages of completion at any one time. Managers overseeing the process tend to look at the functions (or departments) and their problems, more than the product (jobs) themselves.

The high variety of jobs in most service centers or job shops requires a high degree of flexibility in employees and facilities. With such high job variety, operations management can become chaotic. The management challenge is to reduce complexity of operations while still providing the sense of unique service that customers expect or the jobs require.

3. *Batch.* In common usage, batch may be anything from a pan of cookies in your kitchen, to a truck full of concrete, to a massive vessel of chocolate, raw rubber, or molten metal in a factory. Our usage is more restrictive. We consider small-scale baking at home to be a job; production in massive vessels is part of continuous processing. Batch processing falls somewhere in between. Moreover, it is intermittent (like job processing), but output consists of standard, familiar items. As befits its center position in Exhibit 1-5, the three characteristics of focus for batch processing are moderate, moderate, and mixed. In a commercial bakery, for example, bakers and their equipment have enough flexibility to produce several varieties of bread and cookies, perhaps a batch of each type daily; but grilling steaks or creating Caesar salads is outside their skill range. Though batch processing shares some of the difficulties found in job operations, familiarity with the output mix precludes many of the surprises faced by job-processing associates.

*Batch processing at Raleigh Tavern Bakery in Williamsburg, Virginia. A batch process is intermittent and is characterized by moderate volume, variety, and flexibility.*

4. *Repetitive.* In repetitive operations, variety is low; labor is trained for, and equipment designed for, a narrow range of applications; and output volume is high. The uniformity and continuity of processing makes it natural to view repetitive operations as a whole product flow rather than a collection of separate processes or functions. Planning, scheduling, counting, and controlling are by the discrete unit or piece. Repetitive services include forms processing, registrations, and processing customers in a tanning salon. In manufacturing, the assembly industries—from automotive to consumer electronics—provide many examples.

5. *Continuous.* Continuous processors are often referred to as the process industry (short for *continuous-flow process*). Production of fluids, grains, flakes, and pellets, as well as the mining of ores, coal, and so forth, fit the category. Makers of small, discrete items (e.g., nails and toothpicks) are also sometimes considered part of the process industry. Planning, scheduling, and controlling such products is by volume, rather than by unit or piece. Output volume is very high, but variety is low. Like repetitive mode, managers view continuous processing in terms of products more than separable processes or functions. Labor and equipment are specialized, and the industry is capital intensive.

Internet-based exercises at the end of the chapter offer numerous examples of companies using each mode of operations.

Both repetitive and continuous operations require elaborate advance planning, but have innate advantages in operation and control. Simple, rather inflexible rules and rigid standards govern operations.

Regardless of the operations mode, however, the fundamental aim in each environment is to improve all dimensions of performance in ways that customers appreciate. This basic concept—serving the customer—was the subtitle in an earlier edition of this book, and its importance in our overall presentation of operations management has remained at center stage. Customers—better yet, *chains of customers*—is our next topic.

## Chains of Customers

Customers . . . obviously important to any business venture . . . who are they and what do they want? And, how should the operations manager, or *any* manager for that matter, manage provider-customer linkages?

### *Defining the Customer*

One of the quickest ways to describe a chain of customers is to imagine a trip to a fast-food outlet. When we request sandwiches at the counter, for example, the server will relay our order to an associate who is cooking food at a grill. The cook passes the sandwiches out to the server (the internal customer), who in turn passes them on to us, the external customers.

Previously, in our discussion of transformation processes, we noted that many people in organizations perform activities that serve internal customers. As with our cook in the fast-food establishment, all of them have one or more people targeted to receive the results of their efforts. The old view of customer, limited to someone outside the organization, is too narrow. The newer view, however, defines the **customer** as the next process, wherever the work goes next. Whoever is to receive the work that I am doing—my boss, my subordinate, an associate in the purchasing department, a secretary, a company auditor, anyone—is my customer.

Waiters, sales associates, providers of personal services, and others whose jobs bring them into frequent contact with external customers are typically given training in customer relations. They are taught to listen to customers and to pay attention to opportunities for better service. Operations managers should encourage all employees to embrace the next-process-as-customer concept, for such a view allows people deep inside the organization, perhaps far removed from the final user, to also develop sensitivities about what customers want.

The next-process-as-customer idea is owed to the late Kaoru Ishikawa, one of the giants of the quality movement.

## *Basic Customer Wants*

Though customers may, at least in the short run, be unable to fully articulate what they want, their real or underlying requirements may have three components:

1. A statement of recognized need—what is being sought or ordered.
2. The expected manner in which that need should be met.
3. Some idea of the benefits or value accrued by having that need met.[3]

This is the customer's view. The provider's (or supplier's) view of the requirement is called a **specification.** The "spec" is the provider's target, and should match the customer's actual requirement quite closely. Generally, when the provider-customer linkage is a close or familiar one, specs are more likely to match requirements.

Throughout the world of commerce, of course, customers' specific requirements are too numerous to identify. Yet, the number of persistent, general, wants can be narrowed to a short list (see Exhibit 1-6), and they seem to apply universally. Whether the relationship is business-to-consumer or business-to-business, both internal and external customers have six general requirements:

1. *High levels of quality.* From the customers' standpoint, quality has multiple dimensions. Evidence in recent years suggests that quality may be the primary requirement.
2. *A high degree of flexibility.* Customers admire a provider's ability to react easily to shifting requirements and irregular arrival patterns.

**EXHIBIT 1-6 General Customer Requirements**

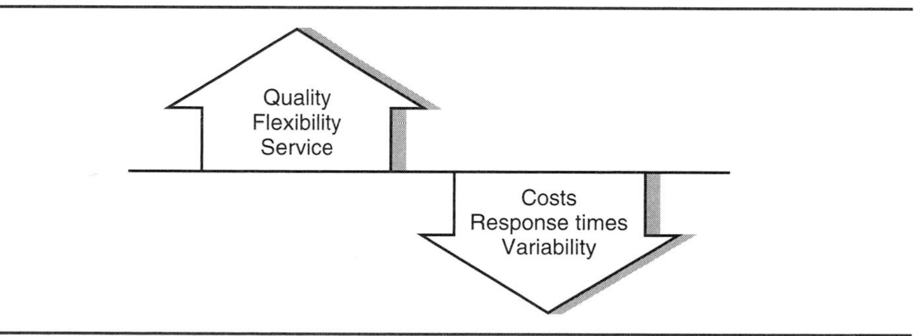

3. *High levels of service.* Subjective measures of customer service include humanity in service delivery; objective measures can include having a required item in stock.
4. *Low costs.* External customers are price conscious; internal customers are concerned when they see costly wastes.
5. *Quick response (speed).* Customers want delay-free service and quick response to changing requirements. The provider aims to satisfy by shortening cycle times and quickly introducing attractive new goods and services.
6. *Little or no variability.* Customers expect consistency; the ideal is zero deviation from targeted or expected results.

These six requirements are part of the foundation of a well-conceived operations management system. Inasmuch as they apply to internal as well as external customers, the requirements have a unifying effect, that is, they permit each employee along the chains of customers to have a common, small set of goals. Being linked to the final customer also gives these goals the stature of being important, not artificial, which can make the work more personally meaningful. Scott Adams, creator of the Dilbert cartoon series, which pokes irreverent fun at popular management concepts, cautions employed people about going overboard on the customer. He tells them,

> You, personally, are No. 1—you!—and then your family and then your co-workers. And somewhere after that is the customer and the stockholder. Of course, it's often in your, your family's, and the stockholders' best interest to treat customers as No. 1.[4]

Don't view the requirements shown in Exhibit 1-6 as potential trade-offs. Customers don't. As consumers, we don't want to settle for quality but at the expense of fast delivery, or for low costs at the expense of good service. We want all of these, and business customers are no different. Customers want increasing performance—in the direction of the arrows in Exhibit 1-6—on all six dimensions. In sum, regarding meeting customer needs, we might state a prescription for better operations management: Excel in one dimension, move on to another and excel in it, then on to a third, and so on. And post results; visible evidence of performance improvement can be quite motivating.

It is challenging for a provider to try to meet multiple customer requirements, but there are plenty of examples of companies who succeed. The Into Practice box "Customers Are the Center of Our Universe" illustrates.

### Value-Building Linkages

As we have seen, provider-customer linkages may be intradepartmental, may transcend departmental walls, or may cross company boundaries. Each link serves as a conduit for the flow of materials, data, instructions, and so forth. Furthermore, there is a cost associated with each link; the connection itself must be operated, maintained, and perhaps upgraded from time to time. Two concerns emerge:

1. Is the linkage an efficient one? Is the customer—the recipient in the linkage—being served correctly?
2. Is the linkage necessary? Is it providing benefits to the organization(s) involved?

INTO PRACTICE

## "Customers Are the Center of Our Universe"

That statement is engraved in the lobby at the Jacksonville, Florida, headquarters of AT&T's Universal Card Services (UCS) Company, a 1992 winner of the Malcolm Baldrige national quality award. UCS has a close partner, Total System Services, Inc. (TSYS), which provides hardware and software support for UCS's credit card operations. Top executives at UCS use a PC-based information system to monitor quality, availability (of hardware to customer service associates), capacity, and inventory. Both partners post daily statistics on accuracy, speed, response time, and customer satisfaction measures throughout their business sites. Average phone response time to customers, for example, is within 2.6 seconds. TSYS keeps its 20 Tandem fault-tolerant processors running 24 hours per day, seven days a week, with 99.5 percent availability.

Source: Chetan S. Sankar, William R. Boulton, Nancy W. Davidson, and Charles A. Snyder, "Building a World-Class Alliance: The Universal Card—TSYS Case," *Academy of Management Executive,* 9, no. 2 (1995), pp. 20–29.

We can resolve the first concern by drawing on insights gained in the preceding section. If requirements are known and properly conveyed to the provider, and if the six basic customer wants are being met, then we can give a thumbs-up to efficiency. If, however, response is delayed or costs escalate, for instance, we know something about the nature of needed corrective action, and can proceed accordingly.

The second concern is more troubling, and not so easy to resolve. It gets at value—the same issue that underscores our fifth definition of operations. Simply put, does the linkage add value that exceeds the costs? The response must look beyond the immediate provider-customer link and consider multiple steps or multiple linkages along the chain. That is, managers must look at the bigger picture and ask, "What do the customers further down the line that includes final consumers think? What value do they assign to these goods and services?"

Equally important is the stability, or lack thereof, attached to the customer perceptions. **Value migration** is the term used to denote changing customer values, changes that can include both *what* customers value (seek most) at a particular time and *where* along the chains of supply they expect to find it. Slywotzky and Morrison, Boston-based consultants specializing in customer- and profit-centric business design, warn managers to look beyond just the immediate provider-customer step:

> In a value migration world, our vision must include two, three, or even four customers along the value chain. So, for example, a component supplier must understand the economic motivations of the manufacturer who buys the components, the distributor who takes the manufacturer's products to sell, and the end-use consumer.[5]

As perhaps additional evidence that the management of service operations is not unlike management of manufacturing operations, we note that concerns surrounding

**Value chain**
A series of transformation processes that move a good or service from inception to final consumer.

value migration go beyond manufacturing. Again, from Slywotzky and Morrison:

> This (value migration) phenomenon stretches across all industries today. Business book publishers, for example, must understand booksellers, *and* corporations that buy books, *and* the individual readers within those companies. Hotel managers must understand travel agents, *and* corporations that have offsite meetings, *and* the human resources people who organize the corporate offsites, *and* the people at the company that will be attending the offsite.[6]

Clearly, the issues of value and its migration are important to operations managers. They must ensure not only that the next-process customers' needs are being served but that—as a whole—the chain continues to meet the changing value expectations of each customer along the way.

### *Value- or Supply-Chain Management*

Keeping an eye on value and its migration is a challenging task. Unfortunately, non-value-adding wastes can emerge at any step along the value chain, and customers—again, somewhere along the line—experience (or at least perceive) a loss in value. Defining waste as anything "that does not add value to the product or service, whether material, equipment, space, time, energy, systems, or human activity of any sort" is a contribution of Robert W. Hall, long a respected voice in the OM field.[7] And while getting rid of wastes in the organization's transformation processes is a principal goal of operations management, doing the same all along the supply chain is a fundamental goal of value-chain or supply-chain management.

In fact, operations management, value-chain management, and supply-chain management share many common objectives. The Contrast box "What's in a Chain?" suggests that name differences may be mostly a matter of discipline. Although we make occasional reference to value and supply chains in this book, we prefer to think in terms of chains of customers, primarily due to a body of knowledge that has been used to help companies strengthen their internal provider-customer linkages.[8] We consider those linkages next.

### *Employees as Customers*

Treat employees like customers? Certainly! At least that's what Colleen Barrett, as the number two executive at Southwest Airlines, expected from company managers in the mid-1990s. In a *Fortune* survey, Southwest was selected at that time as one of the best companies in America to work for. It still is. The company was named to the number two spot in *Fortune*'s latest survey.[9]

Companies that strive for a customer focus soon find that it requires broad changes in the management of their human resources. People must unite across department lines if the organization as a whole is to provide quality and responsive service at low costs. In this cause, OM and organizational behavior (OB) have much to share—OM provides the objectives and OB provides the tools of cooperation and teamwork.

A few years ago, many consultants felt the need to press the case for increasing use of cross-functional teams as effective weapons against organizational waste. Notable successes, however, from well-known corporate giants such as Motorola, Caterpillar, General Electric, Lucent Technologies, Pfizer, and Maytag have left little doubt of the

CONTRAST

## What's in a Chain?

**Value Chain**

- Series of transformation processes that move a good or service from inception to final consumer. Ideally, each step increases the worth or value of the item in the eyes of the next customer.
- Used largely in economics and strategic management disciplines.

**Supply Chain**

- "The supply chain, which is also referred to as the *logistics network,* consists of suppliers, manufacturing centers, warehouses, distribution centers, and retail outlets, as well as raw materials, work-in-process inventory, and finished products that flow between the facilities."[10]
- Used largely in purchasing and materials management disciplines.

**Customer Chain**

- Provider-customer links, extending from origin of a product or service through sale to the end consumer and on to postsale service. Every employee has a customer-the next process, or where the work goes next. Also, each employee *is* a customer of the previous process.
- Used largely in quality assurance, operations management, and marketing disciplines.

power that trained teams of employees can bring to bear in process improvement efforts. Generally, teams are more successful when team members:

1. Understand the value-adding sequences of transformations that occur within their own company, between their company and its suppliers, and between their company and its customers.
2. Are trained in fundamental problem-solving, data-gathering and analysis, and communications tools.
3. Operate in a customer-as-next-process environment.

In the chapters ahead, we have much more to say about teamwork and involving employees in transformation process improvements. For now, we simply note that the next-process idea makes it clear that every employee has a customer. Just as clearly, everyone *is* a customer as well.

When the customer focus is well entrenched, employees strive to provide excellence. How do their companies fare? That's our next topic.

## Competitive Excellence

Teamwork, when properly applied, is now a widely accepted tool for planning, implementing, and improving processes. Likewise, firms today have a better understanding of the positive benefits that can accrue when they properly apply the full breadth of contemporary OM tools.

Success is a complex variable, and as with many other topics, measures of success will emerge in most chapters of this book. Here, we are after an overview, and reemphasize two comments from the chapter's introduction:

1. Successful companies are focused on their customers. They provide goods and services that their customers want, and they do so in ways that attract new customers and compel existing ones to come back for more.
2. Those sought-after goods and services flow from the operations of the successful provider businesses. They are the outputs of carefully planned and executed transformation processes.

And, from our discussion of customer chains, we might add a third point:

3. When the customer focus is extended to include employees, final customers are likely to find a provider that is much more adept at understanding what customers want and finding ways to meet those needs.

The emphasis on customer opinion figures strongly in any general measure of overall company success. Furthermore, continued customer support is crucial in attaining the financial performance necessary for any private-sector firm to survive. In this section, we take a glimpse at two ways by which overall competitive excellence is noted, and conclude with a few comments about success measurement in general.

### *American Customer Satisfaction Index (ACSI)*

A wealth of detail about the ACSI, including annual score trends since its inception in 1994, may be found at its web site: http://acsi.asq.org.

(End-of-chapter exercises suggest specific activities to better understand the ACSI.)

The National Quality Research Center at the University of Michigan's School of Business Administration administers a national customer satisfaction index. Claes Fornell of the center first created the index for Sweden in 1989. Germany set up its own similar index in 1992, and several other countries are at work on theirs.

The U.S. version, called the American Customer Satisfaction Index (ACSI), had its start in 1994. The data come from telephone interviews from a sample of the nation's households. Respondents report on their usage of a company's product, and satisfaction registers on a scale of 0 (lowest) to 100 (highest).[11] From its inception, the ACSI has grown to include companies representing a wide range of private-sector industries and various public administration and government agencies as well. In 1999, the U.S. Internal Revenue Service (IRS) began using the ACSI as a measure of its overall performance in providing service to taxpayers.[12]

The ACSI provides a way for a company to compare itself over time and benchmark against industry averages. It may also help predict future performance and show customer acceptance of a new company initiative. Fornell and his colleagues believe the index also can gauge a sector's and a country's performance better than, say, the consumer price index.[13] Exchange rates, trade, and other factors can push and pull on consumer prices. Marketers may sometimes be able to manipulate customer satisfaction, but not much and not for long.

### *Best Company Surveys*

Business periodicals such as *BusinessWeek, Fortune,* and *IndustryWeek* conduct regular surveys in which respondents are asked to identify companies or plants that stand out on various dimensions of competitive excellence. The Into Practice box "Examples of Excellence" provides some details about three such surveys that were reported at around the turn of the century.

INTO PRACTICE

# Examples of Excellence

- The 10 winners in *IndustryWeek*'s annual America's Best Plant Awards represent the rich diversity of both the Nation's industrial output and regional manufacturing excellence—for example, Dell's computers from Texas, JLG Industries' self-propelled aerial work platforms from Pennsylvania, and Raytheon's aerospace vehicle components from Arizona. These companies report some astounding achievements. Combined performance figures for the past five years include a median productivity increase (value-added per employee) of 55%; a reduction in cycle time (the time from start of production to completion of product) of 54.5%; and a 30.9% return on net assets (profitability divided by average net assets in use). What's the secret?

  > "One facet is a culture of mutual trust and respect. Production teams at these facilities, armed with appropriate training and detailed information on company performance, wage an all-out war on waste."

  —Source: "America's Best Plants," *IndustryWeek,* October 13, 1999.

- San Diego–based Qualcomm, whose superior financial performance in the late 1990s is legendary, credits much of its success to managers who sweat the small stuff, like ball bearings and seconds of assembly time. When the company manufactured its first generation of cellular telephones in 1995, it took a team of 60 employees three hours to build each phone. Qualcomm simplified the design, eliminated component parts such as ball bearings, springs, and pins; and now, 16 employees can turn out a phone in 15 minutes. As for eliminating time waste, Qualcomm engineer Howard Kukla notes, "You may think a second or two doesn't matter . . . but when you're talking about the volume of phones we're making here, it makes a difference."

  —Source: "Secrets of Fastest Growing companies," *Fortune,* September 6, 1999.

- Can companies be outstanding employers and at the same time excel financially? Consider a profile of the 100 best companies to work for in America (as defined by a *Fortune* survey, heavily weighted by survey feedback from over 33,000 randomly selected employees). Headquartered in 30 different states, these 100 companies represent 20 different industry groups with information technology and financial services accounting for just over 40% of the total. But retailing, pipe manufacturing, supermarkets, jam production, and law firms are also represented. Shares of the 58 publicly traded companies in the group have significantly outperformed the S&P 500 in three-year comparisons. For the 49 that have been public for 10 years or longer, the annualized returns are nearly 24% higher than the S&P index over the ten-year period.

  —Source: "The 100 Best Companies to Work For," *Fortune,* January 10, 2000.

Whether the mark of excellence is "best plant," "fastest growing company," "best company to work for," or some other title, the bottom line is that the company has excelled. The examples in the box provide insights, however, about the nature of competitive excellence:

- Higher productivity (value added per employee) and reduced cycle times are hallmarks of improved operations—better transformation processes. Yet, they are accompanied by superior financial performance (return on net assets) as well.
- Teams of employees, and managers, too, "sweat the small stuff"; they wage war on waste. The improvements at Qualcomm—simplified design, fewer parts, and elimination of time waste—are also classic indicators of OM performance enhancement. Yet, again, there are accompanying financial rewards.
- Though not obvious from the box discussion (but noted in the source articles), companies that take care of employees often invest heavily in superior compensation packages, training, and other benefits to improve quality of work life. But, the culture of treating people well apparently pays off on the financial bottom line. ". . . A culture of mutual trust and respect" is mentioned as one reason for success.

True, companies occasionally stumble, let their guards down perhaps, and fall out of favor. Many of these return to excellence, however, and many other companies seem able to exhibit consistently superior performance. As we have noted, there are numerous indicators of organizational success, some more closely associated with OM improvement programs than others. We examine specifics in later chapters, but now let's turn to the big picture.

### *Success Measures in General*

On the one hand, we don't want to suggest that any company owes all of its success solely to improvements in its operations *functional area.* Rather, our prescription is for all functions to render appropriate contributions to overall success by embracing the customer-as-next-process idea. Establish chains of customers within the organization, keep an eye on the needs of the next process, and look down the chain a few steps as well.

On the other hand, when we consider operations as *activities,* that is, as transformation processes that occur throughout the organization, we can make a case that well-managed operations *are* the underlying causes for organizational success. Regardless of the proximate driver—better sales support, more accurate client databases, shorter response times, more favorable financial arrangements, whatever—any success can be traced to customer-oriented employees who are minding the store.

## OM and You

M. Scott Myers, a respected management author and consultant, states that every employee is a manager . . . a manager of his or her immediate workplace.[14] Indeed, the responsibilities inherent in any job include the duty to make effective use of resources under one's control. This inclusive concept of manager dovetails nicely with our belief that every employee is responsible for staying connected with the customer—the next process.

In this, the last section of Chapter 1, we make our case that OM is important to you.

### *Operations Managers*

The job of attacking non-value-adding wastes in an organization's transformation processes is too important to be left up to people with the word *manager* in their titles. It is a job for the entire workforce, who, taken collectively, are the operations managers. They include:

1. *The associates who provide the service or make the product.* These people, sometimes called front-liners, are located throughout the organization. They strive to meet their customers' demands exactly and devise ways to improve outputs and processes. In good companies, these people are seasoned veterans of cross-functional teams and are skilled in data collection and analysis, problem solving, and waste eradication. Moreover, they understand what value adding is all about.
2. *First-line supervisors.* The proper role for these individuals involves little traditional supervision. Rather, they are facilitators who coordinate mixtures of human and physical resources in the cause of customer satisfaction and continuous improvement.
3. *Upper-level managers.* These people manage the training, reward, and recognition systems with an eye to helping junior associates improve their skills. Good managers are teachers and coaches. These people also coordinate allocation of larger amounts of resources, including—but not limited to—the skills of staff personnel.
4. *Staff personnel.* Designers, buyers, trainers, hirers, engineers, schedulers, maintenance technicians, accountants, IT specialists, inspectors, lawyers, and analysts provide necessary expertise throughout any organization. Staff personnel also plan for change and serve on process improvement teams.

White collar or blue, salaried or hourly, line or staff; these distinctions don't mean much in organizations of the type we considered in the preceding section. When all employees are treated as customers, it is much easier for them to be managers as well.

### *Your OM Experience*

Maybe operations management is your major, maybe not. It really doesn't matter, because if you haven't done so already, you will perform operations management activities during your career. As an accountant, for example, you may occupy a staff position if your company is a manufacturer or provider of health care services. But if your company sells accounting or consulting services, you might well be a frontline associate. Similarly, you might put your degree in human resources management to work as a training specialist in a staff position for a telecommunications company, but if your employer makes its money by selling human resources management services, you are likely to be a front-liner. Of course, your career progression might lead to a supervisory or upper management position.

Becoming an operations manager is not so much a matter of your having a position within some company's functional area called "operations" as it is the very real likelihood of your being responsible for transformation processes—wherever in the organization they might occur. Regardless of your degree, job title, company, or industry, your employer will expect you to manage your work area and serve your customers—internal and external.

Moreover, if you and a majority of your associates accept that challenge and embrace the customer focus, your company stands a good change of achieving competitive excellence. And that bodes well for your future!

## Summary Check Points

- ✓ Successful companies provide goods and services that their customers seek out. Those goods and services flow from operations that have been carefully planned and implemented.
- ✓ The word *operations* may refer to total business activities, key income-producing activities, a functional area within an organization, transformation processes, and individual steps within transformation processes.
- ✓ *Management* as an activity consists of three general, overlapping, and iterative sets of duties—creating, implementing, and improving.
- ✓ *Operations management* is the set of activities for creating, implementing, and improving processes that transform resource inputs into output goods and services. OM activities may be appropriately applied anywhere in organizations and may target any level of effort from a single step in a job sequence to the entirety of company activity.
- ✓ As a key functional activity, operations management must exist in all organizations; along with demand management, financial management, and design management, it is a fundamental or *line function.* Supporting activities are called *staff functions.*
- ✓ Outputs form a continuum—most are part good and part service. Despite any differences in outputs, the transformation processes needed to create them are largely similar.
- ✓ There are five general modes of operations that may be found in organizations: project, job, batch, repetitive, and continuous. The modes differ along the dimensions of process overview, output volume, and required variety and flexibility.
- ✓ The *customer* is the next process—wherever one's work goes. Customers may be internal or external.
- ✓ The six basic customer wants are increasing quality, service, and flexibility; along with decreasing cost, response times, and output variability. These are not trade-offs; customers want them all.

- ✓ Customers perceive value increase possibilities all along the supply chain. *Value migration* refers to changes in what customers perceive to be of value and where they expect to find it.
- ✓ *Waste* is anything that does not add value to the product or service, whether material, equipment, space, time, energy, systems, or human activity of any sort.
- ✓ The *employee-as-customer* concept is a cornerstone for attaining superior outputs through cross-functional teams of employees.
- ✓ The *American Customer Satisfaction Index (ACSI)* provides a way for a company to compare its performance changes over time and against industry averages.
- ✓ Top business publications, through surveys and other assessment tools, identify companies or plants that stand out in one or more dimensions of competitive excellence.
- ✓ Operations managers include associates who make products or render services, supervisors, upper-level managers, and staff members.
- ✓ Regardless of your major or intended career path, you will perform operations management activities during your career.

## Exercises

[Note to the student: Additional exercises for each chapter may be found on the CD-ROM that accompanies *Operations Management: Meeting Customers' Demands,* 7th ed.]

1. Pick two organizations—one known primarily as a manufacturer and the other primarily as a services provider—that have a significant commercial interest in each of the following sectors: health care, automotive, education, retailing, travel and leisure, and sports and recreation. For each organization:
   *a.* Define the primary business activity. (Note: You should back up your assessment with data from the organization).
   *b.* Examine financial documents. On the income statement, how are earnings from operations stated? (Hint: Access to financial records might be easier for publicly traded companies.)
   *c.* Review the organizational chart; does it reflect a functional area called *operations*? If so, what are its components? If not, what name is used to identify the operations function?
   *d.* Draw a diagram similar to Exhibit 1-4 denoting key inputs, transformations, and specific outputs for a primary business activity.
2. List the steps that you would have to take in order to perform the tasks listed below. Be thorough; remember travel, cognitive as well as active steps, materials, necessary tools, preparation, cleanup, and so forth. With the end output as a focus, rate each step from 1 to 5, with 1 being "total waste" and 5 being "total value-added." Discuss your assessments with an emphasis on rationale for ratings and possibilities for improvement.
   *a.* Paint the interior walls in the kitchen and bedroom where you currently live.
   *b.* Create and maintain a membership database for an academic or professional organization.
   *c.* Accumulate a wardrobe (on a somewhat modest budget) for wear in your first postgraduation job; business dress will be required.

*d.* Prepare and deliver a 30–40-minute formal class presentation on a research topic assigned by your professor. You will have three classmates as fellow team members.

3. Interview three managers from different organizations; ask them to describe their duties. Construct a list for each manager and classify each duty as (primarily) oriented toward creating, implementing, or improving. Share your findings with two classmates, and develop a collective assessment of the jobs performed by the nine managers in your data set.
4. Chapter 1 identifies four line functions of any organization. Sometimes, however, operations—when viewed as the company's primary business activity—encompasses one of the other functions. Operations in an architectural firm, for instance, might consist of creating building designs. Give an example of this same phenomenon (operations encompassing another function) for the other two line functions and for one staff function.
5. Interview two managers who have experience working within functional organizational structures. Ask them to relate advantages and disadvantages of that form of organization. Share your findings with two classmates, and develop a collective report on your findings.
6. For each employee position listed below, give an example of a next-process customer. Also, give an example in which the listed employee position would be the next-process customer.
   *a.* Cost accountant for a state Department of Natural Resources.
   *b.* Console designer employed by an automobile manufacturer.
   *c.* Market analyst employed by a brokerage firm.
   *d.* Employee benefits counselor for a large bank.
   *e.* Computer software training specialist employed by a university.
   *f.* Civil engineer in a professional engineering firm.
   *g.* Maintenance technician employed by a major airline.
7. For each employee position listed in Exercise 6 (above), extend the customer chain on downstream to a "final" consumer.
8. For each of the following examples, determine the primary mode of operations: project, job, batch, repetitive, or continuous. Briefly explain your decision.
   *a.* Soft-drink bottling plant
   *b.* Dry-cleaning establishment
   *c.* Resort hotel
   *d.* Cafeteria
   *e.* CPA office
   *f.* Highway construction site
   *g.* Laptop computer assembly cell
   *h.* On-line book seller
   *i.* Emergency rescue service facility
   *j.* College or university student advising office
   *k.* Farm at harvest time
   *l.* Commercial bank
9. For each of the examples in Exercise 8 (above), identify any secondary operations mode that might be found. (Hint: There could be more than one secondary mode.)
10. Visit the Operations Management Center (OMC) home page at: http://www.mhhe.com/business/opsci/pom/ Look in the left-center of the screen for the company tours; you will find over 50 virtual tours of company plants and other facilities. Take four tours of your own choosing, and for each tour:
    *a.* Identify the company and the general process style or overview (functional, product, or mixed). What leads you to this classification?
    *b.* Describe the primary operations mode, and briefly describe the output products.
    *c.* Position each of the companies (mentally) along the diagonal of Exhibit 1-5. How well does what you learned on the tour match descriptions offered in your text? Discuss.
11. Fifteen examples (three from each of the common modes of operations) are shown in Exhibit 1-5. Select one example, interview someone who works in your selected job

environment, and prepare a report addressing the following:
   *a.* Describe the nature of the industry; the company or agency mission; the volume, variety, and flexibility characteristics; and the process overview.
   *b.* From your interview data and your own observations and research, describe the various uses of any major tools or equipment employed by the person you interviewed to carry out his or her job.

12. Explain how the six basic customer wants apply in each of the following settings:
    *a.* Air traffic control
    *b.* Database management
    *c.* Pharmaceuticals manufacturing
    *d.* Legal services
    *e.* Commercial shipping and delivery services
13. Define your personal priority sequence (from most important to least important) among the six basic customer wants for two significant products that you plan to buy within the next year. Do the same for two services that you buy on a regular basis. Do you anticipate that your priorities might change in the future for these goods and services? Discuss.
14. Jane told her friends that she was thinking about buying a sweater for $80 at a retail outlet in a mall. Jerry informed her that she should look for it in a discount store; he was sure that she could save $10 or possibly $15. Janet argued that a manufacturer's outlet store would be even cheaper; she guessed that about $55–$60 would be the going price for the sweater. Jack chimed in with a suggestion that Internet shopping would yield the best price, since there were fewer "middlemen" to demand a cut. Joan looked up from her coffee and, in her usual "cut to the chase" style, said that Jane should buy the sweater at whatever place she felt most comfortable with the value she would receive for what she paid.

    Is this a value-added issue? Or a "markup" issue? Is there really a difference? What do you think of Joan's advice? Discuss.
15. Louis bought his desktop computer system from a locally owned computer store for $3,500, a price that included delivery and setup, complete checkout, and free on-site maintenance for six months. Linda bought the identical computer system from a local discount electronics store for $2,900. The store did a complete systems check, but Linda took the computer home and assembled it herself. Her warranty included six months of in-store maintenance. Larry used the Internet to buy the same system for $2,100 directly from the manufacturer (assembler). If problems arose, Larry had benefit of telephone service, but if that could not solve the problem, he would have to ship the computer to a designated repair center.

    How does the concept of value emerge in this example? Consider perception of value- and supply-chain waste in your responses.
16. Sheila is director of purchasing for a regional fast-food outlet chain. She reports directly to the company president. Given her position, should she treat any of her employees as customers? Explain.
17. Visit The American Customer Service Index (ACSI) web site at http://acsi.asq.org
    *a.* Write a brief report that describes the nature, funding, developmental history, and rationale for the ACSI.
    *b.* Explain how the index is constructed and what it reveals about the measured companies.
    *c.* Briefly discuss how the measured companies are selected for inclusion.
18. Visit The American Customer Service Index (ACSI) web site at http://acsi.asq.org
    *a.* Find the index score reports. Then select two industry sectors, and from each sector select two companies whose products or services you use. Record the index scores of these companies for the reported years. Discuss your findings.

   *b.* Do the scores match your personal satisfaction with each company's goods and services? Why or why not?
   *c.* Pick any company (in any sector) that appears to have superior scores on the ACSI. Then, visit that company's web page, look at its annual report, or review its advertisements. To what extent does the company advertise its ACSI score status? Discuss.

19. Obtain a "best companies" report from a recent issue of *BusinessWeek, Fortune, IndustryWeek,* or some other business publication. Prepare a short report on the nature of the accomplishments being praised by the article. To what extent might the accomplishments be attributed to well-managed company operations? Explain.
20. Select three jobs that quite possibly lie in your future career. For each job:
   *a.* List the types of resources that you will most likely be asked to manage.
   *b.* List the outputs that you are likely to be asked to generate.
   *c.* List positions of people who are likely to be on your internal customer list.
   *d.* Extend your influence down the customer chain by listing potential provider-customer links until you reach the final consumer.

CHAPTER 2

# OM STRATEGY: DYNAMIC COMPETITIVENESS

A look back through dictionaries for the word *strategy* or *strategic* is revealing. If we go back to, say, before 1955, we will find the word but the definitions refer to warfare, not business. For example, one of these early dictionaries calls *strategy* "planning and directing of military movements and operations."[1]

Applying the military concept to business, however, was a natural. Both have complex assemblages of resources to plan for and move out against the "enemy," which in business is more politely referred to as the competition. General Electric is credited with being the first company to fashion a strategic plan, in the 1950s. After that, management consultants, business schools, and large organizations of all kinds became advocates and adopters of strategic planning, and today, the subject is a widely accepted field of study. Thompson and Strickland, respected authorities in the field, define **strategy** with an emphasis on its purpose:

> A company's strategy is the "game plan" management has for positioning the company in its chosen market arena, competing successfully, pleasing customers, and achieving good business performance.[2]

We begin this chapter with a general look at the nature of strategy itself and recognize that any OM strategy must be an integral part of the bigger picture—that is, the overall strategy for the organization. Next, we narrow our focus to OM. A brief historical perspective sheds light on some of the notable milestones that help define modern OM strategies. We then turn our attention to forces that drive modern business and shape global competition, emphasizing ways in which OM contributes to the competitiveness and overall economic well-being of the organization. We close the chapter with a reminder that strategic planning alone is not good enough.

Throughout our discussion, bear in mind that the word *dynamic* is in the chapter title for a reason: Strategy is a game plan, but the playing field is a changing one.

## Strategy: The Business Game Plan

The Into Practice box "Strategy—Aims and Actions" presents a small sampling of strategic plans and actions from some well-known corporations. Aims drive actions; Bayer's desire to be the supplier of choice, IBM's plan for enhancing its research capabilities, and GE's e-commerce initiative all cause the companies to, as Bayer puts it,

INTO PRACTICE

## Strategy—Aims and Actions

Two of the 17 guidelines for the strategic alignment of German-based Bayer AG:

> "Our aim is to be our customers' supplier of choice. Customer benefit and satisfaction are paramount, and we act accordingly."
>
> "Our aim is to steadily increase corporate value and obtain an above average return on capital."[3]

* * * * * * * * * *

"IBM is hoping new incentives and a fresh outlook that takes researchers into the field to meet customers will encourage more (of its people to exhibit) entrepreneurial drive. It seems to be working . . . research is turning around . . . the division has soared back to near its all-time high in personnel . . . and opened labs in Austin, Beijing, and Delhi. Chairman Lou Gerstner showcases research as central to IBM's revitalization. . . ."[4]

* * * * * * * * * *

At the beginning of 1999, General Electric CEO Jack Welch declared that e-business would be a major GE strategic initiative. "Welch's initiatives are not flavors of the month; in 19 years as CEO he has announced (but) four." When such an event occurs at General Electric—America's most admired corporation for three years in a row—however, the implementation is companywide and focused. Whether in its plastics distribution business (referred to as Polymerland) or in its Power Systems division, the intent of the new e-commerce is to enhance connections with customers.[5]

* * * * * * * * * *

"AngloDutch consumer-products giant Unilever plans to close 100 plants and shed 25,000 employees—about 10% of its workforce. The company wants to focus on about 400 top brands such as Lipton Tea and Calvin Klein fragrances and lose 1,800 marginal ones."[6]

"act accordingly." Unilever's desire to narrow its product line and focus on its better performers—a worthy objective—serves as a reminder that strategic plans can also drive downsizing and other perhaps unpleasant outcomes. While customers figure prominently in the examples, competitive advantage is a parallel agenda, lurking just below the surface.

Although we would not expect any two companies to have identical strategies, there seem to be some attributes that fit most organizations. First on this list is the degree to which strategy incorporates key elements and addresses key constituents.

### *Ingredients of Strategy*

In the early 1980s, in a simple yet powerful statement on the essence of good strategy, Kenichi Ohmae put the focus on *customers, competitors,* and the *company itself*—the three components of what he called the **strategic triangle.**[7] Ohmae's focus remains valid; we need but flesh out and update the details. A business strategy that is complete and competitive within contemporary business settings must:

- Fit the existing business environment—by addressing customers' needs and competitors' capabilities—yet be capable of anticipating change and responding appropriately.

- Provide a basis for linkages with key partners along the supply or value chain—suppliers, transporters, distributors, wholesalers, retailers, and end consumers.
- Incorporate the activities of *all* of the company's major line functions: finance, design and development, marketing, and operations.
- Extend into staff activities as well, providing clear rationale for development of supporting provider-customer chains throughout the organization.
- Specify dimensions of desired company performance.
- Promote a climate of continuous improvement.

In sum, a sound contemporary strategy keeps customers, competitors, and company at center stage; extends the concept of company resources to incorporate value-chain partners; and recognizes the need to manage change while continuing to meet performance objectives. And, it addresses the need for continuous improvement.

### *Continuous Improvement as Strategy*

To be effective as strategy, continuous improvement must account for the needs of customers and competencies of competitors, and it must build on the organization's capacities and capabilities. Furthermore, it cannot be confined to the ranks of managers and technical experts; it must be woven into the fabric of everyday work for all employees.

The Japanese term for continuous improvement, **kaizen,** is used in some Western firms.

Continuous improvement got its start in leading Japanese export companies, and was adopted by competing companies elsewhere in the world. The idea is to continually, and incrementally, change and improve *everything:* equipment, procedures, employee skills, throughout time, quality, supplier relations, product and service designs, and so on.

Since this idea and many supporting techniques were perfected first at Toyota, they have been called the **Toyota production system.** In an MIT study of worldwide automobile assembly, the system was labeled **lean production.** According to the study's authors,

> [It] is lean because it uses less of everything . . . half the human effort in the factory, half the manufacturing space, half the investment in tools, half the engineering hours to develop a new product in half the time. Also, it requires keeping far less than half the needed inventory on site, results in many fewer defects, and produces a greater and ever growing variety of products.[8]

The lean production approach is so persuasive that it seems to have become the strategic leading edge in some companies. This occurred first within Japan's manufacturing sector, where furious competition reduced the number of motorcycle makers from over 1,000 to a handful. Similar outcomes occurred in many other industries.

The pattern has repeated itself in other countries in response to competition. The enabler is widespread transfer of knowledge on how to generate continuous improvement. A survey of superior manufacturers in the United States, Japan, and Western Europe indicates that the strategic focus among these nations has evolved and, by the early 1990s, had become much alike.

While the survey included only U.S., European, and Japanese plants, there is some evidence that plants elsewhere are focusing on similar pathways to competitiveness. For example, MIT's international automotive study cited Ford's assembly plant in Hermosillo, Mexico, as the world's most efficient.[9]

Eicher Tractors Ltd., operating nine factories in India, is another example. Eicher intensively trains its workforce for continuous improvement. In Eicher's Faridabad tractor assembly plant, evidence of improvements, as well as process controls, is everywhere (see Exhibit 2-1). Output incentive payments have been abolished in favor of producing just in time for use at the next process. Improvement projects are under way in

**EXHIBIT 2-1 Continuous Improvement at Eicher Tractor Ltd.**

*Process specification sheets are posted in each work area at the assembly plant of Eicher Tractor Ltd. These sheets include operating procedures and aid process control, process improvement, and cross-training. Top: Close-up of specs sheets. Bottom: Assembly team in white gloves; specs sheets are above parts trays at either side.*

support departments as well as in the factory. In company transportation, drivers are assuming ownership of vehicle maintenance and have teamed up on a parking lot improvement project. In the finance department, an improvement team has cut the time to issue stock certificates (to investors) from three months to one week.

Eicher Tractor's application of continuous improvement in the back office is a natural extension of doing it in the plant. The same thing has been taking place in the offices of leading manufacturers globally.

Continuous improvement has also become a competitive force among leading organizations in services. Although manufacturers have several names for this strategy (e.g., lean, world-class, or Toyota system), the service industries tend to favor a single term, **total quality management (TQM).** While TQM can take on a narrow definition, it is also used broadly, encompassing organization-wide continuous improvement in meeting customers' requirements. At any rate, continuous improvement has gained prominence as a fundamental component of business strategy in services as well as in manufacturing.

In the early to mid-1990s, some observers attempted to cast continuous improvement in a negative light, arguing that its approach is *evolutionary* in an era when change must be *revolutionary*. That position is unconvincing; it attempts to force an unnecessary trade-off. Successful companies the world over accomplish both; they undergo periods of rapid change—when new technology is acquired or new markets are entered, for example—while simultaneously maintaining ongoing programs of continuous improvement.

People in these organizations realize that changing business environments are the rule rather than the exception. Customers' expectations change, competitors alter their strategies, governments enact new laws affecting commerce, and even Mother Nature reminds us every so often who's really in charge. To a great extent, companies can select the markets in which they wish to compete, but increasingly, they must be prepared to compete in ways defined by those markets. Perhaps good strategy is—at least in part—universal.

## *Universal Strategies*

For some time, business schools taught strategy as a matter of trade-offs. Harvard professor Michael Porter's best-selling 1980 book, *Competitive Strategy,* typified the viewpoint. Porter suggested that a company could effectively pursue only one of the following three strategies: cost leadership, product differentiation, or customer/product focus.[10] That viewpoint began to melt at about the same time as the book was published. We came to realize that companies like Toyota and Canon were beating their Western competitors every which way: on quality, cost, flexibility, and more. The competitiveness of the more successful Japanese companies was rooted mainly in these kinds of customer-sensitive operations strategies, which might be thought of as universal strategies. The proof strengthened when their subsidiaries in North America, and then other Western companies such as Hewlett-Packard, Deere, and Intel, successfully put the same system into practice.

By the mid-1990s, evidence had begun to mount that the universal strategy concept had spread beyond manufacturing and into the service sector. Professor Aleda V. Roth, for example, reported on a research study in which she found a number of health care organizations that "have begun to pioneer new operational models that emphasize quality, service, flexibility, innovation, and cost—simultaneously."[11]

**Differentiation**
A good or service is differentiated when customers perceive that it has some unique value that justifies a premium price. Providers differentiate their outputs with superior quality of design and conformance, responsive (fast) delivery, better service, and so forth.

The trade-off view continues to surface now and then. Current prevalent opinion, however, seems to be that companies can "do it all"—or most of it anyway. Harvard Business School's Professor Pankaj Ghemawat presents a contemporary view of good strategy as one that "embraces the idea that competitive position must consider both relative cost and differentiation, and it recognizes the tension between the two. Positioning, in this view, is an effort to drive the largest possible wedge between cost and differentiation (or price)."[12]

That "wedge" is illustrated in Exhibit 2-2 for a hypothetical industry. Let's assume a single output item—any good or service. Four of the companies that compete in the industry are represented. Average industry performance is illustrated by the competitor at the left; unit cost is $30 and unit selling price is $60, so a unit profit of $30 is obtained. The successful differentiated competitor outperforms the average, however, realizing a profit of $40 per unit. Though its output commands a unit price of $80, its unit cost of $40 is above average as well. The successful low-cost competitor also enjoys a higher-than-average unit profit, $35 in this example. Though it can command a market price of but $55, its low unit costs contribute to its success. The fourth competitor—one that pursues a universal strategy aimed at customer-serving *and* waste-free operations—enjoys *both* high market price and low cost. The unit profit of $60 provides a very distinct competitive advantage in this industry.

What if our hypothetical industry should experience severe downward pressure on prices; say, from a price war, supply glut, or perhaps simply due to demands from increasingly sophisticated and informed customers? Or, suppose there is upward pressure on costs, say from a scarcity of resources? Or—worst-case scenario—what if both occur? The resulting margin squeeze would be devastating to some competitors. While there are no guarantees, the strategy that emphasizes meeting all six basic customer wants appears to have the inside track.

**EXHIBIT 2-2 Competitive Advantage**

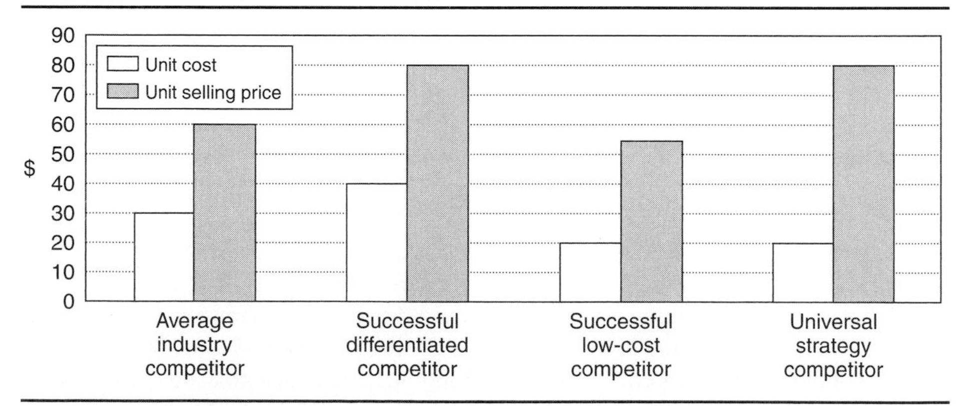


Source: Adapted from Pankaj Ghemawat, *Strategy and the Business Landscape: Text and Cases* (New York: Addison-Wesley, 1999), p. 57. Used with permission.

### *Supportive Functional Strategies*

As we close this section, we are reminded that as a business game plan, sometimes the emphasis of strategy appears to be financial, such as plans for acquiring or merging with other companies. New products or markets are other common targets of business strategies. The input from operations, and the effect on operations, may be unclear. In other cases, the needs of the operations function seem dominant; strategies for supply-chain management and capacity planning come to mind. And, perhaps in these cases the contributions from and effects on financial, design, and marketing activities get blurred. And in all cases, personnel in various staff departments will contribute to strategy execution and will be affected by the outcomes of that strategy.

One of the many contributions of the late W. Edwards Deming is his 14 points. We examine all of them later, but his first point is especially relevant to the present discussion. Deming challenged managers to:

> Create constancy of purpose for the improvement of product and service, with a plan to improve competitive position and stay in business.[13]

In sum, we reiterate that good strategy incorporates everyone. All players—those in the heat of the action and those awaiting their call—must know the game plan. Company-wide constancy of purpose occurs when the overall business strategy is successfully translated down into supportive functional strategies that allow all employees to link their individual activities to company objectives. While strategies for all activities are important, our focus lies with the operations strategy.

## Operations Strategy

Historically, the operations component of business strategy has received less than its share of attention. Too often, executives have concentrated on financial and marketing strategies, and treated product development and operations as after thoughts, or, worse, as givens. Harvard Professor Wickham Skinner perceived this and became a strong voice for giving operations strategy its due. His oft-cited 1969 article, "Manufacturing—Missing Link in Corporate Strategy,"[14] expresses that point of view.

After Skinner sounded the warning, others added their voices, and things began to change. In recent years, operations strategy has evolved rapidly and significantly. In this and the next sections, we consider the past and recent evolution of operations strategy and examine those forces that drive dynamic competitiveness today. To a great extent, a company's capability to plan and execute good operations strategy depends on how well that company has mastered lessons from the past.

### *Evolution of OM Strategy*

Those who craft operations strategy must, of course, be familiar with the tools that exist to carry out that strategy. Evolution of *established or recognized* OM strategies is constrained by the evolution of the OM field itself. Furthermore, *potential new* strategies are likely to be logical extensions to what we now know. Thus, the historical time line showing major concepts, events, and trends that have shaped OM provides useful insight. Exhibit 2-3 presents a brief overview from the industrial revolution through the 20th century.

The entries in the table are not meant to be collectively exhaustive. For one thing, numerous historical achievements that occurred long before the Industrial Revolution exhibited characteristics that suggest sound operations management. Construction projects on a grand scale were completed by early civilizations in Egypt, China, Greece, Rome, and Latin America. Famous military campaigns succeeded (or failed) in large part due to techniques used to allocate resources and manage logistics. And, around 1438, the Arsenal of Venice turned out 10 fully armed warships per day in its assembly-line mode of production. For the most part, however, lessons learned in these early cases were not recorded and passed on.

With the Industrial Revolution, which began in England in about 1760, came better documentation. Concepts and techniques were recorded, taught, and thus passed on to form a growing body of knowledge. That era, lasting some 100 years, was one of increasing mechanization and standardization of parts. It yielded a flood of products, such as the cotton gin; and machines to make other products, such as motor-driven lathes.

The scientific management era might be viewed as an extension of the industrial revolution. Its innovators were Frederick W. Taylor, Frank and Lillian Gilbreth, Henry Gantt, and several others; they brought science to the planning, scheduling, and control of factory work. A bit later, other pioneers extended scientific management into office settings. At the same time, these and related advances laid the cornerstones for modern human resources management and advanced cost accounting. Management of the human element, however, is where Taylor and the Gilbreths had their greatest impact. They documented and timed human work tasks, which, in turn, led to the creation of standards that are essential for training, workforce planning and staffing, budgeting, and job bidding. This era witnessed another significant event that was to have profound effect on production and operations management—Henry Ford applied the assembly line to improve the efficiency of repetitive manufacturing.

The **Hawthorne Effect**—that recognition temporarily raises motivation—still is a well-used term in business and social psychology.

The years between the scientific management era and World War II brought on a variety of events that were to affect OM. The Hawthorne studies at the Western Electric Plant in Cicero, Illinois (near Chicago), revealed that human motivation is complex; people respond to attention as well as pay. These studies and others triggered wholesale changes in management theory and practice and helped launch the field of organizational behavior (OB). Other researchers—called management scientists—began to employ mathematical modeling to study complex business problems such as scheduling and routing; they launched the field of operations research (OR). And, in the mid-1920s, Walter Shewhart and his colleagues at Bell Labs developed the quality control chart and laid the foundation for much of modern statistical process control (SPC).

After World War II, pent-up demand ushered in a period of rapid change as factories shifted production from war materials to peacetime durable and consumer goods. The emphasis was on output quantity, and often, quality took a backseat. War-ravaged economies in Japan and Europe had to be rebuilt, and American industrial expertise accompanied the occupation forces of the Allied nations. In the early 1950s, W. Edwards

### EXHIBIT 2-3 OM Timeline—Major Milestones

| *Date Range* | *Concepts/Trends/Events* |
|---|---|
| 1760–1860 | Industrial Revolution:<br>• Division of labor—Adam Smith<br>• Mechanization of power, steam engine—James Watt<br>• Interchangeable parts—Eli Whitney |
| 1900–1920 | Scientific management:<br>• Training, charting work elements, standards, efficient use of people—F. W. Taylor<br>• Motion and time studies, industrial psychology—Frank and Lillian Gilbreth<br>• Scheduling charts and work control charts—Henry Gantt<br>• Assembly line applied to manufacturing in modern era—Henry Ford |
| 1920–1940 | Pioneering developments in several key disciplines:<br>• Hawthorne studies; showed emotional and social factors to be relevant in work settings; launched organizational behavior as field of study—Elton Mayo<br>• Operations research; quantitative approach to decision making, continued to develop through World War II<br>• Statistical methods for quality assurance—Walter Shewhart |
| 1950s | Rebuilding after World War II:<br>• W. E. Deming and J. M. Juran take their quality improvement messages to Japan<br>• Pioneering use of digital computers in business<br>• Postwar demand surges (for both durable and consumer goods) |
| 1960s | Emergence of revolutionary management concepts and information technology (IT):<br>• Digital computer (3rd generation) gains widespread commercial use<br>• Just-in-time (JIT): lean, short-cycle production methods pioneered by Toyota—Taiichi Ohno<br>• Total quality management (TQM): systematic management of process quality emerges as a competitive force in Japan |
| 1970s | Emerging awareness of OM's role in competitive advantage:<br>• Call for emphasis on operations strategy—Wickham Skinner<br>• OM tools begin to emerge in the service sector<br>• Computer supported production planning; Joseph Orlicky publishes *Materials Requirements Planning (MRP)* in 1975 |
| 1980s | Customers move to "center stage":<br>• JIT and TQM make inroads among North American manufacturers<br>• Customer-as-next-process concept and voice-of-the-customer ideas expand<br>• Quality awards and supplier certifications gain global stature<br>• Time-based competition gains widespread acceptance<br>• Basic principles of OM emerge |
| 1990s | Strategies for global competition:<br>• Heightened emphasis on design and flexibility<br>• Increased globalization of commerce; political and trade barriers fall; new markets emerge (e.g., European Union); trade pacts signed (e.g., NAFTA)<br>• Teaming and partnering; quick order-fulfillment tools and supply-chain management concepts expand (e.g., Enterprise Resource Planning [ERP])<br>• Internet usage; electronic commerce (e-commerce) emerges in both business-to-consumer (B2C) to business-to-business (B2B) arenas |
| 2000 → | ? |

Deming and Joseph M. Juran found fertile ground in Japan for their ideas about paying closer attention to quality. Discussions held during these visits, coupled with emerging expertise among Japan's scientific and engineering community, planted the seeds for revolutionary production methods that would emerge under such titles as lean production, just-in-time, Toyota production methods, and total quality.

The same era spawned the first business computers, which quickly took over mass record keeping and data processing, and were used to help model and analyze complex business problems, largely in operations. The major use of computers in OM, however, lay elsewhere; computer-driven materials requirements planning (MRP), developed in the 1970s, coped with complex material and job planning. Yet another key change in the content of OM studies had been launched. By the early 1980s, some OM textbooks devoted nearly a third of their pages to MRP and related factory and logistics planning and control. Just as OM strategy was beginning to assume its place as a legitimate component of business strategy, OM tools were spreading rapidly into service companies.

In the 1980s, the customer moved to center stage. In Chapter 1, we addressed much of the customer-centric thinking that continues to dominate OM practice today; further examples arise throughout the remainder of the book. Also, numerous awards and registrations aimed at recognition of superior quality gained prominence in the 1980s. By the 1990s, increased global competition had made such terms as "world-class excellence" commonplace. Providers emphasized flexibility, teamwork, and partnerships along value-adding customer chains in order to better meet the needs of a dynamic marketplace. Responsive order fulfillment, driven by increased use of the Internet and electronic commerce, became a business necessity and, therefore, a mandate for operations managers.

Before closing our historical perspective of the development of modern OM, a few comments are in order. In some cases, it is difficult to pinpoint the birth of a contribution, for the incubation period can be long. Also, time can change assessment; some of the more recent influences—say, from the 1980s and 1990s—have not yet played out. Their impact on the field of OM could change in the years ahead. Finally, with all due respect to the persons mentioned in Exhibit 2-3, many other names could certainly be added.

Having taken a glimpse at factors that make OM what it is today, we turn our attention to specific characteristics that we expect to find in any company's OM strategy.

## *Elements of OM Strategy*

When business strategy is translated down into strategy to govern operations, we must keep in mind that the word *operations* refers to a functional area within the company as well as to transformation activities. Thus, OM strategy has two purposes; it must:

1. Address the *functional area of operations*—the part of the company charged with creating and delivering the goods and services destined for external customers.

2. Guide the *operations activities performed by all personnel* working throughout the firm within their respective line or staff departments as members of value-adding chains.

We are *not* suggesting that a company maintain two independent operations management strategies. We are saying that good OM strategy will meet both objectives. In fact, there is much common ground; principles that guide operations within the OM functional area are applicable—with appropriate allowances for work unit composition and purpose—to any other area within the firm.

Very large corporations such as General Electric, Mitsubishi Group, and Philips Electronics have multiple business units competing in various industries, and it usually makes more sense to define OM strategy—and even overall business strategy itself—within each business unit.

**Strategy for the OM Functional Area.** When we consider the operations functional area, the strategic focus is on large-scale or companywide inputs/transformation processes/outputs linkages. OM strategy decisions might be considered within the framework of these linkages.

***Inputs.*** The inputs are the organization's capacity, or operating resources. Strategies with heavy OM focus address such matters as the addition or removal of a unit of capacity, skills and flexibility of the workforce, level of commitment to safety and the environment, and degree of outsourcing.

***Transformation Processes.*** Any strategic decision affecting how inputs become the company's outputs might be considered at least partially under the OM strategy umbrella. Examples include level of investment in product and process development, commitment to standardization, partnership links with other supply-chain members, types of flow-control systems, level and types of automation, degree of incorporation of information technologies, and perhaps general materials management plans.

***Outputs.*** Determining the makeup of company outputs—the line of goods and services—is usually a business-level strategic decision. In any event, operations strategies for outputs should be customer oriented, that is, focused on quality, flexibility, service, cost, responsiveness, and variability (from Exhibit 1-6).

In practice, strategies aimed at one area often affect another. A decision to outsource, for example, say, to buy a component rather than continue to make it in-house, will alter the mix of resource inputs, will create a new supplier partnership or alter an existing one, and might well improve the quality of outputs.

We have identified topics that strategy for the OM function typically covers. But with the exception of the customer orientation suggested for output strategies, we have up to this point been necessarily short on specific recommendations. Investment in process development, for example, might at a given time be "right" for one company and "wrong" for another. Circumstances dictate. However, as we move on to address the second objective of OM strategy—guidance for transformation activities—specific recommendations are the rule.

**Strategy to Guide Transformation Activities.** With operations managers defined as everyone responsible for carrying out value-adding transformation activities (see

Chapter 1), strategic guidance must be quite broad-based. It must have near-universal appeal and be appropriate for the vast majority of situations.

As noted in Exhibit 2-3, during the 1980s a set of principles emerged that appeared to hold promise as such a guide.[15] Refined into 16 **principles of operations management,** they offer a fundamental core list of mandates for sound operations management—applicable throughout the organization. Since their introduction, the principles of operations management have been embraced by hundreds of successful companies around the globe.[16]

The principles of operations management cover a good deal of territory, and serve to guide both strategy formulation and strategy implementation. Collectively, they set the tone for Parts II through V of this book. In order to present the principles with sufficient introductory detail, we have reserved Chapter 3—the final chapter in this introductory part—for that purpose.

At this time, we continue our discussion of OM strategy by turning our attention to output volume—a variable that can significantly affect OM strategy. We look first at relationships between volume, costs, and profit and then consider volume and variety.

## *Volume and Cost Considerations*

A related form of cost-volume analysis may be helpful in crafting strategy for outsourcing (make-or-buy) decisions. We reserve that for a later chapter.

In business, profit is survival. A company's output volume is one key determinant of profits, costs are another, and how customers feel about those outputs—expressed as their willingness to pay for them—is a third. The relationships among these variables offer a quick-look assessment that can be quite helpful in forming OM strategy. The technique is referred to as **cost-volume analysis.**

For simplicity, consider a small company with but one type of output. Equation 2-1 is a general model of the economics of the business.

$$S(Q) = V(Q) + F + P \tag{2-1}$$

Where:

$S$ = selling price of a unit of output
$Q$ = output volume, therefore $(S)(Q)$ is sales revenue
$V$ = unit variable cost, therefore $(V)(Q)$ is total variable costs
$F$ = fixed costs
$P$ = profit (pretax)

Note that total variable costs fluctuate in direct proportion to level of output, while total fixed costs remain constant regardless of output level.[17] The firm's profit is the amount by which sales revenue—the left-hand side of Equation 2-1—exceeds costs. If we rearrange the terms somewhat, we obtain:

$$Q(S - V) = F + P$$

The quantity $(S - V)$, the amount by which selling price exceeds variable cost, is the per-unit contribution margin $(M)$ realized on each unit produced and sold. Performing the substitution, we obtain:

$$Q(M) = F + P \tag{2-2}$$

By setting profit equal to zero, we obtain the **break-even point,** the volume at which sales revenues just cover costs.

$$Q_{BE} = \frac{F}{M} \qquad (2\text{-}3)$$

Example 2-1 illustrates how small business owner-managers might use cost-volume analysis to help formulate strategy.

## Example 2-1: VOLUME-COST ANALYSIS

Amy and Alex own and manage Riverview Antiques & Souvenirs, and are considering changes to their product lines for the upcoming tourist season. One possibility is a T-shirt that would bear a logo that Amy designed to commemorate the town's bicentennial anniversary—an event to be celebrated throughout the season. Equipment needed to custom colorize the logo and imprint the shirts can be leased for $3,000 (a one-year lease is required), blank T-shirts are available for $11each, and Alex estimates that inks, packaging, and other variable-cost items will add $1 per shirt. Amy and Alex decide not to factor in a cost for their labor under the assumption that they will make the shirts during regular hours when not serving customers. To be consistent with the current product pricing ranges, Amy thinks a $20 selling price is appropriate.

*a.* If T-shirt volume is projected to be 1,000 units, what pretax profit will the venture realize?

*b.* What is the break-even volume?

*c.* If Alex and Amy would like to make a profit of at least $7,000 on the T-shirt venture, what volume do they need?

*Solution*

*a.* Adding the unit cost components, we obtain a unit variable cost of $12. Then, substitution into Equation 2-1 yields:

$$(\$20)(1{,}000) = (\$12)(1{,}000) + \$3{,}000 + P$$
$$P = \$5{,}000$$

*b.* From Equation 2-3:

$$\begin{aligned} Q_{BE} &= F \div M \\ &= \$3{,}000 \div (\$20 - \$12) = \$3{,}000 \div \$8 \\ &= 375 \text{ units} \end{aligned}$$

*c.* With the unit contribution margin of $8 as determined in the solution to part *b*, we might use Equation 2-2:

$$\begin{aligned} Q(M) &= F + P \\ Q(\$8) &= \$3{,}000 + \$7{,}000 \\ Q &= \$10{,}000 \div \$8 \\ &= 1{,}250 \text{ units} \end{aligned}$$

Cost-volume analysis summarizes a few key concepts and relationships that managers must keep in mind when formulating and implementing operations strategy:

- The unit contribution margin must be positive for the business to avoid losses on ongoing operations. If a company can't hold its unit variable cost below the selling price that the market—customers—will support, the company cannot compete and production must be discontinued.
- Profit depends on both sales volume and unit margin. Greater earnings occur when the firm sells more units; when the margin is higher; or—the best-case scenario—when both margin and sales volume increase.
- Fixed costs serve as a red flag. They are covered only if margin is positive and sufficient volume is attainable. Since fixed costs are distributed over all production, a higher volume does result in a lower *per-unit* fixed cost. Strategy calling for increased production volume *solely as an attempt to attain lower per-unit fixed costs,* however, is a red herring! Customers may not be interested, and the result is a pile of unmarketable junk!

The closing decades of the 20th century ushered in a broadened (enlightened?) view of the role that operations and operations managers play in cost-volume matters that, in turn, enhance competitiveness. To briefly summarize:

1. Operations managers have traditionally shouldered much of the responsibility for containment of variable costs given the direct relationship of such costs to output-generating transformation processes. A rich array of OM techniques—covered throughout this book—has emerged to help *all* managers make better use of human resources, materials, and other resource inputs.
2. Many traditional "fixed costs" are associated with activities that—though indirect—are strongly affected by direct output-producing operations, and vice versa. Expenses for management and supervision, maintenance, training, design, materials management, purchasing, information processing, energy consumption, and yes, even marketing, are affected, if not by the volume of output itself, then certainly by the nature of the operations that generate that output. The goal is clear . . . eliminate waste wherever it appears; any activity—direct or indirect—that adds cost but no value is a target for elimination.
3. Let's turn to the revenue side of Equation 2-1; does OM contribute to sales? We can answer that question by posing another: What would make customers want more? The answer should come as no surprise: output goods and services that meet the customers' needs.

We have discussed the financial impact of lower fixed and variable costs coupled with higher revenues, but when we put it all together another competitive benefit emerges. Exhibit 2-4A illustrates graphically the basic cost-volume relationships; break-even volume occurs where total sales revenue equals total costs. In Exhibit 2-4B, the former cost lines are dotted and new solid lines represent reductions in variable, fixed, and total costs—results of improvement programs to drive waste from operations.

## EXHIBIT 2-4 Improving Cost-Volume Relationships

**A. Competitive break-even before improvements**

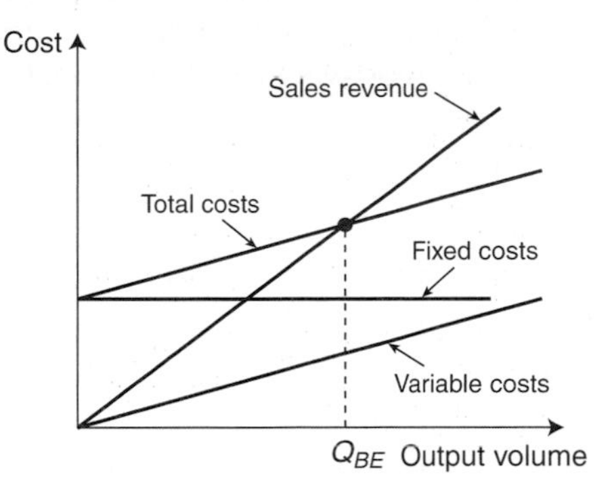


**B. Competitive break-even after cost reductions**

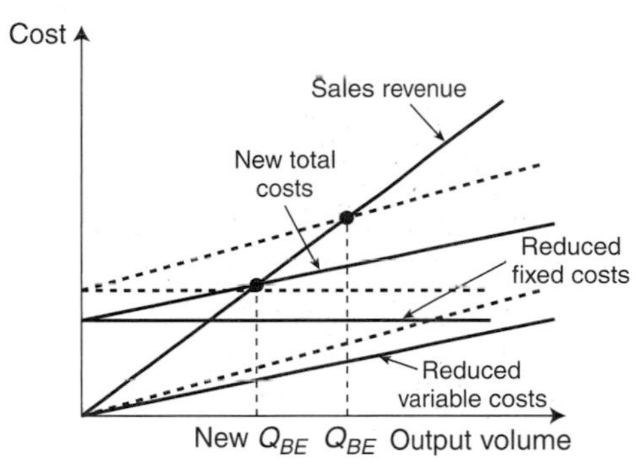


**C. Competitive break-even after cost reductions and output improvements**

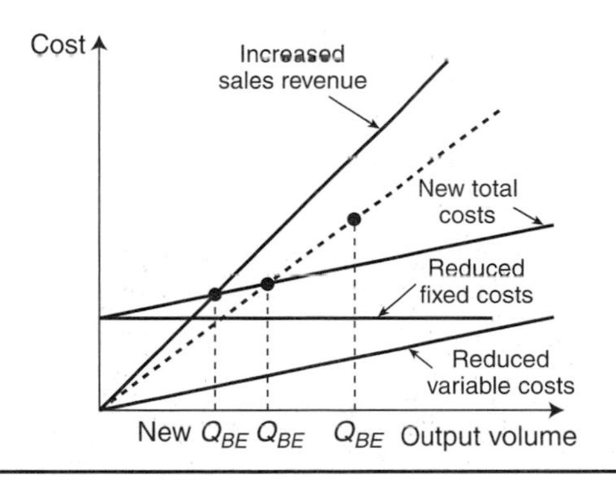


Sales revenue is unchanged. Note that the break-even volume has shifted to the left, indicating that the company can be profitable at lower volumes.

Exhibit 2-4C represents the cost-volume relationships after improvements in outputs have a positive effect on sales; the revenue slope is steeper. Again, the break-even volume has shifted to the left, permitting profitable operations at still lower volume levels.

In sum, by passing the do-it-all thinking of universal strategy down to operations strategy, new opportunities for profitability arise. Smaller-volume markets or specialty products might open up as the firm becomes competitive at lower volumes.

As with the cost-volume relationship, better understanding and management of the interaction between output volumes and variety also affect OM strategy. We take up that topic next.

### *Volume and Variety Considerations*

In Chapter 1, we introduced five general modes of operations, and described them along the dimensions of output volume, output variety, and dominant process (See Exhibit 1-5). Now, we look a bit deeper and see how operations mode, and the desire to shift from one mode to another, can affect strategy. The broad aim is to reap the advantages of streamlining—an objective familiar to savvy drivers.

**Streamlined operations**
Steady flow operations with few delays, stops, starts, and storages.

City driving is harder on a car than highway driving. Mileage is lower, wear and tear is greater, and service is needed more frequently. In addition, the driver's time is wasted on stop-and-go traffic and in the time required for extra auto maintenance. To some extent, city drivers can emulate highway drivers—anticipate traffic light changes, avoid jack-rabbit starts and stops, and so forth.

Operations management is similar: Stop-and-go operations can cause extra waste, inefficiency, high cost, and so on. Like good city driving, astute management can shift irregular stop-and-go operations toward more of a streamlined steady-flow mode. The advantages are considerable. Some are apparent: higher efficiency, consistently higher quality, shorter throughput times, lower inventory, lower labor cost, simpler planning and scheduling, and fewer surprises.

Another kind of benefit of streamlining is more subtle and in the past often not exploited: gaining better visibility of whole products and processes for delivering them. Products are what customers buy, not functions, not separate tasks. Focusing on products, or on customers of those products, has strong appeal as a foundation of total quality management. In other words, today companies have an elevated interest in shifting from modes that dwell on functions to those that focus on products and customers. To better understand mode shifting—toward more product- or customer-focused, streamlined operations, we turn to some notable examples.

**From Custom to Commodity.** Exhibit 2-5 presents a product versus process matrix. The horizontal axis sweeps across a full range of products (goods and services), and the vertical axis does the same for processes. Along the diagonal is a broad band of examples of how products usually pair off with processes.

High and left in the exhibit is one extreme mode of operations. It is the irregular, intermittent (on-and-off) kind of processing that repair services must deal with. The product is **custom** (customized), which means unique. Variety is high, and planning is difficult to say the least. At the other extreme, lower right, is the opposite case. Processing is ultracontinuous, as it must be for a generator of electric power. The product is a **commodity,** very common or undifferentiated. Set it up right—in the design

## Exhibit 2-5 Product versus Process Matrix[18]

*A Federal Express delivery: intermittent process, and somewhat customized service for each client.*
Courtesy Federal Express

*Orange juice bottling is repetitive processing of commodity-like food products.*
© Corbis.

*Manufacturing Portland cement, a commodity product, in the continuous processing mode (mixture of limestone and clay, kiln-heated at 2700°F, ground with gypsum, in 24-hour-a-day, seven-day-a-week operation unchanging for sometimes months).*
Courtesy Portland Cement Association

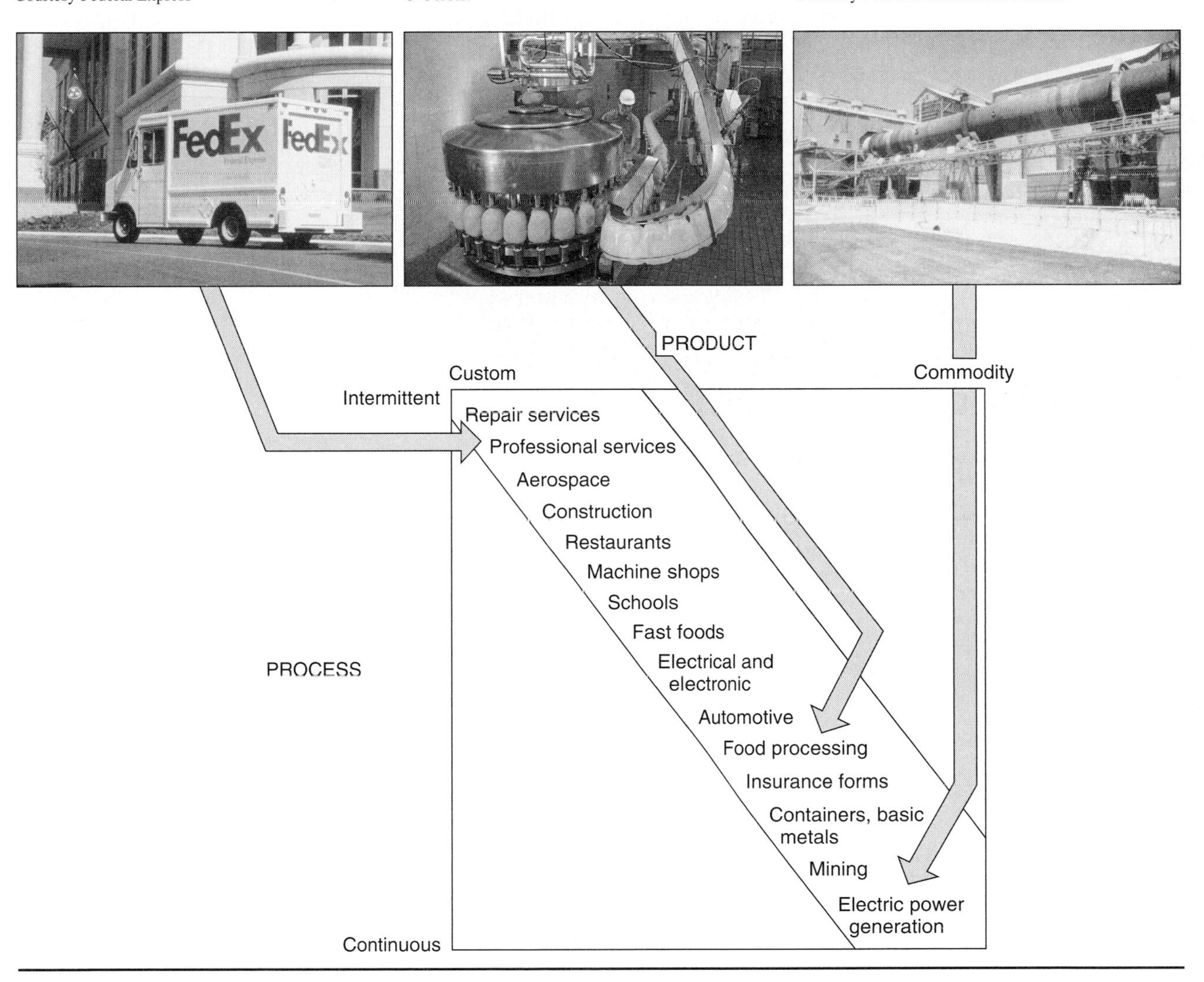

phase—and planning is easy from day to day. All kinds of processes and products are in between the two extremes, as is suggested by the three photo examples in the exhibit.

At one time, all products were provided in the job-processing mode as custom items. For example, put yourself in Placerville, California, in 1849 during the gold rush. Suppose you have a toothache and are lucky enough to find a dentist in the camp. The dentist says you need a tooth filled. He melts down freshly panned gold from the South Fork River and fills your tooth by the light of a lamp burning the oil of a muskrat trapped near the same river. Of course, fuel and gold are commodities today, produced more or less continuously, but they were custom products made in the job mode in 1849.

As demand for any product expands, the low-volume job mode should give way to repetitive or continuous processing, which provides economies of scale. While this applies especially to manufacturing and inventory-related services, there are also examples from human services.

For example, one of the former Soviet Union's first, famed entrepreneurs (in the late 1980s) was Svyatoslav Fyodorov. Dr. Fyodorov's eye surgery clinics annually processed over 200,000 patients suffering from myopia, and were no less than assembly lines:

> Eight beds are arranged around a central axis like spokes in a wheel. A surgeon stands at the head of each bed, on which only the eye of the patient is visible. After each doctor finishes his portion of the task, the wheel makes one-eighth of a turn. The next doctors talk to each other through tiny microphones and headsets. Soft music plays in the background.[19]

Fyodorov accomplished the feat of shifting his specialty out of the job mode into repetitive processing. Other examples of mode shifting cut across process stages.

**Extended Streamlining—Across Process Stages.** Four and one-half decades before Fyodorov, John D. Rockefeller's oil wells steadily pumped product into Rockefeller pipelines and rail tanker cars, which forwarded the product to Rockefeller tank farms. The continuous mode was virtually uninterrupted through three major process stages—extraction, transportation, and storage. Stop-and-go between stages is more typical in the petroleum business. Similarly, Andrew Carnegie's steel manufacturing empire included railroads and lake steamers that moved ore to the great furnaces and then to the finishing mills of Pittsburgh.

Today, one of the purest examples of streamlining across stages may be found in the coal fields of the western United States. The output of lignite mines goes into trucks that drive a mile or so to giant electric power plants and dump their loads onto conveyors. Without stopping, the coal marches forward into furnaces that drive the generators that convert steam to electric power. Still without stopping, the electricity pulses through wires for immediate consumption by millions of users. The operation is continuous from coal through to someone's lamp or refrigerator.

Ford's other quotation: "They can have any color they want, so long as it's black."

Perhaps the most quoted accolade to the efficiencies of streamlined operations comes from a pioneer in the automobile industry. Ford Motor Company once transformed iron ore from its own mines into millions of identical Model T automobiles. As Henry Ford noted, "Our production cycle is about 81 hours from the mine to the finished machine in the freight car, or three days and 9 hours."[20]

**Adding Variety to the Mix.** The products in these examples—gold, muskrat oil, eye surgery, petroleum, steel, electric power, and Model T Fords—could be provided in a more focused repetitive or continuous mode, as long as customers demanded little variety. Indeed, some of history's most skillful entrepreneurs were able to cultivate mass demand and keep it steadily supplied with relatively undifferentiated goods or services. But what happens when customers require variety?

Ford's repetitive-flow mode of manufacture began to unravel when customers started demanding variety. Changing customer tastes affected producers. The auto industry, from assembly plants to parts makers to steel mills, moved well away from repetitive processing and adopted intermittent production—one model at a time, with long **cycle intervals.**

**Cycle Interval**
The time interval between when a particular product or service is made or delivered until the next time it is made or delivered.

Generally, providers want to be able to offer shorter cycle intervals to their customers.

Must an organization choose between satisfying customers' needs for variety and enjoying the benefits of focused, streamlined operations? The conventional view—that only low-variety, high-volume products are likely to reap those benefits—has been the common wisdom. Today's more positive view is that companies with less continuous operations can share the wealth.

A single company, Toyota, deserves much of the credit for the new belief that companies can alter their presumed fate. Over four decades after Ford figured out how to produce automobiles repetitively, Toyota developed methods of doing the same thing but with a variety of models instead of "basic black." Its ability to process mixed models in a repetitive mode, in effect, moves Toyota downward on the product-process matrix displayed in Exhibit 2-5, as the sketch indicates. The shift is toward a more repetitive (continuous) mode, without much rightward movement toward commodity products.

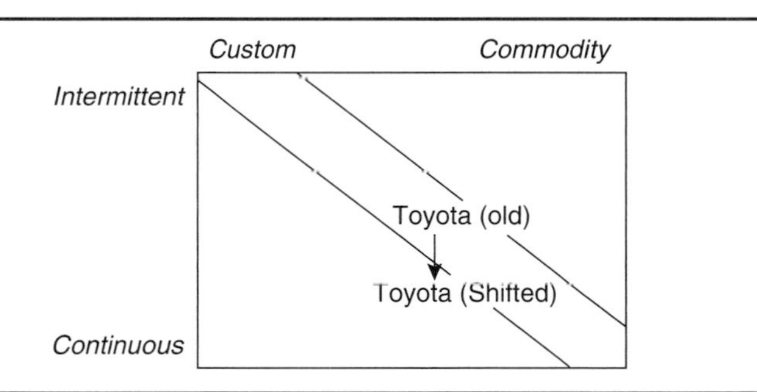


The quest for more continuity without loss of variety, or more variety without loss of continuity, has become strategic and in some cases competitively vital. The ideal is to be in a position to operate competitively at the lower left-hand corner of Exhibit 2-5—reaping the benefits of continuous-mode operations while giving customers all the variety they desire. But can Ford or Toyota—or any manufacturer—do that? Yes, they can. Evidence continues to mount that sweeping changes are occurring in manufacturing economics; customers are truly at center stage and operations strategies are responding to the call.[21]

## Drivers of Dynamic Competitiveness

Thus far, we have made quite a few suggestions about what constitutes effective operations strategy, and we think the basic underlying ideas for those suggestions are sound. However, to reinforce a caveat mentioned at the outset of the chapter: The playing field is a dynamic one. Some observers believe that we are perhaps entering a period of unprecedented and unforeseen change—complete with new paradigms for operations management and even business management itself. Others contend that we are just seeing the fruit of seeds planted in the last 15 or 20 years; today's events, though often spectacular, are and were quite predictable. Perhaps the truth lies somewhere in between.

We won't try to guess the future. What we can do is make note of a few trends or factors that have been, in recent years, key drivers of competitiveness. Though examples cut across functional lines, we limit our focus to those forces that seem especially relevant to operations.

### *Productivity*

**Productivity**—loosely defined as the ratio of outputs to inputs—is an aggregate statistic that is often tied directly to operations. But, is productivity a measure of present and future output-generating capability? Or, is it a statement of past diligence in the creation of effective and efficient resource inputs? Actually, productivity is both; it is a reward and a competitive weapon. And, in recent years the productivity of the U.S. workforce has been on the rise. Labor Department figures show that labor productivity (output per number of hours worked) grew by almost 3 percent in 1999, higher even than 1998's impressive figure of 2.8 percent.[22]

Labor productivity is one component, but we also apply the output-to-input ratio measure to materials, capital, and other resources. In the United States, annual productivity gain hovered around 3 percent from the late 1940s until 1973. From 1973 until 1995, the figure declined significantly, falling below 1 percent in 1995. In the mid-1990s, however, the United States entered a period of rapid productivity growth, referred to by *BusinessWeek* economists as the "New Economy." [23] Through the end of the century, productivity improvements—gained through prior investments in employee training, better tools and technology, and process streamlining—swept across industries and touched most forms of transformation processes. The Into Practice box "Working the Web" provides a few examples.

Faster and better customer service, innovation, and designs, along with lower costs—results that address basic customer wants—improve competitiveness and create strategic options. The box title reflects use of technologies, so let's continue with that theme.

### *E-Commerce*

Clearly, one of the most powerful forces affecting global competitiveness is the explosive growth in electronic commerce, or **e-commerce,** made possible by the Internet.

INTO PRACTICE

## Working the Web

How companies use technology to boost productivity at every stage of the business process.

| PROCESS | EXAMPLE | PAYOFF: |
|---|---|---|
| **INNOVATION** | Royal Dutch/Shell's "GameChanger" teams use the Net to generate new business ideas | New "Light Touch" oil discovery method found 30 million barrels |
| **COLLABORATION** | Ocean Spray's extranet assesses cranberry quality immediately and helps growers get better prices | Growers get higher profits; Ocean Spray cuts waste and boosts productivity |
| **DESIGN** | Honeywell uses the Net to help fashion a customized prototype of anything from a fan blade to a golf club head | Design time cut from six months to 24 hours |
| **PURCHASING** | Ford's AutoXchange creates massive online trading bazaar for its 30,000 suppliers | Could save as much as $8 billion in first few years |
| **MANUFACTURING** | BP Amoco, using Net technology from Honeywell, can quickly identify plant inefficiencies | Stems 2% per day productivity loss in Grangemouth, Scotland, refinery |
| **LOGISTICS** | Cement maker Cemex uses Net-based truck dispatch system to speed deliveries to customers | Cement delivered within 20 minutes, down from 3 hours |
| **MARKETING** | Weyerhaeuser uses the Net to weed out its least valuable customers at Marshfield (Wis.) door plant | Boosted the plant's return on net assets from −2% in 1994 to 27% in 1999 |
| **SERVICE** | GE Power Systems lets customers use the Net to compare the performance of its turbines against other GE turbines in the market | Turbine productivity expected to rise by 1% to 2% annually |

Source: "Why the Productivity Revolution Will Spread" (Segment in *BusinessWeek* Special Report, "The Boom"), *BusinessWeek,* February 14, 2000, p. 116. Used with permission.

Though business-to-consumer (B2C) trade is rising, the biggest volume by far is in the business-to-business (B2B) arena. In an early-2000 report, *The Economist* noted that:

> In business-to-business transactions . . . the advantages and cost savings to be had from dealing on the Internet have caused e-commerce to mushroom. At present, such transactions account for as much as 80% of all e-commerce, which . . . added up to over $150 billion last year (1999) . . . by 2003, that figure could reach $3 trillion.[24]

Several technology companies, including Cisco and Oracle, have transferred almost all of their purchasing (and indeed most of their sales) to the web. And in February 2000, General Motors, Ford, and DaimlerChrysler announced plans to collectively launch an integrated B2B supplier exchange through a single global portal, creating the world's largest virtual market. The three companies plan to open the new venture to all automobile manufacturers around the world and to their suppliers, partners, and dealers.[25]

The potential effects of B2B e-commerce on operations strategies are staggering. Later in this section, we touch on the business-to-consumer aspects of e-commerce and address an even greater array of competitive options for providers who look further down the customer chain.

Maybe you are a consumer completing a $50 business-to-consumer transaction, or a corporate buyer who has just spent $500,000 of your company's money in a business-to-business deal. In either event, you've just clicked on the "enter" key and your e-commerce order is launched. Now what? The ball is in the court of the order fulfillment system.

### *Order Fulfillment*

The web page with customer order-entry is the front end of e-commerce; order fulfillment is the back end—where the work is done. Jim Kalajian, president and COO of Jenkins Group, Inc., a Traverse City, Michigan, distributor of independently published books, sums up some of the frustration in finding web site developers who can see the big picture:

> Everybody and their brother is promising they can build e-commerce sites, but once you peel back the onion you find that they can paint a nice graphic, but all you're getting is the front end. You get a lot of blank stares when you start asking about logistics and integration. . . . I'm going to outsource to a warehouse and I need to make sure my database and business system is compatible.[26]

Providers may fill orders with in-house resources, or—as in the case of Jenkins Group—may contract the work out in varying degrees. A number of big fulfillment houses offer a full range of services. For example, Fingerhut, once a catalog retailer, now handles order fulfillment for Wal-Mart, Macy's, eToys, and many other companies from its facility in St. Cloud, Minnesota. UPS and Federal Express have also entered the order-fulfillment business.[27]

**Original equipment manufacturer (OEM)** The original producer of a product. Used to differentiate from any other company (e.g., wholesaler, distributor, or retailer) in the supply chain.

Companies like Fingerhut have found a strategic niche in taking care of their customers' warehousing, packing, and shipping operations. And retailers like Wal-Mart and Pier 1 understand the strategic importance of linking up with a reliable fulfillment partner. For e-commerce to work for large OEMs with thousands of suppliers, however, an entire network of provider-customer partnerships is necessary.

Consider the "five-day car" objective: A consumer orders a custom-built automobile from a home computer, and is sitting behind the wheel within five days. Toyota introduced the concept in the early 1990s, and by 1995 was placing computer terminals in selected showrooms. In early 2000, North American automakers also offered custom cars—the wait time averaged 64 days.[28] The challenge is great: cut delivery times by 59 days, a 92 percent reduction! Potential payoffs are also huge. Studies suggest that shifting from mass production—based on what manufacturers *think* consumers want—to customized production of exactly what customers want when they want it will cut automakers' unit costs by nearly one-third.

Responding with the correct options from the thousands of possibilities and coordinating the correct parts and supply routes from thousands of suppliers in a just-in-time and just-in-sequence manner are no small tasks. Part of the solution lies in better designs that result in fewer component parts and easier assembly (we address design in Part III), and part of the solution rests in a streamlined order-fulfillment network (examined more closely in Part II). In both cases, teams and partnerships are key ingredients.

## *Teaming and Partnering*

Teaming up internally and externally facilitates fast-paced improvements in quality and customer response. Likewise, external partnerships can secure needed expertise in quick fashion, cutting the time required to establish competitive status.

**Teams.** In General Electric's aircraft-engine assembly facility in Durham, North Carolina; in Dana Corporation's pickup truck chassis plant south of São Paulo, Brazil; in Gates Rubber Company, Siloam Springs, Arkansas; in Logan Regional Hospital, Logan, Utah; and in countless other facilities throughout the world, work teams are an accepted part of business. In each case noted above, dedicated teams of highly motivated associates have accomplished outstanding performance levels on several dimensions of customer-focused outputs. The TQM movement, first in Japan and later in North America, heightened managers' interest as the role of teamwork in creating competitive advantage became better understood. In this book, we are proteam; we are also mindful of caveats that help ensure the best team-situation fit.[29]

Often, the optimal team composition extends outside the firm's boundaries to include suppliers and customers. Securing participation from other members along the supply chain is smoother when strong partnership bonds have been established.

**Partnerships.** Companies gain access to resources (and markets) in a variety of ways; the partnership is but one. Unlike mergers and acquisitions where some change of ownership is the rule, partnership deals are struck when the aim is cooperation without significant realignment of ownership. Partnerships that more directly affect operations management often involve suppliers and/or customers; the previously mentioned integrated supplier chain deal struck by Ford, GM, and DaimlerChrysler is an example. Operations are also affected, of course, when a company elects to make bold changes to its business processes and partners with other companies who have the expertise to help with the transition. Ford, for instance, has partnered with Oracle (for help with software and database management), Cisco (for networking expertise), and Microsoft (for help in getting a consumer driven build-to-order system in place) in its well-publicized move into e-commerce. Ford's strategy is to "use the Net to do everything from ordering a car to linking 30,000 suppliers."[30]

While the ambitious strategies of corporate giants are eye-popping and newsworthy, partnering is no less important to small companies that seek quick access to resources to build their own competitive advantages. Maybe the small firm operates in a local market, or perhaps it is also a source to and partner with a large OEM. Increasingly, outsourcing seems to be the strategy of choice.

### *Outsourcing*

"In 1998, companies farmed out 15% of all manufacturing. In 2000, [the figure had reached] more than 40%."[31] Though outsourcing is nothing new, and every business process is a viable candidate for outsourcing, manufacturing clearly gets at the heart of operations management. Nevertheless, strategies of well-known companies in many industries treat *ownership* of manufacturing facilities as a liability. In the computer industry, Hewlett-Packard, IBM, Silicon Graphics, and others have sold plants to other companies that specialize in manufacturing and then signed the manufacturers on as suppliers.[32] And in the pharmaceuticals industry, the story is much the same:

In 1999, Rhône-Poulenc Rorer merged with Germany's Hoechst, AG, to form Aventis, SA.

> Retaining all manufacturing internally "is not an optimum strategy," says Thomas Kline, vice president for manufacturing at Pfizer. An even more forceful statement comes from former Rhône-Poulenc Rorer Chairman Robert Crawthorn: "Manufacturing is not a key success factor for a pharmaceuticals company. It won't differentiate you unless you screw it up."[33]

Glaxo Wellcome, Eli Lilly, Bristol-Myers Squibb, and Astra are other big-name pharmaceuticals that outsource substantial manufacturing activities.

The story can be repeated for other key industries. Since 1997, Honda, DaimlerChrysler, Toyota, Renault, Volkswagen, Peugeot, General Motors, and Ford have collectively constructed (or have under construction) nine new automobile plants in Brazil.[34] In those state-of-the-art assembly plants, outsourcing is strategic cornerstone. In addition to nearby supplier plants, the automakers rely heavily on vendors' employees who work full-time at the assembly plants themselves.

Outsourcing raises many questions: Just who are the suppliers? Why and how are certain companies selected by the OEMs for partnership status? What can we say about operations strategies that fit those companies? If the reported cost savings that outsourcing bestows on the OEMs are real, are the supplier companies really partners? Or are they economic slaves?

Perhaps there is no definitive set of answers to these and related concerns, but clearly the suppliers have developed their own competitive advantages that make them attractive to their customer-partners. They have developed some distinctive or core competencies. They are sought out because of those competencies.

### *Distinctive and Core Competencies*

**distinctive competency** A strength that sets the organization apart from its competitors.

After a series of biological experiments in 1934, Professor G. F. Gause of Moscow University postulated his principles of competitive exclusion: No two species that make their living the same way can coexist.[35] In strategic terms, the Gause principle says that a firm must strive to distinguish itself from its competitors. The business strategy is to strive for distinctive competency. When purpose gets muddled, indicating a need to restructure or downsize, a cogent strategy is to preserve core competencies.

Sometimes an organization is able to concentrate its entire being around a standout competency. Shouldice Hospital near Toronto, which treats only hernia patients, is an example. Facility layout, medical staff, cafeteria, surgery and recovery rooms, and lounges all cater to that type of patient. By doing numerous hernia repairs each year, and no other surgeries, Shouldice doctors have become proficient. The narrow focus allows nurses to give better care to a greater number of patients, avoids the need for expensive general-purpose equipment that diversified hospitals must have, and, most important, results in higher-quality results. As measured by number of patients needing repeat hernia treatment, Shouldice is 10 times more effective than other hospitals.[36]

Catalytica Pharmaceuticals is another example. It is among the drug industry's largest contract manufacturers. Catalytica's CEO, Gabriel R. Cipau, says the aim for the company's Greenville, North Carolina, plant is to be a "one stop shop" for its customers.[37] In addition to its streamlined production processes, the plant assists with product development, drug formulation research, packaging, and compliance with government regulations. It even manages the inventory levels for two of its major customers. Customers consistently praise Catalytica's ability to meet their needs and demonstrate high levels of service. In 1999, the Catalytica plant was selected as one of *Fortune*'s elite American factories.

An organization's distinctive competency might, like Shouldice Hospital, be a whole focused business unit, complete with financial management, sales and marketing, operations, and other functions. Just as often or more often, it is excellence in some aspect of operations, as is the case at Catalytica. Fast service, very clean premises, and superior quality are examples. While these competencies might be obvious to customers, less apparent factors also qualify. Examples are expert maintenance, low operating costs, and cross-trained labor. These abilities allow the firm, as Professor Gause put it, to make its living a little differently from its competitors in order to survive and succeed.

## Is Strategy Enough?

"Strategy is less than half the battle." That's the clear message in a brutally candid report published by *Fortune* on CEO failures.[38] In the latter years of the 20th century, evidence began to mount that CEO failure is increasingly due to an inability or an unwillingness to mind the operations side of the business. In the majority of cases—the *Fortune* report estimated as many as 70 percent—CEOs fail not for lack of strategy, or even for poor strategy. The problems most often lie in failure to execute the strategy.

For example, the strategies at competitive companies such as Dell Computers, Toyota, and Southwest Airlines are not secrets. Dell's custom marketing/production model is known by all. Toyota will gladly offer tours of its facilities—even to competitors. And Southwest's no-frills strategy has allowed it to be the only airline to make money every year for more than a quarter of a century. In each case, the CEO is quick to acknowledge that the secret of the company's competitive advantage is its execution.

In Chapter 1, we suggested that managers' duties must incorporate creating, implementing, and improving. Strategy formulation gets at the first part but doesn't address parts two and three. Eight of the 10 companies in *Fortune*'s 1999 list of most admired companies did not have a chief operating officer (COO). Rather, each CEO elected to retain responsibilities for operations and adopt a "hands-on" approach. The consensus of opinion seems to be that good strategy is *necessary* for success in a dynamically competitive environment, but it is not *sufficient*.

In a nutshell, managers are admonished to "feel connected to the flow of information about the company and its markets; that includes regular, direct interaction with customers and front-line employees."[39] In Chapter 3, we present a set of principles that will help managers at all levels do exactly that.

## Summary Check Points

✓ Business strategy is the game plan for positioning the company in its chosen markets, competing successfully, pleasing customers, and achieving good business performance.

✓ Kenichi Ohmae defined the *strategic triangle* as customers, competitors, and the company itself; these are the three general determinants of strategy.

✓ *Continuous improvement* (or, *kaizen*) is a strategic foundation in lean production and total quality management (TQM).

✓ *Universal strategy,* in which a company provides both differentiated output and low costs, provides a distinct competitive advantage.

✓ Good business strategy incorporates everyone by creating what W. Edwards Deming referred to as *constancy of purpose* for improvement of outputs and competitive position.

✓ Historically, companies too often overlooked operations strategy; Wickham Skinner—in his classic 1969 article—was an early advocate of correcting that oversight.

✓ Despite earlier human achievements, evolution of modern OM strategies began with the *Industrial Revolution* and has continued to present times; Exhibit 2-3 illustrates major milestones.

✓ Today, operations strategy must serve two purposes: (1) address the functional area of operations with strategic management of the organization's primary input/transformation processes/output links, and (2) guide the operations that occur throughout the organization as employees manage their own individual and group transformations as members of value-adding chains.

✓ *Cost-volume analysis* is one tool that helps determine profitable outputs, and as such affects operations strategy. Operations contributions to profitability include control over variable and fixed costs and creation of output goods and services that command high market prices.

✓ *Lower break-even volume* is another competitive benefit of well-managed operations.

- ✓ The interacting issues of output volume and variety also affect operations strategy. A worthy goal aims at extending the *streamlining* benefits of continuous processing (typically associated with *commodity* production) into the realm of intermittent processing, the typical environment used to provide *custom* products and services.
- ✓ *Competitiveness is dynamic;* its drivers change as customers shift their specific wants and expectations about where value may be obtained.
- ✓ *Productivity,* loosely defined as the ratio of outputs to inputs, can be used as an aggregate measure of operations effectiveness. Productivity is both a reward for past diligence and a statement of present and perhaps future output-generating capability.
- ✓ In the late 1990s and through the turn of the century, *electronic commerce (e-commerce)* emerged as a major factor in business-to-business (B2B) and business-to-consumer (B2C) relationships. The potential effects on operations management strategy formulation and execution are profound.
- ✓ *Order fulfillment,* though not a new activity, is receiving heightened attention in the fast-paced arena of e-commerce; and well-managed operations form an integral link in order-fulfillment systems.
- ✓ In well-run companies, *teams* and *partnerships* are accepted vehicles for establishing, maintaining, and improving competitive advantage.
- ✓ In recent years, *outsourcing*—acquiring goods and services from sources outside the company—has been an increasingly attractive competitive weapon in several industries.
- ✓ Organizations that possess *distinctive or core competencies* are sought out as supplies because of their expertise in providing some unique product or service.
- ✓ While good strategy is necessary for success, it is not sufficient; good execution is more than half the battle.

## Solved Problems

### *Problem 1*

Toni and her brothers own Deck & Grounds, Inc., which offers a wide range of home and landscape improvement products and services. Toni is using cost-volume analysis to help decide whether or not the company should add hot tubs to its product line. Initial cost estimate summaries are:

| | |
|---|---|
| \$21,000 | Truck modifications and new hot tub handling and display equipment |
| \$7,400 | Employee training and required certifications and licenses |
| \$1,800 | Facilities modifications required at Deck & Grounds to create a hot tub display area |
| \$2,300 | Deck & Grounds' average cost for a hot tub* |
| \$1,000 | Materials costs for a basic hot tub installation |
| \$1,100 | Labor costs for a basic hot tub installation |

*Toni will adjust the customer's price up or down by a multiple to reflect variation in tub cost

*a.* If Toni plans to charge an average price of $6,000 for a basic hot tub installation, what will be the break-even volume?
*b.* Suppose Toni wants to break even with 15 installations, what average price must she charge?
*c.* If Toni decides to charge $6,500 for the average tub installation, and if Deck and Grounds completes 20 installations this year, what pretax profit will the company earn from the hot tub product line?

## Solution 1

*a.* Total fixed costs include the first three items in the table, or $30,200.
Variable costs (per installation) include the last three items in the table, or $4,400. Thus, the per-installation margin is ($6,000 − $4,400) = $1,600.
Then, from Equation 2-3:

$$Q_{BE} = \frac{F}{M} = \frac{\$30,200}{\$1,600} = 18.875 \cong 19$$

*b.* Again, Equation 2-3 may be used. Setting $Q_{BE} = 15$, and solving for the unit margin, $M$:

$$Q_{BE} = 15 = \frac{\$30,200}{M}$$

$$M = \frac{\$30,200}{15} = \$2,013.33 \cong \$2,014$$

To have a unit margin of $2,014, Toni's price must exceed unit variable costs by that amount. Thus, unit selling price is ($4,400 + $2,014) = $6,414.
*c.* The profit for this set of conditions may be determined by using Equation 2-1:

$$\$6,500(20) = \$4,400(20) + \$30,200 + P$$

$$P = \$130,000 - (\$88,000 + \$30,200)$$

$$P = \$11,800$$

## Problem 2

Toni takes her cost-volume analysis into her brother Bob's office and says, "Okay, brother dear, it's time to look at the rest of the variables on the hot tub line. My cost estimates are fairly accurate as far as they go, but of course there's more to the story. So, be a good devil's advocate and help me go over the not-so-quantifiable issues."

After some thought as he looked over the cost-volume analysis figures, Bob replied, "I agree. These numbers look good. Okay, time for some brainstorming. Same rules as always; we take turns and me first!"

## Solution 2

*Bob:* After the break-even quantity is achieved—this year or early next year if your volume estimates are close—we will have covered major fixed costs, and profit per installation will increase significantly.

*Toni:* We will have maintenance costs and equipment replacement costs in the future, but you are right . . . unit profits will increase after start-up fixed costs are covered.
*Bob:* What about demand? Can we advertise the new hot tub lines? Should we? Do we want to try to increase volume now? Could we manage, say, two installations per month? Maybe next year we may want to, but . . .
*Toni:* Maybe before we worry about higher volumes, we ought to do more to ensure that the tub supplier is a good one. Maybe I should check around some more. That company is a major distributor for the tub line manufacturer and I did get good recommendations from my sources, however.
*Bob:* The line they carry is a good one, but can this distributor handle us as a customer? Do they have adequate capacity? If things got tight with them, would they go along with our taking delivery directly from the manufacturer? You know me, I always worry about our supply lines.
*Toni:* I know you do, and you know that my worries lie with competitors. We have a great reputation, and I think we can do well against other hot tub installers in the region, but I wonder who else around here might decide to get into the game.

A third voice laughingly interrupted the discussion, "Well, I see my little brother and sister are plotting strategy in my absence again. Clearly, the wisdom of the firstborn is required. The hot tub line, right?"

*Toni:* Join us, Frank. Welcome back. Yes. The cost-volume analysis looks good, but now we're kicking all those "other variables" about.
*Frank:* Toni, I know you are a whiz with the numbers and I know there's no better cost estimator in the country. And Bob, I know you are a genius when it comes to managing new product lines and getting them into black ink quickly. But, I'd like to step back and remind you both of some things we agreed to ask ourselves about any potential new product or service line. . . .

Do we even want to get into the hot tub line? Does it complement our other product and service offerings? Would it play into our competitive strengths? Can we afford to make the commitment? Can we afford not to? Are hot tub sales and installation part of our business game plan?

Bob brewed a fresh pot of coffee and the brainstorming continued. . . .

## Exercises

1. Three companies known for innovations and other accomplishments in the financial services sector are Fidelity Investments (www.fidelity.com), Charles Schwab (www.schwab.com), and E*Trade (www.etrade.com). From visits to the companies' web sites and other sources of information compare and contrast the operations strategies of these three firms.
2. Johnson & Johnson is the world's largest and most diversified health care company. In September of 1999, *The Wall Street Journal* reported that J&J had been named the company with the "best corporate reputation in America." Visit the company's web site (www.johnsonandjohnson.com) and:
   *a.* Review the company credo (North America version). Does the Johnson & Johnson credo suggest a universal strategy? Explain your response.

*b.* Review some of the nearly 200 operating companies (in 51 countries) that make up the Johnson & Johnson corporation and note some of the explicit and implied components of strategy. In your own words, describe the image that Johnson & Johnson is trying to convey. Explain.

3. Find two additional articles on operations strategy by Professor Wickham Skinner. What are his key points?
4. General Electric consistently ranks among the most admired corporations. Visit the General Electric web site at www.ge.com and:
   *a.* Make a list of the major product groups that GE provides.
   *b.* List the services that GE provides.
   *c.* View various parts of the site, and identify statements that reveal strategy or mission of GE business units.
   *d.* Review the GE principles (referred to as "Our Values"). To what extent do those values compare with your text's suggestions about operations strategy? Discuss.
   *e.* Comment on any overall corporate strategy that you detect.
5. In each of the following industries, identify an example of revolutionary—relatively rapid—change and an example of evolutionary—continuous improvement—change. Explain your examples.
   *a.* Telecommunications products
   *b.* Telecommunications services
   *c.* Automobiles
   *d.* Personal computers
   *e.* Commercial banking
6. The music and theater departments at State University will jointly present *The Sound of Music* at six locations around the state during the upcoming season. Two shows, a matinee and an evening performance, will occur at each site.
   *a.* What form of operations mode best describes the 12-production series? Explain your response. (Hint: You might need to review operations modes in Chapter 1.)
   *b.* Discuss the effects of volume (number of performances) and variety. How would your response change if a different musical were to be given at each site?
   *c.* Fred and Freida, the production managers of the show, have asked you for ways in which they might streamline the entire effort. What do you suggest? Why?
7. Planners for the State University musical series discussed in Exercise 6 would like for the performance series to pay for itself and provide a modest amount of extra revenue to support other arts programs. Estimates of expenses that must be born by the school for the upcoming season's musical presentation series are shown in the table below:

| *One-Time Expenses (per Season)* | | *Expenses Incurred at Each Presentation Site* | |
|---|---|---|---|
| Visiting artist expenses | $40,000 | Cast lodging and meals | $4,000 |
| Transportation (vehicle leases & fees) | 3,500 | Site set-up costs | $1,500 |
| Set and costume design and construction | 10,000 | Site promotion expenses | 1,000 |
| Programs (design and set-up costs) | 2,000 | Venue rent and miscellaneous costs | 750 |
| Seasonal promotion expenses | 2,500 | Programs (site-specific printing) | 500 |
| Incidentals and miscellaneous | 1,500 | Site incidentals | 250 |

*a.* If the average ticket price is $20, and if each presentation draws an average of 500 patrons, how many sites will be required for the school to break even on the musical program series? (Note: There are two performances at each site, so assume 1,000 patrons per site.)

*b.* If the school performs its scheduled six-site tour (as described in Exercise 6), what extra revenue will be available to support other university arts programs?

8. State University would like to earn at least $25,000 from the musical series discussed in Exercises 6 and 7 for its arts program. Assuming that average ticket price and expense estimates shown in Exercise 7 remain valid, and that there will be two performances per site, how many patrons must attend at each of the six sites in order for the university to meet its fund-raising goal of $25,000?

9. Professor Beethoven (no relationship) is concerned that a six-site musical program (see Exercises 6, 7, and 8) will take students away from their other studies at State University for an excessive amount of time. He asks if some of the costs might be decreased so that a five-site tour can accomplish perhaps a more modest fund raising goal. Prepare a response for Professor Beethoven that contains two realistic options for a five-site tour, each capable of earning at least $20,000 for the school's arts programs.

10. Alex and Amy, owners of Riverview Antiques & Souvenirs can buy a blank T-shirt of better material quality for $12.50 (as opposed to the $11 shirt described in Example 2-1).

    *a.* If Alex and Amy can command a selling price of $25 for the better shirt, and other costs remain as described in the example, what is the break-even volume?

    *b.* If sales volume for the better quality shirt is 1,000 units during the season, what pretax profit will the company realize on the T-shirt venture?

    *c.* With the better quality shirt and $25 selling price, what volume is required in order for Riverview to earn a $7,000 profit on the shirt product line?

    *d.* Are there any risks associated with the strategy of buying the higher quality T-shirt and pricing the printed shirts at $25? Explain your response.

11. After reviewing the prospect of the alternate shirt (see Exercise 10) Amy tells Alex, "Any strategy that lowers our break-even volume is a good one; such a strategy provides greater competitive advantage." Do you agree with Amy's assessment? Why or why not?

12. After she and her brothers decided to pursue addition of a hot tub product line, Toni (one of the owners of Deck & Grounds, Inc.; see Solved Problems 1 and 2) has done additional research and revised her preliminary cost estimates. The revised figures are shown below:

| | |
|---|---|
| $20,100 | Truck modifications and new hot tub handling and display equipment |
| $6,700 | Employee training and required certifications and licenses |
| $1,900 | Facilities modifications required at Deck & Grounds to create a hot tub display area |
| $2,150 | Deck & Grounds' average cost for a hot tub* |
| $950 | Materials costs for a basic hot tub installation |
| $1,150 | Labor costs for a basic hot tub installation |

*Toni will adjust the customer's price up or down by a multiple to reflect variation in tub cost

*a.* If Toni charges $6,300 for the average tub installation, at what volume will Deck & Grounds break even on the hot tub line?
*b.* To earn a pretax profit of $10,000 on the hot-tub business, how many tubs must the company install (at $6,300) this year?
*c.* What risks are the owners of Deck & Grounds taking by pursuing a strategy of adding the hot tub line? What might be done to lessen the risks? Explain your reasoning.

13. After the brainstorming session (see Solved Problem 2), Frank suggested that Deck & Grounds purchase an initial inventory of four hot tubs for display purposes. Toni and Bob agreed, but felt that the $8,600 ($4 \times$ $2,150) initial display inventory investment should be included in Toni's cost-volume analysis. How might this be accomplished, and what effect would you expect?
14. Discuss how volume-variety issues might be managed in each of the following settings:
    *a.* A concession stand offering several kinds of sandwiches, drinks, candy, and other items.
    *b.* A government office that provides a variety of services for telephone and walk-in customers.
    *c.* A plant that assembles several makes, models, and sizes of television sets.
15. What are the distinctive competencies of the following organizations? Discuss.
    *a.* Holiday Inn
    *b.* Ritz-Carlton
    *c.* The U.S. Marine Corps
    *d.* Boeing
    *e.* L.L. Bean
16. How does competition affect operations management? Consider, for example, some of the most successful firms in the highly competitive fast-food, lodging, and grocery industries. What do the successful firms do in operations management that their less successful competitors (maybe even some companies that went under!) do not do?
17. Pick two examples of North American service providers that that generally have been successful at achieving both cost leadership and differentiation leadership. Explain your selections.
18. Pick two examples of North American product providers that have generally been successful at achieving both cost leadership and differentiation leadership. Explain your selections.
19. Interview two managers who have been with their companies for a few years. Ask them to describe how productivity has changed within their organizations over their terms of employment. Can they identify specific factors that have driven the productivity changes? Have there been any changes in competitiveness? Write a brief essay that details the results of your interviews.
20. Find two examples of retailers that now offer Internet shopping (in addition to traditional retail store and/or catalog shopping). In each case, how has the strategy of adding e-commerce affected company operations? Explain.
21. Each month, many companies announce new partnerships formed to pursue a joint venture or improve competitiveness of ongoing operations. Find three recent examples of these new partnerships and:
    *a.* Note the (stated) purposes of the partnership.
    *b.* Identify the distinctive competence of each of the partnering organizations.
    *c.* Identify the customers who are most likely to benefit by the partnership alliance.

22. Select three prominent companies that provide goods to Internet shoppers. (These may be companies that you deal with yourself.) Inquire about the order-fulfillment procedure that is followed by the company. Where are orders sent? Is fulfillment accomplished by a third party? Where are goods stored prior to shipment to customers? What is the delivery lead time? Write a brief paragraph summarizing your findings for each of the companies.

CHAPTER 3

# PRINCIPLES OF OPERATIONS MANAGEMENT

In Chapter 2, we noted that a company's strategy for operations management must serve two purposes. It must:

1. Address the *functional area of operations*—the part of the company charged with creating and delivering the goods and services destined for external customers.
2. Guide the *operations activities performed by all personnel* working in value-adding chains anywhere within the organization, whether in a line or staff department, on a product or project team, or in an executive position.

In this chapter, our focus is on the second purpose. And, as we saw in Chapter 1, when operations are defined as transformation processes—and deemed to occur wherever value is created throughout the company—breadth of applicability becomes paramount. A set of fundamental principles has emerged to meet that aim.

## Customer-Serving Principles

Elements of operations strategy that seem to apply universally may be thought of as principles of OM. Exhibit 3-1 presents the 16 principles. They have been adopted by hundreds of successful companies the world over as guides for planning, implementing, and improving operations. Just as running and passing are fundamentals for any team in a variety of sports, the principles serve as fundamental strengths upon which a company might build competitive advantage.

The 16 principles are in three broad groups that parallel the duties of management—formulation, implementation, and improvement. Formulation must account for customers, the company, and competitors (the strategic triangle). Implementation principles address four mainstay OM responsibilities—design and organization, capacity, processing, and problem solving and control. Finally, improvement is the focus of principle 16.

Collectively, the principles have a commonsense ring. Further, they hang together in that they are customer focused, employee driven and data (fact) based. We now look more closely at each principle.

1. **Know and Team Up with the Next and Final Customer.** The customer, whether final consumer or next process, is the object of the first and most important

## Exhibit 3-1 Principles of Operations Management

**Operations Strategy—Formulation**

### Customers:

1. Know and team up with the next and final customer.
2. Become dedicated to continual, rapid improvement in quality, cost, response time, flexibility, variability, and service.

### Company:

3. Achieve unified purpose via shared information and team involvement in planning and implementation of change.

### Competitors:

4. Know the competition and the world-class leaders.

**Operations Strategy—Implementation**

### Design and Organization:

5. Cut the number of product or service components or operations and the number of suppliers to a few good ones.
6. Organize resources into multiple chains of customers, each focused on a product, service, or customer family; create workflow teams, cells, and plants-in-a-plant.

### Capacity:

7. Continually invest in human resources through cross training (for mastery of multiple skills); education; job and career-path rotation; and improved health, safety, and security.
8. Maintain and improve present equipment and human work before thinking about new equipment; automate incrementally when process variability cannot otherwise be reduced.
9. Look for simple, flexible, movable, low-cost equipment that can be acquired in multiple copies—each assignable to workflow teams, focused cells, and plants-in-a-plant.

### Processing:

10. Make it easier to make/provide goods or services without error or process variation.
11. Cut flow time (wait time), distance, and inventory all along the chains of customers.
12. Cut setup, changeover, get-ready, and start-up times.
13. Operate at the customer's rate of use (or a smoothed representation of it); decrease cycle interval and lot size.

### Problem solving and control:

14. Record and own quality, process, and problem data at the workplace. Ensure that frontline improvement teams get first chance at problem solving—before staff experts.
15. Cut transactions and reporting; control causes, not symptoms.

**Operations Strategy—Improvement**

16. Market each improvement; share results with employees, suppliers, and customers. Create a foundation for revisions to strategy.

principle. The remaining principles, which follow from this one, concern *how* to serve the customer better.

Getting to know and teaming up with the customer often requires breaking barriers, especially departmental walls. Teaming up can mean moving associates out of functional departments and into teams and cells—that is, organizing associates by how the work flows. If that isn't practical, then organize cross-functional improvement teams. Although these teams do not "live" together, they meet periodically to solve problems.

Geography is often a barrier (e.g., a customer is located miles away). But responses to such barriers can get creative. For example, Globe Metallurgical, supplier of additives to steel mills and foundries, buses its factory associates to customer plants where they get to know their counterparts. This facilitates quick, easy communication, associate to associate, when the customer has a problem, or when Globe people have questions about customer needs. Globe's strong customer focus contributed to its being named the first (1988) recipient of the Malcolm Baldrige National Quality Award in the small business category.

A metal foundry makes castings by pouring hot metal into a mold, letting it set, and breaking the mold.

2. **Become Dedicated to Continual, Rapid Improvement in Quality, Cost, Response Time, Flexibility, Variability, and Service.** Continual improvement means little without an object. The natural objects are the six general customer wants. This principle makes the connection and applies to any organization. Still, each organization is unique. The next two principles aim at tailoring OM strategy to the particular firm and its competitive environment.

3. **Achieve Unified Purpose via Shared Information and Team Involvement in Planning and Implementation of Change.** Information must be shared throughout the organization if employee-driven continuous improvement is to occur. Few companies apply this principle as effectively as Zytec, a producer of power supplies for computing equipment and a 1991 Baldrige quality prize winner. In developing its five-year strategic plan, Zytec involves 20 percent of its workforce, from all corners of the firm; it even has a few key suppliers and customers comment on the plan. Then, every employee and team has a role in translating the plan into action elements with measurable yearly goals.[1]

4. **Know the Competition and the World-Class Leaders.** In many firms, getting to know the competition has been viewed as a sales and marketing function, useful for competitive pricing, product positioning, and promotion. But for superior companies, that approach is insufficient. Operations management associates cannot be effective without competitive information. They need to learn about competitors' designs, capacities, skill base, and supplier/customer linkages—as well as costs, quality, flexibility, and response times.

Old-style competitive analysis is limited to sampling competitors' services and acquiring and "reverse-engineering" their products; continuous improvement requires that and much more. Blue-chip companies conduct benchmarking studies, in which they gather data and exchange visits with other companies, often in totally different industries. They seek to discover the best practices, not just the best services and products. A number of manufacturers have benchmarked Federal Express in order to learn better ways of handling deliveries.

**Benchmarking**
was developed by Xerox Corporation, whose first benchmarking study took place in 1979. Benchmarking was quickly adopted by many other companies.

Failure to learn about the strengths of the competition or about the best performance in any industry (e.g., the ability to deliver better quality or offer quicker response) leads to complacency and decline. But obtaining and using such information helps motivate a company's people to make necessary improvements, which are stated as principles 5 through 15.

5. **Cut the Number of Product or Service Components or Operations and Number of Suppliers to a Few Good Ones.** Having too many components of a product or service or too many suppliers makes it difficult to do justice to any of them. Reducing the number of product components has become a centerpiece of continuous improvement in many top-flight manufacturing companies. Cutting down on the number of suppliers (of component parts or services) is closely related, and it is becoming common practice in both manufacturing and service organizations.

This principle, the first of two in the design and organization category, pertains to *things;* the next deals with *people.*

6. **Organize Resources into Multiple Chains of Customers, Each Focused on a Product, Service, or Customer Family; Create Work-Flow Teams, Focused Cells, and Plants-in-a-Plant.** This principle addresses problems implicit in familiar bureaucratic statements like, "This office is responsible for issuing the permit," or "Our department processes those forms." Department-to-department work flows can be impersonal and invite finger pointing—at the other department—when things go wrong.

*Close proximity promotes teamwork atmosphere during iron assembly at the Sunbeam plant in Coushatta, Louisiana.*

© Philip Gould/Corbis

To ensure good coordination, error prevention, and continuous improvement, a customer—ideally a single person—at the next process should be known and familiar, a real partner or team member. Also needed is a dependable work-flow path. These are among the reasons why many organizations have reengineered themselves: Hospitals have broken up specialty departments and reorganized into patient-focused care units. Insurance companies have broken up underwriting and claims-processing departments and regrouped into multifunctional teams. And factories and their support offices have reengineered to create focused work cells by families of products.

7. **Continually Invest in Human Resources through Cross-Training (for Mastery of Multiple Skills); Education; Job and Career-Path Rotation; and Improved Health, Safety, and Security.** Capacity is high in cost and has long-term impact. That goes not only for physical capacity, treated in principles 8 and 9, but also for human resource capacity.

Human resources are involved in formulating OM strategy and are the driving force for carrying it out. Like all the elements of capacity, the human resource is an object of continuous improvement. Old static approaches won't do.

Old practices: Divide work into jobs so small and simple that any unskilled person, paid minimum wage, could master it the first day. Assign managers, experts, and professionals to a single career track and keep them there for life so they can really learn the function.

Continuous improvement: Each associate continually masters more job and job support skills, problem-solving techniques, and self-(team) management. Through job switching, associates learn the impact of job A on job B; they discover their collective impact on the whole service or product, as well as their effect on customer satisfaction; and they understand their contribution to employee health, safety, and security. Managers and professionals require occasional career-path switching to gain a broader outlook, to increase their value to the company, and to achieve greater personal career security.

8. **Maintain and Improve Present Equipment and Human Work before Thinking about New Equipment; Automate Incrementally When Process Variability Cannot Otherwise Be Reduced.** People are variable, and variability stands in the way of serving the customer. Progress will therefore require new equipment and automation. The easy, cheap way to achieve progress is for associates to tighten up their slack habits and bad practices. This defers the cost and complexity of automation. It also avoids succumbing to the glamour of automation and the tendency to automate for the wrong reasons, such as the following:

- "Replace run-down, poorly maintained present equipment, and cope with quality variation." Automation actually requires a higher degree of attention to equipment care and maintenance and better process controls on quality.
- "Become more flexible." But the most flexible resource is people, not flexible automation.
- "Invest retained earnings." Investing retained earnings in automation sometimes makes sense, but investing in the company's existing human and physical infrastructure is always a good choice.
- "Eliminate the 'labor problem'." Automation causes major workforce changes and potentially even greater labor problems. Such matters (which often are management problems) are best resolved before piling on other major changes.

9. **Look for Simple, Flexible, Movable, Low-Cost Equipment That Can Be Acquired in Multiple Copies—Each Assignable to Work-Flow Teams, Focused Cells, and Plants-in-a-Plant.** How is growing demand to be served? The common tendency is to speed up the existing process: to add more people or to replace a small machine with a bigger, faster, costlier one.

Companies that have followed such practices for several generations of growth may find themselves with serious capacity obstacles. Their single, fast process is not divisible into focused units; it can process only one model at a time in huge amounts, which usually will be out of phase with actual customer demand patterns; it may be in the wrong location and too costly to move. Mainframe computers come to mind.

This plurality principle is the antidote. Planning in multiple-capacity units allows growth to occur at the same time as the firm is becoming product/customer focused. Moreover, focusing equipment and operating teams on narrow families of products/customers helps large and growing companies act like small, customer-service-minded ones. PCs and laptops come to mind.

10. **Make It Easier to Make/Provide Goods or Services without Error or Process Variation.** This and the next three principles involve the processing itself—the transformation of resources into goods and services. The broad principle might be abbreviated as *Do it right the first time.* It enlists concepts and practices stretching from designing for quality, to partnering up with suppliers and customers for quality, to controlling processes for quality, to collecting and analyzing data for removal of the sources of poor quality.

This approach replaces poor but conventional practices in which causes of good and bad quality were not treated. Instead, manufacturing companies had sizable inspection staffs for sorting bad output from good, typically in late processing stages. Service organizations relied on complaint departments. Usually, plenty of bad results still slipped through.

11. **Cut Flow Time (Wait Time), Distance, and Inventory All along the Chain of Customers.** This and the next two principles are closely associated with just-in-time operations, which shorten **cycle time** and improve responsiveness to customers. By cycle time, we mean elapsed time to complete one unit of output in a process that recycles. The output may be one manufactured item, one processed document, or one served client.

In human services, customers' main gripe is usually long waiting lines. One way to cut the waiting time is for the service organization simply to set queue limits in combination with flexible labor. Some banks and retailers are doing this (see further discussion in Chapters 10 and 11). Queue limitation works just as well in processing documents or materials.

Processing inventories can involve multistage waiting lines. The stages from factories to distribution centers to retail storerooms and display counters are typically choked with work-in-process and pipeline inventories. It's a long, loose chain full of waste and delay. Reaction to changes in demand patterns are cumbersome and slow, and the customer may not wait. Mistakes can pile up before they are noted. By then, their causes may be unclear because the trail is cold. Removing excess inventory at each stage might permit delivery while the customer is still interested, and that can preserve or increase sales and market share. Other benefits include reducing delay-related operating costs, such as extra handling, more transactions and documentation, and excess scrap and rework. Often it is possible to achieve quick response by moving process stages closer together—that is, shortening the flow path.

12. **Cut Setup, Changeover, Get-Ready, and Start-up Times.** This principle deals with preparation-to-serve delays of all kinds. For example, if you want to run a

**Setup, changeover, get-ready, or start-up time** The time to switch from useful output in one mode to useful output in the second.

program on your personal computer, you must first get set up. You have to boot the disk, which, on your older model, takes 29 seconds. Then you make a menu selection (19 seconds), instruct the computer to read disk drive A (10 seconds), and call the desired program into memory (12 seconds). After a total of 1 minute and 10 seconds of setup, you are ready to perform useful work. Not so long, perhaps, but what if you need to switch from a word-processing program to a spreadsheet? Would you have to go through another partial setup? And then perhaps another, to use a database program?

Excess setup time on a computer can be a mild annoyance, or it can seriously detract from someone's productivity. Or, if a client is waiting for the computer to process something, it's a real problem of poor service.

In manufacturing, machine setup and production-line changeovers can eat up enormous amounts of costly capacity and render the company unable to change quickly from one product model to another as customer demand patterns change. As just-in-time methods have come into use, many manufacturers have become aggressive about cutting equipment setup times. For example, at Pepsi's bottling plants, bottle size changeovers have been reduced from 90 minutes to 20 minutes.

However, the problem of long preparation time does not have to involve a machine. A customer may fume while a clerk hunts for an order book or a nurse opens cabinets looking for a roll of tape. Such examples of unpreparedness are commonplace and usually easy to fix. Systematic procedures for attacking these problems have migrated from the manufacturing sector to a growing number of service organizations.

13. **Operate at the Customer's Rate of Use (or a Smoothed Representation of It); Decrease Cycle Interval and Lot Size.** That is: Don't go as fast as you can go, only to see the work pile up in front of your customer at the next process. Don't invest in equipment that runs many times faster than the work can be processed downstream. And don't save up large piles of work before sending it on to the next process. Although those practices are common in typically disconnected companies, they are wasteful and stretch out the response time. Customers may not be willing to wait.

14. **Record and Own Quality, Process, and Problem Data at the Workplace. Ensure That Frontline Improvement Teams Get First Chance at Problem Solving—Before Staff Experts.** Problem solving and control, the topic of the last two principles, are ineffective if problem-solving *data* ends up in the wrong place. A common mistake is sending quality, process, and problem data from the front lines to experts in back offices. That leaves frontline associates (the majority of company employees) out of the problem-solving, control, and process ownership loop. Data is what gets them back in. Then they can do plenty, especially in teams in which knowledge, skills, and ideas are readily shared. Staff experts may have more problem-solving skills, but they have less understanding of the processes where problems occur. Also, staff people are not only expensive and relatively scarce, they are often tied up in other projects. This leaves little time for solving ongoing process problems and on-the-spot emergencies, which are the natural responsibility of frontline associates.

15. **Cut Transactions and Reporting: Control Causes, Not Symptoms.** Transactions and reports often deal with symptoms (e.g., our warranty costs are too high, too much overtime last month, etc.). Effective quality control and production control replace transactions and reports (as much as possible) with process data—categorized and detailed as to causes. Those data fuel the continuous improvement effort and need not

end up in a report. In fact, in the continuous process-improvement mode, by the time a report of a problem comes out, a team of associates would probably already be working on it—or may already have solved it.

Transaction cost reduction is especially relevant to services providers. In the 1990s, managers at banks, insurance companies, and hospitals—large consumers of forms and associated paperwork-related supplies—studied their form-dependent reporting systems for cost-cutting possibilities. They discovered that for every dollar the organization spends on forms, it spends an additional $20 filling it out, copying it, routing it, amending it, storing it, and then throwing it out.[2]

16. **Market Each Improvement: Share Results with Employees, Suppliers, and Customers. Create a Foundation for Revisions to Strategy.** Principle 16 encourages the organization to brag; to boast about accomplishments! It extends the information-sharing mandate of principle 3 from planning data and implementation techniques to performance outcomes. Advertising, publication in trade periodicals, and word-of-mouth communications inform customers, suppliers, and even competitors that a new plateau has been reached. Company displays and internal publications allow employees—those largely responsible for the improvements—to keep abreast of progress and share in the glory.

Ardent application of principle 16 has several positive effects: First, heightened market awareness of improvements in *outputs* serves to increase customers' perceptions of value and helps boost company revenues. Second, the formal sharing of improvements in *process performance* throughout the organization—sometimes called institutionalization—often allows other improvement teams to glean useful ideas. Third, knowledge of novel results raises the bar, opens new avenues for competition, and lays the groundwork for new strategies.

**Institutionalization** is a required component in many team excellence award competitions. In the Illinois Manufacturers' Association competition, for example, it accounts for 10 percent of a team's overall score.

Perhaps the ultimate evidence that principle 16 has been effective occurs when demand for the company's outputs far exceeds its capacity, and the company can pick and choose its customers, rather than having the customers do all of the choosing. Though rare, it does happen! Nypro, a large injection molder headquartered in Clinton, Massachusetts, had over 600 customers for its plastic products in the early 1980s. By the mid-1990s, that number had been pruned—by Nypro—to 31.[3] Today, Nypro remains committed to its simple aim, " . . . to be the best in the world in precision injection molding and related manufacturing solutions . . . creating value for our customers, employees and communities."[4]

**Injection molding** Hot liquid plastic is forced through a die (e.g., for drinking straws or tubes) or into the cavity of a mold where it is allowed to harden into the desired shape.

A final comment about principle 16: The degree to which a company will have opportunity to use it depends highly on the degree to which the company has embraced the other 15 principles.

As we prepared previous editions of this book, we were concerned that presentation of the principles of OM in the early chapters might be a case of too much too soon. No longer. The core ideas—if not the principles themselves—have become ingrained in the daily operations of businesses around the globe. Increasingly, OM students have gained, from their experiences as employees and as customers, firsthand knowledge of several of the principles. And they have read or heard about others, for business literature is replete with success stories touting progress in meeting the targets defined by the principles; we've seen a few thus far in this book.

That said, we realize that some of the principles are less well understood, and we will work to develop them as we go. Throughout the book, we restate a given principle as a margin note near to a concept, procedure, or example to which it applies. At this time, we turn our attention to some of the issues that arise when the principles are implemented.

## Incorporating the Principles

For a variety of reasons, some students, and even a few practitioners, get the idea that while the principles of OM seem okay for guiding the work of line employees and maybe clerical personnel, that's as far as it goes. That is, they fail to see the relevance of OM principles to management, especially upper-level management. In short, what does management by principle have to offer . . . to managers? A related concern is how to measure the incorporation of principles. How do we know if we are succeeding? In this section we address these matters.

### *Principles in Perspective*

A few general comments help put the 16 principles of operations management into perspective:

- The principles serve as strategy but they do not cover the whole strategic waterfront. For example, they cannot *completely* guide a decision on where to set up a branch office, suggest an effective marketing campaign, or direct a major research and development (R&D) program. Complex issues like these involve many variables; top-executive strategic planning as well as strategies for key functional activities will still be required. But, principle 3 should govern that planning.
- Although customers' needs are first-order business, the principles also meet the primary needs of other stakeholders such as employees, officers, investors, suppliers, and creditors. As such, the principles serve to reduce conflict. However, dictionaries tell us that principles are fundamental laws, applicable in the vast majority of cases, but perhaps not in every one.
- The principles are not for managers per se; they are for everyone. All employees, from frontline associates to top-level executives can—and should—put them to use in daily activities. Regardless of whether transformation activities occur within the operations functional area, in a sales meeting, on a design team, or while negotiating financial terms of a contract, the principles apply.

At the close of Chapter 2, we noted that successful CEOs stay connected to company operations. They make a habit of direct interaction with customers and employees—actions suggested in principles 1, 3, 14, and 16. The implication, of course, is that such involvement makes them better managers. Thus, it would seem that a case can be made for the principles in the implementation and improvement parts of strategic management, but what about on strategy formulation? Can the OM principles help create strategy? More importantly, can adherence to the principles result in *better* strategy?

## *Giving Strategy an Edge*

With widespread buy-in to the principles, unified purpose—itself the aim of principle 3—begins to emerge. Teams educate one another about what happens in remote corners of company operations, linkages appear, and the "us-versus-them" syndrome begins to fade. A suggestion that funds be invested in training so that technicians might learn how to cut setup times in a test lab, for example, finds wide-ranging support. People know that improvements will come, and eventually, everyone will benefit from the more responsive lab service. A basic customer need will have been addressed.

Former Motorola chairman and CEO Bob Galvin wanted all Motorola employees to have one-month's training every year.

Perhaps the next training need will appear in accounting; maybe new software to help manage accounts receivable in budding e-commerce activities must be learned. Again, when management by principles is in force, all parties see the pending benefits—principles 2, 7, 10, and perhaps 12 will be served. And the people—lab technicians and accountants in these brief examples—gain expertise. They know more. They have more to offer. They understand, arguably better than any outsiders, the capabilities of the company—one-third of the strategic triangle. The prudent CEO, or any other manager, will want to tap these new resources.

When managers recognize and nurture expertise in the workforce, strategy implementation, and even formulation, needn't be a one-way street as depicted in Exhibit 3-2A. Perhaps top managers will—and should—continue to have primary responsibility for making strategy. We leave that debate for others. We can, however, state with confidence that a shared-information environment, represented in Exhibit 3-2B, brings more knowledge to the table. Furthermore, when everyone is unified in purpose—on the same page, so to speak—strategy implementation is streamlined.

## *Measurement of Success*[5]

How does a company know if it has successfully implemented one or more of the principles of operations management? It won't know unless its managers are willing to submit to a candid review of ongoing business activities. When such a review is undertaken, the company is judged on how well it has implemented each of the 16 principles and may be awarded from zero to five points on each. Scoring is objective; quantifiable plateaus define each point level. The composite scoring scale, complete with the stages in the life-cycle metaphor, is shown in Exhibit 3-3.

Prior to about 1980, few if any companies would have scored above 10 points. The many concepts that underlie the 16 principles just were not on anyone's agenda at that time. One of the first reports of large-scale assessment, published in 1996, analyzed 130 manufacturing companies representing four continents and seven industrial sectors. The distribution of composite score ranges, again accompanied by life-stage analogies, are shown in Exhibit 3-4.

Though management by principles experience varied among the sample set, a few of the companies had been working to incorporate the OM principles for about 10 years.

## Exhibit 3-2 New Thinking about Strategy

**A. Top-Down Strategy**

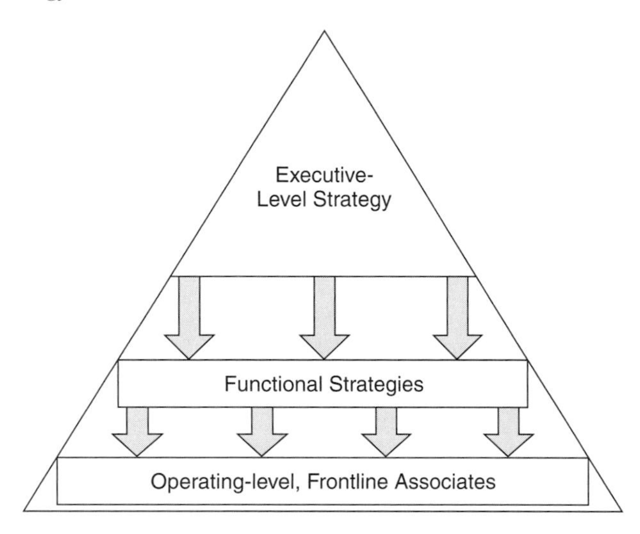


**B. Shared-Information Strategy**

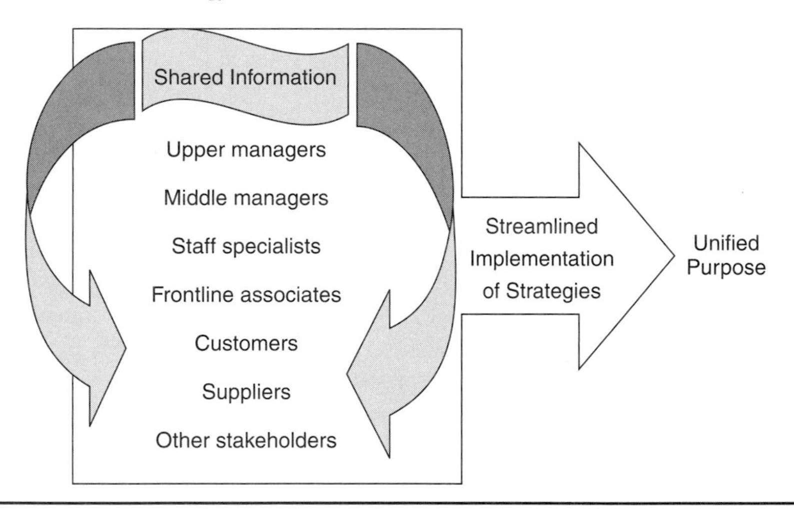


## Exhibit 3-3 Scoring Scale—Principles of Operations Management

**Assessment: 0–5 points awarded for each of the 16 principles**

| | |
|---|---|
| 11–24 points | Eyes open, first steps, early training |
| 25–38 points | Childhood: Trial and error |
| 39–52 points | Adolescence: Checklists and guidelines |
| 53–66 points | Adulthood: Policies |
| 67–80 points | Maturity: Principles |

**EXHIBIT 3-4 Score Distribution—Implementation of OM Principles**

| *Score Range* | *Number of Organizations* |
|---|---|
| Not born yet, 0–10 points | 3 |
| Eyes open, first steps, 11–24 points | 41 |
| Childhood, 25–38 points | 43 |
| Adolescence, 39–52 points | 38 |
| Adulthood, 53–66 points | 5 |
| Maturity, 67–80 points | 0 |

Why are there no "mature" companies? The scoring criteria are tough . . . deliberately so. The aim is to provide a worthy challenge along with guidance for step-by-step continuous improvement. And, over time, that will sharpen competitive advantage.

We have completed our coverage of the foundations of operations management. What lies ahead?

- In Part II, we turn our attention to master planning for demand, capacity, and order fulfillment. These are broad topics that constitute the basis for organization wide transformations.
- In Part III, we look more closely at ways of meeting basic customer wants that were introduced in Chapter 1. "Better, faster, and cheaper" is the theme of Part III.
- Part IV looks at key OM resources—people, materials, and facilities. Output goods and services don't happen unless these factors are carefully managed.
- Finally, in Part V, we return to modes of operations, also introduced in Chapter 1. This time, however, we take a much closer look.

## Summary Check Points

✓ Sixteen principles of operations management serve to guide the activities of all personnel working in value-adding chains throughout any organization. As such, the principles form a strategic foundation upon which competitive advantage can be built.

✓ Collectively, the principles of operations management assist in the (1) formulation or creation of operations strategy, (2) implementation of that strategy in critical organizational duties and elements, and (3) crafting of revisions necessary to maintain continuous improvement in meeting customers' needs.

✓ Although the principles of operations management give priority to customers' needs, the concerns of other organizational stakeholders are addressed as well.

✓ With widespread buy-in to the principles of operations management, sharing of information increases. Strategy creation and implementation are streamlined, and *unity-of-purpose* begins to emerge within the organization.

✓ Progress in implementation of the principles of operations management follows an objective scoring system that, in turn, defines plateaus of accomplishment.

## Exercises

1. According to studies by America's Research Group, 83 percent of women and 91 percent of men say long checkout lines cause them to stop patronizing a store.[6] It is not surprising, therefore, to find that speeding up the checkout process is a major objective for retailing giants such as Wal-Mart, K mart, and Target.
   *a.* What principles of operations management are directly supported by this objective?
   *b.* If you were charged with speeding up the checkout process, what *other* principles of operations management might you follow in accomplishing the task?
2. One element of First City Bank's operations strategy is the opening of 15 new ATM machines in locations around the area.
   *a.* With which principle of operations management does this strategy seem most consistent? Why?
   *b.* Jack Simpson, director of operations at First City, spends several hours each week reading advertisements from competing banks in the area, driving around the area to observe competitors' drive-through banks, and reviewing trade publications for news of banking innovations. What principle of OM is Jack following? Is this work really necessary? Discuss.
   *c.* What other sources of information might First City Bank tap in order to assess its performance? How do these efforts relate to the principles of operations management?
3. Boston-based Teradyne (www.teradyne.com) makes complex instrumentation used to test chips, circuit boards, computerized phone systems, and even software. Teradyne's Catalyst chip tester is priced at $1.5 million to $2 million each.[7]
   *a.* At one time, Teradyne purchased circuit boards from whatever supplier had the capacity to build them. Now, Teradyne buys the boards from only the most competent suppliers. Quality has improved while the cost of the boards decreased by 13 percent, or $6 million per year. What principles of operations management relate to these actions?
   *b.* Formerly, design and manufacturing were conducted separately at Teradyne. On one prototype, assemblers were required to use 20 different types of screws and six different tools to attach those screws.[8] Now, designers and assemblers work together; assemblers assist in design, and designers help assemble prototypes. Product development is faster, far fewer part types and tools are required, and assembly time has decreased by about 38 percent. What principles of OM are supported by these actions?
4. Solectron, winner of two of the prestigious Malcolm Baldrige National Quality Awards, is the world's largest electronics manufacturing services company. Visit the Solectron web site (www.solectron.com) and:
   *a.* Review the company mission statement. What principles of OM are embodied in Solectron's mission? Discuss.
   *b.* Examine other pages in Solectron's web site. What evidence do you find that the company is devoted to meeting basic customer wants as defined in OM principle 2?
   *c.* To what extent does Solectron's web site relate to OM principle 16? Give specific examples of your reasoning.
5. Milwaukee-based Signicast Corporation bills itself as "the world's most advanced investment caster."[9] Visit the Signicast web site (www.signicast.com) and:
   *a.* Review the company history statement. What principles of OM are embodied in the growth and strategy of Signicast? Discuss.
   *b.* How does Signicast define "customer"? How does this relate to the principles of OM?

*c*. Give specific examples of ways the Signicast satisfies customers' needs.
(Note: While at the Signicast site, you have an excellent opportunity to learn about the investment casting process and view some products created in this manner.)

6. What organization that you have dealt with as a customer or client seems best at following principle 11—cutting flow time and travel distance for you (as client) or for your order? How has this been accomplished? (You may need to conduct a small investigation to answer this.)
7. What organization that you have dealt with as a customer or client seems best at following principle 12—being able to switch quickly from one kind of work (or customer) to another without long changeover delays? How has this been accomplished? (You may need to conduct a small investigation to answer this.)
8. What happens when a provider of goods fails to operate at the customer's rate of use (OM principle 13)? (Note: There are two parts to this response.)
9. What happens when a services provider fails to follow principle 13 and operate at the customer's rate of use?
10. Arbor Nurseries does a large business in planting trees for real estate developers who invariably want service "right now." Which four principles of OM must Arbor heed in order to be responsive to this customer want? Discuss.
11. The food and restaurant division of a city health department is under pressure from the department director to improve its performance. The local newspaper has been running a series of exposés on filth in popular restaurants. The stories have criticized the health department for (a) infrequent inspections and (b) long delays in responding to written and telephone complaints about certain restaurants. The division, consisting of five inspectors, 20 clerical employees, and five managerial and supervisory personnel, claims that it doesn't have enough staff and budget to be thorough and quick to respond, as well as make frequent visits. Select four principles of OM that might help the division. Explain your choices.
12. In the 1960s, companywide job announcements at John Deere & Company's headquarters were regularly posted on bulletin boards in the information systems department. Information technology (IT) specialists were encouraged to apply for jobs in marketing, production, and so forth. Four decades later, similar policies were still in force. Today, Deere's IT personnel receive general training on company information systems and specific training from the person that they are replacing. In addition, they are asked to spend two to three months in the functional area that they will most directly support in order to observe processes and activities that are in place.

    Do these sorts of policies relate to any of the principles of OM? Discuss.
13. In your experience as an employee or volunteer, you undoubtedly have encountered annoyance over delays and high error and rework rates at times when these problems are due to separation into departmental specialties. Identify several of the principles of OM that might be followed in order to improve the situation. Discuss how each might be applied.

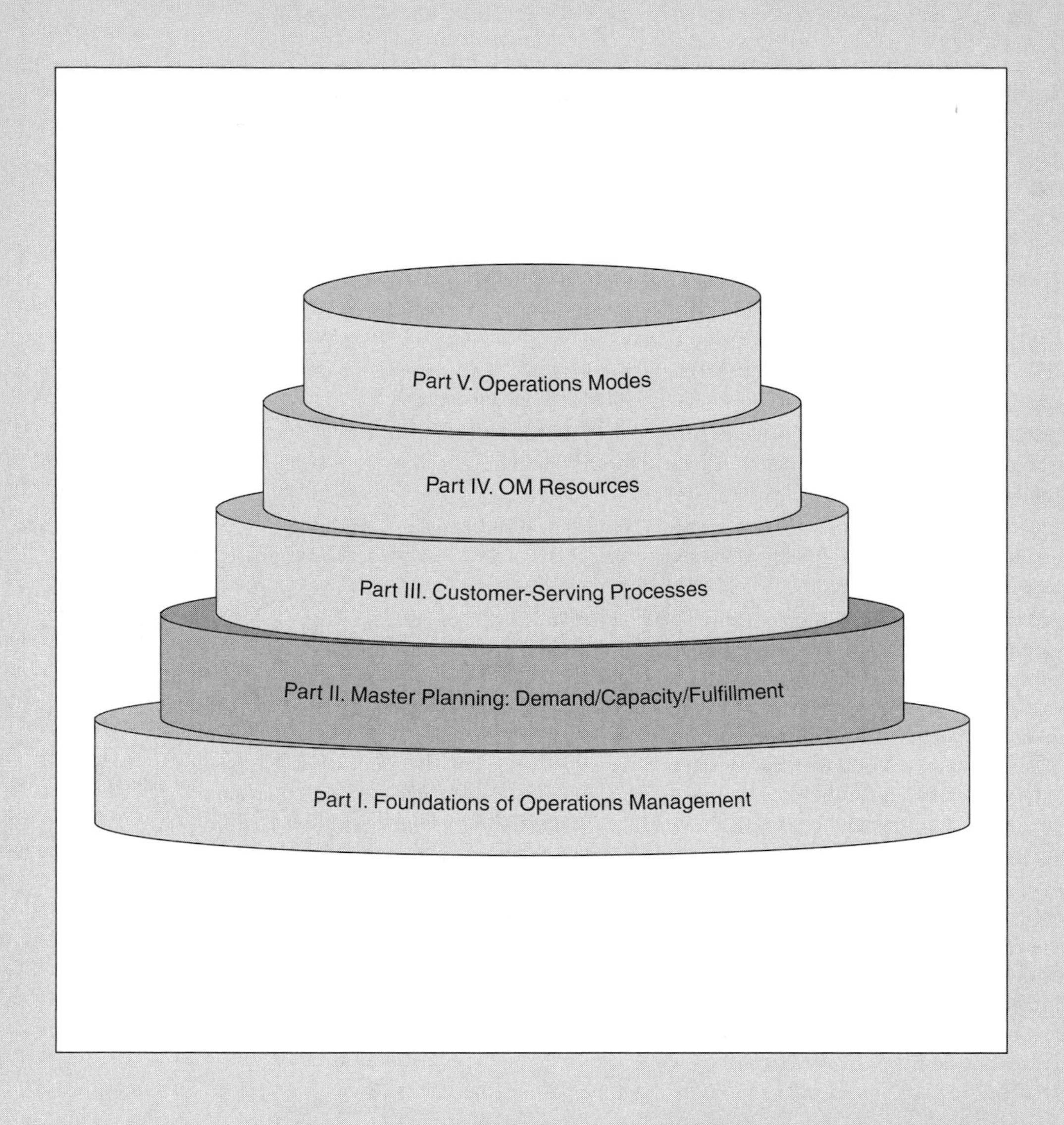
Part V. Operations Modes
Part IV. OM Resources
Part III. Customer-Serving Processes
Part II. Master Planning: Demand/Capacity/Fulfillment
Part I. Foundations of Operations Management

PART II

# MASTER PLANNING: DEMAND/CAPACITY/ FULFILLMENT



Part II is our second-level pass at the field of operations management. Here, we consider what might be referred to as broad-level operations management responsibilities—assessing demand, developing capacity to serve that demand, and crafting a master schedule of planned outputs. Fulfillment of customer orders is the objective, and supplier partnerships figure prominently into the order fulfillment process.

***Points to ponder:*** Just because demand is there doesn't mean that we can or even want to serve it. The business plan (what we *want* to do) and profit potential serve to restrict our choices. The more flexible our capacity, however, the more options we have.

CHAPTER 4

# DEMAND MANAGEMENT AND FORECASTING

Chapters 4 and 5 shift the focus from strategy to the types of planning activities that are needed in order to extend strategic objectives down into the workings of a company's operations. Regardless of the industry, the company, or even the particular choice of strategy, these high-level planning activities—collectively referred to as **master planning**—must occur to guide implementations if customer needs are to be met.

Demand management, the focus of this chapter, is one "half" of master planning. Capacity planning and master scheduling, taken up in Chapter 5, form the other. In practice, demand management, capacity planning, and to some extent master scheduling can occur in a near-simultaneous mode. Distinctions get blurred, since activities that support one often support the others as well. This overlap becomes more apparent as the discussion and examples of Chapters 4 and 5 unfold.

When all parts come together effectively, however, master planning sets the stage for an appropriate balance between supply and demand. That, in turn, enhances competitiveness; costs are lower when resource and processing wastes are minimized, and revenues increase when customer orders are filled. (We examine order fulfillment in Chapter 6.)

Customers' demand for goods and services is the driver, so to speak, so that's the point of departure. Just how *is* demand managed?

## Demand Management in Perspective

Like most of the topics in this book, demand management doesn't "belong" to operations; it affects and is affected by activities throughout an organization. Customer demand is the lifeblood of any enterprise. Though we take an OM perspective and position demand management within the broader umbrella of OM master planning, we view them both within the context of the overall firm. We then narrow the focus and look closely at what makes up demand management.

### *Demand Management in the Organization*

The darker-shaded boxes in Exhibit 4-1 depict core elements of operations management. In a nutshell, business and operations strategies guide master planning, which, in turn, charts the course for transformations that fulfill customer orders. Master planning

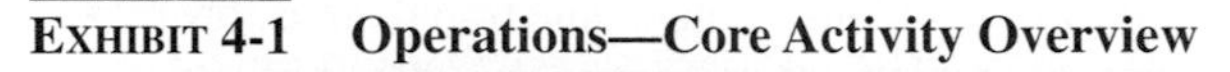

**EXHIBIT 4-1 Operations—Core Activity Overview**

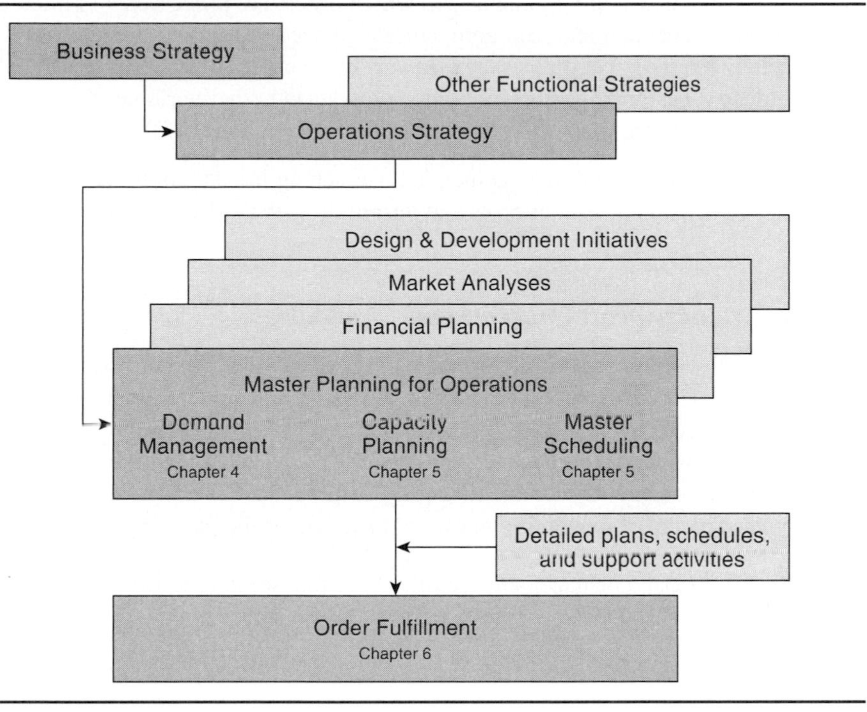


with its three component parts—including demand management—creates the transition link between strategy and results. Lighter shaded elements in Exhibit 4-1 highlight other key relationships that are fundamental to understanding how operations fits within the framework of the organization as a whole. Some points to remember:

- As noted in Chapter 2, operations strategy and other functional strategies ought to be in sync, for collectively, these strategies drive everything else.
- Master planning *is* high-level operations planning. It is equal in importance to financial planning, marketing analyses, and design and development initiatives—the "other" line functions' high-level plans. As with strategies, these plans along with the plans for key staff areas must be mutually supportive.

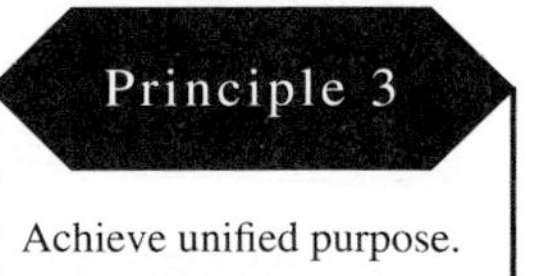


- Demand management, while a critical input to operations planning and pictured within the master planning "box" in Exhibit 4-1, is vital to other parts of the organization as well. It's at the heart of marketing, sets parameters on financial plans, and drives design and development programs. Thus, demand management is a job for multifunctional teams; representatives from marketing, finance and accounting, and design have crucial inputs to offer. (As we shall see in Chapter 5, the same is true for capacity planning and master scheduling.)

- Master plans, buttressed by high-level plans in other functional areas, provide general definition to the manner in which orders are processed and filled in order to meet demand. But companies also need supporting detailed plans and schedules. The specifics of these lower-level activities depend a great deal on industry, customer desires, operations mode, and other variables. Examples of various detailed plans emerge throughout the remainder of the book.

The theme of demand management's far-reaching impact continues when we take a closer look at some of the concepts and terminology that arise when it is carried out in practice.

## *Demand Management: Concepts and Terminology*

As noted in the chapter introduction, demand management is a must-do activity in all organizations. Thus, we expect much variety in its specific application from firm to firm. The Into Practice box "Demand Management in . . ." illustrates but a few of the issues that arise as providers of goods and services craft ways to discover and meet demand. Different approaches to demand management often reflect varying emphases on objectives, type or nature of demand in question, or length of the planning horizon.

**Objectives.** Demand management activities have four somewhat overlapping objectives.

1. *Plan for demand—develop readiness and flexibility.* This relates closely to capacity planning (often the case in manufacturing) or resource planning,

*Under supply creates customer waiting time. As the photo on the left shows, people queue up to buy a hot new product. Oversupply creates large inventories and the costs associated with handling those inventories. The photo on the right shows unsold vehicles in a dealer's lot.*

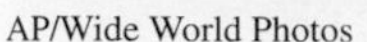

AP/Wide World Photos

© Corbis

INTO PRACTICE

# Demand Management in . . .

### Health Care and Other Public Services:

"There is an increasing challenge to meet the demand for public services that are free at the point of use. Examples in the United Kingdom (in increasing degree of complexity and controversy) include water, higher education, road space, and health care. These are services that we, as a society, all perceive as important and where demand is rising rapidly, and where there are usually significant inefficiencies and inequities in the way they are offered."

Source: "Managing Demand Better," UK Health Service Demand Management Learning Set Web Site, University of Cambridge Clinical School (http://fester.his.path.cam.ac.uk/phealth/demand.htm) [Visited April 2000]

### Personal Products Manufacturing:

"Consumers (are increasingly) demanding gratification from products and services customized to their unique needs. Day Timers, based in Allentown, PA, has responded to this shift by updating the design and manufacture of its standard generic planners. It now allows customers to personalize them by identifying important events or dates, which are then preprinted into the booklets or diary pages."

Source: Peter H. Christian and Emory W. Zimmers, Jr. "Age of Agile Manufacturing Puts Quality to the Test," *Quality Progress,* May 1999, pp. 45–51.

### Transportation:

"The next time you're on an airplane, ask the guy beside you how much his ticket cost; chances are the two of you paid different prices. . . . What sounds like a disservice to full-fare passengers is actually a shrewd strategy that airlines use to maximize profits by forecasting customer demand and charging multiple fares on single flights. Airlines hold as many seats as possible for last minute, full-fare business travelers, but if they miscalculate demand they end up with empty seats. The only way airlines can make that game of chicken profitable is by using a passenger-demand forecasting system to help decide what to charge when."

Source: "Working Smart: United Airlines' Passenger Demand Forecasting System," *CIO Magazine,* July 1, 1999 (http://www.cio.com/archive/070199_smart_content.html)

### Order Fulfillment:

On May 8, 2000, J.D. Edwards & Company announced that it had achieved a new benchmark in B2B order fulfillment capability. In conjunction with Sun Microsystems, the company demonstrated ability to process over 220,000 sales order lines per hour. "The test simulated service for 50,000 buyers ordering more than 5,000 items . . . [over the entire] sale-to-cash process . . . from order placement through fulfillment."

Source: "J.D. Edwards' OneWorld Reaches New B2B Fulfillment Scalability Record" (http://www.prnewswire.com), May 8, 2000.

staffing (in retailing or service organizations), or scheduling (in many types of firms). It might incorporate training, new equipment or technology, new partnerships, and so forth.

2. *Recognize and account for all sources of demand.* This includes keeping track of known orders from external and internal customers, and **demand forecasting**—estimating future demand and potential orders. Forecasting is addressed later in the chapter.
3. *Preprocess demand.* This refers to the initial steps in order processing and fulfillment activities; we take up these topics in Chapter 6.
4. *Influence the timing, quantity, or nature of demand.* Numerous examples of demand manipulation exist: lower prices for matinee movies or "red-eye"

flights (timing), price discounts for purchase of multiple items (quantity), and restaurant "specials" or rebates on specific automobile models (nature).

**Types of Demand.** Demand may be classified along several dimensions. Three are of particular use in operations management. We may speak of independent versus dependent demand, demand for outputs versus inputs, and aggregate versus item demand.

1. *Independent or dependent demand.* An **independent demand** item is desired by customers for use as is; it does not need to go into a larger assembly (called a *parent* item) in order to be used. Desire for a **dependent demand** item, on the other hand, exists solely because of demand for the parent independent demand item. Demand for a table (independent demand item), for example, creates demand for four table legs (dependent demand items). Generally, we forecast independent demand, but calculate demand for dependent items. A forecast demand for 10 tables yields a calculated demand for 40 ($4 \times 10$) legs.

2. *Demand for outputs or inputs.* Demand for outputs—goods and services that external customers want—is familiar to most of us. But operations managers also need to know demand for units of resources such as hours of labor or machine time. Likewise, financial managers must know levels of funds needed to cover operations, design and development efforts, and support activities. In some cases, inputs demand is referred to as *capacity demand,* a topic we reserve for the next chapter. In other instances, managers speak of human resource requirements, budget needs, or facilities requirements.

Demand for inputs may be calculated if the dependency relationship to projected outputs is clear and accurate. For instance, if every new scuba tank requires a 30-minute test at a hydrostatic pressure station, then demand for test-station time (input) is easily calculated from tank (output) demand. When dependency relationships are ill defined, however, people must usually forecast demand for inputs.

3. *Aggregate versus item demand.* **Aggregate demand** is total demand, not broken down by specific item or category. Examples might be tons of steel consumed, total labor hours, and number of pallets of supplies. **Item demand,** as the name suggests, refers to demand for a specific part (perhaps by number), operation (again, by number), or activity (maybe by job code). In a given situation, aggregate or item demand may be independent or dependent, may refer to outputs or inputs, and may be forecast or calculated.

**Length of the Planning Horizon.** Demand management must meet short-, medium-, and long-term needs. The length of term for these intervals varies a great deal by industry, but one general rule applies to all: The demand management effort can be simplified if **lead time**—the time required to get things done—is shortened. (Lead time is referred to as **cycle time** or **throughput time** in some industries.)

Principles 2 &11

Reduce response time and flow time.

1. *Short term.* The short-term focus is item demand. Personnel need to know requirements—stated in natural units—for quantities and timing of each item is the company's mix of output goods and services and for resource items as well. JIT, flexible manufacturing systems, and Internet-based commerce have significantly reduced the

short-term horizon; for some durable goods producers, short-term is but a day or two. In services, short-term time horizons are often daily, hourly, or even 10- to 15-minute intervals in fast-paced operations settings.[1]

2. *Medium term.* The medium-term aim is to project aggregate goods and services demand in order to facilitate capacity planning. The focus is on aggregate labor, machine usage, and inventory. Planners also work with more general units of measure; dollar-volume is one good indicator of overall (aggregate) demand in retailing, for example.

In the service sector, medium-term demand management could cover but a few days; monthly and quarterly time frames are common. In manufacturing, the medium-term horizon varies; 6 to 18 months has been traditional, but a variety of forces have collapsed that time frame. Designs that are easier to build, better supply-chain management, manufacturing process improvements, and technological innovations associated with Internet-based commerce are examples of time-based competition influences. Today, for some manufacturers the medium-term horizon begins a few weeks into the future.

3. *Long term.* Long-term demand management affects planning for buildings, infrastructure, utilities, capital equipment, and product design and development programs. Long-term plans may extend 10 or 20 years into the future for companies that acquire or supply large-scale capital-intensive items or cutting-edge goods. Nuclear power plants, hazardous waste treatment and containment facilities, and new drugs can require extensive hearings and debate, environmental impact studies, licenses, and government approvals. The long-term horizon for services providers, on the other hand, may be but a few months. Monetary volume is the preferred measure for long-term demand management.

In large organizations, demand management activities keep many employees busy. In start-ups and small firms, though the task is spread among fewer people, its importance is every bit as crucial. When demand is known, in the form of customer orders perhaps, the demand management task is challenging enough. When demand is not known—the situation most organizations face to some degree—it must be forecast. The remainder of this chapter is devoted to forecasting and some of the additional challenges it places on demand management teams.

## Issues in Demand Forecasting

Let's be candid: *Forecasting is guessing.* Trying to predict the future is an iffy proposition. Businesses forecast because they have to, not because they want to. The desire to increase competitiveness by being ready for customers—coupled with the reality of lead times—makes forecasting a necessary ingredient in demand management.

But, wouldn't the competitive thing be to simply stock large inventories of outputs and wait for the customer orders to roll in? Not really; there are risks of being stuck with costly inventories when forecasts are too high just as there are risks of lost sales when forecasts have been too low. Insight into the science and art of forecasting comes by understanding lead-time composition, sources of business forecasting data, and forecast error.

### *Lead-Time Composition*

Measurement of lead time can often result in two different values, one from the provider and another from the customer. The difference is explainable at least in part when one considers the long-, medium-, and short-term components of "the time required to get things done." In OM, therefore, it helps to examine the lead-time/forecasting horizon interface from two perspectives, provider's and customer's. Both are captured in Exhibit 4-2.

**Provider's Perspective.** Seven numbered lead-time activities, in rough sequential order from left to right, are generic, but describe major activities that must occur before outputs can be delivered. Portions of the first three occur somewhat simultaneously; they reveal responsibilities of financial and design personnel in addition to capacity-planning activities, where operations and several key support groups have significant impact. Moreover, these three sets of activities might occur but once, with occasional upgrades, for a given product family or market group. The last four activities (4–7) are largely the job for operations supported by purchasing and other specialists. They could be highly repetitive, occurring numerous times during a product's life span. Generally:

1. In start-up operations or whenever new products or processes are introduced, the provider's long-term forecasting horizon must incorporate the time it takes to get all of the lead-time activities accomplished. If it takes five years to acquire financing, design, capacity, and so forth to market a new product, then the forecasting horizon must be *at least* that long.

**EXHIBIT 4-2 Forecasting Lead-Time Requirements**

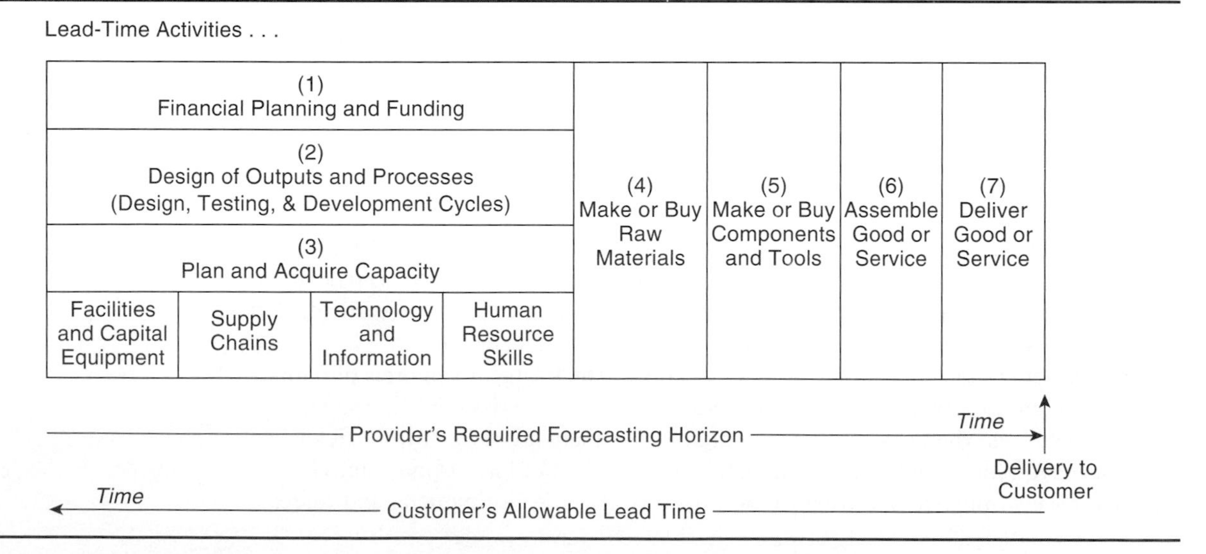

2. After start-up, say during steady-state operations, initial lead-time activities for a product or customer group are completed, and the forecasting horizon can shorten. Medium-term or even short-term forecasting will provide information necessary to marshal resources for materials acquisition, assembly, and delivery obligations.
3. At each stage, forecasters must consider timing requirements of next-process customers, and—as we were reminded in Chapter 1—look on down the line to the needs of end-stage (probably external) customers. Implementation of just-in-time processing with its tight stage-to-stage linkages, however, makes this a natural occurrence.

**Principle 13**

Operate at the customer's rate of use.

**Customer's Perspective.** For customers, allowable lead-time is a statement not only of *how long* they are willing to wait but also of *what they are willing to wait for.* In Exhibit 4-2, the lower arrow extends from right to left and indicates lead-time activities that progressively might be included in allowable lead times. Several categories emerge:

- Some industries have competitive pressures to meet demand immediately upon receipt of an order. Customers expect to wait only for delivery from most service providers and from retail outlets where delivery occurs from stock.
- Next are industries where customers are willing to wait for assembly and delivery. These make-parts-to-stock and assemble-to-order businesses include Subway sandwich shops, mail- or Internet-ordered computer outlets, and custom assembly job providers.
- Job-oriented, make-to-order firms form the next class. After placing orders, customers wait for component (and perhaps materials as well) acquisition in addition to assembly and delivery. Foundries, hospitals, and landscape/nursery companies are in this group. Responsive supply chains minimize the amount of materials these firms must keep on hand.
- Industries with very long planning, design, and manufacturing or installation lead times make up the final class. These firms provide either heavy capital goods or large-scale integrative equipment installation and service work. Examples include shipbuilders and heavy construction companies. Customers know that they are project oriented and make only to order.

Usually, customers are blind to any preceding forecasting and demand management effort; they just expect it to have been done. They judge a provider's competitive timeliness according to *their* definition of allowable lead time—the time from order placement until receipt of goods or services.

To sum up a bit, two fundamental messages for operations managers emerge. First, to reiterate a point made earlier, take action to reduce lead times at every stage. Forecasting is simpler when the horizon can be decreased. Getting rid of process wastes—process streamlining—is the aim. Second, be better prepared to meet demand as it materializes. And as long as lead time is a reality, better forecasts will bear fruit. We now continue along that line with a brief look at major sources of forecast data.

### *Data Sources*

For many people, the wild ride of the stock markets during the 1990s and early 2000s gave new meaning to the timeless human fascination with the future: I wonder what tomorrow will bring? Prudent investors learned that an expanded set of information sources helped them plan their financial futures.

Businesses are no different. They want to chart a course with inputs from a variety of sources. Consequently, demand forecasting is often three-pronged, perhaps coordinated by a corporate planning department. Three major groups of projections help create a demand forecast.

- *Marketing projections.* Planners base marketing projections, typically measured in monetary units, on sales projections, sales force estimates, test market results, other kinds of consumer surveys, and special promotions.
- *Economic projections.* Economists look at how the economy is likely to affect the organization's demand. Economic forecasting based on sets of computer-processed mathematical equations is known as econometrics.
- *Historical demand projections.* Computerized statistical packages help teams project past demand patterns into the future.

Principle 10

Improve accuracy; reduce variation.

While further exploration of marketing and economic projections is beyond our scope, we do recognize their importance. They show the big picture so that planners can sharpen their judgment about future demand and reduce variation between what customers want and what the firm provides. Historical demand projections (taken up later), on the other hand, are at the core of demand management. Regardless of the sources of data for forecasting, a fundamental aim is high forecast accuracy, usually measured by forecast error.

### *Forecast Error*

The popular ways of measuring **forecast error** have this in common: All are after the fact. That is, a manager must wait one period (sometimes longer) to unearth the error in the forecast.

*Forecast error* for a specific item in a given time period is:

$$E_t = D_t - F_t \tag{4-1}$$

where

$E_t$ = Error for period $t$

$D_t$ = Actual demand that occurred in period $t$

$F_t$ = Forecast for period $t$

The period $t$ depends on the purpose of the forecast. It might be a year for forecasting demand for a new facility (e.g., new motel units), or it might be 15 minutes for a hot prepared fast food (e.g., a hamburger) or for trade requests on an Internet brokerage.

Usually, there is little value in knowing the error for just one period. Forecast error over several periods, however, indicates the validity of the forecasting method.

**Mean Absolute Deviation.** Among the ways of calculating average error, one of the simplest and widest used is the **mean absolute deviation (MAD).** The MAD is the sum of the absolute values of the errors divided by the number of forecast periods; that is,

$$MAD = \frac{\sum |E_t|}{n} \tag{4-2}$$

where $n$ is number of periods.

Example 4-1 shows the calculation of the MAD for eight business days in a small service firm.

## Example 4-1: FORECAST ERROR—RÉSUMÉS-A-GLOW, LTD.

Kathy and Kyle have just opened their new business, a résumé preparation service. As part of their business plan, needed to secure start-up financing, they forecast a level daily demand of 10 customers. After the first eight days of business, they evaluated the wisdom of the level forecast. Exhibit 4-3 shows the demand pattern and the error. The table below shows the day, actual demand (number of customers), and forecast in the first three columns. In column 1, −8 is the first business day, −7 is the next, and so on through the eighth business day.

| *(1) Period (day) (t)* | *(2) Demand (customers) ($D_t$)* | *(3) Forecast (customers) ($F_t$)* | *(4) Error ($E_t$)* | *(5) Absolute Error $\lvert E_t \rvert$* |
|---|---|---|---|---|
| −8 | 10 | 10 | 0 | 0 |
| −7 | 8 | 10 | −2 | 2 |
| −6 | 13 | 10 | 3 | 3 |
| −5 | 5 | 10 | −5 | 5 |
| −4 | 9 | 10 | −1 | 1 |
| −3 | 8 | 10 | −2 | 2 |
| −2 | 11 | 10 | 1 | 1 |
| −1 | 12 | 10 | 2 | 2 |
| | | Sum: | −4 | 16 |

Error, in column 4, is column 2 minus column 3, and column 5 is the absolute value (ignore the minus signs) of column 4. The sum of column 5 provides the working figure needed in the formula:

$$MAD = \frac{\sum |E_t|}{n} = \frac{16}{8} = 2.0$$

**EXHIBIT 4-3 Demand and Forecast Plot—Résumés-a-Glow, Ltd.**

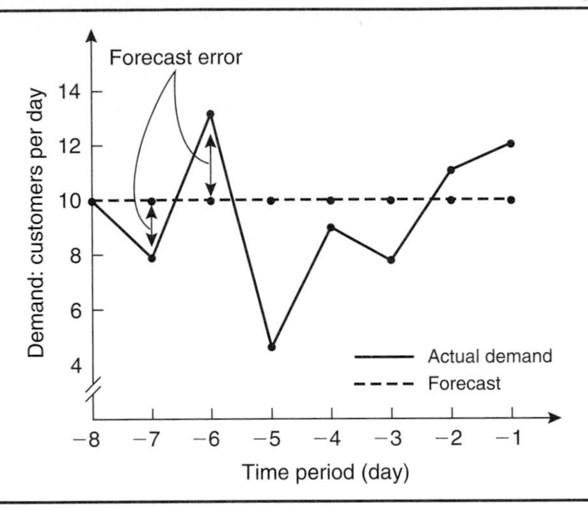


Is a mean absolute error of 2.0 too high? If so, does it suggest changing the forecast or the forecasting method? Kathy and Kyle decide to watch closely for another week or two, then decide.

**Forecasting Specific versus Aggregate Demand.** Forecast error is likely to be high for a specific product such as number of vanity vehicle license plates. Error is less, however, when forecasting the aggregate demand for a group of several related products, such as vanity, common, commercial, and government vehicle plates. The reason is that the high and low forecasts for each product tend to cancel out in the aggregate.

This can affect capacity planning. Example: The human resource department of vehicle licensing is planning labor requirements for the next four quarters. First personnel project historical demand for all types of licenses. Next, they translate the aggregate projection into labor hours and then number of people.

Using aggregate forecasting in this way works fine if employees are flexible. If not, the method is a sham. Say that the licensing agency has four service counters, one for each type of vehicle license. If vanity plates surge in popularity, that service counter and its support people will need help. If employees at the next counter—say, common plates—are cross-trained, no problem. One or more common-plate associates help process the vanity-plate paperwork. Service does not degrade, and the aggregate forecast has done its work well.

**Forecast Error: Near versus Distant Future.** Make an honest effort at answering these three questions: How many hours will you spend reading this week? How about the third week in April next year? The week of your 85th birthday? Obviously, forecasts are more accurate for near-future periods than for more distant ones. This somewhat intuitive point is illustrated in Exhibit 4-4 with data from a picture frame assembly shop.

Initially, the supervisor set a level forecast of 500 frames per week (column 2) for the next two quarters, far enough out for capacity-planning purposes. The cumulative

**EXHIBIT 4-4 Cumulative Forecast Error: Picture Frames**

| (1)<br>Week Number | (2)<br>Weekly Demand Forecast | (3)<br>Cumulative Demand Forecast [(1) × (2)] | (4)<br>Cumulative Actual Demand | (5)<br>Cumulative Absolute Error [\|(4) − (3)\|] |
|---|---|---|---|---|
| 2 | 500 | 1,000 | 1,162 | 162 |
| 5 | 500 | 2,500 | 2,716 | 216 |
| 10 | 500 | 5,000 | 5,488 | 488 |
| 15 | 500 | 7,500 | 8,110 | 610 |
| 20 | 500 | 10,000 | 11,250 | 1,250 |
| 26 | 500 | 13,000 | 14,510 | 1,510 |

forecast for selected weeks (2, 5, 10, 15, 20, and 26) appears in column 3; column 3 equals column 1 times column 2. Column 4 shows cumulative actual demand—for the same selected weekly periods. Cumulative absolute error (column 5) is actual (column 4) minus forecast (column 3). Error rises as the forecast takes in a longer time period.

The picture frame example raises several issues concerning length of forecast period and other more general points:

**Principle 2**

Cut response times.

1. Long-term forecasting, even with the threat of increasing error, is often necessary in order to plan medium-, and long-term capacity. Forecasts must project as far into the future as the firm's lead times.
2. The demand pattern in the picture frame example is actually rather steady, slightly less than 560 frames per week, so the level forecast was the correct move on the supervisor's part. Though a bit low in magnitude, it was a good pattern guess. Furthermore, as we see in later chapters, smooth or level demand is easier to serve.
3. As time passes, interjecting newer data (e.g., recent demands) can refine forecast. The frame-shop supervisor might have examined cumulative error after week 5, for instance, and switched to a weekly forecast of 550 frames (roughly 2,716 ÷ 5) at that point. If so, the cumulative forecast for the 26-week period would have been 14,050 (2,500 through week 5 and 11,550 for weeks 6 through 26)—a figure much closer to actual demand for the two quarters. Alternatively, the supervisor might have elected monthly adjustments.
4. Forecast error analysis is hindsight. We can speak about what the frame shop supervisor should have done because we can see the entire two quarters—the historical demand time series. At the five-week point, however, the supervisor didn't have that knowledge; a guess had to be made.

If the frame shop supervisor asked you now what to forecast for the next two quarters, your response might be, "About 560 frames per week—that is, if the past demand pattern holds true for the future."

You've just used one of several popular projection techniques. We examine others in the sections that follow.

## Historical Demand Projections

Getting a good forecast may require trying out several techniques and selecting the best one—the one with lowest forecast error. The matrix in Exhibit 4-5 relates techniques to forecast horizons and purposes. The techniques group into three categories, all relying on historical demand data. The first two, multiperiod pattern and patternless projections, employ time-series data. The two "No's" in the patternless row indicate that those techniques have limited applicability; their only effective use is for short-term product scheduling. Associative projections, the third group in the matrix, do not involve time series; rather, they track demand against some variable other than time.

**Time series**
A sequential set of observations of a variable, such as demand, taken at regular intervals; useful in both historical analyses and future projections.

By time series, we mean a series of demands over time. The main recognizable time-series components are

1. **Trend,** or slope, defined as the positive or negative shift in series value over a certain time period.
2. **Seasonal variation (seasonality),** usually occurring within one year and recurring annually.
3. **Cyclical pattern,** also recurring, but usually spanning several years.
4. **Random events** of two types:
   *a.* Explained, such as effects of natural disasters or accidents.
   *b.* Unexplained, for which no *known* cause exists.

Each of the first three variations appears in pure form as a separate three-year time series in Exhibit 4-6A. The trend line is positive. In the undulating seasonality series, the seasonal high occurs in the first quarter of each year and the seasonal low is in the third quarter. The cyclical series peaks in about the middle of year 2. Exhibit 4-6B shows how

**EXHIBIT 4-5 Historical Demand Projection Forecasting Techniques**

| | Forecast Horizon | | |
|---|---|---|---|
| *Forecasting Technique* | *Short Term* | *Medium Term* | *Long Term* |
| Multiperiod pattern projection (mean, trend, seasonal) | Yes | Yes | Yes |
| Patternless projection (moving average, exponential smoothing, and simulation) | Yes | No | No |
| Associative projection (leading indicator and correlation) | Yes | Yes | Yes |
| | ↑ Product scheduling | ↑ Labor and inventory planning | ↑ Facilities planning |
| | Forecast Purposes | | |

**EXHIBIT 4-6 Components of a Time Series**

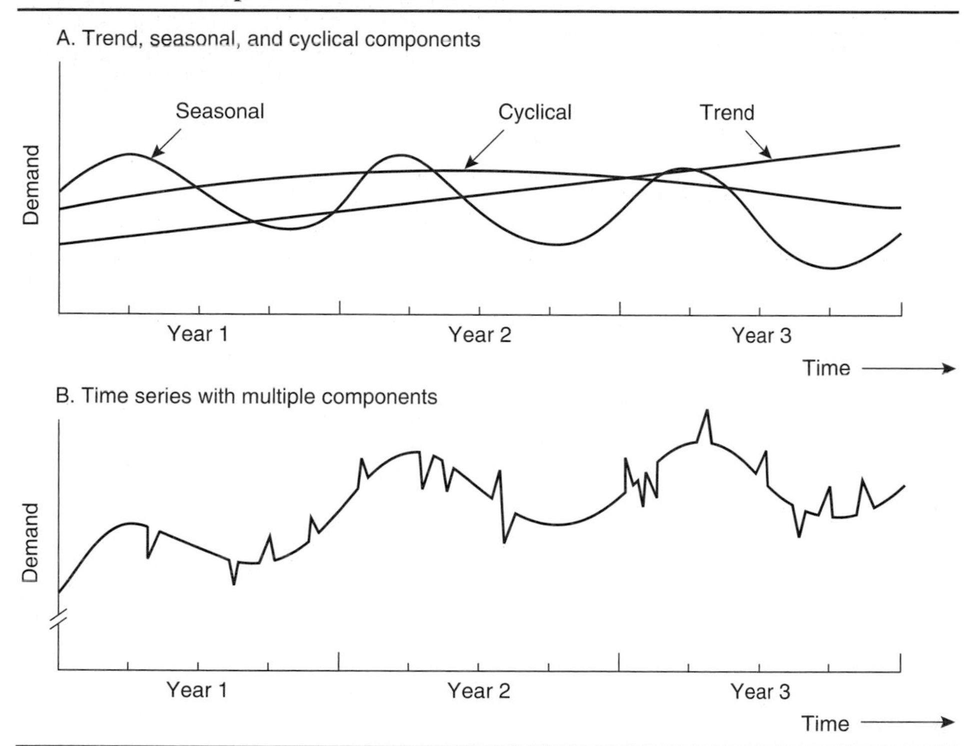


a time series might appear with all three of the pure components along with some random events, shown as spikes.

Forecasting models exist for use with time series containing any or all of these components. Many demand forecasts are rather simple extensions of past series behavior into the future. For example, suppose the demand for tow-truck and jump-start services has peaked in the winter season in the 10 years for which records exist. We would expect this seasonal component to continue, and that would affect the tow-truck firm's planning of service to troubled motorists in the future.

Seasonal effects surround us (the flu season, the tourist season in a given locale, the harvest season), and all usher in demand peaks and valleys for goods and services. The magnitude may vary, but the pattern goes on and on.

# Multiperiod Pattern Projection

Consideration of the historical forecasting models listed in Exhibit 4-5 constitutes most of the remainder of the chapter. First are the three models used in multiperiod pattern projection.

### *Mean and Trend Projections*

The simplest projection of a time series uses the arithmetic mean. When historical demand lacks trend and is not inherently seasonal, the simple mean may serve well. More

**Exhibit 4-7 Arithmetic Mean and Trend Projection—Data Services, Inc.**

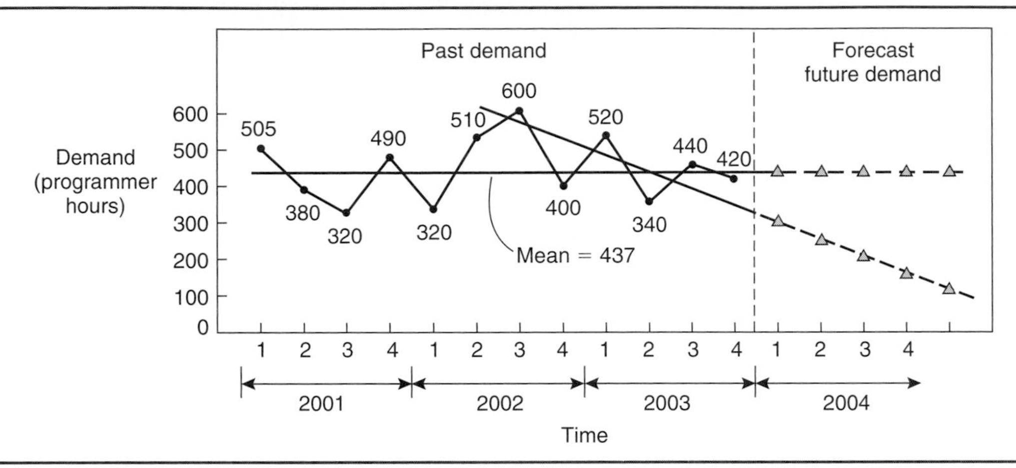


often there is at least some upward or downward trend, which could even be projected as a curve. Exhibit 4-7 illustrates the mean and trend for Data Services, Inc., which offers commercial computer programming.

Three years of past quarterly demand in hours of programmer time are plotted. A first impression might be that there is no strong trend, and a bit of study shows no seasonal pattern either. If a certain quarter's demand is high one year, it looks as likely to be low the next. The up-and-down movement seems random. Also, one would not consider programming to have a seasonal demand pattern. What should the forecast be for upcoming quarters in the year 2004? Perhaps the mean (which works out to be 437) is the best way to minimize forecast error for such a nondescript demand; see the level dashed line.

Alternatively, we might look at only the most recent data, say, the last seven quarters. The trend is downward; see the "eyeball" projection (done by eye with a straightedge) slanting downward in the exhibit. Data Services's analysts may consider the projection to be valid for one or two quarters into the year 2004. They do not accept it for the longer term, since it is trending toward out-of-business status! If they know the business is strong enough to carry on and prosper, the analysts would look for a more realistic way to project the future.

For a better forecast, better demand data might help. Let us assume that 20, not 12, quarters of past demand data are available; see Exhibit 4-8. Quite a different pattern emerges. The long-run trend, projected with a straight edge two years (eight quarters) into the future, is definitely upward. The year 2004 quarterly forecasts are now in the range of 500 programmer-hours instead of the 300 to 200 range resulting from the seven-quarter downward trend projection in Exhibit 4-7.

Another interpretation is that the 20-quarter demand data describe a slow curve. The exhibit shows such a curve projected by the eyeball method through 2004. The 2004–2005 forecast is now between the two previous straight-line forecasts leveling off at about 450.

**Exhibit 4-8 Twenty-Quarter Eyeball Curve—Data Services, Inc.**

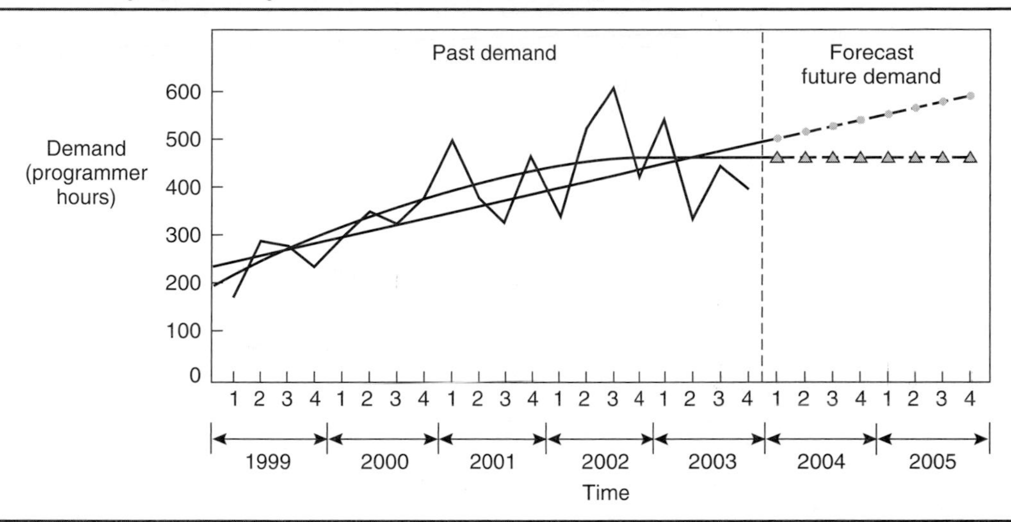


Forecasters may use the graphic projection only to sharpen their own judgment. For example, Data Services's people may know something about their customers that leads them to a more optimistic forecast than the projected 450 programmer hours. As Al Ries and Jack Trout point out, "Trends change very slowly. It's only a fad that is fast-moving."[2] Even where outside information, perhaps about a fad, seems to overrule historical projections, the projections are worth doing. The procedure is quick and simple.

Another method of trend projection is mathematical projection using regression analysis. The least-squares technique of regression analysis, discussed in the chapter supplement, results in an equation of a straight line that best fits the historical demand data. To get a trend projection, teams extend the line into the future. The least-squares method may be modified to yield nonlinear projections as well.

The accuracy of least squares is not its main value. Eyes and straightedge are generally accurate enough for something as speculative as forecasting. But computer-based forecasting routines have an extra benefit: They are usually able to print out mathematical formulas as approximations of the demand pattern, graphic projections, and tabular listings. Thus, least-squares regression is valued not for its forecasting accuracy but because it aids in routinizing some of the forecasting steps.

### *Seasonal Effects*

Often an item showing a trend also has a history of demand seasonality. In fact, perhaps most goods and services exhibit at least some seasonality, which calls for the **seasonal index** method of building seasonality into a demand forecast.

**Seasonal Index: An Example.** The moving business is seasonal, so let's consider how a mover might make use of seasonal indexes. Exhibit 4-9 shows four years of

**EXHIBIT 4-9 Seasonal Demand History—Metro Movers**

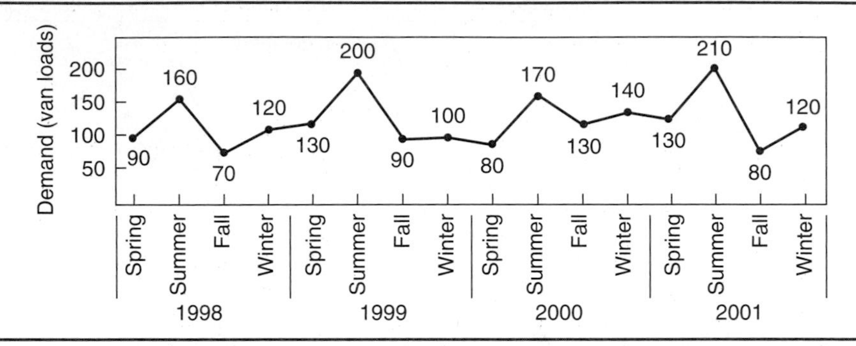


demand data, in van loads, for Metro Movers, Inc. Since moving companies experience heavy demand surges during summer school vacations, Metro groups its demand history into three-month seasons—summer, fall, winter, and spring.

From the demand graph, summer demand is clearly the highest and fall demand is generally the lowest. (Note: Besides seasonality, there appears to be a slight upward trend over the 16 periods, but we'll ignore that for now.)

Using fall 1998 as an example, we calculate the seasonal index as follows:

1. Find the seasonal average. Fall 1998 is in the middle of a year that includes half of spring 1998, all of summer, fall, and winter 1998, and half of spring 1999. Thus, the seasonal average demand for the year that surrounds fall 1998 is

$$\frac{(90/2) + 160 + 70 + 120 + (130/2)}{4} = 115 \text{ van loads}$$

2. Find the seasonal index by dividing actual demand by the seasonal average. Since actual demand for fall 1998 is 70, the seasonal index is

$$\frac{70}{115} = 0.61$$

In other words, the fall 1998 demand was only 61 percent of an average season's demand for the surrounding year.

By the same two-step procedure, the four years of demand history yield the following seasonal indexes:

| | | | |
|---|---|---|---|
| Fall 1998 | 0.61 | Spring 2000 | 0.70 |
| Winter 1998 | 0.96 | Summer 2000 | 1.36 |
| Spring 1999 | 0.98 | Fall 2000 | 0.95 |
| Summer 1999 | 1.51 | Winter 2000 | 0.95 |
| Fall 1999 | 0.73 | Spring 2001 | 0.89 |
| Winter 1999 | 0.88 | Summer 2001 | 1.53 |

3. The final step is to reduce the three indexes for each season to a single average value. For the three summer indexes the average is

   $$\frac{1.51 + 1.36 + 1.53}{3} = 1.47$$

   The other three average seasonal indexes are: 0.85 for spring, 0.76 for fall, and 0.93 for winter. These numbers are rounded so that the four indexes sum to 4.0—exactly four seasons.

Now, Metro's forecasters have what they need to do a seasonally adjusted forecast. Suppose Metro expects to move 480 van loads of goods in 2002, which is simply an arithmetic mean projection of recent past years' demand. It would be foolish to just divide 480 by 4 and project 120 vans per season. Instead, multiply the average-season value, 120 loads, by the seasonal index for each season, yielding seasonally adjustable forecasts. The procedure is as follows:

$120 \times 0.86 = 103$ vans forecast for spring 2002

$120 \times 1.47 = 176$ vans forecast for summer 2002

$120 \times 0.76 = 91$ vans forecast for fall 2002

$120 \times 0.93 = \underline{112}$ vans forecast for winter 2002

Yearly total $= 482$ (not exactly 480 because of upward rounding)

**Seasonally Adjusted Trends.** The seasonal index method may also be applied to projections when a trend component is present. Suppose forecasters at Metro Movers believed that the 2003 moving demand would reflect a 5 percent upward trend over the 2002 demand. On an annual basis, that increase would be calculated as

$$480 \times 1.05 = 504 \text{ vans for 2003}$$

And the average-season demand for 2003 would be:

$$504 \div 4 = 126 \text{ vans}$$

Next, the seasonal indexes may be applied to the value of the average season. The procedure is as follows

$126 \times 0.86 = 107$ vans for spring 2003

$126 \times 1.47 = 185$ vans for summer 2003

$126 \times 0.76 = 96$ vans for fall 2003

$126 \times 0.93 = \underline{117}$ vans for winter 2003

Total $= 506$ vans

Exhibit 4-10 shows the 2002 and 2003 forecasts. The figure shows what might be expected: Trend effects, which are so important over the long run, tend to be overshadowed by seasonality when the short run, say, one year or less, is the focus. For

Steady growth, reflected by an upward trend, is great for business. Seasonal demand ups and downs, however, can give managers fits when they try to plan capacity to meet that demand.

**EXHIBIT 4-10 Seasonal Adjustment of Trend Projection—Metro Movers**

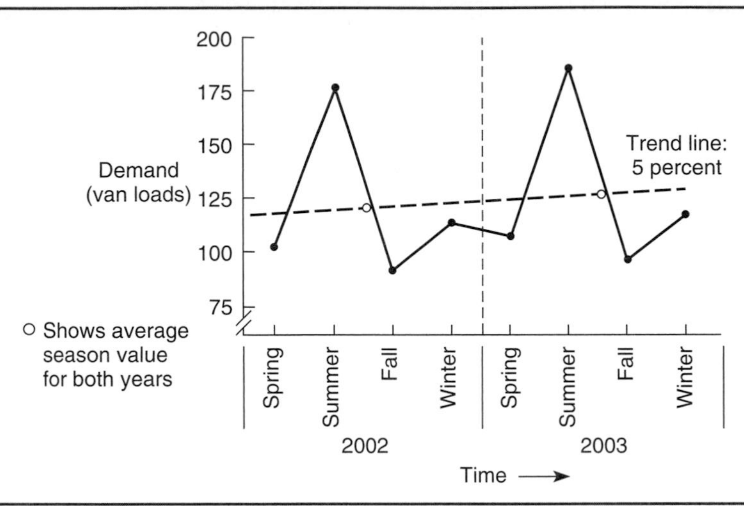


forecasting and capacity management teams, the dominant message of Exhibit 4-10 is the seasonal pattern; the upward trend is secondary.

**Cyclical Patterns—Natural and Induced.** Naturally occurring seasons are sometimes accompanied by extraordinary events that affect the magnitude of seasonal peaks. For example, a summer heat wave might raise temperatures from the seasonally normal high 80s to record 100-degree heat and create unusual demand for electricity. Also, accountants know that every spring is income tax season; newly revised tax laws, however, can further increase the peak demand for their services. In both cases, extra capacity will be needed beyond that associated with the usual seasonal surge. A public accounting firm that saw a 17-percent increase in its tax-related business following the 1986 U.S. tax law change, for instance, might plan on an additional 15 to 20 percent demand surge when new changes occur. Retailers have long known that holiday season sales create demand for more capacity (more clerks, longer store hours, etc.). They also know that extraordinary events, such as a mild winter, new toy or fashion craze, or negative report from a consumer advocacy group, further affect capacity needs in various departments or specialty shops.

*Hockey-stick management,* another name for end-of-period push, reflects the output pattern that resembles a series of hockey sticks placed end-to-end, with the blades extending upward at the end of each period.

Other seasonal patterns are artificial. For example, some firms often fall into a pattern of inflating current sales totals—by various means—to meet some sort of goal. One version, well known in manufacturing circles, is called the *end-of-month push* (also end-of-week, end-of-quarter, and end-of-year push). People relax in the early part of the period and then go into a frenzy at the end to meet the target. Sometimes, the end-of-year demand-surge pattern occurs because customers have money to spend at the end of their fiscal years.

Another artificial pattern is called *channel stuffing,* and arises from pressures to meet sales quotas in selling to wholesalers and retailers. In a few cases, pressures to meet goals have driven people to desperate, sometimes illegal, acts.[3] Though seasonal analysis can and should account for artificial patterns, that should not stop people from attacking the problem directly in an effort to eliminate them.

To summarize the multiperiod pattern projections, keep in mind that their source is historical demand data described as time-series patterns. Finding the patterns can require some computations, but projecting them into the future is direct and simple. If there is evidence suggesting that future conditions will differ markedly from past ones, the forecasting team should avoid the pattern projection techniques or use them with extreme caution.

We now turn to patternless projection.

## Patternless Projection

The patternless projection techniques make no inferences about past demand data but merely react to the most recent demands. These techniques—the moving average, exponential smoothing, and simulation—typically produce a single value, which is the forecast for a single period into the future.

In practice, forecasters extend the projection several additional periods into the future. In the absence of trend and seasonality, extending the single value is appropriate and results in a rolling forecast. In each new period, the previous projection is dropped and the newly computed forecast becomes the new projection. These techniques are best suited to short-term forecasting for scheduling product mix. The forecast period typically is a week, a month, or a quarter.

**rolling forecast**
Forecasts redone or rolled over at intervals—for example, every week, month, quarter, or year.

### *Moving Average*

The **moving average** is simply the arithmetic mean or average of a given number of the most recent actual demands. Formulas and explanations for the moving-average technique are presented in Exhibit 4-11.

The weighted moving average recognizes more important demands by assigning them higher weights. The advantages of weighting are somewhat offset, however, by the added burden of selecting weights: Just how much more important is last month's demand than that from two months ago? From three months ago? Fortunately, exponential smoothing (discussed in the next section) provides an easier way to achieve about the same results as weighted moving averaging. Therefore, we shall limit our discussion of moving-average forecasting to the simple moving-average model, which is derived from the more general model as shown in Exhibit 4-11.

The examples in the remainder of the chapter include much tabled data and calculation. We have, in most cases, rounded to facilitate presentation.

Like other time-series methods, the moving average smooths the actual historical demand fluctuations, as illustrated in Exhibit 4-12. The data are for our moving company, Metro, except this time the demand history is in weekly instead of quarterly increments.

## Exhibit 4-11 Moving Averages: Formulas and Explanation

A general expression for the moving average forecasting model is

$$F_t = \frac{\sum_{i=t-n}^{t-1} (D_i \times W_i)}{\sum_{i=t-n}^{t-1} W_i} \tag{4-3}$$

where

$F_t$ = Moving average forecast for period $t$

$n$ = Time span, the number of demand periods included in the computed average

$D_i$ = Actual demand for period $i$

$W_i$ = Weight value given to data in period $i$

When different weights are used for the various data values, the computed forecast is referred to as the *weighted moving average.* Typically, higher weights are assigned to more recent periods. When the demand for each time period is weighted equally, usually with a weight of 1, we compute a *simple moving average* forecast. The sum of the weights (the denominator in Equation 4-3) will then equal the number of periods in the time span ($n$). The numerator is also simplified for simple moving averages, resulting in

$$F_t = \frac{\sum_{i=t-n}^{t-1} D_i}{n} \quad \text{or, simply, } F_t = \frac{\sum D}{n} \tag{4-4}$$

## Exhibit 4-12 Demand Data and Moving Average—Metro Movers

| Week | Demand (van loads) | Three-Week Moving Average |
|---|---|---|
| −16 | 6 | |
| −15 | 8 | 9.0 |
| −14 | 13 | 10.7 |
| −13 | 11 | 11.7 |
| −12 | 11 | 12.7 |
| −11 | 16 | 12.7 |
| −10 | 11 | 11.7 |
| −9 | 8 | 8.7 |
| −8 | 7 | 10.0 |
| −7 | 15 | 10.7 |
| −6 | 10 | 12.0 |
| −5 | 11 | 8.7 |
| −4 | 5 | 8.3 |
| −3 | 9 | 8.7 |
| −2 | 12 | 11.0 |
| −1 | 12 | |

Demands for the last 16 weeks are shown on the left in Exhibit 4-12, where −1 means one week ago, −2 means two weeks ago, and so forth. On the right in Exhibit 4-12 is a column of three-week moving averages.

In Exhibit 4-13, the three-week moving average for weeks −16, −15, and −14 is projected as the forecast for week −13. The result, 9.0, which smooths the peaks in demand (6, 8, and 13) that actually occurred in the first three periods, can be obtained from Equation 4-4.

$$F_t = \frac{\sum D}{n}$$

$$F_{-13} = \frac{\sum D}{3} = \frac{6 + 8 + 13}{3} = 9.0$$

Since actual demand in week −13 was 11, the forecast error is 11 − 9 = 2. That is a shortage or underestimate of two vans for that week. The moving average for weeks −15, −14, and −13 then becomes the forecast for week −12. The forecast error is 11 − 10.7 = 0.3. The process continues, the average moving (or rolling over) each week, dropping off the oldest week and adding the newest; hence, a moving average.

**EXHIBIT 4-13 Three-Week Moving Average and MAD—Metro Movers**

| *(1)* Week | *(2)* Forecast Demand Actual Demand | *(3)* (three-week moving average) | *(4)* Sum of Absolute Forecast Error [(2) − (3)] | *(5)* Values of Forecast Errors |
|---|---|---|---|---|
| −16 | 6 | | | |
| −15 | 8 | | | |
| −14 | 13 | | | |
| −13 | 11 | 9.0 | 2.0 | 2.0 |
| −12 | 11 | 10.7 | 0.3 | 2.3 |
| −11 | 16 | 11.7 | 4.3 | 6.6 |
| −10 | 11 | 12.7 | −1.7 | 8.3 |
| −9 | 8 | 12.7 | −4.7 | 13.0 |
| −8 | 7 | 11.7 | −4.7 | 17.7 |
| −7 | 15 | 8.7 | 6.3 | 24.0 |
| −6 | 10 | 10.0 | 0.0 | 24.0 |
| −5 | 11 | 10.7 | 0.3 | 24.3 |
| −4 | 5 | 12.0 | −7.0 | 31.3 |
| −3 | 9 | 8.7 | 0.3 | 31.6 |
| −2 | 12 | 8.3 | 3.7 | 35.3 |
| −1 | 12 | 8.7 | 3.3 | 38.6 |

$$MAD = \frac{38.6}{13} = 3.0 \text{ vans per week}$$

**EXHIBIT 4-14 Six-Week Moving Average and MAD—Metro Movers**

| (1) Week | (2) Actual Demand (vans) | (3) Forecast Demand (six-week moving average) (vans) | (4) Forecast Error [(2) − (3)] | (5) Sum of Absolute Values of Forecast Errors |
|---|---|---|---|---|
| −16 | 6 | | | |
| −15 | 8 | | | |
| −14 | 13 | | | |
| −13 | 11 | | | |
| −12 | 11 | | | |
| −11 | 16 | | | |
| −10 | 11 | 10.8 | 0.2 | 0.2 |
| −9 | 8 | 11.7 | −3.7 | 3.9 |
| −8 | 7 | 11.7 | −4.7 | 8.6 |
| −7 | 15 | 10.7 | 4.3 | 12.9 |
| −6 | 10 | 11.3 | −1.3 | 14.2 |
| −5 | 11 | 11.2 | −0.2 | 14.4 |
| −4 | 5 | 10.3 | −5.3 | 19.7 |
| −3 | 9 | 9.3 | −0.3 | 20.0 |
| −2 | 12 | 9.5 | 2.5 | 22.5 |
| −1 | 12 | 10.3 | 1.7 | 24.2 |

$$MAD = \frac{24.2}{10} = 2.4 \text{ vans per week}$$

The three-period moving-average forecast results in a forecast error (MAD) of 3.0 vans per week (see calculation at the bottom of Exhibit 4-13). But the choice of three weeks was arbitrary.

Suppose forecasters decide to try a different time span, say, six weeks. The six-week moving average, forecast errors, and MAD calculations are shown in Exhibit 4-14. The MAD of 2.4 is better than the previous 3.0 value. They could try other moving average time spans and perhaps further reduce the error with the aid of a computer.

Moving average time spans generally should be long where demand is rather stable (e.g., groceries) and short for highly changeable demand (e.g., white-water rafting). Most users of moving average are providers of durable goods, which tend to have stable demand patterns in the short run and time spans of 6 to 12 periods are common.

History-based forecasting methods yield a series of forecast values that are smoother—less variable—than the time series itself. These smoothing effects are illustrated in Exhibit 4-15 for the three-week and six-week data in the moving-average example. The actual demand pattern exhibits some extreme high and low spikes. The three-week moving-average data pattern, from Exhibit 4-13, has spikes that are much less pronounced. The six-week moving-average data pattern, taken from Exhibit 4-14, is smoothed even further.

**EXHIBIT 4-15 Smoothing Effects of the Moving Average**

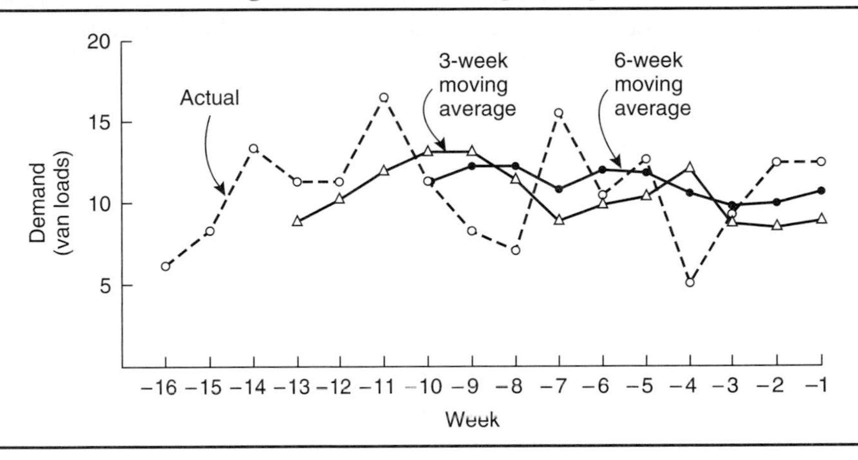


The time span resulting in the lowest MAD is the best choice for actual use in fore casting future demand. But keep in mind that the forecasters relied on past data. As long as they think the future will be similar to the past, that is fine. If the future will be different, however, there is little point in expending much time analyzing past demand.

### *Exponential Smoothing*

Many firms that adopted the moving average technique in the 1950s saw fit to change to **exponential smoothing** in the 1960s and 1970s. Today it is among the most widely used quantitative forecasting techniques.

Simple exponential smoothing smoothes the historical demand time series. However, it assigns a different weight to each period's data and thus is really a weighted moving average. Weight values are obtained by selecting a single smoothing coefficient, $\alpha$, such that $0 \leq \alpha \leq 1.0$. The exponential smoothing formula is:

$$F_{t+1} = F_t + \alpha(D_t - F_t) \tag{4-5}$$

Where

$F_{t+1}$ = Forecast for period $t + 1$

$\alpha$ = Smoothing constant

$D_t$ = Actual demand for period $t$

$F_t$ = Forecast for period $t$

Equation 4-5 shows that each smoothed average has two elements: the most recent demand, $D_t$ (new information), and the historical smoothed average, $F_t$ (old information). The term in parenthesis, $D_t - F_t$, is the forecast error for period $t$. Thus, the exponential smoothing forecast for a period may be thought of as the forecast for the preceding period adjusted by some fraction ($\alpha$) of the forecast error. That is:

$$\text{Next forecast} = \text{Last forecast} + \alpha(\text{Last demand} - \text{Last forecast})$$

For example, assume that the last forecast was for 100 units but demand was only 90. If $\alpha$ is set at 0.2, the exponential smoothing forecast is

$$\begin{aligned}\text{Next forecast} &= 100 + 0.2(90 - 100)\\ &= 100 + 0.2(-10)\\ &= 100 - 2 = 98\end{aligned}$$

This forecast of two fewer units than the forecast for last period makes sense because the last period was overestimated. Thus, exponential smoothing results in lower forecasts where teams have recently overestimated and in higher forecasts where they have underestimated.

Exhibit 4-16 illustrates, again using Metro Movers as the example. In the exhibit, $\alpha$ is set equal to 0.2. In exponential smoothing, there must be a start-up forecast; in this case, it is 10.6 for week −5. Following the suggestions of Brown,[4] the start-up value here is the simple mean of past demand data.

The underestimate for start-up week −5 was slight: only 0.4 units. Multiplying that 0.4 by the 0.2 smoothing constant yields an adjustment of 0.1, rounded off. Adding that 0.1 to the old forecast of 10.6 yields 10.7 as the forecast for week −4.

In week −4, the 10.7 forecast exceeds actual demand of 5; the error is −5.7. That times 0.2 gives an adjustment of −1.1. Thus, the next forecast, for week −3, is cut back by −1.1 to 9.6. And so on.

In testing for the proper value of $\alpha$, the mean absolute deviation is again helpful. Using past demand data, forecasting teams could calculate the MAD for various values of $\alpha$, then adopt the $\alpha$ yielding the lowest MAD. It is common to use an $\alpha$ in the range of 0.1 to 0.3. The reason is the same as that mentioned earlier for using longer moving-average time spans: Most larger firms using exponential smoothing are of durable goods having rather stable short-run demand patterns. A small $\alpha$, such as 0.2, fits this situation

**EXHIBIT 4-16 Exponentially Smoothed Demand Forecasts—Metro Movers**

| (1) Week | (2) Actual Demand | (3) Forecast | (4) Forecast Error [(2) − (3)] | (5) Smoothing Adjustment [(0.2) × (col. 4)] | (6) Exponentially Smoothed Forecast [(3) + (5)] | (7) Sum of Absolute Value of Forecast Errors | |
|---|---|---|---|---|---|---|---|
| −5 | 11 | 10.6 | 0.4 | 0.1 | 10.7 | | Start-up phase |
| −4 | 5 | 10.7 | −5.7 | −1.1 | 9.6 | 5.7 | Forecasting phase |
| −3 | 9 | 9.6 | −0.6 | −0.1 | 9.5 | 6.3 | |
| −2 | 12 | 9.5 | 2.5 | 0.5 | 10.0 | 8.8 | |
| −1 | 12 | 10.0 | 2.0 | | | 10.8 | |

$$MAD = \frac{10.8}{4} = 2.7 \text{ vans per week}$$

well. A small $\alpha$ means a small adjustment for forecast error, and this keeps each successive forecast close to its predecessor. A large $\alpha$, say, 0.7, would result in new forecasts that followed even large up-and-down swings of actual demand. That would be suitable for the less-stable demand pattern of a luxury good or service.

It may appear that the next exponential smoothing forecast is always based solely on what happened last period, with no regard for all preceding demand periods. Not so. Metaphorically, if the forecast for next period, $F_t$, is the child, the parent is $F_{t-1}$, the grandparent is $F_{t-2}$, the great-grandparent is $F_{t-3}$, and so forth. The current offspring, $F_t$, has inherited a portion, $\alpha$, of the error attributable to the parent, $F_{t-1}$, a smaller portion of the error attributable to the grandparent, and so forth.

Consider the manner in which weights are assigned in an exponential smoothing series. In a case where $\alpha = 0.2$, we would get the following results:

0.2 is the weight assigned to the $F_{t-1}$ error.

(0.2)(0.8) is the weight assigned to the $F_{t-2}$ error.

$(0.2)(0.8)^2$ is the weight assigned to the $F_{t-3}$ error.

$(0.2)(0.8)^3$ is the weight assigned to the $F_{t-4}$ error.

In general, $(\alpha)(1-\alpha)^{i-1}$ is the weight assigned to the $F_{t-i}$ error.

The pattern of decreasing weights for $\alpha = 0.2$ is plotted in Exhibit 4-17. Also plotted are the calculated weights for $\alpha = 0.5$. The exponential smoothing weights extend back into the past indefinitely.

It is possible to construct a weighted moving average that closely approximates exponential smoothing. But why bother? Exponential smoothing tends to be more accurate and is simpler and less expensive to perform than moving average. Furthermore, exponential smoothing can be extended to handle forecasting chores for data with trends and seasonality. Such models are beyond our scope, but may be found in forecasting texts.

**EXHIBIT 4-17 Example Weight Patterns for Exponential Smoothing**

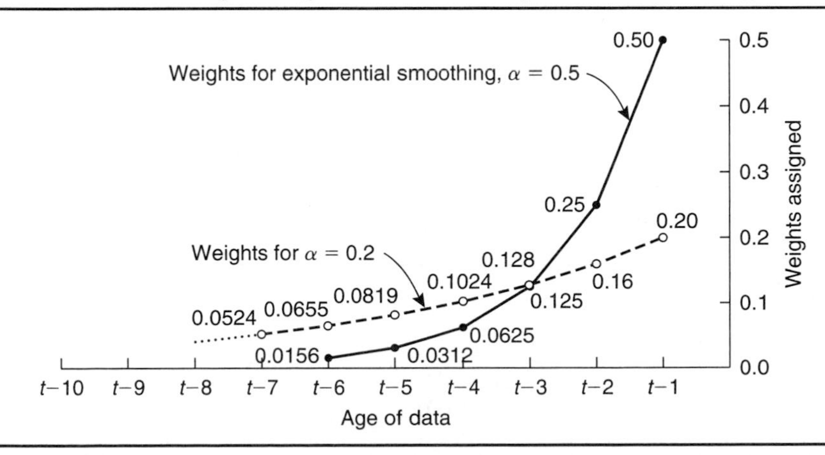

Is forecasting-model simplicity a true advantage? Research evidence suggests that it is. Simple models are not only easier to implement, but they frequently outperform more complicated ones. When two or three simple models are used together (e.g., with results averaged) performance improves even more.[5]

The main weakness of exponential smoothing and moving average bears repeating. The underlying assumption of both models is that past demand data is the best indicator of the future. But what if it isn't? Sometimes the very fact that a good or service has been in very high demand causes demand to drop in the near future. Customers become sated and demand drops. As was observed earlier, wise managers use multiple forecasting sources.

### *Adaptive Smoothing*

**Adaptive smoothing** is usually used as an extension of exponential smoothing, and thus is often called adaptive exponential smoothing. Forecasters may adjust the value of the smoothing coefficient ($\alpha$) if cumulative forecast error gets too large, thus adapting the forecasting model to changing conditions.

Cumulative forecast error is called the running sum of forecast error (RSFE). To signal the need for a change in $\alpha$, the magnitude of RSFE is divided by the MAD to compute what is known as a **tracking signal:**

$$\text{Tracking signal} = \frac{RSFE}{MAD} \tag{4-6}$$

Sustained increase in tracking-signal magnitude reflects bias in the forecasting model, which the forecasting team would want to eliminate. Two bias conditions may arise; fortunately, both are corrected in the same manner:

1. *Tracking signal magnitude increases, positive direction:* The RSFE is getting larger in the positive direction due to underforecasting. The cure is to increase forecast values by increasing $\alpha$, since the forecast errors are positive. A larger $\alpha$ then increases the forecast.
2. *Tracking signal magnitude increases, negative direction:* The RSFE is getting increasingly negative due to overforecasting. The cure is to decrease forecast values by increasing $\alpha$, since forecast errors are negative. A larger $\alpha$ then decreases the forecast.

It is known that when forecast errors are normally distributed, one standard deviation equals approximately 1.25 times the MAD. From the table of areas under the normal curve in Appendix A, we may obtain probabilities associated with various portions of a hypothetical tracking-signal distribution assuming that no forecast model bias exists. The approximate probabilities are:

| *Area* | *Probability* |
|---|---|
| $0 \pm 1$ SD (or $\pm$ 1.25 MAD) | 0.6826 |
| $0 \pm 2$ SD (or $\pm$ 2.50 MAD) | 0.9545 |
| $0 \pm 3$ SD (or $\pm$ 3.75 MAD) | 0.9972 |

Thus, the likelihood of the tracking signal exceeding a value of ±3.75 is very remote if the model is not biased. Continued tracking-signal values with magnitudes less than 3.0, with some alternation in sign, usually denotes an unbiased forecasting model. A helpful rule of thumb is to consider changing the smoothing constant when the tracking signal exceeds 4 for high-value items or 6 for low-value items.

### *Forecasting by Simulation*

Trend and seasonal analysis, moving average, and exponential smoothing are standard forecasting tools, especially for durable-goods manufacturers. Computers provide computational power to run forecasting simulations involving several techniques. Forecasting simulation has the potential to be more accurate than any of the individual forecasting techniques.

In each simulated trial, the forecast values are subtracted from a set of actual demands from the recent past, giving simulated forecast error. The forecast method yielding the least error is selected by the computer, which uses it to make just the next period's forecast. Each successive forecast requires a new simulation, possibly based on a new technique. (In contrast, the search for a time span or a smoothing constant—for a moving average or exponential smoothing—is performed as an occasional review rather than every forecasting period.)

Perhaps the best known forecasting simulation routine is **focus forecasting,** which was devised for use by buyers for hardware stores.[6] In this system, each product is simulated every month for the next three months and seven forecast techniques are tested. Each is simple for buyers and other inventory people in the company to understand. For example, one of the seven forecasting techniques is a simple three-month sum (which is not quite the same as a three-month moving average). The simulation for that method uses historical demand data for only the past six months, which are grouped into two three-month demand periods.

Focus forecasting was developed by Bernard T. Smith, as inventory manager at American Hardware Supply, for use in buying 100,000 hardware products.

## Associative Projection

In all of the preceding techniques, forecasters track demand over time. Associative projection tracks demand, not against time, but against some other known variable, perhaps student enrollment or inches of precipitation. The associative techniques are the leading indicator and correlation.

### *Leading Indicator*

If another variable precedes changes in demand, the other variable is a **leading indicator.** The leading indicator is helpful if the patterns of change in the two variables are similar (i.e., they correlate) and if the lead time is long enough for action to be taken before the demand change occurs.

Few firms are able to discover a variable that changes with demand but leads it significantly. The reason probably is that demand for a given good or service usually depends on (is led by) a number of variables rather than a single dominant one. The search for such a variable can be costly and futile. Therefore, most of the work with leading indicators has centered on national economic forecasting instead of local demand forecasting. Nevertheless, the leading indicator is a valued predictor in those cases where it can be isolated. Example 4-2 illustrates.

## Example 4-2: State Jobs Service and Leading Indicators

Mr. H. Hand, manager of the Metro City office of the State Jobs Service, sees the need for better demand forecasting. The problem has been that surges in clients tend to catch the office off guard. Advance warning of demand is needed in order to plan for staff, desks, phones, forms, and even space.

One element of demand is well known: Many of the job seekers are there as a result of being laid off by Acme Industries, which is by far the largest employer in Metro City. Hand is able to obtain Acme records on layoffs over the past year. He plots the layoff data on a time chart, along with the Jobs Service office's data on job applicants, in Exhibit 4-18. The chart shows the number of job applicants ranging from a high of 145 (period 8) to a low of 45 (period 20). Layoffs at Acme range from a high 60 (periods 6 and 7) to a low of zero (several periods).

Plotting the points seems well worth the effort because Hand notes a striking similarity in the shapes of the two plots. Further, the layoffs plot seems to lead the applicants plot. For example, the high of 145 applicants occurred two weeks after the high of 60 layoffs and the low of 45 applicants occurred two weeks after layoffs spiked downward to zero. Weeks 1, 3, 17, 21, and 22 are other places on the layoff plot in which a two-week lead appears; the lead is close to two weeks in weeks 11 through 15.

Does a two-week lead make sense, or could it be coincidence? Hand feels that it makes sense. He bases this on the impression that laid-off Acme people tend to live off their severance pay for a time—two weeks seems reasonable—before actively seeking other jobs. Hand therefore takes the final steps. First, he establishes an information system. This is simply an agreement that every two weeks Acme will release the number of its laid-off employees to the Jobs Service office. Second, he establishes a forecasting procedure based on that layoff information and the two-week lead pattern in Exhibit 4-18.

**Exhibit 4-18 Layoffs at Acme and Job Applications at Jobs Service, with Time Scale**

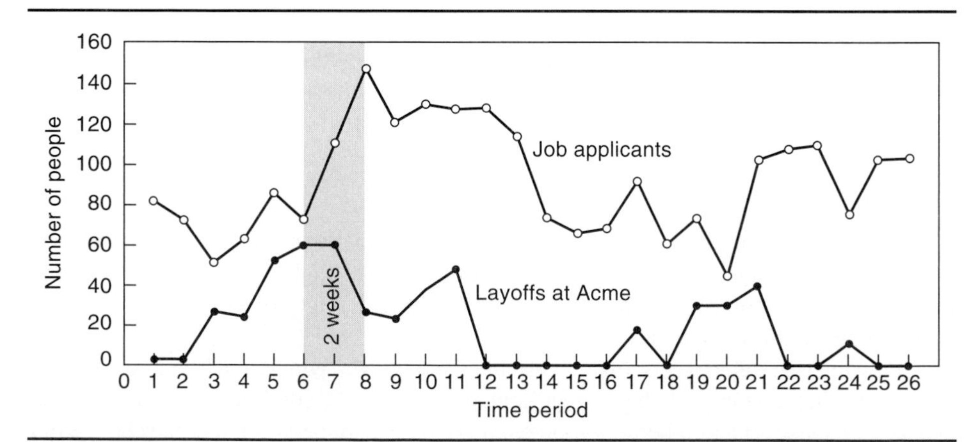

**Exhibit 4-19 Correlation of Layoffs at Acme ($T-2$) with Demand at Jobs Service ($T$)**

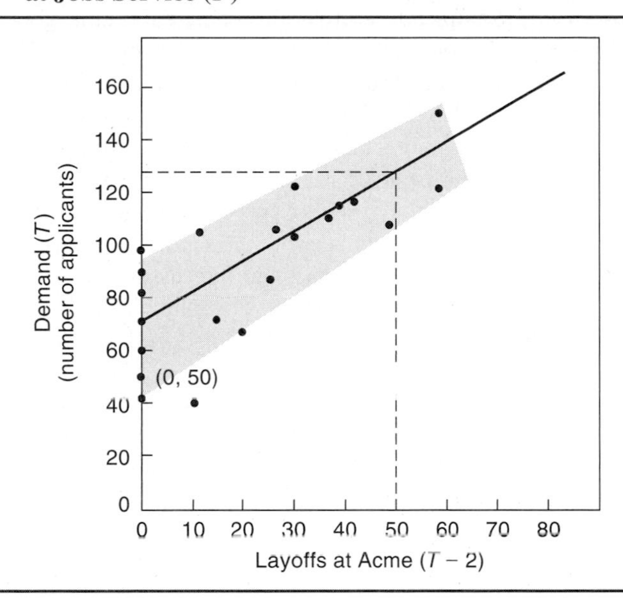


In setting up a forecasting procedure, Hand regraphs the data from Exhibit 4-18. The new graph, shown in Exhibit 4-19, is a scatter diagram. It plots layoffs at Acme for period $T-2$ and applicants at the Jobs Service for period $T$ as the two axes of the graph. For example, the first point plotted is (0,50), which is taken from Exhibit 4-18, where for period 1 layoffs are 0 and two weeks later applicants are 50. Every other point is plotted in the same way. The points tend to go upward left to right, clustering around the solid line (an eyeball regression line).

Hand uses the solid line for forecasting. Suppose, for example, that he learns today that Acme is laying off 50 people this week. In Exhibit 4-19 a dashed vertical line extending from 50 to the solid line and leftward yields a forecast demand of about 125. This tells Hand to plan for 125 applicants in two weeks.

## *Correlation*

**Correlation** means degree of association.

How good is Mr. Hand's leading indicator? By one measure—the supporting information system—it is very good! The layoff data from Acme are cheap to obtain and highly accurate. But in terms of lead time, it is not so good. Two weeks' notice seems insufficient for the purpose of adjusting resources on hand. In terms of validity, the leading indicator seems good, but how may we measure good? One answer is to measure it by the correlation coefficient.

The correlation coefficient, $r$, is a measure of degree of association. The value of $r$ ranges from 1.0 for perfect positive correlation to 0.0 for no correlation at all to $-1.0$ for perfect negative correlation. In positive correlation, a rise in one attribute occurs along with a rise in the other; in negative correlation, a rise in one occurs along with a fall in the other. To calculate $r$, forecasters need a number of pairs of values. The chapter supplement provides a formula and sample calculations.

For the Jobs Service example, the correlation coefficient is quite good (about +0.78, calculations not given), which one can see by looking at Exhibit 4-19. The points tend to cluster along the broad, shaded band running upward at about a 30-degree angle. This is the pattern of a positive correlation. (Negative correlations go downward left to right.)

Zero-lead-time correlation is usually covered in the introductory statistics course.

In the Jobs Service example, the amount of lead was determined visually. The two variables were plotted on the time scale in Exhibit 4-18, and brief inspection showed that the two curves were generally two weeks apart. What about a lead period of zero? That would exist where a pair of events occur at the same time. Even if the correlation is perfect ($r = 1.0$), it appears that it is useless in forecasting. No lead time means no forewarning and, it might seem, no forecasting. This impression is incorrect. Correlation with no lead can be valuable if the indicator (independent variable) is more predictable than is demand.

As an example, phone company planners in a large city may know that new residential phone orders correlate nearly perfectly with new arrivals in the city—with no lead time. There is probably value in knowing this because in most large cities careful studies are done to project population increases. Fairly reliable projections of new residences may be available. The phone company need not spend a lot of money projecting residential telephone installations; instead, forecasters may use the city's data on new residences.

## Demand Forecasting in Practice

A survey by Professors Nada Sanders and Karl Manrodt sheds light on current forecasting practices in U.S. corporations.[7] In this section, we discuss a few of the survey results and then consider an example that reveals a glimpse of a few more forecasting realities.

### *Preference for Simple Techniques*

The Sanders and Manrodt survey included a slightly greater number of service companies than manufacturers and tended more toward large than small companies. Respondents revealed that the more popular methods of demand forecasting include none of the quantitative methods listed in Exhibit 4-5. Rather, the preference is for simpler models. The most popular method, long referred to as the **naïve method,** is simply to use the most recent period's demand (sales, perhaps) as the forecast for next period.

Next most popular are judgmental methods. For medium- and long-term forecasting, which are infrequent and high in impact, the companies tend to rely on the opinions of a number of executives; this method is often called the **jury of executive opinion.** For short-term forecasting, which occurs far more often, a single high-level executive may do the judging.

Why are these nonquantitative methods so widely used? The survey respondents tended to name lack of good demand data as the number-one reason. It suggests that practicing managers often fail on the basics—in this case setting up an infrastructure for data collection.

Precisely how such an infrastructure should be created will depend, of course, on the organization and a host of other variables. The following example, however, illustrates how data requirements might be crafted as part of an overall forecasting plan.

### *Support Service Forecasting: Data Requirements*

Clearly, those responsible for a business's final goods and services—the revenue producing items—ought to forecast. For a nonprofit, the same holds for major mission items such as number of eligible clients. That scope of forecasting is necessary but not sufficient. All managers should forecast, including those responsible for staff services and nonrevenue items. Often a key step in developing better forecasting in these support settings is identification of data requirements; that is, knowing what to forecast. Example 4-3 illustrates.

#### Example 4-3: APEX BUS AND LIMO CHARTERS

O. R. Guy is the new president of Apex. One of his first acts is to create the department of management science and assign corporate forecasting to it. Corporate forecasting applies to the firm's revenue-earning services: its charter bus rentals.

Management science department analysts arrive at a forecast of a 10 percent increase in total bus charter sales for next year. Mr. Guy informs key department heads that they may consider 10 percent increases their targets for planning departmental budgets. Mr. Guy hears the following protests at the next department head meeting:

> *Engineering chief:* O. R., I hate to protest any budget increase. But I'd rather wait until I need it. The engineering workload often goes down when bus charters go up. That's because marketing pressures us less for new bus cabin customization designs when sales are good. But then, in some years of good sales, we have a lot of new design and design modification work. This happens when several bus interiors are in the decline phase of their life cycles. So you can see that our budget should not depend strictly on corporate sales.
> *Director of human resources:* We are the same way, O. R. The personnel workload depends more on things like whether the labor contract is up for renewal. Sure, we need to do more interviewing and training when corporate sales go up. But we have bigger problems when they go down. Layoffs and reassignments are tougher. Also, when sales go down, we may get more grievances.
> *Marketing chief:* Well, I hate to be the crybaby. But it's marketing that bears most of the load in meeting that 10 percent forecast sales increase. I was going to ask for a 20 percent budget increase—mainly for a stepped-up advertising campaign. I don't dispute the management science projection of a 10 percent sales increase. The market is there; we just need to spend more to tap it.

Based on those three comments, Mr. Guy rescinds his note about a 10 percent targeted budget increase. He then informs managers at all levels that they are expected to formally forecast their key workloads. That becomes the basis for their plans and budgets. A management science associate advises those managers requesting help.

To explain what is meant by key workloads, Mr. Guy provides each manager with a simple forecasting plan developed by the director of human resources:

| *Workloads* | *Forecast Basis* |
|---|---|
| 1. Hiring/interviewing. | Number of job openings is based on data from other departments. Number of job applicants is based on trend projection and judgment. |
| 2. Layoffs and reassignments | Number of employees is based on data from other departments. |
| 3. Grievances. | The number of stage 1, 2, and 3 grievances, estimated separately, is based on trend projection and judgment. |
| 4. Training. | The number of classroom hours and the number of on-the-job training hours; both are based on data from other departments. |
| 5. Payroll actions. | Number of payroll actions is based on number of employees and judgment on impact of major changes. |
| 6. Union contract negotiations. | Number of key issues is based on judgment. |
| 7. Miscellaneous—all other workloads. | Not forecast in units; instead, resource needs are are estimated directly based on trends and judgment. |

The data-gathering message of Example 4-3 deserves further comment. Today, the high rate of business failure, especially among start-ups and small firms, is partly owed to record-keeping failures and consequent misjudging (really, mismanaging) demand. A good deal of the problem can be addressed by looking internally—as illustrated in the example—at readily available sources of data. The balance of data for forecasting and demand management must come from outside the firm, of course, and external customers are the prime targets of data-gathering activities.

The desire for more and better demand data is highly visible. Bar-code scanning and point-of-sale data collection from customers exemplify retailing's solution. And some organizations simply buy information about people from other companies or from governmental agencies willing to sell information in their client databases. Unfortunately, there is an ugly side to this desire to know about customers. For example, in early 2000 the "Internet privacy mess"—as *BusinessWeek* calls it—had grown to such proportions that 92 percent of Net users were uncomfortable with the way their personal information had been collected and then disseminated by e-commerce companies.[8]

Resolution of the ethical implications associated with modern data management is beyond our scope. We would hope (expect?) that managers remain mindful of the legal and moral limits to learning about their current and potential customers. On the other hand, until data from both internal and external sources are available, managers will have to rely on judgment and naïve forecasting methods, which can be fraught with error.

### *Growing Competency*

When data are available, managers seem willing to take advantage of the more advanced forecasting models. Among the quantitative demand forecasting models listed in Exhibit 4-5, the Sanders-Manrodt survey revealed moving average to be the most widely used. (For economic forecasting, regression is the favorite.) Comparing their results with previous similar ones, the researchers had cause for cheer: The level of awareness and positive views of advanced forecasting methods is higher than in the past.

Though on average, firms seem not to use advanced techniques, some companies live and die by their sophisticated demand forecasting models. The rental car industry, which has suffered low profitability or losses in recent years, is an example. Demand management in this business is complicated by several factors; notable among them are allowing customers to pick up and return at different locations, and serving business customers who prefer larger cars and airport pickups on weekdays versus leisure customers who prefer small ones and downtown hotel pickups on weekends. Industry-leader Hertz has developed elaborate demand management and forecasting models to cope.[9] Its models try to project needs for number of cars in the fleet, best locations to which to deploy the cars, diversity of types of vehicles, and pricing combinations (one-day rentals, weekend rentals, and so forth).

## Summary Check Points

- ✓ Demand management forms one "half" of master planning; for operations managers, it is both a high-level planning activity and an implementation tool that guides order preprocessing and through which demand quantity and timing may be manipulated.
- ✓ When demand is not known, it must be forecast, and most organizations forecast to some degree. Within the organization, those responsible for revenue-producing outputs, nonrevenue items, and support services all have an obligation to forecast.
- ✓ Demand may be classified along several dimensions: independent or dependent, outputs or inputs (resources), and aggregate or item.
- ✓ Demand management and demand forecasting apply to long-, medium-, and short-term planning horizons; the forecasting horizon must extend beyond composite lead times.
- ✓ By shortening lead-time elements, companies can condense the forecasting horizon.
- ✓ Customers view lead time from their own perspective, and—after placing an order—are willing to wait only for specific lead-time activities; they expect earlier lead-time steps to have already been taken.
- ✓ Marketing projections, economic projections, and historical demand projections are broad categories of forecasting data sources.
- ✓ The quality of a forecast can only be determined after the fact, by computing forecast error; the mean absolute deviation (MAD) is a popular measure of forecast error.

- ✓ Forecasts tend to be more accurate for aggregate demand than for individual item demand, and more accurate for near-future periods than for distant-future ones.
- ✓ Time series, plots of demand over some time interval, may have trend, seasonal, cyclical, and "random event" components.
- ✓ Multiperiod pattern projection forecasting techniques utilize past demand series to (1) determine what if any patterns exist, and (2) project the pattern(s) into the future. Mean, trend, and seasonal patterns might be discovered.
- ✓ Patternless projection techniques make no inference about past demand series; instead, they react to recent demand values. Moving average and exponential smoothing are examples.
- ✓ Adaptive smoothing may be used to correct for bias in a forecasting model.
- ✓ Forecasting by simulation often combines several models and tends to be more accurate than any of the models used alone.
- ✓ Associative projection techniques examine demand not as a time series but as a function of some other predictor variable(s). Leading indicators and correlates are examples.
- ✓ In practice, simple forecasting models are preferred, perhaps due to a lack of data upon which to base more advanced forecasting techniques.
- ✓ Identification of appropriate records (and other data) is a crucial step in developing better forecasting abilities.
- ✓ There is a growing concern over privacy of personal information; data-gathering managers have an obligation to heed legal and moral limits in their pursuit of better demand data.
- ✓ Some evidence suggests that managers are becoming more aware of and more predisposed to use advanced forecasting methods.

## Solved Problems

### *Problem 1*

Historical demand data and forecasts exist for the eight-period time interval shown below:

| Period | −8 | −7 | −6 | −5 | −4 | −3 | −2 | −1 |
|---|---|---|---|---|---|---|---|---|
| Demand | 100 | 110 | 104 | 98 | 106 | 102 | 100 | 98 |
| Forecast | 104 | 102 | 104 | 100 | 100 | 104 | 103 | 102 |

Arrange the information in a table similar to the one in Example 4-1. Compute the forecast error (MAD). Plot the demand and forecasts as time series as in Exhibit 4-3.

### *Solution 1*

The period, demand, and forecasts are shown in the first three columns of Exhibit 4-20. The rest of the table contains the computations necessary for determining the required error measures. The actual historical demand and forecasts for the eight time periods are plotted in Exhibit 4-21.

## Exhibit 4-20 Forecast Error Measured: Solved Problem 1

| *Period* ($t$) | *Demand* ($D_t$) | *Forecast* ($F_t$) | *Error* ($E_t$) | *Absolute Error* $\lvert E_t \rvert$ |
|---|---|---|---|---|
| −8 | 100 | 104 | −4 | 4 |
| −7 | 110 | 102 | 8 | 8 |
| −6 | 104 | 104 | 0 | 0 |
| −5 | 98 | 100 | −2 | 2 |
| −4 | 106 | 100 | 6 | 6 |
| −3 | 102 | 104 | −2 | 2 |
| −2 | 100 | 103 | −3 | 3 |
| −1 | 98 | 102 | −4 | 4 |
| | | Sum: | −1 | 29 |

$$MAD \text{ (from Equation 4-2)} = \frac{29}{8} = 3.625$$

## Exhibit 4-21 Demand and Forecast Plots: Solved Problem 1

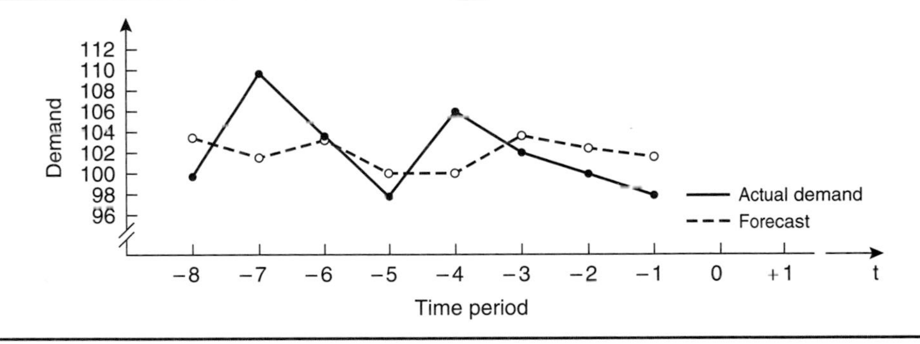


### *Problem 2*

Consider again the historical demand and forecast data in Solved Problem 1. Determine the running sum of the forecast error (RSFE) at the end of each period, and calculate the tracking signal after period −1.

### *Solution 2*

Exhibit 4-22 contains the given data, forecasts, and error calculations in the first five columns. The sixth column contains the RSFE values at the end of each period. The tracking signal at the end of period −1 is calculated below the table.

**EXHIBIT 4-22 Data and Solution Table: Solved Problem 2**

| *Period* ($t$) | *Demand* ($D_t$) | *Forecast* ($F_t$) | *Error* ($E_t$) | *Absolute Error* $\lvert E_t \rvert$ | *RSFE* |
|---|---|---|---|---|---|
| −8 | 100 | 104 | −4 | 4 | −4 |
| −7 | 110 | 102 | 8 | 8 | 4 |
| −6 | 104 | 104 | 0 | 0 | 4 |
| −5 | 98 | 100 | −2 | 2 | 2 |
| −4 | 106 | 100 | 6 | 6 | 8 |
| −3 | 102 | 104 | −2 | 2 | 6 |
| −2 | 100 | 103 | −3 | 3 | 3 |
| −1 | 98 | 102 | −4 | 4 | −1 |
| | | | | Sum = 29 | |

$$MAD = \frac{29}{8} = 3.625$$

$$\text{Tracking signal} = \frac{\text{RSFE}}{\text{MAD}} = \frac{-1}{3.625} = -0.276$$

***Problem 3***

Following are historical demand data for 12 periods:

| Period | −12 | −11 | −10 | −9 | −8 | −7 | −6 | −5 | −4 | −3 | −2 | −1 |
|---|---|---|---|---|---|---|---|---|---|---|---|---|
| Demand | 40 | 42 | 41 | 44 | 40 | 39 | 39 | 41 | 45 | 41 | 38 | 40 |

*a.* Calculate simple-moving-average forecasts and mean absolute deviation for the data, using a time span of 4.

*b.* Plot the demand data and the forecasts on a time axis.

***Solution 3***

The time periods and historical demand data are shown in the first two columns of Exhibit 4-23. Moving average forecasts are in column 3, and error terms are in columns 4 and 5. Sample calculations and MAD values appear below the table.

Sample calculations: simple moving average (from Equation 4-4):

$$F_t = \frac{\sum D}{n} = \frac{40 + 42 + 41 + 44}{4} = \frac{167}{4} = 41.75$$

$$MAD = \frac{17.0}{8} = 2.125$$

The plots of the 12 periods of historical demand data and the moving-average forecasts are shown in Exhibit 4-24. We see how the moving average technique smooths the peaks in the data.

**EXHIBIT 4-23 Data, Forecasts, and Errors: Solved Problem 3**

| (1) Period (t) | (2) Demand ($D_t$) | (3) Simple-Moving-Average Forecast ($F_t$) | (4) Error ($E_t$) | (5) Absolute Error $\|E_t\|$ |
|---|---|---|---|---|
| −12 | 40 | | | |
| −11 | 42 | | | |
| −10 | 41 | | | |
| −9 | 44 | | | |
| −8 | 40 | 41.75 | −1.75 | 1.75 |
| −7 | 39 | 41.75 | −2.75 | 2.75 |
| −6 | 39 | 41.00 | −2.00 | 2.00 |
| −5 | 41 | 40.50 | 0.50 | 0.50 |
| −4 | 45 | 39.75 | 5.25 | 5.25 |
| −3 | 41 | 41.00 | 0.00 | 0.00 |
| −2 | 38 | 41.50 | −3.50 | 3.50 |
| −1 | 40 | 41.25 | −1.25 | 1.25 |
| | | | | Sum = 17.00 |

**EXHIBIT 4-24 Demand Data and Moving-Average Forecasts: Solved Problem 3**

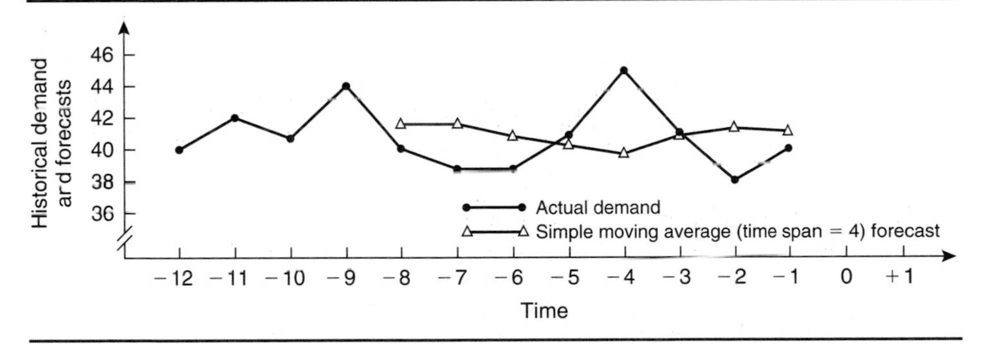


### *Problem 4*

The first five periods of demand data from Solved Problem 3 are shown in the following table. Using a smoothing coefficient, $\alpha = 0.3$, compute simple exponentially smoothed forecasts for periods −4 through −1. Initialize the procedure with a forecast value for period −5 of 41.

| Period | −5 | −4 | −3 | −2 | −1 |
|---|---|---|---|---|---|
| Demand | 40 | 42 | 41 | 44 | 40 |

**EXHIBIT 4-25 Data, Forecasts, and Errors: Solved Problem 4**

| *Period* $(t)$ | *Smoothed Demand* $(D_t)$ | *Exponentially Smoothed Forecast* $(\alpha = 0.3)$ $(F_t)$ | *Error* $(E_t)$ | *Absolute Error* $(\lvert E_t \rvert)$ |
|---|---|---|---|---|
| −5 | 40 | 41.000 | −1.000 | 1.000 |
| −4 | 42 | 40.700 | 1.300 | 1.300 |
| −3 | 41 | 41.090 | −0.090 | 0.090 |
| −2 | 44 | 41.063 | 2.937 | 2.937 |
| −1 | 40 | 41.944 | −1.944 | 1.944 |
| | | | | Sum = 7.271 |

### *Solution 4*

The data, forecasts, and absolute errors for the five-period interval are given in Exhibit 4-25. Sample calculations and the MAD follow.

Sample calculations (from Equation 4-5):

$$F_{t+1} = F_t + \alpha(D_t - F_t)$$

$$F_{-4} = F_{-5} + \alpha(D_{-5} - F_{-5})$$
$$= 41 + 0.3(40 - 41) = 40.700$$

$$F_{-3} = F_{-4} + 0.3(D_{-4} - F_{-4})$$
$$= 40.7 + 0.3(42 - 40.7) = 41.090$$

$$\text{MAD} = \frac{7.271}{5} = 1.454$$

## Exercises

[Note: Students familiar with spreadsheet software will find it helpful for some of the exercises in this chapter. The CD-ROM that accompanies your text has exercises that utilize Microsoft Excel.]

1. Demand management includes forecasting to estimate existing or natural demand, acknowledgment of customer orders, and demand manipulation. For each of the following industries, suggest two methods of demand manipulation.
   *a.* Automobiles
   *b.* Health care services
   *c.* Transportation services
   *d.* Personal computer software
   *e.* Resorts (lodging and entertainment)
   *f.* Books
2. "Past demand is the best predictor for future demand."
   *a.* List three reasons you would offer if called upon to refute that statement.
   *b.* List three reasons that you would suggest if asked to support the statement.
3. Exhibit 4-2 shows that forecast horizons must extend to cover various lead-time activities. For each of the following settings (a) Briefly discuss the long-, medium-, and short-term forecasting needs. (b) For what lead-time activities would a customer be willing to wait?

(Hint: Specify the customer that you have in mind.) Explain your logic.

*a.* Furniture retailer
*b.* Clothing manufacturing
*c.* Highway construction
*d.* Air conditioning/heating installer
e. Hair stylist
*f.* Commercial printing
*g.* Tractor service shop
*h.* Roller-skating rink
*i.* Natural gas distributor
*j.* Orthodontist's office
*k.* Church parish
*l.* Luxury yacht manufacturing
*m.* Small-appliance manufacturing
*n.* Toy designer

4. Planners at Ash County Hospital are preparing two documents for next quarter: a staffing (capacity) plan and a personnel budget. The following table contains a computer printout, by department, of labor data for last quarter, the most recent quarter of record. The forecast was produced prior to last quarter. The planning team also has a printout of departmental labor forecasts for *next quarter,* and those figures are very close to the forecasts for last quarter. Based on your analysis of last quarter's figures, to what extent would you feel comfortable in using the forecast for next quarter as a basis for the two required plans? (Hint: You might want to look at aggregate forecast error and at individual department error.)

| *Department* | *Last Quarter Labor Hours (Actual)* | *Last Quarter Labor Hours (Forecast)* |
|---|---|---|
| Anesthesia | 198 | 150 |
| Cardiopulmonary | 210 | 200 |
| Emergency | 609 | 660 |
| Obstetrics | 464 | 380 |
| Pathology | 75 | 90 |
| Physical therapy | 89 | 100 |
| Radiology | 331 | 360 |
| Surgery | 974 | 950 |

5. At Henry & Henry, Public Accountants, Franklin Henry, as managing partner, is responsible for forecasting demand for professional accounting services. He forecasts both aggregate demand and demand for each group specialty that Henry & Henry provides. His forecast for the estate planning group for the preceding six-month period (made six months before that) was 120 client-days (1 client-day = 8 billing hours) of work per month. Actual demand for these months is shown in the table below:

| *Month* | *Jan* | *Feb* | *Mar* | *Apr* | *May* | *Jun* |
|---|---|---|---|---|---|---|
| **Demand (client-days)** | 100 | 90 | 110 | 115 | 130 | 125 |

*a.* Plot the demand and forecast data on a time axis (similar to Exhibit 4-3).
*b.* Calculate the MAD.
*c.* Suggest a forecasting model that Franklin might find appropriate for the next six-month period. Explain your choice.
*d.* Using your model, what are the forecasts for each of the next six months? Explain.

6. In addition to the estate planning group at H&H (see Exercise 5), Franklin Henry also forecasts demand for an auditing and accounting services group and a business consulting group. His group forecasts for the preceding six-month period (made six months prior to that time) are each based on a level, patternless projection. The following table shows these forecasts and actual demand for each group.

| | **Estate Planning Group (Client-days)** | | **Auditing and Accounting Group (Client-days)** | | **Business Consulting Group (Client-days)** | |
|---|---|---|---|---|---|---|
| *Month* | *Actual Demand* | *Forecast* | *Actual Demand* | *Forecast* | *Actual Demand* | *Forecast* |
| Jan | 100 | 120 | 270 | 250 | 140 | 100 |
| Feb | 90 | 120 | 240 | 250 | 130 | 100 |
| Mar | 110 | 120 | 280 | 250 | 160 | 100 |
| Apr | 115 | 120 | 260 | 250 | 180 | 100 |
| May | 130 | 120 | 300 | 250 | 220 | 100 |
| Jun | 125 | 120 | 220 | 250 | 190 | 100 |

*a.* Calculate the aggregate forecast error for the labor resource at H&H.
*b.* Calculate the forecast error for each of the three groups for the six-month period.
*c.* What forecast would you suggest for the next six months for the auditing and accounting group? Why?
*d.* What forecast would you suggest for the next six months for the business consulting group? Why?
*e.* Discuss the pros and cons of group and aggregate labor forecasts at H&H.

7. The table below shows demand for the most recent eight months for a *service part* (industry's term for a spare or replacement part) that QWQ, Inc., produces. Sarah Nelson, a product manager at QWQ, must forecast demand for the next few months. She notes that a level forecast of 1,600 per month has been in effect.

| *Month* | *−8* | *−7* | *−6* | *−5* | *−4* | *−3* | *−2* | *−1* |
|---|---|---|---|---|---|---|---|---|
| **Demand** (× **100**) | 17 | 20 | 14 | 18 | 14 | 13 | 13 | 12 |
| **Forecast** (× **100**) | 16 | 16 | 16 | 16 | 16 | 16 | 16 | 16 |

*a.* Calculate the mean absolute deviation (MAD) for the 8 months of data.
*b.* Plot the demand and forecast on a graph that has room for you to extend projections several months into the future.
*c.* Use a multiperiod pattern projection technique to forecast demand for six or seven months into the future. Explain your choice of technique.
*d.* If Sarah were to present your forecast to senior management, what types of questions might she face? How might she answer them?

8. Should a manager of a television or radio station forecast demand? Why or why not? What sort of demand are we talking about? (A brief interview with such a manager would be informative.)

9. Gulliver and Dorothy are quite fond of travel and use this hobby to launch a business. They start an Internet-based tour-planning service that targets senior citizens wanting short trips to scenic and historic sites. The client visits the web page, completes and submits a "specification screen," and the service suggests up to three trips for the client's perusal. If the client opts for one of the tours, the service will, for a fee, make all arrangements and deliver schedules, tickets, and so forth. The table below shows the number of trips that the service sold during its first 10 weeks of operation.

| *Week* | *−10* | *−9* | *−8* | *−7* | *−6* | *−5* | *−4* | *−3* | *−2* | *−1* |
|---|---|---|---|---|---|---|---|---|---|---|
| **Tours** | 2 | 4 | 8 | 15 | 14 | 17 | 19 | 18 | 20 | 21 |

   *a.* Plot the demand data as a time series.
   *b.* What method(s) would you use to forecast service demand for the next three or four months? Why?
   *c.* Is the demand pattern what you would expect for a start-up company? Explain your answer.

10. Big Splash, Ltd., sells and installs residential swimming pools. Demand for installations for the last eight quarters is given in the table below.

| *Quarter* | *Winter Year 1* | *Spring Year 1* | *Summer Year 1* | *Fall Year 1* | *Winter Year 2* | *Spring Year 2* | *Summer Year 2* | *Fall Year 2* |
|---|---|---|---|---|---|---|---|---|
| **Pools** | 12 | 22 | 20 | 11 | 13 | 22 | 24 | 12 |

   *a.* Plot the eight quarters of demand as a time series. What is the time series pattern?
   *b.* What value would you forecast for the winter quarter of year 3? Why?
   *c.* What is the average seasonal (quarterly) pool demand based on the eight quarters of data?
   *d.* Using all eight quarters of data, calculate a seasonal index for each of the four quarters.
   *e.* If the *annual* demand for pools at Big Splash, Ltd., is projected to total 80 in year 3, what is the forecast for each quarter in year 3?
   *f.* Does this set of seasonal indexes make sense for the business under consideration? Explain.

11. Recent monthly caseload in a public defender's office was as follows:

| *January* | *February* | *March* | *April* | *May* | *June* |
|---|---|---|---|---|---|
| 180 | 100 | 90 | 110 | 110 | 120 |
| *July* | *August* | *September* | *October* | *November* | *December* |
| 140 | 170 | 150 | 160 | 160 | 170 |

   *a.* Graph the demands as (1) a two-month moving average and (2) a six-month moving average. What do the graphs show about the smoothing effects of different moving-average time spans?

*b.* Calculate a five-month moving average centered on June. Then use that value to calculate a seasonal index for June.

*c.* What factors would determine the usefulness of the seasonal index in question *b*?

12. Service-part demands for lawn mower blades at Lawngirl Manufacturing Company, along with three-week and nine-week moving-average data, are as follows:

| | Week | | | | | | | |
|---|---|---|---|---|---|---|---|---|
| | *−16* | *−15* | *−14* | *−13* | *−12* | *−11* | *−10* | *−9* |
| Demand | 800 | 460 | 630 | 880 | 510 | 910 | 420 | 740 |
| Three-week moving average | | 630 | 657 | 673 | 767 | 613 | 690 | 650 |
| Nine-week moving average | | | | | 682 | 671 | 713 | 710 |

| | Week | | | | | | | |
|---|---|---|---|---|---|---|---|---|
| | *−8* | *−7* | *−6* | *−5* | *−4* | *−3* | *−2* | *−1* |
| Demand | 790 | 700 | 840 | 600 | 930 | 680 | 900 | 800 |
| Three-week moving average | 743 | 777 | 713 | 790 | 737 | 837 | 793 | |
| Nine-week moving average | 716 | 734 | 733 | 776 | | | | |

*a.* For weeks −12 through −5, plot the raw demand data, the three-week moving-average data, and the nine-week moving-average data on one graph. Comment on the smoothing effects of the different time spans (note that the raw data constitute a one-week moving average).

*b.* Assuming a nonseasonal demand, what is the forecast for next week if a one-week moving average is used? If a three-week moving average is used? If a nine-week moving average is used?

*c.* Consider your answers from question *b* and the nature of the product: lawn mower blades. Which moving average time span seems best?

13. The table below shows six periods of demand data, forecasts for those six periods and for the first future period (period +1), and computations used to compute error and tracking signal values. Displayed values are rounded. The table was created using Microsoft Excel. A copy of this table is on your CD-ROM; the file name is FCST-EXP.XLS.

Forecasting: Exponential Smoothing
Alpha = 0.4

| *Period* | *Demand* | *Forecast* | *Error* | *Abs. Error* | *Abs. Err Sum* | *RSFE* | *MAD* | *Track. Sig.* |
|---|---|---|---|---|---|---|---|---|
| −6 | 230 | 225.0 | 5.0 | 5.0 | 5.0 | 5.0 | 5.0 | 1.00 |
| −5 | 205 | 227.0 | −22.0 | 22.0 | 27.0 | −17.0 | 13.5 | −1.26 |
| −4 | 210 | 218.2 | −8.2 | 8.2 | 35.2 | −25.2 | 11.7 | −2.15 |
| −3 | 240 | 214.9 | 25.1 | 25.1 | 60.3 | −0.1 | 15.1 | −0.01 |
| −2 | 235 | 225.0 | 10.0 | 10.0 | 70.3 | 9.9 | 14.1 | 0.71 |
| −1 | 245 | 229.0 | 16.0 | 16.0 | 86.4 | 26.0 | 14.4 | 1.80 |
| +1 | | 235.4 | | | | | | |

*a.* Verify the MAD and the tracking signal after period –1. Comment on the appropriateness of the forecasting model for this demand data.
*b.* Verify the forecast for period +1. Is it appropriate to project a forecast further into the future? Explain your logic.

14. Would another value for the exponential smoothing constant ($\alpha$) be a better choice for the six-period demand data shown in the table in Exercise 13?
*a.* Reconstruct the table using $\alpha = \mathbf{0.6}$ to the extent necessary for you to determine the MAD and tracking signal after period –1.
*b.* Reconstruct the table using $\alpha = \mathbf{0.2}$ to the extent necessary for you to determine the MAD and tracking signal after period –1.
*c.* Discuss the effects of the value of the smoothing constant on these demand data.
*(Note: If you are familiar with Excel, you may wish to use the CD-ROM file and change the value for alpha.)*

15. To assist with budgeting, the materials manager at Citrus Life and Casualty Company forecasts use of office supplies at the company's headquarters facility. He uses exponential smoothing to forecast the aggregate dollar amount of demand by quarter. Recent demand and forecast data are in the table below.

| *Quarter* | *Demand (\$ × 1,000)* | *Forecast (\$ × 1,000)* |
|---|---|---|
| Winter | 12.0 | 11.9 |
| Spring | 11.9 | |
| Summer | 12.1 | |
| Fall | 11.8 | |

*a.* If the manager has been using a smoothing coefficient of 0.4, what will be the forecasts for spring, summer, fall, and next winter?
*b.* Is the manager using a sound approach to forecasting? Explain.

16. The captain of the *Pescado Grande,* a sport fishing boat that docks at Ensenada, Mexico, is trying to develop a plan for crew needs by day of the week. The basis is the number of paying customers per day. Following are data for the last three weeks:

| | *Monday* | *Tuesday* | *Wednesday* | *Thursday* | *Friday* | *Saturday* | *Sunday* |
|---|---|---|---|---|---|---|---|
| Week –3 | 12 | 6 | 10 | 12 | 18 | 30 | 26 |
| Week –2 | 9 | 4 | 5 | 8 | 22 | 32 | 34 |
| Week –1 | 3 | 10 | 8 | 7 | 14 | 27 | 31 |

*a.* Calculate "seasonal" (daily) indexes for Sunday and Monday. Base the calculations on the appropriate seven-day average demand. What index should be used for planning the crew on Sunday and Monday of this week? Explain.
*b.* If the average number of paying customers per day next week is expected to be 16, how many should be forecast for Monday?

17. Q. R. Smith, owner-manager of Smith's Kitchens, Inc., sees some evidence that demand for kitchen cabinets is related to local tax mill rates, which are adjusted twice yearly. Following

are recent data that Smith has collected:

| | Half-Year Period | | | | | | | | | |
|---|---|---|---|---|---|---|---|---|---|---|
| | *−10* | *−9* | *−8* | *−7* | *−6* | *−5* | *−4* | *−3* | *−2* | *−1* |
| Cabinet demand | 55 | 70 | 75 | 70 | 80 | 85 | 90 | 80 | 70 | 75 |
| Mill rate | 110 | 125 | 135 | 145 | 140 | 140 | 160 | 150 | 150 | 140 |

*a.* Develop a graph (scatter diagram) with cabinet demands ($Y_t$) on the vertical axis and mill rates three periods earlier ($X_{t-3}$) on the horizontal axis. Plot each combination of demand and mill rate three periods earlier (i.e., $Y_t$ and $X_{t-3}$) on the graph. For example, the first point would be the demand, 70, for period −7 and the rate, 110, for period −10. Examine your graph. Is there enough association between demand and mill rates three periods (one-and-a-half years) earlier to be useful for forecasting? Explain.

*b.* Calculate the formula for the straight line of best fit for the data in (*a*). Using your formula along with the appropriate mill rate, what is the forecast cabinet demand for the next six-month period?

*c.* Calculate the coefficient of correlation. Is your impression from part (*a*) confirmed?

18. The owner-manager of a convenience store wants to improve her staffing plan to better serve her customers and more effectively manage labor costs. To meet those objectives, she would like to develop better ways to predict demand (sales) at her store. Since her store is a registered lottery ticket outlet, one question concerns the effect that lottery prize level in "Bonanza Behemoth" (a weekly drawing) has on her sales of general merchandise. Payoff levels are widely known in advance of drawings, especially when there is a "rollover" because no one had the winning numbers. The manager collects data for lottery drawings for the last quarter (13 weeks). She records lottery grand prize payoffs—the amount of the jackpot—along with her merchandise register receipts for the 48 hours prior to each drawing. Data are shown in the table below.

| | | | | | | | | | | | | | |
|---|---|---|---|---|---|---|---|---|---|---|---|---|---|
| Payoff ($millions) | 5.0 | 5.0 | 8.5 | 11.0 | 5.0 | 8.5 | 11.0 | 15.0 | 20.0 | 5.0 | 5.0 | 8.5 | 11.0 |
| Receipts ($thousands) | 7.2 | 3.9 | 7.7 | 14.3 | 6.1 | 10.1 | 12.2 | 14.5 | 18.4 | 7.1 | 4.8 | 7.0 | 13.7 |

*a.* Calculate the correlation coefficient between the data sets.

*b.* Is the correlation strong enough for the manager to use upcoming lottery payoff as a predictor of merchandise demand at the store? Explain your logic.

*c.* Is the concept of "leading indicator" a factor in this example? Explain.

*d.* Is "merchandise sales" a good indicator of aggregate demand in a convenience store? Discuss.

19. The chief of planning at North American Hotels, Inc., suspects that convention business may be associated with productivity indexes and tourist business with weather. The graphs in Exhibit 4-26 show two of his attempts to make these associations:

*a.* Based on your inspection of the productivity–convention business graph, what should he conclude? Comment on the usefulness of the analysis for the hotel.

**EXHIBIT 4-26**

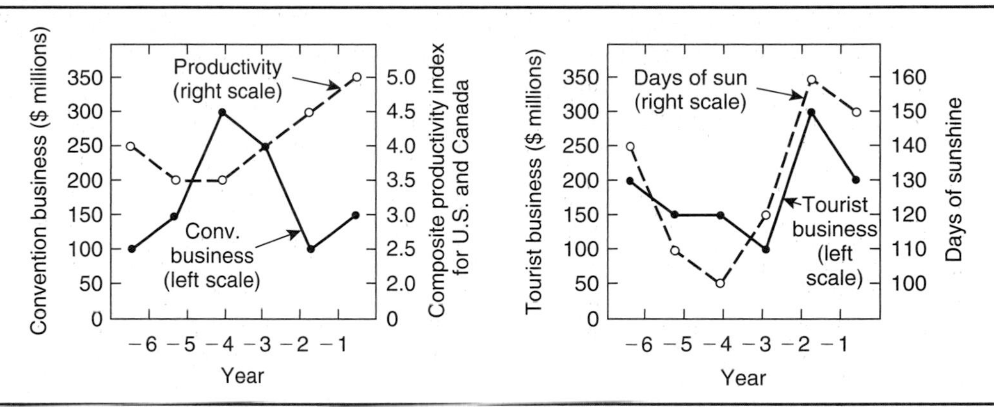


*b.* Based on your inspection of the sunshine–tourist business graph, what should the chief of planning conclude? Comment on the usefulness of the analysis for the hotel.

20. The safety division at Acme Manufacturing Company has written the following numbers of safety citations in the past seven months:

| | Month | | | | | | |
|---|---|---|---|---|---|---|---|
| | *−7* | *6* | *−5* | *−4* | *−3* | *−2* | *−1* |
| Citations | 71 | 63 | 60 | 58 | 61 | 40 | 42 |

*a.* Using the eyeball method, plot the data and project the number of citations that might be expected next month.

*b.* The chief safety inspector suspects that safety citations are related to number of new hires. She has collected the following data on new hires for the same seven months.

| | Month | | | | | | |
|---|---|---|---|---|---|---|---|
| | *−7* | *−6* | *−5* | *−4* | *−3* | *−2* | *−1* |
| New hires | 40 | 31 | 27 | 33 | 10 | 25 | 25 |

Analyze the association between new hires and citations. Look for a leading indicator.

*c.* Calculate the formula for the straight line of best fit (line of regression) for the last seven months of citations. Use the formula to calculate the projected demand for the next two months.

*d.* Calculate the coefficient of correlation between new hires and citations. Make the same calculation but with new hires leading citations by one month. (Base the calculations on citations for months −6 and −1 and new hires for months −7 to −2.) Comment on the difference and on which type of associative forecast is more appropriate.

21. Anderson Theaters owns a chain of movie theaters. In one college town, there are several Anderson Theaters. Anderson wants to find out exactly what influence the college student population has on movie attendance. Student population figures have been obtained from local colleges. These, along with movie attendance figures for the past 12 months, are as shown in the table that follows:
    *a.* What is the correlation coefficient?
    *b.* Is this correlation analysis useful for Anderson Theaters? Discuss fully.

| | Month | | | | | | | | | | | |
|---|---|---|---|---|---|---|---|---|---|---|---|---|
| | *1* | *2* | *3* | *4* | *5* | *6* | *7* | *8* | *9* | *10* | *11* | *12* |
| Students* | 8 | 18 | 18 | 18 | 15 | 9 | 11 | 6 | 17 | 19 | 19 | 13 |
| Attendance* | 14 | 15 | 16 | 12 | 10 | 8 | 9 | 7 | 11 | 13 | 14 | 17 |

*In thousands. The student figures are monthly averages.

## Supplement

# LEAST SQUARES AND CORRELATION COEFFICIENTS

In this supplement we examine two related techniques. Both concern the straight line that most closely fits a set of plotted data points:

1. The least-squares technique, which yields an equation for the straight line of best fit (line of regression).
2. The correlation coefficient, which measures how well a given straight line or line of regression fits a set of plotted data points.

### Least Squares

The general formula for a straight line is:

$$Y = a + bX$$

For any set of plotted data points, the least-squares method may be used to determine values for $a$ and $b$ in the formula that best fits the data points: $a$ is the $Y$ intercept, and $b$ is the slope. Least-squares formulas for $a$ and $b$ follow, first in the general form and then in a simpler form for a special case.

General form:

$$a = \frac{\sum Y}{N} - b\left(\frac{\sum X}{N}\right)$$

$$b = \frac{N\sum XY - \sum X \sum Y}{N\sum X^2 - \left(\sum X\right)^2}$$

Special form (when $\sum X = 0$, i.e., an odd number of periods):

$$a = \frac{\sum Y}{N} \text{ and } b = \frac{\sum XY}{\sum X^2}$$

where

$\sum Y$ = Sum of $Y$-values for all plotted points

$N$ = Total number of plotted points

$\sum XY$ = Sum of product of $X$ value and $Y$ value for all plotted points

$\sum X^2$ = Sum of squares of $X$ values for all plotted points

$\sum X$ = Sum of $X$ values for all plotted points

The least-squares technique is shown in Example S4-1 using the special form of the equation.

## Example S4-1: LEAST SQUARES TREND LINE—DATA SERVICES, INC.

At Data Services, Inc., demand in the last seven quarters in programmer-hours was as follows: 510, 600, 400, 520, 340, 440, and 420. What is the trend line?

*Solution*

The following table simplifies computation of $a$ and $b$ values. The fourth quarter, in which demand was 520, is treated as the base period; it is numbered as period 0. The three previous periods are numbered −1, −2, and −3; the three succeeding periods are numbered +1, +2, and +3. The low numbers simplify calculation and, since their sum is zero—that is, $\sum X = 0$—the simpler least-squares equation apply. The $Y$ values are the seven demand figures.

| $Y$ | $X$ | $X^2$ | $XY$ | |
|---|---|---|---|---|
| 510 | −3 | 9 | −1,530 | |
| 600 | −2 | 4 | −1,200 | |
| 400 | −1 | 1 | −400 | |
| 520 | 0 | 0 | 0 | ← Base period |
| 340 | +1 | 1 | +340 | |
| 440 | +2 | 4 | +880 | |
| 420 | +3 | 9 | +1,260 | |
| Sums = 3,230 | 0 | 28 | −650 | |

Since

$$a = \sum Y/N \text{ and } b = \sum XY/\sum X^2,$$

$$a = \frac{3,230}{7} = 461$$

$$b = \frac{-650}{28} = -23.2$$

The formula for the line of best fit is:

$$Y = 461 - 23.2X$$

The formula may be used to forecast, say, the next quarter. With the base or centermost period numbered 0, the next quarter is numbered +4. Then,

$$Y = 461 - 23.2\,(+4)$$
$$= 368 \text{ programmer-hours}$$

**EXHIBIT S4-1 Seven-Quarter Least-Squares Trend—Data Services, Inc.**

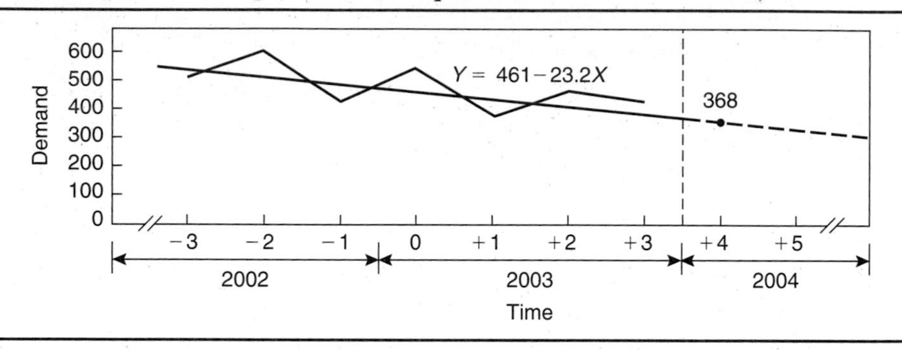


Exhibit S4-1 summarizes the results of the least-squares computations and the forecast for next quarter; note the very close pattern of the demand data here with that in Exhibit 4-7. Dates are added to the figure to make it agree with the dates for 4-7 in the chapter. Clearly the least-squares trend is very nearly the same as the eyeball trend in Exhibit 4-7, as we would expect it to be.

## Correlation Coefficients

The coefficient of correlation ($r$) ranges from $\pm 1.0$ for perfect correlation to 0.0 for no correlation at all. An $r$ of $\pm 1.0$ applies to the case where all plotted points are on the straight line of best fit.

A widely used formula for $r$ is

$$r = \frac{\sum XY - \sum X \sum Y / N}{\sqrt{\left[\sum X^2 - \left(\sum X\right)^2 / N\right]\left[\sum Y^2 - \left(\sum Y\right)^2 / N\right]}}$$

Example S4-2 demonstrates the formula for the State Jobs Service.

### Example S4-2: CORRELATION COEFFICIENT—STATE JOBS SERVICE

Layoffs at Acme two weeks earlier are plotted against job applicants at the Jobs Service office. Exhibit 4-18 in the chapter shows the correlation visually. What is the calculated coefficient of correlation ($r$)?

*Solution*

Exhibit S4-2 provides the necessary totals to solve for $r$. All $X$ and $Y$ values are taken from

**EXHIBIT S4-2 Working Figures for Computing *r*—State Jobs Service**

| *Number of Applicants (Y)* | *Layoffs at Acme (T − 2) (X)* | $Y^2$ | $X^2$ | $XY$ |
|---|---|---|---|---|
| 50 | 0 | 2,500 | 0 | 0 |
| 60 | 0 | 3,600 | 0 | 0 |
| 80 | 25 | 6,400 | 625 | 2,000 |
| 65 | 20 | 4,225 | 400 | 1,300 |
| 110 | 50 | 12,100 | 2,500 | 5,500 |
| 145 | 60 | 21,025 | 3,600 | 8,700 |
| 115 | 60 | 13,225 | 3,600 | 6,900 |
| 125 | 25 | 15,625 | 625 | 3,125 |
| 120 | 20 | 14,400 | 400 | 2,400 |
| 120 | 35 | 14,400 | 1,225 | 4,200 |
| 110 | 45 | 12,100 | 2,025 | 4,950 |
| 70 | 0 | 4,900 | 0 | 0 |
| 60 | 0 | 3,600 | 0 | 0 |
| 65 | 0 | 4,225 | 0 | 0 |
| 90 | 0 | 8,100 | 0 | 0 |
| 55 | 0 | 3,025 | 0 | 0 |
| 70 | 20 | 4,900 | 400 | 1,400 |
| 45 | 0 | 2,025 | 0 | 0 |
| 100 | 30 | 10,000 | 900 | 3,000 |
| 105 | 30 | 11,025 | 900 | 3,150 |
| 105 | 40 | 11,025 | 1,600 | 4,200 |
| 70 | 0 | 4,900 | 0 | 0 |
| 95 | 0 | 9,025 | 0 | 0 |
| 100 | 10 | 10,00 | 100 | 1,000 |
| Sums = 2,130 | 470 | 206,350 | 18,900 | 51,825 |

Example 4-2 in this chapter. Since there are 24 data items, $N = 24$. Calculation of $r$ is as follows:

$$r = \frac{\sum XY - \sum X \sum Y/N}{\sqrt{\left[\sum X^2 - \left(\sum X\right)^2/N\right]\left[\sum Y^2 - \left(\sum Y\right)^2/N\right]}}$$

$$= \frac{51{,}825 - (2{,}130)(470)/24}{\sqrt{18{,}900 - (470)^2/24)(206{,}350 - (2{,}130)^2/24)]}}$$

$$= 0.78$$

An $r$ of 0.78 is rather high. Layoffs at Acme may be considered a good leading indicator.

CHAPTER 5

# CAPACITY PLANNING AND MASTER SCHEDULING

Capacity is a concept that extends beyond the borders of a business or industry and into society's ability to meet the needs of its citizens. The Into Practice box "Gridlock" illustrates. Indeed, as world populations increase, we can expect more such situations. Highway congestion, health care restrictions, and Internet overloads are other reminders. Are those demand problems? Or are they capacity problems? What you are thinking now is the very reason that master planners address the demand/capacity (or demand/supply) partnership together.

In businesses of the past, the partners were often quite uncooperative. Functional separatism was the culprit. Marketing's job was to sell, and production's job was to supply. No need for salespeople to understand production capacity and scheduling concerns, and no need for operations personnel to worry about customer demand issues. The two functions were at odds a great deal of the time, and, of course, the customer was the loser.

Today, competitive pressures in business preclude most of that kind of nonsense. Successful companies rely heavily on multifunctional teams well-versed in the economic realities of commerce and trained to work together to achieve the appropriate supply/demand balance. They know that:

1. When capacity is not sufficient to meet demand, customers won't wait around; they go elsewhere. For the provider, sales revenues are lost.
2. Excesses capacity and output are costly wastes that erode the provider's profit margins. Inevitable price increases also drive customers to competitors.
3. Remedies to capacity excess, such as downsizing, force plant closings and layoffs that create short-term financial burdens and exact substantial human costs as well.

Master planning teams have the job of preventing these problems. In this chapter, we take up we take up the second "half" of master planning—capacity planning and master scheduling. Capacity to meet demands and the schedules for doing so constitute the supply side of the demand/supply partnership.

## Planning for Capacity and Output

In Chapter 4, specifically in Exhibit 4-1, we classified capacity planning and master scheduling as key components of the master planning duties of operations management. In this section, we take a more detailed look at those activities, beginning with a terminology and sequence overview.

INTO PRACTICE

## Gridlock

"Though observers of airline traffic don't agree on much, they all concede that the existing system must be improved. With about 21,000 commercial flight departures each day . . . projected to grow by 2 to 5 percent a year, air planners have moved from lamenting air congestion to invoking the dreaded "G" word . . . *Gridlock.*

A National Civil Aviation Review Commission report warned, "Traffic data and trends indicate that adding just a few minutes of delay to each airline flight in the United States will bring the aviation system to gridlock with dramatic negative impacts on the economy, not to mention alarming safety implications."

The air traffic control system is simply overloaded—and outdated—and is straining to keep up. "Planes simply 'disappear' from controllers' radar screens; in 1998 Air Force One vanished twice. To compensate for such lapses, controllers must increase safety margins by boosting separation distances and holding planes back. As pilot-turned-airline-manager William B. Cotton of United Airlines puts it, 'Safety has always been maintained at the expense of capacity and efficiency.' "

Source: Eric Scigliano, "Delayed Takeoff," *Technology Review,* September–October 1999, pp. 44–52.

*Commercial air travel schedules create the need for capacity planning on the part of airlines, airports, and government agencies.*

© Jacques M. Chenet/Corbis

### *Terminology and Sequence Overview*

Whether referring to national or international public-serving infrastructure such as air transportation systems, equipment and labor resources in a factory, or workstations in a university computer lab, **capacity** is the ability to accommodate. From an OM

**EXHIBIT 5-1 Master Planning: Sequence Overview**

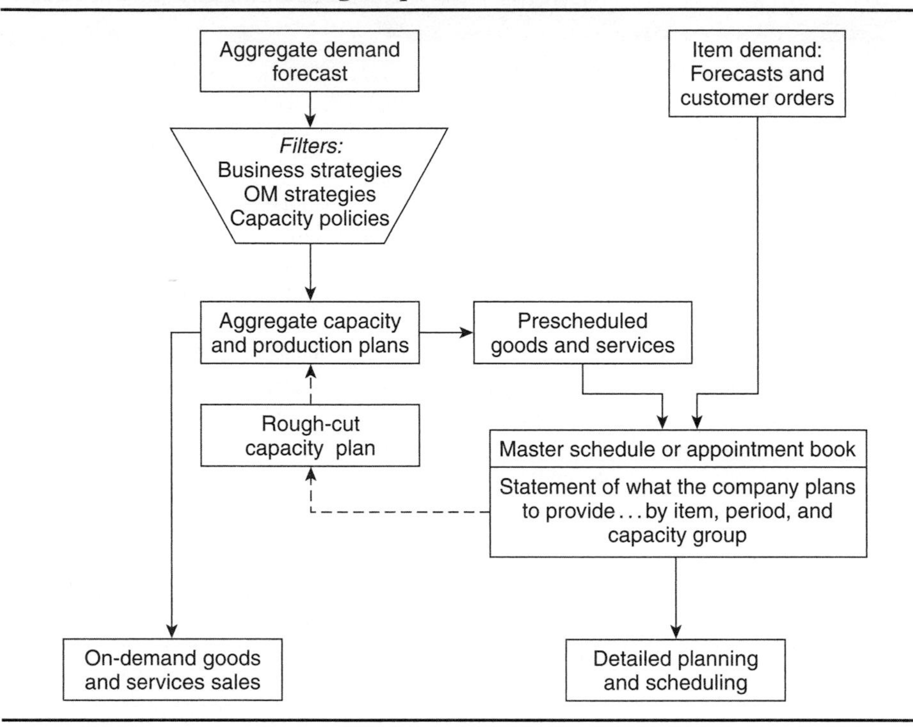


perspective, it refers to a provider's capability of performing the transformations necessary to ensure that goods and services satisfy customers' demands. **Capacity planning** refers to a broad range of activities—all focused on creating and maintaining customer-serving resources and adjusting the levels of those resources as required.

Exhibit 5-1 "explodes" the master planning box of Exhibit 4-1 into greater detail. As we saw in Chapter 4, both aggregate and item demands are incorporated into the master planning sequence. Strategy and policies act as filters, especially for aggregate projections. What the business *wants to do* is a major determinant of eventual plans for outputs. In Part I we took a look at company or business-level strategies, and will address operations strategies and policies later in this chapter.

Capacity planning, like demand management, must include long-, medium-, and short-term horizons. Long-range capacity planning provides facilities and capital equipment. We treat facilities in Chapter 14 and address equipment and other process concerns in Part III. We discuss short-term plans, often referred to as detailed plans or simply *schedules,* in later chapters where they fit well with other topics. The box at left-center of Exhibit 5-1—aggregate capacity and production plans—lies at the heart of medium-term capacity planning and is our focus here.

Two streams of outputs are governed by the aggregate capacity and production plans:

**1. On-demand Outputs.** For on-demand sales and services (e.g., emergency medical treatment, utilities or equipment repairs, or fast foods), the capacity plan aims at providing the right amount of space, equipment, labor, and inventory to do business. The emphasis is on capacity allocation; there may be no production or output plan per se.

**2. Prescheduled Outputs.** Goods and services that lend themselves to prescheduling (e.g., dental appointments, construction, or most manufactured goods), can require three steps: (1) creation of production plans, (2) creation of a master schedule, and (3) the detailed planning and scheduling referred to above (and, again, reserved for later chapters).

The **production plan** specifies levels of output, perhaps by aggregate categories or groups, which will satisfy demand. Broad-level checks ensure that—generally—the production plan and aggregate capacity are balanced and conform to the firm's established strategy and policies.

Next, more specifics are spelled out in the **master schedule**—a statement of what the company will provide according to specific configurations (items), quantities, dates, and capacity groups. In manufacturing, the master schedule is called the **master production schedule (MPS),** but in services it has a more generic name such as the appointment book or facility schedule.

At this stage, the focus has shifted to outputs—the master schedule is, after all, a commitment to produce or serve. Capacity concerns are sometimes checked again, however, especially in complex manufacturing settings. **Rough-cut capacity planning** ensures that a particular master schedule can be accommodated given known capacity constraints and, again, is consistent with policies. If significant master schedule changes are needed, the production and capacity plans might need to be revised as well. The dashed arrows in Exhibit 5-1 indicate this feedback loop. Typically, some degree of master schedule change is the rule rather than the exception, especially as one looks further out on the planning horizon. (That's why, in precomputer times, appointment books were done in pencil rather than pen!)

We now have the basic definitions and sequence overview in mind. The remainder of this section clarifies; first with an example from a small business and then with a glimpse at what capacity planning and master scheduling teams do in larger companies.

### *Small Business Example*

The Anita's Studio example relates to two other chapter examples: Koji Film Co., a manufacturer whose product Anita might use, and FastFotos, Inc., a service business that Anita might turn to for film processing.

Although the more complex tools and most of the terminology evolved in North American manufacturing, all organizations perform capacity planning and master scheduling. Anita's Studio, a small service-oriented business, must consider the same issues—though on a smaller scale—as large multinational manufacturers. Example 5-1 illustrates. The margin notes, positioned beside appropriate text passages, highlight these issues.

Example 5-1: MASTER PLANNING—PHOTOGRAPHY SERVICES, PART I

Anita's Studio is a professional photography business. Anita specializes in individual and family portraits. She shoots in her own studio and does her own developing and printing. Demand may be expressed as the number of customers or, more precisely, the number of photos. But to Anita, demand has another, equally important meaning: demand for capacity. What capacity does she need in order to satisfy the demand for her services?

Demand for outputs. . . . . . .

Demand for capacity. . . . . .

Elements of capacity. . . . . .

The first capacity item is Anita's time, which includes hours in the studio, developing, packaging, record keeping, management, and so forth. Second is the demand for paper, developing chemicals, film, and other supplies. Next, she needs certain tools and equipment, such as cameras, lights, backdrops, enlargers, drying racks, and light meters. Finally, she needs the facility (studio) itself.

Capacity limits. . . . . . .

Further, each item is limited. Anita's time is restricted to something less than 24 hours a day, the enlarger can handle only so many prints per hour, the studio accommodates only certain group sizes, backdrops, and so forth. If Anita knows that demand for her work is relatively stable, she may develop a relatively stable capacity plan.

But what if she wants to change her business plan, say, by expanding into event photography—weddings and other social or sporting events? For one thing, demand for photographs and capacity to process them will grow, which requires further capacity planning.

Complexity created by diversification. . . . . .

Also, while some capacity items are common to both portrait and event photography, others must be separately planned. Event work will require new kinds of capacity: It generates travel and on-site shooting time. Moreover, Anita may have to purchase faster lenses, battery packs, film winders, and other special equipment. Both event and portrait work, however, require capacity for developing and printing.

Capacity strategy and possible capacity plans. . . . . .

Another issue is seasonality. Weddings, anniversaries, graduations, and proms pile up in May and June. Thus, more capacity will be needed in those months. Anita may consider buying more equipment, hiring assistants, and contracting out some developing and printing. On the other hand, she may choose simply to limit the business she accepts, reasoning that any added springtime capacity will be unused during the rest of the year. She might wish to avoid the unpleasant task of dismissing assistants when there is not enough work. The point is that she has options in planning capacity.

Business plan influence. . . . . .

Anita's business plan, including goals, strategies, and policies, will affect her thinking about capacity options. What she wants to do influences what she plans to do.

Master scheduling. . . . . .

Schedule (meeting demand) allocates capacity. . . . . .

In developing an appointment book (master schedule), Anita must consider demand for her services as well as her capacity to provide them. Total (aggregate) demand for all photography services will determine the load on her developing and printing capacity and on her capacity to cover demand for billing and other clerical operations. The mix of portrait and event photography (major subgroups of aggregate demand) will determine the capacity requirements for studio shooting and travel/site-shooting times, respectively. Finally, planning for each capacity item, such as each type of film and each size of printing paper, will require forecasts of each type of photography assignment, including number of shots, size and number of prints desired, and so forth. Actual customer bookings and ensuing print orders will most accurately help predict capacity needed, by type.

Capacity plan affects the master schedule. . . . . .

Master schedule revisions. . . . . .

On the other side of the coin, the capacity plan Anita selects will determine how much and what type of demand she can satisfy. She might have to revise her appointment book, perhaps more than once, as she juggles demand and capacity, seeking a fit.

Effects on service to customers. . . . . .

It is easy to see that inattention to demand for photography services might lead to investment in too much or too little capacity. Likewise, failure to consider capacity could lead to overbooking and promising more than can be delivered. Adverse effects may include delays, customer dissatisfaction, lost business, and overall careless and hurried business practices.

---

Several points emerge from the Anita's Studio example:

1. Capacity is needed in order to meet demand—without panic or shortcuts.
2. The business plan (including plans for expansion or contraction) influences capacity choices (equipment quantity, staff size, etc.).

3. Greater variety of products or services offered (portrait photography, event photography, etc.) complicates capacity planning.
4. Demand planning and capacity planning set limits on what the appointment book (master schedule) can accommodate.
5. In a given period, one or more revisions of the master schedule/appointment book might be required.

We reemphasize that these points also apply to large firms, where the extra difficulty of reaching consensus among the many manager-planners adds further complexity. Two additional issues that affect large organizations were not evident in Anita's Studio; we add them to our list:

6. Flexibility makes master planning easier. Cross-trained personnel may be more readily moved to where demand is greatest, and flexible equipment may be assigned to a variety of jobs. (Proprietors like Anita should keep this point in mind as their businesses grow.)
7. Standard designs—in parts, components, and processes—make it easier to smooth out demands on capacity and also reduce the chance of stock outages or excessive inventory buildups. (Small businesses can benefit here, too. Sticking with the same types of equipment, for example, makes it easier to move jobs and employees around to balance demand and capacity.)

**Principles 7 & 9**

Cross-train employees.

Acquire flexible equipment.

Let's expand our perspective now by looking at master planning in larger organizations. Teams come into play.

## *Master Planning Teams*

In larger companies, master planning requires multiple cross-functional teams to accomplish what a small business owner-manager can do alone. We addressed the demand management activities in Chapter 4; here we look at specific composition and duties of capacity planning and master scheduling teams. First, an important reminder: In well-run companies, there is much information sharing—or even member sharing—among these teams.

Exhibit 5-2 shows typical capacity planning team membership. Often, especially in manufacturing, this team also develops the production plan in conjunction with a capacity plan. As with any team, it is important to get all of the right people on the team. The objectives are broad level demand/capacity balance and production and capacity plans—both shown at the right in Exhibit 5-2. Inspection shows that the plan calls for capacity to meet or exceed forecast demand; the step-up in capacity for March ensures this.

Exhibit 5-3A shows typical master scheduling team actions and outputs. (Recall from Exhibit 5-1 that master scheduling occurs after initial production and capacity planning.) The job is to steer capacity toward supplying actual demand items and toward specific, budgeted, process improvement activities. Master scheduling team outputs, shown at the right, include the various master schedules that we noted earlier along with scheduled time for process improvements.

**EXHIBIT 5-2 Capacity Planning Team and Its Responsibilities**

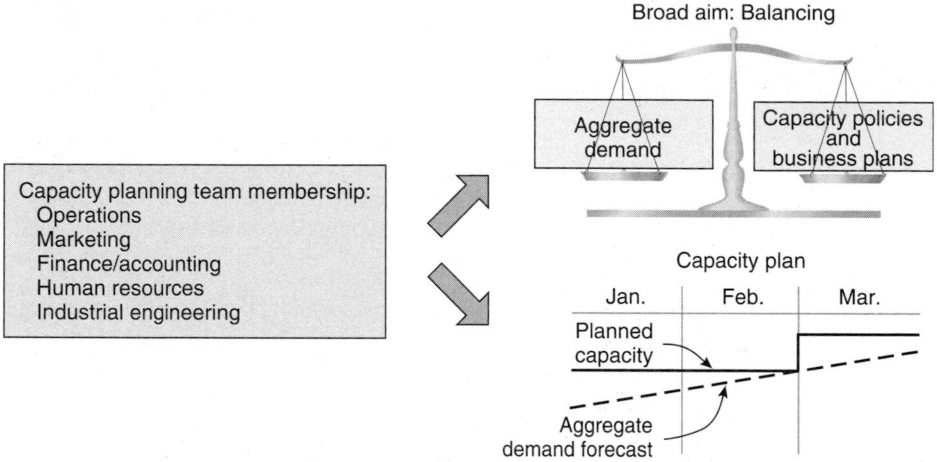

Broad aim: Balancing
Aggregate demand
Capacity policies and business plans

Capacity planning team membership:
Operations
Marketing
Finance/accounting
Human resources
Industrial engineering

Capacity plan
Jan. Feb. Mar.
Planned capacity
Aggregate demand forecast

Exhibit 5-3B provides a typical master scheduling team composition at the left, and examples of master schedules at the right. In the production example, the MPS shows a five-week schedule for three products. The services example might apply to a design firm; four projects are scheduled to be accomplished within the dates shown.

Questions about the plan may arise: What if product X needs components that get delayed? Or, what if the design firm doesn't have enough structural engineers to cover the scheduled work? Indeed, as we noted in the Anita's Studio example, the schedule might need to be changed. Detailed capacity planning and scheduling, topics we have yet to cover, often result in master schedule changes. Also, demand may change and master schedule changes become more likely as product and service offerings and the transformation processes required to provide them become more complex.

At this point, we have an overview under our belt—terms, an example, and specific master planning team duties have been addressed. Now, it is time to backtrack a bit and dig deeper into details. We look first at capacity strategies.

## Capacity Strategies

How do capacity or production strategies differ from operations strategies? Recall from Part I that operations strategies define the ways in which the company or business unit responds to cost-volume, volume-variety, and related issues. OM strategy also sets the tone for incorporation of principles that will guide OM activities at all levels, and—in broad fashion—prescribes how the firm will incorporate technology and other innovations.

Capacity strategy, though defined by OM strategy, is narrower. And as we have mentioned, and as examples later in the chapter will reveal, when outputs can be

**EXHIBIT 5-3 Master Planning: Master Scheduling Team**

A. SCHEDULING TEAM ACTION

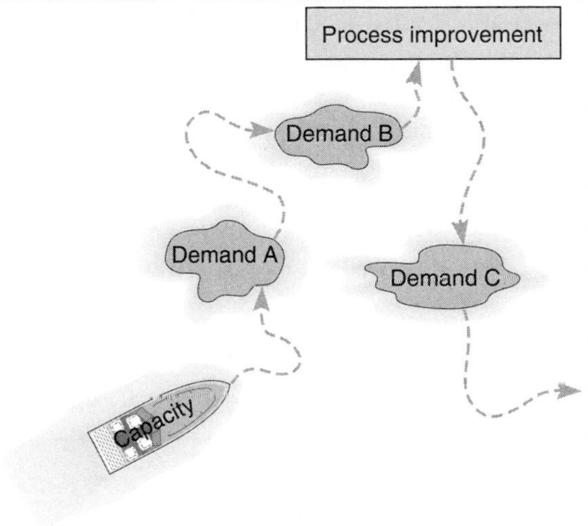

Process improvement

Demand B

Demand A

Demand C

Capacity

RESULTING SCHEDULES

- Master production schedule (MPS)
- Appointment book
- Facility schedule
- Time reserved for process improvements

B. EXAMPLES

Master scheduling team membership:
- Operations
- Production control
- Accounting
- Human resources

Production →

Master production schedule

| | 2001 | | 2002 | | |
|---|---|---|---|---|---|
| | Weeks | | | | |
| Product | 51 | 52 | 1 | 2 | 3 |
| X | 10 | 10 | 10 | 12 | 12 |
| Y | 2 | – | – | 3 | 6 |
| Z | 18 | 18 | 16 | 11 | 9 |

Services →

Design schedule
Mar.–May, 2002

| Job | Schedule |
|---|---|
| County Building | Mar. 15 – Apr. 15 |
| Wild River Bridge | Apr. 1–30 |
| Oak Terrace Apts. | Apr. 10–30 |
| Prairie Mall | May 1–30 |

prescheduled, capacity strategy is usually linked to the production (outputs) strategy. (Actually, in such settings *production/capacity strategy* is a more accurate descriptor of the focus, but in practice, the term *capacity strategy* is often used to include both.)

As a rule, adjustments to capacity levels are costly, and are frequently avoided or delayed even if demand must go unserved; the introductory Into Practice box on air transport gridlock exemplifies. Fortunately for operations managers—and for their customers—a variety of options exist to make efficient use of existing capacity and to enhance that capacity. We treat those topics in the next sections; for now, our focus is overall capacity strategy.

### *Chase-Demand versus Level-Capacity Strategies*

Suppose we have forecast for customer demand for one of our output goods or services—for our purposes, we needn't specify which—for the first six months of next year. The forecast data appear in the bottom row of Exhibit 5-4 and are plotted as the dark triangles on a dashed line graph in the figure. Further, assume that each unit of output requires two hours of labor. The period-by-period demand for labor—capacity—is shown in the second row from the bottom, and plotted as dots on the solid line at the top of the figure.

In a pure **chase-demand strategy,** period output will match demand. In January, 110 units will be provided; 90 in February, and so forth. Furthermore, capacity demands follow the same pattern, but reflect the 2-for-1-consumption requirement. The lighter-shaded bars illustrate; 220 hours of capacity needed in January, 180 in February, and so on.

**EXHIBIT 5-4 Capacity Strategies—Pure Forms**

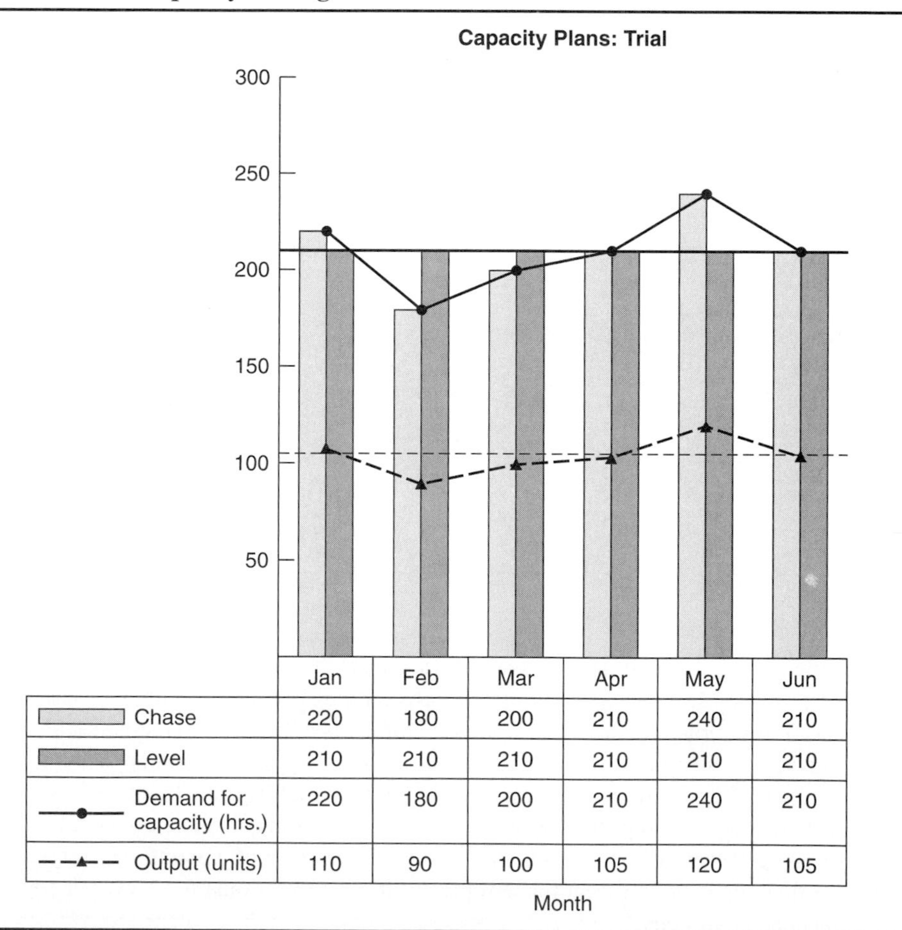


| | Jan | Feb | Mar | Apr | May | Jun |
|---|---|---|---|---|---|---|
| Chase | 220 | 180 | 200 | 210 | 240 | 210 |
| Level | 210 | 210 | 210 | 210 | 210 | 210 |
| Demand for capacity (hrs.) | 220 | 180 | 200 | 210 | 240 | 210 |
| Output (units) | 110 | 90 | 100 | 105 | 120 | 105 |

Another pure-form, the **level-capacity strategy,** holds capacity at (or very near) some fixed amount, regardless of the demand pattern. The output plan and the supporting capacity plan appear level over time. In Exhibit 5-4, the production plan might set period output at 105 units—the level dotted line—the average for the six-month forecast horizon. Thus the capacity plan, again reflecting the two-hours-per-unit requirement, calls for 210 hours per month, shown by the darker-shaded bars.

Chase-demand is found in labor-intensive businesses, especially services, where required skills are low. The labor force fluctuates with demand. Or, in either manufacturing or service, where the level of outsourcing is high, chase-demand is accomplished by simply increasing or decreasing the volume of buying.

Capital-intensive businesses favor level-capacity; the aim is high capacity utilization in order to recover equipment costs. In labor-intensive settings, level capacity is preferred if employees' skill qualifications are high or if skills are scarce. The aim is to retain good people.

The level-capacity strategy sometimes raises inventory levels and order backlogs. In a make-to-stock company, for instance, demand reductions might cause planners to allow inventory levels to increase just to keep capacity level. Or, planners at a make-to-order firm may let order backlogs build rather than change (increase, in this case) the capacity level.

**backlog**
Accumulation of unfinished work or unfilled orders.

Exhibit 5-5 summarizes conditions one might find in pure chase-demand and level-capacity settings. Businesses that employ low-wage, low-skill people tend to use the chase strategy. With low skill levels, training costs are low per employee but could be high per year, since turnover tends to be high. Turnover also means high hire–fire costs and, along with low skills, contributes to high error rates. Forecasting and budgeting may be short term since lead times for adding to or cutting the workforce are short.

Level capacity has opposite features. To attract more skillful people, pay and working conditions must be better. Training costs per employee are high. The attractions of the job are meant to keep turnover and hire–fire costs low, and high labor skills hold down error rates. Forecasting and budgeting must be longer term, since hiring and training skilled people takes time.

**EXHIBIT 5-5 Comparison of Chase-Demand and Level-Capacity Strategies**

| | *Chase Demand* | *Level Capacity* |
|---|---|---|
| Labor skill level | Low | High |
| Wage rate | Low | High |
| Working conditions | Erratic | Pleasant |
| Training required per employee | Low | High |
| Labor turnover | High | Low |
| Hire–fire costs | High | Low |
| Error rate | High | Low |
| Type of budgeting and forecasting required | Short term | Long term |

Although our discussion has emphasized the human component of capacity, facilities, equipment, information channels, and other resources enter the capacity plan as well. Furthermore, in a growing number of companies, a single pure-form capacity strategy won't do, and a mixed or hybrid version is chosen instead. The goal is to capture the benefits but avoid the drawbacks of pure chase-demand or level-capacity. Finally, competitive pressures—many discussed in Part I—have increased the concern for capacity management in strategic-level managerial planning; more proactive options are emerging. One approach requires taking a closer look at demand.

### *Revisiting Demand Composition*

All demand is not equal. Pursuit of greater market share per se can be hazardous to a company's health; rather, *profitable* markets ought to be the target.[1] Indeed, greater attention to profit margin—an issue we addressed in Chapter 2—has benefits that include capacity management and extend into pricing and other strategic concerns.[2] From an OM perspective, however, greater demand selectivity promotes effective capacity use.

Essentially, a multifunctional master scheduling team freed from departmental barriers is able to examine the composition of demand and separate good orders from the not-so-good ones. Exhibit 5-6A shows a situation where demand (the "jagged line") has grown to such an extent that it *consistently* exceeds capacity. The master scheduling team breaks down that demand into three categories: orders for high-profit items, low-profit items, and loss items (see Exhibit 5-6B). The team immediately gives preference to high-profit items by removing some of the loss and lower-profit items from the current demand stream (delaying, canceling, or subcontracting those orders). Longer-term actions might include removing items from the product line; changing pricing, advertising, and promotion; and impressing salespeople with the need to discourage sales of loss items.

Cost systems often don't yield true item cost; the master scheduling team may need to do its own activity-based costing audit to get good cost data for finding true item profitability.

**EXHIBIT 5-6 Analysis of Demand at an Apparent Capacity Constraint**

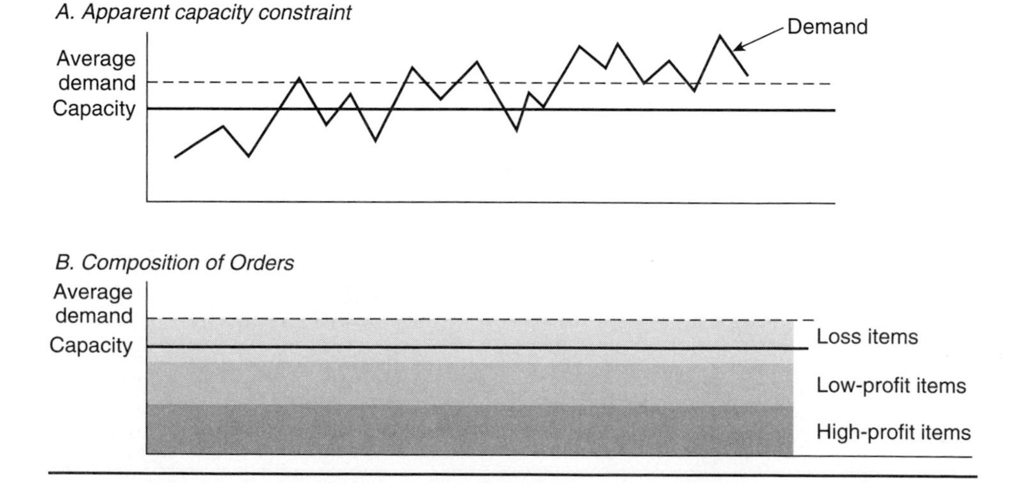

Besides segmenting demand by profitability, the master scheduling team may also segment by type of customer: vital customers, average customers, and difficult customers. Good customers get priority service, but the annoying ones are turned away. Thus, the team rejects the view that "a sale is a sale." It segments demand on overloaded resources and takes commonsense actions to relieve the overloads.

Companies following this strategy include Queen City Treating Company, a small Cincinnati firm specializing in heat-treating metal parts. CEO Ed Stenger says that formerly the company policy was "Be everything to everyone. Compete on price. Quote all comers—regardless of part or process. Promise whatever it takes on delivery. And never tell a customer anything more than he absolutely needs to know." But Stenger had heard a different tune at a meeting on strategy sponsored by the Cincinnati Chamber of Commerce. The message induced Stenger and some of his young managers to rethink their conventional strategy.[3] They studied their customer base and developed a strategy of targeted growth, as opposed to being all things to everyone. Stenger and his team arranged customers into three tiers. First-tier customers: high volume, common processes. Second tier: substantial volume, considerable process commonality. These two tiers are "key accounts." Third tier: low volume, irregular frequency, and little process commonality. A new price and delivery structure strongly favors key-account customers both in dollars and delivery times—at the expense of the third tier.

Stenger explains: "The simple fact is, and always has been, that the lowest tier customer interrupts our ability to service the upper tiers—those who pay the bills. . . . Which doesn't mean we won't service [the third tier]. It just means they'll pay more and wait longer if they want us to do the work."

Other companies going for targeted growth include

- Omni-Circuits, Inc., Glenview, Illinois. Omni has trimmed its customer list from 200 to 20.[4]
- Microelectronics Modules Corp., Milwaukee. Each Friday morning CEO Kenneth A. Hammer and key lieutenants sit down and decide which customers to accept or decline.[5]

Giving preference to best products and best customers is good business anywhere. Why wouldn't every company do it? we might ask. One reason is that companies have lacked team structures for joint planning across departmental lines. Another is that companies often expect too much from their computer scheduling routines. The computer system is unlikely to be able to sort out the best options as to which customer orders or which products to favor when demand is overheated. Prudence calls for involving experienced teams of human decision makers in such matters.

High-level teams have not limited their scrutiny to demand. Again, when all parties are represented, opportunities for a variety of improvements—all with capacity-enhancing potential—begin to emerge from throughout the company.

### *Capacity Enhancement*

Companies are also finding ways to make existing capacity more dependable and versatile. Exhibit 5-7 lists six approaches that teams of associates can take to reduce the

### EXHIBIT 5-7 Toward Capacity Enhancement

1. Less service (and therefore less demand on capacity) for less-profitable items or less-valued customers.
2. Cross-training and faster equipment changeovers to gain capacity, flexibility, and speed.
3. Maintaining capable standby capacity, including trained, on-call labor.
4. High involvement in improvement projects that cut capacity losses due to down equipment, lack of materials or information, rework, scrap, and low process yields.
5. Deliberately cutting stock to create temporary bottlenecks, thereby stimulating the need to solve basic problems.
6. Moving emergency buffer stock offline, thus cutting throughput time while retaining protection against random bottleneck conditions.

firm's vulnerability to overloads. The first item (reducing service and capacity consumption for low-profit items) was addressed previously. And the second (increasing flexibility to gain capacity) is examined throughout the book. But the other four items need some explanation.

**Principle 9**

Multiple units of capacity.

Well-trained standby labor (number 3) is effective as long as there is enough available, not theoretical, physical capacity (equipment and space) for the standby labor to use. Having standby equipment capacity ties in with the ninth principle of operations management, calling for multiple smaller units of capacity. The rationale is simple. If one small unit breaks down, others of the same type keep humming, but if a single, large-capacity unit goes down, production comes to a halt.

Number 4 aims at getting more output from existing capacity through improvement projects. Improvement teams especially focus on eliminating stoppages and preventing losses from bad quality.

In the lore of JIT, one purpose of cutting buffer stocks (number 5) is to stimulate problem solving. The procedure is to cut inventories between a pair of processes until the user process sometimes runs out of work (a stockout). The idea is to create a bottleneck, though not a severe or permanent one. This makes people in the process feel the actual pain of a shortage in order to create the incentive to expose and fix the underlying cause of variability. In other words, you create a small, temporary bottleneck in order to prevent a large, chronic one.

Number 6 is a way of avoiding a trade-off dilemma. Prudent managers have followed the apparently commonsense practice of inserting buffer stocks wherever there is a capacity constraint. The trouble is that buffer stock adds lead time, which has multiple negative effects.

Let's turn this technique around: Where there is a serious but infrequent capacity constraint, move the protective buffer stock offline. For example, an Ontario, Canada, manufacturer keeps one day's supply of six sizes of steel blanks in a low-cost, offline location; historically the blanking equipment breaks down a few times a year. When it does, someone fetches the buffer stock, and operations carry on, avoiding late deliveries, while the equipment is fixed. If the buffer stock was on line, it would add one extra day of lead time all year long, even though it is needed only a few times a year. Furthermore, if on line, it would take up premium space and require constant handling and the usual administrative expenses of work-in-process inventory.

A successful strategy for capacity enhancement requires an organization-wide commitment. Overall, Exhibit 5-7 shows *effects;* in Part III we see more of the *techniques,* especially for items 2, 3, and 4. Our closing capacity strategy topic—capacity cushion—also reflects total company involvement.

### *Capacity Cushion*

While demand scrutiny and capacity enhancement are valuable capacity management tools, some companies attempt to avoid, or at least delay, the need to adjust capacity in the first place. They create a **capacity cushion**—a preplanned capacity excess. Suppose the planners using the data in Exhibit 5-4 provide a 10 percent capacity cushion. Under a level-capacity strategy, for example, planned capacity for each period would be roughly 231 hours (210 × 1.10).

Not investing in enough capacity became common in North America and may have contributed to the productivity crisis of the 1980s. Misguided strategy was to blame: Managers milked cash out of existing facilities and failed to invest to expand capacity. Today, companies such as Merck (pharmaceuticals) and Milliken (textiles and chemicals) exemplify what could be a trend of increased use of reasonable capacity cushion. (See Contrast box "Capacity Management.")

The theme of capacity cushion appears in JIT writings as well—usually referred to as **undercapacity planning** (or, **undercapacity scheduling).** The idea is simple: Don't commit to a schedule that consumes all available capacity; leave a reserve to handle demand spikes, special customer needs, or last-minute problems, and time for improvements to capacity resources. Solectron (a two-time winner of the Baldrige Award) for example, plans its operations "at about 75 percent to 80 percent capacity to accommodate customer order fluctuations due to market volatility." The electronics manufacturer calls the practice "flexible capacity."[6]

CONTRAST

## Capacity Management

**"By the Numbers" Capacity**

Plan for full utilization of capacity—for hours of demand to equal available hours of labor and facilities or even to overutilize capacity (e.g., work overtime on a regular basis).

**Well-Managed Capacity**

Plan for enough capacity to ensure high quality, on-time performance every time, and reasonable time for improvement activities.

In the next section, we see an example of undercapacity scheduling; it illustrates the capacity cushion strategy put to use. In general, any strategy gets implemented through ensuing policies.

## Capacity Policies

**Policy** is guidance or technique used to implement strategy. Obviously, capacity policies should be consistent with strategic business and capacity plans. In practice, the effects of capacity policies reverberate throughout an organization and along customer and supply chains as well.

### *Effects of Capacity Policies*

Recall our photographer in Example 5-1. Suppose Anita chooses to follow a chase-demand strategy. She might adopt a customer-oriented policy of promising portrait proofs within 72 hours after the sitting. To meet that commitment, her capacity policy might be to make extensive use of subcontracting (to a friend's studio) for developing and printing. Other examples of specific policies follow:

- A municipal power company has a strategy of providing high employee security in order to gain a stable workforce. Its enabling policies include (1) maintaining excess linespeople and installers in order to meet surges in demand and (2) subcontracting (to local electric contractors) extraordinary maintenance, especially repair of downed lines.
- A bowling lane proprietor's strategy is one of high utilization of bowling lanes. To act on that strategy, the proprietor offers lower prices for daytime bowling.
- At a food wholesaler, planners have adopted a competitive strategy of very fast service to retail grocers. Its supportive policies include shift work, weekend hours, overtime, cross-trained office associates who can help out in the warehouse or drive delivery vehicles, and large inventories.

Exhibit 5-8 shows examples of these and several other common capacity policies. As illustrated, some apply only labor, others to nonlabor resources, and still others to both.

Top company officers are responsible for setting capacity policies. The Into Practice box "Hewlett-Packard's Flex Force" illustrates. Some capacity policies are general: "Avoid overtime, and keep inventories low." Others are specific, expressed numerically as minimums, maximums, or ranges, and may also be priority ordered. For example, a set of priority-ordered policies aimed at maintaining a level permanent workforce might be

1. For insufficient demand:
   *a.* Keep employees busy by building backlogs—maximum of 10 percent buildup above predicted demand.
   *b.* Lay off employees only after a 10 percent backlog is on hand.

**EXHIBIT 5-8 Capacity Management Policies**

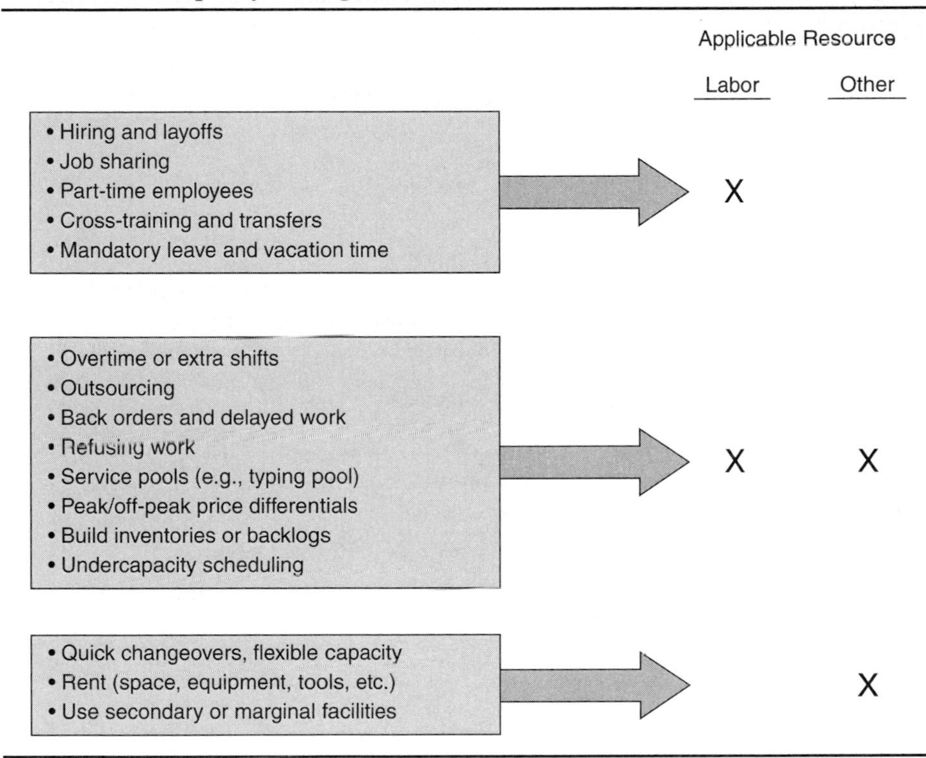


2. For excess demand:
   *a.* Use temporary labor for the first 5 percent of excess demand.
   *b.* Use overtime for the next 5 percent.
   *c.* Reduce customer service (serve best customers fully, but for lesser customers, postpone or even refuse the work, offer partial shipments, etc.).

With such specific policies, master planning is straightforward; managers just follow the policies. Usually, however, a company will not hem itself in so explicitly. Some successful companies throughout the world, of course, can claim with pride that they have never had layoffs. Have they just been lucky? Perhaps fortune has played a role, but then again maybe foresight and attention to detail—a proactive approach to master planning—helped create some of the good fortune.

Capacity policies work best when they're in place before they are needed. But how might a prudent manager anticipate such a need?

### *Policy Options: An Example*

Let's return to Anita's Studio, a few years after we parted company in Example 5-1. Example 5-2, illustrating much of what we've learned thus far about master planning, finds Anita's business booming.

INTO PRACTICE

## Hewlett-Packard's Flex Force: Level Capacity Plus Chase Demand

At Hewlett-Packard's Lake Stevens Instruments division, demand spikes made capacity planning difficult. Their solution: flex force, a permanent pool of on-call temporary employees. At its inception, flex force was designed to meet these six requirements:

1. Provide 20 percent flexibility in the total capacity projections.
2. Assure short-term response (within 48 hours) to changes in capacity requirements.
3. Provide training necessary to maintain quality levels, regardless of changing workloads.
4. Be cost neutral. There should be no perceived cost advantage or disadvantage from using the flex force program.
5. Flex force employees should feel like HP employees and not be treated as second-class citizens. They should be included in departmental meetings, enjoy equal access to the facility, and not be visibly identifiable as flex force employees.
6. Flex force employees should want part-time employment and not accept part-time employment as a means to attaining full-time employment.

Flex force grew from an initial pilot-test group to 80 employees. The six requirements were generally met, and "on-time delivery rates, frequently among the best in the company, have been largely attributed to the ability of the flex force to quickly respond to changing order rates on any product."*

*John Schneider, "Putting the Flex in a Flexible Work Force," *Target,* Special edition (1991), pp. 5–13.

### Example 5-2: MASTER PLANNING—PHOTOGRAPHY SERVICES, PART II

Two years ago, Anita expanded her photography business to include weddings and proms, in addition to her portrait and group photo work. She has found that the expansion has increased her portrait work as well, since many of her former wedding clients want her to take their anniversary portraits, children's pictures, and so on.

Wedding pictures, like portrait photographs, require manual developing in two stages—the proofs and the final prints of the customer's selected poses. Anita prefers to develop these herself, although for the past two springs she has had to hire an assistant to help with developing. Prom photographs, however, are like group photographs; machine developing is sufficient. She contracts all machine development work to FastFotos, Inc., a commercial photofinisher.

Word of Anita's expertise has spread; she enjoys a top reputation, and clients have learned to book her early. Each December, before leaving on her January ski vacation, Anita likes to plan her capacity requirements—especially the requirements for her own time—for the spring, her busy season. As she examines demand for her services, shown in Exhibit 5-9, she realizes just how much business is growing. Group photo, wedding, and prom demands are all in the form of orders; portrait work is a mixture of orders and Anita's forecast based on recent demands for this six-month period, but adjusted upward to reflect this year's projected increase.

**EXHIBIT 5-9 Monthly Job Demand—Anita's Studio**

| *Job Type* | *Feb.* | *March* | *April* | *May* | *June* | *July* |
|---|---|---|---|---|---|---|
| Portrait photo | 18 | 12 | 15 | 40 | 50 | 35 |
| Group photo | 6 | 4 | 8 | 5 | 7 | 5 |
| Wedding | 1 | 2 | 4 | 5 | 10 | 8 |
| Prom | 0 | 0 | 5 | 7 | 1 | 0 |

**Job Details**

- Portrait photo: Requires 1 hour photograph time; manually developed—2 hours proof development time and 5 hours of final print development time.
- Group photo: Requires 2 hours photograph time; machine developed.
- Wedding: Requires 3 hours of photograph time; manually developed—6 hours proof development time, and 10 hours of final print development time.
- Prom: Requires 4 hours of photograph time; machine developed.

**Business Plan**

Anita prefers to limit her photography time to about 25 hours per week even during the spring season. If she goes much above that, time requirements for (manual) photo developing become excessive—especially since she prides herself on rapid turnaround time for her customers. She has found that bookkeeping consumes about five hours of her time each week; maintenance and housekeeping another three hours; and inventory management about one hour. She likes to include personal improvement time—for professional reading, seminars, and so forth—in her schedule as well; two hours each week is her aim.

If Anita uses the demand data in Exhibit 5-9 as a trial master schedule for the six-month period, what capacity planning issues will she face? What options might she pursue?

*Solution*

Since Anita is concerned primarily with capacity requirements for her time, the initial step is to convert the trial master schedule demand data into capacity units—that is, hours of Anita's time. Next, the other capacity demands, things she either has to do to run the business or wants to do for personal improvement, must be factored in. The result will be a rough statement of the demand for her labor (capacity) in hours per month; Exhibit 5-10 illustrates.

Example calculations, May:

$$\begin{aligned}\textit{Photographic hours} &= (\textit{40 portraits} \times \textit{1 hr./sitting}) \\ &\quad + (\textit{5 groups} \times \textit{2 hrs./sitting}) \\ &\quad + (\textit{5 weddings} \times \textit{3 hrs./wedding}) \\ &\quad + (\textit{7 proms} \times \textit{4 hrs./prom}) \\ &= \textit{93 hrs.}\end{aligned}$$

$$\begin{aligned}\textit{Developing hours} &= (\textit{40 portraits} \times \textit{7 hrs./sitting}) \\ &\quad + (\textit{5 wedding} \times \textit{16 hrs./wedding}) \\ &= \textit{360 hrs.}\end{aligned}$$

**EXHIBIT 5-10 Rough Capacity Demand for Owner's Time—Anita's Studio**

| *Job Type* | *Feb.* | *March* | *April* | *May* | *June* | *July* |
|---|---|---|---|---|---|---|
| Portrait photo | 18 | 12 | 15 | 40 | 50 | 35 |
| Group photo | 12 | 8 | 16 | 10 | 14 | 10 |
| Wedding | 3 | 6 | 12 | 15 | 30 | 24 |
| Prom | 0 | 0 | 20 | 28 | 4 | 0 |
| **Total photo hours** | **33** | **26** | **63** | **93** | **98** | **69** |
| Developing hours | 142 | 116 | 169 | 360 | 510 | 373 |
| Bookkeeping | 20 | 20 | 20 | 20 | 20 | 20 |
| Maintenance/housekeeping | 12 | 12 | 12 | 12 | 12 | 12 |
| Inventory management | 4 | 4 | 4 | 4 | 4 | 4 |
| Personal improvement | 8 | 8 | 8 | 8 | 8 | 8 |
| Total hours | 219 | 186 | 276 | 497 | 652 | 486 |

The resulting labor-hour workload is about what Anita expected. She can handle February, March, and—with some long workdays—April loads, *as they are now.* But beginning in May, she will need some help. In addition to her own overtime, Anita has other capacity planning options available. She's interested in four:

1. Hire assistants, for one or more of the following:
   - Most or all of the manual photograph developing work.
   - Some of the photography work and some of the developing.
   - Bookkeeping, maintenance, housekeeping, and inventory management.
2. Outsource more of the developing work; perhaps let FastFotos, Inc., do some of the portrait and wedding proofs and finish print developing. Maybe outsource bookkeeping and maintenance, too.
3. Attempt to alter the master schedule by shifting workload forward or backward in the schedule.
4. Limit future bookings to priority customers—existing clients, for example.

Example 5-2 ends without Anita having selected a particular capacity plan. She will incorporate information about costs, previous experience with these and other capacity options, and perhaps think again about what she *wants to do* before settling on a plan. Regardless of the chosen policies, capacity planners must deal with issues of capacity utilization. [The chapter supplement illustrates aggregate capacity planning using Excel® spreadsheet software.]

### *Capacity Utilization*

**Utilization** refers to intensity of use of capacity. A general expression for it is:

$$\text{Utilization rate} = \frac{\text{Time in use}}{\text{Time available}} \tag{5-1}$$

where availability is the time that a resource is considered ready for use. Utilization planning involves two questions: (1) How shall we define full utilization? (2) What is planned utilization for the upcoming capacity planning period?

Typically, companies define full utilization at some high but attainable level. Usually it is less than 24 hours a day, seven days a week. For example, Anita would probably consider being up and running 24 hours a day to be unreasonable—in terms of both customer and staff expectations. For her business, a reasonable definition of full utilization might be 44 hours per week (five 8-hour days plus Saturday mornings). In some capacity planning periods, she may elect to remain open during those hours, which means 44 hours per week is also her planned utilization. During August, however, suppose she plans to close on Mondays and Saturdays, reducing her planned capacity utilization to 32 hours per week. Then, by equation 5-1, Anita's Studio would operate at a capacity utilization rate of 72.7 percent (32 divided by 44).

At some assembly plants, full capacity is defined as 3 shifts per day, five days a week, or 15 shifts per week. If the planning team sets next quarter's capacity plan (based on the latest demand forecast) at 2 shifts of scheduled assembly per day, or 10 shifts per week, then planned capacity utilization would be 67 percent (10 divided by 15).

For paper and metal processors, because their equipment is so expensive (see Exhibit 5-11), full capacity may mean 21 shifts per week (including scheduled maintenance time). If a paper plant's demand is slack and its master planning committee elects to run only 18 shifts a week, planned capacity utilization is 86 percent (18 divided by 21).

### Over- and Undercapacity Planning

Whatever the definition of full capacity, should the goal be to utilize it fully? It depends. In times of superheated demand, companies will sometimes plan to overuse capacity: Anita, for example, might advertise special Sunday hours during the busiest season. Normally, however, high levels of performance in the eyes of customers require some slack and undercapacity scheduling—defined earlier—is one answer.

Principle 1

Get to know the competition.

A deliberate policy of undercapacity planning may be set forth numerically. A dental clinic, for example, might plan at 15 percent under capacity. If clinic capacity (measured in dentists' time, dental technician time, etc.) is 100 patients per day, the clinic will plan and schedule for 85 patients per day. The extra 15 percent is not to be squandered. Rather, the policy calls for using the time for data analysis; project work; preventive maintenance on equipment; training; and other activities aimed at reducing errors, rework, equipment trouble, and variation of all kinds. The benefits include fewer unplanned stoppages, greater staff efficiency, lower operating costs, time to fit in emergency patients, time for unexpected patient problems, less rework, and happier customers. Well-served customers, in turn, lead to higher customer retention, thus avoiding the costs of patient turnover or, worse, too few patients to keep the staff busy.

Example 5-3 illustrates some of the simple calculations that might be involved in applying undercapacity planning in a manufacturing setting, the planning takes place at the level of a master production schedule.

**EXHIBIT 5-11 Paper Plant Operations**

*Top left—Parent roll of tissue. Top right—Team (amid rolls of tissue) examines partially converted segment. Bottom—Product segment, plus packaged final product (conversion machines in background).*

Source: Courtesy Pope & Talbot, Inc., Consumer Products Division.

## Example 5-3: UNDERCAPACITY SCHEDULING—KOJI FILM CO.

The star of the product line at Koji Co., a photographic film manufacturer, is 135 24-exposure, 100-speed color film. The yield per eight-hour shift has averaged 6,600 rolls, or 825 rolls per hour. Koji's master scheduling team has adopted a rate-based schedule of 6,000 rolls per shift—no more, no less—which is the current sales rate.

Is the schedule attainable? What is the underscheduling policy in percentage terms?

*Solution*

The target of 6,000 should be attainable in one eight-hour shift most of the time. In a shift with average problems, the 6,000 rolls would be produced in about $7\frac{1}{4}$ hours (6,000/825 rolls per hour = 7.27 hours). On a bad day with two or three line stoppages, the 6,000 may still get produced—by working right up to the bell. On a very bad day, the 6,000 might be made by working some overtime.

The underscheduling policy is 6,000/6,600 = 90.9 percent.

---

Though undercapacity planning is designed to work within a given work area, its power is amplified when resources are flexible enough to move among several areas. Resource flexibility also helps when natural work areas—groups or families—are the basis for capacity planning.

## Group (Family) Capacity Planning

Group-based capacity planning is a commonsense partner of aggregate forecasting (discussed in Chapter 4). To some degree, it applies in most types of organizations.

### *Capacity Groups in a Small Business*

Look again at Exhibit 5-10, capacity demand for labor hours at Anita's Studio. Anita might reasonably expect that if she hires an office manager, that person could do the bookkeeping, inventory management, and perhaps some or all of the maintenance and housekeeping chores, but should not be expected to have photography skills. A photography assistant, on the other hand, might be expected to take and develop photographs, but won't necessarily have office management skills.

Thus, Anita could manage the labor component of her capacity as two groups. Indeed, the capacity demand pattern shown in Exhibit 5-10 suggests some wisdom for this grouping: The office management duties (as we shall call them) impose a steady demand on capacity—about 36 hours per month. Perhaps Anita will seek a regular, part-time employee for this job, following a level-capacity strategy. The photography and developing work, however, varies with the season. Maybe outsourcing or temporary employees (with appropriate skills)—implemented on a chase-demand basis—are appropriate options for this group. Her most flexible resource—her own time—is her ace in the hole, available to meet any extra demand surges that come along. Example 5-4 illustrates how Anita might create a capacity plan using these policies.

Example 5-4: GROUP CAPACITY PLANNING—SMALL BUSINESS

---

Anita, a professional photographer and small business owner, has separated demand for labor capacity at her studio into two groups. The first, for office management activities (bookkeeping, inventory management, and maintenance and general housekeeping), is steady, and averages about 36 hours per month. The second is for photography services (taking and developing photographs) and is highly seasonal. Demand for each capacity group (in hours) for an upcoming six-month period is shown below. (These data were obtained from Exhibit 5-10.)

| | Month | | | | | |
|---|---|---|---|---|---|---|
| *Demand for Labor Capacity—By Groups (hrs.)* | *Feb.* | *March* | *April* | *May* | *June* | *July* |
| Office management activities | 36 | 36 | 36 | 36 | 36 | 36 |
| Photography services | 175 | 142 | 232 | 453 | 608 | 442 |

Anita has decided to employ a part-time office manager on a regular basis; she will ask this new employee to work 10 hours each week, or 40 hours per month. Her plan now—in late December—is to get the new office manager on board within the next month. To meet the demand for photography services, she has elected to

- Hire two temporary assistants during April; she wants them both on board by May. They will each work 40 hours per week (160 hours per month).
- Limit her *planned* personal labor commitment to 40 hours per week (160 hours per month). [She knows that she will probably work more, but wishes to hold her own "overtime" in reserve to meet last-minute needs of her regular customers.]
- Outsource photo developing work to FastFotos, Inc., (a commercial photofinisher) whenever demand exceeds capacity available from the two assistants and her own time.

Develop a capacity plan that will meet Anita's capacity planning objectives.

*Solution*

Exhibit 5-12 shows one possible capacity plan that will meet Anita's goals. The plan is based on having one photography assistant working for half of April—an assumption, of course.

Outsourcing (15 hours) is planned for February simply to meet Anita's goal of holding her own planned time to no more than 160 hours per month. Of course, if no last-minute orders arise, she may elect to forgo the outsourcing and do the 15 hours of developing work herself. It's not important for her to make that decision now. What is important, however, is that she has a plan in place and is ready to deal with contingencies that might arise.

**EXHIBIT 5-12 Capacity Plan—Anita's Studio**

| *Capacity Plan—By Group (hrs)* | *Feb.* | *March* | *April* | *May* | *June* | *July* |
|---|---|---|---|---|---|---|
| Office management activities | | | | | | |
| Demand | 36 | 36 | 36 | 36 | 36 | 36 |
| Capacity: New office manager (part-time) | 40 | 40 | 40 | 40 | 40 | 40 |
| Photography service | | | | | | |
| Demand | 175 | 142 | 232 | 453 | 608 | 442 |
| Capacity: Photo assistant #1 | — | — | 80 | 160 | 160 | 160 |
| Capacity: Photo assistant #2 | — | — | — | 160 | 160 | 160 |
| Capacity: Outsourcing (FastFotos, Inc.) | 15 | — | — | — | 130 | — |
| Capacity: Owner (Anita) | 160 | 142 | 152 | 133 | 158 | 122 |

Group capacity planning in larger organizations follows the same three steps. To recap, they are:

1. Group products into natural families and select units for aggregate capacity planning. A family consists of goods/services that employ units of capacity going through roughly the same processes. It is a natural family only if capacity (skills and equipment) is flexible enough to process all the goods/services within the family.
2. Project aggregate customer demand for each capacity group. This forecast is in the units of measure chosen in step 1.
3. Develop a production plan (output units), and convert to capacity units if necessary. This step aims at having the right amount of aggregate resources on hand.

The 1–2–3 capacity planning procedure applies to both on-demand (make-to-order) businesses and make-to-stock production. Our next example is for on-demand commercial photo processing services.

### *On-Demand and Make-to-Order Operations*

Example 5-5 illustrates the 1–2–3 procedure. The idea for the example (but not the data) comes from Ashton Photo, Salem, Oregon. Ashton's professional photo-processing business has been organized into 16 U-shaped photo-finishing cells. Each cell has about nine cross-trained members, focuses on one type of photo (e.g., sports teams or school photos), and processes the entire job from incoming film to outgoing finished work and invoice.

#### Example 5-5: CAPACITY PLANNING—FASTFOTOS, INC.

FastFotos is a large photofinisher, handling both consumer and commercial film processing (including some contract work for Anita's Studios, especially in the school graduation season). It is an on-demand, make-to-order business.

The capacity-planning team (the personnel director and the operations manager) plans capacity a number of weeks in advance. Since there is plenty of equipment capacity, the plan includes labor only. Their day-to day fine-tuning includes reasonable overtime and labor borrowing.

The capacity team uses the three-step method:

*Step 1.* They conclude that consumer and commercial photo processing make up separate capacity groups: Consumer processing is routine; commercial customers usually require special processing. Routine processing and special processing take place in different areas of the building. Number of orders is an appropriate capacity measure for both groups. The team plans capacity for its all-important commercial accounts first.

*Step 2.* The team uses recent past demand (number of orders) as a simple, reasonable projection of demand for the next eight-week capacity planning period.

*Step 3.* Exhibit 5-13 is the capacity-planning work sheet for commercial business. It includes recent demand data (second column) and two capacity options, both tight on capacity (team members are very cost conscious). Option 1 provides enough capacity to process 1,800 orders

Here *orders* is the unit of measure in a production plan and is also a suitable (surrogate) measure of capacity.

**EXHIBIT 5-13 Capacity/Backlog Options at FastFotos, Inc.**

| Recent Demand | | Option 1 Capacity: 1,800 Orders per Week | | | | Option 2 Capacity: 2,100 Orders per Week | | | |
|---|---|---|---|---|---|---|---|---|---|
| *Week* | *Orders* | *Orders* | *Deviation* | *Backlog* | *Excess Capacity* | *Orders* | *Deviation* | *Backlog* | *Excess Capacity* |
| 1 | 1,800 | 1,800 | 0 | | | 2,100 | +300 | | 300 |
| 2 | 1,100 | 1,800 | +700 | | 700 | 2,100 | +1,000 | | 1,000 |
| 3 | 1,800 | 1,800 | 0 | | | 2,100 | +300 | | 300 |
| 4 | 1,950 | 1,800 | −150 | −150 | | 2,100 | +150 | | 150 |
| 5 | 2,300 | 1,800 | −150 | −650 | | 2,100 | −200 | −200 | |
| 6 | 2,800 | 1,800 | −1,000 | −1,650 | | 2,100 | −700 | −900 | |
| 7 | 2,250 | 1,800 | −450 | −2,100 | | 2,100 | −150 | −1,050 | |
| 8 | 1,200 | 1,800 | +600 | −1,500 | | 2,100 | +900 | −150 | |
| Total | 15,200 | | | | | | | | |

$$\text{Mean demand} = \frac{15{,}200}{8} = 1{,}900 \text{ orders per week}$$

per week (100 fewer than the mean recent demand of 1,900 per week). Projected deviations range from +700 (excess capacity) to −1,000 orders per week. Since negative deviations signify backlogged orders, consecutive negative values carry over to the next week. The projected backlog grows to −2,100 orders in week 7, then falls to −1,500 in week 8. The capacity shortage in week 7 is more than one week's backlog (2,100 orders / 1,800 orders per week = 1.17 weeks), which won't do in FastFoto's competitive business.

Option 2 provides for 300 more orders per week than option 1. This results in projected excess capacity in the first four weeks, but insufficient capacity in the second four weeks; the backlog grows to a high of −1,050 orders in week 7. Since 1,050 orders is less than one week's backlog, the capacity planning team considers the plan workable.

Does this method of capacity planning assume that future demand will be like past demand? No. While total demand may be fairly close, the week-to-week demand pattern is sure to be different. Thus, maximum backlogs can be much more or less than projected. Still, the simple method illustrated in Example 5-5 employs existing demand data. It can work quite well *if* overtime, job transfers, and other flexible responses are available in weeks when the plan goes wrong. Put another way, capacity planners generally should reserve their flexible options for when the plan does not work out.

In some businesses, such as transportation, restaurants, and lodging, an unmet order is lost; backlogs are not carryable. The method used in Example 5-5 is modified in those cases to treat demand as noncumulative so that negative deviations are lost sales, not backlogs.

### *Make-to-Stock Operations*

In the make-to-stock case, capacity planning follows the three-step process and often adds a fourth step: Refine the plan to provide for desired inventory levels. There may

*Make-to-Stock Operations. Pill production process to be followed by packaging. Orders will be filled from stocked finished goods.*

© Corbis

also be a fifth step: Further test the feasibility of the plan by examining how it affects critical resources (e.g., a heavily used machine or a specially skilled associate). The five steps are illustrated in Example 5-6.

## Example 5-6: Capacity (Production) Planning—Quark Electronics

Capacity planning at Quark Electronics was once reactive. If work was piling up in Shop A (long customer-order backlogs), a planner in that shop would request more labor, extra shifts, or other reactive capacity changes. Planning capacity based on demand forecasts seemed hopeless because there were too many different products and forecasts were too inaccurate.

However, a capacity-planning team was formed, and they have learned to apply group-based forecasting and capacity planning in four steps.

*Step 1:* The team divided its production processes into three product families, groups 1, 2, and 3. Each group covers a large number of electronic items, including end products, subassemblies, and component parts.

The team studied product routings (flow paths) and found three dominant paths through the four shops (see Exhibit 5-14). A few products do not fit any of these routings, but enough do to provide a solid basis for capacity (production) planning, with groups large enough for aggregate forecast accuracy.

*Step 2:* The capacity team obtains aggregate demand forecasts for each of the three product groupings; the forecast for group 1 is in pieces per week (see Exhibit 5-15).

*Step 3:* The capacity plan is stated in pieces per week and is evaluated to ensure that it is consistent with capacity policies and is realistic. The team's calculations (not shown) ensure that projected aggregate labor-hours in product group 1 are sufficient to meet projected demand each week, with time to spare for improvement work.

## EXHIBIT 5-14 Common Routings—Quark Electronics

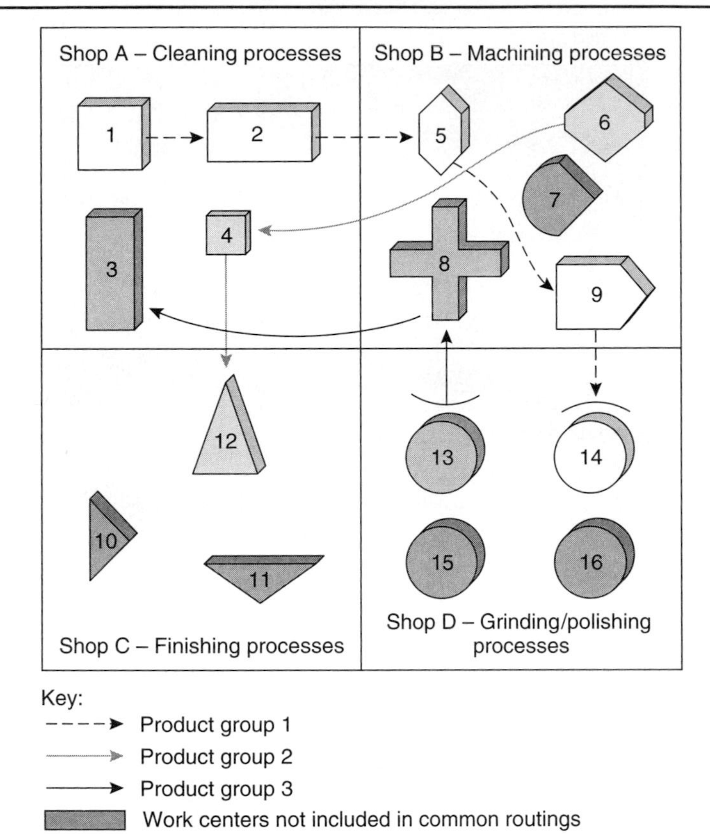


Note: Machines 13, 14, 15, and 16 are identical; thus 15 and 16 could be substituted for 13 and 14, if needed.

## EXHIBIT 5-15 Capacity Plan—Product Group 1

**Quark Electronics: Pieces through Product Group 1**

| | **Forecast** | | **Capacity (Production) Plan** | | |
|---|---|---|---|---|---|
| *Week* | *Pieces per Week (000)* | *Cumulative* | *Pieces per Week (000)* | *Cumulative* | *Inventory* |
| 0 | — | — | — | — | 14.0 |
| 1 | 10.0 | 10.0 | 10.1 | 10.1 | 14.1 |
| 2 | 10.0 | 20.0 | 10.1 | 20.2 | 14.2 |
| 3 | 10.4 | 30.4 | 10.1 | 30.3 | 13.9 |
| 4 | 10.4 | 40.8 | 10.1 | 40.4 | 13.6 |

*Step 4:* Several years ago Quark's senior management decided to follow its competitors and focus, not on direct labor costs (which had fallen to less than 3 percent of production costs), but on intensive management of inventories (over 65 percent of costs). Thus, capacity planners now build inventory reductions into the capacity plans. The current four-week capacity plan shows a decline from 14,000 to 13,600 pieces (see last column in Exhibit 5-15). But each year, just prior to Quark's busy season, the capacity planners allow a buildup of inventories in anticipation of a seasonal surge in demand.

Quark's capacity-planning team must repeat all of these steps for product groups 2 and 3. But is that the end of it? Sometimes not.

*Step 5:* To be on the safe side, the planners want to know that their capacity plan does not overload certain critical resources. For example, Machine 5, a complex machine in Shop B (and in the Product Group 1 routing) is nearly always the first to be overloaded, thereby becoming a bottleneck. Since the capacity plan is stated in pieces per week, which represents a nonspecific mixture of products, the team cannot precisely project the workload of Machine 5. Instead, they use historical average machine-hours per piece as the basis for rough-cut capacity planning. For Machine 5, the data show 0.0075 hours per piece. Thus, for group 1 and week 1:

$$\text{Projected workload} = 10{,}100 \text{ pieces} \times 0.0075 \text{ hours per piece}$$
$$= 75.75 \text{ hours}$$

This is within Quark's upper limit policy of 80 planned hours of workload per week, but the capacity team finds this too close for comfort. It leaves little margin for error, and forecasts are notoriously erroneous.

What to do? The marketing director (a member of the team) says, "No problem." Promotion costs are too high, and sales people have been booking orders from customers whose credit is shaky. His actions to deal with these two problems will, he estimates, cut projected demand by 5 percent. Quick recalculation of all capacity figures yield a plan the whole team likes.

Marketing director's actions show capacity planning is more than translating demand into capacity numbers. If it were only number crunching, it could all be done by a computer—no need for a team.

## *Capacity Planning in Improved Layouts*

The Quark Electronics example represents good capacity planning for a firm that is organized by function. As we have noted, however, the modern movement is toward better forms of organization. The idea is to break up functional departments and group activities into more meaningful layouts—focused on a product group or customer group. In some circles, the term **group technology (GT)** is used as the overall descriptor; in others it might be called **cellular layout** or even **cellular manufacturing.** (We examine these concepts in Chapter 14.)

Often, as is the case at Quark Electronics, dominant **product routings**—the flow paths of products through the facility—suggest natural groupings. Exhibit 5-16 illustrates how the common routings identified in Exhibit 5-14 might be used to create three natural work cells. Employee, equipment, and accessories have been moved into the product-flow-oriented cells, making group-based capacity planning more natural.

This form of organization has other benefits. It creates a natural chains of provider-customer linkages, facilitates cross-training, team-building, and problem solving.

**Principle 6**

Form multiple chains focused on customer or product families.

**Exhibit 5-16 Cells—Quark Electronics**

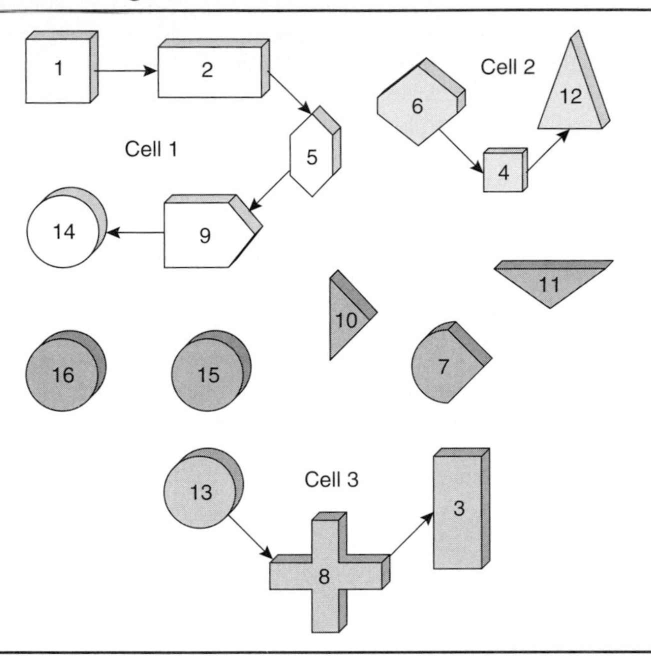


Note: Work centers not organized into cells are shaded dark gray. Centers 15 and 16 are mobile, capable of quick replacement for center 13 or 14.

## Master Scheduling

A capacity plan puts aggregate customer demand into time slots, but the master schedule puts actual orders into time slots. Exhibit 5-10, for example, shows that Anita's Studio has aggregate demand for 98 hours of photography services in June. But we would have to look at the master schedule (appointment book, in this case) to see an actual order: Mr. and Mrs. O'Grady will have their portrait taken on June 20 at 2:00 P.M. in the portrait sitting room.

The scheduled order matches the O'Grady's demand with capacity—in this instance, one hour of photographer's time and a one-hour use (reservation) of the portrait room. If we look deeper and incorporate other capacity elements along with Anita's customer-service policies, we conclude that the master schedule entry actually commits even larger chunks of capacity, including

- Two hours of proof developing time within 72 hours of the O'Grady's June 20 sitting. (See "Job Details" in Example 5-2.)
- Five more hours of developing time for final prints. This requirement could occur immediately after proof delivery if the O'Grady's quickly return the proofs with their selected poses and print order.

- Office time for processing the O'Grady's order, billing, and so forth; plus the nonlabor capacity elements (film, paper, etc.) if developing is done in-house.

In principle, it works much the same way in large manufacturing plants. The capacity plan might show, for instance, that a package wrapper will be required for 100 hours during June, but we must turn to the master schedule—and perhaps to more detailed schedules, as well—to discover when that machine will be preparing a specific completed order for shipment. The detailed schedules also reveal commitment of other capacity elements as the order moves through the plant. In practice, due precisely to the large number of diverse capacity elements required to convert planned orders into actual outputs, master scheduling in manufacturing can become complicated. It may even be "more art than science."[7] Thus, we will save coverage of some of these complexities until we examine specific manufacturing environments in later chapters.

This section focuses on general master scheduling concepts and on how the master schedule relates to capacity planning and demand management. Let's ask the most basic question first: Do all organizations even need master scheduling?

## *Applicability and Scope*

As we've noted, all organizations ought to perform demand management, and all must have some sort of capacity plan. But those organizations that provide on-demand services have no time to plan at the detailed level of a master schedule. That includes organizations catering to walk-in or call-in customers: retailers, fast-food restaurants, emergency rooms, police and fire departments, automobile registration facilities, buses, and so forth.

By contrast, reserved-seat businesses, professional services, and manufacturers draft a detailed master schedule. At Anita's Studios, the appointment book schedules customers into Anita's available time slots. A bigger service business such as a medical clinic would have a separate appointment book for each physician, and might also have appointment books for scarce, high-cost facilities like surgery suites.

Manufacturing is a bit more complicated. A master scheduling team (from operations, production control, sales, accounting, and human resources) weighs the master scheduling alternatives and sets priorities. Good customers, for example, get preferential slots in the master schedule; hence, the need for sales to be represented on the team. High-profit items ought to be preferred over marginal ones; hence, accounting needs a representative.

The master scheduling team may construct the master production schedule (MPS) around major capacity-consuming modules (end items) of the final product. Major modules (e.g., large engines) are costly and warrant careful advance scheduling. Smaller parts may take just a few hours and not cost much. Since each module consumes different resources (capacity) with different timing, each gets its own segment of the MPS. Exhibit 5-17 illustrates with a simple partial MPS covering a five-week period.

With these few examples of a master schedule's scope in mind, let's turn our attention to the process through which master scheduling is accomplished. We begin with a basic example from the services sector.

**EXHIBIT 5-17 Partial Master Production Schedule—Computer Assembly**

| | Weekly Production Schedule | | | | |
|---|---|---|---|---|---|
| *Modules* | *Jan. 13–17* | *Jan. 20–24* | *Jan. 27–31* | *Feb. 3–7* | *Feb. 10–14* |
| **Mother Board:** | | | | | |
| X–121 | 53 | 61 | 57 | 62 | 58 |
| X–221 | 45 | 42 | 50 | 44 | 40 |
| (Etc.) | — | — | — | — | — |
| **Power Supply** | | | | | |
| Y–123 | 100 | 120 | 110 | 95 | 105 |
| Y–223 | 220 | 210 | 240 | 220 | 235 |
| (Etc.) | — | — | — | — | — |
| **Hard Disk:** | | | | | |

## *Master Scheduling: Services Example*

Preparation of the master schedule is a key duty of department heads and other administrators in educational institutions. Example 5-7 illustrates.

Example 5-7: MASTER SCHEDULING IN DEPARTMENT OF MANAGEMENT—FUNK UNIVERSITY

Each department chairperson in the College of Business at Funk University must prepare a master schedule of course offerings. They prepare the schedule twice each term, once based on preregistration, and again after general or final registration has occurred.

The procedure is illustrated in Exhibit 5-18. The Management Department faculty clusters its courses (perhaps 30 to 40 offerings) into three capacity groups (block 2):

1. Quantitative/management information systems (MIS)/operations management (OM)
2. Behavioral/human resources management (HRM)
3. General management/business policy

Although other departments would use the same master scheduling procedure, their aggregate forecast groups would differ. The groupings are not intended to correspond to clusters of demand; rather, the intent is to form natural groups of capacity. At Funk University, the faculty consider courses within each capacity group similar enough so that faculty within that group have necessary expertise to teach most of the courses. While the groupings aren't perfect, they should be all right for the purpose: Arrive at a capacity plan (out of block 3) that matches up reasonably well with total course requirements (block 6), leading to a trial master schedule of course offerings (block 7).

The budget (education plan) and strategies and policies (block 1) are controls on the capacity plan. Policies are for class sizes (faculty–student ratios), classroom space, teaching loads (per faculty member), use of teaching assistants, and utilization of faculty skills (the extent to which faculty teach in stronger or weaker areas of expertise).

While blocks 1 through 3 concern aggregate demand and capacity, blocks 4 through 6 deal with unit demand course by course. Block 4 is actual demand, consisting of registrations by

**EXHIBIT 5-18 Master Scheduling—Department of Management**

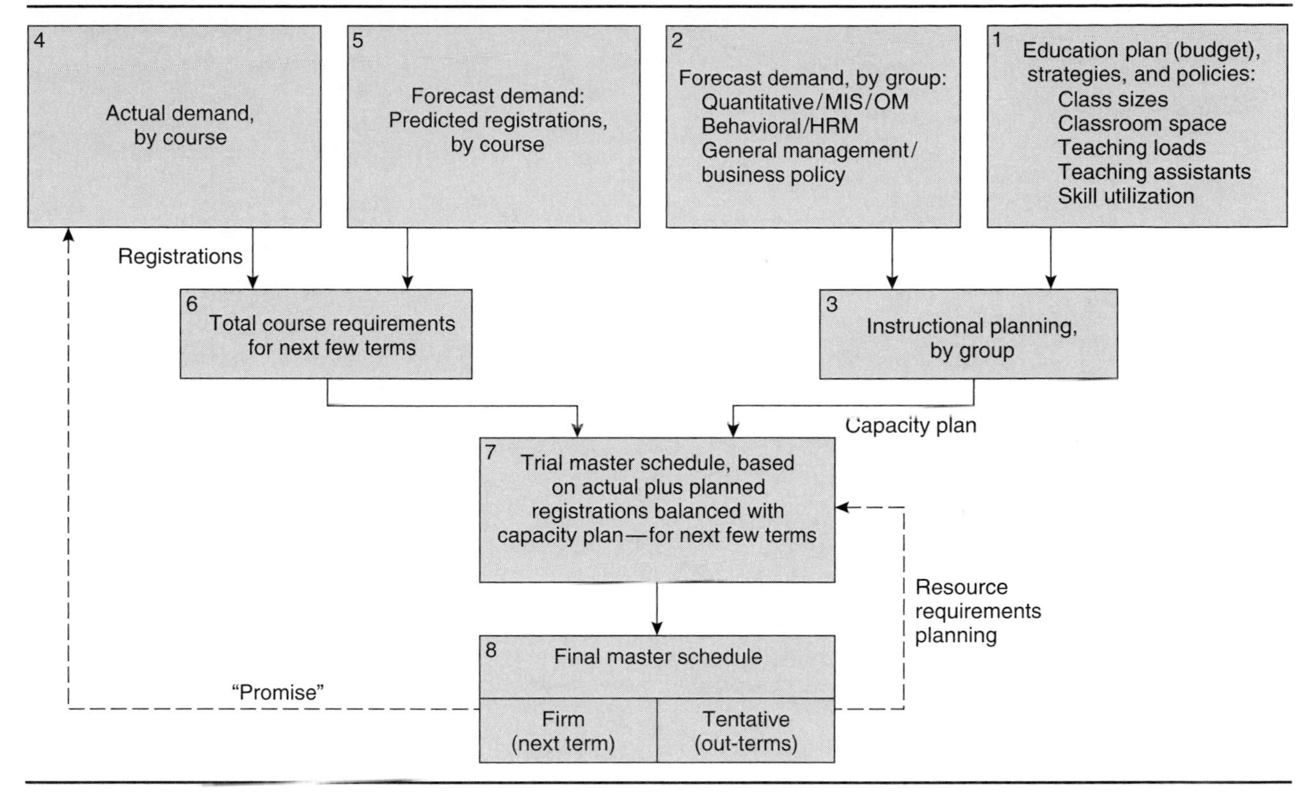


course. Block 5 is forecast demand: predicted registrations, by course, based on historical patterns plus other knowledge.

Next, in block 6, the chairperson assembles course requirements for the next few terms into a list. Then she matches this shopping list against what is available in the capacity plan. The result is the trial master schedule of course offerings for the next few terms. The feedback arrow from block 8 to block 7, resource requirements planning, indicates closed-loop control. It makes the master schedule an accurate reflection of capacity to meet demands by adjusting the master schedule until scarce resource overloads are eliminated.

A final master schedule emerges at block 8. It is firm for the upcoming term and tentative for future terms. At this point, Funk University's registrar sends out an order promise to students who have registered. He either confirms or denies their registration for a given course. If denied, he may offer a substitute.

## *Master Scheduling: Manufacturing Example*

Exhibit 5-18 contains the basics of master planning. Exhibit 5-19, expanding those basics, yields a master planning model for the complex case of a manufacturer that fabricates and assembles in the job or batch mode.

**EXHIBIT 5-19 Capacity-Demand Matching Process**

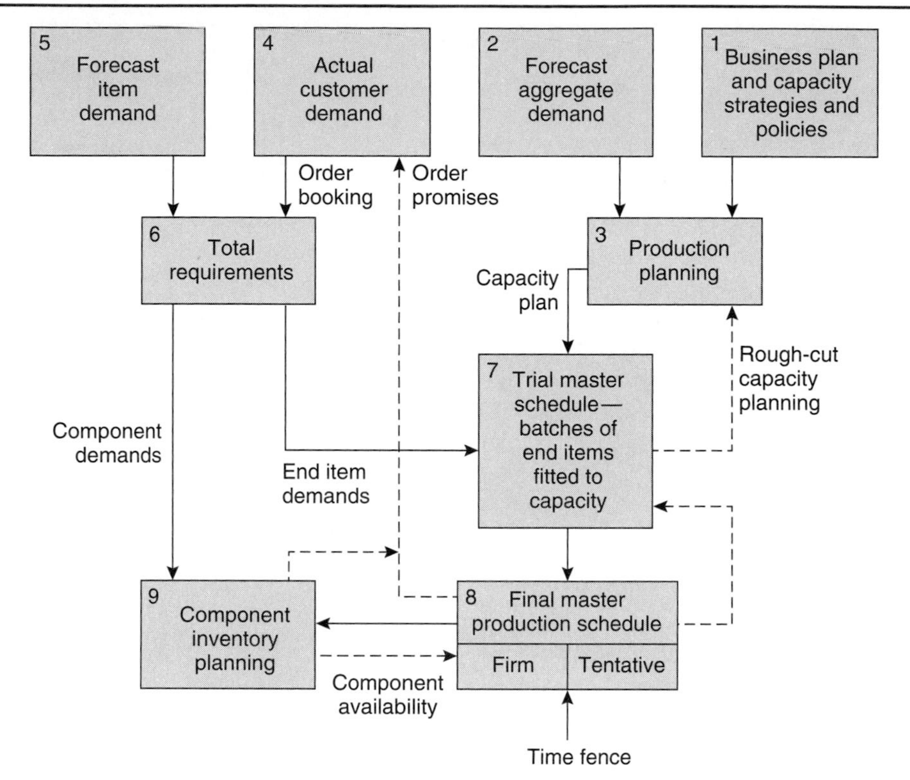


Blocks 1 through 6 are the same for a manufacturer as for a service: A capacity planning team guided by business plans and capacity strategies (box 1) uses aggregate demand forecasts (box 2) to plan overall production activity (box 3), thereby yielding a capacity plan. The sales force goes to work booking orders (box 4), which combine with forecasts of future orders (box 5), adding up to total requirements (box 6).

**Scheduling End Products and Components.** After block 6, there may be a split into two different types of schedules, one for end products and another for component parts. The one for end products is the master production schedule (MPS), block 7 (trial) and block 8 (final). The master scheduling team, in generating the MPS, tries to smooth out lumpy demand streams and may also collect demands for the same products into production lots.

The schedule for component parts includes demands for parts needed to meet the master production schedule, and may also include independently demanded component parts, such as service parts (see arrows from blocks 6 and 8 to block 9 in Exhibit 5-19).

**Time Fence Policies (Avoiding Nervous Schedules).** After suitable trials, the master scheduling team produces a final MPS. The firm portion typically covers the products's cumulative lead time, which ends at a time fence. A different master scheduling policy is needed for the two sides of the time fence. On one side (in the firm zone where work has already begun) schedule changes are generally avoided, because they generate disruptions that ripple through many stages of planning and execution. On the other side of the time fence (in the tentative zone), schedule changes are just on paper. Thus, the firm portion of the schedule is changed only as a last resort, but the tentative portion may be changed frequently.

**cumulative lead time**
Total time from first activity (e.g., drawing materials from stock) to completion of the item.

**time fence**
Point in the future beyond the longest total lead time; separates firm scheduling zone from tentative zone.

**Order Promise.** A primary concern of the customer is an order promise date, which comes from a salesperson. Salespeople must have reliable information from master scheduling so that they can make reliable promises. The importance of having a sales representative on the master scheduling team has already been mentioned.

In an attempt to improve delivery promises some companies install a complete information system that accurately calculates order completions. However, problems can persist under such a system. Better if the firm simplifies and integrates ordering, planning, scheduling, purchasing, and production, and thereby eliminates causes of the usual delays so all jobs get done quickly and predictably. Most importantly, good order-promise practices allow the master schedule to serve the needs of final customers as well as improve utilization of capacity.

**Principle 10**

Make it easy to avoid error or variation.

### *Master Scheduling in Make-to-Order Plants*

A special case of master planning in manufacturing is make-to-order production. An example is a producer of ultrasound machines for hospitals and medical clinics—no production without a firm order. The bane of the make-to-order producer is lack of planning lead time. Clinics order ultrasounds and want them right away. With no lead time, can a master production schedule extend far enough into the future to match demand with capacity reasonably well? The answer is yes. One approach is to use a flexible, customer-oriented procedure that involves what is called **consuming the master schedule** (or consuming the forecast).

The method employs an MPS with three subdivisions: master schedule, actual demand, and available to promise (see Exhibit 5-20). The procedure begins with the

**EXHIBIT 5-20 Consuming the Master Production Schedule**

| | Week | | | | |
|---|---|---|---|---|---|
| | *1* | *2* | *3* | *4* | *5* |
| Ultrasound A: | | | | | |
| Master schedule | 4 | 2 | 0 | 6 | 3 |
| Actual demand | 2 | 0 | 0 | 1 | 0 |
| Available to promise | 2 | 2 | 0 | 5 | 3 |
| Ultrasound B: | | | | | |
| Master schedule | 0 | 7 | 8 | 2 | 0 |
| Actual demand | 0 | 1 | 4 | 2 | 0 |
| Available to promise | 0 | 6 | 4 | 0 | 0 |

master schedule, based on forecasting. As salespeople book orders, the master scheduler enters the quantities in the actual demand row. The term *available to promise* means the computed difference between master schedule and actual demand quantities.

We see in Exhibit 5-20 that in week 4, one unit of ultrasound A has been sold—to be completed or delivered in that week—and five are available to promise. In the same week, both master-scheduled units of ultrasound B have been sold, leaving none available to promise. The master schedule is said to be consumed by actual orders being booked by salespeople. The master schedule keeps sales informed about quantities available to promise so that the sales force will not overconsume the schedule.

## *Rough-Cut Capacity Planning*

The feedback loop from block 7 to block 3 in Exhibit 5-19 refers to rough-cut capacity planning. The aim, as we saw in Exhibit 5-1 and again in Example 5-6, is to assure the capacity-planning team that the production plan will not overload a scarce resource. Typically, a scarce resource is an expensive machine or a hard-to-get skill, such as a graphics designer or a programmer for a numerically controlled cutting machine.

In one sense, every organization does rough-cut capacity planning:

> It might be as simple as saying, "I have a plan that calls for shipping $3 million worth of products this month, and I've always been able to ship $4 million per month. So we have the proven capacity to meet the plan." Alternately, you might say, "Management wants us to ship $7 million a month during the summer season. We have no precedent for being able to do that—management's new plan appears to be unrealistic at this time."[8]

**bill of labor**
States amount (hours) of each skill needed to produce/provide one unit. (Similarly, bill of materials states amount of each material needed to produce one unit.)

Running a rough-cut check requires data that show how much of the scarce resource is required per unit of product to be made or provided. Assume, for example, that a plastics manufacturer has a bill of labor stating that a newly designed plastic case for a computer keyboard requires, on average, 46 hours of mold-making labor. (The firm's senior mold-maker's skills are exceptional—nobody else has those skills.) To improve confidence that aggregate forecast demand will not overload the mold-maker, the capacity-planning team runs a rough-cut check on the amount of mold-making labor required.

Assume that the forecast is for eight new case designs in an upcoming quarter. Then

$$8 \text{ cases} \times 46 \text{ hours per case} = 368 \text{ hours}$$

Since a standard quarter equals 520 hours (13 weeks $\times$ 40 hours per week), the production plan looks doable. Capacity for the scarce resource is adequate.

But providing only 368 hours of molding for the mold-maker in a 520-hour quarter may seem inadequate to keep the expert busy.

Not so. In fact, being well below the 520-hour maximum is comforting at this stage of planning—no work has been scheduled and no orders have been received. When orders do arrive, they are unlikely to spread out evenly over the quarter. When orders pile up, the mold-maker will be quite busy. But when no orders require new mold design, the mold-maker will be occupied with repair and maintenance of existing molds and improvement projects. Vacations and possible illness may also intervene.

### *Perspective*

Early master planning lore emerged in manufacturing, say in the 1970s and 1980s, in North America as companies were trying to get a handle on computers and related technology. Long planning sequences were the rule, and schedules were usually not taken very seriously, because no one expected them to be met. Today, a quarter century later, competitive pressures to make products better, faster, *and* cheaper—along with the explosive growth of the services sector—make paramount two related concerns in the master planning game: (1) capacity must be flexible, and (2) planning horizons are getting shorter.

Capacity plans provide the resources to meet demands for goods and services, and master schedules are our commitments to do so. When we implement or execute the master schedule, orders flow and customer demand is fulfilled. And that's our topic in the next chapter.

## Summary Check Points

✓ Capacity planning and master scheduling collectively constitute the "second half" of master planning; along with demand management, they make up high-level core OM duties.

✓ Capacity in the ability to accommodate; capacity planning refers to a broad range of activities aimed at creating, maintaining, and adjusting customer-serving resources.

✓ In the master-planning sequence, business plans and strategies filter aggregate demand. Aggregate output and capacity plans are crafted and guide creation of the master schedule (MPS in manufacturing)—a statement of what the firm will provide by item, time, and quantity.

✓ Business plans—what the company wants to do—help define capacity choices.

✓ Flexible resources make capacity planning easier; demand/capacity mismatches may be resolved faster and more cheaply when labor and equipment can do multiple tasks.

✓ In large organizations, master planning is for teams; capacity planning teams balance capacity and demand and craft production (output) and capacity plans. Master scheduling teams allocate resources and create master schedules stating output intentions.

✓ General, pure-form capacity strategies include chase-demand and level-capacity, but hybrids are common.

✓ One technique for making better use of capacity calls for revisiting demand—separating demand into categories according to its profitability or ease of service. (A form of demand management).

✓ Capacity enhancement activities serve to make existing capacity more dependable and versatile. Increasingly, successful companies maintain capacity cushion and underschedule capacity as a general policy.

✓ Capacity strategies are implemented through policies that affect labor as well as other resource componcnts; like strategies, policy works better when capacity is flexible.

✓ Utilization defines the rate of use of capacity. Utilization at or over 100 percent of rated capacity may be used in peak demand periods, but sustained operations should be planned at less than rated capacity.

✓ Group-based capacity planning is common in small and large firms; it succeeds when planners:

1. Base capacity groups on natural "families" of goods or services—grouped according to dominant flow route, similarity in production or delivery, or customer.
2. Project aggregate customer demands (outputs) for each capacity group.
3. Develop a production (outputs) plan and then convert to capacity units for each group.

✓ In make-to-stock operations, two additional capacity planning steps are often included:

4. Incorporate inventory management goals into the production and capacity plans.
5. Perform rough-cut capacity planning to ensure that the plans do not overload critical resource components.

✓ Improved layouts—created under such banners as group technology (GT), cellular layout or cellular operations—facilitate group capacity planning and bestow other benefits as well.

✓ The master schedule fits actual orders into capacity slots, on a machine or labor schedule or in an appointment book, for instance. Companies that operate solely in an on-demand mode usually have no need for a master schedule, nor really any way of getting one.

✓ Where outputs can be prescheduled, such as in reserved-seat services and in manufacturing, master scheduling is an essential step in reserving capacity for demands and in allocation demands to capacity resources.

✓ Typically, the master schedule requires iterations; trial schedules must be checked against capacity limits and adjusted for late-arriving demands before the final master schedule is set.

✓ Time fences separate the master schedule horizon into firm (near future) and tentative (distant future) zones. Changes in the firm zone may be prohibitively costly, but changes in the tentative zone are usually "on paper only" and have no real affect on ongoing operations.

✓ In make-to-order plants, the master schedule is "consumed" as prescheduled output is bought by and promised (assigned) to customers.

✓ Two central, and related, capacity planning issues face modern operations managers: the need for more flexibility in capacity and the shrinking planing horizons forced by time-based competition.

## Solved Problems

### *Problem 1*

Jack Sharp, a recent college graduate, seeks an entrepreneurial career. He started a consulting firm that helps small retail establishments and professional offices install microcomputer-based record keeping. Realizing that the only resources he has to sell are his expertise and workaholic tendencies, Jack plans on working about 280 hours per month. (Will all work and no play make Jack Sharp dull?) He has grouped his clients into three types: small retail outlets (such as shopping mall specialty stores), single-principal professional offices, and partnership professional offices. Jack estimates that time requirements for those clients will average 20, 40, and 50 hours, respectively.

Much telephone work and knocking on doors has resulted in a tentative client list for the next six months. Jack wants to match customer demand with available capacity (his time) and develop a trial schedule. The demand for each job type is as follows:

| | | **Demand—Customers/Month (month)** | | | | | |
|---|---|---|---|---|---|---|---|
| *Client Type* | *Time Required (hours)* | *1* | *2* | *3* | *4* | *5* | *6* |
| Retail store | 20 | 4 | — | 6 | 3 | 4 | 2 |
| Single professional | 40 | 2 | 6 | 4 | — | — | 3 |
| Multipartner professional | 50 | 3 | — | — | 4 | — | 5 |

### *Solution 1*

The following table shows Jack's capacity requirements by group (client type) for the six-month planning horizon as well as idle capacity or overload conditions:

| | **Demand—Resources/Month (Hours per client × Number of clients) (months)** | | | | | | |
|---|---|---|---|---|---|---|---|
| *Client Type* | *1* | *2* | *3* | *4* | *5* | *6* | *Cumulative (for group)* |
| Retail store | 80 | — | 120 | 60 | 80 | 40 | 380 |
| Single professional | 80 | 240 | 160 | — | — | 120 | 600 |
| Multipartner professional | 150 | — | — | 200 | — | 250 | 600 |
| Total capacity requirements (hours of time) | 310 | 240 | 280 | 260 | 80 | 410 | 1,580 |
| Capacity available | 280 | 280 | 280 | 280 | 280 | 280 | 1,680 |
| Extra capacity ("−" denotes overload) | −30 | 40 | 0 | 20 | 200 | −130 | 100 |

For the total planning horizon, Jack has not overextended himself. He has 100 hours of excess capacity. He may have to work a few more hours during the first month, if demand estimates are accurate. His problem is months 5 and 6. He might try to entice some customers to use his services a month earlier than planned. But schedules very far out have a way of changing—often several times—prior to when the originally scheduled dates become current.

### Problem 2

Exhibit 5-12, an example capacity plan for Anita's Studio, is based on a projected demand stream and some assumptions (e.g., one new assistant works half of April). As part of her master planning, Anita wonders if she might have to adjust her capacity plan if actual demand on her photography service is, say, 15 percent higher during the six-month planning period?

### Solution 2

The lower part of Exhibit 5-12 is used as the format for the table shown below. Photography service demand (photo taking and developing work) has been increased by 15 percent in each month. Other assumptions, and Anita's desired policy of limiting her own work to 160 hours per month, remain in force.

| *Capacity Plan—By Group (hours)* | *Feb.* | *Mar.* | *Apr.* | *May* | *June* | *July* |
|---|---|---|---|---|---|---|
| Photography service: Demand | 202 | 164 | 267 | 521 | 700 | 509 |
| Capacity: Photo assistant #1 | — | — | 80 | 160 | 160 | 160 |
| Capacity: Photo assistant #2 | — | — | — | 160 | 160 | 160 |
| Capacity: Outsourcing (FastFotos, Inc.) | 42 | 4 | 27 | 41 | 220 | 29 |
| Capacity: Owner (Anita) | 160 | 160 | 160 | 160 | 160 | 160 |

If Anita sticks with her desire to limit her own planned time to no more than 160 hours per month, outsourcing will be used to absorb the extra capacity requirements. As she examines this plan, she sees no urgent need to alter her original strategy. A third photography assistant could be used full time during June if Anita desires to cut down on the amount of outsourcing, but even with a 15-percent demand increase, that person wouldn't be needed during other months. She does note, however, that this plan consumes all 160 hours of her personal (planned) time allocation. Maybe she should begin thinking about a regular, but part-time, assistant to work about 40 to 60 hours per month. That would free up some of her time and might be more flexible than outsourcing. Back to the basic issue in capacity planning: What does she *want* to do?

### Problem 3

An assembly line currently staffed with 10 assemblers produces an average of 190 units per day. The current sales rate for the product is 200 units per day. If the company follows a policy of scheduling at 85 percent of capacity, what should it do? (Options include setting a new production rate or changing capacity.)

### Solution 3

The production rate must be 200 units per day, exactly the number being sold. Then 200 is set equal to 85 percent of capacity, and capacity is solved for algebraically:

$$0.85X = 200$$

Then,

$$X = 235.3 \text{ units per day}$$

Since 10 assemblers can produce 190 on the average, we need to know how many assemblers are needed to produce 235.3. Therefore:

$$\frac{10}{190} = \frac{X}{235.3}$$

$$190X = 2{,}353$$

$$X = 12.38, \text{ or } 13 \text{ assemblers}$$

Thus, the company must assign three more assemblers to the production line.

## Exercises

1. Assume that you are president of a large company and have a strong aversion to laying off employees. Devise a multistep policy governing what your company would do if demand in certain product lines dropped, creating excess labor. Your last step should be employee terminations.
2. Federal Express, the overnight delivery service, has a no-layoff policy. The company is also known for its promote-from-within policy; 16 of its 18 senior vice presidents started in nonmanagerial jobs.[9] Visit the Federal Express Web site (www.federalexpress.com/us/) and review the careers pages. You will find mention of Federal Express's "PSP" program.
   *a.* What is the PSP program?
   *b.* How might such a program, together with other human resource management policies at Federal Express, help facilitate a no-layoff policy?
   *c.* How might such programs facilitate capacity planning?
3. Investigate one company in three of the following types to find out (*a*) what full capacity is in terms of hours or shifts per week, and why, and (*b*) what current capacity utilization is, and why:

| | |
|---|---|
| Supermarket | Overnight mail service |
| Discount store | Manufacturing plant |
| Bank | Certified public accounting firm |
| Art gallery | Charitable institution |

4. Investigate a retailer, a wholesaler, or a manufacturer to learn whether its current capacity plan includes both numeric labor and inventory levels. What are the plan's aims? Why? (If your company does not have a numeric capacity plan, find out why.)
5. City Sod is a small business that sells and lays sod (rolled strips of grass). The owner has devised a forecasting procedure based on demand history from previous years plus projection of demand in recent weeks. The forecast for the next six weeks, in labor hours of sod laying, is

   900 880 1,000 890 950 870

   Currently City Sod has a staff of sod layers consisting of five crew chiefs and 15 laborers. A crew chief lays sod along with the laborers but also directs the crew. The owner has decided on the following staffing policies:

*a.* A two-week backlog will be accumulated before adding staff.

*b.* Plans are based on a 40-hour work week; overtime is used only to absorb weather or other delays and employee absence or resignations.

*c.* The ideal crew size is one crew chief and four laborers.

Devise a hiring plan for the six-week period covered by the forecast. In your answer, assume a current backlog of 1,480 labor hours of sod-laying orders. Does City Sod follow more of a chase-demand or level-capacity strategy of production planning? Explain.

6. Bright Way Janitorial Service has long followed a level-capacity strategy of capacity planning. Now, however, the company is considering a shift from level-capacity to chase-demand. Bright Way managers know that chase demand would greatly simplify production/capacity planning. Explain why this is so. What new management problems would chase demand tend to create?

7. Coast Limited Railways operates a car repair yard in Kansas City to repair its cars. Workload forecasts for the upcoming 7-month horizon are shown below:

| Month | 1 | 2 | 3 | 4 | 5 | 6 | 7 |
|---|---|---|---|---|---|---|---|
| No. of Cars | 81 | 60 | 91 | 56 | 86 | 72 | 58 |

Coast Limited Headquarters has directed the Kansas City managers to plan for a level capacity that will exceed the forecast demand in each month by no more than an amount equal to one-half of the average monthly demand for the seven-month period.

*a.* Prepare a plan that will meet that policy.

*b.* Comment on the demand/capacity imbalance that will result from this plan. Should it be of concern to managers at the Kansas City facility? Explain.

(Note to student: Set the problem up manually so you understand how the planners at Kansas City will satisfy the headquarters' policy. Then, if you are familiar with Excel®, you may wish to review the solution on your CD-ROM and create other forecast scenarios to test the effects on plans resulting from the mandated capacity policy. The next exercise illustrates.)

8. Early in the first month of implementation of the Coast Limited production/capacity plan (see Exercise 7) two customers expressed the need to make substantial changes to the workload they had planned for Coast's Kansas City facility. One, having just declared bankruptcy, canceled a repair order for 50 cars in month 3. The other wants to increase its month-5 order by 12 cars. Revised workload forecasts appear below; shaded cells denote the changes.

| Month | 1 | 2 | 3 | 4 | 5 | 6 | 7 |
|---|---|---|---|---|---|---|---|
| No. of Cars | 81 | 60 | 41 | 56 | 98 | 72 | 58 |

*a.* Prepare a new capacity plan for the seven-month period that will meet Coast Limited's capacity planning policy.

*b.* Comment on any demand/capacity imbalances. Should the new plan concern managers at the Kansas City facility? Explain.

9. The purchasing director and two senior buyers at Windward Sportswear, an apparel manufacturer, jointly prepare the purchasing department's staffing (capacity) plan. They test alternative staffing plans using recent demand data. Demand is measured as the number of purchase orders (POs) per week, based on purchase requests from other Windward departments. Data for the past six weeks follow:

| | Week | | | | | |
|---|---|---|---|---|---|---|
| | *1* | *2* | *3* | *4* | *5* | *6* |
| POs | 128 | 135 | 120 | 140 | 155 | 102 |

*a.* If the team elects to staff the department for 130 POs per week, will purchasing be able to serve its customers adequately? Explain.
*b.* What capacity plan would you recommend? Why?
*c.* If customers require very fast processing of purchase requests, what could the purchasing department do to efficiently accommodate the requirement?

10. Old English Tea Company blends and packages an average of 7,000 boxes of tea per shift. Sixteen people tend the production line, and the company follows a policy of undercapacity scheduling, scheduling labor at 90 percent of capacity. Demand is down, and the production rate must be reduced to meet the demand of 6,500 boxes per shift. How many people should be added or how many assigned to other work? Assume that labor and output rate are linearly related.

11. A computer software company has one production line that copies programs onto floppy disks and packages the disks. The line has been scheduled at full capacity and has been consuming 30 hours of direct labor per day. Demand recently has risen from 1,400 to 1,500 packages per day. Also, managers wish to convert to undercapacity labor scheduling. (Problems in meeting schedules and resulting lost sales have brought about the policy change.) Determine the new labor-hour requirements for a policy of 15 percent undercapacity scheduling.

12. Dominion Envelope Co. produces a variety of paper and light-cardboard envelopes, often with customer-specified printing on them. Dominion formed an order-processing cell for its biggest customer, Bank of North America (BNA). The cell consists of one person each from sales, accounting, materials, and operations. Orders from other customers go from department to department, but BNA orders are processed in the cell, then sent to operations for production, packaging, and shipping.
*a.* How would capacity planning differ for BNA orders versus other orders?
*b.* How could capacity planning be improved for other customers?

13. Concrete Products, Inc., uses molds to make reinforced concrete structural members (trusses, etc.) for large buildings and bridges. Each order is a special design, so no finished-goods inventories are possible. Concrete Products uses a chase-demand strategy of hiring labor to assemble, fill, and disassemble the molds. If it takes a week to hire and train a laborer, how can Concrete Products make the chase-demand strategy work well? What

types of labor (capacity) policies would work? Recent work loads, in labor hours, on the shake tables are as follows:

| Week | 1 | 2 | 3 | 4 | 5 | 6 | 7 | 8 | 9 |
|---|---|---|---|---|---|---|---|---|---|
| Labor hours | 212 | 200 | 170 | 204 | 241 | 194 | 168 | 215 | 225 |

14. At a fiberglass products company, the dominant product line is fiberglass bathtub and shower units, which sell to the high-quality segment of the market. The company's best employees work in tubs and showers, which are treated as a separate capacity group. Forecast demands for this capacity group are in labor hours. For the next three months, demand is forecast at 1,900, 1,200, and 1,400 labor hours. The present inventory is 1,600 labor-hours' worth of tub and shower units, in all sizes and colors. The plan is to reduce the inventory to 1,000 after three months because the slow season is approaching.
    *a.* Prepare a production plan for the next three months that minimizes labor fluctuation.
    *b.* How would the master production schedule differ from the production plan?
15. Gulf Tube and Pipe Company prepares monthly production/capacity plans for three capacity areas, one of which is the pipe-forming, -cutting, and -welding (FCW) processes. The forecast FCW demand for next month is as follows:

| *Week* | *Forecast Lineal Feet (000)* |
|---|---|
| 1 | 6,000 |
| 2 | 5,800 |
| 3 | 5,400 |
| 4 | 4,600 |

The present inventory is 16 million lineal feet.

*a.* Devise a production plan following a chase-demand strategy that results in an ending inventory of 14 million lineal feet.
*b.* Devise a production plan following a level-capacity strategy that results in an ending inventory of 14 million lineal feet.
*c.* The following rule of thumb is used for purposes of capacity planning: two operators are required for every 1 million lineal feet produced. Develop two capacity (i.e., workforce) plans, one using data from (*a*) and the other using data from (*b*).
*d.* Cite data from (*a*) through (*c*) to explain the contrasting effects on inventories and labor of chase-demand and level-capacity strategies.

16. Devise a master scheduling procedure diagram similar to Exhibit 5-18 but for draftspeople in an engineering firm. Explain your diagram.
17. Devise a master scheduling procedure diagram similar to Exhibit 5-18, but for a maintenance department. Assume that maintenance includes janitorial crews, plumbers, and electricians, but does not include construction or remodeling personnel. Explain your diagram.
18. Capacity planning is never easy, and seems especially difficult for providers of on-demand services, where demand varies greatly throughout the day. Four situations are listed below.

Pick any two and write a brief analysis of how each deals with the unpredictability factor in planning capacity. You may need to interview one or more people in a real firm.

- Fast-food restaurant
- Internet service provider
- Bank
- Social services hot-line help desk

19. The supplement to Chapter 5 illustrates capacity planning using Excel® spreadhseet software for Anita's Studio. To generate plans, Anita must complete the demand table that appears in Exhibit S5-2. The table shown below reflects Anita's demand projections by output item for the next year.

**Anita's Studio: Capacity Plan**
Data Sheet

| | Demand: Orders + Forecast | | | | |
|---|---|---|---|---|---|
| *Month* | *Portrait* | *Group Still* | *Wedding* | *Prom/Party* | *Athletic* |
| Jan | 13 | 10 | 7 | 3 | 6 |
| Feb | 36 | 12 | 12 | 8 | 11 |
| Mar | 18 | 10 | 9 | 6 | 16 |
| Apr | 24 | 11 | 20 | 21 | 7 |
| May | 53 | 18 | 25 | 26 | 6 |
| Jun | 54 | 16 | 28 | 11 | 3 |
| Jul | 51 | 17 | 22 | 4 | 2 |
| Aug | 23 | 10 | 15 | 4 | 9 |
| Sep | 28 | 19 | 14 | 10 | 14 |
| Oct | 26 | 18 | 19 | 12 | 15 |
| Nov | 26 | 9 | 10 | 15 | 16 |
| Dec | 33 | 17 | 11 | 16 | 17 |
| Totals | 385 | 167 | 192 | 136 | 122 |

Using the capacity-planning program for Anita's Studio that is on your CD-ROM, enter these demand projections in the appropriate table (light blue shading) on the first sheet (labeled DataSheet) in the workbook. Examine the capacity plans generated on the next three worksheets, labeled CapPlan1, CapPlan2, and CapPlan3. Respectively, they use the following staffing assumptions (the same assumptions as are used for the three plans in the supplement):

1. Two full-time photographers with overtime limited to 60 hours per month.
2. Three full-time photographers with overtime limited to 60 hours per month.
3. Two full-time photographers with a temporary junior associate employed during April, May, June, and July. Overtime is limited to 60 hours per month for these 4 months, and to 40 hours per month for the remaining 8 months of the year.

Salary and other cost data are as defined in the supplement.

*a.* Of these three options, which capacity plans should Anita adopt for the upcoming year?

*b.* Might there be a better plan? To the extent that you feel comfortable using Excel®, feel free to experiment! Just be prepared in case your instructor asks for your logic.

**SUPPLEMENT**

# AGGREGATE CAPACITY PLANNING WITH EXCEL®

After going through the struggles that befall most start-ups, Anita has made a success of her small photography business—Anita's Studio. Her staff consists of two full-time photographers, a full-time office manager, and a half-time clerical and bookkeeping assistant.

Anita's current concern is her photographers. The problem is (what the photographers consider to be) excessive overtime requirements—needed for the in-house developing work that Anita's Studio provides. Both are quite skilled, diligent in their work, and personable; Anita would like to keep them. She has promised to take a look at the next year's plans and try to arrive at a suitable solution. She has also agreed to immediately begin limiting overtime to a maximum of 30 hours per month for each photographer. Fortunately, she can simply increase the outsourcing of developing work to make up any capacity shortfalls. With a fresh cup of coffee at hand, Anita starts her assessment.

Several years ago, she began planning her labor requirements by group—photography and developing work make up one group and office management duties the other. Anita will limit her present analysis to the photography group. First, she reviews demands for photography and developing capacity for each type of output service that Anita's Studio provides. (See Exhibit S5-1.)

Anita sees no need to revise any of the capacity requirements, so she turns her attention to cost and capacity availability data and rethinks some of her policies.

- As owner/manager, Anita has never included her own "salary" in her labor cost estimates. But she does record her planned workload. As her reputation has grown, Anita has an increased set of business, professional, and educational commitments, so she now keeps her *planned* workload to about 20 hours of photography per week for 47 weeks of the

**EXHIBIT S5-1 Capacity Requirements Profile**

| *Product* | *Photography Group Capacity Requirements* |
|---|---|
| Portrait | • 1.0 hour photography (in studio)<br>• 1.5 hours proof developing<br>• 4.0 hours final print developing |
| Group still | • 1.5 hours photography (mostly on site)<br>• 1.0 hours proof selection & developing<br>• 0.5 hours machine developing and "quick framing"* |
| Wedding | • 3.0 hours photography<br>• 5.0 hours proof selection and developing<br>• 7.0 hours final print developing and presentation preparation |
| Prom/Party | • 4.0 hours photography<br>• 1.0 hour final print developing<br>• 2.0 hours machine developing and "quick framing"* |
| Athletic event | • 3.0 hours photography<br>• 1.5 hours machine developing* |

*Machine work is outsourced; Anita keeps track for possible future use.

year. She knows that her "extra time" could be used in a crunch to meet unforeseen contingencies.

- Each of the two photographers is paid an annual salary of $44,000. She figures their capacity at 40 hours times 48 weeks, or 1,920 hours per year. Due to odd-hour assignments, they keep their own hours, and Anita has had no trouble with that arrangement. For overtime work (anything over 40 hours per week), Anita pays them $30 per hour.
- Anita has built her reputation on quality and timely service. She follows a chase-demand strategy, booking appointments when customers desire and maintaining a near-perfect record of "proofs-within-72-hours." Anita sincerely wants to avoid changes in those policies. To ensure quality, she wants her staff to do all photography work, but she will outsource any developing work that exceeds the studio's regular and overtime capacity. (Since she outsources all machine developing work, it won't come into play in her current analysis.) Outsourced manual developing costs $40 per hour.
- Anita will definitely incorporate her promised overtime limit into her planning—no more than 60 hours per month (30 per photographer) can be planned. Even though she pays well, Anita senses that the overtime has become a serious problem. One of her photographers is working on her master's degree and the other is heavily involved in his children's sports programs.

The final piece of the puzzle is Anita's estimates for next year's demand. Due to her reputation, most orders are booked many months in advance. Anita does make a few adjustments—upward in each case—to reflect past years' demands. Her experienced eye makes a quick check of projected demand pattern, and she turns to her computer, where she uses her spreadsheet program to assist in her aggregate planning computations.

Exhibit S5-2 shows Anita's capacity plan data sheet. She enters output item demand estimates for each month in the upper-left table. Required capacity for each output item is shown in a small table beneath the demand estimates. In the upper-right table, results of aggregate capacity requirement calculations appear. The column at the extreme right—aggregate manual hours—is Anita's focus.

Anita wants her first trial capacity plan to reflect things as they are, with the incorporation of the 60-hour-per-month overtime limit. Exhibit S5-3 shows that plan. Moving from left to right we see that aggregate capacity requirements are carried over from the data sheet. Next, available capacity is entered. This figure reflects the two photographers' times and Anita's own contribution; annual capacity is divided over the 12 months:

$$\frac{((1{,}920 \text{ hours/photographer} \times 2 \text{ photographers}) + 940 \text{ hours for Anita})}{12} \cong 398 \text{ hours/month}$$

The next two columns show the demand/capacity imbalance, either as excess capacity or as a capacity shortage. When a shortage exists (e.g., February, April, etc.), the first 60 hours are covered by overtime. Overtime costs, at $30 per hour, are next. When the 60-hour overtime allocation is not sufficient to cover demand (in 9 of 12 months), outsourcing makes up the balance. Outsourcing costs, at $40 per hour, appear in the next column. The last column contains the monthly allocation of salary for the two photographers ($88,000 ÷ 12 ≅ $7,333).

Finally, we see that for this capacity plan, photography group aggregate costs are about $162,545 (the sum of salary, outsourcing, and overtime costs).

Anita notices that for 10 of the 12 months of the coming year, planned overtime for her photographers is at or near the agreed-upon maximum. Maybe it's time to give more thought to something she has been considering—the addition of a third photographer. First, though, another cup of coffee.

## EXHIBIT S5-2 Capacity Planning Data Sheet

**Anita's Studio: Capacity Plan Data Sheet**

**Demand: Orders + Forecast**

| *Month* | *Portrait* | *Group Still* | *Wedding* | *Prom/Party* | *Athletic* |
|---|---|---|---|---|---|
| Jan | 15 | 8 | 8 | 4 | 10 |
| Feb | 35 | 12 | 11 | 9 | 12 |
| Mar | 21 | 9 | 10 | 6 | 14 |
| Apr | 25 | 10 | 18 | 20 | 6 |
| May | 50 | 20 | 23 | 25 | 5 |
| Jun | 60 | 15 | 25 | 10 | 4 |
| Jul | 45 | 16 | 20 | 5 | 1 |
| Aug | 25 | 10 | 15 | 5 | 8 |
| Sep | 30 | 20 | 15 | 9 | 12 |
| Oct | 25 | 20 | 18 | 12 | 14 |
| Nov | 25 | 10 | 10 | 14 | 14 |
| Dec | 35 | 15 | 7 | 15 | 12 |
| Totals | 391 | 165 | 180 | 134 | 112 |

**Aggregate Capacity Requirements: Hours**

| *Month* | *Photo* | Developing *Manual* | Developing *Machine* | *Aggregate Manual Hours* |
|---|---|---|---|---|
| Jan | 97.0 | 190.5 | 27.0 | 287.5 |
| Feb | 158.0 | 345.5 | 42.0 | 503.5 |
| Mar | 130.5 | 250.5 | 37.5 | 381.0 |
| Apr | 192.0 | 383.5 | 54.0 | 575.5 |
| May | 264.0 | 596.0 | 67.5 | 860.0 |
| Jun | 209.5 | 655.0 | 33.5 | 864.5 |
| Jul | 152.0 | 508.5 | 19.5 | 660.5 |
| Aug | 129.0 | 332.5 | 27.0 | 461.5 |
| Sep | 177.0 | 374.0 | 46.0 | 551.0 |
| Oct | 199.0 | 385.5 | 55.0 | 584.5 |
| Nov | 168.0 | 281.5 | 54.0 | 449.5 |
| Dec | 174.5 | 306.5 | 55.5 | 481.0 |
| Totals | 2,050.5 | 4,609.5 | 518.5 | 6,660.0 |

**Capacity (Time) Required: Hours**

| *Item* | *Photo* | Developing *Proof* | Developing *Final* | Developing *(Machine)* |
|---|---|---|---|---|
| Portrait | 1.0 | 1.5 | 4.0 | NA |
| Group Still | 1.5 | 1.0 | NA | 0.5 |
| Wedding | 3.0 | 5.0 | 7.0 | NA |
| Prom/Party | 4.0 | NA | 1.0 | 2.0 |
| Athletic | 3.0 | NA | NA | 1.5 |

Since no changes are needed on the data sheet, Anita goes directly to the "capacity available" column shown in Exhibit S5-3. To reflect inclusion of a third photographer—also working 1,920 hours per year—Anita changes the 398 to 558 for each month. That figure is obtained as follows:

$$\frac{(1{,}920 \times 3) + 940}{12} = \frac{6{,}700}{12} \cong 558$$

Anita also needs to change the salary cost entry to reflect the third photographer's salary. She would prefer to find an experienced person, so she decides to assume that another $44,000 per year is reasonable for her market area. Total salaries ($132,000) spread out over the year yields $11,000 per month. Exhibit S5-4 shows the second trial capacity plan. We do notice that Anita does *not* adjust the maximum allowable overtime. Her logic is that with the third photographer, the 60-hour maximum can be spread over all three people, and a 20-hour-per-month obligation

## EXHIBIT S5-3 Trial Capacity Plan 1 (Current Staff)

**Anita's Studio: Capacity Plan 1: 2 Full-time Photographers**

| *Month* | *Aggregate Capacity Requirement* | *Capacity Available* | *Excess Capacity* | *Capacity Shortage* | *Overtime Hours* | *Overtime Costs ($)* | *Outsource Hours* | *Outsource Costs ($)* | *Salary Costs ($)* |
|---|---|---|---|---|---|---|---|---|---|
| Jan | 287.5 | 398.0 | 110.5 | | | | | | 7,333 |
| Feb | 503.5 | 398.0 | | 105.5 | 60.0 | 1,800 | 45.5 | 1,820 | 7,333 |
| Mar | 381.0 | 398.0 | 17.0 | | | | | | 7,333 |
| Apr | 575.5 | 398.0 | | 177.5 | 60.0 | 1,800 | 117.5 | 4,700 | 7,333 |
| May | 860.0 | 398.0 | | 462.0 | 60.0 | 1,800 | 402.0 | 16,080 | 7,333 |
| Jun | 864.5 | 398.0 | | 466.5 | 60.0 | 1,800 | 406.5 | 16,260 | 7,333 |
| Jul | 660.5 | 398.0 | | 262.5 | 60.0 | 1,800 | 202.5 | 8,100 | 7,333 |
| Aug | 461.5 | 398.0 | | 63.5 | 60.0 | 1,800 | 3.5 | 140 | 7,333 |
| Sep | 551.0 | 398.0 | | 153.0 | 60.0 | 1,800 | 93.0 | 3,720 | 7,333 |
| Oct | 584.5 | 398.0 | | 186.5 | 60.0 | 1,800 | 126.5 | 5,060 | 7,333 |
| Nov | 449.5 | 398.0 | | 51.5 | 51.5 | 1,545 | | | 7,333 |
| Dec | 481.0 | 398.0 | | 83.0 | 60.0 | 1,800 | 23.0 | 920 | 7,333 |
| Totals | 6,660.0 | 4,776.0 | 127.5 | 2,011.5 | | $ 17,745 | | $ 56,800 | $ 88,000 |
| | | | | | | | Total Costs for Plan | | $ 162,545 |

Overtime charged at $30/hr.; up to 30 hours/month/photographer is allowed.
Outsourcing charged at $40/hr.; used after overtime allowance is allocated.

(rather than the current 30-hour one) should please her two current associates. Finally, Anita notices that the total cost associated with Plan 2 is about $159,960—a slight drop from the current conditions shown in Plan 1. Apparently Anita has solved her problem . . . less per-person overtime, less need to rely on outsourcing, and all at a lower cost! On that note, she calls it a day.

Sometimes, the problem with solved problems is that they don't stay that way. After a somewhat restless night's sleep, Anita is back at her computer bright and early . . . with her coffee, of course. As she studies the new plan—the one calling for a third full-time photographer—the latest manifestation of her old worry resurfaces: *What if I can't maintain enough business to support a third photographer?* Anita does not relish the thought of having to lay anyone off. Maybe she should consider a third plan, one a bit more conservative.

A third plan would also require a bit more thought. Going back to Trial Plan 1 (Exhibit S5-3), Anita studies the patterns. Outsourcing costs balloon from April through July due to severe capacity shortage in those months; so, perhaps she could hire a temporary photographer during that interval. Time for some assumptions and some help in making them. Anita makes two quick telephone calls to ask her two photographers if they can do a working lunch—on her, of course—at the studio.

After reviewing Anita's work, her two associates immediately favor the plan calling for the third photographer (Exhibit S5-4). Admitting that the lower per-person overtime is a biasing factor, they point out other advantages: The excess capacity in August and December fits well with vacation and holiday schedules, and all three of them had been making good use of the January–March period for professional development activities. Finally, they note the steady growth in demand for Anita's Studio services over the past few years. Why shouldn't that continue?

## EXHIBIT S5-4 Trial Capacity Plan 2

**Anita's Studio: Capacity Plan 2: 3 Full-time Photographers**

| *Month* | *Aggregate Capacity Requirement* | *Capacity Available* | *Excess Capacity* | *Capacity Shortage* | *Overtime Hours* | *Overtime Costs ($)* | *Outsource Hours* | *Outsource Costs ($)* | *Salary Costs ($)* |
|---|---|---|---|---|---|---|---|---|---|
| Jan | 287.5 | 558.0 | 270.5 | | | | | | 11,000 |
| Feb | 503.5 | 558.0 | 54.5 | | | | | | 11,000 |
| Mar | 381.0 | 558.0 | 177.0 | | | | | | 11,000 |
| Apr | 575.5 | 558.0 | | 17.5 | 17.5 | 525 | | | 11,000 |
| May | 860.0 | 558.0 | | 302.0 | 60.0 | 1,800 | 242.0 | 9,680 | 11,000 |
| Jun | 864.5 | 558.0 | | 306.5 | 60.0 | 1,800 | 246.5 | 9,860 | 11,000 |
| Jul | 660.5 | 558.0 | | 102.5 | 60.0 | 1,800 | 42.5 | 1,700 | 11,000 |
| Aug | 461.5 | 558.0 | 96.5 | | | | | | 11,000 |
| Sep | 551.0 | 558.0 | 7.0 | | | | | | 11,000 |
| Oct | 584.5 | 558.0 | | 26.5 | 26.5 | 795 | | | 11,000 |
| Nov | 449.5 | 558.0 | 108.5 | | | | | | 11,000 |
| Dec | 481.0 | 558.0 | 77.0 | | | | | | 11,000 |
| Totals | 6,660.0 | 6,696.0 | 791.0 | 755.0 | | $ 6,720 | | $ 21,240 | $ 132,000 |
| | | | | | | | | Total Costs for Plan | $ 159,960 |

Overtime charged at $30/hr.; up to 20 hours/month/photographer is allowed.
Outsourcing charged at $40/hr.; used after overtime allowance is allocated.

Anita listens intently, glad to hear her associates arrive at many of the same conclusions that she had reached privately. But still . . . that lingering concern. She isn't surprised when her associates admit that they also understand and appreciate her worry about maintaining sufficient workload to support a new full-time photographer. When Anita raises the prospect of a compromise plan, one calling for a new temporary photographer during the busy months, she meets enthusiastic support.

Over the next few days, the group does some checking and then schedules another working lunch. Plan 3—referred to as the compromise plan—calls for hiring a qualified but junior photographer for the months of April through July, with the prospect (but no promise) of full-time employment at a later date. Anita feels that the chance for a strong recommendation from her will also help attract good candidates. A salary of $2,500 per month is suggested; it is very competitive for the market, especially for a beginning photographer. Anita will add 160 hours per month (four 40-hour weeks) to available capacity in April through July, and add $2,500 to monthly salary costs for those months.

To the delight of her associates, Anita plans to include the new photographer in overtime allocation. Specifically, she will split 60 hours (during April through July) three ways. The icing on the cake occurs, however, when she says that she will craft a plan that limits overtime to 40 hours per month for the other eight months of the year.

Anita's third plan is shown in Exhibit S5-5. In addition to the capacity and salary increases in April through July, Anita has made appropriate overtime adjustments to reflect the 40-hour limit for

## EXHIBIT S5-5 Trial Capacity Plan 3

**Anita's Studio: Capacity Plan 3: 2 Full-/1 Part-time Photographers**

| Month | *Aggregate Capacity Requirement* | *Capacity Available* | *Excess Capacity* | *Capacity Shortage* | *Overtime Hours* | *Overtime Costs ($)* | *Outsource Hours* | *Outsource Costs ($)* | *Salary Costs ($)* |
|---|---|---|---|---|---|---|---|---|---|
| Jan | 287.5 | 398.0 | 110.5 | | | | | | 7,333 |
| Feb | 503.5 | 398.0 | | 105.5 | 40.0 | 1,200 | 65.5 | 2,620 | 7,333 |
| Mar | 381.0 | 398.0 | 17.0 | | | | | | 7,333 |
| Apr | 575.5 | 558.0 | | 17.5 | 17.5 | 525 | | | 9,833 |
| May | 860.0 | 558.0 | | 302.0 | 60.0 | 1,800 | 242.0 | 9,680 | 9,833 |
| Jun | 864.5 | 558.0 | | 306.6 | 60.0 | 1,800 | 246.5 | 9,860 | 9,833 |
| Jul | 660.5 | 558.0 | | 102.5 | 60.0 | 1,800 | 42.5 | 1,700 | 9,833 |
| Aug | 461.5 | 398.0 | | 63.5 | 40.0 | 1,200 | 23.5 | 940 | 7,333 |
| Sep | 551.0 | 398.0 | | 153.0 | 40.0 | 1,200 | 113.0 | 4,520 | 7,333 |
| Oct | 584.5 | 398.0 | | 186.5 | 40.0 | 1,200 | 146.5 | 5,860 | 7,333 |
| Nov | 449.5 | 398.0 | | 51.5 | 40.0 | 1,200 | 11.5 | 460 | 7,333 |
| Dec | 481.0 | 398.0 | | 83.0 | 40.0 | 1,200 | 43.0 | 1,720 | 7,333 |
| Totals | 6,660.0 | 5,416.0 | 127.5 | 1,371.5 | | $ 13,125 | | $ 37,360 | $ 98,000 |
| | | | | | | | Total Costs for Plan | | $ 148,485 |

Overtime charged at $30/hr.; up to 20 hours/month/photographer is allowed.
[Overtime maximums: 60 hours (April–July), 40 hours in other 8 months]
Outsourcing charged at $40/hr.; used after overtime allowance is allocated.

all months except April through July. Total plan costs are $148,485—the lowest of any of the three trial plans.

Anita studies the third trial plan. Another cup . . . more thoughts . . . those assumptions that we made . . .

---

[Note to student: The aggregate capacity planning worksheet used in this supplement is on the CD-ROM that accompanies your text.]

CHAPTER 6

# Order Fulfillment and Purchasing

## Into Practice

### Internet Commerce

"With Internet commerce, you're dealing in lots of 'eaches,' not a truckload of identical products," says Michael A. Schmitt, senior vice president at J.D. Edwards & Co., a large software vendor headquartered in Denver. Schmitt was referring to custom ordering *and production* of automobiles. Each custom order can require a slightly different mix of parts for the final product, and that triggers dozens or even hundreds of purchase orders to parts and materials suppliers. "If you tried to handle all this on paper and over the phone, it would never get done," adds Schmitt. "Computers have to talk to other computers."

Earlier, automakers and other large OEMs tried to automate such transactions with private, expensive electronic data interchange (EDI) networks. Now, the Internet is widely available and cheap enough so that even small job shops can hook up. As a result, predict John J. Fontanella, director of supply-chain research at Boston-based AMR Research, Inc., "we'll see 90% of manufacturing move to the Internet in short order."

Source: Otis Port, "Customers Move Into the Driver's Seat," *BusinesWeek,* October 4, 1999, pp. 103–106.

The opening Into Practice box, "Internet Commerce," provides a glimpse, admittedly a projection, of sweeping change in manufacturing. And clearly, purchasing and order fulfillment play major roles in that change. Our focus in this chapter centers on how operations management supports and is supported by these and other core components of *supply-chain management* (also known as *logistics network management*).[1]

For successful global companies, these topics have been on the front burner since the late 1980s and are still there; and, as the box suggests, technology has opened the door for smaller firms as well. Indeed, several of the key drivers of modern, competitive business and operations strategies (mentioned in Chapter 2) are explored in this chapter.

At the outset of Part II, Exhibit 4-1 defined order fulfillment as a core operations management duty. From a customer's perspective, it is, arguably, the most important duty, so that's where we shall begin.

9 5 T 2 0 1

# Order Fulfillment

As the new millennium began, business news bulletins—especially the Internet-based ones—carried numerous daily announcements about new agreements among companies. The tone was one of outsourcing, partnership, and order fulfillment. A common theme: Large, well-known, and established firm partners with newer (perhaps even start-up) company to outsource order fulfillment.

## *Outsourcing Order Fulfillment*

At first blush, one might wonder what could prompt a large, well-capitalized company to entrust one of its core operations duties to a little firm that "nobody ever heard of." Reasons vary, of course, but consider another common theme: The large company is entering the world of e-commerce and hasn't the foggiest idea of what it is doing, but the little firm does. And, even though the large company has the *financial* resources to develop its own in-house fulfillment "solution," the pressures of time-based competition limit the viability of that strategy . . . for now.

Put another way, the partner firm has the distinctive competency to get the order fulfillment job done faster, better, and cheaper. Outsourcing—purchasing order-fulfillment services in this case—is the competitive strategy for the large firm. Will the large client company ever develop an in-house order-fulfillment capability? That, of course, depends on how well the partner-provider is able to continue to deliver what the client wants.

When order fulfillment is outsourced, doesn't the company doing the order fulfillment gain control over some of the client company's resources? It certainly does! Again, a theme sounded in Chapter 2 and reiterated here—partnerships have become an embedded ingredient in today's competitive arena. Regardless of who processes and fills customer orders, however, the sequence of activities is of concern to operations managers. Let's look closer.

## *Order-Fulfillment Sequence*

The master planning sequence (Exhibit 5-1) reveals two streams of orders, one for on-demand goods and services and the other for outputs that can be prescheduled. Both streams carry over into the order-fulfillment sequence shown in Exhibit 6-1. Since both streams follow capacity planning, we may assume that for the most part order processing and fulfillment take place after a satisfactory demand/capacity balance has been achieved. There will be occasional problems—demand surges, equipment malfunctions, employee strikes, and so forth—but if master planning has been done correctly, most order processing and fulfillment should flow smoothly.

The order-processing and fulfillment sequence applies to demands from both internal and external customers. To meet various types of demand (discussed in Chapter 4) it must be flexible enough to accommodate several possibilities:

1. When it can be served in compressed form, the on-demand stream, reflected by numbers 1, 2, 3, and 10, may happen in near-simultaneous mode. Immediately

10 STEPS

**EXHIBIT 6-1 Order Fulfillment Sequence**

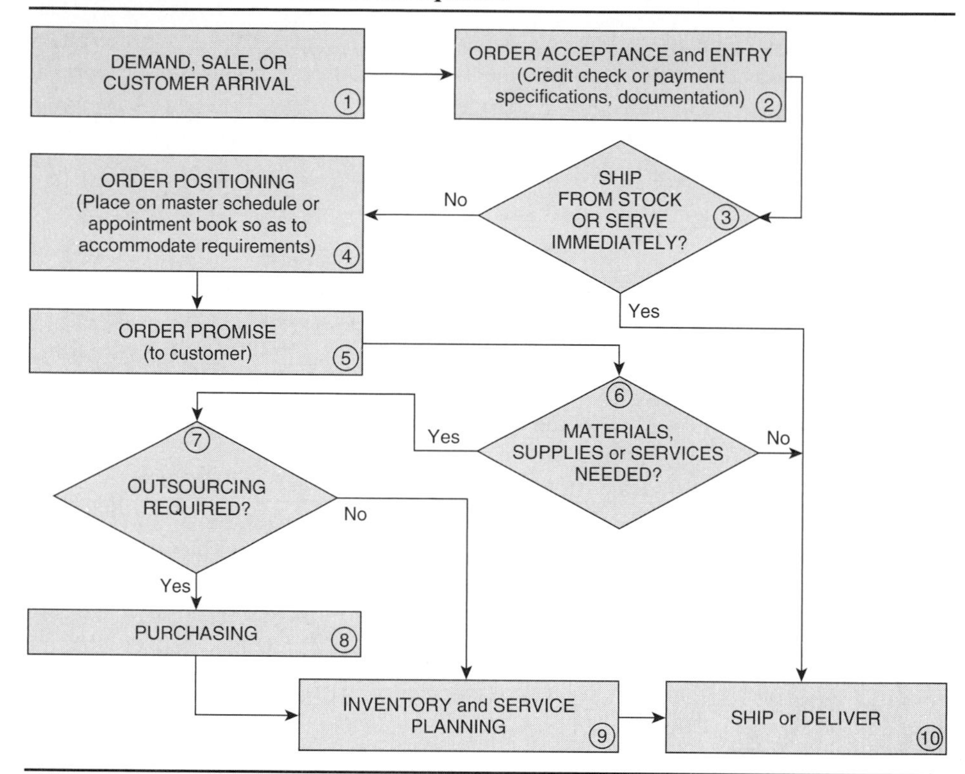


after placing your Internet book or ticket order, for example, you are informed that your order has been filled (or can be filled shortly from stock).

2. A somewhat longer sequence that adds steps 4, 5, and 6 applies to orders that must be scheduled but that can be served with existing materials, supplies, and service capacity; eye exams and drop-off repair work are examples.
3. If additional resources are needed, the question becomes whether in-house supply chains are adequate for order fulfillment. If so, steps 7 and 9 enter the sequence.
4. Finally, if outsourcing is required, appropriate purchasing (step 8) is accomplished. Most manufactured goods and many services adhere to either the third or fourth sequence. Whether for purchased materials or outside services such as medical or legal opinions, many providers must outsource.

The CD-Rom case study "The Office Goes Kanban at Boeing" illustrates visual kanban in practice.

Some organizations make hard work of order fulfillment by stretching it out and failing to be ready for customers or orders. Departmental walls chop up the sequence and hinder unified preparation. Superior firms, however, rely on methods that combine or avoid certain steps. They may employ simple, visual "kanban" methods of triggering action. In addition, they may organize co-located teams, or work cells, to compress steps in the sequence (see Into Practice, "Speedy Order Processing . . .").

Of the 10 steps in the order-fulfillment sequence of Exhibit 6-1, blocks 8 and 9 are major functions in their own right. Block 9, inventory planning, is reserved for later chapters. Block 8, purchasing, is the subject of the remainder of this chapter.

**Principle 2**

Dedicate to continuous, rapid improvement.

## Purchasing: Valued Supplier-Partners

Purchased inventories typically account for some 70 percent of expenses in retailing and 90 percent in wholesaling. In manufacturing, over 60 percent of the final cost of finished goods consists of purchased materials. In addition, organizations of all kinds contract for diverse services—janitorial, consulting, plant operation, information system operations, manufacturing, and, as we have seen, order fulfillment.

Traditional purchasing focused on price—not costs—and in some settings, that is still the case. Commodity buyers, for example, may see little need to stray from this simple but effective buying criterion. And when we buy many retail goods and services, we may justifiably depend heavily on price. For industrial (and many home) buyers, however, emphasis has migrated to *total costs*—purchase price, plus cost of buying, plus cost of having (operating, maintaining, etc.). If we factor in some intangibles such as image or status, we begin to describe an evolution of buying strategy from price orientation to value orientation.

Is the price-to-value shift responsible for the surge in outsourcing in recent years? Perhaps, but we leave that debate for others. Whatever the causes, there have been noticeable changes in the structures (or, *paradigms*) of buyer-source arrangements, the attention placed on supplier selection, and the underlying nature of the customer-supplier relationships.

### *Purchasing Paradigms*

Exhibit 6-2 shows four models of customer-supplier structures. In Model 1, the customer simply buys from each source; the arrows denote flow of goods and services. There are many relationships to maintain, and each relationship adds to the costs of buying. To the extent that the customer can, or will, consolidate sources—Model 2—so as to buy more items from each, the buying costs drop. The supplier may even offer quantity or volume discounts, so buyer's purchase prices decrease as well. During the 1990s, for example, Ford cut the number of its Tier One suppliers (those doing business directly with Ford) from 2,500 to 1,600 and expects to be down to 1,200 within a few years.[2] In 2000, Ford had about 10,000 nonproduction suppliers, less than half the number it had in the early 1990s.[3]

The third model depicts outsourcing of the purchasing function. The customer has a contracted buyer perform those activities. For materials, the contract buyer may also perform a variety of inventory management functions as well, perhaps including holding inventory until it is delivered to the customer's point of use at the time of use. In the spring of 2000, for example, Stanford University School of Medicine's Stanford Hospital and

INTO PRACTICE

## Speedy Order Processing at Atlantic Envelope Company

Atlantic Envelope Company's seven sites had the same back-office problem: slow order entry. It was taking a week or so (nobody had actually measured it) from when salespeople booked a customer order (such as from a retail chain, an office-supplies wholesaler, or perhaps a high-volume mail handler like Federal Express) to the start of envelope production or shipment from stock.

### Stage 1, 1990

Atlantic's effort to streamline order entry began at the company's home plant in Atlanta in the fall of 1990. Earlier, office partitions had been removed so that four order-processing associates (order editor, order typist 1, order typist 2, and order checker) could operate more as a work cell. By itself, working in a common area as an order-processing cell did not result in noticeable changes.

As a base line for improvement, it was necessary to measure the processing time. It averaged five days, but was highly unstable. Moreover, all orders, except those designated for special routing, were treated alike. No rational priority system existed. One quick result: Merely measuring processing time resulted in its being cut to an average of three days, without conscious efforts on the part of the cell associates.

### Stage 2, 1992

Then the team went to work. By fall 1992, they had cut average processing time from five days to about eight hours (and reduced their processing team from four to three associates). They made the following primary improvements:

- An order-entry associate screens incoming orders and puts them into color-coded folders: one color for standard manufacturing orders, a second for rush orders, a third for "jet" orders (overprinting on existing envelope stock using a jet printer), and a fourth for orders filled through purchasing from another Atlantic plant or an outside printer. Color-coding sets the stage for separate, focused treatment of each type of order.
- Jet orders, for example, are processed by a jet coordinator (a new position), who is able to get a sample to the art and composition department in about an hour (formerly it took one day). She determines which jet press to use, assigns the completion date, and returns the jet order to the order-entry cell for final processing (price, commissions, etc.) and forwarding to the jet press department. Jet order processing time is now 5 days (15 days formerly).
- Large, split-lot orders and stock replenishment orders, both involving inventory actions, go directly to the inventory planner for more specialized handling.
- Order-entry associates now hold regular order review meetings with raw materials and scheduling people; these meetings resolve order-processing problems faster and reduce errors.

Clinics announced that Promedix (a Ventro Corporation business unit) would be its buyer for all specialty medical products.[4] Model 4, an extension of Model 3, reflects a buying collective (three customer companies) employing a single contracted buyer. Small organizations sometimes resort to a collective structure to increase their buying leverage.

Other structures and hybrids exist, of course. On the whole, though, Exhibit 6-2 does point out some ways to make purchasing into more of a competitive weapon. Regardless of structure, however, the matter of supplier selection remains. If we can't make a selection based on price alone, what else should we examine?

- Order entry now sends incorrect and incomplete orders to sales service associates, who are better able to take corrective action with salespeople and customers.
- Associates are becoming cross-trained, allowing people to help at another order-processing desk and across department lines as needed in order to handle surges in certain types of orders.

In the spirit of continuous improvement, further innovations are being considered. At the same time, Atlantic's other sites are involved in their own order-entry streamlining, mostly by adapting the Atlanta system.

*Order processing cycle times chart order-entry associates at Atlantic Envelope Company's Atlanta facility. It shows average time to process 47 orders on Thursday, March 5, to be 7.9 hours. Large chart in the center shows average for the first four days in March. To the left are charts for prior months.*

## Supplier Selection

Some well-known companies have "open invitations" for *potential* suppliers. Caterpillar, for example, has a supplier information form on its web page that may be downloaded, completed, and returned to Caterpillar's purchasing services.[5] (An end-of-chapter exercise has more on Cat's supplier qualifications.) Though an initial screening tool, the form invites a prospective supplier to submit information about competencies and past performance . . . one way for Caterpillar to hear about supplier-partner prospects.

**Exhibit 6-2 Purchasing Paradigms**

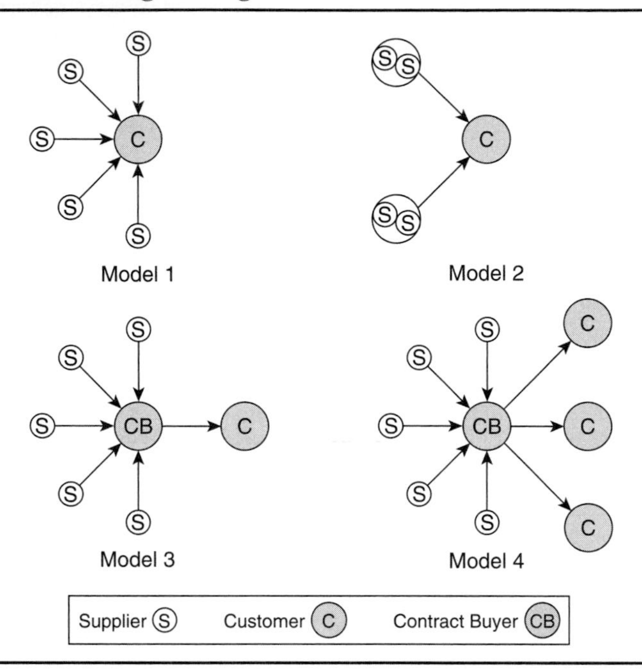


Though initial screenings can be effective starting points, final supplier selection usually involves a more thorough investigation into potential supplier. Many companies, including Caterpillar, have strict quality and other process capability requirements. (We examine them in Part III). Additionally, a wide range of other criteria might be used. Exhibit 6-3 lists some of the primary categories and gives examples of specific factors within each.

The first four general groups address the prospective supplier's line function capabilities. Notice that within the operations area, we mention the six fundamental demands (discussed in Chapter 1) that any customer expects of providers' transformation processes. Situation specifics, of course, will vary.

The next category, information flow and data sharing, is crucial in today's e-commerce world. Compatibility must be ensured. Next, composition of the prospective supplier's own chain of customer connections should be investigated. Competitive concerns demand such a check. Finally, a variety of cultural and ethical factors might have a bearing on the relationship. The last specific concern—trust—is no trivial matter. As John L. Mariotti, former president of Huffy Bicycles and Rubbermaid Office Products and founder and CEO of The Enterprise Group, puts it:

> Why aren't more companies aggressively developing their supply chain capabilities? The problem isn't a lack of technology. Nor is it a difficulty in understanding the basic concept. Instead, the issue comes down to a shortage of trust—that quality that allows cooperation and collaboration to take place both within the organization and across the supply chain partners.[6]

**EXHIBIT 6-3 Example Supplier Selection Criteria**

| *General Criteria Group* | *Examples of Specific Concerns* |
|---|---|
| Financial/Economic | • Overall financial health of prospective supplier<br>• Pricing and cost structures within the industry<br>• Tariffs and other import restrictions |
| Marketing | • Knowledge and competency of sales force<br>• Access to key personnel (e.g., engineers) |
| Design/Development | • Supplier's design and development capabilities<br>• Compatibility and standardization of design protocols<br>• Speed of supplier's design and development processes |
| Operations | • Supplier's transformation processes provide:<br>✓ Quality ↑<br>✓ Service ↑<br>✓ Flexibility ↑<br>✓ Response times ↓<br>✓ Variability ↓<br>✓ Cost factors ↓ |
| Information/Data Flow | • Compatibility of information system components<br>• Data-sharing and security issues |
| Competitive Factors | • Supplier's own suppliers and "other" customers |
| Cultural/Ethical Factors | • Supplier's record and reputation concerning human resource policies, safety, environmental protection, and past delivery performance<br>• Trust |

Note: These are the six general customer wants defined in Chapter 1. Parts III and IV provide more detail.

Regardless of whether the supplier has just been selected or is has been on board for a while, the partnership must be nurtured. Dealing with these multiple issues, to get real value, can require a considerable transition.

### *Transition toward Partnership*

Keki Bhote describes the transition toward partnership as a four-stage evolution:[7]

*Stage 1:* Confrontation with the supplier.

*Stage 2:* Arm's-length relationship, where adversarial attitudes gradually give way to a cautious, tentative working relationship.

*Stage 3:* A congruence of mutual goals, a coming together.

*Stage 4:* A full-blown partnership between customer and supplier.

We shall say no more about the confrontation stage, with its emphasis on price, its squabbling over contracts and compliance, and its occasional law suits. Rather, we examine the arm's-length, goal-congruence, and full-blown partnership stages.

**Arm's-Length Purchasing.** Purchasing is done impersonally, the arm's-length approach. The purchasing department's organization is by commodity group. Each buyer has responsibility for one or a few commodities, such as sportswear, shoes, steel, electronics, paper and supplies, and contracted services. A typical week may bring hundreds of requisitions from other departments to be processed and forwarded to dozens of suppliers. In addition, the buying staff receives voluminous data from the receiving department. Some is for reconciliation—matching the original purchase order with what actually came in. Other data are for evaluating supplier performance, in order to help buyers make decisions on which suppliers to deal with in the future. Buyers keep busy as well in seeking new suppliers, then soliciting and processing bids. All the while, they are handling complaints from unhappy internal and external customers who have unmet materials needs.

Poor quality, wrong quantity, wrong items, and, especially, late deliveries keep requisitioners anxious and buyers busy. Changing delivery dates or quantities, arranging alternative transportation, and attending to the large flow of paperwork keeps buyers from getting to know suppliers.

Management may choose not to know what happens in the supplier's system, in effect, to treat it as a black box (see Exhibit 6-4). Order information (orders, requisitions, inquiries, change requests, etc.) goes into the box, and status information (acknowledgements, responses, etc.) and, eventually, goods and services themselves come out. But what's inside remains a mystery.

Too often, the arm's-length, black-box approach degenerates into an adversarial system: Buying companies distrust suppliers and change them often. In response, suppliers often do not do their best for customers, which makes their replacement by other suppliers likely. And the cycle repeats and degenerates.

**Goal Congruence.** Quality is a good starting point in moving away from an arm's length relationship: Both parties can only benefit from higher levels of quality. An important step is to shift the responsibility for quality from the buyer's inspectors or users to the supplier's processes. Just-in-time processing is another mutually beneficial target of goal congruence: Cut out all the delays—and costly wastes—that stand in both parties' way of delivering just in time for use.

**Full Partnership.** Ultimately, as a step in achieving full partnership, the buying company's purchasing department may need to be streamlined. While a centralized

**Exhibit 6-4 Black Box View of the Supplier's System**

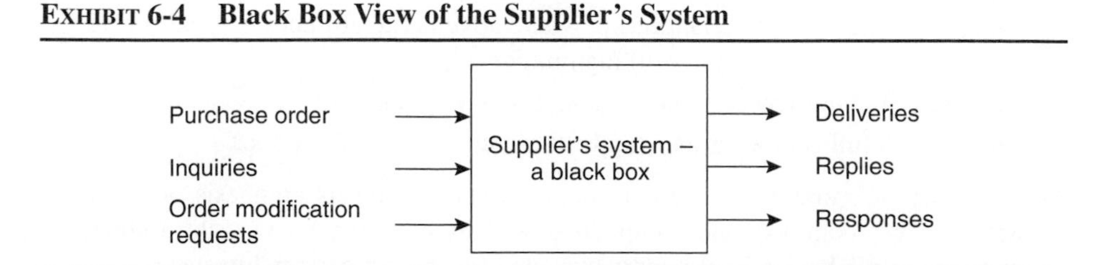

CONTRAST

## The Purchasing Associate

**Traditional**

- Commodity oriented.
- Burdened with paperwork.
- Out of touch with suppliers.

**More Effective**

- Captain of a purchasing team of colleagues and suppliers.
- Quality oriented and challenged by task variety.

Affiliation with the National Association of Purchasing Management (NAPM) provides a window to career opportunities in purchasing and related fields.

purchasing core may be retained, portions of the department may split off to join product or customer-focused teams or cells. The teams may even count supplier representatives among their membership, which is another, strong step in the direction of supplier partnership. (See the Contrast box for a summary of the traditional and more-effective viewpoints.) A modern trend in manufacturing is to create a new job classification called **buyer-planner:** A buyer assumes the added role of job planner, or a job planner takes on buying responsibilities. The buyer becomes an integral member of a production team.

The end-stage results of the transition extend far beyond the purchasing department, however. In the next section, we get a feel for just how pervasive supplier partnership can be.

# Features of Supplier Partnerships

To emphasize a point made throughout this book: Provider-customer chains exist within the organization as well as across the organization's boundaries. Thus, a full partnership must involve internal functions as well as outside suppliers. In this section we examine both.

### *Internal Relationships*

Typically, the internal functions affected by purchasing activities include:

*Purchasing.* Buyers and staff are the main action component of the purchasing effort.

*Product design and development.* This function may be called upon to develop specifications for the products or services to be bought.

*Operations.* Often operations teams or managers requisition, receive, and use the purchased item.

*Material control.* Personnel plan inventory levels, release material, and ensure record accuracy.

*Information systems.* The information system, usually computerized, handles order-processing transactions and related documentation.

*Receiving.* In the case of purchased goods, a separate receiving function may accept and process incoming items before the items make their way to the user.

*Accounts payable.* This section of the accounting department pays the supplier for accepted goods and services.

*Legal.* Purchase orders, even if conveyed orally, are legal contracts, which may need careful scrutiny.

In complex purchasing cases, all of these internal functions are active. The TQM concept of multifunctional teamwork is key to avoiding mistakes and maximizing chances for a successful acquisition.

The trend toward partnerships is strongest among big companies, such as Bank of Boston, Federal Express, and Daimler-Chrysler. Some, such as Harley-Davidson, label their approach "partners in profit," which asserts the buying company's commitment not to skewer the suppliers but to help make them strong. A few companies have even dropped the "purchasing" department label; Frito-Lay, for example, has a vice president, and department, of supplier development. Advanced data communication systems and trade pacts have made partnering possible across borders and oceans. Between quality at the source and supplier teams are a number of other features of supplier partnership, discussed next.

### External Relationships

Exhibit 6-5 contrasts the partnership and adversarial approaches. Most of the points under the partnership column in the exhibit could be called features of just-in-time purchasing, or of total-quality purchasing . . . again, evidence that JIT, total quality, and external partnerships are closely related.

While few companies have been totally adversarial with external suppliers, most have been that way to some degree. In contrast, certain leading-edge companies have embraced nearly all of the partnership items, and many others have adopted them in part. The extremes of adversary and partnership are anchors for discussion of the 12 dimensions in Exhibit 6-5.

**Tenure.** Under the adversarial approach, it's supplier musical chairs. A new supplier's price list might catch a buyer's eye and trigger a switch from the old to the new supplier. For large-volume (or big-ticket) services or items, buyers request bids from several suppliers at least yearly; the low bidder (often not the present supplier) usually gets the contract.

The partnership approach calls for staying with one supplier and letting the learning curve work for the benefit of both parties. Suppliers who get to know a customer's real requirements are valuable participants on continuous-improvement teams.

**Type of Agreement.** In the adversarial approach, sporadic purchase orders for a single item may rotate among 5 or 10 suppliers. Special, one-time buys will probably always

**EXHIBIT 6-5 Supplier Relationships**

| | *Adversary* | *Partnership* |
|---|---|---|
| 1. Tenure | Brief | Long-term, stable |
| 2. Type of agreement | Sporadic purchase orders | Exclusive or semi-exclusive contracts, usually at least one year |
| 3. Number of sources | Several sources per item for protection against risk and for price competition | One or a few good suppliers for each item or commodity group |
| 4. Prices/costs | High on average; low buy-in bids (below costs) can lead to unstable suppliers | Low; scale economies from volume contracts; suppliers can invest in improvements |
| 5. Quality | Uncertain; reliance on receiving inspections | Quality at source; supplier uses statistical process control and total quality management |
| 6. Design | Customer developed | Make use of suppliers' design expertise |
| 7. Delivery frequency/order size | Infrequent, large lots | Frequent (sometimes more than one per day), small lots just in time |
| 8. Order conveyance | Mail | Long-term: contracts. Short-term: kanban, phone, fax, EDI, or Internet |
| 9. Documentation | Packing lists, invoices, and count/inspection forms | Sometimes no count, inspection, or list—just monthly bill |
| 10. Transportation | Late and undependable; stock missing or damaged | Dependably quick, on time, and intact |
| 11. Delivery location | Receiving dock and stockroom | Direct to point of use |
| 12. Openness | Very little; black box | On-site audits of supplier, concurrent design, visits by frontline associates |

require a purchase order. For regularly used items, however, the trend is toward one-year or longer contracts. Five-year contracts have become widespread in the North American auto industry; one-year contracts are more common in the volatile electronics industry.

Some contracts specify the quantity for the next few months and provide a forecast for the rest of the year. Also, the contract may grant exclusivity to a supplier but not stipulate exact quantities.

**Number of Sources.** Having several sources for each purchased item is common practice among adversarially oriented buyers. Government regulations require it for certain classes of goods and services for reasons of price competition and a sense of fairness in public expenditures. In most cases, however, fear of supplier failure accounts for the many-supplier rule.

Over time, multiple sourcing has effects opposite to what is intended. It raises each supplier's costs and thus costs to the customer.[8] But sole- or preferred-supplier sourcing gives the supplier confidence that demand will continue. This encourages supplier investment in process and product improvements that offer economies of scale. Indeed, some believe that widespread multiple sourcing in North America and Europe in recent decades ruined part of the supplier base, which drove buying companies offshore, primarily to the Far East, in search of quality goods from reliable suppliers.

Multiple sources are also costly to buying organizations. They multiply costs of selection, evaluation, certification, data processing, communications, and administrative and clerical activities, for example. A less tangible cost is the loss of the opportunity to get to know and take advantage of suppliers' capabilities.

**Principle 5**

Cut the number of suppliers.

Competitive organizations strive to reduce these wastes, and a total quality or JIT program is often the impetus. A survey of North American companies revealed the average number of suppliers to be 1,096 prior to JIT. The number dropped to 759 after one year of JIT, to 656 after two years, and to 357 after five years. On average, the companies had cut their number of suppliers by over 67 percent in five years.[9] Other companies' programs aim at reducing the number of suppliers as a goal in itself. For example, a 3M factory in New Ulm, Minnesota, trimmed its active vendor list from 2,800 to 600 in the first year, and to 300 in the second year.[10] Furthermore, the trend has spread from manufacturing to fast-food companies, hotels, retailers, and wholesalers. Wallace Company, a distributor of oil-drilling repair parts and a winner of the Malcolm Baldrige Quality Award, cut its number of valve suppliers from 2,500 to 325.[11] Reductions of suppliers usually are competitive rather than arbitrary, and buying companies are usually up-front about their intentions to cut suppliers. [See Into Practice box, "Staying Lean with Low Risk."]

Despite the obvious cost benefits of supplier reductions, some companies fear that the sole supplier might fail. Sole-sourcing is not always the answer; often firms maintain two suppliers for each commodity group but just one for each part within a group. If disaster strikes one supplier, the other is able to help without the expense of developing new supply channels.

INTO PRACTICE

## Staying Lean with Low Risk

"Our inventory levels are at a fraction of where they were in the mid-1980s, but we feel there's no higher risk of shortages developing now than then," said Allen Hagstrand, in charge of purchasing for the Stamford, Connecticut, unit of Schweppes PLC, the London food and beverage producer.

Closer cooperation with a smaller but better-informed assortment of suppliers has helped, according to Mr. Hagstrand. "Today we get close to 80 percent of our glass containers from a single company, whereas seven years ago no one supplier provided more than 30 percent," he said. "We used to play one off against the other and keep them guessing, while now we all work very closely together, providing sales forecasts and other data we once kept to ourselves."

Source: Alfred L. Malabre, Jr., "Firm's Inventories Are Remarkably Lean," *The Wall Street Journal,* November 3, 1992.

**Prices/Costs.** In the adversarial approach, price tends to dominate the buy decision. Again, this may make sense for commodities, but for most items design, quality, delivery, and service also deserve emphasis.

Overemphasis on price can backfire. For example, sometimes a supplier will outbid other suppliers with a discount or a bid price that is below its costs; then, however, it may overcharge on other contracts in order to stay in business. Also, when big customers with clout are able to force suppliers into making recklessly low bids, the suppliers become unstable and financially unable to invest in improvements. That instability, along with frequent changing of suppliers, introduces high change costs for both parties. Thus, while the adversarial approach focuses on getting good prices, it often causes the opposite.

By contrast, the partnership approach, offering stable high-volume contracts with opportunities for economies of scale, is attractive to suppliers. It persuades them to try to improve and do their best for customers.

**Quality.** When suppliers are distrusted, customers must protect themselves. The insurance may be a sizable staff of inspectors at the receiving dock or in a holding area. Sometimes it takes days for goods to clear incoming inspection, while users watch their own schedules slip. For purchased services, the distrusted supplier's work must be checked, reports and claims must be filed and reconciled, and sometimes the service must be redone.

Instead of spending so much time discovering post-receipt errors, firms need to partner up and send customer teams to visit, develop, certify, and then nurture suppliers. Some companies furnish training and technical assistance to suppliers to prevent mistakes (fail-safing) or to help the supplier discover and correct them (process control). Sometimes supplier nurturing extends throughout an industry.

**Principle 10**

Make it easy to provide goods and services without error.

**Design.** If a customer buys out of a catalog or off the shelf, the supplier clearly has control of the design specifications. However, the customer often wants special features or service. In the adversarial approach, the customer typically does the design work, passes the specs on to the supplier, and expects them to be followed. But that approach has come under attack from wise customers. Programs such as early supplier involvement, design-build teams, and quality function deployment tap suppliers' expertise and can reduce design and development time significantly.

**Delivery Frequency/Order Size.** Shipping costs depend partly on whether the volume is great enough to fill a truck (or barge or sea container). Since volume for a certain item traditionally has been split among several suppliers, each supplier must ship less often in order to get full-load freight rates. Thus, it has been normal for customers to have to receive large lots infrequently; many weeks' supply per shipment is common.

Under the partnership approach, in which a smaller number of suppliers each has a greater volume of business, shipping more often—weekly, daily, or even more frequently—becomes economical. If the bulk is insufficient to fill a semitrailer, then a smaller truck or van may make the deliveries.

For remote suppliers, frequent, small-lot deliveries are made economical by what the auto industry calls milk runs. A single truck stops at several suppliers, collecting a small amount from each; when the truck is full, it delivers to one or more customers. Milk runs range from one a week to several loops per day.

Distance need not be a serious problem. One Chrysler milk run, extending from El Paso, Texas, to the Detroit area, takes 56 hours. Small-lot deliveries are even occuring across oceans; for example, a ship departing from a Far Eastern port may carry in a single sea container just a day's worth of several dozen different bulky auto parts; each day another similarly loaded ship departs, and each spends five weeks on the sea, but one arrives at a North American port to offload every day.

**Principle 13**

Operate at the customer's rate of use; decrease cycle interval and order size.

**Order Conveyance.** Exhibit 6-6 illustrates the order conveyance and documentation aspects of purchasing. We deal with order conveyance here and documentation in the next section. In traditional delivery systems, a mailed purchase order from the customer or an order booked by a salesperson starts the ball rolling in the supplier's plant (see the top portion of Exhibit 6-6A).

Modern partnership agreements use up-to-date order conveyance: phone, fax, electronic data interchange (EDI), and, of course, the Internet (see Exhibit 6-6B). Large companies such as automakers, Sears, and Wal-Mart have used EDI systems effectively for a number of years, but they are costly to install and operate; one estimate is that no company ever established EDI links with more than 20 percent of its suppliers.[12] But Internet connections are relatively cheap and available to even the smallest supplier.

Basic kanban is still another communications method. A kanban (identification card) is attached to the container, which is returnable; its return to the supplier is the authorization to forward one more containerful to the customer. Basic kanban is also usable in conjunction with electronic messaging. Standardized returnable containers provide physical discipline and control, while an electronic message or faxed kanban card provides early warning, before the empty container itself is delivered back to the supplier.

**Documentation.** Critical documentation associated with traditional purchasing occurs after the supplier receives the purchase order, completes required transformations, and ships goods to the customer (see Exhibit 6-6A). When the shipment arrives, receiving inspectors verify its correctness: right item, right quantity, and right quality. Receiving associates check the supplier's packing list against the receiving dock's copy of the purchase order and note discrepancies on forms that go to purchasing and accounts payable. After reconciliation, accounts payable issues a request-for-payment (RFP) to the controller's office, which cuts and mails a check.

The partnership approach tries to eliminate or simplify paperwork. In an ideal system based on a master agreement (see Exhibit 6-6B), there is no purchase order, packing list, or receiving report. A bar-coded kanban card identifies standard containers as to contents, quantity, and so forth. Inspection isn't needed; supplier and item are certified. When an associate scans the kanban bar code upon receipt of the order, accounts payable receives payment authorization. A monthly bill and electronic funds transfer may complete the process.

**Principle 15**

Cut transactions and reporting.

**EXHIBIT 6-6 Purchasing—Order Conveyance and Documentation**

A. Traditional approach

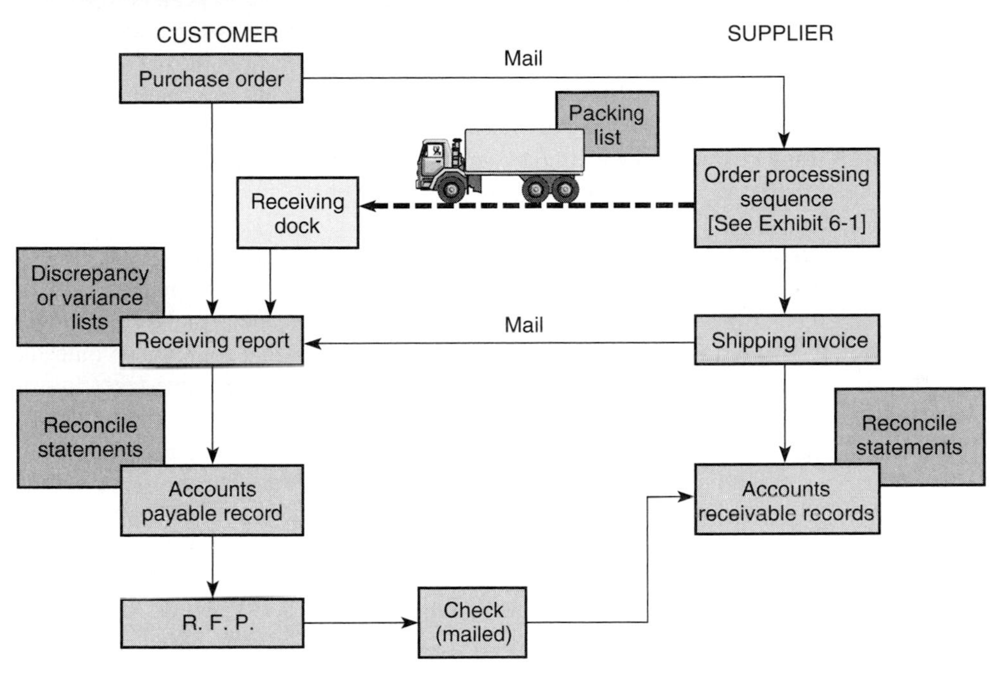


B. Partnership approach

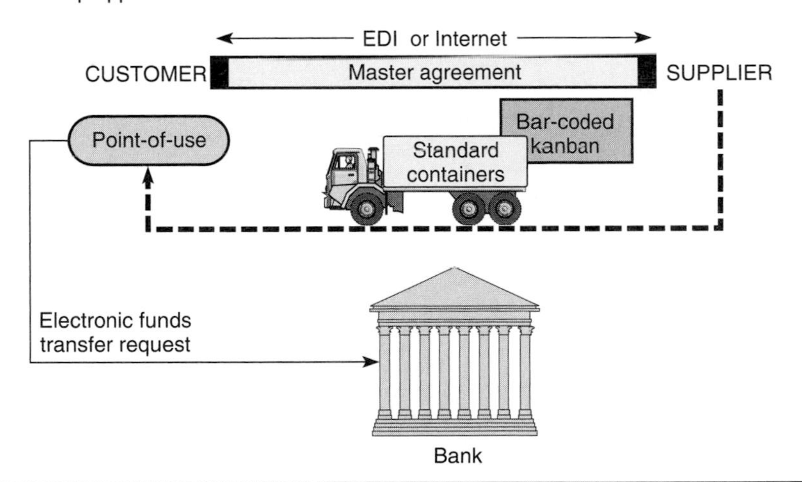

**Transportation.** Prior to the deregulation of trucking (which occurred in the United States in 1980 and in other countries in subsequent years), this dominant mode of transport was slow and unreliable. Along with the resulting keen competition, customers' demands for quality and speed have transformed the transportation industry. While in the old days freight haulers could not guarantee the *day* of delivery, today, sometimes, deliveries are to the *hour*. Truckers increasingly rely on satellite navigation, cellular phones, and personal computers. The increasing demands for quick, on-time, zero-damage transport have thrust the various players in the total transport system into close partnerships and multimodal freight agreements.

**Delivery Location.** Deliveries have historically gone to a single receiving dock (see the top portion of Exhibit 6-7; the vertical arrows depict internal flow of purchased items). The traditional relationship between the customer and Supplier A is costly, time-consuming, and wasteful. Materials may be handled four times: onto the dock for a quick check of contents and quantity, into quality hold in the receiving stockroom for counting and inspection, then to a free-to-use area of the stockroom, and finally to the point of use.

The partnership approach , on the other hand, would employ a quality-certified supplier (reflected as Supplier B in Exhibit 6-7) and would skip all or most of the non-value-adding steps. In industry parlance, items go dock-to-line (or dock-to-use), right to their destination in the plant, lab, kitchen, sales floor, or office. Some companies are remodeling their buildings to provide receiving docks and doors at multiple locations around the building so that trucks can deliver close to use points.

In some cases, the driver is authorized to carry or push a trolley or parts through the dock to an interior user location. This is the case for paper and packaging materials

**EXHIBIT 6-7 Delivery Location: Dock versus Point of Use**

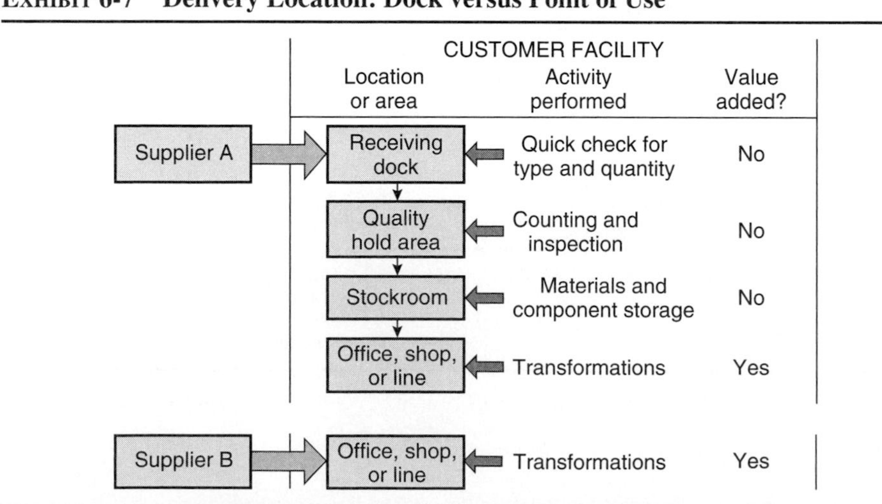

delivered from Smurfit Company, a JIT supplier to Microsoft-Ireland, a Dublin-based plant producing software products for the European market.

**Relationship Openness.** The adversarial approach is one of arm's-length relationship. The buyer, in the office or at trade shows, sifts through many suppliers' offerings and finally selects a few; from then on, communication is by mail and fax (except in times of materials scarcity, when the suppliers put their customers "on allocation"—1,000 electronic games or dolls to this store chain, 1,200 to that one, and so forth).

The partnership approach requires the buying organization to send teams to the supplier's site. That includes sending operations employees who use the purchased items. The visitors get to know people at the supplier's facility and acquire an understanding of the supplier's culture, skills, processes, nagging problems, and potential sources of misunderstanding. They invite the supplier's people to reciprocate the visit.

The buyer's outreach effort usually also includes some kind of supplier evaluation or certification. To some extent, evaluation teams supplement their own efforts with public, industry, or international quality recognition (e.g., ISO 9000 registration). Companies may formally evaluate and certify suppliers of both materials and services.

The buying company that is truly serious about a strong partnership must be a good customer. Motorola, for example,

> conducts quarterly confidential surveys of its main suppliers to evaluate its performance as a customer. Each Motorola plant is rated in nineteen areas that the company feels are important to the buyer–seller partnership. Motorola has established a fifteen-member council of suppliers to rate its practices and offer suggestions for improving, for example, the accuracy of production schedules or design layouts that Motorola gives them.[13]

Failure to visit and perform audits or obtain evaluations from external partners invites misunderstanding, bad feelings, and a return to adversarial relationships. It is perhaps like gardening: Till the soil, or weeds will grow.

## Outsourcing as Strategy

Despite the high levels of expenditures represented by purchased items in most companies, purchasing was historically not thought of as strategic. That has certainly changed, as we noted in Chapter 2. In a never-ending search for competitive advantage, companies recognize limits on their own distinctive competencies and look to outsourcing as the strategy of choice for obtaining needed skills and products. Outsourcing is fast and flexible, offers top quality, and, as more companies are discovering, is quite often cheaper in the long run.

The strategic significance of outsourcing is bolstered when we consider the large number of candidate activities, some of which are shown in Exhibit 6-8. They extend across the gamut of the transformation processes sequence from design to delivery and customer service.

Issues related to outsourcing strategy include vertical integration, make-or-buy cost analysis, standardization, and modular buying. We discuss each next.

**Exhibit 6-8 Candidates for Outsourcing**

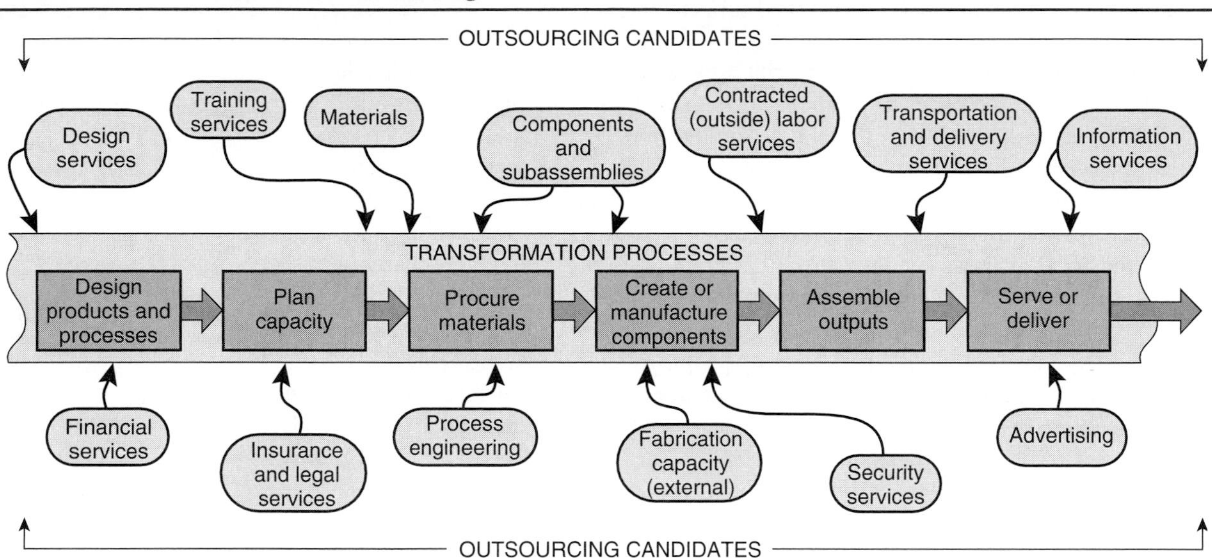


### *Outsourcing versus Vertical Integration*

In **vertical integration,** a company acquires capacity to perform activities that are either upstream or downstream of its current capabilities. **Backward integration** looks upstream to the company's inputs; it refers to the creation or acquisition of supply sources. The company may construct new facilities, for example, or it may simply buy a former supplier. **Forward integration** focuses downstream on outputs; a manufacturer may build its own distribution network complete with warehouses and retail outlets, for instance.

Traditionally, vertical integration seemed the only way to gain control of costs and quality—the "if you want it done right, do it yourself" concept. Today, however, an increasing number of firms are choosing to retain their core competencies—the "stick to your knitting" idea—and outsource the rest. The old fear of losing control has diminished due to successful experiences with supplier partnerships, and frankly, due to the reality that outside suppliers are often the superior option.

The authors of "Managing Our Way to Economic Decline," an acclaimed 1980 article, commented on backward integration. Companies with stable, commodity-like products, such as metals and petroleum, often can gain economies and profit improvements through backward integration. The strategy may backfire, however, for companies in technologically active industries. Backward integration "may provide a quick, short-term boost to ROI figures in the next annual report, but it may also paralyze the long-term ability of a company to keep on top of technological change."[14]

Sometimes, the mere threat of outsourcing can help shape up the inside organization. In a variation on this idea, a number of companies have been bringing operations back to the United States or Canada to cut costs or improve quality—the same reasons for leaving some years earlier. An article on the subject notes further reasons for coming home:[15]

- Automation and "new product designs that shrink the number of parts and simplify assembly."
- Quick response. "What many companies compete on today is service—the ability to produce with lead times of a day or two."
- Fast product development. It is better for the "design and manufacturing folks to be physically close so that they can talk elbow to elbow, modifying continuously."

Any advantages of "stick to your knitting" and outsourcing, of course, depend on having reliable suppliers. The ideal is for the buyer company to exert control over a few vital factors of the supply channels, leaving the supplier free to innovate and keep up with technologies in its area of expertise. Reliable suppliers don't just happen; they must be nurtured.

### *Make-or-Buy Economics*

Make-or-buy analysis is a variant of cost-volume analysis considered in Chapter 2.

The question of whether to outsource or not is often a complex issue, not fully reducible to cost analysis. For an existing service or good, going outside means the firm no longer needs the employees currently doing the work; reducing the workforce is always unpleasant and costly. Moreover, some of the overhead costs connected to the outsourced item may not disconnect easily, thereby reducing the potential savings.

Some of the outsourcing decision, however, is a cost-volume issue. A simple form of break-even analysis captures the basic elements; see Exhibit 6-9.

**EXHIBIT 6-9 Make-or-Buy Break-Even Analysis**

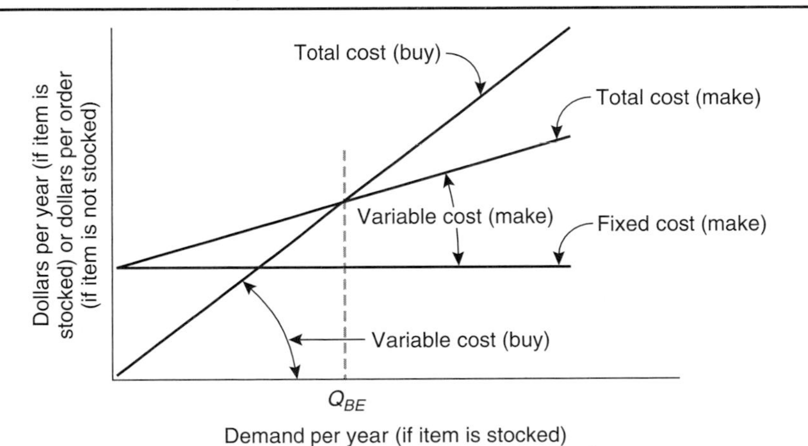

As the exhibit shows, if the item is bought, there is no fixed cost. Instead, the total cost (*TC*) is simply the unit price (*P*) times demand (*D*):

$$TC_{buy} = P \times D \tag{6-1}$$

If the item is made, there is a fixed cost (*FC*) of setting up for production. The other element of total cost is the variable cost of production, which equals the assumed constant unit variable cost (*V*) times demand (*D*). Then

$$TC_{make} = (V \times D) + FC \tag{6-2}$$

We see in Exhibit 6-9 that the break-even demand $Q_{BE}$ occurs where the total costs are equal. For demand less than $Q_{BE}$, the total cost to buy is lower; thus, *buy* is preferred. For demand greater than $Q_{BE}$, offsetting the fixed cost by the lower unit cost results in a lower cost to make; so *make* is preferred. The analysis should be based on annual demand and cost if the item is stocked and is bought year after year. The demand and cost of a single order should be used for a nonstocked item that may or may not be reordered in future years.

Since the total costs are equal at the break-even point, a break-even formula is easily developed. Using $Q_{BE}$ (for break-even demand) instead of *D*, we have

$$TC_{buy} = TC_{make}$$

$$P \times Q_{BE} = (V \times Q_{BE}) + FC$$

Then, by algebraic transformation,

$$Q_{BE} = \frac{FC}{P - V} \tag{6-3}$$

For example, assume you can buy candles at the store for $1 each. Or you can pay $50 for candle-making apparatus and make your own candles for a unit variable cost (wax, wicks, etc.) of $0.75. What volume is necessary in order to recover your fixed cost—that is, break even?

Solution:

$$Q_{BE} = \frac{50}{1 - 0.75} = \frac{50}{0.25} = 200 \text{ candles.}$$

Classical make-or-buy is simple enough, but what about its overall usefulness? Like any model, the make-or-buy model entails certain assumptions. First, both options must be realistic. For the make option, this goes beyond the cost of the candle-making apparatus. To be realistic, there are questions of technical knowledge to be successful in such a new endeavor. And will management resources be spread too thin if candle-making is taken on? Another issue is technological obsolescence. What if a new, lower-cost method of candle-making appears? If you invested in the old method, you're stuck and could be underpriced by a competitor.

Concern over these kinds of questions and assumptions seem trivial in this candle-making example. But what if owners of a shopping mall are considering a $10 million expenditure for installing their own power-generating facilities instead of buying power from the local utility? Now the issues (technical skills, managerial demands, obsolescence, etc.) loom large. The point is that the make-or-buy model does not make the decision but only helps sharpen decision makers' judgment.

The issue of obsolescence is also related to the next two topics, standardization and modular buying.

### *Standardization*

Standardization means settling on a few rather than many sizes, formats, and so forth. A standardization strategy is one way to ward off obsolescence, though that is by no means its only purpose. Standardization may apply to printed materials, software, hardware, methods and processes.

Lee and Dobler state that, in manufacturing, "standardization is the prerequisite to mass production." They credit Eli Whitney's development of standardization (initially of musket parts) as having led ultimately to the emergence of the United States as the world's dominant mass producer in the 20th century.[16] This does not necessarily mean standardized *end products.* The more powerful strategy is being able to make a wide variety of end products from a small number of standardized parts and materials. The same goes for services. For example, serve a wide variety of training needs with a small number of standardized training methods.

The cost savings can be substantial. For one thing, standardization is key to **delayed differentiation**—keeping items in a lower cost state as long as possible by delaying transformation of generic items into differentiated items. Furthermore, fewer items means less purchasing, receiving, inspection, storage, and billing. In manufacturing, standardization reduces the number of different kinds of production equipment and tooling, and production of some parts may be relatively continuous and just in time, instead of inefficient stop-and-go production with intermittent delays and changeover costs.

Some companies, and some industries, have standardization committees. National and world bodies also develop standards. The American National Standards Institute (ANSI) is a federation of over 100 organizations that develop industrial standards. After research and debate, ANSI may approve a recommended standard for adoption nationwide. Perhaps the most vexing standardization issue in America is metrics, since the United States is the only nonmetric country among major industrial countries. However, most American companies with good export markets have gone metric on their own.

### *Modular Buying*

Purchasing in already-put-together modules has special advantages for companies whose products are made from many hundreds or thousands of parts. New automobile plants in Brazil make extensive use of modularization.[17]

How to tell if a plant has too many parts: Have a look. If most of what you see are vehicles, overhead conveyors, and storage systems, the plant is sinking in a sea of parts.

If the firm is adversarial with suppliers, it tries to cope with excessive-part difficulties itself. But partnership companies look to their suppliers for a solution, such as having a supplier acquire and preassemble a collection of loose parts into a module, to be delivered with certified quality just in time for use. Though it takes years to

INTO PRACTICE

## Supplier in Residence

The purchasing department at Bose Corporation, producer of high-end speakers and sound systems, is a pioneer in an extension of the supplier-partnership concept. Their approach, registered under the trademark JIT II, features suppliers in residence at the Bose headquarters facility in Framingham, Massachusetts, as well as at Bose factories. Conceived in 1987, the Bose program has grown to include nine suppliers, of metal, plastics, packaging, printing, stationery, export/import, and transportation goods and services. The supplier representatives are "stationed at the Bose facility at the [supplier's] expense, on a full-time basis, [given] access to customer data, people, and processes, and granted the right to place purchase orders with their own organizations on behalf of Bose. . . . Simply put, JIT II eliminates buyer and salesman, and the [supplier] and customer work closely together."

Source: Adapted from "JIT II: An Inside Story," *APICS—The Performance Advantage,* October 1992, pp. 20–22.

implement, this solution has become attractive to manufacturers of such complex products as automobiles, aircraft, large appliances, and mass spectrometers. (A car has over 13,000 parts, and the Boeing 777 has 132,000 engineered parts and over 3 million fasteners.)

Sometimes the initiative comes from supplier companies. The automotive group at Eagle-Picher Company has proposed to its automotive customers that it supply multipurpose rubber floor mats. The mats would include the underlayment, plus electrical wiring for taillights and accessories. That gets wiring inside the car, for more reliable quality, instead of strung beneath the car where it is exposed to the elements. Eagle-Picher wants to become a stronger, more valuable supplier with business for *more* parts, while helping its customers to become stronger by needing to manage *fewer* parts.

In a still closer kind of partnership, the supplier moves onto the buying organization's premises in order to become almost like "family." The Into Practice box "Supplier in Residence" offers an example of this practice—registered as a trademark, **JIT II.**

The outsourcing-related matters just discussed are of strategic importance. The day-to-day business of carrying out sourcing strategies requires systematic policies and procedures, our next topic.

## Purchasing Policies and Procedures

Commonsense policies relating to value and kind of items bought provide guidance for purchasing professionals. In considering those policies, we look first at ABC analysis and its influence on common buying procedures. Related to this are two final chapter topics: measurement and compliance issues and value analysis.

### *ABC Analysis*

It makes sense to manage costly goods and services tightly and cheap ones loosely. That logic is the basis of **ABC analysis,** an old and still important tool of materials management. Because of the influence that "ABC thinking" exerts on purchasing, however, it is quite relevant to our present discussion.

ABC analysis begins by classifying all stocked items by annual dollar volume, that is, annual demand times cost per unit. Class A items, those needing close control, are the high-dollar-volume group. They may include 80 percent of total purchase cost but only 1 percent of total items bought. Class B is a medium-dollar-volume group, perhaps 15 percent of cost and 30 percent of items. Class C is the rest, say, 5 percent of cost and 69 percent of items. Some firms continue with D and perhaps E categories.

Computer processing makes ABC analysis easy to do. Item cost is available in the inventory master file. Any measure of annual usage may be used, such as actual usage last year, actual usage last month times 12, or a forecast. After the computer provides a list of items in descending dollar-volume order, associates divide the list into A, B, and C, based on the company's category break-point policies.

The resulting ABC listing may be used as follows (the details will vary from firm to firm):

1. *Purchasing.* Have each contract or purchase order for a class A item signed by the president or chief financial officer, for a class B item by a department head, and for a class C item by any buyer.
2. *Physical inventory counting.* Count A items weekly or daily, B items monthly, and C items annually.
3. *Forecasting.* Forecast A items by several methods on the computer with resolution by a forecasting committee, B items by simple trend projection, and C items by buyer's best guess.
4. *Safety stock.* No safety stock for A items, one week's supply for B items, and one month's supply for C items.
5. *Quick response.* Deliver A items frequently, perhaps daily, just in time. Deliver Bs weekly, and Cs monthly.

At a TQM team's suggestion, Microsoft USA provides each group assistant (serving a group of software engineers) with a credit card for buying low-value items, thus bypassing the purchasing department for nearly 40 percent of the firm's purchases.

Class A items are often the best prospects for full JIT treatment because they have the volume to most easily justify frequent small-lot deliveries, perhaps daily. It is no small achievement to switch an item to daily deliveries; typical delivery intervals/lot sizes in the non-JIT mode are monthly or greater. JIT policies for B and C items are more modest: perhaps weekly deliveries for class B items and monthly for class Cs.

Actually, many companies have found ways to do much better than that for some Bs and Cs. For example, a sizable number of manufacturing plants now buy all their hundreds of hardware items (screws, bolts, grommets, etc.) from a single supplier. Commonly, that supplier visits the customer at least once a week, and sometimes even daily, goes right out to the factory floor to fill the bins and trays, and just invoices the customer monthly. While each hardware item is class C in annual value, the whole commodity group adds up to class A value, which makes it economical for the supplier to provide that kind of customer service.

A different twist on the same general idea was discussed earlier: buying completed modules instead of the individual parts. Past practice in automotive assembly, for example, was to buy and receive hundreds of class B parts for instrument panels, doors, and so forth for piece-by-piece installation on the assembly line. The sheer volume of parts made this system a receiving and material-handling nightmare.

The current trend is to have a subcontractor, a specialist in instrument panels or doors, for example, deliver completed modules to the assembly plant. While the individual parts are class B, the modules are class A in value, which makes daily deliveries (sometimes several times a day) economical.

ABC applies as well to inventory-intensive wholesaling and retailing as it does to manufacturing (see Example 6-1).

## Example 6-1: ABC Analysis—Wholesaler

At Universal Motor Supply Company, the buyer has arranged 10 inventory items in order of annual dollar volume. Exhibit 6-10 shows the ordered list, with monetary volume expressed in percentages. The buyer examines the list to arrive at an ABC classification of the items.

Exhibit 6-11 shows the 10 items as the buyer grouped them into classes A, B, and C. The groupings seem natural: The three B items account for over seven (9.8 ÷ 1.3) times as much annual volume as the five C items, and two A items account for about nine times as much as the three B items. It is clear that A items should receive major attention. Have them delivered often in small quantities, store them in flow racks at or near the receiving/shipping docks, and carefully monitor and control them. Class Bs should receive moderate attention, and class Cs little attention; for example, handle them manually and store them in conventional racks in a remote part of the warehouse.

**Exhibit 6-10 Inventory Items in Annual-Dollar-Volume Order—Universal Motor Supply Company**

| *Stock Number* | *Annual Demand* | *Unit Cost* | *Annual Dollar Volume* | *Percent* |
|---|---|---|---|---|
| 407 | 40,000 | $ 35.50 | $1,420,000 | 59.53% |
| 210 | 1,000 | 700.00 | 700,000 | 29.35 |
| 021 | 2,000 | 55.00 | 110,000 | 4.61 |
| 388 | 20,000 | 4.00 | 80,000 | 3.35 |
| 413 | 4,400 | 10.00 | 44,000 | 1.84 |
| 195 | 500 | 36.00 | 18,000 | 0.75 |
| 330 | 40 | 214.00 | 8,560 | 0.36 |
| 114 | 100 | 43.00 | 4,300 | 0.18 |
| 274 | 280 | 1.00 | 280 | 0.01 |
| 359 | 600 | 0.25 | 150 | 0.01 |
| | | Totals | $2,385,290 | ~100.0% |

**EXHIBIT 6-11 ABC Classification—Universal Motor Supply Company**

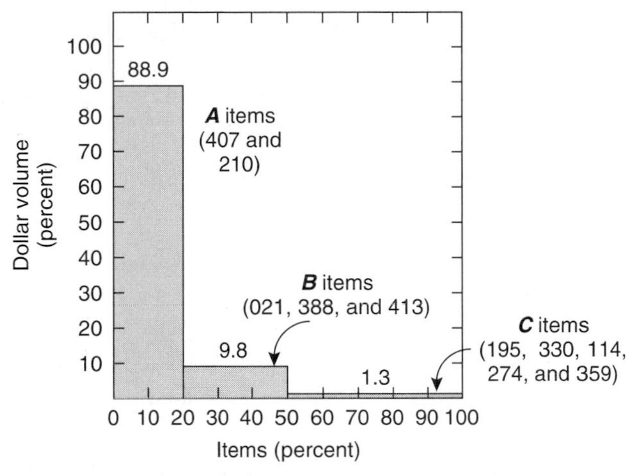


### *Purchasing and Contracting Practices*

Besides ABC analysis, there are other common purchasing practices and terms that managers should know. They have to do with arranging the supplier–buyer agreement and the terms of that agreement, and they group fairly well into the A, B, and C categories.

**Class A Items.** A class A item may be a service contract, an expensive, seldom-ordered item, or a low-cost item that is ordered often or in large quantities. Common purchasing measures are:

**Soliciting competitive bids on specifications.** The buyer mails an invitation to bid or a request for quotation to prospective suppliers. The item to be bought is defined by technical specifications, performance specifications, and procedural specifications. Such detail may be necessary because the item is nonstandard or because the buying firm wishes to exclude low-quality suppliers. Also, specifications can provide a sound basis for determining compliance with the buyer's requirements. Engineers often play a key role in developing specs, and blueprints may be attached. Attorneys may ensure that contractual obligations are legally correct.

Governments, especially the federal government, intermittently buy based on publicly available specs. Regulations require that for many types of purchases the invitation to bid be published in a widely circulated government document.

**Certification.** Quality-conscious companies conduct formal studies to quality-certify suppliers and items bought from them. Older approaches, which rank suppliers rather than certify them, are based on external price data, delivery timeliness, defect rates, and a few other factors. Quality certification sometimes includes such factors as quality of design, training, response time, and delivery performance.

**Negotiation.** Where sources of supply are stable, there may be no need to solicit formal bids. Instead, purchasing teams may just periodically negotiate with the regular source for better price or delivery terms. Typically, negotiation applies to nonstandard class A goods and services.

**Speculative buying.** In this type of purchasing, also called buying down, the buyer will purchase in excess of immediate needs when the price is down. The practice is risky in that price could fall further, and a need for the items bought may never materialize.

**Hedging.** Hedging applies especially to commodities, such as wheat, corn, silver, and lumber. Organized futures markets exist for some commodities. A buyer can pay cash to buy a commodity now and at the same time sell a like amount of a future delivery of the commodity. Price changes will mean that losses on one order are offset by gains on the other.

**Class B Items.** Class B goods and moderate-cost services usually warrant less purchasing effort. That applies to many kinds of standard off-the-shelf goods, such as maintenance, repair, and operating (MRO) supplies as well as standard services, such as those of a plumber or an auto body shop. For nonstandard items in the class B cost range, specifications might be necessary, but the expense of soliciting bids is harder to justify than for class A items. Buying procedures for the class B category include the following:

**Approved supplier lists.** Companies like to buy from proven suppliers. Buyers rely on the approved supplier list, especially for class B items, though it also is used for class A and class C buying. Increasingly, approved supplier means certified supplier.

**Catalog buying.** Perhaps the most common purchasing procedure for off-the-shelf MRO goods is buying out of current catalogs, sometimes with the help of salespeople. Most buyers have shelves full of suppliers' catalogs for this purpose.

**Blanket orders.** An ongoing but varying need for an item with class B annual volume may call for a blanket-order contract with a supplier. The blanket order covers a given time period, and deliveries are arranged by sending a simple release notice to the supplier. Price and other matters are covered in the contract.

**Systems contract.** A systems contract is similar to a blanket order, but it is longer term and more stringently defined. The purchasing department negotiates the systems contract; purchasing then typically monitors, but does not participate in, ordering. The contract may name certain responsible employees who may order, by mail, phone, or other means, directly from the supplier.

**Class C Items.** Class C or low-cost items are worthy of little attention by purchasing specialists. Buying such items from a certified supplier provides a measure of control.

For many items even that is too much control and red tape, and to avoid these, using departments buy out of petty cash funds. Until recently, petty cash buying has been restricted to office employees. Now a few progressive North American companies provide each improvement team with a petty cash fund for purchasing low-cost items that can improve performance.

### *Buying Intangibles*

When teams buy intangibles they must employ different purchasing practices than when buying tangibles. The distinction arises largely because the quality characteristics of tangibles can be measured (variables) or classified and counted (attributes). An intangible item, however, is sometimes difficult to identify, much less specify. Consequently, it may be hard to hold the provider accountable for the buyer's performance/compliance wishes.

Intangibility is relative (see Exhibit 6-12). At the highly tangible end of the scale, quality is generally determined by objective, measurable output standards. At the highly intangible end of the scale are few, if any, measurable output quality characteristics on which to judge compliance with requirements; thus, emphasis shifts to input or procedural factors as surrogate indicators of quality. Specific attention to these two extremes, as well as the intermediate levels of tangibility, is warranted.

- For highly tangible items (screws, diodes, and switches), quality is easily measured.
- Commodities are tangible but may require a certain amount of subjective eyeball judgments to grade quality; thus assessment moves from variables into attributes.

**EXHIBIT 6-12 Tangibility of Purchased Goods**

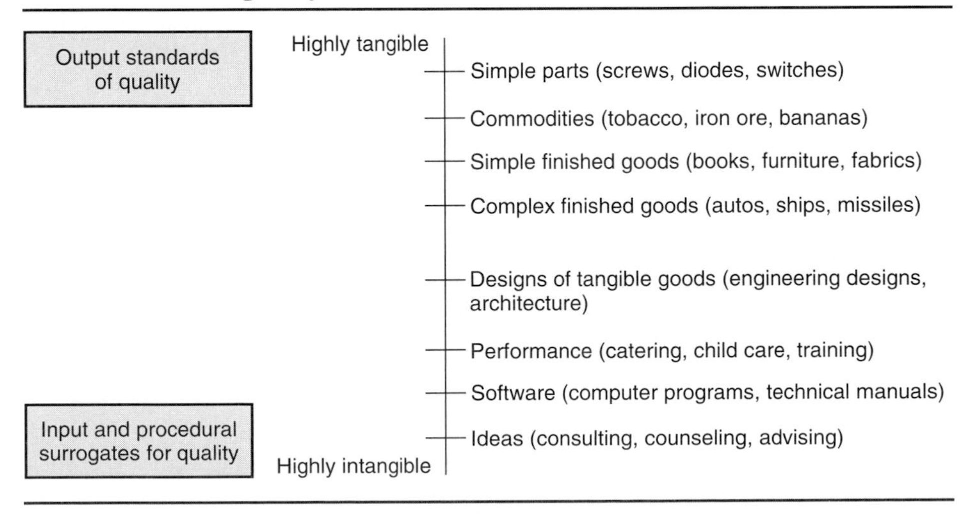

- Simple finished goods have several measurable physical properties, but visual inspection for scratches, flaws, and so on, may be more important. Again, buyers mix attributes assessment and variables assessment.
- Complex finished goods have thousands of measurable physical properties of *form* (e.g., dimensions) and *function* (such as turning radius and speed). Nevertheless, partly subjective judgments of effectiveness (how well a destroyer protects the fleet, or a mobile home keeps the elements out) are also important.
- Designs for tangible goods, are harder to judge until the end result (the tangible good itself) becomes reality. If a bridge caves in or a door handle keeps breaking off, we can (in hindsight) judge the design to be bad. The engineer might even be liable for damages. Perhaps the best *up-front* help for buyers of these items is design expertise on the buying team.
- Contracting for performance is on the upswing. It is difficult to write standards into a contract. Consequently, there is growing use of measures of compliance such as mean number of customer complaints and opinion polling involving customers, experts, or impartial panels using some form of simple rating scale (e.g., 1 to 5, with 5 being "best").
- Software and documentation are slightly more intangible. Buyers of these items must distinguish between the quality of the item specified, a television set, for example, and the quality of the documentation (operating instructions manual) being purchased.
- Highly intangible items, at the bottom of Exhibit 6-12, have no physically measurable properties. Therefore, purchase contracts may be based on input and procedural factors. In a contract with a consultant, input factors may include specifying level of education and years of experience of the consultants sent out on the job; procedural factors may include number of people to be interviewed and number of pages on the final consultant's report. Those do not define the quality of the consultant's services, but they are often treated as surrogates for output quality.

We can conclude that the most serious measurement and compliance assessment problems occur when buying performance, software, and ideas—items at the intangible end of the scale. Buying from certified suppliers, or at least from those with good reputations, helps.

Public and corporate officials rely increasingly on consultants to help them with sticky decisions. But the inability to write tough contracts leaves the officials at the consultants' mercy. Fortunately, most consultants are professionally dedicated and motivated to maintain self-respect. Still, contracting for intangibles is a challenge for buyers, one that permeates all organizational transformations. Clearly, trust, openness, and a few good suppliers are key to meeting the purchasing challenge.

**value analysis (VA)**
Team analysis of existing product design specifications with the aim of improving value; developed in the purchasing department of General Electric in 1947.

### *Value Analysis*

Purchasing means spending money. But purchasing professionals also may become involved in projects that offer long-term substantial savings (making money) for their company. Value analysis projects are of this type.

In large organizations, file cabinets in purchasing and design may be filled with specs developed years ago. New technology outdates some of the old specifications. Each time such items are reordered, the obsolescence becomes more apparent and purchasing takes the heat for not "buying modern." It is no surprise that VA was developed and promoted by purchasing people. As engineers got more involved, the concepts were extended to include new designs as well as old specs.

In some companies and in the federal government, engineers conduct a related type of analysis, calling it **value engineering (VE).** While value analysis is sometimes applied to services, it is mostly associated with goods, especially where material costs and usage rates are high.

The VA step-by-step procedure has been adopted worldwide. The steps are a variation of the scientific method:

1. *Select product.* Select a product that is ripe for improvement.
2. *Gather information.* The team coordinator collects drawings, costs, scrap rates, forecasts, operations sheets, and so forth, before the team first meets. Team members provide whatever information they have.
3. *Define function.* The team, which sometimes includes the customer, meets and defines each function of the product. A function is defined in two words: a verb and a noun (e.g., "A barrel *contains fluid.*"). Only essential functions are included. Next, the team estimates the present cost of each function. That reveals which functions are costing far too much. (Note: Defining functions in this way is unique and sets VA apart from other cost reduction techniques.)
4. *Generate alternatives.* Team members brainstorm to develop ideas for new and different ways to accomplish the functions. Ideas are recorded and later culled to a list of manageable size.
5. *Evaluate alternatives.* The team evaluates alternatives based on feasibility, cost, and other factors, which cuts the list to a few good ideas.
6. *Present proposals.* Refine the final alternatives and present them to a management committee as change proposals.
7. *Implement plan.* Translate the approved change proposal into an engineering change order (ECO) and put it into effect.

In Example 6-2, the description of a real VA study helps show how the procedure works.[18]

## Example 6-2: Value Analysis of Preprinted Quotation Binders

The marketing manager had a problem involving the binders used by her salespeople in making customer quotations: The commercial printer that had been producing the binders notified her that because of increased costs, they would have to charge her $1.75 each instead of $1.25. She mentioned the problem to the value analysis team member from her department.

That afternoon at the VA team meeting, the marketing representative commented on the increase. The team, seeing the effects that the 40 percent price increase would have on the cost of the multitude of quotations sent out by that company, decided to look into the matter.

First, they determined the functions of the binder: "provide advertising," "provide appearance," and "provide protection." Next, they asked some of the salespeople to participate in a VA study. Their task would be to generate creative ideas on different ways of accomplishing the three functions. One of the salespeople noted that the present binders were so thick that when received by customers, clerical assistants removed the quotation materials from the binders so they wouldn't take up so much space in their files; he had seen this done on several occasions. With this information, the team asked the question, Is the binder made by the right process, given the quantities used?

A team member from industrial engineering commented that his department had just purchased some simple binders to cover their master routing sheets. They were a clear plastic folder into which the sheets were inserted; then, a long, plastic clip the length of the folder "zipped" the folder closed on one side to hold the papers in place. The folders costs only $0.10 each.

Following up on this idea, the team obtained a copy of a customer quotation set and tried it out on one of the plastic folders. They found that the folder not only took care of the function, "provide protection", but it also accomplished the function "provide advertising" since the company letterhead showed through the clear plastic, and the function "provide appearance" since the folder looked better than the old binder. The team showed the folder to the marketing manager, who realized that the clear plastic jacket not only solved her cost problem but also was thin enough that it would not be removed by the customer, thus maintaining the appearance and protection of the quotation materials.

Source: Arthur E. Mudge, *Innovative Change: 101 Case Histories* (Pittsburgh, Penn.: J. Pohl Associates, 1989), p. 68.

---

Impressed by the results of VA and VE in private industry, the Department of Defense issued VE regulations applicable to all DOD contracts costing more than $100,000. In 1964, the American Ordnance Association conducted a survey that randomly sampled 124 successful VE changes in the DOD.[19] The survey report showed not only impressive cost savings but also, in many cases, collateral gains in the areas of reliability, maintainability, producibility, human factors, parts availability, production lead time, quality, weight, logistics, performance, and packaging. The DOD then implemented a formula for sharing VE savings (usually 20 percent) with contractors; that gave the contractors' VE teams added incentive to squeeze savings out of the design specifications.

An informal method of value analysis has recently come into use. In a JIT plant a problem might arise that threatens to stop production. That summons a buyer or engineer to the shop floor; a foreman and perhaps an operator will join in the problem analysis. Blueprints may be marked up and taken immediately to the inside or outside maker of the parts that are causing the problem.

Conducting value analysis in that way—on the fly—requires that blueprints and design specs not be too limiting. Design engineers traditionally have tried to specify every dimension, type of material, finish, and so on, which greatly limits options for producing the item. The nonrestrictive specs concept aims at giving the maker latitude over nonessential design attributes so that easy, cheap ways of making the part may be searched for and easily changed when someone sees a better way.

The purist might say that making design decisions on the floor should not be called value analysis because the formal steps (defining functions, generating alternatives, etc.) are bypassed. While that is true, the less formal approach has the advantage of giving more attention to how product design affects producibility, a key element in overall product cost. Also, producibility is a vital concern in just-in-time production in which a production problem can starve later production stages of parts and bring operations to a halt.

**Principle 3**

Achieve team involvement in implementation of change.

## Summary Check Points

✓ Order fulfillment is a core operations management duty, and may be accomplished by drawing on internal and/or external provider-customer supply chains.

✓ The order-fulfillment sequence accommodates internal and external demands as well as on-demand items and goods and service outputs that can be prescheduled.

✓ Purchasing activities often account for a majority of costs in business operations, lending impetus for consideration of purchasing as a strategic weapon.

✓ General structures or paradigms of buyer-supplier relationships have evolved as competitive pressures force companies to seek greater competencies and leverage.

✓ Supplier selection can involve examination of many criteria; they range from technical performance specifications to the basic matter of trust.

✓ Transition towards partnerships with suppliers involves a four-stage evolution: confrontation, arm's-length relationship, goal congruence, and partnership.

✓ Partnership provider-customer relationships ought to exist within organizations as well as across organizational boundaries.

✓ Traditional adversarial supplier relationships may be compared with more enlightened partnership relationships on several key dimensions—Exhibit 6-5 illustrates 12 examples.

✓ Outsourcing, in some ways a "contemporary" term for purchasing, has been shown to offer competitive advantages across a broad range of transformation processes.

✓ Vertical integration refers to a company's acquisition of capacity to perform activities that are either upstream or downstream of its current activities. Backward integration applies to input or supply sources, and forward integration's focus is downstream toward the end consumer.

✓ Make-or-buy analysis, a form of cost-volume analysis, may be helpful in making strategic outsourcing decisions.

✓ Standardization means opting for a few rather than many general types, models, sizes, formats and so on.

✓ Modules are preassembled components comprised of perhaps many small parts; companies that buy modules cut their assembly costs and rely on suppliers for module design and integration.

✓ ABC analysis is a form of discriminating among many items of inventory according to value. It helps determine purchasing policies.

✓ Generally, it is more difficult to buy intangibles than tangibles because quality is more difficult to assess in the former.
✓ Value analysis is a formal, step-by-step procedure designed to enhance buyer's overall value in the purchase of large-scale or high-volume items.

## Solved Problem

### *Problem*

Consider the following list of parts, their unit costs, and annual requirements:

| *Part Number* | *Unit Cost* | *Annual Demand* |
|---|---|---|
| M2 | $ 20.00 | 120 |
| A5 | 2.00 | 155,000 |
| A7 | 8,000.00 | 13 |
| L8 | 950.00 | 6 |
| L4 | 0.30 | 7,000 |
| A6 | 10.00 | 9,400 |
| M9 | 6,000.00 | 70 |
| Q2 | 400.00 | 240 |
| Z1 | 0.50 | 200 |

Compute the annual value and percentage of total value for each part. Arrange the nine parts into ABC categories. Plot cumulative percentages in order from the greatest- to least-valued part.

### *Solution*

First, we compute the annual value for each part, obtain the total annual value of materials, and derive the required percentages, which are shown in the table below.

| *Part Number* | *Annual Value* | *Percentage of Total* | *Cumulative Percentage* |
|---|---|---|---|
| M9 | $ 420,000 | 40.61% | 40.61% |
| A5 | 310,000 | 29.97 | 70.58 |
| A7 | 104,000 | 10.06 | 80.64 |
| Q2 | 96,000 | 9.28 | 89.92 |
| A6 | 94,000 | 9.09 | 99.01 |
| L8 | 5,700 | 0.55 | 99.56 |
| M2 | 2,400 | 0.23 | 99.79 |
| L4 | 2,100 | 0.20 | 99.99 |
| Z1 | 100 | 0.01 | 100.00 |
| | Sum = $1,034,300 | | |

**EXHIBIT 6-13 Cumulative Percentage of Total Annual Inventory Value**

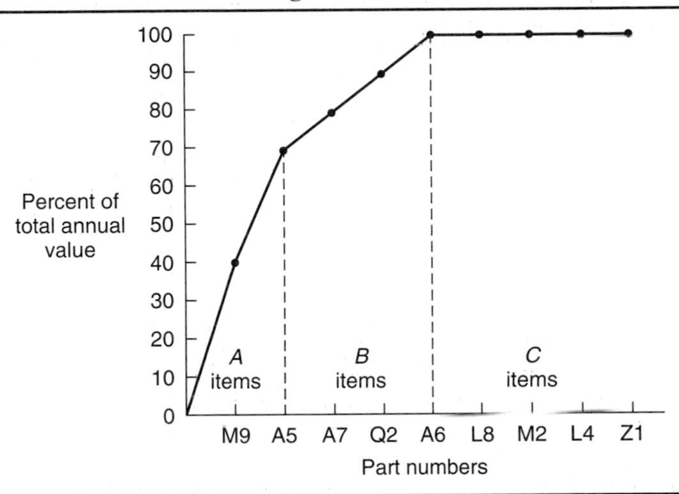


We see that two parts, M9 and A5, account for over 70 percent of the total annual materials value and are likely candidates for treatment as A parts. We might select the next three parts, A7, Q2, and A6, as our class Bs. The remaining items, L8, M2, L4, and Z1, would be the C items. The plot is shown in Exhibit 6-13.

## Exercises

1. Visit Caterpillar's web site (www.cat.com). In the "Shortcuts" window, select the option "Doing Business with Cat" and then download the new supplier questionnaire. Prepare a short report on the types of information that prospective suppliers are asked to provide on the questionnaire.
2. The chapter discussion on partnership versus adversarial buyer–supplier relationships examines 12 dimensions on which the relationship might be rated. A number of organizational types are listed below. For each type, identify the relationship's most crucial dimensions. Explain your reasoning.
   *a.* Aerospace company that is highly project oriented.
   *b.* Chemical company.
   *c.* Foundry.
   *d.* Major accounting firm.
   *e.* U.S. Navy shipyard.
   *f.* Private shipyard faced with severe cost problems.
   *g.* Machine tool manufacturer.
   *h.* Retail hardware store.
   *i.* Integrated circuit manufacturer.
   *j.* Hairstyling salon.

3. You would like to negotiate a long-term (three-year), exclusive contract to sell your grounds mowing and upkeep services to a city government for parks and other public property the city owns. The city's purchasing agent believes that such a contract would not be in the city's best interests because "free competition wouldn't get a chance to work." Prepare a rebuttal, giving specific ways in which the city might benefit from a contract with you.
4. John Revere, operations director at CalComp, Inc., a producer of graphics peripheral products, "was given an ultimatum: Shape up the factory or it would be shipped to Singapore" (Bruce C. P. Rayner, "Made in America: CalComp plots a World-Class Future," *Electronic Business,* August 1, 1988, pp. 28–32). Among Revere's actions to preserve U.S. operations was his challenge to the team designing the new 1023 model pen plotter: Design it with no more than 20 fasteners (screws, bolts, etc.) bought from no more than 20 suppliers located no farther than 20 miles from the CalComp facility in Anaheim, California.

   How would achievement of these three objectives keep production in Anaheim? Cite concepts from the chapter in your answer.
5. David N. Burt reports ("Managing Suppliers up to Speed," *Harvard Business Review,* July–August 1989, pp. 127–35) that Xerox's copier division was in a cost squeeze and losing market share in the 1970s. Corrective actions included reducing its supplier base from 5,000 to 400 companies. Further, "it trained suppliers in statistical quality control (SQC), just-in-time (JIT) manufacturing, and total quality commitment (TQC). Under a program of continuous improvement, it included suppliers in the design of new products, often substituting performance specifications for blueprints in the expectation that suppliers should design final parts themselves."

   Which of the 12 characteristics of supplier partnership given in the chapter was Xerox following in these actions? Explain.
6. A home building contractor presently subcontracts concrete work, mainly pouring driveways, sidewalks, and patios. The average cost for the purchased concrete work at a new home is $2,100. For $29,000 per year, the building contractor can lease equipment (mainly a concrete pumper truck with crane arm) and do the concrete work himself. He will also have to spend about $1,600 to get training for some of his crew. He estimates that if he does the concrete work in-house, his labor and materials costs will average about $1,400 per new house.
   *a.* What will be the break-even volume ($Q_{BE}$) during the first year?
   *b.* Will the break-even volume change in subsequent years? Explain your answer.
   *c.* Draw and fully label the break-even graph for the first year.
7. About Your House (AYH), a real estate agency, posts listings for homes in its "middle and up" bracket on an Internet web page that is maintained by an outside firm; the firm charges $80 per house for a posting of up to three months. Some houses don't sell within the three-month period, and AYH is concerned—as are the house owners who want a sale—when one of these postings "drops off." Recently, one of the office staff at AYH, a computer-savvy part-time university student, suggested that AYH "do its own thing with the web stuff."

   After some checking, the senior partner found that he could get an annual lease for necessary computer equipment, and buy software for $4,200. Further, AYH can lease sufficient web space from a local Internet services provider for $150 per month or for $1,200 annually. Employee training would cost $400. Finally, in-house labor to "post" the details for a house would require two hours, charged at $13 per hour.
   *a.* How many houses would AYH have to post during the first year to break even?
   *b.* Construct and label the break-even graph.

*c.* If AYH decided to continue to "do its own thing," what might change in the second year to affect break-even analysis? Explain.

8. P. Pincher, the purchasing director at Yummy Foods Inc., is examining company travel expenses. Yummy personnel must travel the world over in search of new delicacies to add to Yummy's product lines. Recently, Pincher received an interesting proposal: For an annual fee of $12,000 plus a 4.5 percent commission on all booked travel, a start-up firm offered to make all of Yummy's travel reservations. Through the Internet, Yummy employees need only post their travel requests and specifications, and reservations would be made. Pincher's analysis shows that under the current scheme, each department at Yummy made its travel reservations independently through multiple agencies. Commissions and other fees paid total about 7 percent of the travel costs.
   *a.* What annual dollar volume of travel must Yummy experience in order to break even on the proposed sole-source contract?
   *b.* Construct and label the break-even graph.
   *c.* What other factors might Pincher need to consider in the analysis? Explain.
9. Following are eight items in a firm's inventory. Devise an ABC classification scheme for the items. Show which class each item fits into.

| *Item* | *Unit Cost* | *Annual Demand* |
|---|---|---|
| A | $ 1.35 | 6,200 |
| B | 53.00 | 900 |
| C | 5.20 | 50 |
| D | 92.00 | 120 |
| E | 800.00 | 2 |
| F | 0.25 | 5,000 |
| G | 9,000.00 | 5 |
| H | 15.00 | 18,000 |

10. Several examples of uses of ABC inventory classification were discussed in the chapter. Suggest four more uses and discuss their value.
11. Arrange the following six item numbers into logical A, B, and C classes (put at least one item into each class):

| *Item Number* | *Quantity Demanded Last Year* | *Unit Price* |
|---|---|---|
| 24 | 2 | $ 800 |
| 8 | 10 | 15,000 |
| 37 | 1,000 | 0.05 |
| 92 | 3 | 12 |
| 14 | 80 | 50 |
| 35 | 20 | 1.25 |

12. Arrange the following five item numbers into logical A, B, and C classes (put at least one item into each class):

| *Item Number* | *Quantity Demanded Last Year* | *Unit Cost* |
|---|---|---|
| 109 | 6 | $1,000 |
| 083 | 400 | 0.25 |
| 062 | 10 | 10 |
| 122 | 1 | 280 |
| 030 | 10,000 | 3 |

13. Danielle Weatherby is director of purchasing at Spark-o-Mation. Her company, a producer of sophisticated control and security systems, has had a successful supplier certification program in place for six years; Danielle herself laid much of the groundwork for the program. She attended several good seminars, benchmarked other supplier certification programs, and ensured that her own associates, as well as prospective suppliers, were well trained and informed as the program evolved.

    Spark-o-Mation's supplier base has been reduced to approximately 20 percent of its size since Danielle came on board, and the current suppliers are treated as partners. They've earned it; JIT delivery to the point-of-use is in place, receiving inspection at Spark-o-Mation is a thing of the past, Internet use has reduced the paperwork, and suppliers have active roles in Spark-o-Mation's design efforts. Danielle feels that further reduction in the supplier base would be detrimental to Spark-o-Mation's performance.

    She reads a memo she just received:

    Memo to all Department Heads:

    As you know, earnings have been flat for three quarters, and last quarter's orders were disappointing. Several large customers cite problems with the quality and timely delivery of our product, and some are threatening to go elsewhere for their control systems. I want you all to conduct a thorough (internal) audit of your departmental operations with an eye for change. Let's get together next Tuesday at 8:00 A.M.

    Thanks,
    Mark Smith
    VP, Operations

    Danielle has several thoughts:

    - Clearly, Mark needs help from all of us; I must be a team player on this one.
    - We've already done so much in purchasing. Can we be expected to improve on an already great system?

- I know we're getting good materials; the quality problems must be occurring elsewhere. How can I say that without pointing the finger?
- We get great delivery, but we can't give it. I wonder why?

How should Danielle respond?

14. Adam Pendleton is director of purchasing for THIS Company. THIS (The Healthcare Industry Supply) provides a broad line of MRO items to hospitals and clinics in several western, Rocky Mountain, and Great Plains states and in the western provinces of Canada. One of the best performing of those items is uniforms. THIS offers surgical gowns and laboratory coats in many styles and colors as well as uniforms for nurses, technicians, orderlies, cafeteria employees, and so forth. THIS buys almost all of its uniforms directly from an apparel manufacturer with two plants located in two southeastern states. In both cases, the plant is the town's major employer.

    THIS accounts for approximately 35 percent of the apparel manufacturer's sales. Over the years, THIS has lived with slow but steady price increases. Delivery from the supplier has been adequate, but there is room for improvement. Quality is average at best; often shipments have to be returned for some correction of sizing, color, special insignia, or other mistake.

    Already today, Adam has had to make two calls to the supplier to straighten out details in orders. The uniform supplier stays in his mind as he reads a memo he just received:

    Adam,

    As you know, everyone is screaming about health care costs; our customers are getting hammered to keep their costs down, and the buck is being passed back to us. We've simply got to do two things: First, get our own costs down so we can be more price competitive; second, build up a better quality image. Maybe I've got those two reversed, but you get the idea. I've been wondering about getting rid of some of our poorer suppliers; I think there are better and cheaper sources out there. Any ideas? We can't sit on this; I'd like to get together with you early Tuesday morning if possible.

    Thanks,
    Nell Jones
    Executive VP

    As Adam mulls over Jones's note, several thoughts come to mind:

    - Clearly, Nell needs help and is counting on me to play a key role in this matter.
    - The supplier certification program that I tried to implement three years ago—with little support from upper management—would have made things easier now.
    - If changing suppliers is the answer, the uniform supplier ought to be among the first to go.

    How should Adam respond?

15. The purchasing department at OK Industries uses different buying techniques for various items bought. What are two appropriate buying techniques for each of the following items?
    *a.* Bearings and seals for the factory machinery.
    *b.* Gear assemblies bought as direct materials in quantities of 8,000 per year.
    *c.* A special bottle of drafting ink for the company's one draftperson.
    *d.* Nails used in the maintenance department.

16. Several types of organizations are listed below, each with different kinds of purchases to make:

| | |
|---|---|
| Fashions (apparel) | Car rental company |
| Liquor wholesaler | Glass manufacturer |
| City government | Plastics manufacturer |
| Major home appliance manufacturer | Computer manufacturer |
| Electric power company | Food wholesaler |
| Furniture manufacturer | Shipbuilder |
| Construction contractor | Aerospace company |

   *a.* Discuss some key purchasing techniques that would be useful for four of the organization types.
   *b.* Which types of organizations on the list are most likely to be heavily involved in buying intangibles? Explain.
   *c.* Which types of organizations on the list are more likely to use an approved supplier list? Bid solicitation based on specifications? Blanket orders? Explain.
   *d.* Which types of organizations on the list are most likely to use value analysis? Explain.
17. In recent years public school systems have contracted with private companies to run schools. The contracts may feature incentive payments for raising scores on standardized math and verbal tests. What are some of the pros and cons in these contracts. Discuss.
18. Value analysis often begins by selecting VA projects from old specifications found in the design engineering files. How is value analysis modified in companies using the just-in-time production system? Why?
19. Following is a list of products to be analyzed by value analysis:

   • Home intruder alarm
   • Backpack-style book toter
   • Coaster on which to set drinks
   • Life insurance policy (whole life)
   • Pencil sharpener
   • Mutual fund
   • Bookends
   • Bike handlebars
   • Bike lock
   • Lamp part shown at right

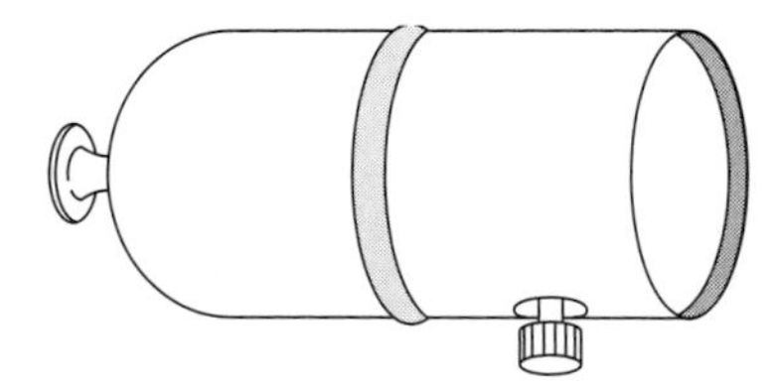

   *a.* Select any four of the above and define their function or functions in two words as discussed in the chapter.
   *b.* Why is function definition an early and precisely done step in value analysis/value engineering? Explain what this step accomplishes, using some of your examples from (*a*).

20. Jane A. Doe has just moved to another city and taken a management job with a company that manufactures patio grills, which was exactly the kind of company she had worked for in her prior city of residence. She finds that her new company has three or four times as many different part numbers going into essentially the same models of grills. What steps might Jane suggest? Discuss.
21. Contact the purchasing department of a service organization in your area. Conduct an interview to determine the level of interest and action on an outsourcing strategy. Write a brief essay in which you evaluate the correctness of the organization's outsourcing activity.

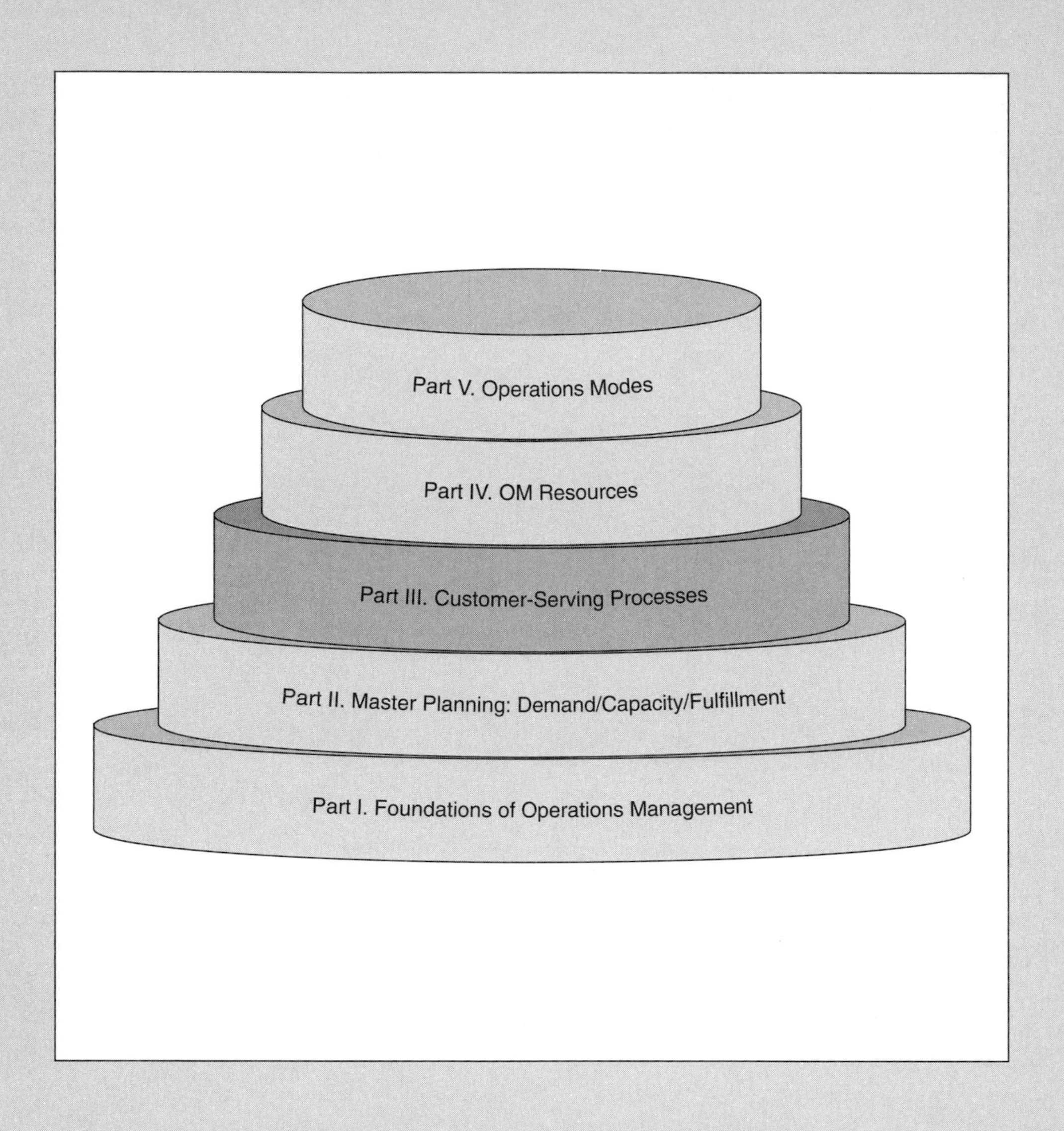
Part V. Operations Modes
Part IV. OM Resources
Part III. Customer-Serving Processes
Part II. Master Planning: Demand/Capacity/Fulfillment
Part I. Foundations of Operations Management

PART

# III CUSTOMER-SERVING PROCESSES



In Part III, we delve deeper into the transformation processes that provide the six basic customer wants—better quality, faster response times, lower costs, greater flexibility, less variability, and better service. Better outputs and better processes for creation of those outputs begin with better designs, but thoughtful implementation and continuous improvement are also needed if the company is to enjoy a competitive advantage. Maintaining the flow and removing process wastes are also prominent themes in this part.

***Points to ponder:*** Actions taken to affect one aspect of a process output—quality, perhaps—often create other effects as well. Moreover, the same processes that give us the outputs we need for company survival can also produce unwanted outputs such as pollution and unsafe conditions.

CHAPTER 7

# DESIGNING FOR CUSTOMERS' NEEDS

The Vancouver division of Hewlett-Packard has realized the benefits of what H-P calls "design for supply-chain management." The division once had made all models of its printers in its factories, then shipped the printers to distribution centers around the world for order processing with customers. Variable demands from different countries, however, created stocking problems: excesses of some printers and shortages of others in the distribution centers. Instead of treating the issue as a forecasting or just an inventory problem, the new idea was to design the printers differently to partially eliminate the problem. Engineers redesigned the printers so that the power-supply module could be attached externally instead of being built in. That permits the factories to ship basic printer models to the distribution centers, who then customize the product for their local markets. This requires that the centers take on new functions: procuring power supply modules and manuals, performing a few final assembly and packing operations, and ensuring quality. While this plan would increase the cost of those operations, it would reduce overall costs and improve customer service.

Source: Hau L. Lee and Corey Billington, "The Evolution of Supply-Chain-Management Models and Practice at Hewlett-Packard," *Interfaces,* September–October 1995, pp. 42–63.

The introductory Hewlett-Packard example illustrates some fundamental points that merit closer attention:

- First, what goes on in one part of an organization usually affects the other parts. In this brief story, we see elements of design, supply-chain management, demand management and forecasting, inventory management, purchasing, assembly, and quality assurance. Did H-P have a design problem? . . . a supply-chain problem? . . . a demand management problem? . . . a quality problem? We needn't go on; the answer to all of those questions is "yes." We might spin the story to emphasize one activity or area (in fact, we do so implicitly just by placing it in the "design chapter") but the unity-of-purpose message—OM Principle 3—is at center stage. Multifunctional teamwork got the job done at H-P.[1]
- The second point is a short but hopefully user-friendly digression: If this is your first exposure to OM, your understanding of the possible impacts of H-P's

power-supply problem on some activities (e.g., forecasting or purchasing) might be greater because those are topics that we have covered. If the impact of the new design on inventory management or quality assurance is not so clear at this time, however, please be patient; those topics lie ahead. OM is a highly integrated field, and discussion of one activity suggests overlap into others as well. Quite frankly, that's what you will find in practice.

- Third, the example reminds us that *designing for customers' needs* (the chapter title) is the aim regardless of where those customers appear along the chain. In the example, the engineers' design efforts first served next-process customers (assemblers and distribution centers) before they served the needs of end consumers. As we shall see, good design takes into account not only the needs of internal and external customers, it addresses broader social and environmental concerns as well.
- Finally, the example also reminds us that design can be a competitive weapon.

In one sense, our look into design is a natural extension of the value analysis and value engineering discussion that closed the last chapter. Just as importantly, though, a new perspective has emerged. In Part III our focus shifts to the processes where customer-serving transformations take place, and design is a major determinant of process success or failure.

## Design: A Core Business Responsibility

A chronic weakness among many companies is undermanagement of design and development. Perhaps part of the fault is that business schools have chronically under-emphasized design as a core business responsibility. Ironically, we probably know more about poor design practices than we do about good ones. But design problems ripple into operations (and into marketing, too, for that matter). Quality deteriorates, processing slows or stops, and costs mount. Customers look elsewhere. In short, competitiveness suffers.

### *Design as a Competitive Weapon*

For an increasing number of companies, however, a lackadaisical attitude about design is a thing of the past. The Into Practice box "Design at Black & Decker" illustrates.

Black & Decker is joined by Apple Computer, Samsung Electronics, Compaq, Hewlett-Packard, Philips Electronics, and Steelcase at the top echelons of consistent corporate winners of the Industrial Design Excellence Awards (IDEA).[2] Although it is an overstatement to suggest that attention to design (alone) saved Black & Decker, it is also reckless to ignore the effects. But the question remains, "Just what is the real business impact of good design?"

To attempt an answer to that question, *BusinessWeek* sponsored a competition run by the Industrial Design Society of America in the closing months of 1999. For the first

INTO PRACTICE

## Design at Black & Decker

Black & Decker, based in Towson, Maryland, is the world's leading producer of power tools, specialty fastening systems, security hardware (lock sets, deadbolts, etc.), and glass container-making equipment. It is also the largest full-line supplier of small household appliances in North America and competes in lawn and garden products, plumbing supplies, and other commercial and industrial product lines.[1] Goods from Black & Decker's 50 manufacturing facilities in the United States and 15 other nations produced revenues of $5.3 billion in 1994. Profits were up by 93 percent from the previous year.[2] Though hard to tell from this description, the mid-1990s found Black & Decker just beginning to emerge from a decade of trouble.

Despite a reputation as the company that defined the power tool industry, Black & Decker's market share began to erode in the mid-1980s. Production costs crept up, product quality slipped, and customer service deteriorated. By 1991, B&D was battling with foreign producers in both professional power-tool and consumer-appliance markets. Professional builders and tradesmen were bypassing B&D in favor of innovative tools from companies like Makita, and they had all but abandoned B&D's DeWalt line—heavy-duty power tools for commercial applications. Likewise, retail consumers rejected B&D's home appliance lines in favor of high-quality, state-of-the-art appliances from Matsushita and Braun.[3]

Black & Decker fought back. Part of its strategy called for a strong design effort, and in 1991 teams from several of B&D's global units banded together to invigorate tired product lines. New designs typically had to meet multiple goals. For example, the DeWalt cordless, pistol-grip drill/screwdriver (shown in Exhibit 7-1A) had to:

- Be compact, easy to carry around, and comfortable for the carpenter who might use it all day.
- Have a cushioned grip, thin enough to grasp yet wide enough to accommodate the battery pack that makes the tool cordless.
- House a motor powerful enough for commercial use. (Designers also opted for a better motor than those available off the shelf.)
- Have a list price in the $170–$200 range.
- Be marketable on a global basis.[4]

The design hallmark of Black & Decker's highly successful SnakeLight (Exhibit 7-1B) is flexibility—in more ways than one. Its tubular, flexible body can be coiled or twisted around objects to provide hands-free illumination in almost any setting. Operational flexibility is further promoted through enhancements to the standard (home model) design: A shop model comes with a mounting bracket, and an automobile model is powered from the vehicle's battery via the cigarette lighter outlet.

Apparently, customers appreciate Black & Decker's design effort; by 1995, the company had reestablished a solid lead in the professional cordless drill market. The design community is also impressed, for both the DeWalt drill and the SnakeLight won gold awards in the 1995 Industrial Design Excellence Award Competition (no company won more than two gold awards).

---

time in formal competition, contestant companies:

> ". . . had to show in quantitative terms the impact that the design had on the bottom line. And the measures were rigorous. . . ." [Judges] wanted to see the connection between the benchmarks [company performance indicators] and the design itself. "What lessons can be drawn from the winners? Good product design in and of itself can have a strong business impact. [but] 'It's not just the product,' says jury chair Charles Jones, director of global product design at Whirlpool Corp. 'The winners unlocked the code of integrating design into the context of the whole business architecture.' "[3]

**EXHIBIT 7-1 Black & Decker's Award-Winning Products**

*A. DeWalt cordless drill/screwdriver. B. Black & Decker Snakelight.*

A

B

Courtesy Black & Decker

Perhaps more importantly, Black & Decker has apparently remained committed to its emphasis on sound design strategy. During the five-year period of 1996–2000, Black & Decker won a total of 12 IDEA competition awards, a number exceeded only by Apple Computer (with 15) and Samsung Electronics (with 14).

Sources: [1]Gary Hoover, Alta Campbell, and Patrick J. Spain, eds. *Hoover's Handbook of American Business* (Austin, TX: The Reference Press, 1995).
[2]"The Fortune 500," *Fortune,* May 15, 1995.
[3]Joseph Weber, "A Better Grip on Hawking Tools," *BusinessWeek,* June 5, 1995, p. 99.
[4]Ibid.
[5]Bruce Nussbaum, "Winners 2000: The Best Product Designs of the Year," *BusinessWeek,* June 12, 2000, pp. 113 ff.

In short, it seems that good product design makes a company more competitive, but when the design effort extends beyond product and into processes, the rewards are even greater.

### *Dual Focus: Outputs and Processes*

Design has two main targets: the outputs (goods and services that customers want) and the processes that provide them. In this chapter, much of our focus will be on the former. As for process design, it is at the core of practically every chapter in the book.

Part III—Chapters 7 through 11—is dedicated to designing and implementing streamlined customer-serving processes. Furthermore, Parts IV and V treat key process components as well.

We hasten to add, however, that several of the topics addressed in this chapter are applicable not only to output design but also to process design. The coverage of reliability later in this chapter, for example, certainly applies to processes. And when we address product design, we include items that can become process equipment, so environmentally friendly design topics (addressed in this chapter) have strong influence on process design.

Both quality analysis (Chapter 9) and methods analysis (Chapter 12) discuss process flowcharts, and other topics in those chapters are almost exclusively process oriented. Positioning of plant and equipment and layout (Chapter 14) also constitute significant process design components. Additional topics in still more chapters take in other elements in a complete process design.

Finally, design of outputs greatly defines choices of process and method. In fact, as we shall see, one criterion of good product and service design is that it bring about ease of processing. Thus, we shall pay particular attention to how design-related activities affect operations and to the contributions operations managers make to design programs. For one thing, we recognize design as the first step in quality.

### *Designed-in Quality*

The problem that plagued Black & Decker—tired product lines—is common to many well-regarded companies. Their goods fare well in the marketplace, which breeds the attitude, "Don't tamper with a winner!" But improved design concepts are taking root. Innovative competitors lurk, ready to beat existing industry standards and crow about it through performance-comparison advertising. For example, computer system hardware and software providers almost always introduce new products by comparing performance of those products with the industry leaders.

Principle 16

Market every improvement.

Since new features stem from market feedback or reflect advances in technology, designs that incorporate those features are likely to advance quality in the eyes of customers. Thus, a strong design program, including one that wins prestigious design awards, is itself one mark of organizational quality.

Design is the first step to quality in another, more specific manner: The quality of output goods and services—and the processes that provide them—begins during the initial design activities. Exhibit 7-2—applicable to products, services, and processes—shows how an iterative action cycle of design, discovery, and improvement provides quality.

In practice, the five phases of the quality action cycle overlap, and sometimes, we're even able to eliminate parts of the third (discovery) phase. Picture it this way: The *ideal* way to attain quality is to have perfectly designed outputs that are created without defect or variation by perfectly functioning processes. When perfection fails to materialize, the next best thing is to discover problems as soon as possible and work quickly to develop remedies for the underlying causes of those problems, before any "bad output" finds its way downstream to customers. Continuous improvement toward the ideal is the hallmark of total quality management.

Reserving analysis of the latter stages of the quality action cycle for Chapter 9, we continue our focus on design by examining some of the strategic issues.

**EXHIBIT 7-2 Quality Action Cycle**

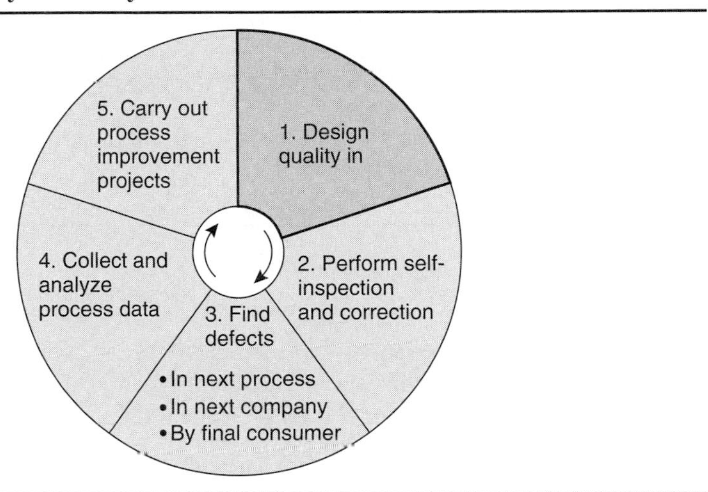


## Research, Design, and Development Strategy

Often, design is financed through a company's research and development (R&D) budget. Regardless of spending levels, however, an effective design strategy for *any* firm is one that overcomes weaknesses inherent in conventional design efforts. But even that is not enough, for contemporary design programs must directly support immediate business needs. Also, customers want faster and better designs that require use of modern design technology. In this section, we explore each of these issues further.

**Research** pushes the boundaries of science, aiming for new products, services, and processes.

**Development** translates those innovations into useful tools for employees (*implementation*) and/or into practical outputs for customers (*commercialization*).

### *Weaknesses of Conventional Design*

Sometimes customers sound off when they encounter poorly designed goods and services. They express themselves on consumer information cards that accompany new products or on feedback forms found on restaurant tables or in bank lobbies; maybe they even write letters. The providers in these cases are fortunate, for they get the feedback necessary to make changes. But more often, customers just take their business elsewhere. Providers don't get the specific details, but—as was the case with Black & Decker—falling revenues signal possible design problems.

Though we applaud attempts to gather customer feedback, some improvements in design programs needn't wait. Many of the problems deserving immediate attention can be traced to one or more of the historical weaknesses of conventional design:

- *Design is slow.* Consequently, a product or service is late to market, arriving after competitors are entrenched. Or, ineffective transformation processes continue to operate because redesigns are delayed. Negative effects ripple through the three other primary line areas: (1) marketing must play catch-up in sales, and advertising can't tout the firm as the innovator; (2) operations also plays catch-up to competitors' postintroduction improvements; and (3) delayed

**EXHIBIT 7-3 Cost of Arriving Late to Market**

| | Number of Months | | | | | |
|---|---|---|---|---|---|---|
| If a company is late to market by: | 6 | 5 | 4 | 3 | 2 | 1 |
| Then average gross profit potential is reduced by: | 33% | 25% | 18% | 13% | 7% | 3% |

Source: McKinsey & Company data, cited in Joseph T. Vesey, "The New Competitors: Thinking in Terms of 'Speed to Market,'" *Manufacturing Engineering,* June 1991, pp. 16–24.

financial returns prolong (or worse, preclude) investment recovery. Exhibit 7-3 shows the financial consequences of being late to market. For example, a company that is late to market by four months can expect an average reduction in gross profits of 18 percent.

- *Design is myopic.* This has been a common blind spot even for Western companies known for commitment to research. Though the problem takes many forms, perhaps the classic example occurs when people take the word *design* to mean *product design,* and pay little or no attention to design of the processes—often made up largely of support services—needed to develop and commercialize discoveries. For service providers, design myopia acts in the same fashion; firms concentrate on the frontline service—the point of customer contact—and give scant attention to design of back-office support services. Resulting problems in those areas detract from any high regard customers might have for the frontline service.
- *Design is staffed-off.* In traditional design settings, designers are a breed apart—literally. They perform their work in isolation from their various customers, including fellow employees who must transform designs into outputs, sell or distribute those outputs, and buy or consume the outputs. Guesses substitute for facts because too many constituencies are not represented at the design table. When designs don't pan out, counterproductive finger pointing ensues.
- *Design is unfocused.* This problem may also appear in several forms, but all suggest the lack of clear guidelines for channeling the design program to remain true to function or purpose. Professors Karl Ulrich and Steven Eppinger note that early European industrial design theory emphasized the importance of precision, simplicity, and economy; it was believed that design should flow from the inside out as form follows function.[4] That is, designers should devote primary attention to the core components that make the "thing" being designed perform its intended function. However, according to Ulrich and Eppinger, dedication to function has not been as strong in the history of North American design strategy. In their haste to embellish external appearance, designers here placed more emphasis on nonfunctional features (e.g., cosmetic add-ons) than on inner workings so critical to functional performance.

Individually, each design weakness is bad enough. When acting in concert, they give customers—internal as well as external—cause to scream. Frequently, the effects of weak design show up as shoddy performance in operations. For example, when a new product or service is a hit and demand exceeds expectations, operations scurries to increase production or service capacity. Undesirable results include poor recruiting, inadequate training, reliance on untested equipment and sources of supply, and postponement of essential maintenance. In these cases, *all* of the right people weren't included during design discussions.

Broadly speaking:

- Whenever a good or service can't be easily built or installed, operated, delivered, or maintained, operations personnel are likely to take the heat for what is actually a manifestation of one or more of the traditional weaknesses of design.
- When it won't sell, marketing gets the blame.
- If it costs too much to provide, accountants feel the pressure to sharpen their pencils.

In general, as industry has begun to recognize the effects of poor design programs, and as employees in all areas of organizations have begun to understand how design has been affecting their work, the reaction has been positive. Comprehensive design programs that attack traditional weaknesses—and do much more—have emerged.

## *Comprehensive Design Program*

Design program specifics differ, of course, but superior companies seem to agree on several common characteristics that describe effective product, service, and process design. Exhibit 7-4 presents a model for a comprehensive design program composed of six integrated and overlapping parts.

The first two parts are strategic planning activities. First, senior managers decide which businesses to pursue and then select products and services to offer within the chosen industries; this determines the overall competitive environment in which the firm will operate. Next, the firm's design strategy must be positioned and implemented within that environment. This requires continuous environmental scanning and analysis—with specific attention to customers' changing wants and competitors' shifting abilities and weaknesses. Since environmental change often evokes modifications in business strategy, some reformulation of design strategy might be needed. (Of course, operations, marketing, and financial strategies might need to be altered as well.)

**Principles 1 & 4**

Get to know the customers and the competitors.

With strategy set, implementation puts that strategy into action. Among companies with leading R&D programs, the multi- or cross-functional team concept is the vehicle of choice for addressing all of the historical design weaknesses. (See the Into Practice box, "One-Coffeepot Teams.") When teams also include customers and suppliers—all close enough to share a coffeepot—design efforts become fully sensitized.

The bottom three boxes in Exhibit 7-4 represent broad categories of design team responsibilities. We've mentioned the collection of customer and competitor data as it affects design strategy, but such information also plays a tactical role during design

**EXHIBIT 7-4 Comprehensive Design Program**

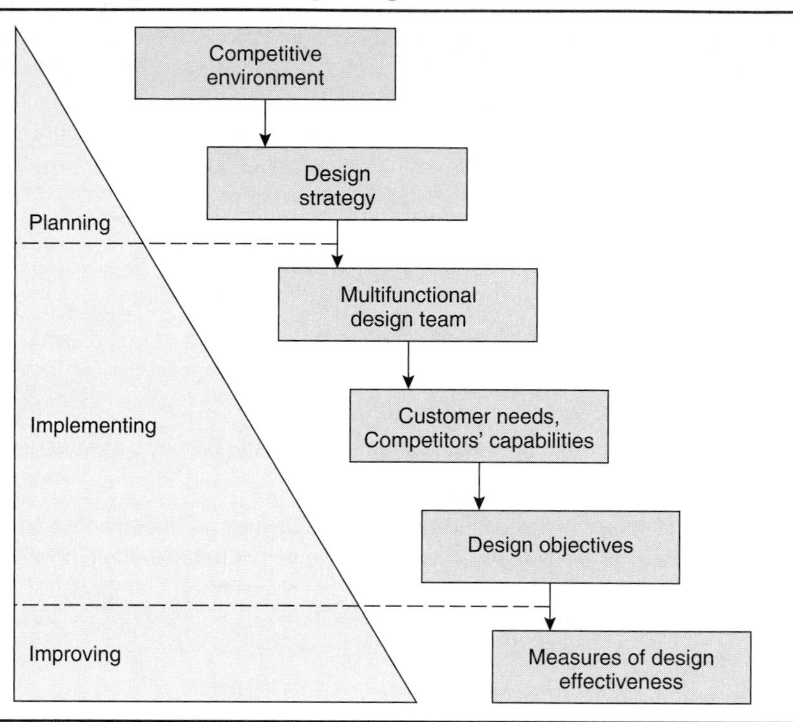


efforts. Later in the chapter, for example, we see how information about customers and competitors is incorporated into quality function deployment.

To overcome the traditional weakness of lack of focus, effective design programs need guidelines and targets, as the next-to-last box in Exhibit 7-4 shows. Objectives will vary from setting to setting, but since our main interest is the design/operations interface, we shall concentrate mostly on operations examples. Finally, represented by the last box, teams must have relevant measures of design program effectiveness. Feedback sparks improvement.

## *Technology in Design*

Arguably, the impact of computer-related technologies is at its most spectacular in the design arena. For decades, increasing processor power (at lower costs) coupled with a vast array of commercial and personal software has made **computer-aided design (CAD)** a natural to even the smallest of companies. The impressive displays of CAD applications in the design of complex durable goods sometimes makes us forget that the personal-computer-based applications for design of business cards, forms, and so forth is really another form of CAD.

For manufacturers of complex products, more specific and powerful **computer-aided engineering (CAE)** applications assist with design concept development and

INTO PRACTICE

## One-Coffeepot Teams

"For your average General Electric Co. researcher accustomed to the quiet, contemplative life in Schenectady, New York, being a member of a 'one-coffeepot' product-development team is no tea party. The teams unite GE researchers, manufacturers, and marketers in a single location, where they can sweep away obstacles to a new lightbulb or locomotive as they swill hot java.

"Lonie Edelheit, GE's senior vice president for research and development says most of the company's researchers have embraced the one-coffeepot concept. In any case, he says, there's no alternative: 'Speed means change. Everybody's got to understand that.' "

Source: Peter Coy, "Blue-Sky Research Comes Down to Earth," *BusinessWeek,* July 3, 1995, pp. 78–80.

specification and analysis of desirable functions. Process design may be enhanced through **computer-aided process planning (CAPP),** often aimed at extending design specifications into the operations activities needed to create the part. More broadly, process design is often accompanied by **process simulation**—trial runs of a computer model of the production flow-control process.

Although further discussion of design technologies is beyond our scope, we can summarize with the caveat: Today, if for no other reason, the shorter lead times demanded by time-based competition mandate that design strategies incorporate some degree of technology.

Thus far in this chapter, we've talked a bit about design strategy. We use the rest of the chapter to examine the remaining elements of the comprehensive design program. Teams are the first topic.

## Design Teams

A theme of this book is the power of teams throughout organizations' activities, but what specifically do multifunctional teams do to improve design? Quite a bit. Furthermore, benefits accrue to both providers and customers: Providers overcome weaknesses in traditional design with powerful design techniques and tools that teams make possible. Customers enjoy improvements evident in final designs, often having made direct contributions to those designs. We will discuss but two of the more significant items in each category. First, teams facilitate concept development and make concurrent design possible. Second, when design is team based, products, services, and processes are more likely to be more socially responsible.

### *Concept Development*

At the heart of any design program lies the notion of *concept development.* Crawford defines a **design concept** as "a combination of verbal and/or prototype form that tells what is going to be changed and how the customer stands to gain (and lose)."[5] Three essential parts must exist for an idea or plan to be elevated to the status of concept:

- *Form.* This is the physical thing itself—its shape, materials content, and so on. In the case of a service, form is often described by the steps needed to provide the service.
- *Technology.* The principles, techniques, equipment, mechanics, policies, and so forth to be employed in creating or attaining the good or service collectively constitute the technology. Examples include a particular assembly sequence or delivery plan. (Perhaps we're not stretching to suggest that Crawford's *technology* is essentially the *process.*)
- *Benefit.* Benefit is the value the customer plans to derive from the good or service.

According to Ulrich and Eppinger, design concept development begins with *concept generation,* itself a procedure. It transforms a set of customer needs and target specifications into a set of possible design concepts from which the team will select the most promising alternative.[6] One part of concept generation is **competitive analysis**—investigation of competitors' offerings.

Benchmarking (discussed in Chapter 8), a newer "sibling" of competitive analysis, seeks out best practices and products anywhere, not just from competitors.

For services, competitive analysis requires going to the competitor, being served, and taking extensive notes for later use by your own service design teams. In manufacturing, the usual procedure is to buy a competitor's product and bring it in for thorough study, perhaps including complete disassembly, which is called *reverse engineering.*

After selection of the most promising design concept, development continues with refinements of specifications, economic analyses, and other fine-tuning activities. As the design nears final form, interest naturally shifts to production and delivery systems. Again, with effective use of team-based design, the transition will be smooth, for those charged with process design and operation will have already been active contributors to the design effort. That is, concurrent design will be ongoing.

## *Concurrent Design*

**Concurrent design,** also known as **simultaneous engineering,** occurs when contributors to an overall design effort provide their expertise at the same time (concurrently) while working as a team instead of as isolated functional specialists working in serial fashion. Concurrent design, sometimes with much input from suppliers, is the norm in many leading companies; the examples from the automobile and the consumer-products industries in the accompanying Into Practice box illustrate.

From an operations perspective, significant benefits stem from getting those who design, operate, and maintain transformation processes included early and on the same team as those who design products. James Lardner, vice president at Deere and Company, maintains that "we can cut capital investment for automation by 50%–60% just by getting the design and manufacturing people together from the beginning."[7] Though our focus is operations, we emphasize that a full concurrent-design team also includes people from marketing, finance, purchasing, human resources, and other inside departments; customers, suppliers, and freight carriers; and perhaps community and regulatory officials.

INTO PRACTICE

## Concurrent Design in the Auto Industry

"Today's suppliers are part and parcel of the process," says Jay Hay, vice president of the Ford program office at Milford, Ohio, based SDRC. "Suppliers are now designing 50% or more of today's cars." Direct communications and common access to shared computer design files among customer-supplier team members are essential. That way, suppliers are always sure that they are viewing the most up-to-date designs. Kathy Gross, CAD designer at ADAC Plastics, Inc. [Grand Rapids, MI] says, "We can go into [the database files] for the newest review of glass or sheet metal design. Other [Ford] suppliers can pull up our part to see how our latch will pick up their rod."

Source: Laurie Ann Toupin, "The Drive to Digital Design," *Design News Online,* February 7, 2000.

## Concurrent Design at Rubbermaid

"Unlike many consumer-product companies, [Rubbermaid] does no test marketing. Instead, [it] has created entrepreneurial teams of five to seven members in each of its four dozen product categories. Each team includes a product manager, research and manufacturing engineers, and financial, sales, and marketing executives. The teams conceive their own products, shepherding them from the design stage to the marketplace."

Source: Valerie Reitman, "Rubbermaid Turns Up Plenty of Profit in the Mundane," *The Wall Street Journal,* March 27, 1992.

When a business is young or small, teaming up for effective design is easy and natural. But as the firm grows, people split off into functional specialties. In that overspecialized system, product designers are accused of "throwing the design over the wall" to manufacturing or service process designers and saying in effect, "Let's see you figure out how to build that!" When process planners need to make changes, the design goes back "over the wall" to product designers, with the implication that, "If you had been smart enough to create a producible design in the first place . . ." Round after round of changes and attempts at production follow, usually creating disruptions and increased costs throughout the organization.

In manufacturing, redesign results in **engineering change orders (ECOs),** each of which can go through many time-consuming and costly approval steps.

Even when product life cycles are long, concurrent design has merit. For one thing, it avoids time-consuming misunderstandings and costly "do-overs" during the design phase. For another, it reduces costly bugs, errors, rework, and warranty claims during production, delivery, and customer use phases. "If a bonus system or orientation program needs to be redesigned because employees could not understand it, this is clearly 'rework.' "[8]

### *Socially Responsible Design*

The team approach has yet another advantage. When we truly think about including *all customer constituencies,* a broader range of design functions emerges and that, in turn,

CONTRAST

## Design

### Over-the-Wall Design

- Becomes common practice as organization grows and splits into functional departments.
- Common, especially, in businesses, with long product lives (little urgency to develop new products).
- Tends to be slow.
- Tends to require several costly rounds of debugging.

### Concurrent (Team) Design

- Tends to be common practice in very small organizations and where product redesigns occur often.
- Elevated competition has made it common in consumer electronics, cars, consumer credit, mortgage loans, and so on.
- Is fast and avoids problems (design rework) stemming from poor coordination and lack of shared information.

suggests more design options. Environmentally friendly designs fall under the umbrella of social responsibility, but we reserve treatment of those issues to later in the chapter.

Sometimes reaction to a social concern opens up a set of promising new design options. For example, in attempting to design products easily operable by disabled consumers, designers have unearthed an attractive new approach called **universal design.**[9] It often turns out that, say, easy-to-open doors or easy-to-access information services are popular with young and old, able and disabled.

The Trace Research and Development Center at the University of Wisconsin (Madison) is widely known for its attention to universal designs. Professor Gregg Vanderheiden, founder and director of the Trace Center, sums up his mission:

> The bottom line for us is not how accessible you can make things, but how accessible and usable you can make standard, mass-market, attractive, money-making, profitable products. If the last string of adjectives isn't true, then we're not interested because it has no relevance to manufacturing or sales of standard products.
>
> The focus of our center is entirely on how to design standard products so that they can be sold to people who may or may not have disabilities, or may or may not acquire them. And how you design [those products] so that people who don't have disabilities would say, "That's the one I want to buy."[10]

Universal designs are good news for the maker because it means greater standardization. Also, design teams can focus their energies on perfecting the fewer designs they work with. Provider and customer benefit; it's a win-win situation.

In this section, we've looked at selected strengths of team-based design. Next, we see how those benefits and others can be integrated within the context of a powerful yet relatively new tool—quality function deployment.

## Quality Function Deployment

**Quality function deployment (QFD)** provides a structured way of viewing the big picture and of organizing the details of both product and process design.[11] The structure comes from a series of matrices. The first and most important matrix spells out customer needs—the "voice of the customer"—and compares the company's and key competitors' abilities to satisfy those needs. When the matrix is filled in and "roofed over," it takes the shape of a house—the **house of quality.**

QFD: Procedure for transforming customer requirements and competitor capabilities into provider targets, extending from design research to operations, marketing, and distribution.

Exhibit 7-5 is a house of quality developed with the aid of the owners of a chain of dry-cleaning stores. The owners might use the matrix for improving one or more of their existing stores or for planning a new one. We interpret the QFD matrix as follows:

Like many quality techniques, QFD got its start in manufacturing; that may change as its uses in services (e.g., Exhibit 7-5) become better known.

- The central portion shows what the customer wants and how to provide it.
- Symbols in the central portion show strong, medium, small, or no relationship between whats and hows. A double circle, strong, worth nine relationship points, appears six times. For example, a "perfect press" strongly depends on "firm press pads" and "good equipment maintenance," which account for two of the double circles.
- The five customer requirements are ranked 1 to 5 in importance. "Completely clean" is the customers' number-one concern; "no delay at counter" gets a 5.
- The ratings in each *how* column add up to an importance weighting. Good training, of medium importance for satisfying all five customer requirements, adds up to 15 points, which is second in importance to equipment maintenance, with 19 points.
- The house's roof correlates each *how* with each other factor. Only four of the combinations show a correlation. The double circle indicates a strong correlation between "good equipment maintenance" and "no rust in steam-press lines," meaning that steam-press components are subject to rust and thus must be cleaned out or replaced regularly.
- Target values, in the "basement" of the house, give a numeric target for each *how:* Change press pads monthly to keep them firm.
- The house's "sub-basement" and right wing show comparisons of the company and key competitors. We see at the bottom that the company is slightly better than competitors A and B in keeping solvent clean, in avoiding rust, and in maintenance. Ratings in the right wing show that both competitors are better in counter delays and quick turnaround.

The tough part for the design team is getting good data to enter into the matrix. Data sources may include focus groups, surveys, studies, comparison shopping, competitive analysis, public information, calculations, and reckoning.

The design team uses the basic house of quality in the product-planning stage. More detailed matrices may be developed for three remaining stages of design—that is, product design, process planning, and process control planning (see Exhibit 7-6).[12]

**EXHIBIT 7-5 "House of Quality" for a Dry Cleaner**

Correlation (roof):

- Good training – Clean D.C. solvent: ○ (Positive)
- Good training – Clean D.C. filters: ○ (Positive)
- Good training – No rust in S.P. lines: ○ (Positive)
- No rust in S.P. lines – Good equipment maintenance: ◎ (Strong positive)

**Correlation:**
◎ Strong positive
○ Positive
× Negative
✳ Strong negative

| Customer requirements (Operating requirements →) | Importance to customer | Good training | Clean D.C. solvent | Clean D.C. filters | No rust in S.P. lines | Firm press pads | Good equipment maintenance | Competitive evaluation (X = Us, A = Comp. A, B = Comp. B. (5 is best)) 1 2 3 4 5 |
|---|---|---|---|---|---|---|---|---|
| Completely clean | 1 | ○ | ◎ | ◎ | ◎ | | ◎ | AB: 3, X: 4 |
| Perfect press | 2 | ○ | | | | ◎ | ◎ | B: 1, A: 2, X: 3 |
| No delay at counter | 5 | ○ | | | | | | X: 2, B: 3, A: 5 |
| Quick turnaround | 3 | ○ | | | | | △ | X: 1, A: 3, B: 4 |
| Friendly service | 4 | ○ | | | | | | AB: 1, X: 2 |
| Importance weighting | | 15 | 9 | 9 | 9 | 9 | 19 | |
| Target values | | 4-hr formal, 2-wk. OJT | Visual daily | Visual daily, clean monthly | Visual daily | Change monthly | Monthly, plus as needed | |
| Technical evaluation (1–5) | | X: 2, A: 1, B: 5 | X: 3, A: 2, B: 1 | X: 2, A: 5, B: 1 | X: 4, B: 3, A: 2 | X: 4, B: 5, A: 3 | X: 5, A: 4, B: 3 | |

**Relationships:**
◎ Strong = 9
○ Medium = 3
△ Small = 1

**EXHIBIT 7-6 QFD Overview**

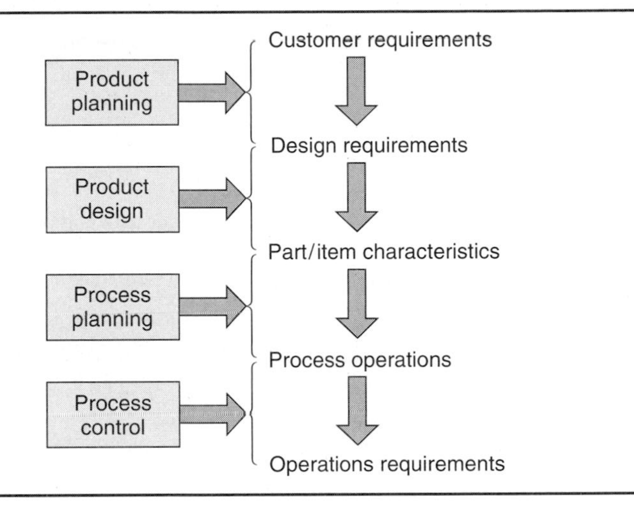


## Design Objectives

Quality function deployment is at its best when the aim is to satisfy a prescribed set of customer needs in the face of rather well-defined competitors' capabilities. Design objectives flow somewhat naturally from specific performance targets. On a broader level, however, general guidelines have emerged and are gaining widespread acceptance by design teams across a variety of industries. Though the guidelines do pose targets for product designs, operations managers can appreciate their substantial emphasis on design of transformation processes as well.

In this section, we examine design-for-operations guidelines and then turn to other design objectives.

### *Design for Operations: Guidelines*

Design lore is replete with examples of what have come to be known as DFX criteria: Design for X, which can mean design for quality, reliability, or other desired ends. Sometimes product designers overlook the realities of frontline operations: the moment of truth with an unpredictable customer or the many sources of surprise, variation, agony, and error in operations. The design team may be able to avoid some of these pitfalls by following design-for-operations guidelines, which have evolved from the works of professors Geoffrey Boothroyd and Peter Dewhurst.[13]

In the early 1980s, Boothroyd and Dewhurst began to publish on design for operations for manufactured products. By the 1990s, tens of thousands of design engineers had studied **design for manufacture and assembly (DFMA).** (For a comprehensive Boothroyd-Dewhurst example, see Solved Problem 2 at the end of the chapter).

Although the DFMA guidelines were aimed at manufacturing, they have proven to be general enough to apply well to services; thus, we use the more general term, **design for operations (DFO).** Exhibit 7-7 lists one version of DFO guidelines.

**EXHIBIT 7-7 Design for Operations Guidelines**

**General Guidelines:**
1. Design to target markets and target costs.
2. Minimize number of parts and number of operations.

**Quality Guidelines:**
3. Ensure that customer requirements are known and design to those requirements.
4. Ensure that process capabilities are known (those in your firm and of your suppliers) and design to those capabilities.
5. Use standard procedures, materials, and processes with already known and proven quality.

**Operability Guidelines:**
6. Design multifunctional/multiuse components and service elements and modules.
7. Design for ease of joining, separating, rejoining (goods) and ease of coupling/uncoupling (services).
8. Design for one-way assembly, one-way travel (avoid backtracking and return visits).
9. Avoid special fasteners and connectors (goods) and off-line or misfit service elements.
10. Avoid fragile designs requiring extraordinary effort or attentiveness—or that otherwise tempt substandard or unsafe performance.

The first two guidelines are general in that they have wide-ranging benefits.

**1. Target Markets and Target Costs.** Customer and marketing representatives bring sales targets, profit data, and competitors' pricing policies to the team. If it looks like, for example, the new product's production costs or the proposed process's operating costs will exceed competitive levels by a great deal, the project gets dropped quickly.[14] If the gap is closer, the team may opt to experiment on ways to reduce build or operating costs and thus salvage the project.

A newer tool approaches costs from a different yet complementary view. By applying the concepts and mathematics associated with the Taguchi loss function (in Chapter 8), the team's engineering and operating experts are able to project savings resulting from designs that reduce product or process variation.[15] Taguchi's broad concept includes losses (e.g., stemming from design deficiencies) to society, not just to the provider or the customer.[16]

Principle 5

A few good product/service components.

**2. Minimize Parts and Operations.** The Boothroyd-Dewhurst methodology focuses especially on this guideline, minimizing the number of parts or, outside of manufacturing, the number of operations. For example, input client data one time, not several times. Exhibit 7-8 illustrates a manufacturing example. The design team is minimizing number of parts as it designs "a better mouse." Each part is analyzed to ascertain the best type of material and the best manufacturing method.

The next three guidelines pertain to quality: quality requirements of the customer (guideline 3), quality capabilities of internal and external processes (guideline 4), and use of standardization to make quality easier to deliver (guideline 5).

**Exhibit 7-8 Designing a Better Mouse**

*DFMA team designs a better mouse. New design cuts screws from seven to zero, assembly adjustments from eight to zero, assembly time from 592 to 277 seconds; also cuts material costs 47 percent, package costs 59 percent.*

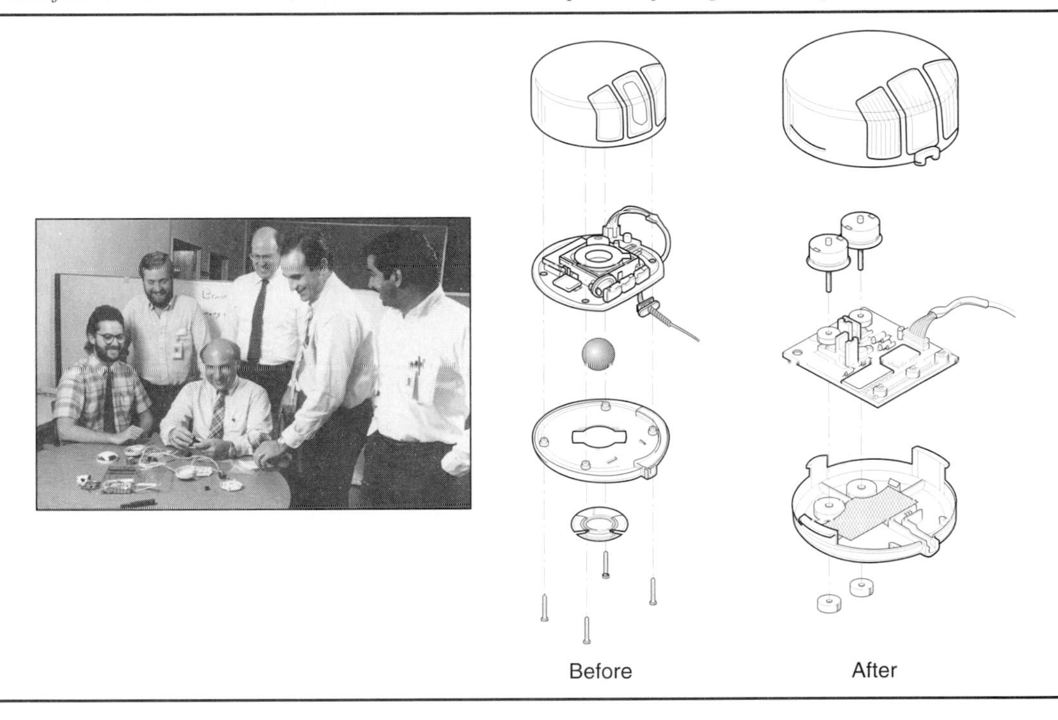


**3. Customer Requirements.** Guideline 3 calls for the design team to discover customers' precise requirements and to keep abreast of changes during the design project. Requirements may specify physical characteristics, operating parameters, or processing needs. The design team must be clear on the matter because one of its jobs is to transform requirements into specifications and tolerances.

**Principle 10**

Eliminate error and process variation.

Good suppliers, inside or outside the firm, do whatever they can to find out their customers' real requirements, avoid misunderstanding, and make their customers look good. When communications are good, design tips flow both ways, and sometimes it's the customer who makes the supplier look good.

**4. Process Capability.** Guideline 4, designing to process capability, affects the design team in two ways. First, the team is held responsible if the design cannot easily be delivered or produced using available processes (including those of the supplier). Second, in being held responsible, the design team must become familiar with process capabilities, which usually are measurable to some degree.

Capability measures might include years of experience, amount of cross-training, and educational attainment of associates; documentation of procedures; safety devices in place; low equipment failure rates; and ability to achieve and hold tolerances. The latter may be measured using the process capability index, $C_{pk}$, which has become important in manufacturing in recent years. (We address $C_{pk}$ in Chapter 9).

**5. Standard Procedures, Materials, and Processes.** The fifth guideline advises designers to favor standard procedures, materials, and processes. Related to standardization are questions about creativity, satisfying customer needs for variety, and new opportunities for global marketing. Each of these issues warrants brief discussion.

***Standardization.*** Nonstandard designs are risky because of lack of knowledge about their performance. Xerox found this out the hard way. One consultant observed that, for lack of competition, the company's large staff of bright engineers developed machines with "incredibly complex technology. . . . Everything inside a Xerox machine was special. You could not go out and use a normal nut. It had to be a specially designed nut. The concept of using as many standard parts as possible was not even thought of."[17] Design complexities led to costly field service to make copiers work properly. High costs opened the door to competition, which actually was good for Xerox.

***Standardization and Creativity.*** Now Xerox—a 1990 Malcolm Baldrige Award winner—along with many other companies, has firm policies on use of standard parts. Some apply the guideline quantitatively. For example, a plastics recycling team at Xerox worked to reduce the 500-odd plastic formulations that its designers had been using. The team initially recommended fewer than 50 formulations—now they are down to about 10.[18]

The "5-day automobile," discussed in Chapter 2, will depend heavily on part and process standardization.

***Standardization and Personalized Design.*** Standardization may be the only way to make personalized design profitable: Carefully design a small number of standard elements that can be delivered in volume at low cost, and have the flexibility to quickly customize them right in front of the customer.

This formula—personalization but with standard components—is the basis for Panasonic's personalized bicycle, which starts out with customer fitting in a retail store.[19] The clerk enters customer measurements, color choice, and other specs (see Exhibit 7-9A) into a computer, and a computer-aided design routine at the factory produces a customized blueprint in three minutes.

While final assembly is still mostly manual, frame welding employs flexible automation. Racks of a limited number of standard frame models surround the automation equipment and are selected following the customer's specs.

Customer-run greeting card machines follow much the same formula (see Exhibit 7-9B). A large variety of customer choices are possible from a few standardized components, such as plain card, envelope, and inks. According to American Greetings Corp. president Edward Fruchtenbaum, the CreataCard machine is the "ultimate combination of just-in-time manufacturing and micro-marketing."[20]

**Principle 16**

Market every improvement.

***Standardization and Globalization.*** Taken in conjunction with guideline 2 (minimize parts and operations), this guideline has strategic implications. As goods and services are designed with fewer, more standardized components and operations, costs go down and quality becomes more dependable. In turn, this increases their appeal, sometimes to the point where people around the globe know about and want the item.

**EXHIBIT 7-9 Personalized Design from Standard Components**

*A. 11,231,862 variations of Panasonic bicycle. Customer fitting in retail store. B. Personalized greeting card machines. C. Online version of personalized card design.*

A

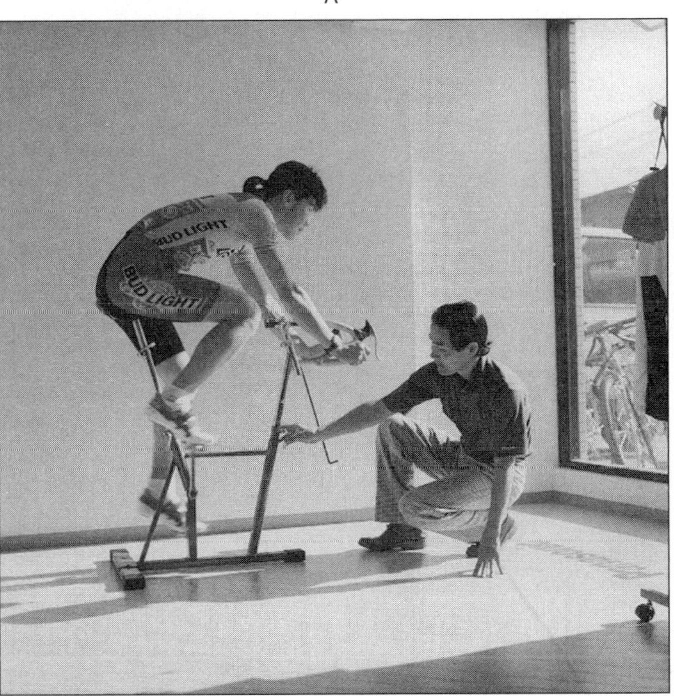


Used by permission of Matrix, Inc.

B

Used by permission of American Greetings Corp.

C

AP/Wide World.

Guidelines 6 through 10 focus on operability—avoiding difficulties in frontline operations.

**6. Multifunctional/Multiuse Elements and Modules.** The do-it-yourself industry is alive and thriving. Buy some plumbing modules, shelving components, or mix-and-match clothing, and combine to taste. Good design in accordance with this guideline makes it possible.

Insurance companies, investment funds, health care, and other service companies do much the same thing: design a self-contained service module (e.g., payroll processing) and offer it to companies that seek ways of cutting their own overhead and getting out of service areas beyond their expertise. For an example of manufacturing modules, see the Into Practice box, "Modular Design . . . at Scania Truck."

**7. Ease of Joining/Separating, Coupling/Uncoupling.** Push, click, snap, whirr. That's the sound of the modern keyboard, clock, or auto dashboard being assembled. It's easy, quick, and if the design team has heeded guideline 7, mostly error-free.

Are snap-together connections hard to notice? That's good—until someone needs to take off a cover for repair, or until the junked unit gets to the recycler to be separated

INTO PRACTICE

## Modular Design with Standardized Parts—Competitive Advantage at Scania Truck

"Scania, the Swedish maker of heavy-duty trucks, buses, and diesel engines, has parlayed a modular design strategy into a robust formula for low costs and sustained profitability." A comparison of Scania and Volvo truck performance in the 1980s is telling. The two companies sold about the same number of trucks in those years. Volvo's trucks, however, required about twice as many part numbers. (Each different part gets a different number, so "part numbers" is widely used in industry to indicate variety of parts.) By designing from half as many part numbers, Scania's product development costs averaged about half of Volvo's costs. Moreover, Scania enjoys a higher customer retention rate than either of its two main European rivals. Scania retains about 80 percent, Volvo about 60 percent, and Mercedes-Benz trucks about 60 percent.

It took Scania's design engineers about 15 years to achieve, by 1980, what they consider to be full-scale modularization and component standardization. Scania's product design route to success is notably different from that of many other manufacturers. The Toyota production system, for example, is based primarily on process simplification and flexibility rather than component design. Leif Östling, Scania's general manager, explains the cost advantages of Scania's design concept: Reducing part numbers results in higher production volumes of each retained part. He maintains that production costs per unit fall about 10 percent when standardization permits the production quantity of the part to double. Furthermore, distribution costs (from ordering and storing) fall about 30 percent when part numbers are cut in half.

Source: H. Thomas Johnson and Anders Bröms, "The Spirit in the Walls: A Pattern for High Performance at Scania," *Target*, May/June 1995, pp. 9–17.

into reusable materials. Today's designer needs extra ingenuity to make disassembly and separation as easy as push-and-snap assembly. (Yet another DFX term: *design for disassembly,* or *DFDA*.)

A salesperson with cellular phone and data diskette can go to work on the road, at home, or in the sales office if process permits easy service coupling/uncoupling as the need arises. Increasingly, facilities (in hotels, airlines, restaurants, etc.) are designed so that people can easily plug in and plug out.

**8. One-Way Assembly and Travel.** Who hasn't had to stand in one line for a certain service element, wait in another line for the next element, and then later go back to the first line? Guideline 8 aims at avoiding that kind of backtracking and in manufacturing is helping to revitalize some assembly plants. For example, IBM was an early convert to designing products for layered assembly. The bottom layer may be the box itself. Then comes a bottom plastic cover for, say, a personal computer. Next are the inside components, then the top cover and loose accessories, and finally the top of the box. Since all assembly motions are up and down, IBM can equip the assembly lines with its own simple pick-and-place robots; no need for elaborate, costly robots with multiple axes of motion.

**9. Avoid Special Fastening and Fitting.** This guideline avoids special steps. In manufacturing, the guideline applies especially to connectors and fasteners (*fasteners* is industry's term for bolts, washers, nuts, screws, etc.). For example, the number of screws in one of IBM's redesigned LaserPrinters was cut from dozens to a handful. A misfit service would include one that requires a server to leave a client in order to fetch a file folder or hunt down a manager for an approval.

**10. Avoid Fragile Designs.** Tendencies or temptations to take unsafe shortcuts, to be careless with sensitive equipment, to be brusque with customers, to steal, or otherwise misperform are partly avoidable by using designs that make such tendencies difficult.

One approach is to design controls into the process. Examples: design the process to maintain strict segregation of personal and business possessions, clearly labeled locations for all files and materials, easy access to backup help, and safety-guard gates to keep associates from blundering into an unsafe area.

Another approach is the use of **robust design** concepts. Examples: shatter-resistant glass, a waterproof watch, carpeting that comes clean even if smeared with black grease, and keyboards you can spill Coke on.

### *Design for Reliability and Serviceability*

The DFO quality guidelines, especially guideline 3, are deliberately quite broad—they must encompass diverse customer needs and they must apply to both product and process quality. We can illustrate how the guidelines are put into practice, however, by looking at reliability and serviceability.

**Reliability** is the probability that an item will function as planned over a given time period. It may be calculated as follows:

$$R = e^{-\lambda t} \qquad (7\text{-}1)$$

where

$R =$ Reliability, a value from 0 to 1.0

$e =$ the base of natural logarithms (approximately 2.718)

$\lambda =$ a constant failure rate

$t =$ specified point in time

**Serviceability** is a bit harder to define; it means different things to various constituencies. One common thread, however, is the degree to which an item may be maintained: either kept in service through preventive maintenance or restored to service after a breakdown. Popular measures that relate to serviceability include:

At process-industry plants (e.g., refineries), where failures can be catastrophic, emphasis is on prevention of failure through planned, regularly scheduled maintenance. Many such facilities place primary interest in *mean time between planned maintenance* (MTBPM) rather than MTBF.

- **Failure rate,** denoted by the Greek letter *lambda* ($\lambda$), is the average number of times an item is expected to fail within a given time period. As we saw in Equation 7-1, lambda is the critical determinant of reliability.
- **Mean time between failures (MTBF)** is the average time between failures of a repairable item, or the average time to first failure of a nonrepairable item. MTBF is usually denoted by the Greek letter *mu* ($\mu$) MTBF is the inverse of failure rate; that is, $\mu = 1/\lambda$.
- **Mean time to repair (MTTR)** is the average time required to repair (or replace) assuming that appropriate parts and sufficient expertise are available. In some circles, MTTR is used almost synonymously with serviceability.
- **Availability** is the proportion of time that a resource is ready for use. One version of availability ($A$) considers only designated operating time (thus excluding planned downtime for preventive maintenance, overhauls, etc.) and combines MTBF and MTTR:

$$A = \frac{\text{MTBF}}{\text{MTBF} + \text{MTTR}} \tag{7-2}$$

Examples 7-1 and 7-2 illustrate how design teams incorporate these measures into their work.

### Example 7-1: Battery Reliability

Westport Communications Systems builds heavy-duty, portable radios for use by emergency service personnel such as firefighters and rescue personnel. The standard rechargeable batteries Westport has been buying to package with its radios have a rated MTBF of 10 hours under conditions of normal use; failure is said to occur when battery charge fails to register at a prescribed point on a test meter. A representative from the battery supplier announced that a design team was working on a new deluxe battery that would have an MTBF rating of 20 hours. What effect would the new battery have on the performance reliability of the radios? What other options might Westport suggest to its customers?

*Solution*

Westport employees can observe the effects on reliability by constructing reliability curves—which demonstrate reliability decline over time—for both the standard and deluxe batteries. They must first invert each MTBF value to obtain the failure rate, $\lambda$, for each battery:

$$\text{Standard battery: } \lambda = 1/\mu = 1/10 = 0.10 \text{ failure per hour}$$

$$\text{Deluxe battery: } \lambda = 1/\mu = 1/20 = 0.05 \text{ failure per hour}$$

Then, from Equation 7-1, reliability values for selected time values are determined. For example, reliability of the standard battery after three hours of service is

$$R = e^{-(\lambda)(t)} = e^{-(0.1 \text{ failure/hr.})(3 \text{ hrs.})} = e^{-0.3} = 0.74$$

Thus, there is a 74 percent chance that a battery will continue to retain the prescribed charge after three hours of operation. A note of caution: This is an average; some batteries will last longer, others not as long. By repeating the calculation for various time points and then doing the same for the deluxe battery, a table of reliability values may be constructed:

| | Reliability Values | | | | | |
|---|---|---|---|---|---|---|
| Time (hours) | 1 | 2 | 3 | 4 | 5 | 6 |
| Standard battery (MTBF = 10 hours) | 0.90 | 0.82 | 0.74 | 0.67 | 0.61 | 0.55 |
| Deluxe battery (MTBF = 20 hours) | 0.95 | 0.90 | 0.86 | 0.82 | 0.78 | 0.74 |

Exhibit 7-10A shows the reliability graphs for the two batteries, plotted from data in the table. The time could be extended, of course, but the general downward trend would continue. If a customer stated that even greater reliability was needed, Westport might suggest that they keep sets of spare batteries and change them at regular intervals, say, every hour. In such a case, reliability would be approximately as shown in Exhibit 7-10B, assuming the customer had elected to use standard batteries.

**EXHIBIT 7-10 Battery Reliability Curves**

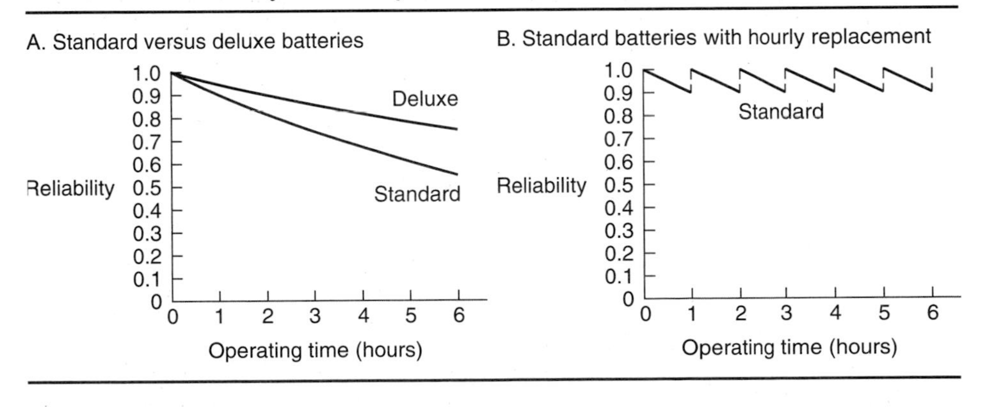

## Example 7-2: Ensuring Resource Availability

A redesign team is planning modifications to a line of its high-speed office photocopiers. A major customer's representative is on the team and has requested that every effort be made to provide an availability rating of at least 0.96. The historical MTBF for that line of photocopiers is 50 hours and the MTTR is 3 hours. What options might the team consider?

*Solution*

Initial availability calculations reveal the magnitude of the problem. From Equation 7-2:

$$A = \frac{50}{50 + 3} = 0.94$$

The customer has requested a higher availability than currently exists, so that problem must be addressed. Team members suggest two approaches: First, the team might try to achieve a higher MTBF rating by designing out failure-prone components. Suppose one design alternative could result in an MTBF of 60 hours. Application of Equation 7-2 reveals:

$$A = \frac{60}{60 + 3} = 0.95$$

Improvement is evident, but more is needed. An alternative approach, suggested by team members who have operated and maintained the photocopiers, focuses on increased parts standardization and easier compartment access; their aim is a shorter repair time. Their estimates show a realistic value of two hours for MTTR. That, in turn, results in an availability rating of $50/52$, or 0.96, the figure specified by the customer. Of course, the team ought to implement both changes, improving availability even more.

---

Example 7-1 showed that designers might be able to increase reliability by choosing a more robust component—in the example, a battery with a larger MTBF. Or, they might suggest that operators replace the component at regular intervals (e.g., change batteries hourly). But what if the best, perhaps state-of-the-art, component is already in place, and changeover is impractical or impossible? Often, the answer lies in improving reliability through redundancy—the backup parachute idea. The technique is popular with process designers stymied by a weak-link (unreliable), but necessary, system component. A simple example borrowed from basic electrical circuit design illustrates.

In circuits, parallel connections allow each circuit branch to operate independently (or very nearly so); loss of one branch doesn't interfere with operation of other branches. Failure of one light bulb, for instance, won't knock out bulbs on other branches, and the overall job (i.e., lighting a space) still gets done. Suppose item $A$ in Exhibit 7-11A (maybe just a lightbulb, but it could be any component, or an entire service process) has a reliability, which can be determined by using Equation 7-1, of 0.9 at time equal to one week. The process reliability between points $X$ and $Y$, then, is simply 0.9 at the end of any one-week operating period.

Now, suppose another $A$ is added, operating independently of (or parallel to) the first. Exhibit 7-11B illustrates. System or process reliability between points $X$ and $Y$ at

**EXHIBIT 7-11 Improving Process Reliability through Redundancy**

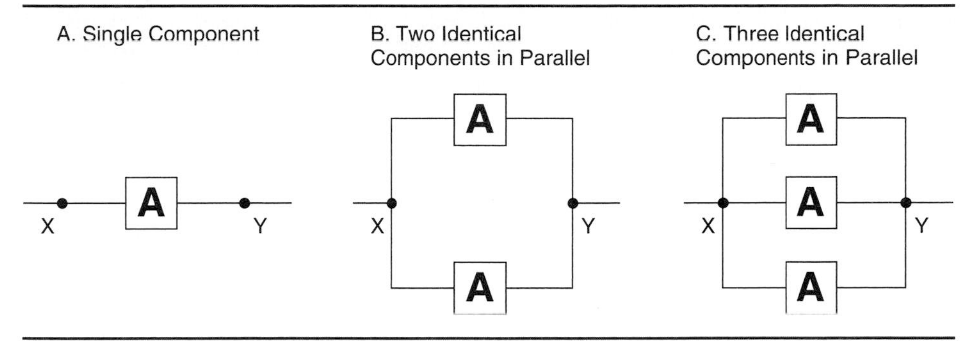


the end of one week may be determined as follows:

$$R_{XY} = 1 - (1 - R_A)^n \tag{7-3}$$

We've used identical components in this discussion, and assumed that reliability decay functions are the same whether the component is experiencing operating life or merely shelf life. Variation of components types or variation of reliability function within type of component doesn't alter the gist of the message; the math just gets more cumbersome.

where

$R_{XY}$ = process reliability

$R_A$ = item or component reliability of an $A$ after a certain time period

$n$ = number of identical redundant items in the process system

Substituting appropriate values for $R_A$ and $n$ yields:

$$\begin{aligned} R_{XY} &= 1 - (1 - R_A)^n \\ &= 1 - (1 - 0.9)^2 = 1 - (0.1)^2 \\ &= 0.99 \end{aligned}$$

Addition of yet a third item $A$ branch is shown in Exhibit 7-11C. The reliability, again of the process contained between points $X$ and $Y$ at the end of a one-week period, may be determined with the same equation:

$$\begin{aligned} R_{XY} &= 1 - (1 - R_A)^n \\ &= 1 - (1 - 0.9)^3 = 1 - (0.1)^3 \\ &= 0.999 \end{aligned}$$

The marginal increase in reliability decreases (by tenfold in this example) for each iteration—clearly an economic consideration that would come into play. Practical physical constraints—such as the weight limits imposed on spacecraft—also restrict the luxury of increased reliability through unbounded redundancy. But even short downtime for repairs can prove catastrophic—say, in nuclear power plant coolant systems, refinery flow control systems, and hospital power supply systems. In such cases, increased reliability through redundancy is often the design team's best bet.

### Design for Automation

Boothroyd and Dewhurst's operability guidelines—6 through 10—are particularly useful as design teams cope with automation, a topic of continuing concern for operations managers. Three broad issues, affecting output and process design efforts, come into play:

- Wasteful or unnecessary processes should not be automated. Clean up the former and eliminate the latter *before* considering automation.
- The theme of the five guidelines is simplification for good reason: The simpler the task, the easier it will be to design equipment to do it. Development will also be faster and cheaper.
- When design teams strive for an easy-to-automate design, they sometimes get an unexpected dividend: Following the operability guidelines might simplify the process to such an extent that the firm can avoid the time and expense needed to acquire and install the automation.

### Design for the Environment

An unfortunate consequence of the operations that create our goods and services is that they also create unwanted outputs—especially waste and pollutants. Industry is not the only polluter of course, but it is a major one. Fortunately, we can do something about that, and the effort begins in design. **Design for the environment (DFE)**—another of the "DFX" set of acronyms—refers to steps taken during the design process to minimize the negative environmental impact of output goods and services and the processes that provide them.

One approach is to incorporate specifications into designs and agreements that define suppliers' environmental responsibilities. Increasingly, the world's large OEMs are requiring their suppliers to register to **ISO 14000,** the Environmental Management Standards defined by the Geneva-based International Organization for Standardization (ISO). In the fall of 1999, for example, Ford and then General Motors announced their timetables for expected supplier registration.[21] Though this sounds a bit dogmatic, we should note that the objective is for all companies to create, enunciate, and activate their own **environmental management systems (EMS),** a key requirement for obtaining ISO 14000 registration. And the "game plan" is global; manufacturers throughout Europe, Asia, and North America are following similar strategies.

Furthermore, the U.S. Environmental Protection Agency (EPA), the European Environment Agency (EEA), and the United Nations Environment Programme (UNEP) are collaborating to create a global multilingual environmental thesaurus to facilitate better communications and understanding throughout global provider-customer chains.

But why the emphasis during design? *Pollution prevention,* or "P2" as the EPA calls it.[22] It's better to prevent pollution from happening than to try to clean it up later. This reduction-at-the-source idea is an extension of the designed-in quality concept that we examined earlier in the chapter: Better design prevents more malfunctions, defects, and other quality problems. In fact, ISO 14000 is itself patterned after ISO 9000, the ISO's quality management standards. (We discuss ISO 9000 and standards in general in Chapter 8.)

## Design Review and Appraisal

Design and development is a loop. Preliminary designs are critiqued, improved, critiqued again, improved again, and so on. This commonly continues after the product designs are in production or services are being delivered, and customers are sampling the results. The inescapable questions remain: "Has quality been designed in?" and "How do we know?"

We don't know. To find out, the extended design team must listen to customers, keep track of competitors, and when necessary, modify the design. External feedback begins to reach the design team as soon as the first customers begin to work with the designs. Quite often, these first customers are operations personnel. Later, marketing and advertising associates get their turn; they must present the new designs to external customers—the final arbiters. Systematic, measurement-based design checking all along the chain (called design review) provides a near-constant flow of design appraisal data.

The tools and guidelines we've covered in this chapter suggest several specific measures of design-team performance. Percentage of standard parts or new parts, attainment of target costs, availability, reliability, design cycle time, frequency and magnitude of design changes, rework, and warranty costs are a few examples. Other more general measures address ergonomics, environmental concerns, and aesthetic factors.

But the list of those who evaluate designs, the criteria they use, and their sophistication all seem to be expanding. Several trends bear watching: First, businesses are increasingly aware of the financial impact of design—in short- and long-term operations and marketing. As such, many are turning to outside expertise—outsourcing their design work. Providing design services is a booming business. Second, customers all along the chain have elevated their willingness to sound off about design. They know more about design, are more demanding of design excellence, and appear to be less intimidated by so-called experts who fail to listen. Perhaps it's fair to say that design appraisal has gone public. Finally, customers not only want design teams to do more—to cover more territory, so to speak—they also want to help.

## Summary Check Points

✓ Design is a core business responsibility; good design programs are an effective competitive weapon, but results of poor ones send unwelcome ripples through the rest of the organization and along the customer chain.

✓ Design has two primary targets: the output goods and services that customers want and the processes that create those outputs.

✓ Designed-in quality refers to the key role that design can play in establishing eventual quality of outputs and processes.

✓ Research, design, and development strategy must overcome traditional weaknesses—design has been slow, myopic, and unfocused. It has also been relegated to out-of-touch specialists.

✓ A comprehensive design program plans, implements, and improves (that is, manages) design efforts through a series of integrated and overlapping elements or stages.
✓ A wide array of computer-based technologies exist to help design teams carry out their work; computer-aided design (CAD), computer-aided engineering (CAE), computer-aided process planning (CAPP), and simulation are examples.
✓ In all but the smallest firms, design is a job for teams.
✓ A design concept is a verbal and prototype explanation of what is to be changed and how the change will affect the customer.
✓ Concurrent design (simultaneous engineering) shortens design by including all relevant parties early in the design sequence.
✓ A good example of socially responsible design effort is universal designs—standard, marketable, items that are intended for and preferred by anyone, not just people with disabilities.
✓ Quality function deployment provides a structured sequence for capturing customer requirements, translating those into design requirements, creating part or item characteristics, matching those characteristics to process operations, and finally identifying the resources to carry out the operations.
✓ Design for operations guidelines focus on operations associates as the customers of the design team; the objective is to assist—through better design—the people who will carry out subsequent work.
✓ Design for reliability and serviceability aims at creating products and processes that will work when needed. Reliability may be enhanced with superior parts and/or through redundancy.
✓ When designing for automation, care should be taken to streamline processes before automating them; get the waste out first, then automate.
✓ Design for the environment (DFE) aims to create outputs and processes that minimize waste and pollution at the source.
✓ Companies who seek to register to ISO 14000, the environmental management standards created by the International Organization for Standardization, must first create and implement an environmental management system.
✓ Greater environmental protection has widespread global support.

## Solved Problems

### *Problem 1*

Betty's daughter will soon open her new advertising agency, and Betty is shopping for a small office gift to present when she visits the agency next week. At an office supply store, Betty finds an electric pencil sharpener she likes. A label on the box informs her that the sharpener has a mean time between failure (MTBF) of two years. A clerk who arrives to assist informs Betty that the

MTBF figure means that after two years, there is a 50-50 chance that the sharpener will still be working. Is the clerk correct?

*Solution 1*

The value of the sharpener's reliability at a time period of two years is the issue. First compute the failure rate (we must assume that it is constant): $\lambda = 1/\mu$, or $\frac{1}{2}$ per year. Then, apply Equation 7-1.

$$R = e^{-\lambda t} = e^{-(1/2)(2)} = e^{-(1)}$$
$$= 1/e = 1/2.718 = 0.368$$

So the clerk is incorrect. A common mistake is to assume that reliability at MTBF is one-half, or 50 percent. The correct value, however, is about 0.37, slightly more than a one-third chance of successful operation.

*Problem 2*

Exhibit 7-12 shows an assembly diagram for a simple product. Redesign the product for ease of assembly and robotics.

*Solution 2*

First, the design team evaluates the present method in terms of the strict and well-defined requirements for assembly by a robot. Then it simplifies the design.

**Step 1: Robotic assembly.** The design team specifies the following robotic assembly method. The robot starts by putting four bolts upright into four pods in a special fixture, one at a time. Then it puts a washer on each bolt. Next, the robot must position the base so the holes line up with the four bolts—a difficult alignment unless the holes are large. The robot's next tasks are to grab a bracket, position it, and secure it at each end with a washer, a lock washer, and a nut. Tightening the nuts requires that the robot return its ordinary gripper to the tool rack, fasten its "wrist" to a special nut-turning device, and then, after the nuts are tight, switch back to the ordinary gripper.

Exhibit 7-13 gives the design team's estimated times for the seven tasks described (some done more than once), plus five more. Their estimate of 12 seconds for assembling the two nuts may be optimistic. They assume that bolts or nuts have special self-alignment features so threads will engage correctly and not bind or get cross-threaded.

## Exhibit 7-12 Assembly Using Common Fasteners

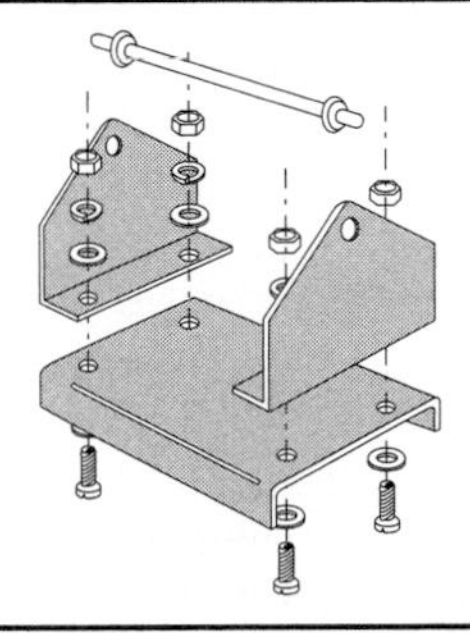

Source: Adapted from G. Boothroyd and P. Dewhurst, "Product Design . . . Key to Successful Robotic Assembly," *Assembly Engineering,* September 1986, pp. 90–93. Used with permission.

**EXHIBIT 7-13 Approximate Robotic Assembly Time—Bracket-and-Spindle Assembly**

| *Part* | *Repeats* | *Time (seconds)* | *Operation* |
|---|---|---|---|
| Screw | 4 | 12 | Place in fixture |
| Washer | 4 | 12 | Place on screw |
| Base | 1 | 3 | Place on screws |
| Bracket | 1 | 3 | Position on base |
| Washer | 2 | 6 | Place on screw |
| Lock washer | 2 | 6 | Place on screw |
| Nut | 2 | 12 | Secure bracket (requires tool change) |
| Spindle | 1 | 3 | Insert one end in bracket (needs holding) |
| Bracket | 1 | 3 | Position on base and locate spindle |
| Washer | 2 | 6 | Place on screw |
| Lock washer | 2 | 6 | Place on screw |
| Nut | 2 | 12 | Secure bracket (requires tool change) |
| **Totals** | **24** | **84** | |

**EXHIBIT 7-14 One-Piece Base and Elimination of Fasteners**

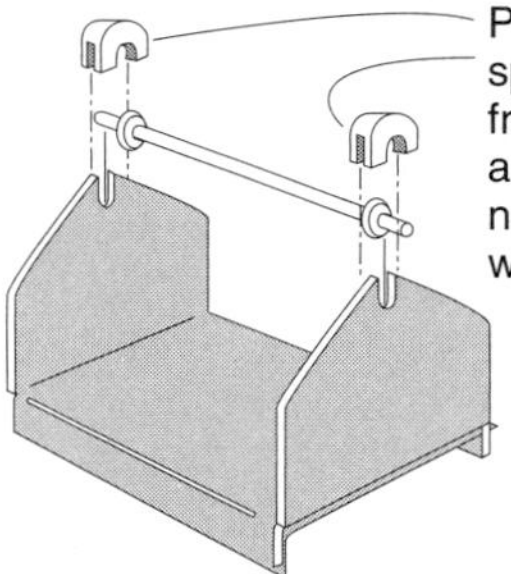


The robot continues by inserting the spindle into one bracket hole and then moving the second bracket to receive the spindle. Since the robot has only one hand, it cannot hold the spindle and move the second bracket into place at the same time. It must move a fixture into place to hold up the spindle momentarily. Finally, the bracket is fastened down with washers and nuts.

The complete set of tasks includes insertions in several directions, which the team agrees would require an elaborate, costly robot. The total assembly time is 84 seconds, of which 86 percent is fastening. Of the 24 parts in the assembly, 20 are just for fastening. Are all those bolts, nuts, and washers really necessary? Perhaps not. But they are common and cheap, and assembly designers routinely choose such means of fastening.

**Step 2: Simplified design.** One way to simplify the design is to look for simpler ways to fasten the brackets. But why fasten them? Isn't it possible to make the brackets and base as one piece? The team believes it is. Their new design is shown in Exhibit 7-14. In that design, plastic

**EXHIBIT 7-15 Design for Push-and-Snap Assembly**

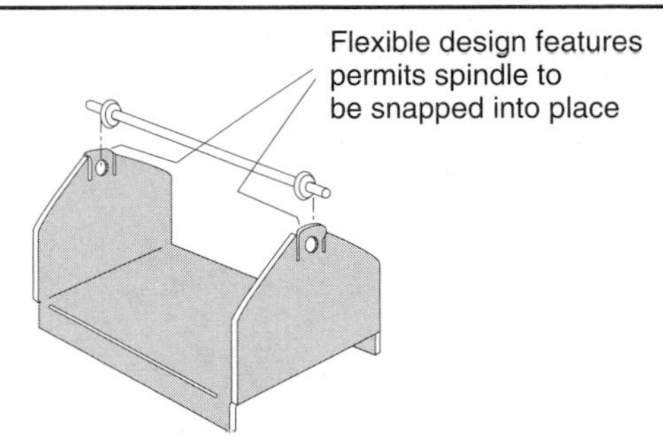


inserts secure the spindle; both spindle and inserts may be assembled from above, which allows use of a simpler, cheaper type of robot with no special grippers or holding fixtures. There are only four parts, and a robot could assemble them in, say, 12 seconds. That improves output and productivity by 600 percent (from 43 to 300 assemblies per hour).

There may be better solutions. If specifications permit, the team realizes, the spindle could be made from material that will bend or flex. Then a two-piece design, as in Exhibit 7-15, will be possible. Now assembly consists of just one step and one motion: Snap spindle downward into place. The simplest of robots may be used.

Now, however, the design team has made assembly so simple that using a robot begins to seem excessive. If a robot were used, the parts would have to be presented to the robot on some sort of carrier—probably loaded by hand. Clearly it is just as easy—or even easier—to do the whole assembly by hand. Save the robot budget for tasks difficult for people.

**Principle 8**

Automate incrementally when process variability cannot otherwise be reduced.

***Problem 3***

Grittelbane Optics grinds special lenses for eyewear and for optical equipment used in medical and scientific laboratories. Almost without exception, the main grinder, an SL-54, gets out of alignment once during each standard five-day (40-hour) workweek. Grittelbane technicians call in a service representative from the manufacturer, SightLines, to realign the grinder, a tedious job that takes an average of four hours. Karl Grittelbane, company president, forecasts business growth and plans to purchase an additional grinder. His call to the sales V.P. (Vice President) at SightLines goes like this, "Except for the alignment problem, your grinder suits me just fine. I'd like to buy another SL-54; it would make my training and maintenance easier, but the downtime is killing me. I've got to look elsewhere if your designers can't come up with a fix . . . and soon." As SightLine's sales V.P., how should you respond?

***Solution 3***

First, whether or not Grittlebane is correct in blaming poor design, SightLine's design team ought to investigate. With access to Grittelbane's failure and repair records, the team can assess the magnitude of the downtime problem by computing availability. From these data, SightLines personnel find that MTBF = 5 days, and MTTR = 0.5, on average. Then from Equation 7-2.

$$A = \frac{\text{MTBF}}{\text{MTBF} + \text{MTTR}} = \frac{5}{5.5} = 0.91$$

With just over 90-percent availability, Grittelbane will feel the loss of capacity—especially if the business is growing. The team *might* set an availability target (e.g., 98 percent or higher) for future redesign work on the SL-54, but there are other issues to address here.

First, Grittelbane needs some quick help. As a temporary fix until further investigation transpires, a preventive-maintenance program might be suggested, with weekly—or more frequently if needed—alignment performed during nonbusiness hours. Meanwhile, the team should study the repair (realignment) process; maybe it can be streamlined, cutting the MTTR value. A permanent solution, however, requires that the cause of the out-of-alignment condition be identified and eliminated. That might involve grinder design changes, operator training (new procedures or manuals might be needed), and site visits to study the operating environment at Grittelbane. If poor design is the culprit, competitive analysis or benchmarking could be warranted. Clearly, this is a team task for SightLine and Grittelbane personnel.

Oh yes, the question about what the *sales* V.P. should do? . . . Write some soothing letters while the design team carries out the work? Not in today's competitive company! With sleeves rolled up, he or she will likely be an active member of the investigation team!

### *Problem 4*

A valve control assembly is part of a chemical company's process design for an upcoming plant addition; its rated MTBF is two years. Due to the inherently unstable nature of some of the chemicals the plant will process, equipment failure could be catastrophic. Typical of process industry operations, long periods of sustained flow—several months to a year, perhaps—will be the norm. As one of the design team's representatives from plant operations, you and fellow team members will evaluate the reliability of the valve control assembly and report back to the team.

### *Solution 4*

You know that the control assembly reliability at two years, the MTBF, is about 0.368; an unacceptably low figure in your judgment. Perhaps you perform a quick reliability calculation for the one-year point, given the duration of some of the plant's processing runs. First, the failure rate (assumed constant) using *year* as the unit of time:

$$\lambda = \frac{1}{\mu} = \frac{1}{2} = 0.5 \text{ failures/yr.}$$

Then, from Equation 7-1, the reliability at the one-year point is:

$$R = e^{-(\lambda)(t)} = e^{-(0.5 \text{ failures/yr.})(1 \text{ yr.})} = e^{-0.5} = 0.607$$

The low reliability figure suggests that a more robust process design is needed. One option is to select control assemblies that have higher reliability (i.e., longer MTBF ratings), *if they are available.* Another possibility is to increase overall reliability through redundancy. For example, if two parallel control assemblies were employed, equation 7-3 is used to find reliability at the one-year point:

$$R = 1 - (1 - R_c)^2 = 1 - (1 - 0.607)^2 \approx 0.85$$

where $R_c$ is the reliability of one control assembly after one year. For three control assemblies in parallel, the reliability—again at the one-year point—is:

$$R = 1 - (1 - R_c)^3 = 1 - (0.393)^3 \approx 0.94$$

You and your colleagues might present to the team a full set of reliability decay curves (similar to those found in Exhibit 7-10) for these and other options, but perhaps it's time to look at cost figures, or maybe brainstorm or benchmark for other ways to control chemical flow.

## Exercises

1. Visit the web site for Delphi Automotive Systems (http://www.delphiauto.com) and investigate what Delphi has to say about environmental responsibility. Also:
   *a.* Cite any instances of Delphi's being recognized or cited for accomplishments as an environmentally friendly company.
   *b.* Classify Delphi's accomplishments as either control of pollution at the source or as activities that clean up and/or recycle. Explain your choices and rationale.
2. Six companies, including Black & Decker, are referred to as consistent corporate winners of the Industrial Design Excellence Awards (IDEA). Pick any two of those companies and:
   *a.* List products that have received awards (maybe other than IDEA awards). Briefly note what unique characteristic or quality resulted in the award.
   *b.* If you were in the market for one of the award-winning products, would its having been recognized by an "award team" affect your decision to buy? Explain.
3. For two of the following McDonald's end products and components, find out who the principle designers/developers were and how the developments took place: sauces for Chicken McNuggets, special chicken for McNuggets, fish sandwich, Egg McMuffin. How does McDonald's deal with the quality of ingredients?
4. A chess clock shown in the accompanying illustration is housed in a molded plastic case that is closed up in the rear with two flat plastic square plates. (Chess clocks contain two identical clocks, one for each player in a timed chess game.) The three pieces are represented below, along with a sample of the special screw that goes into the eight drilled holes that fasten the clocks to the square plates. (Two other holes in the case and four holes and two half-moons in the squares are for clock adjustment. For purposes of this question, ignore them.)

   Suggest two practical design improvements based on the guidelines in Exhibit 7-7. (Mention the specific guidelines you are using as the basis for your suggestions.)

Chess clock

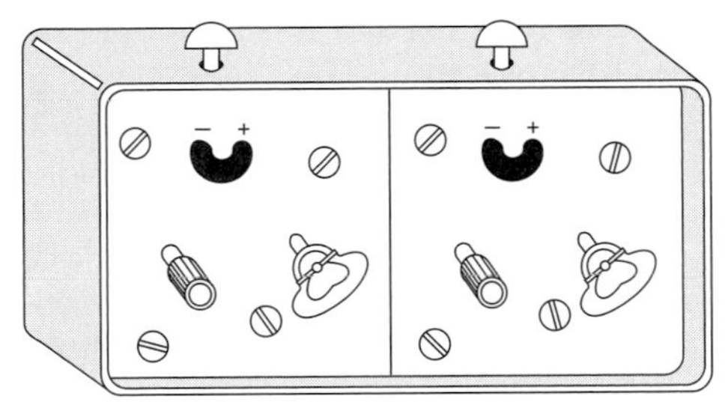


0.3 Inch

Screw specifications:
- Brass
- Flat head with slot
- Threaded on inside

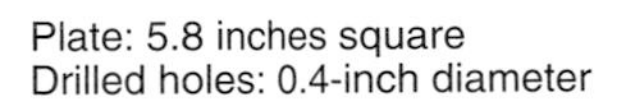

5. Visit the web site for The ISO 14000 Information Center and go to the "What's New" page. The direct URL is (http://www.iso14000.com/WhatsNew/News01.htm)
   *a.* Select two news items that are recent at the time of your visit. Write a brief report summarizing the contents of those articles.

*b.* Should large OEMs such as Ford and General Motors mandate registration to ISO 14000 as a supplier requirement? Why or why not?

6. Faceplates that cover electrical wall outlets and wall switches fasten with one or two screws. Suggest a modification that would eliminate the need for screws. Would the benefits be significant? Explain. Can you offer any arguments against redesign to eliminate screws?
7. Play the role of dietitian, fashion designer, architect, or financial portfolio designer. Describe the problems you can avoid with the proper degree of interaction with your suppliers.
8. At Monitor Manufacturing Company, product development engineers operate under a strict policy of frequent interaction with customers to ensure that designs match customer requirements. Still, customers view Monitor's designs as only average. What can the problem be?
9. Select one of the following processes:
   - Automatic (drive through) car wash.
   - Clothing dry cleaners.
   - Quick oil change and lube service.
   - A weekly shopping trip to buy food and household supplies (e.g., cleaners, over-the-counter medicines, etc.).

   *a.* List possible sources of pollution associated with the process and classify each as pollution at the source or as clean-up/recycle pollution. Explain your logic. (Hint: You may have to think about a few links up or down the supply chain.]

   *b.* Improve the process so as to reduce source pollution. Explain your suggestion.
10. (Group exercise) UPS, based in Greenwich, Connecticut, announced in late 1994 that it was converting 500 of the 888 delivery trucks operating in Connecticut to operate on compressed natural gas (CNG). The reason? The state had recently decided to allow 50 percent of the investment in alternative fueled vehicles to be written off of corporate taxes and to exempt clean-running vehicles from the 31-cent/gallon state gasoline tax.

    As a group, brainstorm to identify a list of design factors that UPS, its suppliers, customers, and other stakeholders might need to consider in such a conversion program. (Hint: Don't limit your thinking to changes on the vehicles.)
11. (Group Exercises) Sony Corporation's 1.5-million-square-foot TV assembly plant in San Diego used to receive cathode ray tubes (CRTs) in cardboard boxes; after the tubes were removed, the boxes were destined for the trash bin. In the mid-1990s, a design team developed alternative packaging for tube transport—a collapsible wire basket that could be stacked and returned to the CRT supplier. John Pion, Sony's director of purchasing, says, "The [design] program was driven not only by environmental consideration, but there was approximately a 2 percent cost reduction in the piece price when all costs are included. We've been able to eliminate 1,700,000 pounds of materials from the waste stream according to this year's [1994] figures." Also, the plant's annual savings in disposal costs is around $300,000.[23]

    Your group has three tasks:

    *a.* Decide whether the basket design represents a product or process design change. Be prepared to present your reasoning.

    *b.* Prepare a list of the functional activities (at Sony and other organizations) that would most likely have input on, or be affected by, the packaging design change. Should all of these parties be on the design team? Explain your logic.

c. Could reusable packaging (e.g., wire or plastic baskets or crates) be used on most or all large home appliances throughout the production, distribution, and retailing cycle—with the end consumer returning the packaging? Prepare a list of the product and process design considerations that would need to be faced.

12. Tokyo Seating Company operates TRI-CON, a subsidiary manufacturing division in the United States. Some years ago, TRI-CON asked an American metal products company to bid on a contract to provide TRI-CON with metal seat pans for motorcycle seats. TRI-CON's request for proposal specified a steel gauge and little else. The American firm was uncomfortable with TRI-CON's minimal specifications and refused to bid. Why would TRI-CON say so little about the kind of seat pan it wanted?
13. Team or individual assignment: A partial QFD matrix is given below for a fast-food hamburger container. Your assignment is (a) to add the house of quality's roof, (b) collect real data from two fast-food hamburger restaurants and use it to complete the QFD matrix, and (c) draw conclusions about the excellence of the two containers.

How

| What | | Design of container | Ergonomics | Insulation | Biodegradability |
|---|---|---|---|---|---|
| | Hold of heat | | | | |
| | Container appeal | | | | |
| | Easc of opening/use | | | | |
| | Environmentally sound | | | | |

14. According to one report, Japanese automakers are talking about building networks of small market-driven factories that will allow fabrication of a car from just 37 snap-together parts. Each such factory would economically produce about 10,000 autos a year, versus a typical break-even volume of over 200,000 in today's auto plants.

    To make this prediction a reality, name and discuss the five most important design principles and guidelines that would need to be employed.
15. From your own experiences, give, and explain, an example of (a) robust design of a service (to reduce chances of misperformance), (b) design of a service to reduce or eliminate backtracking and return visits, and (c) easily plugged-in service modules.
16. From your own experience, give three examples of reducing the number of operations (service steps). Explain.
17. Which of the following is best suited for robotic assembly: (a) assembling a clock consisting of a frame, faceplate, mechanism, backplate, and three screws; or (b) assembling a clock into a plastic box, which requires inserting a bottom liner into the bottom box piece, placing an instruction card, clock, and top liner on top, and snapping the top box piece downward to cngage with thc bottom piecc? Explain.

18. A security system timer controls lights, and other electrical components. The MTBF for the timer is advertised to be 6,000 hours. When should the operator or maintenance associate consider replacing the timer? Discuss your recommendations.
19. Equation 7-2 defined availability in terms of mean time between failure (MTBF) and mean time to repair (MTTR). To what extent are design teams responsible for these two parameters? To what extent are front-liners and maintenance associates responsible?
20. A control valve for a fuel supply system has an average failure rate of one failure per three years. Suppose the fuel supply system is to be used on an upcoming space mission that will last two weeks.
    *a.* Is this part of the vehicle safe enough? (Calculate value of reliability at mission end.)
    *b.* What might be done to improve reliability of this, or any other, component?
21. A design team at a test equipment provider has the following problem: A (potential) new customer wants the availability of any new computer testing units to be at least 0.99; that is a target for the team. Team members (maintenance personnel and the customer's operators) argue that, because of the need to recalibrate, a realistic figure for average repair time (should a breakdown occur in a test unit) is one hour. What options are open to the team?
22. A furnace thermostat has a constant failure rate of one failure per 30 months, and a mean time to repair of two hours.
    *a.* What is the thermostat reliability after 12 months? After 24 months? After 36 months?
    *b.* What is the availability?
    *c.* Should a design team try to streamline the repair process to reduce the MTTR? Explain.
23. A rechargeable electric razor battery provides an average of 50 minutes *of operating time* before the razor's recharge warning light flashes. It takes an average of two hours for the battery to fully recharge. Is it appropriate to compute the razor's availability with Equation 7-2? Why or why not?
24. A coolant line sensor has a reliability of 0.85 after one year of operation. What would the reliability be at the one-year point if
    *a.* Two of the sensors were used in a parallel configuration?
    *b.* Three of the sensors were used in a parallel configuration?
25. The photocopying machine in the management department at Acme University is in nearly constant use. But, breakdowns are frequent, and repairs typically consume a half-day or more. Professors, teaching assistants, secretaries, and student office assistants are starting to grumble, so the department chair promises to find the funds for a new machine. Professor Brown says the new copier ought to have a very high mean time between failures. Professor Green—who disagrees with Professor Brown on just about every topic—argues that a low mean time to repair is more essential. The department chair invites you for coffee and poses the question, "Who is correct, Brown or Green? And, oh yes, please tell me why."

# CHAPTER 8

# THE QUALITY IMPERATIVE

- At First Hawaiian Bank, tellers tend the drive-up windows and lobby counters in much the same way as their counterparts the world over. Between customers and during other free periods, however, First Hawaiian tellers telephone long time depositors to thank them for their business and inquire if service might be improved.
- Members of the 217-person student body of Mt. Edgecumbe High School in Sitka, Alaska, spend 90 minutes weekly in training—learning to apply the tools of continuous process improvement and problem solving. They team up with faculty on improvement projects and have traveled the continent telling their story to managers in blue-chip companies.
- At Mitsubishi Motor Company's plant in Normal, Illinois, a multifunctional team is systematically working its way through automobile warranty claims. In one recent project, the team applied its problem-solving skills to power-window regulators with a goal of complete elimination of faulty window operation and the underlying causes—that is, zero defects. Within a few months, the goal was met and the team moved on to another problem.
- Calgary-based Canadian Airlines International introduced its Service Quality program in 1990, and it's paying off. Mishandled or delayed baggage has been reduced by 75 percent, for example, and speed of telephone response has increased by 79 percent. Kevin J. Jenkins, president and CEO, sums it up this way, "Organizing a basic flight schedule and loosely adhering to that schedule will not make an airline stand out. Having exceptional service quality will."[1]
- Nestlé, headquartered in Vevey, Switzerland, follows a simple strategy: back up top-quality products with top-quality service. Its service operations follow two cherished customer rights: the right to security and the right to information. Accordingly, customer service lines are answered by culinary and nutrition experts, not by public relations specialists. Further, it is company policy that every customer complaint be investigated at the factory level—by the plant manager working with production line associates.

These brief snapshots provide a glimpse of the pervasive, global quality imperative.[2] Although quality appears in every chapter—we addressed designed-in quality in Chapter 7, for example—this chapter begins our more focused treatment on the subject. And, to reiterate an important point from the preceding chapter, quality pertains to output goods and services and to the processes used to create those outputs.

Quality is a driving force in contemporary OM and a potent competitive weapon. In this chapter we consider meanings of quality, explore the relationship between total quality management and OM, examine how quality affects competitiveness, look at quality standards and awards, and offer suggestions for establishing effective employee-driven quality.

## Quality: A Broad View

Shakespeare's eternal question, "What's in a name?" can be asked of quality. Does the word *quality* denote a desirable characteristic in output goods and services? Or, does it describe processes that make and deliver those outputs in ways that please customers? Or, especially when appended with the word *management* and preceded by the word *total,* does it refer to an even bigger picture—an overall approach to running organizations? The answers are *yes, yes,* and *yes*. The quality concept is both comprehensive and complex.

### *Quality Terminology*

Today, it's hard to find a business that doesn't have some manner of formal program for ensuring quality in the goods or services that it provides. Hospitals, schools and universities, and government agencies have also joined the movement. Unique names, acronyms, logos, and company- or customer-specific jargon abound. Thousands of publications (books, articles, films, etc.) on some facet of quality have appeared since the early 1980s.

Although consumers welcome the widespread attention to quality, some observers lament the lack of clear definitions. For example, Philip Crosby and the late W. Edwards Deming, both respected pioneers in the quality movement during the 20th century, avoid the term total quality management (TQM), arguing, respectively, that it lacks clear definition or even meaning. Joseph M. Juran, another respected voice in the quality field, says that part of the problem stems from a failure to distinguish quality goals from the steps taken to reach those goals; that is, quality and total quality management need to be defined separately.[3] First, we consider quality.

**Quality.** As the quality movement has evolved, so has the definition of quality. To keep demanding customers happy, businesses have expanded the concept of quality and at the same time have improved their ability to deliver on a wider array of quality dimensions. Exhibit 8-1 contains two itemized lists that exemplify this broadened view. The first was proposed for services; the second is more goods oriented. Despite

**EXHIBIT 8-1 Dimensions of Quality**

**10 Dimensions of Service Quality***

*Reliability*—consistency of performance and dependability.
*Responsiveness*—willingness or readiness to provide service; timeliness.
*Competence*—possession of the skills and knowledge required to perform the service.
*Access*—approachability and ease of contact.
*Courtesy*—politeness, respect, consideration for property, clean and neat appearance.
*Communication*—educating and informing customers in language they can understand; listening to customers.
*Credibility*—trustworthiness, believability; having customer's best interest at heart.
*Security*—freedom from danger, risk, or doubt.
*Understanding*—making an effort to understand the customer's needs; learning the specific requirements; providing individualized attention; recognizing the regular customer.
*Tangibles*—the physical evidence of service (facilities, tools, equipment).

**8 Dimensions of Quality†**

*Performance*—primary operating characteristics.
*Features*—little extras.
*Reliability*—probability of successful operation (nonfailure) within a given time span.
*Conformance*—meeting preestablished standards.
*Durability*—length of usefulness, economically and technically.
*Serviceability*—speed, courtesy, competence, and ease of repair.
*Aesthetics*—pleasing to the senses.
*Perceived quality*—indirect evaluations of quality (e.g., reputation).

*Adapted from Leonard L. Berry, Valerie A. Zeithaml, and A. Parasuraman, "Quality Counts in Services, Too," *Business Horizons*, May–June 1985, pp. 44–52.
†Adapted from David A. Garvin, *Managing Quality: The Strategic and Competitive Edge* (New York: The Free Press, 1988), p. 49ff.

differences in wording, the lists share two characteristics:

- Both reflect how *customers* think about quality.
- Both suggest action—things managers at all levels need to address if quality is to happen.

Thus, they point the way for quality management.

**Total Quality Management (TQM).** Juran provides a straightforward yet very inclusive definition of TQM: those actions needed to get to world-class quality.[4] The word total is a contribution of Armand Feigenbaum and the late Kaoru Ishikawa—two additional respected quality pioneers: In top organizations, quality management is no longer treated as a staff responsibility or functional speciality tucked away somewhere behind a door labeled "Inspection Department." Instead, it is everybody's business, a total commitment—organizationally as a competitive requirement; collectively as people pool their skills and special talents as members of improvement teams; and singly as each individual performs job tasks.

The term *total quality*, or *TQ* is becoming a popular shortcut to refer both to the characteristic of quality and to quality management.

## *TQM in Practice*

A broad view further manifests itself in the multitude of programs, techniques, and tools being implemented under the banner of TQM and its close cousins. At about the same time some leading Western companies were fashioning their TQM agendas in the early

*Conference on the fly. Multifunctional personnel address quality assurance on the shop floor.*

© Michael Rosenfeld/Tony Stone

1980s, others were placing equal or greater emphasis on just-in-time (JIT) operations. From its inception in Japan, JIT had a strong quality improvement component in addition to its main emphasis on cycle-time reduction. The early view by companies like Toyota was that TQM and JIT are mutually reinforcing. Today, most competitive organizations embrace and extend that notion; they include benchmarking, reengineering, supplier development, total preventive maintenance, quick-response programs, and a host of team-related tools, along with the more "hard-science" quality management techniques such as statistical process control, design of experiments, and scientific problem solving.

Research evidence also supports a broad description of TQM. In one recent study, for example, researchers grouped quality management into four broad dimensions—relationships with suppliers, relationships with customers, product design, and transformation processes. They found that all four dimensions were important contributors to high quality performance.[5]

As they will with any management initiative, however, some people prefer to focus their attention on flaws or failures in TQM implementations. And indeed, there have been many instances when tools that might be considered part of a TQM program haven't worked out. So, how can we know if application of a new (or old) tool or procedure, training program, or process change is sound TQM? GEC Plessey Semiconductors (GPS), headquartered in Wiltshire, England, answers that question with a simple test based on three fundamentals: customers, teamwork, and improvement.[6] GPS personnel evaluate all company programs on the seven dimensions shown in Exhibit 8-2. Using a scale to measure success on each item, GPS employees keep vital opportunities for improvement in focus.

GPS is among the organizations that have grown with TQM. They see it as having evolved into a broad set of teachable practices, a centerpiece of good management, and

**EXHIBIT 8-2 GEC Plessey Semiconductors' TQM Test**

*Is It TQM?*

- Is there a clear link to customers?
- Is there a clear link to company objectives?
- Have improvement measures been defined?
- Are managers and employees involved as a team?
- Is the team using a TQM (scientific problem-solving) process and tools?
- Is the team accomplishing and documenting its work?
- Are team decisions derived from data?

Source: Adapted from Samuel Feinberg, "Overcoming the Real Issues of Implementation," *Quality Progress,* July 1995, pp. 79–81.

an imperative for successful global operations. While much of that evolution has taken place within the last two decades, the roots of TQM are deeper, as we shall see next.

## TQM: History and Heritage

In tracing TQM's development, a few milestones stand out. Some were noted in the OM timeline in Chapter 2 (see Exhibit 2-3). We begin with artisan-based quality assurance, then move forward to note influences of the Industrial Revolution and consumerism. We continue with an overview of the major contributions of 20th century quality pioneers, and conclude with a brief contemporary perspective on the OM–TQM interface.

### *Quality Assurance*

Interest in quality is centuries old. The code of Hammurabi, which dates from 2150 B.C., mandated death for any builder whose work resulted in the death of a customer. Other quality-related codes, often equally harsh, are found in the writings of the ancient Phoenicians, Egyptians, and Aztecs.[7] Despite the harsh codes, however, it was the artisan's pride, not fear, that contributed most significantly to supporting quality assurance for centuries to come.

**Quality assurance,** in the view of George Edwards of Bell Labs, who coined the term in the 1920s, requires deliberate managerial planning and action, interlocked quality activities throughout the firm, and a senior officer in charge companywide.

**The Industrial Revolution.** Long supplier–customer chains are a product of the Industrial Revolution. In order for the masses to enjoy a wider array of goods, production costs had to decrease. New machines allowed production operations to be broken down into minute steps that unskilled labor could utilize. Demand and output increased as production costs decreased. Labor became specialized and disconnected from the big picture. Production people focused on quantity rather than quality; the reward system supported such behavior. In an attempt to stem the tide of deteriorating quality, managers assigned inspectors to check the work of line employees. Inspection, however, merely became another job specialty. Inspectors were unable to improve production quality; they could only find and remove some of the bad output after it had been produced. In many companies, quality fell apart and customers were angry.

The European Community's Product Liability Directive of 1985 called for the passage of strict liability laws in each EC country.

**Consumerism and Liability Laws.** Product quality and safety began to capture public attention in the mid-1960s. Activist Ralph Nader, consumer federations, action-line columns in newspapers, and investigative TV and newspaper journalists all contributed to increasing the public's interest. In 1965, the American Law Institute issued its "Restatement of the Law of Torts," which defined strict liability: making manufacturers liable for product defects even without proof of negligence.

Since the 1980s, physicians, accountants, attorneys, corporate directors, and volunteer members of civic organization boards increasingly became defendants in civil litigation. Liability insurance rates skyrocketed.

Concern for safe consumption of goods and services also led to regulatory action. In 1972, the U.S. Congress passed the Consumer Product Safety Act, which aims at preventing hazardous or defective products from reaching the consumer. Most other Western countries have followed the same pattern. Some companies extended their product warranties in the 1980s and early 1990s, but well-publicized product recalls seemed to say that quality on the warranty paper was not quality in fact. At the same time, in affluent nations large numbers of a new and demanding type of consumer emerged: the consumer of average means, who prefers to do without rather than pay for second best. There was a revival of neglected crafts such as handweaving, stone grinding of flour, and creation of stained-glass windows. Consumers sought the quality of the earlier age of the artisan.

We aren't suggesting that the goods and services of old were superior to modern ones. As customers, we want the convenience, safety, technology, and low cost of modern goods. But we also want to know (or at least feel) that the provider of the goods or services is listening to us, cares about our needs, and will "make it right the first time." The influences of an artisan-based quality taproot linger.

The quality imperative is also rooted in the experiences, research and writings, and teachings of modern era quality pioneers, some of whom we've mentioned in the previous section.

## *Quality Pioneers of the 20th Century*

As the concepts and practice of total quality continue to evolve, the contributions of other leaders of the quality movement will emerge, but for now the work of six individuals stands out: W. Edwards Deming, Joseph M. Juran, Armand V. Feigenbaum, Kaoru Ishikawa, Philip B. Crosby, and Genichi Taguchi. Exhibit 8-3 contains a summary of their more noteworthy contributions to the field of quality. (A chapter supplement provides detailed explanations and suggests reference materials by and about these individuals.)

Though known, respectfully, as quality gurus, their thinking and influence extend well beyond the management of quality alone. They all speak of

- Companywide integration of purpose—a shared culture manifested by a top-down commitment to quality that is embraced at all levels.
- High regard for humans, as individuals and as vital components of teams.

## EXHIBIT 8-3 Quality Pioneers—Major Contributions

**W. Edwards Deming (1900–1993)**
- 14 Points (for obtaining quality)
- Plan-Do-Check-Act cycle for continuing improvement
- Ardent support for training and data-based problem solving

**Joseph M. Juran (1904– )**
- Editor-in-Chief, *The Quality Handbook*
- Management breakthrough (precursor to process reengineering)
- The quality trilogy—planning, control, and improvement

**Armand V. Feigenbaum (1920– )**
- Concept of total quality control
- Clarification of quality costs—those associated with poor quality
- Concept of "hidden plant"—plant capacity required for rework

**Kaoru Ishikawa (1915–1989)**
- Registered the first quality control circle (in 1962)
- Cause–effect diagrams (fishbone charts)
- Elemental statistical method—simple but effective tools for data-based decision making

**Philip B. Crosby (1926– )**
- Concept of zero defects as the only acceptable quality goal
- Published *Quality Is Free;* argued that lack of quality is what costs
- Defined quality as meeting customer requirements

**Genichi Taguchi (1924– )**
- Simplified pathway for greater efficiency in experimental design
- Robust designs to withstand rigors of production and customer use
- Quality loss function; idea that any deviation from target value of a quality characteristic costs society in some way.

---

- Continuous improvement in all facets of operations—a never-ending program of looking for problems (defects, delays, waste, etc.); finding and eliminating root causes of those problems.
- Widespread service to all segments of society through sharing of total quality management ideas, programs, data, and results.

### *OM and TQM: Contemporary Interfaces*

Reflection on the concepts and heritage of TQM along with the principles of OM might prompt the question, "Isn't there a great deal of common ground?" Indeed there is; and the flow of influence goes both ways. Scott Mitchell, director of operations for Troy, Michigan, based Delphi Automotive, puts the operations/quality interface into perspective: ". . . the major quality challenge facing the [automotive] industry is speed, how to get the product to the consumer at a very rapid pace. Automakers are operating with

CONTRAST

## Quality and Speed

**Old View**

Good quality takes time. Speed (e.g., shorter cycle times) makes poor quality.

**New View***

"It may sound absurd, but perhaps the surest way to improve quality is speed—by cutting the cycle time from inception to delivery, be the product a car, a piece of research, or an insurance claim."

James F. Swallow, vice president
A. T. Kearney (consultants)

*Source: Otis Port and John Carey, "Questing for the Best," *BusinessWeek,* October 25, 1991, p. 8–16.

shorter supply chains, or at least quicker ones, and they are putting a lot of emphasis on less inventory, lower costs and lean manufacturing. . . . [B]ut when you reduce the supply base and shorten the reaction time, you cannot tolerate products that are inferior in quality."[8]

Operations in any organization contain primary transformation processes—key targets for obtaining built-in quality improvement. These same processes, however, are also targets for other changes such as increased productivity, greater flexibility, or faster throughput. A change in methods, for example, though initially intended to improve output timing, may surprise implementors by also yielding better output. Rather than quietly accepting the "good luck," today's enlightened firm will eagerly seek to understand the cause of the unforeseen improvement. A second round of changes, perhaps with a quality improvement aim this time, may also result in greater speed or in some other desired outcome. To summarize, long-held beliefs about relationships among variables go by the wayside, as the Contrast box "Quality and Speed" illustrates.

The continuing rounds of change and improvement have competitiveness, our next topic, as a dominant target.

## TQM and Competitiveness

Dictionaries tell us that competition is effort expended by two or more parties to win the favor of a target individual or group. In this section, we look more closely at how TQM efforts can make an organization more competitive.

In the late 1980s, Gabriel Pall, director of the IBM Quality Institute and former line manager, described two primary pathways through which improved quality enhances a company's profitability; Exhibit 8-4 illustrates. Market-route benefits begin when improved quality increases the product's value in the eyes of customers. The provider may

**Exhibit 8-4 Competitive Benefits of TQM**

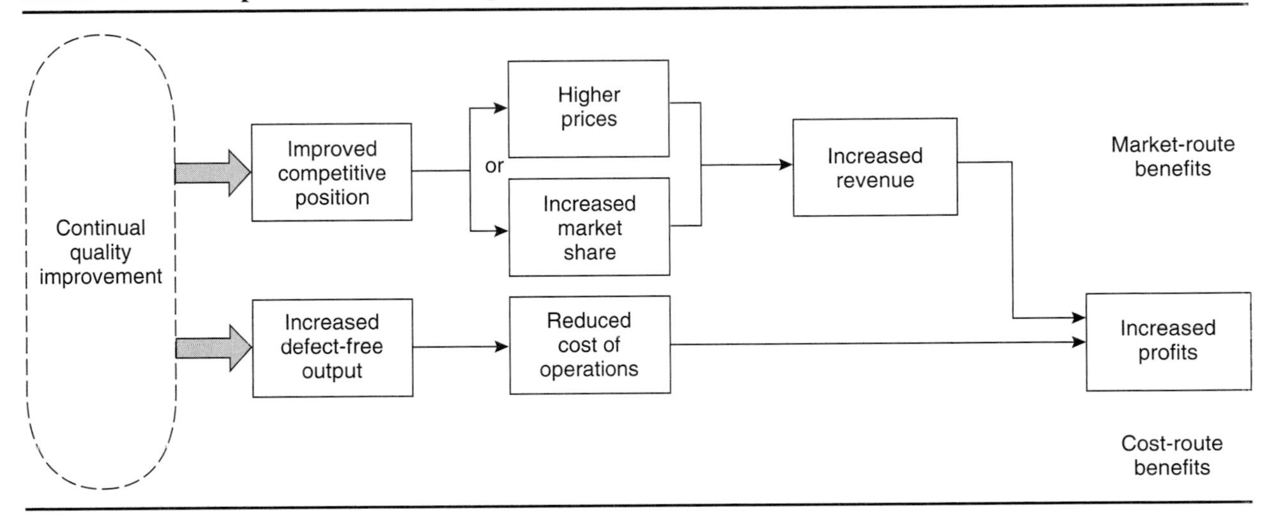


Source: Adapted from Gabriel Pall, *Quality Process Management* (Englewood Cliffs, N. J.: Prentice-Hall, Inc., 1987). chap. 1.

raise prices or—by holding prices steady—realize a gain in market share; revenue increases in either case. Cost-route benefits accrue because increased defect free output cuts operating costs per unit, and lower costs also enhance profits. Remember the margins we discussed in chapter 2?

Profitability is one time-honored indicator that customers are as a whole satisfied with a company's output. Demonstrating linkages from better quality to profits might seem a waste of time to the TQM "believer," but it is often a necessary step in convincing budget-minded managers (who face demanding stockholders) to cough up funds for process improvements. When managers evaluate a pending TQM program, Pall's two pathways define issues of concern: "How will it help us in the marketplace?" and "What will it cost?" Let's look first at costs.

Market and cost route benefits also apply to government agencies, charities, and other not-for-profit groups. Those served by a quality-improving agency are more satisfied and more inclined to make donations or improve tax referendums, thus providing more revenue and resources to the organization.

## *Cost of Quality*

Perhaps the earliest method of trying to incorporate costs of quality into modern managerial decision making was known simply as the **cost-of-quality** approach. Four categories of quality-related costs were identified:

*Internal failure costs.* Costs the provider incurs directly—prior to delivery or shipment to customers—as a result of defective output. Examples are scrap, rework, retest, downtime, and searching for something misplaced.

*External failure costs.* Costs to the provider when defects are discovered after delivery or shipment to customers. Included are returns, warranty expenses, allowances, returned material handling, complaint processing, and service recovery. In extreme cases, liability settlements and legal fees would be included.

*Appraisal costs*. Costs of determining the degree of quality. They include monitoring, materials inspection and testing, maintenance of test equipment, and materials and other resources consumed during inspection and testing (e.g., destructive testing of flash bulbs or food items).

*Prevention costs.* Costs of efforts to minimize appraisal and failure costs. They include quality planning, training, new-products review, reporting, and improvement projects.

Though few firms' cost accounting systems bore expense accounts with these names, the cost-of-quality expenses did receive considerable attention in more theoretical cost-versus-quality debates. And in some instances, these concepts guided quality planning and budgeting efforts. Astute quality pioneers noted, however, that "these costs are associated solely with defective product—the costs of making, finding, repairing, or avoiding defects. The costs of making good products are not a part of quality costs."[9]

In sum, the term *cost-of-quality* is itself misleading. Taguchi's **quality loss function,** shown in Exhibit 8-5, correctly points out that the worrisome costs are those associated with *not* having quality. Furthermore, Taguchi's view accommodates a much broader concept of costs—he considers not just costs to a provider but costs to all of society.

Basically, Taguchi holds that unwelcome costs to some segment of society—producer, customer, end consumer, or even society at large—occur with any deviation

**EXHIBIT 8-5 Taguchi's Quality Loss Function**

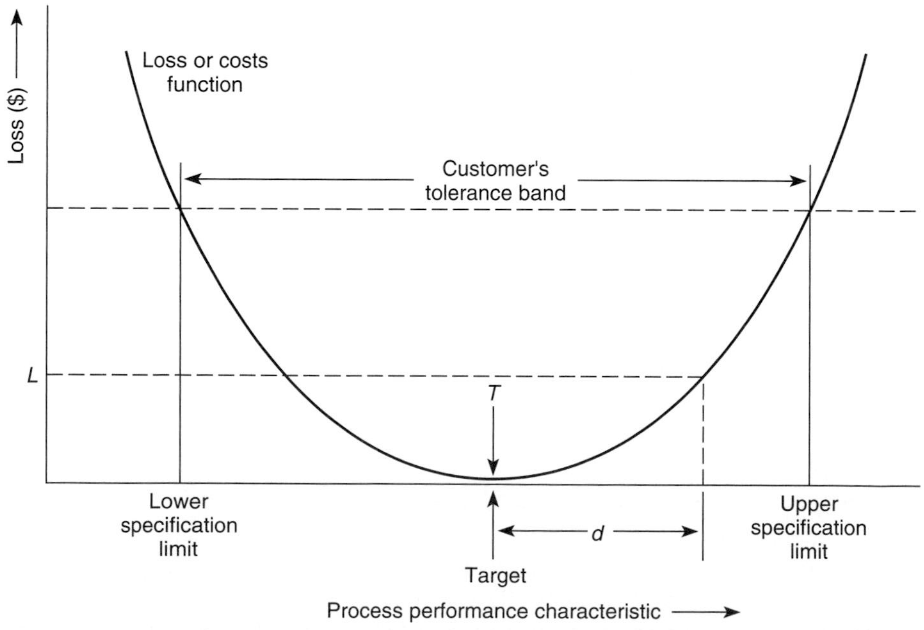

of process performance from the intended or designed target. The smaller the amount of this deviation, the smaller the social cost and the more valuable the product or service.[10]

Just meeting specifications, reflected as the customer's tolerance band in Exhibit 8-5, is not good enough. Taguchi argues for continuing effort to reduce variability. He holds that the loss from performance variation ($L$) is directly related to the square of the deviation ($d$) from the target value ($T$).

Other, more specific examples of costs attributable to poor quality serve to complement Taguchi's broad-range-impact warning. The Into Practice box "Escalating Cost of Defects" illustrates how internal costs can mount when poor quality goes undetected. And, throughout this book we are reminded of the "external" costs should customers reject our outputs.

In the early stages of their TQM efforts, quality advocates in a number of well-known firms (e.g., Motorola, Texas Instruments, and Xerox) used the cost-of-quality argument for shock value. Cost-minded senior managers were often startled to learn that "costs of *un*-quality" in their companies were 10 percent to 20 percent of annual revenue. When other arguments for managerial commitment to quality improvement programs failed, the cost-of-quality speech often got results.

Should firms that already have thriving TQM programs continue doing annual cost-of-quality audits? Probably not. Consider, for example, a process improvement that prevents defective output. In a TQM company, it's a better-than-even bet that the change has other benefits; perhaps it results in faster or better engineering, reduces cycle times, or improves safety. Is the expense of the change a cost of quality? Or of engineering, production, or employee safety? Under TQM, quality is everybody's

Leading Japanese companies, having launched TQM by other means, had little use for cost-of-quality accounts or logic and have avoided this usage.

INTO PRACTICE

## Escalating Cost of Defects

The following rule of thumb has become an article of faith in the electronics industry:

- If a defective part is caught by the supplier (before leaving supplier's plant), then there is no cost to the customer (the manufacturer).
- If that part is caught as it enters the manufacturer's plant, the cost is $0.30.
- If that part is caught at the first stage of assembly (after paperwork, handling, scheduling, and other activities that assume the part is good), the cost is $3.00.
- If that part is caught at the final test (common in electronics manufacture), the cost is $30.00.
- If that part is not discovered until after it leaves the manufacturer's plant, the cost is $300.00. It must be returned, replaced, and so on. (This figure, $300.00, *does not* include certain additional costs such as insurance, warranty, lost business, or loss of customer goodwill.)

Note: Raymond A. Cawsey, vice president of quality, Dickey-john Corp., confirms that these figures are "very close" to the true mark for his employer, an electronics firm.

business; it's woven into the fabric of every job. So, the amount spent to achieve quality is difficult to state precisely. But even if we could find it, it isn't a cost we want to eliminate.

In retrospect, it seems the main value of the cost-of-quality concept was in raising consciousness about quality's competitive importance. Recent studies on quality's impact have been broader. They consider quality-induced performance gains in addition to reductions in costs. As such, they look more at the *value* of TQM.

### *Value of Quality*

As TQM gained momentum, companies began to pour large sums into its implementation. Not surprisingly, critics raised two good questions: "Is quality being improved?" and "If so, are the improvements contributing to the bottom line?" In short, is Pall's model valid? Numerous studies have addressed the question; we consider but a few.

1. The General Accounting Office (GAO), the investigative arm of Congress, studied data from 20 finalists in the 1988 and 1989 (initial years) Malcolm Baldrige National Quality Award competition to ascertain whether TQM improved performance. The results show that, after beginning TQM programs, quality-oriented companies experience general improvements in market share and profitability, customer satisfaction, quality, cost, and employee relations.[11]

   Another survey (reported nearly a decade later) of winners, applicants, and nonapplicants of the Baldrige Award and various state quality awards confirmed the previous results on all except two performance measures.[12]
2. Additional survey data, including the widely quoted PIMS (Profit Impact of Market Strategy) studies, also show positive effects from quality improvement efforts.[13] Exhibit 8-6 summarizes the PIMS analysis of the impact of quality on return on investment (ROI) and return on sales (ROS). As relative quality increases, we notice a strong positive increase in business performance. ROI increases 2.7 times, from a low of 12 percent for firms in the lowest quintile of quality to a high of 32 percent for those in the top quintile. Similarly, ROS increases from a low of 5 percent to a 13 percent for the top quintile group.
3. In 1995, the National Institute of Standards and Technology (NIST), part of the U.S. Department of Commerce, created the "Baldrige Index," a mythical stock fund made up of publicly traded companies who have won the Baldrige Award. NIST "invests" $1,000 in each company's stock on the first business day following announcement of the awards. Another hypothetical $1,000 is simultaneously invested in the S&P 500. As of the end of 1999, the "Baldrige Index" had outperformed the S&P by 4.8 to 1, achieving a 1,101 percent return on investment to a 228 percent for the S&P.[14]
4. Professor James L. Heskett and a team of colleagues, all members of Harvard Business School's service management interest group, studied successful service companies, including Banc One, Intuit, Southwest Airlines,

**EXHIBIT 8-6 Relative Quality and Rates of Return**

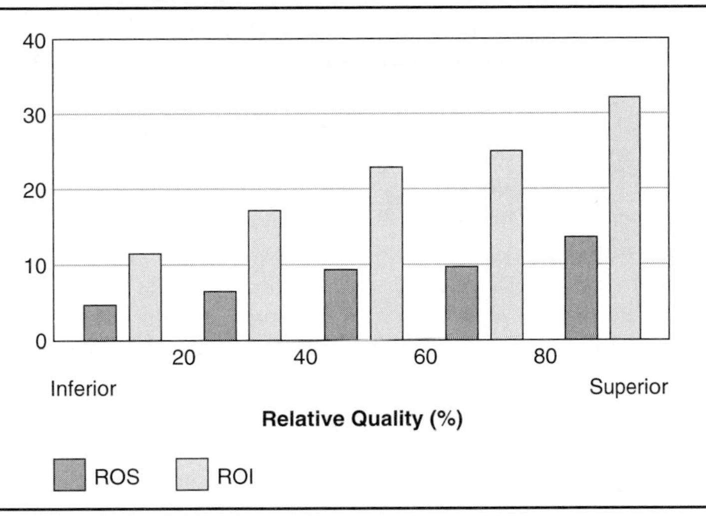


ServiceMaster, USAA, Taco Bell, and MCI. The researchers place special emphasis on the roles played by the human elements—customers and service providers' employees. Working backwards along what they refer to as the **service-profit chain,** they suggest that

> Profit and growth are stimulated primarily by customer loyalty. Loyalty is a direct result of customer satisfaction. Satisfaction is largely influenced by the value of services provided to customers. Value is created by satisfied, loyal, and productive employees. Employee satisfaction, in turn, results primarily from high-quality support services and policies that enable employees to deliver results to customers.[15]

Though they prefer to call these linkages propositions until further study bears them out, the Harvard team appears to support the general idea of Pall's model—quality promotes value. Moreover, their extension and refinements suggest that the reverse might also be true.

In sum, there appears to be ample evidence of a quality–competitiveness linkage. Customers acknowledge quality with their loyalty, but, as the next section shows, quality can also lead to more formal recognition.

## Recognizing Quality

Twenty years ago, most of the topics in this section didn't appear in OM books or elsewhere. As the quality imperative caught on, however, the scramble to discover and recognize excellence in quality was on. Benchmarking, supplier certification programs, ISO 9000 registration, and competition for quality awards have all contributed to global definitions of quality and quality management. They serve to *recognize* quality.

### *Benchmarking*

Benchmarking, developed at Xerox Corporation in the late 1970s, is the systematic search for best practices, from whatever source, to be used in improving a company's own processes.

Competitive benchmarking of **processes** is a relative of a much older technique: competitive analysis of **products,** which is a topic of Chapter 7.

At first, Xerox people called it competitive benchmarking. As the words suggest, they limited its application to finding their direct competitor's best practices. Xerox benchmarking teams boldly contacted competing manufacturers of copiers, computers, and other Xerox products. They asked, "How about we visit you and you visit us? We'll exchange information."

Why would rivals go for such a brazen proposal? Because the two companies would each benefit relative to other competitors not involved. (See the Contrast box, "Benchmarking." But, why restrict benchmarking to competitors? Why not *non*competitive benchmarking—searching for best practices anywhere?

Principle 4

Know the competition and world leaders.

Xerox manager, Robert Camp describes a benchmarking visit to L.L. Bean, the mail-order retailer, to learn what's behind Bean's legendary excellence in customer service.[16] Other companies have followed Xerox to L.L. Bean. Another frequently benchmarked company is Federal Express, for its overnight delivery ability.

Houston's Second Baptist Church, serving 12,000 parishioners weekly, uses benchmarking (e.g., Disney World's parking and people skills) in its own customer quality program.

Now, benchmarking is in wide use by major hotels, accounting firms, transportation companies, banks, manufacturing companies, and others. Marriott Hotels have benchmarked the hiring, training, and pay practices of fast-food companies because hotels hire out of the same labor pool. Corporate attorneys at Motorola have even employed benchmarking. Richard Weise, general counsel at Motorola, says "We began to compile information on how many lawyers and paralegals it takes for each $1 billion in sales. We looked at how other law departments use tools such as computers [and] learned from them. Finally, we determined relative costs of delivering legal services domestically versus internationally."[17]

With so many firms involved in benchmarking—and trying to visit some of the same high-performance firms—the idea of putting benchmarking data into data banks arose. Thus, under the sponsorship of subscribing companies, the American Productivity and Quality Center in Houston has established an International Benchmarking Clearinghouse.

CONTRAST

## Toward Benchmarking

**Keep It a Secret**

Our results, practices, and process knowledge are for our eyes only. Lock the doors, frown on outside visitors.

**Trade It**

Our results, practices, and knowledge are valuable assets; so are those of other good companies. Let's trade.

**EXHIBIT 8-7 The Benchmarking Process: Common Steps**

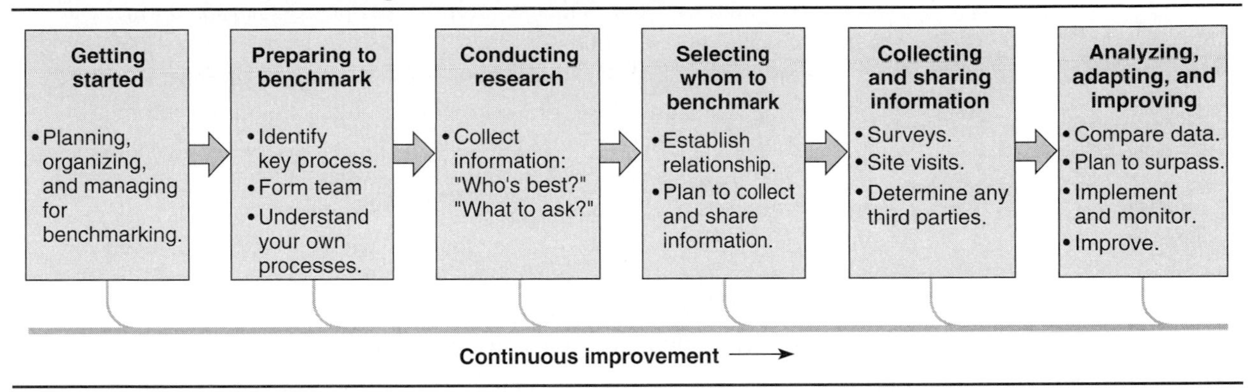


Source: Reprinted with permission from QUALITY (March 1992), a Capital Cities/ABC, Inc., Company.

Xerox divided its initial benchmarking procedure into 10 steps, but Camp and other experts have noted successful programs based on as few as four defined stages. What matters is that all necessary actions are accomplished. Exhibit 8-7 shows one common format.

First comes planning and organization. The next step is all-important; selecting the process to be benchmarked and the team members. However, the team should not immediately set off to benchmark another company. First they need to analyze their *own* processes, in the following terms:

*Metrics* (measurements in numbers). For example, a team from accounts payable may find it takes 18 hours average elapsed time but only 23 minutes of paid labor to process an invoice.

*Practices*. The team documents every step in the process, noting delays, sources of errors, departments and skills involved, and so forth.

The third step is collecting information on whom to benchmark and what questions to ask. The fourth is to gain approval and establish plans for exchange visits.

Fifth is the benchmarking itself, including a visit to the benchmarked firms' sites. Information sought must parallel that already gathered by the team for its own firm—namely, metrics and practices. Last, the benchmarking team analyzes the data, develops plans for change, and follows through.

Benchmarking has spread from its North American origin to many corners of the globe, and like other tools, it has been improved. Benchmarking teams may now tap computer networks and the clearinghouse database for much information, but the site visit remains popular. Camp, assessing benchmarking practice in an update of his earlier (1989) volume, notes other changes, including the following:[18]

- The overall benchmarking task really has two major components: a user process and a management process. The former consists of the steps that actually make up the benchmarking study (e.g., Exhibit 8-7). The latter is much broader, containing all those actions that support the user process before, during, and after the actual investigation.

- To the original (Xerox) benchmarking procedure, Camp adds what he calls a "step zero," to ensure consensus on key facets of benchmarking before it is begun. Camp says that step zero is best described as the quality process. Benchmarking has a greater chance of success when launched in an environment already steeped in TQM philosophy and procedures.
- *Problem-based benchmarking*—reaction to a specific trouble spot—was the right approach for early benchmarking efforts. Now, leading-edge firms realize that *process-based-benchmarking,* which targets those key business-wide processes contributing most to company goals, offers greater payback.

Camp (1995, p. 4) notes that benchmarking is mentioned over 200 times in the 1994 Baldrige Award criteria, and directly or indirectly affects up to 50 percent of the award's scoring.

Most likely, benchmarking will continue to evolve as additional successes emerge. Its place in the TQM toolkit seems secure, however, inasmuch as it is expected of applicants for the Malcolm Baldrige National Quality Award.

### Supplier Certification

Recall from Chapter 6 the reliance on certified suppliers for quality assurance.

We've seen that in the third step, the benchmarking team asks, Who's the best? The team's purchasing associate might suggest taking a look at the company's own certified, high-quality suppliers.

Traditional assessments of supplier performance and capability were not stringent enough for TQM-driven companies. A quality-centered approach, called supplier certification, fills the need. Certification can have several levels. For example, Upright-Ireland, a maker of custom scaffolding, uses four levels (see Exhibit 8-8). As at other companies that certify suppliers, Upright's highest level of certification (registered firm suppliers) means there's no need to inspect the supplier's goods or services; an Upright certification team is satisfied that the supplier has processes capable and under control. Upright has only about 180 employees. But it is one of many small- and medium-sized firms that have extensively implemented total quality management concepts.

Principle 16

Market every improvement.

Receiving an important customer's highest certification is grounds for celebration at any supplier company. But someone should note that awards can also be lost if improvement does not continue. Other customers' certifications are the next challenges. Marketers—always on the lookout for a competitive edge—quickly insert certification information into promotional materials.

Principle 5

Reduce to a few good suppliers.

The growth of certification programs parallels another, related trend: reduction in the number of suppliers. That movement has picked up steam as more companies, service as well as industrial, see the competitive advantages of dealing with but a few good suppliers. What suppliers do they keep? Those that can meet their quality certification requirements.

Suppliers may grumble about coercion, but those that are certified by big customers may find that effort an extra payoff when the time comes for them to seek registration to the ISO 9000 standard.

**EXHIBIT 8-8 Supplier Certification at Upright-Ireland**

*Left: Wall chart listing Upright's certified (just-in-time, with no inspection) suppliers, in four categories.*
*Right: Color-coded bins, which some of Upright's certified suppliers refill daily. Clipboards, one for each supplier, give daily feedback information to suppliers.*

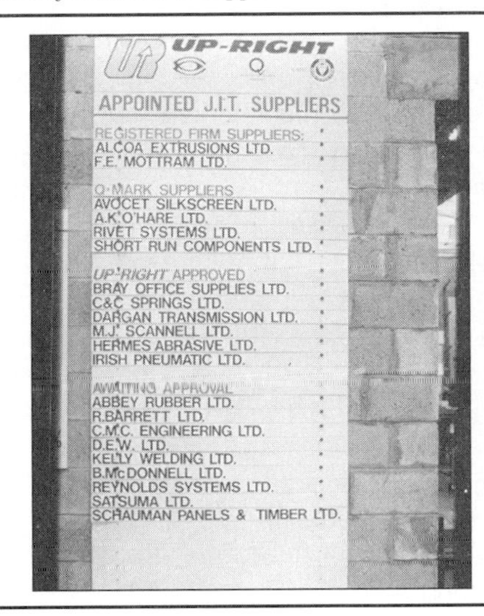

**EXHIBIT 8-9 ISO 9000 Series Standards—2000 Format**

| *Standard* | *Title* |
|---|---|
| ISO 9000 | Quality Management Systems—Fundamentals and Vocabulary |
| ISO 9001 | Quality Management Systems—Requirements |
| ISO 9004 | Quality Management Systems—Guidelines for Performance Improvements |

## *ISO 9000 Series Standards*

The **ISO 9000 Standard** is actually an umbrella name for three separate but related quality standards originally published in 1987 (and revised in 1994 and in 2000) by the International Organization for Standardization, based in Geneva, Switzerland. Though support has been particularly strong within the European community, its use is global. Exhibit 8-9 shows the ISO 9000 standards in their 2000 format.

"ISO" is not an acronym for the International Organization of Standardization; it is Greek for "uniform" and is used as a prefix in words like isobar and isotherm. The intent is that ISO standards are uniform the world over.

Many companies require their suppliers to register to ISO 9000, and expect those suppliers to, in turn, require their own suppliers to register as well. As customers, their rationale is understandable: The quality imperative demands reliable suppliers. Under the ISO 9000 scheme, a company (or a division or plant within a company) arranges to have its *quality systems documentation and implementation* audited by an independent accredited registrar. The phrase "third-party registration" is used to refer to this objective assessment. The particular role(s) to be played by a supplier (design, production, etc.) determine which portions of the standard must be met.

If the quality systems—specifically, the plan, the implementation, and the documentation—are in order, the company is registered, and is permitted to advertise that fact in its promotional materials and other documents. The registrar continues to survey the supplier and makes full reassessments every three or four years.

**QS 9000** is a set of standards based on ISO 9000 but containing additional requirements that are particular to the automotive industry.

Registration isn't cheap. One large international corporation registered 20 of its plants at a per-plant cost of $200,000 to $300,000. When asked how his company could justify such expenditures, one manager replied, "We can't afford not to."[19] But the cost controversy lingers.[20]

Is registration to ISO 9000 standards the ultimate quality performance achievement? No. As mentioned earlier, the standard does not certify quality of goods and services, but rather registers the existence of proper quality plans, programs, documentation, data, and procedures. Some customers may wish to probe deeper and require additional assurances of quality, but they might opt to not bother if a supplier balks at going for ISO registration. Another supplier will want the business.

In the final analysis, registration *is* a form of service to customers. And, managers who have taken companies through ISO 9000 registration offer another perspective; "The only approach to ISO 9000 registration that works is to improve the company's quality system for the benefit of those who function within it; ISO 9000 registration is a by-product of quality system improvement."[21]

### *Deming Prize and Malcolm Baldrige National Quality Award*

Until the late 1980s, the **Deming Prize,** named after W. Edwards Deming and administered by the Union of Japanese Scientists and Engineers (JUSE), was the only quality award of note. First presented in 1951, the Deming Prize was largely unappreciated outside Japan for over 30 years. As the quality of Japanese goods caught the world's attention in the 1970s and 1980s, however, the Deming Prize—along with a wealth of Japanese insight into quality philosophy and technique—gained international acclaim. It is the esteemed grandfather of other quality awards, including the Malcolm Baldrige Award in the United States.

On August 20, 1987, President Ronald Reagan signed Public Law 100–107, the Malcolm Baldrige National Quality Improvement Act. Named after the late secretary of commerce, the legislation reflected growing belief that the U.S. government should take a more active role in promoting quality and established the **Malcolm Baldrige National Quality Award (MBNQA)** that would recognize total quality management in American industry.

Responsibility for managing the award rests with the National Institute of Standards and Technology (NIST) and with the Milwaukee-based American Society for Quality (ASQ). The criteria are applied on an absolute (not relative) scale, and judges have the discretion of giving no awards if applicants fail to measure up. The annual awards for businesses were first given in 1988 and may go to no more than two winners in each of three categories—manufacturing, services, and small business. Exhibit 8-10 contains brief profiles of the 1999 winners along with information for obtaining a historical report of winning companies.

Many more companies ask for award applications than actually apply. In 1991, for example, 235,000 applications were sent out, but only 106 companies applied. Further, only about 10 percent of the applicants merit a site visit by an examination team. Facing such sobering numbers, why even bother with an application?

For some, the motivation comes from a major customer. In 1988, for example, after it won a Baldrige Award, Motorola expected all of its suppliers to apply. Motorola knew that the applications process mandates extensive company introspection; the applications criteria provide an excellent checklist and pathway to total quality improvements. Today, many companies have accepted the premise that self-assessment has rewards of its own.

**EXHIBIT 8-10 Malcolm Baldrige National Quality Award Winners**

**Winning Companies—1999**

**The Ritz-Carlton Hotel Company, L.L.C.**
(Atlanta, GA—service)

The Ritz-Carlton Hotel Company, L.L.C., a wholly owned subsidiary of Marriott International, Inc., manages 36 luxury hotels worldwide. It has about 17,000 employees, and is the only service company to have won the Baldrige Award twice.

**BI**
(Minneapolis, MN—service)

BI employs more than 1,400 associates and helps its customers achieve business goals by enhancing the performance of people. It helps improve communications, training, measurement, and rewards systems.

**STMicroelectronics, Inc.—Region Americas**
(Carrollton, TX—manufacturing)

With over 3,000 employees in 37 North American sites, STMicroelectronics, Inc.—Region Americas designs, develops, manufacturers, and markets semiconductor integrated circuits for global customers in several major industries.

**Sunny Fresh Foods**
(Monticello, MN—small business)

A Wholly owned subsidiary of Cargill, Inc., Sunny Fresh Foods manufacturers further processed egg products. It has about 380 employees.

**History—Winning Companies**

The National Institute of Standards and Technology (NIST) maintains a complete history of the Baldrige Award, including winning companies and their profiles, at its quality web site (www.quality.nist.gov). The brief profiles appearing above (for the 1999 winners) were taken from that source.

*Lobby of the Ritz Carlton Hotel, Boston, Massachusetts. The Ritz Carlton is a two-time winner of the Baldrige Award.*

© Steve Dunwell/Corbis.

Although the basic structure, intent, and procedure associated with the Baldrige Award remain largely as originally designed, the award continues to evolve. The heart of the award is reflected in the core values and concepts, which, in turn, signify evolving ideas about quality of outputs and processes. The core values and concepts in the 2000 criteria were:

1. Visionary Leadership
2. Customer Driven
3. Organizational and Personal Learning
4. Valuing Employees and Partners
5. Agility
6. Focus on the Future
7. Managing for Innovation
8. Management by Fact
9. Public Responsibility and Citizenship
10. Focus on Results and Creating Value
11. Systems Perspective.

The core values and concepts are embodied in seven broad categories containing 19 examination items. Exhibit 8-11 shows the 2000 categories and items along with maximum point scores, reflecting the relative weight given to each item during scoring. J. M. Juran has expressed the opinion that the Baldrige Award criteria are the most comprehensive available list of actions needed to improve quality.[22]

Originally, not-for-profit organizations were ineligible for Baldrige Award competition. Today, however, separate Baldrige Award programs exist for health care and educational organizations. Although there are some differences in terminology to

**EXHIBIT 8-11 MBNQA Examination Criteria—2000**

| *2000 Categories/Items* | | *Point Values* |
|---|---|---|
| **1 Leadership** | | **125** |
| 1.1 Organizational Leadership | 85 | |
| 1.2 Public Responsibility and Citizenship | 40 | |
| **2 Strategic Planning** | | **85** |
| 2.1 Strategy Development | 40 | |
| 2.2 Strategy Deployment | 45 | |
| **3 Customer and Market Focus** | | **85** |
| 3.1 Customer and Market Knowledge | 40 | |
| 3.2 Customer Satisfaction and Relationships | 45 | |
| **4 Information and Analysis** | | **85** |
| 4.1 Measurement of Organizational Performance | 40 | |
| 4.2 Analysis of Organizational Performance | 45 | |
| **5 Human Resource Focus** | | **85** |
| 5.1 Work Systems | 35 | |
| 5.2 Employee Education, Training, and Development | 25 | |
| 5.3 Employee Well-Being and Satisfaction | 25 | |
| **6 Process Management** | | **85** |
| 6.1 Product and Service Processes | 55 | |
| 6.2 Support Processes | 15 | |
| 6.3 Supplier and Partnering Processes | 15 | |
| **7 Business Results** | | **450** |
| 7.1 Customer Focused Results | 115 | |
| 7.2 Financial and Market Results | 115 | |
| 7.3 Human Resource Results | 80 | |
| 7.4 Supplier and Partner Results | 25 | |
| 7.5 Organizational Effectiveness Results | 115 | |
| | **Total Points** | **1,000** |

emphasize fundamental mission objectives, the overall structure and management for these two newer programs closely follow the business model. The NIST Website, www.quality.nist.gov, makes complete criteria for these awards available for downloading.

As with the Deming Prize, the Baldrige has its critics. For example, some people lament the marketability of success that comes from winning the award, or feel that the Baldrige Award mandate for winners to share the secret of success with other companies (even competitors) is unrealistic. Despite the criticisms, however, Baldrige winners continue to attract attention. Perhaps the greatest contribution of the Baldrige Award to date, however, is the fallout in the form of other awards that closely follow its format and the widespread acceptance of its criteria by companies as guidelines for internal improvement efforts, often independent of any award application process.

Winning a quality award is not the signal to relax. In 1990, consultant Richard Dobbins participated in a study of several Deming Prize–winning companies in Japan. The study team members were especially impressed by auto parts supplier Nippondenso. Its proud, highly involved workforce had thoroughly mastered tools of process improvement, and the company made a lot of money and rarely produced a defective part. Dobbins said to a Nippondenso plant manager, "It's easy to see how you won a Deming Prize with a management system like this." The manager replied, "Oh no, we won our Deming Prize in the 1960s; all of this we have learned since then."[23] The learning goes on among Nippondenso's employees. The next section further examines workforce involvement.

## Employee-Driven Quality

We have considered the roots and development of the quality imperative. We now turn to implementation—specifically, the need for broad-based human involvement and commitment. Gaining that commitment requires action on three fronts:

1. *Training.* Everyone needs training in the tools of continuous improvement, problem solving, and statistical process control. In addition, people require training in job skills, plus cross-training for an understanding of the bigger picture.
2. *Organization.* People need to be put into close contact with customers (next process) and suppliers (previous process). This calls for organization of multifunctional customer-, product-, or service-focused cells, teams, and projects.
3. *Local ownership.* The management, control, and reward systems need to be realigned with the goals of employee- and team-driven, customer-centered quality and continuous improvement.

### *Time Out for Training*

Quality is free, Philip Crosby says. It pays its own way—but not without an upfront investment. The investment is for training, the essential catalyst for action.

Amid all the evidence that businesses have taken the quality imperative to heart, the elevated commitment of certain firms to quality-oriented training and cross-training stands out. For example:

Principle 7

Cross-training, mastery, education.

- Banc One Mortgage in Indianapolis has reorganized into teams averaging 17 cross-trained people who work on all aspects of a loan application at once.
- Carolina Power & Light trains all service specialists in two job areas foreign to them.

INTO PRACTICE

## Star-Point System at Miller Brewing Company, Trenton, Ohio

The million-square-foot Trenton brewery produces about the same amount of bottled and canned beer with some 400 production associates as other similarly sized breweries do with 800 employees. A key to the Trenton plant's success is its unique staffing plan: In this three shift, 24-hour-a-day operation, all production associates work nine-hour shifts instead of the usual eight. This adds up to five hours more than the 40-hours-per-week maximum stipulated as regular pay in U.S. wage laws, which means the workforce must receive five hours of "time-and-a-half" overtime pay every week all year long. The extra hour per day per shift, however, offers time for extensive training and for use of that training in the cause of continuous improvement. Within 18 months of being hired, an employee will have advanced through 25 training topics in five modules, called star points: quality, safety, productivity/maintenance, personnel, and administrative. Under quality, for example, the training topics are process improvement, product specifications, housekeeping/good manufacturing practices, raw materials, and records. All employees are on various kinds of teams, and each team designates a member to serve on other teams who deal with matters related to each of the five star points. In sum, the star-point system provides a pathway toward a self-managed team mode of operation.

- A Miller brewery reserves an hour every day for employee training and an array of team-based management activities, even though the plant bottles and cans beer 24 hours a day; see the details in the Into Practice box above.

There are thousands more examples like these. Most come from companies—including large, well-known ones—that had been spending virtually nothing on training frontline employees. The old view was that training is an expense, takes away time from real work, and is down the drain when an employee leaves the company. The new view is that it is a necessary investment.

Lack of training deters teamwork because, at least in Western cultures, people do not seem to be naturally team oriented. Athletic coaches and managers, for example, have to spend years molding lone wolves into wolf packs. In response to the demands of TQM, consultants are out in force providing team-building assistance.

### *Getting Organized—Team Formats*

Team *organization* comes before team building. If a group of angry prisoners received team-building training, they might unite to burn down the jail. The same holds for businesses and agencies. The first priority is getting the right people on the team.

**Quality Circles.** One useful kind of team is the quality circle (which was popularized by Kaoru Ishikawa in Japan, where it is called a quality control [QC] circle). Japan's QC circles contributed as many as 100 times more suggestions per employee than Western

**EXHIBIT 8-12 Quality Circles: Gangs versus Teams**

A. Gangs: Quality circles composed of employees from same department or shop.

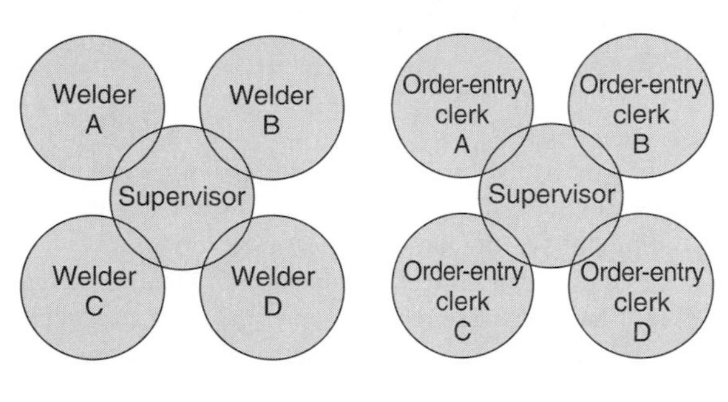


B. Teams: Quality circle composed of a chain of provider user pairs — formally organized into a work cell.

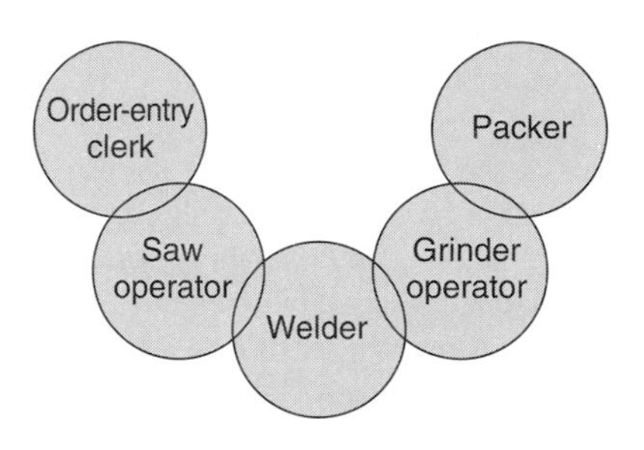


companies could elicit. In short order, quality circles were organized from Melbourne to Calcutta, Cape Town to Oslo, and Montevideo to Anchorage. The results were favorable, but not much more so than certain other programs, such as suggestion plans. It now seems clear that most quality circles were organized in a way that *avoided* a customer focus—that is, they excluded next processes.

Part A of Exhibit 8-12 shows two examples of a quality circle composed of five people in a single department. The first consists of four welders and a supervisor, while the second has four order-entry clerks and a supervisor. Those circles could meet every day and never hear a complaint about the quality of welds or errors in recording customer requirements. Also, the circles would not be inclined to discuss causes of their own delays. Since their customers are not in the circles, the circles will discuss shared annoyances: room temperature, lighting, company recreation and benefits, work hours, and so forth. While all deserve attention, they are only indirectly related to serving a customer. In fact, circles like these may spend much of their time complaining about the demands of customers, instead of teaming up to serve them.

**Cells.** Part B of Exhibit 8-12 shows how to organize quality circles for effective process improvement. This type of circle is hard to organize because it requires moving people and equipment out of functional departments. Here an order-entry clerk is teamed up with the customer who processes the order at the first production operation: a saw operator. The order-entry terminal and the saw are moved close together. Then add more maker–customer pairs from other departments: a welder and welding equipment, a grinder and grinding equipment, and a packer and packing tools and supplies. The five operations become one, a **work cell,** or simply a **cell.** A few companies call it a **natural team.**

Document processing cells and manufacturing cells are rarely organized for the purpose of creating quality circles. Rather, they are formed to quicken response time, cut out many clerical activities and transactions, eliminate bulk handling across long distances, and slash inventories along with potential rework or scrap.

One result, however, is a group of associates who can scarcely avoid some quality circle behaviors. The welder who closes a seam incompletely will hear about it very soon from the grinding machine operator at the adjacent work station. The two are a team whether or not they care to be. A "bad pass" from one cell member to the next gets prompt attention.

**Teams.** As 1980s circles did, teams often employ a facilitator, whose job may include keeping team meetings on track and providing training. One set of team training topics includes team dynamics, communications, and other behavioral matters, including how to interview and choose new employees and how to evaluate one another's performance. Another set aims at general problem-solving tools, such as brainstorming, nominal group techniques, role-playing, and multivoting. Still another set focuses on the "hard sciences" of quality: process flowcharts, Pareto analysis, fishbone and run diagrams, and other process control tools (all discussed in Chapter 9).

To be effective, teams need all three kinds of training. Research by Andersen Consulting and two English universities, however, suggests that Western teams too often emphasize the human issues and neglect process control. In contrast, in Japan, which has more years of experience with teams than the West, the main role of teams is to "support process control and improvement."[24]

To some extent the manufacturing sector already has passed through the phase of teams focused primarily on human issues, as was generally the case during Western industry's first attempts in the early 1980s to implement quality circles. By now, many manufacturers have learned to use the full potential of teams—for both human and quality improvement issues. (See Into Practice box, "Teams, Rocket Science, and Trust.")

INTO PRACTICE

# Teams, Rocket Science, and Trust

Concepts: Multiskilled, cross-functional, self-directed work teams.

Environment: General Electric's jet engine assembly plant in Durham, North Carolina.

"The jet engines are produced by nine teams of people—teams that are given just one basic directive: the day that their next engine must be loaded onto a truck. All other decisions—who does what work; how to balance training, vacations, overtime against work flow; how to make the manufacturing process more efficient; how to handle teammates who slack off—all of that stays within the team.

"And one more thing: Jet engine assembly is rocket science—or rather, something no less difficult than rocket science. In an engine that weighs 8.5 tons and has 10,000 parts, even a nut that weighs less than an ounce is installed with a torque wrench.

"So how can something so complicated, so demanding, so fraught with risk, be trusted to people who answer only to themselves? Trust is a funny thing. It is the mystery—and the genius—of what goes on at GE Durham."

Source: Charles Fishman, "Engines of Democracy," *Fast Company*, October 1999, pp. 175ff.

Service organizations seem to be going through a similar learning process: Early efforts favored human issues and the less effective team membership pattern of Exhibit 8-12A (gangs). Numerous service companies, however, have evolved to more effective forms. An example is Fidelity Investment's "Monetary Gate" team, which, in its own corner of a single building in Texas, is able to process monetary corrections in 24 hours; formerly, corrections went back and forth among offices in dispersed cities and sometimes took months to complete.

### *Local Ownership of TQM*

Unfortunately, smoothly functioning teams don't spring forth directly out of TQM training sessions. Individual behaviors change slowly, and frustration breeds in the void.

It need not be so. An excellent quick outlet for initial TQM enthusiasm is your own *personal quality checksheet,* which is a list of a few standout personal defects that you can record by a simple tally stroke on a checksheet in your pocket or on your desk. In their book *Quality Is Personal,* Harry Roberts and Bernard Sergesketter explain using their own experiences, plus those of colleagues.[25] Sergesketter, a manager for AT&T's Central Region of Business Network Sales, developed the method, and many of his associates quickly picked it up. His initial checksheet is as follows.

On time for meetings.

Answer phone in two rings or less.

Return phone calls same or next day.

Respond to letters in five business days.

Clean desk.

Credenza: only same-day paper.

Sergesketter counted his total number of defects monthly. The total quickly fell from about 100 in spring 1990 to 10, then 5. Also, he has implemented changes, such as date-stamping mail, that help with measuring defects and attaining improved performance.

Roberts, a University of Chicago professor, has found that just making the list has resulted in virtual elimination of some defects. Many of his executive MBA students have taken up the personal quality checksheet habit in their studies and back on their jobs as well. Experience so far suggests the following:

1. Define the defect unambiguously so it can be recognized easily and tallied.
2. No New Year's resolutions. Focus on attainable defects, especially waste reducers and time-savers. Later refine the list, perhaps including activity expanders to make productive use of the time saved.

As personal quality checksheets lead the way and teams follow, everyone needs to feel a sense of ownership of control, of improvements, and of results. It also means less control from on high and fewer levels of management to review improvement proposals. Further, the company must shift toward rewarding specific results at local levels rather than general ones at high levels.

**EXHIBIT 8-13 Drawings Based on Two of the Many Quality Improvement Charts at Florida Power & Light**

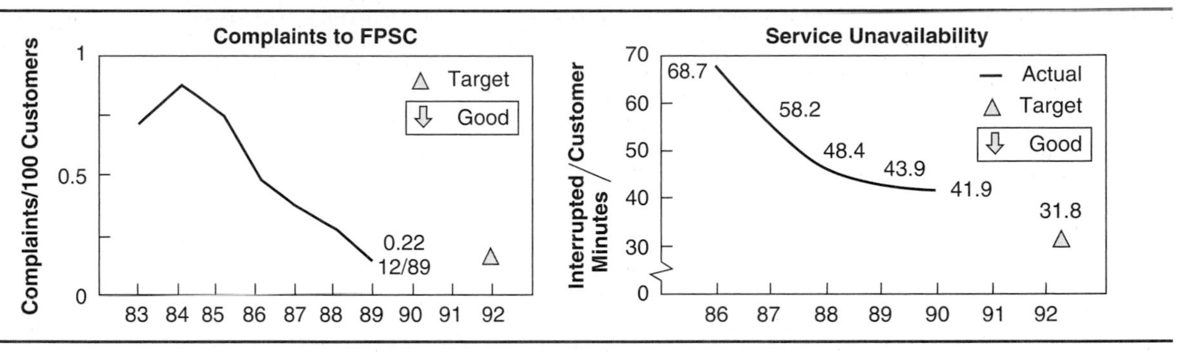


To support local ownership, managers need to be out of their offices and visible locally, where they admire control charts and process experiments, help remove obstacles, and pass out awards. When local ownership has truly taken root, the evidence is likely to include charts of all kinds—on walls, doors, and partitions—*in the workplace* rather than in managers, offices. Exhibit 8-13 shows two examples from Florida Power & Light, 1989 winner of Japan's Deming Prize (the first non-Japanese winner of the prize).

**Principle 14**

Retain local ownership of quality, data, results.

There is much more to be said about local ownership and total quality control. We will continue to explore these topics in detail in the remaining chapters.

## Summary Check Points

- ✓ Quality of output and process is an imperative in contemporary business.
- ✓ Providers should adopt a broad definition of quality, capable of incorporating multiple performance characteristics, and focused on what customers really want.
- ✓ In practice, programs aimed at improving total quality programs exist under a variety of names and incorporate a host of tools from diverse disciplines.
- ✓ Modern quality assurance has evolved; ancient and often harsh codes gave way to artisan pride until the Industrial Revolution served to separate provider from customer.
- ✓ Consumerism movements, government intervention, and tort liability laws have played roles in assuring quality and safety of contemporary goods and services.
- ✓ Quality pioneers of the twentieth century, all known for emphasis on broader management issues, include W. Edwards Deming, Joseph M. Juran, Armand V. Feigenbaum, Kaoru Ishikawa, Philip B. Crosby, and Genichi Taguchi.
- ✓ The total quality movement and development of modern OM have mostly attempted to accomplish the same ends; the process improvement that serves a key OM objective will often serve a quality objective as well.
- ✓ The preponderance of research evidence suggests that companies that invest in total quality improvement programs reap additional benefits in the form of financial returns and greater market (competitive) power.

✓ The *value-of-quality* assumption has mostly supplanted the older *cost-of-quality* argument; the modern concern is for the costs incurred by not having quality.
✓ Quality is recognized through benchmarking, supplier certification, registration to global standards (e.g., ISO 9000), and quality awards (e.g., the Deming Prize and the Malcolm Baldrige National Quality Award).
✓ Employee-driven quality requires an investment in human resources, but the payoff has been demonstrated in numerous organizational settings.
✓ Team formats should favor the provider-customer chain orientation rather than a functional group structure.
✓ Local ownership of TQM often begins with a personal orientation to quality.

## Exercises

1. Interview two managers, one in the private sector and the other from the public sector. Ask the following questions:
   *a.* Is quality increasing or decreasing in importance in your field?
   *b.* Does improved quality pay? Why or why not?

   Discuss your findings.
2. "The only acceptable performance is zero defects." Discuss the application of that phrase to each of the following situations:
   *a.* Surgeons performing elective surgery.
   *b.* Machinists fabricating automobile engines.
   *c.* Lawyers defending accused child molesters.
   *d.* Grocers stocking the supermarket deli display.
   *e.* Investment counselors giving financial advice.
   *f.* Police officers apprehending a suspect.
   *g.* County clerks recording tax payments.
   *h.* Merchants selling exercise equipment.
   *i.* College students typing term papers.
3. How do you determine quality in products? For example, how do you distinguish a good automobile (or barstool, topcoat, aspirin, or golf ball) from a bad one? Does the item's price influence your thinking? What are society's beliefs regarding a relationship between price and quality? Are these beliefs realistic?
4. How do you determine quality in services? For example, how do you distinguish a good lawyer (or accountant, professor, athlete, or barber) from a bad one? Does the service's price—fee charged or salary received—have any influence on your thinking? Does society pay the same attention to price when judging the quality of services as it does in the case of goods? Why or why not?
5. Refer to Exhibit 8-1, "Dimensions of Quality":
   *a.* Explain each of the 10 dimensions of service quality as it applies to one service of your choice.
   *b.* Explain each of Garvin's eight dimensions of quality as it applies to a product of your choice.

6. Apply the Plan-Do-Check-Act cycle (details contained in chapter supplement)—suggest specific actions for each of the four steps—to one of the following problems:
   *a.* Fellow employees (or students) are habitually late or absent from team meetings.
   *b.* Cashier lines at the cafeteria take too much time.
   *c.* Utility bills at home (house, apartment, dorm, or fraternity or sorority house) are too high.
   *d.* The bookstore always runs out of blank computer diskettes.
   *e.* Printer cartridges in the computer lab run out of ink (creating light print).
7. *John:* Hi Jane! How's it going?

   *Jane:* Lousy! My grandmom sent me a sweater for my birthday, but there's a flaw in the weaving. I have to mail it back to her, she has to return it to the store and hope they have another of the same style and color in my size, and then send it back to me. What a pain! She shouldn't have to go through that hassle.

   *John:* Yeah, I've been through that no-questions-asked returns policy too many times myself.
   *a.* List the members of the provider–customer chain in the above story.
   *b.* Where did quality break down?
   *c.* What social costs occurred in the above story?
   *d.* How might situations like the above be prevented?
   *e.* Is a free-returns policy high-quality service? Why or why not?
8. Acme Inc. has just installed a high-efficiency motor-generator set to clean up the electrical power supply (remove unwanted fluctuations) to its precision equipment lab. Results include more accurate readings for tests, longer equipment life with less downtime, lower maintenance costs, shorter turnaround times for lab services for Acme's customers, and more accurate job scheduling due to increased equipment reliability. Is the expenditure for the motor-generator set a cost of quality? Discuss.
9. *Suzy:* Sam, they've reduced our training budget again! How can my people provide the TQM training our company needs in order to achieve preferred supplier certification from Caterpillar? And we're also trying to get ISO 9000/QS 9000 registration!

   *Sam:* I know. I talked to Betty in budgeting this morning. The feeling among the powers that be is that during the current business slump cuts have to come from soft areas—places that aren't value-adding. I guess their feeling about training is, "Adds costs but no proven value." Do you think we might present a convincing argument to change their minds?

   Write a brief essay containing arguments that Suzy and Sam could use in trying to get the training budget restored.
10. At Ace Repair, at the completion of each job, the mechanic uses a prepared checklist to inspect his own work. For large jobs, this can consume up to half an hour. A wall sign informs customers that labor is billed at $45 an hour.
    *a.* Should the mechanics inspect their own work? Why or why not?
    *b.* Is the inspection time a cost of quality? Discuss.
    *c.* Does the value-of-quality notion apply? Why or why not.
    *d.* If "do it right the first time" is a company policy, is the inspection really necessary? Why or why not?
    *e.* Suppose we were talking about maintenance or repairs to commercial jet aircraft; how would your responses to parts *a*, *b*, and *c* change?
11. A young athlete aspires to win an Olympic medal in speedskating. She is well aware of the accomplishments of Bonnie Blair, the United States' gold medalist, and decides that

benchmarking can help. She records Ms. Blair's winning times for each skating event and proclaims, "Those are my benchmarks." Discuss this approach to benchmarking.

12. At Sandwiches-Are-We, the manager of the second shift, which covers the dinner-hour rush, declares: "We have too many customer gripes about cold sandwiches. Any ideas?" One young part-time employee (who happens to be taking an OM course at City University) replies, "Not now, but we can use benchmarking to solve the problem." Discuss the pros and cons of this approach to benchmarking.
13. Abdul and Alice are co-chairs of the University Student Service Club's fundraising committee. For the past few years, fundraising has been on the decline, but Abdul and Alice are determined to reverse that trend. They plan to benchmark other campus organizations, and copy the successful ones. What are the pros and cons of their plan?
14. Review the list of Malcolm Baldrige National Quality Award winners listed on the NIST web site called out in Exhibit 8–10. Pick two of the winners and investigate their performance since winning the award. Discuss your findings.
15. Would quality circles work well in improving the performance of a hockey team? Of a group of students banding together to study? Discuss.
16. After 12 to 19 percent increases in tuition and other fees across the state university system, a group of concerned students, parents, and other friends of higher education formed an ad hoc group to investigate the problem of runaway college costs.
    *a.* Is this group a team as defined in the text? Discuss.
    *b.* Who (what agencies, groups, etc.) ought to be represented in the group to prevent the *gang* syndrome from taking over.
17. At Rocky Mountain Academy, the basketball and skiing coaches have decided to employ the quality circle concept. Each circle will consist of the top five athletes on the team. The coaches' purpose is to try to tap their athletes' intelligence and thereby generate ideas that will improve the teams' effectiveness. Considering what makes quality circles work well or poorly, assess the likely results of the quality circle experiment for each coach.
18. Seven bank tellers volunteered to form the bank's first quality circle. The human resources department conducted an attitude survey just before the quality circle was formed and again after it had been meeting for six months. The survey showed a dramatic improvement in morale and attitude. Further, the circle produced 38 suggestions in the six-month period. Is this quality circle well conceived? Are its results excellent, or not?

## SUPPLEMENT

# QUALITY PIONEERS OF THE 20TH CENTURY

Discounting the ancient artisan's pride in doing the job right, we may place the roots of TQM in the 20th century. Britain's R.A. Fisher's classic agricultural experiments during the first two decades set the stage for the experimental design and statistical process control tools we have today. Walter Shewhart, a physicist at Bell Labs, applied Fisher's concepts directly to manufacturing, and the modern era of quality was off and running[26].

Shewhart, in turn, exerted strong influence over the late W. Edwards Deming and Joseph M. Juran, perhaps the two dominant figures in the quality movement. In this supplement, we present some of the major contributions of Deming and Juran, along with those of Armand V. Feigenbaum, Kaoru Ishikawa, Philip B. Crosby, and Genichi Taguchi.

## W. Edwards Deming

Although relatively unknown in his native country, the late W. Edwards Deming has been a Japanese hero for some 50 years. He began to gain recognition in the United States for his contributions to quality management on June 24, 1980, when NBC broadcast "If Japan Can . . . Why Can't We?" That documentary highlights Deming's role in Japan's industrial ascendancy.

Japan named its top national prize for contributions to quality after Deming and first awarded the Deming Prize in 1951. Deming continued to travel to Japan over the next three decades, sharing his concepts on data-based quality, developing a competitive edge, and management's role in these areas in general.[27]

In his later years, Deming lectured extensively, advocating his 14 points for management (see Exhibit S8-1). He believed that while quality is everyone's job, management must lead the effort.

### EXHIBIT S8-1 Deming's 14 Points

1. Create constancy of purpose for the improvement of product and service with a plan to become competitive, stay in business, and provide jobs. Decide whom top management is responsible to.
2. Adopt the new philosophy. We are in a new economic age. We can no longer live with commonly accepted levels of delays, mistakes, defective materials, and defective workmanship.
3. Cease dependence on mass inspection. Require, instead, statistical evidence that quality is built in. (Prevent defects rather than detect defects.)
4. End the practice of awarding business on the basis of price tag alone. Instead, depend on meaningful measures of quality, along with price. Eliminate suppliers that cannot qualify with statistical evidence of quality.
5. Find problems. It is management's job to work continually on the system (design, incoming materials, composition of material, maintenance, improvement of machine, training, supervision, retraining).
6. Institute modern methods of training on the job.
7. The responsibility of foremen must be changed from sheer numbers to quality . . . [which] will automatically improve productivity. Management must prepare to take immediate action on reports from foremen concerning barriers such as inherited defects, machines not maintained, poor tools, fuzzy operational definitions.
8. Drive out fear, so that everyone may work effectively for the company.
9. Break down barriers between departments. People in research, design, sales, and production must work as a team to foresee problems of production that may be encountered with various materials and specifications.
10. Eliminate numerical goals, posters, and slogans for the workforce asking for new levels of productivity without providing methods.
11. Eliminate work standards that prescribe numerical quotas.
12. Remove barriers that stand between the hourly worker and his or her right to pride of workmanship.
13. Institute a vigorous program of education and retraining.
14. Create a structure in top management that will push every day on the above 13 points.

Source: Adapted from W. Edwards Deming, *Quality Productivity and Competitive Position* (Cambridge, Mass: MIT, Center for Advanced Engineering Study, 1982), pp. 16–17.

Further, he stated that his 14 points apply to both small and large organizations and in the service sector as well as in manufacturing.

Deming was known for his "rough" style in his seminars. He would not let managers off the hook if he sensed that they lacked sufficient commitment to quality.

Deming was an ardent proponent of training. He argued that doing your best simply isn't good enough until you know what you're doing. According to Deming, there is no substitute for knowledge. Classic Deming may be seen in the following excerpt from one of his (self-reported) communications to one organization's management:

> This report is written at your request after study of some of the problems that you have been having with production, high costs, and variable quality, which altogether, as I understand you, have been the cause of considerable worry to you about your competitive position. . . . My opening point is that no permanent impact has ever been accomplished in improvement of quality unless the top management carries out their responsibilities. These responsibilities never cease: they continue forever. No short-cut has ever been discovered. Failure of your own management to accept and act on their responsibilities for quality is, in my opinion, the prime cause of your trouble.[28]

The PDCA cycle is referred to as the Deming cycle by many, perhaps because he is largely responsible for its popularity. Deming, however, gave credit for its creation to his mentor, Walter Shewhart, who also developed the control chart.

As a statistician, Deming was an ardent proponent of the use of process data to make decisions and solve problems: use analysis if the data exist; if not, use experimentation and data collection. He followed an orderly approach to continuous improvement known as the **Plan-Do-Check-Act (PDCA) cycle,** which is among the best-known tools in the TQM arsenal. One form is shown in Exhibit S8-2.

## Joseph M. Juran

Like Deming, Joseph M. Juran was a pioneer of quality education in Japan. He has also been known in the Western world for his textbooks and as editor-in-chief of *The Quality Control Handbook.* Like Deming, Juran was largely ignored by American management until the 1980s.

Juran's research has shown that over 80 percent of quality defects are *management controllable,* and it is therefore management that most needs change. He published *Managerial Breakthrough* in 1964 as a guide for the solution of chronic quality problems.[29] The breakthrough procedure is designed to gain and maintain improvements in quality. The sequence is as follows.[30]

1. Convince others that a breakthrough is needed.
2. Identify the *vital few* projects (involves Pareto analyses, discussed in Chapter 9).

**EXHIBIT S8-2 The Plan-Do-Check-Act Cycle for Continuing Improvement**

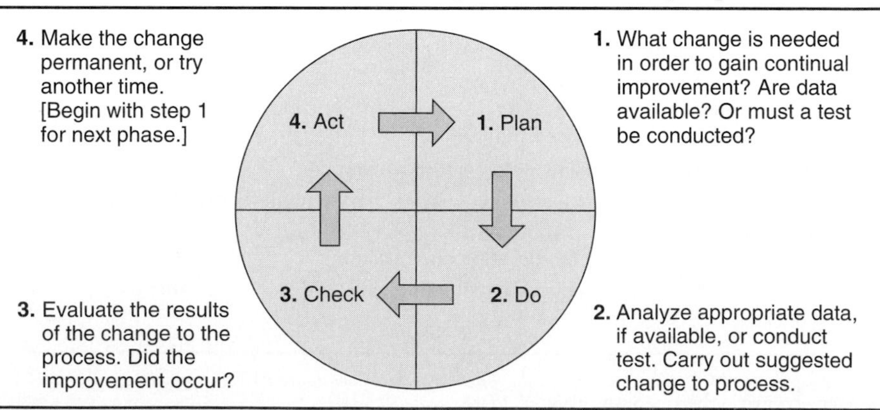

3. Organize for a breakthrough in knowledge.
4. Conduct an analysis to discover the cause(s) of the problem.
5. Determine the effect of the proposed changes on the people involved, and find ways to overcome resistance to these changes.
6. Take action to institute the changes, including training of all personnel involved.
7. Institute appropriate controls that will hold the new, improved quality level but not restrict continued improvement—perhaps through another breakthrough sequence.

Juran's now-classic definition of quality is *fitness for use.* He intends those words to apply broadly, to include such properties as reliability, maintainability, and producibility; also, in certain situations, service response time, service availability, and price.

Juran defines quality management in terms of the *quality trilogy,*[31] which consists of:

Quality planning.
Quality control.
Quality improvement.

Proper quality planning results in processes capable of meeting quality goals under certain operating conditions. Quality control consists of measuring actual quality performance, comparing it with a standard, and acting on any difference. Juran believes that inherent planning deficiencies might result in chronic waste, and it is up to the control process (initially) to keep the waste from getting any worse. Finally, quality improvement is superimposed on quality control. Quality improvement means finding ways to do better than standard and breaking through to unprecedented levels of performance. The desired end results are quality levels that are even higher than planned performance levels.

## Armand V. Feigenbaum

Armand V. Feigenbaum is best known for originating the concept of **total quality control (TQC).** In his book *Total Quality Control* (first published in 1951 under another title), Feigenbaum explains that quality must be attended to through all stages of the industrial cycle and that

> control must start with identification of customer quality requirements and end only when the product has been placed in the hands of a customer who remains satisfied. Total quality control guides the coordinated actions of people, machines, and information to achieve this goal.[32]

To Feigenbaum, responsibility for TQC must be shared and should not rest with the quality assurance (QA) or quality control (QC) function alone. Feigenbaum also clarified the idea of *quality costs*—costs associated with poor quality. He was among the first to argue that better quality is, in the long run, cheaper. He defines "hidden plant" as the proportion of plant capacity that exists in order to rework unsatisfactory parts. This proportion generally ranges from 15 to 40 percent of the plant's capacity.

## Kaoru Ishikawa

Kaoru Ishikawa, the late Japanese quality authority, acknowledged Deming's and Juran's influence on his thinking. However, Ishikawa must be recognized for his own contributions. He was responsible for the initial deployment of **quality control circles**—small groups of employees that meet regularly to plan and (often) carry out process changes to improve quality, productivity, or the work environment.

He also developed Ishikawa cause–effect charts, or "fishbone diagrams," so named because of their structural resemblance to the skeleton of a fish (discussed in Chapter 9). Like Deming, Juran, and Feigenbaum, Ishikawa also emphasized quality as a way of management.

Ishikawa felt that there is not enough reliance on inputs to quality from nonspecialists. In 1968, he began using the term *companywide quality control (CWQC)* to differentiate the broadened approach to TQC from the more specialized view. Today, the terms TQC and CWQC are used almost interchangeably.

Another significant contribution of Ishikawa is his work on taking much of the mystery out of the statistical aspects of quality assurance. Conforming to the belief that without statistical analysis there can be no quality control, Ishikawa divided statistical methods into three categories according to level of difficulty, as shown in Exhibit S8-3.

The intermediate and advanced methods are for engineers and quality specialists and are beyond the scope of our discussion. The elemental statistical method, or the *seven indispensable tools* for process control, however, are for everyone's use and should be mastered by all organization members. Ishikawa intends that to include company presidents, directors, middle managers, supervisors, and front-line employees. His experience suggests that about 95 percent of all problems within a company can be solved with these tools. (We examine them in Chapter 9.)

### Philip B. Crosby

Philip B. Crosby, former corporate vice president and director of quality control at ITT Corp., is the author of the popular book *Quality Is Free: The Art of Making Quality Certain.* In his book,

**EXHIBIT S8-3 Ishikawa's Statistical Methods**

I. Elemental statistical method.
   *a.* Pareto analysis (vital few versus trivial many).
   *b.* Cause-and-effect diagram, also known as the *fishbone chart* (this, Ishikawa points out, is not a true statistical technique).
   *c.* Stratification.
   *d.* Checksheet.
   *e.* Histogram.
   *f.* Scatter diagram.
   *g.* Graph and Shewhart process control chart.

II. Intermediate statistical method.
   *a.* Theory of sampling surveys.
   *b.* Statistical sampling inspection.
   *c.* Various methods of statistical estimation and hypothesis testing.
   *d.* Methods of utilizing sensory tests.
   *e.* Methods of experiment design.

III. Advanced statistical method (using computers).
   *a.* Advanced experimental design.
   *b.* Multivariate analysis.
   *c.* Operations research methods.

Source: Adapted from Kaoru Ishikawa, *What Is Total Quality Control? The Japanese Way,* trans. David J. Lu (Englewood Cliffs, N.J.: Prentice-Hall, 1985), chap. 12 (TSI56.I8313).

Crosby explains that quality is not a gift but is free. What costs money is all the things that prevent jobs from being done right the first time. When quality is made certain, an organization avoids these expenses.

Crosby proposes **zero defects** as the goal for quality. To any who find that goal too ambitious, he simply asks, "If not zero defects, then what goal would you propose?" One often-used figure is the acceptable quality level (AQL), which is used in acceptance inspection. Briefly, AQL allows a certain proportion of defective items. Crosby explains that an AQL is a commitment to a certain amount of defects—before we start! The AQL idea is certainly out of step with a commitment to continuous improvement. Taking the consumer's view, Crosby makes his point bluntly:

> Consider the AQL you would establish on the product you buy. Would you accept an automobile that you knew in advance was 15 percent defective? 5 percent? 1 percent? One half of 1 percent? How about the nurses that care for newborn babies? Would an AQL of 3 percent on mishandling be too rigid?[33]

Crosby says that mistakes are caused by two things: lack of knowledge and lack of attention. Lack of knowledge, he argues, is measurable and can be attacked with well-known means. Lack of attention, however, is an attitude problem and must be changed by the individual. The individual, in turn, has a better chance of making the change if there exists a company commitment to zero defects. Crosby also states that while the tools of quality control are useful and available, they must be put into perspective. The important factor, he insists, is understanding and meeting a customer's requirements.[34]

## Genichi Taguchi

Is it sufficient to control processes, inspect output, identify and remove defects, and rely on customer feedback? Genichi Taguchi says no. To improve quality, he argues, one must look upstream at the design stage because that is where quality begins. Quality must be designed in; it cannot be inspected in later. One fact of obtaining better design is experimentation on variables that contribute to a product's performance. Taguchi's strong belief in this approach has brought **design of experiments (DOE)** into wider use by quality experts, designers, and other members of design-build teams. Taguchi also believes that teams should aim for **robust designs**—designs that can withstand the hard-to-eliminate variabilities that occur in transformation processes or later in customer use.

Little was known of Taguchi's ideas in North America until the American Supplier Institute (formerly a Ford Motor Company training unit) began to offer courses on Taguchi methods to the general public in 1984. Taguchi's short-cut variations on conventional DOE tools are efficient, working only with those variables that are most likely to contribute to large improvements quickly. For example, suppose that a compound is being created from 15 chemicals; each chemical can be purchased from two suppliers, and there is a slight variation in chemical concentrations between the two sources. Classical experimental design, calling for a *full factorial experiment,* would need $2^{15}$ (or 32,768) test runs to determine the mix of suppliers that yields optimal compound performance, with all chemical interactions considered. Taguchi would use a form of *fractional factorial experiment,* referred to as an *orthogonal array,* to perform the experiment in only 16 test runs.[35] The orthogonal array is a balanced plan for experimentation. Only those design variables deemed (by experts) most likely to affect output or performance are included.

While purists have faulted Taguchi's methods on various technical grounds, advocates argue that optimal design is not the important aim. Rather, a design that is nearly optimal and very quickly obtained is preferable.[36] Taguchi's approach tends to appeal to engineers—his customers—who find the presentation understandable and usable.

In addition to his work in design, Taguchi is known for development of the previously discussed quality loss function. Taguchi intends that the loss function remain valid at all times during a product's life. In theory, when process output performance reaches the specification limit, the customer's *economic* interest in the item is neutral; that is, the losses will exactly offset any gain from having the item.

For Taguchi, social loss must affect quality cost management decisions; that is, investments in quality improvement should be compared with savings to society rather than to the firm alone. Ultimately society will reward (or penalize) the firm for its record of societal savings; thus, Taguchi's view is meant to be sound for business.

CHAPTER 9

# Process Control and Improvement

The quality imperative is just that—a demand or mandate from customers. But quality becomes reality through the efforts of skilled people using the tools of their trades and motivated to provide that quality. A. V. Feigenbaum wrote, in his milestone book, *Total Quality Control,* that the burden of proof rests with the maker of the part, not with inspectors.[1] Thus, with sound design as a supporting platform, those who operate the transformation processes that create goods and services must stand ready to assume the responsibility for quality. In this chapter, we look closely at how processes are controlled and improved.

## Improving Outputs and Processes

When people do apply their skills and motivations to the improvement of customer-serving processes—the general topic of Part III—positive results can extend beyond quality improvement and reach into the larger set of customer wants. That is, although improvement in quality per se is a primary aim of process improvement, it is not the only one.

### *Targets: Quality* and . . .

As we have noted in past chapters, process outputs can be many and varied. Improvement efforts may target—and achieve—better quality, faster response (lower times), lower variability, better service, or combinations of these and other customer wants. The Into Practice box "Improving the Process" illustrates with two service examples: better and faster clinical research at Procter & Gamble and improved after-sale service to automobile buyers at Lexus. And, if one accepts the broad definition of quality espoused in Chapter 8, these process improvements also constitute quality improvements.

Sometimes, in fact, our definition of quality is time: That is the case when we stand, fidgeting impatiently, in long lines waiting for service. Usually, however, the time–quality connection is more subtle than that. As Robert Galvin, former CEO of Motorola, put it, "One can focus on time and improve quality" and "one can focus on quality and accomplish time."[2] The following points explain this apparent contradiction:

- *Quick response.* Improving quality eliminates delays for rework, process adjustments, and placating customers, thus providing quick response for a greater percentage of customers.
- *On-time.* Quality the first time—every time—removes a major cause of delays, late completions, and unpredictability, thereby improving on-time performance.

INTO PRACTICE

# Improving the Process

Procter & Gamble wanted its over-the-counter (OTC) clinical trials process to be more effective. It could have focused on quality—measured by "audit findings" or data errors or inconsistencies that must be resolved before a clinical study is approved for release. Instead, the company . . . "focused the improvement on significant reductions in clinical cycle time." This includes the time required for planning, initiating, and reporting clinical studies. (It does not include time when test subjects are on a drug or treatment regimen.) Using plan-do-check-act (PDCA), flowcharts, control charts, and other process improvement tools, the company was, in three years, able to cut study cycle times by 83 percent while improving data quality by over 60 percent.

Source: David A. McCamey, Robert W. Boggs, and Linda M. Bayuk, "More, Better, Faster from Total Quality Effort," *Quality Progress,* August 1999, pp. 43–50.

*Quality Digest (to Richard L. Chitty, vice president of parts, service, and customer satisfaction for Lexus, the luxury car division of Toyota Motor Sales, U.S.A.):* How do you identify and deal with process problems in a service environment?

*Chitty:* We developed Lexus service by flowcharting everything. . . . This forms the basis for our service training. If some problem occurs, you go back and look at the flowchart and say, OK, here's our problem. [For example,] normally, if a customer has a tire problem, they go to the Goodyear or the Firestone store. But Lexus doesn't want that. We want customers to come back to us. That was the problem we identified. The next step was to map out the process. We flowcharted it. We examined the process, took the emotions out of it, determined the right thing to do, and then got the vendor in and figured out a system to deal with the issue.[1]

Source: Dirk Dusharme, "An Interview with Richard L. Chitty," *Quality Digest,* December 1995, pp. 50–51.

*Continuous Process Improvement. Customer discussing service needs with Lexus service department personnel.*

© James Shaffer.

- *Quick feedback.* All efforts to cut out delays (the whole just-in-time, or quick-response, agenda) provide quicker feedback on causes of bad quality, allowing earlier process improvement efforts. To quote from Western Electric's classic handbook on quality control, "It is an axiom in quality control that the time to identify assignable causes is while those causes are active," and further, "delay may mean that the cause of trouble is harder to identify, and in many cases cannot be identified at all."[3] In other words, anything that reduces delays is a powerful technique for process quality improvement.

- *Enough time for quality.* The time saved by removing delays and making quality right must not be squandered. It needs to be reinvested in training, design collaboration, inspection and on-the-spot correction, feedback and consultation with people in earlier and later processes, data collection, and improvement projects. If those activities are neglected, for example, under pressure for more output, quality suffers, and a chain reaction of delays and variations results in *less* output and *slower* response.

**Principle 10**

Make quality easy to achieve.

These interlinkages—time, quality, and problems in general—suggest that improvement should be looked at broadly. Discussion through the rest of the chapter follows through with that idea in mind. Furthermore, in Chapters 10 and 11, where we highlight lower costs and faster times as primary process improvement goals, we shall note concurrent quality improvements as well.

### *Source-Oriented Improvement Cycle*

The quality improvement action cycle (seen first in Chapter 7) appears again in Exhibit 9-1. It is a repeating design-discover-improve sequence, and here we emphasize the process aspect of the design stage. A full description of the cycle follows.

**Design.** The first two steps build quality into the process or stop a wayward process in its tracks.

1. Design a capable, fail-safe process, for the best approach is prevention. **Process capability** means capable of meeting customer requirements or specifications. (We address capability later in the chapter.) Since no design is perfect, add backup protection: fail-safe devices or procedures. The aim of

Some companies refer to fail-safing by its Japanese name, *pokayoke*.

**EXHIBIT 9-1 Quality Action Cycle: Process Orientation**

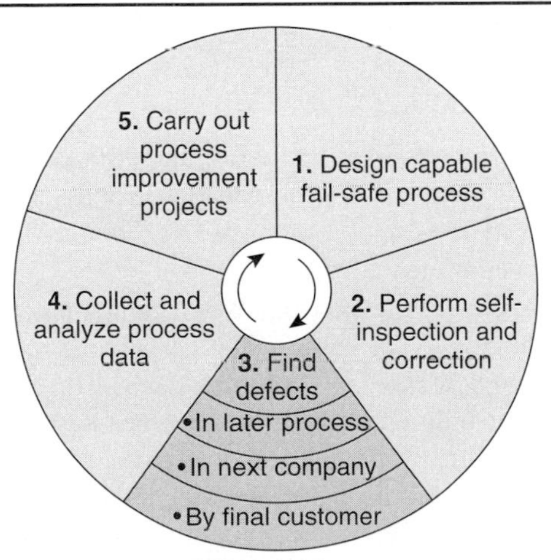

**fail-safing** is to equip a process with features that prevent a mishap from going forward or even happening at all. For example, an invoice-payment computer routine won't write a check for an out-of-bounds amount.

2. If the process is not fail-safe, the next best response is self-inspection and correction. Each frontline associate receives authority to correct a problem, such as placating an angry customer on the spot, or to stop whole production line, to avoid making bad products. And every work group takes responsibility for correcting its own mishaps; no passing problems on to a separate complaint or rework department.

### Detection

3. When problems cannot be fully contained at the source, we are pushed into the poor practice of inspection and discovery at a later stage (dark, shaded zone in Exhibit 9-1). Delayed detection is costly and damaging to reputations. Quick-as-possible feedback provides some damage control. The early-warning system should provide specific feedback from all subsequent error discovery points: in a later process in the same organization, within the next company, and by the final customer.

Principles 2 & 14

Dedicate to continuous improvement. Involve frontline associates in problem solving.

**Improvement.** Process improvement requires collection and use of data about process problems:

4. Collecting process data cannot be a sporadic effort. Supervisors and operators need training in how to measure quality, collect quality data, and analyze quality statistics in order to isolate root causes.
5. The collected data become the raw material for problem solving. Process improvement teams analyze the data and attack the problems. Improvement projects aim at making deficient processes capable and fail-safe, and the quality action cycle begins again.

## *Role of Quality Professionals*

With a quality-at-the-source mind-set and frontline associates assuming primary responsibility for quality, is there still a need for a quality assurance (QA) department? Usually there is, except in very small organizations. However, the quality movement changes the role of that department.

Exhibit 9-2 notes the changes, which are toward greater professionalism and heightened responsibilities for quality professionals. They plan, report, audit, coordinate, train, consult, and develop new methodologies for quality. Instead of merely inspecting someone else's work, they audit entire quality-assurance systems. And, they help with the transition of various quality-assurance activities to the source. Noted quality authority Frank Gryna explains: "By far the best way to implement quality methods is through line organizations rather than through a staff quality department. Isn't it a shame that it took us so long to understand this point?"[4]

**Exhibit 9-2 The Quality Department: Emerging Roles**

- Companywide quality planning.
- Generating executive reports on quality.
- Auditing outgoing quality.
- Auditing quality practices.
- Coordinating and assisting on improvement projects.
- Training for quality.
- Consulting for quality.
- Developing new quality methodologies.
- Transferring activities to line departments.

Source: Adapted from Frank M. Gryna, "The Quality Director of the '90s." *Quality Progress,* April 1991, p. 37.

Kelly Air Force Base, San Antonio, Texas, is making the transition. One hundred seventy-one teams were formed to focus on quality improvement. According to Rodney House, assistant to the base commander, "Inspection has always been a separate operation by certified personnel. We are now trending toward production workers doing their own inspection and we will certify a limited number of them for it."[5] Many businesses and the general public, however, are confused about inspectors and inspection—as we note next.

## *Inspection*

Recall the TV ad of the inspector in the white smock at the end of the production line saying something like, "I do a complete inspection of every [pair of jeans, telephone set, etc.]. Nothing goes out of here without my stamp of approval on it. You can count on it!"

But we cannot count on it. Inspection is the least effective way to control quality. As Exhibit 9-1 shows, we try first to design quality into the process. We want to handle remaining defectives and process variation through process improvement. Still, what do you do when design and improvement are weak? You rely on inspection. The modified quality action cycle, with a much enlarged detection zone, is shown below.

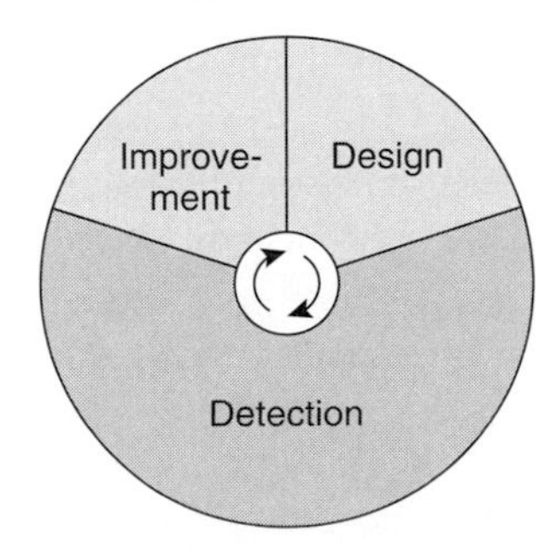

CONTRAST

## Quality-Assurance Staff

### Inspected-in Quality

Quality professionals and inspectors were responsible for quality.

There were never enough inspectors, so:

- Parts sat around for days waiting to be declared good or bad.
- Clients had to wait for an inspector to approve a service (e.g., authorize payment on a check) or review paperwork.

### Built-in Quality

Frontline associates are responsible for their own process integrity and output quality.

Quality professionals serve as expert back-up to line people, giving advice on improvement projects, training, and other quality assurance support.

Inspectors are reassigned and carry their expertise into other line and staff work.

The following are some situations where inspection is likely or necessary:

- To enter an airport concourse, everyone and their hand-carried items goes through security X-ray screening.
- A process for handling nuclear materials is fully capable and under strict process control. Still, to be doubly safe, regulations require inspection.
- The quality- and process-control situation for a brand-new supplier are unknown. It's prudent to inspect the incoming products.
- One of your own processes varies wildly. It's prudent to inspect the output.

Thus, even though quality by design and by improvement is much preferred, inspection cannot be eliminated. The following are five approaches to inspection, all of which aim at catching mishaps efficiently.

*Opinion surveys.* Service clients fill out a form or answer questions about quality of a service. Open-ended questions require judgmental review; answers on, say, a seven-point numeric scale may be reduced to service-quality statistics. Willingness of clients to participate affects survey reliability.

*100 percent inspection.* An associate checks every unit, typically for highly critical quality characteristics, for new suppliers, and for new designs. This approach is subject to inspection errors and fatigue unless automated.

*First-article inspection.* In low-volume operations, after the process is set up, the operator checks the first unit; if the unit is good, the process is thought to be set up right so that it will produce good units. A better approach is for the operator to do a first- and last-article inspection; if the first and last units are good, probably the process did not change and the intervening units are good.

*Destructive testing.* The associate tests an item by destroying it (e.g., running a car into a wall to see how the bumper holds up); destructive testing necessarily is done on a sampling basis.

*Acceptance sampling.* Based on statistical sampling tables, the inspector checks a random or stratified sample from a larger lot. If the sample is within the acceptable quality level (AQL), the lot passes inspection. A bad lot receives a 100 percent rectifying inspection, and bad units are replaced with good ones.

**Acceptance sampling** should not be confused with **statistical process control (SPC).** Both rely on statistical data and both date back to work at Western Electric in the 1920s and 1930s. Drs. W. Edwards Deming and Joseph M. Juran were among the experts in the employ of that company who were in on development of both acceptance sampling and SPC. The big difference is that SPC occurs while a process is running and may provide feedback fast enough to make process adjustments, thus minimizing the amount of "bad" output. Acceptance sampling, on the other hand, merely detects some problem output—after it has been created. As in most things, we prefer prevention to detection, and then early rather than later detection.

While many organizations have not made the transition from detection to prevention, many others have. Usually the prevention of quality deficiencies is part of a large package of improvements and waste elimination. Two examples follow:

- *Jostens Diplomas, Red Wing, Minnesota, a printer of graduation diplomas.* This business unit of Jostens (which also is the leading cap-and-gown and class-ring maker) transferred 45 inspectors from an end-of-line inspection department into positions side by side with printing associates. At the same time, four of six personal computers were moved to the production floor for immediate processing of corrections, cross-training and skills certification programs were established, and cycle times fell from nearly four or five weeks to 24 hours.
- *AMPEX, Colorado Springs, Colorado, a producer of high-end recording products.* This AMPEX facility reduced its number of inspectors from 100 to zero. This improvement was part of a broad package of improvements: Cycle time for one recorder was reduced from 120 days to 18 days, flow distance from a mile to 150 feet, annual scrap and rework from $9.7 million to $1.1 million, and setup time on a key machine from eight hours to 30 minutes. At the same time, yearly training per person was raised from about 6 hours to 20 hours, and operators began ordering material directly from suppliers without the need to go through the purchasing department.[6]

**Principle 11**

Cut flow time and distance.

## The Process Focus

Transformation processes can be quite complex. Thus, in the vast majority of cases, a multiplicity of causes exists for the effects, both good and bad, that we experience with output goods and services. Recognition of this fact has led to strong support for a process focus as the underpinning for TQM. Overall, the process focus has served us well.

**EXHIBIT 9-3 A Transformation Process**

| | |
|---|---|
| Definition: | Process: A unique combination of elements, conditions, or causes that collectively produces a given outcome or set of results. |
| Composition: | Components of a process may be classified according to the "seven M's":<br>Materials (raw materials, components, or documents awaiting processing).<br>Manpower (the human factor; better yet, *people power*).<br>Methods (product and process design and operating procedures).<br>Machines (tools and equipment used in the process).<br>Measurement (techniques and tools used to gather process performance data).<br>Maintenance (the system for providing care for process components, including training of people).<br>Management (policy, work rules, and environment). |
| Performance: | Process performance (output, intended or incidental) depends on how the process has been designed, built or installed, operated, and maintained. |

### *Process Definition, Description, and Performance*

A **process** (see Exhibit 9-3) is the unique set of conditions (seven M's) that creates certain outcomes. Change a process (deliberately or accidentally) and different results (better or worse) are likely to occur. In many processes, not all of the M's are apparent. Some human services, for example, involve virtually no materials. In some cases, maintenance might be considered a part of methods. In other instances, people prefer to use category names that better fit their company or industry; *tooling* might be a category for a manufacturer, *packaging* for a warehouse, and *reservations system* for a resort. Whatever the category names, however, the aim is to understand processes in terms of all the variables that can affect process output.

Process components change over time: one data-entry person replaces another, materials come from a different supplier, a machine or its cutting tool is changed, a different maintenance schedule is started, and so on. This can result in constant process restabilization, with quality losses and costs each time.

TQM provides a better idea: Make process elements easily substitutable with no negative impact on process performance, thereby avoiding the burden of restabilization. Fail-safe designs, training for mastery of multiple jobs, supplier certification, and standardization of equipment and tools are among the ways of pursuing that aim. But how do we know whether a substitution has changed a process or not? We analyze the process output.

### *Process Output Distributions*

In the 1920s, Western Electric's Walter Shewhart and George Edwards pioneered the use of statistical analysis of process output data. They gave us the process control chart, discussed later in the chapter, and they showed what distributions of process output data reveal about how the process is working.

**EXHIBIT 9-4 The Normal Distribution—Shaft Diameter Output Example**

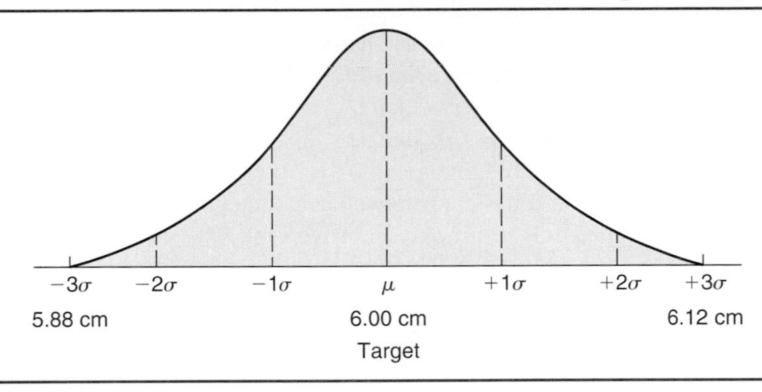


Source: Adapted from Ross Johnson and William O. Winchell, *Production and Quality* (Milwaukee: American Society for Quality Press, 1989), p. 10.

Though not all process output distributions are the same, we can gain insight from looking closer at a frequently occurring one. According to an American Society for Quality (ASQ) training manual:

> It has been well established that most machines and processes yield dimensions or other characteristics in the form of a normal curve [see Exhibit 9-4]. If a machine were set to turn a shaft with a target diameter of 6 cm, we know that all shafts would not be exactly the same. The precision of the machine would determine how close the variation could be held. From past experience we might know that the parts would fall in a distribution with *almost* 100 percent of the items being within ±0.12 cm of the mean value of the process output (here, equal to the target of 6.00 cm). Normal curve theory establishes that about 99.7 percent of the parts will fall within three standard deviations—$3\sigma$, or 3-sigma—of the mean. Here, three standard deviations equal 0.12 cm, thus one sigma equals 0.04 cm.[7]

Shaft diameter might be designated a **quality characteristic,** a performance output of a process that is of particular interest to a customer. If so, the maker would want to know more about the diameter's actual process output distribution. The distribution might be as shown in Exhibit 9-4. Note that the distribution is portrayed as being centered precisely at the target. While centering satisfies one aim, there still is output variation around the target to be concerned about.

**Assignable and Common Causes.** Two kinds of variation affect every process output distribution. **Assignable variation** is attributable to a specific cause. Find this cause, correct it, and the assignable variation is gone. **Common-cause variation** is variation that remains in process output when all assignable variation has been removed.

Imagine yourself driving down the highway trying to stay in your lane. The blowing wind, the crown of the road, and highway imperfections are some of the common causes of variation in your driving. Low tire pressure would be a special cause; fill the

Shewhart coined the term *assignable variation.* Deming, it is said, preferred to call it *special cause variation.* AT&T, where both men once worked, uses the term *unnatural variation.* All three terms refer to the same thing.

tire and the assignable variation goes away. Usually the operator can pinpoint such special causes; it doesn't require the skills of a quality scientist.

Common-cause variation is random and harder to trace. In driving, the multitude of small-chance fluctuations that occur are the source. The process as a whole is the likely culprit. Common-cause reduction may require an administrative decision costing some money: Erect shelter belts of trees to dampen the wind; smooth the roadway. The process itself needs changing if common-cause variation is to be decreased.

Since less variability is a basic customer want, attacking the two types of variation is an excellent approach to process improvement. The general sequence is as follows:

1. Eliminate the special-cause variation by correcting the problems. When a process output distribution is free of all special-cause variation, that process is said to be in a state of **statistical control,** or simply *in control*. Removal of special causes results in a stable, predictable process output. A process that is in control still has common variation in its output, however.
2. Reduce that common variation. Required actions might include product or process redesign or some other substantial investment.

Reduction of common variation is a central concern in process capability improvement, covered later in this chapter.

The variation-reduction sequence gets best results in the hands of a team of people representing elements of the whole process.

**Variables and Attributes.** Process output data, come in two forms: variables data and attributes data. **Variables data** result from measuring or computing the amount of or value of a quality characteristic. The shaft diameter distribution of Exhibit 9-4, for example, would come from measuring shaft diameters. Variables data are continuous; any value within a given output range (5.88 cm to 6.12 cm for the shaft diameters) may occur. Other examples of outputs captured as variables data are packaged weights of foods, times required for county clerks to record documents, density of pollutants, brightness in an office, loudness at a rock concert, price-earnings ratios, and grade point averages.

**Attributes data,** the other type, are simpler than variables data. A measurement isn't required, just a classifying judgment: may be yes-or-no for friendly service; good-or-bad for a car wash; small, medium, and large for farm melons; or AAA, AA, or A for debt obligations in a portfolio. A battery tester with a red zone and a green zone provides an attributes check. Similarly, we test a night light by putting it into a socket and flipping the switch. It either lights or it doesn't. A table setting in a fancy restaurant may be checked by the head waiter. If one fork or glass is out of place, the headwaiter judges the table setting to be defective. Diameters of ball bearings could be checked by rolling them across a hole-filled surface. Those that fall through are too small; their diameters needn't be measured.

We see from these descriptions that variables data must be measured, whereas attributes data are usually counted. And while attributes data are easier to collect, variables data yield more information. Example 9-1, using variables data, presents some of the issues involved in studying a process.

## Example 9-1: Process Focus Applied

Consider a process for the production of bolts (see Exhibit 9-5). Components from each of the seven M's make up the process and create bolts with several quality characteristics. Customers would indicate the following:

1. *Quality characteristics important enough to receive close attention.* For a simple product like a machine bolt, customer-critical characteristics might be length, diameter, and thread depth; each would be represented by a frequency distribution. Here, we look at but one characteristic, bolt length.
2. *A desired value—and thus the maker's target—for each quality characteristic.* Here, assume customers have requested 3-inch-long bolts.

As Exhibit 9-5 shows, the output distribution of bolt lengths has a certain central tendency, or location, and an amount variation (dispersion). Thus, the distribution reveals two useful pieces of process output information: One is whether the process is centered on 3 inches, as the customer wants, or on the high or low side. The other is the amount of variation, or spread—the

**Exhibit 9-5 The Process Focus: Contributing Variables and Performance**

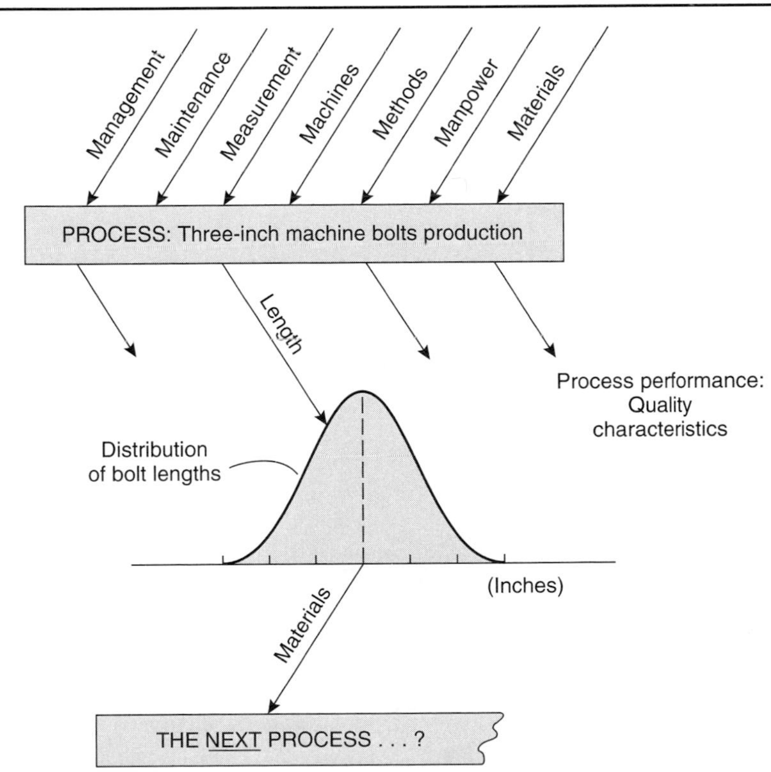

## Exhibit 9-6 Bolt Length Process Output

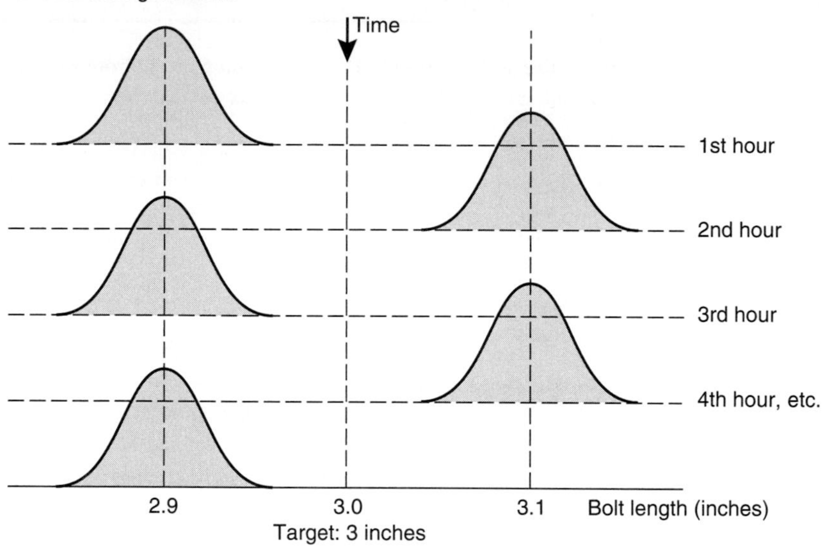


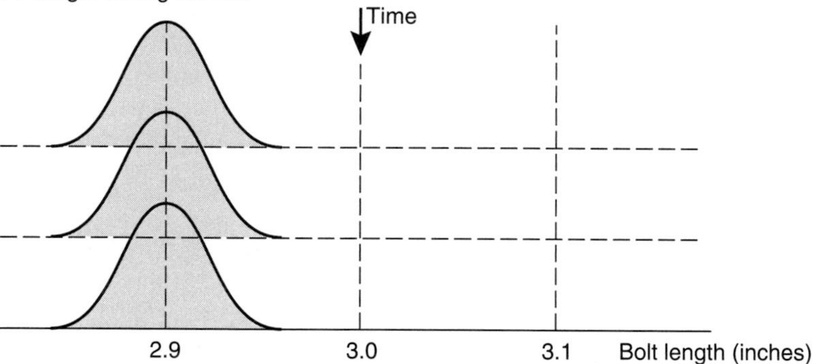


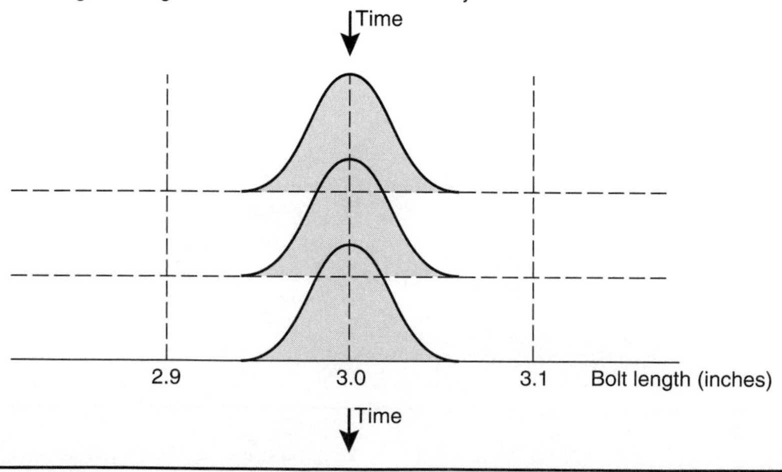

less of it the better. The bolt-making machinist knows that, as shown in Exhibit 9-5, the output of this process is the input to the next. Even if it is not a problem here, bolt-length variation may cause trouble at the next or any other downstream process. Studying the distribution is a simple, cheap, and effective method of understanding quite a bit about the process.

Unfortunately, process output distributions are not always as stable as this bolt-length distribution appears to be; stability requires work. Suppose the machinist draws a random sample of bolts and measures their lengths at intervals of approximately one hour. Let's say the lengths are distributed as shown in the upper section of Exhibit 9-6, that is, centered around 2.9 inches for one hour, around 3.1 inches the next, back to 2.9, and so on. This odd pattern tells the machinist to look for a special cause for the hour-to-hour variation. It may be that the machinist had been switching methods of cutting the bolt bar-stock about every hour. Suspicion falls on cutting method as the special cause.

The machinist stops switching cutting methods and focuses on the method leading to bolts averaging about 2.9 inches. Exhibit 9-6B shows how this *new* process might appear. Continued measurement, say, for several hours, could convince the machinist that the special variation has been eliminated, resulting in a process that is in control. But process control is not enough. A larger issue remains: the bolts are still not meeting the target of 3 inches.

The machinist makes another process change: "I increased the feed of the bar-stock into the cutting tool by 1⁄10 of an inch by moving a stop block. That got the process centered on target." The result, in Exhibit 9-6C, shows that the process is centered on target and stable across time. If there are no other special causes, the process is once again in control. Remember, the main benefit of statistical process control is predictability; as long as control is maintained, process output will be stable. Even better, however, the process now is in control and on target.

---

The machinist in Example 9-1 dealt with two of the three main concerns in process analysis: achieving process control and getting the process on target. But, as is clear from Exhibit 9-6C, the process still exhibits variation in output. Process capability analysis attacks that common variation. We reserve that topic for later in the chapter.

**Principle 10**

Eliminate process variation.

Also, the machinist followed a systematic approach: First, collect process output data and analyze it—what quality control people call listening to the process. Make a change if necessary, and then repeat. In the simple bolt-making example, one person achieved control and (some) improvement. Usually, problems are bigger, more ill-defined, and require the efforts of teams. We look now at a systematic approach to guide those efforts.

### *Improvement Project Overview*

The fifth part of the quality action cycle (Exhibit 9-1) calls for process improvement projects. The systematic approach to those improvement projects follows the scientific method of investigation, familiar from physical or social science studies (see Exhibit 9-7). Briefly, the sequence is to find and study a problem, generate and evaluate possible solutions, implement and review the chosen solution, then repeat for a new problem.

The scientific method provides an overall plan of attack. But process improvement teams still need a set of tools to use at each step.

**Exhibit 9-7 Scientific Method for Process Improvement**

1. Identify and define the problem.
2. Study the existing situation: collect necessary data.
3. Generate possible solution alternatives.
4. Evaluate alternatives and choose the preferred one.
5. Implement the improvement and measure results.
6. Evaluate and revise if required.
7. Otherwise, return to step 1 and start again with a new problem.

**Exhibit 9-8 Tools for Process Improvement**

| General Tools | Coarse-Grained Tools | Fine-Grained Tools |
|---|---|---|
| 1. Team-building and group-interaction tools. | 3. Process flowchart. | 7. Fail-safing. |
| 2. Specific process/technology tools. | 4. Check sheets and histograms. | 8. Design of experiments (DOE). |
| | 5. Pareto analysis. | 9. Scattergrams. |
| | 6. Fishbone charts. | 10. Run diagram. |
| | | 11. Process control chart. |

Exhibit 9-8 lists widely accepted tools for process improvement. The two in the general category require little explanation. Team building and group interaction tools, with deep roots in the social sciences, have a new home in team-based TQM. The specific process and technology tools relate or apply to a certain work specialty. They might include a computer spreadsheet, stethoscope, backhoe, accident claim form, customer satisfaction survey card, or coordinate measuring machine—anything that helps improve process output.

The four coarse-grained and five fine-grained tools are basic techniques of quality science. A growing belief is that every employee should know and regularly use these tools—except for DOE, which requires special statistical analysis skills. Discussion of them makes up most of the remainder of the chapter.

## Coarse-Grained Analysis and Improvement

Tools 3 through 6 are a starting point for listening to the process: process flowchart, check sheet and histogram, Pareto analysis, and fishbone chart. They help sift the data and point to the most promising targets for improvement. Sometimes these tools reveal the root causes clearly enough to make the solution apparent. Other times, they segregate the most promising target for further fine-grained analysis.

**EXHIBIT 9-9 Flow Chart Symbols**

| | | |
|---|---|---|
| ○ | Operation | Activities that might add value to a workpiece or provide a value-adding service to a customer; usually requires a setup. |
| ⇒ | Transportation | Movement of object from one work station to another; movement of customer from one operation to another. |
| □ | Inspection | Work is checked for some characteristic of quality; may call for 100 percent inspection or inspection by sampling. |
| ▽ | Storage | Applies to materials or documents; may be temporary or permanent. |
| D | Delay | Time person, materials, or documents wait for next operation; in *lot* delay, wait is for other items in the lot to be processed; in *process* delay, entire lot waits for workstation or other bottleneck to clear. |

## *Process Flowchart*

A flowchart gets the analysis started. It helps the team visualize the value chain. The **process flowchart** pictures the full process flow in all its complexity.

As they develop the flowchart, team members often are surprised by what they see. Someone might point out that certain sequences were put into effect years before under different conditions. The team may agree that whole sequences no longer are necessary or that certain steps should be eliminated, combined, or rearranged. While the process flowchart is nearly 100 years old, it has elevated stature today in helping identify process activities that add value and others that do not.

Computer program flowcharts reflect another type. Their purpose is to illustrate processing or computational sequence or flow.

Exhibit 9-9 shows and describes widely used flowcharting symbols. Of the five, only the operation symbol denotes *what might be* a **value-adding activity.** Sometimes operations themselves add little or no value and should be removed or improved. The other symbols reflect an addition of cost, not value. The symbols used in computer systems analysis, which are slightly different, can be used instead of or intermixed with these five. Any consistent set of symbols will work. (Exhibit 6-1 shows an order fulfillment flowchart. The diamond is used to indicate option points, because no quality assessment [inspection] is needed.)

Exhibit 9-10 shows how an improvement team might document a company's travel authorization process. The before version, part A, has eight value-adding operations, five transportations, two inspections, and three delays. The streamlined version in part B uses personal computer communication by E-mail. It cuts the operations to five, transports to two, inspections to one (combined with an operation), and delays to one. The reduction from eight to five operations does not mean less value, because value-adding operations also consume costly resources and time. The result is a simpler process that does the job.

As with the other coarse-grained techniques, sometimes the flowchart alone tells the improvement team what it needs to know to complete the project. More often, the flowchart maps the process for further analysis.

## *Check Sheet and Histogram*

A **check sheet** is the simplest of all the data collection tools. Just make a check mark each time the mishap occurs. One form of the check sheet has just a single category,

**EXHIBIT 9-10 Flowchart: Travel Authorization Process**

A. Original travel authorization process

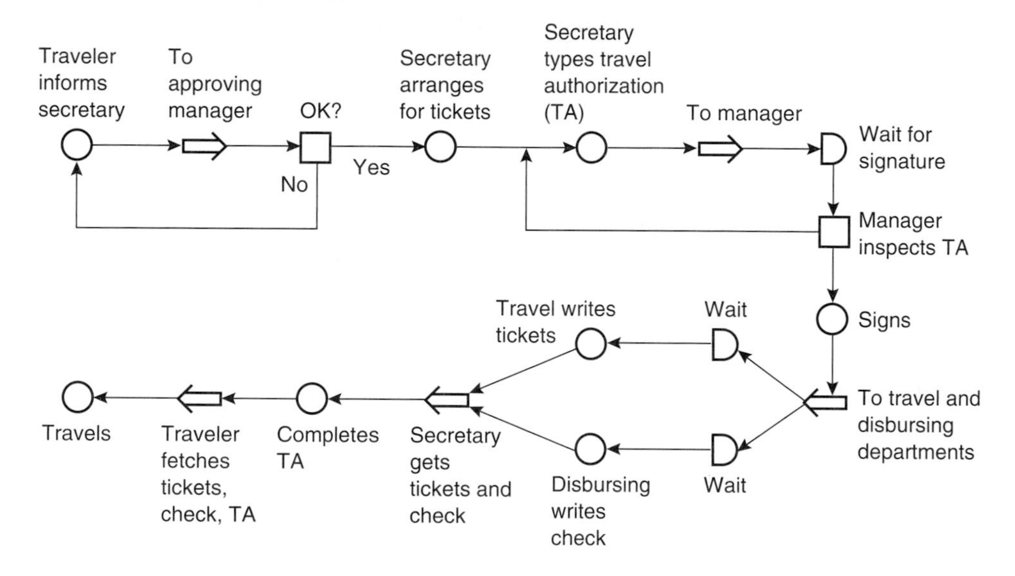


B. Improved travel authorization process—with E-mail

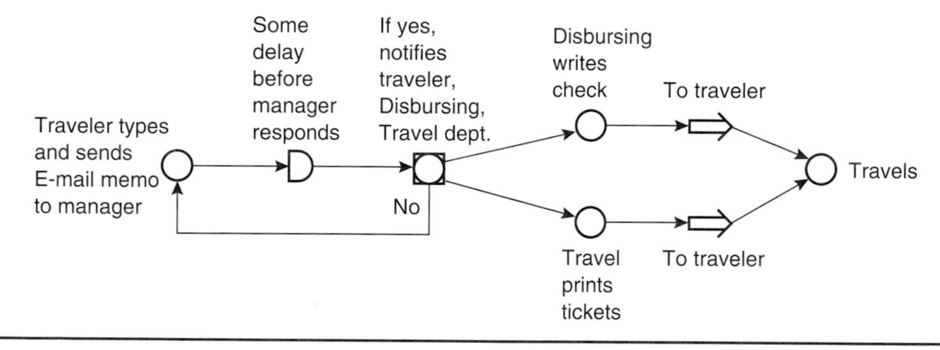


Source: Adapted from Dennis C. Kinlaw, *Continuous Improvement and Measurement for Total Quality* (Burr Ridge, Ill.: Business One Irwin, 1992), pp. 214–15.

such as "meeting started late today." Usually more useful is a multicategory version, which tracks occurrences of problems in more detail. The Into Practice box shows the advantage of more categories at Akron General Medical Center.

**Histograms** offer another way to display frequency data. A histogram, which is more structured than a check sheet, has equal-interval numeric categories on one axis with occurrence frequency shown on the other.

In the example of Exhibit 9-11, the X-axis is in 10-minute time intervals. The improvement team is tracking how long it takes for a hotel crew to do a typical ballroom

INTO PRACTICE

## Check Sheet for Mishap Analysis at Akron General

Quality-data collection is an important first step to isolating root causes of medication errors, says Gayle Joiner. A quality management specialist at the 550-bed Akron General Medical Center, Joiner is also a member of Akron's improvement group and liaison team, comprising clinical nursing and pharmacy staff. The team first began looking at medication errors in 1992. They discovered a variety of systemic problems, including inadequate reporting on the type and severity of errors.

The team's original data collection method provided enough data to plot trends, says Joiner, but it was too vague to be useful for action planning and intervention. For instance, one of the check-boxes on the original form simply said: "Incorrect dose."

The team revised the check sheet to include four subcategories under that heading. They included the following: "Incorrect dose dispensed from pharmacy," "Verbal order taken incorrectly," "Incorrect dose ordered," and "Dosage calculation error." See sample below.

With the new form and more-specific data, the team reduced medication errors by 30 percent. In addition, the information provides useful material for training and orienting new staff.

Source: Adapted from "Hospital Improves Reports," *Quality Digest*, April 1995, p. 9.

| | Frequency of Occurrence | | | |
|---|---|---|---|---|
| | *Week 1* | *Week 2* | *Week 3* | *Week 4* |
| Incorrect dose dispensed from pharmacy | ✓✓✓ | ✓✓ | ✓ | ✓✓✓✓ |
| Verbal order taken incorrectly | ✓ | | ✓✓ | ✓ |
| Incorrect dose ordered | ✓✓ | ✓✓✓✓ | ✓ | ✓ |
| Dosage calculation error | | ✓ | ✓ | |

conversion: Tear down a ballroom that has been set up for a conference, and reset it for a banquet. The histogram shows in some detail what the events department probably was concerned about: high variability, which makes it difficult for the sales people to schedule time for ballroom events. Since 9 of the 17 setups took 50 or more minutes, perhaps the improvement team will want to focus on those worst cases. One solution might be to increase the crew size for some of the more complex tear-down/setup cases.

### *Pareto Analysis*

**Pareto analysis** helps separate the vital few from the trivial many. In process improvement, Pareto analysis proceeds as follows:

1. Identify the factors affecting process variability or product quality.
2. Keep track of how often a measurable defect or nonconformity is related to each factor.

**EXHIBIT 9-11 Histogram: Ballroom Setup Time Requirements**

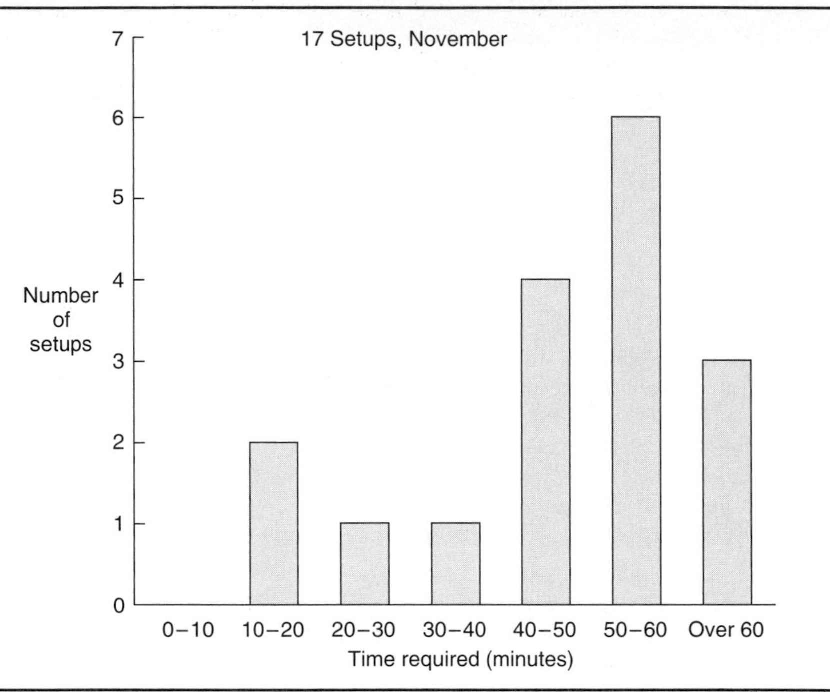


3. Plot the results on a bar chart, where length of a bar stands for (or is proportional to) the number of times the causal factor occurs. Position more serious causes (longest bars) to the left of less serious ones.

Giving an item the degree of attention it deserves has been called the principle of parsimony (parsimony means frugality). The more general principle, widely applicable in society, is the Pareto principle, named after economist Vilfredo Pareto (1848–1923). His observation that most of the wealth is in the hands of a small percentage of the population makes it simple (frugal) to study wealth by studying just the wealthy.

Exhibit 9-12 is a Pareto chart derived from study of the drive-through-window (DTW) operation at a Kentucky Fried Chicken (KFC) restaurant in Oklahoma City. In that region, KFC had been losing market share to other fast-food companies that had quicker DTW service. Automatic timers had collected the data. The Pareto highlights the main cause, window hang time, accounting for 58 percent of the total service time. Hang time is KFC jargon for how long a customer waits—"hangs"—at the window to receive the order, pay, and leave.[8]

Checksheets and Pareto analysis often preceed—and feed problem data to—fishbone analysis (see photo, Exhibit 9-13).

## *Fishbone Chart*

The process analysis continued at KFC Oklahoma City. The team displayed causes and subcauses of service delay at DTW on a **fishbone chart,** so named because it looks like the skeleton of a fish. See Exhibit 9-14.

In fishbone analysis, the team works backwards from the target for improvement on the spine bone, identifying causes down through the **"bone structure."** The lowest level

**EXHIBIT 9-12 Pareto Chart: DTW Time**

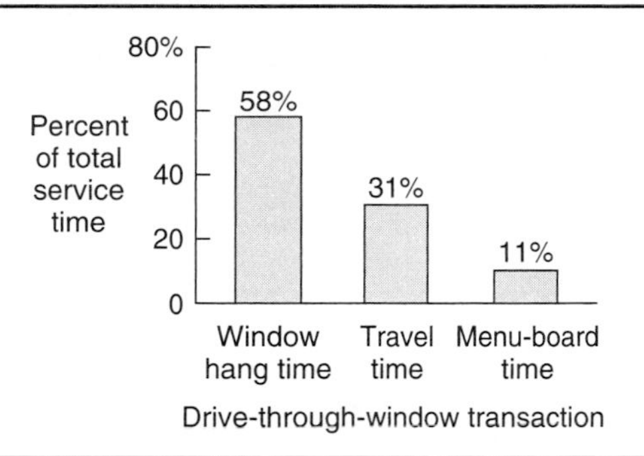


Source: Reprinted by permission, Uday M. Apte and Charles C. Reynolds, "Quality Management at Kentucky Fried Chicken," *Interfaces* 25, No. 3, May–June 1995, pp. 6–21, The Institute for Operations Research and the Management Sciences, 290 Westminster Street, Providence, RI 02903.

**EXHIBIT 9-13 Process Improvement Team in Action**

*Improvement team member at Atlanta's West Paces Ferry Hospital leads team developing a fishbone chart, while another member updates a Pareto chart labeled "Causes of Delay."*

of detail (finest bones) may reveal root causes, which are worthy targets for further problem solving. Exhibit 9-14 shows but two "subbone" levels, but third and fourth levels might be required.

The KFC team set up its fishbone in a typical way: with four general categories—people, equipment, materials, and methods—main causes. (Purists prefer not to use these general categories. Instead they would look for case-specific main causes, such as

**EXHIBIT 9-14 Fishbone Chart: Service Delays at KFC**

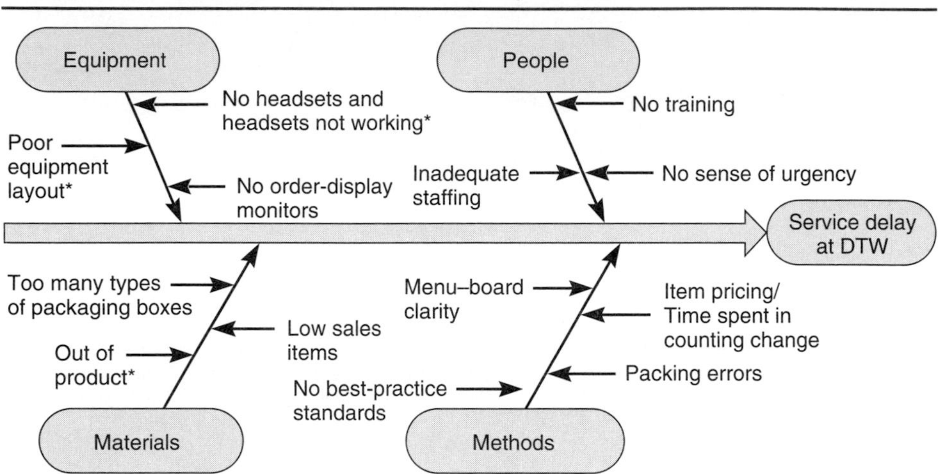


*Most frequent problems/highest impact.

Source: Reprinted by permission, Uday M. Apte and Charles C. Reynolds, "Quality Management at Kentucky Fried Chicken," *Interfaces* 25, No. 3, May–June 1995, pp. 6–21, The Institute for Operations Research and the Management Sciences, 290 Westminster Street, Providence, RI 02903.

"behind-counter confusion," "customer confusion," and "conflicts with KFC corporate standards.")

The next step was to return to check-sheet data. Three of the root causes were the most frequent and highest-impact problems. The three, designated with asterisks, are "No headsets and headsets not working," "Poor equipment layout," and "Out of product." The following are among the team's improvements on these three problems:

Principle 2

Dedicate to continual improvement.

- Instituted a procedure for regular testing of all headsets, and stockpiled supplies of headset batteries and replacement belts.
- Rearranged the packing area, cutting the number of steps a packer had to move from six to two.
- Eliminated certain slow-selling products and replaced low-demand multiple desserts with a single popular dessert item.[9]

## Fine-Grained Analysis and Improvement

We have just seen examples of how the coarse-grained tools can sometimes lead to solutions—without further, more-detailed study. It's like the apple that fell on Sir Isaac Newton's head. He deduced the gravity concept from the coarse-level "analysis."

The five more refined analysis tools from Exhibit 9-8 study one quality characteristic at a time. The purpose might be to further test a good idea, such as Newton's. More often, it is to impose a control on a varying quality characteristic or to find a solution that so far has been elusive. Fail-safing has the latter purpose.

### Fail-Safing

A common fail-safing example for suppliers of boxes of parts is egg-crate box dividers so that only the correct number of parts—no more, no less—can be packed and sent to a user. Unlike other tools of improvement, fail-safing does not rely on any particular sources of process data. Rather, it is a mind-set that can help direct associates, positively, toward a permanent if unrealizable process fix: Expand the improvement zone of the quality action cycle, and shrink the detection zone to nothing.

*Quality action cycle. No detection zone since process is fail-safed*

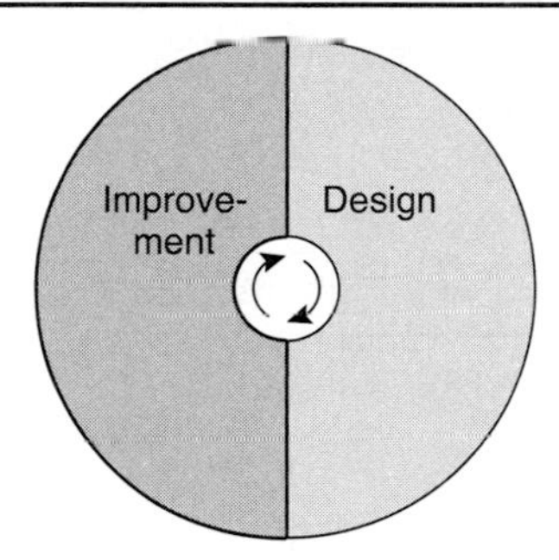


Fail-safing is best applied at the root-cause level of analysis—for example, a third- or fourth-level sub-bone of a fishbone chart. It can prevent, for instance:

- Leaving out parts or steps.
- Fitting components or service elements together improperly.
- Failing to follow the right process sequence.
- Bad process result (e.g., the machine stops itself because of excess tool wear).
- Passing errors along to the next process (because the root cause has been found and eliminated).

Fail-safe devices may be as simple as templates, egg-crate dividers, velcro, glue, and paint, or as fancy as limit switches, electric eyes, scales, locks, probes, timers, and scopes. Exhibit 9-15B illustrates fail-safing achieved with a small notch designed into the insert and housing pieces to prevent upside-down insertion during processing.

Fail-safing embraces a realistic view of people, processes, and errors. It recognizes that people need to be protected from their own naturally variable behaviors. This is an excellent attitude and often leads to the right solution. If people are unaware that processes can and should be fail-safed, their tendency is to hide the mishap when it occurs to avoid the possibility of blame.

**EXHIBIT 9-15 Simple Fail-Safe Design**

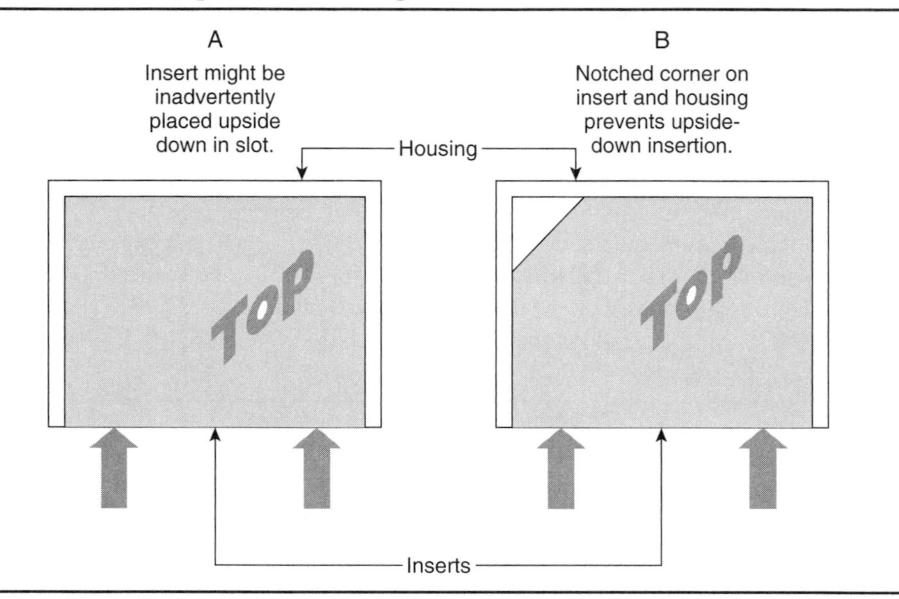


### *Design of Experiments (DOE)*

The statistician may reply with a phrase popular in TQM: Torture the data and it will confess.

Sometimes the improvement team is stumped: flowcharts, Pareto analyses, or fishbone charts have brought too many potential causes to the surface. "Which are the *actual* causes?" Statisticians or engineers who are seasoned veterans in the art and science of experimentation can help.

As noted earlier, the early 1990s witnessed renewed interest in **design of experiments (DOE)** as the quality movement progressed. The intricacies of DOE, including the Taguchi short-cut methods, are beyond the scope of this discussion, but some comments about how to bring experimentation into the improvement process are in order. The best way is to have those with DOE expertise join process improvement teams as consultants. It is important that experts and frontline associates rub shoulders. Experts have much to learn about applications, and front-liners need to learn what they can about advanced methods. Cross-learning is the key to joint ownership of processes and results.

While not everyone should try to master DOE techniques, another experimental tool, the scatter diagram, is easy for everyone to learn and use.

### *Scatter Diagram and Correlation*

As used in TQM, a **scatter diagram** (scattergram for short) plots process output effects against experimental changes in process inputs. The correlation coefficient (discussed in Chapter 4) pins down the relationship in precise numeric terms. Often, we can adequately estimate the strength of the association just by looking at the scattergram.

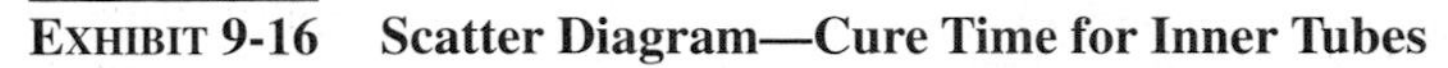

**EXHIBIT 9-16 Scatter Diagram—Cure Time for Inner Tubes**

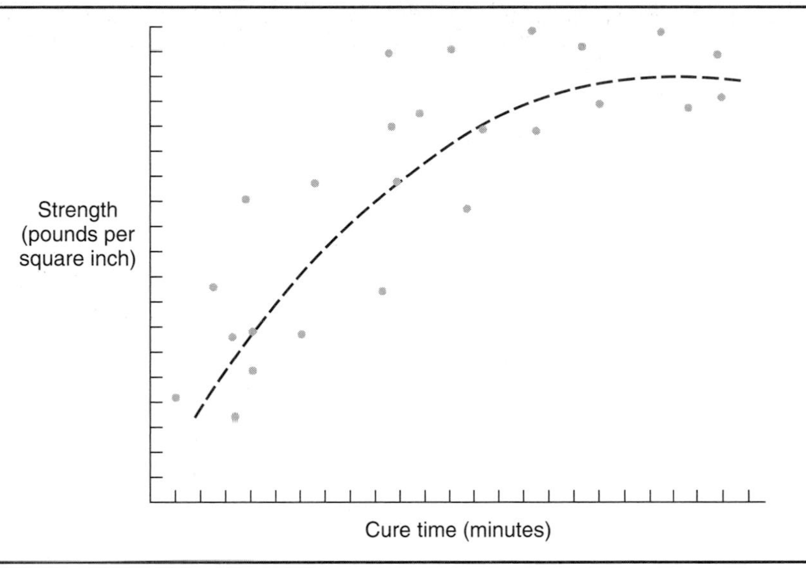


Suppose that associates producing rubber inner tubes have noted wide variation in tube strength, as revealed by overfilling the tubes with air. They run an experiment seeking ways to reduce the variation. At the previous process in their work cell, in which formed tubes are cured in ovens, they vary the curing time. Next, they test the tubes, plot curing times against tube strength on a scatter diagram, and look for a correlation.

Exhibit 9-16 is the resulting scatter diagram. Each point represents one tube. Cure time is a point's horizontal location, and strength is its vertical location. The conclusions:

1. Tube strength correlates well with cure time, as shown by a definite clustering of points about the sketched-in curving line.
2. Tube strength increases with cure time up to a point, after which further cure time does no more good and may even be harmful.

Having found one source of variation, the team presses on, looking for other factors that might correlate with tube strength.

### *Run Diagram*

When we aren't doing experiments or solving problems, what should we be doing—besides the task itself? Watching the process.

Here again we need tools. Relying on impressions won't do. The **run diagram** is the simplest of the process-monitoring tools.

A run diagram is simply a running plot of a certain measured quality characteristic. It could be number of minutes each successive airplane departs late or number of customers visiting the complaint desk of a store each day. In these cases, the company might specify an upper limit, which would be plotted on the run diagram. Any point above the upper specification (spec) limit would be obvious—and perhaps grounds for taking some kind of action.

In injection molding, hot, liquid plastic is injected into a mold containing one or more cavities in the desired shape of parts. The plastic cools and hardens forming the part.

In other cases, there might be both an upper and a lower specification limit. Consider a plastic part made in an injection-molding process. It might be a component for a toy, a home appliance, or a consumer electronics product. The customer's specifications are targets for the operation. Example 9-2 shows how the run diagram works.

## Example 9-2: Run Diagram—Injection-Molded Parts

*Part:* Round plastic part with a target (nominal) diameter of 5.00 cm

*Specification (tolerance band):* 5.00 ± 0.05 cm

*Quality objective:* Continually improve quality and productivity by reducing the fraction of parts that do not meet the specifications, which call for diameters in the range of 4.95 cm to 5.05 cm.

*Analysis phases:* The improvement process follows distinct phases:

*Phase 1:* Operator measures every piece and plots outer diameter on the run diagram. Exhibit 9-17 shows diameters for 30 pieces. Pieces 7 and 23 are larger than the upper limit (5.05 cm), and pieces 17, 25, 26, 29, and 30 are smaller than the lower limit (4.95 cm). Also, there is a discernable drift downward over time. Action is needed.

*Phase 2:* The improvement team looks for causes. Some possibilities are

- The operator suspects machine heat buildup. In that case, a likely root cause is a faulty thermostat. A mechanic pulls out the old thermostat, finds it is indeed bad, and replaces it.
- The supervisor wonders about raw material impurities. A simple, no-cost solution is carried out: A sheet of clear plastic covers the containers of resin, so that passersby won't think the open box is a trash receptacle.

**Exhibit 9-17 Run Diagram—Outer Diameters of 30 Pieces**

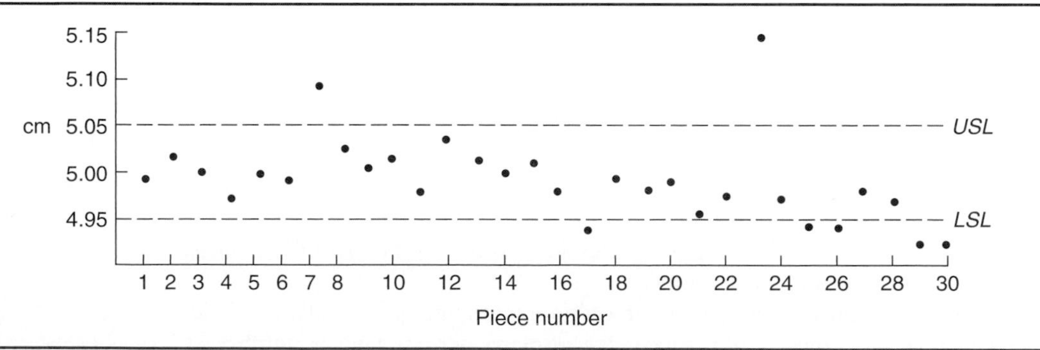

**EXHIBIT 9-18 Run Diagram—Outer Diameters of 30 More Pieces**

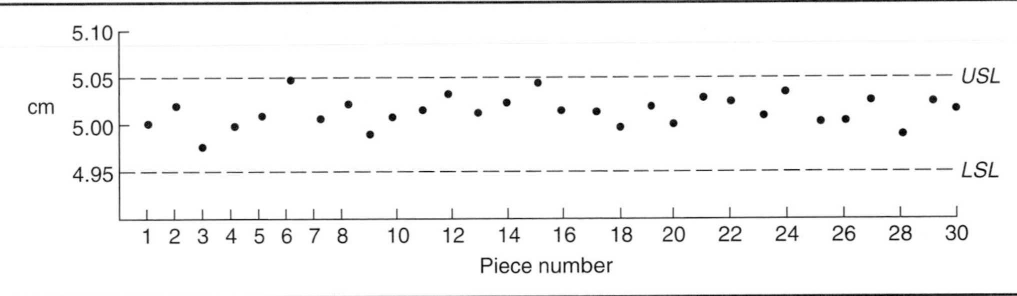


*Phase 3:* The operator again starts producing, measuring diameters, and plotting. Exhibit 9-18 shows that, for 30 more pieces, the diameters fall within specs and exhibit no drift.

*Phase 4:* Output has improved, so measurement frequency may be reduced. Process improvement, however, continues.

### *Process Control Chart*

While the run diagram plots data on every unit, the **process control chart,** less precisely referred to as the quality control chart, relies on sampling. The method requires plotting statistical samples of measured process output for a quality characteristic. The sampling must be done initially to establish trial control limits. Then, sampling continues with the results plotted on the control charts. By watching the plotted points, the observer can monitor process variation, which may call for some kind of corrective action to the process.

Control charts come in several forms.[10] We examine three of the more popular kinds: **mean and range charts,** which operate as a pair; **proportion-defective chart;** and **number-of-defects chart.** The mean and range charts rely on measurements of a continuous variable, such as weight, height, or specific gravity and are therefore referred to as **variables charts.** Both the proportion-defective and the number-of-defects charts, on the other hand, count occurrences of a quality attribute within a sample and are called attribute charts. The underpinnings of the three charts are three different statistical probability distributions: normal distribution for the mean chart, binomial distribution for the proportion-defective chart, and Poisson distribution for the number-of-defects chart.

We consider the mean and range first. The example is a continuation of our injection-molding process, which operators first monitored using run diagrams (Example 9-2). They had concluded that "measurement frequency may be reduced," in this case to statistical samples from which we determine the mean and range. As with the run diagram, mean and range charting has distinct phases, which we follow in Example 9-3.

## Example 9-3: Mean and Range Charts—Injection-Molded Parts

*Phase 1.* Collect and record data. Columns (3) through (6) of Exhibit 9-19 display the measures of diameters for 20 hourly samples of four parts each (that is, $k = 20$ and $n = 4$). Each sample mean, $\overline{X}$ (col. 7), shows process location, and the sample range $R$ (in col. 8) reflects process dispersion or spread at the time the operator drew the sample. (Historically, in order to simplify the calculations, dispersion was measured by the range instead of by standard deviation. For most popular sample sizes ($n = 4$, 5, or 6) the range chart or the standard deviation ($S$) chart work well. If larger sample sizes are used (certainly if $n \geq 10$), the $S$ chart is preferred.)[11]

*Phase 2.* Calculate chart center lines and control limits. This phase has several steps. The first is to compute sample averages and ranges for each of the 20 samples. For the first sample,

$$\overline{X}_1 = \frac{\sum x}{n} = \frac{5.06 + 5.00 + 5.03 + 5.01}{4} = 5.025$$

$$R_1 = 5.06 - 5.00 = 0.06$$

These two calculations, repeated for the other 19 samples, fill out columns (7) and (8) of Exhibit 9-19.

### Exhibit 9-19 Measurements for Designing Mean and Range Charts

| | | Measurements (cm) | | | | | |
|---|---|---|---|---|---|---|---|
| (1) Sample Number | (2) Date | (3) $x_1$ | (4) $x_2$ | (5) $x_3$ | (6) $x_4$ | (7) Mean ($\overline{X}$) | (8) Range ($R$) |
| 1 | 10/10 | 5.01 | 5.00 | 5.03 | 5.06 | 5.025 | 0.06 |
| 2 | | 4.99 | 5.03 | 5.03 | 5.05 | 5.025 | 0.06 |
| 3 | | 5.03 | 5.04 | 4.99 | 4.94 | 5.000 | 0.10 |
| 4 | | 5.05 | 5.03 | 5.00 | 5.01 | 5.022 | 0.05 |
| 5 | | 4.97 | 5.04 | 4.96 | 5.00 | 4.992 | 0.08 |
| 6 | | 4.97 | 5.00 | 4.99 | 5.02 | 4.995 | 0.05 |
| 7 | | 5.06 | 5.00 | 5.02 | 4.96 | 5.010 | 0.10 |
| 8 | | 5.03 | 4.98 | 5.01 | 4.95 | 4.992 | 0.08 |
| 9 | 10/11 | 5.05 | 5.03 | 5.05 | 4.98 | 5.028 | 0.07 |
| 10 | | 4.99 | 5.03 | 5.01 | 4.96 | 4.998 | 0.07 |
| 11 | | 4.98 | 5.05 | 5.05 | 4.94 | 5.005 | 0.11 |
| 12 | | 4.95 | 5.04 | 4.99 | 4.99 | 4.992 | 0.09 |
| 13 | | 5.00 | 5.05 | 5.01 | 4.97 | 5.008 | 0.08 |
| 14 | | 4.96 | 5.03 | 5.05 | 5.00 | 5.010 | 0.09 |
| 15 | | 5.08 | 5.01 | 5.02 | 4.96 | 5.018 | 0.12 |
| 16 | | 5.02 | 4.98 | 5.04 | 4.95 | 4.998 | 0.09 |
| 17 | 10/12 | 5.02 | 4.99 | 4.99 | 5.04 | 5.010 | 0.05 |
| 18 | | 4.99 | 5.00 | 5.05 | 5.05 | 5.022 | 0.06 |
| 19 | | 5.03 | 5.02 | 5.01 | 4.96 | 5.005 | 0.07 |
| 20 | | 5.02 | 5.04 | 5.04 | 5.04 | 5.040 | 0.02 |
| | | | | | Totals | 100.195 | 1.50 |

The center lines for the mean and range charts are the grand average of the sample averages, $\overline{\overline{X}}$ (referred to as "*X*-double-bar") and $\overline{R}$ (referred to as "*R*-bar"). In this case,

$$\overline{\overline{X}} = \frac{\sum \overline{X}}{k} = \frac{100.195}{20} = 5.010 \text{ cm} \tag{9-1}$$

$$\overline{R} = \frac{\sum R}{k} = \frac{1.50}{20} = 0.075 \text{ cm} \tag{9-2}$$

Next, calculate control limits. Typically, the limits are set at three standard errors above and below the center line; they are commonly referred to as three-sigma limits. The *central limit theorem* (a standard topic in statistics studies) applies. The theorem holds that (for our purposes) the sample averages will form a normal (bell-shaped) distribution, regardless of the population from which the samples are taken. Then, approximately 99.72 percent of all sample averages should fall within three standard errors of the mean. That holds *if* the process is in a state of statistical control.

To simplify the calculations, we obtain the control limits by approximation (rather than by actually calculating the standard error). Exhibit 9-20 contains frequently used approximation factors for mean and range charts. The tables are derived from the mathematics of the normal distribution and the distribution of ranges. For the sample mean chart,

$$\text{Upper control limit } (UCL_{\overline{x}}) = \overline{\overline{X}} + (A_2)(\overline{R}) \tag{9-3}$$

$$\text{Lower control limit } (LCL_{\overline{x}}) = \overline{\overline{X}} - (A_2)(\overline{R}) \tag{9-4}$$

From Equations 9-1 and 9-2, $\overline{\overline{X}} = 5.010$ and $\overline{R} = 0.075$. Then, the control limits are

$$UCL_{\overline{x}} = 5.010 + (0.729)(0.075) = 5.010 + 0.055 = 5.065$$

$$LCL_{\overline{x}} = 5.010 - (0.729)(0.075) = 5.010 - 0.055 = 4.955$$

Then, $\overline{R}$ becomes the center line of the range chart. The three-sigma limits for the range chart use the $D_4$ and $D_3$ factors from Exhibit 9-20, with sample size $n = 4$:

$$UCL_R = (D_4)(\overline{R}) = (2.282)(0.075) = 0.171 \tag{9-5}$$

$$LCL_R = (D_3)(\overline{R}) = (0)(0.075) = 0 \tag{9-6}$$

**EXHIBIT 9-20 Process Control Chart Factors**

| *Sample (or subgroup) Size* ($n$) | *Control Limit Factor for Averages (mean charts)* ($A_2$) | *UCL factor for Ranges (range charts)* ($D_4$) | *LCL Factor for Ranges (range charts)* ($D_3$) | *Factor for Estimating Process Sigma* ($\hat{\sigma} = \overline{R}/d_2$) ($d_2$) |
|---|---|---|---|---|
| 2 | 1.880 | 3.267 | 0 | 1.128 |
| 3 | 1.023 | 2.575 | 0 | 1.693 |
| 4 | 0.729 | 2.282 | 0 | 2.059 |
| 5 | 0.577 | 2.115 | 0 | 2.326 |
| 6 | 0.483 | 2.004 | 0 | 2.534 |
| 7 | 0.419 | 1.924 | 0.076 | 2.704 |
| 8 | 0.373 | 1.864 | 0.136 | 2.847 |
| 9 | 0.337 | 1.816 | 0.184 | 2.970 |
| 10 | 0.308 | 1.777 | 0.223 | 3.078 |

**EXHIBIT 9-21 Initial Mean and Range Charts**

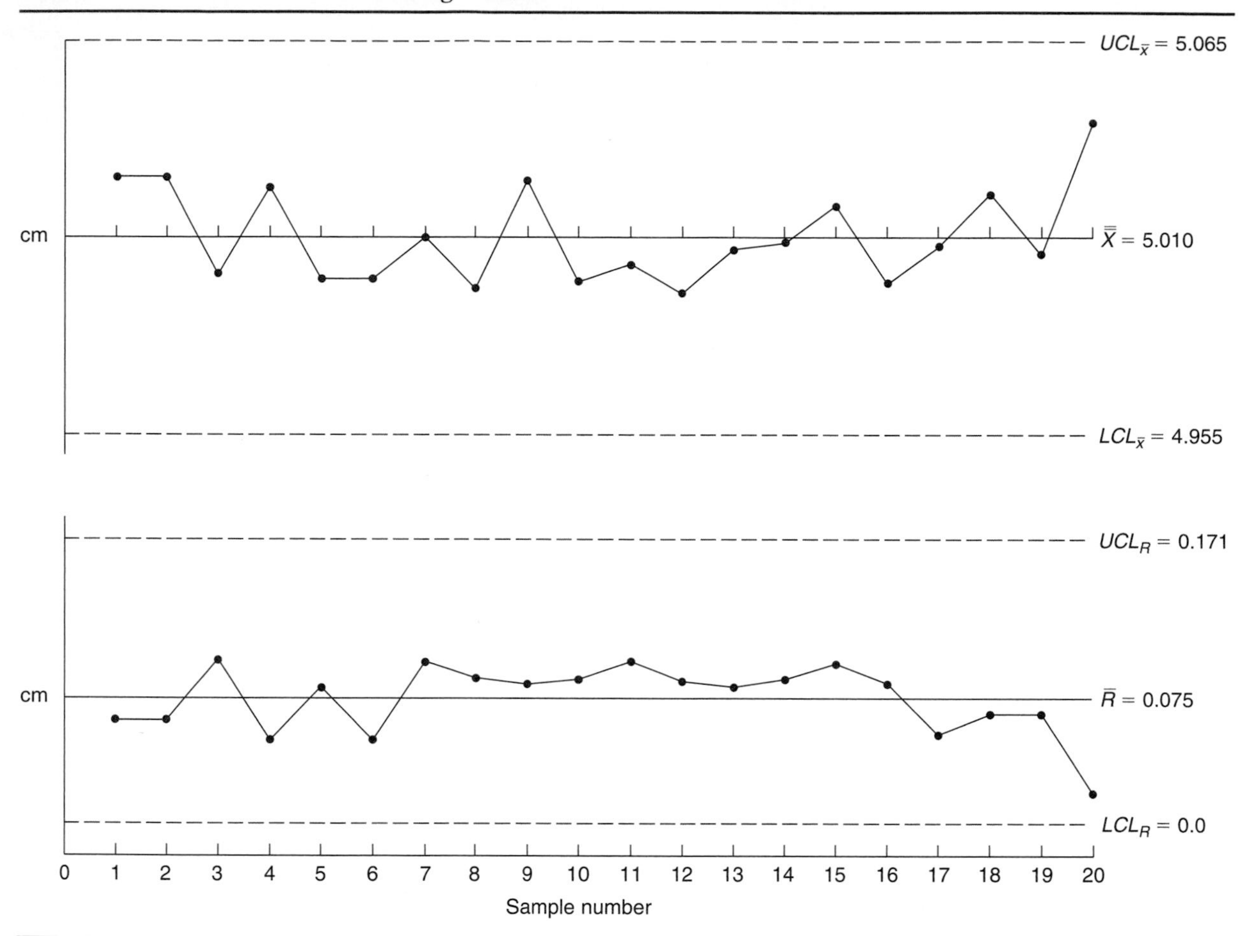


*Phase 3.* Draw the control charts. Most companies use preprinted forms or computerized templates for their control charts. The operator adds center lines and control limits, then plots the data, sample averages and ranges. Exhibit 9-21 shows the resulting mean and range charts.

*Phase 4.* Analysis of control chart data. Is the process in control? The operator does a few tests to answer the question. The obvious test is simple. Are any points outside the control limits? Two other commonly used tests are as follows: Do seven consecutive points either rise or fall? Do eight or more consecutive points fall on the same side of the center line? Failure of any of the tests indicates presence of special variation, unstable output, and an out-of-control process. (Other tests exist, but we defer those to more specialized treatments.)

Process control has nothing whatsoever to do with meeting specifications. A process may be in control and still produce totally unworthy output. Control means consistency only.

The operator inspects the two charts (Exhibit 9-21) and sees that one of the tests fails: On the range chart, 10 successive points are above the center line. That suggests some shift in a process component—special variation.

*Phase 5.* Check for causes of special variation. It might be a new operator, new raw material lot, or a different measurement gauge. A process improvement team must investigate. After dealing with the special causes, they construct new control charts to see if the process is under control. The cycle continues until control is attained.

What's next—after achieving process control? It is investigation of process capability. We shall return to capability analysis for our injection-molding process after examining two kinds of control charts for attributes.

## Example 9-4: PROPORTION DEFECTIVE CHART—ORDER FULFILLMENT

A start-up order-fulfillment company has completed a very busy first month of business. The order proofing and authorization group has done very well; most initial "bugs" seem to have been ironed out. The supervisor wonders, however, if process data might suggest problem areas that he is unaware of. He informs his group of the plan and elicits their help.

*Phase 1:* The first step, as is the case with any improvement project, is to make some decisions. The group decides to look at the proportion of orders, from a random sample of 1,000 per day during the most recent 20 days of business. Exhibit 9-22 summarizes the data.

### EXHIBIT 9-22 Attribute Inspection Data

**Order Fulfillment Errors**

| *Day* | *Defective Orders* | *Proportion Defective (p)* |
|---|---|---|
| 1 | 31 | 0.031 |
| 2 | 24 | 0.024 |
| 3 | 14 | 0.014 |
| 4 | 33 | 0.033 |
| 5 | 12 | 0.012 |
| 6 | 14 | 0.014 |
| 7 | 17 | 0.017 |
| 8 | 19 | 0.019 |
| 9 | 11 | 0.011 |
| 10 | 16 | 0.016 |
| 11 | 9 | 0.009 |
| 12 | 20 | 0.020 |
| 13 | 12 | 0.012 |
| 14 | 15 | 0.015 |
| 15 | 11 | 0.011 |
| 16 | 8 | 0.008 |
| 17 | 12 | 0.012 |
| 18 | 6 | 0.006 |
| 19 | 8 | 0.008 |
| 20 | 5 | 0.005 |
| Sums: | 297 | 0.297 |

$n = 1{,}000$ per day
$p$-bar $= 0.0149$
$UCL = 0.0263$
$LCL = 0.0034$

(Note: Exhibits 9-22 and 9-23 were prepared using Excel-based control chart programs that are available on the CD-ROM that came with your textbook.)

*Phase 2*: Next, a team member calculates the chart center line ($\overline{p}$) and control limits $\pm 3\sigma$ from the center line. Since the chart plots proportion defective, there are only two values for the attribute: good or bad (defective or nondefective). Thus, the binomial (two numbers) distribution applies. The standard deviation, sigma ($\sigma$) in the binomial distribution is

$$\sigma = \sqrt{\frac{\overline{p}(1-\overline{p})}{n}}$$

where

$\overline{p}$ = Average (mean) fraction defective

$n$ = Number in each sample

Therefore, the control limits, at $3\sigma$ from the center line, $\overline{p}$, are

$$UCL = \overline{p} + 3\sqrt{\frac{\overline{p}(1-\overline{p})}{n}} \tag{9-7}$$

$$LCL = \overline{p} - 3\sqrt{\frac{\overline{p}(1-\overline{p})}{n}} \tag{9-8}$$

The average fraction defective, $\overline{p}$, is total defectives divided by total items inspected, where total items inspected equals number of samples, $k$, times sample size, $n$:

$$\overline{p} = \frac{\text{Total defectives found}}{kn} \tag{9-9}$$

Since 297 defectives were found in 20 samples of 1,000 orders,

$$\overline{p} = \frac{297}{(20)(1{,}000)} = 0.0149$$

The control limits are:

$$UCL = \overline{p} + 3\sqrt{\frac{\overline{p}(1-\overline{p})}{n}}$$

$$= 0.0149 + 3\sqrt{\frac{(0.0149)(0.9851)}{1{,}000}}$$

$$= 0.0263$$

$$LCL = 0.0149 - 3\sqrt{\frac{(0.0149)(0.9851)}{1{,}000}}$$

$$= 0.0034$$

*Phase 3:* Data points are added to the chart. Exhibit 9-23 shows the pattern for the 20-day period. Two points exceed the upper control limit and there is a clear process drift downward. Thus the process is "out of control." But is there cause for concern and corrective action? No!

**EXHIBIT 9-23 Proportion Defectives Chart**

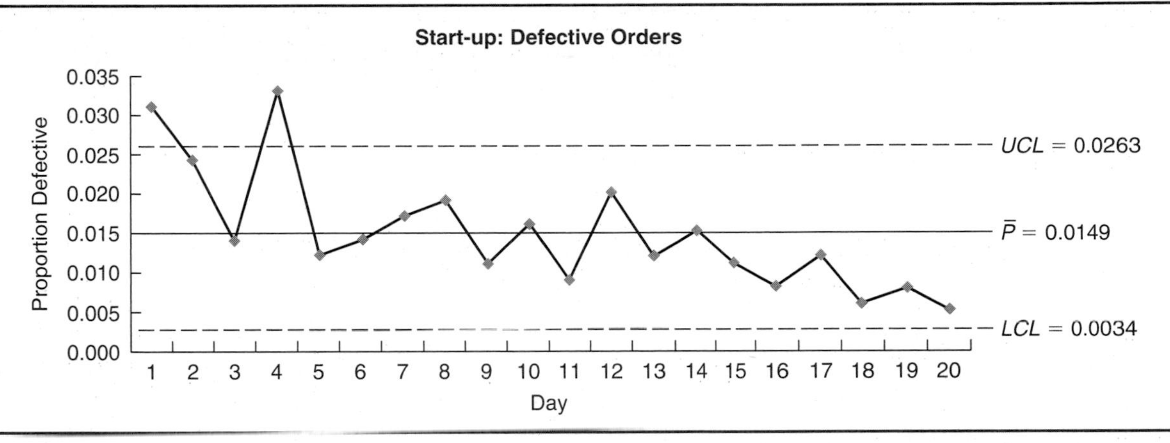


On an attribute chart, where people typically plot some form of error or defect, the aim is to achieve a downward drift, then keep it going. Zero defects—not process control—is the goal.

## Example 9-5: NUMBER-OF-DEFECTS CHART—HOTEL SUITE INSPECTION

A luxury hotel has five suites for visiting dignitaries and other VIPs—like operations management professors. The hotel's TQM effort has a strong advocate, the housekeeping supervisor, who has implemented a quality-check system for those five suites. Housekeeping associates, on a rotating basis, serve as inspectors, checking the suites immediately after completion of housekeeping. They record as defects any deviation from the hotel's standards of excellence (a ruffled towel, wilting flowers, unstocked bar and refrigerator, etc.). Every day the inspector records on a control chart the number of defects, $c$, found.

*Phase 1:* As always, decisions about data collection are mostly defined by the circumstances. In this case, suites may be cleaned only at the guests' convenience, and the inspector must follow shortly thereafter. Defect totals apply to the entire five-suite inspection; Exhibit 9-24 shows those totals for a 26-day period.

*Phase 2:* Calculate center line and control limits. The center line ($\bar{c}$) is the sum of the defects found divided by the number of inspections ($k$, which should be at least 25). Here,

$$\bar{c} = \frac{\sum c}{k} = \frac{39}{26} = 1.50 \qquad (9\text{-}10)$$

To get control limits, the supervisor needs to know the standard deviation. Since the basis for the number-of-defects chart is the Poisson statistical distribution, rather than the binomial or normal, the formula for the standard derivation ($\sigma$) is very simple:

$$\sigma = \sqrt{\bar{c}}$$

**EXHIBIT 9-24 Hotel Suite Inspection—Defects Discovered**

| *Day* | *Defects* | *Day* | *Defects* | *Day* | *Defects* |
|---|---|---|---|---|---|
| 1 | 2 | 10 | 4 | 19 | 1 |
| 2 | 0 | 11 | 2 | 20 | 1 |
| 3 | 3 | 12 | 1 | 21 | 2 |
| 4 | 1 | 13 | 2 | 22 | 1 |
| 5 | 2 | 14 | 3 | 23 | 0 |
| 6 | 3 | 15 | 1 | 24 | 3 |
| 7 | 1 | 16 | 3 | 25 | 0 |
| 8 | 0 | 17 | 2 | 26 | 1 |
| 9 | 0 | 18 | 0 | Total | 39 |

**EXHIBIT 9-25 Number-of-Defects Chart for Hotel Suite Inspection**

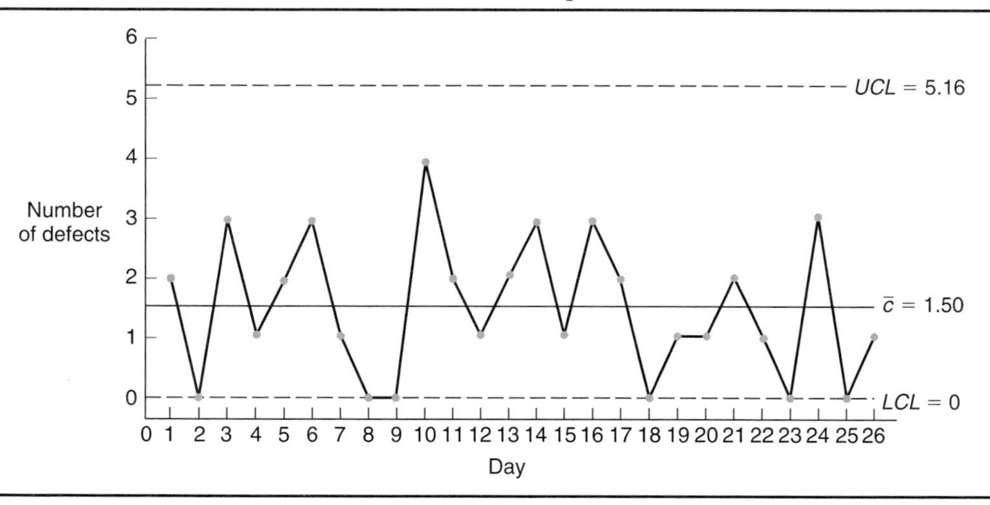


Thus the $3\sigma$ control limits are:

$$UCL = \bar{c} + 3\sqrt{\bar{c}} \tag{9-11}$$
$$= 1.50 + 3(1.22)$$
$$= 5.16$$

$$LCL = \bar{c} - 3\sqrt{\bar{c}} \tag{9-12}$$
$$= -2.16, \text{ or } 0^*$$

Next, the housekeeping staff construct the process control chart (in much the same fashion as for a proportion-defective chart). They draw the center line and control limits and plot the 26 data points. Exhibit 9-25 shows the completed chart. The process is within limits and does

*There cannot be a negative control limit on attribute control charts.

not violate the consecutive-points rule. The group concludes that the process is in control. The housekeeping supervisor and staff, however, aren't satisfied with control; they want perfection.

*Phase 3:* Process improvement efforts continue. The group's ideas might include checklists to avoid forgetting, a closer supplier of freshly cut flowers (maybe just outside the hotel's front door), and prestocked bar and refrigerator shelves that are inserted each day and refilled at night.

## Process Capability Analysis

Process capability refers to the ability of the process to meet specifications. It should not be attempted until process control is achieved, except in special circumstances, which are beyond our scope. Usually, process capability is expressed using one or more **process capability indexes.** The best known index is $C_{pk}$. A process improvement team must know the specification for a quality characteristic and what the process output looks like before it can compute $C_{pk}$. The foundation for capability indexes, and perhaps a better understanding of their meaning, comes from a process capability graph.

### *Process Capability Graph*

To see how an improvement team could develop a process capability graph, we return to the injection-molding process used in Example 9-2 (run diagram) and Example 9-3 ($\overline{X}$ and $R$ control charts). Assuming that injection-molding associates have attained process control, the only variation in process output is the natural (common) variation. That variation, equal to six standard deviations ($6\sigma$), is referred to as the inherent process capability. The team first determines inherent capability.

The standard deviation of process output is unknown but is estimated as follows:

$$\hat{\sigma} = \overline{R}/d_2 \tag{9-13}$$

where

$\hat{o}$ = Estimate for $\sigma$

$d_2$ = Conversion factor found in quality control tables (see Exhibit 9-20); it is a function of sample size

From Exhibit 9-20, for a sample size ($n$) of 4, $d_2$ is 2.059; and from Example 9-3, $\overline{R}$ is 0.075 cm. Then:

$$\sigma = \frac{\overline{R}}{d_2} = \frac{0.075 \text{ cm}}{2.059} = 0.036 \text{ cm}$$

The value for $6\sigma$ becomes:

$$6\sigma = 6(0.036 \text{ cm}) = 0.216 \text{ cm}$$

This inherent capability, 0.216 cm, is a statement of variation only; it makes no claim as to location. Process output location is already known, however. From Example 9-3 the injection-molding process is centered at 5.01 cm—the value of $\overline{\overline{X}}$. Thus the team can

**EXHIBIT 9-26 Process Capability Graph: Injection-Molding Process**

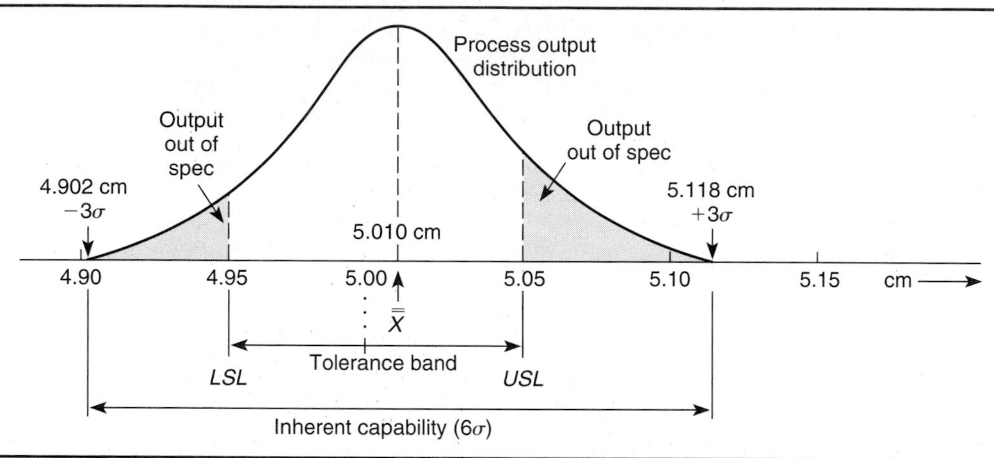


fully describe the expected process output distribution. It is centered at 5.01 cm and extends $3\sigma$ (0.108 cm) above (to 5.118 cm) and below (to 4.902 cm) that center.

To complete the process capability graph, the team adds the specification for the outer diameter of the part. In that specification, $5.00 \pm 0.05$ cm, the tolerance band extends from the center (target) of 5.00 cm down to 4.95 cm and up to 5.05 cm. The allowable tolerance band is just 0.10 cm wide, much less than the inherent capability (0.216 cm) of the process. Exhibit 9-26 shows the process capability graph.

The shaded areas at each end represent molded parts that do not meet specifications. With the normal curve areas table (Appendix A), the team could compute the proportion of output that fails to meet specification. (We leave that for an end-of-chapter solved problem.)

### *Process Capability Indexes*

Improvement teams usually do not need to go to the extreme of constructing a capability graph such as Exhibit 9-26 in order to compare output with specifications. They calculate capability indexes instead.

One popular index, $C_p$, is called simply the **capability index.** It is a ratio of the width of the tolerance band, $(USL - LSL)$, to the inherent process capability, $6\sigma$. That is:

$$C_p = \frac{(USL - LSL)}{6\sigma} \tag{9-14}$$

where:

$USL$ = upper specification limit, and

$LSL$ = lower specification limit.

If the process width is less than the allowable tolerance band, the value of $C_p$ will be greater than unity, and the process is said to be capable, and more accurately should be said to be *potentially* capable. The reason for the caveat lies in the weakness of the $C_p$ index: it considers only variation, and not central tendency or location. Indeed, even if $6\sigma < (USL - LSL)$, there is no way of knowing whether any of the process output meets specification. Some users choose to refer to $C_p$ as the index for use when the process is assumed to be centered at the specification target. Years of theoretical and empirical research have shown, however, that such an assumption is rarely valid.[12]

A better capability index exists, however, and requires just a bit more computation. $\boldsymbol{C_{pk}}$ (pronounce it by saying all three letters) is a single number that conveys most of the information in Exhibit 9-26. $C_{pk}$ is found as shown in Equation 9-15.

$$C_{pk} = \min\left(\frac{USL - \overline{\overline{X}}}{3\sigma}, \frac{\overline{\overline{X}} - LSL}{3\sigma}\right) \tag{9-15}$$

If the process is centered at the specification target, the two ratios are the same and either may be used. As we have noted, however, output is usually not centered. The danger of out-of-specification output is greater at the nearer spec limit, hence the focus on the minimum numerator value. In the injection molding example, the process center ($\overline{\overline{X}} = 5.01$) is nearer the upper spec limit, so $C_{pk}$ is determined to be:

$$C_{pk} = \frac{5.05 - 5.01}{3(0.036)} = \frac{0.04}{0.108} = 0.37$$

What does that value mean? Is it good or bad? Unfortunately, it is bad. It reveals that a large portion of the process output is not meeting customer's specification—something we had determined from the process capability graph in Exhibit 9-26. For process output to be within the specification range (tolerance band), $C_{pk}$ must be at least 1.0. The higher the value the better, for $C_{pk}$ increases when one or both of two desirable outcomes occur: (1) the process is very near the spec target, hence the numerator in the $C_{pk}$ ratio is larger, and (2) process variability is lower, making the denominator ($3\sigma$) smaller. Exhibit 9-27 shows four general $C_{pk}$ conditions in the form of small process capability sketches. To summarize, $C_{pk}$ shows not only whether process output is capable of meeting specifications but whether it *does* meet specs.

When $C_{pk}$ calculations began to loom large in North American industry in the 1980s, OEMs that requested a $C_{pk}$ value of 1.33 from suppliers were known as "tough customers." Few companies (including some of those tough guys themselves) could comply. Today, even as some firms struggle to meet the older 1.33 value, the benchmark keeps moving . . . as we see next.

### *Six-Sigma Quality*

In the 1980s, Motorola (already established at that time as an early leader in the North American quality improvement movement) developed and instituted a program called "six-sigma quality." Process capability, and the $C_{pk}$ index in particular, provide a

## EXHIBIT 9-27 Capability Index $C_{pk}$: Four Examples

- If $C_{pk}$ is negative, then $\overline{\overline{X}}$ is not within tolerance limits, indicating a very high defect rate; process improvement is urgently needed.

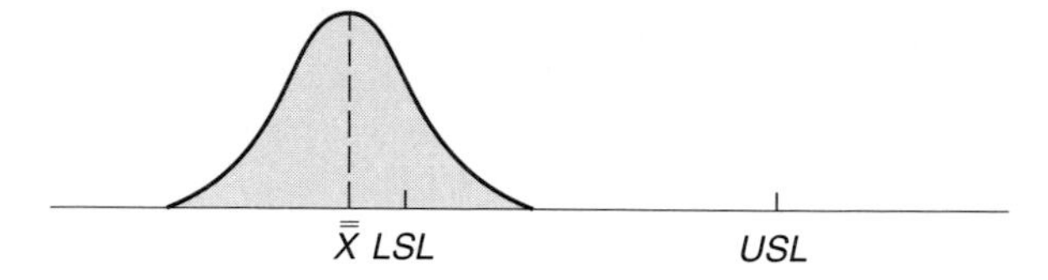


- If $C_{pk}$ is positive but less than 1.0—the case for the injection-molding process—the process is centered somewhere within the tolerance band but its width exceeds the tolerance band; again, serious work is needed, for some output is out of spec.

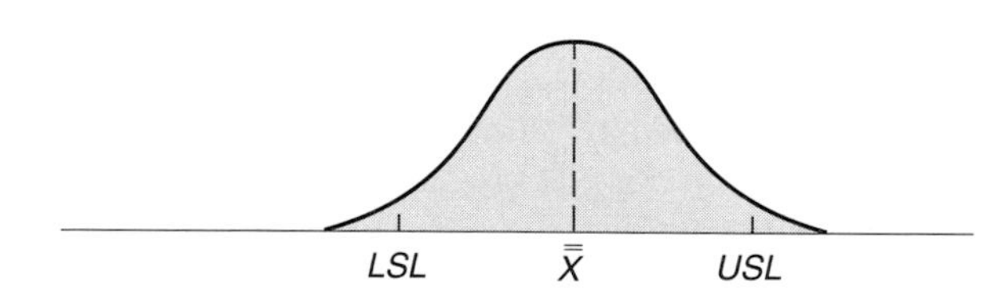


- If $C_{pk}$ equals 1.0, the process just (barely) meets specs; it is centered somewhere within the tolerance band.

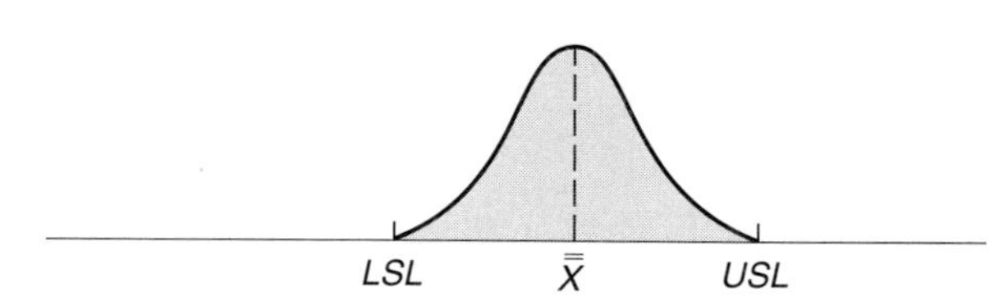


- If $C_{pk}$ is greater than 1.0, all process output is within tolerances; the higher the value of $C_{pk}$, the better.

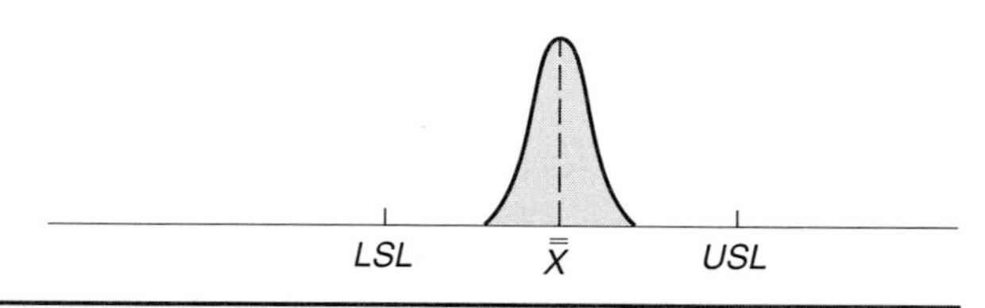


convenient point of departure for us to take a brief look at this popular process improvement tool that is today also ingrained at General Electric, Polaroid, Sony, Texas Instruments, Canon, and other big-name companies.[13] Reported operations and financial successes among such advocates prompted the auto industry to investigate, and in 2000, efforts began at Ford and other automakers to consider how the six-sigma ideas might blend with the already popular QS 9000 standards.[14]

Today's six-sigma quality improvement programs reach far beyond capability analysis, but the program philosophy and measures of success emerge from an understanding of process capability. The name "six sigma" refers to the distance that would have to exist between the center ($\overline{\overline{X}}$) of any process and the nearer spec limit in order to have $C_{pk} = 2.0$. That distance is equal to six of *that process's* standard deviations. However, there is more to the story. The banner headline of six-sigma quality level is no more than 3.4 defects per million opportunities—a quality level that was eye-popping in the early 1980s, and still is for many organizations. That figure, however, translates into a process-center-to-nearest-spec distance of about 4.5 standard deviations, not 6. (Or, into a $C_{pk}$ of 1.5 rather than 2.0.) So what gives?

The answer is long-run process drift. In a nutshell, the process will shift through a range of about 1.5 standard deviations (each way) over the long haul, "robbing" us of some of the short-term process capability.[15] We might say that in order to get the benefits of 4.5 sigma-quality, we must aim for 6-sigma; to count on a $C_{pk}$ value of 1.5, we must aim for 2.0. In the final analysis, however, the ultimate goal isn't the value of $C_{pk}$ or "number of sigmas." Rather, it is defect-free output. And, no matter where one positions the spec limits, improvement can *always* be defined as getting more of the process output closer to the target. Nevertheless, capability analysis and its derivatives give us a handy way to show our customers just how good we are.

Principle 16

Market every improvement.

Yet another reason to pursue continuous improvement and narrower spec limits is a phenomenon caller variation stackup, or tolerance stackup, our next topic.

### Variation Stackup

Output that meets specs may be unsatisfactory when the customer has to put it to use with other outputs. **Variation stackup** occurs when two or more outputs that must be used jointly each lie at the extreme of their spec limits. Consider this example:

Door specifications: 36.0 ± 0.25 inches.
Frame specifications: 36.5 − 0.25 inches.

Even if all doors and frames are within their respective specs, one of the smaller doors placed within one of the larger frames results in gaps through which unwelcome weather passes. The opposite possibility, a larger door in a smaller frame, requires planing and sanding to get the door even to close. Sorting and matching doors to frames is a weak solution; it is costly and it treats symptoms but not underlying problems.

Variation stackup can apply in services as well. Consider a municipal bus system. Specs for the bus drivers might be to arrive at each stop no more than five minutes behind schedule. If the customer is five minutes early and the bus is five minutes late, however, it is bad service. Just-in-time arrival of the customer coupled with an early departing bus is equally poor service.

The best cure for these and other variation stackup problems is reduction of process variability. Make all doors close to 36.0 inches and all frames close to 36.5 inches. Put enough slack in the bus schedule so that buses are rarely late and set a rule that a bus may never leave a stop early.

The variation stackup problem is amplified in the mixing stages of continuous process production. Often several ingredients, not just two, are mixed together. Purities, specific gravities, and fineness of various liquid and solid ingredients may all be within specs, but on the high (or low) side. When mixed and processed, the result might be tacky rubber, cloudy glass, unstable chemicals, rough surfaces, crumbly pills, brittle plastics, or M&Ms that melt in your hands.

## Process Improvement in Perspective

Does anybody besides industry leaders use these quality control and improvement techniques? Students and teachers at the Lower Nazareth Elementary School in Pennsylvania do. Together with business partners from the Martin Guitar Company, they went after behavior problems in the cafeteria. The project team collected baseline statistics, developed improvement options, and put several into effect. Bad behaviors, including shouting, running, and leaving the building, decreased by 56 percent.

Second graders at Western Salisbury (Pennsylvania) School are in the learning mode. Their subject matter includes flowcharts, Paretos, and fishbone diagrams. Using these tools, they developed baseline data on time to make a peanut butter and jelly sandwich. After study and improvement, they cut the sandwich production time from an average of about 3 minutes to 1.4 minutes.[16]

Process improvement is for everybody—but not without tools. Education is the starting point. Making data-based continuous quality improvement a part of everyone's job—or even school life—sustains the improvement pattern, which avoids sinking into a work life of frustration over chronic problems that never get solved. The transition to the process improvement approach is summarized in the Contrast box, "Approach to Quality."

CONTRAST

## Approach to Quality

### Old Approach

- Worry about output volume first, and then worry about quality—when it becomes a problem.
- Produce large lots and rely on sampling inspection to accept or reject; sort to find good ones; scrap or rework bad ones.
- Declare some proportion defective (1–2 percent, perhaps) as acceptable quality level (AQL) and strive to meet that goal.

### Process Improvement (TQM) Approach

- Everyone serves a customer and all customers want quality.
- Aim for fail-safe processes.
- Control processes for consistent output.
- Use capability analysis to guide continued efforts to improve processes.
- They only acceptable goal is zero defects.

## Summary Check Points

- ✓ Process improvement efforts may target quality, speed, or some other customer want, but may end up affecting a wider array of outputs.
- ✓ Improvement at the source is the aim of the quality action cycle; iterations of design, detection, and improvement result in process improvements. If source containment of any poor quality fails, then detection in later processes or by customers will be the first chance to rectify some problems.
- ✓ As frontline operators assume responsibility for quality, quality professionals assume roles as trainers, auditors, improvement consultants, and companywide quality planners.
- ✓ Even in an arena of quality at the source, some inspection will be needed for new product or supplier situations, hazardous or critical goods, and other settings in which public safety and security might be threatened.
- ✓ Statistical process control (SPC) uses inspection while the process transformation activities are taking place, perhaps with rapid feedback in time for quick adjustment if needed.
- ✓ Acceptance sampling (inspection) takes place after the goods are produced. The decision is often to accept or reject a lot by examining a sample from that lot.
- ✓ A transformation process is a unique combination of elements, conditions, or causes that collectively produces a given outcome or set of results.
- ✓ Process performance depends on how the process is designed, built or installed, operated, and maintained.
- ✓ Assignable (special) variation in process output is attributable to a specific cause; find and fix the cause, and the assignable variation disappears.
- ✓ Common or inherent variation remains after all assignable-cause variation has been removed. A process that is in statistical control has only common variation.
- ✓ Variables data result from measurement or computation of some quality characteristic; attributes data come from judging, counting, or assigning events to categories.
- ✓ Improvement projects follow the scientific method of inquiry and employ general tools, coarse-grained tools, and fine-grained tools.
- ✓ Coarse-grained tools include flowcharts, check sheets and histograms, Pareto analysis, and fishbone charts.
- ✓ Fine-grained tools include fail-safing, design-of-experiments (DOE), scattergrams and correlation, run diagrams, and control charts.
- ✓ Variables control charts include the chart for averages ($X$-bar) and ranges ($R$); attributes charts include the proportion defective ($p$) chart, and the number of defects ($c$) chart.

✓ Process control says nothing about meeting specifications; a process may be in control and produce product that is totally unacceptable. In control means stable or consistent.

✓ Process capability means capable of meeting specifications; the $C_{pk}$ index shows whether or not process output does indeed meet specifications.

✓ Six-sigma quality programs extend the process capability concept into a broad program of process improvements.

✓ Variance stackup results when outputs that meet their individual specifications fail to provide quality when used together; reduction in output variability is the solution.

✓ Process improvement is for everybody; education is the starting point.

## Solved Problems

### *Problem 1*

Connector leads for electronic ignition components are produced to a specification of 8.000 ± 0.010 cm. The process has been studied, and the following values have been obtained:

$$\text{Process average} = \overline{\overline{X}} = 8.003 \text{ cm}$$

$$\text{Standard deviation (estimate)} = \hat{\sigma} = 0.002 \text{ cm}$$

Calculate:

*a.* The inherent process capability

*b.* The capability index $C_{pk}$

### *Solution 1*

*a.* Inherent process capability $= 6 \times \hat{\sigma}$

$$= 6 \times 0.002 \text{ cm}$$

$$= 0.012 \text{ cm}$$

*b.* Since the process average (8.003 cm) is closer to the upper spec limit than to the lower, the appropriate form of Equation 9-15 (with values inserted) is:

$$C_{pk} = \frac{USL - \overline{\overline{X}}}{3\sigma} = \frac{8.010 - 8.003}{3(0.002)} = 1.167$$

The value of $C_{pk}$ is greater than 1.0, so all process output meets spec. Some buyers in today's marketplace, however, would not be satisfied with so low a value. A process improvement team needs to take a look.

### *Problem 2*

Samples of 180 units are drawn from production in order to construct a proportion-defective chart. Develop the chart for the following 16 samples of percentages defective. Is the process satisfactory for use on the production line? Explain.

| Sample | Percent Defective | Sample | Percent Defective | Sample | Percent Defective | Sample | Percent Defective |
|---|---|---|---|---|---|---|---|
| 1 | 2 | 5 | 1 | 9 | 6 | 13 | 4 |
| 2 | 5 | 6 | 0 | 10 | 2 | 14 | 3 |
| 3 | 5 | 7 | 2 | 11 | 7 | 15 | 2 |
| 4 | 3 | 8 | 2 | 12 | 1 | 16 | 3 |

### Solution 2

First, calculate $\overline{p}$, $UCL$, and $LCL$, using Equations 9-7 through 9-9.

$$\overline{p} = \frac{\text{Total percent defective}}{k}$$

$$= \frac{2+5+5+3+1+0+2+2+6+2+7+1+4+3+2+3}{16}$$

$$= \frac{48}{16} = 3 \text{ percent, or } 0.03$$

$$UCL = \overline{p} + 3\sqrt{\frac{\overline{p}(1-\overline{p})}{n}} = 0.03 + 3\sqrt{\frac{0.03(0.97)}{180}} = 0.068$$

$$LCL = \overline{p} - 3\sqrt{\frac{\overline{p}(1-\overline{p})}{n}} = 0.03 - 0.038 = -0.08, \text{ or } 0$$

Next, develop a chart and plot the 16 data points on it:

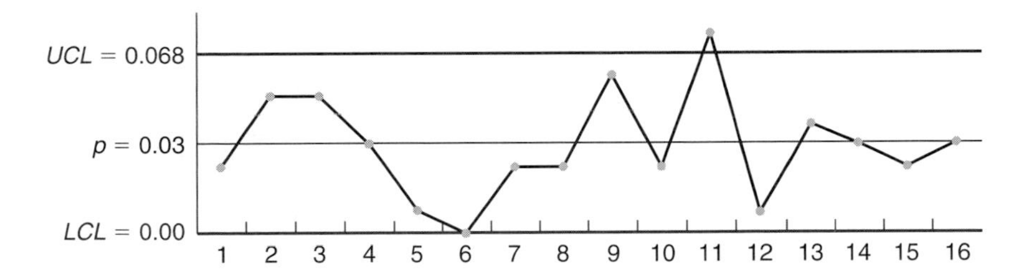


Sample 11 is above the *UCL*, which indicates that the process is unstable, out of statistical control. Look for a special cause, eliminate it, and try again.

### Problem 3

I. B. Poorly is director of Employee Wellness Programs for Alpine Escapes, a chain of winter sports resorts. He knows that Alpine's employee health care costs have risen 78 percent in the last three years. Absenteeism, low productivity, and poor attitudes (especially in the presence of customers) are other symptoms of poor health among employees. I. B. organized a largely volunteer process improvement team to turn things around. The team interviewed and tested a sample of 60 Alpine employees and recorded health problems on a check sheet. Join I. B.'s team and show how process improvement tools might be used to systematically tackle the health improvement task at Alpine.

### *Solution 3*

First, analyze the following check sheet:

| *Health Problem* | *Occurrences* | *Total* | *Health Problem* | *Occurrences* | *Total* |
|---|---|---|---|---|---|
| Poor sleep habits | 卌 \|\|\|\| | 9 | Smoking | 卌 卌 卌 \|\|\| | 18 |
| High cholesterol | 卌 卌 \|\|\|\| | 14 | Overweight | 卌 卌 卌 卌 卌 \| 卌 卌 | 36 |
| High blood pressure | 卌 卌 卌 \|\| | 17 | | | |
| Poor circulation | \|\|\|\| | 4 | Alcohol abuse | 卌 \|\|\| | 8 |
| | | | Other problems | 卌 \| | 6 |

Clearly, some of the 60 members of the sample had more than one health problem, and perhaps there are interrelationships among the listed ills. A Pareto analysis, however, would call for more-detailed study of the most frequently occurring problem. Thus, the team ought to focus on weight by making it the spine of a fishbone chart. Such a chart, including some of the team's brainstorming (possible causes and effects), is sketched here.

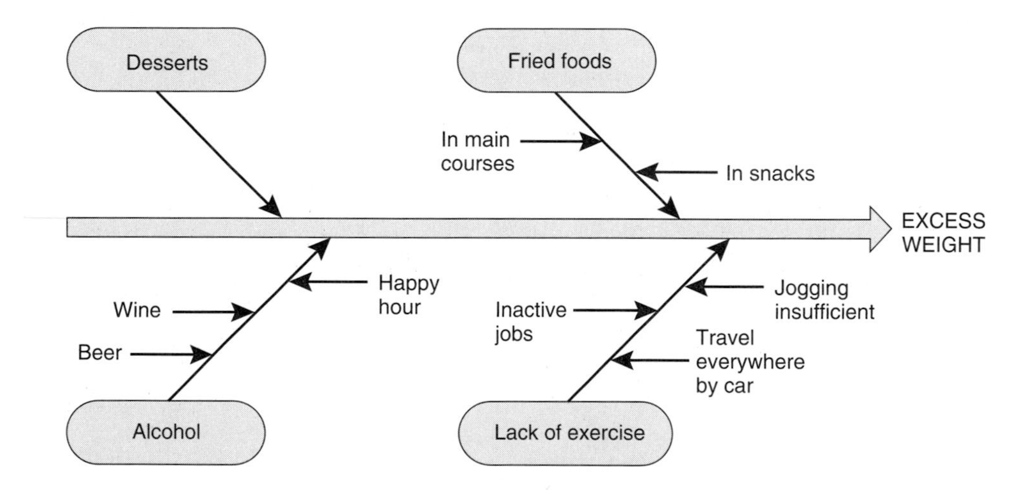


Each end point on the fishbone chart suggests action. The team might use process control charts to track percentage of employees who succumb to various poor health habits (snacks, no exercise, smoking, etc.). Effects of process interventions such as healthy cafeteria food, flexible work hours, exercise periods, and so forth, ought to show up on the charts.

Pareto analysis may again be used for the "jogging insufficient" end point. The accompanying Pareto chart provides concrete data on specific reasons for insufficient jogging. In this case, the dominant cause, "skipped entirely," might be used as the spine for another, finer fishbone analysis indicating reasons for skipping (e.g., bad weather or working late).

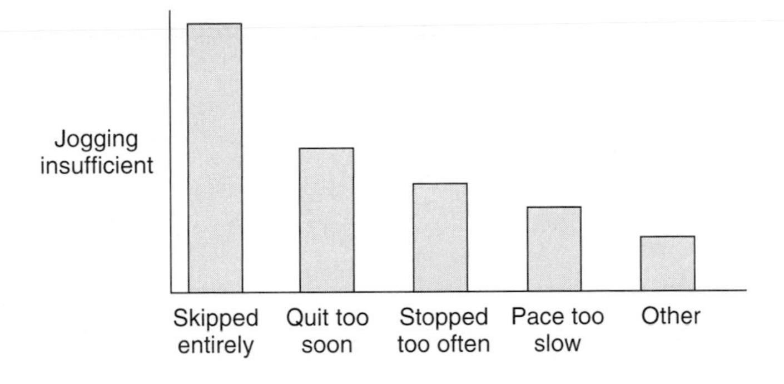


### *Problem 4*

The fill process for 9-ounce bottles of Island Sunscreen Lotion is under scrutiny by a process improvement team. Sample average and ranges from 20 samples of four bottles each are shown in the table below. Construct mean and range charts and analyze the information given by the charts.

| *Sample Number* | *Average (oz.)* | *Range (oz.)* | *Sample Number* | *Average (oz.)* | *Range (oz.)* |
|---|---|---|---|---|---|
| 1 | 9.025 | 0.2 | 11 | 9.025 | 0.3 |
| 2 | 9.050 | 0.1 | 12 | 9.100 | 0.2 |
| 3 | 9.100 | 0.3 | 13 | 9.125 | 0.3 |
| 4 | 9.100 | 0.3 | 14 | 9.150 | 0.5 |
| 5 | 9.000 | 0.5 | 15 | 8.950 | 0.2 |
| 6 | 9.025 | 0.3 | 16 | 9.000 | 0.5 |
| 7 | 9.050 | 0.4 | 17 | 9.025 | 0.2 |
| 8 | 9.075 | 0.1 | 18 | 9.100 | 0.2 |
| 9 | 9.000 | 0.2 | 19 | 9.050 | 0.1 |
| 10 | 8.975 | 0.3 | 20 | 9.075 | 0.4 |

### *Solution 4*

Following the procedure used in Example 9-3, calculate center lines and control limits for both mean and range charts. First, the center line for the mean chart:

$$\overline{\overline{X}} = \frac{\sum \overline{X}}{k} = \frac{181}{20} = 9.05 \text{ oz.}$$

For the range chart:

$$\overline{R} = \frac{\sum R}{k} = \frac{5.6}{20} = 0.28 \text{ oz.}$$

Next, (using factors from Exhibit 9-20) control limits for the mean chart:

$$UCL_{\overline{x}} = \overline{\overline{X}} + A_2\overline{R} = 9.05 + (0.729)(0.28) = 9.25 \text{ oz.}$$

$$LCL_{\overline{x}} = \overline{\overline{X}} - A_2\overline{R} = 9.05 - (0.729)(0.28) = 8.85 \text{ oz.}$$

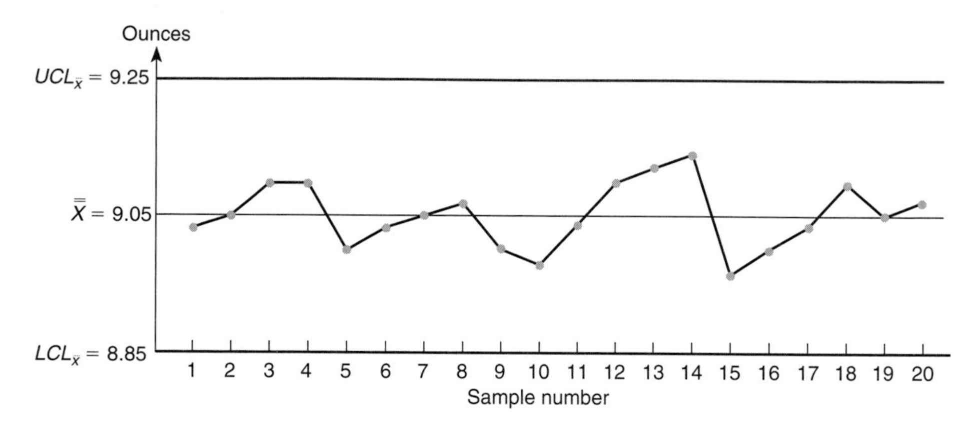


RANGE CHART

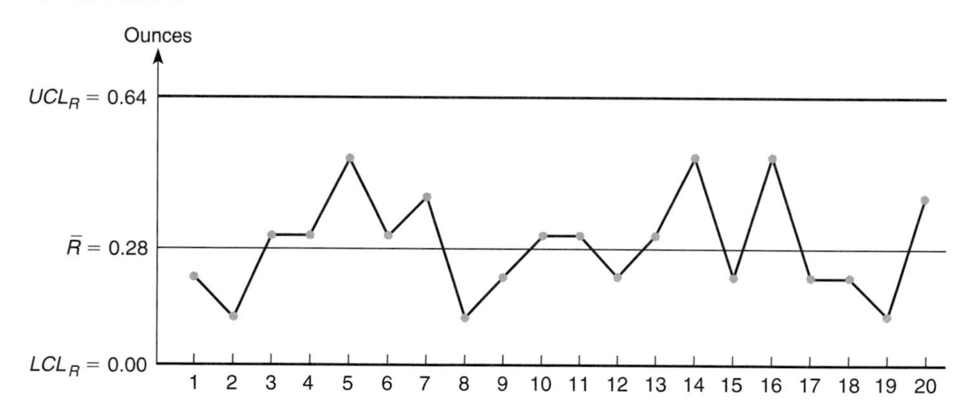


Limits for the range chart:

$$UCL_R = D_4(\overline{R}) = 2.282(0.28) = 0.64 \text{ oz.}$$

$$LCL_R = D_3(\overline{R}) = 0(0.28) = 0$$

Place the center line and control limits on the respective mean and range charts and then plot the sample averages and ranges. The accompanying charts illustrate.

Comparison of chart patterns with tests for process control reveals that all tests pass. Close inspection does show what seems to be a cyclic pattern—high to low about every four or five samples—on the mean chart. The team must investigate. Perhaps they will find that the on-off cycling of large motors such as air conditioners is affecting the lotion-filling machines. If a special cause for the apparent pattern is found, it must be eliminated.

The cycling might disappear on its own after a few more samples, and if stability continues, the team will begin capability analysis by comparing process output with specifications.

### *Problem 5*

Exhibit 9-26 is the process capability graph for the injection-molding process discussed in Example 9-3. The improvement team has asked you to compute the percentage of molding process output that fails to meet specifications and to comment on the implications.

***Solution 5***

Use the normal curve areas (see Table A-1 in Appendix A) to find the proportion of output that lies beyond each spec limit; that is, the areas that are shaded in Exhibit 9-26.

Recall from Example 9-3 that the process center is: $\overline{\overline{X}} = 5.01$ cm

Also, from Equation 9-13, $\sigma = 0.036$ cm

To use Table A-1, find the number of standard deviations (called $z$ values) that each spec limit lies from $\overline{\overline{X}}$, the process average. The formula is:

$$z = \frac{\text{Spec limit} - \overline{\overline{X}}}{\sigma}$$

Two $z$ values are needed, one for each spec limit:

$$z_{LSL} = \frac{4.95 - 5.01}{0.036} = -1.67$$

$$z_{USL} = \frac{5.05 - 5.01}{0.036} = 1.11$$

From Table A-1, read directly the area between the distribution average and the $z$ values. Then subtract each of those areas from 0.5, the area in half the distribution. The remainder is the area or proportion (or, for present purposes, percentage of output) that lies outside the respective spec limit. For the lower spec limit:

$$\text{Table area} = 0.4525\text{, so } (0.5 - 0.4525) = 0.0475\text{, or } 4.75 \text{ percent}$$

For the upper spec limit:

$$\text{Table area} = 0.3665\text{, so } (0.5 - 0.3665) = 0.1335\text{, or } 13.35 \text{ percent}$$

Add the two out-of-spec percentages, to get the total for the molding process:

$$(4.75) + (13.35) = 18.1 \text{ percent of output fails to meet specs}$$

In your report to the improvement team, you might mention something about getting that errant output within specs—a free 18-percent boost in capacity. Tell the team about the key goal in all process improvement: Hit the target, the first time and every time!

## Exercises

1. Fix-M-Up, Inc., is a small chain of stores that clean and repair printers, photocopiers, and other office equipment. Define a process for the company along the lines of that discussed in the chapter for the manufacture of three-inch bolts. Prepare a list of quality characteristics you might wish to use if you were considering using Fix-M-Up as the maintenance contractor for your company's office equipment.
2. Using either the Jostens Diplomas or the Ampex examples in the chapter, fully explain why so many improvements occurred at the same time.
3. A listing of products/services follows. Select two from each column and do the following:
   *a.* For each of your four selections, decide on two attributes and/or variables that you think are most suitable for inspection. Explain your reasoning.

*b.* Discuss whether a formal statistical sampling method or an informal inspection method is more sensible for each selection.

| *Column 1* | *Column 2* |
|---|---|
| Diver's wetsuit | Auto tire mounting |
| Highway road map | Package shipping services |
| Pocket calculator | Bookbinding |
| Frying pan | Internet security services |
| Space heater | Data entry |
| Electric switch | Proofreading |
| Glue | Wallpaper hanging |
| Daily multiple vitamins | Library reference services |
| Watch | Nursing care |
| Handgun | Legal services |
| Cradle alarm for infant | Food catering |
| | Cleanliness of dishes |
| | Bank teller service |
| | Education services |

4. A camping and outdoor recreation goods manufacturer (which employees 1,000 people) is planning to adopt a total quality program. Following are some characteristics of its present production system:
   *a.* There is a quality assurance department of 50 people, including 30 inspectors.
   *b.* Rejected products discovered at the end of final assembly are sent by conveyor to a rework area staffed by 120 people.
   *c.* All purchased raw materials and parts are inspected on the receiving docks using acceptance sampling.
   *d.* All direct laborers are paid by how much they produce, which is measured daily.
   What changes would you suggest? Discuss.
5. Exhibit 9-10 shows flowcharts of a travel authorization process, one before improvements and the other after. What principles of operations management were used to improve the process? State specifically how each principle you list was beneficial.
6. With an attributes chart, such as the $p$-chart and $c$-chart that we studied in this chapter, the ideal situation is an out-of-control situation. Explain what that statement means. You might want to revisit Example 9-4. Be sure that your response includes appropriate definitions and, always a plus, a sketch or two to illustrate your logic.
7. An Into Practice box in the chapter presents check-sheet data for Akron General Medical Center. Those data are reproduced below.

| | **Frequency of Occurrence** | | | |
|---|---|---|---|---|
| | *Week 1* | *Week 2* | *Week 3* | *Week 4* |
| Incorrect dose dispensed from pharmacy | ✓✓ | ✓ | ✓✓ | ✓ |
| Verbal order taken incorrectly | ✓✓✓ | ✓ | ✓✓✓✓ | ✓✓✓ |
| Incorrect dose ordered | ✓✓ | ✓✓✓ | ✓ | ✓✓ |
| Dosage calculation error | ✓ | ✓ | | ✓ |

*a.* Rearrange the data as a Pareto chart.
*b.* The data do not easily rearrange into the form of a histogram. Why not? What raw data would be needed to develop one or more histograms?
*c.* Compare the usefulness of a Pareto analysis with histograms for Akron General's project.

8. American Pen and Pencil (AmPen) has had most of the market for ballpoint pens, but now it is under great pressure from a competitor whose product is clearly superior. AmPen operators have identified several quality problems, including viscosity of ink, which is affected by the temperature of the mixing solution; purity of powdered ink and amount of water; the ballpoint assembly, which is affected by ball diameter, ball roundness, and trueness of the tube opening into which the ball goes; and strength of the clip, which is affected by the thickness of the metal and the correctness of the shape after stamping.
   *a.* Draw a fishbone chart for these ballpoint pen factors. How should the chart be used?
   *b.* An inspection procedure at the ink-mixing stage reveals that 80 percent of bad samples are caused by impurities, 15 percent by wrong temperature, and 5 percent by wrong amount of water. Draw a Pareto chart. How should it be used?
9. A bellman is trying to determine the factors that increase tips. Some of his ideas are how long it takes to reach a guest after being summoned, how many words he speaks to a guest, how long it takes the coat room to retrieve guest luggage, and how much luggage a guest has.
   *a.* Arrange these few factors into a logical fishbone chart. Explain your chart.
   *b.* Which of the factors is likely to plot on a scatter diagram as an upside-down U? Explain.
10. Some social services employees are developing a fishbone chart on how to improve the average attendance at a neighborhood activity center. So far, the chart is as shown below; only one primary bone, "materials and machines," is filled out.
   *a.* Fill out the rest of the primary bones with reasonable cause and subcause arrows.
   *b.* Suggest three actions to be taken next.

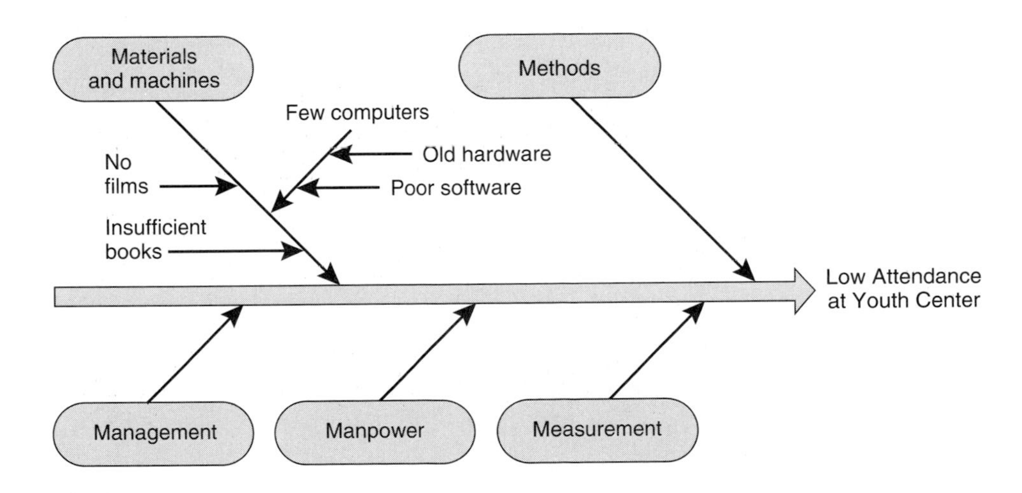


11. Chompo Dog Food, Ltd., has just installed a new filling machine for its 40-pound dry dog food product. The quality characteristic of concern is fill weight; the company would like to average just over 40 pounds per bag—but not by much due to expense.

Initial samples, taken throughout the first day of using the new filling machine are shown in the table below.

**40 # Dog Food Fill Process**

| *Sample #* | *Bag Weight (lbs.)* | | | | *Sample #* | *Bag Weight (lbs.)* | | | |
|---|---|---|---|---|---|---|---|---|---|
| 1 | 40 | 41 | 43 | 43 | 11 | 43 | 44 | 42 | 40 |
| 2 | 41 | 38 | 38 | 37 | 12 | 40 | 40 | 42 | 43 |
| 3 | 39 | 45 | 43 | 40 | 13 | 39 | 38 | 37 | 38 |
| 4 | 43 | 46 | 44 | 43 | 14 | 36 | 37 | 39 | 43 |
| 5 | 39 | 37 | 39 | 40 | 15 | 40 | 42 | 41 | 41 |
| 6 | 44 | 43 | 45 | 42 | 16 | 38 | 39 | 41 | 40 |
| 7 | 38 | 39 | 39 | 43 | 17 | 42 | 43 | 38 | 39 |
| 8 | 41 | 42 | 42 | 41 | 18 | 44 | 47 | 46 | 45 |
| 9 | 43 | 45 | 42 | 44 | 19 | 42 | 37 | 39 | 39 |
| 10 | 45 | 43 | 45 | 37 | 20 | 43 | 45 | 41 | 38 |

*a.* Construct trial control limits on *X*-bar and *R* charts.
*b.* Comment on the characteristics of the filling process.
*c.* What, if anything, should Chompo do next? Explain.
(Note: A helpful Excel spreadsheet program is available on the CD-ROM that came with your book.)

12. Suggest a fail-safing approach for each of the following problems:
    *a.* Forgetting to turn off office equipment at quitting time.
    *b.* Missing appointments.
    *c.* Remembering passwords for Internet web sites.
    *d.* Not having correct change for unattended tollway exit booths.
    *e.* Losing one sock, earring, or glove from a (matching) pair.
13. Following is a scatter diagram showing inches of deviation from the correct length of wooden blinds and humidity in the shop.
    *a.* What does the shape of the scattered points indicate?
    *b.* Sharpness of the saw blade is also known to affect the correctness of blind length. Make a drawing of how the scatter for those two factors (sharpness and deviation of length) would probably look.

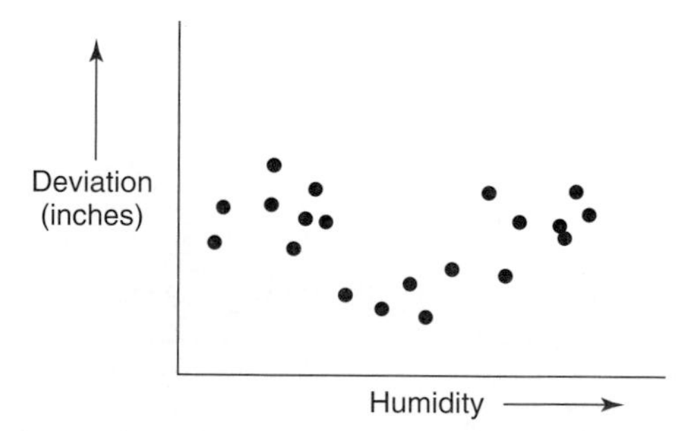


14. You are manager of one of the Oil Can (speedy auto oil change and lubrication) stores. You've been collecting data on time, in minutes, to service cars. Your purpose is to reduce

variability in the completion times, and you believe that job specifications will help. Completion times for one day's business, 25 cars, follow:

6, 10, 14, 14, 9, 11, 13, 8, 16, 15, 19, 15, 9, 18, 15, 16, 15, 17, 12, 17, 17, 15, 18, 14, 9

*a.* Plot the points on a run diagram. What does the diagram reveal about the process?
*b.* Create spec limits and insert them on your run diagram. What investigations are suggested?
*c.* Plot the data as a histogram. What questions does that histogram raise?
*d.* Explain how these data and tools might be used advantageously in your store.

15. An associate measures current loss in a circuit and plots the means of sample measurements on an existing process control chart. Most of the means fall below the lower control limit—less current loss than before. What is the implication of this on such factors as pricing, marketing, purchasing, production, training, design, and control charts?

16. Environmental Control Associates (ECA) supplies monitoring equipment and services to a number of clients that maintain environmentally sensitive facilities. A prospective client suspects environmental control system problems in a facility that it operates four days a week and is considering installation of continuous monitoring and control hardware and the purchase of monitoring service—altogether an expensive proposition. Site personnel have collected electrical consumption readings for each of the four operating days for the last 20 weeks (see data table below). They plan to construct averages and ranges charts using that data. A team from the prospective client's facility is visiting Environmental Control Associates and thinks the control charts might be useful to ECA personnel. (Power consumption analysis is one of the tools that ECA uses, typically from its own continuous monitoring equipment, however.)

**Electrical Usage: Environmental Control**

| *Sample #* | *Consumption (KWH)* | | | | *Sample #* | *Consumption (KWH)* | | | |
|---|---|---|---|---|---|---|---|---|---|
| 1 | 96 | 99 | 101 | 121 | 11 | 99 | 109 | 116 | 101 |
| 2 | 110 | 102 | 94 | 98 | 12 | 108 | 111 | 99 | 102 |
| 3 | 90 | 111 | 102 | 114 | 13 | 97 | 105 | 108 | 104 |
| 4 | 100 | 116 | 112 | 109 | 14 | 109 | 111 | 103 | 106 |
| 5 | 97 | 98 | 108 | 105 | 15 | 102 | 110 | 107 | 98 |
| 6 | 102 | 104 | 117 | 118 | 16 | 103 | 98 | 96 | 105 |
| 7 | 108 | 117 | 112 | 125 | 17 | 108 | 110 | 98 | 97 |
| 8 | 99 | 102 | 100 | 103 | 18 | 98 | 99 | 97 | 95 |
| 9 | 111 | 103 | 104 | 97 | 19 | 108 | 115 | 100 | 99 |
| 10 | 95 | 106 | 98 | 114 | 20 | 106 | 107 | 96 | 98 |

*a.* Construct the averages and ranges charts and prepare a brief report analyzing your findings. Be especially careful to suggest possible explanations for the data.
*b.* One ECA engineer, experienced with the foibles associated with human measurement and data recording, asks, "How trustworthy are these data points?" She goes on to add, "Maybe we should discuss how measurement is part of the process under study." Does she have a point? Respond with references to these data and to human measurement in general.

(Note: The Excel spreadsheet program on your CD-ROM may be used with this exercise.)

17. An improvement team for a medical supply manufacturer subjects hypodermic needles to a bend test, and the results, in grams, are plotted on mean and range charts. A suitable number of samples have been inspected. The resulting $\overline{\overline{X}}$ is 26.1, and the resulting $\overline{R}$ is 5.0.
    *a.* For $n = 8$, calculate the control limits for the control charts.
    *b.* What should be done with the values calculated in question *a*?
    *c.* Assume that process control charts have been developed and that the operator has been using the charts regularly. For one sample of hypodermics, $\overline{X} = 26.08$ and $R = 0.03$. Should there be an investigation for a special cause? Explain.
18. Spark-O-Plenty, Inc., periodically takes random samples, each with a sample size of six, from a production line that manufactures $\frac{1}{2}$ volt batteries. The sampled batteries are tested on a voltmeter. The production line has just been modified, and a new quality control plan must be designed. For that purpose, 10 random samples (of six each) have been taken over a suitable period of time; the test results are as follows:

| | **Test Voltages** | | | | | |
|---|---|---|---|---|---|---|
| *Sample Number* | $V_1$ | $V_2$ | $V_3$ | $V_4$ | $V_5$ | $V_6$ |
| 1 | 0.498 | 0.492 | 0.510 | 0.505 | 0.504 | 0.487 |
| 2 | 0.482 | 0.491 | 0.502 | 0.481 | 0.496 | 0.492 |
| 3 | 0.501 | 0.512 | 0.503 | 0.499 | 0.498 | 0.511 |
| 4 | 0.498 | 0.486 | 0.502 | 0.503 | 0.510 | 0.501 |
| 5 | 0.500 | 0.507 | 0.509 | 0.498 | 0.512 | 0.518 |
| 6 | 0.476 | 0.492 | 0.496 | 0.521 | 0.505 | 0.490 |
| 7 | 0.511 | 0.522 | 0.513 | 0.518 | 0.520 | 0.516 |
| 8 | 0.488 | 0.512 | 0.501 | 0.498 | 0.492 | 0.498 |
| 9 | 0.482 | 0.490 | 0.510 | 0.500 | 0.495 | 0.482 |
| 10 | 0.505 | 0.496 | 0.498 | 0.490 | 0.485 | 0.499 |

    *a.* Compute and draw the appropriate process control chart(s) for the data.
    *b.* What should be done next? Discuss.
19. A process improvement team at Hang-M-High, a manufacturer of coat hangers, decided what constitutes a defective hanger. Samples of 200 hangers were inspected on each of the last 20 days. The numbers of defectives found are given below. Construct a proportion-defective chart for the data. What should the team do next? Explain.
    (Note: You may use the Excel Spreadsheet software on your CD-ROM).

| *Day* | *Number Defective* | *Day* | *Number Defective* | *Day* | *Number Defective* | *Day* | *Number Defective* |
|---|---|---|---|---|---|---|---|
| 1 | 20 | 6 | 19 | 11 | 33 | 16 | 16 |
| 2 | 14 | 7 | 13 | 12 | 8 | 17 | 11 |
| 3 | 32 | 8 | 10 | 13 | 10 | 18 | 10 |
| 4 | 12 | 9 | 18 | 14 | 9 | 19 | 12 |
| 5 | 17 | 10 | 14 | 15 | 7 | 20 | 8 |

20. OK-Mart, a chain retailer, contracts with Electro Corporation to manufacture an OK brand of photo flashbulb. OK-Mart states that it wants an average quality of 99 percent good flashbulbs—that is, 99 percent that actually flash. Electro's marketing manager states that their goal should be for 99.9 percent to flash (better than OK-Mart's stated goal). After production begins at Electro, sampling on the production line over a representative time period shows 0.2 percent defective.
    *a.* Where should the center line be drawn on a process control chart? Why?
    *b.* What, if anything, needs to be done about the difference between goals and actual quality?
21. A pottery manufacturing firm constructs process control charts. Thirty pottery samples are taken, and the mean proportion of pottery samples that fail a strength test is 0.02, which becomes the center line on a proportion-defective chart. Control limits are put in place, and the 30 defect rates are plotted on the chart. Two of the 30 fall above the upper control limit, but all 30 meet the requirements of the major customer, a department store. Explain the situation. What should be done?
22. Rescue Services Training (RST) trains emergency rescue squads for state, county, and municipal police and fire departments. The training program development and improvement group at RST evaluates company training effectiveness, in part, by performance of trainee teams on the Simulated Emergency Rescue Exercise (SERE). During the SERE, trainee teams may err by omitting required steps as well as by committing acts that they shouldn't. The training group records total errors for each team. The table shows error data for the last 25 trainee teams:

| *SERE Team* | *Errors* | *SERE Team* | *Errors* | *SERE Team* | *Errors* | *SERE Team* | *Errors* | *SERE Team* | *Errors* |
|---|---|---|---|---|---|---|---|---|---|
| 1 | 8 | 6 | 3 | 11 | 2 | 16 | 6 | 21 | 4 |
| 2 | 6 | 7 | 1 | 12 | 2 | 17 | 14 | 22 | 2 |
| 3 | 2 | 8 | 5 | 13 | 3 | 18 | 4 | 23 | 7 |
| 4 | 4 | 9 | 7 | 14 | 3 | 19 | 6 | 24 | 6 |
| 5 | 9 | 10 | 3 | 15 | 12 | 20 | 8 | 25 | 5 |

    *a.* Plot the error data on a number-of-defects chart.
    *b.* Analyze the chart and comment on process stability.
    *c.* Prepare a list of recommendations to the training program development and improvement group.
    (Note: A *C*-chart program is available on the CD-ROM that accompanies your textbook.)
23. The training program development and improvement group at RST (see problem 22) suspects that the SERE error rate may depend on experience level—that is, trainee team members' years on-the-job in police or fire departments before coming to RST's program. How might that suspicion be investigated? Be specific in the tools and procedures that you recommend.
24. A food processing company has large tanks that are cleaned daily. Cleaning includes the use of packaged detergents, which dissolve in a solution inside the tanks. The company purchases detergent packages with a fill-weight specification of 12.00 ± 0.08 oz.
    A supplier representative claims that his company uses statistical process control and will promise an inherent process capability of 0.20 oz. for the fill-weight specification. The

brochure says nothing else about the process except that the advertised weight of the detergent packages is 12 oz.

*a.* Should the food processor buy detergent from this supplier? Why or why not?

*b.* If the supplier had control chart evidence that its fill-weight process was in fact centered at 12.00 oz. and was in a state of statistical control, how would your answer to question *a* change? Does all output meet specs?

*c.* Suppose the supplier is a reliable provider of other products and can reasonably be expected to improve the detergent-packaging process. What advice would you offer to the food processor on seeking alternate suppliers? What advice would you offer the supplier regarding the relationship with the food processor?

25. Plug-N-Go, Ltd., makes valve covers to a diameter specification of 0.500 ± 0.020 cm. The normally distributed process is in control, centered at 0.493 cm, and has an inherent process capability of 0.024 cm. The next sketch shows the process distribution.

*a.* Calculate the process capability index $C_{pk}$.

*b.* Should Plug-N-Go be concerned about reducing the variation in the diameter process output? Why or why not? What about location? Explain.

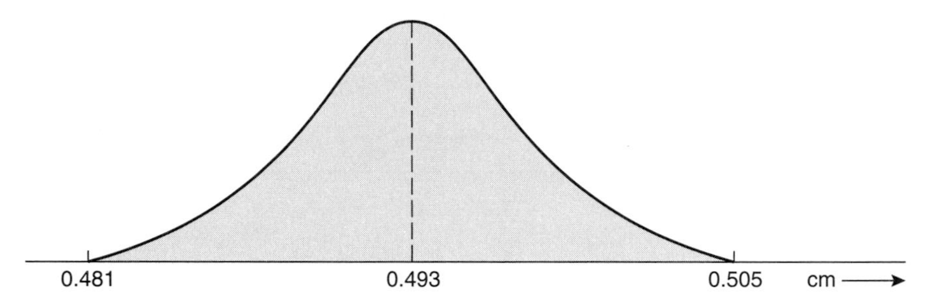


26. Suppose the valve cover process in Exercise 25 is in control but centered at 0.510 cm. The inherent process capability and the diameter specification are as given in Exercise 25. The process would appear as follows:

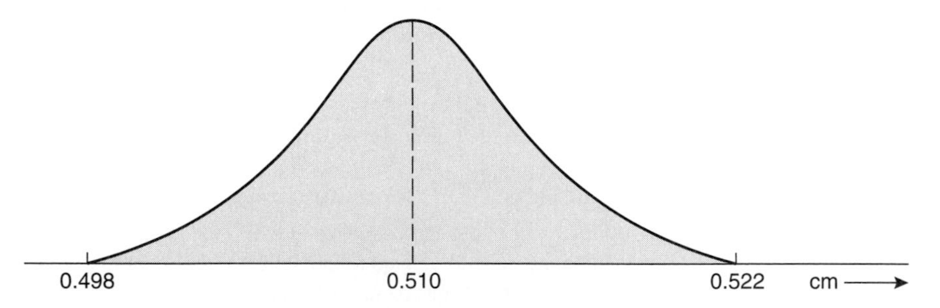


*a.* Calculate $C_{pk}$.

*b.* Use Appendix A (areas under the normal curve) to determine what proportion, if any, of the valve covers would fall outside the specifications.

*c.* What action, if any, should Plug-N-Go take regarding the valve cover process?

27. Give two examples of tolerance stackup for a goods producer.

28. Give two examples of variation stackup for a service provider.

# CHAPTER 10

# FLOW CONTROL: ELIMINATING PROCESS WASTE

Better controls and process improvements are carry-over agendas from Chapter 9 as we continue our Part III discussion of customer-serving processes. Having addressed design and quality, we now focus more directly on incorporating other basic customer wants—lower costs, faster response, and flexibility—into those processes. (Faster response continues as a theme in Chapter 11 as well.)

A sound **flow control system** is central to building and keeping customer-friendly processes; it ensures timely, accurate, value-adding movement of goods, services, or customers themselves through various stages of processing. Better flow control is *one* objective of several popular OM tools—benchmarking, reengineering, design for manufacturability, quick-response manufacturing (QRM), group technology/cellular layout, and just-in-time operations, for instance.

In this chapter, we examine a few ways that good—or bad—flow control can affect operations and we conclude with a brief look at measuring flow-control system effectiveness.

## Flow-Control System Overview

Analogies have a way of being imperfect, but let's try one anyway: The flow-control system in a company is like the operating system in your personal computer. You don't know it's "doing its thing" until it isn't. Put another way, troubles in the flow-control system (or the computer's operating system) remind us that it *is* a part of the picture and that we mustn't take it for granted.

Let's take the analogy a step further: Good flow control crosses all departments, links internal and external provider–customer chains, and facilitates attainment of the common purpose. In similar fashion, the computer's operating system "touches everything" as it fills a linking role; it links hardware, software, and information networks and helps the operator accomplish some purpose. And when they occur, flow-control system breakdowns—like computer operating system faults—tend to produce widely variable effects that can crop up in unpredictable places.

### *Process Variability*

Flow-control problems can be caused by faulty equipment, too little or too much management, wrong materials or wrong quantity—in short, by any of the process components defined in Chapter 9 (see Exhibit 9-3). And, like deviation from a specification

**EXHIBIT 10-1 Variability: Deviation from Target**

*A. Late or early delivery of material. B. After-sale contact with customer, too much (annoying), too little (desertion)*

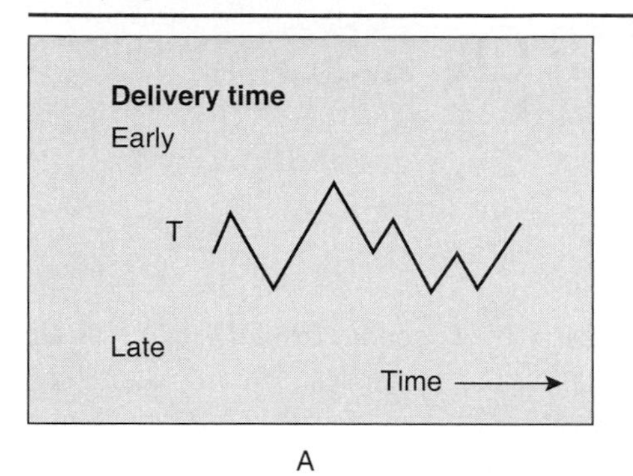


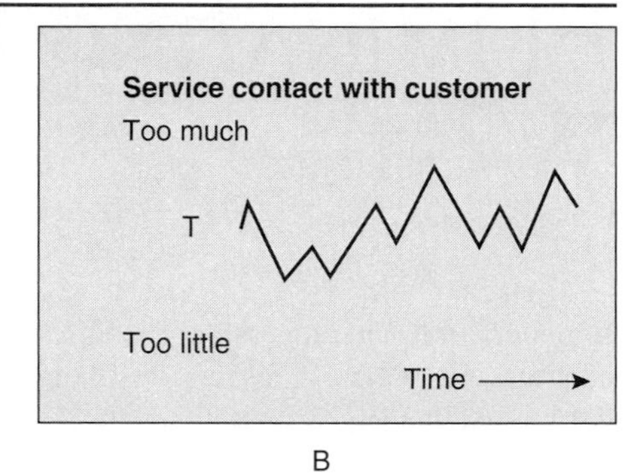


target for an output good, deviation from targeted *process performance* creates costs somewhere along the line. In any organization, multiple process elements can vary at the same time, and the combined variations can result in everything from mild annoyances to failures and delays to complete shutdowns. Exhibit 10-1 illustrates for delivery time and for service to customers.

**Principle 10**

Eliminate process variation.

In the exhibit, the T stands for the performance target: what should happen every time. The variabilities are not pluses (goods) and minuses (bads) that cancel out over the long run: One uncooked cake and one burned cake do not average out to great baking. All variabilities are bad, and combining them only makes matters worse: Bad-quality material is not forgiven if delivery is too early. Ted Waitt, chairman and CEO of Gateway 2000, the computer-by-mail company, has the customer in mind: "I convinced our manufacturing people that an early shipment was as bad as a late shipment, so the 'on-time' [goal of 90 percent on time in less than five days] means just that. No more waiting for a UPS man that doesn't show, or having something show up unexpectedly."[1]

*Variability, variation, uncertainty,* and *undependability,* are used more or less synonymously, as are *invariability, certainty,* and *dependability*.

Process variability annoys, both because it yields bad results and because it equals uncertainty. If a bus is late by 10 minutes dependably, we might be able to live with it. But if it's 10 minutes late on average—sometimes much later, on time, or early—we may give up on bus riding.

Keeping buses on time requires controlling just a few sources of variability. But flow control in a complex organization involves many interacting sources of variability, such as multiple internal processes using many different external materials and other resources. Reducing interacting variability requires a three-pronged attack:

1. System designers avoid complexity so that there are fewer sources of variability.
2. Every associate and team finds ways to control process variation.
3. Cross-functional teams develop ways to detect and plan around or adjust to sources of variability, thus producing a satisfactory result.

Developing the flow-control system requires a basic understanding of key relationships (or linkages) and overall impact.

### *Linkages and Impact*

At the outset of this section, we alluded to the pervasiveness of flow control. There is no single department that can control flows. In some manufacturing companies, a department called something like *production control* has some flow-control responsibility though not the full set. Actually, flow control is as much or more about keeping things moving between those value-adding production processes.

The flow-control system in wholesaling is *mostly* an inventory system; in manufacturing, a production and inventory system; in human services, a customer-processing system; and in telecommunications, an information-processing system. Control does not mean elimination. In any setting work is essential. But the idea is to keep it flowing, as smoothly as possible, with an overall aim of avoiding slacks and gluts or at least reducing their impact.

Any practicing operations manager will agree that flow disruption, especially when unplanned, is costly. The ability of that manager to give an accurate figure for the disruption, however, depends on the assumptions inherent in the company's cost accounting procedures and that manager's understanding of them.

## Causes of Costs

In Chapter 2 we talked about OM's role in enhancing company margins—driving a larger wedge between costs of providing goods and services and the prices we can command for them. As we noted there, process streamlining—getting rid of wastes—is a core ingredient of that effort.

The assumption, of course, is that those wastes are **cost drivers,** or true causes of costs, and thus cut into the company's profit margins. In this section, we examine a few of the difficulties associated with cost-driver classifications by focusing on inventory-related costs. First, though, we very briefly look at a traditional cost analysis tool.

### *Cost Variance*

Unfortunately, not all cost statements reflect operating reality. Numerous respected authorities in the field of cost (managerial) accounting have called for substantive revisions to cost accounting techniques so that they better reflect true cost drivers.[2] For years, standard practice has been to issue periodic **cost variance** reports as a form of feedback and control, and frankly, to serve as a warning to "errant managers."

The system sums up standard and actual costs for all work completed during a period. Standard cost represents what *should have been* spent for normal amounts of direct labor, materials, and so forth; actual cost comes from payroll expenditures, materials accounts payable, and other transaction records. If actual cost exceeds standard cost, a negative cost variance results, and if severe or often enough, can result in pressure for someone to shape up.

In theory, the cost variance makes sense. In practice, often it does not. While a detailed assessment is far beyond our scope, we will note that *in general,* cost variance systems do not adequately account for overhead (fixed costs) and *can* seriously misallocate direct costs as well. Though a bit of a simplification, we might sum up by saying that discretionary cost allocation—though perhaps not malicious—can be deceiving. For this reason, some companies (e.g., Motorola) worry less about trying to compute cost savings associated with an improvement project than about keeping track of other, more objectively measured cost drivers.

Principle 15

Cut reporting; control causes.

When a company abandons detailed, period-cost measures, aren't there some risks? Perhaps so, if the company has no better way to deal with costs and wastes. A better way, however, has proven itself. It is a multifaceted system of identifying and then eliminating the causes of cost, poor quality, delays, and other undesirables.

### *Seven Deadly Wastes*

This system introduces additional, detailed process improvement measures, and it takes aim at the so-called **seven deadly wastes.** Originally formulated for factories,[3] the seven wastes are adapted for any organization as follows:

1. *Waste of doing more than the customer wants or needs.* In an office, this includes too many reports issued too often, too many meetings, too many interruptions. At retail it would include badgering the customer and demonstrating products and models that go beyond the customer's interests. In a factory it is, simply, overproduction.
2. *Waste of waiting.* This is wasting the time of clients, suppliers, or the workforce.
3. *Transport waste.* Ill-planned layouts of facilities can mean long travel distances from process to process for customers, suppliers, the workforce, materials, supplies, mail, tools, and equipment.
4. *Processing waste.* In the value-adding operations themselves, processing wastes can add up: Files are not properly cross-referenced. Procedures are not kept up-to-date. The task sequence is cumbersome or difficult to do.
5. *Inventory waste.* This includes all of the extra costs of holding and monitoring inventories, such as outdated catalogs and records, obsolete materials, and items bought or produced in excessive quantities too early for use.
6. *Waste of motion or energy.* Mere motion or consumption of energy do not equal useful work. The test is, Does it add value to the product? If not, it wastes motion or energy.
7. *Waste of defects and mishaps.* Any defect or any mishap creates a chain reaction of other wastes—potentially all of the preceding six wastes—to "make it right." Included are wasting time, adding transport distance (e.g., return and do it over), inserting extra processing, requiring more inventories, and wasting motions or energy. Poor quality affects nearly everything negatively.

In effectively attacking these wastes, process-improvement teams apply a full array of problem-solving tools (e.g., the eleven basic tools, which were presented in Chapter 9). As results of such efforts draw attention, competitors get interested in driving wastes out of their processes as well. The Into Practice box "Toward Waste-Free

INTO PRACTICE

## Toward Waste-Free Processes

Personnel at John Deere's Horicon, Wisconsin, facility promise their suppliers reduced (faster) manufacturing cycle times, improved margins, and a better understanding of manufacturing operations. In return suppliers attend one of Deere-Horicon's supplier development seminars on QRM.

"Central to QRM (Quick-response manufacturing) is a relentless quest for flow-time reduction. Deere-Horicon QRM practitioners use 'manufacturing cycle time reduction' as a descriptor . . . within standard QRM terminology, 'lead time reduction' is the terminology of choice. For practical purposes, the terms are functional equivalents."

Employees of Fisher Barton, a supplier of cutting blades for Deere's golf green mowers, worked with a Deere-Horicon supplier development team to revise the work cell. Results: Batch size decreased from 500 to 200, cycle time dropped from 11 days to 3, and in-process queue time decreased from 108 hours to 64 hours.

Source: Peter Golden, "Deere on the Run," *IIE Solutions,* July 1999, pp. 26–31.

"In 1997, Delphi Automotive Systems began laying groundwork for a total redesign of all of its 200 plants. The result: faster factories. Today, Delphi's Oak Creek, Wisconsin, plant uses only half of its 1 million square feet of floor space; has eliminated 98% of its powered conveyor system; has cut 230 processes from that system; and has increased productivity by more than 25%."

"In an economy based on mass customization, speed, quality, and flexibility, the assembly line has given way to the biological cell." Today each "U-shaped" cell at Oak Creek requires between one and four employees, consumes parts from small plastic carts loaded into short, portable, gravity-feed conveyors that hold but 30 minutes' worth of inventory. Frequent, small-lot replenishment occurs only as needed. The effect is an elimination of backlogs and further progress towards just-in-time operations. Inventory turns at the plant have tripled.

Source: David Dorsey, "Change Factory," *Fast Company,* June 2000, pp. 210ff.

Processes" offers two examples of successful projects. In both cases, the aim was faster operations.

Success is contagious, and made even more so when competitive forces enter the picture. One spillover effect is that we begin to look at old assumptions—whatever they may be—with a more critical eye. We begin, for example, to see a piece of very necessary work-in-process (WIP) inventory that happens to be waiting in a queue to be fed into a machine in a different light. Yes, traditional accounting tells us that it is an asset, but our knowledge that its costs mount as it sits raises the word "liability" in our thoughts as well. That delay is costing us money!

### *Costs of Delays (Carrying Costs)*

To reiterate, the work must flow. That advice becomes doubly important when cost is considered, for cost is like dust—it tends to settle on anything that is sitting around. Rapid processing allows little time for costs to accumulate. When material is idle, it incurs a cost above and beyond its unit price. That cost is called an **inventory carrying cost.**

Office work collects carrying costs, too. For example, office people sometimes spend more time searching (in-baskets, brief cases, computer files) for a document than working on it. In human services, customers waiting in line or holding the telephone "for the next available service representative" bear their own costs of idleness, which, they may estimate, sometimes exceed the value of the purchase or service sought.

**Costs of Idleness.** What do those delays cost? For a client the cost is hard to judge because most of it is poor-service cost, that is, the cost of the client's involuntary idleness. Likewise, for documents and files the cost of idleness is mostly the cost of slow service to the customer; costs of storing and carrying the documents and files are minor.

What about materials in a hospital, restaurant, or factory? First are the physical costs of holding inventory and the financial costs of having working capital tied up in idle inventory. But those are the obvious carrying costs, which accounting and inventory management writings have always recognized. More recently these writings have paid heed to less obvious and "hidden" costs. Obvious, semiobvious, and hidden inventory carrying costs are listed in Exhibit 10-2.

**Obvious Costs.** In order to be a true inventory carrying cost, a cost must rise with the growth, and fall with the reduction, of inventory. **Capital cost,** first on the list, clearly qualifies. Company financial managers frequently attempt to secure bank loans or lines of credit to pay for more inventory. Banks often use the inventory as collateral for loans.

## EXHIBIT 10-2 Carrying-Cost Elements

Obvious carrying costs:
- Capital cost—interest or opportunity costs of working capital tied up in stock
- Holding cost—stockroom costs of:
  - Space
  - Storage implements (e.g., shelving and stock-picking vehicles)
  - Insurance on space, equipment, and inventories
  - Inventory taxes
  - Stockkeepers' wages
  - Damage and shrinkage while in storage

Semiobvious carrying costs:
- Obsolescence
- Inventory planning and management
- Stock record keeping
- Physical inventory taking

Hidden carrying costs:
- Cost of stock on production floor:
  - Space
  - Storage implements (e.g., racks, pallets, containers)
  - Handling implements (e.g., conveyors, cranes, forklift trucks)
- Inventory transactions and data processing support
- Management and technical support for equipment used in storage, handling, and inventory data processing
- Scrap and rework
- Lot inspections
- Lost sales, lost customers because of slow processing

Only in abnormal situations can a company avoid capital costs. For example, Harley-Davidson people like to crow about the time when they got paid for production before they had to pay for the raw materials. On the books, the effect appears as negative inventory. (The product was not motorcycles but a subassembly they had contracted to make for another company.) The negative inventory situation arose because of Harley's successful just-in-time efforts: Work sped through the plant—raw materials to finished goods—in a day or two versus the weeks that it would have taken in Harley's pre-JIT days.

Next on the list is **holding cost,** which is mainly the cost of running stockrooms. While the accounting system may consider space and storage implements as fixed costs, they exist only to hold stock; therefore, they are true carrying costs. The other more or less obvious holding costs are insurance, taxes, material department wages, damages, and shrinkage.

**Semiobvious Costs.** Semiobvious carrying costs include inventory obsolescence and costs of inventory management and clerical activities (see Exhibit 10-2). People involved in inventory planning, stock record keeping, and physical inventory counting do not actually handle stock, and their offices often are far from stockrooms. Perhaps for these reasons, some companies include those costs as general or operating overhead. Clearly, however, they are inventory carrying costs.

Obsolescence cost is nearly zero when materials arrive just in time for use, but it can be high if companies buy in large batches and then find that the need for the items has dried up. High-fashion stores and high-tech electronics companies should be acutely aware of obsolescence as a cost of carrying inventory. Old-line manufacturers, however, might write off obsolete stock only once every 10 years; if so, they may fail to include obsolescence routinely in their calculated carrying-cost rate.

**Hidden Costs.** Carrying costs that commingle with other costs tend to be hidden. A prime example is stock released from a stockroom to operations (factory, sales floor, kitchen, etc.), where it sits idle between operations, tying up cash and occupying costly space. In manufacturing, idle in-process inventories commonly occupy half or more of factory floor space. Idle stock often sits on racks, conveyors, automatic storage systems, and other costly equipment, and it adds up to a major hidden carrying cost component.

Most companies once invalidly charged those costs as production costs. Today, accountants and operations managers and associates are increasingly asking: Does it add value? Does the activity produce something saleable or directly serve a paying customer? If not, treat it as an inventory carrying cost. Illustration: a conveyor literally carries inventory and adds no value to the product.

Another so-called **non-value-adding (NVA)** activity is processing inventory transactions, including the cost of employees' time for entering inventory usage and scrap data into terminals plus the cost of the terminals, usually treated incorrectly as operating costs. Much greater are the associated central processing costs (hardware, software, and computer operations) and the costs of corrections and report processing. In inventory-intensive firms, inventory management is the dominant computer application; its costs have been conveniently bundled into the information system department's total costs, but they are actually hidden inventory carrying costs. Costs of management and technical support for storage, handling, and data-processing equipment are also carrying costs, but they are rarely treated as such.

Principle 11

Cut inventory.

Scrap and rework costs also fall with decreases in inventories, including decreases in lot sizes. This is true in processing perishables (such as cutting off rot from food items), in wholesaling and retailing (e.g., an entire lot of garments missing a buttonhole), in information processing, and in manufacturing.

Independent inspectors conducting sampling inspections may reject a whole lot based on a bad sample and send the lot back for rectification.

As an information processing example, suppose telephone sales associates send sales orders forward once a day in batches averaging 800 orders. Order entry clerks in the next department might find numerous defects, such as missing quantity, incomplete address, or lack of a promise date. Sometimes, especially for a new promotion, an entire lot of 800 orders will contain the same error. More commonly, errors will occur at some average percentage. Either way, order entry clerks end up sending the faulty forms back to the sales office for rework, probably the next day (see Exhibit 10-3A). Meanwhile, time has passed and sales people are busy with other orders. They are no longer clear

**Exhibit 10-3 Effect of Lot Size on Rework/Scrap**

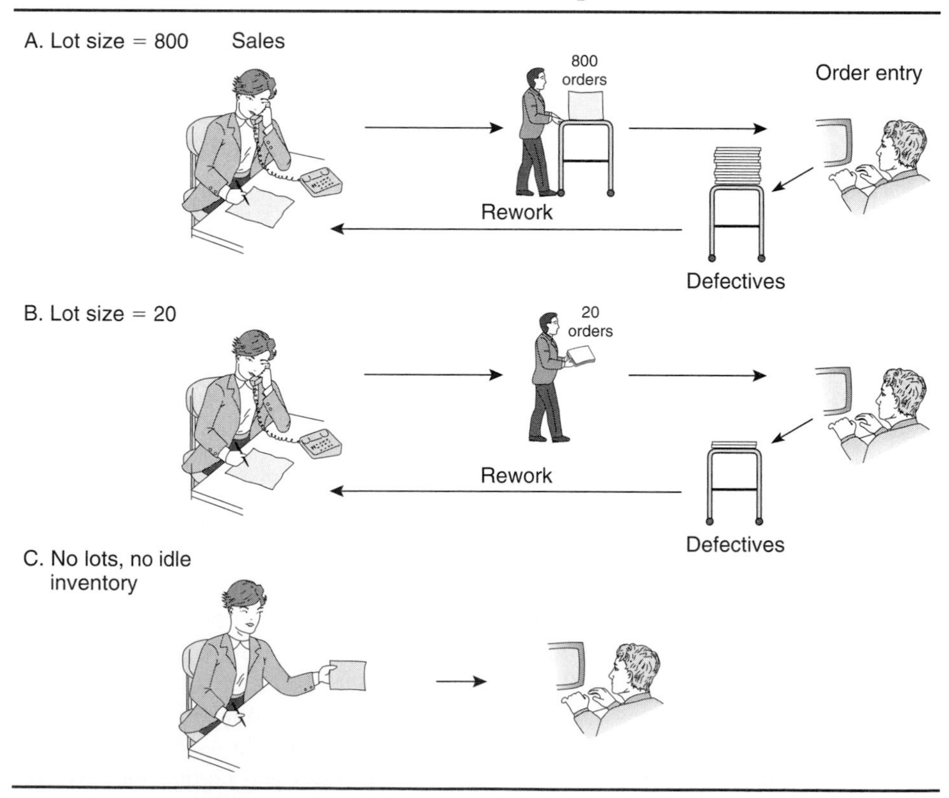

about the details of yesterday's orders and the likely root causes of yesterday's order-processing errors.

If salespeople processed and forwarded orders in lots of 20 instead of 800 (Exhibit 10-3B), maximum damage would be 20, which could be sent back while the trail of causes is still warm.

Much better still would be for a sales associate to hand the order directly to an order entry clerk (Exhibit 10-3C). They become a team, intolerant of errors on order forms. Large defective lots are no longer possible. When an error occurs, the clerk usually discovers it right away while the cause is still obvious. The team finds ways to permanently eliminate the causes, steadily driving down the rate of defective order forms.

Principle 13

Decrease cycle interval and lot size.

Inspection costs merit similar scrutiny. Inspectors facing large lots have the big job of sorting out the bad ones. However, some companies avoid large lots by adopting just-in-time techniques. They avoid large *bad* lots by implementing strict process controls to prevent rather than merely detect defects. The tie-in between inspection costs and lot-size quantities is becoming clear, and the conclusion is that even inspectors may be treated as a carrying cost.

Last and most important are the costs of lost sales and lost customer allegiance when the flow-control system is plagued by stalled orders. Thus, the negative impact of idle inventories on customer responsiveness is also a carrying cost. But by keeping lot sizes, queues, and transport distances short, the firm can ensure that the work flows through the system cleanly and quickly—perhaps surprising, delighting, and retaining the customer.

**Uses of Carrying Costs.** In some organizations inventories are such a dominant cost that virtually every investment proposal has an inventory effect. Therefore, it is important to use a realistic carrying cost when doing a financial analysis for a proposal.

Traditionally, carrying cost has been stated as an annual rate based on the item's value. Older books on inventory management suggested a rate of 25 percent as a good average. Many North American manufacturers still use 25 percent (or 24 percent—2 percent per month). But that rate is based on the obvious carrying costs (Exhibit 10-2) and possibly some of the semiobvious costs.

If all carrying costs are included, as they should be, what is the proper rate? No studies have answered that question definitively. In 1990, Ernst & Young suggested a rate of at least 48 percent. Today, the rate is surely at least 50 percent. Indeed, several manufacturers have upped their rates to 50 percent or higher.[5] When researchers have unearthed all carrying costs, more companies may use higher rates, perhaps as high as 100 percent. To see what 100 percent means, imagine a $50 chair sitting in a stockroom for a year. The owner would be paying another $50 for the chair in the form of the costs of carrying it.

Thinking about moving a machine and its operator across the building to team up with a machine and operator at the next process? How much inventory savings are there, and what carrying-cost rate is being used? Suppose that the cost of moving is $2,000 and that $3,000 of inventory would be eliminated. At a 25 percent rate, the savings are $750 per year (0.25 × $3,000); without doing a discounted cash flow analysis, payback on the investment will take $2\frac{2}{3}$ years ($2,000 ÷ $750 per year)—perhaps not very attractive. At 100 percent, carrying-cost savings are $3,000 per year and the investment pays for itself in less than a year:

$$\text{Simple payback period} = \frac{\text{Investment cost}}{\text{Annual savings}} \tag{10-1}$$

The best-known financial analysis that uses carrying-cost rates is in calculating an economic order quantity (see Chapter 13). Another issue that bears on flow-control systems is the degree to which a company has developed a quick-changeover flexibility, which makes smaller lots more economical.

## Quick-Change Flexibility

How long does it take an Indy 500 pit crew to change four tires, fill the tank, clean the windshield, and squirt Gatorade into the driver's mouth? Fifteen seconds? Less? Regardless of how long, the workings of an efficient pit crew capture many concepts of quick-change teamwork and readiness.

Concern about changeover and readiness is not limited to pit crews. The Ritz-Carlton Hotel Company, a 1992 and 1999 winner of the Malcolm Baldrige National Quality Award, for example, switched from independent room cleaning to team cleaning as part of an effort to reduce the time needed to prepare guest rooms. By more than meeting its goal of a 50 percent reduction in cleaning-cycle time, Ritz-Carlton made a significant reduction in the time guests had to wait at the front desk for check-in.[6]

From the famous racetrack in Indianapolis to the posh suites in some of the world's finest hotels, quick-change tactics are directly responsible for winning operational performances. The underlying concepts are simple and can be expressed as guidelines for action.

### *Guidelines*

A milestone achievement for a quick-changeover team is one-touch setup, meaning virtually no setup time; next best is single-digit setup (less than 10 minutes).

Although some businesses are famous for their quick changeover expertise (e.g., stage crews and airline caterers), most organizations give the matter scant attention. But elevated competition in many businesses demands quicker, error-free service and enhancing the firm's ability to continually reduce changeover and get-ready times. The training materials that address these concerns are based on a few guidelines (see Exhibit 10-4), which we discuss next.

**Changeover Avoidance.** Guideline one is the special case of a single service, product model, or type of customer that gets its own dedicated process. If, say, three quarters of McDonald's customers wanted a Big Mac and a medium Coke, the restaurant would set up a dedicated Mac-and-a-Coke line, with no flexibility or changeovers to worry about. All companies would love to have products that are popular. The simplicity, low cost, and uniformly high quality of this mode of processing yields high profits and large numbers of loyal customers.

## Exhibit 10-4 Quick Changeover, Setup, and Readiness Guidelines

Changeover avoidance:

1. A dedicated, single-purpose process.

Be-ready improvements—developed by teams of associates:

2. External (offline) steps performed while process is active.
3. Setup implements close, clean, in top condition, and ready.
4. For costly equipment, trained crew and clockwork precision.

Modifications—technical assistance on improvement team:

5. Eliminate/immobilize unneeded devices and adjusters.
6. Add positioners and locators.
7. Simplify/standardize software, equipment, fixtures, fasteners, and accessories.
8. Employ externally loadable magazines and work-element holders.

## Exhibit 10-5 Changeover Analysis and Shadow Board at Microsoft-Ireland

*A. Setup steps.* *B. Shadow board*

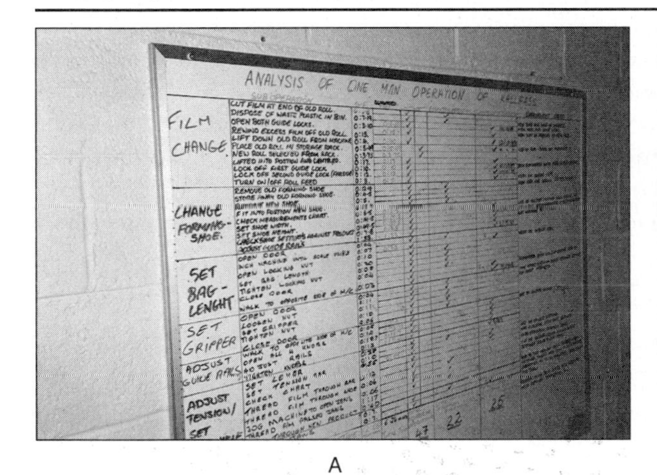


A

B

**Be-Ready Improvements.** The next three guidelines provide natural, low-cost improvement projects for teams of associates.

Guideline two is doing all possible setup steps while the process is engaged on its previous product model, type of customer, or service. That minimizes the time the process is stopped and unproductive. Alternatively stated: Convert internal setup time (while the process is stopped) to external steps (done offline, while the process is running a prior job). At a laundromat, for example, have your next load sorted and the detergent and other additives measured out before the machine stops.

Exhibit 10-5A shows detailed analysis of setup steps on a packing machine at Microsoft, Dublin, Ireland. The analysis includes separate columns for steps to be done

Experience shows that the be-ready improvements can often cut changeover times by 50 percent or more.

**setup** or **changeover**
Timed from end of previous productive output to the start of the next, including all checks for quality and adjustments to get it right.

while the machine is stopped versus those to be done beforehand. Packaging machine changeovers are frequent because this plant duplicates and packages diskettes just in time for many Microsoft products in many different languages for the European market.

Guideline three (an extension of two) provides the discipline of "A place for everything, and everything in its place." Have you had to wait to sign something while a clerk looks for a 49-cent pen? Or has one, but it won't write? By contrast, an Indy pit crew is ready with gasoline hoses, tire-changing devices, and tires correctly positioned and in tip-top shape. And room-cleaning teams at Ritz-Carlton hotels have towels, linens, bar stocks, and cleaning supplies stocked and ready for use long before cleaning activities begin. Surgical teams in operating rooms, rescue team personnel, and firefighters adopt the same kinds of readiness habits and discipline.

In some firms, operators rig pegboards on which to hang tools. A shadow board, with silhouettes of tools painted on, provides better visibility.

In factories, readiness may include hanging precleaned and sharpened hand tools on "shadow boards" at the workplace: no fumbling through a drawer or tool box, or walking to a tool room. Exhibit 10-5B shows a shadow board holding four simple tools used by teams assembling instruction manuals at Microsoft's plant in Dublin, Ireland.

Where equipment is expensive—a race car, a surgical room, or a massive press line that stamps out automobile body parts—a sizable, well-trained changeover crew is justified. Guideline four is deftly applied, for example, in well-managed conference centers: Dozens of employees gather minutes before a conference ends, and quickly and acting in parallel, they dismantle the speaker's platform, remove water pitchers and other tabletop items, fold and stack tables and chairs, clean the area, and set up for an evening banquet or wedding party.

**Principle 7**

Develop human resources through cross-training.

Too often the opposite occurs in factories of well-known companies, such as a $5 million packaging line for a headache remedy halted for four hours while one or two maintenance technicians make hundreds of adjustments, one by one (serially), for the next package size or type of tablet. The JIT movement has caused many manufacturers to change their human resource practices so that such expensive equipment can be set up efficiently.

Experience shows that following be-ready and modification guidelines can often cut total changeover time by 80 or 90 percent.

**Modifications.** Guidelines five through eight generally require that the improvement team call on an expert for technical assistance. Since the modifications may be costly, these guidelines would usually take effect after the be-ready guidelines (two through four).

Guideline five calls for eliminating or immobilizing devices and adjusters that come with the equipment or that were once part of the process but are no longer needed. For example, an overhead projector has a focus knob, but if the projector stays in the same classroom anchored to a table facing the same screen year after year, the focus adjustment unit is an invitation for unnecessary, non-value-adding tampering and variable image quality. In one company, a conference room user had wound strapping tape around the adjustment knob at the right focus setting so that other users could skip the adjustment step.

Why not just order the projector with a fixed focal length to suit the room layout? Because it would be a costly special order, and the manufacturer would have to charge a higher price. Equipment designers usually include many adjustment features, which broadens appeal, increases demand, produces economies of scale, and lowers the price.

INTO PRACTICE

## Quick Setup at . . .

### Kentucky Fried Chicken

Quick-setup techniques are not limited to manufacturing plants. Associates at four Oklahoma City area KFC restaurants studied Shigeo Shingo's SMED (single-minute exchange of die) book and put it to use reorganizing the window service area. Changing from one order to another now involves no lifting, no bending, no more than two steps (down from six), easy reach-up-and-pull-down motions, and only two sizes of packer boxes. These changes, plus a few others (see related Chapter 5 discussion) cut window "hang time" delays, which customer surveys revealed were driving customers away. The four restaurants reduced average hang times from over two minutes to 60 seconds. In the year of the improvements, these restaurants enjoyed 17.5 percent growth in sales and 12.3 percent increases in productivity, as compared with declines of 3.0 percent and 0.4 percent in the same measures for the entire KFC district.

Source: Uday M. Apte and Charles C. Reynolds, "Quality Management at Kentucky Fried Chicken," *Interfaces,* May–June 1995, pp. 6–21.

### General Mills

How do auto-race pit crews change tires and service cars so quickly? Some engineers from General Mills visited Nascar race tracks to find out. For one thing, according to General Mills' chairman Stephen W. Sanger, they learned that "you don't do anything that requires tools if you can figure out a way to do it without them. If you can put a handle on something instead of a wrench, you do it. And you don't do anything during a pit stop that you can do before."

Source: "General Mills Gets in Shape for Turnaround," *The Wall Street Journal,* September 26, 1995, pp. B1 and B4.

After the sale, however, teams of users should work on removing or immobilizing unneeded adjustment devices.

Guideline six is the opposite of five: adding special features not usually provided by the equipment manufacturer. For example, to make recycling easier, a team might come up with a plan to equip all the firm's pop machines with a bin that receives, crushes, and holds empty cans.

In manufacturing, setup teams frequently devise locator pins, stops, air-cushion glides, and guide paths that make it easier to change a mold or a die. Exhibit 10-6 shows huge "sleds" on rails, used for quickly and accurately moving multiton dies in and out of stamping presses.

Guideline seven calls for simplified, standardized designs. Too many brands of word processors computers, typewriters, and drill presses (each obtained at a bargain price) expand exponentially the array of supporting devices and sets of instructions needed for setup and changeover. Standardization also applies to accessories; for example, if all fastening bolts on a machine are the same size, only one size of wrench is needed in machine changeover.

**Exhibit 10-6 Quick-Die-Change Equipment, GM Stamping Plant**

*Die-handling sleds on rails are among the quick-die-change innovations on this six-press tandem stamping line, for auto body parts, at this General Motors stamping plant in Pittsburgh. This plant was the winner in a nationwide competition, called the Die Change Challenge, clocking a single-digit die change at 9 minutes 41 seconds (compared with an average 23 hours at the same plant a few years earlier). The resulting plant flexibility was a key factor in a corporate decision to remove the Pittsburgh facility from GM's plant closure list.*

Source: "Industry News," *Manufacturing Engineering,* July 1992, p. 24.

The other part of this guideline is simplification, which should take place before standardization. Exhibit 10-7 shows three examples of how an accessory might be altered so that its use in a changeover takes much less time:

- A U-shaped washer can be slid against a bolt; no need to remove a nut first.
- Pear-shaped bolt holes allow the head of the bolt to slip through the large hole, then slide into the narrow slot for tightening.
- A bolt with cutaway threads may be inserted all the way down into a hole with similar cutaway threads; then, just a quarter turn of a wrench fastens the bolt tightly.

Quick-change teams worldwide have been trained to make use of these kinds of simplified devices.[7]

Guideline eight specifies having extra holders for the work elements, such as component parts, tools, or paper feedstock. Think of a fondue party where each person loads a backup fondue fork while having another already loaded fork in the hot oil.

**Exhibit 10-7 Washer, Bolt Hole, and Threads Simplified for Quick Installation**

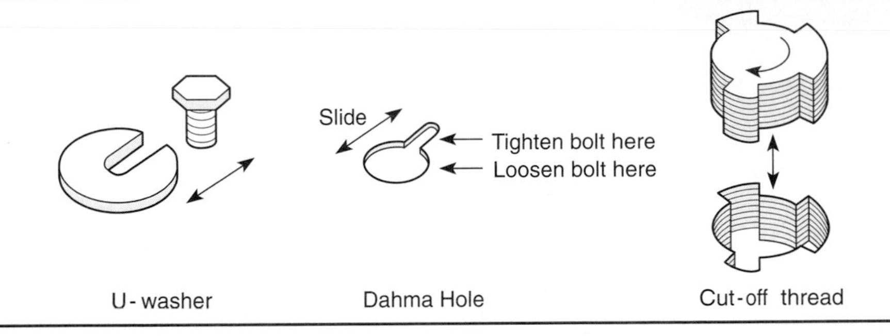


Source: Adapted from Kiyoshi Suzaki, *The New Manufacturing Challenge: Techniques for Continuous Improvement* (New York: Free Press, 1987), p. 38.

### *Quick-Changeover Projects*

The eight guidelines assist project teams organized specifically to improve readiness and cut changeover times. In practice, by cutting setup time, the project team usually also improves process consistency, quality, safety, maintenance, ease of operation, housekeeping, and other factors for the target process. Similarly, a team organized to reduce process variation will often also cut setup time. In other words, many of the goals of continuous improvement and competitiveness overlap and are largely inseparable.

This inseparability can be bothersome to veteran managers and technicians, who are used to seeing the work subdivided into many specialties and allocated to specialty departments: quality issues to a quality department, maintenance to a plant maintenance group, and so on. However, as we have reiterated throughout this book, superior companies have discovered the power of continuous improvement led by cross-trained, frontline teams.

**Principle 14**

Improvement led by frontline teams

## Quick Response: Managing Intersector Flows

QR links different companies in several stages of production, supply, and freight hauling to final points of sale. The ultimate aim is tight synchronization: Pick the cotton that's spun into thread that's woven into cloth that's dyed and finished into fabric that's cut and sewed into a shirt that's delivered to the store just before you walk in to buy it—all of this, and transportation, too, in sync. Synchronization at each stage affects scheduling, purchasing, storage, logistics, capacity, marketing, and cash-flow planning. The accompanying Into Practice box gives examples of QR.

**Principle 13**

Operate at the customer's rate of use.

### *Basic and Enhanced QR*

Quick response's unofficial kickoff was in June 1986 in Chicago. Roger Milliken, chairman of textile manufacturer Milliken & Co., was instrumental in getting together a few dozen retailers and textile and apparel suppliers to discuss foreign competition. The

INTO PRACTICE

## QR at Luxottica Group SpA of Italy

"Luxottica [the world's largest eyeware manufacturer] reorganized its U.S. sales staff and started sharing with customers the advantages of computer power. It is equipping [independent] retailers with software that checks Luxottica's stock and orders goods for overnight delivery. In the past, delivery took days or weeks."

Source: Bill Saporito, "Cutting Out the Middleman," *Fortune,* April 6, 1992, p. 96.

## QR in Apparel

"VF Corporation [maker of Wrangler, Lee, Jantzen, and Vanity Fair apparel] has devised and implemented a Market Response System (MRS), designed to reduce cycle time and inventory, lower costs, and offer retailers and consumers the products they want, when they want them. MRS is executed through a series of simultaneous rather than sequential marketing, production, and supply activities, linked by information technology."

According to Lawrence Pugh, CEO, "If we eliminate organizational barriers and encourage such a free flow of information, we can get a specific product replaced on the retail shelf in less than seven days—in an environment where 60 to 90 days has been considered good practice. . . . [By implementing MRS] we can make it so that the consumer can count on having the right product, size, and color in the store every day."

Source: Advertising supplement, *Fortune,* September 21, 1992.

"Today, when JC Penney sells a Mens Relaxed Fit in Pepper Wash in size 32 × 32, Avondale Mills knows they just moved 2.218 square yards of denim."

Source: Michael A. McEntire, "Consumer Responsive Product Development," Conference Proceedings, Quick Response '94, Automatic Identification Manufacturers, Inc. (AIM USA), 1994, p. 68.

Bennetton's and The Limited's home-grown versions of QR existed before 1986. But the Milliken-led group brought QR into general use.

main issue was how North American fiber-textile-apparel industries could compete with low-wage companies off shore. Participants at this and following meetings wanted to use technology to exploit the proximity of U.S. companies to the American market, and the goal was to set standards so everyone from raw material supplier to the retail store could speak the same electronic language and share data.

QR has rapidly expanded. An annual Quick Response convention and exhibition has emerged to promote the concept and the technology. The photo "Survival of the Quickest" suggests a sports metaphor that expresses the competitive spirit of QR programs.

Basic QR requires point-of-sale (POS) data only from selected stores. This is like predicting election results. Pollsters use voter intentions from key precincts to predict election winners with high accuracy. Similarly, manufacturers—even if several echelons removed from final sales points—can schedule production based on recent POS samples. Conventional scheduling, on the other hand, is always weeks or months out of date.

In an advanced version of quick response, called **vendor-managed inventory (VMI),** retailers confer to producers the management of retail inventories. Retailers

*Survival of the quickest.*

©PhotoDisc

send point-of-sale data to producers daily, and producers have access to retailers' inventory files. Unlike basic QR, which requires scanning data only from a few stores, VMI can provide manufacturers with complete data—from every store.

Still another advanced form of QR is called **efficient customer response (ECR)**. ECR provides additional supply-chain linkages, in four main ways.[8]

- *Efficient replenishment.* These are the practices already described for QR and VMI.
- *Efficient assortment.* Retailers use sophisticated "category management" software to stock store areas with what consumers want most. The twin aims are more sales per square foot and improved customer satisfaction.
- *Efficient promotion.* Order, produce, ship, and stock exactly what sells. Cease forward buying, trade loading, and BOGOs (buy one, get one free), which pay little heed to real customer needs or usage.
- *Efficient product introduction.* Product development is a joint effort. Producers, distributors, brokers, and retailers team up to get the right products to market quickly.

Regarding efficient promotion, Ronald Zarrella, GM's head of sales and marketing, introduced the following: Promote cars throughout their life cycle, instead of spending lavishly in the introductory year, then starving the model after that.

## *QR and JIT: Linking External and Internal Flow Control*

QR is the offspring of just-in-time and it embodies JIT's core concept of final customers "pulling the strings" to cause production and delivery, back through the chain of supply. For QR to work, firms at each echelon in the supply chain must improve their internal

**EXHIBIT 10-8 Smart New Way to Get Goods to Consumers**

*Top row: Consumers lose when manufacturers periodically stuff excess goods into distributors' warehouses (sometimes called trade loading). Here a typical grocery item takes 84 days to go from factory to store shelf. Bottom row: Speeded-up cycle is more efficient, improves company's cash flow, and gives consumers a fresher product at a better price*

The manufacturer stockpiles ingredients and packaging supplies to meet peak production levels.

Plants prepare huge runs. Scheduling is chaotic, with more overtime and temporary workers.

Freight companies charge premium rates for the manufacturer's periodic blow-out shipments.

No more panic purchases are necessary. The company cuts down on inventories, freeing up cash.

Factories run on normal shifts. The company cuts down on overtime pay and supplemental workers.

The manufacturer eliminates peak-and-valley distribution. That helps it save 5% in shipping costs.

Source: Patricia Sellers, "The Dumbest Marketing Ploy," *Fortune,* October 5, 1992, pp. 88–94. Used with permission. Jim McManus, Illustrator.

processes—in office support, distribution, and freight areas, as well as in frontline operations (see Exhibit 10-8). These firms can use a broad array of proven JIT techniques for responding to customers' demands, plus TQM techniques for getting it right.

**Kanban**
A signal (e.g., an empty container or an order card affixable to the container) that more parts are needed.

By involving retailers, QR uses sales scanning data that big retailers had collected for years but never used to good advantage. Before QR's introduction, firm-to-firm JIT arrangements were widespread but mostly limited to manufacturing: processed-material or component suppliers linked (by kanban, fax, EDI, etc.) to fabrication or assembly plants. QR establishes a common basis for sector-to-sector flow control, linking goods and service sectors seamlessly.

JIT was born in Japan and is now practiced worldwide, but QR is a uniquely North American contribution to good management. America's large open market and relatively

Distributors overstock as they binge on short-term discounts. Cartons sit for weeks inside warehouses.

At distribution centers, the goods get overhandled. Damaged items go back to the manufacturer.

Twelve weeks after the items leave the production line, they may not be fresh for the consumer.

Wholesalers' inventories get cut in half. That means storage and handling costs decline 17%.

Retailers receive undamaged products. Their perception of the manufacturer's quality improves.

The consumer gets the goods 25 days earlier, and—even better news—at a 6% lower price.

efficient distribution system offered a favorable environment for QR's development. The necessary alliances have been difficult to attain in Japan with its many layers of middlemen between manufacturers and retailers. In Europe, despite geographical difficulties (national borders), QR is catching on.

### *Logistics: Moving the Goods*

As we've seen, QR and JIT both rely on efficient freight and distribution management, which businesses refer to as **logistics** or more recently, supply-chain management. In fact, logistics has become a high-visibility partner of marketing and operations management, after years of being left to disparate specialists. Producers and retailers increasingly see that they cannot be expert in managing the flow among parties in the

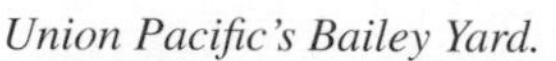

*Union Pacific's Bailey Yard.*

Source: Union Pacific museum collection.

supply chain. They must partner up with freight movers (air, rail, truck, barge) and distributors.

A growing trend is for a single logistics company to take over both freight and some of the management of distribution centers. Federal Express receives and stores personal computer components for IBM and Compaq Computer. Then, when a company (or a person) orders a customized PC system, Federal Express pulls the components, boxes them (with manuals thrown in), and makes the delivery. This role expansion has transformed Federal Express from an overnight mail delivery company into a supplier of order-fulfillment services.

DSC Logistics, with a 1.2-million-square-foot warehouse in Melrose Park, Illinois, got itself into the business by a different route. It had been strictly a warehouser. Ann Drake, who runs the family-owned business, changed its name from Dry Storage Company in 1993.[9]

Trucking companies are metamorphosing into full-service logistics as well:

> Just behind a vast field of corn on Packerland Drive in Green Bay, Wisconsin, stands the brain center of Schneider National. Once strictly a trucking company, Schneider now focuses on its highly profitable logistics business. It has about 140 logistics contracts, ranging from $2 million to $200 million, the last for a deal with GM.
>
> On one giant floor, hundreds of Schneider customer-service representatives in cubicles track freight using electronic data interchange technology. With a satellite system, a Schneider representative can tell customers exactly where its drivers are, and, more importantly, what time a given shipment will be delivered.[10]

Satellite-navigated trucks time their arrival at unloading docks to the hour—or even within a 15-minute window. Producers help by providing advance shipping notices to the freight haulers.

The retailer's distribution centers are shifting their roles as well, sometimes spurning their traditional storage role. Instead, they move incoming goods directly to other docks and outbound trucks. The following describes this no-stop procedure, called **cross-docking:**

> Every truck in industry-leading Schneider National's fleet has sprouted a jaunty little satellite antenna. . . . You look in the cab and see generally not a Teamsters truck driver but an "associate" with a merit pay plan and an on-board computer that links him with headquarters. . . . When Schneider's tractor-trailer pulls up with a cargo of appliances, for example, Sear's home delivery trucks are lined up across the loading dock, scheduled to bring them to customers expecting delivery that day.[11]

Railroads, too, are involved. John Bromley, director of public affairs at Union Pacific, says, "No other country in the world has such a modern rail freight system [as does the United States]. And no other system operates at a profit without government subsidies. We may not have the high-speed passenger trains like Europe and Japan, but we've sure got them beat when it comes to hauling freight." Union Pacific's Bailey Yard in North Platte, Nebraska, is billed in the Guiness Book of World Records as the world's largest train yard. It is 10 miles end to end, has 150 branching, parallel tracks, and handles 120 trains and 9,000 freight cars daily.[12]

## Measuring Flow-Control System Performance

What should a high-performance flow-control group strive to achieve? Exhibit 10-9 summarizes traditional and newer answers to that question. Traditional (and still common) examples of flow-control measures include 95 percent on-time performance against *internal* schedules, 99 percent inventory accuracy, and five inventory turns per year.

**EXHIBIT 10-9 Measurements of Flow-Control Performance**

| | *Traditional* | *New* |
|---|---|---|
| Pipeline control | None | Order-to-receipt time (supplier performance)<br>Advance-shipping-notice-to-receipt time (freight carrier performance)<br>Receipt-to-selling floor time (retailer performance) |
| Operation control | On-time order completion | Cycle time (thoughput time, response time)<br>Response ratio |
| Inventory control | Stock-record accuracy | Invariable quantity of items/containers in fixed locations between each pair of processes |
| | Inventory turnover, company | Joint inventory turnover, company plus suppliers |

Companies still care about each of these factors, but emphasis is shifting from internal due dates, stock records, and inventories to speedy response through the supply chain and customer chain.

### *Pipeline Efficiency*

Quick response programs look beyond the department or company walls. QR-connected firms in the supply pipeline all work from the same scanning data: real customer demand. The supporting information system usually allows suppliers to send advance shipping notices to freight carriers via EDI, fax or Internet transmission.

New pipeline-oriented measurements need to be devised to reflect flow control among suppliers, freight carriers, and retailers. Examples for suppliers include time from ordering to receipt of material by the customer; for carriers, time from receipt of the advance shipping notice to customer receipt of the goods; and for the retailer, time from receipt of the goods to their availability on the sales floor.

### *Cycle Times/Lead Times*

A prominent performance measure within the company walls is cycle time, or lead time, including time to process all information related to production or service. Aside from measuring quickness of response, cycle time serves as an overall indicator of flow control. Long cycle times (e.g., many weeks) are evidence that the work flow is out of control.

Better flow control means a smaller flow-control staff. That is, as cycle times fall and the work flow becomes more tightly controlled, the firm needs fewer expediters, schedulers, dispatchers, and clerical staff.

**defibrillator**
medical emergency device that electrically stimulates a failing heart.

For example, JIT implementation teams at Physio Control (a manufacturer of defibrillators) were able to create 11 JIT cells (or *team-built* lines, as they are called at Physio). The focused cells used daily rate scheduling, revised monthly, thus eliminating thousands of work orders. Work-in-process (WIP) inventories plunged, emptied WIP stock rooms were torn out, and remaining small stocks became the property of each team-built line. Physio's 10-member production control department had no scheduling or inventory management to do and was abolished, and the 10 people were retrained for other duties, such as supplier certification and supplier development.

### *Response Ratios*

Cycle time is a fine measurement of overall flow through several processes, but what about measurements within each of those processes? The **response ratio** fills the need.

The three response ratios are cycle time to work content, process speed to use rate, and pieces to work stations or operators. The ideal ratio for each is 1 to 1, but in practice it is typically 5, 10, 100, or 1,000 to 1. What does a ratio of, say, 100 to 1 mean? Examples for each ratio serve to illustrate:

- In a drop-and-add line (at registration for college classes), there is an average of 99 minutes of delay for a 1-minute transaction to have a form signed. The

99 minutes of delay plus the 1 minute for signature yield a ratio of 100 minutes of total cycle time to 1 minute of value-adding work content.

- A wire-cutting machine currently is cutting 1,000 pieces of electrical power cord per hour for a certain model of lamp. Lamp assembly, the next process, installs that model of cut cord at only 10 per hour. The ratio or process speed to use rate, thus, is 1,000 to 10, or 100 to 1.
- A clerk in a purchasing department typically has a stack of 99 invoices in an in-basket and just 1 invoice being worked on. This constitutes a pieces-to-operator ratio of 100 to 1.

In each case, high ratios mean long queues of customers, documents, idle materials, or projects. Team members may calculate the ratio, post it in the workplace, and then work to lower it. But they cannot do so without making improvements that we have covered in this and previous chapters: cut changeover times, limit the queues, have a system for borrowing labor when lines get too long, eliminate disruptive rework by doing it right the first time, keep all areas clean and well organized, run equipment at the use rate instead of at maximum speed, and so forth.

A main advantage of the response ratio is that it is unitless, devoid of numbers of minutes, clients, truckloads, and so forth. The goal of 1 to 1 or 2 to 1 is the same for any kind of work, and it enables comparison of improvement rates across the enterprise. In short, the ratio is promising as a universal measure of service speed, flow control, and, conversely, nonvalue-added wastes and delays.[13]

### *Inventory Control and Turnover*

The last flow-control measures listed in Exhibit 10-9 are inventory control and **inventory turnover.** We shall defer inventory control to Chapter 13 and focus here on inventory turnover.

For manufacturers, wholesalers, and retailers, inventory turnover remains a good overall measure accounting for many of the wastes tied up in inventory. Corporate management or improvement teams can use it to assess site performance, and site managers/teams can use inventory turnover, or turnover improvement, to measure their own performance. Low inventory turnover normally indicates poor performance, symptomatic of waste and inflexibility; high and increasing inventory turns indicate good performance and continuous improvement.

**special case**
Retail stores maintain what is known as *presentation stock*, which means excess inventory whose purpose is to convey an image of having plenty. Without such stocks customers may think the store is in trouble. Presentation stock puts a limit on how much the store can increase its inventory turnover.

Moreover, research evidence suggests that long-term trend in inventory turnover may be as good or better an indicator of company strength than the usual financial measures, such as profitability and sales revenue. This suggestion is based on a study of inventory turnover for well-known manufacturers in the United States and the United Kingdom over a 45-year period beginning in 1950; partial supporting evidence comes from France and Australia.[14] The research shows declining turnovers for about 25 years. Then, many manufacturers began to react. They learned about lean production concepts and put them to work. One result of all of these improvement methodologies is less dependence on inventories as a cover for problems, so inventory turnovers improve.

**EXHIBIT 10-10 Inventory Turnover**

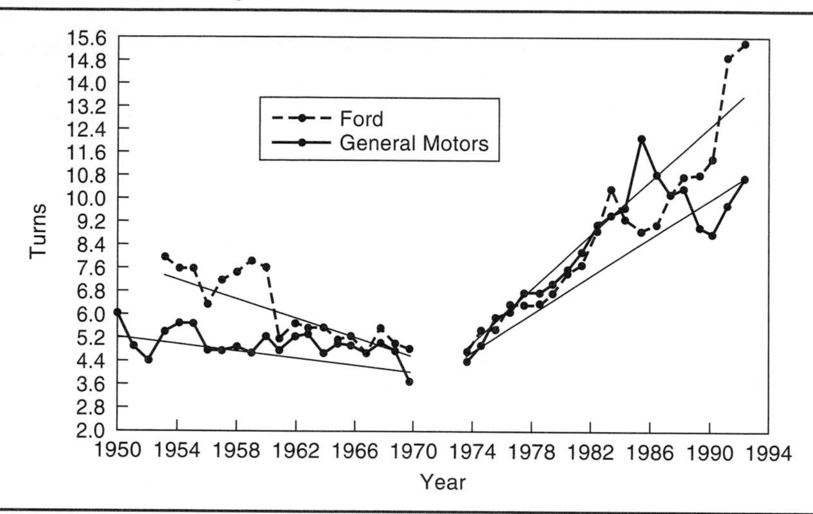


Source: Schonberger & Associates, Inc.

Exhibit 10-10 shows the decline-incline pattern in inventory turns for Ford and General Motors. Ford's annual rate of improvement since 1994 was 3.6 percent; GM's was 3.3 percent. Other data from the study show roughly the same many-year pattern of decline-incline for Caterpillar, Emerson Electric, Eaton, Cummins Engine, Outboard Marine, and other U.S. companies, as well as similar firms in the other countries.

Annual inventory turnover is cost of goods sold divided by the value of average inventory:

$$T = \frac{CGS}{I} \tag{10-2}$$

where

$$T = \text{Turnover}$$
$$CGS = \text{Cost of goods sold (annual)}$$
$$I = \text{Average inventory value}$$

To illustrate, assume that a modem costs \$30 to produce, is selling at a rate of 1,000 per year, and average inventory is worth \$6,000. What is the inventory turnover?

$$\text{Cost of goods sold (CGS)} = \text{Unit cost} \times \text{Annual sales}$$
$$= \$30 \times 1{,}000 = \$30{,}000$$
$$T = \frac{CGS}{I} = \frac{\$30{,}000}{\$6{,}000} = 5 \text{ turns per year}$$

The firm is selling its inventory, or turning it over, five times per year. Compared with an average of between three and four turns for North American industry, that's not bad. (The industry average is much higher in high-volume, continuous production and lower in one-of-a-kind production.) However, some North American plants that used to turn their inventories 3 or 4 times have, through lean practices, improved that to 10, 20, 30—even 100—turns.

A poor turnover (below three) could arise from flow times stretching out over many weeks or months. It could also result when demand response is fast but achieved with high inventories. Thus, turnover is a good measure of flow-control system performance.

It may be useful to calculate turnover by category: raw materials, work-in-process, finished goods, and total inventory. Extending the example of the modem manufacturer, assume that $1,500 of the $6,000 average inventory is finished goods, $1,500 is raw materials, and $3,000 is WIP. Assume further that the cost of labor and overhead to convert raw materials to finished goods is $12,000, which is used in calculating WIP turnover as follows:

$$T_{WIP} = \frac{\text{Manufacturing costs}}{WIP}$$

$$= \frac{\$12{,}000}{\$3{,}000} = 4 \text{ WIP turns per year} \quad (10\text{-}3)$$

To calculate raw material (RM) and finished goods inventory (FGI) turnover, we may assume the price of purchased materials plus purchasing overhead to be $14,000 and the overhead cost to carry finished goods to be $4,000. Then,

$$T_{RM} = \frac{\text{Purchasing costs}}{RM}$$

$$= \frac{\$14{,}000}{\$1{,}500} = 9.3 \text{ RM turns per year} \quad (10\text{-}4)$$

$$T_{FGI} = \frac{\text{Finished goods overhead costs}}{FGI}$$

$$= \frac{\$4{,}000}{\$1{,}500} = 2.7 \text{ FGI turns per year} \quad (10\text{-}5)$$

Some firms also compute an RIP turnover, which includes both raw materials and WIP. One company that uses the RIP measure is TRW's Mission Products Division in Texas. The division, one of the more successful JIT converts, improved its RIP turnover from 3 to about 35 per year.

## Summary Check Points

✓ The flow-control system ensures timely, accurate, value-adding movement of goods, services, or customers themselves through various stages of processing.

✓ The flow-control system may run unnoticed when all is well, but flow-control problems can produce variable and unpredictable effects throughout the organization.

✓ Deviation from a process performance target works the same way as a deviation from a product specification target, costs to some segment of society will increase. Slacks and gluts do not "cancel out" to yield acceptable performance.

✓ Flow-control doesn't belong to a department; it touches all parts of the organization.

- ✓ Cost drivers are causes of costs.
- ✓ A cost variance exists when actual cost differs from standard cost; a negative variance (i.e., actual cost exceeds standard cost) may result in pressure for change on the part of the manager who is responsible for the activity.
- ✓ Traditional costing systems tend to apply overhead costs in ways that do not accurately reflect true absorption of those costs.
- ✓ One well-known list of causes of costs is the seven deadly wastes.
- ✓ Inventory carrying costs exemplify costs of delays in the flow-control systems; these may be obvious, semiobvious, or hidden.
- ✓ Generally, smaller lot sizes are easier for the flow-control system to manage.
- ✓ Quick-change flexibility is a tool for rapid switching of resources from one mode to another.
- ✓ Quick changeover guidelines suggest (in order) changeover avoidance, be-ready improvements, and process modifications.
- ✓ Quick response (QR) programs assist in management of intersector flow control.
- ✓ Vendor-managed inventory (VMI) is the name applied when retailers outsource their inventory management to their suppliers.
- ✓ QR and JIT link together to create seamless internal and external flow-control.
- ✓ Logistics (supply-chain management) is a vital link in flow-control systems.
- ✓ Cross-docking occurs when goods from a supplier's truck go directly to a distributor's or customer's vehicle without entering inventory.
- ✓ Flow-control system performance may be measured by examining pipeline efficiency, cycle or lead times, response ratios, and inventory turnover ratios.
- ✓ The *ideal* value for a response ratio is 1:1; any value over 1:1 signifies delay in the flow-control system.
- ✓ Inventory turnover ratios indicate the number of times inventory (or a category of inventory) was replaced (usually annually). They are measures of the speed of goods; higher ratios are usually a sign of a smooth-running flow-control system.

## Solved Problems

### *Problem 1*

A print shop often has numerous jobs stacked up before the huge paper slicing machine. Even by running the slicer overtime and with extra shifts, some days the slicer cannot keep up with the workload. What is a JIT solution to the problem? What solutions would be consistent with the *theory-of-constraints* concept?

### *Solution 1*

The JIT approach, based on continuous improvement, would be to seek permanent solutions to the capacity limitations. An improvement team might recommend acquiring one or two small, simple paper-cutting machines that could provide backup and ease the bottleneck. Other techniques favored under JIT are quick setup to reduce the machine time lost in changing from one paper size to another, high levels of preventive maintenance on the machine to keep it from breaking down in the middle of a busy day, high levels of quality control so that the machine's limited capacity will not be eaten up by rework, and moving materials from process to process in small quantities.

Usable theory-of-constraints concepts include (1) consolidating similar orders (e.g., same paper sizes) into a large production batch, thus minimizing setup frequency, and (2) moving small transfer batches forward from the slicer to the next processes rather than waiting for completion of an entire production run (same as one of the JIT solutions). Both concepts help get more work per day through the bottleneck machine during busy times.

### *Problem 2*

At Computer Services, Inc., small software jobs start at the chief analyst's desk, where each job is assigned to one of the 10 systems analysts. On average, a job sits in the chief's in-basket for $7\frac{3}{4}$ hours before the chief starts processing it. Average processing time is 15 minutes. In systems analysis, there typically are 60 active jobs.

Use the appropriate response ratios to analyze the delay situation at the chief's desk and in systems analysis.

### *Solution 2*

Chief: Lead time to work content is the proper ratio:

$$\begin{aligned}\text{Total cycle time} &= 7\tfrac{3}{4}\text{ hours delay} + \tfrac{1}{4}\text{ hours work content}\\ &= 8\text{ hours}\end{aligned}$$

Then:

$$\text{Ratio (cycle time to work content)} = 8\text{ to }\tfrac{1}{4}\text{, or 32 to 1}$$

Analysts: Pieces to operators is the proper ratio:

$$\begin{aligned}\text{Number of pieces} &= 60\text{ jobs}\\ \text{Number of operators} &= 10\text{ analysts}\end{aligned}$$

Then:

$$\text{Ratio (pieces to operators)} = 60\text{ to }10\text{, or 6 to 1}$$

### *Problem 3*

One division of J. W., Inc., produces detergent. Its current RIP inventory turnover is 9. Another division, producing a line of electronic timing devices for home and industrial use, has an RIP turnover of 4. Both divisions have about the same annual costs of purchased materials plus cost to convert them to finished goods: $2 million.

*a.* What is the average total of raw materials and WIP for each division?
*b.* Should the turnovers be used for comparing the two divisions or for some other purpose?

### *Solution 3*

*a.* The turnover formula must be inverted from

$$T_{RIP} = \frac{\text{Purchasing and manufacturing costs}}{RIP}$$

to

$$RIP = \frac{\text{Purchasing and manufacturing costs}}{T_{RIP}}$$

Then:

For detergent: $RIP = \$2{,}000{,}000/9 = \$222{,}222$

For timers: $RIP = \$2{,}000{,}000/4 = \$500{,}000$

*b.* It is unreasonable to compare turnovers. Detergent is made in a continuous process, which should not give rise to nearly as much idle inventory as do timers. It is reasonable to regularly assess the trends in RIP turnover separately for each product. Higher RIP turnover is an overall sign of improvement in division performance.

## Exercises

1. Process variabilities induce firms to carry protective excess inventories; the greater the excess, the greater the inventory carrying cost. Process variabilities also can result in inventory shortages. The greater the shortage, the greater which costs? Explain.
2. Iota Company produces bicycle reflectors. Currently Iota buys the main raw material, bags of plastic pellets, in large quantities about three times a year. Its policy is to order another lot when stock on hand falls to five days' worth (the reorder point). Now Iota is considering a just-in-time purchasing approach: small quantities ordered frequently, perhaps as often as every two weeks.

   There is a risk that the supplier will deliver late. Will JIT purchasing increase or decrease the risk? Should the reorder point be changed? Explain.
3. A plant specializing in precision machining is considering buying a numerical control (NC) machine with an installed cost of $200,000. The NC machine can perform multiple metal-cutting operations by successively rotating a mounted metal work piece and selecting cutting tools from a magazine. Thus, it would incorporate operations now done at scattered machine centers and would eliminate idle materials between machine and stockroom. Average inventory reduction from using the NC machine is estimated at $60,000. Also, the single machine will cost less to set up and operate than the present multiple machines, an additional savings of $50,000 per year.
   *a.* If 20 percent is used as the inventory carrying cost, how quickly can the investment pay for itself (what is the payback period)?
   *b.* Suggest four more important kinds of savings that are likely but less obvious than savings from materials and direct labor. Recalculate the payback period using a larger, more realistic carrying cost (your best estimate).
4. When Hewlett-Packard's Boise division converted to JIT, it eliminated all work orders. One result was 100,000 fewer computer transactions per month.
   *a.* In what sense may those eliminated transactions be considered as non-value-adding? An element of inventory carrying cost?
   *b.* This story is detailed in Rick Hunt, Linda Garrett, and C. Mike Merz, "Direct Labor Cost Not Always Relevant at H-P," *Management Accounting,* February 1985, pp. 58–62. Find this article and explain how the transactions were eliminated.
5. Jack is an assembler at Penrod Pen Company. His job is to pack a gold-plated pen and pencil set, plus guarantee card, into a gift box. He puts the completed box on a chute, which

feeds a machine that applies an outer wrap. (The chute holds a maximum of five boxes.) As an employee, Jack exhibits normal human failings, especially these:

> Occasionally he drops a pen, pencil, or card and while he searches for it on the floor, the outer-wrap machine runs out of boxes to wrap and stops. Several times the machine has lost 50 to 100 cycles while Jack was searching.
>
> Every few hours the assembly line is changed to produce a different model of pen and pencil set, which requires a different guarantee card. But Jack sometimes forgets to change to the correct card. (Inspectors discover the error through random sampling.) As many as 1,000 boxes may have to be torn open and reworked, and when that happens an order for an important customer is usually late.

The supervisor has a solution to Jack's variable performance: extra inventory.

*a.* Explain exactly how extra inventory could be worked into the process to serve as a solution.

*b.* Jack has ideas for certain types of fixtures and automatic checkers that, he feels sure, would immediately catch either of his chronic errors. The devices, installed at his end of the feeder chute, would eliminate the need for the extra inventory that his supervisor has proposed. The supervisor weighs the cost of the devices against the savings on inventory carrying costs using Penrod's usual carrying cost rate of 25 percent. Jack feels the rate is too low. Is Jack right? Be specific in your answer.

6. The director of purchasing and materials management at Ivy Memorial Hospital wants her hospital to be the first in the area to implement a quick-response program with its suppliers of medical devices. How should she proceed?
7. Rate the following four types of businesses, one (poor) to four (good), as to the applicability of quick-response systems in the business. Explain your ratings.
   *a.* Welfare agency.
   *b.* Fast-food restaurant.
   *c.* Producer of pigments.
   *d.* Trucking company.
8. Clerks at your local post office must be prepared to sell stamps, weigh and post several types of letters and parcels, insure mail, and perform dozens of other operations. Find out about and discuss two of the quick-changeover guidelines that seem to be followed by post office clerks to enable them to quickly switch from one operation to another.
9. Over-Nite Mail Corporation experienced two serious problems as business grew in the past 18 months: (1) Over 10 percent of its service orders take three days or more for successful delivery; (2) record accuracy (showing where orders are in its delivery system) is poor; random sampling shows that 30 percent of the records are inaccurate (e.g., a log book shows that a piece of mail is in the delivery truck while it is really still in the sorting room). A recent investment in a computerized order-tracking system has improved record accuracy to 99.5 percent. Should that give the company a significant competitive edge over competing overnight delivery companies? Explain. In your explanation, describe how the company should measure the effectiveness of its order control system.
10. A plant that produces industrial thermostats has successfully implemented MRP. One result is that mean production cycle time (from raw material to finished goods) has improved modestly, from 9.3 to 8.7 weeks. Two large improvements are (1) stock-record accuracy has risen from 68 to 99.2 percent, and (2) on-time completion of work orders is up from 60 to 97 percent. Plant management and the consulting company that assisted in the conversion to MRP are delighted; they claim that inventory control and production control are approaching perfection. They expect the results to stem some of their business losses to

domestic and foreign competitors. Are their expectations realistic? Are the inventory and production control really so good? Discuss.

11. The following are examples of complex, delay-prone intersector material flows. For each one, recommend changes that employ advanced logistics concepts.
    *a.* A manufacturer of auto parts for the "after market" (i.e., replacement parts used in automotive repair) currently sends its production—over 2,000 different parts—to its own warehouse. The warehouse receives and fills orders from 25 distributors disbursed around Canada, the United States, and Mexico and forwards the ordered items to the distributors in its own trucks. The distributors receive and fill orders from several hundred auto parts stores and forward the items to the stores in their own trucks. Late deliveries, wrong shipments, and stockouts are common in the distribution centers and in the stores.
    *b.* A high-end furniture manufacturer in Michigan has learned, through market research, of large potential sales of its product in markets it has not tapped in the past: the U.S. and Canadian West Coast and most of Europe. The company has always shipped by independent truckers to its traditional markets in the Great Lakes area. The question is, can the new markets pay off, given the increased transportation challenges?
    *c.* Headquarters of a chain of dress shops contracts locally for design of private-label dresses and also contracts to local apparel makers to have the dresses made and delivered. However, sales have been falling and retail store managers in scattered markets are rebelling, saying the dresses cost too much and must be ordered too far in advance of each season. Company managers know that some competitors go "off shore" to have work done. They wonder if that option is practical, given the new logistics issues.
12. The chapter discussion of quick-change flexibility includes as an Into Practice box, "Quick Setup at Kentucky Fried Chicken and at General Mills." Review the example and relate each improvement to one of the eight guidelines for quick changeover listed in Exhibit 10-4. (Example: For General Mills, "You don't do anything during a pit stop that you can do before"; which of the eight guidelines does that statement refer to?) Discuss your answers.
13. The equipment used in a campus testing service includes order-entry terminals, optical scanning equipment, computers, and printers. At certain times, one or more of the machines has days' worth of jobs queued up. What do you recommend? Why?
14. Elmo's Burger Shoppe sells $50,000 worth of plain burgers per month. The profit margin is 10 percent. Total inventory on hand averages $12,000. What is the inventory turnover? Should Elmo separately calculate turnovers for purchased materials, WIP, and finished goods? Explain.
15. ABC Specialties, Inc., produces a wide variety of office and home products, one of which is a small mail scale. Annual cost of goods sold for the scale is $100,000, which includes $60,000 to purchase raw materials and $35,000 to convert them to finished goods. The average value of recently purchased plastic and metal parts and materials, plus fasteners, is $10,000; the value of partially completed production is $5,000; and the value of completed finished goods is $15,000. Compute separate and total inventory turnovers. Is ABC managing scale production well? Explain.
16. Exhibit 10-1 shows variability in relation to target performance. The point was made in the chapter that positive and negative variations do not cancel one another out. How does these ideas compare with Taguchi's social loss concept (discussed in Chapter 8)?
17. From your own experience as a client or customer, give an example of especially good server readiness and especially poor server readiness.

# CHAPTER 11

# TIMING—ANOTHER IMPERATIVE

"Thank you for calling ______, your full-service provider of ______. You might be interested to know that we have expanded our line of ______ to include ______ and ______. To obtain more information about this new product line, please call 1-800-________.

"Please listen closely to the following options as they may have recently changed: If you would like to inquire about ______, please press 1; if you would like to question a bill, please press 2; if . . . or, you may stay on the line to speak directly to a customer service representative."

(After a few seconds, then ringing . . .) "All of our customer service representatives are currently busy serving other customers. Please stay on the line, your call is important to us and it will be answered in the order received.

(After 30 seconds of music, or another advertisement . . . ) "All of our representatives are still busy serving other customers. Please continue to hold. Your call is important to us. . . ."

(After a few(?) more reminders to stay on the line, spaced at 30-second intervals . . . ) "Hello, my name is ________. We are sorry about your wait. How may I help you?"

Does the introductory example constitute good service? Perhaps so, for it *might* be available 24 hours per day, seven days a week. Also, perhaps most of the calling customers' needs can be addressed within what they might consider to be a reasonable waiting time. The emphasis is on the word *perhaps,* however, for the pace of life has increased consumers' distaste for waiting.

Though it certainly matters in the end, we needn't get into the issue of whether the customer service representative was able to provide a fast, accurate solution once contact had been established in order to render one judgment: The customer had to wait. He or she had entered a waiting line, or queue, even though fellow queue members might be miles or even continents away.

When we recall (from Chapter 10) that waiting is one of the seven deadly wastes, we understand why in businesses the distaste for waiting can be even greater, in that managers often can and will place a cost on waiting or delay time. It might include employees' salaries, equipment rental fees, inventory carrying costs, utility costs (or any of numerous other fixed costs), and so forth. Quite literally, *"Time is money."*

In Chapter 1, we saw that timing, like quality and cost, is a basic customer demand. In this concluding chapter on customer-serving processes, our focus is on timing—another imperative. We look briefly at some mechanics of waiting lines, and then consider ways to limit those lines. We consider newer concepts like kanban and pull-system operations that have widespread applicability for improving timing in both goods production and service delivery.

## Timing—Impact on OM

In 1990, Joseph D. Blackburn published *Time-Based Competition: The Next Battleground in American Manufacturing,* in which he warned that the battle for better quality, clearly under way at that time, should not be viewed as the final struggle in the war for competitive position.[1] He reminded us that timing is also very much on the mind of customers.

Through the 1990s, time-based competition emerged into the reality that Blackburn had predicted, and today it is fair to say that all organizations face timing problems of one form or another. Moreover, operations managers find themselves in the thick of the timing battle.

### *Dual Output Requirements*

*Faster response times,* suggested between the lines in the opening vignette, is one time-related requirement, but customers also want *on-time performance.* The Into Practice box illustrates faster turnaround (response) time at Dun & Bradstreet and better on-time performance at Canadian Airlines. We can toss in another requirement, perhaps better viewed as an extension of the first two: Customers also want consistently fast and consistently on-time performance. In other words, the basic requirement of *less variability* is very much a part of the timing requirement as well.

Greater customer awareness of timing performance is playing a role. Public transportation companies, government agencies, and other high-visibility organizations must publish schedules of their operations, meetings, projects, and so forth. Even a casual observer can compare what was promised to what was delivered. Being late or taking too long shows up quickly. And of course, consumer groups have a powerful communications link in the Internet—word spreads rapidly. Thus, the timing of an organization's grand outputs—those goods and services destined for external customers—can cast a positive or negative light on overall company operations. "Quick-look" analyses of outputs, however, fail to reveal the depth of impact that timing has on support operations.

### *Timing in Support Operations*

Whenever people or materials are late, carefully crafted schedules go awry, and the negative effects ripple up and down chains of provider–customer linkages throughout the organization. Waiting, unplanned downtime, extra handling of materials and equipment, expensive rescheduling actions, personnel shuffling, and inventory excesses or outages

INTO PRACTICE

## Turnaround Time at Dun & Bradstreet

Millions of times a year, companies go to Dun & Bradstreet for information they need about other firms they might want to do business with. In 1991, it was taking Dun & Bradstreet an average of about five days to provide the information a client company requested. Since that beat its own turnaround standard of seven days, Dun & Bradstreet thought it was doing a good job. Customer surveys, however, revealed that though clients were satisfied with accuracy of the research reports and clarity of presentation, they were dissatisfied with turnaround time; often they wanted the reports in no more than three days.

The company launched Operation Clean Slate in a pilot project in its Greensboro, North Carolina, site, one of the largest and most productive of its 71 regional offices. Seven team members, who called themselves the Greensboro Groundbreakers, went to work. Within two weeks the Groundbreakers had developed dozens of time-saving ideas, which cut turnaround time to three days. The improvements included such changes as eliminating duplicate steps and not allowing offices to build up backlogs of work. Within a year, the team had driven the time down to 1.85 days. After implementing the best ideas in all offices, average turnaround nationwide fell to 2.6 days, with improved quality level and no additional staff or other resources.

Source: Michael E. Berkin, "Dun & Bradstreet Conducts 'Operation Clean Slate,' " *Quality Progress*, November 1993, pp. 105–07.

## On-time Performance at Canadian Airlines

"Research has indicated that the most important factor to an air traveler is on-time performance. The industry measures on time [as] whether a flight leaves within 15 minutes of the scheduled departure time and, in fact, even later than that if the reason why it's late relates to bad weather, mechanical difficulties, or congested air traffic.

"But that's not how customers define 'on time.' They think on time means just that, not give or take 15 minutes. . . . So we decided that we were going to start measuring on-time performance by the customer's watch.

"Getting an airplane out on time is quite interesting because it requires a major cross-functional effort . . . The coordination of the airport, which directs customers to the proper gate; the pilot who flies the plane; the flight attendant who makes sure that all safety requirements are met; the people who load the luggage and cargo; and the caterers who load the food. Both suppliers and employees have to be committed, so teamwork and partnering with suppliers are very important.

"We developed a process on how to count down to flight departures. By using this process, each person . . . involved . . . knows when he or she must complete the work in order for the flight to depart on time.

"Our on-time performance, as measured by the customer's watch, has gone from 57 percent to 74 percent. This includes all departures, whether the reason for the delay was controllable or not. This countdown process has resulted in a savings of about $35 million each year."

Source: Kevin J. Jenkins, president and CEO of Canadian Airlines International, in an interview by Karen Bemowski, "Quality Is Helping Canadian Airlines International Get off the Ground," *Quality Progress*, October 1995, pp. 33–35.

add costs and thus serve to negatively impact operations effectiveness and financial performance.

Actually, timing affects most facets of operations management, and thus factors into nearly every chapter of this book. Exhibit 11-1 illustrates some of the more concentrated discussions of timing-related material. The listing in Exhibit 11-1 is not meant

**EXHIBIT 11-1 Timing Issues in Operations**

| General Area | Example Topics | Material |
|---|---|---|
| Operations strategy | Timing objectives | Ch. 3 |
| Meeting general customer requirements | Faster response time<br>On-time delivery<br>Reducing timing variation | Most chapters |
| Resource reliability | Available time<br>Repair time (down time) | Ch. 7 |
| Forecasting | Lead time<br>Forecast time horizon | Ch. 4 |
| Customer and materials flow | Quick response<br>Materials order timing<br>Queue time limits<br>Customer throughput time | Ch. 10, 11, and 13 |
| Setups and changeovers | Quick-changeover/setup time | Ch. 10 |
| Continuous operations | Cycle time<br>Throughput time<br>Work-content time<br>Takt time | Ch. 15 |
| Job and batch operations | Lead time<br>Queue time<br>Run time<br>Setup/changeover time<br>Inspection time<br>Move/transport time | Ch. 16 |
| Time standards | Elemental time<br>Normal (rated) time<br>Standard time | Ch. 12 |
| Maintenance | PM time | Ch. 14 |

to be exhaustive; perhaps it is best viewed as a general statement of the many opportunities that operations managers have to positively affect timing.

In the remainder of this chapter, we focus on tools and techniques. We begin with a timing problem that is familiar to most of us—the ubiquitous waiting line.

## Waiting Lines—Delays for the Customer

It may not be obvious at first, but waiting lines are a problem for goods providers as well as for those in the services industries. In the last chapter, we considered several delay and timing problems that crop up in inventory-related operations. Indeed, much of the purpose of flow control might be viewed from the perspective of avoiding costs associated with waiting lines or queues that can develop in any setting.

Waiting lines are clearly an ever-present concern for services providers. Unfortunately, we sometimes hear stories of serious injuries or even death caused by crowds

**EXHIBIT 11-2 Waiting-Line Components**

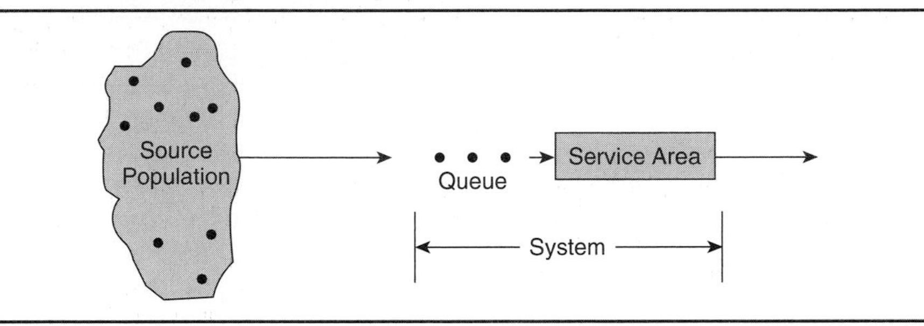


grown impatient with waiting. Are we too impatient as a society? Maybe so, but we shall leave that debate to the sociologists.

It is within our scope, though, to recognize situations that create waiting lines, understand some of the reactions that we might expect from humans confronted by waiting-line situations, and discuss ways to minimize negative effects caused by the waste of waiting. We begin by looking at some fundamental waiting line issues.

## *Waiting-Line Basics*

Exhibit 11-2 shows a general model of the waiting-line problem. The source population represents the group from which waiting-line system participants will be drawn; it may be infinite or finite. A **finite-source population** has limited members, and removal of even one has a noticeable effect on the likelihood that another will emerge into the queue. Suppose, for example, an electronic test lab has four oscilloscopes that might require calibration. If one scope is in calibration, the likelihood of another emerging is different than if all four had been in operation. In an **infinite-source population,** emergence of one member (or even several) does not noticeably alter the likelihood that another will emerge. Automobiles arriving at the tollbooth on the Golden Gate Bridge, or e-commerce orders placed on a busy web page, for example, reflect infinite-source populations. We will limit further discussion to infinite-source populations, as they lend themselves to less cumbersome mathematics yet illustrate the waiting-line problem quite effectively.

The total *waiting-line system* consists of the queue and the service area. We shall assume that the **queue discipline,** that is, the priority for moving from line to service, is first-come-first-served. In some settings other queue disciplines are in effect. The hospital emergency room is a classic example—the more severely injured patients move to the head of the line. For most business settings, however, first-come-first-served is appropriate.

The pattern of arrivals may be constant, say, in a machine-paced setting. In most instances, however, arrivals are random (no pattern). In the latter case, we may predict arrivals—often quite closely—by using the Poisson probability distribution. The statistic of interest is average **arrival rate** (average number of arrivals per time period) and is denoted by the lowercase Greek letter lambda, $\lambda$.

Service times are yet another concern. Constant service times exist in instances of (again) machine pacing; industrial assembly operations may use constant service times even if arrivals are irregular. An automatic car wash is a service sector example. Irregular service times are the rule in most instances, however. Frequently, we use the negative exponential probability distribution to describe service times. But our interest lies in approximating the average **service rate,** and the negative exponential service time distribution converts into a Poisson distribution for service rate. We denote service rate (average number served per time period) with the lowercase Greek letter mu, $\mu$.[2]

There are four basic waiting-line system configurations. They are shown in Exhibit 11-3 along with examples of each type. Formulas (usually referred to as *queuing*

**EXHIBIT 11-3 Basic Waiting-Line and Service Facility Patterns**

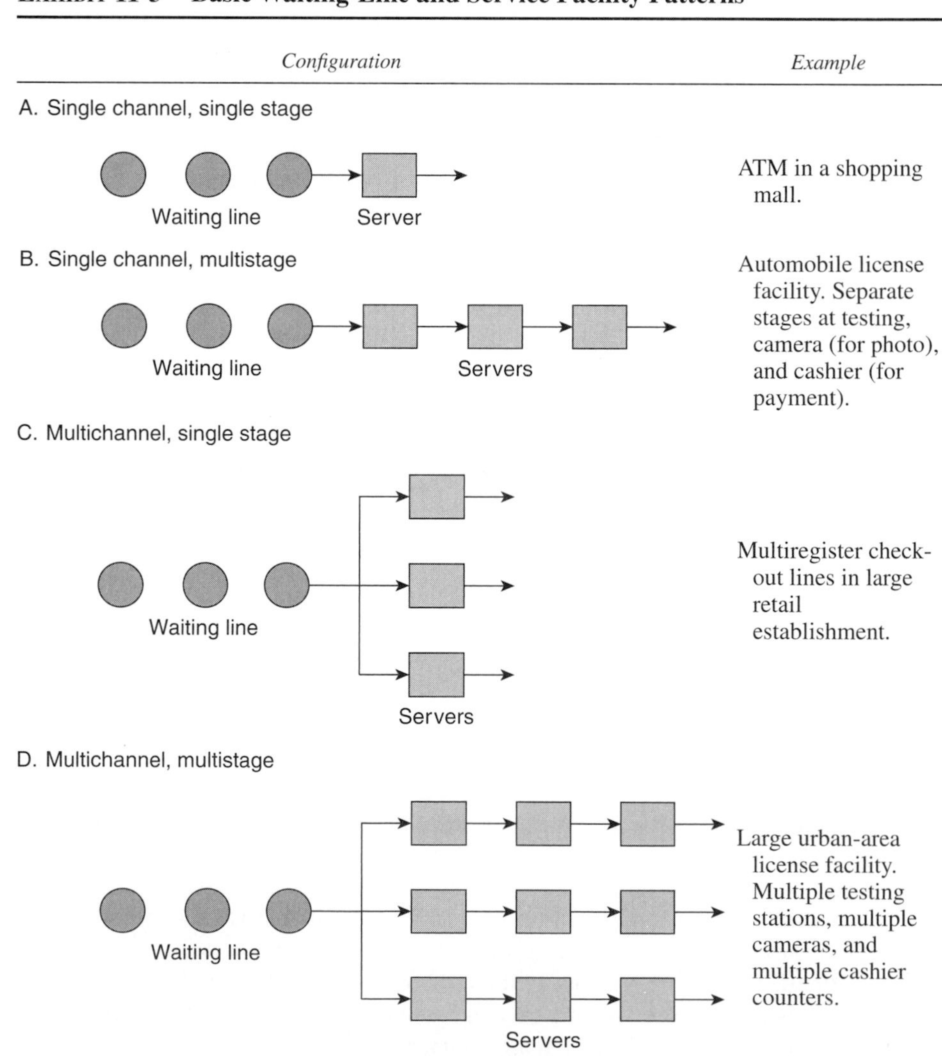

**EXHIBIT 11-4 Queuing Formulas for Single-Channel, Single-Stage Service Facility**

| *Performance Characteristic* | *Formula* | *Equation Number* |
|---|---|---|
| Server utilization | $U = \frac{\lambda}{\mu}$ | (11-1) |
| Server idleness | $I = 1 - \frac{\lambda}{\mu}$ | (11-2) |
| Mean waiting time in queue | $T_q = \frac{\lambda}{\mu(\mu - \lambda)}$ | (11-3) |
| Mean time in system | $T_s = \frac{1}{\mu - \lambda}$ | (11-4) |
| Mean number in queue | $N_q = \frac{\lambda^2}{\mu(\mu - \lambda)}$ | (11-5) |
| Mean number in system | $N_s = \frac{\lambda}{(\mu - \lambda)}$ | (11-6) |
| Probability of $n$ units in system | $P_n = \left(1 - \frac{\lambda}{\mu}\right)\left(\frac{\lambda}{\mu}\right)^n$ | (11-7) |
| Mean time in queue ($\mu$ constant) | $T_{qc} = \frac{\lambda}{2\mu(\mu - \lambda)}$ | (11-8) |
| Mean number in queue ($\mu$ constant) | $N_{qc} = \frac{\lambda^2}{2\mu(\mu - \lambda)}$ | (11-9) |

*formulas*) exist for determining performance characteristics in each of the four basic configurations. The single-channel, single-stage formulas are the simplest and are the ones we shall explore further.

Exhibit 11-4 shows nine formulas that yield variables of interest. With the exception of the last two, Equation 11-8 and Equation 11-9, we are assuming Poisson arrivals and negative exponential service times, as discussed earlier. In these last two equations, we assume a constant service pattern. In all cases, we must assume that the service rate exceeds the arrival rate (that is, $\mu > \lambda$); else, the system is unstable, and among other things, an infinite queue will build *in theory*. Finally, we assume steady-state operation; start-up and wind-down effects are ignored.

Example 11-1 illustrates how the queuing formulas are used to make a general assessment of a waiting-line situation.

### Example 11-1: WAITING-LINE ANALYSIS OF DO-IT-YOURSELF COUNTER

Saturday is known as do-it-yourself day at Hammer Hardware. Joe Hammer is thinking about setting up a special counter for the do-it-yourself customers at which they can get not only help with where to find products in the store but also some quick advice about the best way to handle their upcoming projects. Experience has taught Joe that three minutes is a good figure to allow for average time required to serve a "do-it-yourselfer" and that these customers will arrive about every 10 minutes throughout the day.

*a.* If Joe sets up the counter under these conditions, what operating characteristics might he expect?

*b.* What might Joe do to avoid costs of idleness?

*c.* What is the likelihood that two or more people will be at the counter, either waiting or being served, at any one time?

*Solution*

*a.* First, we convert the service and arrival time estimates into service and arrival rates. Service rate is 20 per hour (60 minutes ÷ 3 minutes), and arrival rate is 6 per hour (60 minutes ÷ 10 minutes). Now, we can apply Equations 11-1 through 11-6 from Exhibit 11-4 to compute performance characteristics for the service counter.

Utilization: $$U = \frac{\lambda}{\mu} = \frac{6}{20} = 0.30 \quad \text{or, 30 percent}$$

Idleness: $$I = 1 - \frac{\lambda}{\mu} = 1 - 0.3 = 0.7 \quad \text{or, 70 percent}$$

Average time in queue: $$T_q = \frac{\lambda}{\mu(\mu - \lambda)} = \frac{6}{20(20 - 6)} = \frac{6}{280}$$
$$= 0.0214 \text{ hrs. or, 1.29 minutes}$$

Average time in system: $$T_s = \frac{1}{(\mu - \lambda)} = \frac{1}{14} = 0.071 \text{ hrs. or, 4.29 minutes}$$

Average number in queue: $$N_q = \frac{\lambda^2}{\mu(\mu - \lambda)} = \frac{36}{20(14)} = \frac{36}{280} \cong 0.13$$

Average number in system: $$N_s = \frac{\lambda}{(\mu - \lambda)} = \frac{6}{14} \cong 0.43$$

From this assessment, Joe might conclude that his customers will not have to wait an excessive amount of time. The idleness factor, at 70 percent, might cause him some concern.

*b.* Joe might ensure that the person(s) staffing the new counter have other work to do during idle periods. Cross-training (OM Principle 7) makes this option easier to implement.

*c.* The probability that *two or more people* will be in the counter system at the same time is equal to one minus the probability that there will be *either zero or one person* in the system. From Equation 11-7, we determine the probability of zero and the probability of one, sum those two values, and then subtract from one.

Probability of zero: $$P_0 = \left(1 - \frac{\lambda}{\mu}\right)\left(\frac{\lambda}{\mu}\right)^0 = \left(1 - \frac{6}{20}\right)\left(\frac{6}{20}\right)^0$$
$$= (0.7)(0.3)^0 = (0.7)(1) = 0.70$$

Probability of one: $$P_1 = \left(1 - \frac{\lambda}{\mu}\right)\left(\frac{\lambda}{\mu}\right)^1 = \left(1 - \frac{6}{20}\right)\left(\frac{6}{20}\right)^1$$
$$= (0.7)(0.3)^1 = (0.7)(0.3) = 0.21$$

We add to get the probability that there is either zero or one in the system; that sum is 0.91. So, we may conclude that the probability of having two or more people in the system is 0.09—not a very likely event. Joe need not worry about the counter getting overloaded with customers.

---

## *Economic Factors of Waiting Lines*

Does the do-it-yourself counter make good business sense for Joe? Any attempt to answer that question imposes some sort of cost/benefit analysis. Joe might easily determine his costs (e.g., installation, staffing, and so forth), but what figures should he use to put in the "benefits column"? He hopes, of course, that the counter will improve his business by attracting more customers who buy more materials. Joe might install the new counter, track his register receipts for a few weeks or months, maybe do some quick customer surveys, and then be able to make a better estimate of any financial benefits that stem from the counter. But this sort of analysis would go on whether waiting lines were involved or not.

Direct economic implications *of waiting lines themselves* focus on costs of waiting and costs associated with idle (or underutilized) facilities. In Example 11-1, the hardware service counter installation and operating expenses may be allocated over a larger range of store operations, but only if:

1. The counter attendant is cross-trained and has other work to do during idle periods on Saturday. (*OM Principle 7*)
2. The counter itself is flexible, and can be easily converted to other uses on other days of the week if Saturday is to remain the only do-it-yourself help day. (*OM Principles 12 and 9*)

At the service counter itself, Joe has no waiting costs, but his customers do. Having to wait in line for just over one minute (on average), they probably would not complain. But, what if the new counter is such a success that more customers begin to show up? What if the mean arrival rate doubles to 12 per hour, or grows even more? Will customers begin to complain then, or worse, will they take their business elsewhere? (Solved Problem 1 at the end of this chapter explores the performance of the service counter under other conditions.)

But as we have seen, businesses *do* incur waiting costs throughout their operations. In Chapter 10, we considered costs associated with waiting or delay, especially for nonhuman resources such as inventory. Moreover, we saw that those costs can be difficult to accurately gauge. When humans are doing the waiting—whether they are internal or external customers—further complications arise. Employee wage or salary level data offer a start on human waiting cost estimates if the customer is an internal one. But for an overall figure, an educated guess must often suffice. (Solved Problem 2 at the end of this chapter provides additional details.)

Costs associated with various intangibles such as frustration, loss of motivation, or worse are even more elusive, but just as real. For as we suggested earlier, humans don't like to wait.

### *Human Reactions to Waiting Lines*

How long would you continue to hold if you were the caller in the chapter-opening vignette? How long would you wait to use an office photocopier or scanner at work? How long must the line of cars be at your favorite fast-food establishment before you just keep on driving past and seek food elsewhere? Now let's make you the provider . . . what is your reaction when a rush of customers hits your workstation? Don't you speed up, trying to adjust your pace—at least for the short run—to better keep up with demand?

The realities of waiting lines disrupt steady-state assumptions and serve to limit the applicability of queuing models. First, let's look at what is called queue behavior. When a person enters a queue, grows tired of waiting and exits, that person is said to have **reneged.** A person who intends to enter a queue, but upon seeing its length turns away and refuses to enter, is said to have **balked.** If multiple service channels exist, and queue members can change lines, **line jockeying** occurs; people seek the "faster-moving" line or lane.

Businesses sometimes resort to clever (devious?) measures to control these behaviors: Hidden queues at amusement parks and drive-up lanes that loop behind buildings are examples. Also, physical barriers prevent line jockeying (and reneging, in some instances). Other companies adopt a more customer-friendly posture; they keep customers appraised of queue status. Signs at Walt Disney World in Orlando, for example, advise patrons of approximate waiting time (from this spot) to the ride or attraction. And at USAA Insurance, when all service agents are occupied, calling customers are told the approximate time that they will wait for an agent. Whenever multiple servers (channels) are involved, the single-queue approach gives customers a sense of fairness . . . everyone waits the same "for the next available counter or agent." No need to try and guess which line will be shorter.

Although we applaud the efforts to instill fairness and keep customers informed, they may not reduce balking and reneging. When we factor in the (very human) tendency for servers to speed up or slow down as demand varies, steady-state conditions erode further. All told, the human impact in waiting lines is very real and warns us to treat queuing model results as estimates only.

To summarize, waiting lines are common and merit study. And despite their limitations, queuing models do provide the operations manager a good quick-look approximation of waiting-line operating characteristics. The Into Practice box "Speeding Up Checkout" offers a brief glimpse into the priority that better waiting-line management is receiving, in this case, among retailers and their suppliers.

Contemporary competitive waiting-line strategy seems to boil down to "Queues—if you can't prevent them, then limit them." That's our next topic.

## Queue Limitation

A powerful set of tools for queue limitation exists. They incorporate the latest technologies, yet they also draw from much simpler, time-honored, customer-oriented "good business" practices. They work in manufacturing as well as in services. We need say

INTO PRACTICE

## Speeding Up Checkout

At a time when Internet rivals offer shopping with no lines at all, retailers face more pressure than ever to speed customers along. . . . Many are also realizing that "register rage"—customer irritation over long lines and slow clerks—can be a real threat to business. According to studies by America's Research Group, 83% of women and 91% of men say long lines prompted them to stop patronizing a particular store.

"The least we can do is give customers a good checkout," says Kevin Turner, chief information officer for Wal-Mart Stores, Inc., which is testing several new technologies in its stores. K-Mart is also spending large sums on improvements such as faster scanners and portable cash registers. Wal-mart uses a technique it calls "line buster" in which associates armed with hand held scanners and portable computers scan items in a customer's cart and hand over a reusable card containing item data that the cashier merely swipes to accomplish checkout and payment.

The dream is *smart packaging* in which products are fixed with a small tag (chip) that emits a signal for store registers to pick up and register the sale and tally the bill. Procter & Gamble and other consumer-products companies are working together to devise a standard for the smart tags.

The allure for consumer-products makers isn't just speedier checkout. They'll be able to get constant readings from the tags so they can tightly manage production and store deliveries, and collect more-detailed sales records.

To go along with the smart packaging, Kevin Ashton, a brand manager for P & G's Oil of Olay line, has designed smart shelving. The shelves read and transmit data via the Internet to the store manager and to the manufacturer, notifying them when they run low. The manager doesn't have to take inventory and the manufacturer can produce and ship refills.

Source: Emily Nelson, "Big Retailers Try to Speed Up Checkout," *The Wall Street Journal,* March 13, 2000, Section B, p. 1.

little about some of the more obvious ones . . . for example, when a line forms at a checkout counter, open another register. Others require more explanation and more planning to implement. Time-based competition and competitive cost-control mandates leave little room for debate as to their necessity, however.

At the broadest, anything that serves to decrease delays—especially those attributed to some type of waiting line—may qualify. We have addressed many of these tools thus far in our discussions of planning and strategy, order fulfillment, and process improvements. In this section, we home in on the queue-limiting capabilities of kanban and pull-system operations. Then, in the last section of the chapter, we take a broader look at push versus pull philosophies at work in operations.

### *Kanban as Queue Limiter*

Kanban methodology and the pull-system concept have their roots in the just-in-time family of tools. Born in manufacturing, they are today equally at home in service settings as well. **Kanban,** from the Japanese, literally means card or visible record. An ancient meaning of kanban is, however, shop sign, and Exhibit 11-5 is a kimono shop example. The colorful, artistic shop sign conveyed simple, accurate information about a shop's product or service to passing shoppers in Japanese villages hundreds of years

**Exhibit 11-5 Japanese Shop Sign (Kanban) for Kimono Shop**

Source: Dana Levy, Lea Sneider, and Frank B. Gibney, *Kanban: The Art of the Japanese Shop Sign* (San Francisco: Chronicle Books, 1983), p. 75.

ago. Less artistically, but just as simply and effectively, today's kanban tells a provider what and how much to forward to a customer. And—more important—it tells the provider *when* to act, using visual signals and simple rules.

How does kanban work? Many variations exist, but let's look at classic kanban—a card system. In such a system, kanbans recirculate; any container with parts in it must have a kanban attached. Kanban cards contain such information as item name, stock or part number, quantity in the container, user, provider, and card number.[3]

Exhibit 11-6 illustrates this version of kanban for an item, Part A, that might be a desk drawer going from a desk drawer manufacturing cell (maker) to desk assembly (user). In this example each of three carts holds five desk drawers, and has its own kanban card; the kanbans are numbered 1 of 3, 2 of 3, and 3 of 3. When an assembler takes the first desk drawer from the cart, the card is pulled, to be collected by (or sent to) the desk drawer production associates.

At the drawer production cell, the card is the signal to act; specifically, it instructs the provider to make five more desk drawers of type A, and make them now. Thus, if the cell makes a family of parts, say, several types of drawers, shelves, and roll-tops, the kanban specifies which to produce. Two key points: (1) The user drives production. Had the desk assembler not needed the drawer, the card would not have been taken from the cart and returned to the drawer-making cell. And at the cell, the rule is (2) No card, no production. Thus, customer demand pulls work along the supply chain—the defining characteristics of the **pull system,** or **pull-mode operations.** We shall say more about pull systems later in this chapter.

As the desk drawer example illustrates, kanban keeps the provider attuned to customer usage. Thus, kanban is a queue limiter, a device that limits the length of the queue (waiting line) and thus the waiting time of items—or people—waiting for service.

**Exhibit 11-6 Card (Kanban) System**

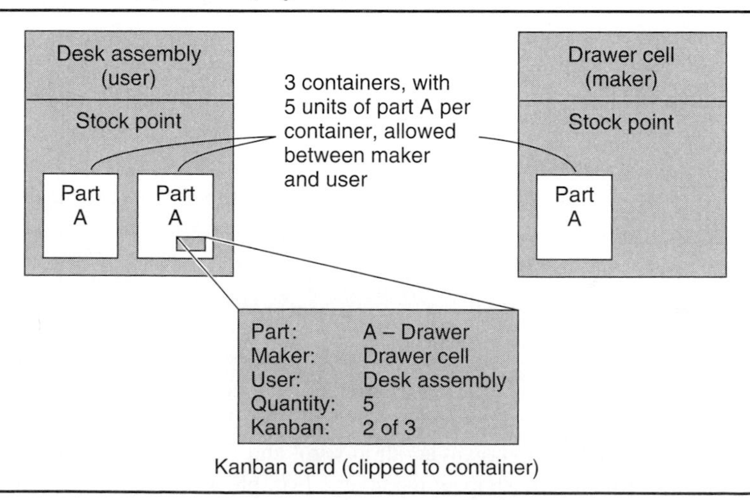

**EXHIBIT 11-7 Queue Limiter (Kanban) Variations**

- Classical card kanban: Recirculating containers with detachable cards.
- Labeled containers: Recirculating containers and carts, permanent kanban identifying labels attached.
- Unlabeled containers or kanban squares: Contents of flow path obvious, so no identifying label (card) necessary.
- Timer or warning light or bell: Queue *time* limitation, instead of *quantity* limitation.
- Queue limit policy: Prominently displayed, hard-to-ignore queue limit.
- Colored golf balls, poker chips, abacus beads, discs, flags and so on: Queue depletion below queue limit signaled by a colored indicator.
- Electronic: Notification of queue depletion below queue limit via electronic communication.
- Automatic queue limiter: In automated system, notification of queue depletion, below queue limit, via automatic device.

Queue limitation replaces lax flow control with discipline. Throughput times, along with variation in throughput times, decrease, as customer satisfaction and competitive position increase. Exhibit 11-7 lists various queue limitation methods, but is not intended to be an exhaustive list. We've discussed classical card kanban; the remaining types listed in the exhibit are considered below.

**Labeled Containers.** Here the card is permanently affixed to recirculating kanban containers, carts, dollies, trolleys—a limited number per item. At Harley-Davidson's engine and transmission plant in Milwaukee, nearly all component parts are controlled this way. Kanban for a certain gear, going from a machining cell to transmission assembly, might be set at four recirculating parts boxes (kanban = 4), each holding exactly 20 gears, and each having a plate riveted to it on which the usual kanban information is written. The rule: No box, no production (of that part) at the cell.

**Unlabeled Containers or Spaces (Kanban Squares).** Some firms use unlabeled recirculating kanban containers (carts, dollies, trolleys, etc.) or kanban squares (spaces on the floor or a table). An identifying label is unneeded under each of the following conditions:

- The container holds only one (homogeneous) item, such as a certain size gas tank. Exhibit 11-8 illustrates two special containers for defibrillators, made by Physio Control Company. The three-level container—queue limit (kanban) = 3—was devised for one of Physio's products in its first assembly-and-test cell. Associates assembling a similar product in Physio's second cell, seeking an improvement, adopted a one-unit version of the container (queue limit = 1).

**EXHIBIT 11-8 Kanban Containers at Physio Control Company**

*Top: Three-level cabinet container. Bottom: Slide-out tray on one level.*

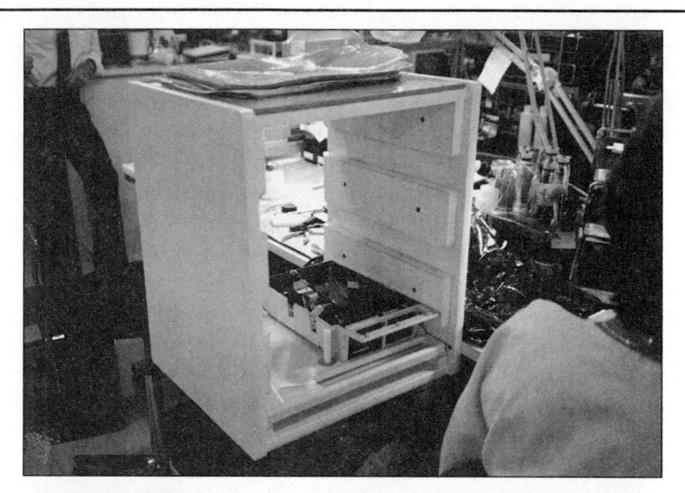

- Various (nonhomogeneous) items are flowing through the same process sequence, such as different customer orders through order processing, or successive 10-person groups of tourists on a fixed-sequence guided tour.
- The empty square signals the need for production. For example, unlabeled kanban squares are common in electronic assembly plants. Typically, one square is taped off on each table on an assembly line (kanban = 1). Each assembler looks to the square at the next table for the customer's signal—an empty kanban square—that more work is needed. For big units, the kanban square is on the floor, and some kind of lifting/moving apparatus is usually needed for transport to the next process.

**Exhibit 11-9 "Three-Person Promise" at Ernst Home and Garden Stores**

**Timer or Warning Light or Bell.** Each Seafirst Bank has a clock and a sign, where customers queue up for a teller, that says the bank will pay \$5 to anyone who waits more than five minutes for a teller (queue limit = 5 minutes). Since customer arrivals are extremely uneven, Seafirst uses part-time and flexible labor to keep queues below the limit. Some tellers work only the noon rush, some only on Mondays, Fridays, paydays for the area's biggest employer, and so forth. (See further discussion in the case study, "5 Minutes, \$5—Seafirst Bank" contained on your CD-ROM.)

**Queue-Limit Policy.** Ernst Home and Garden stores put up signs above cashier stations proclaiming the Three-Person Promise (queue limit = 3; see Exhibit 11-9). The sign explains that if a fourth person enters a line, an Ernst clerk comes immediately to open another cashier station.

**Colored Golf Balls, Poker Chips, and Abacus Beads.** At a Kawasaki engine plant, when a certain part in subassembly is down to its queue limit, the assembler rolls a colored golf ball down a pipe to a machine center, which tells the operator what part to run next. Associates at a Seagate disk drive plant in Minneapolis came up with red and blue poker chips and abacus heads, one row for each product, where red means don't make it (we still have some), and blue means make it (we are down to the queue limit).

**Electronic Signal.** Some users convey usage data, or notification of having reached the queue limit, electronically. Bar-code scanning of kanbans can capture the usage. From there, the data goes to a provider process internal to the organization or to an outside supplier. Internal transmission may employ radio frequency signaling or other wireless messaging.[4] External notification goes by fax, Internet or satellite. As noted in earlier chapters, these kinds of external communication are elemental in quick-response partnerships that link retailers, wholesalers, and manufacturers.

**Exhibit 11-10 Automated Queue Limitation (Kanban) Example**

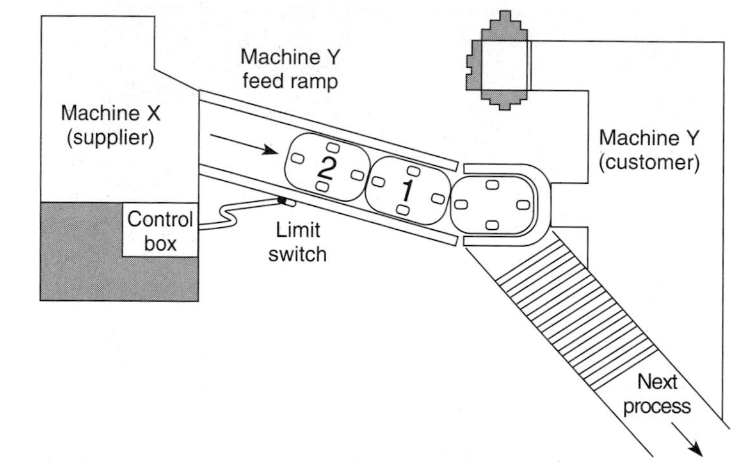


**Automatic Queue Limiter.** When automated conveyor systems link processes, limit switches governing each feeder machine can keep the queues short before each user machine. Exhibit 11-10 is a schematic illustration. The limit switch, positioned in the conveyor or feed mechanism of Machine Y, limits the queue. When piece 2 slides into a position where it blocks the switch (queue limit = 2), a signal halts Machine X. When Machine Y pulls the next unit forward for processing, the switch is tripped and Machine X gets a signal to make and forward another piece.

At the other extreme from electronic and automated signaling, the notification could be just a shout to a provider at a nearby process. It doesn't matter how the message is conveyed. What is important is that the kanban system be disciplined: Send no more parts, or clients, until the current queue is below the limit.

## *Queue Limits and Dependable Service*

In each of the previous examples, queue limitation serves two basic customer needs: short lead time and invariability. It shortens the lead time by bringing average waiting delays below the queue (kanban) limit, and it prevents extreme wait-time variations.

Exhibit 11-11 shows eight customer experiences with a certain business, perhaps a bank. In part A, with no queue limits, the customer's total time commitment (wait time plus service time) is highly variable, ranging from a low of 3 minutes (fourth instance) to a high of 28 minutes (eighth instance). The average is 16 minutes. In part B, with a queue limit of 5 minutes, the variation is slight, ranging from 3 to 7 minutes, and the average is 5.25 minutes.

A high ratio of queue time to production or service time, as in Exhibit 11-11A, is the norm in manufacturing and office work as well as in human services. Therefore, queue limitation is the key to greatly improved response times.

**EXHIBIT 11-11 Effects of Queue Limit on Total Customer Time**

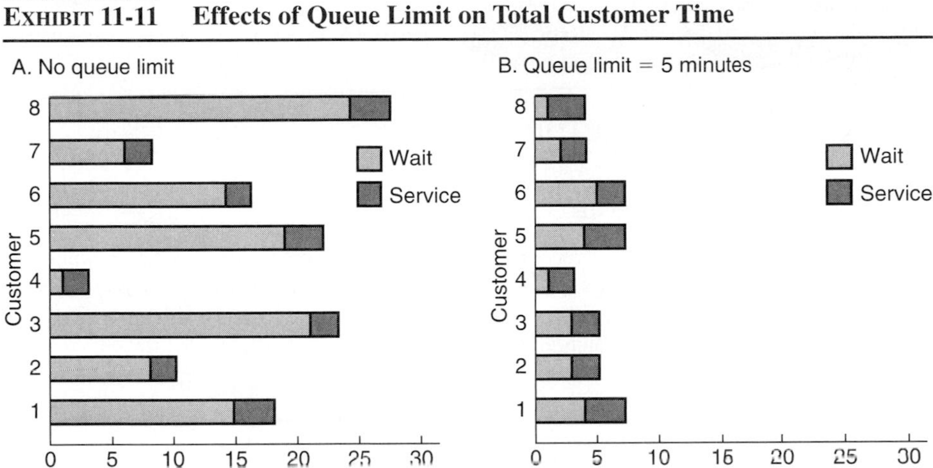


In some companies, success with queue limitation in the direction of Exhibit 11-11B has led to the following results:

- The guesswork is removed. Rob Henderson, plant manager of Corning's ceramic filters business in Corning, New York, says: "We used to negotiate on the request date. We don't do that anymore." With a known, dependably fast throughput time, the Corning salesperson and customer needn't negotiate, which partly explains why this Corning plant was chosen "one of America's best plants" by *Industry Week*.[5]
- Reliable order promise dates are easy to set. At Ahlstrom Pump (Finland and U.S. facilities), the multifunctional product strategy team has worked out an order-promise policy they call "rules of the game," which is based on its dependably quick time to produce any pump, large or small. Nearly all parts, made or bought, are kanban controlled.
- On-time performance improves. In extensively employing kanban, Baldor Electric, a specialty (high-mix) electric-motor manufacturer, has cut its throughput time from an unstable average of four weeks to a fixed five days.[6] As a result, in March 1991, associates at Baldor's Westville, Oklahoma, plant celebrated a full year of on-time deliveries.

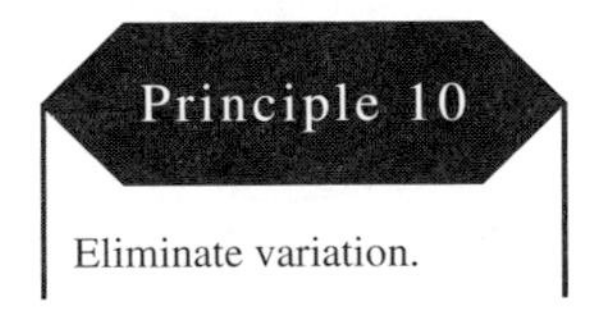

Eliminate variation.

In each of these examples, kanban system designers paid special attention to labeled stock locations, exact counts, and special containers. Then, with proper training, people can operate the kanban system effectively without cumbersome records; see Contrast box, "Materials Management."

Maintaining discipline with regard to physical stocks is one requirement of dependable kanban operations. Another is a high degree of human resource flexibility. Without it, a surge in business at Physio Control, Ernst Home and Garden, or Seafirst

CONTRAST

## Materials Management

| Conventional Stocking Systems | Kanban |
|---|---|
| Failure prone: Rely on fallible stock records, separated from actual stocks; stocks often poorly segregated, counted, contained, and susceptible to damage and unauthorized usage. | Few failures: Stock location and count well defined, easily verified; stocks well packaged or "containered"; simple, visual, disciplined. |

Bank will create long waiting lines of partially complete defibrillators (Physio) or customers (Ernst and Seafirst). These companies keep the queues short—within their kanban limits—by having backup labor options to meet the crunch. At Physio, the backup labor can include temporary transfers of people from other parts of the plant; working extra hours, extra shifts, and weekends; and bringing in temporary employees. Ernst and Seafirst rely on cross-trained employees who can restock shelves, unload incoming trucks in the back room, or work the cash registers; and on-call casual labor.

### *Continuous Improvement (Kanban Removal)*

A special attraction of kanban, as described in early writings on it, is the kanban removal feature, a simple way of decrementally reducing the queue (See Example 11-2).

Example 11-2: KANBAN/EDI SERVICE AGREEMENT—MEDIVICE, INC., AND MUNY HOSPITAL

Last year, Muny Hospital contracted with Medivice, Inc., to provide medical devices under a kanban/electronic data interchange (EDI) contract. The initial, trial agreement included 30 high-use items—for example, bar-coded cartons of H1 disposable hypodermic needles.

For that item Muny Hospital's stores manager and a Medivice salesperson agreed to an initial kanban quantity of eight cartoons. Whenever Muny's demands for H1 needles requires a stores clerk to break open another carton, the clerk uses a wand to scan the carton's bar code. An EDI message goes to Medivice, authorizing shipment of one carton next time the truck goes to the hospital. If the hospital has used, say, three cartons since the previous delivery, Medivice learns about it through EDI and ships three cartons instead of one.

But was eight the right kanban quantity? Experience soon provided the answer. In the midst of a serious flu epidemic, Muny Hospital quickly went through all eight cartons of H1s and experienced a stockout. The medical staff was in a panic until Medivice made a special midnight needle delivery. That seemed like an isolated exception, but several more stockouts occurred in the next two months, caused by various system failures (miscount of cartons, a late truck, a stockout at Medivice's warehouse, and a defective lot of H1 disposable needles). As a result, the stores manager and the salesperson increased the kanban quantity of H1 needles to 10 cartons.

On I1 intravenous (IV) solution bags, the opposite happened. The initial kanban quantity, 14 containers, proved to be more than enough. Despite a few start-up problems in getting I1 IV bags on kanban, they were always available at the hospital. The service rate on this item was 100 percent, which spelled too much inventory to the stores manager and called for kanban removal. The manager and the salesperson reduced the kanban quantity to 10 containers of IV bags. More reduction followed, primarily because hospital improvement teams, including representatives from the freight carrier and the supplier, implemented overall improvements in the kanban system.

**service rate or fill rate** Percentage of demands (items) filled out of existing stock (or immediate production).

Stores employees wanted a simple, easily noticed record of stockout incidence for H1 needles, I1 bags, and the 28 other kanban-controlled items. They developed a large visible wall-chart check sheet with preprinted categories of problem causes. A stores clerk makes a check mark beside the probable cause whenever a stockout occurs. Improvement teams later investigate the most frequently checked causes.

**Principle 11**

Cut wait time and inventory.

Stores associates treat reduction of kanban quantities as one measure of success; response ratios, in pieces rather than boxes, are another useful measure. Associates make check marks for stockouts, and they track kanban reductions on the same wall chart, shown in part in Exhibit 11-12. Out of Muny's several thousand stockkeeping units (SKUs), only 30 are currently under kanban, so it's feasible to chart them all.

**stockkeeping unit (SKU)** An item at a particular geographic location; a stocked item requiring separate management. SKU is used in retailing, manufacturing, and elsewhere.

### EXHIBIT 11-12 Kanban Status and Stockout Check Sheet—Hospital

| *Items on Kanban* | *Last Year* | *This Year* | | | | | | | | | |
|---|---|---|---|---|---|---|---|---|---|---|---|
| Hypodermic needle, H1 | | J | F | M | A | M | J | J | A | S | . . . |
| Kanbans | 8→ 10 → 8 | 8 | 8 | 7 | 6 | 6 | 6 | 6 | | | |
| Stockouts | 5 | | | | // | | | | | | |
| Comments: April problem (damaged needle packages—two stockouts) quickly resolved by supplier; no need to increase kanban quantity. | | | | | | | | | | | |
| . . . | | | | | | | | | | | |
| IV bags. I1 | | | | | | | | | | | |
| Kanbans | 14 → 10 | 10 | 10 | 10 | 9 | 8 | 8 | 7 | | | |
| Stockouts | 0 | | | | | | | | | | |
| Comments: No stockouts last year or this year to date. | | | | | | | | | | | |
| . . . | | | | | | | | | | | |
| Nurserver carts | | | | | | | | | | | |
| Kanbans | 30 → 25 | 25 | 25 | 25 | 22 | 22 | 22 | 22 | | | |
| Stockouts | | | | | | / | | | | | |
| Comments: June late delivery (8:30 A.M. instead of 5:30) due to large turnover of drivers (e.g., graduation of student drivers). Freight company has set up backup driver system, so no change in kanbans. | | | | | | | | | | | |

Note: Data shown for only 3 of 30 kanban items.

The exhibit includes two *individual* SKUs (H1 hypodermic needles and I1-IV bags) and the Nurserver cart, a shelved cart filled with common supplies (tape, swabs, tongue depressors, etc.). Medivice takes Nurserver carts away each day for restocking and return.

Exhibit 11-12 shows a pattern of few stockouts (high fill rates), which is to be expected since kanban is a disciplined, highly reliable system. The exhibit shows that last year, the kanban quantity for H1 needles increased from 8 to 10 (as explained earlier) but then fell back to 8, with further reductions—from 8 to 6—occurring this year. The stockout problem that occurred twice in April this year was quickly resolved, but Muny's cautious associates agreed to keep kanban at six cartons for awhile. Good service experience has led to intermittent kanban removal for both I1 IVs (14 to 10 to 7 kanbans) and Nurserver carts (30 to 25 to 22 kanbans; a single late Nurserver delivery problem causing the June stockout was successfully resolved.)

## Pull- and Push-Mode Operations

As noted earlier, just-in-time and kanban are often associated with pull-system, or pull-mode, operations. The distinction between pull- or push-mode operations lies in determining whether the provider or the customer controls the flow. In this section we examine some of the differences between the two modes, consider why push-mode often dominates, and close with some observations regarding increased pull-mode operations.

### *Push-Pull Distinctions*

In **pull-mode operations,** the recipient's signal is required before the provider sends the work along; that is, the customer controls the flow of work. Kanban signals—whether in the form of a card, container, or human being in a waiting line—tell the provider of good or service that it is time for action. Pull-mode governs many machine-dispensed goods and services; vending machines, ATMs, and car washes are common examples. Also, most personal human services are (almost) pure pull operations; no action is taken until the customer presents the request for service. Many government services also qualify . . . response to fire alarms is a classic case of pull-mode.

In **push-mode operations,** the provider sends work along in the absence of any call from the customer. In push-mode, the provider determines when (and often what) work flows . . . "Ready or not, here it comes!" Some services have considerable push-mode components. Radio and television stations, for example, broadcast (literally) to the cosmos even if (in the short run, at least) no one is tuned in. And, many manufactured goods flow because the provider chooses to produce them, not because a customer has ordered them. To be fair, push-mode providers usually act in anticipation of demand being "out there," but that demand is a far cry from being a firm customer order.

Numerous hybrid situations may be identified. Utility services (electricity, water, etc.) are pushed into the distribution channels, but the customer's flip of a switch or turn of a faucet is required to start the meter running and thus make the final (pull-signal) determination of flow control. Some fast-food outlets keep a small quantity of prepared sandwiches in a short slide chute; push-mode up to say, kanban = 3, but not more. If these are top-sellers, they move rather quickly so food freshness is assured and response times are lowered.[7] In Chapter 5, we considered a hybrid manufacturing situation when we discussed consuming as part of the master schedule. Providers produce to a schedule—in response to some combination of aggregate demand and specific orders—but specific customer orders pull (consume) the products from the master schedule, leaving an amount still available to promise.

Most will agree that pull-mode operations appear to be more customer oriented. Let the next stage drive the flow. However, push-mode has been dominant.

### *Dominance of Push Systems*

Signs of push-mode dominance appear in nearly every type of operations. Factories have conveyors, pallets, and storage racks filled with goods being pushed out with no queue limits in place. The mounds of unsought goods move out into distribution channels, to warehouses, and on to retailers where they clutter storefronts until "special sales" are required to move them along—often at a loss. In services, long lines form and providers have no response plans in place to, again, limit the queues . . . servers just keep chugging along at the built-in pace. Response times—time in queue or in system—get extended.

Although apparently wasteful and insensitive to customer wants, push-mode operations have dominated for several reasons:

1. *Inflexibility.* A surge in customers or order arrivals will cause a queue to lengthen unless the provider can muster resources. Insufficient physical capacity, lack of cross-trained labor or a backup labor supply, and no outsourcing partners are frequently the culprits.
2. *Geographical distances.* In manufacturing or distribution, providers and users are often quite separated, and that tempts the supplier to keep producing and push product forward. Poor contact with customers down the line is to blame.
3. *Erroneous costing.* As we saw in Chapter 10, costs of producing an item in advance of need and carrying that item until it is needed are often grossly underestimated.
4. *Period quotas.* When managers feel pressure to attain period production or sales quotas, the result can be an end-of-period push to get goods out the door. Often described as *"hockey-stick management,"* the flow pattern resembles a series of hockey sticks lying end to end with the blades extended upward to reflect increased output near period end.
5. *Capacity/budget justification.* Even if production or sales quotas aren't involved, the desire to "show high levels of resource utilization" as a way of justifying existing budget levels or capacity allocations can prompt managers to push unneeded work onto society. End-of-fiscal-year spending—perhaps to fund frivolous projects or research studies—by public and not-for-profit organizations is a classic example of push-mode waste.

Competitive forces are making continued disregard for customer desires a hazardous game. In response, many steps have been taken to improve operations so that they can be accomplished in a more pull-mode manner.

### Toward Pull Operations

What can companies that have a conveyor-paced production lines—say for bottling, canning, tableting, or assembly—do to instill pull-mode operations? Increasingly, they are installing stop or slow-down switches so that any line employee has the ability to make the line more "pull" and less "push." The idea is to treat each person like the customer that he or she is and build in the ability to say, "I'm having a problem here, stop sending me any more work until I can get this taken care of." Exhibit 11-13 illustrates a line-stop button in use at a Ford assembly plant.

When teams of associates, including key technical support people and process engineers, are handy, the problems get resolved quickly and work can begin again. When cross-training is the rule, people have multiple skills and are more likely to be able to help neighbors on the line. When undercapacity scheduling is the policy, time for problem solving is available for teams to devise permanent, preventive fixes. When flexible, movable, equipment is available, quick replacement or substitution is an option. When flow distances are short, simple but effective visual signals provide timely feedback from colleagues and from process equipment. We could go on, but in sum, when principles of operations management have been followed, pull-mode operations are more likely to find a fit.

And, to carry this point further—into a chapter and part conclusion—we note that the ability to carry out just-in-time operations (or, lean manufacturing, total quality

**Exhibit 11-13 Operator Ownership of the Process-Line Start/Stop Switches**

*Operator hitting line-stop button at Ford assembly plant, Louisville, Kentucky.*

Source: *Manufacturing Engineering Magazine,* Society of Manufacturing Engineers. Photo courtesy of Mid-West Conveyor Co., Kansas City, Kansas.

management, or whatever name one chooses to apply to improved processes) must be earned. Toyota worked for over 20 years just to develop its just-in-time system, and improvements continue to this day.

To conclude, we note that competitive operations are accomplished through good customer-oriented processes—aimed, as we have seen in Part III, at giving customers better quality, faster and more consistent response times, less variation, lower costs, more flexibility, and better service. Processes capable of delivering those results, in turn, depend on how the company manages its resources—our topic in Part IV.

## Summary Check Points

✓ Timing, a basic customer requirement, takes two forms: Customers want *faster*, more responsive service, and they want *on-time* service.

✓ Costs of waiting, identified as one of the seven deadly wastes, include time wasted by internal and external customers and delays encountered by queues of materials, documents, and other nonhuman work flows.

✓ Time-based competition heightens the need for greater flexibility, lower variability, and better quality (no time for do-overs). Dependable service and lower costs along the supply route are the results.

✓ Timing is a common theme in most OM activities, a constant reminder of its importance.

✓ Waiting lines, or queues, create flow-control problems for service providers and goods producers alike.

✓ The waiting-line system is comprised of a queue and a service area; the queue forms from a source population that may be infinite or finite.

✓ Queue discipline governs the priority rules for moving from queue to service; first-come-first-served is common in businesses.

✓ Average arrival rate ($\lambda$) and average service rate ($\mu$) are key statistics used to perform waiting-line analyses.

✓ Basic waiting-line configurations include single or multiple channels and single or multiple stages. Queuing formulas exist that provide estimates of various relevant waiting-line performance characteristics.

✓ Human behaviors affect waiting-line system stability; balking, reneging, and line jockeying are common customer behaviors, and speed-up and slow-down may be exhibited by servers.

✓ Kanban may serve as effective queue-limiting tools. When coupled with an overall pull-mode philosophy, they help place top priority on customer needs.

✓ Several variations of kanban exist; they are found in manufacturing and service settings.

✓ Queue limits have been shown to reduce guesswork in operations, promote more accurate order-promise dates, cut throughput times, and improve on-time deliveries.

✓ Systematic kanban removal is a form of continuous improvement; each iteration stresses the flow-control system and helps identify weak links that become the targets for improvement projects.
✓ In pull-mode operations, the customer controls the flow of work; in push-mode, the provider determines when (and maybe what) work is to be done.
✓ Despite the customer-friendly attractiveness of pull-mode operations, push-mode has dominated for a variety of reasons.
✓ Leading companies have recognized the competitive benefit of increased pull-mode influence in operations.

## Solved Problems

### *Problem 1*

Joe worries that his do-it-yourself help counter may be a success. More precisely, his concern is that increased usage may overload the system and result in longer customer waits. What performance characteristics might he expect if the average customer arrival rate doubles? Triples? For now, he will assume the same server rate (no speed-up), and stable queues (no balking or reneging). Other data are as given in Example 11-1.

### *Solution 1*

Equations 11-1 through 11-6 may be applied to determine operating characteristics for the counter waiting line system. The mean arrival rate, $\lambda$, will change from 6 to 12 for one set of calculations and to 18 for the second set. Results for $\lambda = 6$, 12 and 18, as well as for integer values in that range, are shown in the table on the next page. (These results were determined with the Excel spreadsheet for single-channel, single-stage waiting lines that is available on your CD-ROM.)

Among other performance characteristics, Joe's "quick-look" analysis shows that if average arrival rate reaches 12, for example, customer line wait time is about 4.8 minutes (0.08 hours $\times$ 60 minutes/hr.). At $\lambda = 18$, that figure will increase to about 27 minutes. Though his counter utilization will increase *in theory,* Joe knows that in reality, customers won't put up with such long waiting times. Instability will be the result, and queuing formula estimates suggest that Joe must consider queue-limiting steps should the counter prove successful.

### *Problem 2*

In a large commercial painting shop, painters are highly skilled and can perform a wide variety of intricate paint jobs. Each job requires a unique blend of paints, adhesives, and other chemicals. Painters present blending specs at the service counter of the company blending shop and wait while a special crew does the blending in a mostly manual mode. Business is up; more jobs are coming in, and the owner has noticed a bottleneck at the blending counter. Painter arrivals average 10 per hour, and blending requires an average of 5 minutes ($\mu = 12$/hour). Standard Poisson assumptions apply.

The owner is considering installing a computerized blending process. The manufacturer's claim is that the blending crew can blend at a constant rate and produce more consistent results,

| Single-Stage, Single-Channel (M/M/1) Queuing Model: "Quick-Look" | | | | | | | |
|---|---|---|---|---|---|---|---|
| | | (Mu Fixed, Various Lambda Values) | | | | | |
| Mu = | 20 | | | | | | |
| | | | | | | | |
| Lambda: | Min = | 6 | Max = | 18 | | | |
| | | | | | | | |
| | | *Utilization* | *Idleness* | *Mean Time in Queue* | *Mean Time in System* | *Mean Number in Queue* | *Mean Number in System* |
| *Lambda* | *Mu* | *U* | *I* | $T_q$ | $T_s$ | $N_q$ | $N_s$ |
| 6 | 20 | 0.30 | 0.70 | 0.02 | 0.07 | 0.13 | 0.43 |
| 7 | 20 | 0.35 | 0.65 | 0.03 | 0.08 | 0.19 | 0.54 |
| 8 | 20 | 0.40 | 0.60 | 0.03 | 0.08 | 0.27 | 0.67 |
| 9 | 20 | 0.45 | 0.55 | 0.04 | 0.09 | 0.37 | 0.82 |
| 10 | 20 | 0.50 | 0.50 | 0.05 | 0.10 | 0.50 | 1.00 |
| 11 | 20 | 0.55 | 0.45 | 0.06 | 0.11 | 0.67 | 1.22 |
| 12 | 20 | 0.60 | 0.40 | 0.08 | 0.13 | 0.90 | 1.50 |
| 13 | 20 | 0.65 | 0.35 | 0.09 | 0.14 | 1.21 | 1.86 |
| 14 | 20 | 0.70 | 0.30 | 0.12 | 0.17 | 1.63 | 2.33 |
| 15 | 20 | 0.75 | 0.25 | 0.15 | 0.20 | 2.25 | 3.00 |
| 16 | 20 | 0.80 | 0.20 | 0.20 | 0.25 | 3.20 | 4.00 |
| 17 | 20 | 0.85 | 0.15 | 0.28 | 0.33 | 4.82 | 5.67 |
| 18 | 20 | 0.90 | 0.10 | 0.45 | 0.50 | 8.10 | 9.00 |
| | | | | | | | |

ensuring a better quality job. Equipment brochures advertise "5-minute blending." Knowing that he pays his painters an average of $25 per hour, the owner wonders if savings in waiting time costs will be enough to justify the new equipment.

***Solution 2***

At this point, the objective is to compute estimated waiting-line cost savings. Using the values of $\lambda = 10$ and $\mu = 12$, we use Equation 11-5 to compute the mean number of painters in queue during the day with manual blending, and then use Equation 11-9 to compute mean number in queue with the constant-rate service assumption in effect. First, for manual blending:

$$N_q = \frac{\lambda^2}{\mu(\mu - \lambda)} = \frac{10^2}{12(12 - 10)} = \frac{100}{24} = 4.17$$

Now, for machine-assisted blending:

$$N_{qc} = \frac{\lambda^2}{2\mu(\mu - \lambda)} = \frac{10^2}{24(12 - 10)} = \frac{100}{48} = 2.08$$

The constant-service-rate blending will cut the average number of waiting painters from about 4.17 to about 2.08. Let's round off and assume the line is reduced by two people. For an eight-hour day, the waiting cost saving is about:

$$(\$25/\text{hr.} \times 8 \text{ hr./day} \times 2 \text{ painter-days}) = \$400$$

Thus far, the analysis has considered reduced waiting costs for painters only, but that is our focus here. Before any final decision, of course, the owner must gather additional data and make further estimates. Will there be lower or higher personnel costs required to staff the new blending system, for instance? And it goes without saying that blending system purchase or rental costs (for acquisition and operation) constitute the "other side of the issue."

### *Problem 3*

At Computer Services, Inc., small software jobs start at the desk of the chief analyst, who assigns each job to one of the 10 systems analysts. On average, a job sits in the chief's in-basket for $7\frac{3}{4}$ hours before the chief starts processing it. Average processing time is 15 minutes. In systems analysis, there typically are 60 active jobs. Is queue limitation (kanban) usable at either work center? Explain.

### *Solution 3*

Queue limitation could be used in several ways. For the chief, the rule could be to have zero jobs in the in-basket (queue limit = 0) at the end of the day and stay late, if necessary, to meet the rule. Another possibility is to set the queue limit = 5; if the in-basket ever has more than five jobs, call for help from the most senior analyst.

For the analysts, a general queue limitation policy is one possibility. For example, set an overall response ratio at 2 to 1, with no more than 20 jobs assigned to the 10 analysts. Stay late, borrow programmers for use as analysts, or subcontract work to avoid exceeding the ratio. A rule such as queue limit = 2 at each analyst's desk will yield the same overall ratio. It is hard to say whether the overall ratio or queue limit = 2 at each analyst's desk would work better.

The result of using queue limitation is to speed work through in much less total cycle time (but the same work content time per job). In the office, queue limitation forces people to start one job and finish it instead of starting many jobs, switching among them and stretching all of them out.

## Exercises

1. Metro pollution control moves about the city with a mobile unit checking auto exhaust emissions. Metro officers block the road, stop all cars, and attach an exhaust-sampling device. There are two new exhaust-sampling devices on the market. One has a fixed test time of one minute. The other has a variable time; the manufacturer claims that the average is 0.85 minutes. If cars arrive at the roadblock at an average rate of 40 per hour, which device is better if the objective is to minimize citizens' total delay at the check? Does your answer change if the average arrival rate is only 10 cars per hour? Explain.

2. A frozen dessert outlet makes several labor-intensive cool treats. Although the treats are available year round, they are especially popular during the summer months. If customers arrive at a rate of 10 per hour during the busy season, and it takes an average of four minutes to make and serve one of the treats:
   *a.* What is the utilization of the treat-serving counter?
   *b.* What is the probability that a customer will not have to wait in line but can enter the serving area immediately upon arrival at the outlet?
   *c.* What is the mean time a customer will spend in queue?
   *d.* What is the mean time that a customer will spend in the system?
   *e.* What is the mean number of customers that might be expected to be in queue at any time?
   *f.* What is the mean number of customers that might be expected to be in the system at any time?
   *g.* What is the probability of finding two or more customers in the system at any time?
3. Computers arrive at a constant rate of 18 per hour at a wrapping station for packaging prior to shipment. The automatic packaging equipment requires a constant three minutes to package a computer. Discuss the performance characteristics of this system. Be sure to explain any waiting-line problems that are encountered.
4. Suppose the computers in Exercise 3 arrive at an average rate of 18 per hour, and the packaging is done manually in an average time of three minutes. (Assume Poisson distributions.)
   *a.* What are the performance characteristics of the waiting-line system?
   *b.* How would you compute the costs of the delays in this system? (You should describe your analysis procedure, and you *may* wish to create some costs and other values for illustrative purposes.)
5. Scuba tanks arrive at a pressure test station for testing prior to shipment. The arrival rate is eight per hour and the station test time averages five minutes. Poisson distributions are assumed.
   *a.* What is the utilization of the test station?
   *b.* What is the probability that a tank have to wait in queue prior to testing?
   *c.* What is the mean time a tank will spend in queue?
   *d.* What is the mean time that a tank will spend in the system?
   *e.* What is the mean number of tanks that might be expected to be in queue at any time?
   *f.* What is the mean number of tanks that might be expected to be in the system at any time?
   *g.* What is the probability of finding three or more tanks in the system at any time?
6. If the test performed on the scuba tanks in Exercise 5 requires a fixed amount of time—exactly five minutes—and if arrival rate and pattern remain as described in Exercise 5:
   *a.* What is the mean time a tank will spend in queue?
   *b.* What is the mean time that a tank will spend in the system?
   *c.* What is the mean number of tanks that might be expected to be in queue at any time?
   *d.* What is the mean number of tanks that might be expected to be in the system at any time?
   *e.* What, if any, effects will the constant service rate have on the overall costs of scuba tank production? Explain your response.
   *f.* What criteria, in addition to throughput time, will be relevant to any decision about changing the procedures or resources employed in the tank testing?
7. An insurance company has hired you to improve the "waiting-line problems" associated with its telephone callers. One number is given to customers for their use in reporting accidents and/or making claims. A second number is supposed to be used for billing questions, and a third is (again) supposed to be for new customers or current customers

making policy changes. In practice, people call any of the numbers for any of the reasons, and their calls get routed to the appropriate company personnel. Many clients complain about the waits . . . hey, that's why you got the job!

*a.* What recommendations would you make? Why?

*b.* Your new boss says, "Reading from a letter I got from an irate customer, 'Why don't you bozos tell your customers when they call how long they are going to wait on the %$#@* telephone when you can't give immediate service!' Maybe this person has a point. We can always make a recording, but how can we predict how long a person might wait?"

How would you respond to your boss?

8. A returns counter in the customer service department of a large retail outlet is staffed by as many as four or as few as one depending on the expected volume of customers who wish to return goods. Despite good intentions, however, sometimes demand projections are off, and the counter is either overstaffed or understaffed.
   *a.* Devise a plan that will increase counter utilization and also limit customer queues.
   *b.* What systems (programs, policies, and so on) must be in place before your plan can be implemented? Explain fully.
9. What is the purpose of a "take-a-number" service system, in which customers are served in numerical order? Is it a form of queue limiter? Explain your answers.
10. Is a buffet line an example of pull-mode or push-mode operations? Explain your response.
11. Is the production and distribution of a daily newspaper in a major metropolitan area an example of pull-mode or push-mode operations? Explain your answer.
12. Sentrol, Inc., maker of premier sensor products for the security industry, employs nearly every kind of queue limiter in its plant operations, which has cut its average production throughput time to four hours. A remaining problem is cutting the time to refill assembly teams' kanban containers with purchased components from the stockroom next door. Most containers are about the size of a one-quart ice cream carton and hold lightweight resisters, wire sets, screws, and so on. It takes about 50 minutes for a stockroom associate pushing a trolley of full kanban containers to make a complete circuit around the assembly floor; the circuit includes collecting empty kanban containers.

    On a trial basis, a stockroom associate on roller skates (with crash helmet and knee pads) has been making the circuit, carrying two or three cartons at a time. Does this idea sound feasible? What would its advantages be? How would they be measured? Are there disadvantages?
13. Sentrol, Inc., maker of premier sensor products for the security industry (motion detectors, door and window entry detectors, etc.), receives hundreds of orders and other inquiries from resellers and final users by phone each day. Sentrol's customer strategy team has rejected the use of an automatic answering system. The team believes that good service requires real people answering the phones within four rings every time. The trouble is, the calls arrive unevenly, sometimes 5 per hour and sometimes 50 per hour. Is the customer strategy team's four-rings policy practical? If so, how can it be made to work? (Note: Four rings is a queue-limitation policy.)
14. An accounts payable office consists of three people. Their work flow includes passing piles of invoices among them in the process of authorizing payment. Recently, the average number of invoices on the three desks was 150 and the typical time an invoice spent in the office was three days. Select a response ratio, and explain how it might be used to improve the operation. What results might be expected?

15. A manufacturer of X-ray machines presently has partially completed machines scattered around the assembly areas, with only a few actually being worked on by the department's five assemblers. The units accumulate in assembly because parts and subassemblies from other departments arrive whenever the departments happen to complete them.
    *a.* Is the current system push or pull? Explain.
    *b.* Suggest an improved system.
16. Four ways to limit queues are (1) kanban squares, (2) special-purpose containers, (3) general-purpose containers with kanban (cards) attached, and (4) a powered assembly conveyor with no container or card necessary. Which of the four should be used in each of the following situations? Explain your answers.
    *a.* A book printer; books are printed and bound in a route through four different departments.
    *b.* Final assembly of 13-inch TV sets.
    *c.* Production of vitreous china products (sinks of all sizes, toilets, tubs, etc.); involves molding, glazing, firing in kilns, and so forth.
    *d.* Repetitive production of several different large, highly polished precision metal parts.
    *e.* Internal mail delivery in a large office building.

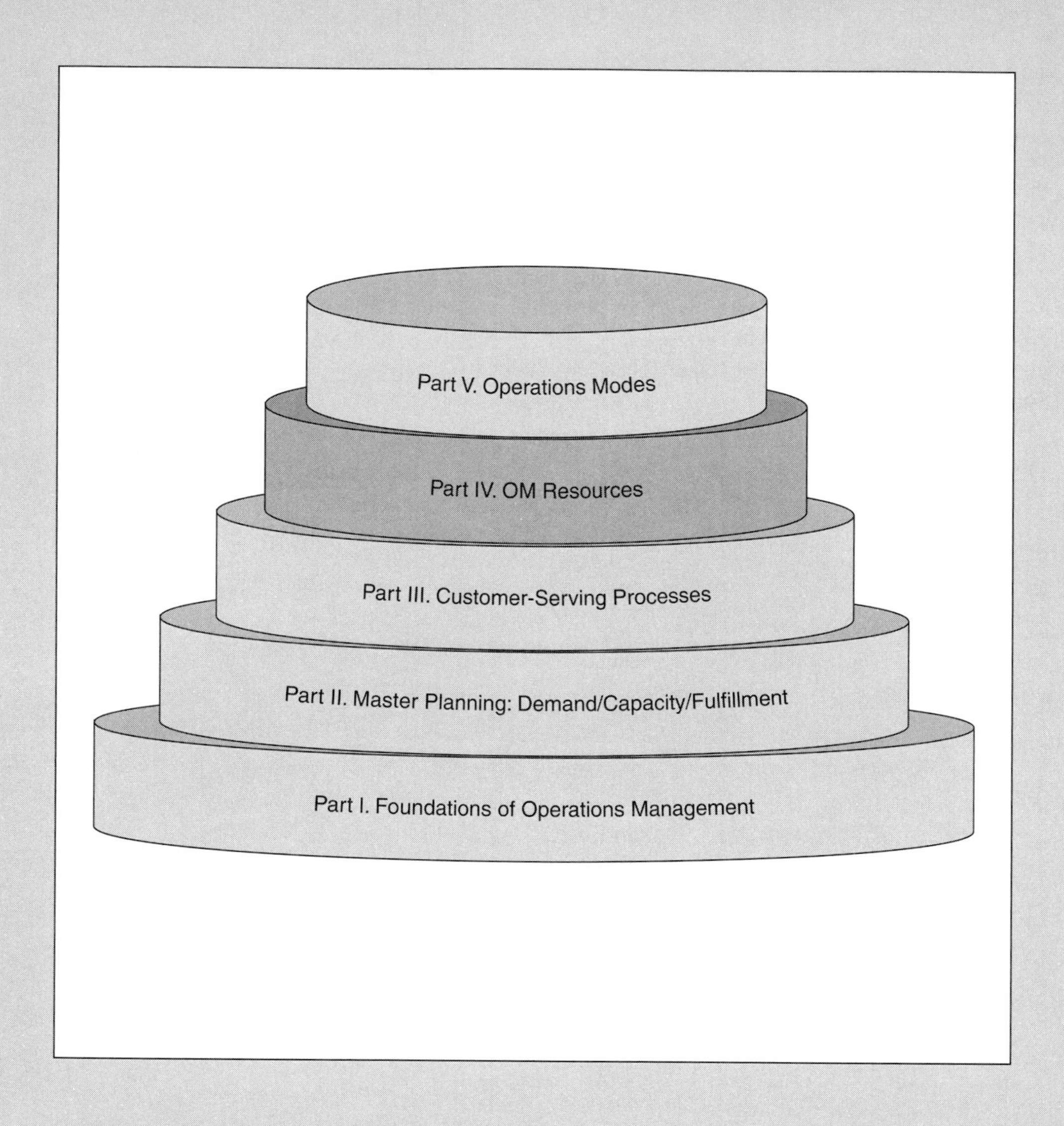
Part V. Operations Modes
Part IV. OM Resources
Part III. Customer-Serving Processes
Part II. Master Planning: Demand/Capacity/Fulfillment
Part I. Foundations of Operations Management

# OM RESOURCES



In Part IV, we progress to yet another level of depth; but this time, the spotlight is on three fundamental types of resources that form key inputs to the transformation processes discussed in Part III. Specifically, we address human resources, materials, and facilities. Productivity, standards, and compensation are notable issues we address in Chapter 12. Lot-sizing and materials requirements planning are major topics in Chapter 13. Facility location, layout, and maintenance are concepts covered in Chapter 14.

***Points to ponder:*** Good resources are needed if we are to have good processes and good outputs. Competitive resource positioning is a big step in the right direction. However, taking care of those resources—through training and maintenance—is just as important.

# CHAPTER 12

# PEOPLE AND PRODUCTIVITY

As we noted in Chapter 2, **productivity** is broadly defined as the outputs to inputs ratio. It applies to all assets—capital, facilities, materials, information, and yes, labor. As an isolated number, a productivity ratio or index means little. When compared to a similar ratio of a competitor, however, or when examined repeatedly over time, it reveals considerably more information. In fact, most companies measure it, and managers fret over it. It is a driver of competitiveness.

U.S. government productivity reporting emphasizes labor productivity.[1] And to many businesspeople, the word *productivity* is limited to mean productivity of labor. And while we do not advocate that narrow view, we readily acknowledge that labor productivity is a vital concern for operations management. Moreover, the issues of human resources management and productivity have been inexorably intertwined in popular press and (sometimes) professional writings as well. When productivity drops, labor takes the blame.

In this chapter—the first in our Part IV treatment of operations resources—we examine the people–productivity interface. Perhaps the marriage is indeed fitting, for even though productivity can flow from nonhuman assets, people make it happen. Also, just as the so-called new economy has opened the door to new paradigms of productivity enhancement,[2] new rules appear to govern the relationship between companies and their human assets.

## New Economy, New Games, New Rules

To the "old warhorse" who entered the workforce in the 1960s, there's a lot of "new" in the new economy. The new millennium began on the heels of a decade of change: The cold war ended; the Berlin Wall came down in late 1989. The longest sustained economic expansion period in U.S. history began in the early 1990s. The European Union solidified further, and introduced a common currency in January 1999. And, in 1991, the National Science Foundation privatized the Internet.

These and other notable events and trends of the 1990s might be viewed simply as the latest wave of change, however, for the 1980s exhibited their own turbulence. We need not repeat Chapter 2's OM timeline to make the point that today's competitive dynamics have been brewing for decades. Returns on previous technology investments, payoff from employee training, new partnerships, better understanding of true cost drivers and wastes, and better management have all contributed to the productivity "boom."[3]

### *Productivity: Payoff and Promise*

Customers—business and consumer—demand better, and faster, and cheaper. In one sense, these demands are all reflected in the productivity ratio:

$$P = \frac{\text{Outputs}}{\text{Inputs}} \tag{12-1}$$

Mandates for quality and timing performance, coupled with flexibility and service, are calls for more, that is, for enhanced outputs. On the flip side is the demand for lower prices, which—if margins are to remain—translates to lower costs, and that exerts downward pressure on the denominator. In sum, do more with less, or perhaps more appetizingly stated . . . use the resource inputs more efficiently and effectively.

Providers who are able to deliver increase the pressure on those who aren't. The productivity payoffs for those companies who have paid their dues, so to speak, remain but promises for those who have yet to take advantage. Familiar old-line companies like GM, Ford, DaimlerChrysler, Royal Dutch/Shell Group, Honeywell International, and General Electric are emulating their smaller, younger counterparts in incorporating new technologies to bolster their existing strengths. But, unlike previous spurts of technology spending, redesigned processes accompany this one.[4]

In other words, smarter management of technology is afoot. More managers have caught on . . . you can't gain improvement in productivity by automating or speeding up bad processes. The proper sequence is clear: Set the sights on getting quality and timing in and costly wastes out, then—and only then—open the purse to spending for technology that will help meet these aims. The productivity potential is there: At Corning, average procurement cost per product dropped from $140 to $10. At NCR Corp., the order-to-delivery lead time dropped from three days to just a few hours.[5] Lower the denominator, raise the numerator.

**Principle 8**

Improve existing processes before thinking about new equipment.

### *The Wild New Workforce*

Productivity is climbing, but what does the new economy say about people? Perhaps the word is transition. The "old warhorse" we mentioned earlier has witnessed profound shifts in people/employer expectations. Consider the three short reports in the Into Practice box "Will the Real Human Resource Please Stand Up?" While stories of loyalty and teamwork continue to appear, especially from successful companies such as Baldrige Award winner Wainwright Industries, the last two vignettes in the box suggest that other trends are emerging.

Frankly, it has always been difficult to speak of human resources as a singular entity. It should, therefore, came as no surprise to find diversity in human resources management policies. Indeed, one set of rules seems to apply to high-talent knowledge

*A casual, relaxed environment has been shown to promote productivity in increasing numbers of organizations.*

AP/Wide World.

employees who are in great demand across most industries, and another set exists for the rest of the workforce. That, of course, is a formula for tension.

> These tensions between the haves and the have-nots are fueling a lot of new resentments. At workplaces everywhere, new hires with no experience are swaggering into the office with pay packages far bigger than those of veteran staffers. Elite employees are making so much money so quickly and are juggling so many job offers that they live in constant fear of making the wrong decision and blowing their chance of getting their "two commas" and retiring at age 40.[6]

The scramble for top talent is expensive. To hold *overall* human resource costs in check, a growing number of companies are:

- Asking people to work more (260 more hours per year in 1999 than in 1989).
- Using temporary employees (to avoid costly permanent staff).
- Using variable pay (to avoid getting locked in to long-term fixed salaries).
- Resorting to frequent layoffs (more in 1999 than at any other time in the 1990s).
- Pushing work offshore, or demanding that suppliers do so.[7]

**Principle 7**

Invest in human resources with job and career rotation.

Other firms are going in another direction. Sometimes, retaining top employees boils down to giving them opportunities for new jobs within the company. The employee benefits, for career progression does not depend on switching employers. Employers win too; recruiting from inside the company saves time, money, and talent. Apparently, this policy holds promise, but there is room for improvement. *The Wall Street Journal* recently noted that "In most industries it takes employees two weeks to find a job outside the company and two months to find a job within the company."[8]

And despite the fact that in the United States real wages rose but 0.8 percent during 1999, financial incentives *for the talented* soar to new heights. According to some, employee stock options are the biggest change in employer-employee relations in the

INTO PRACTICE

## Will the Real Human Resource Please Stand Up?

"When geese fly in their characteristic 'V' formation, the flapping motion of each member of the flock creates an aerodynamic lift for the bird immediately behind. When the lead bird tires, it falls back and another one moves up to take its place at the point. This collaborative effort increases the flying range of the geese by at least 70 percent over what it would be if they flew alone or in random formation.

"Everyone here knows that story," says Mike Simms, plant manager at Wainwright Industries, a 1994 winner of a Baldrige Award. "It's an important emotional lesson about teamwork."

Source: Les Landes, "Leading the Duck at Mission Control," *Quality Progress,* July 1995, pp. 43–48.

"Just as the new economy is dismantling the old rules of commerce, the new workforce is shredding the contracts between employers and employees. Employers are giving up rigid wage scales in favor of flexible compensation. They are learning to live with high turnover and abolishing seniority-based pay. 'We're in a dramatic transformation,' says Hewitt Associates LLC compensation consultant Paul Shafer. 'We're moving toward personalized pay.'

"In this environment, an employee who remains loyal to an organization is penalized. After all, if the woman in the next cubicle can jump to another company for a 20% raise, a signing bonus, and stock options, why should you wait around for that 4% merit hike?"

Source: "The Wild New Workforce" (Cover Story), *BusinessWeek,* December 6, 1999, pp. 39ff.

"Then there's a younger generation—those people who are coming out of college. They're not as willing as veterans are to work 18-hour days for what could be a financial crapshoot. At the same time, they do expect to hit it big. KPMG did a poll of college seniors about their work expectations. Fully 74% of those students said that they expect to become millionaires."

Source: "How to Play the Talent Game" (Interview with Ms. Colleen Aylward, founder of Devon James Associates, Inc., a Seattle-based recruiting firm), *Fast Company,* June 2000, pp. 363ff.

1990s, affecting not just what people are worth but how and why they work; and the pace of options is accelerating.[9] The authors of *Fortune*'s 2000 annual report of the best companies to work for, however, point to other perks: "The big story is that these companies are trying to help employees balance their home and work lives. More and more offer perks such as flexible schedules and day care."[10]

To sum up, demand for productivity puts pressures on companies to ask more from employees and to seek employees who have more to give. Employees, in turn, are demanding more from their employers, and those who possess the knowledge and skills are getting it. Loyalty, from either direction, may be becoming a rare commodity.

### *The Road Ahead*

We won't attempt to resolve the human resource management issues confronting modern business; it lies far beyond our scope. We will, however, briefly acknowledge prominent suggestions—for employers and employees—that could prove useful in coming years.

Increased workforce flexibility, in line with OM Principle 7 and a basic customer requirement, holds promise as a "win-win" rule for the road. Flexibility breeds responsiveness, reducing the time customers must wait while providers get the right mix of human resources together. In addition, as Edward Lawler puts it, a "broad perspective helps employees to be innovative in improving operations. Thus, they become more effective in a quality circle, or any other problem-solving group."[11] For example, a buyer with receiving or stockroom experience will be not only a better buyer but also better able to work with receiving and stockroom associates on work-flow improvement projects. Similarly, a salesperson who takes an inside operations job is likely to bring to the job an outside customer view and total business success vision.

Lawler makes the related point that since high-performance organizations have been flattening their organization structures, they need to create "new career tracks that do not depend on upward mobility" and that provide "a new 'nonlinear' way for people to grow and to succeed in their careers."[12]

The large baby-boom population exerts pressures in the same direction: many associates seeking few vertical advancement openings. Since the baby boomers will remain in the labor force for nearly two more decades, employers will not soon escape from the need for policy changes such as horizontal promotions.

Employees also have responsibilities. Whether one is based in operations management or not, the value of understanding other specialties cannot be overemphasized. Signs suggest that employers will continue to be attracted to employees who build breadth of skills. Perhaps the advice of Ralph Waldo Emerson, published in 1841, is most appropriate today. Exhibit 12-1 illustrates.

When labor productivity is low, the root cause may be quite a bit deeper than simply underperforming human resources. More likely, the management system is deficient . . . failing to provide timely information, good component and process design, up-to-date

### EXHIBIT 12-1 "Self-Reliance" Revisited

Over 150 years ago, Ralph Waldo Emerson wrote his classic essay, "Self Reliance." His theme, "trust thyself," is perhaps the best advice available today as individuals cope with new rules of employment. The future belongs to those who try to control their own destinies, who commit to a lifetime of learning. Richard Nelson Bolles (author of the job-hunter's bible, *What Color Is Your Parachute?*) advises everyone to inventory his or her skills, add to them every single year, and always have a ready answer to the question, what would you do if you lost your job tomorrow?

Experts agree that "the most employable people will be flexible folk who can move easily from one function to another, integrating diverse disciplines and perspectives." Competitive businesses know this. Although many have undergone deep downsizing, they are taking steps to ensure they keep the employees they want. There is also the hope that after a period of perhaps painful demolition of outdated workplace structures and ideas, jobholders will have more respect, responsibility, challenge, and fun.

Anyone who wants to be retained should start adapting now. Abraham Zaleznik, psychoanalyst and professor emeritus at the Harvard business school, feels that "the theme of the dawning era is greater accountability on the part of individuals and corporations." He says, "We're all up against a relentless, impersonal reality called the marketplace, which will reward those who do good jobs and punish those who don't."

Source: Adapted from Stratford Sherman, "A Brave New Darwinian Workplace," *Fortune,* January 25, 1993, pp. 51–56.

training, technical support, strategy and policy guidance, healthy work environment, and supportive culture. Labor's ability to work up to potential—intellectually or physically—hinges on these and related factors. Although we touch on some of these issues in this chapter, they also relate to discussions found elsewhere in the book.

In the remainder of this chapter, the scope is more narrowly focused. We look into the history and evolution of productivity improvement, pay and other rewards, contemporary productivity issues, and the use of time standards.

## Roots: Productivity and Scientific Management

The first organized approach to improving the productivity of labor arose in the United States at the end of the 19th century from the work of the pioneers of **scientific management.** Prominent among them were Frederick W. Taylor, Frank and Lillian Gilbreth, and others, including Harrington Emerson, who specialized in office processes. Their approach was to standardize the labor element of operations: standard methods and standard times. Nonstandard labor practices were simply too expensive and wasteful.

Scientific management, so named by U.S. Supreme Court Justice Louis Brandeis, was born in a period of transition and could be thought of as the last phase of the Industrial Revolution. Earlier phases concerned invention, mechanization, standardization of parts, division of labor, and the factory system. Machines and parts were standardized, and labor was divided into narrow specialties. Prior to scientific management, however, labor productivity was controlled more by supervisors' skill than by design. Taylor's and the Gilbreths' techniques for methods study (or motion study) and time study extended science into the realm of the line employee.

Briefly stated (and paraphrasing Taylor), the four principles of scientific management are:

1. Develop a science for each element of a person's work, which replaces the old rule-of-thumb method.
2. Scientifically select and then train, teach, and develop the work force, instead of—as in the past—having employees choose their own work and having them train themselves as best as they can.
3. Heartily cooperate with the employees so as to ensure all of the work being done is in accordance with the principles of science.
4. Ensure that there is an almost equal division of work and responsibility between the management and the employee. The management takes over all work for which they are better fitted than the employees, while in the past almost all of the work and the greater part of the responsibility were thrown upon the employees.[13]

### *Impact of Scientific Management*

While putting the finishing touches on the Industrial Revolution, scientific management ushered in the beginnings of the modern manufacturing era. Since the United States was the birthplace of scientific management, it enjoyed the first benefits. Methods and standards programs spread rapidly in U.S. manufacturing firms between 1900 and 1950, which may help explain the phenomenal growth of industrial output in the United States in the first half of the century.

Beginning in the 1940s, comparable programs found their way into hospitals, food service, hotels, transportation, and other services. So carefully industrially engineered is the McDonald's hamburger that Levitt calls it "the technocratic hamburger."[14] By the early 1980s, the industrial engineering department at United Parcel Service (UPS) had grown to 3,000 people and "had so perfected manual package handling that UPS had the industry's lowest costs."[15] In many industries, it has been hard to compete without good methods design and labor standards.

Scientific management is not without its critics. Labor unions often have resisted time standards. Some believe that under work measurement a person is treated like a microcomputer memory chip. At the first sign of performance deterioration, discard or replace the chip; it's just not cost-effective to attempt to repair or recycle it. Often the ultimate plan is to replace the entire memory system, and even the computer itself, with faster memory and more powerful equipment.

Some of the criticisms focus more on "Taylorism" (referring to Frederick W. Taylor, the "father" of scientific management) than on the movement itself. One of Taylor's ideas was that each function should have its own specialist-managers, so that a production associate might have one boss for training, another for quality, another for scheduling, and so forth. After decades of building up separate functional entities, companies in the 1980s began to see the folly: little communication or cooperation across the functions. Reengineering would be required to reunite the firm.

Whether Taylor, who died in 1915, should be held responsible for the excesses of seven or more decades is debatable. There is, however, no question about Taylor's central role in the development of methods study and time standards, which, as was noted in Chapter 2, have been instrumental in providing the documentation for training. Time standards have been maligned, but nevertheless they have a valued role in time-based competition and in modern-day total quality management and process improvement.

Employers have long sought solutions to the human problems associated with the application of methods and time standards. The most promising approaches, past and present, lie in putting variety and meaning back into the task or job.

## *Tasks, Jobs, and Job Design*

The design of work and work systems has evolved through three phases. First was scientific management, which focuses on the task itself. Next came job design, which aims at improving the job and therefore the life of a jobholder. Today's approach, emphasized throughout this book, is on service to the next and final customer and related feelings of satisfaction by the server. A review of the three phases follows.

**Tasks.** Division of labor, performed scientifically using methods-study techniques, yields a well-engineered task. Consider the task of scraping food leavings off a stainless steel tray into a garbage can. Is that task also a job; that is, can the firm define it as a job and hire someone to do just that task over and over? The answer is yes. Such narrow tasks are sometimes treated as a whole job.

**Jobs.** If all jobs were developed like the plate-scraping one, wouldn't work life be intolerable? A collection of concepts called **job design** attempts to avoid such a fate for working people.

Best known among the job-design ideas are job enlargement and job enrichment. Job enlargement dates back to the 1950s, when Thomas Watson, founder of IBM, promoted the effort out of his strong belief in providing people with meaningful work. Job enlargement means expanding the number of tasks included in a person's job—for example, cooking, serving, and scraping plates; it offers horizontal variety. Job enrichment, a later development with roots at Texas Instruments and AT&T, expands on the job enlargement idea. Enlargement means more tasks; enrichment means more meaningful, satisfying, and fulfilling tasks or responsibilities; for example, an enriched job may entail use of mental and interpersonal skill—scraping plates and teaming up with others to select new dishes, scrapers, and dishwashing equipment.

The liberating effects of enlargement/enrichment are not necessarily in conflict with the restrictions of prescribed methods and time standards. In fact, one could argue that without standards, an enlarged/enriched job might be poorly defined, exposing the employee to frustration and criticism. Existence of job standards offers a guidepath for avoiding problems, thereby offering more freedom for the associate to work on process improvements, which translate into still better job standards.

**Customers, Internal and External.** Enlargement and enrichment, as originally conceived, were oriented to the individual, not to the team and not to the next or final customer. The following corrects this deficiency:

- Ensure that enlargement is directed toward mastery of the jobs of fellow team members—that is, cross-training.
- Ensure that enrichment is customer oriented. Specifically, this calls for associates to acquire the data collection, analysis, problem-solving, and teamwork skills and responsibilities required in total quality management.

An obstacle in the way of learning more skills is the job classification system, or work rules.

How could the Buick division of General Motors have turned itself around so dramatically, from among GM's sickest divisions in the mid-1980s to having car models in the J. D. Powers top-10 auto quality listing by 1990? Perhaps this had something to do with it: A cooperative agreement between Buick management and the United Auto Workers union that reduced the number of job classifications from hundreds to just three. Pay for skills, replacing the seniority pay system, also was part of the deal.[16] **Skill-based pay** fits with the new requirement for associates to master multiple skills. It is often palatable to the employee, union or nonunion, because the common concern has shifted somewhat from job security to work-life security; each new skill mastered becomes another line on the employee's résumé, should a résumé be needed sometime.

### *Process Improvement and Productivity*

Modern improvement tools, presented in Chapter 9, are a mixture of old and new: process flowcharting from the Taylor/Gilbreth era, plus several newer tools that originated in connection with quality improvement (see the 11 tools for process improvement, Exhibit 9-8). Here we take a second look, from a productivity angle.

Systematic productivity improvement, as developed by Taylor, the Gilbreths, and other pioneers of scientific management, involved **methods study,** with **flowcharting** at the core. Methods study always has been aimed at improving not only productivity but also safety and ease of performing the work. Making the work easier to do safely increasingly gets into issues of human physiology, stress, and bodily limitations, and has spawned a subfield of process improvement called **ergonomics.** Because of escalating worker's compensation and litigation costs, interest in ergonomics has never been higher. "A single case of carpal tunnel syndrome, a painful condition involving compression of the wrist's median nerve, costs up to $30,000. . . . Eliminating this type of ergonomics problem sometimes requires less than $1,000."[17]

Methods study takes place at the job level and at the process level. As Exhibit 12-2 shows, each application has a different set of before-and-after flowcharts.

One type of analysis at the job level is **motion study,** which is limited to the work of an immobile employee at a desk or work bench. The analyst flowcharts what the left and right hands are doing. The other type of job-level study is for a mobile employee tending more than one machine; the analyst flowcharts both the person's and the machine's activities.

Job-level methods study pertains to the productivity and ergonomic conditions of direct labor, but not to overall productivity, which includes typically out-of-control overhead costs. Improvement teams may use process-level analysis in directly attacking the high overhead costs and wastes, along with some direct-labor wastes.

Unlike job-level flowcharts, process flowcharts (see Exhibits 6-1 and 9-10 for examples) do not have a time scale and thus do not readily reveal how much productivity improvement is achieved. Industrial engineers, who've used process flowcharts for decades, have rarely found it necessary to translate improvements into before and after costs. It is clear that productivity improves with the elimination of non-value-adding steps.

**EXHIBIT 12-2 Methods Study: Job and Process Improvement**

| *Type* | *Application* | *Flowchart* |
|---|---|---|
| *Job level:* | | |
| Motion study | Manual task at work bench or desk | Left-and-right-hand time chart |
| Operator-machine analysis | Operator tending machines | Operator-machine time chart |
| *Process level:* | Mobile employee, product, or customer | Process flowchart |

While these process improvement techniques have generally been effective when administered by specialists such as industrial engineers, they have been shown to be even more so in the hands of empowered line operations employees.

## Pay and Other Incentives

As we have seen, new rules ushered in by dynamic competitiveness have had a profound impact on the ways that companies compensate employees—especially the more cherished ones. Given companies' hesitation to establish a high (fixed cost) salary base, and given employees' demands for less traditional forms of compensation (e.g., flextime, shorter hours, education costs reimbursement, and so forth), pay in the traditional sense *may* be less important than in previous generations. The jury is still out on that question.

Nevertheless, for the foreseeable future at least, wages and salaries will continue to be a key part of the compensation scheme. In this section we look at some concepts about what constitutes fair pay (wages and salaries) and then turn our attention briefly to other forms of compensation.

### *Fair Pay*

Exhibit 12-3 lists eight views of what constitutes fair pay, the rationale for each, and traditional advocates of each type. Note that number 8, gainsharing, is a group pay scheme that may have a variety of names. Types 1 through 7 are for an individual's pay.

The list in Exhibit 12-3 is not necessarily exhaustive, nor are the categories completely exclusive. One might argue, for example, that pay according to supply and demand (category 5) and pay for knowledge or skills (category 6) overlap. Collectively, however, the list provides insight into what we as a society think about how we are paid for our labors.

### *Other Forms of Compensation*

In a word, *benefits*. Just prior to the beginning of the new millennium, *Worth* magazine collected data from a variety of sources on the benefits question. Exhibit 12-4 shows the most effective (top five) benefits in helping to retain employees, the most common benefits (again, top five) that companies offer, and the top five benefits that are the most desirable ones for employees to receive. The latter rankings are according to John Challenger, CEO of the Chicago-based recruiter Challenger, Gray, and Christmas.

We note that items 1, 2, and 4 are common in the three columns of Exhibit 12-4, indicating that companies and employees are in sync with giving and wanting what have been determined to be in employees' best interests. Differences in items 3 and 5 suggest that companies are offering relative inexpensive perks (in most areas) when employees desire items that might reasonably be expected to cost their employers more. Regarding stock options, deemed to be (third) in employees' best interests, we note that options might play a lesser role in *retaining* employees than in *attracting* them in the first place.

When Congress limited the amount of an employee's salary a company could claim as a deduction to $1 million, it added the proviso that compensation above the $1 million mark that is tied to performance would also qualify. Thus, there is likely to be increased

**Exhibit 12-3 Concepts of Fair Pay**

| *What Is Fair Pay?* | *Who Subscribes to This?* |
|---|---|
| **1. Everyone Paid the Same.**<br>Rationale: We are all created equal; we are all products of our environments and partners in society.<br>Means: High minimum wage applied equally to all. | Organized labor<br>Socialists |
| **2. Pay by the Hour (or Week, Month, Year).**<br>Rationale: Though we are products of our environment, society's work must be done, and work is most easily measured in time units.<br>Means: Have employees punch time clocks, and reprimand them for tardiness. | Supervisors (easy to figure out pay)<br>Organized labor (employees like to "put in their time"—or their time and a half) |
| **3. Pay According to Job Content.**<br>Rationale: It is not the person who should be paid but the position; "heavy" positions should be paid heavily, "light"positions lightly.<br>Means: Job evaluation, using job ranking/classification, point plan, factor comparison. | Personnel managers (requires a large pay-and-classification staff)<br>Bureaucrats; (seems rational and impersonal; fits concept of rank or hierarchy) |
| **4. Pay According to Output.**<br>Rationale: Though we are products of our environment, society's work must be done, and work should be measured in output (not merely time on the job). Output efficiency is based on a count of actual units produced as comparedwith a standard.<br>Means: Piecework, incentive pay, gainsharing. | Industrial engineers<br>Economists |
| **5. Pay According to Supply and Demand.**<br>Rationale: Society's messiest jobs must be done too, and more pay for less desirable jobs is necessary to attract employees.<br>Means: Let the labor market function (or list jobs needing to be done, and set pay according to willingness to do each job—the *Walden II* method). | Some economists (e.g., those advocating below-minimum wages for teenagers)<br>B. F. Skinner (see his book *Walden II*) |
| **6. Pay for Skills and/or Knowledge.**<br>Rationale: Pay system should encourage learning so employees can take "ownership" of their processes and can quickly fix problems.<br>Means: Extra pay for passing tests of mastery of more skills and knowledge. | Many of the best-known companies |
| **7. Incentive Bonus.**<br>Rationale: Signing bonus is necessary in order to secure top talent.<br>Means: One-time extra compensation at initiation of employment. | Many of the best-known companies, especially when timely filling of a key position is critical, or when an executive is recruited |
| **8. Gainsharing Program.**<br>Rationale: Group effort created an organizational gain, so all group members should receive a share in the company's gain.<br>Means: Extra compensation for a limited duration; amount tied to amount of company gain and rules for distribution. | Companies with heavy use of teams and group commitment programs |

**Exhibit 12-4 Employee Benefits**

| *Most Effective Benefits for Retaining Employees* | *Most Common Benefits Offered by Employers* | *Most Desirable Benefits for Employees to Receive* |
|---|---|---|
| 1. Health care | 1. Health care | 1. Health and dental program |
| 2. 401(k) or 403(b) | 2. 401(k) or 403(b) | 2. 401(k) matching |
| 3. Flexible work schedule | 3. On-site parking | 3. Stock options |
| 4. Training cost reimbursement | 4. Training cost reimbursement | 4. Tuition reimbursement |
| 5. Pension | 5. Casual dress | 5. Extra time off |

Source: Adapted from Reshma Memon Yaqub, "Perking Right Along," *Worth Guide to Benefits, Compensation, and Perks*, Winter 1999, pp. 14–19.

emphasis on closer links between performance—or, productivity—and compensation. Indeed, as we mentioned earlier in the chapter, there already exists a broad-level connection between productivity and costs. We look more closely at that relationship next.

## Productivity and Cost

As colorful center for the Los Angeles Lakers, Shaquille O'Neal scores some 30 points per game. He is productive per number of minutes played and, probably, per dollar that he is paid: a quality asset, a bottom-line player. Sports fans judge a basketball player's productivity according to O'Neal's kind of output units (points, rebounds) but are savvy enough also to weigh input units such as game minutes and salary. The National Basketball Association might prefer to judge the productivity of a "Shaq" in number of fans per game who come to see him and his team; Shaq's team fills arenas all around the league.

Whether you consider the din of shouting fans, clanking factory machines, humming office equipment, or babbling customers, the bottom line for operations management is usually output units compared with input units. The measures are used for performance appraisal, recognition, reward, and motivation for continual improvement. Therefore, getting the units right is important to every department, team, and associate.

### *Misplaced Blame*

A modern view is that far too much blame—for cost, scrap, rework, delays, and so forth—has been heaped on frontline employees. In manufacturing, direct labor now averages less than 15 percent of operating cost. A century ago, when direct labor amounted to over 50 percent of operating cost on average, emphasis on labor variance made more sense. Today, overhead costs are commonly over five times the cost of direct labor. While a complete cost-variance system includes overhead cost, overhead includes too many diverse elements for an overhead variance to have much impact; managers therefore have fixed their attention on the labor-variance data.

There are other reasons, besides the shrinking direct-labor cost component, for questioning the classic cost-variance measurement system. One is the realization that quality, not just output, is a key to competitive advantage. Another is the wholesale reorganization of resources (reengineering) that has been taking place in many businesses: away from fragmented and toward product- or customer-focused. This paves the way to simpler, more meaningful measures of performance. A third is overlapping job responsibilities: Front-liners are assuming first responsibility for quality, good workplace organization, upkeep of equipment, data collection and diagnosis, problem solving, and, sometimes, interviewing and training new employees. Formerly, those activities were treated as indirect labor, supervision, and overhead. Fourth, conventional productivity systems require an extensive amount of data. For example, some systems require expenses to be assigned to minute budgetary codes. Others require data on when an associate starts and completes work for a given client or job, and commonly the associate works for several clients or jobs every day.

An alternative outlook favors lumping together all labor costs, not tracking labor job by job, or separating direct labor from other payroll costs. As frontline associates team up with experts and managers, dividing lines blur, and so do the old labor-cost categories. For example, a Westinghouse plant in North Carolina was reorganized into several product-focused miniplants, each of which became a new, smaller, more-focused cost center. Employees' pay is automatically charged to the miniplants to which each is assigned; once a week supervisors simply turn in an exception report noting any absenteeism or overtime hours.[18]

### *More Effective Productivity Measures*

While productivity measurement has often become cumbersome, costly, and ineffective, there are plenty of examples of simple, useful ones. (See "New Productivity" in the Contrast box.)

• *Retailers.* A widely used measure is sales per square foot. Stu Leonard's food stores and Circuit City electronic stores rate exceptionally high on this scale. Under this measure, store managers and sales associates become more attuned to customer needs—for example, for quality, quick service, and attentiveness—because these factors bring

CONTRAST

## Productivity

| **Old Productivity** | **New Productivity** |
|---|---|
| Narrow, fractionated: On the output side, emphasis is on operations (rather than whole products). On the input side, focus is on direct-labor cost, charged to operations and departments (not to products or customers). | Broad, integrated: On the output side, focus is on whole products or subproducts. On the input side, all human-resource and other operating costs are included and related to whole products or specific customers. |

in business. On the other hand, if stores are rated on sales per salesperson, managers might tend to cut staff, resulting in declining service and, finally, less business.

• *Accounting, legal, and consultancy firms.* A common measure is billable hours (an hour of time billable to the client) per professional associate. This measure, again, reflects ability to attract customers. Moreover, it gives managers and professionals room to be real operations managers, that is, to weigh the value of different types of staffing, equipment, training, thoroughness, after-sale service, and so forth.

• *Manufacturers.* Harley-Davidson, the motorcycle manufacturer, is among the vanguard of producers shifting toward new, team-oriented productivity and quality measures. Two of the company's new measures are motorcycles per employee and total conversion cost per bike.[19] Formerly, like most other manufacturers, Harley computed productivity separately for each of its many work centers and departments. The new, simple, overall measures encourage these units to work together, and they support Harley's extensive efforts to eliminate inventories between departments and to merge the formerly separated processes into product focused cells. Effects of these improvements show up clearly and directly in the new measures of performance for a whole motorcycle.

These examples illustrate measures that are effective, unifying, and simple:

• *Effective.* The measures are directed toward business activity, customers, and the products or services themselves. Less effective are measures of resource activity instead of business activity, and functions rather than products and customer allegiance.

• *Unifying.* The aim is to include not just frontline labor but all operations and operating costs.

• *Simple.* The new thinking: Complex data collection, person by person, job by job, function by function, is out; using already-available data is in.

Even the best single measures of performance, however, are insufficient. In superior companies, the expectation is that each employee will contribute in many more ways than just "doing the job." The idea is to directly control the causes of cost, rather than monitor costs after the fact . . . a point we made in Chapter 10.

## Productive Resources

We have identified some common, noncost ways of evaluating the productivity of various resources. Terms like *efficiency, busyness* and *idleness,* and *utilization* can be used loosely; they also have precise meanings and can be measured numerically. Examples follow, first for equipment and other nonhuman resources; then for people.

### *Equipment Utilization*

A general formula for **utilization** of labor or equipment is:

$$\text{Utilization} = \frac{\text{Time in use}}{\text{Time available}} \tag{12-2}$$

**EXHIBIT 12-5 Equipment Utilization Trend Report**

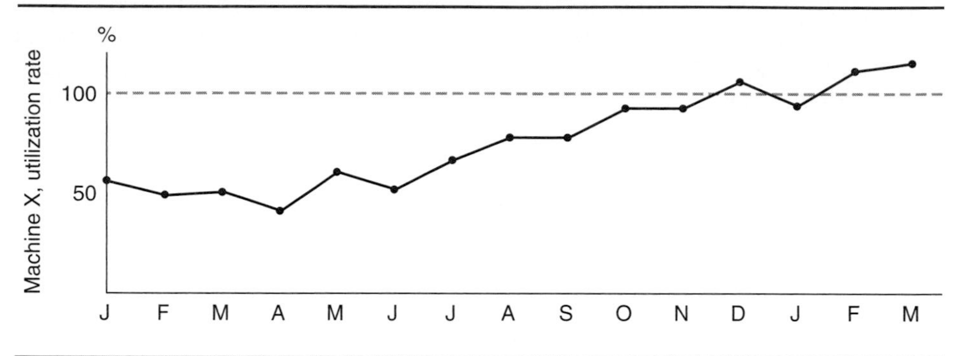


Equipment utilization reports, expressing Equation 12-2 as a percentage, are common in larger companies. For some equipment, 40 hours (one shift operation) is used as available hours per week. Sometimes two or more shifts are the basis. Data for the reports sometimes can be collected automatically by timers in the vehicle, conveyor line, data terminal, medical device, or other equipment.

The machine utilization report has at least three purposes. First, it serves as a check on how well the plant and the company plan in advance for the right capacity. Second, trends in utilization suggest when more capacity will be needed so that equipment can be ordered in advance. Third, when the report shows decreasing utilization, that suggests the need for sales promotions or for rethinking the purpose for having the unutilized capacity.

Exhibit 12-5 shows a machine utilized over 100 percent on a one-shift basis; that means the machine is run on overtime, extra shifts, or weekends, which may require payment of overtime wages. The company might have seen the trend months earlier so that another machine or a larger machine was put on order and is due in soon.

With today's mood of questioning virtually everything in operations management, the utilization report has come under fire. Harley-Davidson has simply eliminated equipment utilization reports. Why? Because the reports can cover up certain faults and result in treating symptoms, not causes. The next list points out potential weaknesses in equipment utilization reports or the way the reports are used:

- High utilization can be achieved by disposing of slow equipment and running all jobs on new, fast machines. But old, slow equipment can be valuable when considering moving equipment into cells or other focused zones within a building.
- Utilization may include bad time (e.g., a copier making blank or wrinkled copies) or get-ready and setup times. If the firm adds capacity when equipment is engaged in such ineffective activities, poor habits set in.
- High utilization may be achieved by running very large lots, which produce unneeded inventories and lengthen cycle times.
- Utilization reports can encourage dabbling in peripheral services to keep equipment busy; over time, the facility becomes unfocused.

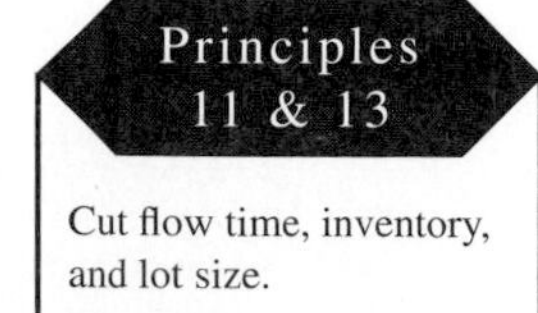


Cut flow time, inventory, and lot size.

- Utilization is usually measured in hours, when the real concern should be utilization of capital (return on investment).
- Finally, and perhaps most important, 100-percent utilization is not even desirable. For example, no computer center wants its mainframe to be 100 percent utilized, because the effect would be long backlogs, interminable delays in getting jobs run, and anxious customers squabbling for priority.

### *Labor Utilization*

For the labor resource, it is common to keep track of absences resulting from illness, jury duty, military duty, labor-union activities, tardiness, and so forth. Each of these eats into productive time.

More specifically, the utilization formula, Equation 12-2, also works for the human resource.

Assume, for example, that a five-person office group spends 2,000 minutes at work on an assortment of 38 jobs (such as letters and reports) in an eight-hour day, which for five people is 2,400 minutes ($8 \times 60 \times 5$). The utilization, from Equation 12-2, is

$$\text{Utilization} = \frac{\text{Time working}}{\text{Time available for work}}$$

$$= \frac{2{,}000}{2{,}400} = 0.83, \text{ or } 83 \text{ percent}$$

And what about the other 400 minutes of the 2,400-minute day? We should not be too quick to label it idleness. The five office associates might use that time for worthwhile activities such as cross-training or teaming up on improvement projects.

The utilization formula is simple, but it requires data on time working. An efficient, proven approach for getting those data is work sampling.

### *Work Sampling*

A **work-sampling study** yields data on percentage of time working, idled, or delayed. Further, the study team can subdivide the idleness into categories, thereby showing process bottlenecks. Example 12-1 illustrates.

#### Example 12-1: WORK SAMPLING—PATHOLOGY LAB

The director of Midtown Pathological Labs is concerned. Costs are going up rapidly; the staff has plenty to do, yet is often idled by assorted problems. The director decides to probe the sources of delay by conducting a one-week work-sampling study. Of special interest are lab equipment failures, supply shortages, delays waiting for instructions, excessive coffee breaks, and lab technicians absent from the work area. The director prepares a work-sampling data sheet that includes those five categories of delay (plus an *other* category); she also works up a schedule for taking 100 sample observations (20 per day).

The schedule and completed form are shown in Exhibit 12-6. The results, the staff not working 35 percent of the time, confirm the director's impression of serious delay problems. The breakdown into categories of delay yields insight as to causes.

**EXHIBIT 12-6 Work-Sampling Data Sheets—Midtown Pathological Labs**

SCHEDULE OF OBSERVATION TIMES

| Mon. | Tues. | Wed. | Thurs. | Fri. |
|---|---|---|---|---|
| 8:01 | | | | |
| 8:13 | | | | |
| 9:47 | | | | |
| 9:59 | | | | |
| 10:12 | | | | |
| 10:59 | | | | |
| 11:16 | | | | |
| 11:32 | | | | |
| 1:00 | | | | |
| 1:15 | | | | |
| 1:19 | | | | |
| 2:52 | | | | |
| 2:55 | | | | |
| 2:56 | | | | |
| 2:57 | | | | |
| 3:02 | | | | |
| 3:29 | | | | |
| 3:37 | | | | |
| 4:07 | | | | |
| 4:32 | | | | |

WORK-SAMPLING FORM

| Category of activity | Observations (tallies) | Percentages |
|---|---|---|
| Working | 65 | 65% |
| Not working: | | |
| • Equipment failure | 3 | 3% |
| • Supplies shortage | 6 | 6% |
| • Wait for instructions | 9 | 9% |
| • Coffee break | 13 | 13% |
| • Out of area | 2 | 2% |
| • Other | 2 | 2% |
| Total | 100 | 100% |

The management system can be blamed for the first 18 percent of nonworking time. Equipment failure (3 percent), supply shortages (6 percent), and wait for instructions (9 percent) are management failures to provide technicians with resources for keeping busy.

The 13 percent of delay for coffee breaks is an employee problem. Authorized coffee breaks are a 15-minute morning break and a 15-minute afternoon break. This amounts to 30 minutes or, in percent of an eight-hour day:

$$\frac{30\text{ min}}{8\text{ hr.} \times 60\text{ mins./hr.}} = 0.0625 \approx 6\text{ percent}$$

The coffee-break abuses may be dealt with immediately. The data on resource shortages do not offer a solution, but they do tip off the director on where to look.

Besides delay statistics, work sampling yields the complement, utilization rate. As we have seen, utilization (65 percent in the example) means busyness—hours busy divided by hours available. But most of us are very busy at times and not so busy at others. To avoid bias, the analyst doing work sampling must take care to do the study in a representative time period—representative of average conditions, if that is the goal, or representative of very busy conditions if peak periods are being examined. Ways of avoiding other types of bias, including insufficient sample size, can be found in basic industrial engineering books.

### Labor Efficiency

Human labor is a unique resource that is not merely utilized. Unlike the nonhuman kind (e.g., equipment and materials), the human resource has a will; it can choose to work at a normal pace or much faster or slower than that. Later, we shall see how to find out what normal, or standard, pace is. For now, we'll examine one of the uses of standard time—determining **labor efficiency,** which is done in one of two ways:

**standard time**
The time a fully qualified person is expected to need to complete a task under normal conditions.

$$\text{Efficiency} = \frac{\text{Standard time per unit}}{\text{Actual time per unit}} \quad \text{or, simply,} \quad \frac{\text{Standard time}}{\text{Actual time}} \tag{12-3}$$

$$\text{Efficiency} = \frac{\text{Actual units per time period}}{\text{Standard units per time period}} \quad \text{or, simply,} \quad \frac{\text{Actual units}}{\text{Standard units}} \tag{12-4}$$

Note that the two versions are mathematically equivalent; each is an inversion of the other.

**Efficiency for Nonuniform and Uniform Products.** We may illustrate by returning to our five-person office team, which turned out 38 jobs yesterday. Assume that 34 is the standard output per day (for five people). According to Equation 12-4,

$$\begin{aligned}\text{Efficiency} &= \frac{38 \text{ actual units/day}}{34 \text{ standard units/day}} \\ &= 1.12, \text{ or } 112 \text{ percent}\end{aligned}$$

To use Equation 12-3, the data must be converted to time per unit. Say that in their 2,400 minutes, the office staff actually spends 1,900 minutes at work on the 38 completed jobs. The other 500 minutes include coffee breaks, cleanup, improvement meetings, and time off for someone to visit a dentist. Then,

$$\begin{aligned}\text{Standard time} &= \frac{1{,}900 \text{ minutes/day}}{34 \text{ standard units/day}} \\ &= 55.9 \text{ minutes/unit}\end{aligned}$$

and

$$\begin{aligned}\text{Actual time} &= \frac{1{,}900 \text{ minutes/day}}{38 \text{ actual units/day}} \\ &= 50.0 \text{ minutes/unit}\end{aligned}$$

Then, by Equation 12-3,

$$\begin{aligned}\text{Efficiency} &= \frac{55.9 \text{ minutes/unit}}{50.0 \text{ minutes/unit}} \\ &= 1.12 \text{ or } 112 \text{ percent}\end{aligned}$$

In this example, the 38 jobs (letters, reports, etc.) are not uniform. Thus, the standard time of 55.9 minutes represents an average job, but of course some jobs could take all day and others just a few minutes. With such a nonuniform product, an efficiency measure still can be meaningful, but only if it covers a sufficiently long time period, in which the mix of complex and simple jobs would tend to even out. One day and 38 jobs are not enough for a fair efficiency reading. Monthly reporting would be more acceptable. (See other examples for nonuniform operations in the Into Practice box "Efficiency . . .")

Fairness becomes less of an issue when the output units are high in volume and uniform, or nearly so, such as stuffing envelopes in a mass political mailing. A fair efficiency rating, using Equations 12-3 or 12-4, could even be turned out daily (although it is hard to think of reasons for doing so that often).

The matter of uniformity or type of output is itself a productivity measurement issue.

**Measures of Output.** Measuring productive output is not always just a matter of counting envelopes or completed letters and reports. A few other output measures are commonly used in other kinds of operations. Exhibit 12-7 summarizes the measures for the three basic types of operation. (We consider these in Part V.)

As the exhibit shows, in repetitive or continuous operations measuring output simply requires counting completed units that meet minimum quality standards. The count may be in units per day, and the unit of measurement may be pieces, gallons, yards, or numbers of clients. The count may be transformed into yield (good units completed divided by total units started) or variance from (amount short of) quantity scheduled.

In job production, output measurement can be costly and difficult. A parts order may be routed through multiple work centers, with output measured at each. As is shown in Exhibit 12-7, the measurement may include a unit count of clients or documents processed or parts successfully produced (not scrapped). Time of completion is also reported so priorities may be recomputed for upcoming work centers. Periodically, perhaps every two weeks, a report may summarize work moved out after successful completion as compared with work moved into each work center. Another report may show job-order due dates met, which measures the success for all the work centers put together. Percent of completion is a suitable measure where processing time at a given

**EXHIBIT 12-7 Output Measures, by Type of Operations**

| *Type of Operation* | *Output Measures* |
|---|---|
| Continuous or repetitive | Unit count |
| Job | Unit count (work center)<br>Due dates met (job orders)<br>Percent of completion |
| Project | Percent of completion<br>Milestones completed on time<br>Events completed on time |

INTO PRACTICE

## Efficiency and Time Standards for Nonuniform Operation

**Example:** The U.S. Air Force Logistics Command, which operates very large job-shops for aircraft repair, compares accumulated standard times against accumulated clock hours for most of its repair-shop crews (and calculates efficiency using Equation 16-3). The reporting period of two weeks is long enough to include perhaps hundreds of task time standards.

**Example:** Most college libraries use computers to produce catalog cards. A cataloging aide with book in hand enters data about a new book at a terminal, and the data are transmitted to a central library cataloging service center. The center's computer database is searched to find (in the United States) a Library of Congress catalog number for the book. For the search to be successful, the cataloging aide must enter the right data. This can be difficult, for example, for foreign-language books, musical compositions, and government documents.

Managers at one college library set a monthly standard rate (historical) of 300 books per cataloging aide. Aides deeply resented the standard rate because some aides arrived early in the morning in order to fill their carts with easy books, which allowed them to easily exceed 300 books per month. Other aides who liked the challenge of the tough books actually looked worse when the monthly report came out. The solution: distribute books to cataloging aides at random each morning. That way, each receives about the same variety of types of books over a period of months.

work center is long (days or weeks) and the output is not readily countable. Examples are major overhauls and renovations.

Three kinds of output measures listed in Exhibit 12-7 for project operations are percent of completion, milestones completed on time, and events completed on time. Those measures are discussed in connection with project management and the PERT/CPM technique in Chapter 17.

### *Productivity Reporting in Perspective*

Reports on resource productivity tend to proliferate and get out of hand, sometimes to the point where as much is spent on reporting as on paying for the resources. This happened at a Tektronix plant producing portable oscilloscopes. A study revealed that the labor reporting, including data entry, computer processing, error correction, and other steps, was costing as much as the total payroll the labor reports were supposed to control! Needless to say, Tektronix canceled the labor reporting, which eliminated about 35,000 computer transactions per month.[20]

It is staff organizations, such as purchasing, human resources, and accounting, that generate resource reports. Those organizations are input oriented, but they exist only for serving line operations, which are output oriented and customer oriented. But preservation, growth, and power instincts can conflict with the ideal of providing only the resources necessary for use in serving customers. Those instincts tend to result in too much resource management and too many reports. When large organizations fall on hard times, regaining economic health may include cutting staff employees and many of their reports.

Thus far, we have considered cost and noncost approaches to productivity management. Next we examine the time standard, a key source of data for these approaches.

## Time Standards and Their Uses

Work is simply a form of exertion. But a unit of work (such as a job, task, or project) is defined more specifically, including the time taken to perform it.

Sometimes work time is estimated in advance. For example, in a two-person operation, if person B must wait for person A to finish a job, B will want an advance estimate of how long A's job will take. A and B as an improvement team may want to time their operations as part of a process-improvement project. Others may want time estimates in order to judge whether A and B can handle the work or will need help (more staff). Still others may use these times in preparing an estimate or bid. In addition, the existence of time estimates is likely to have motivational value—a target for A and B to shoot for.

To summarize, we have identified five purposes of time standards (time estimates): coordination and scheduling, process improvement, staffing, estimating and bidding, and motivation. In the remainder of this section, we examine these five topics.

### *Coordination and Scheduling*

The primary use of time standards is in coordination and scheduling. Actually, by definition, a schedule is a time standard, with proper adjustments for efficiency and utilization; that is, the time between the scheduled start and the scheduled finish of a task equals standard time—the time it should take under normal assumptions:

1. Adjusted downward for a fast employee or upward for a slow employee.
2. Adjusted downward for less than 100 percent labor utilization (i.e., for expected idleness).

Mathematically, scheduled output for a given time period is

$$\text{Scheduled output} = \frac{\text{Efficiency} \times \text{Utilization}}{\text{Standard time per unit}} \tag{12-5}$$

or

$$\text{Scheduled output} = \frac{\text{Standard units}}{\text{per time period}} \times \text{Efficiency} \times \text{Utilization} \tag{12-6}$$

where (from Equation 12-2)

$$\text{Utilization} = \frac{\text{Time working}}{\text{Time available for work}}$$

A useful inversion of Equation 12-5 is

$$\text{Scheduled time} = \frac{\text{Standard time per unit}}{\text{Efficiency} \times \text{Utilization}} \tag{12-7}$$

As Equation 12-7 shows, when efficiency or utilization improve (denominator), scheduled time is reduced.

Where coordination demands are light, formal scheduling of work units may be unnecessary. But there is nearly always at least a vague time plan for starting and finishing an upcoming task.

### *Analysis, Planning, and Motivation*

A second set of uses of time standards includes:

- *Analysis of alternative methods and equipment.* Improvement teams may use time standards in estimating amount of labor required for each alternative.
- *Staffing.* Staff (labor) needed is the product of units forecast times standard time per unit. Labor budgeting goes a step further. Labor budget equals staff needed times average wage.
- *Estimating and bidding.* The staff component of an estimate or bid is computed the same way as the staff budget. Accurate bidding is critical to profitability in project work. Estimates or bids are also important in many kinds of services such as medicine, law, consultancy, and automotive repair.
- *Motivation.* Without a deadline, people tend to put things off. A time standard acts like a deadline, helping to keep people motivated to meet the standard. A weakness is that the time standard may not seem like a real need to employees. People are more likely to respond to a known, valid customer need date or quantity, which itself could be based on a time standard. The motivational value of a time standard also depends on whether people believe it is valid, which depends on the techniques used in developing the standard, our next topic.

## Time Standards Techniques

Exhibit 12-8 lists six ways of developing a time standard. The first four are engineered, which means rigorously developed to a high level of validity. The last two are nonengineered. In this section we consider the differences and go through the details for time study, the most prevalent technique. Discussion of the remaining five techniques is reserved for the chapter supplement.

### *Engineered and Nonengineered Standards*

Four techniques may result in engineered time standards. Engineered standards are prepared at some expense following the scientific methods of the industrial engineer. The expense of an engineered time standard may be worthwhile if precision is needed, for example, in highly repetitive processes, where small gains add up fast. The following steps lead to an engineered standard:

1. Clearly specify the method.
2. Obtain time values via a proper sampling procedure or from validated tables.

**Exhibit 12-8 Techniques for Setting Time Standards**

| *Technique* | *Source of Times* | *Timing Role of Analyst* |
|---|---|---|
| **Engineered** | | |
| 1. Time study | Stopwatch (or film) | Direct observation: Record times for several cycles of the task; judge and record pace. |
| 2. Work sampling | Percent of study period busy at given task divided by number of units produced | Direct observation: Randomly check employee status; keep tallies of employee activities and pace; obtain production count. |
| 3. Predetermined | Table lookup | Define task in basic body motions; look up time values in basic motion tables. |
| 4. Standard data | Table lookup | Define task in small, common elements (e.g., pound nail); look up time value in standard-data tables. |
| **Nonengineered** | | |
| 5. Historical (statistical) | Past records on actual task times | Determine arithmetic mean and/or other useful statistics. |
| 6. Technical estimate (guesstimate) | Experienced judgment | Experienced person estimates times, preferably after breaking task into operations. |

3. Adjust for employee pace.
4. Include allowances for personal, rest, and delay time.

Each step adds precision. A precise time standard is associated with a known standard, preferably improved, method. One way to get precise time values is to use direct observation and a proper sampling procedure; direct observation is avoided by use of a synthetic time value from validated tables. Where direct observation is used, the time value should be adjusted for employee pace, but validated tables for time values have built-in pace adjustments. Finally, the pace-adjusted time is further adjusted by adding reasonable allowances for employees' personal and rest time and for unavoidable delay.

**guesstimate**
Also known as WAG or SWAG, common abbreviations for slightly salty phrases some readers may be familiar with.

The nonengineered techniques, based on history or guesstimates, control none of the above four factors of precision. Even the first four techniques in Exhibit 12-8 are worthy of the term *engineered* only if they are precisely developed following the four steps. In the following discussions, we see how the steps apply for each technique.

### *Time Study*

World War II was the heyday of film analysis. Almost anything that might help the war effort received funding.

The most direct approach to time standards is timing an employee who is performing the task. A stopwatch is the usual timing device, but motion picture film or videotape also works. **Time study** is best for shorter-cycle tasks. The cost of having an analyst at the worksite and timing a proper number of cycles of the task tends to rule out time study for longer-cycle tasks. The four time-study steps are explained next and illustrated in Solved Problem 2 in this chapter.

1. *Select task and define method.* There are choices to be made here. For example, packing and crating a large refrigeration unit consists of packing the unit into a carton, placing the carton on a pallet, building a wooden crate around the carton and pallet, stenciling, and steelstrapping. A single time study of the whole series of tasks is one possibility. Alternatively, analysts could separately time-study each major task, but each of those involves lesser tasks, which could be separately time-studied. Pounding a single nail into a crate could be the task chosen for study.

Once the task has been chosen, the analyst defines the method and its elements. The definition must clearly specify the actions that constitute the start and the end of each element, which is how the analyst knows when to take each stopwatch reading.

2. *Elemental time.* Tools of the time-study analyst include a clipboard, a preprinted time-study data sheet, and a stopwatch. The watch is mounted on the clipboard. Before timing, the analyst observes for a while to be sure the operator is following the prescribed method.

In the timing phase, the analyst records a stopwatch reading for each element. Several cycles of the task should be timed so that effects of early or late readings can be averaged out. Multiple cycles also provide a better basis for judging pace and observing unavoidable delays and irregular activities. Comments on irregularities are entered in a remarks section on the data sheet.

The number of cycles to time could be calculated based on the statistical dispersion of individual element readings. However, most firms pay more attention to the cost of multiple cycles than to the statistical dispersion of readings. For example, General Electric has established a table as a guide to the number of cycles.[21] The table calls for timing only 3 cycles if the cycle time is 40 minutes or more, but it calls for timing 200 cycles if the cycle time is as short as 0.1 minutes. Since 200 cycles at 0.1 minutes adds up to only 20 minutes of observer time, the 200-cycle study may cost less to do than the 3-cycle study of a 40-minute task.

The result of timing is an average **elemental time (ET),** a raw time value.

3. *Pace rating.* If the analyst times a slow person, the average cycle time will be excessive—*loose* is the term usually used; if a faster person is timed, the ET will be tight. To avoid loose or tight standards, the analyst judges the employee's pace during the study. The *pace rating* is then used mathematically to adjust ET to yield a *normal time.* This is called *normalizing.* The normal pace is 100 percent, a 125 percent pace is 25 percent faster, and so on.

Common benchmarks of normal (100 percent) pace:

- Hand motions: Deal four hands of 13 cards in 30 seconds.
- Walking, normal person, unloaded, level surface: three miles an hour.

Pace rating is the most judgmental part of setting time standards, but it need not be pure guesswork. Films from the American Management Association and other sources provide training in pace rating. The films show a variety of factory and office tasks. The same task is shown at different speeds, and the viewer writes down the apparent pace for each speed. Then, with the projector shut off, the viewer's ratings are compared with an answer key. Correct answers have been decided upon by experts or measured by film speed.

Most people can become good enough at pace rating to be able to come within ±5 percent of the correct ratings. It is easier to rate a person who is close to normal than one who is very slow or fast. Because of this, it is a good idea for the analyst to try to find a normal employee to observe in doing a time study (or work-sampling study). Sometimes pace rating is omitted by preselecting an employee who is performing at normal; the omission is illusory since the rating is done in the employee selection step.

4. *Personal, rest, and delay (PR&D).* The normalized time per unit is not the standard time, because we can't expect a person to produce at that normal rate hour after hour without stopping. Personal time allowances (rest room, etc.) and rest allowances (e.g., coffee breaks) may be set by company policy or union contract. In industrial shops, the rest allowance may be for more than coffee; it may go as high as 50 percent for tasks performed in a freezer or near a furnace.

Strictly speaking, unavoidable delay—for example, difficulty in meeting tight tolerances or small variations in materials or equipment—is inherent in the method. Some companies also include certain delays that are beyond the method, such as unbalanced work flows, lack of work, or breakdowns. Unavoidable delays are sometimes determined by a work-sampling study in which occurrences of various types of delay are tallied.

The allowances are usually combined as a percentage, referred to as the *personal, rest, and delay (PR&D) allowance.* The combined allowance is then added to the normalized time, resulting in a standard time.

In the chapter supplement, we briefly discuss four other approaches to determining a time standard: work sampling, predetermined, standard data, and historical. The four basic steps—obtain method, obtain time values, adjust for pace, and add allowances—are common to all the approaches. The main difference is in the way of obtaining the time values.

## Summary Check Points

✓ Productivity is broadly defined as the ratio of outputs to inputs; it is more meaningful if used in comparative fashion or examined over time.

✓ U.S. government reports as well as many business interests see labor productivity as the dominant concern in productivity analysis.

✓ Productivity is a reward for past investments in people and processes, and it is also a promise of things to come.

✓ Many old-line companies are adapting new technology to their existing processes in an attempt to bolster productivity.

✓ The new economy has led to greater tension among employees; talented "in-demand" people seem to have a different set of rules.

✓ To hold down overall labor costs, some companies are asking employees to work longer, using temporary employees, using variable pay, resorting to layoffs, and pushing work offshore.

✓ Job rotation may help companies keep talented personnel who seek career progression.

✓ Increased workforce flexibility appears to be a win-win strategy for employers and employees alike.

- ✓ Formal productivity assessment had its roots in the scientific management era; Frederick W. Taylor, Frank and Lillian Gilbreth, Henry Gantt, and Harrington Emerson made key contributions during that period.
- ✓ Scientific management made many positive contributions to modern-day process improvement.
- ✓ The design of work systems has progressed through three phases: scientific management, job design, and customer serving.
- ✓ A systematic productivity improvement involves job-level and process-level analyses.
- ✓ There are at least eight concepts of what constitutes fair pay; each has its advocates.
- ✓ Employee benefits constitute the "other half" of compensation.
- ✓ Too much blame for productivity problems has been heaped on frontline employees.
- ✓ Cost and labor variance reports have been popular tools for assessment of productivity, but there are more effective measures available.
- ✓ Utilization—time in use over time available—may be applied to equipment or labor.
- ✓ Work sampling is a simple tool for collecting work-status data.
- ✓ Labor efficiency is standard time over actual time, or actual units over standard units.
- ✓ In general, productivity reporting has required too many status reports.
- ✓ Time standards are needed for coordination and scheduling, process improvements, staffing, estimating and bidding, and motivation.
- ✓ Time standards may be engineered (set formally) or nonengineered.
- ✓ Time study is a formal, four-step procedure for setting engineered standards.

## Solved Problems

### *Problem 1*

Gate City Tire sells and installs tires, some by appointment and the rest to drop-in customers. Appointments are carefully scheduled so that (1) the customer may be told when the car will be ready and (2) installers are kept busy. The manager knows that under normal conditions a four-tire installation takes about 20 minutes. The time varies depending on the installer's speed (efficiency) and the delay (utilization) encountered. Gate City follows the concept of under-capacity scheduling: For an 8-hour paid shift, the company schedules 7.3 hours of tire installing.

During the 7.3 hours of assigned work, efficiency has been found to be 90 percent; it is low because the present crew lacks experience. Utilization, again during the 7.3 assigned hours, is 80 percent. Delays arise from tool breakdowns, parts shortages, special customer requests, and two authorized 15-minute coffee breaks; these, plus miscellaneous delays, account for the 20-percent nonutilization time.

Regardless of expected daily output, each daily job may be separately scheduled. For example, the third job of the day, a phoned appointment, is assigned to Jeff, who has been only 80 percent efficient. But, the manager expects no delays for lack of materials, tool breakdowns, or other problems, and it is not near coffee-break time; thus, he expects utilization on this job to be 100 percent.

*a.* Calculate the current scheduled daily output.

*b.* What is the scheduled installation time of the third job of the day, assuming Jeff is given the job?

***Solution 1***

*a.* From Equation 12-6,

$$\text{Scheduled output} = \frac{7.3 \text{ hours} \times 60 \text{ minutes/hour}}{20 \text{ minutes/installation}} \times \frac{90 \text{ percent}}{\text{efficiency}} \times \frac{80 \text{ percent}}{\text{utilization}}$$

$$= 15.768, \text{ or approximately 16 installations per day}$$

*b.* The scheduled installation time, from Equation 12-7 is

$$\text{Scheduled time} = \frac{20 \text{ minutes/installation}}{80 \text{ percent} \times 100 \text{ percent}} = 25 \text{ minutes}$$

***Problem 2***

A proposed bolt-washer-nut assembly method was approved, and a time-study analyst was assigned to develop a time standard for the task. After observation, the analyst has reduced the task to four timable elements. Six cycles are timed by the continuous stopwatch method, and each element is pace rated. Calculate the standard time. (For a short-cycle task like bolt-washer-nut assembly, it would take less than an hour to time, say, 30 cycles, but our six-cycle example is sufficient to illustrate the procedure.)

***Solution 2***

The time-study data sheet is shown in Exhibit 12-9. The analyst reads the stopwatch in hundredths of a minute and does not insert decimal points until after the last computation. The stopwatch begins at zero and runs continuously for 7.55 minutes. The analyst enters continuous readings below the diagonal line, and then computes elemental times by successive subtraction.

Average elemental time (ET) is the sum of elemental times divided by 6; for element 2, ET is divided by 5 because one irregular elemental time was thrown out. The average goes below the diagonal line in the ET column. The analyst judges pace and enters pace ratings in the rating factor (RF) column, with decimal points not included. Normalized time (NT) equals ET times RF. The NT column adds up to 110, or 1.10 minutes per cycle.

The analyst adds a PR&D allowance, which has been negotiated with the labor union. It provides 3 percent personal time (e.g., blow nose), two 15-minute rest (coffee) breaks, and 2 percent unavoidable delay allowance. These are minimum allowances; the contract allows rest time to be set higher for highly fatiguing work, and the delay allowance may be set higher for tasks involving abnormal delays.

The two 15-minute breaks convert to percentage of an eight-hour, or 480-minute, day by

$$\frac{30 \text{ minutes}}{480 \text{ minutes}} = 0.0625, \text{ or } 6.25\%$$

$$\text{Total PR\&D allowance} = 3\% + 6.25\% + 2\%$$

$$= 11.25\%$$

**EXHIBIT 12-9 Time-Study Data Sheet-Bolt—Washer-Nut Assembly**

| | Cycles | | | | | | | | | |
|---|---|---|---|---|---|---|---|---|---|---|
| *Element* | *1* | *2* | *3* | *4* | *5* | *6* | *ET* | *RF* | *NT* | *Remarks* |
| 1. Get bolts and place in fixture. | 12<br>12 | 10<br>116 | 13<br>240 | 11<br>349 | 16<br>468 | 10<br>656 | 72<br>12 | 110 | 13.2 | |
| 2. Get Washers and place on bolts. | 14<br>26 | 16<br>132 | 15<br>255 | 14<br>363 | 93<br>561 | 14<br>670 | 73<br>14.6 | 100 | 14.6 | 5th cycle: Blew nose |
| 3. Get nuts and assemble onto bolts. | 75<br>101 | 86<br>218 | 77<br>332 | 82<br>445 | 79<br>640 | 78<br>748 | 477<br>79.5 | 95 | 75.5 | |
| 4. Drop assemblies down chutes. | 05<br>106 | 09<br>227 | 06<br>338 | 07<br>452 | 06<br>646 | 07<br>755 | 40<br>6.7 | 100 | 6.7 | |

| **Calculations** | | |
|---|---|---|
| | Total normalized time | 110.0 |
| | × (PR&D allowance + 100%): | × 111.25% |
| | **Standard time** | 122.375, or 1.22 minutes/unit |

In a final computation, the analyst multiplies the total normalized time by the PR&D allowance of 11.25 percent plus 100 percent (which is mathematically the same as adding 11.25 percent of the total normalized time). The result is the standard time of 1.22 minutes per unit.

## Exercises

1. The president of Universal Service Corp. is concerned. His company is in serious financial trouble, even though its cost system (roughly the same system most other firms use) shows that labor costs have been going down significantly for months. How would you advise the president?
2. Visit the web site for the U.S. Bureau of Labor Statistics and review the Quarterly Labor Productivity frequently asked questions (http://stats.bls.gov/lprfaq.htm). What difficulties does the BLS have in measuring productivity? Discuss.
3. Laws in many countries require division of company employees into management and labor, with different employment laws for each. For decision-making purposes, however, some companies have abolished these categories. Hewlett-Packard, for example, considers everyone overhead, with no separate category called direct labor.
   *a.* What is the effect of this practice on measuring labor productivity?
   *b.* Discuss the advantages and/or disadvantages of this practice.

4. "Equal pay for equal work" was the hot pay issue in an earlier era. Next came "Equal pay for comparable work." With which concept(s) of fair pay (from Exhibit 12-3) does the comparable-work idea seem most consistent? Explain.
5. You report to your new job where your boss says, "Keep your equipment utilization up . . . 95 percent or better if you can." What concerns would you have about this policy? Explain fully.
6. Thumb's Tax Service has grown by 45 percent per year for the last three years, and now has 42 tax offices supported by a company headquarters of 13 people (tax specialists, computer programmers, marketers, etc.) along with a range of computer equipment. Thumb's profits, however, have been weak to nonexistent. Everyone suspects the reason is Thumb's costing, which leads to pricing in which difficult private and commercial clients pay an average of only 35 percent more than easy ones.
   *a.* What operating decisions at a tax service like Thumb's require good cost data? In your answer, explain what costs are needed.
   *b.* How can Thumb's management team resolve the costing problem?
7. At International Express Company, professionals and technicians from the industrial engineering, (IE) department and the quality assurance (QA) department are engaged in a turf battle. The IEs are claiming that they are the experts in flowcharting and methods improvement and should retain that responsibility. The QA specialists are claiming they should now have the responsibility. Who is right? Explain.
8. Three key monthly reports reviewed by officers at Nanosoft Inc., a software development firm, are (1) utilization of Nanosoft's six copying machines; (2) utilization of labor, including clerical, machine operators, analysts, and programmers, based on work sampling studies covering a different office area each month; and (3) utilization of books, reports, and documents in the Nanosoft library. Discuss the probable effectiveness of these reports. Should anything be changed in this reporting system? Explain.
9. (See MTM discussion in this chapter supplement.) A salesperson has an order for 1,000 candles in the shape of an athletic team's mascot. Production control assembles the following data from the candlemaking shop, to be used in setting a price (direct cost and overhead plus markup):

| | |
|---|---|
| Elemental time | 20,000 TMUs |
| Allowance for personal time and unavoidable delay | 9% |
| Authorized break time | 20 minutes per day |

   Recent candlemaking statistics are

| | |
|---|---|
| Total clock hours for candlemakers | 350 hours |
| Standard hours' worth of candles produced | 380 hours |

   *a.* What standard time should be used in computing standard cost?
   *b.* If there are two employees in candlemaking, how many hours should be scheduled for them to complete the order for the 1,000 special candles?

*c.* Assume the candle order has been finished and took 190 hours to complete. What rate of efficiency did a crew attain?

10. The director of a social agency is preparing next year's budget. The agency's caseload averaged 42 clients per day last year, but it has been increasing at an annual rate of 18 percent. The director and caseworkers agree that it takes 3.5 hours on average to handle each client properly.
    *a.* How many caseworkers should be requested as the staff component of next year's budget assuming the 18-percent increase in caseload? Assume that caseworkers work an average 250 days per year (which allows for vacation days, sick days, etc.) at eight hours per workday.
    *b.* What kind of time standard is the agency using? Is there any way to improve this?
    *c.* What other reasonable uses exist for the time standard?
11. Assume your boss is supervisor of the packing and crating department and has just sent you the following memo: "The president wants all shops, including ours, covered by time standards. I'd like you to do a preliminary study to see if reasonable time standards can be set for our type of work. Everything we pack is of a different size. So how can we have standard times?"
    *a.* Respond to the boss's memo.
    *b.* What technique for setting time standards is best for this type of work? Explain.
12. In an automobile plant, a time-standards analyst finds that the average elemental time for mounting tires onto rims is 3.6 minutes. If the personal, rest, and delay allowance is 12 percent and the pace rating 111 percent, what is the standard time?
13. An MTM analyst predicts that installing a cord on a proposed new telephone set will take 4,250 TMUs.
    *a.* What is the standard time in minutes if the shop allows a 20 percent PR&D allowance? (See MTM discussion in chapter supplement.)
    *b.* How can the analyst set a standard on a proposed telephone set? Doesn't the item have to actually exist? Discuss.
14. An employee in an electronics plant is using a lugging machine to attach a connector onto the end of a wire. (The machine automatically kicks the wire into a chute once the connector has been attached.) The following data are provided by a time-study analyst. Stopwatch readings are in hundredths of a minute and cumulative from element to element and cycle to cycle.

| | **Cycle** | | | | |
|---|---|---|---|---|---|
| *Job Element* | *1* | *2* | *3* | *4* | *Pace Rating* |
| Cut length of wire | 21 | 48 | 74 | 103 | 100 |
| Insert into lugger and press start button | 30 | 58 | 86 | 112 | 90 |

*a.* What is the standard time? Assume a personal time allowance of 5 percent, a delay allowance of 3 percent, and two 20-minute coffee breaks per eight-hour day.
*b.* What would be the advantage in using methods-time-measurement (MTM) instead of stopwatch time study? (See MTM discussion in chapter supplement.)

15. A work sampling study has been conducted for the job of spray-painting a set of parts. The job consists of mounting the parts on hangers, then spraying them. The PR&D allowance is 20 percent. The analyst's tally sheet is shown below:

Job: Spray painting — Time period: Five 8-hour days

| *Activities Sampled* | *Tallies* | *Total* | *Work Count* | *Pace Rating* |
|---|---|---|---|---|
| 1. Mount | 𝍸 𝍸 𝍸 𝍸 𝍸 𝍸 | 30 | 20 | 110 |
| 2. Spray | 𝍸 𝍸 𝍸 𝍸 𝍸 𝍸<br>𝍸 𝍸 𝍸 𝍸 | 50 | 20 | 120 |
| 3. Nonwork | 𝍸 𝍸 𝍸 𝍸 | 20 | | |
| | Total | 100 | | |

*a.* What is the elemental time for each task? (See work-sampling discussion in chapter supplement.)
*b.* What is the rated time for each task?
*c.* What is the standard time for each task?
*d.* What is the value of the data on nonwork time? How could the data be improved to make them more useful?

16. A supervisor has done a work-sampling study of a subordinate, a clerk-typist. The purpose was to set time standards for typing letters and retrieving letters on file. Therefore, those two tasks were tallied on the work-sampling tally sheet, along with a miscellaneous category for all other clerk-typist activities. The complete tally sheet is as follows:

Subject: Typist — Tasks: Typing letters and retrieving letters on file
Dates: November 29–December 10 (10 working days) — Analyst: Clerical supervisor

| *Activities Sampled* | *Tallies* | *Total Count* | *Percentage Rating* | *Work Count* | *Pace Rating* |
|---|---|---|---|---|---|
| 1. Type letters | 𝍸 𝍸 𝍸 𝍸 𝍸 𝍸 𝍸 𝍸 𝍸 𝍸 𝍸<br>𝍸 𝍸 𝍸 𝍸 𝍸 𝍸 𝍸 𝍸 𝍸 𝍸 𝍸 | 110 | 55% | 60 | 90 |
| 2. Retrieve letters | 𝍸 𝍸 𝍸 𝍸 𝍸 𝍸 | 30 | 15 | 150 | 80 |
| 3. Miscellaneous | 𝍸 𝍸 𝍸 𝍸 𝍸 𝍸 𝍸 𝍸 𝍸<br>𝍸 𝍸 𝍸 | 60 | 30% | — | — |
| | Totals | 200 | 100% | | |

*a.* PR&D allowance is 10 percent. Compute elemental time, rated time, and standard time for each task. (See work-sampling discussion in chapter supplement.)
*b.* Discuss the possible uses of these time standards.
*c.* Comment on the fairness and/or validity of these time standards. Are they engineered?

17. Mailroom associates at an insurance company prepare all of the company's premiums and letters for mailing. A time study has been done on the job of enclosing premium statements

*Solution*

Serum test:
From Equation 12-8:

$$\text{Elemental time} = \frac{0.30 \times 5 \text{ days} \times 480 \text{ minutes/technician-day} \times 2 \text{ technicians}}{48 \text{ tests}}$$

$$= 30 \text{ minutes per test}$$

From Equation 12-9:

$$\text{Standard time} = \text{ET} \times \text{RF} \times (100 \text{ percent} + \text{PR\&D})$$
$$= 30 \times 90 \text{ percent} \times 113 \text{ percent}$$
$$= 30.51 \text{ minutes per test (per technician)}$$

Whole-blood test:

$$\text{Elemental time} = \frac{0.25 \times 5 \text{ days} \times 480 \text{ minutes/technician-day}}{32 \text{ tests}}$$
$$= 18.75 \text{ minutes}$$

$$\text{Standard time} = \text{ET} \times \text{RF} \times (100 \text{ percent} + \text{PR\&D})$$
$$= 18.75 \times 105 \text{ percent} \times 113 \text{ percent}$$
$$= 22.25 \text{ minutes per test}$$

Are these precise (engineered) time standards? The technicians in the chemistry lab don't think theirs is. They point out to the director that their method is to run the serum tests in batches and as a two-person team. There could be one or many samples in a batch, but the time to run a batch does not directly depend on the number of samples in it. The time standard for serum testing is imprecise, indeed, invalid, because the work-sampling study was not precise as to method.

The hematology technician has a milder objection: A mere 25 observations of the whole-blood testing were extrapolated into an assumed 600 minutes of testing time during the week. While the sample size seems rather small, the technician and the director decide that the standard time of 22.25 minutes per test is usable for short-term capacity adjustments. These include scheduling overtime, using part-time help, and subcontracting to other labs.

For example, on a given day, perhaps 30 blood samples will arrive and require testing in hematology. At 22.25 minutes per test, the workload is $22.25 \times 30 = 667.5$ minutes of testing. Since an eight-hour day is only 480 minutes, the director had better tell the technician to plan on some overtime that evening. Part-time help and subcontracting are other options.

## Predetermined Standards

Predetermined time standards really are only partially predetermined. The predetermined part is the tables of time values for basic motions. The other part is properly selecting basic-motion time values in order to build a time standard for a larger task.

Basic-motion tables were Frank Gilbreth's idea, but it took some 35 years of effort by many researchers to develop them, mostly through film analysis. The best-known tables are those of the

MTM (Methods-Time Measurement) Association.[22] Our limited discussion focuses on **methods-time measurement (MTM).** MTM and other synthetic techniques have several advantages:

1. No need to time; the data are in tables.
2. No need to observe; the standard may be set before the job is ever performed and without disrupting the employee.
3. No need to rate pace; the time data in the tables were normalized when the tables were created.

Other predetermined time systems not requiring so much detail:

- Work-Factor.
- MODAPTS.

A disadvantage of MTM is the great amount of detail involved in building a standard from the tables. Basic MTM motions are tiny; motions are measured in *time measurement units (TMUs),* and one TMU is only 0.0006 minutes. A 1.0-minute cycle time equals 1,667 TMUs. One MTM motion usually takes 10 to 20 TMUs; thus, about 80 to 160 basic motions would be identified in the 1.0-minute period. Although much training is required of the analyst to achieve that detail, MTM is preceived as a fair approach to time standards and is widely used.

The MTM Association has developed tables for the following types of basic motions: reach; move; turn and apply pressure; grasp; position; release; disengage; eye travel and eye focus; body, leg, and foot motions; and simultaneous motions. Again, most times were developed by film analysis.

One of the tables, the reach table, is shown in Exhibit S12-1. From the table we see, for example, that reaching 16 inches to an "object jumbled with other objects in a group so that search and select occur" takes 17 TMUs. That motion, abbreviated as an *RC16* motion, takes about 0.01 minutes or less than a second.

In an MTM study, the analyst enters each motion on a simultaneous motion (SIMO) chart, which is a left-and-right-hand chart. The total TMUs on the chart are converted to minutes. The total is the rated (leveled) time, not the elemental time, because 100 percent pace is built into the tables. Add a PR&D allowance, and you have the standard time.

## Standard Data

**Standard-data** standards, like predetermined (e.g., MTM) standards, are synthetically produced from tables. But standard-data tables are for larger units of work. An example is the flat-rate manuals used in the auto-repair industry. Flat-rate tables list times for repair tasks such as "replace spark plugs" and "change oil." Auto manufacturers produce such tables for repairs on new cars. Flat-rate manuals for older cars, which take more time to repair, are available from independent companies. Best known are the Chilton manuals.

If precise time study, work sampling, or MTM is the basis for the tables, the standard data may be considered to be engineered. It is normal for a firm to keep time standards on file, and it is just one more step to assemble standards from the files into standard-data tables. The next step is to assemble standard data for a whole trade or industry. This has been done in auto repair and other common trades, notably machining and maintenance trades.

The standard-data tables come in several levels. Basic motions (e.g., MTM) are the most detailed level. Next come combinations of basic data (e.g., MTM Association's general-purpose data), such as a joint time for reach-grasp-release. Then come elemental standard data for common elements, like gauging and marking. Standard data for still larger units of work are at the level of whole tasks, such as those of auto repair mechanics or electricians.

Variable working conditions and lack of common methods from firm to firm may compromise the built-in precision of standard data. Still, standard data are efficient in that they bring time standards down to the level of the planner, the supervisor, and the operator. Experts create the tables, but we all can use them.

**Exhibit S12-1 Reach Table for MTM Analysis**

| | Time in TMUs* | | | | Hand in Motion (TMU) | | |
|---|---|---|---|---|---|---|---|
| *Length of Reach in Inches* | *Case A* | *Case B* | *Case C or D* | *Case E* | *A* | *B* | *Case and Description* |
| $\frac{3}{4}$ or less | 2.0 | 2.0 | 2.0 | 2.0 | 1.6 | 1.6 | A—Reach to object in a fixed location or to object in other hand or on which the other hand rests. |
| 1 | 2.5 | 2.5 | 3.6 | 2.4 | 2.3 | 2.3 | B—Reach to single object in location that may vary slightly from cycle to cycle. |
| 2 | 4.0 | 4.0 | 5.9 | 3.8 | 3.5 | 2.7 | C—Reach to object jumbled with other objects in a group so that search and select occur. |
| 3 | 5.3 | 5.3 | 7.3 | 5.3 | 4.5 | 3.6 | D—Reach to a very small object or where accurate grasp is required. |
| 4 | 6.1 | 6.4 | 8.4 | 6.8 | 4.9 | 4.3 | E—Reach to indefinite position to get hand in position for body balance, next motion, or out of way. |
| 5 | 6.5 | 7.8 | 9.4 | 7.4 | 5.3 | 5.0 | |
| 6 | 7.0 | 8.6 | 10.1 | 8.0 | 5.7 | 5.7 | |
| 7 | 7.4 | 9.3 | 10.8 | 8.7 | 6.1 | 6.5 | |
| 8 | 7.9 | 10.1 | 11.5 | 9.3 | 6.5 | 7.2 | |
| 9 | 8.3 | 10.8 | 12.2 | 9.9 | 6.9 | 7.9 | |
| 10 | 8.7 | 11.5 | 12.9 | 10.5 | 7.3 | 8.6 | |
| 12 | 9.6 | 12.9 | 14.2 | 11.8 | 8.1 | 10.1 | |
| 14 | 10.5 | 14.4 | 15.6 | 13.0 | 8.9 | 11.5 | |
| 16 | 11.4 | 15.8 | 17.0 | 14.2 | 9.7 | 12.9 | |
| 18 | 12.3 | 17.2 | 18.4 | 15.5 | 10.5 | 14.4 | |
| 20 | 13.1 | 18.6 | 19.8 | 16.7 | 11.3 | 15.8 | |
| 22 | 14.0 | 20.1 | 21.2 | 18.0 | 12.1 | 17.3 | |
| 24 | 14.9 | 21.5 | 22.5 | 19.2 | 12.9 | 18.8 | |
| 26 | 15.8 | 22.9 | 23.9 | 20.4 | 13.7 | 20.2 | |
| 28 | 16.7 | 24.4 | 25.3 | 21.7 | 14.5 | 21.7 | |
| 30 | 17.5 | 25.8 | 26.7 | 22.9 | 15.3 | 23.2 | |

*One time measurement unit (TMU) represents 0.00001 hour.

Source: MTM Association for Standards and Research. Copyrighted by the MTM Association for Standards and Research. No reprint permission without written consent from the MTM Association, 16–01 Broadway, Fair Lawn, New Jersey 07410.

## Historical Standards and Technical Estimates

Nonengineered techniques—historical and technical estimates—are far more widely used than engineered techniques, and rightly so. Most of our work (or play) is variable, and the cost to measure it with precision is prohibitive. Still, explicit time estimates help improve management, and nonengineered techniques serve the purpose. Historical standards and technical estimates are simple to develop and need not be explained further.

CHAPTER 13

# MANAGING MATERIALS: TIMING AND QUANTITIES

In this chapter, we continue our Part IV discussion of operations resources but shift our focus from human resources to materials. **Materials management** incorporates a broad set of activities related to acquiring, moving or handling, storage, and control or monitoring of materials. Thus, purchasing, distribution, and other supply-chain management duties could be included.

We have considered purchasing relationships in Chapter 6 and supply-chain management in several chapters, and touch on those topics lightly in this chapter. The bulk of our focus here, however, lies on **inventory management**—actions taken to manage the company's materials assets after the contractual relationships with suppliers are in place, but (generally) prior to distribution downstream. Inventory management is, of course, a major component of materials management. We start with some basics.

## Inventory Management Fundamentals

Because inventories are essential to operations, most chapters in this book contain some inventory-related terms or concepts. We will save topics that relate more directly to type of operations environment for Part V, but let's briefly summarize what we have covered thus far and add a few more fundamentals.

In our discussion of demand management in Chapter 4, we learned that an inventory may be **independent** or **dependent.** We address both kinds in the pages ahead. We also spoke of **aggregate** versus **item demand;** our primary focus in this chapter is on items—the specific part numbers, if you will. In Chapter 6, we also addressed classification of inventory items according to aggregate value—the **"ABC" system.** And, in Chapter 10, we considered **inventory turnover ratios** as indicators of flow-control system performance. Recall that flow-through inventories—those destined to move on to downstream customers—are classified as **raw materials,** then as **work-in-process (WIP),** and finally as **finished goods** as they move through the transformation processes. The final class of inventory—maintenance, repair, and operations **(MRO) items**—is for internal consumption.

In some organizations (warehouses and retail outlets, for instance), inventory control consumes a great deal of management's attention. Clearly, many inventory issues related to stocking, display, stock rotation, security, and so on are relevant in those settings, but specific "how-to" discussion of those matters is beyond our scope. Two fundamental decisions are part of *every* inventory management system, however, and as the chapter title reflects, *are* squarely within our focus:

1. **Inventory timing**—deciding when to place an order for replenishment of an item, and
2. **Lot-sizing**—deciding the quantity, that is, how many of that item to order.

Inventory timing and quantity decisions are influenced by other factors that we have covered: push- or pull-mode operations, process flexibility and responsiveness, demand pattern stability, quality, and design. Effects of these and related OM factors emerge throughout the remainder of the chapter.

Finally, as the techniques that we examine in this chapter reveal, inventory timing and quantity concerns are themselves related. We start with an older but highly valued tool in which quantity refers not so much to size of order as to how much is left in stock when an order is placed.

## Reorder Point (ROP)

Inventory timing with **reorder point (ROP)** is probably as old as humanity (maybe older; some animals, such as squirrels, also replenish low stocks). The ROP provides for replenishing stocks when they reach some low level. Let's look at some ROP variations.

### *Perpetual Inventory System*

The classic use of the reorder point occurs in a **perpetual inventory system.** Perpetually—every time an issue is made—the stock on hand is checked to see whether it is down to the ROP. If it is, someone places an order. In the informal case, stock clerks perpetually examine the physical stock level itself. More formally, a records clerk or a computer examines the balance on a stock record.

Reorder points are part of our personal lives. We may reorder (go out to get) postage stamps when we have only three left, or we may buy a new half gallon of milk when there is about two inches left in the old container. Sometimes we get reminders from the manufacturer: the desk calendar or box of personal checks containing a reorder notice.

### *Two-Bin System*

A version of the perpetual reorder point called the two-bin system is often used in small stockrooms. Two adjacent storage bins hold a single item, and users are told to withdraw from bin 1 first. The rule is this: When the first bin empties, place an order. The second bin contains the ROP, a quantity that covers the lead time for filling the order and may allow for some additional buffer or safety stock.

There are many variations. A colored sheet of paper may be inserted in a stack of forms on a shelf to show when the ROP (the second bin) has been reached. Indirect material, such as washers, screws, and nails, is often placed in trays on assemblers' workbenches; a painted line partway down inside the tray can designate the ROP. Transistors, diodes, and so on, are often stored in corrugated boxes on shelves; a small box

**EXHIBIT 13-1 Two-Bin (Kanban) System at Upright-Ireland**

in the larger box may be used to contain the ROP (the second bin). Exhibit 13-1 shows two component parts (left side and right side of a bin) controlled by a two-bin system at Upright-Ireland. At Upright, the two-bin system is an element of JIT, which covers virtually all of Upright's parts, bought or made. When an associate breaks into the second bin, that is the kanban signal to order another package.

The two-bin system works best when one person is in charge of the stockroom or is in charge of a daily check to see which items are down to the ROP. Otherwise, people can get too busy to note the need for an order; associates can blame each other if the second bin is emptied but no one has reordered.

In firms with partial computer control of inventories, a bar code strip can be affixed to bin 2. Then, when bin 2 is entered, it is easy to initiate the reorder. Just scan the bar code, which holds identifying data. People are less likely to forget to order when ordering is so simple.

## *ROP Calculation*

Planners and buyers may set the reorder point (the quantity in bin 2) by judgment and experience or by an ROP formula. Judgment would tend to follow the concepts embodied in the basic ROP formula:

$$ROP = DLT + SS = (D)(LT) + SS \qquad (13\text{-}1)$$

where

$ROP$ = Reorder point (a quantity on hand when order is made)

$DLT$ = Demand during lead time

$SS$ = Safety stock (or buffer stock)

$D$ = Average demand per time period

$LT$ = Average lead time (from order placement to receipt of goods)

ROP calculation is simple, but it does require reliable numbers if it is to be trusted. The planner or buyer often uses recent averages for demand rate and replenishment lead time. Safety stock could be set judgmentally or by using a formula; more on how to do that after we consider two ROP examples.

### Example 13-1: ROP CALCULATION—FUEL OIL EXAMPLE

Assume that a building heated by fuel oil consumes an average of 600 gallons per year and the average lead time is two weeks. Thus:

$$D = 600 \text{ gallons per year}$$
$$LT = 2 \text{ weeks/52 weeks per year} = 0.04 \text{ year}$$
$$DLT = (D)(LT) = (600)(0.04) = 24 \text{ gallons}$$

Then, if desired safety stock is 40 gallons:

$$ROP = DLT + SS = 24 + 40$$
$$= 64 \text{ gallons}$$

## *Replenishment Cycle*

In Example 13-1 an average demand rate of about 24 gallons is based on an average replenishment lead time of two weeks. Average values tend to smooth things out, masking the existence of stock outages and inventory peaks. Example 13-2 provides a more realistic picture of ROP replenishment cycles.

### Example 13-2: REPLENISHMENT CYCLES FOR DISCRETE DEMAND—RADIATOR CAP EXAMPLE

Radiator caps are issued in discrete units; that is, you cannot issue half a radiator cap. (In contrast, a continuous item like fuel oil can be issued in fractions of a gallon.) Exhibit 13-2 shows two replenishment cycles for radiator caps. The graph shows a stairstep depletion pattern. It also shows early and late order arrivals, including a case in which backordering occurs.

In the first cycle, radiator caps start out being issued at a slow pace (i.e., slower than past average demand). In the fourth time period there is a spurt, and at the end of the period stock on hand drops below the ROP. An order is placed. During lead time, stock issues begin slowly, then speed up in periods 6 and 7. All radiator caps are gone by the beginning of period 7, and orders still come in.

The shaded zone below the zero line indicates orders unfilled because of the stockout condition, caused by the combination of slow delivery (greater-than-average lead time) and a late spurt in demand.

The second cycle begins when the order arrives in period 7. The order quantity (lot size) brings the stock level up from zero to $Q$ units, and the backorders are immediately filled, dropping the stock level somewhat. The stock depletion rate is about average through period 10. In period 11, demand for radiator caps surges. The surge continues into period 12, and it reduces stock to below the ROP. An order is placed.

**backorder**
Order accepted when stock is out.

**EXHIBIT 13-2 ROP Replenishment Cycles—Radiator Cap Example**

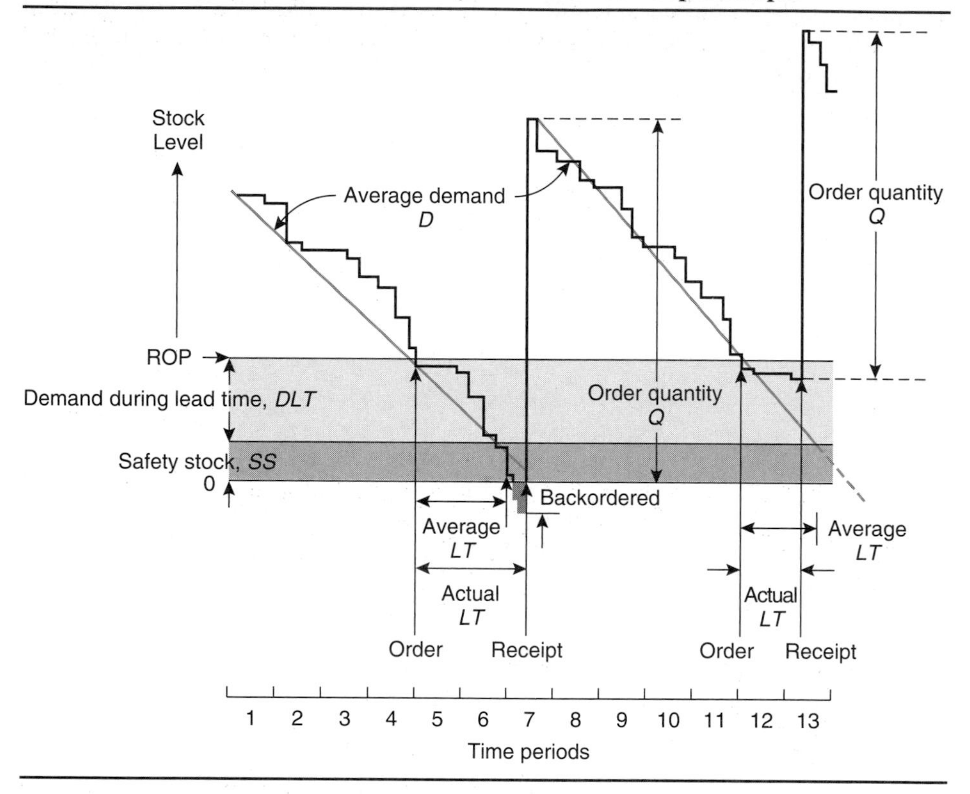


This time, delivery is faster than average (see actual *LT* as compared with average *LT*), and there is little demand during the lead-time period. The result is little use of the *DLT* quantity and no use of the *SS* amount. Stock is high when the order quantity ($Q$) arrives. The order arrival pushes up the stock level to near the maximum possible, which is the ROP plus $Q$.

## *Periodic System*

The ROP method of replenishment requires perpetual checking of the balance on hand. Why not just check the balance at fixed time intervals? The periodic system does just that. The regularity in order intervals makes the periodic system popular with retailers, who often set up a schedule of checking stock levels in slack periods each day, once a week, or perhaps monthly.

Often the periodic system of timing orders is combined with maximum–minimum quantity criteria. For example, a grocery store might periodically reorder laundry soaps, with two days as the order interval. The maximum shelf space, and therefore maximum inventory, for one item—say, Whiter-White Detergent—might be four cases, and the desired minimum, one case. The periodic system works like this:

1. Check stock of Whiter-White on Monday, Wednesday, Friday, and so on.
2. If shelf stock is below one case, reorder enough to bring the stock as close to four cases as possible without exceeding that amount.
3. If stock is above one case, don't reorder.

Note that the minimum is really a reorder-point quantity used in conjunction with the reorder-point interval; the maximum governs what the lot size must be in order to bring stock up to the maximum level.

## Buffer Stock (Safety Stock)

Regardless of the system used for inventory timing, keeping customers well served is difficult. Consumption and output rates vary, and stoppages, accidents, and natural disasters sometimes disrupt operations. These difficulties lead managers to rely on protection in the form of buffer stocks, also called safety stocks.

Factory people tend to call it buffer stock: a buffer between one machine and the next. To retailers and wholesalers, where reorder points are most common, it's safety stock.

Even well-run just-in-time operations and quick-response programs must rely somewhat on buffer stocks. Buffer stock, a special class of inventory, is like the spare tire in your auto or your homeowner's insurance policy: You hope you don't need it, but you don't dare operate without it. Buffer stock is expensive, however, and needs careful management.

In Chapter 5, we introduced the concept of offline buffer stock, which provides protection but does not consume throughput time. Sometimes it is appropriate to calculate the quantity of buffer stock; the calculation procedure and comments about its limitations round out our discussion of careful buffer-stock management.

### *Statistical Safety Stock*

In retailing and wholesaling, safety (buffer) stock must be far greater than in dependent demand situations. Customers must be served, but their demands for a given item tend to be highly variable. Fortunately, demand variability and customer service can be expressed in numbers. Manipulate the two numbers (the desired customer-service level and the demand-variation level) in a certain way, and the result is a calculated statistical safety stock.

The first step is to decide on the desired customer **service level.** Among the many possible definitions of service levels, the following is popular: the percentage of orders filled from stock on hand, also called **fill rate.** That, plus its converse, the **stockout rate,** must equal 100 percent. For example, a planned service level of 0.98 means that customer orders would be filled 98 percent of the time, with a stockout the remaining 2 percent of the time.

Safety stock is calculated from service level by the following formula (assuming independent demands, normally distributed):

$$SS = z\sqrt{LT(SD)^2} \tag{13-2}$$

where

$SS$ = Safety stock

$z$ = Value from normal distribution table (see Appendix A), based on service level

$LT$ = Lead time

$SD$ = Standard deviation of demand

(Note: *LT* and *SD* must be stated in the same time units; for example, if *SD* is calculated based on variability over one-month time periods, *LT* must be expressed in months.) Example 13-3 illustrates.

### Example 13-3: Safety Stock—Loaves of Bread

Assume that mean demand for bread at your house is 100 slices per week and that demand varies by a standard deviation of 40 slices per week. The desired service level is 97.72 percent. It takes just one day to replenish the bread supply. How much safety stock should you carry? What is the reorder point?

*Solution*

All data must be in the same time units. Thus, replenishment lead time of one day is converted to 1/7 week.

The service level, 0.9772, represents a probability: 0.50 (the left half of the area under the normal curve) plus 0.4772. We look for 0.4772 in Appendix A and find it where $z = 2.00$. From Equation 13-2:

$$SS = z\sqrt{LT(SD)^2}$$
$$= 2.00\sqrt{1/7(40)^2} = 30.2 \text{ slices.}$$

and, from Equation 13-1:

$$ROP = (D)(LT) + SS$$
$$= (100)(1/7) + 30.2 = 44.5 \text{ slices}$$

## *Perspective on Buffer Stock*

Unfortunately, the statistical safety stock method omits factors that affect safety stock. One is the effect of lot size. Large lot sizes act as buffer stock; if the lot size is very large, a calculated statistical safety stock will be insignificant (compared with the buffering effects of the large lots) and not worth calculating. Small lot sizes have the opposite effect, which suggests keeping larger safety stocks on hand than the calculated statistical quantity.

In retailing and wholesaling, lot sizes normally are moderate, which means that the statistical model is valid enough. Exceptions are hard-to-get items or items from undependable suppliers. In those cases, the main concern may be with variable supply, but the statistical model focuses on variable demand.

The same types of limitations restrict use of the statistical model in setting buffer stocks for semifinished factory materials and other dependent-demand items. The big problems are the variabilities in supply (the maker).

Other miscellaneous factors that affect buffer stock are:

*Cost.* For very costly items, keep very little (even zero) buffer stock on hand. For low-cost items (washers, paper clips), keep perhaps as much as a year's worth.

*Space.* If the item is very bulky, keep the buffer stock small, and vice versa.

*Consequences of a stockout.* Sometimes a wide variety of options, such as substitute items, are available in the event of a stockout; in such cases, keep the buffer stock small.

*Obsolescence.* In high-tech industries, large buffer stocks mean large obsolescence costs; thus, keep buffer stocks small.

With so many factors not present in the model, how can the model be effectively used? To answer this question, let's consider a company that takes particular pride in its high service level. The centerpiece of Frito-Lay's corporate culture is its ability to provide its customers with a 99.5 percent service level.[1] Current-demand data (captured by bar-code scanning or collected by Frito-Lay's 10,000 store representatives) go into company computers, which calculate demand, standard deviation of demand, safety stock, and reorder point for each product. Armed with computer listings of calculated ROPs for each item, product managers can decide whether to change any ROPs in light of other safety-stock factors such as cost and space.

The reorder point technique can be an effective tool for timing decisions. And as we noted with the detergent example, lot size (quantity ordered) range may be determined by the situation, shelf space in that example. In other instances, however, we desire more freedom in determining how many to order at any one time. That is, we want more lot-sizing flexibility.

## Lot Sizing: Fundamentals

A **lot** is a group of items processed, transported, and/or tracked as a unit. In manufacturing, items within a lot are typically meant to be identical. In services, lot items may differ from one another to a greater degree, but they usually share a common flow sequence. In this section, we first see how lots form and examine the specifics of lot-size effects on throughput times. Then we explore benefits of lot-for-lot operations, look at examples of how lot sizing might be used, and conclude with an overview of lot sizing in practice.

We've already noted some of the ways lot sizes affect operations. In Chapter 10, for example, we saw how lot size can affect work flows, quality, and costs.

### *Lots and Throughput Times*

Often, people create lots purposefully, but on other occasions lots just seem to appear. The grouping of items into lots is a reality in both manufacturing and service operations.

**Lots in Manufacturing.** Sometimes, a manufacturing order quantity is deliberately set at a specific size, say 500 units. Justification for that lot size hinges on the economics of production; it goes something like this: Item X is produced in a 500-unit vat, so whenever we issue a production order for Item X, the lot size will be 500 units, regardless of how many we actually need at the time. The higher the setup time and cost—that is, the *less* quick-change flexibility a company enjoys—the more sense this sort of thinking seems to make.

**Lots in Services.** Lot sizing issues are also plentiful in the offices of Poge, Poge, Perry, and Wacker. In accounts receivable, Cheryl typically spends mornings on problem accounts. In the afternoon, she turns her attention to the ever-present pile of new invoices in her in-basket and completes as many as she can. Just before quitting time, she drops the finished invoices off at Jim's desk—in his in-basket—for subsequent processing. And so it goes throughout the company: Each employee sensibly accumulates a reasonable pile of items to work on before attacking the pile, and sensibly accumulates a reasonable load before passing it to the next stop.

**throughput time**
Time required to complete a processing sequence.

Regardless of how or why lots are created, however, they can have adverse effects on operations and on customer service. First, lots generally increase throughput time. Exhibit 13-3 illustrates, using three different lot sizes, in a simple process that could fit either manufacturing or service situations.

*Case 1, Six Pieces:* In the first case assume that a lot of six pieces moves as a unit through the three-station process from left to right. In stations I and III, processing is sequential, one piece at a time. In station II, the entire lot may be processed simultaneously. For simplicity, assume processing time is two minutes at each station, and transport times between stations and to the final customer are each one minute. Therefore,

**EXHIBIT 13-3 Lot Size and Throughput Time**

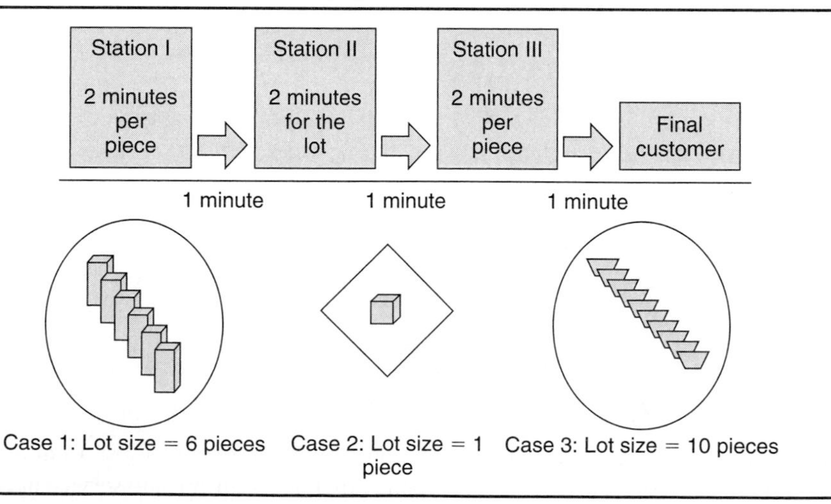

each piece in the lot has a throughput time of 29 minutes, consisting of

- 6 minutes processing (2 minutes at each of the three stations).
- 3 minutes transport (1 minute for each of three transports).
- 10 minutes waiting time, station I (2 minutes for each of the other 5 pieces in the lot to be processed).
- 10 minutes waiting time, station III (again, 2 minutes for each of the 5 other pieces in the lot).

*Case 2, One Piece:* Suppose the lot size was one rather than six. The piece could move through the process to the final customer in nine minutes—no waiting at stations I and III for processing of other pieces.

*Case 3, Ten Pieces:* Now, let's go the other way, and increase the lot size, to say, 10 pieces. Piece processing times and transport times are unaffected, but total waiting time increases from 20 minutes to 36 minutes, that is, 18 minutes each at station I and at station III. This waiting time—36 minutes when the lot size is 10—is attributable to our decision to process and transport work pieces in lots, and is referred to as **lot delay.**[2] Here, lot delay increases throughput time to 45 minutes (6 + 3 + 36).

Large lot sizes also increase throughput times in other ways. Examine Exhibit 13-3 again. Suppose a lot, *Y*, arrives at station III for processing, but must be held up while another lot, *X*, is being finished. Lot *Y* is undergoing **process delay.** Although the *occurrence* of this process delay might be the result of poor planning or schedule mix-ups, its *duration* will depend on the size of the lot being worked on in station III. So, a portion of process delay may also be attributed to lot sizes.

Let's summarize: In sequential processing environments, lots increase throughput times. Thus, the Poge, Poge, Perry, and Wacker employees are missing the consequences of their so-called reasonableness. Lot and process delays emerge due to the in-basket piles. Lengthened throughput times for order processing drive customers to competitors. Moreover, delayed invoice processing creates unwanted disruptions in cash flow—customers can't be expected to pay until they know what they owe. Unfortunately, these inefficient practices are common in firms such as law offices, banks, insurance companies, government agencies, hospitals, and manufacturing companies. The necessary remedy? Cut process and transfer lot sizes—aim to smooth the flow of work. In Exhibit 13-3, the eventual goal might be to process one piece at station I then pass it on to station II while the second piece starts at station I.

**process lot**
Lot undergoing a value-adding transformation.

**transfer lot**
Lot being transferred (moved) to the next value-adding transformation.

But what about simultaneous processing situations, like station II in Exhibit 13-3 or the vat used to produce Item X? As we see next, lots can cause a different kind of trouble in these cases.

## *Lot-for-Lot Operations*

In **lot-for-lot processing,** demand drives lot sizes. More specifically, the lot size produced for a period equals the net demand for that period. As we shall see later in the chapter, lot-for-lot works well in the parent–component dependency chains of materials requirements planning (MRP). It is also an effective lot-sizing policy for JIT environments.

Furthermore, lot-for-lot may be passed down through several stages of supply: "The customer bought four premium tires, so we pulled four from stores, and they ordered four from our distributor, who ordered four from the manufacturer." With no batching into larger lots, orders are frequent. Internet buying can keep ordering costs low; inventories are low and supplier activities closely match real demand. Also, the synchronizing and smoothing effects of lot-for-lot, as compared with batching, stand out. Consider, for example, two sizes of canned food items, apple juice and apple sauce, and two layers of components going into those end products.

Exhibit 13-4A shows a smooth demand pattern for the four products at the canning level. The smooth pattern is carried downward to apple processing and to apple picking.

**Exhibit 13-4 Lot-for-Lot versus Batched Ordering**

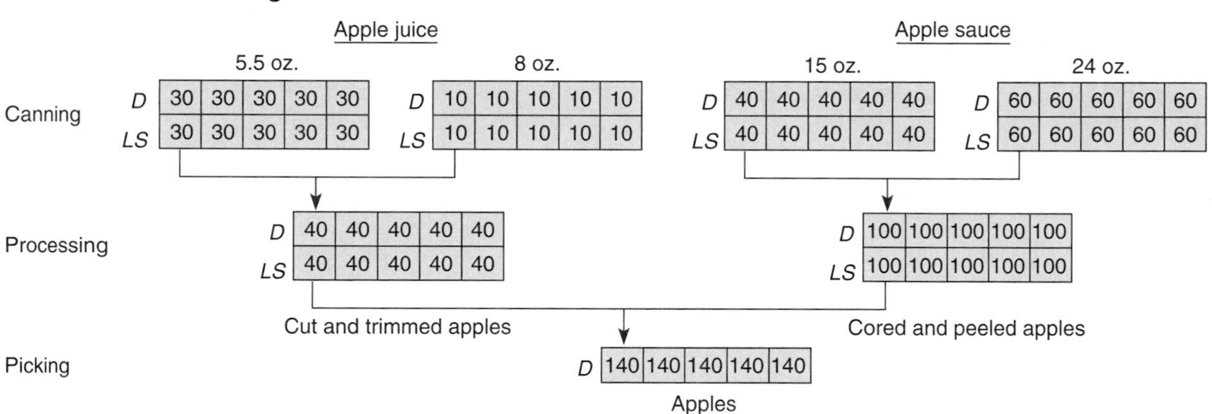


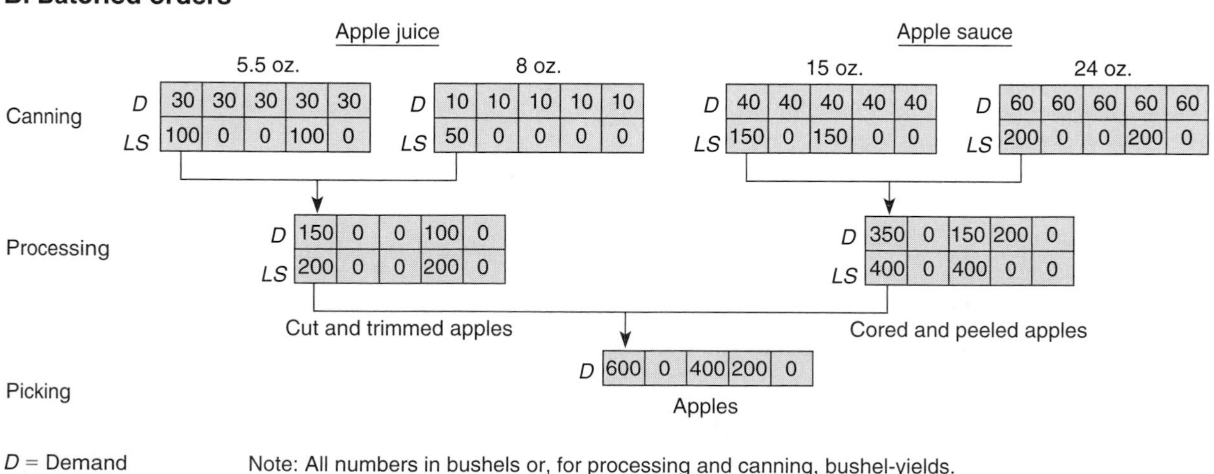


*D* = Demand
*LS* = Lot size

Note: All numbers in bushels or, for processing and canning, bushel-yields.

INTO PRACTICE

## When Large Lots Are Required

Firms such as drug and medical-device manufacturers are required by government regulations to conduct lot-acceptance sampling inspections. This involves testing a statistical sample drawn at random from a larger lot. According to statistical sampling tables, as lot size increases, the percent sampled from the lot gets smaller; therefore, larger lots save on inspection costs. Thus, inspection department managers are motivated to delay sampling until a large lot accumulates.

However, this practice can be frustrating to other managers striving for the just-in-time ideal of making and forwarding items in small lots at the customer's use rate. Gradually, regulations and policies are being rewritten in favor of on-line process control, which is more effective in controlling quality than acceptance sampling, and more JIT friendly.

An obvious benefit is the uniform workload for apple pickers, apple processing associates and equipment, and apple canning line operators and equipment; capacity planning is simple, and capacity may be kept uniformly busy, with little or no overtime or idleness.

The buying of cans, labels, boxes, sugar, and other ingredients and supplies is also uniform. Scheduling and purchasing may be greatly simplified, perhaps to the point where schedules are simply a daily rate, with no need for separate orders and order follow-up for each lot. Queue limitation and kanban might be easily introduced. When even demand is passed back to outside suppliers, they can pass it back through some of their own operations, thus cutting their costs, which can mean price reductions to our apple company.

In Exhibit 13-4B we see a much different pattern. The canning is done in batches, which are fixed in quantity and in excess of daily demand. Maybe somebody has decreed, "Let's can on Monday, Wednesday, and Thursday, and try to save Tuesday and Friday for maintenance on the canning line." But what may be good policy for canning certainly is not good for apple processing, which now has lumpy demands (150, 0, 0, 100, and 0 for cut and trim; 350, 0, 150, 200, 0 for core and peel).

Processing also decides on fixed-batch lot sizes (200 and 400, respectively) that are larger than, and unsynchronized with, parent demands. Those lot sizes become an even lumpier demand pattern for the apple pickers (600 on Monday, none on Tuesday, 400 on Wednesday, 200 on Thursday, and none on Friday). If the pickers can find steadier work, they will surely leave.

This example makes a strong case for keeping lot sizes from growing (but see the Into Practice box for a qualified exception), and for trying to maintain the synchronization inherent in the lot-for-lot approach.

### *Economic Order Quantity*

Unlike lot-for-lot ordering, which uses actual period demand, other lot-sizing models depend on demand forecasts, which are, in turn, often based on past average demand. The economic order quantity (EOQ) is such a model, and may be appropriate for management of a single inventory item. The reorder point, presented earlier, also depends on past average demand. While EOQ and ROP are sometimes studied as a set, we prefer to point out that EOQ may be used with a variety of order-timing methods, and in turn, ROP is usable with various lot-sizing methods.

A little rusty on EOQ formulas? The chapter supplement provides some help, as do end-of-chapter solved problems.

In this section, two examples demonstrate how the EOQ might be applied. The first uses the basic model and the second incorporates quantity discounts.

### Example 13-4: ECONOMIC ORDER QUANTITY—BOOKSTORE

B. K. White, manager of Suburban Books, is thinking of purchasing best-selling titles in economic order quantities. White has assembled the following data:

| | |
|---|---|
| Inventory on hand (books): | |
| Estimated average last year | 18,000 |
| Estimated average cost per book | $10 |
| Average inventory value | $180,000 |
| Annual holding cost: | |
| Rental: Building and fixtures | $36,000 |
| Estimated shrinkage loses | 3,500 |
| Insurance | 2,500 |
| Total | $42,000 |
| Annual capital cost: | |
| Capital invested (tied up in books) | $180,000 |
| Interest rate | 15% |
| Total | $27,000 |
| Annual carrying cost (Annual holding cost + Annual capital cost) $42,000 + $27,000 | $69,000 |
| Carrying cost rate, $I$ (Annual carrying cost ÷ Inventory value) $69,000/$180,000 | 0.38 |
| Purchase order processing cost, $S$ | $12 per order |

*Solution*

Now White has the cost data needed to calculate EOQs. He selects his biggest seller as the first book to be ordered by EOQ—*Gone with the Wind,* which is enjoying a burst of renewed popularity in the store. The paperback recently sold at a rate of 80 copies per month and wholesales for $5 per copy. Thus, for the EOQ equation:

$$C = \$5 \text{ per unit}$$
$$D = 80 \text{ units/month} \times 12 \text{ months/year} = 960 \text{ units/year}$$
$$I = 0.38$$
$$S = \$12$$

Then, using Equation S13-2 (from supplement),

$$EOQ = \sqrt{\frac{2DS}{IC}} = \sqrt{\frac{2(960)12}{0.38(5)}} = 110 \text{ copies/order}$$

White's assistant, M. B. Ainsworth, cannot resist pointing out to her boss a fallacy in this policy. She puts it this way: "Mr. White, I'm not so sure that *Gone with the Wind* is the right book to order by EOQ. The EOQ is based on last month's demand of 80. But demand might be 120 next month and 150 the month after. Maybe we should use EOQ only on our stable sellers in hardcover. How about Webster's *New Collegiate Dictionary?*"

Users may employ variations on the basic EOQ to offset some of the model's limiting assumptions. One variation incorporates quantity discounts as Example 13-5 shows.

## Example 13-5: EOQ WITH QUANTITY DISCOUNT—PETSTORE

U.R. Spot, manager of Happy Pets, has applied basic EOQ to dog leashes, but didn't allow for quantity discounts. Dogworld, Inc., offers the following price breaks for leashes.

| *Quantity Range* | *Price per Leash* |
|---|---|
| 1–48 | $5.00 |
| 49–96 | 4.70 |
| 97 and up | 4.40 |

Other data include:

$$I = 0.25$$

$$S = \$4 \text{ per order}$$

$$D = 960 \text{ units/year } (12 \times 80)$$

*Solution*

Following the procedure from Example S13-2 in the supplement, Spot's first step is to calculate the EOQ using the best available price—$4.40 in this case:

$$EOQ_{4.40} = \sqrt{\frac{2DS}{IC}} = \sqrt{\frac{2(960)(4)}{(0.25)(4.40)}} = 84$$

Since 84 is not within the appropriate quantity range (97 or more), Spot computes the EOQ with the next price option, $4.70:

$$EOQ_{4.70} = \sqrt{\frac{2DS}{IC}} = \sqrt{\frac{2(960)(4)}{(0.25)(4.70)}} = 81$$

The order quantity, 81, is within the appropriate range of 49–96, so Spot is ready to calculate total annual cost, first at the EOQ of 81 and then at the order quantity that would allow him to take advantage of the next price break. Using Equation S13-1 from the chapter supplement:

$$\text{Total annual cost} = \frac{\text{Annual order}}{\text{processing cost}} + \frac{\text{Annual}}{\text{carrying cost}} + \frac{\text{Annual}}{\text{purchase price}}$$

$$= \frac{D}{Q}(S) + IC\left(\frac{Q}{2}\right) + DC$$

$$\text{Total annual cost}_{81} = \frac{960}{81}(4) + 0.25(4.70)\left(\frac{81}{2}\right) + 960(4.70)$$

$$= 47.41 + 47.59 + 4{,}512 = \$4{,}607.00$$

$$\text{Total annual cost}_{97} = \frac{960}{97}(4) + 0.25(4.40)\left(\frac{97}{2}\right) + 960(4.40)$$

$$= 39.59 + 53.35 + 4{,}224 = \$4{,}316.94$$

Thus, the true economic order quantity is 97, since its total annual cost, \$4,316.94, is less than the total of \$4,607.00 for a quantity of 81.

Exhibit 13-5 is a sketch of the cost–volume pattern. It shows that annual order-processing cost drops smoothly and is not affected by the quantity discounts. The annual carrying-cost line

**EXHIBIT 13-5 Annual Cost Graph of Lot Sizes with Quantity Discounts**

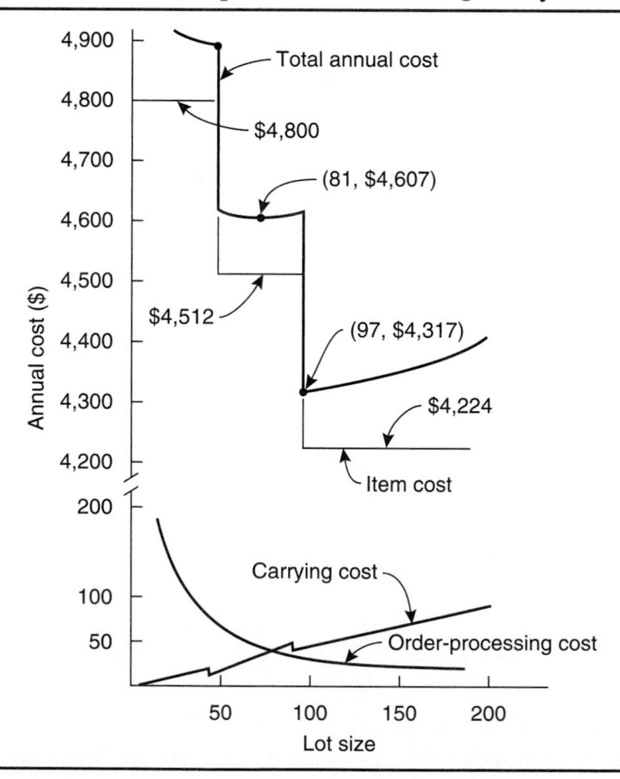

has two small bumps, one at each price break. The annual item cost plunges at each price break, and those effects are dominant in the makeup of total annual cost. The feasible EOQ of 81 at a unit price of $4.70 is not economical compared with the true economic order quantity of 97 at the $4.40 price break.

### *Preference for Simpler Models*

There are more elaborate lot-sizing algorithms than those just discussed. The problem with some of the models that look good on paper, however, is that they require cost calculations for future periods, which means reaching into the future for a demand forecast. But we saw in Chapter 4 that forecasting accuracy drops the further into the future one projects.

Ready access to computers allows any of the lot-sizing models to be run dynamically; that is, lot sizes can be recomputed every time demand projections change. The effect, however, is unstable planned lot sizes. Ever-changing forecasting signals cause the entire inventory planning and control system to become nervous. Costs of replanning, rescheduling, and other shuffling of resources generally outweigh any apparent lot-sizing savings.

Thus, many feel that one lot-sizing method is as good as another. Historically, the simpler models, such as lot-for-lot and basic EOQ, have been preferred in business. The preference for simpler models continues today and probably will in the future, judging by the findings of a large-scale survey.[3] Researchers surveyed firms that provide MRP software to over 25,000 worldwide manufacturing locations. They found that lot-for-lot is the most commonly used lot-sizing technique, fixed-order-quantity is second, fixed-period-quantity is third, and EOQ fourth. The users' rationale for choosing the simple models includes (1) simplicity, (2) employee acceptance, (3) recognition that real-world conditions tend to deny any savings predicted by more complicated optimization models, and (4) realization that lot sizing is not nearly so important as taking steps to drive lot sizes down.

**fixed-period-quantity**
A lot-sizing model that sets order quantity equal to projected net requirements for a given time period.

## Lot Sizing under Attack

Today, with just-in-time and total-quality-management zealots looking for waste under every rock, some rethinking about lot-sizing models is taking place. Instead of asking, What is the economic lot? the new question is, What must be changed to move toward piece-for-piece, or lotless, operations? As we consider that question, we must bear in mind that some of the business world and much of the nonprofit world still is not very JIT/TQM-minded, and therefore some of the fundamentals of lot sizing continue to have a useful role.

We begin our discussion of the pursuit of lotless operations by taking a look at reducing transfer lots. Next, we consider some of the benefits and methods of lot-size reduction and conclude with a synopsis of contemporary thinking about lot-sizing economics.

### *Transfer Lot Reduction*

While process lot sizing has received plenty of attention, transfer lot sizing tends to be overlooked. Actually, though, much of the logic that supports process lot-size reduction (OM Principle 13) also applies to transfer lots.

The rationale for transfer lot-size reduction is simple. Recall from the discussion of Exhibit 13-3, we suggested an improvement target that went something like this: After the first piece is processed at station I, send it on—apart from the rest of its lot—to station II. Were the logic followed throughout the process, a rushed customer could receive output in nine minutes, before the process lot (now down to five pieces) had left station I.

In Exhibit 13-4A, lot-for-lot is the policy for process lots. The transfer lots, however, can be larger or smaller than the process lots. For example, the process lot of 140 bushels per day in picking might be transferred to processing in sublot quantities of 20 bushels every two hours, assuming two seven-hour shifts.

Large tour groups are often handled in much the same way. If a group of 100 college freshmen are to tour the library, the tour leader will break them up into, say, five groups of 20, and stagger the start times as several tour guides lead the groups through the building.

Would transfer of apples from the orchard to processing every two hours be reasonable? It depends on the distance, the content of the lot, and the mode of transport. For apples, a golf cart or other small vehicle might be efficient for delivering 20 bushels every two hours from orchard to plant. If competition requires cutting the transfer lots even more, how about a processing unit on the back of a truck, which follows the pickers through the orchards? Even some railroad freight haulers are striving for smaller lots; see the Into Practice box "Smaller Trains at Conrail."

To summarize,

1. The economic justification for cutting transfer lots is innovation-based reduction of handling costs, which is similar to reducing the cost of changeovers in the case of process lots.
2. Typical innovations involve simplifying the method of transfer (usually toward a less costly mode) and cutting transfer distances by moving people or processing units close together.

INTO PRACTICE

## Smaller Trains at Conrail

In a strategic shift, Conrail is putting fast freight movement, a requirement of its just-in-time customers, ahead of productivity. The key change is keeping trains shorter. "Although longer trains saved on crew and locomotive costs, they resulted in freight sitting in yards and missing connections."

Source: Daniel Machalaba, "Highballing Along: New Conrail Resembles a Growth Company." *The Wall Street Journal,* November 20, 1992.

### *Benefits of Smaller Lots*

For many years, experts advised manufacturers, wholesalers, and retailers to employ economic order quantity models in lot sizing. That advice was widely heeded, especially by professional managers. EOQ models became one of the most used of all management science tools.

However, many who once favored use of EOQ models now support the principle of driving lot sizes down continuously.[4] Benefits of smaller lots cut across departments and reach out to customers, and thus might not be apparent to an isolated inventory manager or model builder. They include the following:

1. Smaller lots get used up sooner; hence, defectives are caught earlier. This reduces scrap and rework and allows sources of problems to be quickly caught and corrected while the evidence of possible causes is still fresh.
2. Small lots decrease throughput time. As we've seen in this chapter, lot-size reductions directly reduce lot delay and indirectly reduce process delay.
3. With small lots, floor space to hold inventory can be cut and work stations can be positioned very close together. Then employees can see and talk to one another, learn one another's job (which improves staffing flexibility), and function as a team.
4. Small lots allow tasks to be closely linked in time. A problem at one work station or supplier firm has a ripple effect; subsequent operations are starved of inventory. Provider and user must treat the problem as a joint problem, and a team attack on such problems becomes natural and common.
5. Activity control is simplified, and costs of support staff, handling and storage devices, control systems, and so forth are reduced.
6. Most important, customers are served more quickly and flexibly, and that increases revenue and avoids the expense of attracting new customers when present customers exit.

The benefits become more pronounced as lot size decreases. The limit? An ideal lot size of one, requiring three key actions:

1. *Reduce setup and changeover costs.* Quick-change tools presented in this chapter point the way.
2. *Reduce order-processing costs.* Kanban, rate-based scheduling, blanket contracts, and customer–supplier partnerships help meet this goal.
3. *Sever ties between process lots and transfer lots.* This chapter showed the effects on throughput time, and later, in Chapter 16, we see how separation of process and transfer lots helps smooth job and batch operations.

In the past, OM students studied a host of lot-sizing models and then grappled with the realities—the difficulties in actually realizing any of the cost savings the models promised. Today, revised thinking about lot-sizing savings provides a sharp contrast, as the box "Capturing Lot-Sizing Savings" illustrates.

CONTRAST

## Capturing Lot-Sizing Savings

| Old Wisdom | New Wisdom |
|---|---|
| **Space** | |
| Storage space not easily converted, so smaller EOQ lots will capture capital-cost savings but not holding-cost savings. | Within a few months, space will be reemployed; until then, cordon it off and cease charging it as inventory-carrying cost. |
| **Money** | |
| Business plan may limit investment in inventory, so if EOQ calls for larger lots, financial policy may not allow them. | Follow Principle 13, ever smaller lot sizes, which further encourages simplifying and cutting costs of processing orders (e.g., via kanban and setup time reduction). |
| **Price/Delivery** | |
| Smaller lot sizes preclude taking advantage of quantity discount price breaks, so large purchase lots are a necessary part of operations. | Follow Principle 5 to establish partnerships with suppliers; negotiate favorable price and delivery schedules for mutual long-term benefit. |
| **Staff** | |
| People who process orders and set up processes may not be easily retrained/reassigned, so larger EOQ lots may fail to capture staff-reduction savings. | Follow Principle 7, cross-training all associates; also, if ordering is reduced, or "order-less" processing employed, buyers/order processors have more time for process improvement; setup people have more time to attack setup times and help train operators to set up their own jobs. |

### *New Economics of Lot Sizing*

Exhibit 13-6A illustrates the economic order quantity concept in graphical form. As continuous improvement programs grounded on the principles of operations management take effect, however, the factors which drive EOQ computations change.

First, drive down setup and order processing costs—the $S$ in the EOQ formula's numerator—so that the cost of ordering frequently in small lots is not much more than ordering infrequently in large lots. How? For items produced in-house, engineer setup and changeover times downward, first to single-digit setup times and finally to one-touch setup. For purchased items, implement kanban, which simplifies ordering, and thus reduces order costs. Stable contracts with a few good (perhaps nearby) suppliers also serve to reduce ordering costs.

## EXHIBIT 13-6 Modifying the EOQ Concept

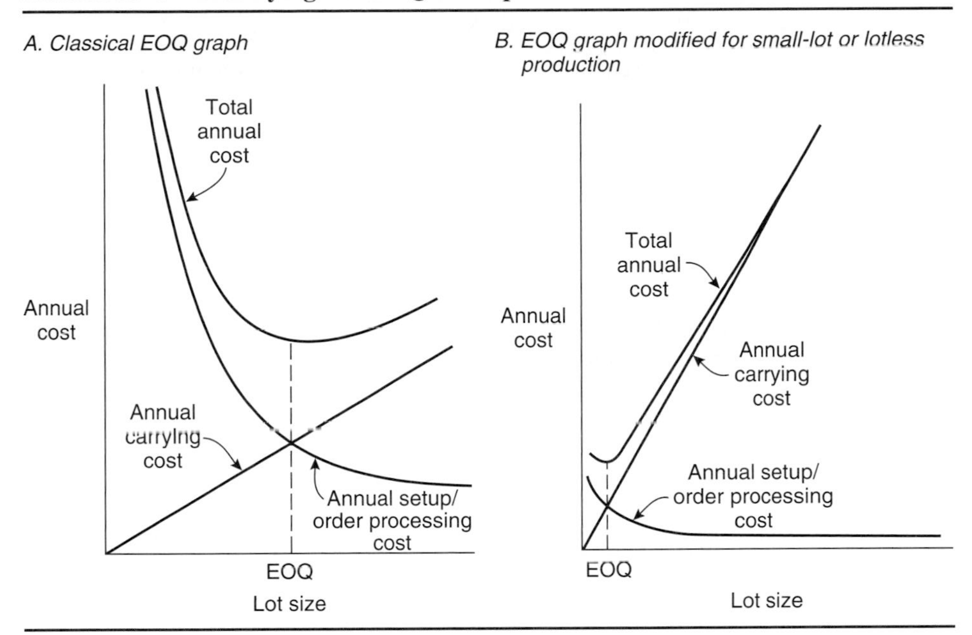


Second, annual carrying costs—expressed by the carrying cost rate, $I$, in the EOQ denominator—get a more thorough assessment than has been the case in the past. Today's value-oriented analysts are inclined to dig out more of the internal costs that truly stem from carrying inventory; the cost categories defined in Exhibit 10-2 guide their efforts. The magnitude of carrying costs increases further when they factor in the external costs of carrying large inventories—namely, customer-and quality-related costs associated with *not* reaping the six benefits of small lots defined in the last section. The result is a much steeper carrying-cost curve.

The effects of these changes are shown graphically in Exhibit 13-6B. The lower setup/order-processing curve, coupled with the steeper carrying-cost curve, acts to drive the economic order quantity to the left, that is, toward lower values. Efforts to define a theoretical minimum value for the EOQ are probably unwarranted. Practical people, at least, seem not to care. They have simply set forth a goal of continuous improvement—in large steps or small—toward piece-for-piece or lotless operations.

To this point, we have discussed techniques for planning largely independent-demand inventory items. But for manufacturers, and a few service organizations, the bulk of inventory items are component parts and subassemblies—dependent-demand items—that are destined to go into a far smaller number of independent demand end items.

When third-generation digital computers exploded into business applications during the late 1960s and early 1970s, the tool for more efficient management of large inventory databases was available. Software followed shortly, and for the last quarter century materials requirements planning and its derivatives have been a dominant feature in operations management.

## Material Requirements Planning (MRP)

**Material requirements planning (MRP),** perfected in North America in the 1970s, harnessed computer power to carry out complex manufacturing planning. Its first applications were in assisting order planners to determine parts needed to meet a known master schedule for end items.

At its inception, MRP combined two old procedures, bill of materials (BOM) explosion and netting, with a new one, backscheduling. New in that the computerization made it feasible, backscheduling means subtracting required lead time from the due date to find when a required item should be started into production or ordered from a supplier.

Through the years, MRP has been updated to include planning for more than materials. Later in this section, we consider some of the extensions. First, however, we take a look at MRP in its basic form and progress through some of its primary features.

### *Basic MRP*

MRP is said to be a push system, but that is an oversimplification. Though MRP usually does plan a push schedule for a week at a time, it may include a production activity control subroutine to adjust the work flow somewhat every day in response to the latest customer needs (pull signals). Also, MRP can be set to plan everything daily or even hourly instead of weekly.

Example 13-6, for a food product, illustrates basic MRP graphically. Since MRP is easier to grasp graphically than in words, some MRP computer systems even show MRP results in graphical form. Two new terms are introduced: **planned order release,** which is found by backscheduling from the date of need, and **residual inventory,** which is inventory left over when an order is canceled or reduced in quantity.

#### Example 13-6: MRP FOR A CATERER

Imagine you are a caterer and have a master schedule of parties to cater every night for the next two weeks. Your policy is zero stock (except for incidentals like seasonings). To plan for zero inventory, you consult menus for every food dish to be provided for each catering order in the next two weeks. Menu quantities times number of servings equals gross requirements. Let us say (without showing calculations) that gross requirements for salami are as shown in part A of Exhibit 13-7. Salami is required in the quantities shown on days 3, 6, 11, and 13.

You normally order salami from a deli two days ahead of time (purchase lead time for salami is two days). Therefore, you plan to release salami orders as shown in part B of Exhibit 13-7. Each planned order release is two days in advance of the gross requirement shown in part A. Backing up by the amount of required lead time is called **back-scheduling.**

The schedule of planned order releases is correctly timed and in the exact quantities needed. It is a material requirements plan for one of the components that go into the foods to be catered. It is a plan for zero inventory and is achieved if the deli delivers the salami orders in the planned two days. If deliveries come a day early, inventory builds. Also, if an order of salami arrives on time but a customer cancels the catering order, residual (leftover) inventory

**EXHIBIT 13-7 Planned Order Release Determination—Salami**

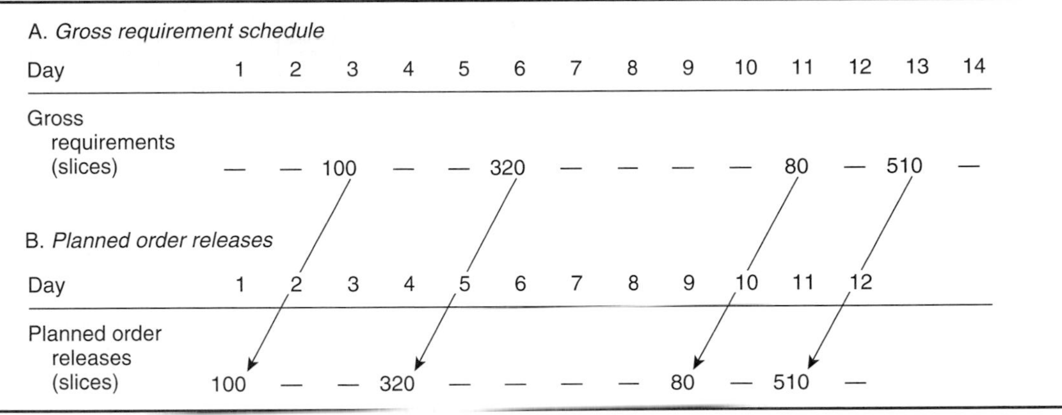

A. *Gross requirement schedule*

| Day | 1 | 2 | 3 | 4 | 5 | 6 | 7 | 8 | 9 | 10 | 11 | 12 | 13 | 14 |
|---|---|---|---|---|---|---|---|---|---|---|---|---|---|---|
| Gross requirements (slices) | — | — | 100 | — | — | 320 | — | — | — | — | 80 | — | 510 | — |

B. *Planned order releases*

| Day | 1 | 2 | 3 | 4 | 5 | 6 | 7 | 8 | 9 | 10 | 11 | 12 |
|---|---|---|---|---|---|---|---|---|---|---|---|---|
| Planned order releases (slices) | 100 | — | — | 320 | — | — | — | — | 80 | — | 510 | — |

builds. Such supply and demand uncertainties create some inventory when MRP is used, but MRP cuts inventory considerably from what it is when the producer (caterer) *plans* to keep components in stock.

## *MRP Computer Processing*

The MRP calculations for salami (Exhibit 13-7) are easy because from salami slices to a master schedule of catered food dishes is only a single level of dependency. Now consider the partial product structure in Exhibit 13-8. (A product structure visually depicts a bill of materials and sometimes is used as a synonym for *bill of materials.*) It is a dependent-demand chain having five levels below the end item, an automobile. The end item typically is designated the zero level in a computer file storing a bill of materials. The figure shows raw metal (5) cut into a gear (4), fitted onto a shaft (3), placed in a gear box (2), installed in an engine (1), and assembled into an auto (0).

The timing and quantities of parts to be ordered at each level depend on needs for parts by the parent item directly above. Planned-order-release calculations must cascade, that is, proceed from the first level to the second, to the third, and so on. Cascading calculations are complex, however, and a good reason for planners to use computers, especially for products having thousands of parts.

But cascading or level-by-level netting is not the only complication. The same raw metal that is cut into a gear might also go into other parent items that ultimately become the vehicle. Moreover, the raw metal (and, perhaps, the gear, shaft, gear box, and engine) may go into other parent items that become other types of vehicles. Finally, dependent demands (i.e., demands that descend from parent items) for parts at any level must be combined with independent demands. Independent demands arise, for example, from orders for spare parts (service parts). Computers are needed to total and properly time-phase all those requirements.

**Exhibit 13-8 Partial Product Structure Showing Dependency Chain**

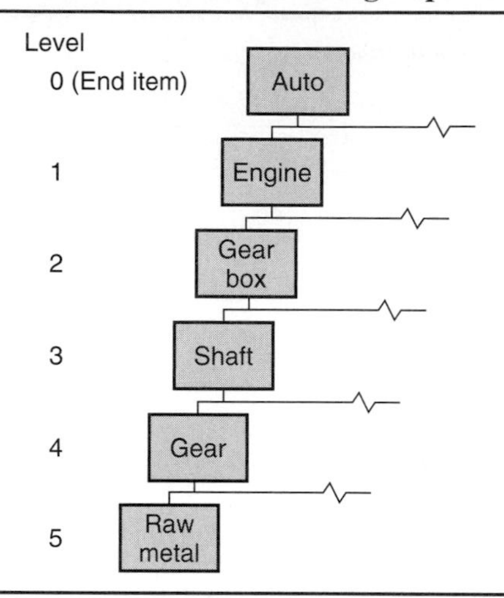


**Exhibit 13-9 MRP Computer Run**

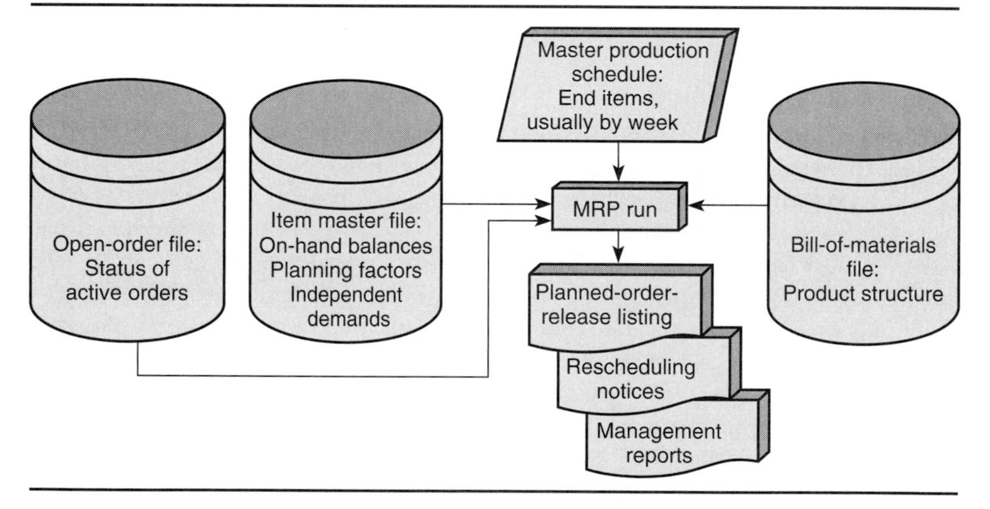


Exhibit 13-9 shows the necessary inputs and outputs of an MRP computer run. The inputs are a master production schedule, an item master file, a bill-of-materials file, and an open-order file. The outputs include a planned-order-release listing, rescheduling notices, and management reports.

**Master Production Schedule.** Recall from Chapter 5 that the master schedule is a statement of the company's intended output. The end-item schedule (of the MPS) drives

MRP. In most MRP-using firms, the master scheduling team plans in weekly time buckets (periods) extending perhaps a year into the future. As time passes, the master production schedule gets increasingly out of date; that is, some of the scheduled quantities are out of line with sales orders being booked. Often, the master scheduling team deals with inaccuracies via more frequent MRP runs, by component parts schedule changes, and by activity control measures on the shop floor.

**Item Master File.** The **item master file** holds reference and control data, including on-hand stock balances and planning factors for every component item. The on-hand balance is simply the quantity that is supposed to be in stock.

The on-hand balance is used by MRP to compute planned orders. First, the system computes gross requirements for a given part. Then it calculates projected stock balances to see if there is a net requirement, which would indicate a need for a planned order; that calculation is called **netting.** A net requirement is the same as a negative projected stock balance, where

$$\begin{matrix}\text{Projected} \\ \text{stock balance}\end{matrix} = \begin{matrix}\text{Previous} \\ \text{stock balance}\end{matrix} - \begin{matrix}\text{Gross} \\ \text{requirements}\end{matrix} + \begin{matrix}\text{Planned and} \\ \text{scheduled receipts}\end{matrix} \qquad (13\text{-}3)$$

Example 13-7 extends Example 13-6 to allow for an on-hand stock balance. Also, let's change salami into salamite, a hypothetical chemical compound. In keeping with the usual industry practice of scheduling in weeks, gross requirements for salamite are stated as a 14-week rather than 14-day schedule.

## Example 13-7: MRP for a Chemical Product

Let us say that 220 units of salamite is the on-hand balance at time zero (the start of week 1). Gross requirements are as shown in Exhibit 13-7 (for salami), but with days changed to weeks. For week 3,

$$\text{Projected stock balance} = 220 - 100 + 0 = 120$$

The positive projected stock balance of 120 shows that there is no need for an order. The projected balance stays at 120 in weeks 4 and 5. In week 6,

$$\text{Projected balance} = 120 - 320 + 0 = -200$$

Now the projected stock balance is a negative 200, which is a net requirement. In MRP, a net requirement is covered by a planned order. The planned order quantity is 200, and the planned order release, obtained by back scheduling, is two weeks earlier, since the planned lead time ($LT$) is two weeks.

Exhibit 13-10 shows MRP results as a four-row display. This type of display might be available for viewing on a video terminal or as printed output. (The scheduled-receipts row, which is empty in this example, is explained later.)

A planned order release of 200 in week 4 covers the net requirement of 200 in week 6. A negative stock balance is thus averted; therefore, the −200 is crossed out and replaced by a zero

**EXHIBIT 13-10 MRP Computations—Salamite**

| *LT* (lead time) = 2<br>Week | | 1 | 2 | 3 | 4 | 5 | 6 | 7 | 8 | 9 | 10 | 11 | 12 | 13 | 14 |
|---|---|---|---|---|---|---|---|---|---|---|---|---|---|---|---|
| Gross requirements | | | | 100 | | | 320 | | | | | 80 | | 510 | |
| Scheduled receipts | | | | | | | | | | | | | | | |
| Projected stock balance | 220 | 220 | 220 | 120 | 120 | 120 | 0<br>~~−200~~ | 0 | 0 | 0 | 0 | 0<br>~~−80~~ | 0 | 0<br>~~−510~~ | 0 |
| Planned order releases | | | | | 200 | | | | | 80 | | 510 | | | |
| | | | | | ↑*LT* = 2 | | | | | ↑*LT* = 2 | | ↑*LT* = 2 | | | |

balance. Recomputation of the stock balance in week 6 to account for the planned receipt of 200 is accomplished with Equation 13-3:

$$\text{Projected stock balance} = 120 - 320 + 200 = 0$$

The projected balance goes negative twice more, in weeks 11 and 13. Planned orders cover the net requirements; thus, the negative quantities are crossed out and replaced by zeros.

Planning factors stored in the item master file include lead time, lot size, safety stock, and so forth. Those factors need less updating than stock balances. In Example 13-7, the lead time (*LT*) of two weeks would have been extracted from the item master file.

So far we have assumed that the planned-order-release quantity is the same as the net requirement. That policy is known as lot-for-lot (i.e., production lot size exactly equals lot quantity required). Sometimes the item master file specifies a preset order quantity or lot size, $Q$ (for quantity). Example 13-8, adapted from Example 13-7, provides for a fixed $Q$.

### Example 13-8: MRP FOR A CHEMICAL PRODUCT—FIXED ORDER QUANTITY

Fixed order quantities compromise the MRP goal of low (or zero) inventories.

Assume that salamite is produced in a vat that holds 500 units. Even though 500 is unlikely to be the net requirement, it seems economical to make the salamite in full 500-unit batches. The excess is carried as a stock balance.

Exhibit 13-11 shows the MRP computations for the case of a fixed order quantity, $Q$, equal to 500 units. A net requirement of 200 arises when the computed stock balance goes negative by 200 in week 6. The computer covers the net requirement with a planned order two weeks earlier (since $LT = 2$). The order is for $Q = 500$, the fixed order quantity, which brings projected stock

**EXHIBIT 13-11 MRP with Fixed Order Quantity—Salamite**

| $LT = 2$ $Q = 500$<br>Week | | 1 | 2 | 3 | 4 | 5 | 6 | 7 | 8 | 9 | 10 | 11 | 12 | 13 | 14 |
|---|---|---|---|---|---|---|---|---|---|---|---|---|---|---|---|
| Gross requirements | | | | 100 | | | 320 | | | | | 80 | | 510 | |
| Scheduled receipts | | | | | | | | | | | | | | | |
| On hand | 220 | 220 | 220 | 120 | 120 | 120 | 300<br>~~−200~~ | 300 | 300 | 300 | 300 | 220 | 220 | 210<br>~~−290~~ | 210 |
| Planned order releases | | | | | 500 | | | | | | | 500 | | | |

balance in week 6 to +300. The balance drops to 220 in week 11 and to −290, indicating a net requirement, in week 13. To prevent the negative balance in week 13, the computer plans an order for 500. The planned order release is in week 11, which eliminates the negative balance in week 13 and leaves 210 units to spare.

**Bill-of-Materials File.** A bill of materials (BOM) is industry's term for a list (often a structured list) of component parts that go into a product. The BOM names the parts detailed on the engineer's blueprints. Like the item master file, the computerized BOM file serves as a reference file for MRP processing.

The BOM file keeps track of which component parts, and how many of each, go into a unit of the parent item. In each MRP run, the computer (1) calculates planned order timing and quantity for the parent item, (2) consults the BOM file to see what goes into the parent, and (3) translates the parent's planned order requirement into gross requirements for each component. This sequence is known as **bill of materials explosion.** For example, if there are three of a certain component per parent, the gross requirement for that component will be equal to triple the planned order quantity for the parent. The grand total of gross requirements for the component would also include requirements derived from other parents and from independent demands. Example 13-9 continues the salamite example to demonstrate the role of the BOM file.

### Example 13-9: MRP FOR A CHEMICAL PRODUCT WITH TWO LEVELS

Planned order releases for salamite have been calculated. The computer consults the BOM file to find what goes into salamite. The first ingredient is a chemical compound known as *sal*. There are two grams of sal per unit of salamite. Therefore, the planned order quantities for salamite are doubled to equal gross requirements for sal. The simple translation of salamite orders into sal needs is shown in Exhibit 13-12. (The salamite data are from Exhibit 13-11.)

**EXHIBIT 13-12 BOM Reference Data and Scheduled Receipts in MRP**

| Week | 1 | 2 | 3 | 4 | 5 | 6 | 7 | 8 | 9 | 10 | 11 | 12 | 13 | 14 |
|---|---|---|---|---|---|---|---|---|---|---|---|---|---|---|
| Parent—Salamite<br>Planned order releases | | | | 500 × 2 ↓ | | | | | | | 500 × 2 ↓ | | | |
| Component—Sal<br>$LT = 5$<br>Gross requirements | | | | 1,000 | | | | | | | 1,000 | | | |
| Scheduled receipts | | | | 1,000 | | | | | | | | | | |
| On hand 0 | 0 | 0 | 0 | 0<br>~~–1,000~~ | 0 | 0 | 0 | 0 | 0 | 0 | 0<br>~~–1,000~~ | 0 | 0 | 0 |
| Planned order releases | | | | | | 1,000 ↑ | | $LT = 5$ | | | | | | |

Projected stock balances and planned order releases may now be calculated for sal as shown in the figure. Then the computer does the same for the next ingredient or component of salamite.

**Computer Runs.** MRP computer runs are usually weekly; a total regeneration of material requirements generally is performed over the weekend. Some companies use regenerative MRP processing every two or three days or even daily. An alternative to regeneration is net-change MRP. Net-change computer software is designed to update only items affected by a change in quantity or timing for a related item. Since not all part numbers need be regenerated, net change saves on volume of output data presented to planners for review.[5]

### *Scheduled Receipts and the Open-Order File*

Another MRP factor is scheduled receipts. Returning to Exhibit 13-12, we see a scheduled receipt of 1,000, which is the gross-requirement quantity in week 4. A scheduled receipt represents an **open order** instead of a planned order. In this case, an order for 1,000 *has already been released,* for make or buy, and is scheduled to be delivered in week 4. Since the lead time is five weeks, the order would have been released and scheduled two weeks ago. (Remember, we're at time zero, the beginning of week 1.)

Let's examine the events that change a planned order into a scheduled receipt. The table on the next page is a partial MRP for sal as it might have appeared on Monday morning two weeks ago.

| Lead time = 5 | | 1 | 2 | 3 | 4 | 5 | 6 |
|---|---|---|---|---|---|---|---|
| Gross requirements | | | | | | | 1,000 |
| Scheduled receipts | | | | | | | |
| On hand | 0 | 0 | 0 | 0 | 0 | 0 | −0<br>~~1,000~~ |
| Planned order releases | | 1,000 | | | | | |

Any time a planned order release appears in the first time-bucket, action to schedule the order is called for. Therefore, sometime on Monday the scheduler writes a shop order to make 1,000 grams of sal. The effect of scheduling the order is to remove it from the planned-order-release row and convert it to a scheduled receipt, as follows:

| Lead time = 5 | | 1 | 2 | 3 | 4 | 5 | 6 |
|---|---|---|---|---|---|---|---|
| Gross requirements | | | | | | | 1,000 |
| Scheduled receipts | | | | | | | 1,000 |
| On hand | 0 | 0 | 0 | 0 | 0 | 0 | 0 |
| Planned order releases | | | | | | | |

On the next MRP run, the scheduled receipt for 1,000 grams will be included. The order is shown as a scheduled receipt each week until the shop delivers the 1,000 grams. But the scheduler could cancel the order or change its quantity or timing. Also, the shop may successfully produce more or less than the planned quantity of 1,000 grams; the *actual amount* delivered is entered as the gain to on-hand inventory.

Referring back to the system flowchart of MRP computer processing in Exhibit 13-9, we see that MRP makes use of an open-order file, which holds data on open orders (scheduled receipts). Each time a scheduler releases a shop order or a buyer releases a purchase order, the order is noted in the open-order file. (Alternatively, item master file records may contain fields indicating if there is an open order for a given item.) When orders are received (or canceled), they are closed and removed from the file.

One step in an MRP computer run, usually after calculation of planned order releases, is to evaluate open orders. The computer checks to see whether quantities and timing for each order in the open-order file are still correct. The check may show that a certain open order is still needed, but perhaps a week later or in a different quantity; or perhaps the order is no longer needed at all. The system issues **rescheduling notices,** which highlight the difference between present revised requirements and open orders. (Order changes and rescheduling notices are normal; the disruption resulting from reacting to every rescheduling notice is often called *system nervousness.*)

**EXHIBIT 13-13 Partial Bill of Materials for a Bicycle**

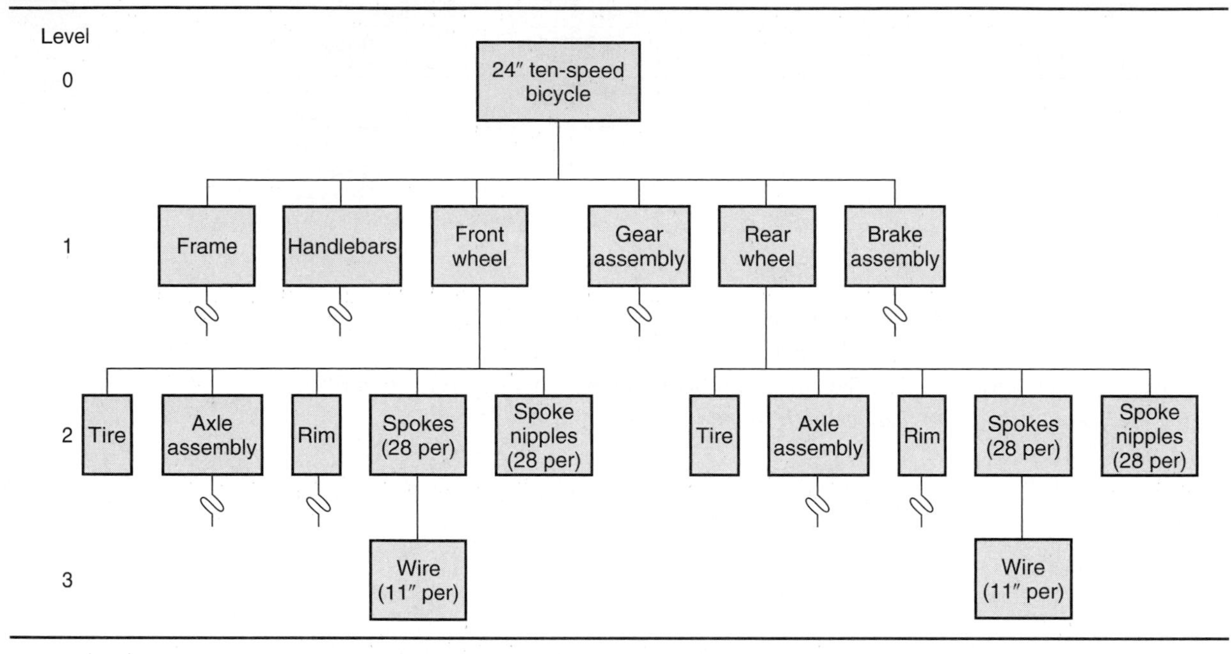


### *Multiple Parents and Scrap Allowances*

So far, we've examined simplified MRP examples. MRP is at its best, however, for complex product structures that can benefit from the computer's sorting powers. Exhibit 13-13 is a partial bill of materials for a bicycle. There is enough room to show only a sample of the bicycle's 300-odd component parts. The complete BOM breaks down into as many levels as are necessary to get to the purchased part. Take the breakdown of the front and rear wheels. Each wheel has a tire, an axle assembly, a rim assembly, 28 spokes, and 28 nipples; each spoke is fabricated (cut, bent, and threaded) from 11 inches of raw wire stock. The nipple is a second-level purchased item and the wire is a third-level purchased item. Spoke nipples and wire stock appear at two locations in the BOM; they also would occur in the BOMs for other bicycle sizes. The computer is efficient for totaling the quantities needed for parts occurring in multiple locations, which is a step in exploding the BOM. (Before computers and MRP were available, BOM explosion was done by legions of clerks using index cards and adding machines.)

Example 13-10 uses some of the bicycle components to show how MRP treats multiple parents and scrap calculations. In the example, netting with scrap allowance included is done as follows:

$$\text{Net requirement} = \frac{\text{Shortage amount}}{1 - \text{Scrap rate}} \tag{13-4}$$

## Example 13-10: MRP Processing—Bicycle Spoke Nipples

Exhibit 13-14 shows generation of gross requirements for spoke nipples and their translation into planned order releases. Planned order releases for front and rear wheels are given for three sizes of bicycle: 20-inch, 24-inch, and 26-inch. Requirements for wheels would have been derived from master production schedules (level 0) for all bike models. Planned order releases for spoke nipples emerge after higher levels of MRP processing have been completed.

In the exhibit, orders for more than one parent are consolidated to become gross requirement for a next-lower-level part. The requirement for nipples in week 5 is based on $84 + 60 + 24 + 24 = 192$ wheels. At 28 nipples per wheel, the gross requirement is $192 \times 28 = 5{,}376$. For week 6, the basis is $36 + 36 + 72 + 84 = 228$ wheels: the gross requirement is $228 \times 28$,which equals 6,384. (Front-wheel and rear-wheel planned orders may be unequal, because there may be extra demand for one or the other as service parts, to make up for scrap losses, etc.)

The 2,500 nipples on hand at week 0 are projected to stay on hand (in stock) through four weeks. In week 5, 5,376 are needed but only 2,500 are available; there is a projected shortage of 2,876. The possibility of a shortage triggers the following: The MRP program subtracts the purchase lead time ($LT$), three weeks, from week 5, giving a planned order date of week 2. The lot size is lot-for-lot. Thus, from Equation 13-4, the computer calculates the planned purchase order

**Exhibit 13-14 MRP Generation of Planned Order Releases—Spoke Nipple Example**

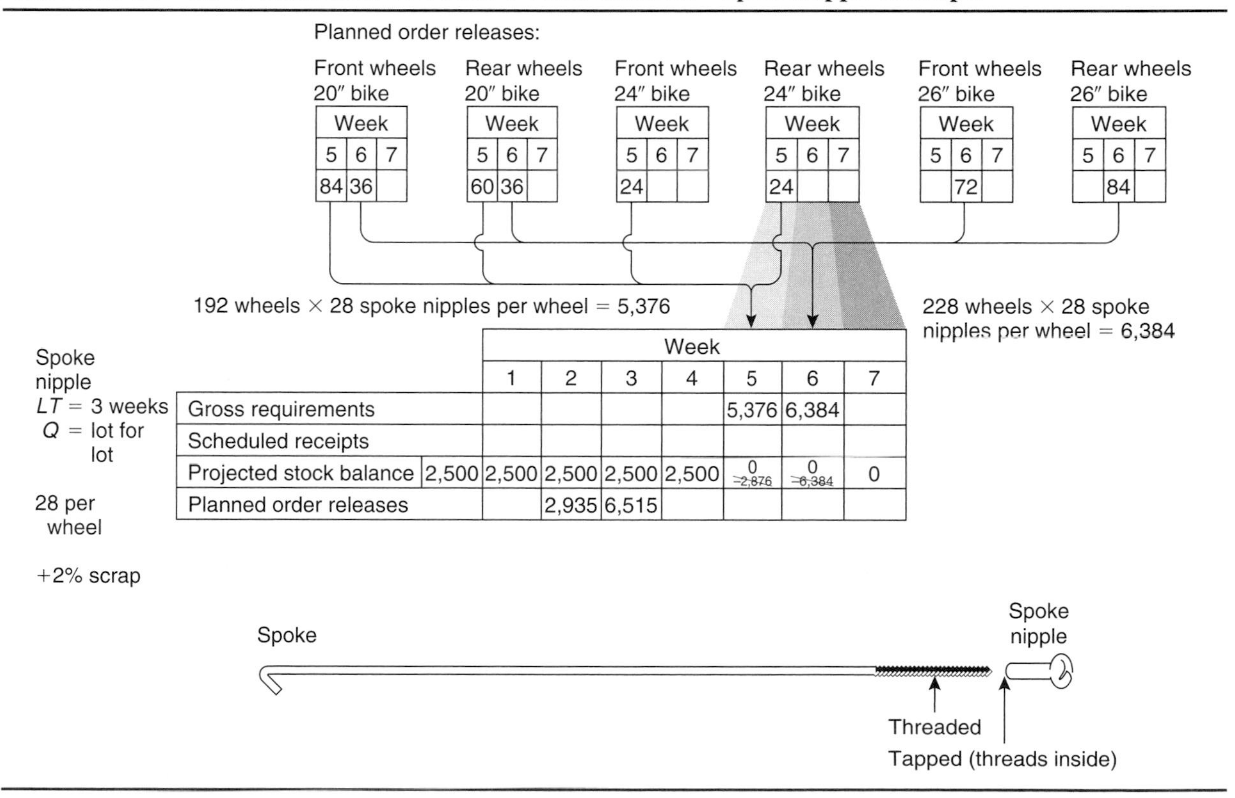


| | | Week 1 | 2 | 3 | 4 | 5 | 6 | 7 |
|---|---|---|---|---|---|---|---|---|
| Gross requirements | | | | | | 5,376 | 6,384 | |
| Scheduled receipts | | | | | | | | |
| Projected stock balance | 2,500 | 2,500 | 2,500 | 2,500 | 2,500 | 0 −2,876 | 0 −6,384 | 0 |
| Planned order releases | | | 2,935 | 6,515 | | | | |

size of 2,935 units, a quantity that covers the projected shortage of 2,876 and allows for a 2 percent scrap rate. Similarly, the projected shortage of 6,384 in week 6 is covered by a planned order back-scheduled to week 3. The order quantity (6,515) again allows for 2 percent scrap.

Note the treatment of the scrap factor. The planned-order-release amount includes the 2 percent so that the extra amount will be placed on order. Planned receipts do not include it, since 2 percent is expected to be scrapped.

### *Independent Demands for Component Parts*

Independent demands for component parts may be entered into the item master file. The subset of MRP for handling independent demands is often called **time-phased order point (TPOP).** TPOP requires that the independent demands be forecast since they cannot be computed; there are no parent demands from which to compute.

The main difference between MRP and TPOP is this: Dependent demands are calculated based on parent-item needs (MRP), while independent demands are forecast. TPOP actually loses its identity when the independent demand is merged with demands derived from MRP; MRP takes over from there. Example 13-11 illustrates the method.

#### Example 13-11: INDEPENDENT DEMANDS—BICYCLE SPOKES

For a bicycle manufacturer, most of the gross demands for spokes are dependent demands derived from planned orders for wheels. Some independent demands for spokes come from parts wholesalers and other bicycle manufacturers that do not make their own spokes.

The independent sources do not make their demands known very far in advance. Thus, independent spoke demand is forecast. The most recent forecast for 11-inch spokes is for 800 units. That quantity is used as the forecast for the next 52 weeks. Exhibit 13-15 shows the 800-per-week projection at the upper left. The upper right shows a dependent demand for 672 spokes in

**EXHIBIT 13-15 TPOP—Spoke Example**

TPOP demand—
forecast for 11-inch spokes

| week | | | | | | |
|---|---|---|---|---|---|---|
| 1 | 2 | 3 | 4 | 5 | 6 | 7 |
| 800 | 800 | 800 | 800 | 800 | 800 | 800 |

MRP demand–planned order
release for 24-inch bike wheels

| week | | | | | | |
|---|---|---|---|---|---|---|
| 1 | 2 | 3 | 4 | 5 | 6 | 7 |
| | | | | 24 | | |

24 wheels × 28 spokes
per wheel = 672

Spoke:
$LT$ = 1 week
$Q$ = 4,800
28 per wheel

| | | | | | | | | |
|---|---|---|---|---|---|---|---|---|
| Gross requirements | | 800 | 800 | 800 | 800 | 1,472 | 800 | 800 |
| Scheduled receipts | | 4,800 | | | | | | |
| Projected stock balance | 200 | 4,200 | 3,400 | 2,600 | 1,800 | 328 | 4,328 ~~-472~~ | 3,528 |
| Planned order releases | | | | | | 4,800 | | |

week 5; that demand is derived from MRP processing at the level of the parent item, 24-inch bike wheels.

The two sources of demand merge into gross requirements for spokes. The independent-demand quantities, 800 per period, are extended directly; the single dependent demand of 672 is computed from the planned order of 24 wheels times 28 spokes per wheel. From this point, MRP logic takes over; the figure shows a net requirement in week 6 covered by a planned order release with a fixed quantity of 4,800 a week earlier.

---

## *Evolution of MRP*

The logic inherent in MRP processing seems so straightforward that some students are prone to ask, "Why didn't manufacturers always use it?" The answer is also straightforward: MRP is a tool born of computer technology; the hardware needed for MRP in even a medium-sized company simply didn't exist until the mid-1960s and the software wasn't available until the early 1970s. The sharp growth in MRP applications occurred in the late 1970s. In its life, however, MRP has evolved and its logic has been extended.

**Closed-Loop MRP.** Early MRP systems were one-way streets. They fed plans to production associates but received no feedback as to the success (or lack thereof) in executing those plans. MRP generates valid schedules in that they are logical extensions of parent demand, but once orders are launched, some of the planning factors stray off course.

In closed-loop MRP, three general types of activities help restore order: close file control ensures that the data files from which MRP draws its information are accurate; production activity control routines provide the scheduler with timely updates as to the status of orders as they move through the plant; and rescheduling actions ensure that revised plans, based on updated information, are known to all (including customers and suppliers).

**Distribution Requirements Planning.** Distribution requirements planning (DRP) extends MRP logic to independent demands from, say, company-operated distribution centers. Traditionally, finished-goods inventories were planned independently of manufacturing; each distribution center would place its order as needed to replenish its shelves. Under DRP, however, demand forecasts for finished goods at the distribution centers become entries to the manufacturing plant's master production schedule.

Since requirements are based on need, customer service levels improve even as overall inventory levels are reduced. For the manufacturer, early warning in the form of realistic needs captured on the master schedule aids production planning and helps prevent crises brought on by "suddenly empty" shelves at a distribution center.

While basic MRP is well defined (standard files and subroutines), the meaning and composition of MRP II is fuzzier (many possible configurations) and not easily illustrated with a few tables.

**Manufacturing Resource Planning (MRP II).** Perhaps the most noteworthy extension of closed-loop MRP to date is manufacturing resource planning, or MRP II—which is intended to incorporate all resources of a manufacturing company. Early MRP II applications used the master production schedule to plan capacity, shipments, tool changes, design work, and cash flows. MRP II software vendors kept adding modules, however, to stay ahead of competitors. Maintenance management, quality, field service and warranty tracking, marketing support, and engineering change control are among the applications one might find in today's MRP II systems.[6]

But that's not all. Some packages incorporate a simulation module, enabling the computer to test prospective schedules before the company commits to a plan. A finite scheduling module, capable of incorporating capacity constraints into the planning mix, is also frequently available. And, to put these tools where they are most needed—in the hands of the operator—client/server technology, or distributed computing, brings MRP II to the desktop PC.[7] Some observers maintain that a fully configured MRP II system, such as we've described here, will continue to be cutting-edge technology for some time.[8]

**Other Extensions of or Alternatives to MRP II.** MRP II, however, is attracting competition. Some of the emergent alternative systems attempt to establish better connections with customers and suppliers. **Enterprise resource planning (ERP),** for example, is a term coined by The Gartner Group of Stamford, Connecticut, and—though not revolutionary in concept—purports to ensure that planning decisions do consider both upstream and downstream members of the supply chain.[9] From published descriptions, however, ERP includes most of the modules attributed to a "loaded" MRP II system.

Find more on managing ERP in Chapter 16 where we focus on job and batch operations.

Major software companies—SAP, Baan, PeopleSoft, and Oracle, for example—have packages marketed under the label of ERP or "enhanced MRP II" that can be tailored to a variety of settings, even public libraries.[10] Some also produce supply-chain management suites that are said to be compatible with their own ERP modules and "front office" suites, leaving the impression that ERP does not always include supply-chain management modules.[11] In general, there appears to be a great deal of variety in what might be included in ERP.

While MRP was fashioned for the manufacturing sector, and its partner DRP for distribution, there have been some efforts to extend it elsewhere. A promising example is MRP's use in hospitals. Many surgeries are elective and therefore scheduled in advance. Adding those to a history-based forecast of nonelective surgeries produces a master schedule, which could drive a computer routine that will plan the required medical devices, instruments, supplies, surgical rooms, staff, and so forth.

Another approach to hospital applications has been developed by researchers Aleda Roth and Roland van Dierdonck. In a research report, they describe their system, called hospital resource planning (HRP), and tests of its feasibility:

> We gathered longitudinal data from two hospitals, one 300-bed community hospital and one 1,100-bed teaching hospital. Our exploratory study indicated that while the concept of MRP II can be transferred to hospitals, the traditional MRP logic has shortcomings. HRP advanced prior research in three ways: (1) consideration of DRGs [diagnostic-related groups] as products with a bill of resources structure that simultaneously incorporates both capacity and materials resources, (2) implementation of a hospital-wide (versus a functional) planning and control system, and (3) gross-to-net requirements logic based on notions of treatment stages.[12]

Whether ERP, HRP, and other extensions of MRP II stick and flourish remains to be seen. They all, however, aim toward a similar set of benefits, discussed next.

## *Benefits of MRP and MRP II*[13]

How valuable is MRP or MRP II? As to overall impact, respected authorities have differing opinions. The late Oliver Wight stated that, "MRP II results in management finally having the numbers to run the business." And when "everybody uses the same set of numbers," MRP II serves as "a company game plan."[14] George Plossl, however, has a different view: MRP II "ignores execution and control activities and has produced more confusion than benefits."[15]

In the narrow sense, the chief benefit of MRP/MRPII is its ability to generate valid schedules and keep them that way. A valid schedule has broad benefits for the entire company, including the following, roughly in order of importance:

1. *Improves on-time completions.* Industry calls this improving customer service, and on-time completion is one good way to measure it. MRP/MRP II companies typically achieve 95 percent or more on-time completions, because completion of a parent item is less apt to be delayed for lack of a component part.
2. *Cuts inventories.* With MRP/MRP II, inventories can be reduced at the same time customer service is improved. Stocks are cut because parts are not ordered if not needed to meet requirements for parent items. Typical gains are 20 to 35 percent.
3. *Provides data (future orders) for planning work center capacity requirements.* This benefit is attainable if basic MRP is enhanced by a capacity requirements planning (CRP) routine (discussed in Chapter 16).
4. *Improves direct-labor productivity.* There is less lost time and overtime because of shortages and less need to waste time halting one job to set up for a shortage-list job. Reduction in lost time tends to be from 5 to 10 percent in fabrication and from 25 to 40 percent in assembly. Overtime cuts are greater, on the order of 50 to 90 percent.
5. *Improves productivity of support staff.* MRP/MRP II cuts expediting ("firefighting"), which allows more time for planning. Purchasing can spend time saving money and selecting good suppliers. Materials management can maintain valid records and better plan inventory needs. Production control can keep priorities up-to-date. Supervisors can better plan capacity and assign jobs. In some cases, fewer support staff are needed.
6. *Facilitates closing the loop with total business planning.* That includes planning capacity and cash flow, which is the chief purpose and benefit of MRP II.

While these are impressive, it should be noted that JIT yields the first five benefits but much more so. Some firms combine the two approaches by overlaying JIT upon an existing MRP system; other firms treat JIT as a replacement for certain MRP subroutines (see the Contrast box, "MRP Coverage").

CONTRAST

## MRP Coverage

In Oliver Wight's 1970s-vintage classification scheme, Class A MRP is the most advanced level.

**Wide MRP Coverage**

A goal of Class A MRP requiring

- High record accuracy.
- All MRP subroutines in use.
- All part numbers on MRP.

**Reduced MRP Coverage**

A goal of disciplined simplicity requiring

- Exact stock placement and standard quantities.
- Reduction of subroutines, except for data files.
- Migration of parts off MRP and onto JIT, regular-use parts first.

## Summary Check Points

✓ Materials management includes a broad set of activities related to acquiring, moving, storing, and control of materials resources. Inventory management is a key component.

✓ Timing and quantity are two fundamental inventory management decisions.

✓ Reorder point systems are used to time replenishment order placement based on the quantity of an item in stock when the order is to be placed; that quantity is the reorder point.

✓ "Two-bin" systems use simple devices to reveal reorder point inventory levels.

✓ Safety stock (buffer stock) is used to protect against stock outages (usually during a replenishment lead-time) due to variations in demand rate or other unforeseen contingencies.

✓ Lot-sizing decisions determine the quantity of an item to be ordered when an order is launched.

✓ In lot-for-lot operations, lot size acquired for a period equals net demand for that period.

✓ Order batching typically results in more unsynchronized and unstable operations.

✓ The economic order quantity (EOQ) is an example of fixed-quantity lot-sizing; the order quantity seeks to minimize inventory policy costs (carrying plus ordering) so long as some rather stringent assumptions are valid. It is best to think of EOQ as a general quantity zone.

✓ Evidence shows that industry prefers the simpler lot-sizing models.

✓ Lot sizing assumptions are "under attack"; the idea is to drive lot sizes down; lot size of one is the target.

- ✓ Smaller lots yield several benefits: better quality, faster throughput time, reduced floor space requirements, close task linking in time, simplified activity control, and faster and more flexible customer service.
- ✓ Material requirements planning (MRP) is a proven tool for planning dependent-demand inventories through its bill-of-materials (BOM) explosion process that results in planned order releases for components of master-scheduled end items.
- ✓ Essential MRP input files include the MPS, BOM, open-order file, and item master (or, inventory status) file. The outputs are planned order listings, rescheduling notices, and other management reports.
- ✓ When lot-for-lot rules are in place, MRP aims at zero excess (carried) inventories. Safety stock requirements, fixed-quantity lot sizes, and lead-time variability, however, serve to make MRP less efficient in meeting that target.
- ✓ Independent demand for component parts is incorporated into MRP with time-phased order point (TPOP) routines.
- ✓ MRP has evolved into several extensions, each attempting to incorporate more of the resource management activity: manufacturing resources planning (MRPII), distribution requirements planning (DRP), capacity requirements planning (CRP), and enterprise resources planning (ERP) are examples.
- ✓ The chief benefit of MRP/MRPII and extensions is to generate valid schedules and keep them that way. Other benefits can include improved on-time completions, reduced inventory levels, better demand data for capacity planning in work cells, improved labor (direct and staff) productivity, and integrating OM with other business functions.

## Solved Problems

***Problem 1***

A wholesaler's computer records show the following for one of its inventory items:

Mean monthly demand = 8,000
Standard deviation of demand = 1,000 per month
Replenishment lead time = 1 month

If the desired service level is 95 percent, what is the statistical safety stock? What is the reorder point?

***Solution 1***

The service level, 0.95, represents a probability: 0.50 (the left half of the zone under the normal curve) plus 0.45. We find 0.45 in Appendix A where, by interpolation, $z = 1.645$. Then, from Equation 13-2:

$$\begin{aligned} SS &= z\sqrt{LT(SD)^2} \\ &= 1.645\sqrt{1(1{,}000)^2} \\ &= 1{,}645 \end{aligned}$$

Next, compute mean demand for the lead time period:

$$DLT = 8{,}000 \text{ per month} \times 1 \text{ month} = 8{,}000$$

Then, from Equation 13-1:

$$\begin{aligned} ROP &= DLT + SS \\ &= 8{,}000 + 1{,}645 = 9{,}645 \end{aligned}$$

***Problem 2***

A manufacturer of industrial solvents has been buying for its own use about 18,000 bottles of solution X4X annually for several years. The cost is $10 per bottle, and $100 is the approximate cost of placing an order for X4X. The firm uses a carrying-cost rate of 30 percent. Calculate the EOQ, the annual ordering cost, and the annual carrying cost for this item.

What would you expect to occur if lot sizes were made larger than the EOQ? Smaller? (Hint: Base your answer to these questions on Exhibit S13-2 in the chapter supplement.)

***Solution 2***

The EOQ may be found using Equation S13-2

$$\begin{aligned} EOQ &= \sqrt{\frac{2DS}{IC}} = \sqrt{\frac{2(18{,}000)(\$100)}{(0.3)(\$10)}} \\ &= \sqrt{1{,}200{,}000} = 1{,}095.45 \text{ bottles} \end{aligned}$$

Equation S13-1 contains the annual ordering and carrying cost terms. Thus,

$$\text{Annual ordering costs} = \left(\frac{D}{Q}\right)(S) = \left(\frac{18{,}000}{1{,}095.45}\right)(\$100) = \$1{,}643.16$$

And

$$\text{Annual carrying costs} = \left(\frac{Q}{2}\right)(IC) = \left(\frac{1{,}095.45}{2}\right)(0.3)(\$10) = \$1{,}643.18$$

Thus, we see that at the EOQ, the annual ordering cost and the annual carrying cost are equal, the very slight difference due to rounding. Exhibit S13-2 shows the equality of the two costs graphically.

At any lot size other than the EOQ, the total annual cost will increase, as shown by the total cost curve in Exhibit S13-2. If the lot size were increased, we would expect carrying cost to increase and ordering cost to decrease. A lot size of less than the EOQ will result in a reduced carrying cost but a higher ordering cost. Overall, however, minor changes in lot size have minimal impacts on total inventory policy costs, so it makes sense to think of the EOQ as a zone or range of lot-size values.

***Problem 3***

T-Square, Ltd., an engineering firm, uses packages of plastic tape of different patterns, widths, and shading to create layouts and other design drawings. About 2,000 packages are consumed each year. The supplier, an office supply company, offers quantity discounts as follows:

| *Quantity/Order* | *Unit Price* |
|---|---|
| 1–99 | $10.00 |
| 100–499 | 9.50 |
| 500 and up | 9.00 |

T-Square uses a 35 percent carrying-cost rate and spends about $30 placing a tape order. Use the EOQ with quantity discount procedure, as demonstrated in Example 13-5, to determine the appropriate tape lot size.

***Solution 3***

First, calculate the EOQ for the lowest available price:

$$EOQ_{9.00} = \sqrt{\frac{2(2{,}000)(\$30)}{(0.35)(\$9.00)}} = 195.18$$

This value is not within the applicable quantity range (500 and up), so repeat using the next available price:

$$EOQ_{9.50} = \sqrt{\frac{2(2{,}000)(\$30)}{(0.35)(\$9.50)}} = 189.97$$

This value is within the appropriate range (100–499), so it is a possible EOQ.

Next, calculate the total annual cost associated with the only feasible EOQ, (approximately) 190 packages, using Equation S13-1:

$$\begin{aligned} TC &= \left(\frac{D}{Q}\right)(S) + (IC)\left(\frac{Q}{2}\right) + DC \\ &= \left(\frac{2{,}000}{190}\right)(\$30) + (0.35)(\$9.50)\left(\frac{190}{2}\right) + (2{,}000)(\$9.50) \\ &= \$315.79 + \$315.88 + \$19{,}000.00 = \$19{,}631.67 \end{aligned}$$

Now calculate the total cost if the lot size were made equal to the next quantity break point, 500 units in this case:

$$\begin{aligned} TC &= \left(\frac{D}{Q}\right)(S) + (IC)\left(\frac{Q}{2}\right) + DC \\ &= \left(\frac{2{,}000}{500}\right)(\$30) + (0.35)(\$9)\left(\frac{500}{2}\right) + (2{,}000)(\$9) \\ &= \$120.00 + \$787.50 + \$18{,}000.00 = \$18{,}907.50 \end{aligned}$$

Since the total annual cost of ordering at the best quantity discount amount, 500 units, is less than that associated with the EOQ, the more economical lot size for T-square is 500 packages.

### *Problem 4*

The same extruded plastic case is used for three different colors of highlighter felt-tipped pen, A, B, and C. Demand for each color for the next five weeks is as follows (numbers are in thousands):

| | **Week** | | | | |
|---|---|---|---|---|---|
| | *1* | *2* | *3* | *4* | *5* |
| A | 10 | | | 10 | |
| B | 18 | | 18 | | 18 |
| C | 8 | 8 | 8 | 8 | 8 |

*a.* What is a plausible reason for demands for A and B to occur in alternate periods whereas demands for C occur in every period?
*b.* Calculate gross requirements for the plastic case. Then, given an on-hand balance of 70,000 at time 0, a lead time of two weeks, and an order quantity of 20,000, calculate planned order releases.

### *Solution 4*

*a.* Demand for colors A and B appears to come from planned orders for a higher-level parent item, perhaps a package containing both colors of highlighter pen. Color C's demand could be independent, perhaps direct orders from a wholesaler or retailer.
*b.*

| | **Week** | | | | | |
|---|---|---|---|---|---|---|
| | *0* | *1* | *2* | *3* | *4* | *5* |
| Gross requirements | | 36 | 8 | 26 | 18 | 26 |
| Scheduled receipts | | | | | | |
| Projected stock balance | 70 | 34 | 26 | 0 | 2<br>−~~18~~ | 16<br>−~~24~~ |
| Planned order releases | | | 20 | 40 | | |

*Explanation:* The projected −18 in week 4 requires a planned order of 20 backscheduled by 2 weeks to week 2. The projected −24 in week 5 requires a double lot size—40 instead of 20—backscheduled to week 3.

## Exercises

1. A beer distributor reorders when a stock item drops to a reorder point. Reorder points include statistical safety stocks with the service level set at 95 percent. For MGD beer, the forecast usage for the next two weeks is 600 cases and the standard deviation of demand has been 100 cases (for a two-week period). Purchase lead time is one week (a five-day workweek).

*a.* What is the safety stock? How many working days' supply is it?
*b.* What is the ROP?
*c.* How many times larger would the safety stock have to be provide 99 percent service to MGD customers? How many working days' supply does the 99 percent level provide?
*d.* Statistical safety stock protects against demand variability. What other two factors do you think are especially important influences on size of safety stock for MGD beer? Explain.

2. Brown Instrument Company replenishes replacement (service) parts based on statistical reorder point. One part is a 40-mm thumbscrew. Relevant data for the thumbscrew are

$$\text{Planned stockout frequency} = \text{One per year}$$
$$\text{Planned lead time} = 1 \text{ week}$$
$$\text{Forecast for next week} = 100$$
$$\text{Batch size} = 300$$
$$\text{Standard deviation of demand} = 25 \text{ (per week)}$$

*a.* What is the reorder point? (Hint: Convert planned stockout frequency, in weeks, to service level.)
*b.* What would be the effect on ROP if lead time were four weeks instead of one? (Just discuss the effect; don't try to calculate it.)

3. An auto muffler shop reorders all common mufflers, and the like, every Tuesday morning. (Rarely needed mufflers are not stocked.) Two of the biggest-selling models are muffler A and muffler B. Each is ordered if stock is below 3, and enough are ordered to bring the supply up to 10; under this reordering system, the average inventory of each is about 8. It takes two days to replenish.

A reorder-point policy with a service level of 90 percent is being considered as a replacement for the present policy. To see whether ROP would reduce costly inventories, the following data are provided:

| | *Muffler A* | *Muffler B* |
|---|---|---|
| Item cost | $7 | $39 |
| Daily usage (average) | 2 | 2 |
| Standard deviation of daily usage | 1.5 | 1.5 |

*a.* What kind of reorder policy is the present one? Are there names for it?
*b.* What safety stocks and ROPs would there be for mufflers A and B under a perpetual system?
*c.* Should the muffler shop go to a perpetual system? Stay with the present system? Devise a hybrid system? Discuss, including pros and cons.

4. One storeroom item has an average demand of 1,200 per year. Demand variability, as measured by standard deviation, is 25 (based on monthly calculations).
*a.* If the desired service level is 95 percent and the lead time is 1.5 months, what is the statistical safety stock?
*b.* The item is bulky, costs over $1,000 per unit, and is bought from a variety of suppliers. What effects should these factors have on the safety stock? Explain.

5. Star City Tool and Die has been using a certain 2-inch-square metal insert at an average rate of 300 per day with a standard deviation of 50. Star City makes the inserts itself on its punch press. Only one day is needed to make more of them.
   *a.* The insert is so critical that management wants the item to be available (in stock) 99.9 percent of the time. What is the statistical safety stock? What is the statistical reorder point?
   *b.* The insert has been required for only the past six weeks and is inexpensive to make. Should these factors affect safety stock and reorder point? Explain. Could a more permanent plan be developed? Should it?
6. Fuel oil is one source of heat in a northern university. Average fuel demand in winter is 10,000 gallons per month. The reorder point is 6,400 gallons, the average lead time is two weeks, and the order quantity is 12,000 gallons.
   *a.* How many orders are there in an average five-month winter season?
   *b.* What is the demand during lead time? What is the safety stock?
7. Would the comparison between lot-for-lot and batch (Exhibit 13-4) make sense if clients were being processed instead of apples? If so, develop a brief example and explain. If not, explain why not.
8. The master scheduling team at a plant producing steel chain is considering a lot-for-lot policy instead of batching into larger lots. The following is their partially completed analysis for three levels of chain making (final chain making, fed by fabrication of cut steel pieces, fed by purchased steel rods).

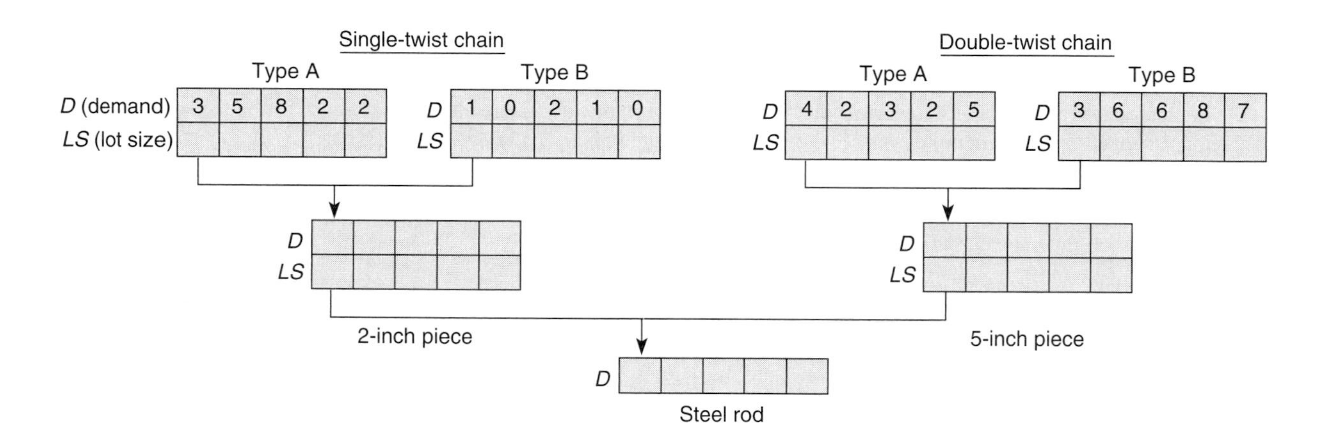


   *a.* Complete the lot-for-lot analysis, following the method of Exhibit 13-4A.
   *b.* Now construct a similar analysis, following the method of Exhibit 13-4B; assume a lot size of 10 for type A and 5 for type B single-twist chain making, 15 for type A and 20 for type B double-twist chain making, 20 for 2-inch-piece fabrication and 40 for 5-inch-piece fabrication.
   *c.* Does your analysis demonstrate the benefits of lot-for-lot in this example of uneven end-product (finished chain) demand? Discuss.
9. The provincial government uses massive quantities of computer printer paper, which it buys centrally. The purchasing department calculates an economic order quantity based on an assumed carrying-cost rate of 30 percent per year. A box of printer paper costs $45, it costs $80 to process an order, and annual demand is for 44,000 boxes of paper.

*a.* What is the EOQ?

*b.* The buyer finds that 800 boxes would be a whole truckload. Should she simply order one truckload? Think about this carefully, and explain your answer.

10. Continental Plate and Boiler Company has one storeroom that holds various sizes of pipe and steel plate. Following are costs and other data associated with pipe and plate buying and storage:

| | |
|---|---|
| Average inventory on hand | $2.0 million |
| Purchasing department wages and overhead | $105,000/year |
| Purchases of pipe and plate | $4.5 million/year |
| Number of purchase orders processed | 800/year |
| Interest rate | 18 percent per year |
| Depreciation on storeroom and its storage racks | $31,000/year |
| Overhead and expenses (including taxes and insurance to operate store (room) | $88,000/year |
| Storeroom salaries | $32,000/year |

*a.* What is the average cost of processing a purchase order ($S$)?

*b.* What is the annual capital cost? Annual holding cost? What is the carrying cost rate ($I$)?

*c.* What are some other, less tangible costs of carrying inventory? How might those costs affect inventory policy at Continental?

11. Maple Tree Insurance Company uses 2,000 boxes of staples per year. The boxes are priced at $3 in quantities of 0 to 299 boxes or $2.60 in quantities of 300 boxes or more. If it costs $15 to process an order and the annual carrying cost rate is 0.30, how many boxes should be ordered at one time? Explain your reasoning and support with a cost analysis.

12. A chemical plant consumes sulfuric acid in a certain process at a uniform rate. Total annual consumption is 25,000 gallons. The plant produces its own sulfuric acid and can set up a production run for a cost of $4,000. The acid can be stored for $21 per gallon per year, including all carrying costs (cost of capital as well as cost to hold in storage). The production rate is so rapid that inventory depletion during production may be ignored.

    *a.* What is the economic order quantity?

    *b.* How many times per year should the acid be produced?

13. A cannery buys knocked-down cardboard boxes from a box company. Demand is 40,000 boxes per year. The inventory carrying-cost rate is 0.25 per year, and the cannery's purchasing department estimates order processing cost at $20. The box company prices the boxes as follows:

    For a purchase of 100 to 3,999 boxes: $0.60 each (minimum order = 100)

    For a purchase of 4,000 or more boxes: $0.50 each

    *a.* Determine the economic order quantity.

    *b.* Express your EOQ in months' supply, and then in dollars.

14. Among other things, Marksman Industries makes 10 different models of gun-cleaning rods. Presently, the 10 models are manufactured one at a time, each for about one week's worth of production (average). The schedule is supposed to provide enough of a given model during the weeklong production run to satisfy about 10 weeks of consumer demand (it will not be made again for 10 weeks). The problem is that by the end of the 10-week cycle for a model, expected consumer demand may have changed. By the time of the next production run, Marksman may have run out of a given model or accumulated a large excess. How can Marksman be more responsive to actual consumer demand? Explain. (Note: You may need to draw from topics you've covered in previous chapters.)

15. Federal Time Corporation makes and sells clocks. Plastic lenses for clock faces are molded in Federal's own facilities. One popular table model has an annual demand of 50,000 clocks; its lens costs $0.90 to make. Setup to mold the lens, consisting of inserting and clamping the correct mold in the injection-molding equipment, costs $120 per production run. (Setup time is about four hours.)
   *a.* Federal has been using EOQ to determine number of lenses per production run. It uses an inventory carrying cost rate of 0.40. What is the EOQ for this lens?
   *b.* The plant manager has become convinced that there are benefits in running lenses in much smaller lots than EOQs. The four-hour setup time must be reduced in order to make small lots economical. What kinds of improvements does Federal need in order to achieve single-digit setup? To achieve one-touch setup?

16. A well-known phenomenon in the semiconductor industry (making microprocessors and memory chips) is that fast processing of a production lot has a higher process yield than slow processing. (*Process yield* means number of good chips from a wafer—i.e., chips that pass electronic tests of quality.) The reason is that the wafers are susceptible to handling, dust, and other kinds of damage that are reduced if the production run is completed and the chips sealed over quickly.

   One semiconductor manufacturer has several models of memory chip to run, one at a time. A production run of a given model normally takes five weeks, but a few small, special runs have been completed in as little as two weeks, with high process yields. How can a manufacturer gain these advantages all the time instead of only in special cases?

17. A bill of materials (BOM) for end item A is shown below. The numbers indicate quantities of each part number required in the parent assembly; for example, each A requires 2 Bs, 2 Cs, and 4 Ds.

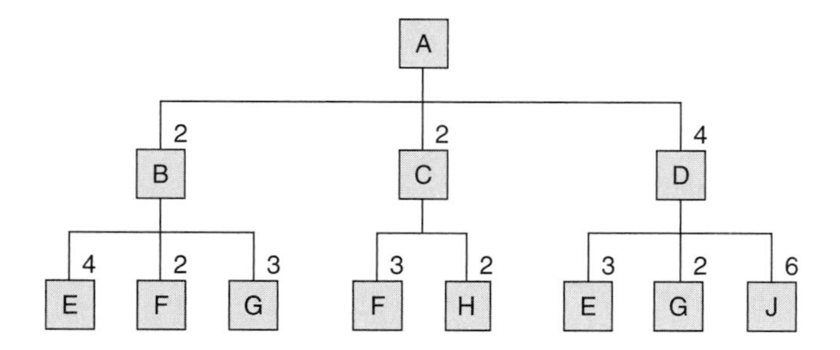


   *a.* If 20 As are to be made, what is the gross number of Fs that will be consumed?
   *b.* Suppose that the correct answer to part *a* exactly equals the number of Fs that are currently in stock. Will that quantity be sufficient for the production of the 20 As? Explain your response?
   *c.* If 15 As are to be made and total on-hand inventory consists of 30 Ds, how many Es will need to be obtained?
   *d.* If 15 As are to be made and total on-hand inventory consists of 6 Cs and 60 Es, what will be the net requirement for Es?
   *e.* Which of the items (A through J) shown in the figure is most likely to be an independent demand item? Why?

18. Partially completed MRP planning records for three of the items contained in the bill of materials (BOM) in Exercise 17 are shown below. *Considering these three items only,* use

the BOM figure to answer the following questions. You may wish to make additional entries on the records, and you will need to refer to the BOM. Assume *lot-for-lot* orders.

| | Time Periods | | | | | | | |
|---|---|---|---|---|---|---|---|---|
| A: Lead time =1 | 1 | 2 | 3 | 4 | 5 | 6 | 7 | 8 |
| Gross requirements | | | | | 80 | | | |
| Scheduled receipts | | | | 20 | | | | |
| On-hand inventory 50 | | | | | | | | |
| Planned orders | | | | | | | | |

| D: Lead time = 2 | | | | | | | | |
|---|---|---|---|---|---|---|---|---|
| Gross requirements | 40 | | 30 | | | | 300 | |
| Scheduled receipts | | | | | | | | |
| On-hand inventory 60 | | | | | | | | |
| Planned orders | | | | | | | | |

| J: Lead time = 1 | | | | | | | | |
|---|---|---|---|---|---|---|---|---|
| Gross requirements | | | | | | | | |
| Scheduled receipts | | | | | | | | |
| On hand inventory 100 | | | | | | | | |
| Planned orders | | | | | | | | |

*a.* The first planned order for A's should be placed in what period?
*b.* How many D's should be ordered in period 2?
*c.* The first gross requirement for J's occurs in what period?
*d.* The first planned order for J's will be in what quantity?
*e.* The first order for J's will be planned for what period?

19. The following matrix shows partial MRP data for a component part. Scheduled receipts and the planned order release row are missing. Lead time is 2 weeks, and a fixed quantity ordering rule is in effect.

| | Week | | | | | |
|---|---|---|---|---|---|---|
| | *0* | *1* | *2* | *3* | *4* | *5* |
| Gross requirements | | 80 | 120 | 90 | 100 | 90 |
| Scheduled receipts | | | | | | |
| Projected stock balance | 190 | 110 | 120 | 30 | 60 | 100 |

What fixed order quantity is used? When is a scheduled receipt due in? In what period is there a planned order release?

20. A partial master production schedule and material requirements plans for a bicycle manufacturer are shown in the accompanying figure.

0-level
Master schedule—26-inch bicycles

| | Weeks | | | | | | | |
|---|---|---|---|---|---|---|---|---|
| | 1 | 2 | 3 | 4 | 5 | 6 | 7 | 8 |
| Master schedule—26-inch bicycles | 40 | 0 | 50 | 0 | 0 | 60 | 0 | 60 |

First-level MRP
Handlebars—1 per bicycle
$LT = 4$, $Q = 100$

| | | 1 | 2 | 3 | 4 | 5 | 6 | 7 | 8 |
|---|---|---|---|---|---|---|---|---|---|
| Gross requirements | | 40 | 0 | 50 | 0 | 0 | 60 | 0 | 60 |
| Scheduled receipts | | | | 100 | | | | | |
| Projected stock balance | 80 | | | | | | | | |
| Planned order release | | | | | | | | | |

From first-level MRP—24-inch bike
From first-level MRP—27-inch bike

Second-level MRP
Cut tubes

1/4 tube per handlebar
$LT = 5$, $Q = 200$

| | | 1 | 2 | 3 | 4 | 5 | 6 | 7 | 8 |
|---|---|---|---|---|---|---|---|---|---|
| Gross requirements | | 50 | | | | | | 120 | |
| Scheduled receipts | | | | | | | | | |
| Projected stock balance | 190 | | | | | | | | |
| Planned order release | | | | | | | | | |

*a.* Complete the calculations of gross requirements, projected stock balances, and planned order releases for handlebars and cut tubes.

*b.* Recalculate the planned order release for cut tubing given a scrap allowance of 3 percent.

21. Six companies produce and sell irrigation equipment in the same region of the country. Company A has a reorder point system. Company B uses MRP, but only to launch orders. Company C has full closed-loop MRP. Company D uses MRP plus distribution requirements planning. Company E has an MRP II system (including DRP). Company F produces orders as they are booked, with each assembly triggering pull signals back through all processes and small kanban quantities of all parts kept on the plant floor. Discuss each company's *likely* competitive strengths and weaknesses.
22. Acme Wood Products Corporation makes wooden picture frames. The 10-by-12-inch size is made with three finishes: oak stained, walnut stained, and mahogany stained. The parts needed for final assembly and finishing for each frame are two 10-inch and two 12-inch wood pieces and four corner brackets. Inventory planning is by MRP. Lot sizes are 2,000 for wood parts and 5,000 for brackets.
    *a.* Construct the BOM structure. You need not limit yourself to the given data.
    *b.* What should go into the item master file? Be as specific as possible given the above data, but you need not limit yourself to these data.
    *c.* Assume that for every oak-stained frame, two walnut-stained and three mahogany-stained frames are made. Also assume that gross requirements for 10-inch wood pieces in the next five weeks are 0, 1200, 0, 480, and 600. Compute all parent-item gross requirements based on these gross requirements for the wood pieces (work backward).
    *d.* Based on the gross requirements information from (*c*), compute the planned-order-release schedule for 10-inch wood pieces only. Assume a current on-hand balance of zero and a lead time of one week.
23. The following sketch shows the two main parts of a transparent-tape dispenser: molded plastic housing and roll of tape. A master production schedule for the dispenser (sold with a roll of tape mounted) is shown below the sketch.

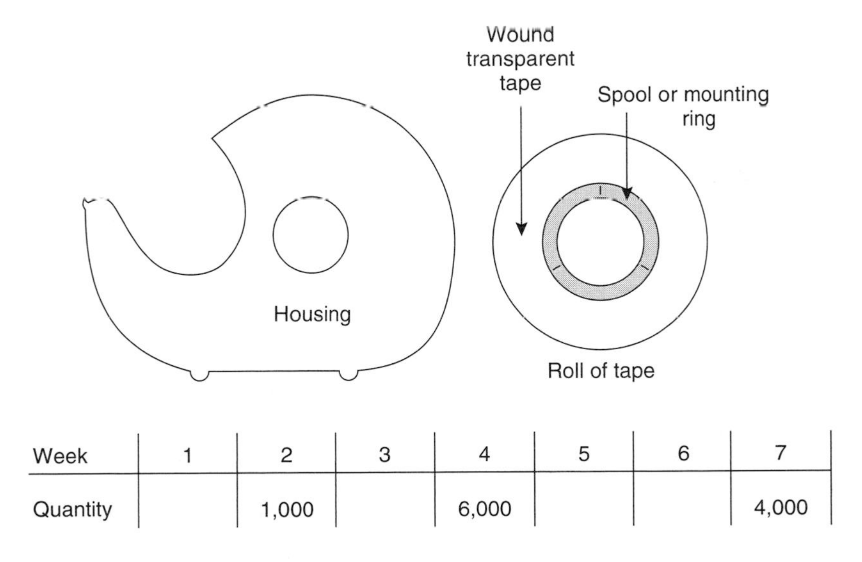


| Week | 1 | 2 | 3 | 4 | 5 | 6 | 7 |
|---|---|---|---|---|---|---|---|
| Quantity | | 1,000 | | 6,000 | | | 4,000 |

    *a.* Draw a structured bill of materials for the tape dispenser. Include the main parts and one level of parts below that.
    *b.* Assume that lead times are one week for the roll of tape and two weeks for the spool (mounting ring). Beginning on-hand balances are 1,200 for the roll of tape and 3,000 for

the spool. Draw the MPS, with MRPs for the roll of tape and the spool below it. (Do not include housing and wound transparent tape.) Compute gross requirements, scheduled receipts (if any), on-hand balances, and planned order releases for the roll of tape and the spool. Use lot-for-lot order quantities. Show your results in the usual MRP display format.

*c.* Explain your entries or lack of entries in the scheduled-receipts row for both the roll of tape and the spool.

*d.* Assume that the rolls of tape are sold separately as well as being a component of the tape dispenser. Make up a forecast of independent (external) demand for rolls of tape for each of the seven time buckets. Merge your forecast of independent demand with the dependent demand from the parent item. Also, assume an on-hand balance of 2,000 for the roll of tape and a scheduled receipt of 4,000 in week 2 for the spool. Recompute MRPs as in (*b*). What could explain the quantity 4,000 as a scheduled receipt in week 2?

24. Assume you are employed by a company that makes a type of simple chair (you decide on the chair's design). MRP is to be the method of inventory planning for the chair.
    *a.* Draw a bill-of-materials structure for the chair. Briefly explain or sketch the type of chair.
    *b.* Develop an 8-to 10-week MPS for the chair.
    *c.* Develop MRPs for three or four of the chair's components, with the following restrictions:
    (1) Include level 1 and level 2 components (e.g., a chair arm might be level 1 and the raw material for making it level 2).
    (2) Make your own assumptions about lead times, order quantities, and beginning inventories.

    Your answer should be realistic; no two students should have the same answer.

25. Follow the instructions of Exercise 24, but use a pair of scissors that has molded-plastic finger and thumb pieces attached to the blade extensions as your product.

26. Select a product composed of fabricated parts (not one referred to in the text explanation of MRP or in preceding MRP problems). In one page, develop an MPS for the product, plus a level 1 MRP for a major module and a level 2 MRP for a part that goes into the level 1 module. (Hint: See Exercise 18.)
    *a.* Develop an 8- to 10-week planning period.
    *b.* Draw the MPS at the top of your page, with time buckets for the two levels of parts MRPs lined up below it. The material requirements plans for the parts should include four rows: one for gross requirements, one for scheduled receipts, one for projected stock balance, and one for planned order releases. Make up the following data: realistic quantities for the MPS; beginning on-hand balances, lead times, and order quantities for each part (make one order quantity fixed and the other lot-for-lot); and one or more scheduled receipts based on a previous, already-released order (be careful about the timing and quantity of scheduled receipts).
    *c.* For level 1 and level 2 parts, calculate the timing and quantities of gross requirements, scheduled receipts, on-hand balance, and planned order releases. Display results on your charts, and
    (1) Include a safety stock for one of the parts.
    (2) Include a scrap allowance for one of the parts.
    (3) Include demands from an external source (rather than from parent planned order releases) for one of the parts.

27. Below are bills of materials for two sizes of kitchen knife. Two parts are common to both knives: rivets and 8-foot wood bars. Also, a 6-inch cut wood block is common to two different parents (handle, left, and handle, right) for the medium-size knife. Currently, there are no parts of any kind on hand or on order. Order quantities are lot-for-lot rather than fixed. The master schedule for the next seven weeks is given below.

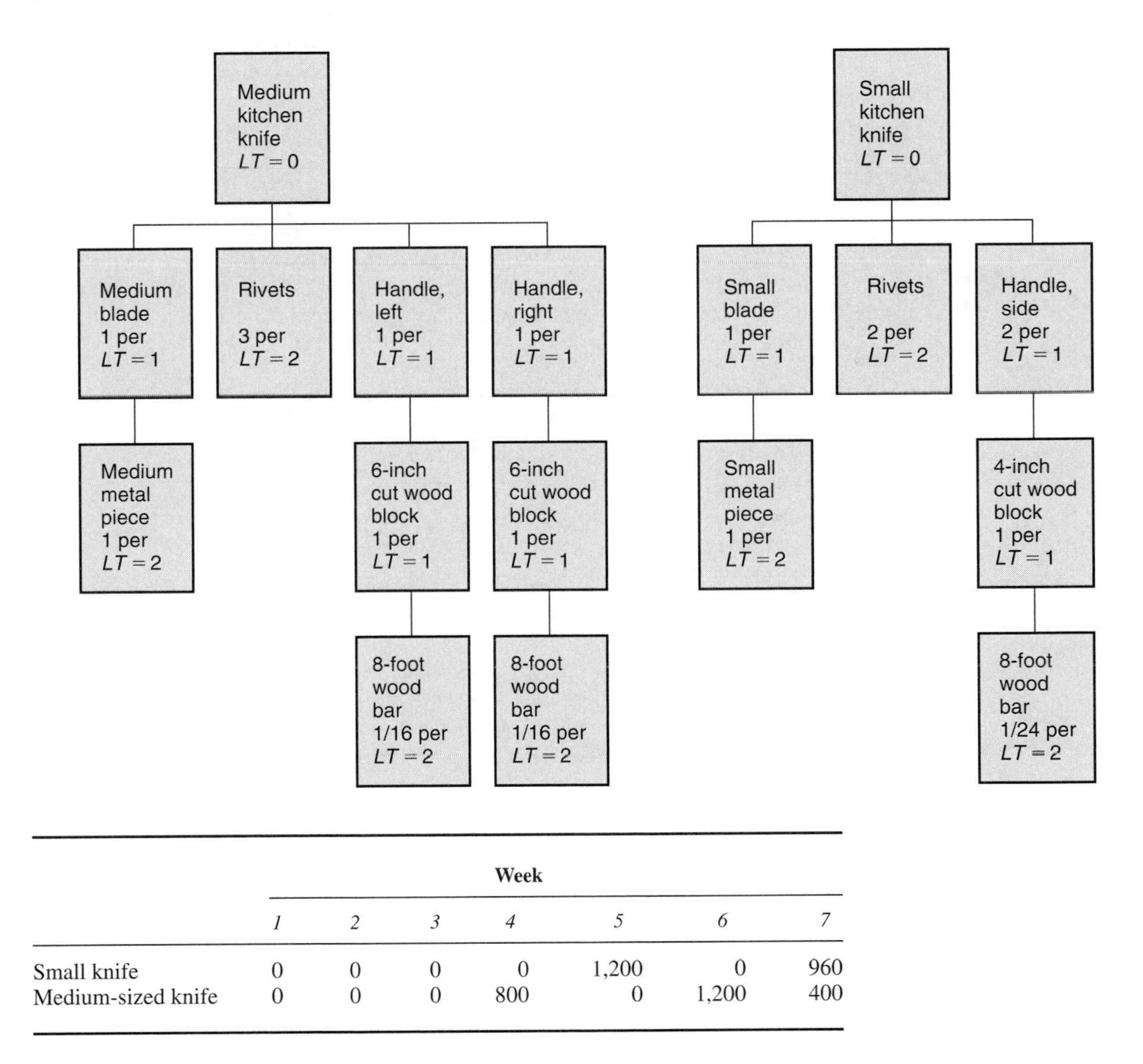


| | Week | | | | | | |
|---|---|---|---|---|---|---|---|
| | *1* | *2* | *3* | *4* | *5* | *6* | *7* |
| Small knife | 0 | 0 | 0 | 0 | 1,200 | 0 | 960 |
| Medium-sized knife | 0 | 0 | 0 | 800 | 0 | 1,200 | 400 |

*a.* What is the first planned order release for rivets? Calculate quantity and week.

*b.* What is the total number of 4-inch cut wood blocks that should be ordered to cover MPS demand in weeks 1 through 5?

*c.* How many 8-foot wood bars should be ordered in week 3?

**SUPPLEMENT**

# ECONOMIC ORDER QUANTITY: THEORY AND DERIVATIONS

The economic order quantity (EOQ) is one of the oldest tools of management science: In 1915, F. W. Harris developed a basic EOQ model. The EOQ is the number of units of a single item that should be planned whenever an order is placed so as to minimize the inventory management costs of that single item during a given time period, usually one year. In this supplement, we first address EOQ assumptions, take a look at categories of costs that arise in inventory management, and then put everything together to determine the EOQ and other related order quantities.

## EOQ Assumptions

Like most models, the basic EOQ makes a few simplifying assumptions. While the real world never quite matches the assumptions, sometimes the matchup is close enough for EOQ concepts to be helpful. Assumptions that pertain to the *basic* EOQ model include:

1. Demand is known and constant, without seasonality. Past demand is used to forecast future period demand.
2. Order processing (or setup) costs are known and constant—they don't vary with quantity ordered.
3. Cost per unit (e.g., purchase price or production cost) is constant; there are no quantity discounts or economies of scale. (Later in this supplement, we extend EOQ concepts to include quantity discounts.)
4. The entire lot is delivered at one time (instantaneous acquisition). This is commonly the case for purchased goods, but not for items produced by the user.
5. The carrying-cost rate is known and constant. Total carrying costs are a linear function and depend on carrying-cost rate and quantity ordered.
6. The inventory depletion rate is constant throughout the order cycle; the average inventory equals one-half the quantity ordered.

## Costs of Inventory

EOQ logic seeks to minimize three types of period inventory costs: order processing cost, carrying cost, and item cost.

**1. Order Processing Cost.** In a given time period (say, a year), an item may be reordered once, twice, three times, or more, even daily in some JIT cases. If it is ordered once, the lot size is large enough to cover the whole year's demand; if ordered twice, a half-year's demand is the lot size; and so on.

The costs of processing an order include the clerical costs of preparing the purchase order or work order. If it is a purchase order, costs of order expediting and processing the invoice are included; if it is a work order, the main cost may be process setup cost. If $S$ is the average cost of processing an order, $Q$ is the lot size (quantity ordered), and $D$ is the forecast annual demand for a given item, then

$$\frac{D}{Q} = \text{Number of orders per year}$$

$$S\left(\frac{D}{Q}\right) = \text{Annual cost of processing orders}$$

Forecast demand ($D$) could cover a period other than a year. For example, if $D$ represents monthly demand, $S(D/Q)$ equals the monthly cost of processing orders.

**2. Carrying Cost.** Carrying cost (discussed at length in Chapter 10) is the cost to finance inventory and hold it in idleness. Thus, carrying cost increases as number of idle units increases. If an item is reordered infrequently in large lots, its carrying costs will be large; if ordered often in small lots, its carrying costs will be small.

Total carrying costs per period divided by value of all inventory items yields what is known as the annual inventory-carrying-cost rate ($I$). Cost analysts may set one rate for all items carried in a given firm. To compute annual carrying cost for a single item, we need the unit cost ($C$) for the item. Then:

$$IC = \text{Cost to carry one unit for one year}$$

For any given lot size ($Q$), annual carrying cost equals annual cost to carry one unit times average number of idle units, ($Q/2$). Symbolically, for a given item we have:

$$IC\left(\frac{Q}{2}\right) = \text{Annual carrying cost}$$

Why is the average inventory equal to $Q/2$? Exhibit S13-1 illustrates the repetition of EOQ order cycles during the year. Inventory increases from 0 to $Q$ (the EOQ) on receipt of each order. Demands during the order cycle reduce inventory from $Q$ to 0. The average amount of inventory, then, is simply the average of the maximum amount ($Q$), and the minimum amount (0), or $Q/2$. (The mathematically inclined might prefer to make the point with a geometrical proof that triangles I and II in Exhibit S13-1 are identical.)

**3. Item Cost.** Item cost comes into play, for instance, when the buyer may obtain price discounts by buying in quantity. But recall that an assumption of the basic EOQ model is constant

**EXHIBIT S13-1 EOQ Order Cycles over Time**

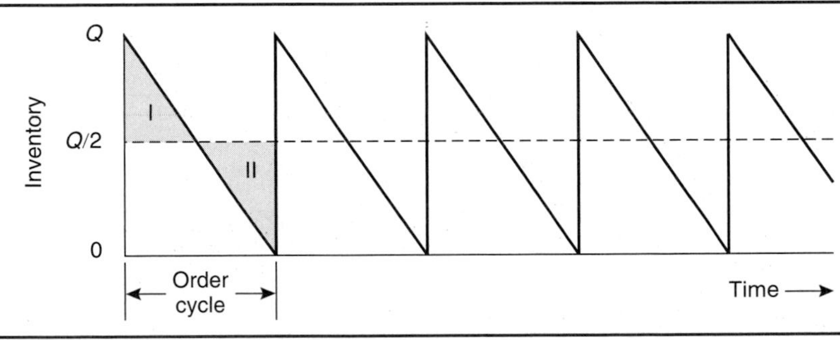

item cost or price; it is unaffected by quantity ordered. The annual item cost, therefore, is annual demand ($D$) times unit cost ($C$). Though necessary for materials budgeting, item cost is mathematically removed from consideration in basic EOQ computations.

We may compute a total annual cost for the item by summing the order-processing costs, carrying costs, and item costs:

$$\text{Total cost} = TC = \left(\frac{D}{Q}\right)(S) + (IC)\left(\frac{Q}{2}\right) + (DC) \qquad \text{(S13-1)}$$

## Basic EOQ Formula Derivation

Exhibit S13-2 shows a plot of the cost elements contained in Equation S13-1 as they would vary with lot size. Item costs, independent of lot size, needn't be plotted. The EOQ is the order quantity that minimizes total annual costs—that is, where the slope of the total cost curve is zero. Also, as the vertical dashed line shows, annual order-processing costs equal annual carrying costs at the EOQ.

Thus, by taking the derivative of the total cost function with respect to $Q$ and setting it equal to the slope (zero), we obtain an expression for the EOQ:

$$\frac{d(TC)}{d(Q)} = \frac{d\left[\left(\frac{D}{Q}\right)(S) + (IC)\left(\frac{Q}{2}\right) + (D)(C)\right]}{d(Q)} = 0$$

$$= -\frac{DS}{Q^2} + \frac{IC}{2} = 0$$

Rearranging the terms, we obtain

$$Q^2 = \frac{2DS}{IC}$$

**EXHIBIT S13-2 Graph of Annual Inventory Policy Cost and Lot Sizes**

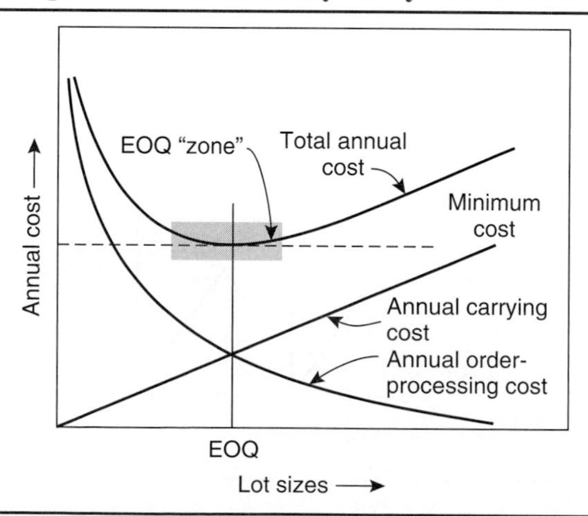

By taking the square roots of both sides,

$$Q = \sqrt{\frac{2DS}{IC}} \tag{S13-2}$$

Equation S13-2 is the classic EOQ formula. Example S13-1 demonstrates the computations, and Example 13-4 in the chapter illustrates how the EOQ model might work in practice. Before turning to extensions of the basic model, two practical reminders are in order:

## Example S13-1: Basic EOQ Computations

Annual demand for an item with a unit cost of $4.00 is 5,000 units. The carrying-cost rate is 50 percent, and it costs $100 to process an order. Compute EOQ and total annual inventory costs for the item.

*Solution*

EOQ is determined with Equation S13-2:

$$EOQ = \sqrt{\frac{2DS}{IC}} = \sqrt{\frac{2(5{,}000)(\$100)}{0.5(\$4)}} = 707$$

Substitute values into Equation S13-1 to obtain total annual inventory costs:

$$\begin{aligned} TC &= \left(\frac{D}{Q}\right)(S) + (IC)\left(\frac{Q}{2}\right) + DC \\ &= \frac{5{,}000}{707}(\$100) + (0.5)(\$4)\left(\frac{707}{2}\right) + 5{,}000(\$4) \\ &= \$707 + \$707 + \$20{,}000 = \$21{,}414 \end{aligned}$$

- In Exhibit S13-2, a shaded zone contains the minimum cost point. In that zone, which is fairly large horizontally, total annual cost does not deviate much from the minimum. Thus, in a practical sense, EOQ may be thought of as a zone or range of lot sizes, rather than as an exact quantity.
- The total cost curve shown in Exhibit S13-2 reflects inventory *policy* costs only. In practice, item costs ($D \times C$), though not considered in *basic* EOQ determination, can be considerably more than the annual policy costs.

### EOQ with Quantity Discounts

Sometimes the cost for purchased items varies due to quantity discounts—price breaks offered by a supplier for volume purchases. Item cost then becomes a relevant factor (along with annual carrying and order-processing costs) in total inventory costs. In the quantity discount situation, we use Equation S13-2 to compute an EOQ. But if the price break afforded at the next (larger) order quantity point reduces total annual costs, then that larger order quantity is the true economic order quantity. A procedure for finding the true EOQ and total annual inventory costs is

1. With Equation S13-2, compute the EOQ using the lowest offered price as item cost ($C$). If the EOQ falls within the quantity range that applies to the lowest feasible price, it is the true EOQ. Use Equation S13-1 to find total annual costs.
2. If the EOQ falls below the lowest-price quantity range, use the next higher price as the value for $C$ and recompute the EOQ. If the (newly) computed EOQ is not within the relevant quantity range for that price, move to the next higher price, and so on.
3. When the computed EOQ is within the appropriate quantity range, use equation S13-1 to find total annual costs at that order quantity and at the order quantity that would permit the next price break. The lower of the two costs identifies the true economic order quantity.

Example S13-2 explains the procedure and illustrates the computations. In the body of the chapter, Example 13-5 shows how EOQ with quantity discounts might be applied by a small business.

## Example S13-2: EOQ WITH QUANTITY DISCOUNT COMPUTATIONS

Annual demand for an item is 5,000 units. The carrying-cost rate is 50 percent, and it costs $100 to process an order. Quantity price breaks are available as shown in the table below:

| *Quantity Range* | *Price per Unit ($)* |
|---|---|
| 0–99 | 4.00 |
| 100–499 | 3.80 |
| 500–999 | 3.60 |
| 1,000 and up | 3.40 |

Compute EOQ and total annual inventory costs for the item.

*Solution*

First, use Equation S13-2 to compute EOQ with the lowest possible price, $3.40, as the item cost:

$$EOQ = \sqrt{\frac{2DS}{IC}} = \sqrt{\frac{2(5{,}000)(\$100)}{0.5\,(\$3.40)}} = 767$$

Since the computed EOQ, 767, is not within the appropriate quantity range of 1,000 or more, move to the next price and recompute the EOQ:

$$EOQ = \sqrt{\frac{2DS}{IC}} = \sqrt{\frac{2(5{,}000)(\$100)}{0.5\,(\$3.60)}} = 745$$

This EOQ is within the applicable quantity range (500–999), so move on to computation of total costs. At the computed EOQ, Equation S13-1 yields

$$
\begin{aligned}
TC_{745} &= \frac{D}{Q}(S) + IC\left(\frac{Q}{2}\right) + DC \\
&= \frac{5{,}000}{745}(\$100) + (0.5)(\$3.60)\left(\frac{745}{2}\right) + 5{,}000(\$3.60) \\
&= \$671 + \$671 + \$18{,}000 = \$19{,}342
\end{aligned}
$$

Total costs for the next price-break point—that is, order quantity of 1,000 at a unit price of \$3.40:

$$
\begin{aligned}
TC_{1,000} &= \frac{D}{Q}(S) + IC\left(\frac{Q}{2}\right) + DC \\
&- \frac{5{,}000}{1{,}000}(\$100) + (0.5)(\$3.40)\left(\frac{1{,}000}{2}\right) + 5{,}000\,(\$3.40) \\
&= \$500 + \$850 + \$17{,}000 = \$18{,}350
\end{aligned}
$$

Thus, 1,000 is the true EOQ since total annual costs are less at that order quantity. Item cost reduction with the price break more than offsets the slightly higher inventory policy costs.

## Economic Manufacturing Quantity

Basic EOQ is suitable for purchased items—an economic purchase quantity—in which the whole lot is usually delivered at one time. When an item is made instead of bought, the quantity ordered is available in trickles as it comes off the production line. This complicates figuring average inventory, on which annual carrying cost is based, and results in a modified EOQ formula. The modification may be called an **economic manufacturing quantity (EMQ)** formula.

EMQ formula also applies to the rare case in which a purchased lot is delivered in trickles, instead of all at once.

The EMQ calls for one new term, the production rate ($P$). $P$ is measured in the same units as $D$ (demand rate), typically in units per year. $P$ must be greater than $D$ in order for the demand to be covered. $P - D$ is the rate of inventory buildup; that is, producing at rate $P$ and using at rate $D$. The difference equals the rate of increase in stock. (Some prefer to use weekly or monthly build-and-use rates, which work just as well in the EMQ model.)

To develop the model, consider that a lot is made in time $T$:

$$Inv_{\max} = Q_{\max} = \text{Build rate} \times \text{Time} = (P - D)(T)$$

Since $Q_{\max}$ is maximum planned inventory and $Q_{\max}/2$ is average inventory,

$$\text{Average inventory} = \frac{Q_{\max}}{2} = \frac{(P - D)(T)}{2}$$

The term $T$ may be eliminated by substitution. The time needed to produce a lot, $Q$, is

$$T = \frac{\text{Quantity}}{\text{Rate}} = \frac{Q}{P}$$

Thus,

$$\text{Average inventory} = \left(\frac{P-Q}{2}\right)\left(\frac{Q}{P}\right) \quad \text{or} \quad \left(\frac{P-D}{P}\right)\left(\frac{Q}{2}\right)$$

And

$$\text{Annual carrying costs} = (IC)\left(\frac{P-D}{P}\right)\left(\frac{Q}{2}\right)$$

Using this expression for carrying costs to replace the carrying cost element in Equation S13-1, again taking the first derivative with respect to $Q$, and rearranging the terms as we did when deriving the basic EOQ formula, we obtain

$$\frac{DS}{Q^2} = \left(\frac{IC}{2}\right)\left(\frac{P-D}{P}\right)$$

Or,

$$Q = \sqrt{\frac{2DS}{IC}\left(\frac{P}{P-D}\right)}$$

Alternatively,

$$EMQ = \sqrt{\frac{2DS}{(IC)(1-D/P)}} \qquad \text{(S13-3)}$$

Differences between basic EOQ and EMQ may be shown graphically. Exhibit S13-3A shows the general pattern of usage and replenishment for basic EOQ. It looks like a ripsaw blade. The vertical line represents the increase in stock that occurs when the whole EOQ is received at one time (instantaneous replenishment). The downward-sloping line is the average demand rate ($D$). Maximum quantity ($Q_{\text{max.}}$) is equal to $Q$, and average quantity ($Q_{\text{ave.}}$) is equal to $Q_{\text{max.}}/2$.

Exhibit S13-3B shows the general inventory pattern for EMQ. It looks like a cross-cut saw blade. The upward-sloping solid line represents the rate of inventory buildup ($P - D$); the production rate ($P$) is shown as a dashed line for reference purposes. The downward-sloping line is the average demand rate ($D$). Maximum inventory ($Q_{\text{max.}}$) is not equal to $Q$; the stock level never

**EXHIBIT S13-3 Basic EOQ and EMQ Replenishment Patterns**

A. Basic EOQ pattern of instantaneous replenishment

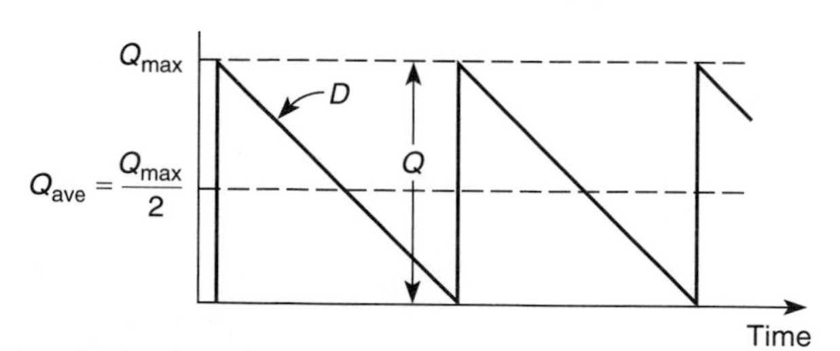


B. EMQ pattern of noninstantaneous replenishment

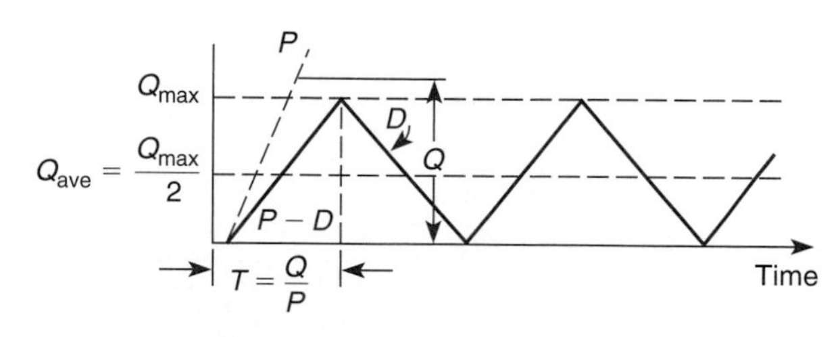

reaches $Q$ because some of $Q$ is being used up (delivered) as it is being produced. $Q_{max.}$ is, instead, equal to $(P - D)(T)$ or $(P - D)(Q/P)$, as was shown earlier, and $Q_{ave.}$ equals half of $Q_{max.}$

Note that for otherwise equal conditions, EMQ is larger than basic EOQ. Inspection of the EMQ formula shows this to be mathematically obvious, because the factor $1 - D/P$ in the denominator makes the denominator smaller and the EMQ larger. The logical reason is that with EMQ there is less stock to carry since part of $Q$ is used as it is produced; with less to carry, it is economical to produce a bit more per lot.

Example S13-3 illustrates the EMQ procedure.

## Example S13-3: EMQ Computations

Annual demand for an item produced in-house with a unit cost of $4.00 is 5,000 units. The carrying-cost rate is 50 percent, and it costs $100 to process an order. Production rate is 500 per week, and demand is constant throughout the year. Compute EMQ and total annual inventory costs for the item.

*Solution*

Constant demand translates into approximately 100 units per week (5,000 ÷ 50). Thus, the $D$:$P$ ratio required in the EMQ formula denominator is 100:500, or 0.2. With this and other supplied information, Equation S13-3 provides the EMQ:

$$EMQ = \sqrt{\frac{2DS}{IC(1 - D/P)}} = \sqrt{\frac{2(5{,}000)(\$100)}{0.5\,(\$4)(1 - 100/500)}} = 791$$

We determine total annual costs from Equation S13-1; the carrying cost element is modified to reflect non-instantaneous acquisition of inventory:

$$TC = \frac{D}{Q}(S) + IC\left(\frac{P - D}{P}\right)\left(\frac{Q}{2}\right) + DC$$

$$= \frac{5{,}000}{791}(\$100) + (0.5)(\$4)\left(\frac{500 - 100}{500}\right)\left(\frac{791}{2}\right) + 5{,}000(\$4)$$

$$= \$632 + \$632 + \$20{,}000 = \$21{,}264$$

CHAPTER 14

# FACILITIES MANAGEMENT

"The new Dana Corp building near Curitiba, 300 miles south of São Paulo supports a high, pitched roof designed to help keep it cool in the Brazilian summer and retain heat in winter."

Inside, employees build "the biggest module yet for an automotive industry that is turning to its suppliers for bigger and bigger subassemblies. It is nothing less than an entire chassis for a pickup truck, complete with steering equipment, fuel tank, drive shaft, suspension, brakes, and wheels already mounted with inflated tires. Every 42 minutes, three of these megamodules are lifted onto a truck that caries them about four miles up the highway to a new Daimler Chrysler plant."

"The bigger the module . . . the bigger the freight headache. Add to that the desire to reduce packing materials and still avoid transport damage, and the solution is obvious: beckon major suppliers closer to the customer's assembly line."

Source: Philip Seikman, "Building 'Em Better in Brazil," *Fortune,* September 6, 1999, pp. 246[C]ff.

On the phone to your Fidelity Investments advisor, you ask about the firm's global-growth fund. "I'd be happy to send you our brochure, which gives the fund's performance and other details," your advisor says.

But the prospectus doesn't come from your advisor. There are more efficient ways to serve Fidelity's customers, who request some millions of "kits" of informational materials and statements annually. To do this well, Fidelity has opened a huge printing and mailing facility in Covington, Kentucky. Using tracking and storage techniques perfected by manufacturers, "the nation's largest nutual-fund company has tried to reinvent the inglorious task of sorting, stuffing, and stamping mail. . . . Fidelity promises that when a customer calls seeking written information, it will be in the mail the next day. Each day's requests are sent electronically to Covington the following morning at 2 A.M. E.S.T. Fidelity has already pulled often-requested materials. For much of the mail, the company downloads the names and addresses into machines that 'ink-jet' the data on the cover and apply metered postage. The machines then optically read the ZIP Code, spray on a Postal Service bar code, sort the letters and spit them into different trays. About 90 percent of the shipments never see the inside of a post office [but are] hauled away by Postal Service trucks and taken directly to the airport."

Source: James S. Hirsch, "A High-Tech System for Sending the Mail Unfolds at Fidelity," *The Wall Street Journal,* March 20, 1996, pp. A1, A6.

In this final chapter of Part IV's coverage of operations management resources, the spotlight shifts to facilities and equipment. As we have done with other important business topics, we shall concentrate on the interfaces with OM, and caution the student that there is much more that needs to be studied about these critical components of transformation processes.

We begin with facilities location, then move on to consider layout. Next comes the all-important issue of plant and equipment maintenance. And we close the chapter with a brief look at handling and transportation issues. First, an overview.

## Facilities Management Overview

Dynamic competitiveness—a term that has appeared several times in earlier chapters—applies to this one as well. The "rules of the game" are changing. The opening vignettes provide a glimpse of how competitive dynamics have affected the operations management/location interface. Pressures to reduce handling and transportation costs and provide timely delivery bring supplier plants close to their durable-goods manufacturing customers. But when the product is a packet of information about a mutual fund, advances in communications, information processing, handling, and transportation technologies make location almost irrelevant as far as company operations are concerned.

Clearly, Fidelity must make use of facilities *somewhere*—either its own or those of a supplier—in order to provide the customer with the required information and thus accomplish business. The location, however, is not nearly so important as having the proper equipment, well-maintained and ready to carry out the order fulfillment activity. Perhaps, it is time to broaden the concept of facilities.

### *Broadened View of Facilities*

Traditionally, we thought of facilities as relatively permanent assets, fixed in place for many months if not for years. But contemporary realities that we have noted in earlier chapters, along with some newer ideas about layout that we address later in this chapter, act to alter that thinking. For one thing, time-based competition makes flexibility a mandate; long-term commitments to facilities are giving way to less permanent ones. Leasing replaces ownership, for instance.

Furthermore, where we work and what we work with have changed. Commuting is a way of life, as are work-at-home arrangements. For an increasing number of talented people, the building that keeps the elements away is not as important as the database that must be accessed. And who can work without the Internet, supported, of course, by the utilities infrastructure? So, just what are facilities?

Let's start with tangible, and then eliminate human resources and flow-through inventory (raw materials, WIP, and finished goods). What we have left might be considered facilities. Structures count of course, as do pieces of equipment, communications and transportation networks, databases, and utilities. What about MRO inventories—large tooling, for instance? Lines get blurry here, so perhaps we should leave those on the fence, so to speak. Manage them as facilities in some circumstances and as inventory in others. But MRO items needn't cause turf battles; there's plenty of responsibility to go around. And, as companies are becoming increasingly aware, responsibility for facilities extends up and down the supply chain.

### *Facility Requirements Pyramid*

Regardless of position in the supply chain, where the using organization does not have the needed facilities itself, it must rely on those of suppliers. Every organization does so to some extent. Furthermore, the company and its chain of suppliers depend on infrastructure, which consists of facilities for communication, transportation, and intermediate storage; utilities; and protective systems such as dams and environmental controls.

In partnering up with a supplier, it is important to certify that the supplier has the right facilities and that they are in good condition.

Exhibit 14-1 illustrates this dependency in the form of a facilities pyramid. Usually a company's own facilities are the first order of business, but failure of a supplier's facilities or infrastructure problems can weaken the pyramid's base. To maintain a high level of customer service, a company might have to provide more facility support than anticipated. For example, firms that move plants into low-cost, perhaps rural, locations sometimes have to build roads, drill wells, or pay to expand sewer systems—public facilities. Lack of infrastructure is often a problem in less-developed countries, while crumbling infrastructure might be the concern in developed ones.

We can illustrate the facilities pyramid by considering a catalog and Internet shopping business. First, it needs facilities for processing orders. It might have its own warehousing and shipping facilities, and it might also have facilities to design, produce, and mail catalogs. But it probably would rely on suppliers' facilities for manufacturing of products advertised in its catalogs. And of course, it might outsource order processing and fulfillment as well.

Beyond that, the business would have to rely considerably on public facilities, or infrastructure. Order conveyance depends on the mail and communication systems. Goods would arrive and be shipped via streets, highways, rails, bridges, airports, ports, and navigable waterways. Inadequate public water systems, sewage treatment plants, and flood-control facilities in the business's zone of operations could greatly increase costs for the mail-order house or any of its suppliers.

Consider the top of the pyramid in Exhibit 14-1: When a company answers the question What facilities are needed? it must include those required for planning and design,

**Exhibit 14-1 The Facility Requirements Pyramid**

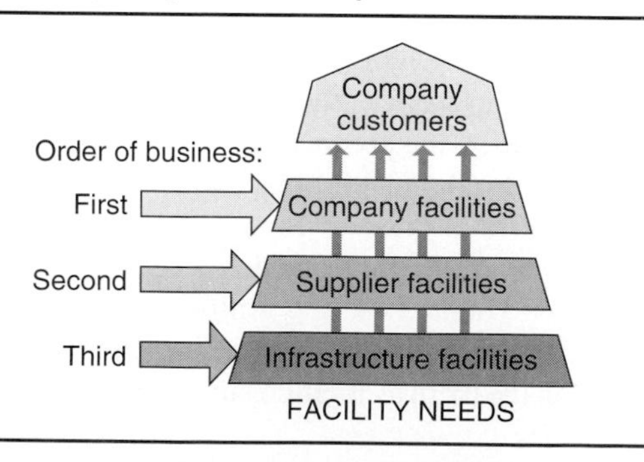

INTO PRACTICE

## Facilities: Competitive and Responsible

"In Amsterdam the headquarters of ING Bank, one of Holland's largest banks, uses one-fifth as much energy per square meter as a nearby bank, even though the buildings cost the same to construct." Efficiency in facilities and equipment design and deployment is both environmentally friendly and financially astute. "Xerox, Compaq, and 3M are among the many firms that have recognized they can cut their greenhouse-gas emissions in half—and enjoy 50% and higher returns on investment—through improved facility efficiency, better lighting and insulation, and smarter motors and building design."

Source: Mark Hertsgaard, "A Global Green Deal," *Time* (Special Edition), April–May 2000, pp. 84–85.

Even in the rust-belt regions of the upper Midwest where economic development is likely to be welcomed, people have a natural suspicion to facility developments, especially when matters of the environment are concerned. According to Pete Battaglia, principal in charge of the Columbus, Ohio, based office of architectural and engineering consulting firm LJB Group, Inc., "More and more, we've been seeing municipalities and planning people insisting that the developer meet with local groups.

"Developers today have learned to see the value of being able to go to a public hearing and say 'We have met with local groups, heard what their concerns were, and tried to accommodate them.'" Some citizens will understand, some won't, he concedes. "But if they see you trying to confront those issues up front, it sets a positive tone and is an important step toward achieving your end goal."

Source: Peter Salwen, "Green Planning Makes Good Neighbors," *IIE Solutions,* April 1999, pp. 31–34.

production, transportation, marketing, service, and the communications and information links that tie them all together and connect the company with its customers. Cutting across all of these facilities elements are concerns for safety and protection of the environment.

The old facilities management view went something like this: "We can be competitive or we can be socially responsible, but not both." Numerous companies that have found ways to do both have debunked that trade-off thinking. The Into practice box "Facilities: Competitive and Responsible" illustrates.

In Chapter 7, we addressed socially and environmentally responsible design, and at this point will simply note that designs are great, but alone they aren't sufficient. ISO 14000 calls for an environmental management system that incorporates all three fundamental duties of management—planning or design, implementation, and improvement. The pollution prevention initiatives of design efforts aim squarely at facilities operations and maintenance activities.

For many people, however environmental protection issues are more a matter of location. And when we toss economics into the mix, facilities location debates can get quite noisy.

## Facilities Location

Are facility location decisions as important as they used to be? More so? The answer often depends on who gets asked. Some developers continue to insist on "greenfield" sites, pristine, previously undeveloped real estate. They fear what former tenants might have left behind on "used" sites. Others find a sense of accomplishment in successful completion of a "brownfield" development—one that involves building or renovating in an old, run-down or abandoned industrial site.[1]

Indeed, some former "enemies" in location battles are joining forces and calling for a greater government and public role in helping developers carry the recycling philosophy into plant location decisions. As with many human endeavors, though, economic factors weigh heavily.

### *Location and Its Economics*

Facility location decisions attract public attention and "get the press," frankly due to the economic and environmental impacts that new or expanded facilities are projected to have on targeted locales. Of course, when the location is a relocation, citizens in the losing community, state, or province are well aware of the negative economic and environmental impacts. Jobs and tax-base revenues depart, and as a species, humans don't have a very good record of cleaning up after themselves. Those "brownfield" sites were formerly bustling shops or factories.

Technology and increased outstanding have tended to confound the issue, however, as physical or web site storefronts may be but windows that trigger operations located continents away. Work here, but live and spend your money there. Nevertheless, on the grand scale, the ebb and flow of money associated with facility locations tends to separate the haves among cities, states, and nations, from the have-nots. Communities recognize this and keep increasing what they are willing to spend to attract businesses and jobs. According to Robert Reich, former U.S. Secretary of Labor, "In 1980 Tennessee paid the equivalent of $11,000 per job to entice Nissan" to locate in the state, and "by 1986 Indiana had to spend $50,000 per job to induce Subaru-Isuzu to set up shop" there. South Carolina's tab for bringing in BMW "is the equivalent of about $100,000 per job."[2]

Until recently, research, design, and management jobs generally stayed in highly developed countries, and lower-skilled jobs were relegated to underdeveloped or emerging nations. But look at some recent examples of who's doing what:[3]

- Hewlett-Packard's new portable inkjet printer business is run from Singapore. The design, manufacture, and profit responsibility are all Singapore based.
- In the village of Fermoy, County Cork, Ireland, 150 Metropolitan Life Insurance Company employees analyze medical insurance claims to determine eligibility for reimbursement in the United States. The work requires knowledge of medicine, the American medical system, and the insurance business.
- In 1990, General Electric bought Tungsram, the Budapest, Hungary, lightbulb manufacturer. In the bargain, GE got a workforce that turned out to be among the world's best at designing and making advanced lighting systems.

The migration of work to new locales usually is preceded by extensive analysis of alternatives, sometimes including a systematic rating procedure. We discuss one such system next.

## *Location Rating System*

The first of three steps is to comparatively rate the importance of a large number of location factors. Exhibit 14-2 is an abbreviated example (many more factors could be included in a location study).

The figure shows that each of 14 factors (A through N) is compared with each other one; ratings are inserted on the matrix. Take, for example, the intersection of factors G and K, "other technology-related companies in area" and "access to suppliers." The

**EXHIBIT 14-2 Evaluation Matrix for Relative Weighting of Location Factors***

**Criteria**

- **A** Stable and experienced labor pool
- **B** High quality of life/reasonable cost of living
- **C** Nearness to customer
- **D** Labor cost
- **E** Utility/tax costs
- **F** Availability of higher education
- **G** Other technology-related companies in area
- **H** Favorable business/community relationships
- **I** Availability of industrial sites
- **J** Air transportation
- **K** Access to suppliers
- **L** Adequate freight lines
- **M** Adequate highway systems
- **N** State aid

**Importance:**

4 – Major preference
3 – Medium preference
2 – Minor preference
I – Letter/letter no preference, each scored one point

Relative weighting

3A
4A
2B 2A
B/D 3A
3D 2B A/F
2E 3F 2A
3D 3F B/G 3A
2D 3G 2B A/I
2F D/G C/H 2I 2A
2G 3D 3I 2B 3A
2F 3E 2D 2J 3B 2A
4F 3I 3D 2C 2B 2A
4G 2F 2J 3D 2L 2B 3A
2G 2F 2K 3D 2M 3B
3I 2G 3F 2L 3D 2C
3J 3G 4F 2M 4D
2I 2K 2G 3F 3E
I/K 2L 3G 4F
2J 3I 2H 3G
3J 3I 2H
3L 3J 2I
2K 3J
L/M 2K
3L
3M

| Factor letter | N | M | L | K | J | I | H | G | F | E | D | C | B | A |
|---|---|---|---|---|---|---|---|---|---|---|---|---|---|---|
| Total weighting raw score | 0 | 8 | 13 | 9 | 18 | 23 | 5 | 26 | 33 | 8 | 31 | 5 | 20 | 31 |

*Not a comprehensive list.

Source: Adapted from Eugene Bauchner, "Making the Most of Your Company's Resources," *Expansion Management,* 1989 Directory, pp. 20–25.

rating in the diamond-shaped box is 3G. Checking the "importance" scale, we see that 3 means "medium preference," in this case, a medium preference of G over K.

The bottom row in Exhibit 14-2 contains total weighting raw scores: The sums of the times each letter appears in the matrix. By studying the scores, we might be able to guess what kind of facility this matrix represents. Availability of higher education (F) is number one in importance; nearness to customer (C) and access to suppliers (K) are near the bottom. Could the facility be a design center?

Step 2 is to rate the locations under consideration against the location factors, A through N in this case. Exhibit 14-3A is a partial matrix (listing just 6 of the 14 factors) showing the site ratings on a 10-point scale for seven locations; in a real study, place names rather than colors would be on the matrix. We see that location Red gets the highest rating, 10, on factor F, higher education. In fact, all of location Red's ratings (for the factors shown) are fairly high. But these are not the final ratings. A third stage is needed.

The third matrix, Exhibit 14-3B, combines ratings from the first and second steps. Location Red got 10 points for higher education, and higher education was rated 33 in importance; 10 times 33 is 330, which goes into the upper-left corner in Exhibit 14-3B. The rest of the matrix gets the same treatment, column totals are added, and total weighted scores are compared. Location Purple is the preferred choice with 1,227 points; locations Blue and Red are not far behind.

## EXHIBIT 14-3 Rating Prospective Locations

**A. Rating Locations by Factors**

| *Factor* | *Red* | *Yellow* | *Green* | *Orange* | *Blue* | *Purple* | *White* |
|---|---|---|---|---|---|---|---|
| F. Higher education | 10 | 5 | 4 | 7 | 8 | 6 | 9 |
| G. Other technology-related companies | 6 | 5 | 4 | 7 | 8 | 9 | 10 |
| A. Stable, experienced labor pool | 6 | 5 | 4 | 7 | 8 | 9 | 7 |
| D. Labor cost | 9 | 6 | 7 | 4 | 8 | 10 | 5 |
| E. Utility/tax cost | 7 | 6 | 5 | 3 | 8 | 10 | 9 |
| J. Air transportation | 10 | 6 | 5 | 8 | 9 | 7 | 4 |

**B. Weighted Location Scores**

| *Factor* | *Red* | *Yellow* | *Green* | *Orange* | *Blue* | *Purple* | *White* |
|---|---|---|---|---|---|---|---|
| F. Higher education (33) | 330 | 165 | 132 | 231 | 264 | 198 | 297 |
| G. Other technology-related companies (26) | 156 | 130 | 104 | 182 | 208 | 234 | 260 |
| A. Stable, experienced labor (31) | 186 | 155 | 124 | 217 | 248 | 279 | 217 |
| D. Labor cost (31) | 279 | 186 | 217 | 124 | 248 | 310 | 155 |
| E. Utility/tax cost (8) | 56 | 48 | 40 | 24 | 64 | 80 | 72 |
| J. Air transportation (18) | 180 | 108 | 90 | 144 | 162 | 126 | 72 |
| Total weighted score | 1,187 | 792 | 707 | 922 | 1,194 | 1,227 | 1,073 |
| Ranking | 3 | 6 | 7 | 5 | 2 | 1 | 4 |

Source: Adapted from Eugene Bauchner, "Making the Most of Your Company's Resources," *Expansion Management,* 1989 Directory, pp. 20–25.

Intangibles, such as the whim of a CEO, could change the decision, or politics could intervene. In any case, systematic analysis is valuable because it reduces a lot of data to a few numbers, which can be used to influence the final decision. Regardless of the location decision, however, or even of the rationale upon which it was based, facilities deployment continues when we look inside the company.

## Facilities Layout

Layout decisions bridge or link facilities and equipment and may extend up or down supply chains. How equipment (and other resources, for that matter) are positioned within facilities is determined to a great extent by the company's dominant mode of operations, a topic we addressed in Chapter 1. The operations management masterminds at the Arsenal of Venice in the 15th century understood the importance of **layout,** the physical organization or geography found at a facility.

> And as one enters the gate there is a great street on either hand with the sea in the middle, and on one side are windows opening out of the houses of the arsenal, and the same on the other side, and out came a galley towed by a boat, and from the windows they handed out to them, from one the cordage, from another the bread, from another the arms, and from another the balistas and mortars, and so from all sides everything which was required, and when the galley had reached the end of the street all the men required were on board, together with the complement of oars, and she was equipped from end to end. In this manner there came out ten galleys full armed, between the hours of three and nine. I know not how to describe what I saw there, whether in the manner of its construction or in the management of the workpeople, and I do not think there is anything finer in the world.[4]

That description identifies the Arsenal of Venice as having a product layout. In this section, we examine basic layouts and their features.

### *Layout Types*

There are four basic types of facilities layout: functional, product, cellular, and fixed position.

1. **Functional layout.** The **functional layout** groups like facilities or functions together: human resource people in the HR department, sheet-metal equipment and people grouped in the sheet-metal shop, and so forth. As we noted in Chapter 1, the functional layout tends to emerge as small organizations grow and functional groups appear. Functional layouts tend to go with the job-processing mode.

Putting people with like functions together may create a climate for mutual support and learning. However, the functional layout has a substantial disadvantage: It puts distance between provider and customer. For example, the accounts receivable clerk usually has frequent business with the sales clerk, but the accounting and sales departments may be at opposite ends of the building.

2. **Product layout.** Facilities line up along the flow of the product in the **product layout.** The customer (next process) is adjacent to, or very near, the provider. Cafeterias,

packing and shipping, and assembly lines are examples. Often, product layouts require substantial investment for lining up equipment and hooking up utilities along the flow path, which may be ill-advised if product volumes fall off or never materialize. The major disadvantage of product layouts, however, is in how they usually are managed. If associates along a flow line are allowed to do only one small job day in and day out, they can hardly be expected to grasp the overall operation or gain a sense of fulfillment. Their worth is diminished, boredom sets in, and morale drops. With cross-training and job rotation in flexible product-flow cells, however, those deficiencies fade.

**Principle 6**

Organize resources into multiple "chains of customers."

3. **Cellular layout.** In the **cellular layout** the idea is to arrange labor, work stations, and equipment into work cells that process families of goods or services that follow similar flow paths. Cells perform better in concert with a number of complementary concepts: Deliberately design items to have as many common features as possible, locate high-use data and accessories within the cell, and cross-train cell operators. A cellular layout is similar to a product layout, although most people think of product layouts (flow lines) as handling only one or just a few products instead of a family. Cellular layout became one of the more important operations management concepts in the 1980s, partly because of its close association with just-in-time applications. We saw in Chapter 5 how cellular layout can facilitate capacity planning.

Cells are often the objective and the result when companies elect to break up functional layouts. For example, a company might form complete design, budget, and buy cells by relocating buyers and accountants next to product designers. Or a manufacturer might transfer a stamping press from the "press room" to where it can make and feed a single part to a using station on a production line.

4. **Fixed-position layout.** In the **fixed-position layout,** it is the product whose position is fixed, and resources (people, machines, materials, and so on) must come to it. Construction is a good example. Another is the manufacture of items too large to be easily moved, such as aircraft and locomotives. Still others are patients in hospital beds, or an actor being dressed, made up, and coached before the performance.

**Mixed layouts**—two or more layout types in a single facility—are common, if not the norm. An example is a restaurant that sets up a buffet brunch line on Sundays. The patron has the choice of going through the buffet line or sitting down and ordering from the menu. Thus the restaurant processes patrons through two types of facilities layout. The buffet customer goes through a product or cellular layout (hard to narrow it down to one or the other). It is a flow line. The menu customer receives service in a fixed layout: Menu, waiter, food, drinks, and check come to the fixed position.

Exhibit 14-4 is a sketch of such a restaurant, identifying the product layout and fixed layout. It also shows that the restaurant includes a functional layout in the kitchen. There foods, not patrons, are the products being transformed. Functional areas include grill, salads, range, desserts, ovens, freezer, and pantry. Arrows show the jumbled flow patterns.

Compared with a single-layout facility, a mixed-layout facility is more difficult to plan, more costly to equip, and more troublesome to maintain. But it may be easier to keep busy because it offers a wider variety of products or services to an enlarged pool of potential customers.

**EXHIBIT 14-4 Mixed Layout in a Restaurant**

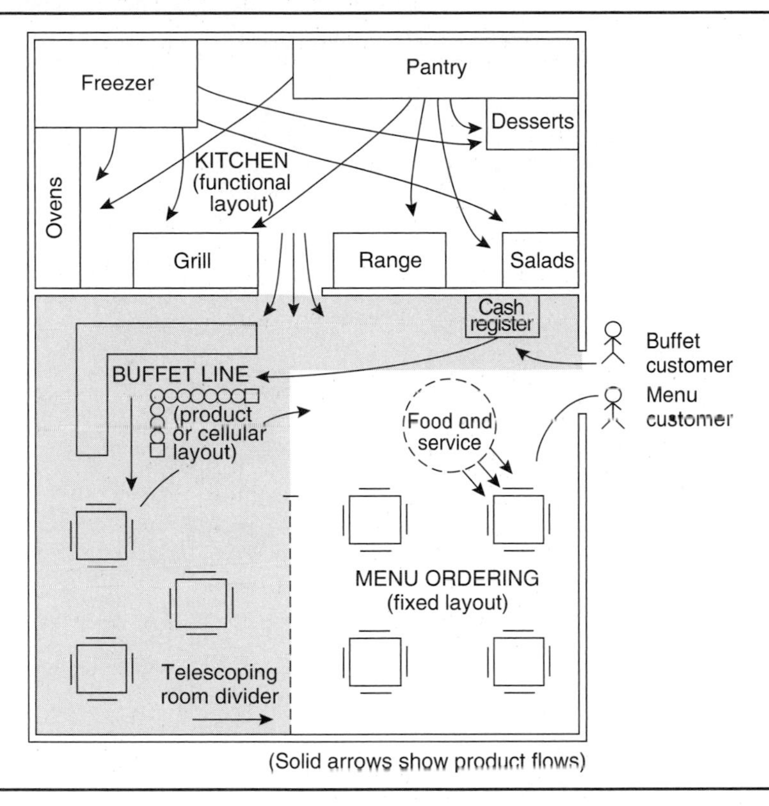


## *U-Shaped Layout*

The main feature of both flow lines and work cells is the close proximity of work stations, which speeds up flow and reduces in-process queuing. Usually, for even better results, the stations are laid out into a U shape. At least six advantages for cells or lines may result from **U-shaped layout.**

1. *Staff flexibility and balance.* The U shape allows one associate to tend several work stations adjacent or across the U, since walking distance is short. Also, more options for balancing work among personnel exist: As demand increases, labor may be added until every station in the cell is tended by an associate.

   Exhibit 14-5 shows a typical U-shaped layout for a manufacturer. As many as eight employees, or as few as one, might tend the machines, depending on demand. Also note that kanban squares link each station with its customer station.
2. *Teamwork.* Getting all staff into a cluster enhances teamwork and joint problem solving. Slowdowns or stoppages quickly ripple through the cell, and cell members form a natural team that must collectively solve the problems

**Principle 1**

Team up with the customer—the next process.

**Exhibit 14-5 U-Shaped Layout—Manufacturing Cell**

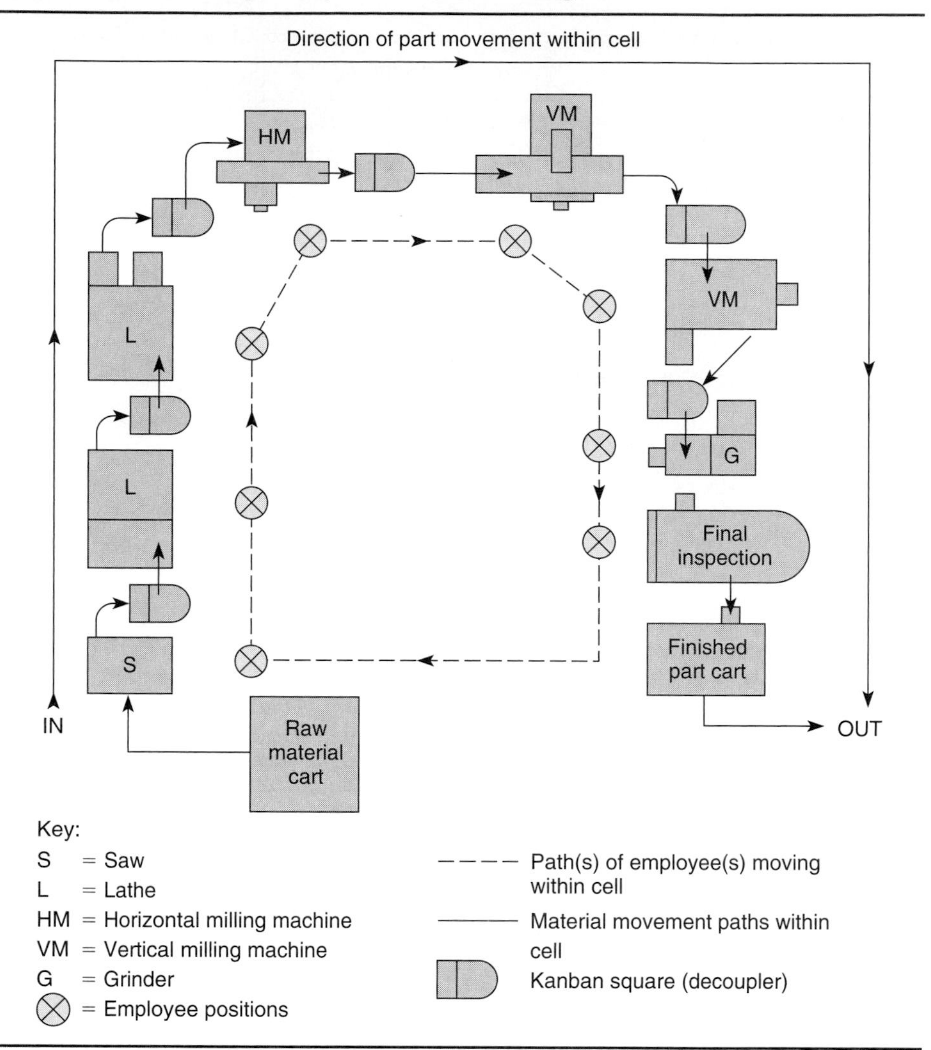


Source: Adapted from J. T. Black, *The Design of the Factory with a Future* (New York: McGraw-Hill, 1991), p. 67. Used with permission.

and get the process going again. Natural teams can hardly form, much less work effectively, if employees are strung out along long lines or dispersed and separated by walls of inventory.

3. *Rework.* When a mistake occurs, a common policy is to send the customer to the complaint department or the item to a separate rework group. But a tenet of total quality management is quality at the source, which calls for correcting mistakes right where they occurred. In the U-shaped layout, the distance to return a mistake is short, making it easier to follow the TQM tenet.

4. *Passage.* A long, straight line interferes with travel of employees, customers, vehicles, and supplies. We object when supermarket aisles are too long, and people protest when a freeway cuts through a neighborhood. A long, straight production line may be a similar imposition.
5. *Work and tool distribution.* Since all stations in a U are immediately accessible from the center, it is easier to distribute materials, parts, instruction sheets, and so on. A single person may be able to handle distribution tasks while also tending a starting or ending station in the U. In unmanned cells, a robot at the center may distribute work and tools and also perform assembly operations.
6. *Linking with other U-shaped layouts.* The U shape provides many arrangement options for linking feeder and user cells. Exhibit 14-6 shows a linked-cell system consisting of final assembly, subassembly, and fabrication cells—all U-shaped. Each fabrication cell might resemble the one shown in Exhibit 14-5 and would provide a different parts family to the subassembly and assembly cells at the appropriate point of use. In a well-balanced system, fabrication

**EXHIBIT 14-6 Linked-Cell Manufacturing System**

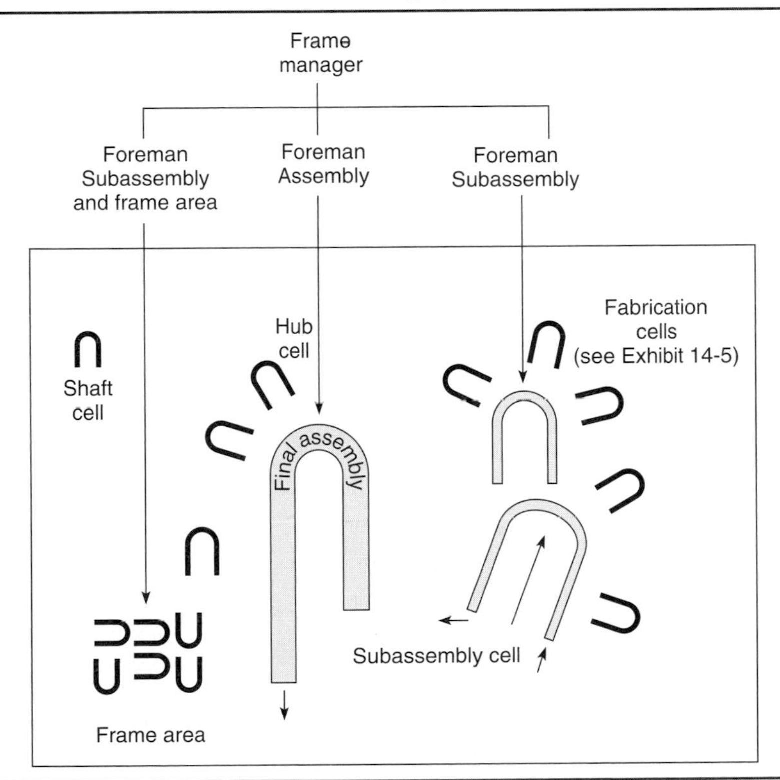


Source: Adapted from Richard J. Schonberger, "The World Class Manufacturing Company," Tape 4 of 12-tape videotape set, 1990; and J. T. Black, *The Design of the Factory with a Future* (New York: McGraw-Hill, 1991), p. 66. Used with permission.

cells would have the same degree of demand-mix and volume flexibility as the subassembly and assembly cells. Note, also, the partial organization chart above the layout diagram: no functional departments. The management hierarchy is cellular to match the layout of facilities.

There are cases where these advantages of the U shape do not fully apply. For example, with a high degree of automation and few parts or tools to be handled, the teamwork benefits are absent. Also, a line processing wide sheets of steel, aluminum, glass, and so on, perhaps should run straight because transfer between machines is simpler if there are no changes in direction.

### *Layout Features*

Some of the distinguishing features of the primary layout types are shown in Exhibit 14-7. It lists eight resource factors and the common treatments for each layout type.

The first factor, facilities arrangement, states the main differences among the layout types. They have already been discussed.

Type of operations is the second factor. Functional layout is dominant in job and batch operations; product layout is typical in repetitive and continuous operations. Continuous improvement calls for identifying all items that have the potential for more or less repetitive operations and to organize product layouts for those items. Cellular layout is suitable for small lots of first one part in a family and then another. Fixed layout is common in construction and industrial projects, for production of large-scale products, and for cases of special human services such as surgery.

**EXHIBIT 14-7 Resources and Layouts—Common Characteristics**

| | **Types of Layout** | | |
|---|---|---|---|
| *Resource Factors* | *Functional* | *Product or Cellular* | *Fixed* |
| 1. Facilities arrangement | Facilities grouped by specialty | Facilities placed along product-flow lines | Facilities arranged for ease of movement to fixed product |
| 2. Type of operations | Job and batch | Continuous and repetitive | Construction and industrial projects; large-scale products, special human services |
| 3. Cost of layout/re-layout | Moderate to low | Moderate to high | Moderate to low |
| 4. Facility utilization | Usually low | High | Moderate |
| 5. Type of operating facilities | General purpose | Special purpose | Mostly general purpose |
| 6. Handling equipment | Variable path | Fixed path | Variable path |
| 7. Handling distance | Long | Short | Moderate |
| 8. Employee skill level | Skilled | Unskilled | Unskilled to skilled |

Cost of layout/re-layout is third. Functional layout, where machines, desks, and the like generally are not tightly linked, is not costly. For a product or cellular layout, the cost is high if pieces of equipment are closely interlinked as in automated lines; the cost may be moderate if production is more labor intensive (i.e., one person hands work to the next). Fixed layout of a construction site requires temporary parking and storage space for operating resources, which usually are not costly. Fixed layout for goods production and for special human services may require a well-equipped bay for assembling a missile or aligning wheels, or a well-equipped operating room. The layout cost can be low if the facilities are mainly general-purpose hand tools, but can be higher (moderate) if special lighting, holding fixtures, work pits, and so forth, are involved.

Fourth is facility utilization. In functional layouts, facilities tend toward low utilization. That is not desirable, but it is typical because the job mix changes all the time and different jobs use different facilities. High facility utilization is a goal of product layout. Line balancing helps achieve it. Fixed layouts tend to have moderate facility utilization because the product mix is not very diverse.

The fifth factor is type of operating facilities. Functional layouts usually hold standard, general-purpose equipment, tools, handling aids, and so forth. Special-purpose facilities are worth investing in if the volume is high, as it normally is with product layouts. In fixed layouts, special products call for some special-purpose facilities, such as an overhead crane or a mounting fixture, but most of the facilities will be general purpose since production volume is not high.

Sixth is handling equipment. In functional layouts, variable-path equipment (hand-carry or on wheels) provides needed handling flexibility. Fixed-path handling equipment (conveyors, elevators, chutes, etc.) helps cut handling time in product layouts. In fixed layouts, a variety of resources come to the site from different places; hence, variable-path handling equipment.

Seventh is handling distance. Functional layouts stretch out over vast areas. In product and cellular layouts, the opposite is true. In fact, a purpose is to tightly cluster the facilities in order to cut distance and handling time. Fixed layouts are in between. The product stays put, but the resources do not flow to the product by fixed routes; resources move to the product from various locations over moderate handling distances.

The eighth factor is employee skill level. In functional layouts, employees tend to be skilled. Machinists, computer operators, nurses, and accountants fit the category. If the skill is based on higher education or apprenticeship, the pay tends to be high; if based on vocational training, the pay tends to be moderate or low. Employees positioned along product layouts may become adept, but they are classed as unskilled because they are easily replaced from an unskilled labor market. In fixed layouts, skilled craftspeople, such as carpenters and welders, often work alongside unskilled laborers, such as shovelers or riveters.

While many more operating-resource factors could be discussed, these eight are enough to show the basic nature of each layout type. Exhibit 14-7 is not intended as an if–then analysis device; that is, we would not conclude that if people are skilled, facility utilization is low, and so on, then a functional layout should be developed. There are better ways to plan the right kind of layout. We consider some of them next.

### *Flexibility in Layout*

New facilities require new layouts. Existing facilities get out-of-date and require re-layout. The type of operations facilities affects flexibility and thus the likelihood of successful re-layout should conditions dictate. We consider four general types.

1. In mechanized production lines, original layout planning had better be good because of the high cost of repositioning large machinery and related facilities. In a petrochemical plant, for example, the layout of tanks, chambers, valves, pipes, and other equipment is so much a part of the plant itself that major re-layout may never be feasible. In steel manufacturing, the cost of major re-layout is also enormous, and steel mills may close rather than retool and re-layout to improve efficiency, meet pollution control regulations, and so on. In such cases, the initial layout choices restrict the ability to respond to major changes in product line or technology for years to come.
2. Assembly lines (manual, not robotic) are less fixed. Assemblers and their tools are mobile. Thus, initial layout planning is not so critical; the focus is on re-layout, which has its own costs. These include costs of planning, line balancing, retraining, and rearranging benches, storage facilities, material handling aids, and large pieces of equipment.
3. Job and batch production often entails large machines and storage and handling aids. Re-layout may be attractive, however, because the equipment used tends to be general purpose, loosely coupled, and movable. A pump manufacturer in South Carolina has constructed a plant with very thick concrete floors so that heavy equipment can be moved anywhere. Exhibit 14-8 shows two large drill presses on casters, with detailed blowups of the casters and mountings themselves.

Principle 9

Flexible, movable equipment.

These kinds of devices for flexible layout and re-layout are important; otherwise the ability to change and continually improve may be thwarted. Symptoms of the need include bottlenecks, backtracking, overcrowding, poor utilization of capacity (including space), poor housekeeping, missed due dates, too much queue time, and a high or growing ratio of total cycle time to actual work content.

4. Labor-intensive services undergo frequent re-layout. Office employees may begin to "wonder where my desk will be on Monday morning." The desk may be across town in newly rented office space. Physical obstacles are few; most offices can move overnight if telephone hookups can be arranged. With few physical problems, office re-layout commonly focuses on people and work climate.

Perhaps people and work climate should be central concerns in all layout and re-layout work. Certainly, many layout jobs are more complex than that faced by Woodsmith (see Into Practice box, "Re-layout . . ."), yet human needs often can be accommodated.

### *Layout-Planning Steps*

In a complex layout situation, hundreds or thousands of jobs may be in progress at any given time. Repetitive, job, and project work may be included, with products and resources moving to work stations via many routings.

When routes are so diverse, how work areas are arranged in a building makes a difference. Dominant flow patterns from makers to customers are there among the apparent jumble of routings, and layout analysis helps to find those patterns.

**EXHIBIT 14-8 Equipment on Wheels**

*Machines on casters.*

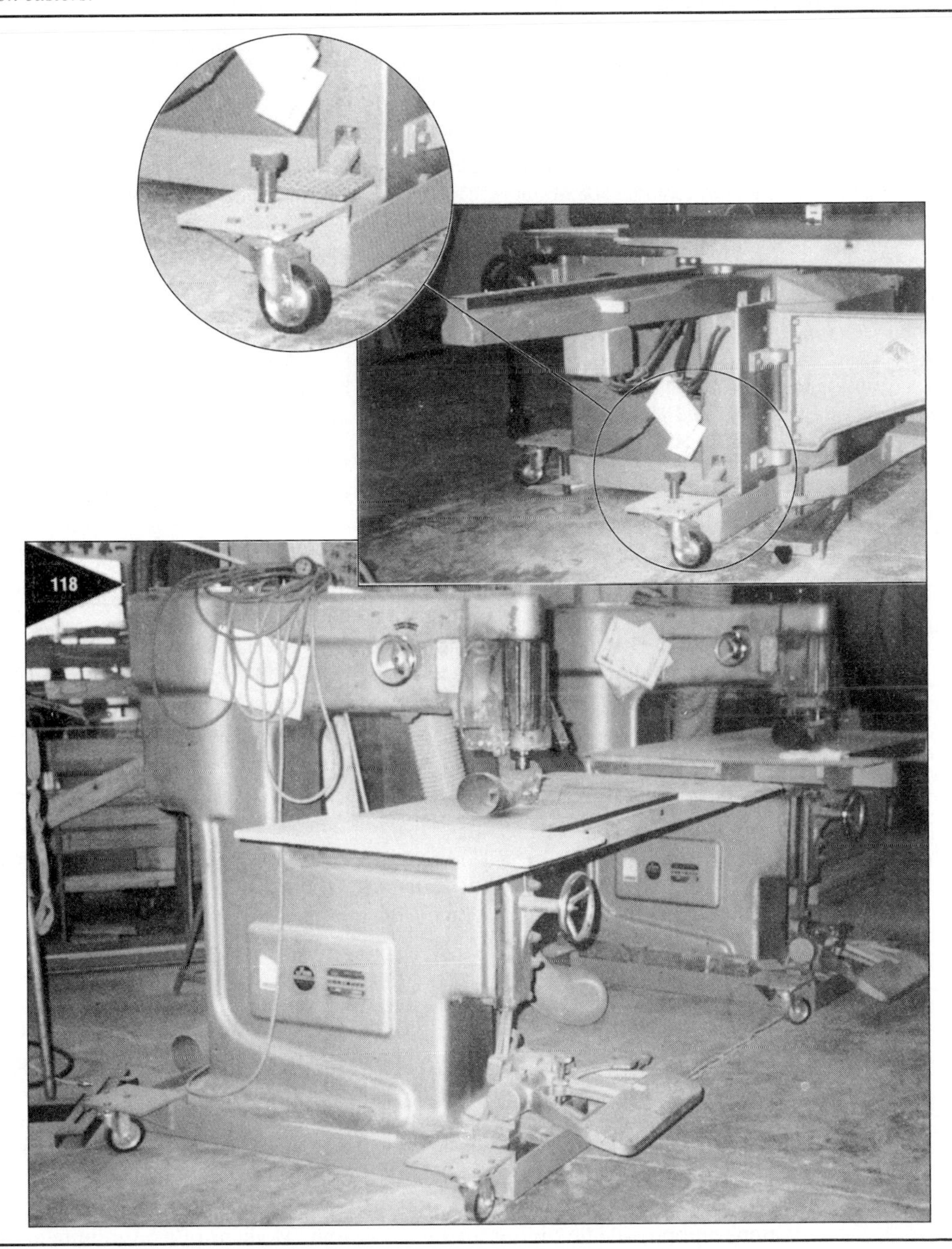


Reprinted from Hiroyuki Hirano, ed., *JIT Factory Revolution: A Pictorial Guide to Factory Design of the Future* (Portland Ore.: Productivity Press, 1988), p. 118. English translation copyright © 1988 by Productivity Press. Reprinted by permission.

INTO PRACTICE

## Re-layout: Employees Pitch in

When Woodsmith, a Des Moines–based publisher of catalogs for do-it-yourself carpenters, recently redesigned its offices, CEO Donald Peshke chose to forgo the use of outside contractors and instead asked each of the 35-person staff to do his or her own area. Peshke's goal was not so much to save money as to save time.

Outside installers would have required over a week to break down the office's movable wall panels and modular furniture and transform the office. With a Friday evening kickoff pizza party, the Woodsmith staff launched the weekend stint, and by Monday morning had the walls redone, furniture installed, and equipment relocated.

With help from a local Herman Miller dealer, each employee had designed a layout for his or her work area, deciding where to locate work surfaces and position computers, file cabinets, and other equipment. Peshke explained: "Our approach was to get them involved in the design so they'd understand what couldn't be done. They accept limitations a lot better that way, instead of the boss saying, 'This is what you're going to live with, like it or not.'" But the best part of the whole experience, according to Peshke, "turned out to be the camaraderie it developed."

Source: Robert A. Mamis, "Employees as Contractors," *Inc.*, November 1992, p. 53.

One layout principle is to arrange work areas in the order of dominant flow. A goal is to get work or resources into, through, and out of each work center in minimum time at reasonable cost. The less time spent in the flow pattern, the less chance of collecting labor and overhead charges and the faster the immediate and final customers are served.

Other factors besides flows may be important. If so, the nonflow factors (e.g., teamwork) may be combined with flow data. The combined data will suggest how close work areas should be to one another, and a rough layout can be developed. The next step is to determine the space requirements for a rough layout. The last step in layout planning is to fit the rough layout into the available space, that is, the proposed or existing building. Several layout plans can be developed for managers to choose from.

The layout planning steps just described are listed in Exhibit 14-9, along with planning aids usable in each step. The chapter supplement contains an example illustrating layout planning for a county office facility.

### *Open Layouts*

One of the special influences on office layout is the **open-office concept.** The concept eliminates many floor-to-ceiling walls and de-emphasizes functional compartmentalization of people. One key advantage is that the open-office concept is more customer friendly, especially in establishments that are trying to promote customer service. By opening up to customers, providers remove some of the mystery or secrecy from their operations. Banks are good examples.

Other advantages of open layouts are that they foster better employee communications and provide flexibility for easy re-layout. Modular office furniture and movable, partial-height partitions aid in achieving these goals.

**Exhibit 14-9 Layout Planning—Steps and Possible Tools**

| *Steps* | *Possible Tools* |
|---|---|
| 1. Analyze work flows. | Flow diagram<br>From–to chart |
| 2. Identify and include nonflow factors, where significant. | Activity-relationship (REL) chart<br>Combined REL chart |
| 3. Assess data and arrange work areas. | Activity arrangement diagram |
| 4. Determine space arrangement plan. | Space relationship diagram |
| 5. Fit space arrangement into available space. | Floor plan<br>Detailed layout models. |

Open offices in Japan, where the concept is deeply ingrained, often are truly wide open. North Americans, in contrast, have emphasized maintaining a degree of privacy and cutting noise. Interior designers use wall carpeting, sound-absorbent panels, acoustical screens, fabric-wrapped desktop risers, and freestanding padded partitions. Office landscaping (use of plants) is also commonplace. In fact, plants are so prominent in the office of Mars (candy bars) in Veghel, Holland, that people there call it the office-garden concept.

Location and layout decisions, though very important, occur infrequently. On the other hand, keeping the facilities in high-quality condition requires ongoing maintenance, our next topic.

## Maintaining Facilities

Suppose one of the following occurs at your computer terminal at work:

- As you are working, your screen suddenly goes blank. When you call computer operations you are told, "Sorry, the system failed again. We're fixing it now."
- As you log on one morning, a message warns you that the system will be shut down at a specified time that day for periodic maintenance. This happens four or five times a month, seemingly at random and for varying lengths of downtime.
- During log-on, the system maintenance downtime schedule for the next several months is displayed, showing short downtime periods that occur on the same dates and at the same time each month.

The three events describe different levels of performance and thus quality of service to customers. Quality is worst in the first example, and it improves as we move from one to another. In the third example, except for a short downtime maintenance period that occurs regularly and predictably, the network should be ready whenever you need to use it.

In Exhibit 9-3, we learned that process performance depends on how well the process has been designed, built or installed, operated, and maintained. Here, we examine maintenance, where the goal is to keep operating resources in good working order, safe, and ready for use when needed. Part of meeting that goal is prevention: Stop trouble before it happens. Doing this well requires a broad-based attack on causes—a program of total preventive maintenance, which is the facility-maintenance counterpart of total quality.

### *Total Preventive Maintenance*

Total productive maintenance is the term often used in manufacturing; we use total preventive maintenance, which is more type-of-business neutral.

When you take your car in for complete service, you get an oil change and lubrication, vacuumed interior, cleaned windows, and a sticker applied to the door frame or window corner reminding you when to return for the next service. Beyond that, the mechanics rotate tires or tune up the engine—if the maintenance schedule calls for it—and replace key components or overhaul certain systems if necessary to avoid failure or unsafe operation. In combination, these services include the three main elements of total preventive maintenance (TPM):

- Regular preventive maintenance, including housekeeping.
- Periodic prefailure replacement or overhauls.
- Intolerance for breakdowns or unsafe conditions (see Into Practice, ". . . La Victoria Foods").

INTO PRACTICE

## Maintainability at La Victoria Foods

"KISS—Keep It Simple Son—that is what I tell myself," grins Wes Guthrie, purchasing expediter at La Victoria Foods. The company's single plant, in Industry, California, produces salsas, jalapeños, nachos, and tomatillo entero.

"The simpler it is in a food plant, the better efficiency you have because there is less to break down. . . . When the chilis are here and when the tomatoes are here, we have to run. We cannot have breakdowns—none of this produce keeps."

Maintenance superintendent Andy Zamberlin notes that when he came to La Victoria 13 years before, the place was a nightmare. It had "too much complicated machinery such as stop/starts [switches], electric motors, and electric eyes that just did not run right." Some component was always breaking down and it often took hours to determine what had broken.

Zamberlin and his staff eliminated much of the assorted conventional electromechanical controls. Today, "almost all of La Victoria's equipment is run by PLC's [programmable logic controllers, a type of computer]. Several PLCs control the batching process. Some control the steam process, which is the 'breaking' or peeling of the tomatoes. Others control the fillers themselves. . . . These are programmed so that the drive motors are in step with the capping machines so they do not speed one up and slow one down." There are few parts on the food-processing equipment to break, and when a fault does occur, computers quickly identify the program.

But, as Guthrie points out, this kind of process control requires a good deal of human involvement. "We've got tomatoes of different sizes and textures. They might be mushy, they might be hard, they might not peel. . . . There are so many variables." He adds, "These PLCs have to be user-controllable. You program parameters, but the operator has to be able to control it."

Source: Adapted from Blake Svenson, "Keeping It Simple to Reduce Spoiled Efficiency in the Food Industry," *Industrial Engineering,* June 1992, pp. 29–32.

Intolerance for facility deficiencies, the third goal, is a hallmark of the Walt Disney culture. Every Disney amusement park employee must continually maintain and clean the premises as well as write up and call in problems requiring maintenance expertise. Disney World in Florida has become a popular destination not only for vacationers but also for benchmarking teams wanting to study Disney's fault-intolerant total maintenance program.

Another example of ardent attention to TPM is the aircraft industry: In aircraft maintenance, prevention is everything; waiting for failure to identify a maintenance need is unacceptable. The Air Force bomber B-52 is a good example of the payoff: decades of continued flight. Even more remarkable is the 70-plus-year-old DC-3; the military version, the C-47, is affectionately known as the "Gooney Bird." A few hundred of these venerable aircraft are still logging miles, thanks to good design and thorough preventive maintenance practices.

On a lesser scale, the conscientious automobile owner also follows the TPM philosophy seriously: Commit a little time and money for regular oil changes and less-frequent but necessary overhauls in order to prevent having to spend even greater amounts of time and money on a breakdown. By giving a little, we gain a lot: a resource that remains in a high state of readiness.

The centerpiece of total preventive maintenance is operator ownership backed up by special maintenance expertise to handle nonroutine problems. The wisdom of this approach becomes apparent as we consider traditional types of maintenance-related procedures.

## *Types of Maintenance*

We classify maintenance operations into two general categories:

- *Periodic maintenance.* Periodic maintenance occurs at some regular interval (e.g., custodial activities are often performed daily). Of course, periodic maintenance forms the core of a preventive maintenance (PM) program. There are three popular versions of PM:
  1. PM based on calendar or clock time—maintenance at regular intervals. An example is the hourly change of a filter on a clean room's air-conditioning unit.
  2. PM based on time of usage, perhaps based on number of cycles. For example, change the cartridge in a laser printer after every 4,000 pages of print. This is often called **predictive maintenance;** the idea is to do maintenance before the predicted time of failure.
  3. PM based on regular inspection. A maintenance requirement may be revealed by planned (perhaps daily or weekly) inspections. The U.S. Air Force refers to this as IRAN (*i*nspect and *r*epair *a*s *n*ecessary) maintenance.
- *Irregular maintenance.* This includes repairs, overhauls, irregular custodial work (e.g., cleaning up spills), irregular PM (e.g., prefailure replacement of components based on control-chart deviations, tests, unusual equipment noises, etc.), installation and relocation of equipment, and minor construction.

**periodic maintenance**
Discretionary regular-interval maintenance aimed at forestalling breakdowns and ensuing work stoppages; sometimes is *preventive* periodic maintenance.

**irregular maintenance**
Maintenance necessary because of a breakdown or a facility alteration.

Maintenance work has traditionally been assigned to associates housed in a central maintenance department, perhaps called plant or facilities maintenance, or (as in many hospitals) in a unit within the facilities engineering group. Typical types of maintenance associates include

- *Millwrights.* These are skilled people who move and install equipment, an irregular, hard-to-manage maintenance activity.
- *Repair technicians.* These are skilled, well-paid troubleshooters who have sharp diagnostic skills.
- *Custodians.* Typically, these people are charged with housekeeping and perhaps minor repairs, light painting, and so forth.
- *Preventive maintenance associates.* This category is hardest to define, for in addition to associates regularly scheduled for PM duties (perhaps on a special maintenance shift), available millwrights and repair personnel also perform PM duties, though typically at higher labor costs.

Now that we have a basic grasp of what maintenance is supposed to do, we can consider how this might better be accomplished. Effective maintenance management focuses on

1. Achieving the right mix of periodic and irregular maintenance.
2. Improving planning, scheduling, and staffing of irregular maintenance, and improving the effectiveness of periodic maintenance.

Flexibility, regularity, and simplification—possible when maintenance becomes a frontline operator's responsibility—help to meet these ends.

### Employee-Centered Maintenance

**Principle 7**

Cross-train for mastery of multiple skills.

The phrase *employee ownership* refers to employees believing that equipment condition is their responsibility and that maintenance, engineering, and outside service representatives are backups. This parallels the shift in responsibility for quality from quality professionals to frontline associates. TPM and TQM are cut from the same cloth. Exhibit 14-10 shows one manner of dispersing the maintenance function. As earlier chapters have noted, in the product- or customer-focused organization associates not only perform value-adding transformations, but they are also cross-trained to perform some of their own operations support. Maintenance specialists and other experts are often assigned to the group to provide on-the-spot training and technical support.

The case for employee-centered maintenance is multifaceted. Frontline associates learn their equipment better, gain fuller control over their own processes, and take greater pride in their workplace when they assume cleanup tasks and responsibility for minor repairs. This cuts repair time since there is less waiting around for someone from maintenance to come and change a bulb, for instance. Furthermore, the trend toward multiple, smaller, more mobile equipment and furnishings makes frontline associates less dependent on millwright availability; they can perform much of the relocation and installation themselves.

**Principle 9**

Look for flexible, movable equipment.

In addition, the involved employee is more likely to develop ideas for fail-safing, which is a superior form of failure prevention (see discussion in Chapter 9). Finally, workforce scheduling is easier because maintenance can often be performed at times

**EXHIBIT 14-10 Modern Maintenance Organization**

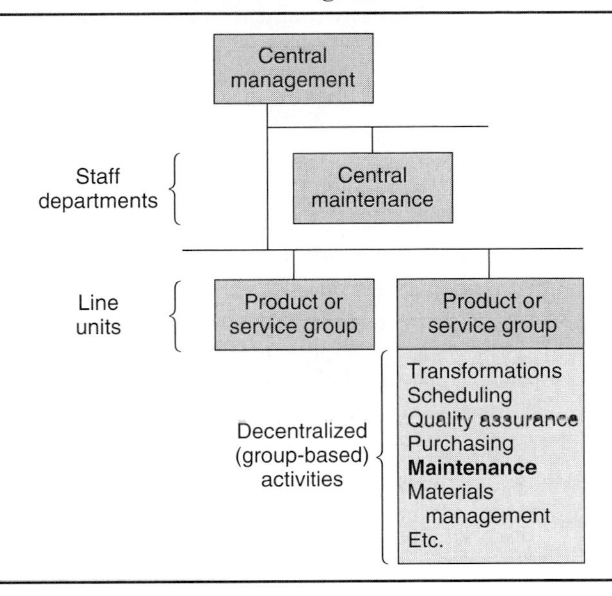


CONTRAST

## Maintenance Responsibilities

### Traditional

- Maintenance is a functional support activity; employees rely on specialists (typically) in the central maintenance department for custodial services, preventive and repair maintenance, and millwright work.

### Employee Ownership/TPM

- Frontline associates have first responsibility for maintenance in their workplaces.
- Specialists from a maintenance department or on cross-functional teams have backup responsibility to handle difficult or unusual problems.

when scheduled work has been completed early; this is true at least under JIT, which calls for associates to perform maintenance and other improvements rather than overproducing.

Shifting primary maintenance responsibility to frontline associates doesn't put the maintenance department out of business; in fact, its responsibilities can become more focused and better defined; see the Contrast box. As responsibilities shift, it is important that frontline associates acquire more than how-to maintenance skills; they also need the support of a stimulating, disciplined environment to ensure that critical activities get carried out. The 5 S's provide some of this support.

### *5 S's plus Safety Management*

The 5-S concept, originated in Japan, calls for regularly scoring each area within a facility on five characteristics related to good housekeeping and organization of work space. The S's stand for five Japanese words, but Western companies seem to be choosing their own meanings. Boeing's version of the S's is as follows: *sorting, sweeping, simplifying, standardizing,* and *self-discipline.* Other companies' S's generally are similar. While the S's may seem to deal with rather trivial matters, they tend to add up to big problems if not controlled. As an example, the fourth Boeing "S" is *standardizing,* which includes ensuring that every team member follows the standard, prescribed method. If in a hospital every nurse has a different way of hooking up an IV to a patient, the results could endanger some patients' lives. The consequences of salespeople who all write up orders differently include added cost and confusion in processing the orders and occasional foul-ups that lead to defection of a customer.

The 5-S system usually entails some kind of public display of scoring against the S's. At Boeing's welded duct plant in Auburn, Washington (see Exhibit 14-11) display boards in every work area extol the S's and show photo examples of good and bad practices.

**EXHIBIT 14-11 5 S's at Boeing's Welded Duct Facility, Auburn, Washington**

*Below left: Typical plant scene before the 5 S's—disorderly, jumbled, undisciplined. Below right: Scene from Welded Duct plant after implementation of the 5 S's showing everything well sorted (designated locations are marked off by white and yellow lines on floor), swept, simplified, and standardized, all of which facilitate self-discipline by team members.*

Photos courtesy of Boeing.

**EXHIBIT 14-12 Spider Diagram Displaying Scores against the 5 S's**

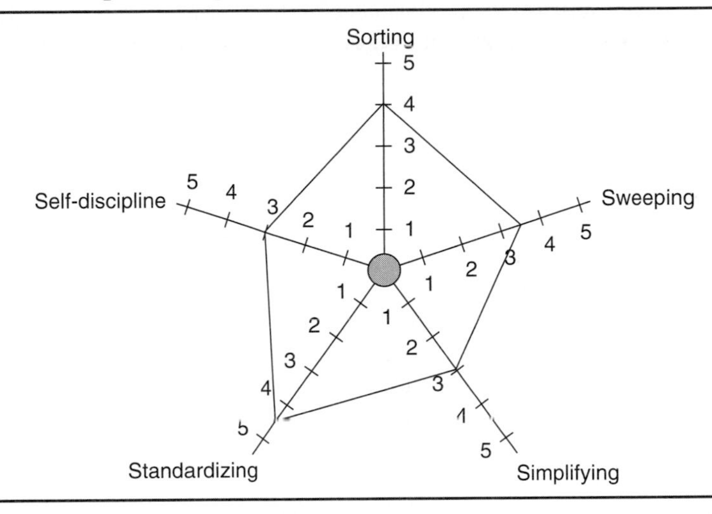


Some companies and hospitals employ **spider diagrams** as the display device. Exhibit 14-12 is an example. The raw diagram is five arms extending outward from a central point, each arm representing one of the S's and scaled off from zero to five points, where zero at the center is the target of perfection. Periodically—commonly once a week—a designated outside rater scores each unit. The rater could be a higher-level manager (e.g., a head nurse or department head) or perhaps a maintenance manager or quality engineer. The scores plot as dots on the arms, and the rater connects the dots to look like a simple web. Next week the web had better be smaller—scores closer to the zero target at the center.

A sixth S, *safety,* may easily be added to the spider diagram, and it easily deserves that kind of intensive management. In some industrialized states, high worker's compensation insurance costs steadily drive away new businesses and send away existing ones. Other costs include potential law suits, interrupted production, and loss of key people and costs of hiring and training a replacement.

Along with the discipline of the S's, it is often a good idea to dedicate certain people as responsible for certain facilities.

## *Dedicated Maintenance*

A company much admired for its commitment to maintenance is United Parcel Service, which keeps most of its over-the-road and delivery vehicles operating and looking as good as new for 20 years or more. A feature of the UPS program is dedicated mechanics and drivers. A driver operates the same vehicle every day, and a mechanic maintains the same group of vehicles. Many military aircraft maintenance programs also use dedicated operator/mechanic programs. Sometimes the names of both the pilot and the maintenance crew chief are painted on the aircraft. Both individuals proudly claim ownership and are responsible for the performance of the aircraft.

Principle 6

Organize resources into focused family groupings.

At UPS, mechanics work at night on delivery vehicles driven mostly during the day, but drivers and mechanics stay closely in touch. Drivers complete a post-trip vehicle inspection report every day, noting any problems. The mechanic goes to work on those problems that evening, and records completed work on the form. Then, the driver uses the form in conducting a pretrip inspection every morning. Similar interactions and documentation between pilots and maintenance crew chiefs have long been standard in military and, in some cases, commercial aircraft maintenance programs.

The interdependency of driver, vehicles, and mechanic keeps responsibilities focused and avoids blaming. In the more typical situation of changing mechanics, operators, and equipment, any of the individuals can become lax, fail to keep good records, and leave problems for the next person or shift.

### *Maintenance Inventories*

Typically, failure of one of the many MRO (maintenance, repair, and operating) parts causes most of the maintenance headaches. Recall from Chapter 6 that MRO inventory is classified as a class B item, indicating that it is not typically among the most costly inventory (class A items), but that neither is it considered part of the "trivial many" (class C items). In a TPM environment, with the focus on increased operator involvement and rapid response, location and care of MRO inventories deserve careful attention. Also, in JIT operations distances must shrink. This includes MRO inventory storage space, which must be close to the action and efficiently used.

It is common for even a medium-sized plant to have hundreds, even thousands, of MRO items, despite standardization and component-part reduction programs. Many are like household hardware items we buy, small and available only in quantities of 10s or even 100s. Exhibit 14-13 shows how people at the Macomb, Illinois, plant of NTN–Bower Corporation contain the parts. Drawer cabinets located near the point of usage (Exhibit 14-13A) consume less than half the space of shelving and facilitate storage of small items like brackets, sleeves, and pins (see Exhibit 14-13B). Adjacent part-location records and clear labeling on drawers make retrieval of even the most obscure item easy. The results? Lower failure rates and less downtime.

### *PM Time*

When equipment runs day and night, people may not be able to get at it to perform necessary maintenance, and breakdowns follow. TPM's solution calls for setting aside time each day for PM. The following are two examples of how this may be done, even in continuous operations.

- As noted in Chapter 8 in an Into Practice box, Miller Brewing Company in Trenton, Ohio, operates three shifts, 24 hours a day, which seems not to allow time for preventive maintenance. The plant's unique staffing plan

**Exhibit 14-13 The Little Parts—Managing MRO Items**

*Below left: Small-part storage drawer cabinets. Below right: Open storage cabinet drawer.*

Source: Courtesy of NTN–Bower Corporation. Used with permission.

overcomes this apparent deficiency: All production associates work nine-hour shifts instead of the usual eight. Part of the extra hour per shift is for preventive maintenance, renovating canning lines (millwright work), and housekeeping. In addition, the nine-hour shifts create a one-hour overlap during which crews from each shift meet together. This provides shift-to-shift continuity—usually missing in multishift operations—and opportunity to inform next-shift people of maintenance or other problems.

- At a U.S. particle-board plant, the large mix-mold-bake-cool line was run 24 hours a day, seven days a week, except for 1 hour of maintenance per week. For lack of regular PM, the line produced much scrap and defective particle board. When asked why there was no daily maintenance shutdown, the reply was, "We have start-up problems." The general manager of several Brazilian particle-board plants heard that story and offered this comment: "We *do* shut down for maintenance every day, and we *don't* have start-up problems." By having to face start-up each day, they had learned how to make it an easy routine.

Old accounting high-utilization logic creates a tendency to want to run very expensive machines continuously. But the enlightened view asks, Don't our most expensive machines deserve our best care rather than our worst? This view is gaining ground in industry, especially as total quality and JIT success elevate the importance of reliability, availability, and maintainability.

The final kind of facilities taken up in the chapter, handling and transportation systems, are included as objects needing TPM-level care.

## Handling and Transportation

Transportation and handling facilities add cost but not value, yet they are needed for work to move through operations and out into customers' hands. In this section we examine handling concepts and analysis, and containerization, one of the techniques for reducing handling while goods are being moved.

### *Unit Load versus Piece by Piece*

Principle 13

Decrease cycle interval and lot size.

A well-established practice that is supposed to hold down handling cost is the **unit-load concept.** The idea is simple: Avoid moving piece by piece; instead, accumulate enough pieces to move them as a unit load. Examples are truckloads and railcar loads between sites, and a loaded pallet, skid, drum, tote box, hand truck, and carton within a facility.

While the unit-load idea has long been popular, it can conflict with such customer-focused objectives as speedier, more flexible response. The latter can call for moving items piece by piece with no extra stock in a state of idleness and no delay for building up a load.

Principle 11

Decrease flow distances.

Actually, the unit-load concept and piece-by-piece viewpoints can converge. If functional layouts are broken up and work centers grouped into work cells, handling distances collapse. Without distance to span, the economical unit-load size is pushed downward and may approach one piece. This course of action is easiest to accomplish when the processing equipment consists of multiple smaller machines, each of which can be a member of a different cell.

Principle 9

Install multiple copies of small, simple machines.

### *Distance–Quantity Analysis*

Handling analysis requires two steps: (1) analyzing resource flows (materials and other resources that require handling, e.g., tools and mail), and (2) prescribing handling methods. If the first step is done well, the second is relatively easy.

Data collected on each product or resource can be plotted on a distance–quantity (DQ) chart or, if products/resources are dissimilar, on a distance–intensity (DI) chart. Intensity of flow, a measure developed by Muther, equals quantity times transportability. Transportability is an artificial measure that may include size, density or bulk, shape, risk of damage, condition, and sometimes value of the given item.[5]

The DQ or DI chart helps show the types of handling methods needed. Exhibit 14-14, serving as a guide, has four quadrants. A low-distance, high-volume product would plot in the first quadrant, which suggests complex handling equipment such as conveyors. Low distance, low volume calls for simple handling (second quadrant) such as hand-carry. High distance, low volume calls for simple transport equipment (any of the vehicle types in the third quadrant). High distance, high volume (fourth quadrant) suggests poor layout; handling distances are too great. If re-layout is impractical right away, the need is for complex transport equipment, such as a railroad.

The solid line cutting through the chart makes another distinction. Above the line are fixed-path types of handling equipment; below it are variable-path types. It is well

**EXHIBIT 14-14 DQ or DI Chart Indicating Preferred Handling Methods**

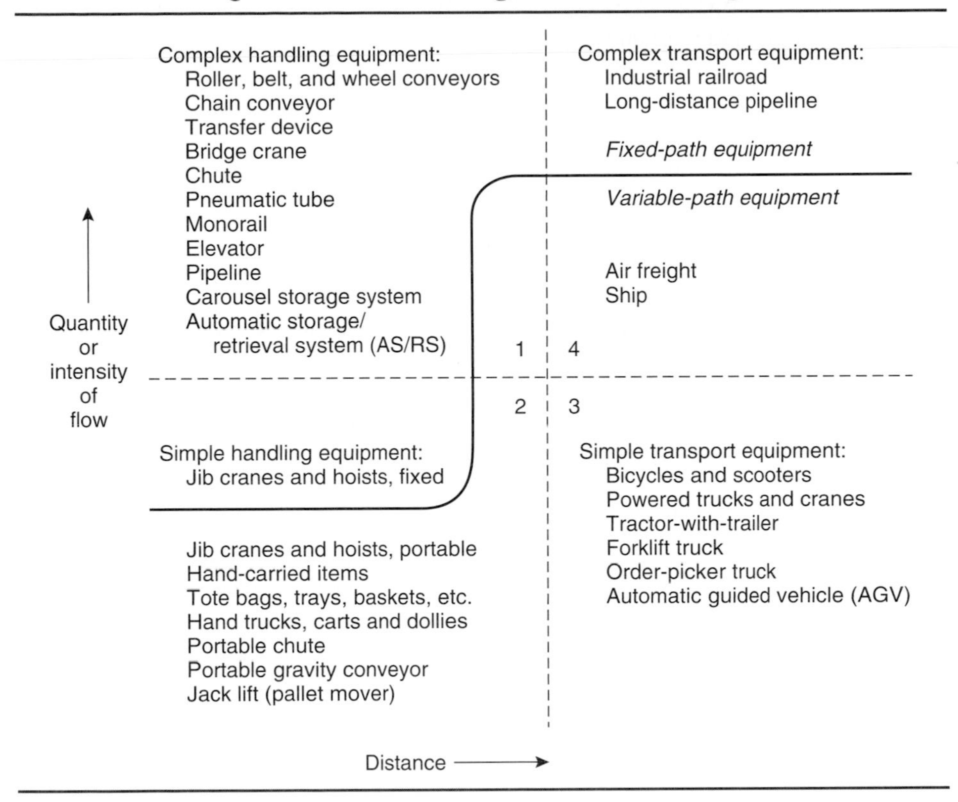


to be cautious about investing in the fixed-path variety; it may be too costly to relocate or modify fixed equipment when needs change.

Some equipment has both handling and storage functions. One example is carousel systems, which are rotatable racks holding small parts, tools, documents, dry cleaning, and so forth. Another example, the automatic storage/retrieval system (AS/RS) consists of rows of racks with automated, computer-controlled, devices to put away and later select baskets or pallets of stock. Both types of equipment were widely installed in North America in the late 1970s and the 1980s. Recently, many companies have been figuring out ways to dismantle some of them; the racks conflict with the goal of avoiding storage. The AS/RS is fine in distribution centers, but when used for storing work-in-process inventories, it is usually a symptom of coordination problems. An exception is a newer type of "mini" AS/RS, which is small enough to be placed at the location where parts or tools are made or used.

Forklift trucks have also lost some of their popularity as a means of handling in-process materials. If machines are close together, as in cells or product layout, materials may be moved by hand, conveyor, transfer device (transfer between adjacent stations), robot, or chute.

The equipment in quadrant 4 and some of the equipment in quadrant 3 of Exhibit 14-14 serve a transportation as well as a handling function. Such equipment tends to be costly enough to warrant special cost analyses.

### *Containerization*

Container design, though usually neglected, can be an essential element of effective handling and transportation. The goals are to protect the goods, ensure exact counts, and simplify loading and unloading.

The Automotive Industry Action Group's containerization task force has developed standard reusable collapsible containers for auto parts usable by competing suppliers and auto assembly plants. The containers avoid throwaway materials, especially cardboard, which cuts costs by a surprisingly large amount—over $50 per car already, according to the manager of one auto assembly plant. Other industries are also plunging into containerization, but mostly with each firm doing its own.

The new containers often are designed to hold an exact, easily verifiable quantity, perhaps through use of partitions or "egg-crate" molded bottoms or inserts. That helps solve a chronic problem. Outside suppliers would deliberately ship too much, hoping to be paid for the excess, or, where the supplier had a stock shortage, ship less than the ordered quantity. Over- and undershipment led to costly delays (to count every piece upon receipt) and generated ill will. The new designs allow for counting containers (e.g., with a bar-code scanner) not pieces; or not counting at all, except on an audit basis. Containerization is all the more necessary in just-in-time operations; JIT lowers inventories and available storage space to the point where receipt of too little or too much can't be tolerated.

On a larger scale, containerization includes semitrailers or large seagoing cargo containers that can also move by rail or be trucked. Cargo containers avoid costly handling of diverse small crates and boxes.

JIT shippers load the cargo boxes with small amounts of multiple components, called kits, rather than loading a huge lot of just one item into the container. Some plants use the transport-kit technique to receive just one day's supply of mixed parts every day from across an ocean.

## Summary Check Points

- ✓ A broadened concept of facilities includes tangible resources excluding human resources and flow-through inventories.
- ✓ The facility requirements pyramid outlines a company's responsibility priorities in securing facilities it needs to conduct business.
- ✓ Leading companies manage facilities in ways that are both competitive and socially responsible.
- ✓ "Brownfield" development is a way of carrying the recycling philosophy into facility-location decisions.
- ✓ Of all facility-management decisions, location is the more "newsworthy" due to economic and environmental impact on target locales.

- ✓ Communities and states have demonstrated a willingness to spend large sums in efforts to attract business.
- ✓ A formal site location rating system will: (1) rate the importance of location factors, (2) rate the locations under consideration against the location factors, and (3) consolidate the results of the first two steps into a final site preference listing.
- ✓ Facility layout—the physical organization or format at a facility—extends facility deployment into the company.
- ✓ The four basic layout types are functional, product, cellular, and fixed position.
- ✓ Mixed layouts (combining two or more of the basic types) are common if not the norm.
- ✓ U-shaped layouts are effective formats for flow lines and work cells; they provide greater staff flexibility and balance, enhanced teamwork, efficient rework (close to the source), easier passage of work, smoother tool and work distribution, and connectivity with other U-shaped cells.
- ✓ Resource factors typically receive different management depending on the dominant layout type in the facility.
- ✓ Flexible layouts offer distinct advantages in fast-paced, dynamic business environments.
- ✓ Dominant flow patterns are initial concerns in layout planning; then nonflow factors are considered, relationship assessments are made, spatial requirements are incorporated; and finally, the rough layout is fit into available space.
- ✓ Open layouts provide greater freedom of flow for resources and customers; fewer barriers also invite teamwork and less secrecy.
- ✓ Proper facilities maintenance is the key to responsive resources; total preventive maintenance is the facility maintenance counterpart to total quality.
- ✓ Total preventive maintenance consists of regular preventive maintenance, periodic prefailure replacements, and intolerance for breakdowns or unsafe conditions.
- ✓ Maintenance activities are classified into two general types: periodic and irregular.
- ✓ Employee-centered maintenance shifts responsibility for workplace cleanliness and general maintenance to line employees and away from staff experts.
- ✓ The 5-S system, perhaps accompanied by spider diagrams, is one tool for maintaining good workplace orderliness and safety.
- ✓ Dedicated maintenance, as exemplified by UPS and the U.S. Air Force, pairs operator and maintenance crew to a specific vehicle.
- ✓ Making time for PM time may decrease short-run utilization, but it enhances overall performance.
- ✓ The unit-load concept is giving way to speedier transport of smaller, maybe piece-by-piece loads.
- ✓ Distance–quantity analysis considers flow volume and distance as key determinants of handling facility selection.
- ✓ Reusable containers not only protect goods, they also provide more efficient control of stock and facilitate JIT operations.

## Solved Problem

### *Problem*

The five departments of a warehouse with their approximate square-footage requirements and activity relationships are as follows:

| DEPARTMENT | AREA (square feet) | ACTIVITY RELATIONSHIPS |
|---|---|---|
| 1. Materials scheduling | 1,000 | |
| 2. Packaging and crating | 1,500 | |
| 3. Materials control supervisor | 500 | |
| 4. Shipping and receiving | 3,000 | |
| 5. Warehouse (storage) | 6,000 | |
| TOTAL | 12,000 square feet | |

| Pair | 1–2 | 1–3 | 1–4 | 1–5 | 2–3 | 2–4 | 2–5 | 3–4 | 3–5 | 4–5 |
|---|---|---|---|---|---|---|---|---|---|---|
| Relationship | E | A | A | I | O | E | I | I | O | A |

*a.* Develop an activity arrangement diagram based on the REL chart data.

*b.* Develop a space relationship diagram for the five departmental areas.

*c.* Fit the five departments into a 100-foot by 150-foot building, and try to maintain 10-foot aisles between departments.

### *Solution*

*a.* Activity arrangement diagram: *b.* Space relationship diagram:

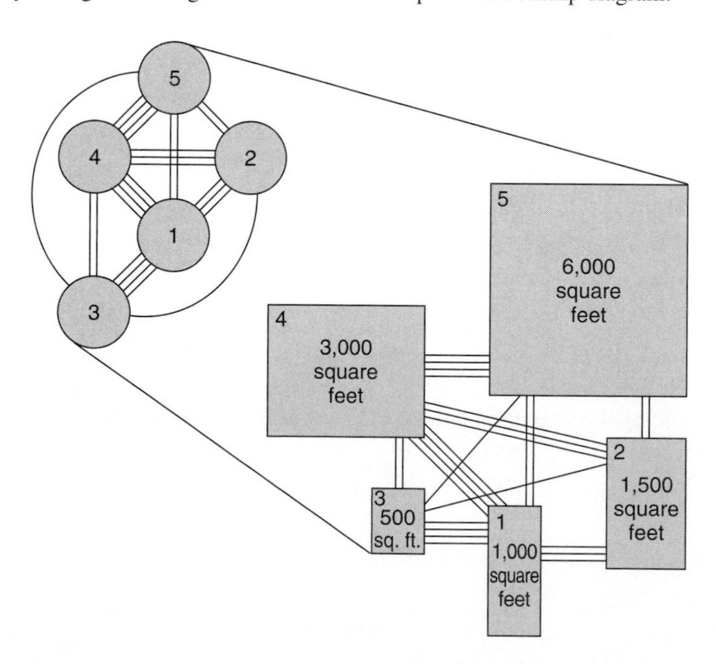

c. Following is a sample departmental layout in a 100-foot by 150-foot building, maintaining 10-foot aisles. (Note: Department 1 has more space than required; all others have the required amount.)

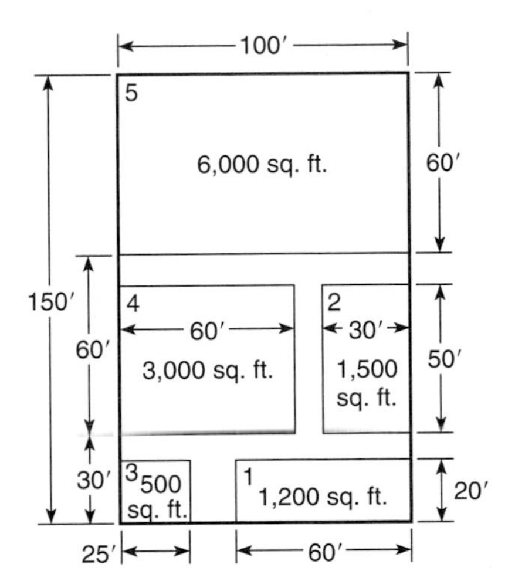


## Exercises

1. Interview an official at your local or state chamber of commerce and find out what incentives are offered to private-sector companies who might wish to locate in the area. Prepare a short report on your findings.
2. Identify the major employer in your city or in the city of your instructor's choosing. Gather information about the economic impact that employer has on the local area. Prepare a brief report of your findings.
3. Visit the web site of the United States Environmental Protection Agency (EPA) and gather information about "Pollution Prevention" or "P2," (http://www.epa.gov/p2/aboutp2.htm). To what extent is P2 a factor in site location decisions? In facility management in general? Discuss.
4. Visit the Information Center for ISO 14000 (http://www.iso14000.com/WhatsNew/News01.htm) and gather information about the role that pollution prevention plays in facility management activities that could become part of a company's environmental management system (EMS).
5. Gather information about "brownfield" development in your area or in an area of your instructor's choosing. Prepare a list of "extra problems" that a developer would encounter in a brownfield development that would not be factors if the development were "greenfield."
6. Which of the 16 Principles of Operations Management most directly relate to facilities management? Why?
7. Amanda's Gift Emporium is famous for its unique year-round "Holiday Season" shopping atmosphere. In addition to a wide variety of gifts on display, Amanda's has custom gift-wrapping services that guarantee no two gifts will be wrapped the same. Business is

booming, and Amanda is thinking about adding some new features to her Emporium. She wants to open a coffee and dessert counter with a few tables and chairs where her customers can enjoy refreshments, and also install a small work area complete with three or four computers so her customers can design their own cards to accompany the gifts that they purchase. She is working on a layout plan. Her planned activity and minimum space requirements are as shown below:

| *Activity Area* | *Space Requirement (Square Feet)* |
|---|---|
| Floor display area | 8,500 |
| Gift wrapping | 1,000 |
| Checkout (cashiers) | 800 |
| Coffee/dessert center | 1,200 |
| Computer card generating area | 1,000 |
| Rest rooms | 400 |
| Employee break room | 300 |
| Shipping, receiving, inventory storage | 1,100 |
| Offices | 1,000 |
| Customer service area (layaway, returns, exchanges, etc.) | 1,600 |
| Total | 16,900 |

*a.* Prepare an activity relationship chart for those areas. Explain your logic, that is, the reasons for your "closeness" ratings.
*b.* Construct an activity-arrangement diagram for the area relationships.
*c.* Construct a sketch of how you would arrange the activity areas in a building that measured 100 feet by 190 feet.

8. The five zones areas for a design office are listed below along with the required area for each. Activity relationship codes are shown at the right.

| Area | Required Space (Square feet) |
|---|---|
| Zone 1 | 2,000 |
| Zone 2 | 500 |
| Zone 3 | 1,000 |
| Zone 4 | 3,000 |
| Zone 5 | 500 |

Activity Relationships

| Pair | Code |
|---|---|
| Zone 1–Zone 2 | I |
| Zone 1–Zone 3 | A |
| Zone 1–Zone 4 | O |
| Zone 1–Zone 5 | O |
| Zone 2–Zone 3 | E |
| Zone 2–Zone 4 | A |
| Zone 2–Zone 5 | E |
| Zone 3–Zone 4 | E |
| Zone 3–Zone 5 | E |
| Zone 4–Zone 5 | I |

*a.* Develop an activity-arrangement diagram based on the REL chart data.
*b.* Develop a space-relationship diagram for the five-zone company.
*c.* Fit the five zones into a building that has outer dimensions of 80 × 110 feet, and try to maintain suitable aisle space between departments.

9. What is the basic layout of the college or university in which you are enrolled? What are the advantages of such a layout? The disadvantages?

10. For each of the following settings, suggest which types of layout (functional, product, cellular, fixed, and mixed) are likely to apply. Some types may have more than one likely type of layout. Explain your choices briefly.

    Auto assembly.
    Auto repair.
    Shipbuilding.
    Machine shop.
    Cafeteria.
    Restaurant.
    Medical clinic.
    Hospital.
    Military physical exams.
    Small-airplane manufacturing.
    Small-airplane overhaul and repair.
    Large airplane overhaul and repair.
    Shoe manufacturing.
    Shoe repair.
    Central processing of insurance forms.
    Packing and crating.

11. Draw a layout of a dentists' office (group practice with three dentists). Label the areas as to whether they are functional, product, cellular, or fixed. Explain.
12. Develop an REL chart for a large discount or department store that you are familiar with. (You may need to visit the store for firsthand information.) Use the store's different departments as activities. Is the REL chart likely to be helpful in layout or re-layout of such a store? How about a flow diagram or a from–to chart? Explain.
13. Automatic Controls Corporation is building a new plant. Eight departments are involved. As part of a plant layout analysis, the activity relationships and square-footage needs for the departments are shown on the combined REL chart (combined flow analysis and nonflow analysis) below.

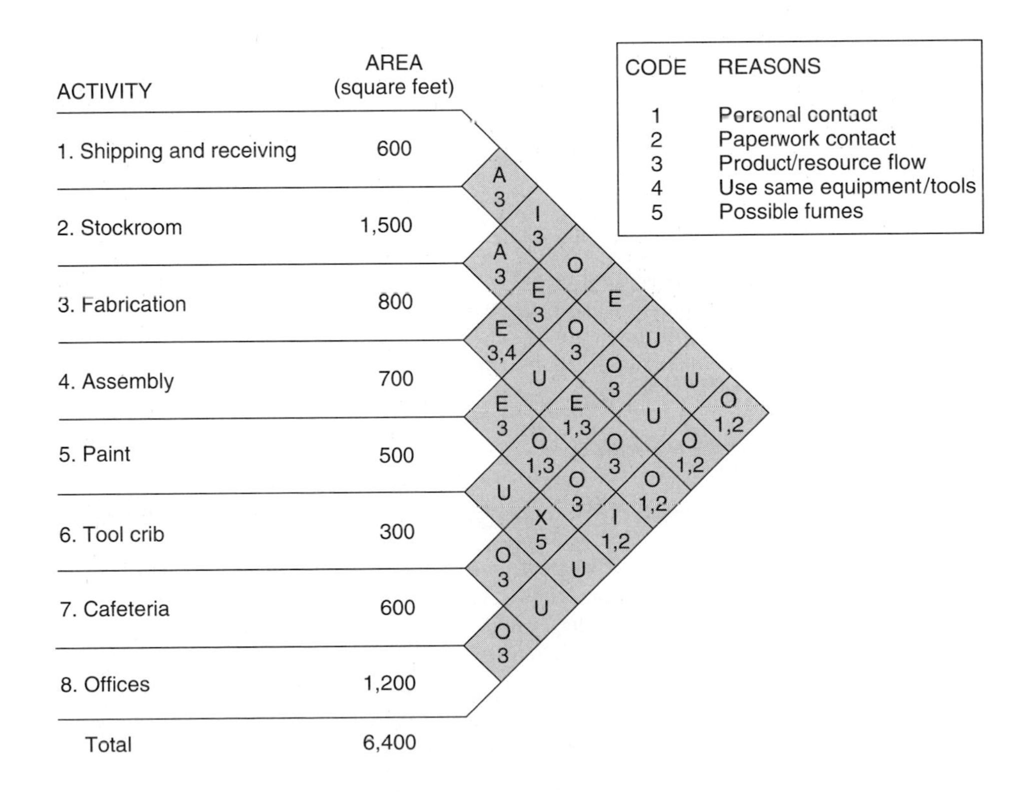

*a.* Develop an activity-arrangement diagram based on the REL-chart data.
*b.* Develop a space-relationship diagram for the eight departmental areas.
*c.* Fit the eight departments into a 100-foot by 80-foot building in as close to an optimal layout as you can. Include aisles between departments on your layout.
*d.* How necessary is the combined REL chart in this case? If it were not included in the analysis, what would the analysis steps be? Explain. (Hint: Note the pattern of reasons for relationships.)

14. Pharmaco, Inc., manufacturer of a drug line in liquid and tablet form, is considering moving to a new building. Layout planning is in process. The following data have been collected on material movements in the drug manufacturing process.

| | *Unit Loads per Month* | *Move Distances (feet) in Present Building* |
|---|---|---|
| **Raw-Material Movements** | | |
| Receiving to raw-material storage: | | 180 |
| 1. Powder in drums. | 800 | |
| 2. Powder in sacks on pallets. | 1,100 | |
| 3. Liquid in drums. | 100 | |
| 4. Controlled substance (heroin) in cans in cartons. | 10 | |
| 5. Empty bottles in cartons on pallets. | 8,000 | |
| 6. Water piped into granulating and liquid mixing (gallons). | 3,000 | |
| **In-Process Movements** | | |
| Raw-material storage to granulating: | | 410 |
| 7. Powder in drums. | 800 | |
| 8. Powder in sacks. | 1,000 | |
| 9. Controlled substance in cans. | 50 | |
| Raw-material storage to liquid mixing: | | 300 |
| 10. Powder in sacks. | 100 | |
| 11. Liquid in drums. | 100 | |
| 12. Controlled substance in cans. | 10 | |
| 13. Granulating to tableting (granules in drums). | 1,500 | 290 |
| 14. Tableting to fill and pack (tables in tubs). | 6,000 | 180 |
| 15. Liquid mixing to fill and pack (gallons piped). | 4,000 | 370 |
| 16. Raw-material storage to fill and pack (empty bottles). | 8,000 | 260 |
| 17. Fill and pack to finished storage (cartons of bottles and of tablet packs on pallets). | 10,000 | 320 |

*a.* Convert the given flow-volume data to a vowel-rating scale; that is, identify which activity pairs (routes) should be rated A, E, I, O, and U.
*b.* Develop an activity arrangement diagram.
*c.* The layout planners see little need for a from–to chart or an REL chart. Explain why.

15. The SLP example (Globe County Offices, chapter supplement) includes only a partial combined REL chart (Exhibit S14-3) and omits the space-relationship diagram. Using the given data in the example, follow the method of the Solved Problem and

*a.* Construct a complete combined REL chart to include all offices. (Use your best judgment along with available information in the example to assign "closeness values" and likely "reasons behind the closeness values.")

*b.* Construct a space-relationship diagram based on the activity-arrangement diagram (Exhibit S14-4) and given space requirements (Exhibit S14-1).

16. The woodshop building of E-Z Window Company is undergoing major re-layout in order to reduce backtracking and decrease flow distances. A flow diagram of the frame-manufacturing operation and an REL chart for nonflow factors in the operation is shown below.

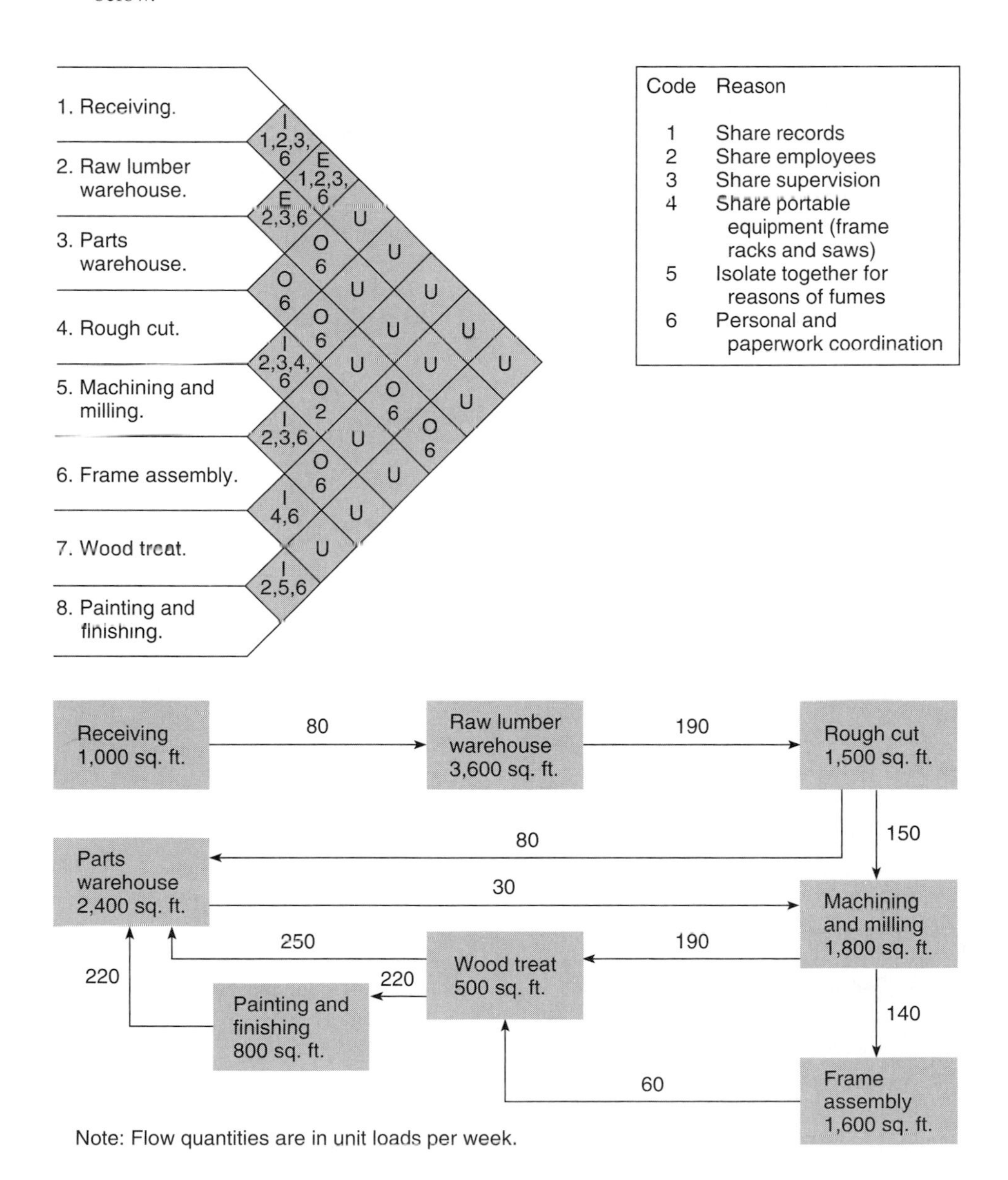

*a.* Construct a from–to chart based on flow-diagram data. What is the meaning of the notation that quantities are in unit loads? Explain by referring to a few examples on the chart.
*b.* What proportion of total flow on your from–to chart represents backtracking? How does that proportion depend on your chosen order of listing activities on the chart? What does your chosen order of listing activities imply about the final layout arrangement?
*c.* Convert the flow volume data in your from–to chart to a vowel-rating scale; that is, identify which activity pairs (routes) should be rated A, E, I, O, and U.
*d.* Combine your vowel-rating data representing flow volumes with the non-flow-factor vowel ratings on the REL chart. Express the result in a new, combined REL chart.
*e.* Convert your combined REL chart into an activity-arrangement diagram.
*f.* Develop a space-relationship diagram for the eight activity areas.
*g.* Fit the eight activity areas into a square building without allowances for aisles, and so on. Make your layout as nearly optimal as you can.

17. Examine the "Principles of Operations Management" in Chapter 3. Which principles seem most directly affected by layout and re-layout decisions? Discuss.
18. Devise a way that you, or you and your partner or living or working associates, might use a version of the spider diagram and 5 S's to eliminate small aggravations that sometimes expand into big ones. Discuss your plan.
19. With computers (microprocessors) now in common use as automobile control devices, they sometimes serve a preventive maintenance purpose. A dash panel could be used to input into a computer every maintenance operation performed on the car, and mileage data could be entered into the computer automatically. A screen could then recommend preventive maintenance whenever a program determines a need.
    *a.* To what extent is this idea in use right now? What are some obstacles in the way of implementing or improving on such a PM system?
    *b.* What are some important items of historical data that would need to be programmed into the auto's computer? Where would such data come from? Explain.
    *c.* Large numbers of nearly identical autos are sold, which provides a sizable potential database for gathering failure and wear-out data. For almost any type of factory machine, there is a smaller potential database; that is, there are far fewer copies of the same machine. Yet good factory PM is based on good failure records. How can a good database be developed for factory machines?
20. Joe Black is head of the maintenance operations division of the plant engineering department at Wexco, Inc. Rumors have been flying around his division. The buzzing is regarding the company's plan to launch a new program called Operator Ownership. The program is aimed at the problem of machine undependability and would place more responsibility for machine performance on the machine operators—a step backwards, in the minds of Black and his subordinates.

    Part of the worry is that operator ownership is budget cutting (slashing the maintenance budget) in disguise, which equals losses of jobs in maintenance operations. Black also harbors natural concerns regarding losses of personal prestige and power.

    Are those worries really justified? Discuss.
21. Captain Henry Harrison has spent much of his career in navy shipyards. In the last 10 years, he has held three positions of authority over shops that build and repair ships. He has been a firm believer in conducting frequent inspections of shop facilities and is a stickler for

having everything neat, clean, and painted. Some people think Captain Harrison spends too much time on this. What do you think?

22. Acme Corporation has invested $5 million in storage and handling gear: $1 million in pallet racks, $1 million in an operatorless wire-guided vehicle delivery system, $1 million in carousel storage (three carousels), $1 million in an AS/RS, and $1 million in a transporter (moving parts from person to person in production cells and lines).

    Evaluate these five handling/storage systems. Rank them in worst-to-best order for a plant pursuing just-in-time production with continual improvement. Explain.
23. Examine the "Principles of Operations Management" in Chapter 3. Which seem most directly affected by handling and transportation issues? Discuss.
24. The chapter suggests that wise customers choose supplier partners that have facilities in good condition. Does it work in the other direction as well? Should suppliers be concerned about their customers' facilities? Discuss.
25. The next drawing shows a "JIT pack" devised by engineers at Texas Instruments' Automotive Electronics unit, which conveys sets of parts between TI and major automotive customers. When filled, the box weighs not more than 40 pounds. Its flexible, built-in spacers hold tubes, trays, and reels of semiconductors or other electronic components; on average, 95 percent of the materials are recyclable and/or reusable.

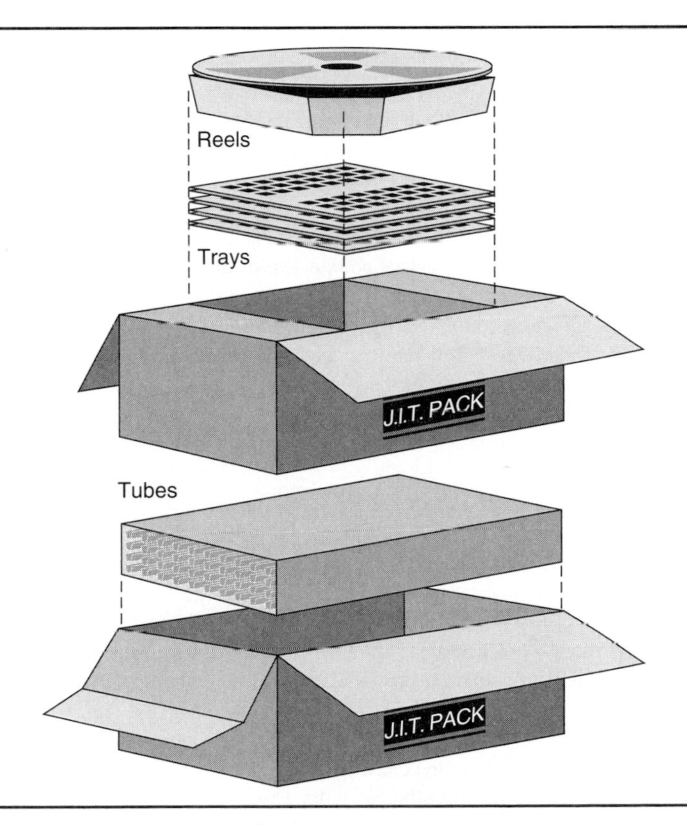


Source: Elizabeth Franklin, "Environment: Thinking 'Outside the Box,'" *Semisphere,* June 1995, pp. 8–9. Courtesy, Texas Instruments Semiconductor Group.

*a.* Based on what you've learned about just-in-time, how does this container support JIT objectives?
*b.* What other benefits can be derived from the JIT pack?
*c.* Which principles of operations management does the JIT pack relate to?

**SUPPLEMENT**

# SYSTEMATIC LAYOUT PLANNING (SLP)[6] EXAMPLE

This supplement demonstrates systematic layout planning using the setps identified in the chapter. The method and some of the tools were developed by R.R. Muther, who calls the approach **systematic layout planning (SLP).** SLP is respected for its practicality, is widely referenced, and is widely used. Though developed in an earlier era, SLP works well in support of a modern, customer-oriented approach to layout.

## Layout Planning—Globe County Offices

Citizens' main contact with Globe County offices is in registering and licensing vehicles. Many people complain because the three county offices involved have not consolidated their services. On busy days there are waiting lines at all three offices. Many vehicle owners must visit all three, and it is common for a citizen to find out, after shuffling forward for awhile, that it is the wrong line.

The elected officials who run the three offices have decided to consolidate. Mr. Ross, a consultant, has been hired to conduct layout analysis using SLP.

Ross's analysis reveals that 12 activities are to be located in the available space and that four of those have significant flows: three service counters, plus the office copier (see Exhibit S14-1). The space requirements are based on careful measurement of desks, files, and so forth, plus use of widely available industry space standards (e.g., 300 square feet per auto in a parking lot).

*Flow analysis.* For those four activities, Ross gathers flow data, which he enters on a from-to chart (which resembles the distance chart found on many road maps), as shown in Exhibit S14-2A. Numbers above the diagonal represent flows of patrons from one activity to another; numbers below the diagonal reflect backtracking by patrons who find themselves in the wrong office, and round-trips to and from the copiers.

Exhibit S14-2B is a conversion chart, which Ross develops for displaying from–to data in order of descending flow volume. Ross then judgmentally inserts horizontal lines that divide the flow-volume bars into five zones, labeled A, E, I, O, and U, which are the standard SLP symbols for flow volume.

*Nonflow factors.* Next, Ross lists nonflow factors, such as the need for employees to be near their supervisor, and rates them using the same five vowel designators. He combines flow and nonflow factors on an activity relationship (REL) chart, a segment of which is shown in Exhibit S14-3.

The REL chart is easy to interpret. The single A in the chart indicates that it is absolutely necessary for customer service people in the clerk and treasurer offices to be close together. Reasons are "work flow" (1), "employee sharing (between departments)" (3), and "share counter" (4). The same reasons apply to the E, for especially important, in the box connecting customer service counter people in the assessor and treasurer offices.

## EXHIBIT S14-1 Major Work Areas—County Offices

| Activity | Space Requirements (square feet) |
|---|---|
| 1. County assessor's office: | |
| *a.* Management | 600 |
| *b.* Motor vehicle—counter* | 300 |
| *c.* Motor vehicle—clerical | 240 |
| *d.* Assessors | 960 |
| 2. County clerk's office: | |
| *e.* Management | 840 |
| *f.* Recording and filing—counter | 240 |
| *g.* Recording and filing—clerical | 960 |
| *h.* Motor vehicle—counter-clerical* | 960 |
| 3. County treasurer's office: | |
| *i.* Management | 420 |
| *j.* Motor vehicle—counter-clerical* | 1,600 |
| 4. Support areas: | |
| *k.* Mail and copier* | 240 |
| *l.* Conference room | 160 |
| Total | 7,520 |

*Significant flows.

Source: This is adapted from a real case. Thanks go to Ross Greathouse of Greathouse-Flanders Associates, Lincoln, Nebraska, for providing original case data.

*Activity arrangement.* Now Ross converts the combined REL chart to an activity arrangement diagram, which shows the arrangement of all activities but without indicating requirements for space, utilities, halls, and so on (see Exhibit S14-4). In this diagram, number of lines between activities stands for flow volume: Four lines corresponds to an A rating on the REL chart, three lines stands for an E rating, and so forth. Distances between circles are set according to desired degree of closeness, as much as possible. Activities 2, 6, 8, and 10, at the core, are all service-counter activities, which earlier ratings showed should be placed close together.

*Space arrangement.* Ross's next-to-last chart (not shown) includes the space data from Exhibit S14-1. The result is a diagram that is in the generally rectangular shape of the space into which the activities must fit; activity blocks are sized according to space needed. The space relationship diagram may be regarded as a rough layout. (See Solved Problem at the end of Chapter 14 for an example.)

*Layout into available space.* Finally, Ross is ready to draw some final layouts, complete with walls, halls, aisles, and other needed elements.

Exhibit S14-5 shows what Ross might have developed. Part A is an actual layout of the county office renovation that is the basis for this example. Part B shows the main feature of that layout, the shared counter. The layout was developed by an architectural firm (though the systematic layout planning process, as presented here, was not fully used) and approved and implemented by newly elected Lancaster County officials in Lincoln, Nebraska.

## EXHIBIT S14-2 Flow Volume (People per Day)—County Offices

A. From–to chart

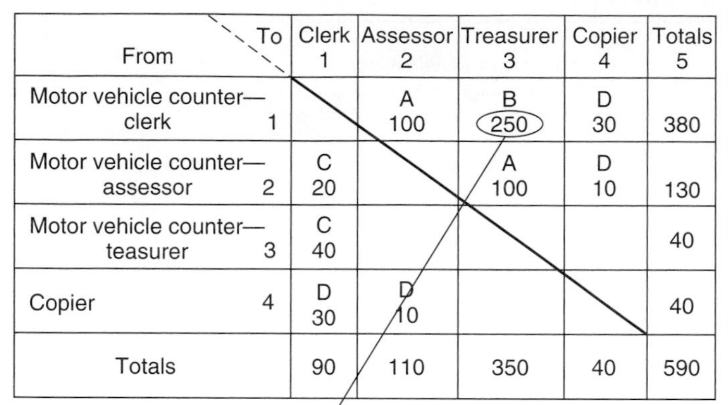

| From \ To | Clerk 1 | Assessor 2 | Treasurer 3 | Copier 4 | Totals 5 |
|---|---|---|---|---|---|
| Motor vehicle counter—clerk 1 | | A 100 | B 250 | D 30 | 380 |
| Motor vehicle counter—assessor 2 | C 20 | | A 100 | D 10 | 130 |
| Motor vehicle counter—teasurer 3 | C 40 | | | | 40 |
| Copier 4 | D 30 | D 10 | | | 40 |
| Totals | 90 | 110 | 350 | 40 | 590 |

Types of product flow:

A Patrons licensing newly purchased vehicles.

B Patrons licensing same-owner vehicles.

C Patrons to wrong office—backtrack to correct office.

D Round-trips to copier.

B. Conversion to vowel ratings on bar chart

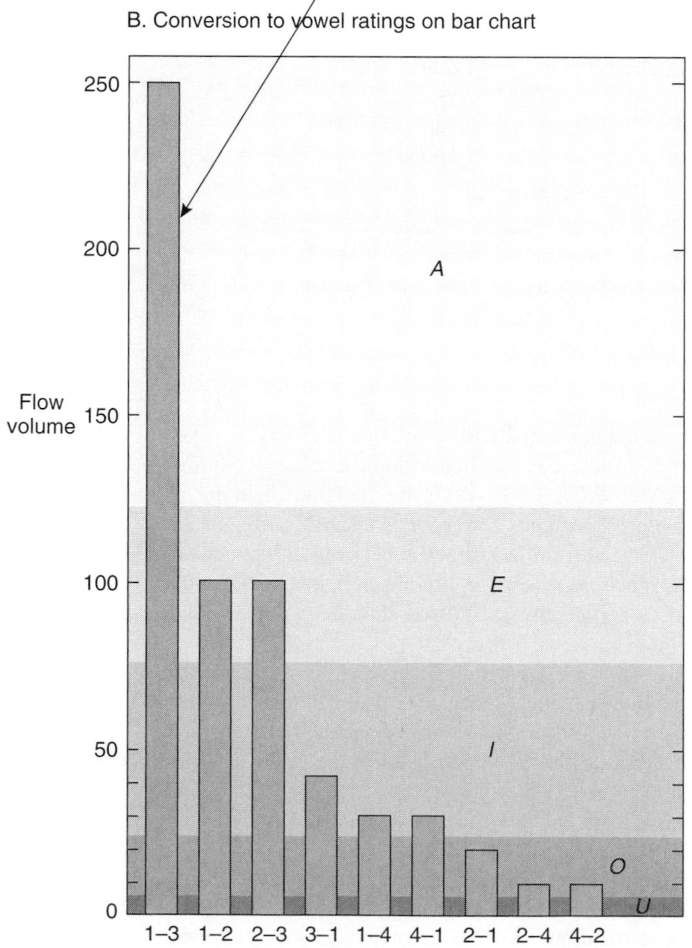


Key:

*A* for *a*bnormally high flow

*E* for *e*specially high flow

*I* for *i*mportant flow

*O* for *o*rdinary flow

*U* for *u*nimportant moves of negligible flow volume

## EXHIBIT S14-3 Combined Activity Relationship (REL) Chart—County Offices

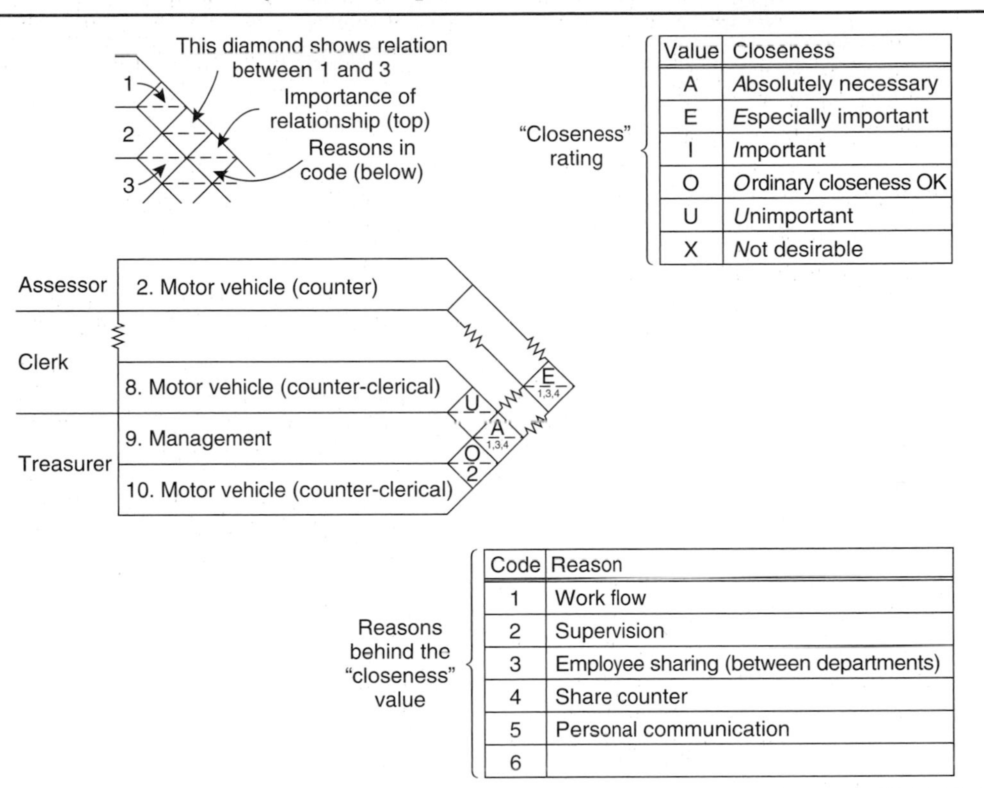


| Value | Closeness |
|---|---|
| A | *A*bsolutely necessary |
| E | *E*specially important |
| I | *I*mportant |
| O | *O*rdinary closeness OK |
| U | *U*nimportant |
| X | *N*ot desirable |

| Code | Reason |
|---|---|
| 1 | Work flow |
| 2 | Supervision |
| 3 | Employee sharing (between departments) |
| 4 | Share counter |
| 5 | Personal communication |
| 6 | |

Source of REL chart form: Richard Muther and Associates, Kansas City, Missouri. Used with permission.s

## EXHIBIT S14-4 Activity-Arrangement Diagram—County Offices

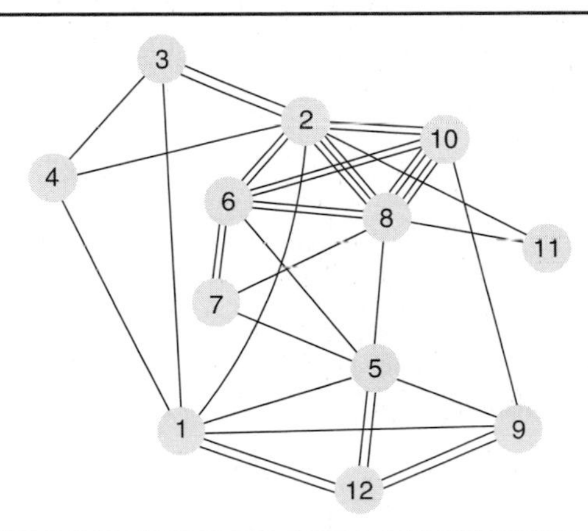

**Exhibit S14-5 New Layout and Motor Vehicle Licensing Counter**

*A. Final layout—county offices. B. Vehicle licensing counter shared by employees of the county assessor, clerk, and treasurer.*

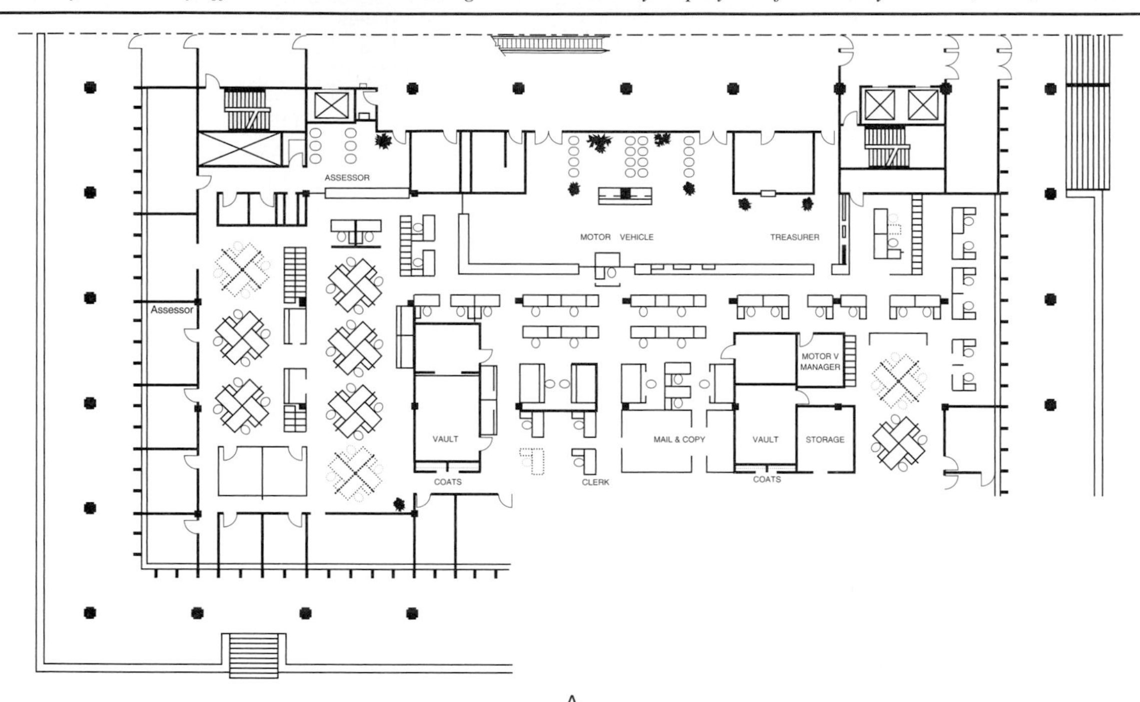


A

B

The Globe County Offices example is fairly simple. In large, complex layouts, analysis within each activity area could include the full SLP treatment—that is, all the SLP steps. In later steps, various two- and three-dimensional models (manual or computer graphic) can be manipulated to produce workable layout options. In the Globe County example, we also glossed over all the trial and error usually involved in the diagramming.

Another layout planning tool that takes a similar approach to the SLP method used in this example is referred to as strategic facility planning (SFP).[7] In that technique, one begins by identifying what are called space planning indentifiers (SPIs). An SPI represents some feature (e.g., function or department) that requires space or has a flow or nonflow relationship with other space planning identifiers. As with the SLP method, affinity diagrams and relationship charts indicate flow volumes and desirability of nearness.

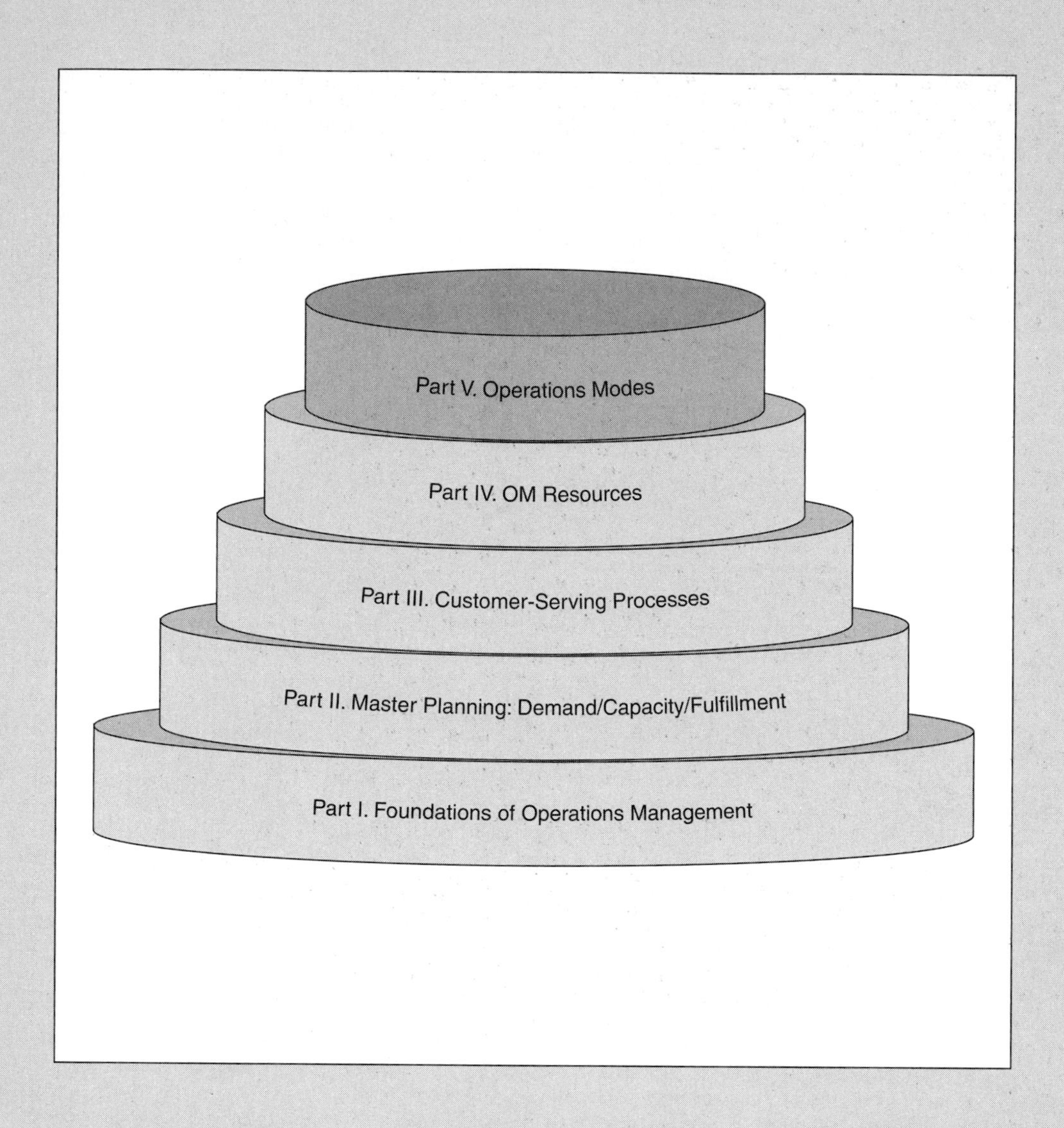
Part V. Operations Modes
Part IV. OM Resources
Part III. Customer-Serving Processes
Part II. Master Planning: Demand/Capacity/Fulfillment
Part I. Foundations of Operations Management

PART

V

# OPERATIONS MODES: IN-DEPTH ANALYSIS



In Part V, we revisit operations modes that were introduced in Chapter 1, but now we take a much more detailed look at the concepts. From the high volumes and low variety associated with continuous flows to the singular output but high-variety arenas of jobs and projects, we explore the tools that successful operations managers use to ensure competitiveness in various types of operations environments.

***Points to ponder:*** Operations management is a field of interrelationships and overlaps. As you study Part V, expect to see traces of design, quality assurance, scheduling, forecasting, strategy, timing, and other topics that we addressed in earlier parts of the book. If you find yourself recalling previously covered material . . . good! That's what we hoped would happen.

CHAPTER 15

# Managing Continuous and Repetitive Operations

> "Catalytica produces the famous anti-AIDS drug AZT and other products for Glaxo; Sudafed for Warner-Lambert (now part of Pfizer); and Elimite, a skin-soothing cream for Allergan. It makes more than 50 other chemicals and pharmaceuticals in pills, capsules, powder, injection doses, suspensions, and solutions for [most of the well-known pharmaceutical companies]. It also manufactures for "virtual" drug companies . . . which have no plants of their own.
>
> "Once a client signs a contract, Catalytica's work starts at the Greenville (NC) "fine chemicals" facility. This 24-hour-a-day operation makes so-called intermediates, which are transformed chemically into organic molecules, the Lego blocks of drug production. The plant offers facilities for grinding, screening, and blending as well as for complex chemical synthesis. Its reactors can cook compounds in 2,000-gallon batches.
>
> "Making the pharmaceuticals comes next. The plant's machines stamp out and package tablets and caplets and fill tubes and bottles with ointments, creams, and liquids. Productions is highly-automated and computer-controlled."
>
> Source: Gene Bylinsky, "America's Elite Factories," *Fortune,* August 16, 1999, pp. 136[C]ff.

High-volume, continuous-flow operations conjure up images of liquids flowing from large vats through mazes of pipes until forced through nozzles into bottles, tubes, or cans. Or, perhaps we think of small discrete objects like pills or pieces of candy zipping down conveyors to be scooped into packages or containers for subsequent capping, sealing, and labeling operations. Such is the "stuff" of the **process industry**—the name we apply to these kinds of transformations.

The Catalytica plant described in the opening vignette is a classic example of process industry operations: Chemicals are mixed, blended, and/or cooked in large vats or tanks, and then flow—as a continuous stream of product—into subsequent stages where repetitive operations prepare the discrete units of finished drugs for distribution. We should add, moreover, that Catalytica does the job in superior style, and has been designated by *Fortune* as one of America's Elite Factories.[1]

This chapter begins Part V, our detailed study of operating environments, with a look at managing continuous and repetitive operations. Technically, as we noted in Chapter 1, *process industry* refers to continuous flow products—powders, pellets, grains, ores, electricity, and other commodities. (Though historically not included, perhaps some services, banking for instance, share some process industry characteristics?) Repetitive operations share many of the characteristics found in continuous-flow processes, but differ in some ways that have an effect on the management of operations, as we shall see in the pages ahead.

## Process Industries—and Hybrids

There are not many purely continuous process industries. Perhaps the one that comes closest is electric power generation. In Wyoming's coal fields, giant shovels dump lignite into huge trucks that move trainlike to dump their loads onto conveyors that carry the fuel into the furnaces of a 500 megawatt energy plant. The coal burns and the turbines spin, generating the power that flows through wires to a million homes and businesses. Nothing stops. The output is not stored. The same goes for hydroelectric power, with slight variation in a few steps.

Far more common is hybrid processing: both continuous and repetitive in the same plant. Typically, the front end is continuous—raw materials start as flows—but the end products emerge as units; we saw this pattern in the Catalytica plant vignette. In candy factories, sugar, chocolate, water, and other ingredients flow in, and cartons of candy bars or boxed candy come out. Potatoes, salt, vegetable oil, and so forth, flow into a potato chip plant, and cartons of sacked chips emerge. Exhibit 15-1 illustrates typical production of food items. Continuous flow of dough through the mixing stage gives way to individual pieces for subsequent freezing and packaging in highly repetitive fashion.

**EXHIBIT 15-1 Typical Production of Food Items**

*Pepperidge Farm® cookie line.*

Courtesy Pepperidge Farm®. Used with permission.

Principles 9 and 12

Use simple, flexible equipment. Cut changeover times.

A critical operations strategy for the hybrids is streamlined processing in both the continuous and repetitive stages. Sometimes, however, the market, the competition, equipment, and other factors gang up to push a firm away from streamlining. The Pepperidge Farm division of Campbell Soup is an example.[2] Pepperidge's dilemma was the same as that of many food processors: a growing variety of products and package sizes and types vying for too few production lines. The schedule for any given product was intermittent with long intervals between production runs—a far cry from streamlined, continuous flows.

One solution was faster changeovers from production of one product to another. This permitted more frequent production of all items. Pepperidge scoured the world to find equipment that could be quickly changed over, allowing a single plant to produce nearly 10 times the number of products per day as was previously possible. With more frequent production—more continuous—the company moved closer to synchronizing baking with store sales. Bake-to-store cycle times for cookies and breads were roughly halved. This is a sizable competitive advantage, since the product on the shelf is fresher. Thus, the operations strategy of becoming more streamlined dovetailed with the business strategy of gaining competitive advantage from providing fresher products closer matched to sales rates.

This strategy applies not only to Pepperidge. It has general application in the process industries. The Pepperidge success formula, plus other factors critical for continuous processors are our next topic.

## Key Success Factors

> The Cypress Plant was built with quality, just-in-time, and total employee involvement in mind; the plant was designed internally, and those who designed it run it. All associates are cross-trained on every task, and a weekly job rotation includes every facet of the plant. Obvious benefits include flexibility and enhanced problem solving. Rapid response to customer requirements has been attained through an 80 percent reduction in changeover times, receipt of materials in the exact (containerized) quantity needed and at the point-of-use, process streamlining, buffer inventory reductions, and quick-response shipping. Brainstorming, partnerships with suppliers, benchmarking, and elimination of non-value-adding steps are other activities contributing to success.[3]

These comments, describing Milliken & Company's Cypress chemical plant in Blacksburg, Virginia, show that many of the themes of this book apply to the chemical industry, too. Success in chemicals, as in other businesses, comes from giving customers quality, flexibility, and responsive just-in-time service with short cycle times and eliminating wastes to drive down costs.

Chemical companies and other process-industry organizations, however, have their own ways of pursuing the general success formula. Exhibit 15-2 identifies nine key success factors that apply especially to process-industry operations. Those nine are joined by five additional success factors to form a broader list that is applicable to repetitive operations. We shall defer discussion of the latter five factors until later in the chapter, and consider only those that pertain to process industry operations at this time. Each of the nine is explained in two parts: the factor itself and contemporary examples of how to apply it.

**Exhibit 15-2 Success Factors for Continuous and Repetitive Operations**

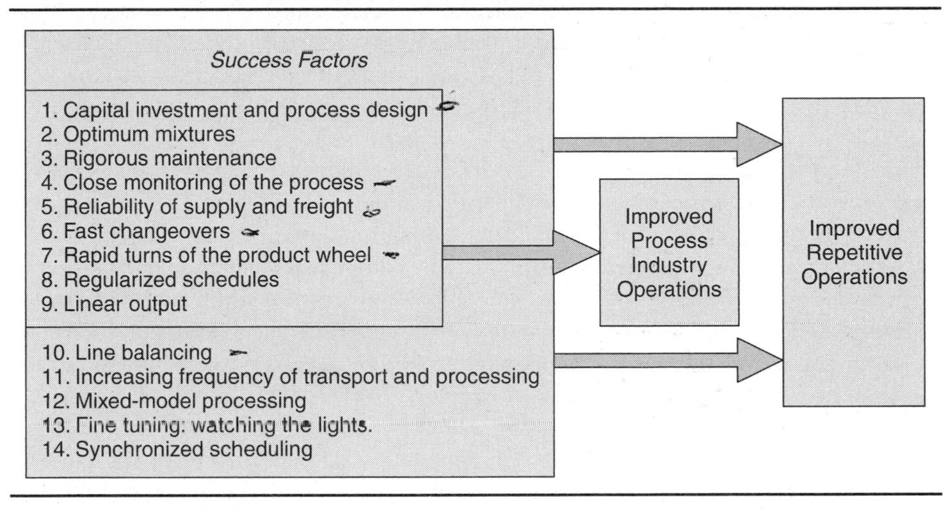


**Capital Investment and Process Design.** Usually continuous processors are capital intensive. Their plants bristle with high-cost automation. Often, competitive advantage comes from having the most modern equipment and from keeping it running close to 168 hours per week ("24/7"). Since this strategy—keep the plants running—tends to produce excessive inventories of certain items, it calls for a companion strategy in sales and marketing: Promote, advertise, and cut deals to move the inventory. Overall, profit margins suffer.

*Application.* Equally important is for the plants to be designed for fail-safe, high-yield operation. Multifunctional product–process design teams can apply their breadth of experience to this goal. Milliken's Cypress plant, designed with operator involvement, is a case in point. The plant features two separate reactor groups, one for large orders and the other for small ones. Conventionally, chemical plants have a single large reactor group, which forces dominant products to compete for processing time with small-volume products. Customer service on both large and small orders suffers.

**Optimum Mixtures.** Some process industries rely heavily on linear programming for finding optimum (best) mixtures of ingredients. An example is production of pet food and livestock feed. Product planners use LP to select the lowest-cost mix of ingredients that will meet nutrition and other standards. Since volumes are usually large, savings of a few cents per bag can add up quickly.

*Application.* Optimizing the mix begins in preproduction planning. Product-development personnel search for better ingredients and involve suppliers in process and materials improvement. Sourcing teams aim for supplier certification.

**Rigorous Maintenance.** An equipment breakdown idles an entire process. In the case of a food or drug company, for example, a whole mixing or bottling line may shut down. When the product is perishable, avoiding breakdowns is all the more critical;

perishability disallows buffer stocks between process stages as protection against breakdowns. The process itself must be capable and well maintained.

*Application.* As we saw in Chapter 14, the highest form of process maintenance is called total preventive maintenance (TPM) and involves every operator. A goal is to eliminate costly downtime caused by equipment malfunctions and failures.

**Close Monitoring of the Process.** In the process industries, laws or industrywide standards often govern product quality, purity, sanitation, and waste. Process monitoring must be rigorous to ensure that standards are met and products are safe and salable.

*Application.* Much of the monitoring may be automated. Programmable logic controllers, a rugged, special-purpose type of computer processor, guide much of the monitoring. (See Into Practice, "Maintainability at La Victoria Foods," in Chapter 14.) Just as important are operator uses of data-based tools for discovery of malfunctions and root causes and their rapid correction.

**Reliability of Supply and Freight.** This includes selection of a plant site close to markets and supplies of materials. Raw materials are the lifeline of process industries. Thus, regardless of plant location, the freight haulers bringing in material must be reliable. (See Exhibit 15-3.) Stockpiling as protection for shaky supply or freight is a limited option. Most of the process industry produces in such large volumes that even a few days' supply of ingredients would make a mountain.

**Exhibit 15-3 Seed Potato Processing in the Netherlands**

*A. Seed potatos move to elevation conveyor in preparation for bagging operation in ZPC plant near Leeuwarden, The Netherlands. B. ZPC truck loaded with seed potatos bound for destination in Eastern Europe. The company logo also reflects rail shipment options.*

A

B

*Application.* Strong supplier relations are critical. The quest is for partnerships with a few good suppliers. Ideally, they deliver just in time direct to points of use closely synchronized with production schedules. For disaster protection, it may be best to store extra stock offline where it will not interfere with the continuity and speed of flow.

**Fast Changeovers.** Producing different blends and container sizes requires changing production lines. Some line changeovers take several days, which may include completely cleaning out all equipment. Fast changeovers make it easier to fit more jobs, large and small, into the schedule in a given time period.

*Application.* The guidelines for quick changeover (Chapter 10), perfected for sheet-metal fabrication and machining, apply as well in the process industries. Flexible, cross-trained associates participate in changeover improvement projects and also execute the improvements. An objective is to schedule more products per time period closer to actual demand patterns. Example: Monsanto Plastics in Cincinnati cut its time to change color in its plastic products from 10 to 12 hours to $1\frac{1}{2}$ hours. The method was to prepare a duplicate color module offline, then stop the process to quickly swap the color modules.

**Rapid Turns of the Product Wheel.** Many companies in the process industries produce assorted products on a single high-capacity production line. Figuratively, the assortment arranges itself on what industry people call the **product wheel.** See Exhibit 15-4. Make the first product, change the process, make the second, change, and so on around the wheel. **Product wheel turn time,** therefore, is the required production cycle time for any member of the product family. Conventionally, companies turn the wheel slowly. That is, they produce huge quantities in long production runs between changeovers. Their aim is to increase the ratio of production time to changeover time. The downside is that customers wanting product E must wait through production runs of products A through D. A more customer-sensitive practice is to speed up the wheel turns.

**EXHIBIT 15-4 Product Wheel**

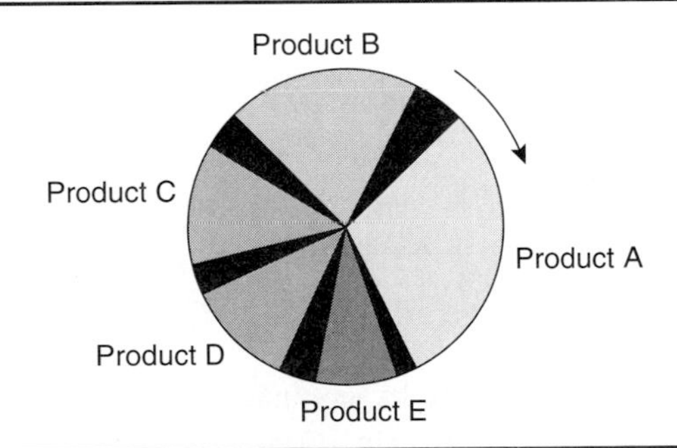


Note: The wedges between products represent process changeovers.

Source: Adapted from Wayne K. Smith, James L. Ingraham, and David M. Rurak, "Time and Pull: A DuPont Case History," *Target* (January/February 1993), pp. 27–12.

*Application.* The usual practice produces large amounts of inventory out of synch with demand rates. While a faster wheel turn reduces equipment utilization, it also cuts lot-size inventories. Speeding the wheel thus may be cost neutral. Example: At Esso Chemical's Sarnia, Ontario, plant (producing polyvinyl chloride, polyethylene, etc.) the wheel turn time was reduced from 80 days to 30. Quicker changeovers paved the way.[4]

DuPont has developed a method of calculating wheel turn time.[5] Data required are downtime attributable to changeovers, outage time, production rate, and demand rate. The DuPont formula is

$$W = \sum C \Big/ \left(1 - O - \frac{\sum D}{P}\right) \tag{15-1}$$

where

$W$ = Wheel turn time

$C$ = Downtime attributable to changeovers (not including changeovers done offline or "on the fly")

$O$ = Outage time, as a decimal

$P$ = Production rate, expressed as a composite average for all products represented by the wheel

$\sum D$ = Average quantity demanded (ordered), summed up for all products on the wheel, for a given time period

*Assumptions:* Production rate $P$ must exceed demand rate $D$, and outage $O$ plus the composite demand-to-production ratio ($\sum D/P$) must be less than 1.0.

Finding the wheel turn time is important for product scheduling. It is even more important for salespeople, who need the information for order promising to customers. An example demonstrates the calculation.

## Example 15-1: WHEEL TURN TIME, EXTRUDER

*Given*

A DuPont plant operates an extruder 24 hours a day. The following are characteristics of the operation:

- Five products varying in color from white (A) to black (E).
- 15-minute changeovers (done on the fly while extruding continues) between colors.
- An eight-hour cleanout between E (black) and A (white).
- 8 percent outage for maintenance.
- 5 percent operator unavailability (breaks, meetings, etc.).
- Required to be produced and shipped daily: 20,000 pounds.
- Production rate of 1,000 pounds per hour or 24,000 pounds per day.

What is the wheel turn time?

*Solution*

Omitting the 15-minute changeovers, since they are on the fly and do not affect $\sum C$, we have,

$$\sum C = \text{Sum of the changeover times} = 8 \text{ hours}$$
$$O = 0.08 + 0.05 = 0.13$$
$$W = 8 \text{ hours} \Big/ \left[1 - 0.13 - \left(\frac{20{,}000}{24{,}000}\right)\right] = 219 \text{ hours, or about 9 days}$$

Thus, sales must allow for up to nine days production cycle time in making order promises to customers.

---

**Regularized Schedules.** Dominant products (say, the 10 most popular of 200 fabrics woven in a textile plant) deserve special treatment. One approach is to fit these products into regularly scheduled processing time slots based on average demand rates. Nondominant products do not have enough volume to make this approach feasible; thus, those products (the other 190 fabrics) may be scheduled irregularly as demands dictate.

*Application.* This may call for two scheduling systems in a single plant. One is for dominant products based on demand rates. (The rate is usually a smoothed representation of actual up-and-down demand patterns.) The second is for low-volume, high-variety products. At Milliken's Cypress plant the separate reactor group for large orders provides an ideal situation for scheduling to a rate.

**Linear Output.** A goal for the process industry is exceptional predictability of output, linear with the schedule. A regularized schedule provides a plan. On the execution side, the company must achieve stable yields per production run. In the process industries, yield means percentage of planned output actually achieved. Say that a fabric producer achieves a yield of 95 percent in one production run, 70 percent in the next, and then 98 percent. This yield pattern is decidedly unstable, which causes supply and demand problems both forward to the customer and backward through the supply chain.

*Application.* The process industries tend toward a fixation on maximizing output volume. Often rather little attention is paid to **linearity.** (Linearity means make to a number—the demand rate—and stop, rather than "Let's see how much we can make today.") Overcommitting equipment and people usually dooms linearity. The antidote is to put some slack—a capacity cushion—into the schedule; that is, schedule production for somewhat less than 168 hours a week. This provides time to address likely process problems and to allow time for process maintenance. Undercapacity scheduling can often increase average output by eliminating causes of severe stoppages.

Conventional practice in the process industry gives emphasis to items 1 through 5 in Exhibit 15-2. Recently, companies have begun to address item 6, quick changeover, and item 7, its companion, fast wheel turns, as well. Few companies, however, have paid heed to items 8 and 9, regularized schedules and linearity, which we consider in more detail next.

## *Regularized Scheduling and Linearity*

Improvement in continuous processing and high-volume repetitive operations often hinges on better scheduling and on greater accuracy in providing the scheduled amount (hitting the target) consistently. Proven techniques for accomplishing these and other aims include processing with regularized schedules and linear output. To fully appreciate their usefulness, the negative consequences of irregular schedules and output need to be understood.

## *Consequences of Irregular Processing*

The bar chart in Exhibit 15-5 represents what a typical process-industry production schedule for item X might look like. Item X is one model or size in a family of products. It might be standard-size 60-watt lightbulbs; 8-oz. cans of tomato sauce; type-AAA batteries; rolls of 35 mm 24-exposure, 100-speed color film; twin-bed-size white percale sheets; half-gallon cartons of cherry nut ice cream; bottles of 50 decongestant tablets; or four-by-eight-foot sheets of 3/8″ plywood.

The exhibit follows the tendency to schedule not in pieces or volume but in work shifts. Now, notice the variabilities. The number of shifts (length) of each production run varies: 2, 3, 1, 1, 3, 4, and 2. The interval between production runs also varies: 18 shifts, then 17, 9, 23, 23, and 14. Between production runs, other models of the same basic product occupy the schedule: other types or sizes of lightbulbs, canned tomato products, batteries, and so on. Normal sales variations, special marketing promotions, and the end-of-the-month push to meet a sales quota cause demand variability, to which the production schedule must react.

Actual output is another source of variability that doesn't show up in Exhibit 15-5. The schedule is reasonably definite as to number of shifts but often rough as to units. For example, consider the first bar in Exhibit 15-5, a production run of two shifts. If Item X is standard 60-watt lightbulbs and an average of 10,000 can be produced in a shift, the bar is interpreted as follows: The production run is two shifts, which might yield 20,000 bulbs. But the yield varies. If all goes well 20,400 may be produced, but

**EXHIBIT 15-5 Schedule, in Work Shifts, for Item X**

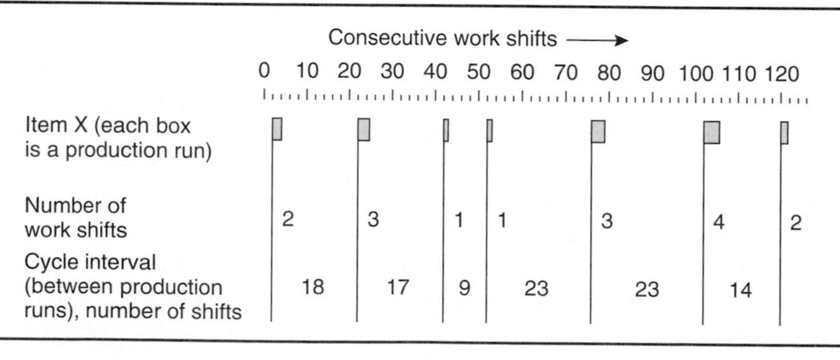

INTO PRACTICE

## Irregular Output: From Record High to New Low

At a South African brewery senior management keenly watched the weekly production total (amount of beer packaged). When the total hit a new record, management threw a "barbey" and beer party for all employees. So employees would occasionally summon a special effort to achieve that. But, "in the week following the record, everyone was so tired that they approached new lows. Management was stimulating their own instability."

Source: Tongue-in-cheek report from Dr. Norman Faull, partner in the Faull and van der Riet consulting firm, specializing in consulting for brewing, paper-making, and other process-industry businesses. Their approach is built around the "success factors for process industries" in Exhibit 15-2.

on a poor day, only 18,500. Once in a while there will be a serious equipment or raw-material failure, and output may be only 8,000, risking a stockout and lost sales. Thus, 60-watt bulbs will need to be fitted into the schedule again quite soon. The whole schedule gets adjusted now and then for such reasons. (See Into Practice box "Irregular Output: From Record High to New Low" for still another cause of variability.)

Overtime or extra shifts are a possibility if the plant is not running at or near full capacity. Traditional accounting systems, however, can nudge manufacturing managers into making poor decisions. They may run costly equipment near to full capacity and skimp on maintenance, inviting later stoppages. If sales fall, managers may lower capacity (shut down a production line) just to ensure that the accounting records show high capacity utilization without large cost variances.

To sum up, irregular production intervals, run times, and output release clouds of uncertainty. Since sales is uncertain about how much product to expect from operations, it tries to keep protective, and costly, buffer stocks in the distribution system. The greater costs are at the supplier side: What supplies of all the ingredients should be kept on hand? When and how much should each supplier deliver? How can suppliers ever achieve regular production schedules and thereby hold down their own wasteful buffer stocks and costs? Irregularities pass backward through all prior stages of supply and production. In short, there is a crying need for regularity and stability.

### *Regular-Slot Processing*

Giving the stars in the product line regular slots in the schedule is one fairly easy way to gain some regularity and stability. The stars are the models or sizes that sell in some quantity every day and earn a high proportion of total revenue. If they sell every day, the ideal is to make some every day, from 8 to 9 A.M., perhaps. The slots should be equal in hours of run time, should be changed when the demand rate changes, and should be spaced at regular intervals.

Principle 2

Reduce variability.

The superstar (the number one revenue earner) gets first claim at regular slots in the schedule; some of the starlets follow. Example 15-2 illustrates.

## Example 15-2: Regular-Slot Scheduling, Photographic Film

Jmart contracts to buy its branded photographic film from a major film manufacturer. Jmart has informed the manufacturer that past service on fast-moving film products has been unsatisfactory. The three products are 100-, 200-, and 400-speed 35 mm 24-exposure film. After some soul-searching, a planning team at the factory has developed a response. It will adopt regular-slot scheduling for the three products of concern by Jmart, its most important customer. These are its top three products, representing about 15 percent of total production volume. Seventy-seven lesser products account for remaining production volume.

**Exhibit 15-6 Three Products with Regularized Schedules**

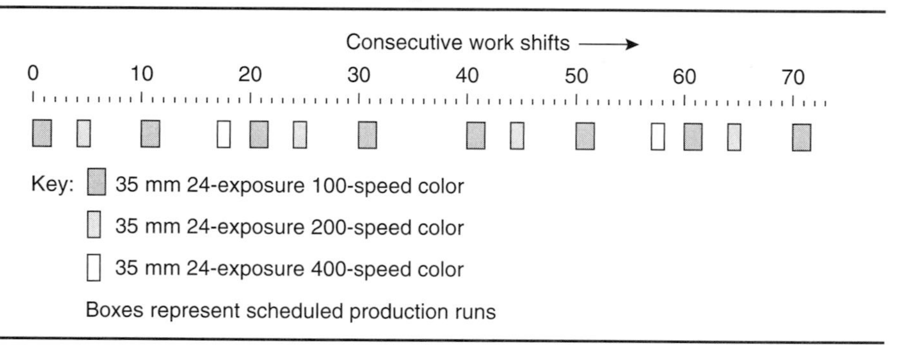


The present schedule, in shifts per production run, is like that shown in Exhibit 15-5: Cycle intervals and production shifts per run are both irregular. The new schedule is shown in Exhibit 15-6. The superstar product, 100-speed film, is in the schedule for $1\frac{1}{2}$ shifts out of every 10 and at a regular interval of every 10 shifts. The 200-speed film's schedule is 1 shift out of every 20, and 400-speed's schedule is 1 shift out of every 40. Those production-run lengths and cycle intervals were not set capriciously. They are based on recent average demand from Jmart plus other customers together with information about average production rates per shift. The plan for the 77 other products is to fit them into the schedule irregularly, as in the past.

In Example 15-2, we were told that regular-slot scheduling yields a production interval for 100-speed film of 10 shifts and that meeting the production rate requires $1\frac{1}{2}$ shifts of capacity each production run. We were not told how to compute those numbers, which is our next topic.

### *Takt Time and Capacity Determination*

In regular-slot scheduling, the demand-driven production interval, called **takt time,** is calculated as follows:

$$\text{Takt time} = \frac{\text{Available time}}{\text{Customer demand rate}} \tag{15-2}$$

Takt time is the maximum interval between successive production units that will still allow the producer to meet a given demand rate. Takt time is the inverse of the minimum allowable production rate and—by itself—is independent of both

- Actual or possible production cycle time.
- The amount of capacity needed to meet the customer demand rate.

Equation 15-3 employs the computed takt time plus a known per-unit cycle time in order to determine amount of capacity needed:

$$\text{Modules of capacity needed} = \frac{\text{Cycle time}}{\text{Takt time}} \tag{15-3}$$

The following example illustrates these concepts.

### Example 15-3: Determining Takt Time and Needed Capacity

An automatic machine at Writing Materials, Inc., produces cuneiform writing instruments in a one-shift-per-day operation. Customer demand is 2,700 pieces per 450-minute day (a 480-minute shift, less 30 minutes for breaks). Production cycle time per piece is 20 seconds. What is the takt time, and how many modules of capacity are needed to meet customer demand?

*Solution*

From Equation 15-2,

$$\text{Takt time} = \frac{450}{2{,}700} = 0.167 \text{ minutes per piece, or 10 seconds per piece}$$

From Equation 15-3,

$$\text{Modules of capacity} = \frac{20 \text{ seconds}}{10 \text{ seconds}} = 2 \text{ modules}$$

This result means that the company needs two automatic machines, each producing at 20-second cycle time rate. An alternative is increasing to two shifts per day on the single automatic machine.

## *Linearity*

Regular slots improve predictability, but yield per run still can be quite variable. In many cases, regular schedule slots should be combined with a policy of linear output. That means setting an attainable output target, running production until it is achieved, and not allowing overproduction.

**linearity index**
Measure of consistency in hitting output target quantity, expressed as a percentage.

No matter how attainable the target quantity is supposed to be, it cannot be met every time. A good way to monitor degree of success is with a linearity index.[6] The index equals 100 percent minus the mean percent deviation, which is the sum of absolute percentage deviations from schedule quantity divided by number of production runs. Mathematically, it is

$$L = 100\% - \frac{\sum |D|}{N} \tag{15-4}$$

where

$L =$ Linearity index

$D =$ Deviation from schedule quantity as a percentage of schedule quantity per run

$N =$ Number of production runs

Typically, associates calculate the index monthly, and number of production runs ($N$) equals number of working days in the month. Calculation of the index is more simply illustrated, assuming only one production run per week, in Example 15-4.

### Example 15-4: CALCULATION OF LINEARITY INDEX

*Given*

500 units of a certain model of a product are to be run one shift a week on Mondays. Actual production last month was 500, 490, 510, and 500. Compute the linearity index for the month.

*Solution*

The deviations from schedule, in units, are 0, −10, +10, and 0. To convert to percent, associates divide each deviation by the schedule quantity per run, 500. That yields 0, −2, +2, and 0 percent, respectively. By Equation 15-4 (ignoring minus signs, since the sum of the absolute deviations is used),

$$
\begin{aligned}
L &= 100\% - \frac{\sum |D|}{N} \\
&= 100\% - \frac{0\% + 2\% + 2\% + 0\%}{4} = 99 \text{ percent}
\end{aligned}
$$

The linearity index reflects that any deviation, over or under schedule, is undesirable; both over- and underproduction cause problems for suppliers and uncertainty for users. In Example 15-4, the shortfall of 10 units in week 2 was made up by deliberate overproduction of 10 in week 3 to get back on target. (The index does not reward getting back on target. However, an alternate form of the index, calculated based on a cumulative schedule, does encourage getting back on schedule; the cumulative basis might be useful in some cases.) Note too that the index will always be 100 percent if the schedule is met every time.

The linearity index is usable in continuous processes, but it seems to have been first used in repetitive operations, our next topic.

## Repetitive Operations

Once the product's state changes from continuous flow to discrete units, we call it repetitive rather than continuous. Of course, a good share of the world's products are discrete from start to finish. In producing discrete units, a worthy goal is to increase repetitiveness and get away from lots—considered in Chapter 16.

INTO PRACTICE

## Transit Banking at First National Bank of Chicago

They come to O'Hare International in aircraft ranging from jumbo passenger planes to chartered two-seater pleasure craft. In trays, boxes, and bags, they head into the city by truck. Their destination is a block-square, 57-story downtown building on Dearborn between Madison and Monroe: First National Bank of Chicago.

The cargo is checks, some 3 million per day. First Chicago (as it often calls itself)* performs contract check clearing for some 12,000 coast-to-coast businesses. A big customer, in, say, Los Angeles—Wilshire Petroleum, perhaps—accumulates checks drawn on banks from all over the country every day. Wilshire wants its money fast. First Chicago has the horsepower—and nearby access to 24-hour-a-day O'Hare airport—to get the job done.

First Chicago clears checks round the clock, seven days a week. Six major deadlines per day dictate cyclic activity for the staff in the Deposit Services department. The deadlines and per-check prices are negotiated with customers. In some cases the deadline is just one hour after receipt of the checks. Processing is in four stages: receiving (including unwrapping and encoding, using 80 encoding machines), sorting (using nine high-speed reader-sorters), wrapping, and final posting. Crews of cross-trained employees migrate from receiving early in the day to wrapping later on. Nearly 200 full- and part-time employees keep the checks moving—and customers happy.

*In 1998, First Chicago merged with Bank One. The new entity, headquartered in Chicago, is Bank One Corporation.

The repetitive mode encompasses more than just manufactured products. High-volume financial, postal, transport, and clerical operations also are in the repetitive category. See the Into Practice box for an example from banking.[7]

Repetitive operations offer a wealth of targets for continuous improvement. One vital factor is good facility layout, as discussed in Chapter 14. Building upon good layout are the nine factors listed in Exhibit 15-2 as success factors for the process industries. Fast changeovers, regularized schedules, and linear output—numbers 6, 8, and 9 in that exhibit—are especially relevant in the repetitive case.

And as mentioned earlier, we add five more that are uniquely important in repetitive processing.

### *Line Balancing*

After a product or cellular layout has been developed, task assignments must be divided among the work stations. Dividing the tasks evenly results in a balanced line. When products or processes change, line *re*balancing becomes necessary. Even simple line-balancing analyses can become quite detailed, and we reserve most of the procedural specifics for an example later in the chapter. Here, we focus on a general overview of line balancing.

Part of **line balancing** analysis is determining number of workstations or number of assemblers, or both. This requires a specified demand rate and data on time standards, work methods, and process flow. Industrial engineers are often the analysts in charge of such information.

To illustrate, suppose demand is such that a line is to provide a unit of work every 3.5 minutes (the takt time). The analyst wants to assign each workstation precisely 3.5 minutes of work. That balances the workload, and it synchronizes tasks so that each pass to the next station occurs just as the assembler completes the task and is ready for the next piece. That 3.5 minutes is the desired **station cycle time.**

Perhaps time standards show that the total **work content time** to make one unit is 35 minutes. Then, with each station working 3.5 minutes, 10 workstations are needed *if perfect balance and time utilization can be achieved.*

For a piece having 35 minutes of work content, however, the throughput time is unlikely to be 35 minutes. Handling among stations and various delays may add time. Also, there may be small buffer stocks between some processes. For example, most high-volume production lines assembling TVs, cameras, videocassette players, keyboards, and the like have several units between stations. If there are two idle units between stations for every one being worked on (a 3:1 pieces-to-stations response ratio), the throughput time is 3 times 35 minutes, or 105 minutes. That is, a unit gets 3.5 minutes of work at station 1, then waits for 7 minutes. It gets 3.5 minutes more work at station 2, then 7 minutes' wait time, and so on, through 10 stations. Raw material enters every 3.5 minutes, but each unit spends 105 minutes in the system. The production rate is 17.14 units per hour (60 minutes/hour ÷ 3.5 minutes).

In this situation, an obvious improvement target is the difference between the throughput time of 105 minutes and the work content time of 35 minutes. The extra 70 minutes is non-value-adding waste, measured as delay time. Eliminating that waste cuts inventory, floor space, time lag until discovery of errors, and time to effect design and demand changes. It also brings about closer dependencies between each provider–customer pair, which creates a better climate for teamwork. The narrow efficiency approach to improvement focuses on work content times and employs methods and time study. The broader effectiveness approach concentrates especially on the non-value-adding delays.

### *Increasing Frequency of Transport and Processing*

There are numerous examples of businesses that achieve roughly repetitive operations in final assembly but are far from it in earlier processes. The term *roughly repetitive* allows for variety within limits. In a Mr. Steak restaurant, the cook who grills steaks has a repetitive job, but the steaks vary in size and quality of meat. Routine purchase orders (POs) in a purchasing department are similar. Each PO is slightly different, but processing them is basically a repetitive operation.

If a Mr. Steak restaurant currently receives steaks every three days, improvement would be receiving in smaller (more repetitive) daily amounts. Obvious advantages are less cold storage, better control of aging, and less forecast error. In the case of POs, a modern improvement is electronic communication. Receive requisitions by e-mail. Send orders to suppliers the same way, one at a time, immediately as needs are known. That gets the supplier working on the order sooner.

Steaks and POs have what are called shallow bills of materials. (For grilled steaks there are just two BOM levels: raw and grilled.) Many products with deep BOMs are, like steaks and invoices, roughly repetitive in the last process, final assembly, but not in earlier processes (lower levels on the BOM). Examples are cars, trucks, tractors, and small aircraft. In final assembly, each successive unit may have its own set of options, but the assemblers perform almost the same operations over and over.

For such products, a way to improve operations is to extend the repetitiveness backward into subassembly, fabrication, and purchasing. The easy way is to cut transfer-lot quantities: smaller loads moved more frequently, ideally with the discipline of kanban. Next, cut process lot size and cycle interval (interval between production runs); this often requires reducing setup or changeover times. These topics were addressed in previous chapters and need no further discussion here.

## *Mixed-Model Processing*

The production schedule interval for the film in Example 15-2 was shown in work shifts, such as 10, 20, and 40. Schedules can be repetitive in much longer or shorter cycle intervals. A very short cycle interval (a day or even a few hours) may call for mixed-model processing.

**mixed-model processing** Short cycle–interval production of a variety of types, sizes, or models of a product family on the same line or within a single cell.

Consider the irregular, long cycle–interval schedule for products L, M, and N shown in Exhibit 15-7A. The boxes represent production runs; they vary in duration, as do the intervals between them. For example, in February and March, nearly two months pass between production runs of product N. Suppose that L, M, and N are standard products that enjoy regular, perhaps daily, sales; thus, they show good potential for repetitive regularized production.

Exhibit 15-7B shows a regularized repetitive schedule with a fairly short cycle interval (one day) between repetitions. Let's examine how a scheduler might determine the mixed-model processing cycle. The objectives are to match production to demand with a regularized schedule that gives star products priority status.

**EXHIBIT 15-7 Irregular, Repetitive, and Mixed-Model Schedules**

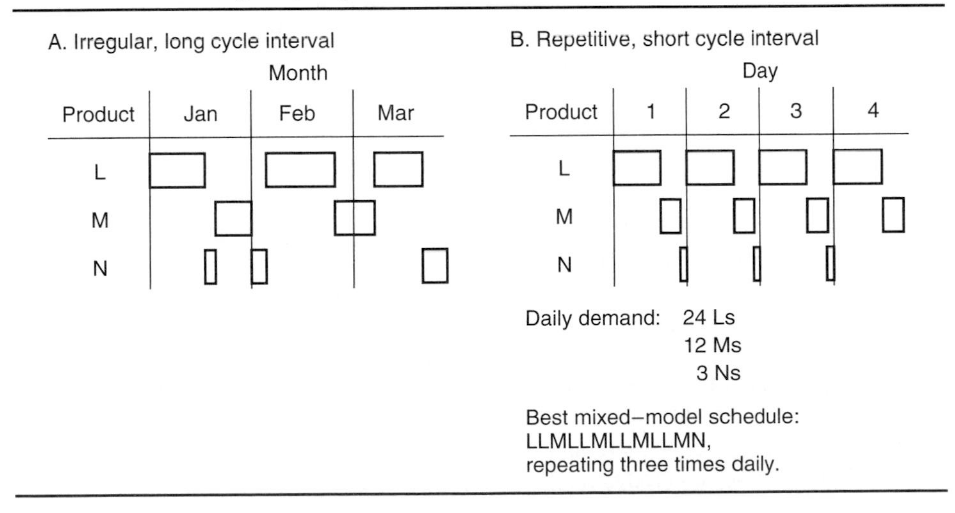

Assume that daily sales average 24 Ls, 12 Ms, and 3 Ns, for a total of 39 units. First, reduce those requirements to the minimum ratio. Dividing each demand amount by 3, the least common denominator, yields 8, 4, and 1. Second, sum the minimum ratios, obtaining the number 13. That becomes the number of units in the repeating processing cycle. That is, every cycle will contain 13 units; 8 will be Ls, 4 will be Ms, and 1 will be N. To meet daily demand, the cycle will repeat three times each day. Third, find the mix of the 13 units that is most repetitive, minimizing the interval between production of each type of product.

This last step might require trial and error, but one or two simple passes may suffice. Consider two possible solutions that meet the daily demand requirement:

There are two levels of repetition in mixed-model processing: (1) cycle repetition during the processing period (day or shift) and (2) repetition within the cycle itself.

1. LLLLLLLLMMMMN—Repeat three times per day. Assessment: Not repetitive within cycle; must wait through up to five units for next L, up to nine units for next M.
2. LLMLLMLLMLLMN—Repeat three times per day. Assessment: Repetitive within cycle, four repeating triplets followed by singleton; maximum wait to next L is two units, and maximum wait to next M is three units. (This is the best schedule for this product mix.)

One advantage of going to the lowest-ratio, most-repetitive mix is that it allows providers of component parts to consider low-capacity processes and cheap equipment. Assume that the products L, M, and N in Exhibit 15-7 are (respectively) 24-, 20-, and 18-inch bicycle wheels, which are made from cut metal strips. If the whole day's requirement of each size is cut in one batch, what cutting equipment is appropriate? A good choice might be a costly, semiautomatic cutting machine that takes an hour to adjust for length changes (setup) but then cuts pieces fast.

On the other hand, if production of each size wheel is spaced out in the lowest-ratio model mix, the need for cut metal strips is also spaced out. Instead of the costly, high-speed cutter, why not use a simple band saw? It is much slower, but it takes virtually no time for a length change, and the low-ratio mixed-model schedule requires many length changes per day. In our example, the band saw would cut two 24-inch strips, one 20-inch strip, two 24s, one 20, two 24s, one 20, two 24s, one 20, and, finally, one 18-inch strip. That 13-unit sequence repeats two additional times throughout the day, exactly matching demand at the next processes, which are rim forming and wheel assembly.

What if the high-speed cutter is already owned and the producer, as part of a continuous improvement effort, is changing the schedule from a daily batch to lowest-ratio mix? An attractive option is to treat 24-inch wheels as the star. Set up the high-speed cutter permanently for that length and cut two at a time intermittently throughout the day. This has the advantages of speed, no more one-hour length changes, and perfect stockless synchronization with the next process. Buy a band saw, if one is not already owned, to cut the 20- and 18-inch lengths.

**Principle 9**

Look for simple, flexible, low-cost equipment.

The benefit of being able to use cheaper, simpler equipment as a result of low-ratio mixed-model scheduling may seem small, or rarely applicable. Not so! Toyota Motors has followed this scheduling and frugal equipment policy (capital expenditure avoidance) perhaps more extensively and longer than any other manufacturer. As a result, Toyota finds itself with massive retained earnings.

Thus far, our discussion of mixed-model processing has been limited to issues and benefits associated with scheduling. Line-balancing algorithms have also been developed for mixed-model assembly lines. For example, in a mixed-model doll clothing line, male dolls, female dolls, large dolls, small dolls, and so forth, may be clothed in a mixed sequence.

Mixed-model line balancing involves (1) determining the sequence of products (model numbers) moving down the line and (2) balancing the line. Some line-balancing methods allow for restrictions and special conditions: subassembly lines that feed main lines, distance and direction requirements, safety needs, special groupings of elements, zoning restrictions, maximum and minimum conveyor speeds, and so forth.

Example 15-5 illustrates some factors involved in mixed-model line balancing.

### Example 15-5: Mixed Models—Boring Holes in Pump Housings

A machine center bores holes in pump housings. It used to take twice as long to set up and run a lot of large pump housings as it did small housings. After a vigorous improvement effort, the setup times are now nearly zero for either size of housing. With negligible setup times, it seems reasonable to run mixed models down a mini-production line composed of machines that bore the holes.

The schedule calls for 22 large (L) and 88 small (S) pump housings per day. Run times are 12 minutes per large unit and 2 minutes per small unit. What cycle of mixed models will produce the scheduled quantity with balanced production?

*Solution*

| Model sequence: | L | S | S | S | S | L | S | S | S | S | . . . |
|---|---|---|---|---|---|---|---|---|---|---|---|
| Operation time: | 12 | 2 | 2 | 2 | 2 | 12 | 2 | 2 | 2 | 2 | . . . |
| | | | 20 | | | | | 20 | | | |

This cycle takes 20 minutes and repeats 22 times per day. The production requires $20 \times 22 = 440$ minutes out of a 480-minute workday, which leaves 40 extra minutes for problem solving, equipment care, and so forth.

## *Fine-Tuning: Watching the Lights*

Line balancing seems precise and accurate, but it isn't. Fine-tuning is needed. A novel method called watching the lights serves to make fine-tuning a bit easier.

It is fairly common for trouble lights to be mounted above production lines to alert troubleshooters and supervisors when there is a slowdown or line stoppage. Typically, a red light signals shutdown and a yellow signals trouble. Yellow lights may also aid in fine-tuning the line balancing. Here is how it works:

1. A new production schedule is issued, rough line balancing takes place, and work begins.
2. Anyone who has trouble keeping up will turn on the yellow light frequently. Those who have no trouble keeping up will not turn on their yellow lights. The

message is clear: Take a few small duties away from those with too much to do and reassign them to those whose lights have not been coming on. When everyone's yellow lights are coming on at about the same frequency, the line is balanced, and no one is pushed into making errors out of haste.

3. With the line balanced, yellow lights no longer suggest line imbalance; they indicate trouble. For the remaining days or weeks of the schedule, the problem signaled by a yellow light is recorded so that there are good data for problem solving.

When industry veterans first hear about this approach, they tend to be dubious or full of questions: "But some people will have much more to do than others. Is that fair? Won't the faster operators complain? Or won't they deliberately go slow and push the yellow button in order to avoid getting more tasks to do?"

The first question is not so hard. It is true that the fast people will end up with more tasks to do, but surely that is more fair, not less. The system should not mask the abilities of the fast employees, nor should it unduly pressure the slower ones. There will be complaints from some of the faster people. The complaints may be resolved in two ways:

1. Give the faster employees bonuses, incentive pay, merit wage increases, pay for knowledge, or special training or other rewards.
2. Evolve a performance appraisal approach that rewards for problem solving, quality control, and work improvement. These activities focus on innovativeness, leadership, and communication skills. Make sure that enough labor is available to make it possible to meet the schedule every day and on most days still allow time for problem solving, quality control, work improvement, and maintenance.

## Line-Balancing Example

A heuristic is a search procedure that may give an optimal solution to a problem but offers no guarantee of doing so. If it can be proven that an exact solution exists, the method becomes an algorithm.

Any of several line-balancing methods may be used in the rough, or initial, balancing stage. They include trial and error, as well as heuristics, algorithms, and mathematical models. Here, we look at a manual heuristic line-balancing procedure, which begins, like other line-balancing methods, with a precedence diagram.

### *Precedence Diagram*

The **precedence diagram** charts the work elements and their required sequence. To get the work elements, the entire process is divided into tasks and subtasks.

One popular type of precedence diagram shows the earliest stage of production where each work element may be done. Element durations, numbers, and sometimes descriptions go on the diagram; arrows show which elements must come before which others.

Example 15-6 demonstrates precedence diagramming. The assembly task is clothing a male doll. In real doll making, all of the work elements for such assembly would probably be done by a single assembler because the element times are very short. But for the sake of illustration, we shall assume progressive, rather than autonomous, assembly. Precedence diagramming can allow for a variety of special restrictions, but this example is kept simple.

## Example 15-6: PRECEDENCE DIAGRAM FOR LINE BALANCING—DOLL ASSEMBLY[8]

A toy company is coming out with a new male doll. The doll is to be clothed on an assembly line, with different items of clothing put on at different stations. The company wants a balanced assembly line.

Methods engineers have broken up the whole job into 13 separate items of clothing, each of which is a work element, with element times as follows:

| *Element* | *Element Time t (in 0.01 minutes)* |
|---|---|
| A. Put on undershorts. | 10 |
| B. Put on undershirt. | 11 |
| C. Put on left sock. | 9 |
| D. Put on right sock. | 9 |
| E. Put on slacks. | 22 |
| F. Put on shirt. | 42 |
| G. Put on left shoe. | 26 |
| H. Put on right shoe. | 26 |
| I. Put on belt. | 30 |
| J. Insert pocket items (wallet, keys, and handkerchief). | 20 |
| K. Put on tie. | 63 |
| L. Put on coat. | 32 |
| M. Put on hat. | 6 |
| Total work content time, $\sum t$, | 306 |

*Solution*

Using the elemental data, associates develop the precedence diagram shown in Exhibit 15-8. Work elements are in the circles and element times are beside the circles. Four elements (A, B, C, and D) have no predecessors and can be started any time. No other elements may begin until their predecessors have been completed.

**EXHIBIT 15-8 Precedence Diagram—Clothing a Doll**

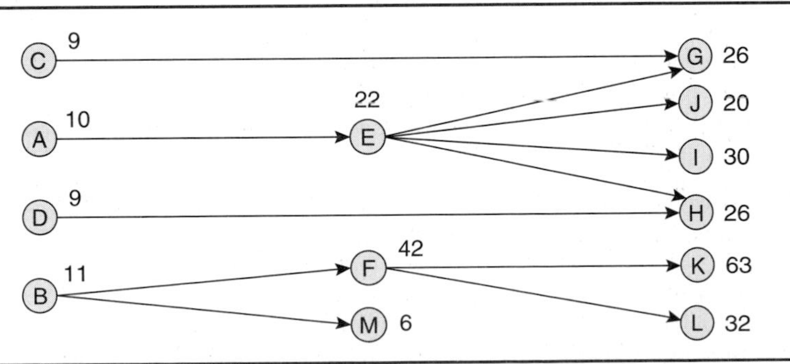

### *Line-Balancing Analysis*

Once the precedence diagram has been completed, actual line balancing may begin. A perfectly balanced line has zero balance delay, which means no wait time at any workstation. **Balance delay,** *d*, is

$$d = \frac{nc - \sum t}{nc} \tag{15-5}$$

where

$$n = \text{Number of workstations}$$
$$c = \text{Station cycle time}$$
$$\sum t = \text{Total work content time for one unit}$$

The result of a line-balancing study is a certain number of workstations, each performing assigned work elements. The goal is not a balanced line that produces as much as possible. Rather, it is a balanced line that produces to the demand rate, no more, no less. The following is an easy-to-use heuristic line-balancing method:

1. Develop the precedence diagram.
2. Determine the station cycle time ($c$) that will yield the per-shift output required to meet demand. The formula is

$$c = \frac{\text{Available production time per day}}{\text{Required output per day (in units)}} \tag{15-6}$$

   (Note: This is the same as takt time; Equation 15-2.)
3. With the station cycle time ($c$) as an upper limit, find the minimum number of stations ($n$)

$$n = \frac{\text{Total work content time}}{\text{Cycle time}} = \frac{\sum t}{c} \tag{15-7}$$

4. Develop the first workstation by assigning elements, one at a time, until the sum of the element times equals the cycle time, or until no feasible elements remain under the precedence restrictions. The rule is, give preference to elements that have the largest element time. (An alternate rule, not so applicable for this simple precedence diagram, is assign elements that have the most following elements.) Repeat for the second workstation, the third, and so forth, until all work elements have been assigned to a station.
5. Calculate balance delay, based on minimum station cycle time, and evaluate. If unsatisfactory, investigate possibilities for altering the process technology to allow more flexibility in balancing the line.

The following example demonstrates this line-balancing method using the doll assembly data from Example 15-6.

## Example 15-7: Balancing a Doll Assembly Line

The sales plan requires an output rate of 450 dolls per day on a one-shift-per-day assembly line. Total assembly time per day, allowing for breaks and other activities, is 420 minutes. How many workstations should there be, and which work elements should be assigned to each station to yield a well-balanced line?

*Solution*

1. Precedence diagram. Given in Exhibit 15-8.
2. Station cycle time. In the numerator, convert minutes to hundredths of a minute.

$$c = \frac{\text{Production time}}{\text{Required output (in units)}} = \frac{420 \text{ min} \times 100}{450 \text{ dolls}} = 93.3 \text{ rounded to } 93$$

3. Minimum number of workstations. Express both numerator and denominator in hundredths of a minute. Total work content ($\sum t$) is 306 hundredths of a minute (from Example 15-6). Then,

$$n = \frac{\sum t}{c} = \frac{306}{93} = 3.3 \text{ rounded to 4 stations}$$

4. Assign work elements to create workstations. Exhibit 15-9 shows how the procedure allocates work elements to the four workstations.
5. Balance delay. All workstations have remaining unassigned times. We can reduce station cycle time by the minimum amount of this unassigned time, which in this case is 2 at the first and second stations. So the minimum station cycle time ($c$) is $93 - 2 = 91$. Then,

$$d = \frac{nc - \sum t}{nc} = \frac{(4 \times 91) - 306}{4 \times 91} = 0.159$$

The 0.159 balance delay indicates 15.9-percent idleness among the four stations, mostly concentrated at station 4. Also, the plan has the assemblers completing the scheduled 450 dolls in 409 minutes (calculation: $91 \times 450/100$), which is 11 minutes less than the planned 420-minute day. What should be done about the idleness and the extra time?

One answer is to make good use of the balance delay: A single person at station 4 could load the pocket items. This would take only 20 hundredths of a minute (12 seconds) in each cycle of 306 hundredths of a minute (3.06 minutes). It might be a good job for a team leader. With so light a task, the leader would have time to help others, coach new employees, record data, perform inspections, fetch materials, and so forth. Alternatively, seek to improve the balance by shifting certain elements from work stations 3 and 4 to 1 and 2. (Various other heuristics, not included in this book, are available for seeking to improve upon a line-balancing alternative.) The extra 11 minutes per day provides extra time for employee projects, training, and so forth. What should not be done is use the 11 minutes to eke out more production, which would just be overproduction . . . one of the seven deadly wastes identified in Chapter 10.

## Exhibit 15-9 Balancing Procedure and Results

**A. Line-Balancing Steps**

| | *Element Assigned* | *Element Time (in 0.01 minutes)* | *Remaining Unassigned Time (in 0.01 minutes)* | *Permissible Remaining Elements* | *Task with Greatest Element Time* |
|---|---|---|---|---|---|
| *Start* | | | 93 | A, B, C, D | B |
| Station 1 | B | 11 | 82 | A, C, D, F, M | F |
| | F | 42 | 40 | A, C, D, L, M | L |
| | L | 32 | 8 | M | M |
| | M | 6 | 2 | None | |
| *Start* | | | 93 | A, C, D, K | K |
| Station 2 | K | 63 | 30 | A, C, D | A |
| | A | 10 | 20 | C, D, E | C or D |
| | C | 9 | 11 | D | D |
| | D | 9 | 2 | None | |
| *Start* | | | 93 | E | E |
| Station 3 | E | 22 | 71 | G, H, I, J | I |
| | I | 30 | 41 | G, H, J | G or H |
| | G | 26 | 15 | None | |
| *Start* | | | 93 | H, J | H |
| Station 4 | H | 26 | 67 | J | J |
| | J | 20 | 47 | None | |

**B. Results: Four Workstations**

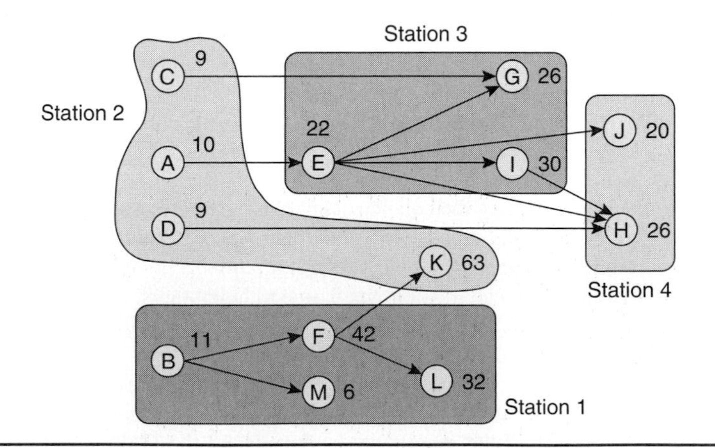

### *Line Balancing in Perspective*

The heuristic method yields good, but not necessarily optimal, results, and development of optimizing algorithms and models continues. Though a variety of line-balancing computer software is available to ease the computational burden, manual heuristic and trial-and-error line balancing efforts are widespread.

For one thing, line balancing is not easily reduced to simple models or algorithms; there are simply too many choices, given the flexibility and variability of humans. Employees can run one machine or several, push a broom or wield a paintbrush between machine cycles, handle machine setup and inspection duties or leave those chores for special crews, speed up or loaf, stay at their work or wander off, fix broken equipment and suggest improvements or leave it up to the specialists, and file documents or sit around waiting for file clerks to do it.

How can balance be designed into a process with those uncertainties? The answer is: One can design only a roughly balanced line. Supervisors and the work group itself need to fine-tune it and redo it often as customer demand rates change.

**Principles 1 and 13**

Get to know the customer. Operate at the customer's rate of use.

## Scope of Application

The techniques of transforming irregular operations into repetitive, synchronized operations apply not only to high-volume production; they may also apply to building, say, one ship every two weeks or one passenger aircraft every three days. If each ship or plane is a special order for a different customer, that is only a partial obstacle to repetitive operations. In manufacture of ships and planes, thousands of parts are the same from unit to unit and are therefore unaffected by special orders. Those thousands of standard parts may be made to highly repetitive schedules—repeating only every two weeks or every three days—with some levels synchronized with the level directly above. The massive problem of scheduling all those parts thus can be partly simplified, and some flows of parts can be put on kanban.

One of the most pressing needs in operations management is extending the benefits of continuous and highly repetitive processing (the stuff of this chapter) into job and batch operations. We take up that challenge in the next chapter.

## Summary Check Points

✓ High-volume, continuous-flow operations characterize what we refer to as the process industry.

✓ Continuous and repetitive operations often occur together, the former term applicable in earlier process stages with the latter more aptly describing finishing stages.

- ✓ In addition to good layout, there are at least nine success factors that can promote improved continuous operations:

    1. Capital investment and process design
    2. Optimum mixtures
    3. Rigorous maintenance
    4. Close monitoring of the process
    5. Reliability of supply and freight
    6. Fast changeovers
    7. Rapid turns of the product wheel
    8. Regularized schedules
    9. Linear output

- ✓ Another five can be added to that list for improving repetitive operations:

    10. Line balancing
    11. Increasing frequency of transport and processing
    12. Mixed-model processing
    13. Fine-tuning: watching the lights.
    14. Synchronized scheduling

- ✓ Faster turns of the product wheel and regularized schedules increase availability of product to customers by cutting cycle times (especially relevant for high-demand items).
- ✓ Linear output helps salespeople make credible delivery date promises to customers.
- ✓ Takt time is the maximum time that may elapse between successive production units in order to meet a period demand requirement.
- ✓ Linearity reveals how closely a provider can hit period production target quantities.
- ✓ The objective of line balancing is to divide job tasks among several workstations so that output requirements may be met with little time waste.
- ✓ More frequent transport and processing of smaller lots yields several benefits; it requires reduced setup and changeover times, good layout, and product quality.
- ✓ Mixed-model processing calls for short cycle-interval production of a variety of items on the same resource facility (e.g., line or cell).
- ✓ Line balancing is not an exact science. One should aim for a close balance and then be prepared to make adjustments by reacting to visual signals (e.g., trouble lights) from associates working at the line stations.
- ✓ One of the most pressing needs in OM is extending the techniques of continuous and repetitive operations into the environment of job and batch operations.

## Solved Problems

### Problem 1

The accompanying table shows 22 working days of production against a regularized schedule for a somewhat new product. The schedule rate, seven per day, was set on the 15th of the prior month. It gets changed in midmonth only when actual orders are greatly deviating from plan, as happened on August 22 to 26. Calculate the linearity index.

| *Date* | *Working Day* | *Pack Schedule* | *Actual Pack* | *Comments* |
|---|---|---|---|---|
| 8–1 | 1 | 7 | 3 | No card cages |
| 2 | 2 | 7 | 3 | |
| 5 | 3 | 7 | 10 | |
| 6 | 4 | 7 | 11 | |
| 7 | 5 | 7 | 4 | Door latch problems |
| 8 | 6 | 7 | 9 | Two people short |
| 9 | 7 | 7 | 9 | |
| 12 | 8 | 7 | 1 | No drives |
| 13 | 9 | 7 | 5 | Rework required |
| 14 | 10 | 7 | 4 | Rework required |
| 15 | 11 | 7 | 5 | Rework required |
| 16 | 12 | 7 | 6 | Rework required |
| 19 | 13 | 7 | 10 | |
| 20 | 14 | 7 | 7 | |
| 21 | 15 | 7 | 10 | |
| 22 | 16 | 0 | 0 | No orders |
| 23 | 17 | 0 | 0 | No orders |
| 26 | 18 | 0 | 0 | No orders |
| 27 | 19 | 7 | 5 | |
| 28 | 20 | 7 | 2 | |
| 29 | 21 | 7 | 3 | |
| 30 | 22 | 7 | 1 | |

### Solution 1

*Step 1:* Insert working columns for calculation of absolute deviation (ignore minus signs) and percent deviation:

| *Working Day* | *Pack Schedule* | *Actual Pack* | *Absolute Deviation* | *Percent Deviation* |
|---|---|---|---|---|
| 1 | 7 | 3 | 4 | 4/7 = 57% |
| 2 | 7 | 3 | 4 | 4/7 = 57 |
| 3 | 7 | 10 | 3 | 3/7 = 43 |
| 4 | 7 | 11 | 4 | 4/7 = 57 |
| 5 | 7 | 4 | 3 | 3/7 = 43 |
| 6 | 7 | 9 | 2 | 2/7 = 29 |

*(Continued)*

*(Concluded)*

| *Working Day* | *Pack Schedule* | *Actual Pack* | *Absolute Deviation* | *Percent Deviation* |
|---|---|---|---|---|
| 7 | 7 | 9 | 2 | 2/7 = 29% |
| 8 | 7 | 1 | 6 | 6/7 = 86 |
| 9 | 7 | 5 | 2 | 2/7 = 29 |
| 10 | 7 | 4 | 3 | 3/7 = 43 |
| 11 | 7 | 5 | 2 | 2/7 = 29 |
| 12 | 7 | 6 | 1 | 1/7 = 14 |
| 13 | 7 | 10 | 3 | 3/7 = 43 |
| 14 | 7 | 7 | 0 | 0/7 = 0 |
| 15 | 7 | 10 | 3 | 3/7 = 43 |
| | —Omit zero schedule days— | | | |
| 19 | 7 | 5 | 2 | 2/7 = 29 |
| 20 | 7 | 2 | 5 | 5/7 = 71 |
| 21 | 7 | 3 | 4 | 4/7 = 57 |
| 22 | 7 | 1 | 6 | 6/7 = 86 |
| Total = 19 working days | | | | Total = 845% |

*Step 2:* Calculate the linearity index ($L$):

$$L = 100\% - \frac{845\%}{19} = 100\% - 44.5\% = 55.5\%$$

***Problem 2***

Consider the following elemental precedence diagram (element times are in units of 0.01 minutes):

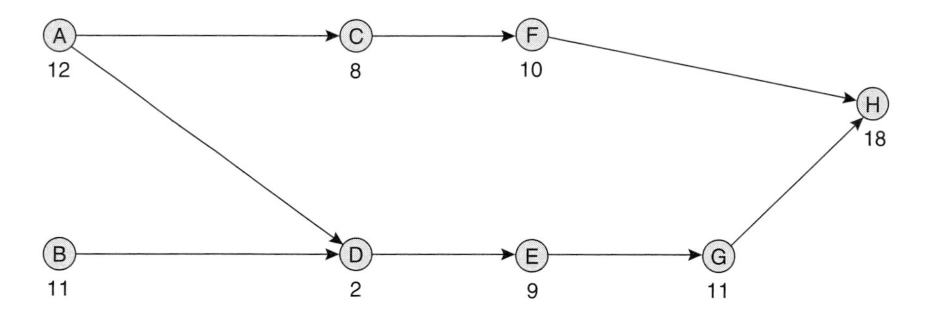


*a.* What would be the cycle times for a line with one workstation (autonomous production)?

*b.* What would be the maximum daily capacity of such a line assuming 420 minutes of work time per day?

*c.* What is the shortest possible cycle time?

*d.* Assuming we used this shortest cycle time, what would daily line capacity be?

*e.* Plan a balanced line for the assembly operation using a cycle time of 0.29 minutes. Compute the balance delay for your solution. What will be the approximate capacity of the line assuming a 420-minute workday?

### *Solution 2*

*a.* With one workstation, the sum of the element times would be a reasonable estimate for the cycle time. In this case, the sum is 0.81 minutes.

*b.* With 420 minutes of available work time per day, the maximum capacity possible with a cycle time of 0.81 minutes would be: 420/0.81 = 519 units.

*c.* The shortest possible cycle time equals the time of the longest element, or 0.18 minutes. We would not necessarily want to use this as the cycle time, but it is possible to do so.

*d.* For a station cycle time of 0.18 minutes and 420-minute workday, the maximum capacity may be obtained by transposing equation (15-6) to

$$\text{Output} = \frac{\text{Production time}}{c} = \frac{420}{0.18} = 2{,}333 \text{ units}$$

*e.* Line-Balancing Steps

| | *Element Assigned* | *Element Time (in 0.01 minutes)* | *Remaining Unassigned Time (in 0.01 minutes)* | *Permissible Remaining Elements* | *Task with Greatest Element Time* |
|---|---|---|---|---|---|
| *Start* | | | 29 | A, B | A |
| Station 1 | A | 12 | 17 | B, C | B |
| | B | 11 | 6 | D | D |
| | D | 2 | 4 | None | |
| *Start* | | | 29 | C, E | E |
| Station 2 | E | 9 | 20 | C, G | G |
| | G | 11 | 9 | C | C |
| | C | 8 | 1 | None | |
| *Start* | | | 29 | F | F |
| Station 3 | F | 10 | 19 | H | H |
| | H | 18 | 1 | None | |

Since remaining unassigned time at workstations 2 and 3 (the most nearly balanced stations) is 1, station cycle time may be reduced; that is, 29 − 1 = 28. Then,

$$\text{Balance delay } (d) = \frac{nc - \sum t}{nc} = \frac{3(28) - 81}{3(28)} = 0.036$$

$$\text{Line capacity} = 420/0.28 = 1{,}500 \text{ units per day}$$

## Exercises

1. In the chapter discussion of repetitive processing, refer to the box entitled, "Transit Banking at First National Bank of Chicago." Which of the success factors discussed in the chapter apply well to the bank's processing? Explain.
2. In the following examples, which stages of processing are best considered as continuous flow and which as repetitive? Discuss.
   *a.* Iced Cappuccino manufacturer.
   *b.* Aspirin tablet producer.
   *c.* Breakfast cereal producer.
   *d.* Nursing care for hospitalized patient.
   *e.* Banking (account maintenance).
   *f.* Facility security services.

3. Modesto Farms operates a high-volume cannery for tomato products: canned whole tomatoes, tomato sauce, tomato paste, and the like. Discuss three vital success factors in the area of manufacturing for this company. Be as specific as you can, even though you have to speculate on the nature of this type of company.
4. Detergent is manufactured in a continuous process through a network of pipes, vessels, and pressure chambers. First, petroleum is distilled into paraffin, which is oxidized and then catalytically hydrogenated under pressure to form fat alcohols. Sulphuric acid is added, and water cools the mixture to yield fat alcohol esters. Bleaching agents and alkalies are injected, and an emerging paste of fat alcohol sulphate is processed through a "spray tower" into finished detergent. Discuss two vital manufacturing success factors for a detergent manufacturer; be as specific as you can.
5. Edsom, Inc., a maker of keyboards for computer products, has a department in which instruction manuals are assembled into three-ring binders and another in which the pages are printed. There are four stages of production for the complete binders:
   *a.* The print shop slices large sheets of paper to size. It prefers to run as many jobs as possible on a recently acquired heavy-duty slicer, which runs faster than two older model slicers still in the shop. All the slicers require some setup time for any job.
   *b.* The printshop prints pages for manuals. Because of long setup times, print jobs for manuals compete with other print jobs for slots in the schedule.
   *c.* A high-speed collator collates the pages. The collator, a dedicated machine in the assembly department, is only used for manuals.
   *d.* Human assemblers open binders, insert sets of pages, and close binders.
   Elsewhere in the plant, the keyboard assembly line runs to a daily rate and achieves nearly perfect linearity.

   Can the four stages of manual production be synchronized to the assembly rate for the keyboards? Should they be synchronized? Discuss fully, giving an example with sample numbers.
6. Building A delivers several kinds of bulky component parts to building B four miles away. The components are made in three production stages in building A. Setup times on some of the equipment and parts assembly lines have been driven down nearly to zero. Building B houses final assembly and packing, each with negligible setup time from model to model of the family of end products.

   Can five production stages in two buildings, plus deliveries between, be completely synchronized to the sales rate? Is a fully mixed-model synchronized schedule feasible?
7. Line 1 at the East Texas plant of Feast Frozen Foods has been troublesome. Its average production has been 5,000 twelve-ounce packages of frozen vegetables per shift, which is equal to average sales. But the variation around the average has been unacceptable. For the 10 shifts last week (a typical week), output was 4,528, 4,780, 5,009, 4,822, 5,860, 5,321, 5,618, 4,699, 4,620, and 4,900.

   About 35 percent of line 1's output consists of Feast's top-selling product, frozen young peas. A production run of peas usually is one shift, but sometimes a half-shift run is scheduled; peas are packaged three or four times per week. The other 65 percent of production is split among 17 other products. Recently, the line 1 crew has been working overtime on about half its shifts. Changing the speeds of the tray-filling and packaging equipment is no problem.
   *a.* Calculate the linearity for last week.
   *b.* Recommend a plan for increasing predictability of output on line 1.

8. Faiko Time Company produces grandfather clocks. Customers (mostly retailers) can select from over 100 styles of fine wood and glass outer enclosures, which are made in Faiko's wood and glass shops. In contrast, only three types of clock mechanisms can be ordered; these are assembled in another Faiko shop.

   The past two week's production orders have been as follows, in numbers of clocks ordered each day: 8, 9, 5, 7, 7, 9, 7, 4, 6, 10. Can Faiko adopt a workable production plan with a regularized production schedule and linear output? Explain why, why not, or to what extent.

9. Almost Blind Co. (ABC) produces metallic blinds for windows in 10 basic colors. The basic process is an extruder, on which color changes take an average of 40 minutes. Since the extruder is a very high-cost machine, ABC runs it seven days a week, 24 hours a day, except for daily maintenance averaging 30 minutes. ABC must produce and ship daily; recent daily amount shipped (including all 10 colors of blinds) has been averaging 1,800 lineal feet. The extruder's production rate is 100 lineal feet per hour. Determine the wheel turn time for the extruder and comment on its uses.

10. Conduct an investigation to determine three different kinds of products that would be produced sequentially in a version of the product wheel. Explain your choices.

11. A bicycle manufacturer has implemented a schedule of assembling each of its three bike models every day (instead of long production runs for individual models). Can it use the same repetitive daily schedule in making handlebars, frames, and wheel assemblies? If so, can the repetitive schedule extend downward to tires, wheels, and spokes? Can it go further downward to wire extruders that make reels of spoke wire and to the steel plant that makes the commodity steel that is drawn into wire? Discuss the possibilities, obstacles, and benefits.

12. As a first step in a line-balancing analysis, the precedence diagram shown below has been developed. All task time units are in 0.01 minutes.
    *a.* Calculate $\sum t$. What station cycle time is required for a daily demand of 1,500 units? What is the minimum required number of work stations? Assume a workday of 420 minutes.
    *b.* Balance the line using longest task time as the criterion for the next assignment. Calculate the resulting balance delay. If the delay is excessive, what is your advice (options include seeking a better balance or living with the imbalance)?

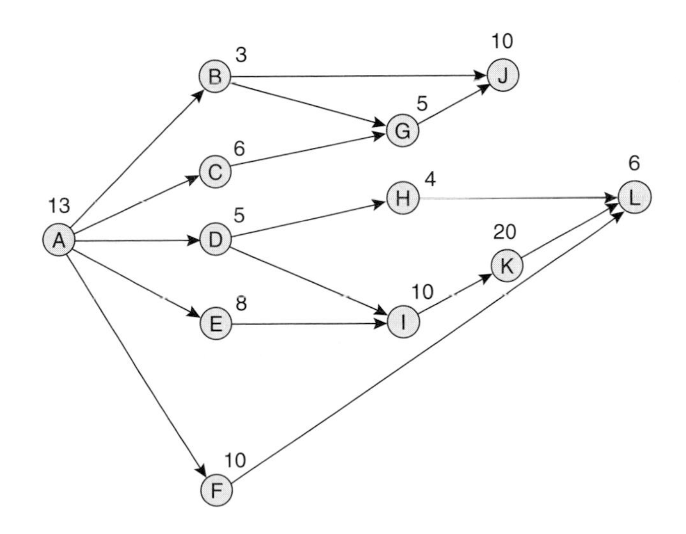

13. The processing of worker's compensation claim forms in a state office is being organized as a production line. Work elements have been divided as far as possible and have been organized into the following precedence diagram. (All element times are in minutes.) If the line must process 50 claims a week, what is the best way to balance the line? The state allows 40 minutes in an eight-hour workday for coffee breaks.

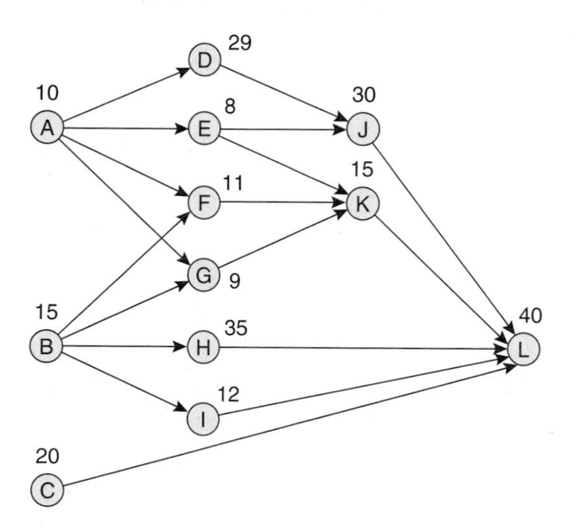


14. Crow's Eye Foods, Inc., has patent rights to a special type of segmented dish for perfect warming of foods in a microwave oven. The dish permits Crow's to launch a new line of frozen breakfasts. Crow's kitchens are planning for the first breakfast: two strips of bacon, one egg, and two slices of buttered toast.
    *a.* Develop a precedence diagram for use in balancing the production line for this breakfast. Make your own (reasonable) assumptions about work elements and element times. Explain your diagram.
    *b.* Make an assumption about demand and production time. Then, balance your line.
15. Zeus, Inc., makes three models of personal computers: large, medium, and small. One purchased part is an internal cooling fan: a large fan for the large computer, medium fan for the medium, and small fan for the small. Zeus produces and buys components purely just-in-time.The end-product schedule calls for producing one large, two medium, and four small computers every 10 minutes during the day, and the schedule is frozen for four weeks into the future. Suppliers deliver component parts (such as fans) once a day.
    *a.* What are the advantages of the daily mixed-model delivery schedule for the fan supplier? (One supplier provides all three sizes.)
    *b.* During one five-day period, Zeus has trouble meeting its daily schedule, falling short by 30 units the first day, 5 units on the second, 2 on the third, 25 on the fourth, and 8 on the fifth. What difficulties does this create for the just-in-time supplier?
    *c.* Zeus's schedule works out to 48 large, 96 medium, and 192 small computers per eight-hour day. What is wrong with the schedule (a possible contributor to the schedule problems described in part *b*)?
16. A production call assembles two models of hair dryer: standard (S) and deluxe (D). Each S requires 4 minutes of assembly time and each D 12 minutes. Customers buy twice as many Ss as Ds. Develop a mixed-model sequence for the two dryers. Make it as well balanced as

possible. What is the cycle time, and how many times can it repeat in a 480-minute day? How would demand for 100 deluxe dryers per day be satisfied?

17. Parts A and B must be heat treated. The heat-treat time for part A is 8 minutes; for part B, it is 10 minutes. The schedule calls for 36 As and 12 Bs per day. Develop a balanced mixed-model sequence for the two parts. How many hours will it take to produce the scheduled amount?
18. Demand for a certain product averages 250 units per day. The product is made and sold in three styles; recently the split among them has been as follows: style 1, 50 percent; style 2, 30 percent; and style 3, 20 percent. Devise a mixed-model schedule with minimum cycle interval for this product line.
19. Find the lowest-ratio mixed-model schedule for four models of computer tables, where daily market requirements are 6 model Ds, 18 model Es, 12 model Fs, and 24 model Gs.
20. When production volume is high and product variety low, dedicated production facilities may be used to run a streamlined make-to-a-number operation. What can be done to streamline production of medium-volume products?
21. In a hospital, customers arrive irregularly. Are there any processes in a hospital that can escape from that basic customer-driven irregularity and get onto a repetitive schedule? Discuss, including any possible benefits.
22. In a department store, customers arrive irregularly. Are there any processes in a store that are important to customer service but that can be put onto a regularized schedule? If so, what are the benefits?

CHAPTER 16

# MANAGING JOB AND BATCH OPERATIONS

"If the [flight] schedule doesn't work, nothing else can work," says David Siegel, a scheduling expert at Continental Airlines. To get a workable schedule, Continental had to force cooperation between marketing, which makes up the schedule, and operations, which flies the schedule. Previously, the two departments "never talked," says Greg Brennerman, chief operating officer for the airline. Marketing would change the schedule so often that the airline could not publish a timetable for several years. Moreover, marketing never consulted with operations as to the feasibility of each schedule.

"We were really just shooting our foot off in the past," says Deborah McCoy, a captain flying DC-10 aircraft and senior director of operational performance. "We knew what was wrong and we were very frustrated."

The new cooperative scheduling effort involved teamwork between marketing and operations. The teams studied the most common connections at its hubs and grouped those flights' gates and times close together. They found insufficient gate times and flying times on some flights and too much on others and made the proper adjustments. Those changes, plus various operational improvements and monetary incentives nudged Continental's on-time performance record up from near the bottom, according to the U.S. Department of Transportation, to near the top. As a bonus, Continental has been able to schedule and fly more flights per day with the same aircraft and crews. "Being on time makes you more productive," says Mr. Brennerman.

Source: Scott McCartney, "How to Make an Airline Run on Schedule," *The Wall Street Journal,* December 22, 1995, pp. B1 and B7.

Even though airlines usually fly repetitive schedules from city to city, many of the crews do not. Job assignment rotations and standby call status, especially among the more junior employees, tend to make each flight a unique job—and often, an obstacle course standing in the way of on-time performance.

In this chapter we continue our study of operations environments, but shift the focus from continuous and repetitive processing modes to intermittent ones—specifically, to jobs and batches. Frankly, operations management presents some of its more unique challenges to those who earn their keep in the job domain.

## The Job Domain

Much of life's work consists of **jobs**—activities requiring allocation of a somewhat predictable collection of resources to a moderately discrete task, and having a defined end point and relatively tangible or at least identifiable results. The job mode of operations covers nearly all human services, most office work, and the vast array of industrial job shops: a widespread, diverse, and hard-to-manage domain. This section highlights key characteristics, suggests a strategy for improving job management, presents a job operations system overview, and concludes with an example.

### *Key Characteristics*

The job environment has been intensively studied, and a bountiful terminology relates to it, especially in the manufacturing sector.[1] The vocabulary grows when we include the service sector. We needn't concern ourselves with most of these terms at this time, but a few characteristics help define the scope of our study. In particular, we must address output volume, task magnitude, and task variety.

**Output Volume.** A job might yield a single unit of output, a dozen units, or even a few thousand. When output consists of multiple units, we refer to it as a lot or job lot. A **batch** is a certain type of job lot, usually a standard lot size or container quantity. Batch processing involves mixing a prescribed set and quantity of ingredients to create the desired output, typically measured by volume or weight: a yard of concrete, a pound of butter, or a liter of sulfuric acid. We treat jobs, batches, and lots together because they require similar management. For convenience, we use the term *job* when referring to any of these low-to-moderate volume modes of intermittent processing.

Lots and effects of lot size have been discussed in Chapters 10 and 13.

**Task Magnitude.** When a job is expected to last for many months or years and calls for large commitments of resources—many people assigned to the team, dedicated facilities and equipment, big budgets, and so forth—we call it a **project** and manage it with special tools discussed in Chapter 17. So, in this chapter, we're not concerned with the very-large-scale efforts. Though smaller than a project, a job still requires a certain level of effort; it must encompass the whole work activity needed to fill some customer's request. That request is an **order**—perhaps called a service order, job order, work order, or shop order. In practice, the work needed to complete an order—the transformations of inputs into outputs—is carried out in a series of steps called **operations.** And as we saw in Chapter 1, each operation usually requires a new setup or changeover. Thus, orders, operations, and setups *are* very much a part of our concern in this chapter.

The order fulfillment sequence was discussed in Chapter 6.

**Task Variety.** Variety—the typically large number of variables one must control—is what makes job management difficult. Consider these jobs: a broken fence repaired, six photostat copies made, 20 tennis rackets strung, a process flowcharted, a patient's disease diagnosed and treated, a computer program written and tested, and a training program delivered. The first three jobs are simple enough; the last four, on the other hand, could require considerable resources, get quite complicated and time-consuming, and produce a combination of tangible and intangible results.

Irregular and/or inconsistent colors, sizes, styles, and materials; varying lot quantities, routings or process steps, waiting and setup times; changing regulations; special requests; and heightened customer expectations are among the many nuances that add spice to job operations. Managing such a jumble of jobs requires a concerted effort—and the right approach.

## *Managing Jobs: A Dual Approach*

Successful job-operations management occurs when people focus attention on two broad sets of activities:

1. *Job planning, scheduling, and control.* This approach, grounded in information systems, has been highly developed, especially in North America. It essentially follows the dictum that job settings are complex, so people need sophisticated tools to manage them. Computerized work planning and scheduling, resource management, factory floor activity control, and simulation of planned operations are key components of these systems.
2. *Simplification, focus, elimination of non-value-adding steps, and streamlining of value-adding steps.* This approach, on the other hand, entails less information system support. Following the logic that job environments need not be as complicated as they have become, this strategy reduces the number of variables to be managed *and* reduces the variation in those (variables) which can't be eliminated.

Principles 5 and 12

Cut number of operations.
Cut setup times.

Today, there is considerable debate about the value of one approach over the other.[2] In the eyes of some observers, the issue is "high-tech" versus "low-tech." Unfortunately, semantics and jargon can confound the issue, especially in one's first exposure to OM. Too often, anything that contains a chip or a line of code gets tossed into the same category and labeled "technology." So let us be more specific: In the first approach, we are talking about the software, hardware, and databases used for production planning and control. Examples include MRP and its extensions—topics that we addressed in Chapter 13.

The second approach embodies many of the concepts presented in this book. In some circles, it is referred to simply as "lean," in deference to Toyota's lean production system, which as we have observed, is the cradle for many of the ideas.[3] But, computers and information processing technologies play vital roles in the lean approach as well. Responsive, in-process data collection and analysis by frontline associates and Internet connections with partner suppliers are examples.

Before we dig deeper into more detailed discussion of the two broad approaches, we need to know more about the job operations system and its variables.

## *Job Operations Systems Overview*

Any time a story about superior customer service appears, we wonder how the provider accomplished the feat. That is, what parts or jobs in the "normal" scheduling process are

**EXHIBIT 16-1 Job Planning, Scheduling, and Control**

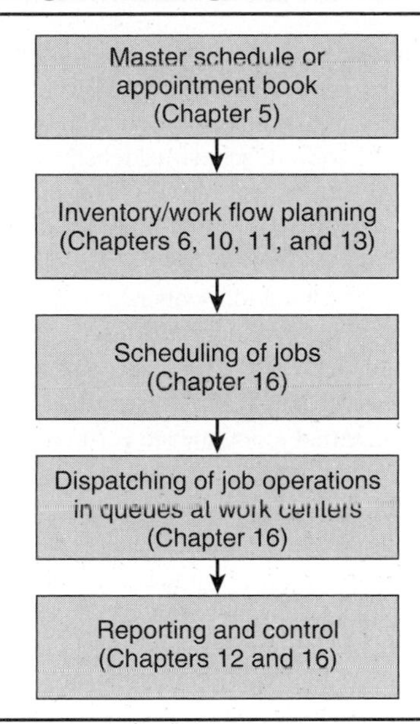


declared nonessential in such instances? Or, is every job still accomplished, but faster, say by cutting out or streamlining some wasteful operations?

Answers to these questions begin by examining just what it takes to plan, and control jobs. Exhibit 16-1 shows a general job-processing sequence applicable to manufacturing or service operations, along with the chapter(s) that contain material relevant to each step. First, master scheduling positions the work in a master schedule or appointment book, sometimes with other similar work. Inventory and work-flow planning, as necessary, come next. Even in pure services, some inventory actions are generally needed so that the job will not be halted for lack of a certain item—say, a special tax form.

If all required inventories are on hand or due in, scheduling at a detailed job-by-job level may take place; for a multi-operation job, this may involve a scheduler's putting start and completion dates on each operation. In the dispatching step, jobs in progress get positioned one more time; dispatching is what we call prioritizing jobs in queue at a given work center. Finally, during or after the transformation, comes reporting and corrective control.

Well-known use of dispatching: Phone for a taxi, and a dispatcher assigns you to a cab, or a cab to you.

From Exhibit 16-1, we see that scheduling takes place at multiple levels, from master scheduling to job dispatching. It can go even lower, on down to the operations level. We consider the distinction between jobs and operations next.

### *Introductory Example: Jobs and Operations*

Example 16-1 describes some of the details associated with even a relatively simple manufacturing job.

### Example 16-1: Jobs and Operations—Bookcase Example

Upon appearing on the master schedule, an order for production of a certain model of bookcases triggers the explosion of the bookcase bill of materials (BOM) into component parts. These parts are dependent demand items, one of which is the shelf. If adequate shelf inventory does not exist and is not anticipated in the form of scheduled receipts, an order will be launched to produce shelf net requirements. Executing that order involves planning, scheduling, and controlling one job through the several operations required for its completion.

Exhibit 16-2 shows Job Number 4444, calling for production of 10 units of the shelf, part number 777. The job consists of a five-operation sequence. The figure shows the operations, numbered 10, 20, 30, 40, and 50, and the inventory conditions between them. Each operation takes place at a separate work center, including the stockroom, so the job routing requires inventory movement *and order tracking and control* through five centers.

As depicted in Exhibit 16-2, the actual job sequence is straightforward: Operation 10: Withdraw boards from the stockroom. Operation 20: Saw boards. Operation 30: Plane boards. Operation 40: Sand boards. Operation 50: Apply finish to sanded boards. The result is 10 finished shelves, component parts that go into the next higher-level item on the BOM for the bookcase.

What we cannot see in Exhibit 16-2 are the troublesome realities of job environments: Each operation requires setup time; installing the proper saw blade, setting the depth of cut on the plane, and so forth. And, after each operation, work-in-process inventories form and sit idle, ready for transport to the next work center. We don't see the queues of other jobs waiting their turn at each work center—for example, orders for frames or cabinets. Also, routings vary; some jobs might require only sawing and planing before they are shipped out. Although we note the intentional scrap—the excess trimmed from boards—at the sawing operation, we don't see piles of unintentional scrap that happen when tools get dull, machines get out of alignment, specifications change, or instructions and other order-documentation paperwork get mixed up. Nor do we see the stacks of jobs returned for rework.

Finally, we do not see the human interactions. A dispatcher might be available to help the wood shop supervisor schedule and control operations—identifying "hot" jobs that are holding up work in assembly areas halfway across the plant. But, the due date for the entire shelf job, we are reminded, was set days or weeks earlier by a scheduler in a distant production control office.

The bookcase example exposes a few of the common complications in job management: multiple routings, setups, moves, queues, inventories, scrap, maintenance, and capacity management.

In a nutshell, many variables require attention, and the information system gets bogged down keeping track of problems. On the other hand, each complication is an improvement target—again, something we take up later in the chapter. At this time, let's focus on what is often the biggest complication of all—scheduling.

## Scheduling

In common usage, the word schedule usually refers to a completion time or date and perhaps to a start time, as well. Master schedules—the first level of job scheduling mentioned in Exhibit 16-1—state the quantity needed and the completion day, week, or

**EXHIBIT 16-2 Job and Operations for 10 Bookcase Shelves**

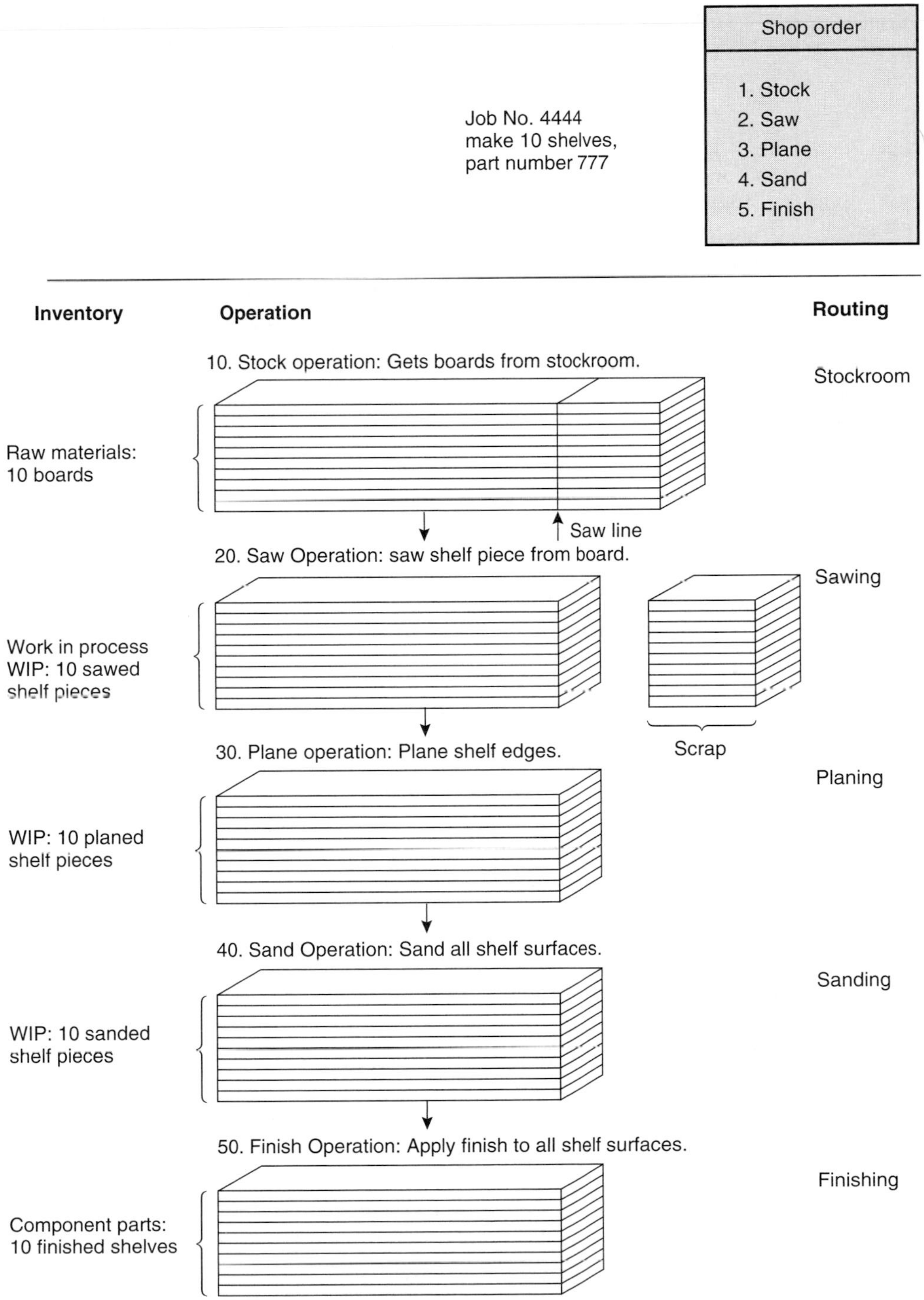

month, but usually not start times. We addressed master scheduling in Chapters 5 and 13. Detailed scheduling, at the job, component, or operation level, is our concern here.

We begin with a brief discussion of output versus resource scheduling, move on to address lead time and work in process, which are two basic causes of job scheduling problems, and conclude with examples of basic scheduling tools and techniques.

## *Output and Resource Scheduling*

Actually, detailed-level scheduling in job environments involves more than deciding about needed completion dates and possible start times for the jobs and operations themselves. In those instances, we are usually fitting potential outputs to resources; schedule Job ABC to work center XYZ on such-and-such date. In some cases, however, it makes more sense to talk about scheduling the resource; for example, surgery suite C has been scheduled from 0800 to 1100 on Thursday.

In services, reservations serve as advance schedules and often more clearly define the resources to be used than does an appointment. In both manufacturing and services, however, the main concern is that the schedules for jobs and operations stay in sync with schedules for the resources needed for transformations.

## *Lead Time*

**Lead time,** as cycle time is generally called in MRP and production-control circles, is the elapsed time required to perform a task or job. We get an idea of the trouble caused by lead time when we consider its components or elements and the uncertainty associated with it.

**Lead Time Elements.** In job operations, lead time to produce or deliver something or provide a service usually contains much more delay time than actual work; that is, the part, client, or document spends far more time idle than being processed. In manufacturing, according to Orlicky,[4] the elements of production lead time for a given part are as follows, in descending order of significance:

1. Queue time.
2. Run time or service time: value-adding time during which the item is being produced or the service is being delivered.
3. Setup time.
4. Wait time (wait for instructions, transportation, tools, etc.).
5. Inspection time.
6. Move time.
7. Other.

Orlicky and others maintain that queue time (the first element) in metal fabrication shops normally accounts for about 90 percent of total lead time. It's often the same for customers buying tickets or paying tolls. Other delays (items 3 through 7 in the above list) take up part of the remaining 10 percent, which leaves run time (value-adding operations) with a very small percentage of total lead time.

**Lead-Time Uncertainty.** Run time may be precisely measured using standard time techniques described in Chapter 12. But queue time for an average job is hard to predict because the average varies with the changing mix of jobs in the system. Queue time for a particular job is even harder to predict, because the job may queue up at several work centers as it completes its routing. Therefore, some schedulers have a habit of simply adding a fixed number of days for queue time and other delays.

Dynamic scheduling is another option, the complexity of which requires that the system be computerized. In this approach, queue time includes an extra allowance for current or projected congestion. One simple measure of congestion is the number of open job orders (jobs in "the shop"), which the computer can find in the open-order file.

Largely due to queue-time uncertainty, total lead time is also hard to predict. Accurate estimates of lead times, and therefore accurate schedules are likely only when work centers are uncongested; only then can the typical job sail through without long and variable work-center queue times. Two questions come to mind: First, with so much uncertainty and use of fudge factors in estimating lead times, is it possible to do a reasonable job of scheduling job operations anyway? Second, what can we do to improve the accuracy of lead-time estimates?

The answer to the first question is yes. In closed-loop MRP, work flows are monitored and schedulers and dispatchers are kept informed of job movement. If they discover that lead-time estimates—and therefore the schedules based on those lead times—are wrong, they can make adjustments; perhaps the scheduler changes the due date for a job, or maybe the dispatcher adjusts priorities for releasing jobs into work centers.

The answer to the second question, can we improve lead-time accuracy, is also yes. Since more accurate lead-time estimates depend on having less shop congestion, the solution is to reduce that congestion; that is, reduce work in process.

## *Work in Process*

The work-in-process (WIP) problem is attacked directly with just-in-time techniques.[5] But the evils of WIP were receiving attention in Western industry well before JIT found its way across the Pacific. For 20 years or more, production-control books and dinner speakers at professional meetings for production-control people preached the following benefits of keeping WIP low:

"Real" meaning of WIP? Work in procrastination.

1. *Service.* Low WIP means less queue time and quicker response to customers; also, with less queue time there is less uncertainty in the schedule and customers may be given better status information.
2. *Forecasts.* We know that forecasts are more accurate for shorter periods into the future—that is, for the shorter lead times that result from smaller amounts of WIP.

3. *Production-control work-force.* Less congestion means less need for control by expediters and dispatchers.
4. *Floor-space and inventory costs.* These are lower when fewer jobs are in process.
5. *Customer satisfaction.* Customers are happy when they don't have to wait in long lines (here the customers are the WIP). They get angry and may take their business elsewhere if lines get too long.

Principle 11

Cut wait time and inventory.

Despite the advantages of low WIP, it can also make managers nervous and fearful that some work centers will run out of work. Each job in the work stream usually will require different operation times at each work center it visits. This causes work to pile up and overload some work centers and, potentially, underload others. As the job mix changes, and it often changes quickly, the pattern of over- and underloading changes. The scheduler is under pressure to overload on the average in order to hold down the number of underloaded work centers. Supervisors get nervous about cost variances when workloads get low.

Having taken a look at job scheduling difficulties created by lead times and work in process, let's turn our attention to some basic scheduling tools. We start with the venerable Gantt Chart.

### Gantt Charts

Henry Gantt's name is attached to a family of widely used scheduling charts. A few examples appear in Exhibit 16-3. In the basic **Gantt chart** form, much like Exhibit 16-3A, vertical divisions represent time, and horizontal rows, the jobs or resources to be scheduled. Lines, bars, brackets, shading, and other devices mark the start, duration, and end of a scheduled entity. The purpose of the charts, as with any visual aid, is to clarify, improve comprehension, and serve as a focus for discussion.

The charts in Exhibit 16-3 are for scheduling three different resource types: equipment, space, and employees. Each also identifies the jobs to be performed by the resources. Note too that each is a services example. While Gantt's original chart was for the control of repetitive manufacturing, today simpler forms of Gantt charts are more widely used in services, where routings are short and queues have few chances to form.[6]

In goods production, Gantt charts may be usable if:

1. *There are not many work centers.* With many work centers, a carefully developed Gantt display of schedules tends to be a piece of gross fiction, because queuing effects (discussed earlier) make lead times unpredictable. Keeping the chart up-to-date under such conditions would be time-consuming and pointless.
2. *Job times are long—days or weeks rather than hours.* One example is a construction project. Drywallers, painters, cement crews, roofers, and so on, may each spend several days or weeks at a work site. With such a long job time, a schedule on a Gantt chart will hold still and not become instantly out-of-date as it would with very short jobs.

## Exhibit 16-3 Common Forms of Gantt Charts

A. Schedule for machine

| Scheduled computer jobs | M | T | W | T | F | S | S | M | T | W | T | F | S | S | M | T | W | T |
|---|---|---|---|---|---|---|---|---|---|---|---|---|---|---|---|---|---|---|
| Payroll | | | ■ | | | | | | | ■ | | | | | | | ■ | |
| Accounts receivable | | | | ■ | | | | | | | ■ | | | | | | | ■ |
| MRP | | | | | ■ | ■ | | | | | | ■ | ■ | | | | | |
| | | | | | | | | | | | | | | | | | | |

B. Schedule for space

| Classroom schedule (Monday) Hour | 6 | 7 | 8 | 9 | 10 | 11 | 12 | 1 |
|---|---|---|---|---|---|---|---|---|
| BA 101 | | | | MGM 331 | ACCT 101 | | MGM | |
| BA 102 | | ECON 205 | | | ECON 400 | | FIN 394 | |

C. Schedule for labor and/or customers

| | | Dentist's appointments |
|---|---|---|
| Mon. | 8:00 | Mrs. Harrison |
| | 8:30 | ↓ |
| | 9:00 | J. Peters |
| | 0:30 | Steve Smith |
| | 10:00 | ↓ |
| | 10:30 | ↓ |
| | 11:00 | ↓ |

3. *Job routings are short*. In parts manufacturing, routings can be long. A single job may pass through 5, 10, or even 15 work centers, with unpredictable queue time at each stop. With so much unpredictability, the Gantt schedule is not believable and thus not worth displaying.

Sometimes a Gantt chart is used for both scheduling and schedule control. This is especially the case in renovation or maintenance work. Exhibit 16-4 shows a Gantt control chart for renovation work. Part A is an initial schedule for three crews. An arrow at the top of each chart identifies the current day.

Maintenance is a service. Thus, it's not surprising that maintenance, like other services, may benefit from Gantt scheduling.

Exhibit 16-4B shows progress after one day. The shading indicates amount of work done, which probably is estimated by the crew chief, in percent of completion. Two-thirds of the first paint job was scheduled for Monday, but the paint crew got the whole job done that day. While the paint crew is one half-day ahead of schedule, drywall is one quarter-day behind. Carpentry did Monday's scheduled work on Monday and is on schedule.

**EXHIBIT 16-4 Gantt Control Chart—Renovation Work**

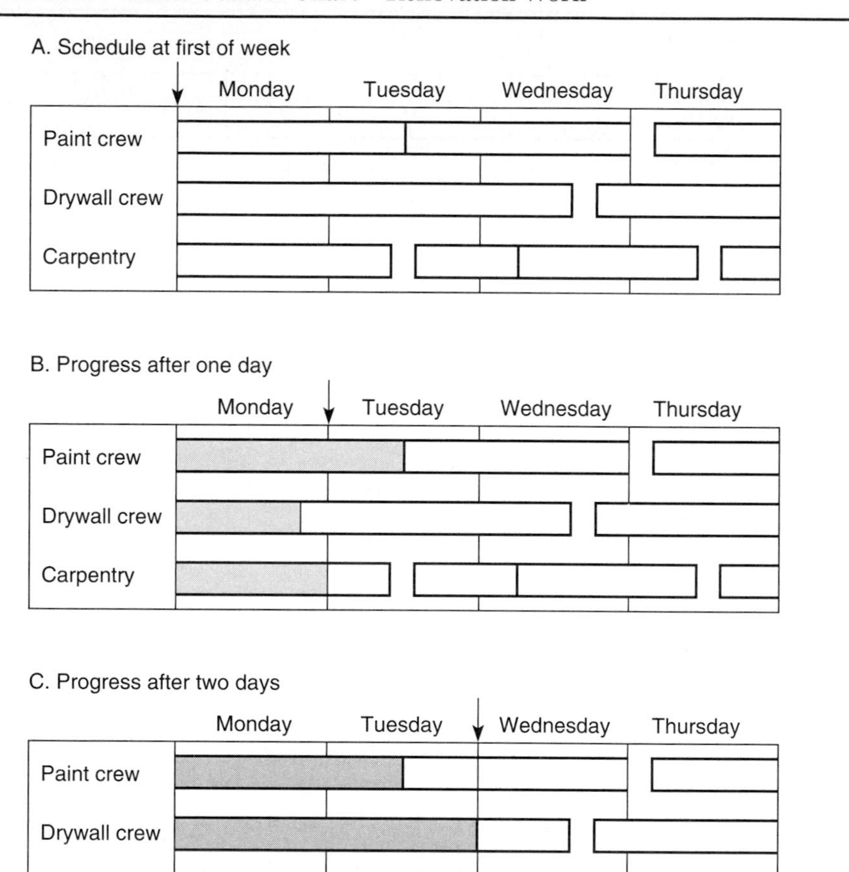


Exhibit 16-4C for Tuesday shows painting falling behind, drywall on schedule, and carpentry ahead.

The visual display offered by Gantt charts is a plus. But when things get complicated—for example, when there are many jobs, many routings, many work centers, and so forth—visual charts must give way to number- and word-based schedules. Also, while Gantt charts may be constructed from a need date backward or from a start date forward, backward scheduling is more likely to be the case in complex job settings. We take up these and related issues next.

## *Forward and Backward Scheduling*

For services offered on demand, the customer need time is typically "as soon as possible" (ASAP is the well-known abbreviation). Using **forward scheduling,** the scheduler begins with the current time or date or with some other planned starting date, adds the successive duration times for various job operations, and arrives at an anticipated order completion date.

For services provided by appointment, **backward scheduling** may be used. An example is deliveries of checks and deposit slips from a small bank to a larger bank's computer service center. The service center may require delivery by 9 P.M. each day. If so, each delivery stop is backward scheduled; that is, the scheduler successively subtracts operation and transport times from 9 P.M. The resulting schedule might appear as shown in the accompanying diagram.

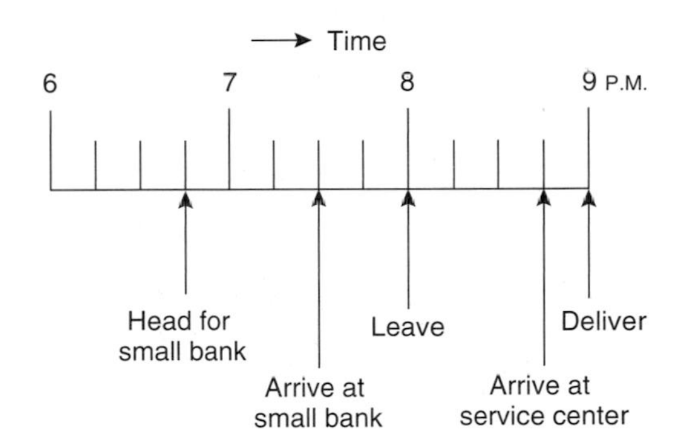


Goods producers, wholesalers, and retailers use both forward and backward scheduling. Generally, inventories that are replenished by reorder point (ROP) are forward scheduled. Goods needed for a parent item or for a special event such as a wedding may be backward scheduled from the date of the net requirement—the MRP approach. Actually, in most MRP systems the planned-order-release date is not the scheduled start day. The computer backward schedules to determine the start *week*, which the scheduler uses to calculate the start *day*. Example 16-2 illustrates.

## Example 16-2: Scheduling a Shop Order—QUIDCO, Inc.

The weekly MRP run at QUIDCO, Inc., shows a planned order in the current time bucket for part number 1005CX. The part is due on Monday of time bucket (week) 3, which is shop calendar date 105 (see Exhibit 16-5A).

The scheduler finds the part number in the routing file, and the routing and time standards for each operation on a PC monitor. She prepares a shop order using the data from the routing file (see Exhibit 16-5B). She uses backward scheduling, along with QUIDCO's rules for computing operation lead times:[7]

1. Allow eight standard hours per day; round upward to whole days.
2. Allow one day between operations for move/queue time and other delays.
3. Allow two days to inspect.
4. Release shop order to the stockroom five days before the job is to be started into production.
5. All dates are treated as end of the eight-hour day.

## EXHIBIT 16-5 Generating Shop Order from Current Planned Order Listing

*A. MRP Listing of Planned Orders Due for Scheduling*

Week of 90
Orders Planned for Release This Week
QUIDCO Inc.

| *Part Number* | *Due Date* |
|---|---|
| 0052X | 110 |
| 0077AX | 115 |
| . | . |
| . | . |
| . | . |
| 1005CX | 105 |
| . | . |
| . | . |
| . | . |

*B. Shop Order, Backward Scheduled*

Shop Order Number 9925
Part Number 1005CX    Quantity: 50    Release Date: 92

| *Operation* | *Description* | *Work Center* | *Setup* | *Cycle Time* | *Standard Hours* | *Due Date* |
|---|---|---|---|---|---|---|
| 20 | Bend rod | 16 | 4.2 | 0.05 | 6.7 | 99 |
| 30 | Finish rod | 85 | 0.4 | 0.18 | 9.4 | 102 |
| 40 | Inspect rod | 52 | | | | 105 |

Due Date: 105

Note: Monday is shop day 90; the listing is for the week beginning with day 90.

A shop calender of consecutively numbered workdays, omitting weekends and holidays, is common among manufacturing firms, because it makes computation easy.

She begins backward scheduling with the due date, 105, in the lower right corner. That is the finish date for the last operation, inspect. She subtracts two days for inspect and one day between operations, which makes 102 the due date for the finish operation. Finish takes 9.4 standard hours [$0.4 + (0.18 \times 50$ pieces)], which rounds upward to two days. Subtracting that plus one day between operations equals 99 as the due date for the bend operation. Finally, she subtracts one day (6.7 hours rounded upward) for bend, five days for stockroom actions, and one day between operations, which makes day 92 the release date. The scheduler therefore holds shop order 9925 in her *hold-for-release* file on Monday and Tuesday (days 90 and 91) and releases it on Wednesday (day 92).

A week goes by. The inventory planner notifies the scheduler that part number 1005CX has a new need date: 110 instead of 105. (The latest MRP run informed him of the later date.) The scheduler recomputes operation due dates and enters them into the computer. The computer uses the new dates in printing out a daily dispatch list. Copies of the list go to the three work center supervisors to tell them about the changes in operations due dates.

In the QUIDCO example, we had the scheduler performing the backward scheduling manually, in order to illustrate the procedure. Obviously, in a real setting computers perform computations of this nature, following any prescribed set of lead-time rules. Also, under the influence of time-based competition, more companies are having MRP systems plan in days rather than weeks; schedulers may then plan in hours rather than days. The net effects are faster throughput and lower WIP, both acting to strengthen the financial posture of the firm.

Although the QUIDCO example provides details about scheduling a single job, what happens when several jobs need to be scheduled into the same work center at the same time? How does one determine the best sequence? Some sort of system for prioritizing is required. That is our next topic.

Work flow drives cash flow; speed up the former to speed up the latter.

### Priority Rules

Priority systems come into play when multiple jobs or operations, typically in a queue, are competing for the same capacity. In retail settings, the priority system is simply first come, first served. In this democratic system, customers are considered homogeneous, one is not more important than another. First come, first served runs itself; no need to pay someone to pick and choose among customers.

Personal service settings might use first come, first served for their walk-in customers, while at the same time giving priority to customers with appointments. The priority rule is a simple one, but some differentiation among customers occurs.

Wholesalers, factories, and offices are blessed with such simplicity only if work can be processed quickly with no queuing or other delays at each work center. If jobs or orders can be processed in, say, a day or less, the company probably will elect just to handle them as they come in. An exception might be an urgent job, which can receive high-priority treatment, such as hand carrying.

Some jobs shops (wholesalers, offices, labs, and so forth, as well as factories) are striving for delay-free processing but are still far from it. If it takes many days or weeks to process an order, the orders may need to be sorted by priority. Factors to consider in setting priorities for jobs include

1. Customer importance.
2. Order urgency.
3. Order profitability.
4. Impact on capacity utilization.
5. Shop performance.

Customer importance, order urgency, and order profitability are rather self-explanatory, and need not be further discussed. The fourth factor, impact on capacity utilization, often requires somewhat detailed analysis of capacity, work load projections, and activity control. We will leave those topics for more advanced studies. That leaves the final factor—shop or system performance.

Earlier, we saw that long lead times and facility congestion, in the form of work in process, are key variables that reduce the responsiveness of job operations. It comes as no surprise, therefore, that schedulers aim at reducing WIP and speeding up the flow of jobs through the system. Thus, average throughput time and average number of jobs in the system—as an indicator of WIP levels—are popular performance indicators. Emphasis on customer service adds another indicator—usually some measure of lateness, such as average time late. Several prioritizing rules exist to help the scheduler pick a job sequence that best meets one or more of these performance criteria. We shall consider four of the most popular:

- *First come, first served (FCFS).* This rule has been discussed within the context of retail operations. In service or manufacturing, the scheduler releases jobs in the order they arrive at the work center.
- *Shortest processing time (SPT).* Under the SPT rule, the scheduler prioritizes jobs in order of their required processing times; the job with the shortest time goes first.
- *Earliest due date (EDD).* Here, the customer with the earliest need date gets the priority, regardless of job arrival order or processing times.
- *Least slack (LS).* Defined as time remaining minus work time required or needed. The job with the least slack is released first.

Example 16-3 illustrates how these rules work.

## Example 16-3: Scheduling Multiple Jobs From a Queue

Five jobs are in a queue waiting to be released into a work center. These jobs, their required processing times, and their due dates are given in the table below. They are listed in the order of their arrival at the work center.

| *Job* | *Required Time (days)* | *Due Date (days hence)* |
|---|---|---|
| A | 3 | 5 |
| B | 6 | 8 |
| C | 2 | 6 |
| D | 4 | 4 |
| E | 1 | 2 |

Determine the proper job sequence using each of the following prioritizing rules: FCFS, SPT, EDD, and LS. For each solution, compute the average throughput time, the average number of jobs in the work center, and the average late time.

*Solution*

The first column in Exhibit 16-6 parts A through D shows the correct job sequence under each of the priority rules. In each table, the column "Processing Period" shows the time a particular job will be worked on. For example, In Exhibit 16-6A, Job A will be accomplished in the first three days, then Job B will require the next six days and be completed on day 9; Job C is next, requiring two days ending on day 11, and so on. In Exhibit 16-6D, the solution under the least-slack rule, we've inserted an extra column to show the slack time. (Again, slack is available time

## EXHIBIT 16-6 Job Scheduling

**A. First-Come-First-Served (FCFS) Rule**

| Job | *Required Time (days)* | *Due date (days hence)* | *Processing Period (start + req'd)* | *Completion Date* | *Days Late* |
|---|---|---|---|---|---|
| A | 3 | 5 | 0 + 3 | 3 | 0 |
| B | 6 | 8 | 3 + 6 | 9 | 1 |
| C | 2 | 6 | 9 + 2 | 11 | 5 |
| D | 4 | 4 | 11 + 4 | 15 | 11 |
| E | 1 | 2 | 15 + 1 | 16 | 14 |
| Sums | 16 | | | 54 | 31 |

Average throughput time = 54 ÷ 5 = 10.8 days.
Average number of jobs in the work center = 54 ÷ 16 = 3.38 jobs.
Average number of days late = 31 ÷ 5 = 6.2 days.

**B. Shortest Processing Time (SPT) Rule**

| Job | *Required Time (days)* | *Due Date (days hence)* | *Processing Period (start + req'd)* | *Completion Date* | *Days Late* |
|---|---|---|---|---|---|
| E | 1 | 2 | 0 + 1 | 1 | 0 |
| C | 2 | 6 | 1 + 2 | 3 | 0 |
| A | 3 | 5 | 3 + 3 | 6 | 1 |
| D | 4 | 4 | 6 + 4 | 10 | 6 |
| B | 6 | 8 | 10 + 6 | 16 | 8 |
| Sums | 16 | | | 36 | 15 |

Average throughput time = 36 ÷ 5 = 7.2 days.
Average number of jobs in the work center = 36 ÷ 16 = 2.25 jobs.
Average number of days late = 15 ÷ 5 = 3.0 days.

**C. Earliest Due Date (EDD) Rule**

| Job | *Required Time (days)* | *Due Date (days hence)* | *Processing Period (start + req'd)* | *Completion Date* | *Days Late* |
|---|---|---|---|---|---|
| E | 1 | 2 | 0 + 1 | 1 | 0 |
| D | 4 | 4 | 1 + 4 | 5 | 1 |
| A | 3 | 5 | 5 + 3 | 8 | 3 |
| C | 2 | 6 | 8 + 2 | 10 | 4 |
| B | 6 | 8 | 10 + 6 | 16 | 8 |
| Sums | 16 | | | 40 | 16 |

Average throughput time = 40 ÷ 5 = 8.0 days.
Average number of jobs in the work center = 40 ÷ 16 = 2.5 jobs.
Average number of days late = 16 ÷ 5 = 3.2 days.

**D. Least Slack (LS) Rule**

| Job | *Required Time (days)* | *Due Date (days hence)* | *Slack (days)* | *Processing Period (start + req'd)* | *Completion Date* | *Days Late* |
|---|---|---|---|---|---|---|
| D | 4 | 4 | 0 | 0 + 4 | 4 | 0 |
| E | 1 | 2 | 1 | 4 + 1 | 5 | 3 |
| A | 3 | 5 | 2 | 5 + 3 | 8 | 3 |
| B | 6 | 8 | 2 | 8 + 6 | 14 | 6 |
| C | 2 | 6 | 4 | 14 + 2 | 16 | 10 |
| Sums | 16 | | | | 47 | 22 |

Average throughput time = 47 ÷ 5 = 9.4 days.
Average number of jobs in the work center = 47 ÷ 16 = 2.94 jobs.
Average number of days late = 22 ÷ 5 = 4.4 days.

**EXHIBIT 16-7 Summary Table—Scheduling with Priority Rules**

| *Performance Dimension* | *FCFS* | *SPT* | *EDD* | *LS* |
|---|---|---|---|---|
| Average throughput time (days) | 10.8 | 7.2 | 8.0 | 9.4 |
| Average number of jobs in the work center | 3.38 | 2.25 | 2.5 | 2.94 |
| Average time late (days) | 6.2 | 3.0 | 3.2 | 4.4 |

minus required time.) The lower portion of each table contains expected shop performance figures—average job throughput time, average number of jobs in the work center, and average number of days late.

The summary table, Exhibit 16-7, compares performance of the four prioritizing rules in this problem. Shortest processing time (SPT) outperforms the other priority rules in all three of the performance dimensions.

Research has shown SPT to be a good rule to follow for job scheduling if a job queue has already formed, as is the case in Example 16-3. It will often minimize the average throughput time and result in the lowest average number of jobs in the system. Why, then, doesn't SPT become gospel? The answers lie in a deeper understanding of actual job operation settings.

First, scheduling occurs each day or perhaps each shift. As new jobs come along, the queue composition changes. Reapplication of SPT would serve to keep longer jobs in lower priorities; they get delayed even further. Customers lose patience. Second, a queue must already exist in order for SPT to be applied. If we keep queues from forming in the first place, FCFS becomes the only practical scheduling rule. Third, SPT is fine as long as performance of one work center is the concern. But if jobs must meet up with other outputs later in an assembly sequence, for instance, EDD might be preferred.

Job-level scheduling, what Example 16-3 is all about, is the second level of scheduling addressed in Exhibit 16-1 (the third box in the figure). Still, many companies find it necessary to schedule at an even more detailed level—operations dispatching.

### *Operations Dispatching*

Recall our discussion of lead-time uncertainty. Since SPT relies directly on knowledge of processing times (as does the LS rule, for that matter), its credibility drops as the possibility of processing-time uncertainty increases. When jobs contain long routings and therefore many operations, *job* processing times are really aggregate estimates that combine the individual times associated with the operations that make up those jobs.

For example, a scheduler might use SPT to release the bookshelf job described in Example 16-1 into the gateway work center—the stockroom in this case—based on its priority position in a job queue. Suppose many other jobs are currently in process, and several have routings that demand time at the planing work station. Quite possibly, a queue forms. Priority rules might also be employed to dispatch work through planing—a third level of scheduling and reflected as the fourth box in Exhibit 16-1.

Sometimes, the job scheduler also handles dispatching, but in complex settings, another individual, called a *dispatcher,* performs the work. In addition to managing **hot-list jobs,** orders for parts not available but needed immediately for open jobs currently in process on the shop floor, dispatchers often handle the **daily priority report** (also called the *dispatch list*).

A hot-listed job getting priority *dispatching* at a single work center may also be a hot job being *expedited* (e.g., hand-carried) through many work centers.

A different priority report goes to each work center supervisor every day, only for jobs already in progress, not for those still in a planned-order state. Priorities are established by using one or more of the priority rules we considered for job scheduling. To illustrate, this time using the least-slack (LS) rule, let's assume that on day 101 four jobs are in queue waiting operations at work center 16, which is the punch press center where metal is punched. Consider the data shown in Exhibit 16-8A; (the first shop order, 9925, is from the QUIDCO example of Exhibit 16 5 recall that operation due dates are derived by back scheduling from the job due date). The slack for the four jobs is given in Exhibit 16-8B, which is roughly in the form of a daily priority report for work center 16. In the figure, slack values show that shop order 9925 is four days behind, 9938 and 9918 are each two days behind, and 9916 is two days ahead; the jobs should be run in work center 16 in that order.

In job operations, dispatching and related activities occur at the junction where planning and scheduling give way to control activities—keeping work moving on schedule and taking corrective action when required. The next section addresses other aspects of control.

**EXHIBIT 16-8 Planning Data and Priority Report for Work Center 16**

**A. Planning and Routing Data**

| *Shop Order* | *Move/Queue Time* | *Punch Press Processing Time (Setup + Run)* | *Operation Due Date* |
|---|---|---|---|
| 9925 | 1 day | 6.7 hours, or 1 day rounded | Day 99 |
| 9938 | 1 day | 15.8 hours, or 2 days rounded | Day 102 |
| 9918 | 1 day | 1.8 hours, or 1 day rounded | Day 101 |
| 9916 | 1 day | 0.8 hours, or 1 day rounded | Day 105 |

**B. Daily Priority Report, by Operation Slack**

| *Shop Order* | *Demand Time (Due Date − Today)* | *Supply Time (Move/Queue + Processing)* | *Operation Slack* |
|---|---|---|---|
| 9925 | 99 − 101 | 1 + 1 | −4 |
| 9938 | 102 − 101 | 1 + 2 | −2 |
| 9918 | 101 − 101 | 1 + 1 | −2 |
| 9916 | 105 − 101 | 1 + 1 | +2 |

## Job and Operations Control

Too many variables to manage—the main problem with job and operations scheduling—also makes controlling in these environments more difficult. As mentioned above, much of what dispatchers do to smooth and redirect work also serves to control jobs and operations. Steps at better control can begin earlier, in the planning stage—when work is loaded onto (i.e., assigned to) work centers. Other actions include capacity control and activity control.

### *Work Center Loading*

*Scheduler:* "In a nutshell, what is your advice on how we should load your work centers?"

*Supervisor:* "Keep 'em busy. But not too busy."

**loading**
Assigning workload to a work center.

The above exchange describes one concern of schedulers: loading the work centers. Whereas a multifunctional team plans overall capacity in light of predicted aggregate workload (Chapter 5), the scheduler has the task of fitting jobs into the schedule so as not to overload or underload work centers day to day and week to week. In some companies, especially those that have implemented material requirements planning, the scheduler may perform loading with the aid of an MRP subroutine, capacity requirements planning (mentioned in Chapter 13).

**Capacity requirements planning (CRP)** is a computer-based method of revealing work center loads. A CRP run requires three inputs. One is planned order releases for component parts. Planned order releases are calculated by the computer in an MRP run (see Chapter 13). The second is open orders for component parts. These are orders released by scheduling (or purchasing) in an earlier period and still in process. The third input is routing data that tell which work centers each component-parts order goes through and how long it takes. Both the open-order file and the routing file must be computerized in order to run CRP.

Schedulers would want to apply CRP where it can do the most good: to work centers that have trouble achieving planned output, thus becoming bottlenecks. CRP projections in those work centers can warn of insufficient capacity far enough in advance for schedulers to do something about it. There is little sense in asking the computer to run CRP projections for all work centers and for 52 weeks into the future, because the real problems are in the near future and likely only in certain work centers. With CRP's potential to alert managers so as to keep work center capacities reasonably close to planned loads, the usual chaotic atmosphere in the job shop may give way to reasonable order and tranquility.

### *Capacity Control*

While capacity planning deals with blocks of jobs and capacity grouping, **capacity control** operates at the level of single jobs and single work centers. The capacity control problem is to make on-the-spot capacity adjustments in order to get a certain job through. Special capacity adjustments may stem from the press to get one or more hot jobs through the system. One way, considered here, is for expediters to push the work through. Another way, discussed in the final section of the chapter, is to select from a range of tools that simplify the processing or the handling so that special push activities are unnecessary—in other words, solve the root causes.

When a job is late or a key customer is getting impatient, our usual reaction is to **expedite:** do whatever is necessary to push the job through and never mind the chaos and interruptions that might ensue. In almost any line of work, unexpected hot jobs and processing obstacles make expediting necessary at least once in a while.

It's easy to see how expediting works in the case of an emergency patient at a clinic or hospital. Medical staffers simply make a triage judgment as to criticality and process more-critical patients before others who had earlier positions in the queues.

## *Activity Control*

The workplace is out of control if it is choked with partly completed jobs. That is true for a restaurant, clinic, or bank as well as for a goods producer. There are two steps to be taken in the quest for balanced loads in work centers. Dispatching, discussed earlier, is one. The other involves input control of work releases into either gateway or bottleneck work centers. Together, these activities make up **activity control**—sometimes called **shop floor control.**

The first half of the scheduler's job is to set due dates for each operation and a release date for the whole job. The second half is to release orders in trickles so as not to overload the work centers. This is often referred to as **input control.** Two techniques of input control are load leveling and firm planned order.

**Load Leveling.** The scheduler typically maintains some form of hold-for-release file. In an auto service shop, a form of "hold for release" file may be visible to all . . . job tickets in a large, slotted wall rack. As a particular auto work bay is free from the previous job (e.g., front-end alignment), the supervisor releases the next alignment job to a mechanic.

In manufacturing the file contains jobs with a mix of priorities. It may also include orders that were due for release on a previous day but were withheld because something (e.g., instructions or materials) was missing, or in order to avoid overloading certain work centers. The scheduler is attempting input **load leveling;** as the term suggests, the purpose is to release a level load, which is a mix of orders that neither overloads nor underloads a work center. Load leveling works well only for gateway work centers, those at the input end of the operation sequence. The foundry that produces castings is a common gateway in metal fabrication, a component sequencing machine used in printed circuit board assembly may be a gateway in electronics, and order entry or customer arrival is a gateway in many service businesses.

**Firm Planned Order.** The **firm planned order** is an MRP tool that may be used to overrule the automatic rescheduling feature of MRP and thus help in load leveling. A firm planned order may be scheduled earlier than the actual need to get the order into a

**EXHIBIT 16-9 Firm Planned Order for Load Leveling in Gateway Work Center**

*Action taken: Job order 688 is scheduled as a firm planned order in week 2 instead of week 3, its MRP-generated date of need.*

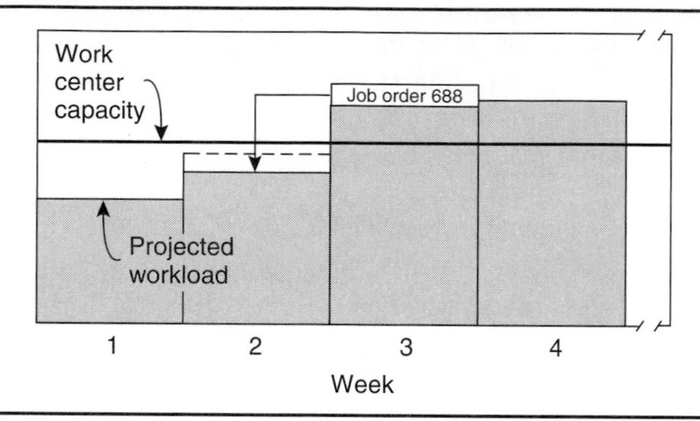


gateway work center in a slack (underloaded) week (see Exhibit 16-9). To invoke the firm planned order, the scheduler instructs the computer to flag a particular planned order and move it to a given time bucket. In the figure, planned order 688 is moved from week 3, its calculated date of need, to week 2, which helps level the load imbalance in weeks 2 and 3. The next MRP run will not reschedule the flagged job back to its need date. It will issue a reschedule message, which may be ignored.

These control tools, along with the planning and scheduling actions considered earlier in the chapter, create a complex system that itself resists control. Efforts to simplify job and batch operations, thus making the system easier to manage, are the next topic.

## Simplification: Reduction of Variables

Crisscrossed flow paths, high error rates, piled-high in-baskets, bulging stock rooms of items not needed yet, shelves full of thick instruction manuals, frequent rescheduling, high overtime and undertime costs, poor on-time service rates, long cycle times, and large backlogs: These are symptoms of overly complex job operations and high-cost, ineffective attempts to cope.

Assorted antidotes are available. In this final section, we review an assortment of simplification methods (presented in previous chapters) that apply to job environments, look at a powerful team-based improvement tool, and conclude with an example of job shop reform.

### *Improvement Perspective*

First, good job environment management does not reduce down to a one-two sequence: simplify, then schedule and control. Rather, it must embody an iterative process of continuous improvement. A *permanent or persistent* bottleneck should not be allowed to exist; find the cause and eliminate it—a Kaizen Blitz team (considered later) is an effective tool. Given the high variability associated with job operations, however, *temporary* bottlenecks will emerge from time to time and must be dealt with. Flexible capacity is a good first line of defense against these nuisances.

Second, better management of job environments should not become a "high-tech" versus "low-tech" contest. As with any operations environment, however, it is about meeting customer wants . . . keeping work flowing and keeping costly wastes out. Lean techniques clean up processes; they help simplify designs, identify and fix trouble spots, and orient the job environment to focus on next-process (customer) requirements and not on esoteric production schedules.

Third, planning and control technology is expensive and should be managed accordingly. It can be effective when used to keep *already improved* processes in control and on schedule. And when large amounts of data *must* be managed, no one suggests uplugging the computers. The emphasized words provide the temporal hint. Improve and simplify first, and you have increased the return-on-investment potential of subsequent scheduling and control technology expenditures.

Much of the disenchantment with ERP systems seems to come from practitioners who have heard horror stories about installations that were being relied on to solve process problems and failed to meet that goal. It may be simply a matter of getting the cart before the horse, so to speak:

> Some manufacturers spent millions of dollars putting in company-wide ERP systems without first redesigning their manufacturing processes. . . . Why rush to institutionalize a wasteful process by laying and ERP system over it? Yet many manufacturers did—and are still doing just that, consultants say. Asked how many clients bothered to redesign their processes before installing ERP systems, Roger Sherrard, marketing and communications manager with IBM Global Services, responds, "None. Not a one"[8]

Others seem convinced that ERP is a drawback simply because it does what it was designed to do best—track process flow. "ERP gives information, but it does not necessarily add value to the bottom line of a company. The problems it introduces—or perpetuates from the days of MRP—include complex bills of materials, inefficient workflows, and unnecessary data collection."[9] Indeed, each of the scheduling and control techniques addressed in this chapter add more paperwork and computer transactions into the system. Is there a better way?

## *Paperless and Visual Systems*

Sometimes it seems that the job in a job environment is controlling the control system; that is, try to keep the work, and the client, form getting buried under piles of reports. Moreover, as time-based competition has taken root, fast-moving job processing is the objective; no one wants to slow down so the paperwork can catch up. One process manager whose company has gone to a complete demand-flow operation sums it up this way: "We do no inventory transactions or labor reporting—nothing. . . . If you have your process correct, there's nothing to track—it's moving too fast."[10] It would seem that "too many transactions" has itself emerged as a sign of waste.

**Principle 15**

Cut transactions and reporting.

Advanced communications and computer technology can create a paperless office or plant. Such facilities already exist. Data-entry terminals in planning offices or, better yet, in customers' own facilities, display screens in work centers, bar codes on all parts containers or mail-distribution tubs, and bar-code readers to track the work flow all help make paper reduction possible. The scheduling and activity control procedures may be just as described above. The difference is that job orders, priority reports, and other notices and files are called up on screens instead of from printed pages.

Another way to deal with transactions and paper is to create the visual office or plant. It is not hard to conceive of this for repetitive or continuous operations. No data screens are needed to tell people what to do when the same work units follow the same flow path sometimes pulled by conveyors.

Can the scheduling and dispatching paper possibly be eliminated in a job shop? The answer is yes, at least partly. A few differences between visual and written work authorization are summarized in Exhibit 16-10. Note that the written system may include a job order, a pick list, and a priority report. The visual system may require an identification card in a slot, but that is fixed information, not transactions generated for each job; process instructions are also fixed information.

Visual system usage for job shops and offices is increasing, and its potential for application is almost limitless. The visual system is potent because it copes with the explosive growth of overhead costs, especially those of processing transactions and of material handling and storage.

**EXHIBIT 16-10 Work Authorization in Job Operations**

| | *Visual* | *Written* |
|---|---|---|
| Work in process | Exact small quantity located next to work center | Large shelf space in stockroom; may be full, partly full, or empty |
| Delivery | Empty slot tells associate to get next unprocessed unit from rack; cards identify units in rack spaces | Written job order is transformed into pick list; tells stockroom what items to pick and deliver to work centers |
| Dispatching | Emptiest slot is next job | Daily priority report tells work center the order of working on the jobs in queue |
| Process instructions | In a file at the work center | Part of work package accompanying the job order |

CONTRAST

## Getting the Hot Jobs Done

**Expediting**

- Expediter selects hot jobs from overdue list; uses lot splitting, overlapping, hand-carry, air freight, "cannibalization" of other jobs, and so forth, to push hot jobs through.

**Planning**

- MRP creates planned orders.
- CRP identifies capacity shortfall.
- Scheduling/rescheduling assigns dates.
- Dispatching reprioritizes—latest jobs first.

**Simplifying**

- Quick setup so that hot jobs scarcely disrupt.
- Cells process similar jobs with natural overlapping and few transactions.
- Flexible capacity—human and equipment resources—to eliminate bottleneck effects.

### *Other Antidotes*

Complementing the shift toward simpler information processing are other complexity antidotes that have been discussed in other chapters. They are reviewed below in two groups, one general and the other specific to this chapter's topics. Also see the Contrast box for a broad comparison of approaches.

**General Simplifications.** These general items apply to all kinds of operations but are especially valuable in job and batch operations where complexity problems tend to be severe.

- Get focused: Strategically limit the variety of businesses per organizational unit (Chapters 1 and 2).
- Reduce, simplify, and standardize designs for the line of goods and services (Chapter 7).
- Control processes at the source, rather than discovering mishaps downstream (Chapter 9).
- Stay tuned to the pulse of the market via comprehensive demand forecasting (Chapter 4).
- Employ a cross-functional master planning team to plan capacity and master schedules so that demand and supply are a reasonably close fit (Chapter 5).
- Adopt quick-response and just-in-time flow controls to remove sources of non-value-adding delay and stay close to the actual demand changes (Chapter 10).

- Cut to a few good supplier-partners (Chapter 6), thus shrinking purchasing complications while creating reliable outsourcing options for use in meeting demand spikes.
- Adopt simple queue-limitation and kanban flow controls (Chapter 11), thereby avoiding flow-control transactions.
- Cut job, lot, and batch sizes so that materials are ordered or produced based on current demand, thus avoiding problems of having too many of the wrong items and being out of the right ones (Chapters 10 and 13).

**Special Simplifications.** The following items relate to expediting and capacity/activity control.

- Cut changeover and setup times (Chapter 10) so that lot splitting into smaller transfer lots does not elevate costs.
- Position facilities the way the work flows, thus avoiding long, jumbled flow paths (Chapters 5 and 14). A hot job then may go directly to the cell or flow line that is focused on similar items (goods, documents, or human services), where it may fit right in without special paperwork, setups, handling, or disruption.
- Keep physical resources in tip-top working condition (Chapter 14), thereby avoiding stoppages and rescheduling.
- Invest in training to enhance employee flexibility (Chapter 12).
- Where there is flow distance to span (e.g., to and from a cell or in the absence of cells), downsize to lower-cost handling methods so that expediting is still affordable (Chapter 14).

The rich array of antidotes makes it seem that a diversity of talent would be required to keep job environments from getting cluttered. That is exactly the case. Furthermore, the teams of people who solve these sorts of problems must do so rapidly. Otherwise, the queues began to form. Fortunately, an effective solution has been developed.

## *Kaizen Blitz Teams*

Kaizen Blitz is a registered service mark of the Association of Manufacturing Excellence (AME).

The Association of Manufacturing Excellence has developed an approach for rapid, action-oriented process improvement efforts that it calls **Kaizen Blitz teams.**[11] As we learned in Chapter 2, *kaizen* is a Japanese term for continuous improvement. *Blitz* is German for flash, or lightening. An Americanization of *blitz,* however, refers to a rapid (lightening-fast) rush of defenders in a football game in an attempt to quickly tackle the opposing quarterback. Thus, Kaizen Blitz teams attack problems that emerge and quickly affect improvement solutions before little problems can become larger ones.

The Kaizen Blitz team has *at most* five days (most use but three) in which to do its work. It is action oriented; team members will create, test, and implement their solution within the five-day time frame. Kaizen Blitz is a low-budget tool; even if unlimited funds were available, the team would not use them. Time does not permit acquisition and installation of new capital equipment or elaborate information system software. Teams must be dedicated to rapid improvements that draw heavily on techniques that eliminate process wastes and place priority on meeting next-process requirements—topics that we have addressed throughout this book.

Kaizen Blitz teams are cross-functional and multilevel (managers—even company officers—work alongside machine operators); usually contain from 6 to 12 members; work 12 to 14 hours a day; and expect to get dirty. The teams include people who regularly work at the process that is to be improved complemented by various specialists as needed for a particular project. Although the teams are capable of taking on a wide range of projects, each individual effort is quite focused . . . say on a single machine, cell, or queue. A specific target or objective typically accompanies the narrow focus: reduce setup time by 90 percent—from one hour down to six minutes (or less), for example.

Kaizen Blitz teams form quickly, take care of business quickly, and disband quickly. Continuous improvement, especially in a job environment, cannot be a long, drawn-out planning-oriented affair. But, though the action is fast, the proven improvements are impressive and lasting:[12]

- Efficiency increases of 20 to 50 percent.
- Immediate inventory reductions of 20 to 80 percent.
- Flow distances cut by 50 to 90 percent.
- Setup time reductions of 50 to 90 percent.
- Productivity increases from 10 to 50 percent.

In sum, the Kaizen Blitz can be a powerful competitive weapon that brings together many of the principles of operations management and focuses them on job operations improvement. In the next section, we take a more in-depth look at one such improvement program that took place in the early years of job-shop reform. Perhaps, the fact that it did take place so early is testament to the pioneering spirit of the managers involved. The story has become a bit of a classic.

## *Reforming the Job Shop: An Example*

In this chapter, we have examined a sophisticated, many-faceted system of managing complex job operations, a system perfected in North America, largely in the 1970s. We've also emphasized simplification, an approach that is highly attractive in view of the high costs and complexity of job operations. We close with a real-life summary (see Into Practice, "Reforming the Job Shop") of what can be done to improve a job shop. The message applies as well to job-oriented offices and, to some extent, human service operations.

INTO PRACTICE

## Reforming the Job Shop

In the summer of 1985 [Schlumberger's Houston downhole sensors (HDS) division] was struggling. Operations were costly, chaotic, and falling short of acceptable standards. Customers were dissatisfied. About 15 percent of the logging tools produced by HDS failed on final acceptance test. Most products were built to schedules established far in advance, but on-time delivery was no better than 70 percent. The average lead times exceeded 12 months. Senior management was also dissatisfied. Cost of sales was unacceptably high, and the plant was bulging with inventories. WIP alone averaged five months of output.

What explains the chronic and intractable problems afflicting job shops? The answer lies in the manufacturing philosophy. At HDS, most products were batched for final assembly and tested in lots that usually represented two or three months' requirements. Therefore, lead times on orders were at least two to three months (in reality much longer) even though many logging tools could be assembled and tested in two weeks.

So why batch? Because management wanted to be as efficient as possible, with efficiency defined as minimizing direct labor charges. Batching generated short-term savings in virtually every phase of the production process. Setup costs are a good example. Parts needed for final assembly must be "kitted" in a warehouse before arriving at the assembly area. Management believed that pulling kits in large lots, rather than as orders arrived, saved money. Batching also meant that workers had to learn how to assemble and test a product only once per batch. Batching minimized the unit costs of configuring test equipment and debugging completed products. Finally, moving products in large batches was combined with the use of queues to smooth work flows and adjust to ever-present parts shortages. Batching in effect, allowed all the factory's workers to be busy all the time.

In the long term, however, batching becomes a big obstacle to the very efficiencies it seeks to achieve. The long-lead-time, large-lot, long-queue philosophy invariably results in split lots, broken setups, lost and defective parts, late deliveries, and large WIP. The results are visible in job shops everywhere: the monthly hockey stick shipments, where a large volume of product leaves the factory at the end of each measurement period; relaxation of quality standards under pressure to make quotas; secret high-rework jobs hidden in WIP; ever-changing production priorities; and daily crises on the shop floor.

We believe the real solution lies in eliminating batching, smoothing, and artificial economies of scale, and organizing a job shop that can quickly and efficiently "change over" from one product to another without incurring large delays and cost penalties.

HDS adopted such a production philosophy. It emphasizes shorter lead times (down from an average of three months to two weeks today), small to nonexistent queues, low inventories, and quick recognition and correction of defects.

Getting control over the shop floor has allowed us to slash overhead. In the summer of 1985, 520 of the division's 830 employees were salaried or indirect personnel. The overhead count now stands at 220 employees. The largest reductions came from three departments—quality control; shipping, receiving, and warehousing; and production control (expediters, dispatchers)—whose roles diminish as quality and on-time performance improves.

These dramatic results did not require large capital expenditures. The management team initially cut the capital budget by 50 percent; annual spending has since run at less than half of depreciation. Those results did not require sophisticated computer applications. In fact, we turned off our shop floor computer, adopted a manual floor-control approach, and canceled a $400,000 automation project.

Source: Adapted from James E. Ashton and Frank X. Cook, Jr., "Time to Reform Job-Shop Manufacturing," *Harvard Business Review,* March–April 1989, pp. 106–11. Used with permission.

## Summary Check Points

✓ Job and batch operations are intermittent and are characterized by low-to-moderate output volume, low-to-moderate task magnitude, and great variety. Most human services fall into the job category.

✓ Jobs are triggered by orders (examples include work, shop, purchase, service, and job orders); job completion is part of the order-fulfillment sequence described in Chapter 6.

✓ Jobs are comprised of a series of steps called operations, each of which typically requires a setup or changeover. Operations may be managed as separate work units within the overall job management scheme.

✓ Job-operations management is accomplished with a dual approach:

1. *Computerized job planning, scheduling, and control that may incorporate resource management.* The idea is that job environments are complex, so complex control systems are necessary.
2. *Process simplification, focus on next-process requirements, elimination of non-value-adding steps and streamlining of value-adding ones.* This approach may be called *lean,* and follows the thinking that job environments have become too complex but needn't be left that way.

✓ Routes are paths that jobs follow from work center to work center. Despite planning efforts, variability often causes queues to form at overloaded or bottleneck work centers.

✓ Lead time, the elapsed time required to perform a job, often consists mostly of queue time; thus lead-time uncertainty is itself driven by uncertainties associated with queues.

✓ Lower WIP translates into better customer service and satisfaction, shorter lead times, more accurate forecasts, lower staff costs, and lower costs for floor-space and inventory.

✓ Gantt charts are effective for job scheduling and control when routings are short, job times are relatively long (days or weeks rather than hours), and there are few work centers.

✓ Both forward and backward scheduling are prevalent in job environments.

✓ Priority rules are used to sequence jobs or operations (often those in a queue); first-come-first-served, shortest-processing-time, earliest-due-date, and least-slack are popular rules.

✓ Job and operations control is accomplished by attention to work center loading, capacity control, and activity control. The latter may include load leveling and firm planned orders.

✓ The simplification approach to job environment management demands continuous improvement iterations; when needed, planning and control technology is more effective if applied to already streamlined processes.

✓ Paperless and visual flow-control systems can eliminate much of the transactions and reporting burden that has bogged down many MRP-based installations.

✓ General simplifications embody principles of OM that we have covered throughout this text; more specific simplifications relate to expediting and capacity/activity management.

✓ Kaizen Blitz teams exemplify the rapid-response efforts needed to keep job operations flowing and drive costly process wastes out.

## Solved Problems

### *Problem 1*

The framing department has an order for 20-pound frames. The operations and standard times for producing one frame are:

| *Operation* | *Standard Time* |
|---|---|
| Cut | 4 hours |
| Weld | 8 hours |
| Grind | 3 hours |
| Finish | 18 hours |

*a.* If it is a hot job, how quickly (in eight-hour days) can it be completed allowing one extra day for material movement and delays?

*b.* The MRP system sets lead times for component parts by a formula: standard hours times five, plus two weeks, rounded upward to full weeks. What lead time does the MRP system use?

*c.* The above two answers are far apart, but both may be fairly realistic. Explain what happens when a planned system accommodates both.

### *Solution 1*

*a.*

$$\begin{aligned}\text{Total work content} &= 4 + 8 + 3 + 18 = 33 \text{ standard hours}\\ &= 4.125 \text{ days, rounded up to 5 days}\\ \text{Total expedited lead time} &= 5 + 1 \text{ extra day}\\ &= 6 \text{ days}\end{aligned}$$

*b.* From (*a*)

$$\text{Total hours} = 33 \text{ hours}$$

Then

$$\begin{aligned}\text{Lead time} &= 165\ (33 \text{ hours} \times 5) + 2 \text{ weeks}\\ &= 165 \text{ hours (or 4.125 weeks)} + 2 \text{ weeks}\\ &= 6.125, \text{ rounded up to 7 weeks}\end{aligned}$$

*c.* The MRP system must back schedule using normal time estimates. The result is a fairly realistic week of need, seven weeks prior to the week due for the frame order. It is nearly eight times greater than the expedite time of six days, which is to be expected since in conventional job shops work spends most of its total lead time in various kinds of delay. The few hot jobs interrupt the routine ones, causing the latter to be delayed still more. (While that situation has been normal in job shops, simplified operations management systems are eliminating delays in some companies.)

### Problem 2

Today is day 11 on the shop calendar, and three jobs are awaiting processing in work center 67, as shown in the following table:

| *Jobs in Work Center 67* | *Scheduled Operation Start Date* | *Scheduled Operation Due Date* |
|---|---|---|
| A | 12 | 18 |
| B | 8 | 16 |
| C | 13 | 17 |

Calculate operation slack for the three jobs. Arrange the jobs in priority order, and indicate which should be done first.

### Solution 2

Slack is equal to available time minus required time, where

$$\text{Available time} = \text{Operation due date} - \text{Today's date}$$

and

$$\text{Required time} = \text{Scheduled due date} - \text{Scheduled start date}$$

Then

| *Job* | *Available Time (Due − Today)* | *Required Time (Due − Start)* | *Operation Slack (Available − Required)* |
|---|---|---|---|
| A | $18 - 11 = 7$ | $18 - 12 = 6$ | $7 - 6 = +1$ |
| B | $16 - 11 = 5$ | $16 - 8 = 8$ | $5 - 8 = -3$ |
| C | $17 - 11 = 6$ | $17 - 13 = 4$ | $6 - 4 = +2$ |
| | First: | B | |
| | Second: | A | |
| | Third: | C | |

## Exercises

1. A manufacturer of stereo speakers produces five main types of high-quality speaker. The company considers itself a job shop. The single production line produces lots of each type of speaker on an irregular schedule. Price competition has been severe, and the company's profits have eroded. A conglomerate is buying the stereo manufacturer and intends to invest

a considerable amount of cash to improve production control and cut production costs. What should the money be invested in?

2. An advertising agency has 12 departments. Every small ad job must pass through at least 6 of them, medium-sized ads through 9 of the departments, and large ads for major clients through all 12 departments. Typically, over 100 ad jobs (each a separate ad for a separate customer's product) are in process at any one time. Most are late, a contributing reason why the agency has lost a few long-standing clients. What should be done to improve on-time performance?
3. A scheduler at QUIDCO, Inc., is working up a schedule for making 20 of part number 0077AX. The inventory planner advises that the order be released this week, week of day 90, and that the order is due on the week of day 115, when it will be needed to go into a parent item. QUIDCO employs closed-loop MRP.
   *a.* How would the inventory planner have determined the week due and the week of release? If the inventory planner has determined these dates, doesn't that constitute rescheduling and eliminate the need for the scheduler to do anything? Discuss.
   *b.* The A in the part number signifies a costly item. For A items, the following rules are used for computing operation lead times:
      (1) Allow eight standard hours per day: round upward to whole (eight-hour) days.
      (2) Allow no time between operations. A items receive priority material handling.
      (3) Allow one day to inspect.
      (4) Release the job to the stockroom four days before it is to be started into production.
      (5) All dates are treated as end of the eight-hour day.

   Schedule a shop order for the item, assuming that the part goes through three operations plus inspection. You make up the setup times and operation times such that the schedule will fit between days 90 and 115. Explain.
   *c.* Compare the operation lead-time rules for part number 0077AX with the rules in Example 16-2 for part number 1005CX. Why should a more expensive item have different lead-time rules? (Hint: WIP has something to do with it.)
4. The maintenance department has two renovation orders that are being scheduled. Order 1 requires these three jobs or tasks: 20 days of wiring, 7 days of drywall work, and 10 days of painting. Order 2 takes 11 days of drywall followed by 8 days of painting.
   *a.* Draw a Gantt chart showing the workloads (backlogs) for each of the three jobs (wiring, drywall, and paint).
   *b.* Draw a Gantt chart showing the two orders back-scheduled, the first with completion due at the end of day 40 and the second due at the end of day 20.
   *c.* Draw a Gantt chart with the two orders forward scheduled. In what situation would forward scheduling for these three trades be useful?
5. Four jobs are on the desk of the scheduler for a firm's minor construction department. Each job begins with masonry, followed by carpentry and wiring. Work-order data are as follows:

| *Work Order* | *Estimated Task Time—Masonry* | *Estimated Task Time—Carpentry* | *Estimated Task Time—Wiring* |
|---|---|---|---|
| 58 | 2 weeks | 3 weeks | $1\frac{1}{2}$ weeks |
| 59 | 1 week | $1\frac{1}{2}$ weeks | 1 week |
| 60 | 3 weeks | 2 weeks | 4 weeks |
| 61 | 5 weeks | $\frac{1}{2}$ week | 2 weeks |

*a.* Prepare a Gantt chart scheduling the four jobs through the three crafts (crafts are rows on your chart). Use first come, first served as the priority rule for scheduling (first *job* first—the whole job). Assume that a craft cannot divide its time between two work orders. How many weeks do the four jobs take?

*b.* Repeat (*a*) but use the shortest processing-time rule instead of first come, first served. Now how many weeks are required?

*c.* Three weeks pass. The following progress is reported to the scheduler:

Masonry completed on WO 58.

Masonry not started on WO 59, 60, or 61.

Carpentry half completed on WO 58.

Show the progress on a Gantt control chart (using part *a* data).

*d.* In this problem situation, each shop is fully loaded as the jobs are sequenced and scheduled. It is finite-capacity loading. What is there about minor construction work of this kind that makes scheduling and loading so uncomplicated (relative to job-lot parts fabrication)?

6. The following Gantt chart shows a scheduled project task and progress as of a given date:

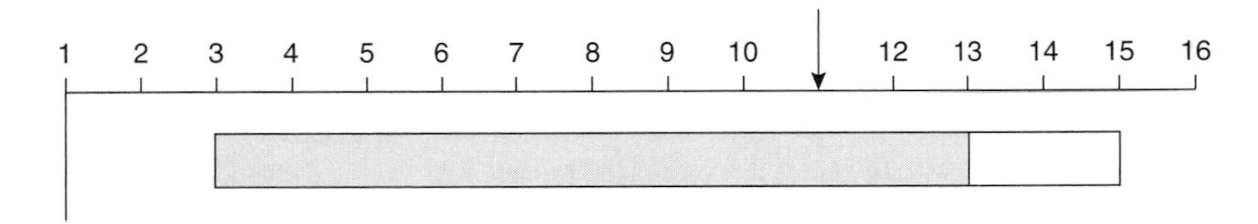


*a.* What is the present date, and what is the percent of completion for the task? How many days ahead or behind schedule are shown?

*b.* Redraw the chart as it will look tomorrow if the entire task is completed. How many days ahead or behind schedule does your chart represent?

*c.* Saturdays and Sundays are not worked and are not identified on the chart. Explain how the dating system treats holidays.

7. Open Air Furniture Company makes patio furniture. There are just three work centers: rough saw, finish saw, and assemble.

Production control keeps track of total workloads for use in short-term scheduling and capacity management. Each week's component-parts orders are translated into machine hours in rough saw and finish saw and into labor hours in assembly. Current machine-hour and labor-hour loads are as follows:

| | *Rough Saw* | *Finish Saw* | *Assemble* |
|---|---|---|---|
| Current week | 270 | 470 | 410 |
| Week 2 | 40 | 110 | 100 |
| Week 3 | — | 40 | 50 |
| Week 4 | — | 30 | 15 |
| Weekly capacity | 150 | 225 | 190 |

*a.* Is operations dispatching likely to be required at any work centers? Explain.

*b.* Is this the type of firm that is likely to rely heavily on expediting? Explain.

8. The following chart shows projected loads for one work center:

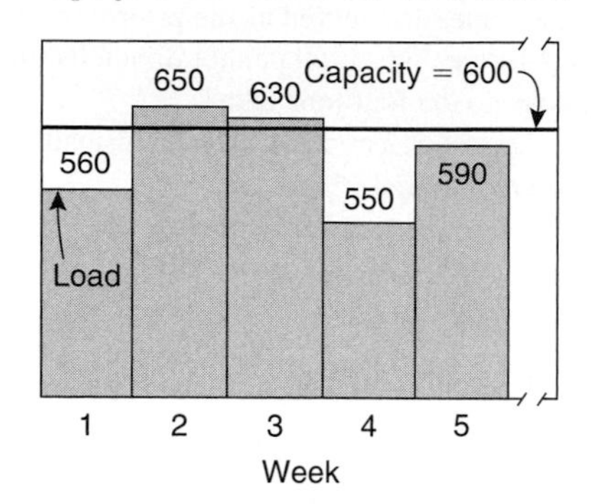


*a.* What may the scheduler do to help correct the imbalance between load and capacity in some weeks? Discuss, including any limitations or difficulties in correcting the imbalance.

*b.* How would the load report be produced?

9. On day 280, the daily priority report for the nickel-plating work center includes job number 2228. That job is due out of plating on day 278, and its planned run time is one day. If an additional day is allowed for move and queue time, what is the operation slack? Show your calculation. How should these calculated results be interpreted?

10. Jerrybuilt Machines, Inc., uses the least-slack priority rule. On shop calendar day 62, the following shop orders will be in work center 30:

| *Shop Order* | *Move/Queue Allowance* | *Operation Time* | *Operation Due Date* |
|---|---|---|---|
| 889 | 2 days | 3 days | 68 |
| 916 | 2 days | 1 day | 64 |
| 901 | 2 days | 1 day | 69 |
| 894 | 1 day | 2 days | 62 |

Calculate the slack for each shop order, and arrange your calculated results in list form as they would appear on a daily dispatch list.

11. Five jobs are in a queue waiting to be released into a work center. These jobs, their required processing times, and their due dates are given in the table below. They are listed in the order of their arrival at the work center.

| *Job* | *Required Time (days)* | *Due Date (days hence)* |
|---|---|---|
| A | 3 | 7 |
| B | 6 | 9 |
| C | 2 | 10 |
| D | 4 | 3 |
| E | 1 | 4 |

Determine the proper job sequence using each of the following prioritizing rules: FCFS, SPT, EDD, and LS. For each solution, compute the average throughput time, the average number of jobs in the work center, and the average late time.

12. Five jobs are in a queue waiting to be released into a work center. These jobs, their required processing times, and their due dates are given in the table below. They are listed in the order of their arrival at the work center.

| *Job* | *Required Time (days)* | *Due Date (days hence)* |
|---|---|---|
| A | 5 | 7 |
| B | 8 | 12 |
| C | 10 | 11 |
| D | 4 | 8 |
| E | 6 | 9 |

Determine the proper job sequence using each of the following prioritizing rules: FCFS, SPT, EDD, and LS. For each solution, compute the average throughput time, the average number of jobs in the work center, and the average late time.

13. The following data apply to three shop orders that happen to end up in work center 17 on day 120:

| *Shop Order* | *Preceding Work Center* | *Day Arrival in Work Center 17* | *Queue Time plus Run Time in Work Center 17* | *Date Due Out of Work Center 17* |
|---|---|---|---|---|
| 300 | 28 | 119 | 5 days | 124 |
| 310 | 14 | 117 | 6 days | 130 |
| 290 | 13 | 118 | 4 days | 125 |

Moves from one work center to another take one day. Calculate operation slack for the three jobs, and arrange them in priority order, first to last.

14. On day 12, shop order number 222 is in the blanking work center; it requires two days in blanking (including all waits, setups, moves, etc.) and is due out of blanking on day 15. Also on day 12, shop order 333 is in the same work center; it requires three days in blanking and is due out on day 17. Finally, on day 12, shop order 444 is in the work center; it requires one day and is due out on day 12.

    Determine which order should be run first, which second, and which third. Calculate slack for each order to prove your answer. What is the meaning of the slack value you get for order 444?

15. For *a*, *b*, and *c*, explain the applicability and describe a suitable approach to (1) scheduling, (2) dispatching, including a priority control rule, and (3) expediting.
    *a*. Getting a driver's license, four stops: written test, driving test, photo, and payment of fee and receipt of license.
    *b*. Getting your car repaired at a large auto dealer: wheel alignment, electrical system, and installation of a new bumper.

*c*. Manufacturing of a wide variety of models of metal office furniture, all models passing through four manufacturing areas: metal shop for cutting and forming the component parts, welding, painting, and final assembly.

16. A central sales office has seen its expediting (hand-carried orders) increase from 2 to 5 to over 10 percent in the last two years. Nonexpedited orders take at least a week to be processed. Suggest improvements in the priority and order-processing system.
17. The city planning department processes all requests for building and construction permits. The permit process, involving eight departments, has been unsatisfactory, and the mayor has appointed a new planning department administrator, who has stated his intention to install a computer system for logging and tracking the flow of all orders. The assistant administrator is arguing against the plan. She says it will be costly, add no value, and may not work. Elaborate upon her argument, including suggestions for an alternative approach.
18. In the diagram shown below, Work Center 22 is a persistent bottleneck. A scheduler has two jobs, to release into gateway (input) work centers as shown—job #115 into Work Center 3 and job #106 into Work Center 5. Routings reveal that each of the jobs must travel to one intermediate work center before reaching Work Center 22. Dotted lines indicate that other job routings also include the two intermediate work centers (12 and 19).

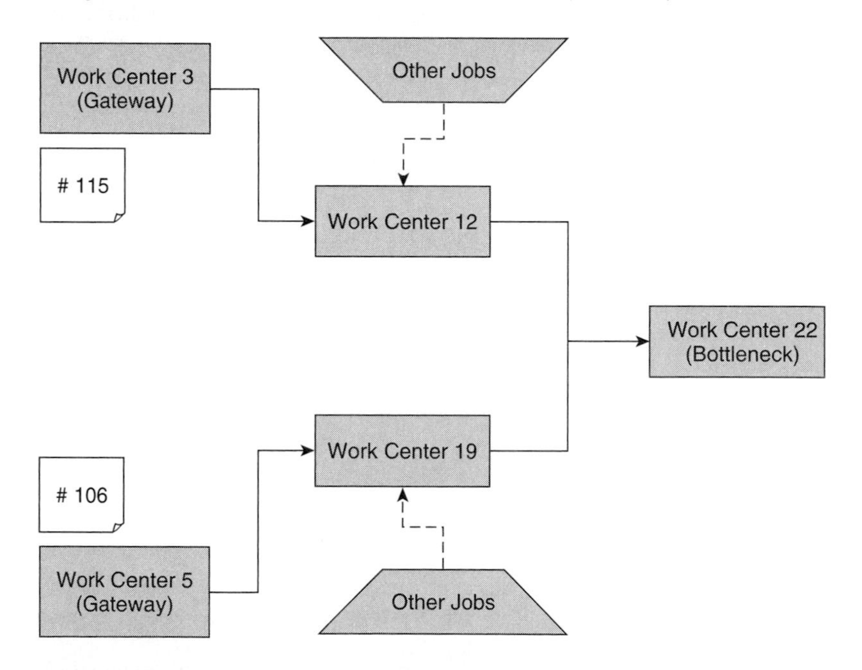


Suppose the scheduler knows that each of the two jobs should require one-half day (4 hours) in Work Center 22 and that both can be scheduled to arrive in Work Center 22 on day 203.

*a*. If the scheduler releases the jobs into the respective gateway work centers today, can we expect them both to be completed in Work Center 22 on day 203 as scheduled? Explain your response. (Hint: A "yes" or a "no" response might work nicely; your grade depends on your explanation.)

*b*. If you were responsible for operations in this company, what steps might you take (short and long term) to ensure that a "yes" response to part *a* is the correct response? Briefly explain your rationale and the results that you expect.

CHAPTER 17

# MANAGING PROJECTS

> "Concorde was the first of an important new breed of aerospace projects: those built through international cooperation [i.e., Britain and France, 1962–1973]. It was a huge technology-push 'spearhead' project, whose basic requirement was simply to carry passengers safely and supersonically. Its development represented a continual struggle to reconcile two entirely different requirements: sustained supersonic flight and subsonic approach. Its cost escalation and schedule delays were huge. This occasioned much public criticism and governmental chagrin. The British governmental psyche was so traumatized that its response to suggestions for high-risk major projects for many decades subsequently was invariably one of nervous disinclination.
>
> "In the end, Concorde proved to be a commercial disaster for its developers . . . a technological triumph yet a plane designed on the massive misconception that speed was the principal criterion for airliner success; an aircraft project that was set up with no regard to the most basic rules of project management, such as a clearly identified owner organization, and one which experienced severe problems of design and technology mismanagement; a project whose chances of success were severely compromised by the two external factors of changes in fuel prices and environmental opposition."[1]

The opening comments on the Concorde come from Peter Morris in his 1994 masterwork, *The Management of Projects.* Morris calls the discipline "deceptively simple." It is, he says, "*integrating* everything that needs to be done (typically utilizing a number of special project management tools and techniques) as the project evolves through its *life cycle* in order to ensure that all objectives are achieved."[2] He notes, however, that while project management "is now comparatively mature, and recognized by thousands if not millions of managers as vitally important, it is in many respects still stuck in a 1960s time warp." By that, Morris means that practitioners and academics mostly take a tools and techniques view of the subject. "Few address the larger, more strategic issues that crucially affect the success of projects."[3]

This third and concluding chapter in our study of types of OM environments examines the complex, unique nature of projects. We shall consider, in order, six aspects of effective project management:

**project**
Large-scale, one-of-a-kind endeavor; employs large amounts of diverse resources.

1. Strategic implications of projects.
2. High-performance project teams.

3. Project organization structures.
4. Information sharing.
5. Tools and techniques.
6. Continuous improvement in projects.

## Projects and Strategy

Morris's assessment of the current lack of strategic focus in much of project management is noteworthy on two fronts: First, contemporary organizations have a crucial need for projects *as vehicles* for accomplishing strategic objectives. Second, failure to consider the overall strategic impact of a particular project on the organization's environment is nothing short of negligence, especially in this era of heightened social awareness of corporate conduct.

### *Projects: Vehicles for Improvement*

Numerous large-scale activities that successful companies must pursue in order to meet strategic objectives call for project management. Projects demand large resource inputs, they incorporate countless value-adding operations, and their effects (ought to) cut wide swaths across organization departments.

For example, we recall a point from Chapter 8's discussion of benchmarking: Robert Camp identifies the targets of process-based benchmarking as business-wide processes that contribute most to company goals.[4] Camp goes on to list an array of 28 tools and techniques, old and new, that Xerox uses in its 10-step benchmarking efforts. Project management—the only technique to span all 10 steps—ties the whole system together.[5] ISO 9000 registration is another popular, large-scale effort of widespread organizational impact; it, too, demands project management (see the Into Practice box "Project Management Applied . . .").

Later in this chapter, we consider a small-scale construction example, and in Chapter 7, we examined issues relating to product design and development. We could also make strong cases for project management in many other facets of contemporary operations management: developing quick-response systems (Chapter 10), supplier partnership networks (Chapter 6), quick-changeover projects (Chapter 10), and facility and process re-layout efforts (Chapter 14). In sum, whenever the task at hand is relatively large, complex, or inclusive, operations managers and their colleagues throughout the firm ought to be thinking project.

### *Environmental Impact*

Projects are expensive and invite internal and external scrutiny. Inside the organization, favorite projects can get the lion's share of resources; employees not on a high-impact project team may feel slighted, perhaps with good reason. Early in the project planning sequence, managers must ask, How will this project affect the organization as a whole?

INTO PRACTICE

## Project Management Applied—ISO 9000 Registration

Skillful management of a project—that's what ISO 9000-series registration is all about. AT&T Global Information Systems' Network Products Division achieved ISO 9001 registration in 13 months after approval of its registration project plan.

Addressing the early planning stages, David S. Huyink, project manager of the AT&T effort, and Craig Westover, who conducted the project's early benchmarking efforts, contend that ISO 9000 project planning must put a "... boundary around the process. ... your documented project plan defines the system. It defines the output (ISO 9000 registration), it defines the process (the actions the organization must take to achieve registration), and it defines the input (the resources required to support the necessary and sufficient actions)."

Source: David Stevenson Huyink and Craig Westover, *ISO 9000: Motivating the People, Mastering the Process, Achieving Registration!* (Burr Ridge, Ill.: Irwin Professional Publishing, 1994), pp. 52 and 280.

External scrutiny occurs when outsiders ask similar questions about the project's impact beyond the organization's boundaries.

Like the MRP systems discussed in Chapter 13, project management tools (considered later in this chapter) are products of the computer era, with formative development paralleling the rise of business computing in the 1960s. Morris observes that many of these early (1960s) projects experienced difficulties because interest was drawn to the excitement of developing the computer tools. Little attention went to management issues like technical uncertainly and contract strategy, or to the emergence of a new class of external factors such as community opposition and environmental impact.[6]

But after a decade or so, evidence suggesting the need for a broader outlook by project managers had begun to accumulate. Morris notes:

> The projects of the early-to-mid-1970s were in fact pointing to a much fuller view of projects management, i.e., that
>
> (a) The impact of projects on their environment is an essential dimension of their chances of success.
>
> (b) This "environmental" impact is measured along several dimensions—economic, political, community, ecological.
>
> (c) Therefore, those responsible for the initiation or accomplishment of such projects should strive to influence the project's chances of success along these "external" environmental dimensions, as well as ensuring that the internal project management functions are being carried out effectively.[7]

By the 1980s, large-scale growth in the project form of management in most companies stretched experienced project managers and their tools thin. As a result, project management is back in the limelight in the research community, as well as in the business world. Greg Hutchins, a principal with Quality Plus Engineering, a Portland,

Oregon, based consulting firm, notes that in recent years, the demand for project management services has skyrocketed.

> What's driving the overwhelming interest in and application of project management? Several things . . .
>
> Many companies are replacing their paper processes with collaborative, often Web-based, digital processes. Companies want things done faster, easier, better—and, of course, cheaper. Customers want companies to react faster to problems and opportunities.
>
> Companies want to differentiate themselves from the competition. The best way is to provide better service and products . . . through project managing processes, people, and information.[8]

Nor surprisingly, the need for faster response applies to project management as it does to other OM settings. By the end of the 1990s, many project-savvy companies had cut their project completion times by half or more. Though tackling jobs much larger than their Kaizen Blitz counterparts that we studied in Chapter 16, today's project managers seem to share the obsession for faster results.

Main advances in project management lie not so much in new tools or techniques as in concentrated efforts to ensure better fit for projects within the overall business strategy and mission. Indeed, "better, faster, and cheaper" are familiar themes for strategic competitiveness that we have sounded often throughout this book. While the full story of project management effectiveness probably has not yet been written, we spell out what is known of it in the rest of the chapter.

## Project Management: Teamwork and Organization

As in many other aspects of operations management, high-performance teamwork deserves a prominent place in effective project management. Teamwork performance, in turn, is affected by how the project is organized and by the flow of information.

### *High-Performance Teamwork*

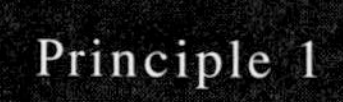


Team up with next and final customer.

Coincident with increasing reliance on projects to carry out company strategies, more people appear to be spending more time in project work. That includes early and continuing involvement of people who formerly had late involvement or no involvement in new-product projects: suppliers; customers; quality specialists; equipment, tool, and materials people; frontline supervisors and associates; and others. Including these people greatly improves the quality of project outcomes, especially if they collect data on mishaps and hold team meetings to improve processes and prevent the mishaps from happening again. Improved project quality is reflected by less project rework and scrap, in addition to speeding up project completion.

While broad representation on project teams is desirable, more people working more hours on a single project may not necessarily lead to quicker project completion time (see the Into Practice box "The More the Messier").

INTO PRACTICE

## The More the Messier

Marvin Patterson, director of corporate engineering at Hewlett-Packard Company, offers evidence on the drawbacks of having too many people on a project team:

> We observed this . . . in the completion of two projects sequentially. [The first was] a project requiring 127 new mechanical parts [and] six mechanical engineers over a period of three years. In a follow-up project, a low-cost roll of the same product, the task was to reduce the number of mechanical parts by two-thirds, thereby reducing the manufacturing costs. That job took 17 [mechanical engineers] four years. What happened? When we asked, the answer came back, "We had so many meetings, we had to talk so much to coordinate the design over 17 people, that the communications burden became onerous."

Source: Marvin L. Patterson with Sam Lightman, *Accelerating Innovation: Improving the Process of Product Development* (New York: Van Nostrand Reinhold, 1993), pp. 184–85 (TS176.P367)

### *Project Organization Structures*

Amount of time that people spend on projects versus working in their functional departments is partly determined by positioning in the organization. The extent of project emphasis in the organization structure can range from zero to total. Three degrees of project organization are shown in Exhibit 17-1, numbered 1 through 3; they are flanked by two nonproject forms, numbered 0 and 00. The five structures are explained below.

0. *Pure functional organization.* In this structure there is no project activity; everyone in every functional department is engaged in ongoing operations. In some slow-to-change organizations, such as a government agency out of the public eye or a monopolistic business in a remote area, this lack of projects may persist for years.
1. *Project coordinator.* This is the weakest approach to project management: A coordinator has a short-term assignment but no project budget or staff. The project coordinator's limited activities revolve around arranging meetings, working out schedules, and expediting. The effective coordinator tries to achieve teamwork by working closely with liaison people in the functional organization, where the real power rests.
2. *Product/commodity/brand manager or project engineer.* This second project form involves a career-track manager or engineer, sometimes with a small staff and limited budgetary authority. Responsibility is for an evolving product family (e.g., commercial loans), brand (e.g., Yellow Pages), or succession of small engineering projects (e.g., civil engineering/construction). To be effective, the management or project engineering team must develop and work closely with a cohesive processing team from the functional base, where most of the work is performed.

**EXHIBIT 17-1 Project Management Organization Structures**

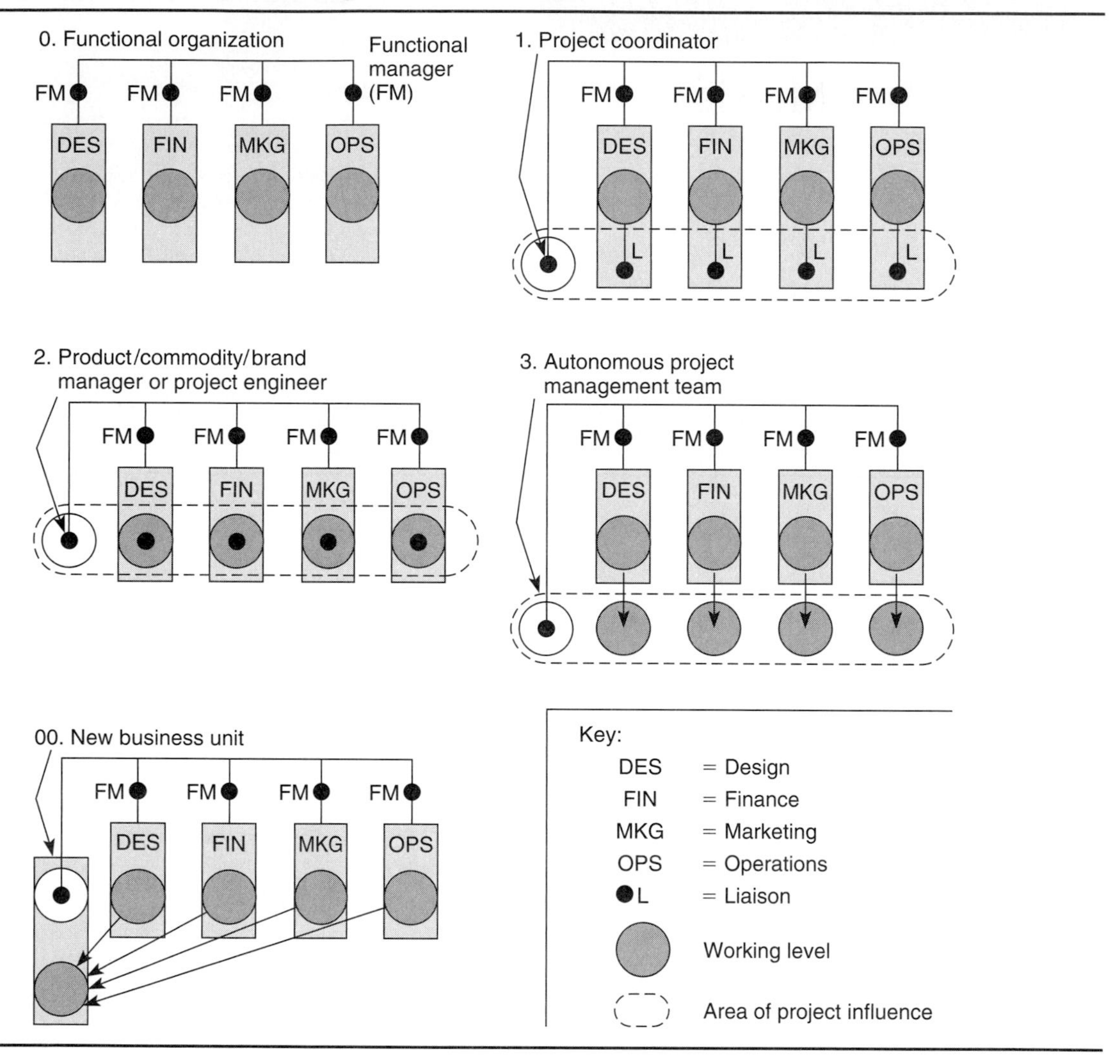


Source: Adapted from Steven C. Wheelwright and Kim B. Clark, *Revolutionizing Product Development: Quantum Leaps in Speed, Efficiency, and Quality* (New York: The Free Press, 1992), p. 191 (HF5415.153.W44).

3. *Autonomous project management team.* Here, the project manager has money to hire a full team out of the functional base or from outside the firm to perform the work in its own space with its own equipment and other resources. The project manager is usually a high-level person who may even outrank the functional managers. Newer versions of this form of project management have been called "tiger" or "bandit" teams because of their aggressive, focused approach and disregard for practices standard in the rest of the firm.

INTO PRACTICE

## Three Types of Projects—Chaparral Steel

Wheelwright and Clark's research suggests that most companies force-fit a standard approach to all projects, which leads to underpowered big projects and overkilled small ones. Chaparral Steel (which appears often on lists of world-class companies) avoids these problems by having three different project management approaches:

- Incremental projects in the $100,000 to $200,000 cost range lasting about two months. These projects (40 or more likely to be in progress on average) are performed by functional subgroups and a lightweight project manager.
- Platform projects in the $500,000 to $1 million range requiring 12–24 months to complete. These projects (three to five under way on average) are led by heavyweight project managers, who usually have moved from a department head position and will return to that position after project completion.
- Major advanced-development projects in the $3 million to $5 million expenditure range requiring three to five years to complete. These projects (usually only about two in progress at any given time) are led by one of seven general foremen.

Source: Adapted from Steven C. Wheelwright and Kim B. Clark, *Revolutionizing Product Development: Quantum Leaps in Speed, Efficiency, and Quality* (New York: The Free Press 1992), pp. 216–17 (HF5415.153.W44).

00. *New business unit.* Occasionally a super project is established as, or grows into, a separate division or business unit. In effect, it becomes a minicompany, a new subsidiary perhaps.

The three project management types in Exhibit 17-1 are general categories, not an exhaustive list. There are other ways to organize, staff, and fund projects, and many companies devise their own variations. See, for example, Chaparral Steel's three approaches (Into Practice box), which are variants of the three project management forms in Exhibit 17-1.

Project teams organized in any of the project management forms in Exhibit 17-1 may look outside the firm for team members. Outside teams could include fully staffed supplier or customer projects; for best results, the inside project group should establish cross-memberships with the outside project teams.

An excellent example of a company that gets maximum service from outside project teams is McDonald's Corporation. Out of a long string of McDonald's products that met its requirements for quality, speed, efficiency, production in a squeezed space, popularity, and profit, only one, the Quarter Pounder, was developed by an inside project team. All the rest were developed by franchised restaurant owners (the customers of McDonald's Corp.) and hard-charging, innovative suppliers.

One of McDonald's successes, Chicken McNuggets, was launched in 1980. The basic nuggets idea emerged after an inside project team had spent 10 years working toward a chicken product. But the nuggets still had to be developed. Bud Sweeney, an account executive at Gorton's (the frozen fish company) came to the rescue. On loan from Gorton's, Sweeney organized and led a chicken SWAT team (like a tiger team), which found help from several sources. Gorton's provided the unique tempura coating. McDonald's product development and quality assurance people handled specifications and test marketing. A chef on loan from a Chicago hotel came up with four dips. Keystone Foods, a frozen beef patty supplier, developed production lines to debone chicken and equipment to cut it into random-looking chunks. And Tyson Foods, a chicken processor, developed a special new breed of bird, called Mr. McDonald, that was almost twice the weight of an ordinary fryer, which made deboning easier.[9]

### *Information Sharing*

Members of the project team can do little without information, which may be likened to raw materials in a factory. However, sharing information goes against the grain of most people in Western cultures.

While we applaud the Western spirit of individualism—a healthful source of innovation—we do not want team members to withhold information from other team members. Information is power, and project teams with wide access to information, including each other's, are powerful and effective.

But what is the mechanism for pulling knowledge out of people's heads, personal files, desk drawers, and other hiding places? Jeffrey Funk details systematic procedures for information sharing at Mitsubishi Electric Company in Japan, based upon his two-year assignment working as a project engineer at that company.[10] Every scrap of information gleaned from visits to libraries, customers, trade shows, conferences, committee meetings, and so forth, is required to be written up and inserted into common files, fully cross referenced. Newly hired engineers at Mitsubishi spend a good deal of their orientation period getting to know the filing system and the rules for its use. The box "Ownership of Information" sums up these points about team ownership of information in contrast to private ownership.

**Principle 3**

Gain unified purpose via shared information.

CONTRAST

## Ownership of Information

**Private Property**

Task-related information retained by the holder of the position in the holder's personal space. Experience and training belong to the individual.

**Team Ownership**

Task-related information, experience, and training belong to the team and the company and should reside in files easily accessible to all team members.

At Mitsubishi, the information generally went into common file cabinets. The concept applies equally well to computer files. Marvin Patterson describes a project team at three geographically disbursed Hewlett-Packard sites: Waldbronn, Germany; Avondale, Pennsylvania; and Palo Alto, California. Each group was working on different parts of an operating system software project.

> The Palo Alto group agreed to maintain the current version of the total operating system and make it remotely accessible to the other sites through a WAN [wide-area network]. The next version . . . would then . . . be made available for remote access. Within minutes both the Avondale and Waldbronn teams would have the current system running at their sites, and development could continue with all teams once again synchronized. This development effort progressed well and resulted in a successful product.
>
> In contrast, an earlier effort, before the age of WANs, attempted . . . the same thing through shipment of magnetic tapes. Shipment delays and time lost passing through customs hampered engineering efforts immensely. Engineers in the three sites were only rarely working with the same version of the operating system. Often as not, recently designed code would prove to be incompatible with operating system updates that had been two weeks or more in transit.[11]

The information sharing referred to so far is mainly what is used to create project outcomes. Besides the *operating information,* the project group must manage project *planning and control information,* our next topic.

## Project Representation

The size and complexity of project operations translate into a sizable project management task. A set of tools and techniques having the abbreviations CPM and PERT is tailor-made for the job.

The **critical path method (CPM)** was developed by Catalytic Construction Company in 1957 as a method for improving planning and control of a project to construct a plant for Du Pont Corporation. CPM was credited with having saved time and money on that project, and today it is well known and widely used in the construction industry.

The **program evaluation and review technique (PERT)** was developed in 1958 by Booz Allen & Hamilton Inc., a large consulting firm, along with U.S. Navy Special Projects Office. PERT was developed to provide more intensive management of the Polaris missile project—one of the largest research and development projects ever undertaken. Nevertheless, it was completed in record time, about four years. PERT got much of the credit and soon was widely adopted in the R&D industry as a tool for intensive project management.

A few early differences between CPM and PERT have mostly disappeared, and it is convenient to think of PERT and CPM as being one and the same, going by the combined term PERT/CPM. The construction industry still calls it CPM, and R&D people, PERT; a few other terminological differences are noted later.

PERT/CPM begins with the work breakdown structure and the network, graphical models that represent (model or mimic) the project itself.

### *Work Breakdown Structure*

The **work breakdown structure** is for a project what the bill of materials is for a job. It is a representation of the building-block structure of the end product: major project modules, secondary components, and so on. To illustrate, we shall use a familiar example: home construction.

A work breakdown structure for building a house is shown in Exhibit 17-2. Part A is a preferred way to develop a work breakdown structure; break down the project into tangible ends or outputs at levels 2 and 3. Part B is a functional-oriented way to draw it and is *not* recommended. The functional-oriented chart does not have tangible products whose completion may be assigned as a unit to a single manager or team. Carpentry, for example, is a function that results in several tangible outcomes: forms for footings, the house's frame, finished cabinets, and so forth. Painting, landscaping, and masonry also are found throughout the project and also result in several clearly identifiable outcomes. When the project is delayed or resources are idled, painters can conveniently blame carpenters, and so forth. If managers supervise given parts of the *project,* they can work to secure cooperation from the various crafts. The idea is to get each craft closely

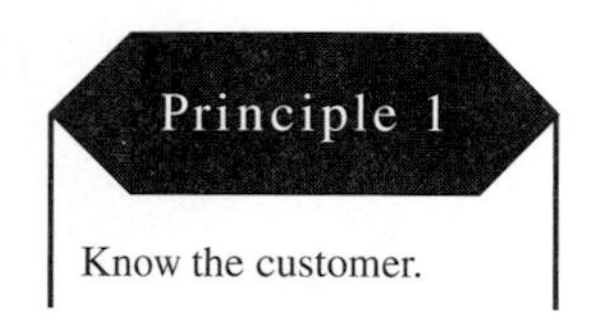


**Exhibit 17-2 Work Breakdown Structures for a House-Building Project**

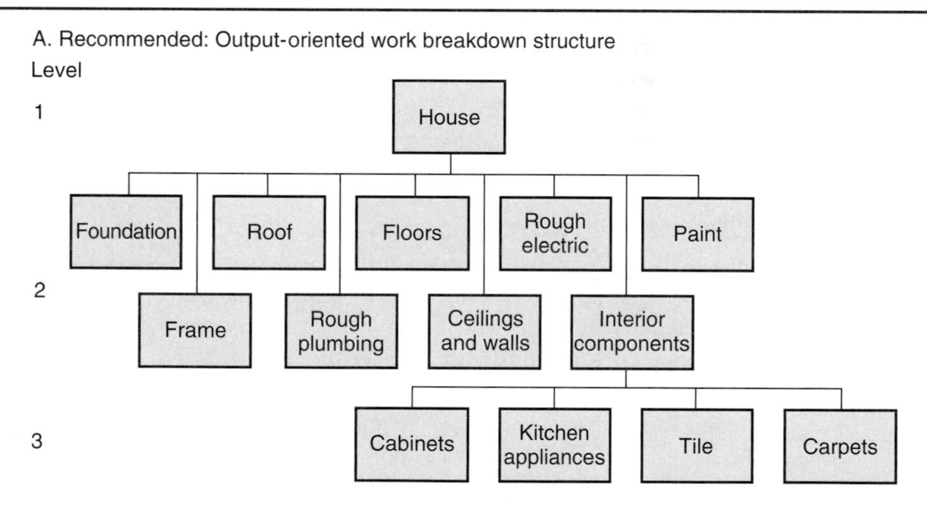


B. Not recommended: Functional-oriented work breakdown structure

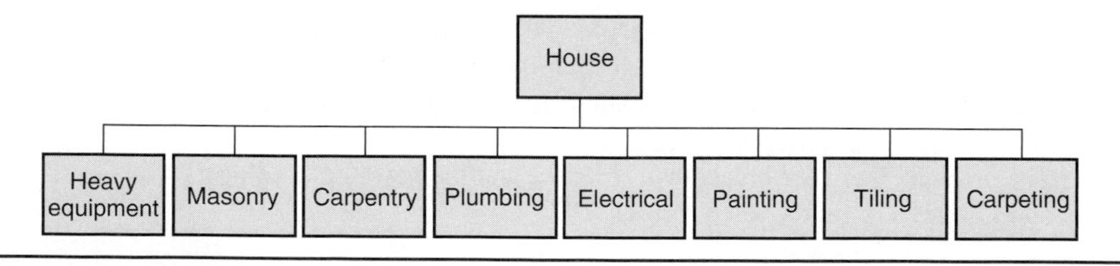

connected to a customer, the next craft, in a joint effort to complete a segment of the house correctly with no delays or wasted resources.

### *Network*

A project consists of dozens, or even hundreds or thousands, of related tasks that must be performed in some sequence. PERT/CPM requires the sequence to be carefully defined in the form of a project **network** (see Exhibit 17-3). The starting and ending nodes of the network are joined by a series of arrows and intermediate nodes that collectively reveal the sequence and relationships of the project tasks.

Networks facilitate project management in at least two ways. First, the immensity of most projects makes it hard to remember and visualize the day-to-day and task-level activities, but a computerized network model remembers with ease. Second, the network aids in managing a large project as a system, consisting of subprojects (subsystems), sub-subprojects, and so on. For example, two of the successive nodes in Exhibit 17-3 could represent the start and end nodes of a subproject, for which a separate, more detailed network could be drawn. Alternatively, the network in Exhibit 17-3 might represent one subproject in an even larger project.

Although networks are valuable project management tools, they must be kept in perspective. First, as the project unfolds, initial planning networks go by the wayside; in large projects, hundreds of network changes can occur every month. Second, just as forecasts are more dubious for distant time periods, time estimates and even sequencing for distant network activities are at best educated guesses. Detailed analysis of an initial planning network—especially of its latter portions—is often unwarranted. Drawing again from the work of Morris:

> One pattern that has emerged for virtually all projects is that once "downstream implementation" begins—after project definition is basically completed and contracts for implementation are let—the amount of work and management control and coordination will increase substantially.[12]

**EXHIBIT 17-3 A PERT/CPM Network**

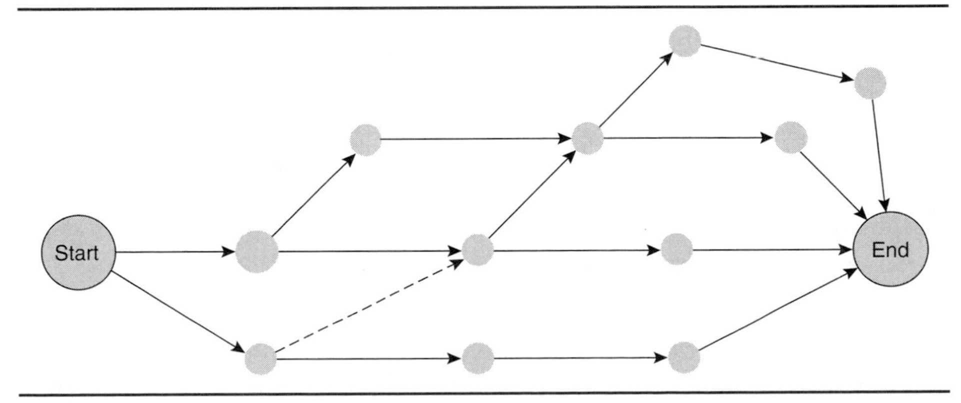

This shift from planning to control and coordination puts project managers in the driver's seat. If they don't like what the network shows about the project status, they shuffle resources or acquire new ones to move the project in a direction more to their liking. After all, they're managing the project, not the network.

## Phased PERT/CPM

Once the project team gets the PERT/CPM models built, members may use the models for capacity planning, task sequencing, projecting completions, identifying most-critical tasks, simulating project change alternatives, scheduling, and controlling. These multiple uses of PERT/CPM tend to group into four phases of project management:

1. *Project planning and sequencing.* Activities in this phase resemble product/service design, process planning, and routing activities in repetitive and job operations.
2. *Time estimating and path analysis.* Time estimating for projects is like time estimating for job operations, but path analysis is unique to project management.
3. *Project scheduling.* Scheduling projects has some elements of both repetitive and job scheduling. But since a project is a single complex endeavor, schedulers must contend with many scheduling dependencies.
4. *Reporting and updating.* Treating the project as a single, large unit of work permits project managers to intensively control using the management-by-exception principle.

**management-by-exception**
Tightly manage what is straying off course—the exceptions—and ignore the rest.

With all four phases, PERT/CPM is more than just tools and techniques. It becomes a management system, with each of the four phases as subsystems. While most projects are not complex enough to warrant the expense of the full system treatment, very large scale projects often qualify. We examine each of the four subsystems next.

### *Project Planning and Sequencing*

In the first subsystem, the project management staff holds meetings with those who will be carrying out the project tasks. In one set of meetings, they develop the work breakdown structure; from that, in a second set of meetings, they complete the network. Using the work breakdown structure of Exhibit 17-2 as our example, we'll proceed with the second set of meetings of the project staff and frontline construction people.

**Task Lists, Network Segments, and Whole Networks.** Exhibit 17-4 shows how the project staff gets started on network development: Starting with one of the bottom-level elements of the work breakdown structure, the frontline experts make lists of tasks necessary to complete the element. Part A shows three of the project elements (cabinets, kitchen appliances, and tile) with tasks listed underneath each. Connecting the tasks into a logical sequence, forming a network segment as shown in Part B, is next. Kitchen wall

**EXHIBIT 17-4 Translating Task Lists into Network Segments**

A. Task lists for project elements

| Cabinets (1) | Kitchen appliances (2) | Tile (3) |
|---|---|---|
| Install kitchen wall cabinets | Install range | Lay kitchen tile |
| Install kitchen floor cabinets | Install dishwasher | Lay bathroom tile |
| Install bathroom vanity | Install hood/fan | Lay hall tile |

B. Network segments

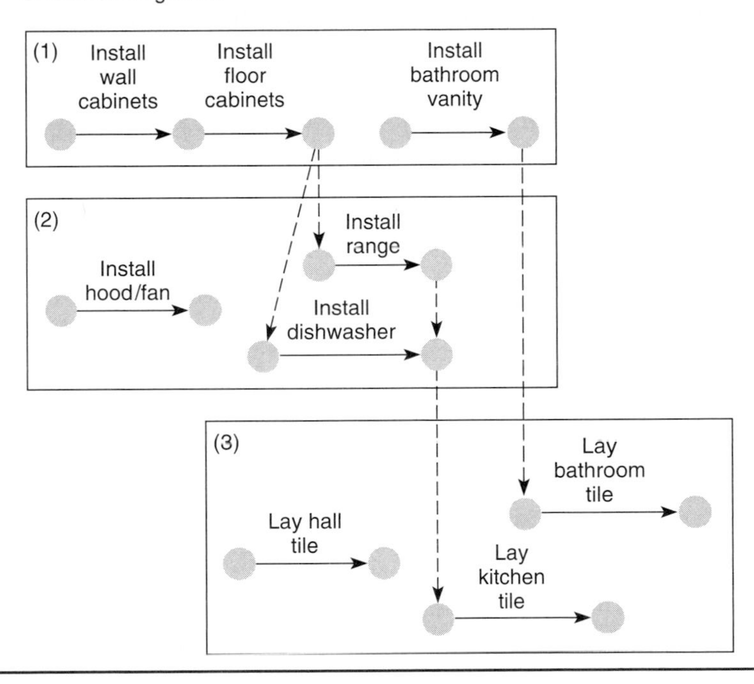


Source: Adapted from Fred Luthans, *Introduction to Management: A Contingency Approach* (Richard J. Schonberger, contributing author) (New York: McGraw-Hill, 1976), p. 88 (HD31.L86). Used with permission.

cabinets go up early, since they are easier to install if the lower cabinets are not in the way. Floor cabinets are installed with gaps for the range and dishwasher, which are put in place next. Kitchen tile is laid after the kitchen cabinet and appliances have been installed; if laid sooner, the tile might not butt closely against the cabinets and appliances and also might get marred. Bathroom tile follows the bathroom vanity for the same reason. Since there appears to be no reason why the hood/fan and thc hall tile should come either before or after the other tasks shown, the project staff temporarily draws them unlinked to other tasks. Later, when they put the full network together, they'll find the logical place in which to fit the hood/fan and hall tile.

The rectangles numbered 1, 2, and 3 in Exhibit 17-4B are not essential; they merely show craft groupings. Note that it would serve no purpose to group all kitchen activities together, all bathroom activities together, and so forth; the kitchen is a room, but it is neither a product to be separately managed nor the responsibility of a separate craft. More important than the craft groupings in the rectangles are the dashed lines between the rectangles. They signify connections between the task of one craft and the task of the following craft.

Finally, the project staff combines the network segments into the full project network. Exhibit 17-5 is the result, except that, for study purposes, we've simplified it; for example, this house has no tile, carpets, or bathroom vanity. This completes the first subsystem. The project management staff has a reasonable representation of the sequence of project activities. It is a useful tool for coordinating and monitoring completions.

**Networking Conventions.** A few rules and conventions of networking follow.

1. *One destination.* A PERT/CPM network (except segments) has only one start event and one end event. (In Exhibit 17-5, these are numbered 1 and 18.) To bring this

**EXHIBIT 17-5 Network for House Construction**

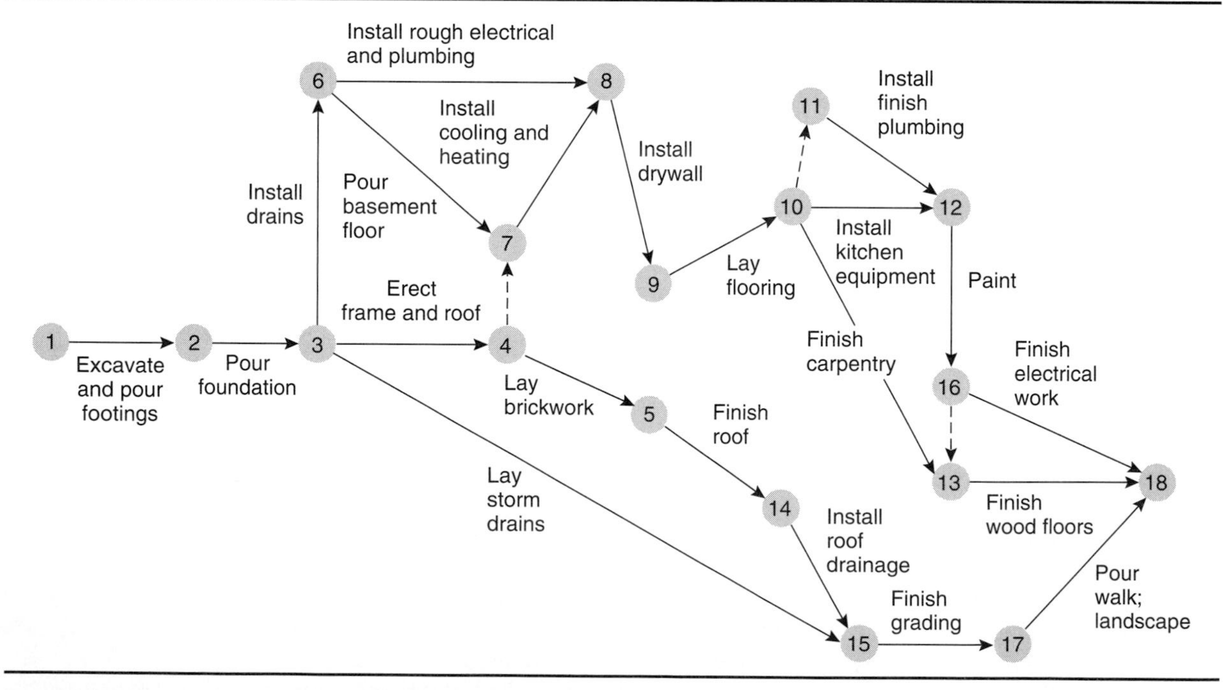


Source: Adapted from Jerome D. Wiest and Ferdinand K. Levy, *A Management Guide PERT/CPM* (Englewood Cliffs, N.J.: Prentice-Hall, Inc., 1969), p. 16. Used with permission.

about, all arrows must progress toward the end, and there can be no doubling back or loops. Exhibit 17-6 shows those two no-no's.

2. *Event completion.* A network *event* stands for the completion of all activities leading into it. Further, in PERT/CPM logic, no activity may begin at an event until all activities leading into that event have been completed. For example, consider event 8 in Exhibit 17-5, completion of rough electrical and plumbling, plus cooling and heating, presumably including an outdoor cooling compressor. We could question that network logic because it says that the next activity (after event 8), install drywall, depends on completion even of the outdoor compressor. In fact, the drywall is intended to cover up only the interior rough work. If the change could seriously affect project flow, the segment of the network in the event 8 vicinity would need to be drawn differently, with activities relabeled.

**event (node)**
Point at which one or more activities (tasks) are completed, and, often, at which others are started; consumes no time or resources but merely marks a key point in time.

Let us generalize to make an important point: Network logic should accurately reflect intended project-flow logic! Typically, managers who spend extra time and effort in network creation are rewarded during project implementation.

3. *Dummy activity.* A **dummy activity** takes no time and consumes no resources. Four of the five dummies (shown as dashed arrows) in Exhibit 17-4 merely connect subnetworks. The project staff will probably omit them when the full network is drawn.

**activity (arrow)**
Basic unit of work in a project.

In Exhibit 17-5, two of the three dummies, 4–7 and 16–13, are necessary for project logic. Activity 4–7 is there to ensure that both 3–4 and 6–7 precede 7–8 but that only 3–4 precedes 4–5. The logic is as follows. We want cooling and heating to be installed on top of a basement floor (6–7) and through holes drilled in the frame (3–4). We want brickwork to go up against the frame (3–4), but it need not wait for a basement floor (6–7) to be poured. The dummy, 4–7, decouples the two merging and the two bursting activities to correctly show the logic. There is no other way to show it. Dummy activity 16–13 has the same purpose.

**EXHIBIT 17-6 Networking Errors**

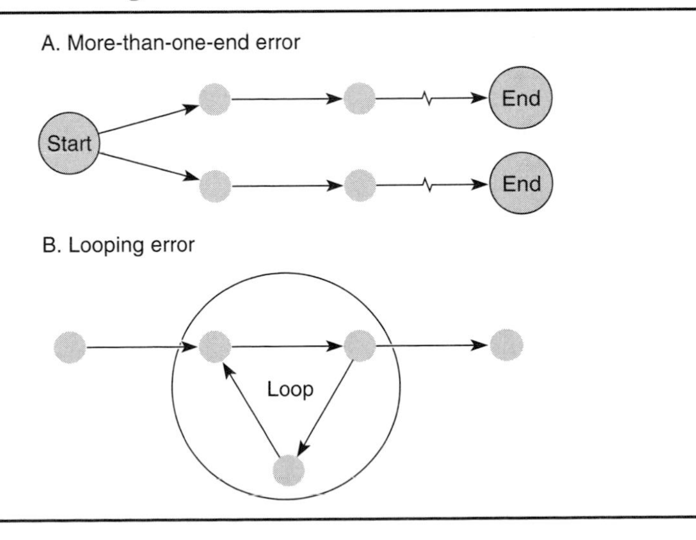

**Exhibit 17-7 Use of a Dummy Activity**

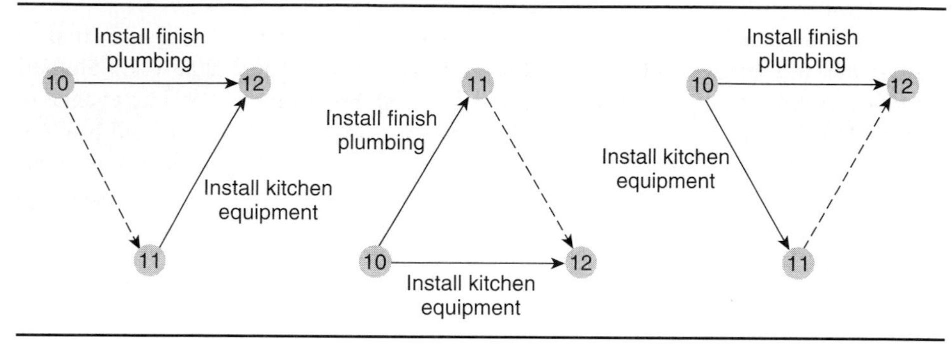


Dummy activity 10–11 exists only to avoid confusing the computer, if the network is computerized. The problem is that two different activities occur between events 10 and 12. In Exhibit 17-5 an extra event (11) creates a dummy activity, 10–11. This ensures that "finish plumbing" and "kitchen equipment" will have unique numbers. Three equivalent ways to do this are shown in Exhibit 17-7.

PERT/CPM computer software identifies activities and their sequence by predecessor and successor event numbers—for example, dummy activity 10–11 goes *from* 10 *to* 11.

4. *Event numbering.* Most computer software for PERT/CPM does not require that event numbers go from smaller to larger. Larger to smaller (e.g., 16 to 13 in Exhibit 17-5) is all right, because the *from* event (16) is entered into the predecessor field in the computer record and the *to* event (13) into the successor field. Thus, the computer has no difficulty keeping the sequence straight.

5. *Level of detail.* Every activity in Exhibit 17-5 could be divided into subactivities. In addition to the burden that more activities impose, however, there is no need to plan for a level of detail beyond what a manager would want to control. On the other hand, there should be enough detail to show when one activity should precede another.

6. *Plan versus actual.* The network is only a plan; it is unlikely to be followed exactly. For example, maybe walks and landscapes will get poured (17-18 in Exhibit 17-5) before finish grading (15–17). Or maybe money will run out and finish grading will be cut from the project. Thus, the network is not an imperative, and it is not violated when not followed. The network is just a best estimate of how the project team expects to do the project. A best estimate is far better than no plan at all and can even have value in small projects; see the accompanying photo of a network on display at Bright Star, a division of Sierra On-Line.

Also, activity-oriented networks in this chapter are activity-on-arrow (or on-arc), in which the task is represented by the arrow (arc). Some people prefer activity-on-node networks, in which the node or circle represents the task and the arrow just shows sequence.

**Events and Milestones.** Most of the network examples in this chapter are activity oriented. It is a form that frontline people can relate to; that is, it describes the work activities themselves. Upper managers are more interested in completions, or *events,* and an event-oriented network that they can use to review project completions. The project staff creates the event-oriented network from an activity-oriented network.

Exhibit 17-8 shows two forms of event-oriented networks. Exhibit 17-8A is a segment of the construction-project example stated as an event-oriented network. Nodes

*Networks are sometimes used even for small projects in small firms. This one is for a project under development at Bright Star, a 15-person company specializing in children's educational computer software.*

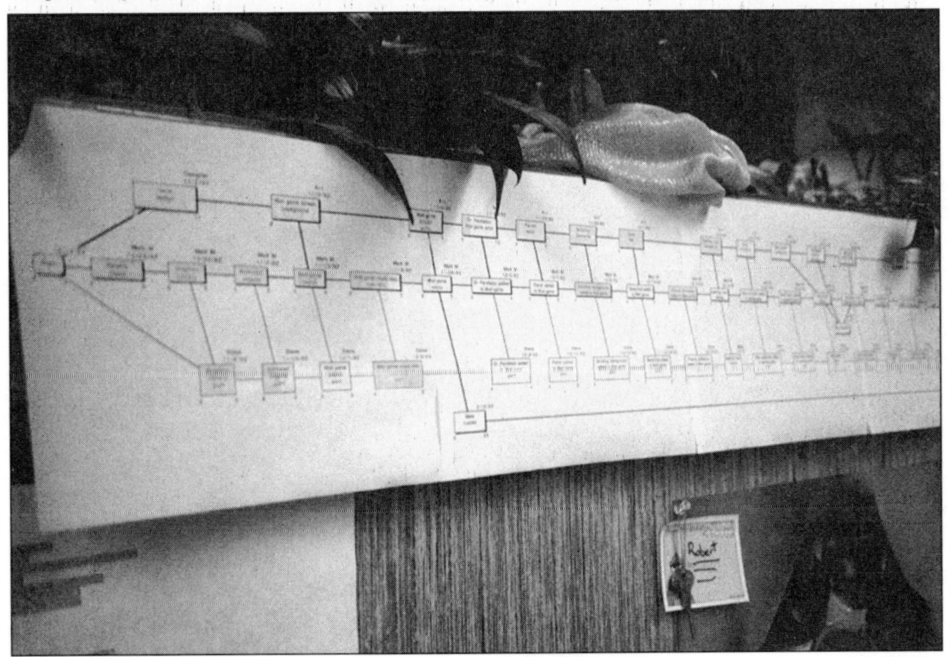


are drawn large in order to hold event descriptions. Descriptions use present-tense verb forms in activity-oriented networks but past-tense forms in event-oriented networks. For example, "pour basement floor" becomes "basement floor poured" in Exhibit 17-8A. At merge points (nodes where two or more activities converge), the event description can get cumbersome. For example, event 8 is "rough plumbing, cooling, and heating installed."

Networks for big projects may include tens or even hundreds of thousands of events. Upper managers surely do not care to review the project event by event. Instead, project managers commonly create a summary network for upper managers. The summary network may be limited to certain key events, called **milestones.** As an example, events 4 and 10 in Exhibit 17-8B are shown to be a condensation of a five-event segment, events 4–7–8–9–10, from Exhibit 17-8A. The best way to construct a milestone chart is to make milestones out of events that signify the end of major project stages. In house construction, most people would think of completion of framing and completion of rough interior work as major stages; these are milestones 4 and 10 in Exhibit 17-8B.

Some sequential accuracy is lost in condensing a network. For example, milestone event 4 subsumes events 2 and 3 (from Exhibit 17-5). But in cutting out event 3, two branches of the tree at that point—branches 3–6 and 3–15—are unceremoniously

**EXHIBIT 17-8 Events and Milestones**

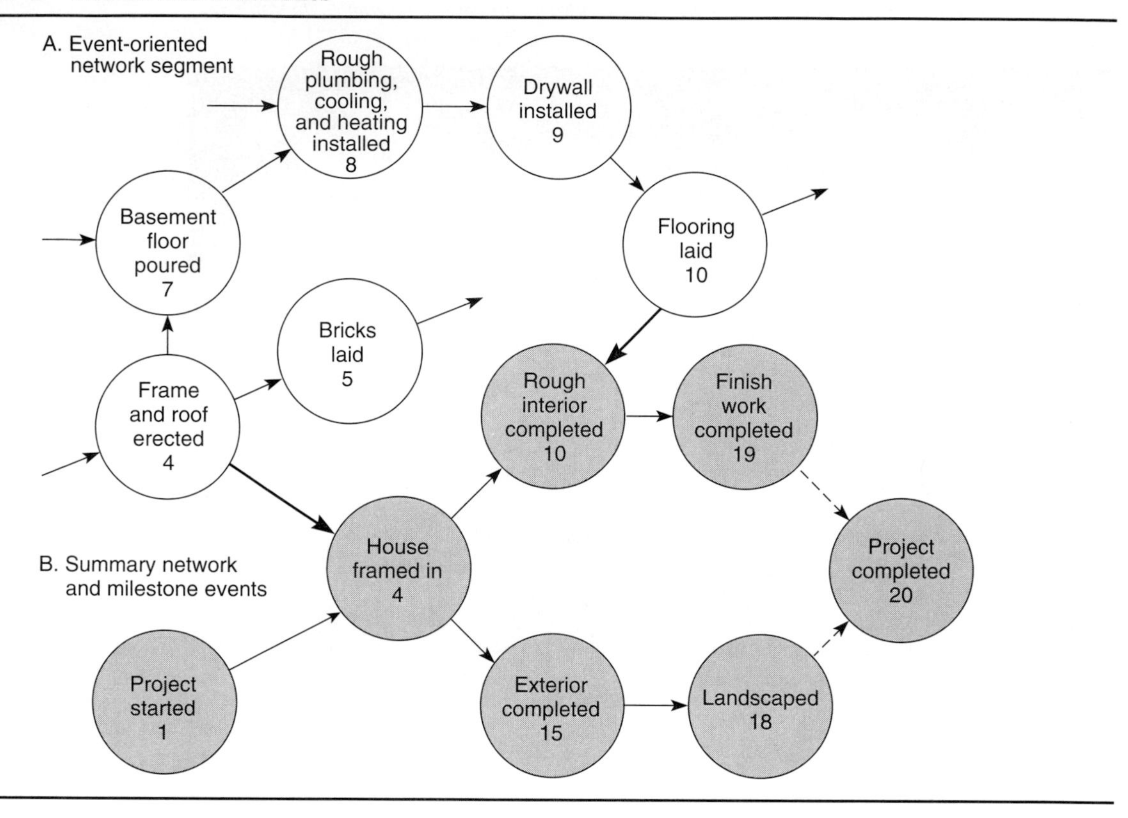


chopped off, as shown in the following illustration. From an upper-management perspective, however, the inaccuracy is of little concern.

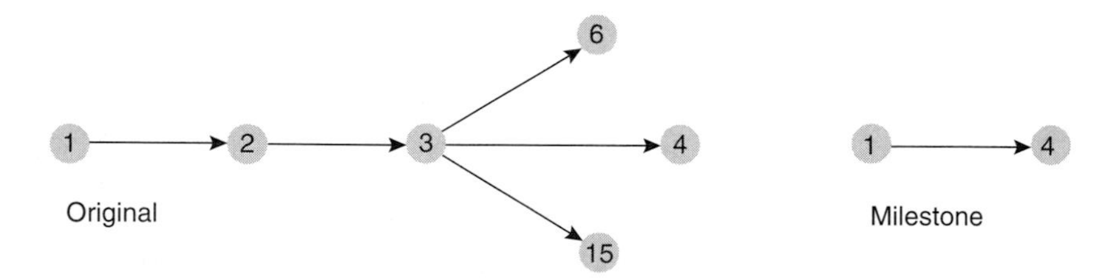


### *Time Estimating and Critical Path*

The second subsystem involves putting time estimates on each network activity so that the project management team can identify critical and slack paths through the network. Critical path activities warrant intensive management; slack path activities usually do not.

**Activity Times.** It is harder to accurately estimate times for projects than for repetitive and job operations because of project uncertainly and task variability. Engineered time standards are unlikely for project activities, except for those that tend to recur from project to project. Instead, the project manager obtains technical estimates from those in charge of each project activity.

**technical estimate**
A type of historical, nonengineered (not carefully defined and timed) time standard; see Chapter sixteen.

The human tendency to pad time estimates in order to arrive at a more attainable goal is somewhat counteracted in construction projects. Typically, enough experience and historical data exist to keep estimators honest. Unfortunately, that is not always the case with research and development projects.

R&D projects often include advanced, state-of-the-art activities; historical benchmark data are scarce. Because of this, PERT, the R&D-oriented half of PERT/CPM, was originally designed to require not just one activity time estimate but three: a most likely, an optimistic, and a pessimistic estimate. Next, the three time estimates were converted into most likely times and variances, and the probability of completing any given event by a given data could be calculated.

The technical logic of the statistical procedure has been confounded in practice by human behavioral tendencies. First, for an activity never done before, it is hard to pry one time estimate out of people, much less three. A request for three estimates may result in drawn-out discussion of the definitions of *most likely, optimistic,* and *pessimistic.* Second, the estimators for R&D activities often are scientists, engineers, and other professionals. They tend to be strong-willed and unafraid to withhold their cooperation. If pressed to provide three estimates, they may give meaningless ones such as 5–10–15 or 8–10–12.

As early as 1961, when NASA adopted PERT, it dropped the requirement for three activity time estimates.

Furthermore, to reiterate a point made earlier, the network will change as the project unfolds; people who have used PERT/CPM in practice know this. Seasoned managers also know that developing flexible capacity options to meet the likely-to-emerge contingencies is a much more productive use of their time than worrying about computer-calculated activity variances that are just as fickle as the three time estimates upon which they are based.

For these reasons, the PERT three-time-estimating procedure has mostly fallen into disuse. Today, in both PERT and CPM, a single best estimate is the norm, where *best estimate* is defined simply as how long the activity is expected to take under typical conditions and with normal resources.

**Path Analysis.** The most time-consuming path is the **critical path.** The path is time critical because a delay in completing any of its activities delays the whole project; see Into Practice, "Turkey Time." We continue the house construction exercise to demonstrate path criticality.

The house construction network of Exhibit 17-5 is reproduced in Exhibit 17-9, with estimates for each activity added. Path durations are given below the network. Although this network is very small, for illustrative purposes, there are still 17 paths to add up. Computers are efficient at adding path times, and path analysis subroutines are basic in PERT/CPM software.

In Exhibit 17-9, path 12 is critical, at 34 days. Several other paths—6, 7, 8, 9, 10, 11, 13, 14, and 15—are nearly critical, at 31 to 33 days. The critical path and nearly

INTO PRACTICE

## Turkey Time

John Battle, scion of an Old South political family and holder of a graduate degree in literature, was construction boss of the 62-story AT&T Gateway Tower in Seattle. "Estimates are done in heaven," says Battle. "The project is run in hell."

Battle likens the critical path to the turkey at a Thanksgiving dinner. Almost any other item on the menu can be done too soon, too late, or not at all, and its effect on the dinner will be marginal. But if the turkey gets delayed, so does dinner.

The critical elements on the path toward Gateway's completion included the "digging and pouring of the foundation, erection of the frame, installation of the elevators, application of the granite and glass skin, and . . . the testing of all the electrical, mechanical and safety systems."

Source: Adapted from Terry McDermott, "High Rise: When a Tower Goes Up, Risk Is as Substantial as the Steel Itself," *Sunday Seattle Times and Post-Intelligencer,* March 25, 1990.

critical path activities deserve close managerial attention. Other activities have more slack or float time and need not be managed so closely.

**slack (slack time)**
The amount of time an activity may be delayed without delaying the project schedule; usually changes as the project progresses.

**Activity Slack.** Calculating slack time by comparing the critical path with noncritical paths seems fairly simple, at least in the networks discussed thus far. However, it becomes tedious, even impossible, for larger, more realistic project networks. Consequently, a three-step algorithm has been developed for finding slack time.

First, we continue with our house construction example to gain an intuitive feel for the concept of slack, especially as it pertains to paths and activities. Then, we can use the three-step algorithm to formally calculate slack for activities in a network segment.

In Exhibit 17-9, paths 7, 11, and 14 take 33 days, or 1 day less than the critical path. This means that relative to the critical path, paths 7, 11, and 14 contain a day of slack (in PERT lingo) or float (in CPM lingo). The day of slack applies not to the whole path but just to certain path activities. Consider path 7 first.

Path 7 is identical to critical path 12 except in the segment from event 3 to event 7. The critical path segment from 3 to 4 to 7 takes four days; the slack path segment from 3 to 6 to 7 takes three days. Activities 3–6 and 6–7 are said to have one day of slack. This means that 3–6 or 6–7 (but not both) could be delayed by one day without affecting the planned project duration. By like reasoning, activity 16–18 on path 11 and activity 10–12 on path 14 have a day of slack.

Slack analysis is complicated when an activity is on more than one slack path segment. Activity 3–6, for example, is on slack path segments 3–6–7 and 3–6–8. Segment 3–6–8 takes four days as compared with eight days for critical path segment 3–4–7–8. It may seem that activities 3–6 and 6–8 have four days of slack and that either could be delayed four days without affecting the planned project duration. But we learned above that activity 3–6, on slack segment 3–6–7, may be delayed no more than one day. Slack

## EXHIBIT 17-9 Path Analysis

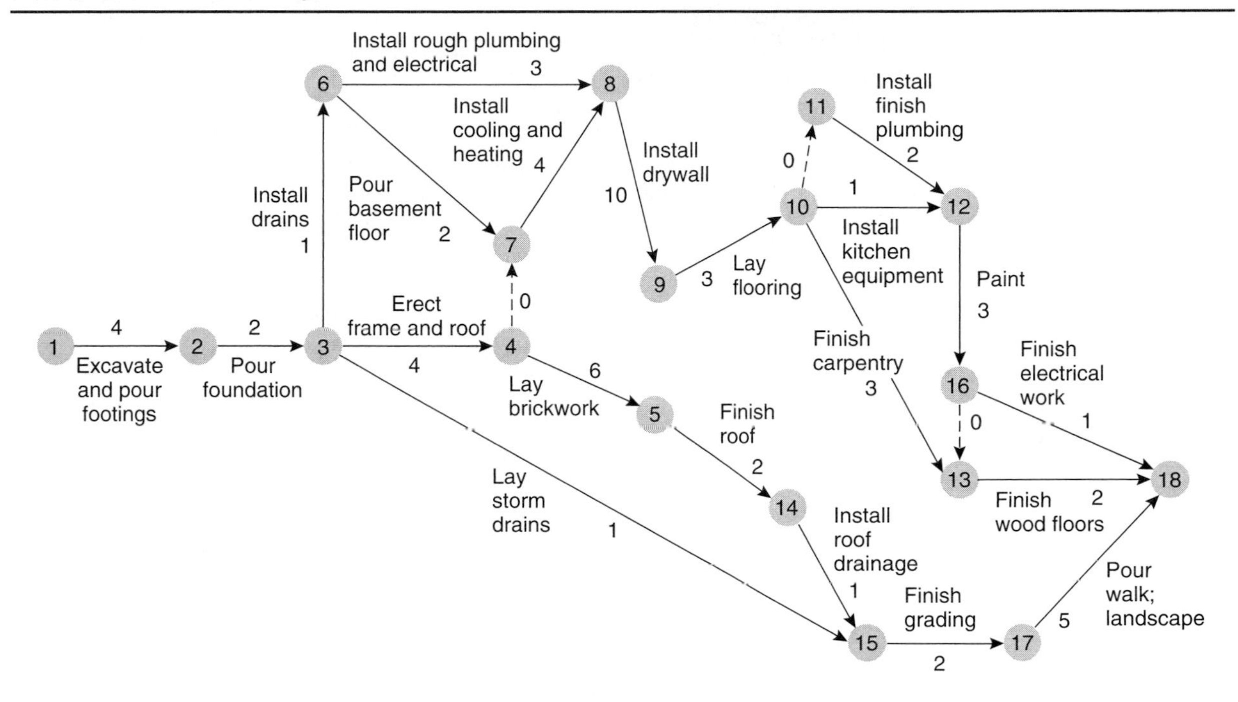


| Path Number | Paths | Path Time | |
|---|---|---|---|
| 1 | 1–2–3–6–8–9–10–11–12–16–18 | 29 days | |
| 2 | 1–2–3–6–8–9–10–11–12–16–13–18 | 30 | |
| 3 | 1–2–3–6–8–9–10–12–16–18 | 28 | |
| 4 | 1–2–3–6–8–9–10–12–16–13–18 | 29 | |
| 5 | 1–2–3–6–8–9–10–13–18 | 28 | Nearly critical paths |
| 6 | 1–2–3–6–7–8–9–10–11–12–16–18 | 32 | Nearly critical paths |
| 7 | 1–2–3–6–7–8–9–10–11–12–16–13–18 | 33 | Nearly critical paths |
| 8 | 1–2–3–6–7–8–9–10–12–16–18 | 31 | Nearly critical paths |
| 9 | 1–2–3–6–7–8–9–10–12–16–13–18 | 31 | Nearly critical paths |
| 10 | 1–2–3–6–7–8–9–10–13–18 | 31 | Nearly critical paths |
| 11 | 1–2–3–4–7–8–9–10–11–12–16–18 | 33 | Nearly critical paths |
| 12 | 1–2–3–4–7–8–9–10–11–12–16–13–18 | 34 | ← Critical path |
| 13 | 1–2–3–4–7–8–9–10–12–16–18 | 32 | Nearly critical paths |
| 14 | 1–2–3–4–7–8–9–10–12–16–13–18 | 33 | Nearly critical paths |
| 15 | 1–2–3–4–7–8–9–10–13–18 | 32 | Nearly critical paths |
| 16 | 1–2–3–4–5–14–15–17–18 | 26 | |
| 17 | 1–2–3–15–17–18 | 14 | |

on 3–6 is therefore one day, not four days; the larger value is rejected. Activity 6–8, however, does have four days of slack.

The formal calculation of slack time may, in three steps, now be demonstrated for the activities shown in Exhibit 17-10.

1. *Earliest start and earliest finish.* Each activity has an **earliest start (ES)** and an **earliest finish (EF)** time, expressed in days for our project. They are determined by a forward pass through the network. We begin with activity 1–2 and set its *ES* to zero, the start of the project. The *EF* for an activity is equal to its *ES* plus its duration, *t*. Thus, the *EF* for activity 1–2 is

$$EF_{1\text{–}2} = ES_{1\text{–}2} + t_{1\text{–}2} = 0 + 4 = 4 \text{ (or day 4)}$$

The *ES* for each successive activity is equal to the largest *EF* of all predecessor activities. We see that node 2, the origin of activity 2–3, has but one predecessor: activity 1–2. Therefore, the *ES* for activity 2–3 is equal to the *EF* for activity 1–2 and has a value of 4. Continuing, we find the *EF* for activity 2–3 as follows:

$$EF_{2\text{–}3} = ES_{2\text{–}3} + t_{2\text{–}3} = 4 + 2 = 6$$

Exhibit 17-10 shows the remainder of the *ES* and *EF* values. The largest *EF* (14 in this case) is taken as the project duration, which is also the duration of the critical path.

2. *Latest start and latest finish.* Each network activity also has a **latest start (LS)** and a **latest finish (LF)** time, again expressed in days for our project. Values for *LS* and *LF* are found by a backward pass through the network. Beginning at node 8, we use the project duration ($EF_{7\text{–}8} = 14$) as the *LF* of all activities ending on node 8. Then we find the *LS* for each activity by subtracting its duration (*t*) from its *LF*. For example, the *LS* for activity 7–8 is

$$LS_{7\text{–}8} = LF_{7\text{–}8} - t_{7\text{–}8} = 14 - 4 = 10 \text{ (or day 10)}$$

And for activity 6–8

$$LS_{6\text{–}8} = LF_{6\text{–}8} - t_{6\text{–}8} = 14 - 3 = 11$$

As we move backward through the network, each successive activity has its *LF* defined as the earliest *LS* of all activities that immediately follow. For example, the *LF* of activity 3–6 is 8, since 8 is the smaller of the *LS* values for activities 6–7 and 6–8. Exhibit 17-10 shows *LF* and *LS* values for the remaining activities.

3. *Slack calculation.* Slack for each activity is simply $LS - ES$ or $LF - EF$.

**Negative Slack.** If *LS* is less than *ES*, negative slack results. Negative slack means the activity is late. Not only is this possible, it is almost the norm, at least for critical path activities. It is so rare for projects to be on time that *The Wall Street Journal* published a front-page story some years ago with headlines proclaiming that a certain large construction project was completed on time. (The project was the domed stadium in Pontiac, Michigan, which also met targeted costs!)

**Exhibit 17-10 Calculating Activity Slack—Summary Table**

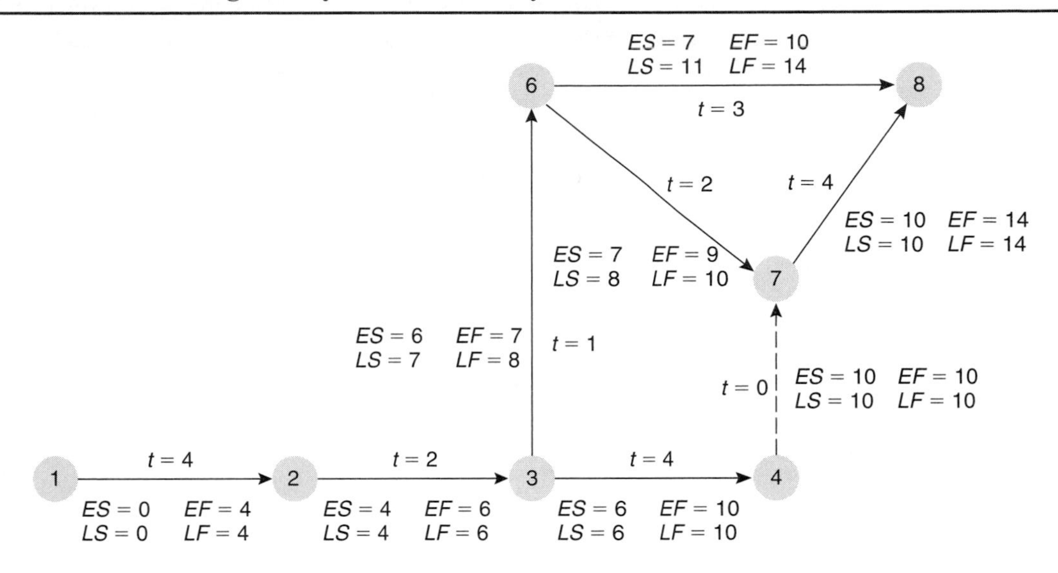


| *Activity* | *(LF–EF)* | *(LS–ES)* | *Slack* | |
|---|---|---|---|---|
| 1–2 | (4–4) | (0–0) | 0 | Critical activity |
| 2–3 | (6–6) | (4–4) | 0 | Critical activity |
| 3–4 | (10–10) | (6–6) | 0 | Critical activity |
| 3–6 | (8–7) | (7–6) | 1 | |
| 4–7 | (10–10) | (10–10) | 0 | Critical activity |
| 6–7 | (10–9) | (8–7) | 1 | |
| 6–8 | (14–10) | (11–7) | 4 | |
| 7–8 | (14–14) | (10–10) | 0 | Critical activity |

Critical path: 1–2–3–4–7–8.
Critical path duration: 14 days.

Suppose that in Exhibit 17-10 the due date had been day 11. For activity 7–8, for example, computations reveal

$$LS_{7\text{–}8} = 11 - 4 = 7$$

$$\text{Slack}_{7\text{–}8} = LS_{7\text{–}8} - ES_{7\text{–}8} = 7 - 10 = -3 \text{ (negative slack)}$$

Each of the other critical path activities would have slack of −3 days, which means the project is three days late while still in the planning stage! Two clear options exist. First, the schedule could be relaxed—push out the due date to 14, for example—to avoid negative slack at the outset. Second, and often the case with large projects, the project could start out late with hopes of catching up.

**Slack-Sort Computer Listing.** The most common PERT/CPM computer output is a slack-sort report of all project activities. Slack sort means sorting or listing activities in order of their degree of slack. Critical path activities have the least slack and therefore appear first; near-critical activities, usually from more than one path, appear next; and so on.

Exhibit 17-11 illustrates this, again using the house-building example. Note that the top activities have negative slack and are most critical. Bottom-most activities are least critical; the last one, activity 3–15, has +17 days of slack, which means that it may be delayed 17 days without affecting the project due date.

The slack-sorted computer listing helps a manager more than a network does. Indeed, most managers rely on this type of listing and never need to see a network.[13]

## *Project Scheduling*

The time data generated in the second PERT/CPM phase is a required input for the third phase, project scheduling. The first step is to compare the projected project duration with allowable duration. If projected duration fails to meet company commitments, choices have to be made before the schedule is set in concrete. Company managers may consider spending more on resources to **crash** the network, literally buying some project time reduction. Managers will want to examine cost and time options provided by the project management staff. Crashing and the time–cost trade-off procedure are explained next, followed by discussion of final project and work center scheduling.

**EXHIBIT 17-11 Computer Listing for Path Analysis**

**Slack-Sorted Activity Report**

| *Activity Number* | *Description* | *Time* | *Earliest Start* | *Latest Start* | *Activity Slack* | |
|---|---|---|---|---|---|---|
| 1–2 | Excavate, pour footings | 4 | 0 | −3 | −3 | Critical path |
| 2–3 | Pour foundation | 2 | 4 | 1 | −3 | |
| 3–4 | Erect frame and roof | 4 | 6 | 3 | −3 | |
| 4–7 | Dummy | 0 | 10 | 7 | −3 | |
| . | . | . | . | . | . | |
| . | . | . | . | . | . | |
| . | . | . | . | . | . | |
| 13–18 | Lay flooring | 2 | 32 | 29 | −3 | |
| 3–6 | Install drains | 1 | 6 | 4 | −2 | |
| 6–7 | Pour basement floor | 2 | 7 | 5 | −2 | |
| 10–12 | Install kitchen equipment | 1 | 27 | 25 | −2 | |
| 16–18 | Finish electrical work | 1 | 32 | 30 | −2 | |
| 10–13 | Finish carpentry | 3 | 27 | 26 | −1 | |
| . | . | . | . | . | . | |
| . | . | . | . | . | . | |
| . | . | . | . | . | . | |
| 15–17 | Finish grading | 2 | 19 | 24 | +5 | |
| 17–18 | Pour walks and landscape | 5 | 21 | 26 | +5 | |
| 3–15 | Lay storm drains | 1 | 6 | 23 | +17 | |

**Crashing and Time–Cost Trade-offs.** If managers elect to spend more on resources to cut project time, they had better apply extra resources to critical path activities since that path determines project completion time. As the critical path is crashed, new critical paths may emerge. The cost to further reduce the project duration may then involve extra resource costs to reduce activity times on multiple paths. The analysis can get complicated.

If resource costs are inconvenient to collect, the choice of which critical path activity to crash is not clear-cut. Crashing an early activity on the critical path may seem wise because the reduction will apply to other paths that could become critical later; but money spent early is gone. The opposite wait-and-see approach seems wise for another reason: Perhaps some critical path activities will be completed earlier than expected, thus averting the need to crash at all; but if that does not happen, late options for crashing may be few and costly.

We explain time–cost trade-off analysis, using the small network and related data of Exhibit 17-12. The critical path is B–D–E, eight days long, at a cost of $390. Project managers may want to spend more money for extra shifts, air freight, and so on, to

**EXHIBIT 17-12 Network and Time—Cost Data**

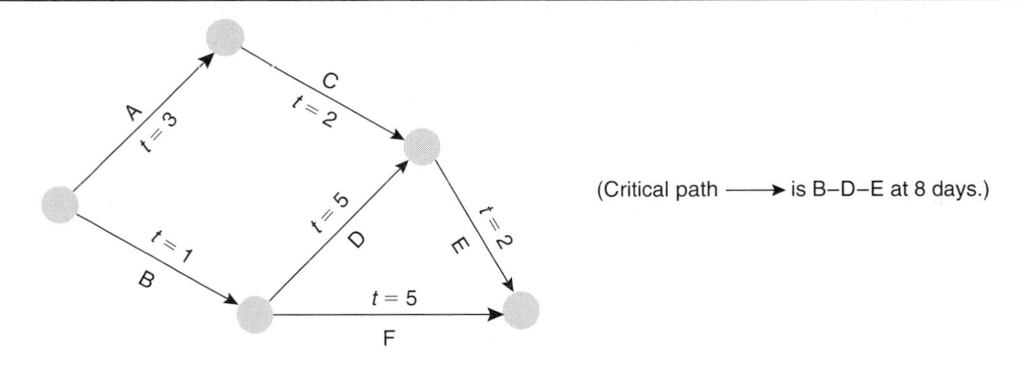


| | Normal | | Crash | | |
|---|---|---|---|---|---|
| *Activity* | *Time* | *Cost* | *Time* | *Cost* | *Cost per Day* |
| A | 3 | $ 50 | 1 | $100 | $25 |
| B | 1 | 40 | 1 | 40 | — |
| C | 2 | 40 | 1 | 80 | 40 |
| D | 5 | 100 | 3 | 160 | 30 |
| E | 2 | 70 | 1 | 160 | 90 |
| F | 5 | 90 | 2 | 300 | 70 |
| | | $390 | | | |

Source: Adapted from Fred Luthans, *Introduction to Management: A Contingency Approach* (Richard J. Schonberger, contributing author) (New York: McGraw-Hill, 1976), p. 378 (HD31.L86). Used with permission.

reduce the time required to complete various tasks. For example, activity A costs $50 to do in three days (normal), $75 to do in two days (paying for overtime, perhaps), and $100 to do in one day (paying still more, perhaps for extra shifts). The linear assumption, $25 for each day reduced, is generally accurate enough for planning purposes.

The normal and crash costs are often engineers' or managers' estimates based on established direct labor and overhead rates; a careful cost accounting estimate may not be necessary. Also, the estimates may be incremental rather then full costs.

The method of calculating average cost per day may be expressed as a formula:

$$\text{Cost per time period} = \frac{\text{Crash cost} - \text{Normal cost}}{\text{Normal time} - \text{Crash time}} \qquad (17\text{-}1)$$

For activity A, the calculation is

$$\frac{\$100 - \$50}{3 \text{ days} - 1 \text{ day}} = \frac{\$50}{2 \text{ days}} = \$25 \text{ per day}$$

Cost per day for each of the other activities is calculated the same way. Activity B cannot be crashed and thus does not have a cost-per-day entry.

The question is: If it costs $390 to do the project in eight days, what would it cost to do it in seven? If we should pick the lowest total in the cost-per-day column, $25 for A, we would be wrong. Spending $25 more on A would reduce A from three to two days, but it would not affect the eight-day projected duration. A critical path activity—B, D, or E—must be selected. B is out because its crash time is no better than its normal time. The choice between D and E favors D, at an extra cost of $30, as opposed to $90 for E. Thus, doing the project in seven days requires $30 more for a total cost of $420.

The next step is to investigate doing the project in six days. But the above reduction of D to four days results in two critical paths, B–D–E and A–C–E, both seven days long. Reducing the project duration to six days is possible by crashing A and D together at a cost of $55, D and C together at $70, or E alone at $90. The first option is cheapest; thus, it is selected, bringing the total project cost up to $475.

Next, try for five days. After the above step, all paths are critical at six days. The only choice (since B and D are already crashed to their minimum times) is to crash E and F by one day. The added cost is $160, with a total project cost of $635. No further time reductions are possible, since the B–D–E path is fully crashed.

If this were a construction project with a penalty of $100 for every day beyond a six-day project duration, alternative 3 below would look best since it has the lowest total cost, $475.

| *Alternative* | *Time (days)* | *Construction Cost* | *Penalty Cost* | *Total Cost* | |
|---|---|---|---|---|---|
| 1 | 8 | $390 | $200 | $590 | |
| 2 | 7 | 420 | 100 | 520 | |
| 3 | 6 | 475 | 0 | 475 | ← Minimum |
| 4 | 5 | 635 | 0 | 635 | |

INTO PRACTICE

## Bridging the Profit Gap

"At the rate of one a day, crews racing to rebuild the Mercer Island bridge have started sinking giant pontoon anchors weighing up to 300 tons each to the bottom of Lake Washington.

"Hundreds more workers at waterfront sites on Commencement Bay in Tacoma and on the Duwamish Waterway in Seattle are assembling the first pontoons, four of which are longer than a football field and so massive they'll have to be floated from their cradles on a high tide."

What's the rush? For General Construction Company and its partner, Rainier Steel Inc., the hurry is "about a $6 million bonus for finishing the job a year ahead of schedule. The state has agreed to pay the joint venture $18,500 a day for every day it finished early. . . . The bonus money 'is the majority of the profit on the project,' according to Scott McKellar, General Construction's vice president of operations."

Source: Adapted from Mark Higgins. "Ready, Set, Build: Crews Race to Finish Bridge Ahead of Schedule," *Seattle Post Intelligencer*, Monday, May 26, 1992.

Time–cost trade-off analysis originated with the CPM people in the construction industry. (For a construction example, see Into Practice, "Bridging the Profit Gap.") It remains more suited for use in construction projects than in R&D efforts for at least two reasons. First, costs and times are easier to estimate in construction. Second, the frequent use of late penalties in construction projects serves as extra incentive for managers in construction to consider time–cost trade-off analysis.

In less-certain project environments (R&D, information systems, disaster relief, etc.) the need to crash projects is just as great as in construction. While the time–cost trade-off procedure is generally not appropriate (the cost uncertainty problem), there are several other approaches for crashing; discussion of them is reserved for the final section in the chapter.

**Event Scheduling.** Event scheduling, the assigning of dates to events in the final network, follows selection of a time–cost alternative. Final activity times, with holidays and weekends considered, form the basis for event dates. An event-dating subroutine in PERT/CPM software accepts as input the planned date of the first event and computes the others. A typical listing shows time-earliest (*TE*) and time-latest (*TL*) to complete each event along with the event slack (*TL* – *TE*).

A normal complication in project scheduling is meshing project schedules with work center schedules. Each subcontractor, department, or work center involved in a given project is likely to be in on other projects, jobs, and repetitive operations. Fitting work center activities into project networks and fitting project activities into work center schedules is a tricky balancing act.

Exhibit 17-13 illustrates this concern. The work center, a grading crew, has developed a Gantt chart showing three upcoming activities that are on the PERT/CPM networks for three different projects. The activities are identified in their respective

**Exhibit 17-13 Decomposition of Network Activities into Work Center Schedules**

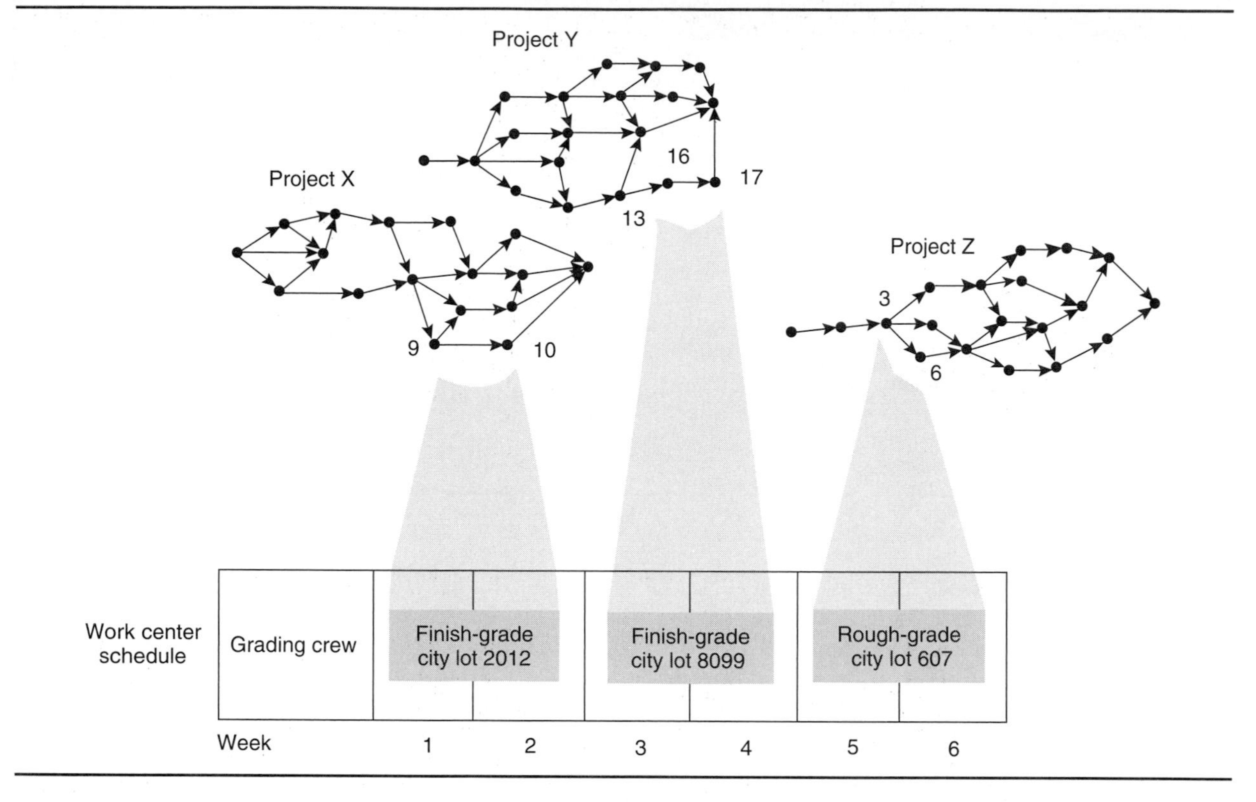


networks (the project managers' schedules) and on the work center schedule, which is the work center manager's concern. Consider activity 9–10 in project X, finish grading of city lot 2012. Obviously the project manager would like the grading crew on the job site at the right time. If activity 9–10 is a critical path activity, any delay on the grading crew's part will affect project X's completion. Any delay will also reflect negatively on the project X manager's performance, especially if late penalties are assessed.

The work center manager, on the other hand, strives for utilization of the work center's resources. After the grading of lot 2012, the work center manager might wish to proceed immediately to lot 8099 to avoid any work center idle time. The manager of project Y would probably have to veto the idea, however, if the predecessor activity for activity 16–17 (lot 8099 grading) has not been completed. Suppose the predecessor activity, shown as 13–16 in the project Y network, is removing a dead tree. Even the work center manager would agree with the project manager's logic: Grading simply cannot begin. Is the grading crew to remain idle for several work days?

Another common problem is when project schedules create demand for work crews to be in two places (perhaps on two projects, each with a different manager) at the same time. Suppose the manager of project Z decides to advance the schedule for activity 3–6, grading of city lot 607, by one week (five workdays). Obviously this will create a problem on the work center schedule during the fourth week. These kinds of conflicts are common and require compromise.

### *Reporting and Updating*

Reporting and updating is the fourth and final subsystem. It extends PERT/CPM management beyond planning and scheduling and into the project control phase. PERT/CPM control revolves around periodic reports, which generally are issued every two weeks or monthly.

Exhibit 17-14 shows a typical reporting scheme. The partial network at the top of the figure divides into monthly reporting periods. At the end of each reporting period, event completion data are entered into the computer. In Exhibit 17-14, the current month is February and February-planned events 1, 2, 3, 5, and 6 have been completed. A data entry record is prepared for each; on the first record, for example, an 01 is placed in the event field and the completion date, 02042002 for February 4, 2002 entered in another field (shown as mm/dd/yyyy in the exhibit).

**EXHIBIT 17-14 PERT/CPM Periodic Reporting**

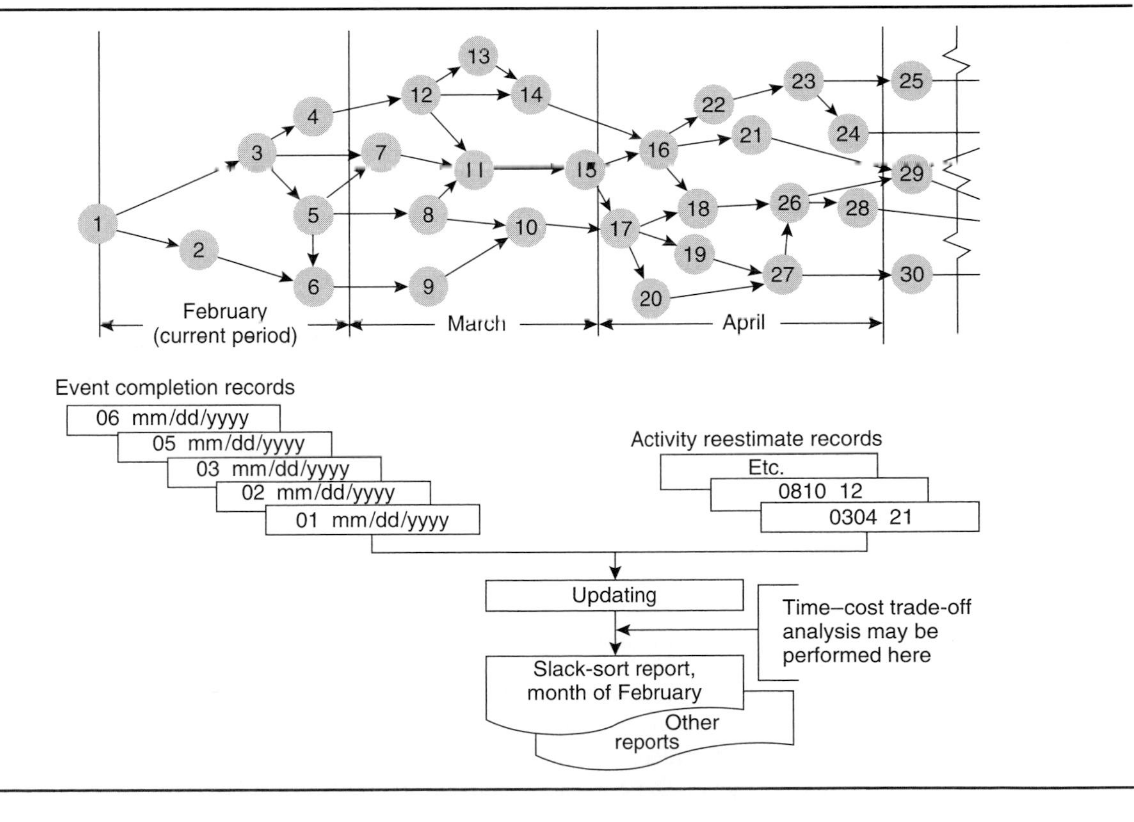

Event 4 was scheduled for February, but no notice of completion has been received. Instead, the project manager has received an activity reestimate notice. The reestimate pertains to why event 4 has not been completed: Event 3, completed (let's assume) on February 12, plus 21 days for activity 3–4, pushes the planned completion date for event 4 into March. Future activities may also be reestimated, as 08–10 has been in Exhibit 17-14.

With event completions and activity reestimates as inputs, the computer updates the PERT/CPM network. A new slack-sort report is produced, showing the new slack status of each activity. The report is like Exhibit 17-11, except that it gives start and due dates for events. The report tells all parties about the new project schedule for all events.

Replanning is inherent to control. It is possible to rerun a time–cost trade-off analysis each month after the network has been updated, using event completion data and activity reestimates. Major replanning may also occur by altering the network. The project staff may add or subtract activities or change the project sequence by adding, removing, or changing a few records. The ease of making such changes is a key asset of PERT/CPM, because project uncertainty demands planning flexibility.

### *Fitting PERT/CPM to the Situation*

PERT/CPM is expensive. Fully computerized PERT/CPM may eat up an additional 2 or 3 percent of total project cost, because it is not a replacement for conventional management. Conventional forecasting, scheduling, inventory control, quality control, budgeting, and so forth, are still done in each functional area. A project management group and PERT/CPM systems hardware and software are additional costs.

Some organizations have tried out and abandoned PERT/CPM because it seemed not to pay for itself. In some cases, the problem is in trying to apply fully computerized PERT/CPM to small-scale projects. Exhibit 17-15 reemphasizes a point partially made early in the chapter: PERT/CPM consists of distinct and separable subsystems. The exhibit further suggests that only projects that are grand in scope warrant the full PERT/CPM treatment. At the other extreme, projects of modest scope may justify the expense of only the first subsystem.

Project scope is expressed in Exhibit 17-15 in terms of four characteristics: size, uncertainty, urgency, and complexity. Size and urgency are self-explanatory. Project uncertainty is of two types:

1. Task uncertainty: doubts about what is to be done.
2. Time uncertainty: doubts about activity time estimates.

Similarly, complexity may be thought of in two ways:

1. Organizational complexity: many organizations involved in the project.
2. Activity complexity: many activities in progress at the same time.

To illustrate, consider the kinds of construction projects managed by a typical (for the United States) Army Corps of Engineers district: dams, man-made lakes, dredging, channel straightening, levees, bridges, and riverbank stabilization, to name a few. The district may have perhaps 100 projects in progress at a given time.

**EXHIBIT 17-15 Matching PERT/CPM Subsystems to Project Scope**

CONTINUUM OF PROJECT CHARACTERISTICS

Small ← Size → Large
Low ← Uncertainty → High
Low ← Urgency → High
Low ← Complexity → High

| PERT/CPM subsystems | | | | |
|---|---|---|---|---|
| 1. Plan project and design network | Yes | Yes | Yes | Yes |
| 2. Time estimation and path analysis | No | Yes | Yes | Yes |
| 3. Network scheduling | No | No | Yes | Yes |
| 4. Reporting and updating | No | No | No | Yes |

A project such as a major dam may be only moderately urgent and uncertain, but it is likely to be very large and complex. In sum, the project characteristics seem to be far enough to the right in Exhibit 17-15 to warrant full, computer-based PERT/CPM, including all four subsystems (four yeses in the exhibit). Without computer-based scheduling, reporting, and control, coordinating the many simultaneous activities of the numerous participating organizations might be chaotic.

Most bridge construction jobs are much smaller and less complex. For such intermediate-scope projects, the project engineer probably should design networks, conduct path analysis, and perhaps use a computer to schedule project events, which may include time–cost trade-off analysis (two or three yeses). But subsystem 4, reporting and updating, may not be warranted. It is the costliest subsystem to administer; it probably costs a lot more than subsystems 1, 2, and 3 combined. A typical bridge is not so urgent as to require the tight time controls of subsystem 4.

Channeling and riverbank stabilization projects are still less urgent and rarely are large, complex, or uncertain. The project engineer may expend a small amount of time, effort, and cost to accomplish subsystem 1, designing PERT/CPM networks (one yes, left column of the figure). The benefits (seeing who has to do what and in what order) are large for the modest cost. There seems little reason to perform path analysis and the other subsystems.

In R&D projects, the model seems equally valid. Designing a major aircraft, such as the Boeing 777 or the Concorde, is a project of massive scope and urgency as well, in view of the capital it ties up. Full PERT/CPM is easily justified. Redesign of a horizontal stabilizer for an existing aircraft, on the other hand, is a modest project; subsystem 1 may be sufficient.

While the logic of this situational approach to the use of PERT/CPM is clear, many managers have not followed it. Attempts to view PERT/CPM as a single indivisible system for use in every project result in disappointment. In such instances, the source of failure is not the PERT/CPM technique.

## Continuous Improvement in Projects

The high degree of complexity and uncertainty inherent in project work is good reason for stressing continuous improvement in project management. Part of the problem is chronic project lateness.

The project management staff can work toward reducing the lateness by controlling its causes. Basically, the causes have to do with unnecessary project complexity and uncertainty. The *unnecessary* category includes having the wrong size and type of project management team and lack of information sharing (common files), topics discussed earlier in the chapter. Related factors are high turnover of team members, poor communication, task unfamiliarity, and too many changes.

**Principle 11**

Cut start-up time.

Project teams typically disband when the project ends. Some members join new teams with new members and others return to a functional home, such as the mortgage loan department or human resources. Each time a new project forms, it can take weeks or months for team members to become well-enough acquainted to be able to work well together. Through at least the early project phases, communication is poor, even when the team is multifunctional and working concurrently. Moreover, the skills of each team member are not fully known.

To avoid these common problems, some firms are keeping team members somewhat intact from one project to the next. For example, Florida-based Harris Corp. does this in its government systems division. As one government contract winds down, the team gets started on the next contract, taking it from concept through completion.

Examples of other means of controlling causes of lateness are drawn from other chapters:

**Principle 10**

Eliminate error and process variation.

- *Total quality management.* Effective project management includes collection of data on mishaps, followed by improvement projects to develop solutions to prevent those mishaps on following projects. Continuous improvement seems to be late in gaining a foothold in project management, even though project work is badly in need of it to combat uncertainty and lateness.
- *Design guidelines* (from Chapter 7). These guidelines call for using standard, already proven designs. This reduces not only complexity but also project uncertainty. That is, with standard designs, activity time estimates will have lower margins of error, making critical-path estimates more accurate.

- *Benchmarking* (from Chapter 8). Project managers are no different from any other manager when it comes to using ideas from "the best." Even when the overall project is blanketed in uncertainty, there are usually many activities or even subprojects that can be speeded up by applying ideas garnered from benchmarking clearinghouses or from direct benchmarking efforts.
- *Quick-response techniques* (from Chapter 10). Project logistics can be mind boggling. The grand scale of operations associated with projects affords ample opportunities for time (and cost) savings through quick-response programs.
- *Supplier partnerships* (from Chapter 6). Relying on unknown and perhaps unreliable suppliers can add significantly to project duration. Though projects are complex—often requiring materials and knowledge from diverse sources—buying from established performers reduces risk.

## Summary Check Points

✓ Projects are large-scale, typically expensive, one-of-a-kind endeavors that may require months or years to complete and involve major portions of an organization's resources.

✓ Modern project management techniques have evolved since the late 1950s when network project models were developed.

✓ Today, project management is in demand, but the emphasis falls more on strategic and environmental implications of projects than on the tools of project management.

✓ Registration to ISO 9000 or to ISO 14000 along with a great variety of construction, information/communication system modification, or facility location/relocation efforts might be effectively managed in a project environment.

✓ Companies vary a great deal in project usage. Purely functional organizations that have no projects are at one extreme, and new business units (perhaps having evolved from successful project efforts) are at the other. Project coordinator, project manager or engineer, and autonomous project teams are intermediate forms.

✓ Projects are represented by a work breakdown structure, which may be converted into a network showing sequential relationships among project activities.

✓ Program evaluation and review technique (PERT) and critical path method (CPM) are two network management tools that originated separately in the 1950s but have evolved so that early differences between the two have mostly disappeared.

✓ PERT/CPM activities group into four phases: project planning and sequencing, time estimating and path analysis, project scheduling, and reporting and updating.

✓ Project sequence networks may be summarized into key event or milestone diagrams for senior management review.

✓ Path analysis (almost always computerized) includes a forward pass through the network to define expected project duration and a backward pass through the network to establish activity slack times. Critical activities have zero slack in initial planning.

✓ Critical and near-critical activities are managed more closely than those with large amounts of slack; multiple critical or near-critical paths are common.

✓ Time-cost analysis—part of project scheduling and rescheduling—for may involve committing additional funds in order to crash activities to shorten planned project duration.

✓ Event scheduling occurs when project activities are placed on departmental or work center activity or job calendars.

✓ Reporting and updating, PERT/CPM's final phase, is also its most expensive; activity status reports form the basis for project replanning and rescheduling activities.

✓ Most effective use of PERT/CPM comes when the tool is properly fit to the magnitude of the project. Project size and cost, complexity, urgency, and uncertainty determine which PERT/CPM subsystems are appropriate.

✓ Continuous improvement in projects comes through controlling causes for lateness—largely matters of unnecessary project complexity and uncertainty.

✓ Total quality management, benchmarking, application of design guidelines, quick response techniques, and partnerships with reliable suppliers are among the key factors that improve project management.

## Solved Problems

### *Problem 1*

If there is negative slack of three months on the upper path for the network shown

*a.* Will the project be completed on time?

*b.* What is the slack on the lower path?

*c.* Is there any need for crashing? Explain.

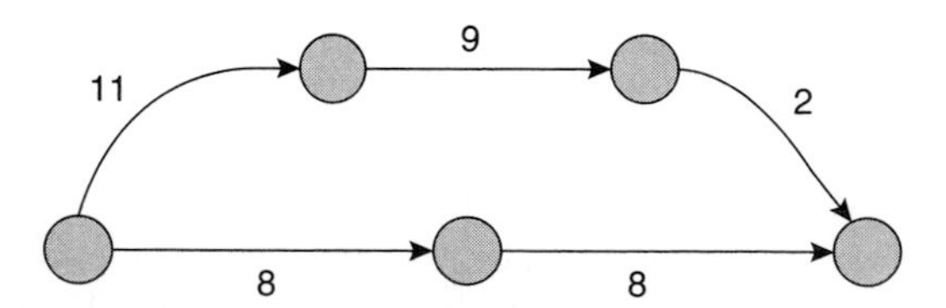


### *Solution 1*

While the problem may be solved with the aid of *ES*/*EF*/*LS*/*LF* calculations, there is no need to do so for this uncomplicated network (it is uncomplicated in that the upper and lower paths each lead straight from first to last event with no interconnections). Further, avoiding the mechanical

*ES*/*LS*/*EF*/*LF* tables forces us to think about what the critical path, the project schedule, and slack really mean.

*a.* Simple addition yields total duration on the two paths:

$$\text{Upper path: } 11 + 9 + 2 = 22 \text{ months}$$
$$\text{Lower path: } 8 + 8 = 16 \text{ months}$$

Since the lower path is less time-consuming, the upper is the critical path. And when there is negative slack on the critical path, that means the project is late, in this case, by 3 months.

*b.* Since slack on the upper path is −3 and its duration is 22 months, that means that the project's scheduled completion is 19 months. Since the lower path takes 16 months, and 19 months are available in the schedule, slack on the lower path is +3.

*c.* The top path is late by three months and thus must be crashed by three months; the bottom path takes three months less than the schedule calls for and thus does not need crashing.

***Problem 2***

Exhibit 17-16 shows a project network with activity times given in weeks.

**EXHIBIT 17-16 Project Network with Activity Times**

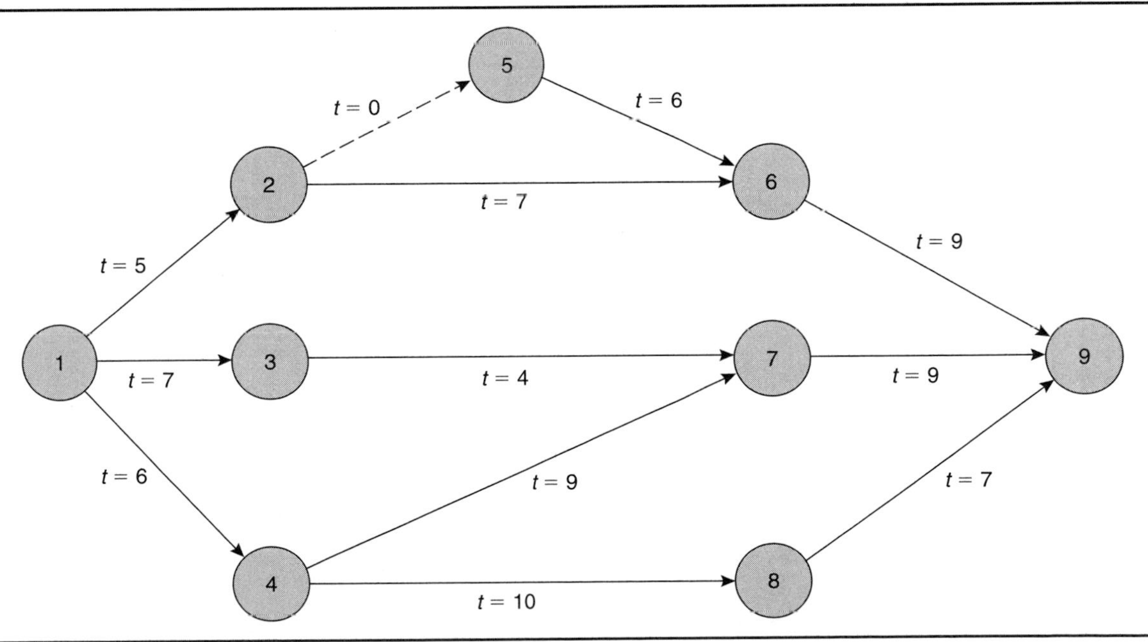

*a.* What are the paths in the network? What is the critical path? Its duration?

*b.* Compute the *ES*, *EF*, *LS*, and *LF* times and the slack for each activity.

*c.* Use the data in the time–cost information table to select appropriate time–cost alternatives for reducing the project duration by:
(1) One week.
(2) Two weeks.
(3) Three weeks.

***Solution 2***

*a.* In this simple network, it is easy to identify all paths. (In more realistic networks, the task becomes impossible to accomplish without a computer.) Paths in this example network are:

| | | |
|---|---|---|
| 1–2–5–6–9 | 20 weeks' duration | |
| 1–2–6–9 | 21 weeks' duration | |
| 1–3–7–9 | 20 weeks' duration | |
| 1–4–7–9 | 24 weeks' duration | (critical path) |
| 1–4–8–9 | 23 weeks' duration | |

*b.* The following table contains the information requested in *b*:

| *Activity* | *Duration (weeks)* | *ES* | *EF* | *LS* | *LF* | *Slack* |
|---|---|---|---|---|---|---|
| 1–2 | 5 | 0 | 5 | 3 | 8 | 3 |
| 1–3 | 7 | 0 | 7 | 4 | 11 | 4 |
| 1–4 | 6 | 0 | 6 | 0 | 6 | 0* |
| 2–5 | 0 | 5 | 5 | 9 | 9 | 4 |
| 2–6 | 7 | 5 | 12 | 8 | 15 | 3 |
| 3–7 | 4 | 7 | 11 | 11 | 15 | 4 |
| 4–7 | 9 | 6 | 15 | 6 | 15 | 0* |
| 4–8 | 10 | 6 | 16 | 7 | 17 | 1 |
| 5–6 | 6 | 5 | 11 | 9 | 15 | 4 |
| 6–9 | 9 | 12 | 21 | 15 | 24 | 3 |
| 7–9 | 9 | 15 | 24 | 15 | 24 | 0* |
| 8–9 | 7 | 16 | 23 | 17 | 24 | 1 |

Notes: Activity 2–5 is a dummy, required to clarify the network because there are two separate activities between nodes 2 and 6.

Critical activities, marked with an * are determined through slack analysis. Recall that $LF - EF = LS - ES =$ Slack.

*ES* for activity 6–9 is the larger of the *EF* for 2–6 and the *EF* for 5–6. Of these values (12 and 11, respectively), 12 governs. The *ES* for activity 7–9 is determined in the same manner.

*LF* for activity 1–2 is the smaller of the *LS* for 2–5 and the *LS* for 2–6. Of these values, 9 and 8, 8 is used. The *LF* activity 1–4 is found by comparing the *LS* values for activities 4–7 and 4–8.

*c.* The time–cost information for the project is contained in the following table:

| Activity | Normal Duration (weeks) | Normal Cost ($) | Crash Duration (weeks) | Crash Cost ($) | Crash Cost ($/week) |
|---|---|---|---|---|---|
| 1–2 | 5 | 800 | 3 | 1,100 | 150 |
| 1–3 | 7 | 950 | 3 | 2,150 | 300 |
| 1–4 | 6 | 600 | 4 | 1,400 | 400 |
| 2–5 | 0 | — | 0 | — | — |
| 2–6 | 7 | 1,100 | 5 | 1,500 | 200 |
| 3–7 | 4 | 750 | 4 | 750 | — |
| 4–7 | 9 | 1,600 | 8 | 1,800 | 200 |
| 4–8 | 10 | 1,000 | 9 | 1,300 | 300 |
| 5–6 | 6 | 1,300 | 4 | 2,200 | 450 |
| 6–9 | 9 | 2,000 | 8 | 2,500 | 500 |
| 7–9 | 9 | 1,500 | 7 | 2,000 | 250 |
| 8–9 | 7 | 900 | 5 | 1,600 | 350 |

(1) In order to achieve a one-week project time reduction, one of the critical activities (1–4, 4–7, and 7–9) must be crashed. Of the three, activity 4–7 has the lowest weekly crash cost, $200, and is therefore our selection.

(2) The two-week reduction cannot be found by considering only the *original* critical path. After 4–7 is crashed one week, there are *two* critical paths: 1–4–7–9 and 1–4–8–9. Also, note that 4–7 may not be crashed further. Since both (new) critical paths must be reduced in order to shorten the project, we might consider crashing 7–9 and 4–8 one week each. This costs $250 + $300 = $550, which is cheaper than the $600 cost of crashing 7–9 and 8–9.

Another alternative is to crash activity 1–4, which has the admirable effect of reducing time on both of our critical paths. While activity 1–4's crash cost seems high at $400, in this case it is a bargain, since it beats the $550 cost of crashing 7–9 and 4–8. Thus, our choice is to crash activity 1–4.

(3) Again look at activity 1 4. It may be crashed a second week for an additional $400. That should be done to obtain the desired three-week reduction in project duration.

## Exercises

1. Which of the five project management organizational structures shown in Exhibit 17-1 would be suitable for each of the following? Explain your answers.
   *a.* Putting on a world's fair.
   *b.* Installing Internet banking for a State bank.
   *c.* New-car contracting for a major rental-car agency.
   *d.* Starting up and running a retailer's new e-commerce division.
   *e.* A curb-and-gutter project in a large city.

2. Contact a local construction company, information systems company (or department), public works agency, market research group, advertising agency, or research and development department (laboratory).
   *a.* Find out what form of project management is in dominant use and why.
   *b.* Find out if PERT/CPM is used, and which subsystems, and why.
3. Develop an output- or outcome-oriented work breakdown structure for a nonconstruction project of your choice. (Examples are a market research project, a political campaign, a disaster-relief project, a research and development project, and a large-scale, computer-based information system development.) You may need to speculate about the nature of your chosen project if you have not had actual experience in a large project. In addition to drawing the work breakdown structure, explain the nature of your project. Show part of at least three levels on your structure.
4. Explain the purpose of activity 4–7 in Exhibit 17-5.
5. Your social organization committee has decided that in order to obtain additional funds for operating expenses, it will produce a play. You have been asked to submit a plan for the next meeting. The plan is to include all the activities or tasks that will have to be accomplished up to the opening of the show. Publicity, tickets, printed programs, and so on, as well as staging for the production, should be part of the plan. The scenery will be constructed in a member's garage and the costumes will be rented.

   To facilitate presentation of the plan, draw a network diagram of about 20 activities. Include brief descriptions of the activities.
6. A manufacturer of CD players buys disk magazines from outside contractors. A new contract is to be awarded for a new style of disk magazine. The company has developed an activity-on-node network for the project. The accompanying network includes an initial contract for magazine development and a second contract for magazine (assuming that the disk magazine tests are OK) for production. Redraw the network in the activity-on-arrow form.

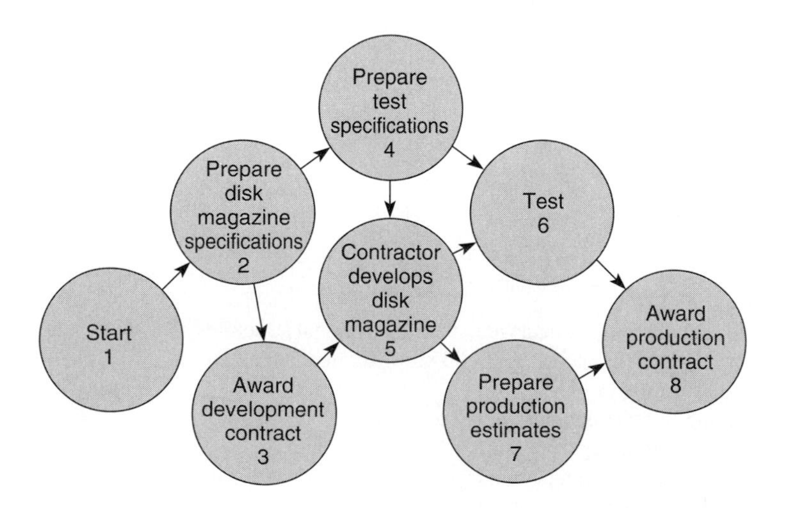

7. In the PERT network shown below, activity times (in weeks) are shown on the arrows.

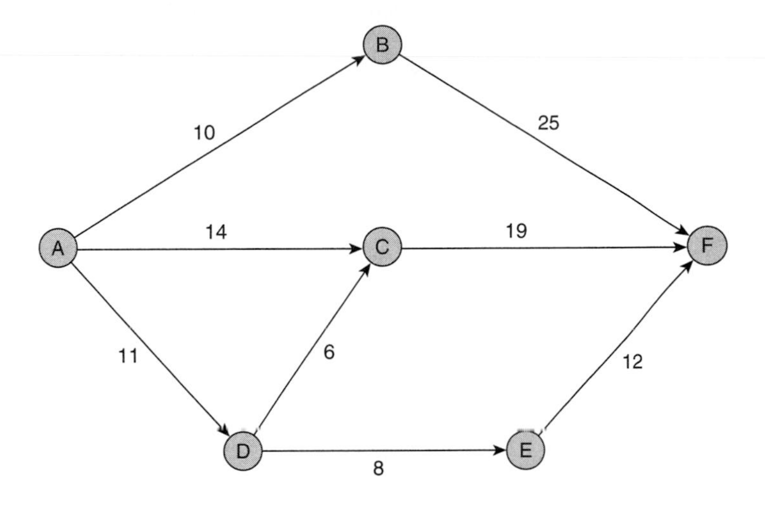


*a.* The early finish time for activity A–C is what?
*b.* The early start time for activity C–F is what?
*c.* What is the slack on activity C–F?
*d.* What is the early finish time for activity B–F?
*e.* The late finish time for activity E–F is what?
*f.* If activity A–C gets delayed so that its early finish becomes 16, how will that affect expected project completion time?

8. Aeropa, Inc., has a contract to develop a guided missile. A PERT/CPM network and activity times are given in the following illustration. Times are in weeks.

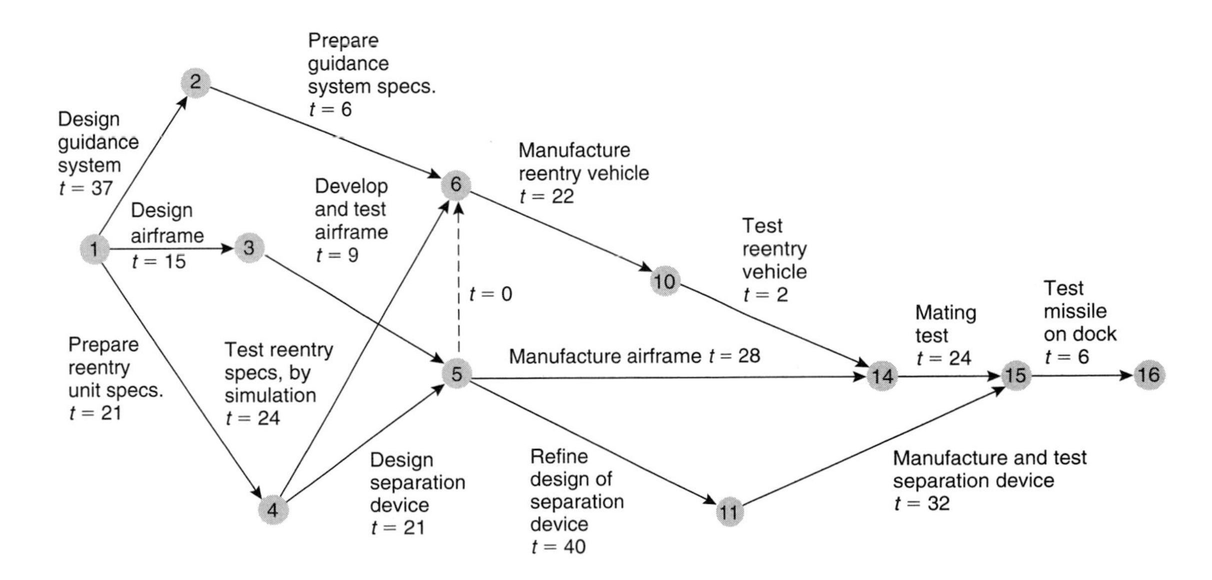

*a.* Compute *ES*, *LS*, *EF*, *LF*, and slack for each activity. Assume that slack = 0 on the critical path. Identify the critical path activities and the critical path duration.

*b.* Draw a condensed event-oriented network with only five milestone events. The five events should be designated as follows: 1. Start. 5. Shell specs completed. 6. Guidance specs completed. 14. Modules completed. 16. Missile tested.

Put activity times on the arrows between your events. Compute *ES*, *LS*, *EF*, *LF*, and slack for each activity. Verify that the critical path duration is the same as in (*a*). What activity time goes on arrow 1–6? Explain the difficulty in deciding on a time for this activity.

*c.* Assume the following project status at the end of week 50:

| *Activity* | *Actual Duration* |
|---|---|
| 1–2 | 39 |
| 1–3 | 17 |
| 1–4 | 20 |
| 2–6 | 7 |
| 3–5 | 9 |
| 4–5 | 28 |
| 4–6 | 20 |

No other activities have been completed.

Develop a slack-sorted activity report similar to Exhibit 17-11 for the project as of the end of week 50. What is the new projected project duration?

9. The following data have been collected for a certain project:

| **Activity** | | **Normal** | | **Crash** | |
|---|---|---|---|---|---|
| *Predecessor Event* | *Successor Event* | *Time (months)* | *Cost ($1,000)* | *Time (months)* | *Cost ($1,000)* |
| 1 | 2 | 6 | 250 | 5 | 360 |
| 2 | 3 | 2 | 300 | 1 | 480 |
| 2 | 4 | 1 | 100 | 1 | 100 |
| 2 | 5 | 7 | 270 | 6 | 470 |
| 3 | 4 | 2 | 120 | 1 | 200 |
| 4 | 5 | 5 | 200 | 1 | 440 |

*a.* Draw the network.

*b.* Compute and indicate the critical path and the normal project cost.

*c.* Compute slack time for each activity in the network, using 12 months as the project due date.

*d.* Perform time–cost trade-off analysis, crashing down to the minimum possible project duration. Display each time–cost alternative.

10. Normal and crash data for the accompanying network are given below. Compute all time–cost options. Which is best if there is a $4,000-per-week penalty for every week beyond a seven-week project duration?[14]

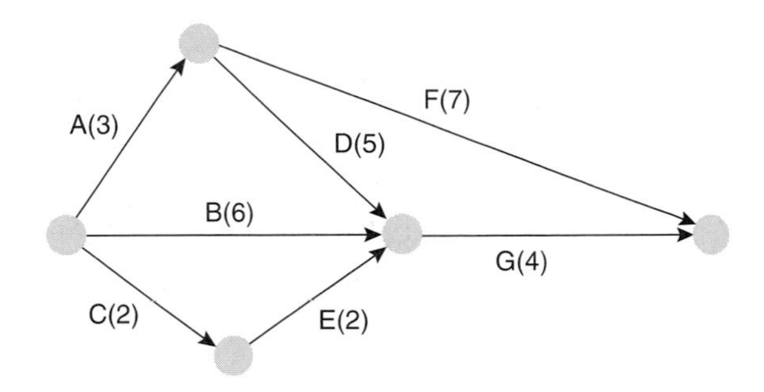


| | Normal | | Crash | |
|---|---|---|---|---|
| *Activity* | *Weeks* | *Cost ($100)* | *Weeks* | *Cost ($100)* |
| A | 3 | $ 50 | 2 | $ 100 |
| B | 6 | 140 | 4 | 260 |
| C | 2 | 25 | 1 | 50 |
| D | 5 | 100 | 3 | 180 |
| E | 2 | 80 | 2 | 80 |
| F | 7 | 115 | 5 | 175 |
| G | 4 | 100 | 2 | 240 |
| | | $610 | | $1,085 |

11. *a.* For the accompanying network, what is the critical path and expected project duration? What is the second most critical path and its duration? (Times are in months).
    *b.* What can the largest time value for activity 3–4 be to ensure that it is not a critical path activity? (Ignore the present time of five months for that activity in answering the question.)

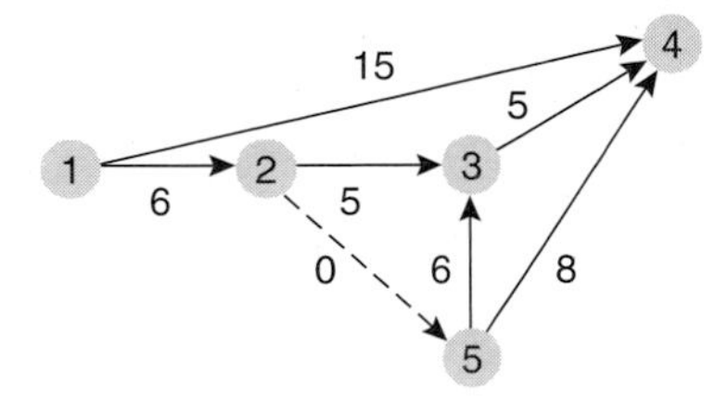

12. In the project network diagram shown below, activity times are in months.

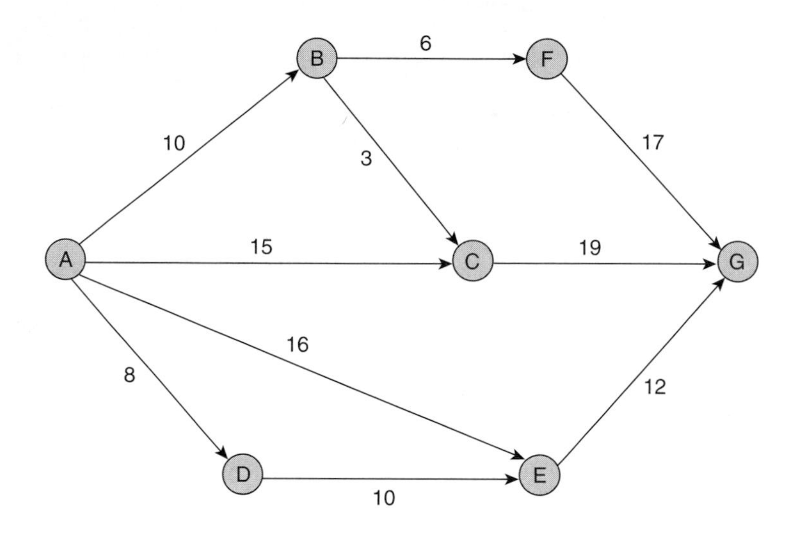


*a.* The early-start (*ES*) time for activity C–G is what?
*b.* The early start for activity E–G is what?
*c.* Which project activity has the latest early-finish time? What is that time?
*d.* What is the slack on activity D–E?
*e.* The late-finish time for activity B–C is what?
*f.* The late-finish time for activity A–E is what?
*g.* Suppose activity E–G has the cheapest crash cost of all project activities. Under what circumstances should E–G be crashed?

13. *a.* For the accompanying network, if there is slack of +5 on the lower path, what is the slack on the upper path?
*b.* If there is slack of +1 on the upper path, what is the slack on the lower path?

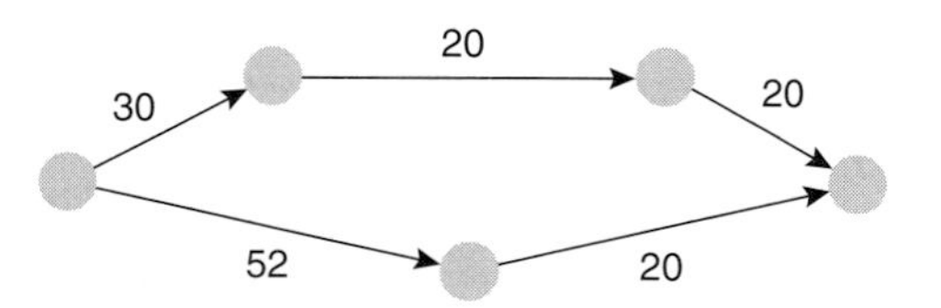


14. *a.* For the accompanying time-and-cost table, what is the least costly way to reduce the project time by one month? (You may wish to draw the network for better visualization of the problem.)
*b.* What is the least costly way to reduce the expected project duration (i.e., crash the project) by three months?

| | Normal | | Crash | |
|---|---|---|---|---|
| *Activity* | *Time (months)* | *Cost ($1,000)* | *Time (months)* | *Cost ($1,000)* |
| 1–2 | 2 | $10 | 1 | $15 |
| 2–3 | 6 | 8 | 5 | 18 |
| 2–4 | 2 | 15 | 1 | 21 |
| 2–5 | 8 | 30 | 6 | 52 |
| 4–3 | 2 | 7 | 2 | 7 |
| 3–5 | 3 | 21 | 1 | 33 |
| 1–5 | 8 | 20 | 5 | 41 |

15. *a.* For the accompanying network and time-and-cost table, what is the least costly way to reduce (crash) the project by one month?

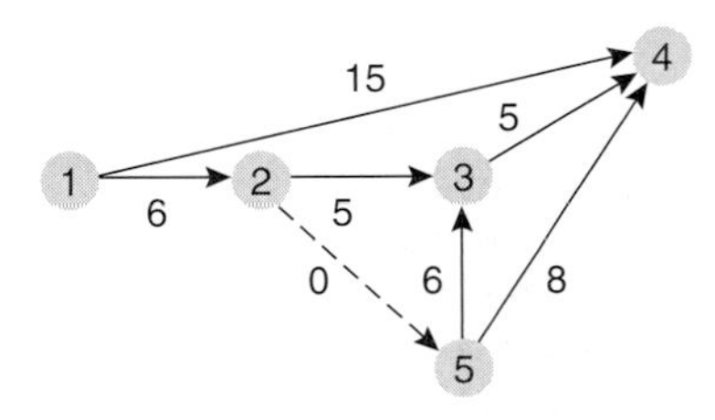


*b.* What is the fastest the project could be done if you used crash times?

| | Normal | | Crash | |
|---|---|---|---|---|
| *Activity* | *Time* | *Cost ($100)* | *Time* | *Cost ($100)* |
| 1–2 | 6 | $100 | 5 | $205 |
| 1–4 | 15 | 200 | 12 | 600 |
| 2–3 | 5 | 100 | 4 | 190 |
| 3–4 | 5 | 150 | 3 | 360 |
| 5–3 | 6 | 80 | 5 | 185 |
| 5–4 | 8 | 300 | 7 | 360 |

16. A number of project types are listed below, ranging from small and simple to grand. As indicated in Exhibit 17-15, modest projects warrant only the first PERT/CPM subsystem, whereas grand projects justify all four subsystems; in-between projects warrant subsystems 1 and 2 or subsystems 1, 2, and 3. Decide which subsystems should apply for each project listed. Explain each.
    *a.* Computer network selection and installation for company of 200 employees.
    *b.* Moving the computer facility for a large bank to a new building in a major city.

*c.* Upgrading 30 classrooms for multimedia capability in a college of business building at a major university.
*d.* Community project to attract new industry in three large, abandoned factory buildings (town of 10,000 people).
*e.* Five-year overhaul of a nuclear submarine.
*f.* Implementing MRP in a manufacturing company of 1,000 employees.
*g.* New-product development testing (including market research) for a major food company.
*h.* Moving a toxic waste containment vessel from one storage facility to a new one in another state.
*i.* Launching a new drug for treatment of arthritis.
*j.* Building a 500-room hotel in Lincoln, Nebraska.
*k.* Building a 500-room hotel in Manhattan.

17. The accompanying network segments are all part of the same home-construction project. Where is a dummy activity needed, and why?

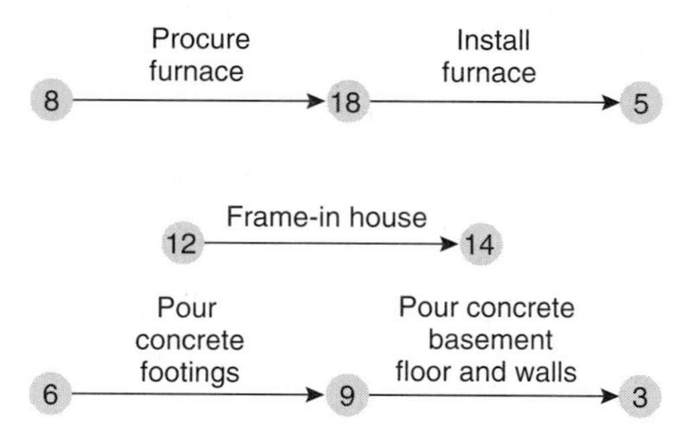


18. The network diagram shown below shows activity duration times in months.

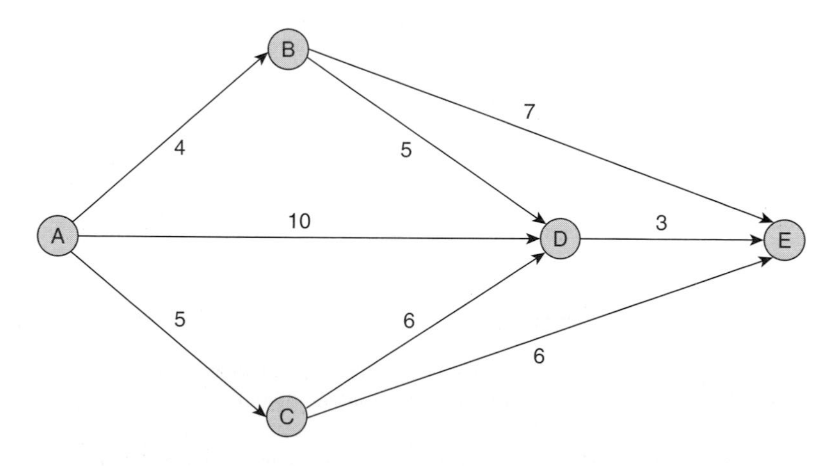


*a.* With a forward pass through the network, compute *ES* and *EF* times for each activity to determine the expected project completion time.
*b.* With a backward pass through the network, compute *LF* and *LS* times for each activity and compute the planned activity slack times.

*c.* Identify the critical activities that exist in this project.

*d.* Suppose that during the project, activity A–B is delayed so that its early finish (*EF*) becomes 7. In that case, the slack for activity D–E would become what?

19. The table below contains time/cost crash data for the network shown in Exercise 18. Assume that activity-crashing costs apply in a linear fashion across the entire possible crashing range, for example, activity B–E costs $20,000/month to crash.

**Table 1: Project Network Time–Cost Data**

| *Activity* | *Normal Time (months)* | *Normal Cost ($ × 1,000)* | *Crash Time (months)* | *Crash Cost ($ × 1,000)* |
|---|---|---|---|---|
| A–B | 4 | 170 | 4 | NA |
| A–C | 5 | 120 | 4 | 180 |
| A–D | 10 | 500 | 9 | 550 |
| B–D | 5 | 180 | 4 | 280 |
| B–E | 7 | 200 | 5 | 240 |
| C–D | 6 | 100 | 3 | 190 |
| C–E | 6 | 300 | 6 | NA |
| D–E | 3 | 50 | 2 | 120 |

*a.* If the project needs to be shortened by one month, the activity that should be crashed is what? Explain your choice.

*b.* If the project needs to be crashed a *second* month, which activity should be crashed?

*c.* As the project is planned now, what is the shortest possible duration? What is the planned cost at the shortest duration?

*d.* How are crashing options affected by project progress?

20. Develop an example of how each of the following tools of process improvement—fishbone chart, Pareto chart, check sheet—might be used in a construction project. Focus your examples on ways to reduce project uncertainty and lateness.

APPENDIX 

# AREAS UNDER THE NORMAL CURVE

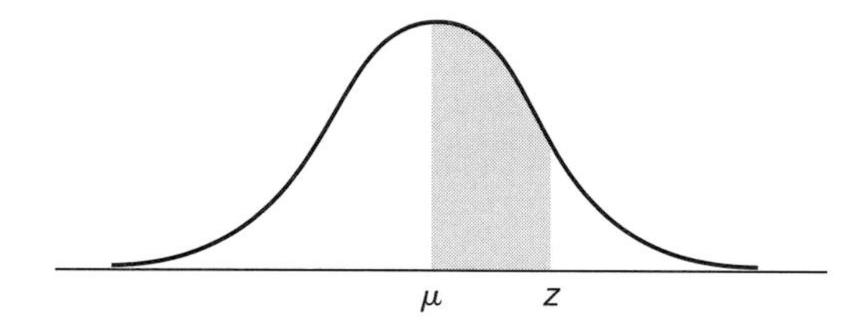


### Example

The area between the mean ($\mu$) and the point one standard deviation above the mean ($z = 1.00$) is 0.3413, or 34.13 percent of the total area under the curve. The area between $z = -1.00$ and $z = 1.00$ is $0.3413 + 0.3413 = 0.6826$.

**TABLE A-1 Areas of Standard Normal Distribution**

| $z$ | 0.00 | 0.01 | 0.02 | 0.03 | 0.04 | 0.05 | 0.06 | 0.07 | 0.08 | 0.09 |
|---|---|---|---|---|---|---|---|---|---|---|
| 0.0 | 0.0000 | 0.0040 | 0.0080 | 0.0120 | 0.0160 | 0.0199 | 0.0239 | 0.0279 | 0.0319 | 0.0359 |
| 0.1 | 0.0398 | 0.0438 | 0.0478 | 0.0517 | 0.0557 | 0.0596 | 0.0636 | 0.0675 | 0.0714 | 0.0753 |
| 0.2 | 0.0793 | 0.0832 | 0.0871 | 0.0910 | 0.0948 | 0.0987 | 0.1026 | 0.1064 | 0.1103 | 0.1141 |
| 0.3 | 0.1179 | 0.1217 | 0.1255 | 0.1293 | 0.1331 | 0.1368 | 0.1406 | 0.1443 | 0.1480 | 0.1517 |
| 0.4 | 0.1554 | 0.1591 | 0.1628 | 0.1664 | 0.1700 | 0.1736 | 0.1772 | 0.1808 | 0.1844 | 0.1879 |
| 0.5 | 0.1915 | 0.1950 | 0.1985 | 0.2019 | 0.2054 | 0.2088 | 0.2123 | 0.2157 | 0.2190 | 0.2224 |
| 0.6 | 0.2257 | 0.2291 | 0.2324 | 0.2357 | 0.2389 | 0.2422 | 0.2454 | 0.2486 | 0.2518 | 0.2549 |
| 0.7 | 0.2580 | 0.2612 | 0.2642 | 0.2673 | 0.2704 | 0.2734 | 0.2764 | 0.2794 | 0.2823 | 0.2852 |
| 0.8 | 0.2881 | 0.2910 | 0.2939 | 0.2967 | 0.2995 | 0.3023 | 0.3051 | 0.3078 | 0.3106 | 0.3133 |
| 0.9 | 0.3159 | 0.3186 | 0.3212 | 0.3238 | 0.3264 | 0.3289 | 0.3315 | 0.3340 | 0.3365 | 0.3389 |
| 1.0 | 0.3413 | 0.3438 | 0.3461 | 0.3485 | 0.3508 | 0.3531 | 0.3554 | 0.3577 | 0.3599 | 0.3621 |
| 1.1 | 0.3643 | 0.3665 | 0.3686 | 0.3708 | 0.3729 | 0.3749 | 0.3770 | 0.3790 | 0.3810 | 0.3830 |
| 1.2 | 0.3849 | 0.3869 | 0.3888 | 0.3907 | 0.3925 | 0.3944 | 0.3962 | 0.3980 | 0.3997 | 0.4015 |
| 1.3 | 0.4032 | 0.4049 | 0.4066 | 0.4082 | 0.4099 | 0.4115 | 0.4131 | 0.4147 | 0.4162 | 0.4177 |
| 1.4 | 0.4192 | 0.4207 | 0.4222 | 0.4236 | 0.4251 | 0.4265 | 0.4279 | 0.4292 | 0.4306 | 0.4319 |

*(continued)*

**TABLE A-1 Areas of Standard Normal Distribution (*contd.*)**

| *z* | *0.00* | *0.01* | *0.02* | *0.03* | *0.04* | *0.05* | *0.06* | *0.07* | *0.08* | *0.09* |
|---|---|---|---|---|---|---|---|---|---|---|
| 1.5 | 0.4332 | 0.4345 | 0.4357 | 0.4370 | 0.4382 | 0.4394 | 0.4406 | 0.4418 | 0.4429 | 0.4441 |
| 1.6 | 0.4452 | 0.4463 | 0.4474 | 0.4484 | 0.4495 | 0.4505 | 0.4515 | 0.4525 | 0.4535 | 0.4545 |
| 1.7 | 0.4554 | 0.4564 | 0.4573 | 0.4582 | 0.4591 | 0.4599 | 0.4608 | 0.4616 | 0.4625 | 0.4633 |
| 1.8 | 0.4641 | 0.4649 | 0.4656 | 0.4664 | 0.4671 | 0.4678 | 0.4686 | 0.4693 | 0.4699 | 0.4706 |
| 1.9 | 0.4713 | 0.4719 | 0.4726 | 0.4732 | 0.4738 | 0.4744 | 0.4750 | 0.4756 | 0.4761 | 0.4767 |
| 2.0 | 0.4772 | 0.4778 | 0.4783 | 0.4788 | 0.4793 | 0.4798 | 0.4803 | 0.4808 | 0.4812 | 0.4817 |
| 2.1 | 0.4821 | 0.4826 | 0.4830 | 0.4834 | 0.4838 | 0.4842 | 0.4846 | 0.4850 | 0.4854 | 0.4857 |
| 2.2 | 0.4861 | 0.4864 | 0.4868 | 0.4871 | 0.4875 | 0.4878 | 0.4881 | 0.4884 | 0.4887 | 0.4890 |
| 2.3 | 0.4893 | 0.4896 | 0.4898 | 0.4901 | 0.4904 | 0.4906 | 0.4909 | 0.4911 | 0.4913 | 0.4916 |
| 2.4 | 0.4918 | 0.4920 | 0.4922 | 0.4925 | 0.4927 | 0.4929 | 0.4931 | 0.4932 | 0.4934 | 0.4936 |
| 2.5 | 0.4938 | 0.4940 | 0.4941 | 0.4943 | 0.4945 | 0.4946 | 0.4948 | 0.4949 | 0.4951 | 0.4952 |
| 2.6 | 0.4953 | 0.4955 | 0.4956 | 0.4957 | 0.4959 | 0.4960 | 0.4961 | 0.4962 | 0.4963 | 0.4964 |
| 2.7 | 0.4965 | 0.4966 | 0.4967 | 0.4968 | 0.4969 | 0.4970 | 0.4971 | 0.4972 | 0.4973 | 0.4974 |
| 2.8 | 0.4974 | 0.4975 | 0.4976 | 0.4977 | 0.4977 | 0.4978 | 0.4979 | 0.4979 | 0.4980 | 0.4981 |
| 2.9 | 0.4981 | 0.4982 | 0.4982 | 0.4983 | 0.4984 | 0.4984 | 0.4985 | 0.4985 | 0.4986 | 0.4986 |
| 3.0 | 0.4986 | 0.4987 | 0.4987 | 0.4988 | 0.4988 | 0.4989 | 0.4989 | 0.4989 | 0.4990 | 0.4990 |
| 3.1 | 0.4990 | 0.4991 | 0.4991 | 0.4991 | 0.4992 | 0.4992 | 0.4992 | 0.4992 | 0.4993 | 0.4993 |
| 3.2 | 0.4993 | 0.4993 | 0.4994 | 0.4994 | 0.4994 | 0.4994 | 0.4994 | 0.4995 | 0.4995 | 0.4995 |
| 3.3 | 0.4995 | 0.4995 | 0.4995 | 0.4996 | 0.4996 | 0.4996 | 0.4996 | 0.4996 | 0.4996 | 0.4997 |
| 3.4 | 0.4997 | 0.4997 | 0.4997 | 0.4997 | 0.4997 | 0.4997 | 0.4997 | 0.4997 | 0.4998 | 0.4998 |
| 3.5 | 0.4998 | 0.4998 | 0.4998 | 0.4998 | 0.4998 | 0.4998 | 0.4998 | 0.4998 | 0.4998 | 0.4998 |
| 3.6 | 0.4998 | 0.4998 | 0.4999 | 0.4999 | 0.4999 | 0.4999 | 0.4999 | 0.4999 | 0.4999 | 0.4999 |
| 3.7 | 0.4999 | 0.4999 | 0.4999 | 0.4999 | 0.4999 | 0.4999 | 0.4999 | 0.4999 | 0.4999 | 0.4999 |
| 3.8 | 0.4999 | 0.4999 | 0.4999 | 0.4999 | 0.4999 | 0.4999 | 0.4999 | 0.5000 | 0.5000 | 0.5000 |
| 3.9 | 0.5000 | 0.5000 | 0.5000 | 0.5000 | 0.5000 | 0.5000 | 0.5000 | 0.5000 | 0.5000 | 0.5000 |

APPENDIX 

# ANSWERS TO SELECTED EXERCISES

## Chapter 1

4. (Operations and other line functions)

   General examples—line:

   - Marketing services company (e.g., advertising agency)
   - Financial services company (e.g., billing and collections service company)

   General example—staff:

   - Inspection services company (e.g., weld X-ray inspection company)

6. (Next-process customer examples)

| *Employee Position* | *Next-Process Customer* | *Previous Process (supplier)* |
|---|---|---|
| Cost accountant | Director of natural resources dept. | DNR field agent (data source) |
| Console designer | Automobile interior designer | Display instrument supplier |
| Market analyst | Financial adviser in the firm | Government data sources |
| Benefits counselor | Employee nearing retirement | Estate planner (e.g., attorney) |
| Software trainer | University employees | Software manufacturer |
| Civil engineer | Managing project engineer | Field survey crew |
| Maintenance technician | Aircrew (pilot and first officer) | Manufacturer (service bulletins) |

8. (Operations modes: Partial response)

| *Organization* | *Type of Operation* | *Explanation or Example* |
|---|---|---|
| Bottling plant | Continuous/Repetitive | Liquid flow, then repetitive at packaging |
| Dry cleaner | Job | Each customer's clothes taken in as a job |
| Resort hotel | Repetitive | Posting daily charges to guests' accounts |
| Cafeteria | Repetitive | Customers flow through food service lines |
| Public accountant | Job or project | Personal tax return (job); company audit (project) |
| Highway construction | Project | Singular, large-scale endeavor |

10. (Operations management Center [OMC] plant tours)

    Note: OMC page format and contents are subject to change, but at any time, 50 or more plant tours are available.

12. (Application of six basic customer wants: Examples)

    Air traffic control:

    *Quality:* Flight safety; e.g., clarity of communications with aircrews.

    *Flexibility:* Knowledge of runway and secondary airport options in case of need.

    *Service:* Capacity planning to further improve safety and on-time performance.

    *Cost:* Efficient training facilities and employee benefits for air traffic controllers to reduce employee turnover.

    *Response time:* Timely weather and airport status information for aircrews.

    *Variability:* Consistent operating procedures among all ATC centers.

14. (Jane's sweater purchase)

    The concept of value chains represents a more contemporary presentation of the older "middle-man mark-up" idea. At each stage in a customer or supply chain, some added value (e.g., parts added, packaging supplied, or service performed) must be perceived by the customer *and wanted by the customer* if that stage is to survive in the long run. The notion of *value migration* suggests that these customer wants and perceptions are dynamic. In this exercise, Joan's advice reflects a benefit-to-cost-ratio way of thinking—arguably the most popular model in our personal and business consumption habits.

16. (Sheila, Director of Purchasing)

    The employee-as-customer concept has grown in popularity; it is a hallmark of an increasing number of successful companies. It is especially important in periods of low unemployment such as that experienced in the United States in recent years. Benefits are numerous: For example, people form habits that carry over to dealings with external customers, workplace animosity decreases, understanding of flow relationships increases, and problem-solving teams become more efficient.

18. (Visit to American Customer Satisfaction Index [ACSI] web site)

    The ASCI is still in its infancy, so widespread use of the data maintained by the National Quality Research Center continues to expand. As more companies become a part of the effort, expect marketing personnel to gain additional insight into its potential for implementing OM Principle 16 . . . the essence of which encourages companies to advertise every improvement in company operations.

## Chapter 2

6. (State University musical presentations)

   *a.* Each site might be considered a project, but not a very complicated one. Actors, musicians, props, and other people and resources will assemble at the site to create the performance. In all performances, however—and certainly during the two performances at each site—the presentation (*The Sound of Music*) remains the same, so we expect repetition of not only the performance but of the setups and take-downs as well.

   *b.* Volume (12 performances overall) will allow for learning effects; operations at later presentations will be more streamlined. Site variety will limit the gains in efficiency, however. If different musicals were to be presented at each site, volume benefits would decrease even further.

   *c.* (Assuming same musical at each site) Design is crucial. Setup and takedown should be major concerns during set and prop design (even during scripting to a lesser extent). Checklists (to cover all details and to assign responsibilities) help prevent oversights. Training (practice) in all facets of the operation—not just performance delivery—will also help ensure that no last-second "surprises" develop.

8. (State University musical presentations, continued)

   Each site must average 1,105 patrons, about 553 for each of the two shows at the site.

10. (Riverview Antiques & Souvenirs)

    *a.* $Q_{BE} = 261$

    *b.* Profit = \$8,500

    *c.* $Q = 870$

    *d.* The obvious risk associated with a higher asking price and customers' value expectations.

12. (Deck and Grounds, Inc.)

    *a.* $Q_{BE} = 14$

    *b.* $Q = 19$

14. (Volume-variety issues at various settings)
    *a. Concession stand.* Set up special lines for high-volume items or combos (e.g., hot dog, fries, and a soft drink). Have patrons buy tickets for food and drink items at a separate cashier's window to avoid having to make change in the food service area.
    *b. Government office.* Design special flow lines for high-volume transactions (e.g., driver's license renewal) but rely on general-purpose counters for low-volume transactions (e.g., requests for special, one-time services or permits).
    *c. Television set assembly plant.* Dedicated line or cell to make the high-volume (high demand) set model and more general-purpose lines or cells for other models.

    (Note the similarity in the way high-volume requirements are managed in manufacturing and in service settings.)
16. (Competition and OM)

    In a nutshell, successful companies keep the customer—the next process—and the customer's requirements in focus at all times. This is carried out in many ways, of course, and we explore them throughout this book. In general, successful companies increase quality, flexibility and service while decreasing variability, response time, and cost. Continuous improvement in meeting these requirements is the mandate.
17. & 18. (Examples of cost leadership and differentiation)

    *Service:* Southwest Airlines is low cost and reliable, known for excellent point-to-point transportation, but no frills.

    *Product:* Dell Computers is very price-competitive but is also known for high-quality components, fast delivery, custom assembly options, and dependable after-sale service.
20. (Addition of Internet shopping to ongoing operations)

    In general, order-fulfillment operations have become more complicated. Outsourcing the order fulfillment activities (e.g., receipt and processing or order information, item "picking" from warehouses, packaging, labeling, and shipping and tracking) has been a frequent option as companies scramble to gain expertise in these areas. Logistics network expertise is a high-demand skill area.

## Chapter 3

2. (First City Bank—operations strategy)
    *a.* The OM strategy suggests a business strategy to attract and retain personal and small-business accounts. It is clearly consistent with OM Principles 1 (get to know the customer), 2 (improve service/reduce response time), 8 (automate incrementally), and 9 (flexible, movable, lower-cost equipment).
    *b.* Simpson's work supports OM Principle 4 (know the competition). This idea is a cornerstone in contemporary strategy, operations, marketing, design, and financial services.
    *c.* Examples of other sources of information include customer surveys, industry data, and regional economic data. Efforts show a direct relationship with all four strategy-formulation OM Principles (1 through 4), and with several capacity and processing principles (7, 10, and 12 in particular).
6. (Cutting flow time and distance: example responses)
    - (A bank) placed ATM machines in select spots on campus to cut travel time and distance for students' financial transactions.
    - The pizza service at (name of company) lets you place orders for up to a week in advance. So you can just make one call and have several meals planned for the week. And they deliver, of course.
    - (Name of florist) opened a shop in the student union. Now it's much easier to get "floral obligations" taken care of in less time. And you get to see what you are ordering.
8. (Provider's failure to operate at customer's use rate)

    If a provider operates faster than the customer's use rate, the result is an inventory accumulation between the two stages. If the provider operates slower than the customer requires, there is a constant series of stock outages at customer's work area.
10. (Arbor Nurseries, Inc.—Principles of OM)
    - Principle 7 (cross-trained employees)
    - Principle 9 (simple, movable equipment in multiple units)
    - Principle 11 (cut flow time, especially in processing of orders)
    - Principle 12 (cut changeover times . . . required to go from one work mode to another)

12. (John Deere and Company—Principles of OM)
    - Principle 7 (cross-train employees for mastery of multiple jobs)
    - Principle 1 (get to know the customer)
    - Principle 10 (make it easier to provide goods and services without error)

## Chapter 4

4. (Planning at Ash County Hospital)

   *Total deviation* for last quarter = 60 hours, for an *average departmental deviation* of 7.5 hours. The MAD is 34 hours, with *departmental absolute deviations* ranging from 10 to 84 hours. In sum, the aggregate labor forecast is fairly accurate, but the departmental specialty forecasts are not. Use of next quarter's labor forecast as a budget planning document is warranted, but better departmental projections are needed for departmental staffing (capacity) planning.

6. (Henry & Henry—group and aggregate forecasts)
   *a.* Aggregate forecast error = 440 client-days.
   *b.* EP = −50 client-days; AA = +70 client-days; BC = +420 client-days.
   *c.* Level at about 260 client-days per month.
   *d.* For the next few months, plan on an upward trend with slope in the range of 10–15 client-days per month. Track actual demand and revise forecast perhaps quarterly or semi-annually.

10. (Big Splash, Ltd.)
    *a.* Seasonal
    *b.* About 12 or 13
    *c.* Average quarter demand = 136 ÷ 8 = 17
    *d.* Winter = 0.74; spring = 1.29; summer = 1.29; fall = 0.68
    *e.* Winter = 14.8; spring = 25.8; summer = 25.8; fall = 13.6
    *f.* Yes, this is a seasonal business.

12. (Lawngirl Manufacturing Company—service parts demand)
    *a.* The greater the time span, the greater the smoothing effects.
    *b.* One-week MA forecast = 800
    Three-week MA forecast = 793
    Nine-week MA forecast = 776
    *c.* Longer time spans are better for stable products with widely dispersed markets—the case for lawnmower replacement (service) parts.

14. (Exponential Smoothing & Tracking Signal)
    *a.* MAD = 13.2; Tracking signal = 1.89
    *b.* MAD = 14.8; Tracking signal = 1.58
    *c.* Larger smoothing coefficient reduces MAD; MAD and TS are inversely related in the three trials (Exercises 4-13 and 4-14), but the data set is too small for conclusions.

16. (Pescado Grande—seasonal index)
    *a.* Seasonal index for Sunday = 1.87; for Monday = 0.405
    *b.* Forecast for Monday = 16 × 0.405 = 6.5

18. (Convenience Store—correlation)
    *a.* Correlation coefficient = 0.93 (Note: Excel example on your CD-ROM).
    *b.* Yes, the correlation is quite strong, definitely worth using lottery payoff as a predictor of 48-hour-period sales.
    *c.* Yes, the amount of lead is approximately five days before the 48-hour period for which sales data have been recorded. This lead might be sufficient for scheduling in a convenience store, especially if part-timers normally work irregular hours.
    *d.* Yes, it is an excellent indicator of overall demand for the store's wares.

20. (Acme Manufacturing Company)
    *a.* Approximately 35 citations for next month
    *b.* Appears that citations pattern follows new hires pattern by one month.
    *c.* $Y = 75.29 - 4.71\ (X)$, where 75.29 is the intercept at period −8 (assumed $X = 0$ point). $Y_8 = 37.57$; $Y_9 = 32.86$
    *d.* Correlation between citations and new hires = 0.33
    Correlation between citations and new hires previous month = 0.86

## Chapter 5

2. (Federal Express)
   *c.* In general, any program that enhances workforce stability also enhances capacity planning by removing uncertainties associated with employee turnover.

6. (Bright Way)

   With a chase-demand strategy, Bright Way becomes more like a typical janitorial service. It would rely more on a transient workforce for adjustable capacity, so there would be less need to plan capacity far into the future.

New management problems would be in the human resources management arena; hiring/firing, scheduling, and supervisory concerns.

8. (Coast Limited—revised demands)

 *a.* Excess capacity allowed in each month $= (466 \div 7) \div 2 = 33.3$ cars. So, month 3 with its demand for 41 cars becomes the constraint. Level capacity will be for $(41 + 33.3) = 74.3$ cars per month.

 *b.* Backlogs occur in month 1 (6.7 cars) and 5 (23.7 cars). The excess capacity available in month 2 is sufficient to cover month one's backlog within a week or two (into month 2). The backlog in month 5 poses a greater problem. As the level-capacity plan stands—at 74.3 cars per month—this backlog will create disruptions through the end of this planning horizon (month 7) and perhaps longer. Maybe some overtime should be planned for months 5 and 6, and of course, appropriate budgets for that overtime must also be planned.

10. (Old English Tea Company)

 The company will need 14.85, rounded up to 15 people to meet production of 6,500 boxes per shift, so one person should be reassigned to other work.

12. (Dominion Envelope Company)

 *a.* In the BNA cell, cross-trained employees can smooth disruptions that the functional organization of the non-BNA work areas is near powerless to correct.

 *b.* Organize more cells, one for each family of similar products or similar customers; that is, implement OM Principle 6.

14. (Fiberglass Products—production plan)

 *a.* Beginning inventory + Production − Sales = Ending Inventory
 1,600 + Production − 4,500 = 1,000
 Production = 3,900; or 1,300 per month

 *b.* The production plan is an aggregate grouping for all tub and shower units. The MPS shows schedule for each item (e.g., size and model). Also, the MPS will plan in weeks or days rather than in months.

## Chapter 6

3. (Buyer-Supplier Relationships—example responses)

 *b.* Chemical company

 - *Number of suppliers.* Typically few suppliers (e.g., wells, mines) promotes partnerships.
 - *Quality.* Process controls needed at the source to avoid the huge expense of removing impurities during processing.
 - *Transportation.* The industry is concentrated (e.g., Gulf of Mexico), but customers are dispersed and highly dependent on assured supply; hence a need for reliable logistics.

 *h.* Retail hardware store

 - *Delivery frequency/order size and Order Conveyance.* Point-of-sale data are timely for triggering small-lot JIT shelf replenishment deliveries rather than large-lot resupply of stockrooms.
 - *Transportation.* Quick, reliable transport can spell the difference between profit and loss in this competitive, low-margin business.

6. (Home building contractor—break-even analysis)

 *a.* $Q_{BE} = 44$

 *b.* Most likely, all costs will be subject to change.

8. (Yummy Foods—break-even analysis)

 *a.* $Q_{BE} = \$480{,}000$

 *c.* As expected, Pincher's analysis considers only expenses paid by Yummy Foods, not fees and commissions that might be paid (to any agent) by travel-related service providers such as airlines and hotels. Could Yummy get lower costs by going directly to airlines and hotel chains and seeking sole-source arrangements? Obviously, travel patterns and requirements of Yummy's personnel weigh heavily in the assessment.

10. (ABC uses)

 Example: Make or buy analysis/decisions. *A* items, done by executive committee; *B* items, done by product or materials manager; *C* items, done by inventory planner.

12. (ABC classes)

| *Item Number* | *Dollar Usage Last Year* | *Class* |
|---|---|---|
| 030 | $30,000 | A |
| 109 | 6,000 | B |
| All others | | C |

14. (THIS Company)

 As conditions stand, loss of THIS Company business could well be the death blow to the uniform supplier.

One critical issue facing Adam, however, is time: Does Adam have enough time to bring the uniform supplier up to quick-response partnership status? Of course, the supplier's willingness and ability to cooperate is a big factor.

16. (Organizational purchasing) Examples:
    *a.* Use of competitive bids; city government for road work, computer manufacturer for components.
    *b.* The city is heavily into buying intangibles; examples include consultant's services and software.
    *c.* Approved supplier lists: all except liquor wholesaler (liquor quality is a "given"). Blanket orders: for commodity items such as the fuel oil that an electric power company might buy.
    *d.* Value analysis (VA) is likely for manufacturers who use large volumes of certain parts. Manufacturers of home appliances, computers, furniture, ships, and aerospace products all qualify.
18. (Value Analysis in JIT companies)

    JIT requires on-the-spot problem solving that includes any needed design changes. For VA to be accomplished in such quick fashion ("on the fly"), specifications must be kept to a minimum. Typically, only performance specifications are included.
20. (Jane Doe—patio grills)

    The excessive parts list shows a lack of standardization. Jane should act to reduce the number of component parts in accordance with OM Principle 5.

## Chapter 7

2. (Design Excellence Awards—influence on buying behavior)

   Example response: To the extent that the design award was given in recognition for characteristics that I valued in the product, then yes, it would influence my buying decision. But I really don't recall seeing where companies have used IDEA awards in their advertising, so I probably would not know if the product had won an award.

   (Note: This student's response blends the concepts of "value in the eyes of the customer" with the message of OM Principle 16—market every improvement.)
4. (Chess clock—design improvements)

   Reduce the number of screws (Guideline 7) and replace the special fasteners with standard ones (Guideline 9).
6. (Electrical outlet and switch plates—design improvements)

   Design for snap-in installation. Benefits include elimination of millions of screw-downs each year by highly paid construction employees. Plastic boxes that may be nailed to wall studs have replaced older, metal boxes that had to be screwed to the studs. If metal studs replace wooden ones, as is happening in some areas, perhaps an insulated, universal joining feature will become prevalent.
8. (Monitor Manufacturing Company)

   Follow the design guidelines, notable Guideline 6—modular designs.
10. (UPS—design changes)

    In addition to vehicle redesigns needed to accommodate natural gas fuel systems, other factors that will require new designs include maintenance training; fuel purchase, delivery, and storage systems; and possible even route layouts.
12. (TRI-CON—specifications)

    Minimal specifications promote producibility and encourage customers' designers to work closely with supplier.
15. (Modular car assembly)

    Relevant guidelines: 2 (minimize parts), 6 (use modules), 7 (ease of assembly), 8 (one-way assembly), 9 (avoid special fasteners).
16. (Reducing number of operations) Examples:
    - Avoiding data reentry: At video rental outlets and automobile "quick-lube" establishments, for instance, the customer's telephone or license plate number pulls up complete customer identification information and maintenance history or customer preferences (e.g., movie preferences or type of motor oil preferred).
    - Some states allow motorists with safe driving records to renew driver's licenses by telephone or via Internet, saving the motorist travel time and reducing the operations required by state personnel.
18. (Security system timer—reliability)

    Reliability at one-half year (26 weeks) is about 0.483; at 4 weeks (approximately one month), about 0.894; and at 2 weeks, about 0.946. Many modern plant-monitoring systems provide data (e.g., emissions, radiation, temperature, etc.) that is required for the plant to operate and to maintain its certifications or even license to operate. Depending on what is being secured in this instance, changeover at the two-week interval may even be too risky.

20. (Fuel system control valve—reliability)

    *a.* At the end of two weeks, $R = 0.987$

    *b.* Reliability can be enhanced through redundancy—a backup (parallel) valve.

22. (Furnace thermostat—reliability and availability)

    *a.* $R_{12\text{ months}} = 0.670$; $R_{24\text{ months}} = 0.449$; $R_{36\text{ months}} = 0.301$

    *b.* Availability $\cong 0.99991$

    *c.* No. Availability is very high and the possible discomfort that a two-hour downtime (average) might cause is minimal.

24. (Coolant line sensor—system reliability)

    *a.* $R_2 \cong 0.978$

    *b.* $R_3 \cong 0.997$

## Chapter 8

2. (Zero defects)

   As you move down the list, pause to consider the potential consequences of a mistake by each provider. None of us wants to be on the receiving end of defects; our aim should be to avoid providing any. The last item on the list helps reveal how committed you are to achieving that aim . . . it's the sort of thing recruiters ask about.

4. (Price versus quality)

   The perception that higher price denotes higher quality service is the issue. Though increasingly challenged by cost-effective and high-quality providers, that perception still permeates some sectors.

6. (PDCA cycle) Example response: Inkless printer cartridges

   *Plan.* Establish a print darkness standard and design a printer sampling plan.

   *Do.* Implement regular printer inspection and cartridge replacement as required.

   *Check.* Check by random or spot testing and survey users for feedback.

   *Act.* Formalize the Inspect and Replace as Necessary (IRAN) scheme, or if printers get approximately equal usage, implement a group-replacement policy.

8. (Acme motor-generator set)

   It is an operating expense (perhaps a capital investment) needed to accomplish a variety of desirable outcomes: better productivity, better service, faster response times, lower operating costs, better quality, and perhaps improved safety.

10. (Ace Auto Repair)

    *a.* Yes, front-liners should take responsibility for quality; also, before the job leaves the work area is the best time to make any necessary corrections.

    *b.* Yes, it is a part of appraisal and prevention of subsequent defects.

    *c.* Yes, even though the mechanic will try to do the job right the first time, the check adds value in the form of an assurance that there are no related problems.

    *d.* Yes, to continue with the logic of part *c*, inspection of the work is a part of doing the job right the first time. And, if properly designed, the inspection and test procedure will be quick and efficient.

    *e.* No change. The consequences of careful inspection just become more obvious.

12. (Sandwiches-Are-We—benchmarking)

    The idea to use benchmarking is a good one. The best place to start (whether or not benchmarking will be used) is a thorough analysis of existing procedures—including some collection of time, distance, and quality data. Often, some possibilities for quick and cheap improvements emerge from that exercise.

14. (Malcolm Baldrige National Quality Award winners)

    Though there has been wide variation, overall, the winners have enjoyed a high level of success over a wide range of organizational performance indicators.

16. (Tuition increase study group)

    *a.* This interest group is not a team as defined in the text. With sustained effort and growing membership, along with some goals or an agenda, it might evolve into one.

    *b.* Customers, providers, and those empowered to enact change should be represented.

18. (Bank tellers)

    It is a poorly designed circle since all participants are from the same work area and, in this case, have the same job title. Diversity among membership (cross functions, job titles, groups, work areas, etc.) is a better scheme.

## Chapter 9

2. (Jostens/Ampex—improvements)

   *Jostens.* Responsibility for quality was transferred to frontline associates. Requisite tools (e.g., computers) and necessary information were placed under frontline control, and cross-training programs were implemented. (OM Principles 2, 7, and 14).

   *Ampex.* Direct effort went into cutting cycle time and reducing flow distance (OM Principles 11 and 13). Scrap was cut (Principle 10), as were setup times (12). Employee training (7) and front-liners' assumption of purchasing responsibilities (14) also contributed.

4. (Camping/Recreation Goods producer—improvements)
   - Review and revise designs in accordance with guidelines in Chapter 7.
   - Emphasize building quality into products rather than after-the-fact inspection; redesign processes to facilitate that aim (see Exhibit 9-1).
   - Train personnel—producers and support employees—in SPC. Also on the subject of training, cross-train employees so that they have mastery of multiple jobs.
   - Establish partnership relationships with a few good suppliers; involve those suppliers in quality improvements.
   - Make sure that the focus shifts from *output* to *good output* all along the supply chain.

6. (Attributes charts—ideal situation)

   The ideal state is zero defects, and on attributes charts that would plot as a flat line at zero on the vertical axis—definitely not a random pattern.

8. (AmPen—fishbone diagram and Pareto chart)
   *a.* The fishbone diagram emphasizes potential causes of error—alerting people as to cause-effect relationships.
   *b.* The Pareto chart shows the relative importance, by some form of numerical relationship, of various types of problems or defects. Attack the most important (e.g., most frequently occurring, most costly, etc.) first.

10. (Social services youth activity center—fishbone diagram)
    *a.* The fishbone skeleton shows five major categories of process variables that could contribute to low attendance at the youth activity center. (You may wish to add others.) Under "methods," for example, you might put a subbone "inconvenient operating hours," and as a sub-subbone "closes too early on weekends" and "no hours on Sunday."
    *b.* Brainstorm to discover which subbones are the most likely causes of poor attendance. Also, other similar centers—successful ones—around the country might be benchmarked. Maybe some experimentation with new activities is in order as well.

12. (Fail-safing approach to common problems)
    *a.* *Office equipment.* Checklist with sign-off, or automatic timers.
    *b.* *Appointments.* Set reminders on computer, or use watch with alarm.
    *c.* *Internet passwords.* Have sites store password, maintain separate passwords file (with a single password itself), or avoid leaving sensitive material (e.g., credit card numbers) on site or in file and use common password such as anniversary date.
    *d.* *Tollway change.* Quit smoking and carry change in automobile ashtray.
    *e.* *One-of-a-pair.* Never separate the pair; always tie or clip together.

14. (Oil Can—run diagram)
    *a.* Assuming that the 25 observations constitute a "fair test," the run diagram shows a rather high degree of variability in service times. The first eight jobs required less than 15 minutes, but subsequent ones took longer. Fatigue may be a factor.
    *b.* Trial spec limits should represent what the process can do and what customers will tolerate. Several possibilities exist; we explore two:
       - The value "12" is an eyeball average; we might arbitrarily set specs at $12 \pm 5$ minutes. Now, what can we find out about the four outliers (the 6, 18, 18, and 19)?
       - We may believe that the early jobs are rushed (early arrivals in a hurry to get to work, perhaps) and that jobs from 9 on are more realistic. A spec of $15 \pm 3$ minutes, for example, might be tried under this assumption.
    *c.* The histogram reveals two "bumps" in the distribution of service times, a small one at 9 minutes and a larger one in the 15–17 minutes range. Perhaps smaller cars require less time? Maybe one mechanic is noticeably faster than the others are?
    *d.* Both may be used to design and implement employee training. Explain that any job that exceeds specs is a reason for discussion as to cause, but avoid the word

"blame." The idea is to learn from the data . . . it is the window into the heart of the process.

16. (Environmental Control Associates—X-bar and R charts)
    *a.* X-double-bar = 104.45; $UCL_X$ = 114.47; $LCL_X$ = 94.43; R-bar = 13.75; $UCL_R$ = 31.38
    *b.* To answer this question, do what the engineer has done—look closely at the data, especially sample 7. Does she suspect a measurement error in the fourth observation? Could the "125" have been misread, or misrecorded? Is a value of 105 or 115 more in line with what the process has revealed about itself? Here, if either 105 or 115 is the correct reading, we come to a different conclusion about our process. In SPC work, we do not casually "toss out" readings we don't like, but we are quite ready to acknowledge that measurement is a part of the process and is just as apt as any other part to give us problems.

18. (Spark-O-Plenty—X-bar and R charts)
    *a.* X-double-bar ≅ 0.500 volts; $UCL_X$ = 0.511; $LCL_X$ = 0.489
    R-bar = 0.023; $UCL_R$ = 0.046
    *b.* Process is out of control. Find and eliminate assignable cause and start over.

20. (OK-Mart & Electro Corp.—*p* chart)
    *a.* Center line on the *p*-chart: *p*-bar = 0.002 (corresponding to 0.2 percent defective)
    *b.* The process output, regardless of whether or not it is in control, does not meet either output standard, so there is work to be done. If assignable causes exist, eliminate them and then prepare another chart. When control is obtained, perhaps substantial process redesign will be required in order to meet the standard.

22. (Rescue Service Training—c chart)
    *a.* C-bar = 5.28; $UCL_C$ = 12.17; $LCL_C$ = 0
    *b.* The process is not in control.
    *c.* Two types of corrections are needed:
    - The error variation among the classes results in the out-of-control situation. Why are some classes so much better (worse) than others? The cause for this variation needs to be rooted out.
    - On a grander scale, how can error rates overall be decreased? The objective is not to obtain process control but to reduce errors to zero. Error classification, perhaps accomplished with a check sheet, might be a good start.

24. (Food processing company—process capability)
    *a.* Total tolerance band = 0.16 oz.; supplier's inherent capability (0.20 oz.) is not good enough, so don't buy.
    *b.* No change. The supplier's problem is excess variation in process output; a change in location and process control can't change that fact.
    *c.* Advise both to work together to determine and eliminate cause of excess variation.

26. (Plug-N-Go—process capability)
    *a.* $C_{pk}$ = 0.833
    *b.* About 0.62 percent of the valve covers are out of spec.
    *c.* Two actions: First, always strive to reduce variation in process output; second, shift process downward toward target specification of 0.50 cm.

28. (Variation stackup—services provider)
    *a.* Classes meet on the hour and last for 50 minutes. Professor Mean holds her marketing class over into the 10-minute break and Professor Meaner starts his accounting class early.
    *b.* A travel agent books a connecting flight scheduled to depart 30 minutes after the first leg flight lands, but the first flight often runs between 20 and 40 minutes late.

## Chapter 10

1. (Iota Company)
   Increase the risk. Raise the reorder point.

4. (Hewlett-Packard)
   *a.* The computer transactions add no value to the goods and services destined for customers. Excess documentation, like the work orders here, is a hidden cost associated with having inventories.
   *b.* Student exercise.

6. (Ivy Memorial Hospital) Example items
   - Involve suppliers early and inform them of the QR effort; explain that demand will be "pulling the string" for hospital services and thus for their services as suppliers.
   - Try to separate demands into independent and dependent items; that will help determine how much lead time the hospital can give its suppliers.
   - Streamline processes all along the provider-customer supply chain.

8. (Post Office—readiness and changeover) Examples:
   - Workplace arrangement (Guideline 3), everything near and in a standard position.
   - Externally loadable stamp drawers (Guideline 8).
10. (MRP for an industrial thermostat producer)

    Cycle time is still very bad. The company has not attacked and reduced non-value-adding wastes.
12. (Quick Setup at KFC and at general Mills) Example responses:
   - At the KFC restaurants, materials were positioned closer to the window (Guideline 3) and packer box sizes were standardized (Guideline 7).
   - Addition of handles to avoid having to find a grasp, and position a tool when an adjustment must be made (Guideline 6) and do as much before the changeover (pit stop) as can be done (guideline 2).
14. (Elmo's Burger Shoppe—inventory turnover)

    Annual sales = \$50,000 per month × 12 months per year = \$600,000

    Annual CGS: CGS + (0.1) CGS = \$600,000
    ∴ CGS = \$545,454 per year

    Inventory turnover: $T$ = \$545,454 ÷ \$12,000 = 45.5 turns per year.

    No, Elmo's should not calculate partial turns because there is no WIP and no finished goods inventory.
16. (Variabilities and Taguchi's social loss concept)

    Both messages: "On-target" performance is the goal. Deviations detract from customer service and result in loss to *some* segment of society.

## Chapter 11

2. (Frozen dessert outlet—queuing models)
   *a.* Utilization = 0.67
   *b.* Probability of no wait = Idleness = 0.33
   *c.* Mean time in queue = 0.133 hours
   *d.* Mean time in the system = 0.20 hours
   *e.* Mean number in queue = 1.33
   *f.* Mean number in the system = 2.0
   *g.* Probability of 2 or more customers in the system = 0.44
4. (Computers at wrapping station—queuing models)
   *a.* System characteristics:
   - Utilization = 0.90
   - Idleness = 0.10
   - Mean time in queue = 0.45 hours
   - Mean time in the system = 0.50 hours
   - Mean number in queue = 8.1
   - Mean number in the system = 9.0

   *b.* The focus is on delay costs, so WIP inventory costs are a major concern. If we value a finished computer (waiting wrapping) at \$1,000, there is \$9,000 worth of goods inventory in the wrapping station alone. If other stations have a similar queue, perhaps several hundred thousand dollars sits in lines . . . waiting.
6. (Scuba Tanks—constant test time)
   *a.* Mean time in queue = 0.083 hours (or, 5 minutes)
   *b.* Mean time in the system = mean time in queue + $1/\mu$ = 0.167 hours (or, 10 minutes)
   *c.* Mean number in queue = 0.67
   *d.* Mean number in the system = mean number in queue + $\lambda/\mu$ = 1.33
   *e.* Lower costs due to shorter throughput times.
   *f.* Quality of the test and cost of the process.
8. (Returns counter staffing)
   *a.* Cross-train area supervisors and other personnel to staff the returns counter and then institute a queue-limit program—maybe when the line reaches three, another employee moves to serve returns counter customers.
   *b.* Cross training and the queue limit policy.
10. (Buffet line—pull or push?)

    Pull in the sense that as customer select and remove items, the buffet staff replaces those items. Push in the (short-term) sense that the provider places the daily selections on the line without a signal from customer as to what food items are preferred. In the long term, however, customer preferences will affect the menu.
12. (Sentrol, Inc.—parts delivery by roller skate)

    Sentrol has been using this system for years. More frequent deliveries of smaller quantities are critical for successful JIT operations. Large items (there are few at Sentrol) would still require a cart for delivery, but since most parts (items) would not be on the cart, even the cart runs occur faster.
14. (Accounts payable office—response ratio)

    An invoices-to-desks ratio (or, pieces to people) is the best option. Thus:

    Response ratio = 150 : 3 = 50 : 1

16. (Queue limitation—methods)
    *a.* *Book printer*. Kanban squares on the floor.
    *b.* *TV set assembly*. Powered conveyor.
    *c.* *Vitreous china products production*. General-purpose containers (e.g., wheeled dollies) with attached kanbans.
    *d.* *Large polished precision metal parts*. Special customized containers.
    *e.* *Internal mail delivery*. General or special-purpose push carts.

## Chapter 12

4. (Comparable Work and Fair Pay)

   Comparable work requires that work content be measured, so the pay-according-to-job content concept applies—item 3 in Exhibit 12-3.

6. (Thumb's Tax Service—possible costing inaccuracy)
   *a.* Good cost data are needed for:
   - Market positioning decisions
   - Line-of-services (product line) decisions
   - Sales growth policies
   - Make-or-buy decisions

   *b.* Break the business into cells, one for personal tax accounts and one for business accounts. Average costs per customer served will be more readily available. Unallocated overhead costs may be parceled out to the two units according to activity levels.

8. (Nanosoft, Inc.—utilization reports)
   *a.* Utilization of large copiers is important, but should be well below 100 %; otherwise urgent jobs will suffer delays. Take random samples a few times each year—not monthly tabulations that nobody reads.
   *b.* There is no point in doing the labor utilization studies every month. Do an annual estimate, or better yet, collect work-sampling data if needed by an improvement team working to eliminate non-value-adding activities.
   *c.* No need for monthly reports. Automation available in modern libraries makes usage figures easy to put together if needed for an improvement effort.

10. (Social services agency)
    *a.* Staff needed = (42 clients/day) × (3.5 hours/client) × (1 employee day/8 hours) × 1.18 = 21.7 ≅ 22 employees
    *b.* Historical standard

12. (Automobile plant—standard time)

    $$\text{Standard time} = 3.6 \text{ minutes} \times 1.11 \times 1.12 = 4.48 \text{ minutes}$$

14. (Lugging machine—standard time)
    *a.* Standard time = 0.314 minutes
    *b.* MTM data are already normalized, so pace rating is not necessary.

16. (Typing—work sampling): Assume a 480-minute workday.
    a. Typing:

    $$\text{Elemental time} = 55\% \text{ of } 4{,}800 \text{ minutes} \div 60 \text{ letters} = 44.0 \text{ minutes/letter}$$

    $$\text{Rated time} = 44.0 \times 0.90 = 39.6 \text{ minutes/letter}$$

    $$\text{Standard time} = 39.6 \times 1.10 = 43.56 \text{ minutes}$$

    Retrieving:

    $$\text{Elemental time} = 15\% \text{ of } 4{,}800 \text{ minutes} \div 150 = 4.8 \text{ minutes/letter}$$

    $$\text{Rated time} = 4.8 \times 0.8 = 3.84 \text{ minutes/letter}$$

    $$\text{Standard time} = 3.84 \times 1.10 = 4.22 \text{ minutes/letter}$$

    *b.* Uses include staffing, scheduling, and evaluation of equipment and methods.
    *c.* Yes, they are engineered standards. If any biases (e.g., easy vs. hard jobs, old vs. new equipment, etc.) are controlled, the standards may be used for personnel evaluation.

18. (Wabash Airways)
    *a.* Standard output per flight = 2 attendants × 70 minutes/flight ÷ 2 minutes/meal = 70 meals per flight

    Efficiency (80 meal flight) = 80 ÷ 70 = 114%

    *b.* 550 meals × 2 minutes/meal ÷ 100 minutes = 11 attendants

20. (Setting time standards—examples)
    *a.* Mowing grass. Historical or standard data
    *b.* Soldering connections. Time study or predetermined standards
    *c.* Drafting. Historical.

## Chapter 13

2. (Brown Instrument Company—ROP)
   *a.* Service level = 1 − (1 ÷ 52) = 0.9808, or 98.08%; and $z \cong 2.07$ (from Appendix A)
   $SS = z(\sqrt{LT})(\sigma) = 2.07(1)(25) = 51.75$
   $ROP = DLT + SS = 100 + 51.75$
   $= 151.75 \cong 152$ thumbscrews
   *b.* Both SS and DLT will increase if leadtime is four weeks, so ROP increases.
4. (Storeroom item—service level and safety stock)
   *a.* For 95% service level, $z \cong 1.645$ (from Appendix A)
   $SS = z(\sqrt{LT})(\sigma) = 1.645(\sqrt{(1.5)})(25) = 50.4 \cong 51$
   *b.* All three factors act to lower the safety stock level.
6. (Fuel oil for university—ROP calculations)
   *a.* Orders per month = 10,000 ÷ 12,000 = 0.83
   Orders in an average five-month season = 5 (0.83) = 4.15
   *b.* Lead time = 2 weeks (approx. $\frac{1}{2}$ month), so $DLT \cong 10{,}000(0.5) = 5{,}000$ gallons
   Safety stock = ROP − DLT = 6,400 − 5,000 = 1,400 gallons
8. (Chain—lot-for-lot versus fixed quantity)
   *a.* Lot-for-lot, steel rod demand

| *Period* | *1* | *2* | *3* | *4* | *5* |
|---|---|---|---|---|---|
| Demand | 11 | 13 | 19 | 13 | 14 |

   *b.* Fixed-order-quantity, steel rod demand

| *Period* | *1* | *2* | *3* | *4* | *5* |
|---|---|---|---|---|---|
| Demand | 60 | 0 | 20 | 40 | 0 |

   *c.* Yes, with a fixed-quantity system, small variations in end-product demand are amplified into large variations in component demand.
10. (Continental Plate and Boiler Company—carrying cost)
   *a.* Order processing cost: S = Annual purchasing dept. costs ÷ Annual # of purchase orders
   S = \$105,000 ÷ 800 = \$131.25 per order
   *b.* Annual capital cost = \$2.0 million × 0.18 = \$360,000
   Annual holding cost = \$31,000 + \$88,000 + \$32,000 = \$151,000
   Carrying cost rate = I = \$511,000 ÷ \$2,000,000 = 0.256, or 25.6%
12. (Chemical plant—EOQ and number of orders)
   *a.* EOQ = 3,086
   *b.* Number of orders = D ÷ EOQ = 25,000 ÷ 3,086 = 8.1
14. (Marksman Industries—responsiveness and lot size)
   Produce smaller lot sizes more frequently; streamline setups to shorten and reduce costs.
16. (Semiconductors—Benefits of small lots)
   Run small lots. If there are star products (high-demand models), use dedicated lines or cells for their production—effectively reducing changeover times to zero.
18. (Partial MRP records)
   *a.* Period 4, an order for 10 units.
   *b.* Plan an order for 40 D's in period 2.
   *c.* First gross requirement for 60 J's occurs in period 1.
   *d.* First planned order for J's is for 200 units.
   *e.* Plan an order for 200 J's in period 1.
20. (Bicycle manufacturer—MRP)
   *a.* Plan an order for 100 handlebars in week 4 and an order for 200 cut tubes in week 2.
   *b.* Net requirement = 206.18, so plan an order for 207 cut tubes in week 2.
22. (Acme Wood Products—MRP calculations)
   *a.* Hint: Your drawing should have three zero-level items (finished goods).
   *b.* Item master file must contain each part number, name of part, on-hand balance, lead time, and lot size. It may also include safety-stock requirements and scrap allowance.
   *c.* Example: Parent item requirements for week 2: 100 oak, 200 walnut, and 300 mahogany frames.
   *d.* Planned order release for 2,000 10-inch pieces in weeks 1 and 4.
27. (Kitchen knives—MRP calculations)
   *a.* Order 2,400 rivets in week 2.
   *b.* Order 2,400 blocks in week 3.
   *c.* Order 130 wood bars in week 3.

## Chapter 14

4. (ISO 14000—pollution prevention)

   Note: As you do your study, try to differentiate activities that *prevent* pollution from happening at the source (e.g., cleaner-burning fuels; more efficient motors; higher yields, and thus less scrap, in production processes) from those that are after-the-fact. The latter types either: (1) reduce or eliminate pollution after it has occurred (e.g., use of filters or scrubbers), or (2) clean up polluted areas (e.g., removal of leaking underground chemical storage tanks and contaminated soil).

6. (OM Principles—facilities management)

   All of the operations strategy formulation principles (numbers 1 through 4) apply. Also, Principle 10 (make products without error) and Principle 14 (record and own process data at the workplace and ensure that front line people get first crack at solving problems) are especially relevant.

8. (Design office—layout)

   In the diagrams, zones 1 and 3 should have *absolutely close* (4-line) relationship, as should zones 2 and 4. There are also four *especially close* (3-line) relationships, two *important* (2-line) ones, and two *ordinary closeness* (1-line) ones.

10. (Industry settings—type of layout) Example responses:
    - *Auto assembly*. Product.
    - *Machine shop*. Cell (if modern); functional if older or traditional shop.
    - *Large aircraft overhaul*. Fixed position.

18. (Spider Diagram—problem solving)

    Example response: Each member of the group might list five personal failings or bad habits that annoy one or more other members of the group. These become the arms for the spider diagram. The most important part, however, is a plan of action that can be implemented to move toward the center of the diagram on each of the arms.

20. (Wexco, Inc.—operator ownership)

    Loss of staff size need not equate to loss of prestige. Black and his personnel should find their expertise in even greater demand.

22. (Acme Corp.—storage and handling gear)

    Worst-to-best listing: AS/RS, carousel, pallet racks, wire-guided system, and transporter.

24. (Customers' facilities—suppliers' concern)

    Absolutely! The customers' competitiveness depends on facilities. There may be little that the supplier can do other than offer to assist, but the supplier should follow Principle 1—especially the part about knowing what customers on down the value chain are thinking.

## Chapter 15

2. (Continuous versus repetitive operations)
   a. *Iced cappuccino manufacturing*. Syrup processing (coffee, milk, water, flavorings, etc.) is continuous; bottling and packaging of finished product are repetitive.
   b. *Aspirin tablet manufacturing*. Tableting is continuous; packaging is repetitive. Mixing—prior to tableting—is batch processing that is roughly repetitive in that batches repeat.
   c. *Breakfast cereal manufacturing*. Continuous processing until packaging, when it becomes repetitive.
   d. *Nursing care for hospitalized patient*. Continuous monitoring (electronic, but with regular personal checks). Hourly or daily activities (medication dispensing, therapy, etc.) are repetitive.
   e. *Banking (account maintenance)*. Check processing and statement preparation activities are repetitive (bordering on continuous); cashing checks, posting deposits, opening and closing accounts are rather repetitive activities. Large-customer account openings and closings and audits may constitute unique jobs—addressed in Chapter 16.
   f. *Facility security services*. Continuous (electronic) monitoring coupled with repetitive visual inspection by guards. Also, repetitive change-out of batteries, sensors, and other components. Initial system design and installation would constitute a job, again, the subject of Chapter 16.

4. (Detergent manufacturing—success factors)
   - Process design and capital investment, much automation and process engineering. Also, automated and continuous process monitoring.
   - Reliability of supply; firm, long-term contracts with key suppliers and dependable transportation (e.g., an owned or controlled pipeline).

6. (Synchronized mixed-model schedule)

   A fully synchronized schedule that covers both buildings is unlikely. Building A should strive for mixed-model schedules.

8. (Faiko Time company)

   Faiko should regularize mechanism assembly to about seven per day (for example, four of type A, two of type B, and one of type C). Check the demand every two weeks and adjust the schedule as required. Enclosures are less amenable to regularizing, but if there is a dominant (demand) type, then it should get regularized production.

10. (Product wheel—example responses)

    - Process-industry products such as chemicals that have a relatively low, intermittent demand individually but are collectively enough to keep the facility busy.
    - Families of parts with near-identical processing steps but with variations in color, size, or shape. Examples include a product line of plastic containers for home use or a line of plastic mugs and glasses that display colors and logos of various universities.

12. (Line balancing analysis)

    *a.* $\sum t = 100$ hundredths, or 1.00 minute

    Cycle time (maximum allowable):
    $c = 420$ minutes/day $\div$ 1,500 units/day
    $= 0.28$ minutes

    Minimum number of stations:
    $n = \sum t \div c = 1.00 \div 0.28 = 3.57$ rounded up to 4.

    *b.* Example balance, using 0.28 minutes as the cycle time, with stations and tasks in order of assignment:

    | | |
    |---|---|
    | Station 1: Tasks A, F, and D | Idle time = 0 |
    | Station 2: Tasks E, I, C, and H | Idle time = 0 |
    | Station 3: Tasks K and L | Idle time = 2 hundredths |
    | Station 4: Tasks B, G, and J | Idle time = 10 hundredths |

    Balance delay: $d = (nc - \sum t) \div nc = 0.12 \div 1.12 = 0.107$, or 10.7%

    The balance delay of just over 10 percent is not so troubling as the imbalance among the stations. Perhaps an early task in the sequence that follows what we see in the precedence diagram could be accomplished in Station 4; that would redefine the job somewhat, however.

16. (Hair dryers—mixed-model line balancing)

    OM Principle 13 suggests that we plan for one cycle to yield two standard and one deluxe model (e.g., SSD). Production time requirements result in a cycle time of $4 + 4 + 12 = 20$ minutes. With a 480-minute workday, the cycle can repeat $480 \div 20 = 24$ times. But that assumes full utilization—a risky schedule in that it allows no undercapacity scheduling benefits.

    If 100 deluxe dryers are demanded per day, there must be $100 \div 24 = 4.17$ lines or cells producing the dryers. That may be obtained by using 4 lines and adding 10 minutes of overtime, but again, that uses 100% of capacity. A better plan is to use 5 lines or cells, each operating at an average capacity of $20 \div 24 = 0.83$, or 83%. That leaves time for maintenance, training, emergency demand surges, and so forth.

18. (Mixed-model product demand)

    Daily requirements:

    Style 1–125 units, Style 2–75 units, Style 3–50 units

    Divide by LCD (25) to determine within-cycle mix:

    Style 1–5 units, Style 2–3 units, Style 3–2 units

    Cycle pattern: 1-2-1-3-1-2-1-3-1-2; repeating 25 times each day

20. (Medium-volume products)

    Take the top 5 or 10 medium-volume products (by revenue or sales quantity) and slot into a repeating cycle schedule that is run every three to five days; the idea is to always have these products on a short-lead-time availability. Fit remaining products in as possible.

22. (Regularized schedules—department store)

    Shelf stocking, ordering, and account processing are but a few activities that can be regularized. Prior processes for shelf stocking (e.g., unboxing, sorting, tagging) should be synchronized to the shelf-stocking schedule.

## Chapter 16

2. (Advertising agency—late job completions)

   In a nutshell, get rid of the queues to speed jobs through the routing—queue limitation and better flow-control procedures are definitely needed. Maybe focus the business to concentrate on fewer job types. Maybe establish cells (with members from relevant departments, but 12 are overkill) to handle ads by type or by industry or by customer. Too much oversight and departmental "check-off" suggests an environment where turf wars are the norm.

4. (Maintenance department—Gantt schedule charts) Partial response:

   *a.* Workload for the two orders in three job areas.

| Day | 5 | 10 | 15 | 20 | 25 | 30 | 35 |
|---|---|---|---|---|---|---|---|
| | | | | | | | |
| Wiring | | | | | | | |
| | | | | | | | |
| Drywall | | | | | | | |
| | | | | | | | |
| Painting | | | | | | | |
| | | | | | | | |

Order 1
Order 2

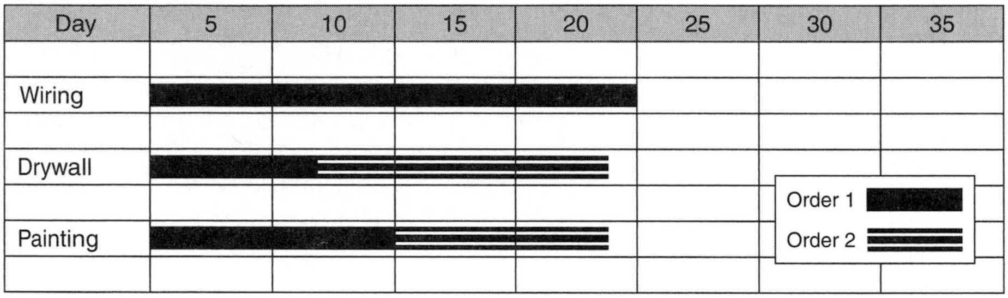

6. (Gantt Chart)

   *a.* Day 11; percent completion = 10 ÷ 12 = 0.83, or 83%. Bar shows status is two days ahead of schedule.

   *b.* Tomorrow, the arrow will show day 12, the bar will be solid (black) and three days beyond day 12, reflecting three days ahead of schedule.

   *c.* Consecutive number shop calendar skips nonwork days.

8. (Workcenter load imbalance)

   *a.* If the workcenter is a gateway, leveling techniques such as firm planned orders may be used. In extreme cases, the master scheduler may be asked to change the MPS.

   *b.* The computer processes the open order file, accumulating loads by time bucket (period) for each workcenter. Next, the same thing occurs for planned orders via CRP software. The combination yields the load report.

10. (Jerrybuilt Machines, Inc.)

    Job release sequence, with slack time:

    894, slack = −3
    916, slack = −1
    889, slack = +1
    901, slack = +4

12. (Job release sequence—prioritizing rules)
    - FCFS: A, B, C, D, E
    - SPT: D, A, E, B, C
    - EDD: A, D, E, C, B
    - LS: C, A, E, B, D (B & D tie)

14. (Blanking center—job priority list)

    Job release sequence, with slack time:

    444, slack = −1
    222, slack = +1
    333, slack = +2

    Negative slack means that the order is behind schedule; required time exceeds available time as planned. In some cases the job can be expedited and completed on schedule, but better management aims at keeping jobs from becoming late in the first place.

16. (Central sales office—hand carry)

    The best solution is to streamline the office so that all jobs are processed as fast as the hand carry ones are today. The benchmark (today's hand-carry processing speed) is there, now meet it. Queue limitation, flexible capacity, flow lines (by family, for example), and Internet links are among the possibilities.

18. (Scheduling for bottleneck workcenter)

    This kind of problem can develop when there is too much focus on just the "known" bottleneck workcenter. The intermediate centers along the routings (12 and 19 in this example) can prove to be the trouble spots, especially as job queues develop. In all work centers, practice queue limitation, reduce setups and changeovers, ensure adequate and flexible capacity, and look for ways to form flow lines or cells of common process families.

## Chapter 17

4. (Rationale for a dummy activity)

   Dummy activity 16–13 assures that both 12–16 and 10–13 precede 13–18 but that only 12–16 precedes 16–18. The idea is for the network to mirror the actual project sequence.

6. (Disk magazines—activity-on-arrow diagram)

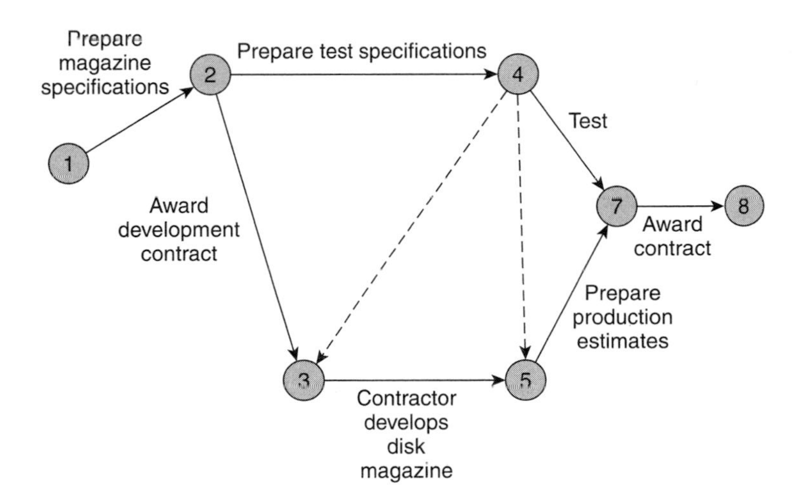


8. (Aeropa, Inc.—PERT/CPM)
   *a.* Critical path: 1–4–5–11–15–16;
   Time estimate = 120 weeks
   *b.* (Individual response)
   *c.* Critical path estimate is now 126 weeks.

10. (PERT/CPM—crashing the network, Partial response)

    Critical path is A-D-G at 12 weeks and at a normal cost of $61,000.

    To cut to 11 weeks, crash D at $4,000; new cost is $65,000.

    To cut to 10 weeks, crash D another week; new cost id $69,000.

    Now there are three critical paths.

12. (PERT/CPM—network analysis)
    *a.* The early start (Es) time for activity **C–G** is 15.
    *b.* The early start for activity **E–G** is 18.
    *c.* Activity **C–G** has the latest early finish time at 34 months.
    *d.* The slack on activity **D–E** is 4.
    *e.* The late finish time for activity **B–C** is 15.
    *f.* The late finish time for activity **A–E** is 22.
    *g.* Activity **E–G** should be crashed if it becomes a critical activity (and there is need to shorten the project).

14. (PERT/CPM—project crashing)
    *a.* Critical activities are 1–2, 2–3, and 3–5 for a total time of 11 months

    Activity 1–2 costs $5,000 to crash one month; next cheapest is activity 3–5 at $6,000 per month.

    *b.* Reduce 1–2 by one month, 2–5 by one month, and 3–5 by two months (not in that order).

16. (PERT/CPM subsystems—example responses)
    *a.* *Computer network selection and installation.* Urgency may be present, but size, uncertainty, and complexity are not factors in this type of job today. System 1 is sufficient.

*h. Moving a toxic waste containment vessel.* Size (distances) may be large geographically—many jurisdictions to cross—but overall complexity, urgency, and uncertainty are relatively modest.

*i. Launching a new drug for arthritis treatment.* (Presumably, research and testing have been completed and FDA approval has been granted since the project is defined as "launching.") Thus, the project boils down to a marketing campaign to educate health care professionals (if a prescription drug) and/or the public it is an over-the-counter remedy. No complexity, little uncertainty, maybe some urgency to beat competitors, and moderate size.

18. (PERT/CPM—network change during implementation)

*a.* Expected project completion time = $E_f$ for activity **D–E** = 14 months.

*b.* (Start with $L_f = 14$ for activities **B–E, D–E,** and **C–E.**)

*c.* Critical activities are **A–C**, **C–D**, and **D–E.**

*d.* If $E_f$ for activity **A–B** becomes 7, then—assuming no other changes—the $E_s$ for activity **D–E** becomes 12 and the $E_f$ for **D–E** becomes 15 (12 + 3). Therefore, **D–E** has slack of (14 − 15) = −1 month. Negative slack is common during projects; the management *might* wish to consider crashing options, but in this case the long advance warning time (since the problem occurred early in the project) provides time for flexible capacity to get the project back on track.

20. (Process improvement tools in construction project)

- *Check sheet.* Record causes for mishaps or problem. Look for patterns that can be used to guide improvement efforts.
- *Fishbone chart.* For major or chronic problems, brainstorm the cause-effect linkages with the help of the fishbone chart. Again, the aim is to discover guidance for improvement.
- *Pareto chart.* Check sheet data on frequencies of problems flows naturally into a Pareto-type chart. The most frequent (or most costly) problem is attacked first.

# END NOTES

## Chapter 1

[1]*Fortune* magazine's most-admired-company status is awarded on the basis of scores on eight criteria. See, for example, "America's Most Admired Companies," *Fortune,* March 1, 1999, pp. 68ff. Excellence among small companies is also recognized; see the cover story in the November 8, 1999, issue of *IW Growing Companies.*

[2]By convention, operations are denoted on the flowchart as small circles and the inspection by a small square. Other standard flowcharting symbols are covered in later chapters. We briefly note at this time, however, that the flowchart is a proven tool in process design and improvement.

[3]Gabriel A. Pall, *Quality Process Management* (Englewood Cliffs, NJ: Prentice-Hall, 1987), pp. 18–19.

[4]Tom Brown, "Decoding the 'Clueless' Manager," an interview with Scott Adams, *Industry Week,* July 3, 1995, pp. 14–18.

[5]Adrian J. Slywotzky and David J. Morrison, *The Profit Zone* (New York: Random House, 1997), p. 29.

[6]Ibid.

[7]Robert W. Hall, *Attaining Manufacturing Excellence: Just In Time, Total Quality, Total People Involvement* (Burr Ridge, IL: Dow Jones–Irwin, 1987), p. 24.

[8]Richard J. Schonberger, *Building a Chain of Customers: Linking Business Functions to Create the World Class Company* (New York: The Free Press, 1990).

[9]Robert Levering and Milton Moskowitz, "The 100 Best Companies to Work For," *Fortune,* January 10, 2000, pp. 83ff.

[10]David Simchi-Levi, Philip Kaminsky, and Edith Simchi-Levi, *Designing and Managing the Supply Chain* (Burr Ridge, IL: Irwin/McGraw-Hill, 2000), p. 1.

[11]Jon Brecka, "The American Customer Satisfaction Index," *Quality Progress,* October 1994, pp. 41–44.

[12]"Tax Man Adds ACSI to Measure Service," *Quality Progress,* May 1999, p. 14.

[13]Ronald E. Yates, "A New Way to Gauge Economy," *Chicago Tribune,* September 18, 1994, p. 1ff.

[14]M. Scott Myers, *Every Employee a Manager,* 3rd ed. (San Diego, CA: University Associates, 1991).

## Chapter 2

[1]*Thorndike-Barnhart Comprehensive Desk Dictionary* (Garden City, NY: The Country Life Press, 1951); in the same source, *strategic* is "pertaining to raw material necessary for warfare . . . [and] of an air force or bombing. . . ." *The New Encyclopedia Britannica* (Chicago: Encyclopedia Britannica, Inc.: 1989) still lists only military references to strategy and related words—an entire column of them in the index.

[2]Arthur A Thompson, Jr. and A. J. Strickland III, *Crafting and Implementing Strategy: Text and Readings,* 10th ed. (Burr Ridge, IL: Irwin/McGraw-Hill, 1998), p. 2.

[3]Guidelines for the Strategic Alignment of the Bayer Group (http://www.bayer.com) [Site visited January 2000].

[4]Robert Buderi, "Into the Big Blue Yonder," *Technology Review,* July–August, 1999, pp. 46–53.

[5]Geoffrey Colvin, "America's Most Admired Companies," *Fortune,* February 21, 2000, pp. 108ff.

[6]Anne Newman, ed., "In Business This Week," *BusinessWeek,* March 6, 2000, p. 54.

[7]Kenichi Ohmae, *The Mind of the Strategist: Business Planning for Competitive Advantage* (New York: McGraw-Hill, 1982), Chapter 8.

[8]James P. Womack, Daniel T. Jones, and Daniel Roos, *The Machine That Changed the World* (New York: Rawson Associates, 1990), p. 13.

[9]Ibid.

[10]Michael E. Porter, *Competitive Strategy: Techniques for Analyzing Industries and Competitors* (New York: The Free Press, 1980), pp. 35–40.

[11]Aleda V. Roth, "World Class Operations: A Paradigm for OM Research in the Strategic Management of Health Care Services," *Decision Line,* July 1995, pp. 5–7.

[12]Pankaj Ghemawat, *Strategy and the Business Landscape: Text and Cases* (New York: Addison-Wesley, 1999), p. 57.

[13]Howard S. Gitlow and Shelly J. Gitlow, *The Deming Guide to Quality and Competitive Position* (Englewood Cliffs, NJ: Prentice-Hall, 1987), p. 20.

[14]Wickham Skinner, "Manufacturing—Missing Link in Corporate Strategy," *Harvard Business Review,* May–June, 1969, pp. 136–45.

[15]Richard J. Schonberger, *World Class Manufacturing: The Lessons of Simplicity Applied* (New York: The Free Press, 1986), pp. 217–18.
[16]Richard J. Schonberger, *World Class Manufacturing: The Next Decade* (New York: The Free Press, 1996).
[17]While a discussion of cost elements is beyond our scope, we will note that specific cost components are seldom completely variable or fixed. For a thorough explanation and examples of typical variable and fixed costs, see Garrison, Ray H. and Eric W. Noreen, *Managerial Accounting,* 9th ed. (Burr Ridge, IL: Irwin/McGraw-Hill, 1999), Chapter 2.
[18]The original idea for the matrix comes from Robert H. Hayes and Steven C. Wheelwright, "Link Manufacturing Product and Process Life Cycles," *Harvard Business Review,* January–February 1979, pp. 133–40. This version of the matrix is adapted from Sam C. Taylor, Samuel M. Seward, and Steven F. Bolander, "Why the Process Industries are Different," *Production and Inventory Management,* Fourth Quarter 1981, pp. 9–24.
[19]Pierre Pean, "How to Get Rich off Perestroika," *Fortune,* May 8, 1989, pp. 145–50.
[20]Henry Ford, *Today and Tomorrow* (Garden City, NY: Doubleday, 1926), p. 115.
[21]Otis Port, "Customers Move into the Driver's Seat," *BusinessWeek,* October 4, 1999, pp. 103–06.
[22]Stephan Franklin, "Productivity of U.S. Workers On a Roll," *Chicago Tribune,* February 9, 2000, Section 3, p. 1.
[23]Michael J. Mandel, "How Fast Can This Hot-Rod Go?" *BusinessWeek,* November 29, 1999, pp. 40–42.
[24]"Survey of E-Commerce: Shopping Around the Web," *The Economist,* February 26, 2000, p. 5.
[25]"Ford, General Motors, and DaimlerChrysler Create World's Largest Internet-Based Virtual Marketplace," AOL News: PRN Newswire (http://www.prnewswire.com), February 25, 2000.
[26]Judith Silverstein, "Desperately Seeking E-fulfillment," *Digital Chicago,* Nov/Dec 1999, p. 4.
[27]Ibid.
[28]Kathleen Kerwin, Marcia Stepanek, and David Welch, "At Ford, E-Commerce Is Job 1," *BusinessWeek,* February 28, 2000, pp. 74–78.
[29]For example, see Richard L. Ratliff, Stephen M. Beckstead, and Steven H. Hanks, "The Use and Management of Teams: A How-To Guide," *Quality Progress,* June 1999, pp. 31–38.
[30]Kerwin et. al., "At Ford, E-Commerce is Job 1," p. 78.
[31]Otis Port, "Customers Move into the Driver's Seat," p. 106.
[32]Ibid.
[33]Gene Bylinsky, "America's Elite Factories," *Fortune,* August 16, 1999, pp. 136A–T.
[34]Philip Siekman, "Building 'em Better in Brazil," *Fortune,* September 6, 1999, pp. 246C–V.
[35]Cited in Bruce D. Henderson, "The Origin of Strategy," *Harvard Business Review,* November–December 1989, pp. 139–43.
[36]William H. Davidow and Bro Uttal, "Service Companies: Focus or Falter," *Harvard Business Review,* July–August, 1989, pp. 77–85.
[37]Gene Bylinsky, "America's Elite factories," p. 136C.
[38]Ram Charan and Geoffrey Colvin, "Why CEOs Fail," *Fortune,* June 21, 1999, pp. 69ff.
[39]Ibid., p. 70.

## Chapter 3

[1]Karen Bemowski, "Three Electronics Firms Win 1991 Baldrige Award," *Quality Progress,* November 1991, pp. 39–41.
[2]Adrian J. Slywotzky and David J. Morrison, *The Profit Zone* (New York: Random House, 1997), p. 27.
[3]Richard J. Schonberger, *World Class Manufacturing: The Next Decade* (New York: The Free Press, 1996), p. 46.
[4]Nypro, Inc. Home Page (http://www.nypro.com/), [Visited March 20, 2000].
[5]This section presents but a brief glimpse of the scoring system that is used to measure success in achieving management by principles. For a complete description and discussion, see J. Schonberger, *World Class Manufacturing: The Next Decade,* Chapters 2 and 3.
[6]Emily Nelson, "Big Retailers Try to Speed Up Checkout," *The Wall Street Journal,* March 31, 2000, p. B1.
[7]Gene Bylinsky, "America's Elite Factories," *Fortune,* August 16, 1999, p. 136P.
[8]Ibid., p. 136T.
[9]Signicast Corporation Home Page (www.signicast.com), [Visited April 2000].

## Chapter 4

[1]Jim Browne, "Scheduling Employees for Round-the-Clock Operations," *IIE Solutions,* February 2000, pp. 30–33.
[2]AI Ries and Jack Trout, *Bottom-Up Marketing* (New York: McGraw-Hill, 1989), p. xii.
[3]Andy Zipster, "How Pressure to Raise Sales Led Miniscribe to Falsify Numbers," *The Wall Street Journal,* September 11, 1989.
[4]Robert Goodell Brown, *Smoothing, Forecasting, and Prediction of Discrete Time Series* (Englewood Cliffs, NJ: Prentice-Hall, 1963), p. 102.
[5]Nada R. Sanders, "The Dollar Considerations of Forecasting with Technique Combinations," *Production and Inventory Management Journal* 33, no. 2 (1992), pp. 47–50.
[6]Bernard T. Smith, *Focus Forecasting: Computer Techniques for Inventory Control* (Boston: CBI Publishing, 1978).
[7]Nada R. Sanders and Karl B. Manrodt, "Forecasting Practices in U.S. Corporations: Survey Results," *Interfaces,* 24, no. 2 (March–April 1994), pp. 92–100.
[8]Heather Green, Mike France, Marcia Stepanek, and Amy Borrus, "It's Time for Rules in Wonderland," *BusinessWeek,* March 20, 2000, pp. 82ff.
[9]William J. Carroll and William C. Grimes, "Evolutionary Change in Product Management: Experiences in the Car Rental Industry," *Interfaces,* September–October 1995, pp. 84–104.

## Chapter 5

[1]Adrian J. Slywotzky and David J. Morrison, *The Profit Zone* (Times Business Random House, 1997), Chapter 1.

[2]"The Power of Smart Pricing," *BusinessWeek,* April 10, 2000, pp. 160–64.

[3]Interview with Ed Stenger, August 1994.

[4]Jim Treece, "The Supplier Is Sometimes Right," *Production,* May 1995, p. 16.

[5]Ibid.

[6]Gary S. Vasilash and Robin Yale Bergstrom, "Customer Obsession at Solectron," *Production,* May 1995, pp. 56–58.

[7]John F. Proud, "Master Scheduling: More Art than Science," *Industrial Engineering Solutions,* September 1995, pp. 38–42.

[8]John F. Proud, "Rough-Cut Capacity Planning: The 'How To' of It," *APICS—The Performance Advantage,* February 1992, pp. 46–49.

[9]Robert Levering and Milton Moskowitz, "The 100 Best Companies to Work For," *Fortune,* January 10, 2000, p. 102.

## Chapter 6

[1]David Simchi-Levi, Philip Kaminsky, and Edith Simchi-Levi, *Designing and Managing the Supply Chain* (Burr Ridge, IL: Irwin/McGraw-Hill, 2000), p. 3.

[2]Stakeholders, Suppliers. Ford Motor Company web site. (www.Ford.com )—visited May 2000.

[3]Ibid.

[4]"Stanford Hospital and Clinics Selects Promedix as Single Source for All Specialty Medical Products," AOL News, America Online News Profiles, May 10, 2000.

[5]"Supplier Questionnaire," Doing Business with Cat. Caterpillar web site (www.cat.com)—visited May 2000.

[6]John L. Mariotti, "The Trust Factor in Supply Chain Management," *Supply Chain Management Review,* Spring 1999, pp. 70–77.

[7]Keki R. Bhote, *Strategic Supply Management: A Blueprint for Revitalizing the Manufacturing–Supplier Partnership* (New York: American Management Association, 1989), p. 13.

[8]James P. Womack, Daniel T. Jones, and Daniel Roos, *The Machine That Changed the World* (New York: Rawson Associates, 1990), Chapter 6.

[9]Larry C. Giunipero, "AME Survey Report: A Survey of JIT Purchasing in American Industry," *Target,* Winter 1988, pp. 25–28.

[10]Roy L. Harmon, *Reinventing the Factory II* (New York: The Free Press, 1992), p. 126.

[11]Michael Barrier, "Overcoming Adversity," *Nation's Business,* June 1991, pp. 25–29.

[12]Otis Port, "Customers Move Into the Driver's Seat," *Business Week,* October 4, 1999, pp. 103–06.

[13]Building Buyer–Seller Partnerships," *Management Accounting Guideline* 32, Hamilton, Ontario, Canada: The Society of Management Accountants of Canada, 1955, p. 33.

[14]Robert H. Hayes and William J. Abernathy, "Managing Our Way to Economic Decline," *Harvard Business Review,* July–August 1980, pp. 67–77.

[15]Edmund Faltermayer, "U.S. Companies Come Back Home," *Fortune,* December 30, 1991, pp. 106–12.

[16]Lamer Lee, Jr., and Donald W. Dobler, *Purchasing and Materials Management: Text and Cases,* 3rd ed. (New York: McGraw-Hill, 1977), pp. 54–55 (HD52.5.L4).

[17]Philip Siekman, "Building 'em Better in Brazil," *Fortune,* September 6, 1999, pp. 246ff.

[18]Based on Arthur E. Mudge, *Value Engineering: A Systematic Approach* (New York: McGraw-Hill, 1971), pp. 263–64 (TS168.M83).

[19]*Reduce Costs and Improve Equipment through Value Engineering,* Directorate of Value Engineering, Office of the Assistant Secretary of Defense for Installations and Logistics, Washington, D.C., January 1967 (TS168,U5).

## Chapter 7

[1]Hau L. Lee and Corey Billington, " The Evolution of Supply-Chain-Management Models and Practice at Hewlett-Packard," *Interfaces,* September–October 1995, pp. 42–63.

[2]Bruce Nussbaum, "Winners 2000: The Best Product Designs of the Year," *BusinessWeek,* June 12, 2000, pp. 113ff.

[3]"A Decade of Design: How Great Products Can Boost the Bottom Line," *BusinessWeek,* November 29, 1999, pp. 85ff.

[4]Karl T. Ulrich and Steven D. Eppinger, *Product Design and Development,* 2d ed. (Burr Ridge, IL: Irwin/McGraw-Hill, 2000), p. 212.

[5]C. Merle Crawford, *New Products Management* (Burr Ridge, IL: Irwin, 1994), p. 80.

[6]Ulrich and Eppinger, *Product Design and Development,* Chapter 6.

[7]Cited in presentation materials by International TechneGroup, Inc., Spring 1991.

[8]David E. Bowen and Edward E. Lawler III, "Total Quality-Oriented Human Resources Management," *Academy of Management Executive,* Spring 1992, pp. 29–41.

[9]Bruce Nussbaum, "What Works for One works for All," *BusinessWeek,* April 20, 1992, pp. 112–13.

[10]Erin O'Briant, "Better Designs for All People," *IIE Solutions,* November 1999, pp. 22–27.

[11]For a critique of QFD, see Edward M. Knod, Jr. and Ann Dietzel, "Quality Function Deployment: Potential Pitfalls," *P/OM Proceedings,* Midwest Business Administration Association, March 1992, pp. 33–40.

[12]Detailed Matrices are discussed in Bob King, *Better Designs in Half the Time: Implementing QFD, Quality Function Deployment in America* (Methuen, MA: GOAL/QPC, 1987).

[13]Geoffrey Boothroyd and Peter Dewhurst, *Design for Assembly* (Wakefield, R.I.: Boothroyd Dewhurst, Inc., 1987).

[14]Yutaka Kato, Germain Boër, and Chee W. Chow, "Target Costing: An Integrative Management Process," *Journal of Cost Management,* Spring 1995, pp. 39–50.

[15]Ranjit Roy, *A Primer on the Taguchi Method.* (New York: Van Nostrand Reinhold, 1990), Chap. 7.

[16]Thomas B. Barker, *Engineering Quality by Design: Interpreting the Taguchi Approach* (New York: Marcel Dekker, Inc., 1990), Chap. 1.
[17]Gary Jacobson and John Hillkirk, *Xerox, American Samurai* (New York: MacMillan, 1986), pp. 178–79.
[18]Robin Yale Bergstrom, "The Quality/Environment Curve," *Production*, June 1995, pp. 62–63.
[19]Susan Moffat, "Japan's New Personalized Production." *Fortune*, October 22, 1990, pp. 132–35.
[20]Joseph F. McKenna, "From JIT, with Love," *Industry Week*, August 17, 1992, pp. 45–51.
[21]"Ford Requires Suppliers to Achieve ISO 14001 Certification," *The ISO 14000 Information Center: What's New*, September 23, 1999. And "GM Requires Suppliers to Achieve ISO 14001 Certification by 2002," *The ISO 14000 Information Center: What's New*, September 24, 1999. (http://www.iso14000.com/WhatsNew/News01.htm)
[22]"About P2," *Pollution Prevention*. United States Environmental Protection Agency, Office of Pollution Prevention and Toxics. (http://www.epa.gov/p2/aboutp2.htm)
[23]Jerome Goldstein, "What's a Matchmaker Doing at a TV Assembly Plant?" *In Business* 16, no. 3 (May–June, 1994).

## Chapter 8

[1]Karen Bemowski, "Quality Is Helping Canadian Airlines International Get off the Ground," *Quality Progress*, October 1995, pp. 33–35.
[2]See *The Quality Imperative* (New York: McGraw-Hill, 1994) [HF5415.157.B87]. This *BusinessWeek* guide, a collaborative work of more than 100 *BusinessWeek* reporters, is an outgrowth of the classic October 1991 issue with the same title.
[3]J. M. Juran, "The Upcoming Century of Quality," *Quality Progress* 27, no. 8 (August 1994), pp. 29–37.
[4]Ibid., p. 32.
[5]Barbara B. Flynn, Roger Schroeder, and Sadao Sakakibara, "Determinants of Quality Performance in High- and Low-Quality Plants," *Quality Management Journal* 2, no. 2 (Winter 1995), pp. 8–25.
[6]Samuel Feinberg, "Overcoming the Real Issues of TQM Implementation," *Quality Progress* 28, no. 5 (July 1995), pp. 79–81.
[7]H. Gitlow, S. Gitlow, A. Oppenheim, and R. Oppenheim, *Tools and Methods for the Improvement of Quality* (Burr Ridge, Ill.: Richard D. Irwin, Inc., 1989), Chap. 1.
[8]Scott Mitchell, "The Major Challenge is Speed," *Quality Progress*, May 2000, p. 38.
[9]J. M. Juran and Frank Gryna, *Quality Planning and Analysis*, 2nd ed. (New York: McGraw-Hill, 1980), p. 13.
[10]Genichi Taguchi, Elsayed A. Elsayed, and Thomas Hsiang, *Quality Engineering in Production Systems* (New York: McGraw-Hill, 1989), Chapter 2.
[11]U.S. General Accounting Office, *Management Practices: U.S. Companies Improve Performance through Quality Efforts* (Gaithersburg, Md: U.S. General Accounting Office, Report GAO/NSIAD–91–190, 1991).
[12]Timothy M. Berquist and Kenneth D. Ramsing, "Measuring Performance after Meeting Award Criteria, *Quality Progress*, September 1999, pp. 66–72.
[13]Robert D. Buzzell and Bradley T. Gale, *The PIMS Principles: Linking Strategy to Performance* (New York: The Free Press, 1987), pp. 107–11.
[14]"Criteria and Their Impact," National Institute of Standards and Technology web site (www.quality.nist.gov/crit2.htm), February 25, 2000.
[15]James L. Heskett, Thomas O. Jones, Gary W. Loveman, W. Earl Sasser, Jr., and Leonard A. Schlesinger, "Putting the Service-Profit Chain to Work," *Harvard Business Review* 72, no. 2 (March–April 1994), pp. 164–74.
[16]Robert C. Camp, *Benchmarking: The Search for Industry Best Practices That Lead to Superior Performance* (Milwaukee: ASQC Quality Press, 1989).
[17]Ronald E. Yates, "Lawyers Not Exempt from Quality Crusade," *Chicago Tribune*, December 1, 1991.
[18]Robert C. Camp, *Business Process Benchmarking* (Milwaukee: ASQC Quality Press, 1995).
[19]George Q. Lofgren, "Quality System Registration: A Guide to Q90/ISO 9000 Series Registration," *Quality Progress*, May 1991, p. 37.
[20]Dan Reid, "Why QS-9000 Was Developed and What's in Its Future," *Quality Progress*, April 2000, pp. 115–17. (Additionally, the July 1999 issue of *Quality Progress* is addressed to the topic of standards and their future.)
[21]Davis S. Huyink and Craig Westover, *ISO 9000: Motivating People, Mastering the Process, and Achieving Registration!* (Burr Ridge, Ill.: Irwin Professional Publishing, 1994), p. 34.
[22]Juran, "The Upcoming Century of Quality," p. 32.
[23]Richard D. Dobbins, "A Failure of Methods, Not Philosophy," *Quality Progress*, July 1995, pp. 31–33.
[24]"The Second Lean Enterprise Report: Executive Summary," Torrance, Calif: Anderson Consulting, 1994.
[25]Harry V. Roberts and Bernard F. Sergesketter, *Quality Is Personal: A Foundation for Total Quality Management* (New York: The Free Press, 1993).
[26]*The Quality Imperative*. A *BusinessWeek* guide. The Editors of *BusinessWeek* with Cynthia Green. New York: McGraw-Hill, 1994 (HF5415.157.B87).
[27]America's discovery of Deming has been traced to Clare Crawford-Mason, a television producer. Working on a documentary on the decline of American industry in the 1970s. Crawford-Mason heard of Deming's work in Japan and pursued her journalistic instincts. See Mary Walton, *The Deming Management Method* (New York: Dodd, Mead, 1986), Chap. 1 (HD38.W36). Also, a series of articles on Deming and the impact of his contribution appears in *Quality Progress*, December 1995.
[28]W. Edwards Deming, *Quality, Productivity, and Competitive Position* (Cambridge, Mass.: MIT Center for Advanced Engineering Study, 1982), p. 316.
[29]J. M. Juran, *Managerial Breakthrough* (New York: McGraw-Hill, 1964).

[30]For a detailed presentation of this sequence, see J. M. Juran and Frank M. Gryna, Jr., *Quality Planning and Analysis,* 2nd ed. (New York: McGraw-Hill, 1980), Chap. 5 (TS156.J86).
[31]J. M. Juran, "The Quality Trilogy," *Quality Progress* 19, no. 8 (August 1986), pp. 19–24.
[32]Armand V. Feigenbaum, *Total Quality Control,* 3rd ed. (New York: McGraw-Hill, 1983), p. 11 (TS156.F44).
[33]Philip B. Crosby, *Quality Is Free: The Art of Making Quality Certain* (New York: McGraw-Hill, 1979), p. 146 (TS156.6.C76).
[34]Philip B. Crosby, *Let's Talk Quality* (New York: McGraw-Hill, 1989), p. 181.
[35]Ranjit Roy, *A Primer on the Taguchi Method* (New York: Van Nostrand Reinhold, 1990), pp. 31–32.
[36]Robert H. Lochner, "Pros and Cons of Taguchi," *Quality Engineering* 3, no. 4 (1991), pp. 537–49.

## Chapter 9

[1]Armand V. Feigenbaum, *Total quality Control: Engineering and Management* (New York: McGraw-Hill, 1961).
[2]Lloyed Dobyns and Clare Crawford-Mason, *Quality or Else: The Revolution in World Business* (Boston: Houghton Mifflin, 1991), p. 139.
[3]*Statistical Quality Control Handbook,* 2nd ed. (Indianapolis: AT&T Technologies, 1956), p. 217.
[4]Frank M. Gryna, "The Quality Director of the '90s," *Quality Progress,* April 1991, p. 37.
[5]"When You Discover Things You Don't Like to Hear About," *Industry Week,* April 17, 1989, p. 54.
[6]*Oliver Wight Operations Consulting and Education,* a newsletter, February 1995.
[7]Adapted from Ross Johnson and William O. Winchell, *Production and Quality* (Milwaukee, WI: American Society for Quality Control Press, 1989), p. 10.
[8]Uday M. Apte and Charles C. Reynolds, "Quality Management at Kentucky Fried Chicken," *Interfaces,* May–June 1995, pp. 6–21.
[9]Ibid.
[10]For examples of other types of control charts, see Donna C. S. Summers, *Quality,* 2d ed. (Upper Saddle River, NJ: Prentice-Hall, 2000), Chapter 5.
[11]Ibid., p. 236.
[12]Mikel Harry and Richard Schroeder, *Six Sigma* (New York: Doubleday, 2000), pp. 141–43.
[13]Ibid., p. viii.
[14]Roderick A. Munro, "Linking Six Sigma with QS-9000," *Quality Progress,* May 2000, pp. 47–53.
[15]Harry and Schroeder, *Six Sigma,* p. 144.
[16]Connie R. Faylor, "Pennsylvania Builds Tomorrow's Workforce," *Quality Progress,* June 1995, pp. 71–73.

## Chapter 10

[1]"A Letter from Ted," *GW2k Gateway Magazine,* Fall 1995, p. 2.
[2]See for example, H. Thomas Johnson, "Managing Costs: An Outmoded Model," *Manufacturing Engineering,* May 1989, p. 44.
[3]Kiyoshi Suzaki, *The New Manufacturing Challenge: Techniques for Continuous Improvement* (New York: The Free Press, 1987), pp. 12–18.
[4]*Total Quality: An Executive's Guide for the 1990s* (Burr Ridge, IL: Dow Jones–Irwin, 1990), p. 185.
[5]For over 15 years, Richard Schonberger has been asking his seminar audiences what their companies use as a carrying cost rate. In recent years, some are citing figures in the 65–67 percent range.
[6]Robert C. Camp, *Business Process Benchmarking: Finding and Implementing Best Practices* (Milwaukee, WI: ASQ Quality Press, 1995), Chapter 11.
[7]A basic reference for manufacturing processes is Shigeo Shingo, *A Revolution in Manufacturing: The SMED [Single-Minute Exchange of Die] System* (Portland, OR: Productivity Press, 1985).
[8]Myron Magnet, "Meet the New Revolutionaries," *Fortune,* February 24, 1992, pp. 94–101.
[9]David Young, "Logistics Revolution Spreads Stealthily," *Chicago Tribune,* November 12, 1995, pp. 5-1, 6.
[10]Jon Bigness, "In Today's Economy, There Is Big Money to be Made in Logistics," *The Wall Street Journal,* September 6, 1995, pp. Al and A9.
[11]Myron Magnet, "Meet the New Revolutionaries," pp. 94–101.
[12]Per Ola and Emily d' Aulaire, "Freight Trains are Back and They're on a Roll," *Smithsonian,* June 1995, pp. 36–49.
[13]Examples of use as well as more on the response ratio technique may be found in Richard J. Schonberger, *World-Class Manufacturing Casebook: Implementing JIT and TQC* (New York: Free Press, 1987).
[14]Richard J. Schonberger, *World-Class Manufacturing: The Next Decade* (New York: Free Press 1996), Chapter 1.

## Chapter 11

[1]Joseph D. Blackburn. *Time-Based Competition: The Next Battleground in American Manufacturing* (Burr Ridge, IL: Richard D. Irwin, 1990).
[2]A more thorough discussion of the relationship between the Poisson probability distribution and the exponential probability distribution in queuing applications may be found in Charles P. Bonini, Warren H. Hausman, and Harold Bierman, Jr. *Quantitative Analysis for Management,* 9th ed. (Burr Ridge, IL: Irwin, 1997), Chapter 9.
[3]For details on kanban variations and rules of use, see Yashuhiro Monden, *Toyota Production System* (Norcross, GA: Industrial Engineering and Management Press, 1983).
[4]A. Ansari and Batoul Modarress, "Wireless Kanban," *Production and Inventory Management Journal,* First Quarter, 1995, pp. 60–64.
[5]"America's Best Plants," *Industry Week,* October 20, 1990.
[6]Joseph C. Quinlan, "The Remaking of Baldor Electric," *Quality in Manufacturing,* September–October 1995, pp. 36–37.
[7]By the late 1990s, some fast-food companies had reengineered their service processes to such an extent that, except during rush times, even the short push-mode chute operation was abandoned in favor of near-total pull-mode operations.

## Chapter 12

[1]"Quarterly Labor Productivity: Frequently Asked Questions" U.S. Department of Labor, Bureau of labor Statistics (http://stats.bls.gov/lprfaq.htm), September 9, 1998. (Site visited June 20, 2000)

[2]Michael J. Mandel, "How Fast Can This Hot-Rod Go?" *BusinessWeek,* November 29, 1999, pp. 40–42.

[3]"The Boom," (Cover Story), *Business Week,* February 14, 2000, pp. 99ff.

[4]Jennifer Reingold, Marcia Stepanek, and Diane Brady, "Why the Productivity Revolution Will Spread," *BusinessWeek,* February 14, 2000, pp. 112–118.

[5]Ibid., p. 114.

[6]"The Wild New Workforce" (Cover Story), *BusinessWeek,* December 6, 1999, pp. 38–42.

[7]Ibid., pp. 40 and 42. Also see Aaron Bernstein, "Welch's March to the South," *BusinessWeek,* December 6, 1999, pp. 74–78.

[8]"Tech Companies Want Talented Employees to Switch Jobs—Not Companies" (Work Week Report), *The Wall Street Journal,* August 3, 1999, p. A1.

[9]Scott Burns, "Better Living through Equity: Why Employee Stock Options Have Become Corporate America's Most Sought-After Perk," *Guide to Benefits, Compensation, and Perks; Worth* (Special Issue), Winter 1999, pp. 21–23.

[10]Robert Levering and Milton Moskowitz, "The 100 Best Companies to Work For," *Fortune,* January 10, 2000, pp. 82ff.

[11]Edward E. Lawler III, "Pay the Person, Not the Job," *Industry Week,* December 7, 1992, pp. 19–24.

[12]Ibid.

[13]F. W. Taylor, *The Principles of Scientific Management* (New York: Harper & Row, 1911), pp. 36–37.

[14]Theodore Levitt, "Productin-Line Approach to Service," *Harvard Business Review,* September–October 1972, pp. 41–52.

[15]Peter Coy and Chuck Hawkins, "UPS: Up from the Stone Age," *BusinessWeek,* June 15, 1992, p. 132.

[16]Brian S. Moskal, "The Wizards of Buick City," *Industry Week,* May 7, 1990, pp. 22–27.

[17]Paula M. Noaker, "Ergonomics on Site," *Manufacturing Engineering,* June 1992, pp. 63–66.

[18]S. S. Cherukuri, "Westinghouse Electric Corporation Asheville's Focused Factories Make a Difference—the 'Village' Concept," *Target,* Fall 1988, pp. 30–32.

[19]John A. Saathoff, "Maintaining Excellence through Change," *Target,* Spring 1989, pp. 13–20.

[20]Peter B. B. Turney and Burce Anderson, "Accounting for Continuous Improvement," *Sloan Management Review,* Winter 1989, pp. 37–47.

[21]Benjamin W. Niebel, *Motion and Time Study,* 9th ed. (Burr Ridge, Ill.: Richard D. Irwin, 1993), p. 389; also see a more elaborate table from Westinghouse on the same page (T60.N54).

[22]The tables were originally developed by H. B. Maynard and associates. See Harold B. Maynard, G. J. Stegemerten, and John L. Schwab, *Methods-Time Measurement* (New York: McGraw-Hill, 1948), (T60.T5M3).

## Chapter 13

[1]Thomas J. Peters and Robert H. Waterman, *In Search of Excellence* (New York: Harper & Row, 1982), pp. 164–65

[2]Shigeo Shingo, *Non-Stock Production: The Shingo System for Continuous Improvement* (Portland, Ore.: Productivity Press, 1988), p. 9.

[3]Jorge Haddock and Donald E. Hubricki, "Which Lot-Sizing Techniques Are Used in Material Requirements Planning?" *Production and Inventory Management,* Third Quarter 1989, pp. 53–56.

[4]Gene Woolsey, well known in the management science community for his colorful "reality check" writings, wrote an editorial attacking the EOQ model's unrealistic assumptions: "A Requiem for the EOQ: An Editorial," *Production and Inventory Management,* Third Quarter 1988, pp. 68–72.

[5]See Joseph Orlicky, *Material Requirements Planning* (New York: McGraw-Hill, 1975), Chapter 10, "Product Definition" [TS155-8.O74].

[6]David A. Turbide, "MRP II: Still Number One!" *IIE Solutions,* July 1995, pp. 28–31.

[7]Paul Hoy, "Client/Server MRP II Comes of Age," *APICS—The Performance Advantage,* June 1995, pp. 38–41.

[8]Himanshu Kumar and Ram Rachamadugu, "Is MRP II Dead?" *APICS—The Performance Advantage,* September 1995, pp. 24–27.

[9]Ronald A. Hicks and Kathryn E. Stecke, "The ERP Maze," *IIE Solutions,* August 1995, pp. 12–16.

[10]"Grant Thornton Completes First Ever Sap Implementation at a U.S. Public Library, "*AOL News* (http://www.prnewswire.com), August 9, 1999.

[11]"Baan Global Unveils Global Supply Chain Offering for E-Business at Annual Supply Chain Conference, Velocity'99," *AOL News* (http://www.prnewswire.com), August 18, 1999.

[12]Aleda V. Roth and Roland van Dierdonck, "Hospital Resource Planning: Concepts, Feasibility, and Framework," Production and Operations Management, Winter 1995, pp. 2–29.

[13]Data on MRP/MRP II gains are drawn from two sources: Wight, *MRP II,* Chapter 4, and Roger G. Schroeder, John C. Anderson, Sharon E. Tupy, and Edna M. White, "A Study of MRP Benefits and Costs" (Working Paper, Graduate School of Business Administration, University of Minnesota, May 1980).

[14]Oliver W. Wight, *MRP II: Unlocking America's Productivity Potential* (Williston, VT: Oliver Wight Limited Publications, 1981), p. 58 [TS161.W5x].

[15]George W. Plossl, *Managing in the New World of Manufacturing* (Englewood Cliffs, NJ: Prentice Hall, 1991), p. 177.

## Chapter 14

[1]Peter Salwen, "Green Planning Makes Good Neighbors," *IIE Solutions,* April 1999, pp. 31–34.

[2]Robert B. Reich, "Toward a New Economic Development," *Industry Week,* October 5, 1992, pp. 37–44.

[3]Brian O'Reilly, "Your New Global Workforce," *Fortune,* December 14, 1992, pp. 52–66.

[4]This description is from Pero Tafur, *Travels and Adventures* (London: G. Routledge & Sons, Ltd., 1926) p. 1435, cited in R. Burlingame, *Backgrounds of power* (New York: Charles Scribner's Sons, 1949).

[5]A method for determining transportability may be found in Richard Mathur, *Systematic Handling Analysis* (Management and Industrial Research Publications, 1969).

[6]Richard R. Mathur, *Systematic Layout Planning* (Boston: Cahners, 1973), pp. 3-1 through 3-8.

[7]Frank Kerns, "Facilities Can Support Strategic Intent," *IIE Solutions,* June 1999, pp. 30–34.

## Chapter 15

[1]Gene Bylinsky, "America's Elite Factories," *Fortune,* August 16, 1999, pp. 136[C]ff.

[2]"A Smart Cookie at Pepperidge," *Fortune,* December 22, 1986, pp. 67–74.

[3]This description of Milliken's Cypress plant was supplied by Mr. Sam P. Gambrell, director of Milliken Industrial Engineering Services, in a personal correspondence, December 1990.

[4]Tupper Cawsey, "The Sarnia Polymers Department, Esso Chemical Canada," in *Case Studies in Accountability,* vol. I of monograph series, January 1991 (Hamilton, Ontario: The Society of Management Accountants of Canada), pp. 52–60.

[5]The method and the example are adapted from Wayne K. Smith, James L. Ingraham, and David M. Rurak, "Time and Pull: A DuPont Case History," *Target,* January/February 1993, pp. 27–42.

[6]The linearity index was devised by Hewlett-Packard Company.

[7]This example is a segment of a case study prepared by Richard Schonberger, June 1994, with the assistance of Patrick O'Malley, vice president for Deposit Services at First Chicago.

[8]Adapted from Theodore O. Prenting and Nicholas T. Thomopoulos, *Humanism and Technology in Assembly Line Systems* (Rochelle Park, N.J.: Spartan Books, 1974), pp. 131–32.

## Chapter 16

[1]For example, see J. F. Cox III, J. H. Blackstone, Jr., and M. S. Spencer, Editors *APICS Dictionary,* 8th ed. (falls Church, VA: American Production and Inventory Control Society, 1995). The dictionary contains 16 entries relating to *job,* 8 entries relating to *batch,* and 15 entries relating to *lot.*

[2]Doug Bartholomew, "Lean vs. ERP," *Industry Week,* July 19, 1999.

[3]For example, see the Lean Enterprise Institute homepage (www.lean.com) and view the content on The Reader's Corner. (Registration as a user is required, but is free.) The site provides access to numerous lean manufacturing articles and ongoing discussions of timely topics.

[4]Joseph Orlicky, *Material Requirements Planning* (New York: McGraw-Hill, 1975), p. 83 (TS155.8.O74).

[5]See, for example, O. Kermit Hobbs, Jr., "Application of JIT Techniques in a Discrete Batch Job Shop," *Production and Inventory Management Journal* 35, no. 1 (First Quarter), 1994. (This article won the *Production and Inventory Management Journal's* Romey Everdell Best Article Award for 1994.)

[6]The original purpose was to display variances from planned production rates in repetitive production.

[7]Adapted from Oliver W. Wight, *Production and Inventory Management and the Computer Age* (Boston: CBI Publishing, 1974), pp. 81–82 (TS155.W533). Note that operation lead times are detailed, whereas job-order lead times, discussed earlier for computing planned order releases, are gross.

[8]Bartholomew, "Lean vs. ERP."

[9]Ibid.

[10]Ibid.

[11]Anthony C. Laraia, Patricia E. Moody, and Robert W. Hall, *The Kaizen Blitz* (New York: John Wiley & Sons, Inc., 1999). (Our discussion of Kaizen Blitz teams draws heavily from this source.)

[12]Ibid., p. xix.

## Chapter 17

[1]Peter W. G. Morris, *The Management of Projects* (London: Thomas Telford, 1994), pp. 90–92.

[2]Ibid., p. viii.

[3]Ibid., p. 217.

[4]Robert C. Camp, *Business Process Benchmarking* (Milwaukee: ASQC Quality Press, 1995), Chap. 1.

[5]Ibid., p. 137.

[6]Morris, *The Management of Projects,* p. 78.

[7]Ibid., p. 104.

[8]Greg Hutchins, "Project Management Is Still Hot," *IIE Solutions,* September 1999, p. 19.

[9]John F. Love, *McDonald's: Behind the Arches* (Toronto: Bantam Books, 1986).

[10]Jeffrey L. Funk, "Case Study: Managing the Organizational Complexity of Applying CIM to Semiconductor Manufacturing in the Mitsubishi Corporation," *Manufacturing Review,* March 1991, pp. 5–17.

[11]Marvin L. Patterson, *Accelerating Innovation: Improving the Process of Product Development* (New York: Van Nostrand Reinhold, 1993), pp. 149–50 (TS176.P367).

[12]Morris, *The Management of Projects,* p. 249.

[13]Often the listing is event oriented rather than activity oriented; for example, instead of earliest- and latest-start activity times (*ES* and *LS*), there will be time-earliest and time-latest event times ($T_E$ and $T_L$).

[14]Adapted from J. S. Sayer, J. E. Kelly, Jr., and M. R. Walker, "Critical Path Scheduling," *Factory,* July 1960.

# GLOSSARY

**ABC (inventory) analysis** Materials classification system in which all stocked items are classified by annual dollar volume. The high-value A items receive close control; medium-value B items get intermediate control; low-value C items receive lowest priority.

**Acceptance sampling** Quality inspection technique in which a sample is taken from a completed production lot and tested. If the sample passes, the lot is assumed good, if the sample fails, the entire lot is inspected.

**Activity** Basic unit of work in a project.

**Activity-based costing (ABC)** A method of costing whereby a job, product, or service is assigned overhead costs only if overhead activity is actually expended to support it; replaces the old methods of allocating overhead costs, typically in proportion to direct labor costs.

**Activity control** Term usually meant to include dispatching along with input control of work releases into either gateway or bottleneck work centers.

**Activity-on-arrow network** A PERT/CPM network form in which activities are shown as arrows.

**Activity-on-node network** A PERT/CPM network form in which activities are shown as nodes.

**Adaptive smoothing** Technique for automatic adjustment of time-series smoothing coefficients based on some function of forecast error, commonly the tracking signal.

**Aggregate demand** Long- and medium-range demand expressed in collective terms rather than broken down by type of product or service or specific model.

**Aggregate demand forecast** Forecast for whole-product or capacity groups; long- or medium-term focus.

**Agile manufacturing** Streamlined, flexible approach that shortens the supply chain between manufacturing and the final consumer; responsiveness enhanced by information system linkages from retail setting to manufacturing cell.

**American Customer Satisfaction Index (ACSI)** A quarterly index that measures customer satisfaction, initially in seven economic sectors made up of 40 industries that are, in turn, represented by 200 organizations.

**Appointment book** A master schedule for the provision of services; a statement of the services to be provided.

**Approved supplier** A supplier given preferential treatment in purchasing decisions by earning high ratings on quality, delivery, price, and service.

**Arrival rate ($\lambda$)** In a waiting line system, the average number of arrivals per time period.

**Assignable-cause variation** See **Special-cause variation.**

**Attribute inspection** Inspection requiring only a yes–no, pass–fail, or good–bad judgment.

**Attributes (control) charts** Statistical process control charts that reflect counted or categorized process data; number of defects ($c$) charts and proportion defective ($p$) charts are examples.

**Attributes data** Data obtained through a classifying judgment (e.g., yes/no, go/no-go, pass/fail) as to the nature of the quality characteristic in question.

**Automatic storage and retrieval system (AS/RS)** Automated equipment, such as racks, bins, forklifts, and computerized location records, collectively designed to hold and retrieve inventory.

**Autonomous operations** The assignment of all work in certain products to a single work station; work is not passed from station to station.

**Availability** Proportion of time a resource is ready for use. Time over which the proportion is determined may exclude planned time for maintenance.

**Backflush** A post-deduction method of accounting for component stock usage at the time of end-product completion. Uses **BOM** explosion to identify quantity of components to deduct from inventory record balances.

**Backlog** Collection of orders awaiting processing.

**Backorder** An order accepted when stock is out; usually filled when stock arrives.

**Backscheduling** Subtracting lead time (or throughput time) from the due date to find the time to start processing or to place an order with a supplier; a basic MRP calculation.

**Backward integration** Setting up to provide goods or services formerly purchased; (sometimes) buying a supplier company, making it a subsidiary.

**Backward scheduling** See **Backscheduling.**

**Balance delay** Ratio of waiting or idle time to total available time per cycle in an assembly line.

**Balk** Arrive at a waiting line but refuse to enter (typically) due to queue length.

**Batch** A large quantity (a lot) of a single item.

**Batch processing** A type of operations in which multiple units of a single item are treated as one processing unit (batch).

**Benchmarking** Investigating best practices anywhere in the world for a given process; basis for comparing benchmarked practice with that of one's own organization in order to inspire improvement.

**Bill of labor** Labor requirements (type and quantity) to produce a product or provide a service; analogous to a **BOM.**

**Bill of materials (BOM)** Product structure for an assembly; shows required components and their quantity at each level of fabrication and assembly.

**Bill of materials (BOM) explosion** Breaking down an order for end products into major, secondary, tertiary, and so forth, components for the purpose of finding gross requirements for all component items.

**Blanket orders** A contract covering purchase of relatively low-cost items for which there is continuous but varying need; specifies price and other matters, but delivery is usually triggered by simple release orders issued as required.

**Bottleneck** Work station or facility for which demand exceeds service capacity; same as a constraint.

**Break-even point** Output volume for a good or service at which sales revenues just cover costs.

**Buffer stock** Inventory maintained to provide customer service in the face of demand and production uncertainty; also known as safety stock. See also **Offline buffer stock**.

**Buying down** Attempting to buy an item with historical price swings at a time when the price is down.

**Capability index ($C_p$)** Process capability index defined as the ratio of the width of the tolerance band to six times the process standard deviation; that is $(USL - LSL) \div 6\sigma$.

**Capability index ($C_{pk}$)** Process capability index defined as the distance from process center to the nearer specification limit divided by three times the process standard deviation.

**Capacity** The ability to accommodate.

**Capacity control** Keeping work centers busy but not overloaded; takes place after work-center loading and may include expediting.

**Capacity cushion** A preplanned excess amount of capacity designed to increase the company's ability to meet demand surges. (See **undercapacity scheduling** for a companion policy that mandates schedules that do not plan to use all available capacity.)

**Capacity planning** Broad range of activities focused on creating and maintaining customer-serving resources and adjusting levels of those resources as required.

**Capacity planning team** The master planning team charged with balancing the company's capacity policies with aggregate customer demand.

**Capacity requirements planning (CRP)** A computer-based method of revealing work-center loads; determines labor and machine resources needed to achieve planned outputs.

**Capital cost** Cost (e.g., interest rate) of acquiring money; a component of **Inventory carrying cost.**

**Carrying cost** The cost, above and beyond unit price, to carry or hold an inventory item in a state of idleness.

**Catalog buying** Purchasing from current supplier catalogs; the common purchasing procedure, for example, for off-the-shelf maintenance, repair, and operating (MRO) items.

**Cause–effect diagram** See **Fishbone diagram.**

**Cell** A linkage of maker–customer pairs, created by drawing people and machines from functional areas and placing them in the same work area to reduce movement distances, inventory, and throughput time and to improve coordination.

**Cellular layout** A layout in which work stations and machines are arranged into cells that provide families of goods or services that follow similar flow paths; very similar to product layout.

**Certification** Formal approval of a supplier as a source for purchased goods and services; typically bestowed after a supplier exhibits process control, design and delivery standards, and other desirable traits. See **supplier certification.**

**Changeover** Changing the setup on a machine, production line, or process in order to produce a new product or service; also called **setup.**

**Chase demand (strategy)** A capacity management strategy in which sufficient capacity is maintained to meet current demand; capacity levels chase (respond to) demand fluctuations.

**Check sheet** A simple data-recording tool on which the user records observations with a check or tic mark. Over time, the marks reveal the underlying frequency distribution.

**Closed-loop MRP** An MRP system with feedback loops aimed at maintaining valid schedules; includes file control, rescheduling actions, and production activity control.

**Commodity product** An undifferentiated product.

**Common cause** Cause for common variation in process output (after specific or assignable causes have been removed).

**Common variation** Variation remaining in process output after all special variation has been removed; may be thought of as the natural variation in a process that is in statistical control.

**Competitor** A rival seeking the same objectives that you seek; a person or another organization vying with you or your company for sales and customers, or perhaps for employees, permits, funding, partnership with good suppliers, and so on.

**Competitive analysis** Thorough study ("reverse engineering") of a competitor's product or service; aimed at generating usable ideas and, sometimes, for lowering complacency about competitors.

**Complete physical inventory** An actual count of all inventory items.

**Component item** An item that goes into the assembly of the parent item; for example, a bulb is a component of a flashlight.

**Composition of demand** Refers to the varying degree of importance of each order in a group awaiting processing; of interest to a master planning committee, especially when demand exceeds capacity, so that more important demands (for preferred customers, or earning higher profit) can receive priority.

**Computer-aided design (CAD)** Incorporation of computers and related technology into the design of processes and outputs.

**Computer-aided engineering (CAE)** Subsets of CAD that are designed to assist in design concept development and testing and analysis of desirable functions and features.

**Computer-aided process planning (CAPP)** Subsets of CAD focused on extending design specifications for outputs into the processes required to create the outputs.

**Computer-integrated manufacturing (CIM)** Computer assistance or direct control of manufacturing from product and process design to scheduling to production and material handling; may include FMS, CAD, and CAM.

**Concurrency** Technique for reducing cycle times in projects by doing design and production of later stages at the same time as, and coordinated with, earlier activities.

**Concurrent design** Design strategy based on simultaneous rather than sequential design; employs multifunctional teams to simultaneously design outputs along with processes that will produce, deliver, and service those outputs.

**Constraint** See **Bottleneck.**

**Consuming the master schedule** Procedure by which master scheduled (planned) quantity of output is allocated (consumed) as orders arrive leaving a net available-to-promise quantity (i.e., produced amount − allocated amount = available to promise amount).

**Continuous operations** Perpetual production of goods that flow; may include production of one batch after another.

**Continuous process** See **Continuous operations.**

**Core competencies** Key business outputs or processes through which an organization distinguishes itself positively. See **Distinctive competency.**

**Correlation coefficient** A measure of the degree of association between two or more variables.

**Cost drivers** True causes of costs; resources or activities that consume financial resources.

**Cost variance** Productivity measure computed by subtracting actual costs of inputs from standard costs of outputs for a given operating unit or job.

**Cost-volume analysis** Study of the relationships among the volume of a company's output goods and services, the costs of providing those outputs, and the amount customers are willing to pay for those outputs.

**Crash (crashing)** Reducing an activity's time by adding resources; crashing critical activities reduces project time.

**Critical path** The path (activity sequence) through a project network that is estimated to consume the most time.

**Critical path method (CPM)** A network-based project management technique initially used on construction projects; about the same as **PERT.**

**Cross-docking** Technique for improving responsiveness by skipping storage time at distribution centers. Material from suppliers' vehicles is moved directly into customers' vehicles for (sometimes) immediate delivery to final consumer.

**Cross-functional team** See **Multi-functional team.**

**Custom product** A highly differentiated, unique, special-purpose, or one-of-a-kind product.

**Customer** The next process (where the work goes next); also, the end user or consumer.

**Cycle counting** An inventory counting plan in which a small fraction of items are counted each day; an alternative to complete physical inventory.

**Cycle interval** The time interval (minutes, hours, days, or weeks) between when a certain product or service is made or delivered until the next time it is made or delivered.

**Cycle time** (1) Raw average time between completion of two successive units of output; for example, an ice maker that dumps six trays of ice per hour operates at a cycle time of 10 minutes. (2) Length of time, including delays, required for materials or a customer to move through a defined value-adding process. Synonym: **Throughput time.**

**Cyclical pattern** Recurring pattern in a time series; generally, each occurrence spans several years.

**Daily priority report** (Also called **dispatch list**) Job priority listing for a given shift or day; lists jobs in the order they are to be released into a work center.

**Delayed differentiation** Retaining standard forms or parts further along the assembly sequence; waiting as long as possible to transform common- or general-purpose items into special-purpose parts. Synonym: Postponement.

**Demand forecasting** Estimating future demand for goods and services.

**Demand management** Recognizing and managing all demands for products and services in accordance with the master plan.

**Deming Prize** Japan's most prestigious award for individual or organizational achievement in the field of quality; named after the late W. Edwards Deming.

**Dependent-demand item** An item for which demand results from demand for a parent item; for example, demand for mower blades is dependent on demand for mowers.

**Derating** Running a machine or production line at less than rated (maximum) capacity to forestall breakdowns, deteriorating quality, and early wear-out.

**Design concept** A combination of verbal and prototype forms telling what is going to change, how it is going to be changed, and how the customer will be affected by the change.

**Design-build team** Team consisting of product-design and process-development people, whose aim is a producible product design.

**Design for operations (DFO)** Concept of designing a product or service to be easy to produce or provide; a manufacturing version is design for manufacture and assembly (DFMA).

**Design for the environment (DFE)** Design efforts aimed at environmental protection during the manufacture, installation, operation, delivery, maintenance, and disposal of processes and outputs.

**Design of experiments (DOE)** A family of techniques used to plan and conduct experiments. In OM, the term is often used in reference to quality improvement activities.

**Design review** A check on engineering designs to ensure satisfaction of customers' requirements and producibility.

**Destructive testing** Product inspection that destroys the product's usefulness, rendering it unfit for sale; may be used, for example, in inspecting a sample of flashbulbs.

**Differentiation strategy** Strategy that seeks to impart distinguishing features—perceived valuable by customers—to output goods and services.

**Dispatcher** A person whose responsibility is to release jobs into work centers or, sometimes, resources to jobs.

**Distinctive competency** A strength that sets an organization apart from its competition.

**Distribution requirements planning (DRP)** Incorporation of distribution requirements into master production schedules; requirements are based on actual forecast needs, not just shelf replacement.

**Dummy activity** A PERT/CPM network activity that consumes no time or resources; used to clarify a network diagram.

**Earliest finish (EF)** The earliest possible time when a project activity may be completed; *EF* equals *ES* plus activity duration ($t$).

**Earliest start (ES)** The earliest possible starting time for a project activity; if an activity has multiple predecessors, its *ES* is equal to the latest predecessors' *EF.*

**Early-life failure** Mortality upon startup for a component or product; often caused by improper assembly or rough handling.

**Early supplier involvement** A program for getting a supplier's personnel involved early in new development or changes affecting items the supplier provides.

**Earnings from operations** Revenue from the sale of a company's primary output goods and services less the cost of providing those goods and services.

**E-commerce** Electronic commerce made possible through the Internet and related technologies.

**Economic order quantity (EOQ)** The (fixed) quantity to be ordered in each order cycle that will minimize total inventory costs.

**Efficiency** Standard time divided by actual time or actual output (units) divided by standard output (units).

**Efficient customer response (ECR)** Advanced form of quick response designed to speed up replenishment, assortment selection, promotion, and product introduction.

**Electronic data interchange (EDI)** A standardized computer-to-computer messaging system used to transmit orders, billing information, and perhaps funds among organizations.

**Elemental time** In time study, the average observed job element time before performance rating and allowance adjustments are included.

**Engineering change orders (ECOs)** Formal changes in product or process design that alter bills of materials, routing, or production technique.

**Enterprise resource planning (ERP)** A term coined by the Gartner Group of Stamford, Connecticut; generally refers to extension of manufacturing resource planning concepts to both upstream and downstream members of the supply chain.

**Environmental management system (EMS)** That portion of an organization's overall management structure that addresses the immediate and long-term impact of the organization's products, services, and processes on the environment.

**Ergonomics** Study of a work environment with emphasis on human physiological concerns; efforts to "fit the job to the person" are examples of ergonomics in practice.

**Event (node)** Point signifying completion of one or more project activities and sometimes the beginning of others; consumes no time or resources but merely marks a point in time.

**Expediting (Expediter)** Actions aimed at pulling urgent jobs, purchases, or customers through more quickly; expediters also called parts chasers.

**Exponential smoothing** A form of weighted moving-average forecasting that uses a smoothing coefficient to assign an aged weight to each period of historical data.

**Facilitator** An individual with overall responsibility for formation, training, and leadership of improvement teams.

**Facilities** Plant and equipment that are generally fixed and unalterable for months to years.

**Fail-safing** Equipping or designing a process to be incapable of (*a*) allowing an error to be passed on to the next process, or (*b*) allowing an error at all.

**Failure rate** Average number of failures in a given time period; the inverse of **Mean time between failures.**

**Fill rate** Proportion or percentage of orders that can be filled from stock on hand; synonymous with *service level.*

**Finished goods (inventory)** At any stage of the supply chain, completed products that are waiting transport or delivery to next-process customers.

**Finite source population** Small drawing or source population in a waiting line system such that the emergence or arrival of one member affects the probability of emergence or arrival of another member.

**Finite-capacity planning** Workload planning methods that consider the limited (finite) capacity of work stations in each scheduling period and assign work to scheduling periods accordingly.

**Firm planned order** An MRP tool for overriding the automatic rescheduling feature of MRP; useful for getting a job into a gateway work center at a convenient time, even if different from the calculated order due date.

**Fishbone chart** A chart resembling the skeleton of a fish in which the spine bone represents the major cause of quality problems and connecting bones, contributing causes; reveals cause–effect linkages. (Also known as **cause–effect diagram** and **Ishikawa diagram.**)

**Fixed-period quantity** Lot-sizing order quantity equal to projected net requirements for a specific time period.

**Fixed-position layout** A facility layout in which the product is kept in one place and facilities come to it; examples include construction and production of very large items.

**Flowcharts** A family of charts showing work sequence; used in data collection and analysis in an improvement study.

**Flow-control system** Interrelated set of activities, equipment, and software used to plan and regulate movement of materials, information, and/or customers through a processing sequence.

**Focus forecasting** A form of simulation-based forecasting; involves selection of the most accurate of several forecasting models as the basis for the next forecast.

**Focused factory** Concept that stresses doing one or a few things well at a given plant.

**Forecast error** For a given time period, actual demand minus forecast demand.

**Forward integration** Acquisition of capacity or capabilities that formerly existed further downstream in the supply chain; for example, a manufacturer might buy its distributor or perhaps build retail outlets.

**Forward scheduling** Beginning with current date or expected start date, adding throughput (lead) time, thus arriving at a scheduled order completion date.

**Functional layout** A form of layout in which similar facilities and functions are grouped together in one place, usually meaning that all people working within each functional area are also grouped together.

**Gain sharing** An incentive pay system in which everyone receives a share of the value of productivity increases.
**Gantt chart** A widely used scheduling chart, with horizontal rows representing jobs or resources to be scheduled and vertical divisions representing time periods.
**Gantt control chart** A chart used to control certain types of jobs with stable priorities—for example, renovation and major maintenance.
**Gross requirements** The total amount of each component needed to produce the ordered quantity of the parent item.
**Group-based capacity planning** Creating aggregate capacity plans with product and service groups or families as core requirement components and a cross-trained labor force available for assignment.
**Group technology (GT)** Operations and layout strategy based on physical and processing similarity for a group of outputs; typically results in a common-routing for the group with cellular layout.
**Hawthorne effect** Recognition or attention temporarily raises motivation to excel; first documented in the 1920s at the Western Electric Plant near Chicago, Illinois.
**Hedging** A form of purchasing that offers some protection from price changes; applies especially to commodities and includes trading on futures markets.
**Histogram** A graphical data summary tool for recording and displaying data into predefined categories; used to study location and dispersion of observations.
**Holding cost** An element of inventory carrying cost; generally associated with stockroom costs, insurance, inventory taxes, and damage or shrinkage during storage.
**Hot-list jobs** Jobs involving parts not available but needed immediately for open orders currently in progress.
**House of quality** Name given to the basic QFD matrix, which includes a house-like roof showing correlations between process factors. See also **Quality function deployment.**
**Idleness rate** Percentage of time that a facility is idle; computed as 1 minus the utilization rate.
**Incentive pay** Pay based on work output; in its purest form, a piece rate.
**Independent-demand item** An item that does not go into a parent item.
**Infinite-capacity planning** A workload planning system that assumes the availability of resources required to provide needed parts and services in each scheduling period and assigns work accordingly; relies on an activity control subroutine to adjust priorities when bottlenecks arise.
**Infinite source population** Drawing population in a waiting-line system that is sufficiently large such that emergence of one member does not appreciably affect the probability of emergence of another member.
**Input control** Control of work releases to gateway or bottleneck work centers.
**Inventory carrying cost** See **Carrying cost.**
**Inventory turnover** Annual cost of goods sold divided by value of average inventory.
**Irregular maintenance** Unscheduled repairs, machine installations (millwright work), and minor construction.
**Ishikawa diagram** See **Fishbone diagram.**
**ISO 9000 Standards** Series of quality systems standards developed and maintained by Geneva-based International Organization for Standardization. The ISO 9000 family is intended to provide a generic core of quality systems standards applicable across a broad range of industry and economic sectors.
**ISO 14000 Standards** Series of standards that provide guidance on the development and implementation of environmental management systems and principles, and on their coordination with other management systems; developed and maintained by the Geneva-based International Organization for Standardization.
**Item demand** Demand broken down into specific types or models of products or services.
**Item master file** An inventory file containing records for each component and assembly; holds on-hand balances, planning factors, and independent-demand data.
**Job** A task of limited size and complexity, usually resulting in something tangible; the whole work activity required to fill a service order or produce a component.
**Job design** The function of fitting tasks together to form a job that can be assigned to a person; emphasis is on creating useful jobs that people can and want to do. Job enlargement, job enrichment, and cross-training are associated with theories of job design.
**Job operations** Intermittent processing, frequently one at a time; characterized by extreme variation in output and process; type of operations in a job shop.
**Jury of executive opinion** Forecasting technique that relies on the collective judgment of a group of knowledgeable executives.
**Just-in-time (JIT) operations** A system of managing operations with little or no delay time or idle inventories between one process and the next.
**Just-in-time II (JIT II)** Trademark registered by Bose Corporation referring to an arrangement by which some suppliers' employees are assigned to work full-time at a customer's facility.
**Kaizen** Continuous improvement.

**Kaizen Blitz Team** Name registered by the Association for Manufacturing Excellence to describe quick-response, multifunctional teams that complete process improvements in focused, concentrated fashion, typically within three to four days.

**Kanban** A communication or signal from the user to the maker (or supplier) for more work; from the Japanese word for "card" or "visible record"; a queue-limitation device.

**Labor efficiency** The ratio of standard time allowed to actual time consumed per unit of work; alternatively, the ratio of actual units completed per time period to standard units for that time period.

**Latest finish (LF)** The latest possible completion time for a project activity to avoid project delay; if the activity has multiple successor activities, its *LF* equals the successors' earliest *LS*.

**Latest start (LS)** The latest possible starting time for a project activity to avoid project delay; $LS = LF -$ Activity duration ($t$).

**Layout** The physical organization or geography found in a facility. Basic types include product, cellular, functional, and fixed-position.

**Lead time** See **Cycle time.**

**Leading indicator** A variable that correlates with demand one or more periods later, giving some signal of magnitude and direction of pending demand change.

**Lean production** See **Toyota production system.**

**Learning curve** Graphical representation of the economy-of-scale concept: greater volume yields lower unit cost; the curve plots resource consumption as a function of lot quantity.

**Level-by-level MRP processing** The MRP way of calculating planned order release quantities and dates, top (zero) level of the BOM first, then subsequent lower levels; ensures complete capture of all requirements.

**Level capacity (strategy)** A capacity management strategy that seeks to retain a stable or constant amount of capacity, especially labor.

**Leveling (normalizing)** In setting time standards, adjusting the elemental time to reflect the pace (level of effort) of the person observed, which yields the leveled (normalized) time.

**Line balancing** A procedure for dividing tasks evenly among employees or work stations in a product or cellular layout; also known as assembly-line balancing.

**Line jockeying** Willful shifting from line to line or lane to lane in an attempt to reduce waiting time.

**Linear output** Production of the same quantity, sometimes in the same mix, each time period; also may mean meeting a variable schedule every day.

**Linearity index** A measure of the success in attaining targeted production or processing quantities; mathematically, it is 100 percent minus the mean percent deviation from scheduled production quantity.

**Load leveling** Scheduler's attempt to release a mix of orders that neither overloads nor underloads work centers.

**Load profile** Future work-center capacity requirements for open and planned orders.

**Loading (load, workload)** Assigning workload to a work center.

**Logistics** Activities associated with the management of freight and distribution systems.

**Lot** Large purchase or production quantity of the same item; often has its own identifying number.

**Lot delay** Delay incurred in sequential processing settings when a piece sits idle during the processing of other pieces in the lot.

**Lot-for-lot processing** The simplest approach to lot sizing; the exact order quantity required by the parent item or ordered by the customer.

**Lot size** Quantity of an item produced, serviced, or transported at one time.

**Lot sizing** Planning order quantities.

**Lot splitting** Splitting a lot quantity into multiple sublots, traditionally for expediting reasons: stop (split up) a current lot already on a machine so a hot job can replace it. Under JIT, lot splitting is fairly normal practice (not expediting), especially if a lot can be split among several of the same type of machine or work station.

**Lumpy workload (demand)** Highly variable pattern of workload (demand).

**Maintainability** Features that make equipment or products easy to maintain.

**Maintenance, repair, and operations (MRO) inventory** Inventory items that are not destined for next-process customers; items that are used in the operations of the owner.

**Make-to-order production** Production is accomplished in response to specific customer orders; output will normally be shipped immediately rather than stored as finished goods.

**Make-to-stock production** Upon completion, production output is destined to be stored as finished goods inventory.

**Malcolm Baldrige National Quality Award (MBNQA)** The United States' most prestigious award for organizational achievement in the field of quality; named after the late Secretary of Commerce Malcolm Baldrige.

**Manufacturability** See **Producibility.**

**Manufacturing resource planning (MRPII)** A comprehensive planning and control system that uses the master production schedule as a basis for scheduling production, capacity, shipments, tool changes, design work, and cash flow.

**Master planning** Broadly, matching aggregate demand with capacity. Narrowly, steering the firm's capacity so as to meet item demands as they materialize. Master planning contains elements of demand management, capacity planning, and master scheduling.

**Master production schedule (MPS)** Master schedule for a goods-producing company.

**Master schedule** A statement of what the firm plans to produce (goods) and/or provide (services), broken down by product model or service type.

**Master scheduling team** The master planning team with responsibility for steering the firm's capacity toward actual demand items and toward specific, budgeted, process-improvement activities.

**Material requirements planning (MRP)** A computer-based system of planning orders to meet the requirements of an MPS, and of tracking inventory flows.

**Materials management** Broad set of activities for acquiring, moving or handling, storing, and controlling materials resources.

**Mean absolute deviation (MAD)** A measure of forecast model accuracy; the sum of absolute values of forecast errors over a number of periods divided by the number of periods.

**Mean chart** A process control chart for variables inspection showing the sample averages for a number of samples or subgroups and thus revealing between-sample variations.

**Mean time between failures (MTBF)** Average time elapsing between failure of a repairable item, or average time to first failure of a nonrepairable item; the inverse of **Failure rate.**

**Mean time to repair (MTTR)** Average time to effect repair or replacement.

**Measured daywork** A nominal incentive-wage system in which standard output serves as a target for an employee.

**Methods study** Procedure for improving the way work is done; follows the scientific method of inquiry.

**Methods-time measurement (MTM)** Procedure for developing synthetic time standards by referring to tables of standards for basic motions.

**Milestone** A key event in a project; one type of upper management–oriented network consists solely of milestone events.

**Mixed-model assembly lines** Assembly lines on which more than one model of a product is made.

**Mixed-model processing** Production schedule that is repetitive in short cycles; conducive to supplying some of each needed model each day closely in line with customer requirements.

**Model** A likeness (mental, graphic, mathematical, or procedural) of a reality.

**Modular design** Design strategy that relies on relatively few universal components which may be assembled in various configurations in order to provide flexibility (e.g., different models or types) to customers.

**Motion study** Methods-improvement approach focusing on basic hand and body motions called **Therbligs.**

**Moving average** In forecasting, the mean or average of a given number of the most recent demand amounts, which becomes the forecast for the next (first future) period; the procedure repeats each period by dropping the oldest, and adding the newest, demand.

**Multi-functional team** Team consisting of individuals drawn from across a spectrum of functional disciplines. Synonym: **Cross-functional team.**

**Multiple regression/correlation** A mathematical model allowing for investigation of a number of causal variables in order to determine their simultaneous effect on a predicted variable such as demand.

**Naïve method (of forecasting)** Popular forecasting technique in which the most recent available demand is used as the next forecast.

**Natural team** See **Cell.**

**Negotiation** A form of purchasing without competitive bidding, typically in a stable supply situation; usually applies to high-dollar-volume items produced to a buyer's specs.

**Net requirement** For an item, its gross requirement minus current or projected stock on hand.

**Netting** A procedure for determining the net requirement for an item; a basic MRP calculation.

**Network** In project management, a diagram showing sequencing of activities that constitute the project.

**Non-value-adding (NVA)** Having the quality of adding cost but no value to goods or services.

**Normal time** Time for accomplishment of a work task after the elemental time has been adjusted to reflect pace rating. See also **Pace rating.**

**Number-of-defects chart** A process control chart for attributes inspection based on the number of defective items in each sample.

**Offline buffer stock** Buffer stock that is kept out of active storage and handling; its purpose is to provide low-cost protection against infrequent, unpredictable process stoppages or surges in demand without consuming throughput time.

**Open-office concept** An office arrangement plan that eliminates most floor-to-ceiling walls; stresses use of modular furniture and movable, partial-height partitions; and deemphasizes compartmentalization of people.

**Open order** An order that has been placed but not completed.

**Operation** Part of a job; one step or task that requires a new setup, often at a different work center.

**Operations** (1) Overall business or organizational activity. (2) Primary or principal revenue-producing business activity. (3) Area or department within an organization charged with responsibility for creation and delivery of output goods and services. (4) Processes in which resource inputs are transformed into outputs. (5) Elemental steps in a job sequence, potentially value adding and usually requiring a setup or changeover.

**Operations management** Broad set of activities that create, implement, or improve an organization's transformations and allied processes.

**Operations strategy** Component of overall business or organizational strategy that governs and guides transformation activities that, in turn, create output goods and services.

**Order** A request from a customer accepted for fulfillment by a provider.

**Order entry** Organizational acceptance of an order into the order-processing system; includes credit checks, customer documentation, translation into operations terms, stock queries, and order number assignment.

**Order fulfillment** Broad set of activities that collectively ensure delivery of goods or services in response to a specific customer order.

**Order promising** Making a commitment to a customer to ship or deliver an order.

**Original equipment manufacturer (OEM)** The original producer of a product; used to distinguish producer from other members of the supply chain (e.g., distributors, retailers, etc.)

**Outsourcing** Finding an outside source of a good or service, instead of making or providing it internally.

**Overlapped production** Condition in which a lot is in production at two or more work centers at the same time, typically because some of the lot is rushed forward on a hot basis; normal practice within work cells.

**Pace rating** Judging the pace of the subject of a time-standards study, where 100 percent is considered normal; yields a factor used in normalizing or leveling the elemental time.

**Parent item** For a component, its next higher level assembly; the part into which a component goes.

**Pareto chart** A chart showing items in any population grouped by category from most to least frequently occurring; useful in categorizing data in order to set priorities for process improvement.

**Pay for skills** Remuneration system in which employees are paid more for acquiring additional skills and greater knowledge; also known as skill-based pay, or pay for knowledge.

**Periodic maintenance** Regularly scheduled custodial services and preventive maintenance.

**Perpetual inventory system** A system in which every issue from inventory triggers a check of on-hand stock to see if the reorder point has been reached.

**Personal, rest, and delay (PR&D) allowance** Amount of time added to normal time to yield standard time; accommodates personal needs and unavoidable delay when setting time standards.

**Planned order (planned order release)** Anticipated order placement; indicated by item, date, and quantity.

**Planning horizon** Period of time covered by a certain type of plan; for example, a long-range forecast might, in a certain kind of business, have a planning horizon of five years.

**Pokayoke** See **Fail-safing.**

**Policy** Directive used to guide implementation of strategy.

**Precedence diagram** A chart showing a repetitive job broken into sequenced flow lines; used in assembly-line balancing.

**Predictive maintenance** Maintenance in advance of failure or wear out, based on predicted life of the component to be maintained.

**Preventive maintenance (PM)** Any actions, including adjustments, replacements, and basic cleanliness, that forestall equipment failure; may be based on calendar time, time of usage, or faults revealed in an inspection.

**Principles of Operations Management** A set of 16 fundamental guidelines for improving operations throughout an organization.

**Priority report** A (typically) daily list of job priorities sent to a work center; also called a dispatch list.

**Process** A unique set of interrelated elements that act together to determine performance; categories from which the specific elements are taken include labor, materials, methods, machines, measurement, maintenance, and management.

**Process capability** In general, a statement of the ability of process output to meet specifications; inherent capability is the width (approximately six standard deviations) of the distribution of process output.

**Process capability index** A numerical expression of the degree to which a process output meets a given specification. The $C_{pk}$ index is a commonly used process capability index.

**Process control** A condition signifying that all special or assignable variation has been removed from process output; only common or chance variation remains. Also known as statistical control.

**Process control chart** Statistical control chart on which to record samples of measured process outputs; the purpose is to note whether the process is statistically stable or changing, so that adjustments can be made as needed.

**Process delay** Delay incurred as a result of a bottleneck; for example, an entire lot is stalled due to insufficient capacity at the next work center in the job routing.

**Process flowchart** See **Flowcharts.**

**Process industry** An industry that produces goods that flow, pour, or mix together; also called continuous-flow process industry.

**Process lot** A number of units treated as one lot for processing; may be subdivided or combined with other lots into a different-sized transfer lot for handling and transport.

**Producible** or **producibility** Easy to make without error and undue cost with present or planned equipment and people; a desirable product design characteristic; also, manufacturability or operability.

**Product layout** A type of layout in which facilities are placed along product flow lines, with the customer (next process) next to the provider.

**Product planning** Developing lines of goods and services.

**Product routing** See **Routing.**

**Product wheel** Metaphor reflecting all products (in a family) that are produced with the same facility or set of resources.

**Product wheel turn time** Required production cycle time (or, interval between product availability) for any product in the family produced on the single resource represented by the "product wheel."

**Product structure** See **Bill of materials (BOM).**

**Production activity control** Keeping work on schedule on the shop floor, using progress information (feedback), which is compared with schedules; sometimes employs daily priority report, which gives priority based on relative lateness.

**Production control** Directing or regulating the flow of work through the production cycle, from purchase of materials to delivery of finished items; flow control. A production control department may include operations planning, scheduling, dispatching, and expediting.

**Production line** Multiple sequential processes arranged into one grand process to produce a product or narrow family of products.

**Production/operations management (POM)** See **Operations management.**

**Production plan** Total planned production, or production rate; unspecific as to product model or type of service.

**Production rate** Pace of production output, expressed in units per time period.

**Productivity** In general, output divided by input; in various forms, may apply to labor, materials, or other resources.

**Program evaluation and review technique (PERT)** A network-based project management technique originally developed for R&D projects; about the same as CPM.

**Progressive operations** Production in which material being worked on is passed from work station to work station; alternative to autonomous production.

**Project** A large-scale, one-of-a-kind endeavor; generally employs large amounts of diverse resources.

**Project manager** A manager or management team having responsibility for a project, not a function. Various project manager types include project manager, commodity manager, project coordinator, project engineer, and brand manager, each having a different degree of authority over the project.

**Project team** Multi-functional team assembled to plan and carry out a project.

**Proportion-defective chart** A process control chart for attributes, which shows the proportion or fraction defective in each sample.

**Pull system/pull-mode operations** A system in which the user pulls work from the maker or provider by some kind of signal (called kanban); pull signals should be issued at rate of actual usage.

**Push system** A system in which the maker pushes work forward into storage or onto the next process with little regard for rate of use; rate of pushing out the work often is preset by schedule.

**Quality** Perception of value in the eyes of the customer.

**Quality action cycle** Iterative program for ensuring quality that places primary emphasis on defect prevention but also incorporates detection as a back-up. Steps include design, self-inspection and correction, defect discovery, process analysis, and continuous improvement.

**Quality assurance** In general, the activities associated with making sure that the customer receives quality goods and services; often, the name given to a department charged with carrying out these responsibilities.

**Quality characteristic** A process performance (output) property of a product or service deemed important enough to control.

**Quality control circle (quality circle)** A small work group that meets periodically to discuss ways to improve quality, productivity, or the work environment.

**Quality cost** (1) *Traditional.* Costs directly attributable to activities performed to prevent and/or detect defective output, and to correct and/or recover from the effects of defective output. (2) *Modern.* Cost or loss to society of any deviation from target.

**Quality function deployment (QFD)** Matrix-based procedure for displaying customers' requirements, processes for meeting them, and competitors' versus one's own company's capabilities on each process; basic QFD matrix may be supplemented with other, more detailed process matrices. See also **House of quality.**

**Quality value** Competitive benefits of quality outputs; they may accrue through marketing advantages and through reduced costs of operations.

**Queue discipline** Priority for moving from queue into service in a waiting-line system; for example, first-come-first-served is a popular queue discipline for service counters.

**Queue limiter (queue limitation)** Device that places an upper limit on number of units waiting (or time waiting) for processing. See also **Kanban.**

**Quick response (QR)** System of linking final retail sales with production and shipping schedules back through the chain of supply; usually employs point-of-sale scanning plus electronic communication and may employ direct shipment from a factory, thus avoiding distribution warehousing.

**Random events** In a time series, patternless occurrences, such as jumps or drops in demand, for which there is no apparent cause.

**Range chart** A process control chart for variables; shows range of each sample—that is, within-sample variation.

**Regularized schedule** A schedule in which certain items are produced at regular intervals.

**Reliability** Probability that an item will work at a given time.

**Renege** Act of entering a queue but exiting before receiving service, typically after having grown tired of waiting.

**Reorder point (ROP)** Quantity of on-hand inventory that serves as a trigger for placing an order for more.

**Repetitive operations** Producing the same item or providing the same service over and over.

**Requisition** An internal request to have something purchased; usually goes to a purchasing department, which uses it in preparing a purchase order.

**Rescheduling notice** A notice (usually from an MRP system) that an order for a component part needs to be rescheduled; stems from a change in due dates or quantities for one or more parent items.

**Residual inventory** Inventory left over when an order is canceled or reduced in quantity.

**Resource requirements planning** A gross check to see if items in the master schedule will overload a scarce resource; also known as rough-cut capacity planning on the trial master schedule.

**Response ratio** A measure of idle work in work centers using ratios of lead time to work content, process speed to use rate, and pieces to work stations or operators; process improvements are reflected in smaller ratios.

**Robust design** Design that is able to withstand unfavorable operating conditions and hostile operating environments.

**Rolling forecast** A forecast that is redone at intervals, typically dropping oldest data and replacing it with most recent data.

**Rough-cut capacity planning** Conversion of an operations plan into capacity needs for key resources. The purpose is to evaluate a plan before trying to implement it.

**Routing** Path from work center to work center that work follows in its transformation into a finished item or complete service; standard routings may be kept in records.

**Run diagram** A running plot of measurements of some process or quality characteristic, piece by piece as a process continues.

**Scatter (correlation) diagram** A plot of effects (e.g., quality changes) against experimental changes in process inputs.

**Scientific management** School of management developed in the late nineteenth century by Frederick Winslow Taylor and contemporaries; incorporates close regimentation and measurement of work, ergonomics, training as to prescribed procedures, and reliance on standard methods and times.

**Seasonal index** Ratio of demand for a particular season to demand for the average season.

**Seasonal variation (seasonality)** Recurring pattern in a time series; occurring within one year and repeating annually.

**Service level** Percentage of orders filled from stock on hand.

**Service parts** Parts or components produced to supply the after-sales service market.

**Service–profit chain** A series of causal links suggesting that profit and growth flow from customer loyalty, which is a result of customer satisfaction. Customer satisfaction stems from perceived value of goods and services received. That value is created by satisfied, loyal, and productive employees. Employee satisfaction, in turn, flows from high-quality support services and policies that empower employees. See also **Value chain.**

**Service rate ($\mu$)** In a waiting line system, the average number that can be served per time period.

**Serviceability** Degree to which an item may be maintained—either kept in service through preventive maintenance or restored to service after a breakdown.

**Setup** See **Changeover.**

**Seven deadly wastes** Basic or root categories of undesirable outcomes (wastes) due to poor process design or faulty operations. Wastes stem from over-production, waiting, transport, processing, inventory, motion, and poor quality.

**Shop calendar** A scheduling calendar with workdays as sequentially numbered days; sometimes numbered 000 to 999.

**Shop floor control** See **Activity control.**

**Simultaneous engineering** Inclusion of supplier, process, and manufacturing engineers early in product design stages; aims for shorter lead times, better quality, and better coordination. See also **Concurrent design.**

**Six-sigma quality** (1) Broadly: A popular program for quality improvement throughout a company's operations. (2) Narrowly: Output quality level that equates to a $C_{pk}$ index value of 1.5, roughly no more than 3.4 defects per million opportunities.

**Skill-based pay** Compensation system in which employees are paid primarily for attainment of skills. Also called **Pay for knowledge.**

**Slack (slack time)** (1) In project management, slack is the amount of time an activity may be delayed without delaying the project schedule; usually changes as the project progresses. (2) In job scheduling and dispatching, slack is available time (time until job is due) minus required time (time needed to perform the job).

**Social loss (of bad quality)** A concept introduced by Genichi Taguchi stating that there is a cost imparted to society whenever process output deviates from the target.

**Soliciting competitive bids** Inviting prospective suppliers to bid (offer a price) on a contract to provide goods or services according to specifications.

**Special-cause variation** A type of variation in process output that can be traced to a specific cause such as a fault or malfunction, removal of which removes the variation.

**Specification** Process output description commonly in two parts: the target (nominal) and the tolerances.

**Speculation (speculative) buying** Purchasing to get an attractive price rather than because of need.

**Spider diagram** Graphical display used to portray changing status of selected group performance factors which are depicted as lines radiating outward from a central point; better performance is reflected as a plot closer to the center.

**Standard data** Tables of time-standard values used to construct synthetic standards.

**Standard deviation (SD)** A measure of dispersion in a distribution; equal to the square root of the variance; in forecasting, defined as the square root of the mean-square error.

**Standard time** The time a qualified person is expected to take to complete a task; the normal time plus an allowance factor.

**Standardization** Settling on a few, rather than many, variations of a given part, product, or service.

**Statistical control** A process is in a state of statistical control if it is free of special-cause (assignable-cause) variation.

**Statistical process control (SPC)** (1) Broadly: Application of a collection of coarse- and fine-grained process analysis techniques to improve process output over time. (2) Narrowly: Application of process control charts to first establish statistical control and then monitor subsequent process improvement efforts.

**Stockkeeping unit (SKU)** An item of inventory at a particular geographic location. For example, if six packs of canned Classic Coca Cola are in a special display near the checkout counters and also stocked with the other soft drinks, that constitutes two SKUs.

**Stockout** Failure to deliver from stock upon receipt of a customer order.

**Stockout rate** Proportion or percentage of orders that cannot be filled from stock on hand.

**Strategic triangle** Attributed to Kenichi Ohmae; the three main component concerns of a company's strategy—customers, competitors, and the company itself.

**Strategy** Management's game plan for positioning the company in its chosen market arena, competing successfully, pleasing customers, and achieving good business performance.

**Streamlined operations** Steady-flow operations with few delays, stops, starts, or storages.

**Supplier certification** See **Certification.**

**Supply chain** (See **Service-profit chain** and **Value chain.**)

**Supply chain management (SCM)** Actions taken to integrate suppliers, operations, and distribution networks so as to keep goods and services flowing in such a way as to meet next-process customers' requirements. (Synonym: **Value-chain management.**)

**Synchronized scheduling (synchronized processing)** Processing with schedules in which the timing of delivery or production of a component is meshed with the use rate of the parent item.

**Systematic layout planning (SLP)** A multistep approach to layout planning based on flow and relationship data.

**Systems contract** A contract with a supplier for a defined set of items, often allowing orders to be placed by line managers without going through the purchasing department.

**Takt time** Demand-driven production interval; the ratio of available work time to customer demand rate (for that work time interval).

**Technical estimate** A nonengineered, experience-based, time standard.

**Theory of constraints** Approach to operations that attempts to schedule and feed work so as to maximize work-flow rate (and therefore cash flow as well) through bottlenecks and constraints.

**Throughput time** See **Cycle time.**

**Time fence** A point on a company's planning horizon that separates the firm portion (typically, the near future) from the tentative portion (more distant future).

**Time measurement unit (TMU)** A time unit in MTM analysis: 1 TMU = 0.0006 minutes, or 0.00001 hours.

**Time-phased order point (TPOP)** A subset of MRP for handling independent-demand items.

**Time series** A sequential set of observations of a variable taken at regular intervals over time.

**Time standard** See **Standard time.**

**Time study** A direct approach for obtaining the cycle time to be used in setting a time standard; obtained by stopwatch or film analysis.

**Tolerance stackup** See **Variation stackup.**

**Total preventive maintenance (TPM)** A full agenda of procedures that improve dependability of equipment, with emphasis on maintaining equipment before it breaks down; bestows primary responsibility for PM on equipment operator.

**Total quality (TQ)** Comprehensive management approach to ensure quality throughout an organization; includes planning and design, supplier and user/processor interface, self-inspection for control, and continual improvement in customer service through process monitoring and feedback; places primary responsibility for quality at the source (i.e., the maker or provider).

**Total quality control (TQC)** See **Total quality.**

**Total quality management (TQM)** (1) Deliberate actions taken to ensure total quality. (2) In manufacturing circles, sometimes used synonymously with Toyota production system or lean manufacturing.

**Toyota production system** A system of management first perfected at Toyota Motor Company. Key characteristics include total quality, just-in-time operations, total preventive maintenance, minimization of wastes, empowerment of cross-trained employees, and great emphasis on continuous improvement throughout all facets of company operations.

**Tracking signal** Typically, the cumulative forecast error in a time series divided by the MAD; used as a limit to trigger adjustment in smoothing coefficients in adaptive smoothing models.

**Transfer lot** A number of units treated as one lot for transport; may be larger or smaller than lots sized for processing (**process lots**).

**Trend** A long-term shift, positive or negative, in the value of a time series; also known as slope.

**Undercapacity scheduling** Scheduling output at less than full capacity; allows schedule to be met on most days and allows times for operators to work on quality and maintenance.

**Unit-load concept** A concept calling for accumulation of enough pieces to make a "full load" before moving any pieces.

**Universal design** A design that is flexible enough to appeal to a broad cross-section of the market.

**Universal strategy** Strategy that seeks to differentiate outputs through high quality, rapid response, and superior service while simultaneously seeking a cost-leadership position through waste-free operations.

**U-shaped layout** A popular variant of product or cellular layout; improves flexibility, teamwork, equipment and tool use, and work flow by arranging work stations into a semi-circular or U-shaped pattern.

**Utilization** Ratio of time in use to time available.

**Value-adding activities** Activities in which value is added to the resource undergoing transformation; does not include non-value-adding transactions, inspections, handling, delays, and so on.

**Value analysis (VA)** Examination of existing product design specifications with the aim of lowering cost; typically centered in the purchasing department.

**Value chain** Series of transformation processes that move a good or service from inception to final consumer; major activity groups include funding, design, testing, production, distribution, marketing, and delivery. Ideally, each step increases the worth (or, value) of the item in the eyes of the next customer. See also **Service–profit chain.**

**Value engineering (VE)** Same as **value analysis,** but typically centered in the engineering organization.

**Value migration** The changes in either (1) priorities for what a customer requires from time to time, or (2) places in the supply chain at which the customer expects to find what is sought.

**Variables (control) chart** Statistical process control chart for recording measured process output data; mean and range (X-bar and R) charts are examples.

**Variables data** Data obtained through measurement of some underlying (usually) continuous distribution (e.g., physical dimensions, weight, time).

**Variables inspection** A test in which measurements of an output (quality) characteristic are taken.

**Variation stackup** The output that results when two or more components at extreme edges within tolerance (specification) limits are assembled or mixed together; often the result is an assembly, batch, or service that performs poorly or is out of specification limits.

**Vendor-managed inventory (VMI)** An advanced version of quick response in which customers confer to their suppliers those activities necessary to manage customers' inventory.

**Vertical integration** Acquisition of capacity to perform activities that were formerly accomplished either upstream or downstream in the supply chain.

**Work breakdown structure (WBS)** Product-oriented list and definition of major modules and secondary components in a project.

**Work cell** See **Cell.**

**Work content time** Time required to make a complete assembly or perform a job; usually the sum of the times of all tasks needed.

**Work in process (WIP)** Partly completed work that is either waiting between processes or is in process.

**Work-sampling study** Work measurement technique in which the analyst makes random, direct observations of subject employee's activity, records output volume, and uses these data to create an engineered time standard.

**Zero defects (ZD)** Proposed as the proper goal of a quality program; an alternative to the past practice of setting an acceptable quality (defect) level.

# INDEX